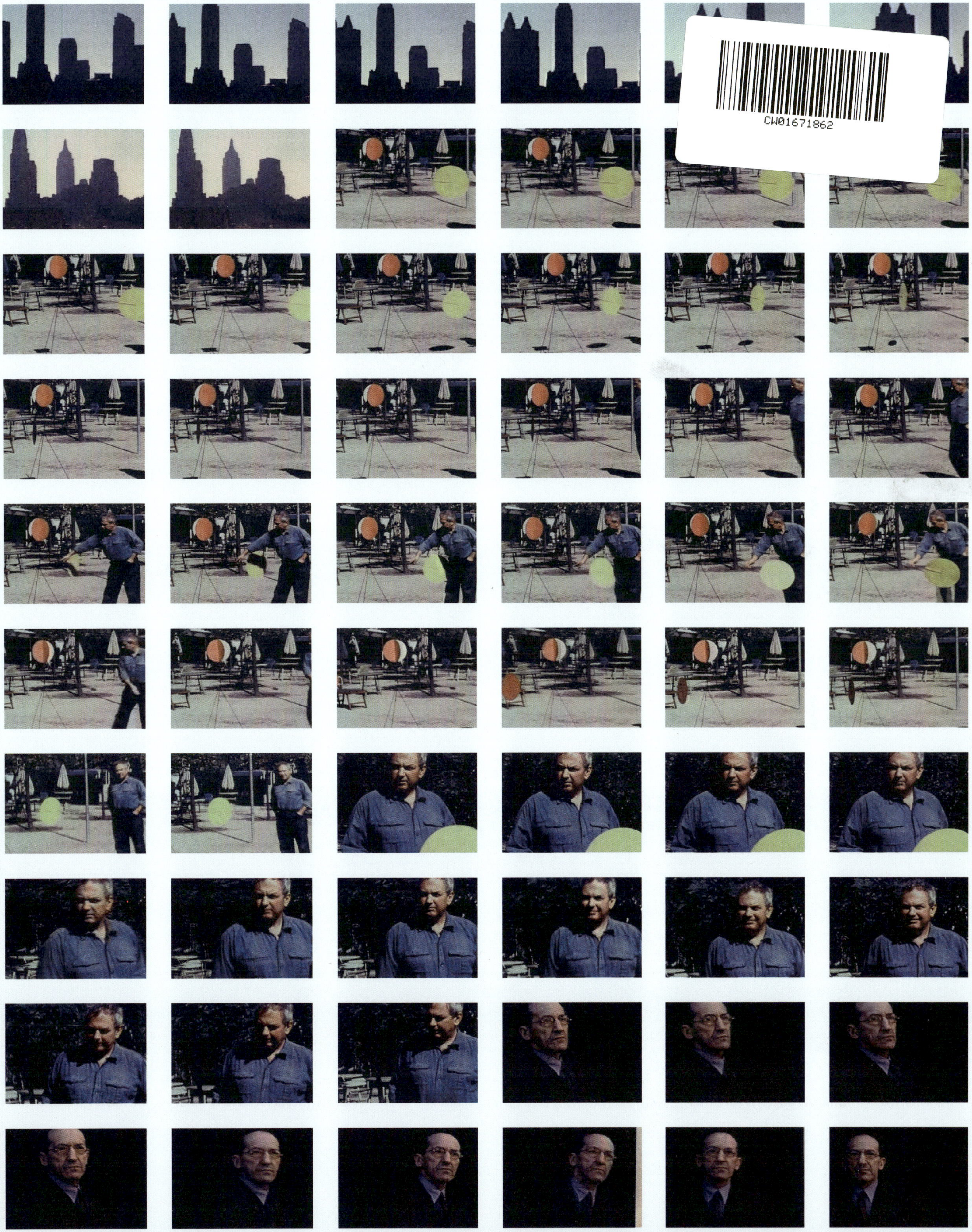

CW01671862

Alexander Calder

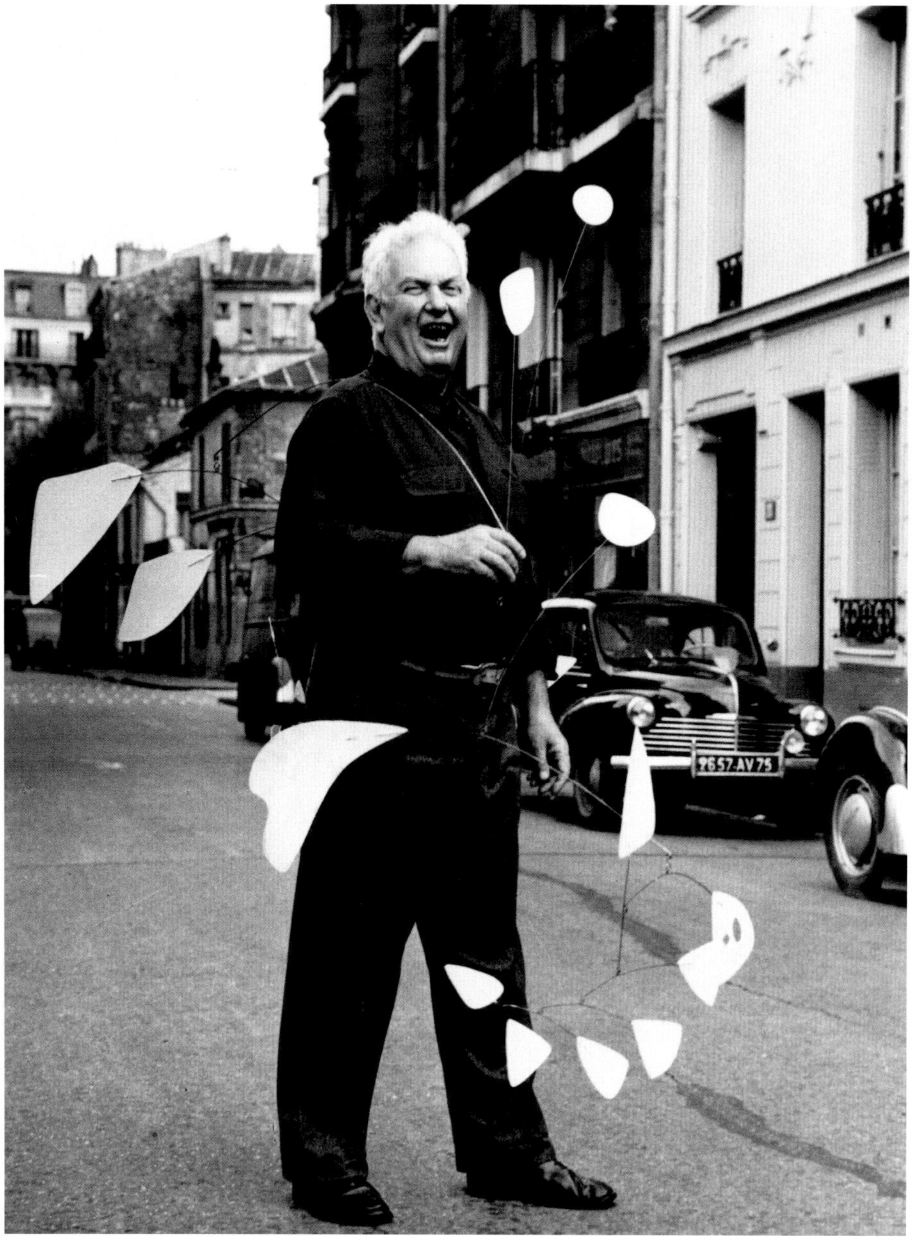

Alexander Calder

Performing Sculpture

Edited by
Achim Borchardt-Hume

With contributions by
Ann Coxon
Penelope Curtis
Marko Daniel
Thomas Fichter
Sérgio B. Martins
Vassilis Oikonomopoulos
Alexander S.C. Rower
Alex J. Taylor

Tate Publishing

First published 2015 by order of the Tate Trustees by Tate Publishing,
a division of Tate Enterprises Ltd, Millbank, London SW1P 4RG
www.tate.org.uk/publishing

on the occasion of the exhibition
Alexander Calder: Performing Sculpture

Tate Modern, London
11 November 2015 – 3 April 2016

Supported by

TERRA
FOUNDATION FOR AMERICAN ART

with additional support from the Performing Sculpture Supporters
Circle: Lydia and Manfred Gorvy; and Tate Patrons

© Tate Enterprises Ltd 2015

All works by and likenesses of Alexander Calder © 2015 Calder
Foundation, New York/DACS, London

Select Chronology © 2015 Alexander S.C. Rower, New York

All rights reserved. No part of this book may be reprinted or
reproduced or utilised in any form or by any electronic, mechanical
or other means, now known or hereafter invented, including
photocopying and recording, or in any information storage or retrieval
system, without permission in writing from the publishers or
a licence from the Copyright Licensing Agency Ltd, www.cla.co.uk

A catalogue record for this book is available from the British Library

ISBN 978 1 84976 344 8 (pbk)
ISBN 978 1 84976 396 7 (hbk)

Designed by Why Not Associates
Colour reproduction by DL Imaging, London
Printed in Belgium by die Keure

Front cover: Alexander Calder, *Antennae with Red and Blue Dots*
c.1953 (detail, see pp.206–7)
Endpapers and inside cover: Alexander Calder with Piet Mondrian,
Marcel Duchamp and Herbert Matter during the installation of
Alexander Calder's retrospective at The Museum of Modern Art,
New York, 1943: film stills from *Calder: Sculpteur de l'air* 2009 by
Elizabeth Goodspeed Chapman, courtesy Robert Storr
Frontispiece: Alexander Calder with *21 feuilles blanches* 1953,
Paris 1954

All artworks are by Alexander Calder unless stated otherwise

Measurements of artworks are given in centimetres,
height before width and depth

FSC
www.fsc.org
MIX
Paper from
responsible sources
FSC® C009115

Contents

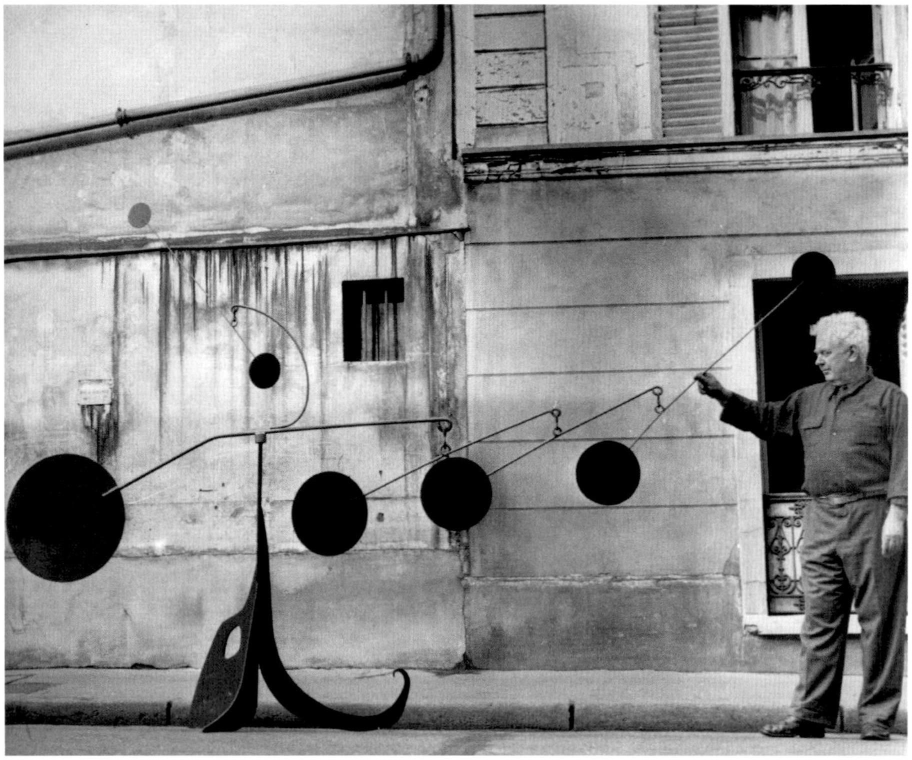

Calder with *Myxomatose* 1953, Paris 1954

Foreword

The term 'sculpture' usually evokes the idea of a static object that asks viewers to walk around it in order to experience its three-dimensionality. Whereas painting historically sought to construct a space for the viewer to look into, sculpture shared the latter's real space instead. However, just as many of Calder's painter friends such as Fernand Léger, Joan Miró and Piet Mondrian contested the dominance of central perspective to make their audience appreciate the reality of painting itself, so a great many avant-garde sculptors from Jean Arp and Alexander Archipenko to Constantin Brancusi and Pablo Picasso began to break down the historic binaries of sculpture – volume and void, surface and mass, gravity and lightness. Setting sculpture into motion became the ultimate frontier.

Credited with inventing the mobile (a term coined by his friend, Marcel Duchamp) Alexander Calder opened up a panoply of new possibilities for sculpture and the relationship between object and viewer. The works brought together for *Alexander Calder: Performing Sculpture* reflect the persistent energy and inventiveness that marked Calder's work ever since his experiments with mechanical and airborne movement during the 1930s. They also show his abiding interest in theatricality and performance, an interest that was sparked through his early experiences of the cabaret and the circus in the 1920s. Calder's desire to incorporate elements of movement and performativity provided a seedbed for a new understanding of art that not only inhabited the audience's space but also created a joint experience of time.

The contribution of Calder's 'performing sculpture' to the continued evolution of art is therefore considerable, yet is often overlooked because of the seeming simplicity and familiarity of the objects he created and showed on the world stage. In 1962 the Arts Council of Great Britain organised a first retrospective exhibition of Alexander Calder at the Tate Gallery. Over half a century later, this exhibition at Tate Modern – Calder's largest to date in the UK – asks us to look afresh at a body of work that is never quite fixed, that moves us by moving itself and that continues to act upon our vision.

This exhibition would not have been possible without the support and collaboration of the Calder Foundation. Their tireless efforts to research, collate, archive, exhibit and support the work of Alexander Calder well into the twenty-first century has made the research and coordination of this exhibition not only a smoother task, but also a far more enjoyable one. In particular we would like to extend our gratitude to Alexander S.C. Rower, Director of the Calder Foundation and grandson of the artist. Sandy's vision, imagination and energy as well as his dedication are unparalleled. In addition, we would like to thank Lily Lyons, Director of Exhibitions and External Affairs; Melissa Claus, Exhibition Coordinator; Alexis Marotta, Director of Archives; John Sapp, Archivist; Susan Braeuer Dam, Director of Research and Publications and Kevin Barry, Registrar for their hard work and commitment to making this exhibition a reality, not least by lending an unprecedented number of key works.

We are acutely conscious of the trust placed in our institution by anybody who temporarily allows us to safeguard their works for the benefit of the public. So we want to express our profound gratitude to all the lenders, institutional and private, and all those who have contributed to the making of the exhibition. In particular we acknowledge the Art Institute of Chicago; the Centre Pompidou, Paris; the Hirshhorn Museum and Sculpture Garden, Smithsonian Institution, Washington DC; the Menil Collection, Houston; Moderna Museet, Stockholm; MACBA, Barcelona; the

Museum of Contemporary Art, Chicago; the Museum of Modern Art, New York; the National Gallery of Art, Washington DC; the Philadelphia Museum of Art; the Scottish National Gallery of Modern Art, Edinburgh; Wadsworth Atheneum, Hartford; and the Whitney Museum of American Art, New York. Private lenders to the exhibition include Galerie Larock-Granoff, Paris; Galerie Natalie Seroussi, Paris; Jonathan O'Hara Gallery, New York; the Lipman Family Foundation, James Mayor and Mayor Gallery, the Jon A. Shirley Collection; as well as lenders who have preferred to remain anonymous. At Pace London we would like to mention Arne Glimcher, Mark Glimcher and Mollie Dent-Brocklehurst as well as salute Tamara Corm for her ceaseless enthusiasm.

We are especially grateful to José Armenio de Brito Cruz, President, and the Board of Directors of the Institute of Brazilian Architects (IAB), Department of São Paulo for generously participating in this exhibition and for enabling people to experience *Black Widow*, an outstanding example of Calder's large-scale mobiles, for the first time outside Brazil. We would also like to acknowledge the more than generous help we have received from Roberta Saraiva Coutinho who worked indefatigably on the details of this complex loan as well as mention our colleague, Flavia Frigeri, Curator who aided this conversation at a crucial point.

Special thanks go to Nancy and Peter Meinig who have generously supported the exhibition not only by parting temporarily with *Chef d'orchestre*, a cherished work in their collection, but by allowing us to reawaken it in a series of performances that bring back to life Calder's original ideas as well as those of his collaborator, Earle Brown. Aside from the helping hand lent by Edward Nahem who facilitated the early stages of this conversation, the presentation and performance of *Chef d'orchestre* owes much to the support of the Earle Brown Foundation, Thomas Fichter, Executive Director and Susan Sollins-Brown who sadly passed away during the course of research for the exhibition. Their generosity, devotion and commitment to our project were remarkable. We gratefully acknowledge the collaboration of Richard Bernas and Richard Benjafield, Head of Wind, Brass and Percussion at the Guildhall School of Music and Drama and the many musicians – too many to mention by name – who worked with us on the realisation of the performance. We would like to extend our thanks to Suzy Upton, Resources Manager, the Martha Graham Centre and all those that have assisted at the various stages of our research, not least Tate's Public Programme convenor Marko Daniel and Joseph Kendra, Assistant Curator Public Programmes, who acted as congenial custodians to this project.

Developing the exhibition concept and installation at a time when the museum is undergoing a period of significant change compelled us to look afresh at the architecture of the exhibition galleries we have made use of for over fifteen years now, designed by Jacques Herzog and Pierre de Meuron within the former Bankside Power Station. Working closely with the curators of *Alexander Calder: Performing Sculpture*, Ascan Mergenthaler, John O'Mara, Rebecca Roberts and the team at Herzog & de Meuron have helped to rationalise the exhibition design in such a way that Calder's works are the stars of the show while revealing the continuous strength and versatility of the building we have become so familiar with. We are also deeply grateful to Matt Castle and his team for sharing their technical expertise in installing Calder's often complex constructions.

We are indebted to the contributors to the catalogue: Penelope Curtis, Marko Daniel, Thomas Fichter, Sérgio Martins and Alex J. Taylor, as well as the exhibition co-curators Ann Coxon and Vassilis Oikonomopoulos for shining the spotlight on facets of Calder's rich career that particularly chime with the exhibition's curatorial argument. The catalogue greatly benefited from the expertise and dedication of the in-house and external Tate Publishing team: Nicola Bion, Juliette Dupire, Deborah Metherell and Faye Robson. If the book captures the spirit of the exhibition this is due to the design expertise and sensitivity of Andrew Altmann and Daniel McGhee of Why Not Associates. We are hugely thankful to the Calder Foundation and all those photographers who have allowed us to reproduce their photographs.

Alexander Calder: Performing Sculpture has been made possible by the provision of insurance through the UK Government Indemnity Scheme. We would like to thank the Department of Culture, Media and Sport and the Arts Council England for providing and arranging this indemnity. The exhibition has been generously sponsored by the Terra Foundation for American Art, a long-standing friend to Tate and one for whom our affection and respect only continue to grow.

This exhibition has been conceived and realised by a small team of curators at Tate Modern who have had the vision to present Calder's work in a new light. Achim Borchardt-Hume, Director of Exhibitions started the conversations and has overseen the process throughout, developing the exhibition in close collaboration with Ann Coxon, Curator and Vassilis Oikonomopoulos, Assistant Curator, whose passion, curiosity and dedication at times appeared inexhaustible. Matthew Gale, Head of Displays, acted as a continuous fount of support in the background. We would also like to mention Iria Candela, Estrellita B. Brodsky, Curator of Latin American Art, Metropolitan Museum of Art, New York and former Curator, International Art, Tate Modern, who worked on the early stages of exhibition research.

The curatorial team has been ably assisted by Stephanie Busson, PA to Director of Exhibitions and Helen O'Malley, Exhibitions Administrator. Helen Sainsbury, Head of Programme Realisation continually offered help and advice on countless matters, as did Rachel Kent, Programme Manager. Caroline McCarthy, Registrar rose to the challenge of coordinating the transport of the work with an equal mix of efficiency and good humour, vital qualities shared by Phil Monk, Art Installation Manager and his assistant Rhona O'Brien, Alex Maroon, Senior Art Handling Technician and their team of excellent technicians. Patricia Smithen, Head of Conservation and her colleagues once again ensured that the trust placed in Tate by lenders would be done full justice. Many thanks are due also to our colleagues in Tate Learning, the TMS Group, the ever-committed Press and Marketing teams, Tate Media and especially Visitor Services.

In a museum of the twenty-first century where live art takes on an ever greater importance we are proud to present with this survey of Calder's work one of the uncontested pioneers of art in motion.

Chris Dercon
Director, Tate Modern

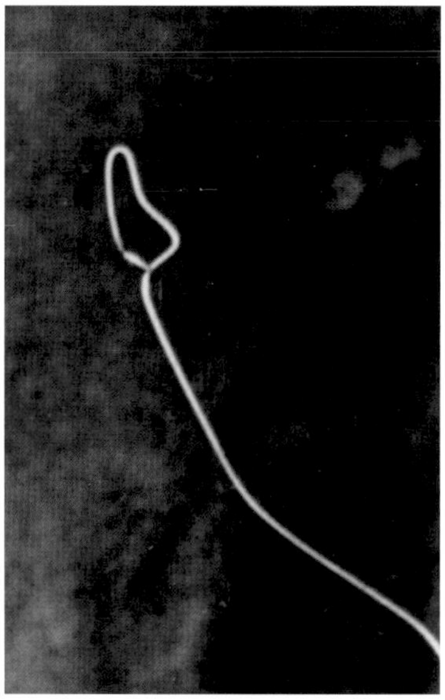

Performance or Post-performance

Penelope Curtis

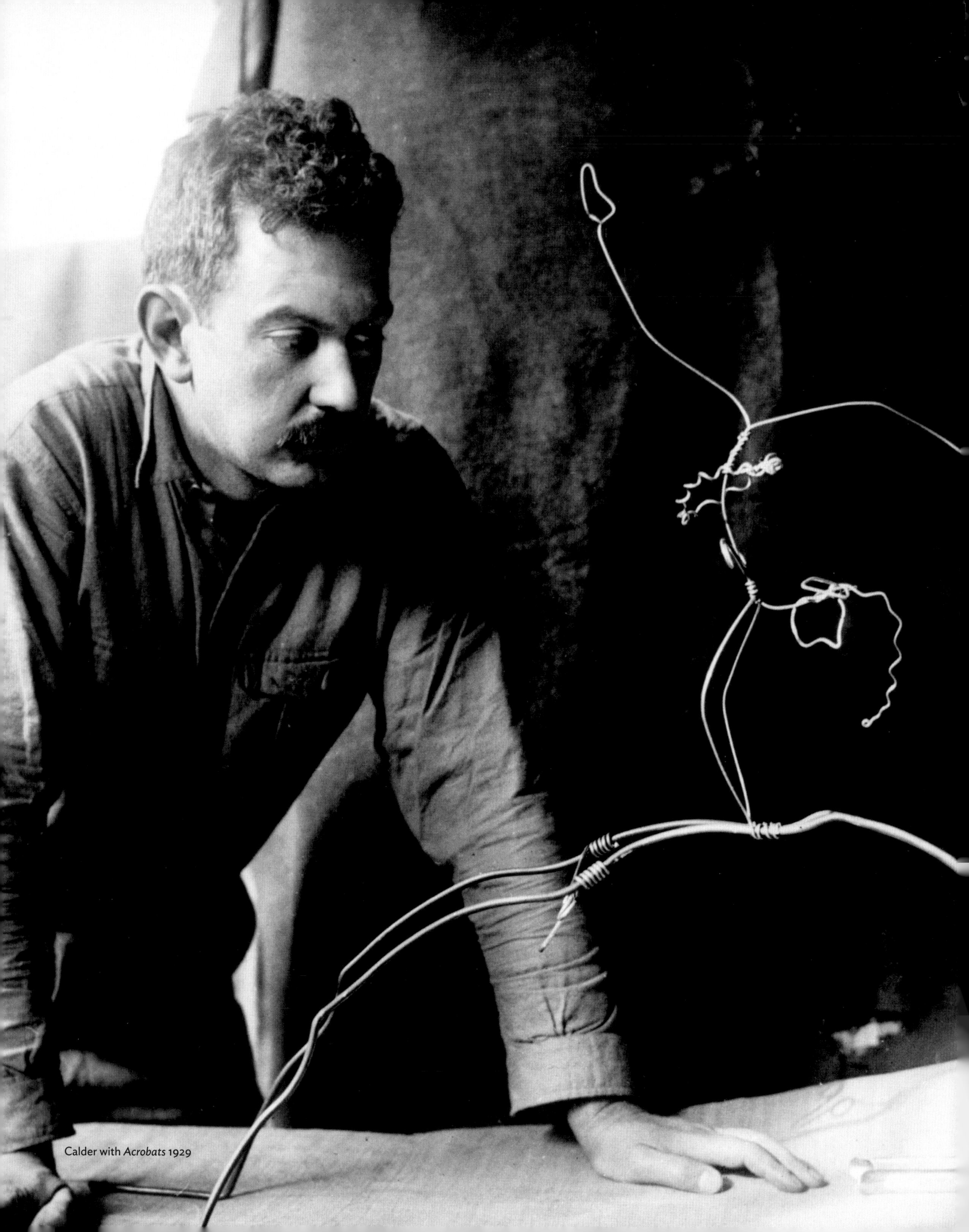

Calder with *Acrobats* 1929

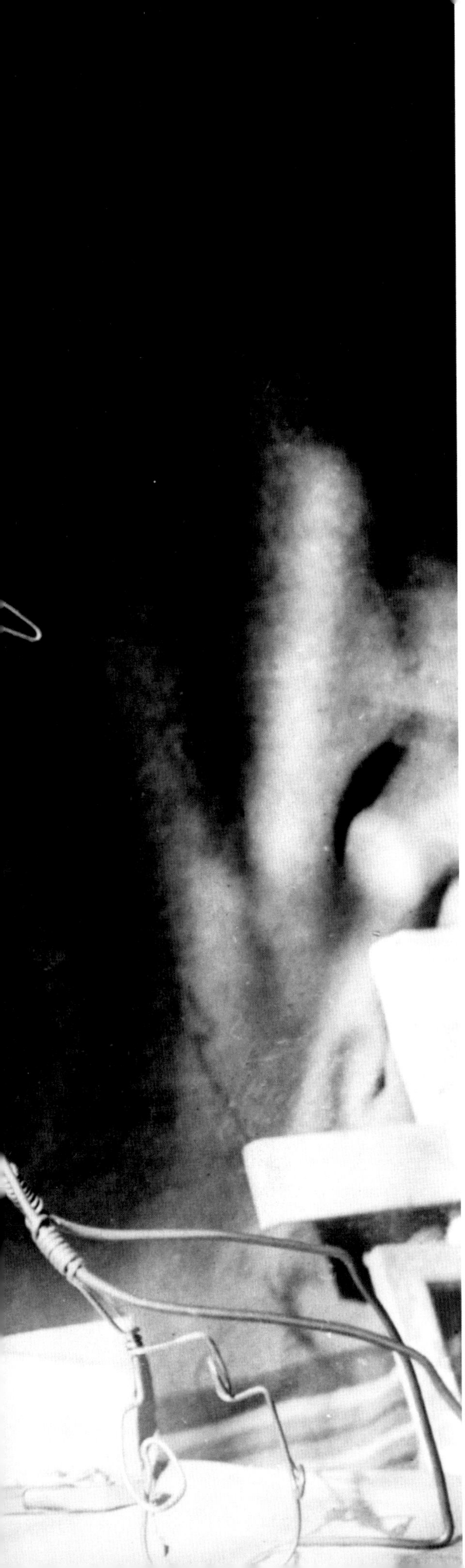

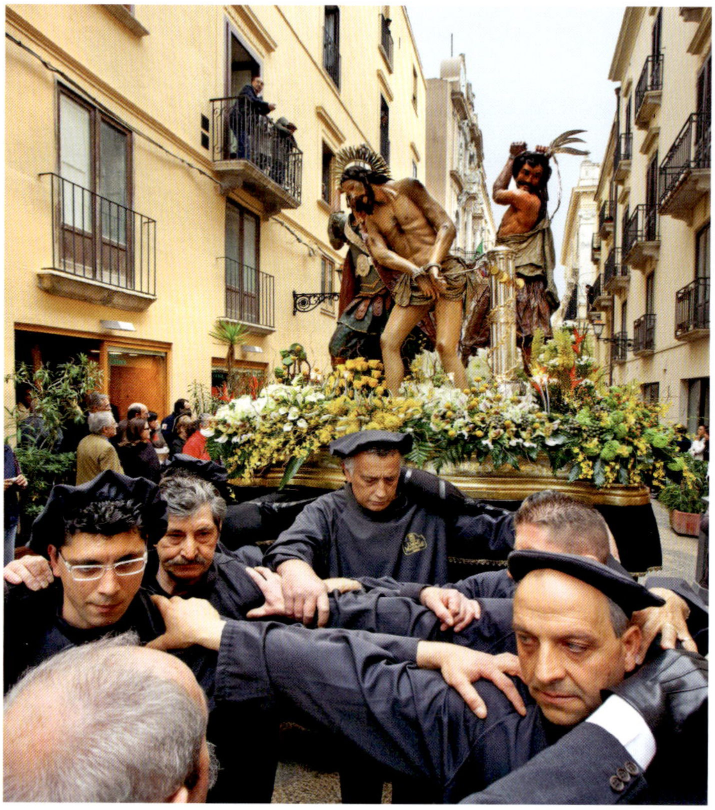

Good Friday procession, Trapani, Sicily

'Performing Sculpture' clearly has a double sense, and perhaps both meanings can be applied to the work of Alexander Calder. On the one hand it is a category of sculpture that performs; on the other it is a state of being, an act of transformation, a moment in which sculpture becomes sculptural. In this short essay I shall consider both senses individually, as well as moments of their coincidence, and suggest that we might see Calder as moving, across his career, from performance in the one sense, to performance in the other. If we think about how sculpture has performed, over time, such a lineage may also allow the question of effectiveness to emerge, as well as that of status or quality, which the word 'performance' connotes today (in our sense of 'high performance' or 'performance appraisal').

Sculpture has long had a role to play, quite literally. Sculptures, historically, very often had two states, both inert and active, depending on the religious calendar. Figures that were so much wood or stone came into their own when dressed, anointed, bejewelled, made-up and activated. Pagan or Christian, depicting god or saint, sculpture has long been required to perform. Sometimes static, at the centre of the temple, but just as often mobile – paraded through the town, as is still the case in the Holy Week processions of Spain and Italy – sculpture is made to perform a narrative role and to be seen in this context. The significance of such moments is attested to by the unwonted activity of the statue, and the unusual access granted to its audience, whether in terms of actual touching, or of vicarious touching, via a mirror. This kind of fulfilment, with shared expectations and required terms, is the most straightforward way of understanding performance, and it is an interpretation entirely appropriate to an understanding of what a subscribing audience wants from their sculptures. This is a knowing performance, one that is entirely complicit and necessarily shared – judged by its conformity to convention. The sculpture acts a part, its role is duly fulfilled, and success is judged as much by propriety and precedent as by the transcendent – i.e. by what has been done before, rather than what is being done for the first time.

Sculptures, especially figurative sculptures (and most sculpture was figurative, at least until recently), very often stand in for something (or someone) else. They are representative at best, imposters at worst. The crucifix stands in for the crucified, and the wooden effigy may very usefully stand in for the real body – especially if that body is fragile, vulnerable or decomposing. In the Museum of Westminster Abbey, London, are the royal mannequins that have taken the place of deceased kings and queens of England, and other public figures, during their funeral processions, and which later stood by their tombs – a kind of colloquial reminder of the more earthly qualities of those now translated to their nearby mausolea. Such a tradition was and is carried on through the waxworks fashioned by Madame Tussauds of London, which play famous people, performing celebrity by means of verisimilitude and marking its changing fortunes.[1]

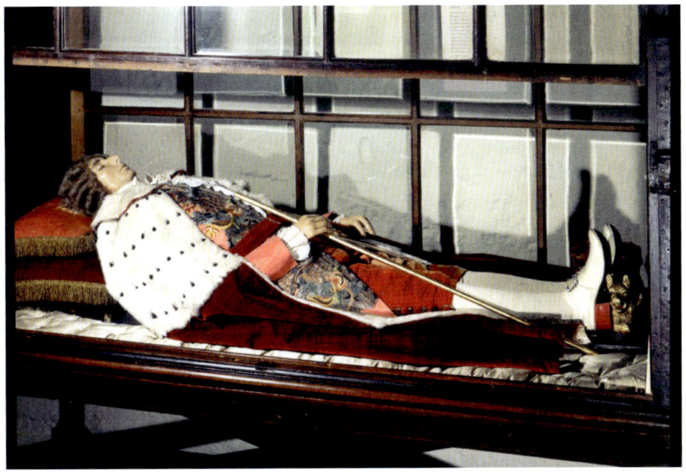

Wax effigy of Edmund, Duke of Buckingham, Westminster Abbey Museum

The idea of the waxwork playing the actor, as is often the case at Tussauds, is perhaps ironic. It seems like a reversal of foundation stories from ancient cultures, in which a statue is brought to life by the erotic fixation of its maker. This is the story of Pandora, the first woman, made by Hephaestus the smith in Ancient Greek mythology, and, more famously, of Pygmalion's love for his ivory creation, Galatea. The interplay between the artist and his figurative creation has engendered countless variations on the story of maker and made, male and female, artist and object, material and inspiration, since its early narration by Ovid. In many of these stories it would seem that the sculpture goes beyond performance, and that, instead, we are faced with a kind of trespass.

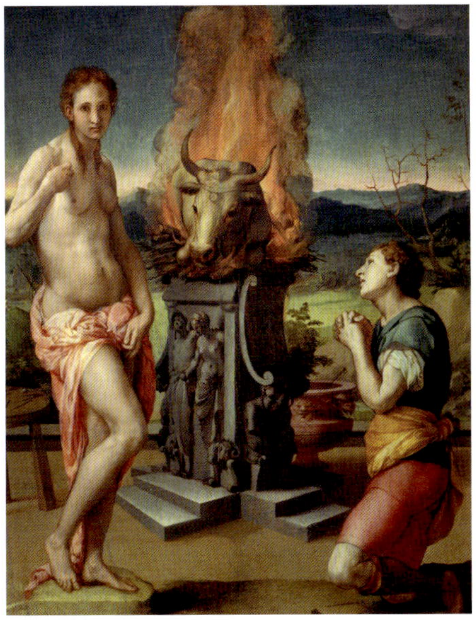

Bronzino (Agnolo di Cosimo Tori) (1503–72), *Pygmalion and Galatea* 1530, Galleria degli Uffizi, Florence

Performance, on the other hand, I would argue, is more to do with behaving properly. As such, it is much less closely connected to Pygmalionism, and is tied, rather, to duty, and to objects and tools that do a job, but do not overstep the mark of expectation. 'Performance' is largely routine and only occasionally exceptional. In sculpture, it generally denotes something rather limited – or crudely figurative – as in the waxworks, dolls and automata that sometimes stand in for human and sacred figures. Such figures generally exist beyond the confines of 'fine art'. Performance has its parameters; its beginning and its end, its props and accessories, its costume and its audience.[2]

The middle ground represented by the theatrical stage, in which props are sculpture or vice versa, has been explored in recent years by artists such as Gerard Byrne, Graham Fagen and Céline Condorelli, who make trees for Samuel Beckett's plays (Byrne, see p.16, and Fagen), or podia for actors (Condorelli). They are building on a modernist practice whose protagonists include Barbara Hepworth and Isamu Noguchi, who made sculptural forms that acquired mobility and even a voice through their association with the modern dancer, composer or playwright. Such artists apparently assert that we are wrong to place performance in opposition to sculpture – that this is a category mistake. Indeed the interest of their work lies in the elision of sculpture and performance, which, as we have seen, is true to a longer tradition.

Such sculptural props are generally abstract, but others, notably those in the form of the ventriloquist's dummy, seem to blend sculpture, prop and performance in

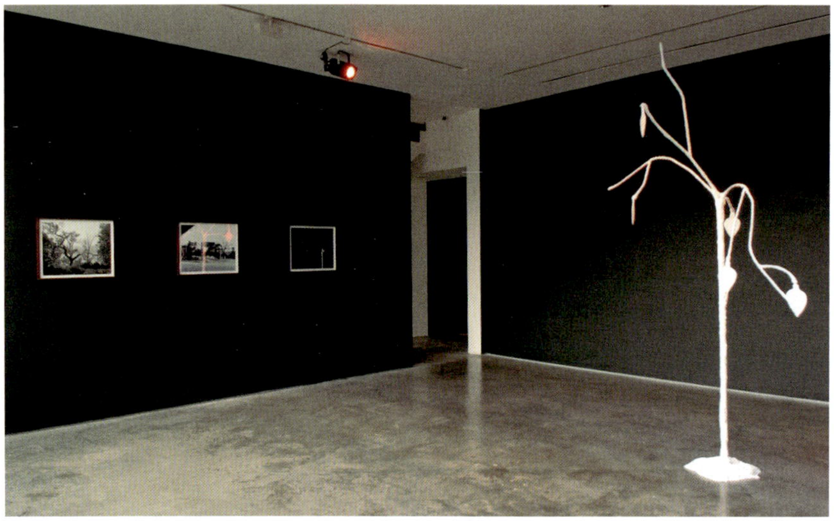

Gerard Byrne, installation: Lisson Gallery, London, 23 March – 4 May 2007

their very make-up. When brought to life by a deceptive 'inner voice', thrown by their manipulator, such figures embody the 'uncanny', the very quality or feeling that accounts for our fascination with this art. When an artist, as is the case with Asta Gröting, makes her own dummy, and writes its script, before handing it over to a professional ventriloquist, we are in a space of even deeper deception – the audience is deceived into thinking that the actor is speaking for himself.

The category of 'speaking sculptures' has evolved, over the centuries, in Rome, where sculptures like 'Pasquino' (and 'Marforio') have traditionally been used as noticeboards for messages critical of the establishment.[3] Though written down, the texts attached (by anonymous authors) to these figures were styled in the voice of the statue, as if they were a script. These mouthed or ventriloquised utterances, hung on the statues, who acted as the mouthpieces for what could not otherwise be said, have come to be known as 'Pasquinades'.[4] The speaking sculptures performed their role, and continue to do so; mute but eloquent, anonymous but highly personal.

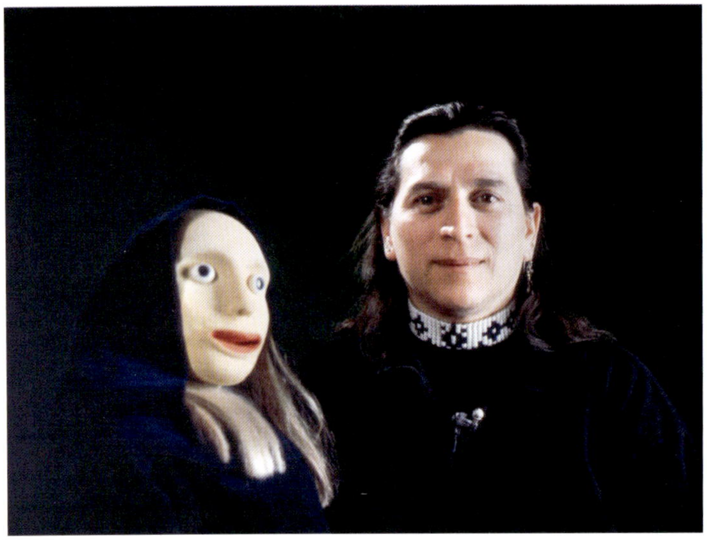

Asta Gröting, *The Inner Voice/You're good* 1999 with Buddy Big Mountain (Los Angeles), digital video, 3.58 min

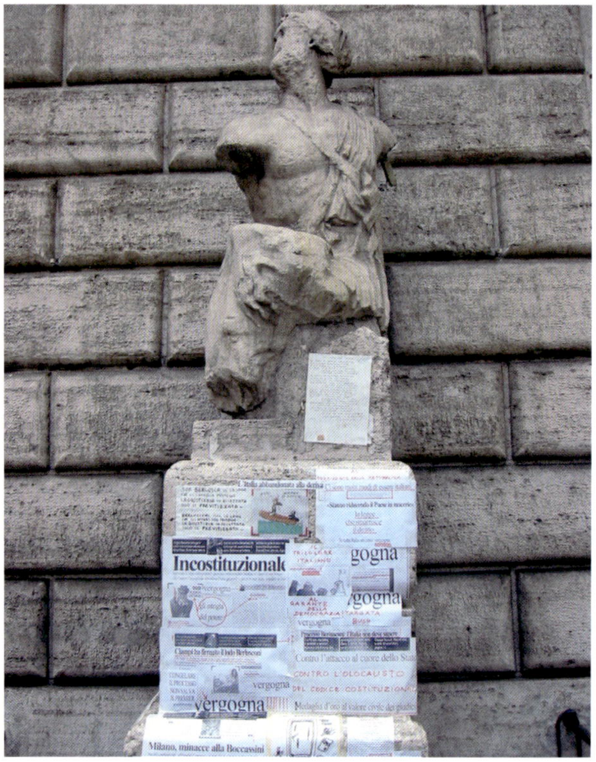

Pasquino, near the Piazza Navona, Rome

Artists have, in recent years, looked to the myths linked to figurative statuary – both its form and subjects – to draw upon deep reserves of associative meaning. This may be done by allusion to named figures who represent foundational myths,[5] or simply, formally, by creating illusory animation out of inanimate materials. Figurative works like those of Tony Oursler can still occupy that in-between space that we know they must have in common with statues of religious and cult figures; they can move in and out of life – animated with sound and moving image, and then suddenly inert. They cast a spell – believable and, then, unbelievable; suddenly just a bundle of sticks and rags again. They perform, and they stop performing; they work, and then they don't. The contrast between these two states is often quite extreme. When the figure is not performing it rapidly falls from grace, becoming base material. In between these two states, one might suggest, is the place occupied by sculpture proper, a condition which is not dependent on performance as such, and which is not so inconstant.

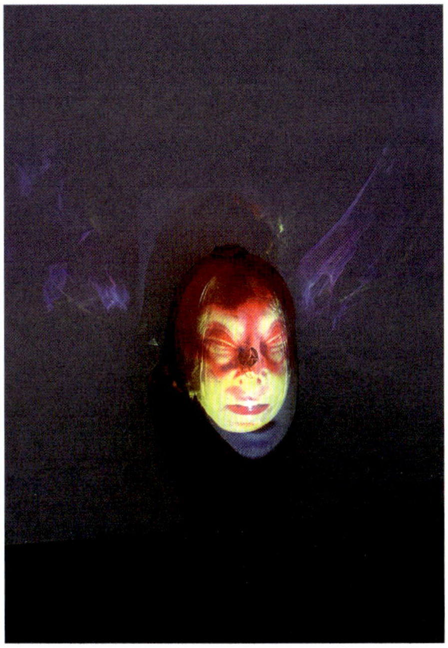

Tony Oursler, *Drift* 2001, glass resin, metal, video projection, 76.2 × 40.6 × 25.4

So what does this mean for a consideration of Calder? What does the category of 'performing sculpture' bring to an understanding of his work? Is it a part of a larger story, or is this a story which is particular to him, a story which 'performs sculpture' for us? If some of his work – notably the *Cirque Calder* 1926–31 and his theatrical design – does indeed come alive and then fall inert, most of his work has much less clearly defined beginnings and ends. His mobiles, and 'stabiles', will move, when certain conditions obtain, but their performances are unfixed in duration, and indeed, marginal to their presence. These works exist in any case, whatever the conditions. However, with their roots in the Big Top, in clockwork, celluloid and curtain calls, there is surely something more to Calder's 'performing sculpture'. If we understand this term as an action, as describing a quality – 'performing' – rather than any one sculpture, then we start to effect the shift in perception necessary to understanding this. Rather than focusing on figures and forms, we might take Calder's jump from figurative to abstract – from sculpture depicting performers, to sculpture that performs – as a jump that carried him, and us, into a new sculptural space. He leaves the figure behind, and he also leaves behind the momentary illusion. Calder will find a way of making the spell last, embedding the unpredictable, contradictory (and often syncopated) movements of animals and people into his works.

How does 'sculpture' happen? It happens when we see it, when it is not subservient to painting, when it does not require a timetable. Sculpture happens when we take notice; when it is not merely decorative, but when it fixes us, and when we, engaged by its own self-absorption, take the time to get to know it. We walk around it, or under it, claimed by its sequential and differing views, aware of its changeability, but also of its centre. Unlike many of his peers, Calder's multi-part works nonetheless become increasingly unified across his career.[6] He effects a shift that is the more dramatic because of the simplicity of his components and the fact that they move and shift in unpredictable and unprescribed ways.

Using very reduced means – the simple flat forms deployed by many of his painter colleagues, unmodulated colours, matt finishes – Calder nonetheless finds the assurance to assert that here we have sculpture.[7] This is done partly through continuity of expression (this is not a one-off or exceptional occurrence) and partly through simplicity, which makes repetition, or repeatability, both possible and necessary. Calder creates a form language that is about itself, and reads itself. It is not about subjects or stories, or even really about place.[8] This is a language that is consistent, coherent and autonomous. (It is also, one might say, consensual. Far from its more radical or marginalised roots, this type of performance occupies civic space in a largely uncontentious manner.)

Thus, I suggest, that even if Calder's career is easily premised upon a modern understanding of performance (something dressed, staged, put on), and even if he was contemporary with artists like Alexander Archipenko, Fernand Léger, and Oskar Schlemmer – who were exploring the movement of colour, very often in performance – Calder's distinction was, in fact, in allowing his sculpture to perform by itself.[9] It is not time-limited, it does not shout, or even narrate. Its presence is animate but softly modulated, speaking a language that no one shares, but which we sense. It is a kind of perpetual activity, which lies at the periphery of our sight, the boundaries of our senses, neither declamatory nor abstaining, but communicable, communicating and within human grasp. His sculptures do not depend on performance, but they do perform as sculpture. Even when we cannot see them move as much as they might, these works are, of course, full of potential movement – some pieces are even set up to tantalise and frustrate, suggesting results (such as the sound of a gong or a clash of parts) that never actually materialise.

There is no elaborate *vraisemblance* in such works, no pretence at reality. There is no known story, mythological or simply emotional. Without such platforms, Calder nonetheless makes us believe that sets of coloured elements are sculpture, and behave like sculpture. His works perform in the sense that they accomplish and bring to pass. They pull us towards them, round them and into them. In this they are uncannily like such famously compelling works as Gianlorenzo Bernini's *Apollo and Daphne* 1622–5 or Auguste Rodin's *The Kiss* 1899, and it is in this arena, and on these terms, that Calder's works become sculpture. They absorb into themselves the movement and the passage of time that eighteenth-century art historian G.E. Lessing had famously sought when examining the sculpture *Laocoön and His Sons* (first century AD). If the story of Laocoön's dreadful predicament is connoted in its entirety by this sculpture, with Calder we experience progression without narrative.[10] There is no metamorphosis other than that wrought by the artist, who has made a sculpture that works, and the embrace of one part by another is held in a continuous play that will always exclude us, just as it includes us.

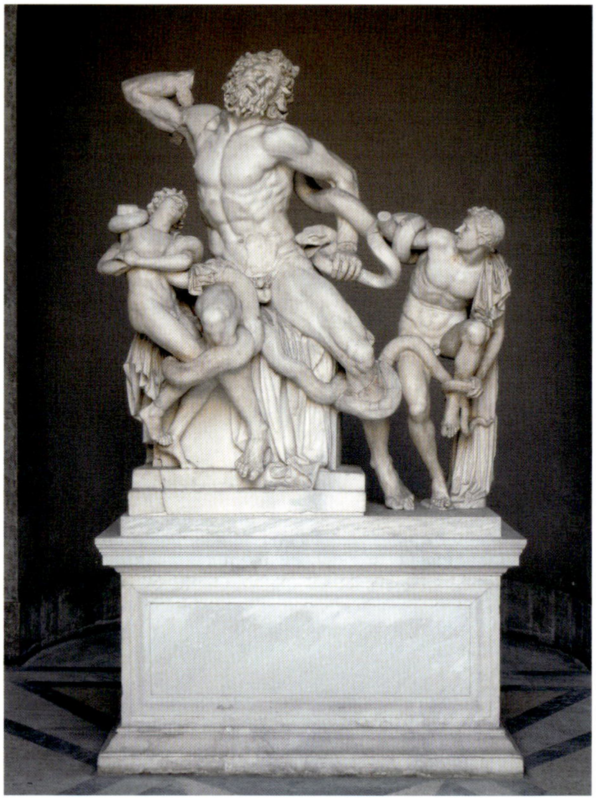

Laocoön and His Sons, Museo Pio-Clementino, Vatican City

Notes

1 The practice of carrying royal effigies in funeral processions lasted from the fourteenth century until 1625, but the making of effigies – often by female craftworkers, skilled at working with wax and cloth – continued into the early nineteenth century, as a way for the Abbey to increase its tourist trade.

2 To a degree, the same can be said of Calder's performances, which depended on his activation of the sculptures, and which lasted for a finite amount of time.

3 The stump of a torso known as 'Pasquino' was excavated in 1501 and set up near the Piazza Navona, where in an annual festival it was dressed up and saluted with Latin verses, which became increasingly satirical.

4 The sculptures were sufficiently well-known to be used as mouthpieces in print, and abroad, as in the 1748 anonymous pamphlet 'Pasquin and Marforio on the Peace: being a discussion, by these celebrated statues at Rome, of the general conduct of England but particularly pending the late war, and in negociating [sic] the present peace', trans. from Italian, London, 1748.

5 As, for example, with the figure of the Golem, as deployed by Canadian artist Jana Sterbak.

6 One can trace his passage from the multi-part, 'gameboard'-type of sculpture used also by Jean Arp, Alberto Giacometti, Barbara Hepworth and Henry Moore, and on to the use of an aerial centre.

7 These 'simple' means are not entirely simple, and photographs do not fully convey the double-sided forms, with different (often complementary) colours on each side, or the unpainted, shiny elements of his works. The shapes and colours that Calder chose for his sculptural components are often close to those used by his painter-friends: notably Jean Hélion and Joan Miró, but perhaps also George L.K. Morris and Hans Erni.

8 A few works do have titles (e.g. *Spring*, *Romulus and Remus* and *Hercules and Lion*, all 1928) that might suggest allegorical subjects, but the sculptures are still primarily about delineation, movement and scale, and seem in many ways to allude to the circus as much as to the ancient world.

9 In this it might be usefully compared to the work of Arp, Lucio Fontana and Fausto Melotti. It is increasingly clear to me the way in which his sculpture was designed to be performed by the artist and by private clients, who could set the works shivering, shaking and trembling, and in conditions where light and breeze might set up reflections and shadows that all too often are absent in the museum.

10 See Calder's own *Laocoön* 1947 for a demonstration of this point. See also the exhibition catalogue *Towards a New Laocoön* (ed. by Penelope Curtis and Stephen Feeke, Henry Moore Institute, Leeds 2007), which paraphrased the title of Clement Greenberg's article (Partisan Review, no.7, July–August 1940, pp.296–310) to group modern British sculpture on the same theme.

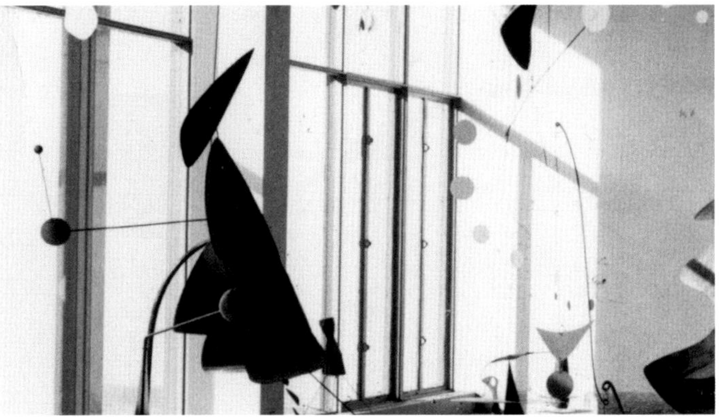

Composing Motions: Staging Calder's 'Performing Sculpture'

Ann Coxon

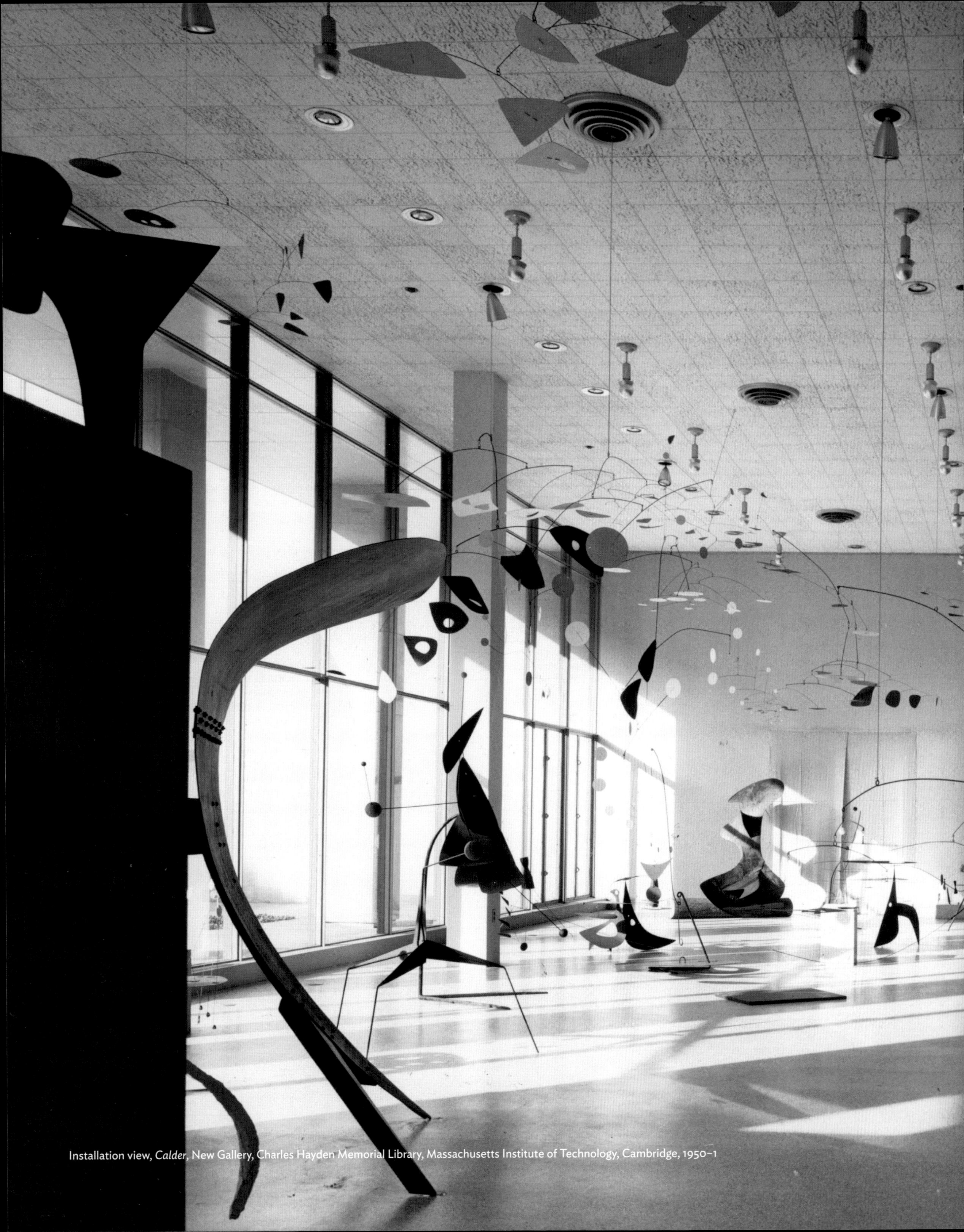

Installation view, *Calder*, New Gallery, Charles Hayden Memorial Library, Massachusetts Institute of Technology, Cambridge, 1950–1

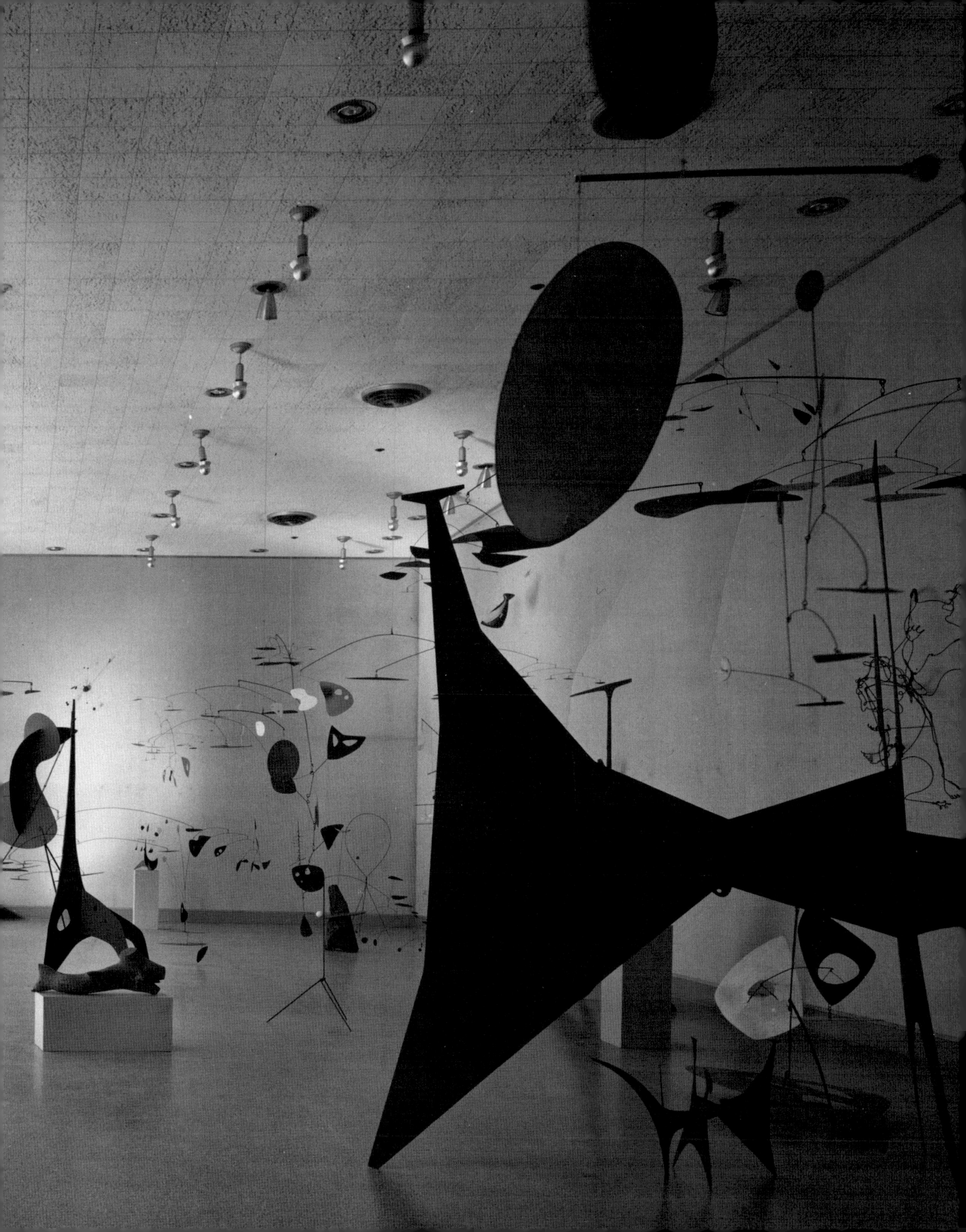

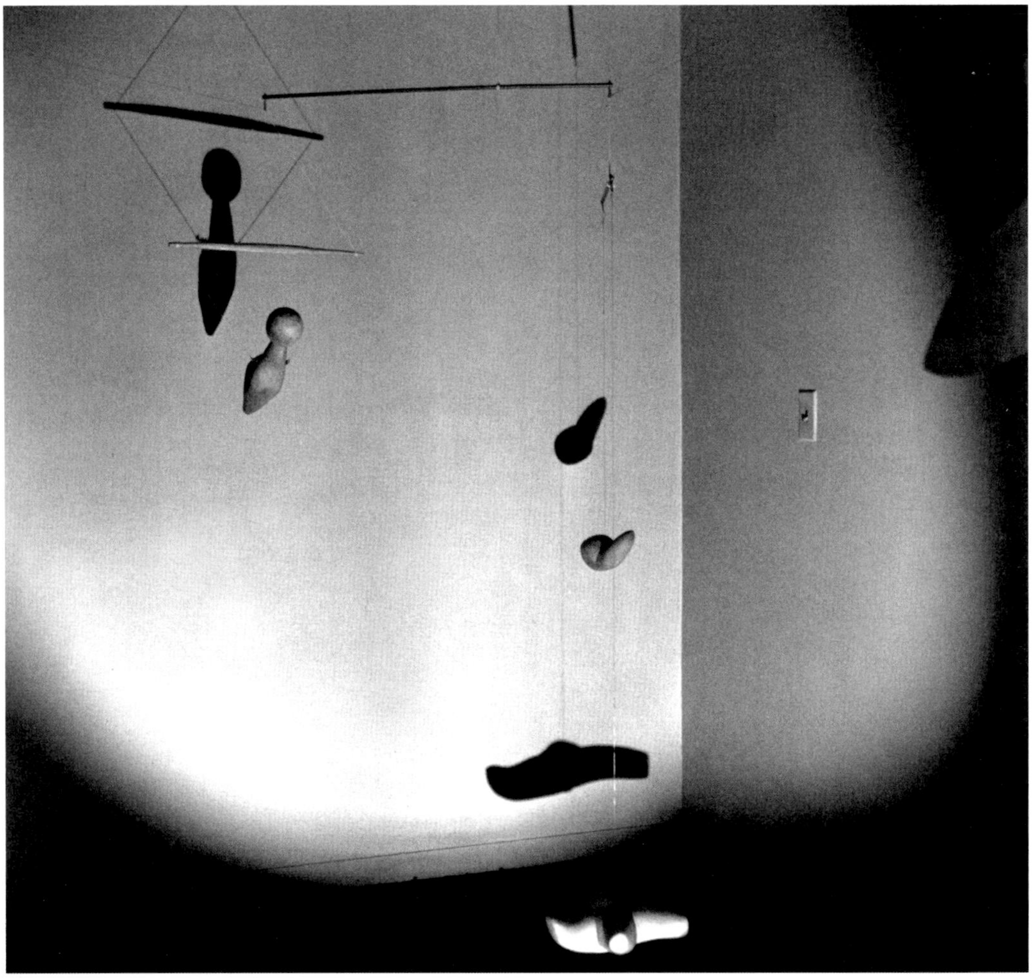

Starfish 1934 (installation view, *Calder: Stabiles & Mobiles*, Pierre Matisse Gallery, New York, 1937), wood, rod, string and wire, 221 × 144.8 × 144.8

> *... why not plastic forms in motion? Not a simple translatory or rotary motion but several motions of different types, speeds and amplitudes composing to make a resultant whole. Just as one can compose colors, [sic] or forms, so one can compose motions.* [1]

In 1936, the Swiss émigré, designer and photographer Herbert Matter arrived in New York. He developed a friendship with Alexander Calder, who invited him into the storefront studio he occupied, near his apartment on East 86th Street. By this time, Calder had become known in transatlantic art circles for his pioneering sculptures, embracing both movement and abstraction. Matter's response to these works is documented by the extraordinary body of photographs he created in Calder's studios as the sculptor prepared for his exhibitions at the Pierre Matisse Gallery in the late 1930s, and in his pictures of the resulting exhibition installations. In a similar manner to the photographs of Picasso's studio created by Brassaï in the 1930s and '40s, Matter and Calder's images play with the use of dramatic lighting effects, heightening the Surrealist atmosphere.

A photograph from the Pierre Matisse Gallery in 1937 shows *Starfish* 1934 – a hanging piece with three simple, carved wooden elements – set into the corner of the room and lit by a strong directional spotlight, causing the three elements to cast dark shadows against the wall. The starfish-shaped carving, which hangs low to the ground and is allowed to spin, is balanced by an anthropomorphic figure with a simple head and tail, hanging, at a much higher level, from a trapeze-like crossbar. The figure recalls the acrobats that so enthralled Calder on his visits to the circus in the mid-1920s and which inspired his famous *Cirque Calder* 1926–31. As with other photographs

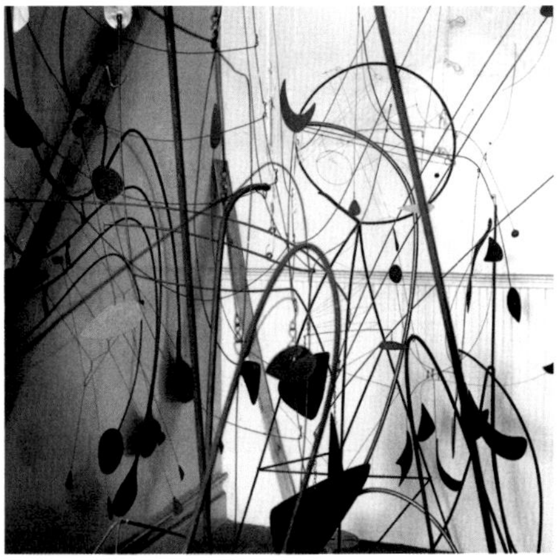

Storefront studio, New York, 1940. Works shown: *Fish Bones* 1939; *The Spider* 1940; *Sphere Pierced by Cylinders* 1939; and *The Hairpins* 1939

that Matter made of Calder's works – sculptures such as *Tightrope* 1936 or *The Brass Family* 1929, which make more direct reference to the circus – the image of *Starfish* captures the drama and tension of the performance, which Calder was able to distil and translate into sculptural form. As the artist stated:

> *There's another thing I like. That's the spotlight that concentrates on a certain area of the circus... There was a performer, Lillian Leitzel; she would come out with the light all on her, and then she did a hundred flops hanging by her wrist from a wire. There was a tall man who stood by her and held her red cape. What I loved was the spotlight on her and the rest in obscurity... I've always been delighted by the way things are hooked together... It's just like a diagram of force. I love the mechanics of the thing – and the vast space – and the spotlight.* [2]

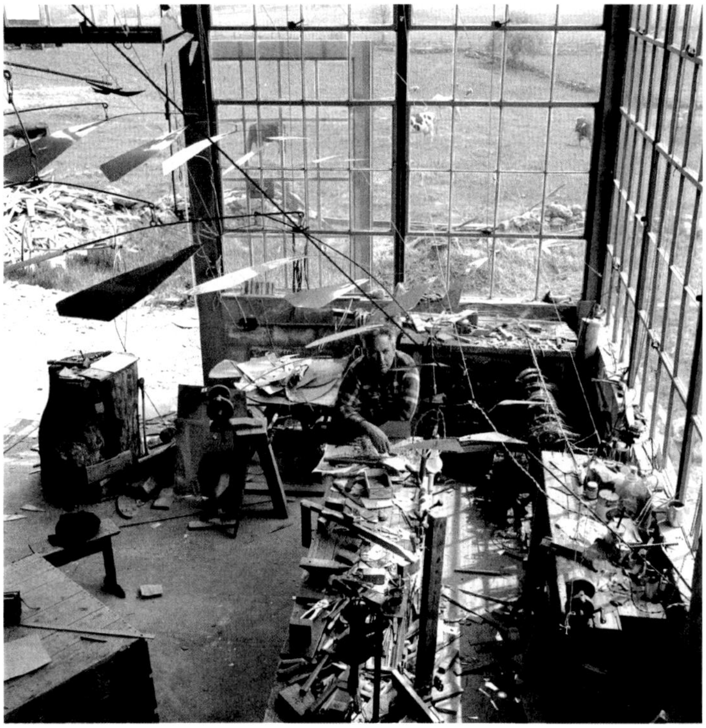

Calder in his Roxbury studio, Connecticut, with the mobile commissioned for the ballroom of Hotel Ávila in Caracas, Venezuela, 1941

In other photographs, Matter's lens focuses on corners of Calder's studio in which works are stored together, creating a tangle of wires that only those very familiar with his body of work could separate out into component parts and pieces. At his large studio in Roxbury, Connecticut, Calder created a pulley system, making use of the cavernous space and full-height windows to hoist his larger mobiles up above the workshop floor. There was a very practical character to this system, with Calder able to lower particular mobiles as and when he needed them, despite the apparent clutter. Looking down, from the vantage point of the mobiles, Matter's photographs of the Roxbury studio capture the tangle of wires and the creative chaos below, as well as the view out through the windows to the rural landscape beyond.

A drawing from 1925 shows Calder's early interest in the system of cables, anchors and guy ropes, visible in the gloom above the spotlights, at the circus tents he visited as a young artist. Combined with his training in engineering, this interest in the mechanics of the circus – the literal staging of the spectacle – clearly influenced the construction of Calder's mobiles and other complex, balanced pieces, but it may also have played a part in the way the artist saw the relationships between his works as they were placed in the spaces of the gallery and studio, and in other contexts.

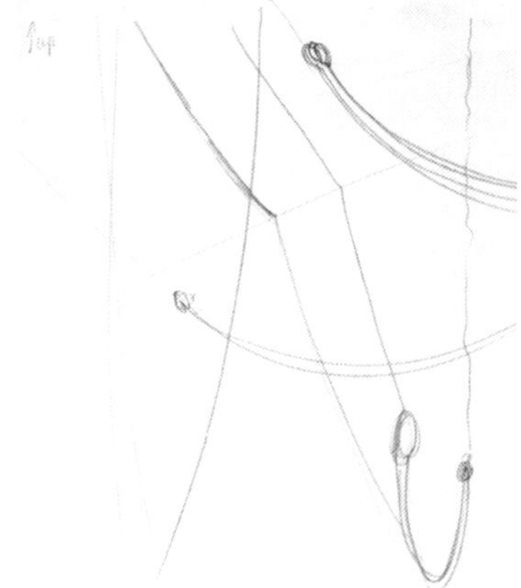

Untitled (Rigging) 1925, pencil on paper, 27.8 × 21.1, Calder Foundation, New York

In 1934, Calder wrote to art collector Albert E. Gallatin, describing himself as an 'illuminating engineer'.[3] The dramatic spotlighting captured in Matter's studio photographs was also employed in Calder's 1937 exhibition at The Mayor Gallery in London. Calder described this in retrospect: 'We darkened the room ... and used a spotlight for dramatic effect. The light cast shadows on the wall, and for the first time I became aware of their value.'[4] In 1943, dramatic lighting was again employed in the presentation of Calder's work, when Matter was invited to act as consultant on the installation of Calder's retrospective (curated by James Johnson Sweeney, in collaboration with Marcel Duchamp) at the Museum of Modern Art (MoMA), New York. Photographs documenting the exhibition show works spotlit, so that they throw shadows onto the walls. Dark painted walls and sections of wall form backdrops for groups of lighter-coloured or delicate mobiles and floor-based pieces. Making use of the capacity for *mise en scène* within the enclosed exhibition space, the installation emphasised the theatricality of the sculptures, presenting them as performers moving in real time before a collective audience.

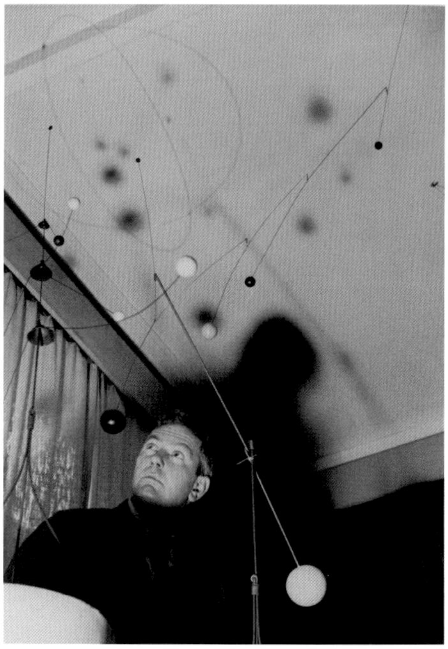

Calder at the installation of *Calder: Mobiles and Stabiles*, The Mayor Gallery, London, 1937

A later exhibition (1950–1) at the Massachusetts Institute of Technology (MIT), Cambridge, presented a densely spaced selection of Calder's mobiles and floor-based works in a large, open gallery with floor-to-ceiling windows letting in natural light – an approach that stands in contrast to the carefully constructed backdrops and dramatic spotlighting at MoMA. Installation photographs looking down the length of the gallery show how difficult it is for the eye to separate the wires and component parts of each individual sculpture when they are shown together in this way. The photographs also show a large portion of the gallery ceiling with its lights and vents, to which the eye would be drawn when looking up at mobiles overhead.

In the exhibition catalogue for the 1943 MoMA retrospective – *Alexander Calder: Sculptures and Constructions* – which included graphic design and photographs by Matter, one page shows a set of six 'spirit photographs'. These are studies of a mobile (*Untitled* 1936), lit up against a dark background and then set into motion so that each picture – created at a slow shutter speed and using stroboscopic lighting – records the arcs, spirals and wobbles described by the sculpture's eight branches and discs. Matter's photographs from 1936 to 1950, published together in book form in 2013, seem to articulate for later generations of curators and scholars the problems of presenting Calder's works from this period:[5] how to show the range of motion inherent in the mobiles and mechanical pieces when the means to do so directly may not always be available (due to their fragility or the need to protect works shown in an exhibition context)? Whether to make use of the drama and shadow-play that fascinated Matter and which he exaggerated through his use of photographic lighting equipment. Equally, how to do justice to the flat planes, simple shapes and bold colours that so clearly link Calder's work to a particular history of abstract modernist art? How to tease apart the mess of wires that were prevalent in Calder's working spaces – how to enable the viewer to see these delicately balanced works against their various settings and backgrounds (and in relation to each other), yet isolate and offset the unique elements of an individual piece? Matter's photographs and designs have set some precedents, in terms of the way we view and display Calder's sculptures, that curators have been grappling with ever since.

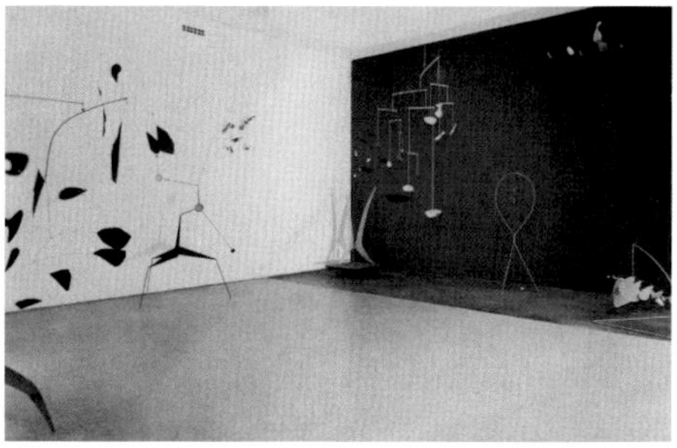

Installation view, *Alexander Calder: Sculptures and Constructions*, The Museum of Modern Art, New York, 1943–4

Matter designed the exhibition catalogue for Calder's 1964 retrospective at the Solomon R. Guggenheim Museum, New York. Installation shots from that exhibition show the large-scale mobile (*The Ghost* 1964) hanging in the central gallery space created by the museum's famous spiralling ramp. An unusual set of photographs taken during this exhibition by photographer Larry Fink show a group of children exploring and interacting with certain sculptures. The children can be seen blowing on the mobiles to prompt them to rotate, or peering through and around sculptures – kneeling and crouching and pressing their bodies against them. Similarly, pictures from the Stedelijk Museum, Amsterdam, in 1959 – when the exhibition *Alexander Calder, Stabilen, Mobilen* was held – show groups of people reaching up to gently touch a mobile. These photographs remind us that many of Calder's sculptures – from the wire works onwards – were originally intended to be set in motion by the air currents created by passers-by or even by the viewer's gentle touch. In 1943, Calder wrote:

> *A mobile in motion leaves an invisible wake behind it, or rather, each element leaves an individual wake behind its individual self. Sometimes these wakes are contracted within each other, and sometimes they are deployed ... In their handling, ie. setting them in motion by a touch of the hand, consideration should be had for the direction in which the object is designed to move, and for the inertia of the mass involved ... A slow gentle impulse, as though one were moving a barge is almost infallible. In any case, gentle is the word.* [6]

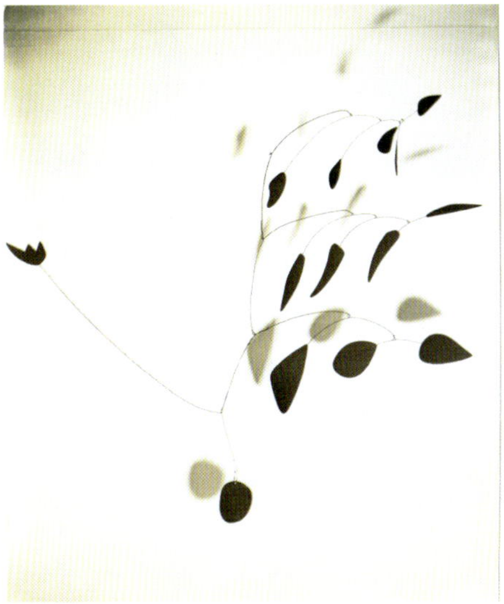

Black Flower 1940, sheet metal, wire and paint, approx. 167.6 × 152.4

Fink's photographs of the exhibition at the Guggenheim were taken just three years before the art critic Michael Fried wrote his seminal essay 'Art and Objecthood', attacking what he saw as a move towards theatricality in art. As he wrote: 'The concepts of quality and value – and to the extent that these are central to art, the concept of art itself – are meaningful, or wholly meaningful, only within the individual arts. What lies between is theatre.'[7]

Fried's essay was prompted by the minimalist sculptors' turn towards a phenomenological encounter with sculpture, which invites the viewer to consider his or her relation to the work, the surrounding space, and the movement and placement of his or her own body. With hindsight, his argument reads as a last-ditch attempt to adhere to high modernist principles and to deny an overwhelming shift in art, throughout the twentieth century, towards temporality, theatricality and interaction with the viewer. Considering Fried's position, Rosalind Krauss discussed the theatricality of mechanical, light-based or mobile pieces from the first half of the twentieth century in her book *Passages in Modern Sculpture* (first published in 1977), in the chapter titled 'Mechanical Ballets: light, motion, theater'. While, for the minimalist sculptors of the late 1960s (to whom Fried was responding), theatricality implicates the viewer, asking him or her to take an increasingly active position, Krauss describes a different relationship between the sculpture and viewer – as played out through works such as László Moholy-Nagy's *Lichtrequisit einer elektrischen Bühne* (Light Prop for an Electric Stage) 1923–30 – in which the sculpture itself is the active element in the 'drama':

> *In the event that the work did not attempt to transform the whole of its ambient space into a theatrical or dramatic context, it would often internalize a sense of theatricality – by projecting, as its* raison d'etre, *a sense of itself as an actor, as an agent of movement. In this sense, the entire range of kinetic sculpture can be seen as tied to the concept of theatricality.* [8]

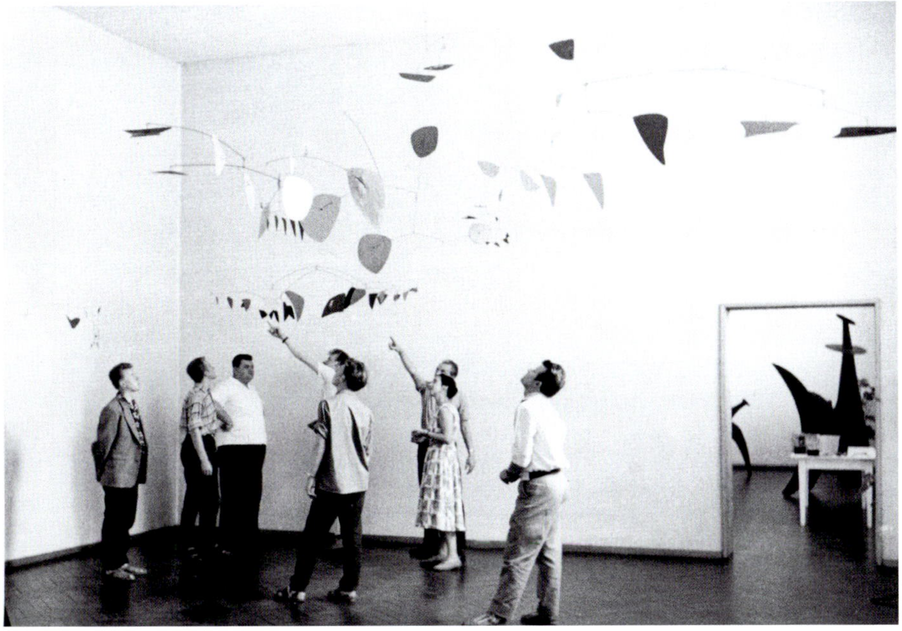

Installation view, *Alexander Calder, Stabilen, Mobilen*, Stedelijk Museum, Amsterdam, 1959

And later, using Calder's mobiles as a key example:

> *In that it is a description of aspects of the body, in that its motion is intermittent rather than mechanically continuous, in that one feels impelled to set it in motion in order for it to 'perform' the role of filling out and inhabiting its own spatiality, the mobile locates its sculptural meaning as a kind of actor.* [9]

In describing the mobiles as 'a kind of actor' (or, by extension, a kind of dancer), Krauss echoes Calder's own description of his works as a form of mechanical ballet of parts (he even referred to specific works as 'ballet objects'[10]), and her point has been taken up by those writing on Calder's works more recently, who have revisited his lifelong desire to stage a drama, or ballet, of moving, sculptural, plastic elements, which culminated in the production of *Work in Progress* in 1968 (see Oikonomopoulos, pp.76–87). If Calder's mobiles and mechanical sculptures locate their meaning as actors (or dancers), the importance of 'staging' them or articulating them in relation to one another within the exhibition context therefore becomes all the more pertinent. In his lifetime, Calder collaborated with others on the design of his exhibitions and on several theatrical productions – composing motions and expanding the definition and context in which sculpture may be seen and encountered. The challenge for curators of Calder exhibitions is to present his 'performing sculptures' in such a way as to explore his interest in movement and theatricality, while protecting the often-fragile works.

Many, and varied, attempts have been made in recent exhibitions to revisit Calder's sculpture in terms of its theatricality. Exhibition designs have employed specially constructed architectural features to frame and isolate the sculptures; or have employed dramatic lighting, or mirrored plinths, to heighten a sense of drama. Many of Calder's sculptures, particularly the mobiles, seem to ask of the viewer that he or she slows down in order to fully appreciate the range of motion. Calder's works do benefit from being seen both in isolation and in interesting juxtapositions, just as the elements within them describe a range of shifting motions within complex compositions. The question is always how to isolate each work, or each part, yet see them in relation to each other and their context: how to simulate the 'spotlight' that highlights certain 'acts' and throws others into temporary darkness.

As much as he spoke of gentleness, Calder loved the drama and chaos of the circus – simultaneous acts, overhead wires, shifting spotlights, the staging of the spectacle. He created a body of work that describes its virtual volume by moving through the viewing space; he took sculpture off the pedestal and presented his works as actors in a 'theatre in the round', where there is no fixed viewpoint and no frontal presentation. The circus may also turn out to be the most useful metaphor yet for thinking about exhibiting Calder – understanding the exhibition space as an expanded stage, with some actions occurring overhead and others within the floor-space. The exhibition needs to strike a careful balance between moments of drama and those of contemplation, to focus the spotlights (both literal and metaphorical), to compose the motions, and to choreograph the production in ways that do justice to Calder's extraordinary body of work.

Notes

1 Alexander Calder, artist statement, in *Modern Painting and Sculpture: Alexander Calder, George L.K. Morris, Calvert Coggeshall, Alma de Gersdorff Morgan*, exh. cat., Berkshire Museum, Pittsfield, MA 1933.

2 Cleve Gray, 'Calder's Circus', *Art in America*, vol.52, no.5, October 1964, p.25.

3 Alexander Calder, letter to Albert E. Gallatin, 4 November 1934, Calder Foundation archives.

4 Dorothy Grafly, 'Alexander Calder: Creator of Moving Forms in Space', *American Artist*, vol.15, no.8, October 1951, p.39.

5 Alexander S.C. Rower (ed.), *Calder by Matter*, Paris 2013.

6 Alexander Calder, 'A Propos of Measuring a Mobile', 1943, Archives of American Art, Smithsonian Institution, http://www.calder.org/life/system/downloads/1943-A-Propos.pdf.

7 Michael Fried, 'Art and Objecthood', *Artforum*, vol.5, no.10, Summer 1967, pp.12–23.

8 Rosalind E. Krauss, 'Mechanical Ballets: light, motion, theater' in Rosalind E. Krauss, *Passages in Modern Sculpture*, New York 1977, p.204.

9 Ibid., p.216.

10 Calder writes about the 'ballet object' in, for example, 'Mobiles', in Myfanwy Evans (ed.), *The Painter's Object*, London 1937, pp.62–7. S ee http://www.calder.org/life/system/downloads/texts/1937-Mobiles-P0301.pdf.

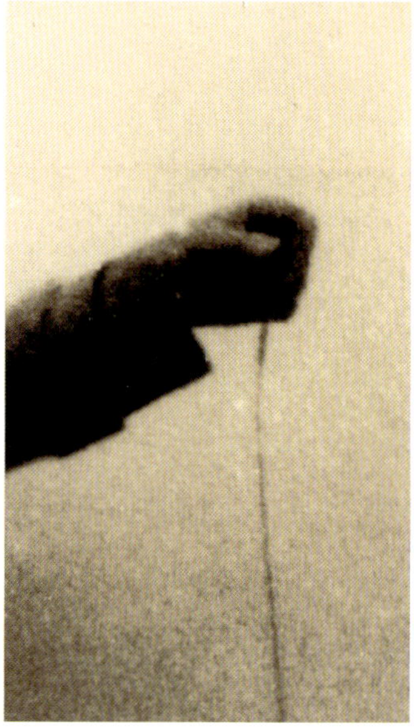

Calder's Carnival

Alex J. Taylor

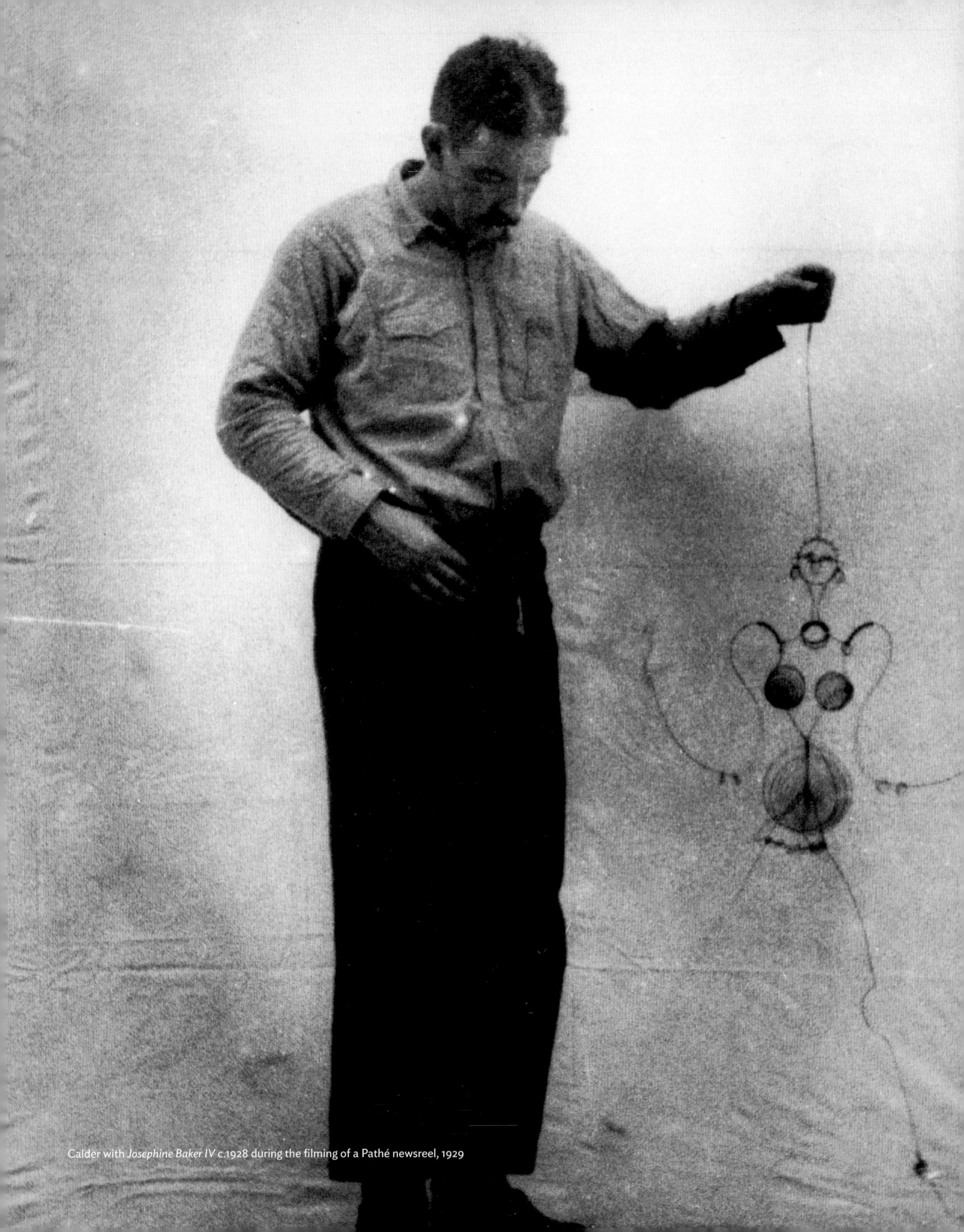

Calder with *Josephine Baker IV* c.1928 during the filming of a Pathé newsreel, 1929

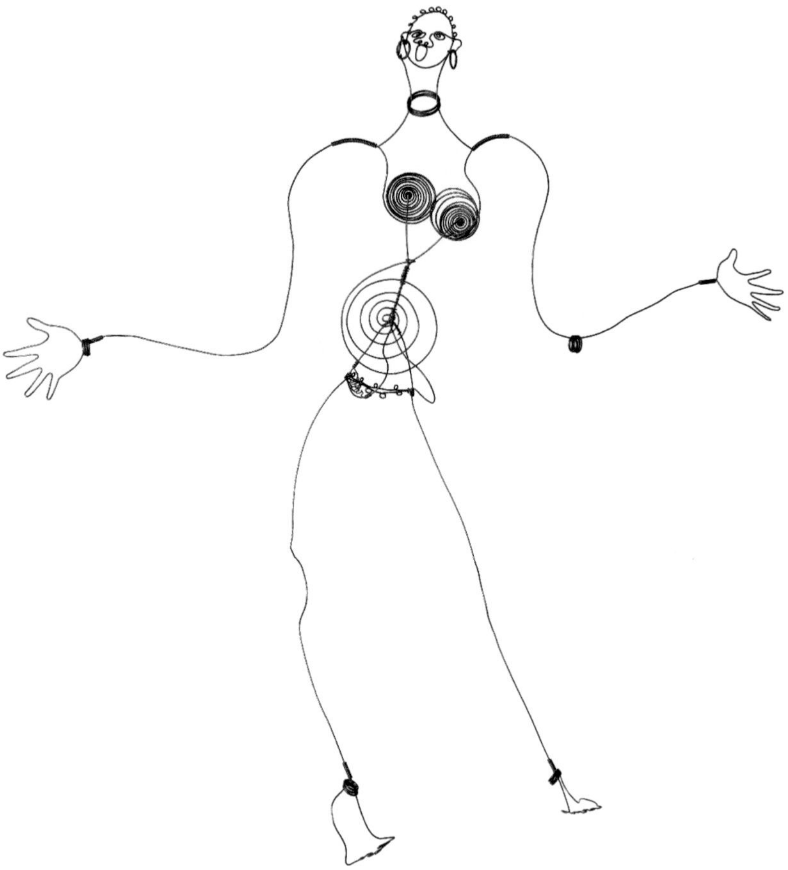

Josephine Baker IV c.1928, wire, 100.5 × 84 × 21, Centre Pompidou, Paris – Musée national d'art moderne – Centre de création industrielle

What are we to make of the densely coiled spirals that decorate Calder's sculptures of African-American dancer Josephine Baker? Calder frequently used the spiral shape in the jewellery he made, and it was once even suggested that he patent the form, but they hardly read here as mere decorative flourishes in the art deco mode.[1] Nor does it seem right to regard the swirls as a stand-in for Baker's costume, even if they do serve to locate the breasts that his subject had so scandalously exposed on the Parisian stage. Given Calder's often-prurient attention to such anatomical details in other wire figures, with their dangling genitals and pinched nipples, Baker's dense wire bustier appears to mask more than it reveals. In this sense, the spiral forms represent an uncharacteristically reserved gesture from a sculptor who, as we shall see, could happily embrace the lewd and the salacious.

There is certainly no such concealment in Calder's *La Négresse* 1929, a figure whose drooping breasts and large buttocks veer uncomfortably close to the tropes associated with sideshow displays such as the 'Hottentot Venus'. The curlicues on Baker's torso, like the oversized earrings and bangles in this sculpture, may hold primitivist significance: the artist thought that 'wire lends itself very well to barbaric ornamentation', and later told art critic Giovanni Carandente that the spiral was the first decorative gesture of primitive cultures.[2] In *Aztec Josephine Baker* 1930, Calder seems especially attentive to the crude stereotypes on which Baker's own freewheeling cultural eclecticism relied; but even in this, the most exoticised of Calder's renditions of Baker, the chief function of the spiral is, I think, to stand as a sign for motion itself. Calder's wire figures always move, but the addition of these twirling forms amplifies the sensations conveyed by Baker's dizzying performances, intensifying the gyrating hips and rolling eyes that had turned the black dancer into a mass media sensation.

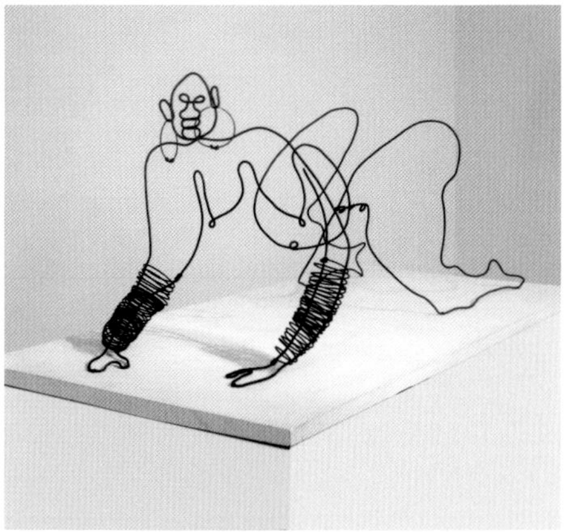

La Négresse 1929, wire, 43 × 100, private collection

The shocking motion of Baker's dance provided Calder with an image of the pace and excitement of modern life at its most unrestrained extreme. Baker's wild shows were everything the mechanical precision of the Tiller Girls dance troupes was not, blending avant-garde dance with jazz-age gymnastics and jungle-themed primitivism – an unruly mix of the erotic and the exotic that, as Sieglinde Lemke has explained, 'not only appealed to audiences across class lines but also constituted an unprecedented crossover between high and low culture'.[3] In choosing Baker as the subject for several early wire figures in Paris, Calder marked out an approach to modernist sculpture that also straddled the elite and the popular equally, willfully combining the fragmentary and abbreviated qualities of his lines with the racy sensationalism of popular entertainment.

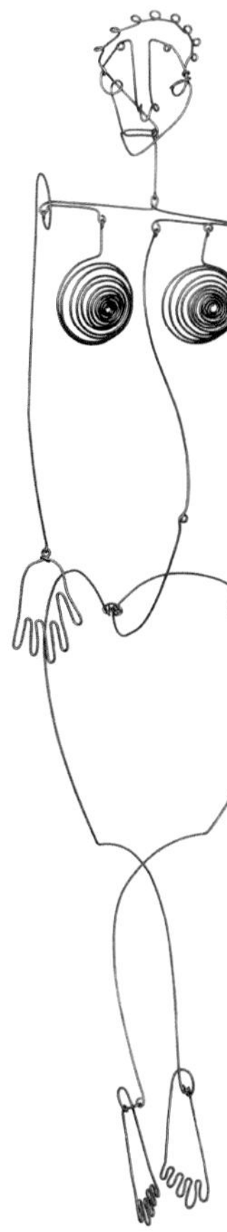

Aztec Josephine Baker 1930, wire, 134.6 × 25.4 × 22.9, Calder Foundation, New York

Long before Calder's monumental sculptures helped add colour and movement to modern urban life, it was the spectacle of the street itself to which his art was first attracted. His early paintings persistently focus on the hubbub of New York City. Studying with painters like John Sloan and George Luks in the 1920s, Calder was influenced by their efforts to capture public life in the metropolis, seeking to evoke on canvas the giant billboards and artificial lights of the city streets as seen on evening excursions.[4] In his commercial illustrations from this period, Calder's subjects included crowds at Madison Square Garden and at a New York Giants baseball game, as well as photo booths, ice cream parlours and Coca Cola stands. Calder was particularly fond of sketching on the subway and, in his 1926 book *Animal Sketching*, recommended drawing on 'public conveyances' (in the absence of a zoo), as most people already 'look like some sort of animal'.[5]

His 'lines in action', as the *National Police Gazette* (for whom he worked from 1924 to 1925) termed them, frequently recorded his experience of public spectacles. Many of the illustrations were of sporting events, but the attraction of exotic animals was most potently felt, as can be seen in his sketch of the Ringling Brothers and Barnum and Bailey circus. These were observations he would go on to miniaturise in his very own transatlantic theatrical spectacular, the sculptural performance *Cirque Calder* 1926–31. Other sketches sought to capture modern dance, experiences that no doubt informed Calder's subsequent attentiveness to the movements of Josephine Baker. Here too, Calder made the most of the erotic possibilities of his subject. In drawings of Spanish starlet Trinidad 'Trini' Ramos, for instance, Calder daringly captioned a tango move as 'rough stuff', while his impressions of an afternoon in the dancing school of Ned Wayburn depict the revealing 'whoopee' moves of the Broadway hopefuls to whom the Ziegfeld choreographer was teaching 'the modern speed of acrobatic and tap dancing'.[6] As his publisher felt the need to explain, regarding such apparently meagre sketches, Calder was 'essentially a "modern" in his work', whose style sought to capture, the 'dancing figures in a few strikingly expressive lines'.[7] That is to say, these skimpy images were modern in their technique as well as their subject, suggesting fleeting motion in their fast-and-loose style and also the heel-kicking expressive freedom of the movements represented.

The sizzle of such imagery owed something to the tabloid context for which it was made. When Calder chose to accompany one drawing of a tightrope walker with the caption 'direct by wire', he drew attention to such relationships, punning on the use of telegraph lines, which had sped up the reporting of current events, but also unwittingly anticipating the medium to which he would soon turn. Such connections remained relevant to Calder's wire figures. Announcing his innovation in 1928, under the headline 'Wonders of Our Age: Portraits by Wire!', one magazine declared that Calder's animated wire portraits had 'out-televisioned television'.[8] (John Logie Baird's first television broadcast in 1926 had, in fact, also involved a sculptural portrait of sorts: the plaster face of a ventriloquist's dummy named Stookie Bill serving as the invention's first broadcast image.) Again, when a 1928 British Pathé film showed Calder at work on a wire portrait, they declared him 'the telephone wire sculptor'.[9] Calder's use of wire tapped into the significance of the material for the media accelerations that would transform twentieth-century popular culture.

To suggest that Calder had 'out-televisioned television' was to locate the effects of his art in its synthesis of entertainment and speed. Even more than his commercial

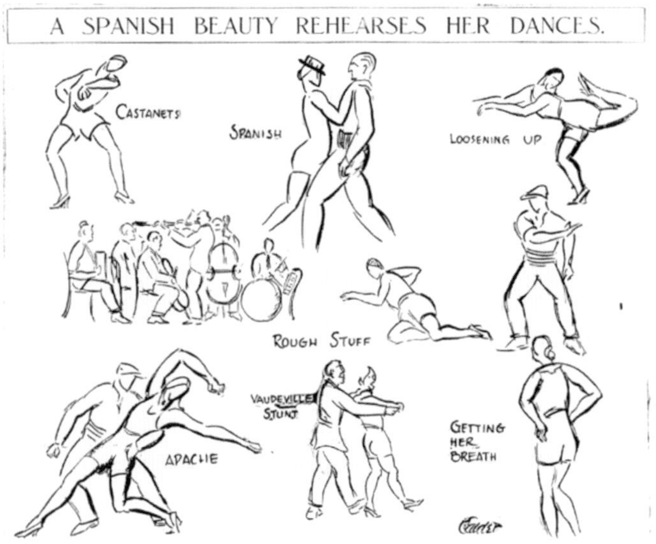

'A Spanish Beauty Rehearses Her Dances', *National Police Gazette*, 21 March 1925

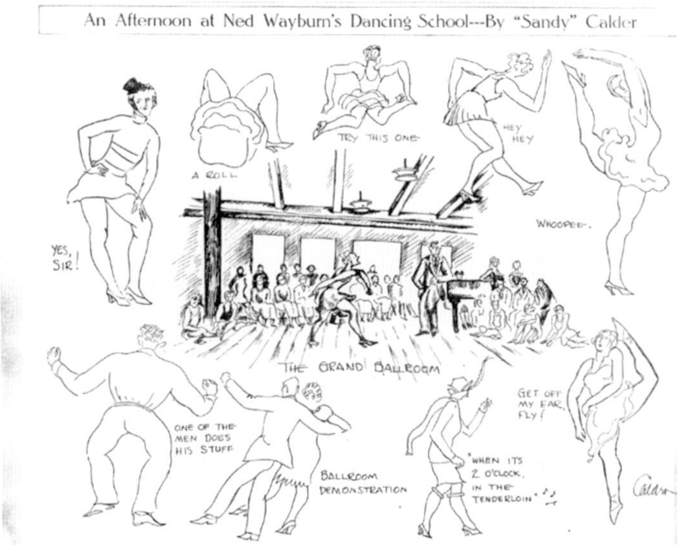

'An Afternoon at Ned Wayburn's Dancing School – By 'Sandy' Calder', *National Police Gazette*, 3 July 1926

drawings, Calder's wire figures were telegraphic both in style and in content. Calder himself understood the importance of such media networks for his success: for his 1929 show at the Galerie Neumann-Nierendorf in Berlin, his dealer apparently sent fake telegrams to publicise the show, and Calder later boasted that he had been 'bracketed on a news-service matrix with Charlie Chaplin and Yehudi Menuhin'.[10] His motley crew of public figures and stock types, as represented in his sculptures, seems to be lifted straight from the newspaper pictorial page: octogenarian industrialist and amateur golfer John D. Rockefeller – who had made the news by dancing a jig to celebrate his best round in twenty years – or the mugging comic James 'Jimmy' Durante, rendered with no less 'mad and frenzied' energy than was shown in his latest Broadway appearance.[11] Other subjects, such as Baker and Alice Prin (aka Kiki de Montparnasse, whose salacious biography, published 1929, had just been banned in America), belonged to the who's who of Parisian bohemia and, in depicting them, Calder sought to demonstrate his own proximity to the same. As Thomas Messer later observed, the wire figures represented 'a gallery of fame in our time'.[12]

If it was the ever-changing stuff of modern life that propelled Calder's early sculpture, his artistic adversary was the lifeless corpse of traditional sculpture. In *Cirque Calder*, the artist's tongue-in-cheek attitude to classical subjects is suggested by a merry-go-round of four figures made from old-fashioned clothes pegs, unveiled alongside a sign indicating that they represent 'The Four Seasons'. When one figure is removed, the scene is swiftly renamed 'The Three Graces' and, again, as 'Dawn and Dusk', when they are reduced to two. For his art world audience, the target of this joke was clear: the boring conventions of neoclassical statuary, and the seemingly endless repetition of largely identical maidens within an endless stream of predictable allegories. When Calder unveiled the show's gyrating 'hoochie-koochie' dancer, cheekily named Fanni, there could be little doubt that this was an artist who required no classical pretext to perform the erotic.

Given the kind of sculpture Calder sought to defy, it is hard not to think of the grandiose monuments made by the artist's father, Stirling. 'I should like to do a fellow on horseback', Calder mused in an interview in 1959, but 'no one thinks of me when they have to make a horse.'[13] Calder had, in fact, made several horses in wire, but this reference undoubtedly targets the stiff equestrian statuary of the past. Elsewhere, Calder would object to bronze sculptures that looked like 'mud piled up on the ground', or marble concoctions whose surfaces resembled 'shaving cream'.[14] On the cusp of his own triumph as America's leading public sculptor, Calder's remark about wanting to sculpt horses is less a lament than it is a gesture of self-definition, a declaration of his own commitment to the motion and agility of modern subjects and his opposition to the dead, solid forms and ideas of the sculptural past.

Calder's rendering of the so-called 'Ebony Venus', Josephine Baker, can, I think, be understood within this programme, ignoring the kinds of nudes ordinarily deemed suitable for sculptural representation.[15] These were tropes that Baker herself had also tackled. Once, at a party, she improvised a dance before a nude sculpture by the neoclassical sculptor Aristide Maillol, copying its pose and resting against it, apparently even talking to it, adopting 'extravagantly grandiose gestures, the picture of a priestess frolicking like a child and making fun of herself and her goddess'.[16] In Baker, Calder found a modern muse whose own mimicry of the tropes of the nude – whether primitive or, in this instance, classical – made her eminently suited to the satirical edge of his early figurative experiments.

Calder's self-positioning was not defined solely against the grand effigies of neoclassical sculpture. As curator James Johnson Sweeney saw it, Calder's efforts to deflate the pompous and self-important opposed all 'false seriousness in art', seeking to dethrone both 'the advance guard painter, as well as the academician'.[17] Much has been made of the inspiration provided by his visit to Piet Mondrian's Paris studio in 1930, but Calder's suggestion that Mondrian's carefully arranged cardboard rectangles should 'oscillate' can equally be understood as a dig at the apparent solemnity of the Dutchman's ascetic studio environment. Unsurprisingly, Mondrian 'objected' to the idea in 1930, before he made the move to America. Perhaps the sight of New York was necessary to imagine an abstraction more in tune with the tempos of the jazz age.[18]

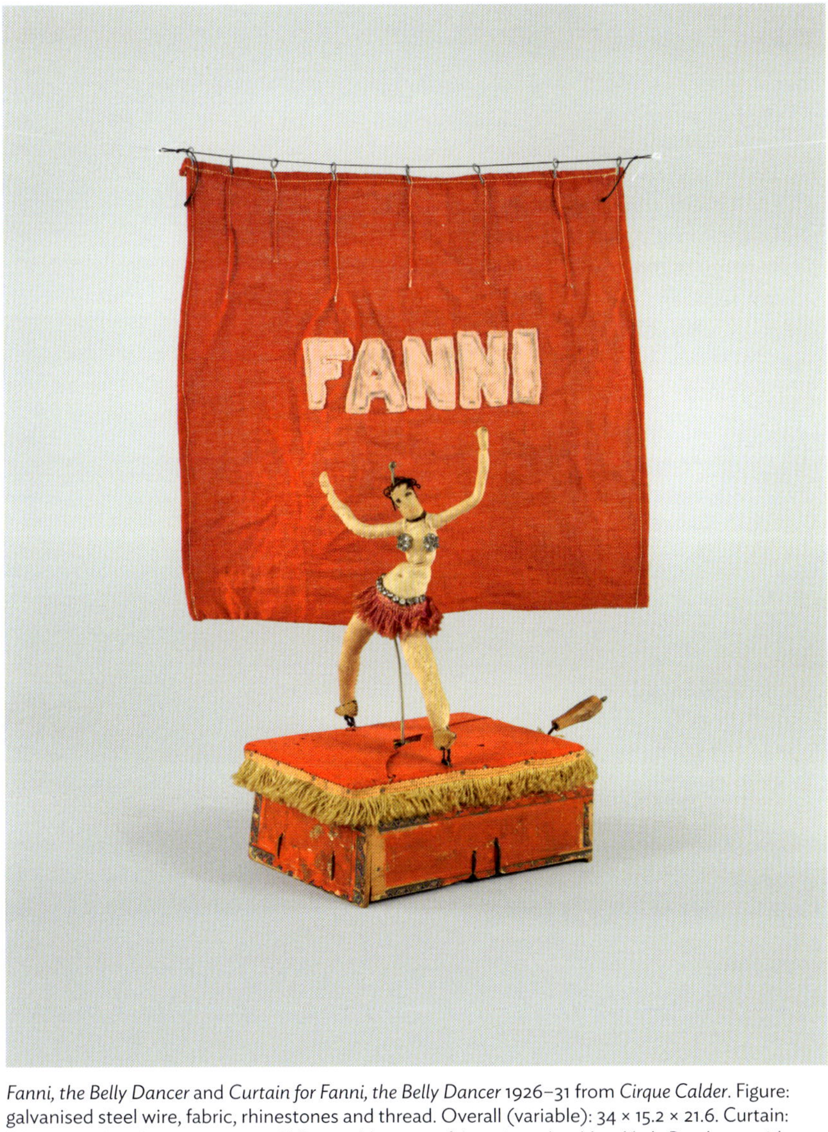

Fanni, the Belly Dancer and *Curtain for Fanni, the Belly Dancer* 1926–31 from *Cirque Calder*. Figure: galvanised steel wire, fabric, rhinestones and thread. Overall (variable): 34 × 15.2 × 21.6. Curtain: fabric, metal and string, 32.1 × 34. Whitney Museum of American Art, New York. Purchase, with funds from a public fundraising campaign in May 1982

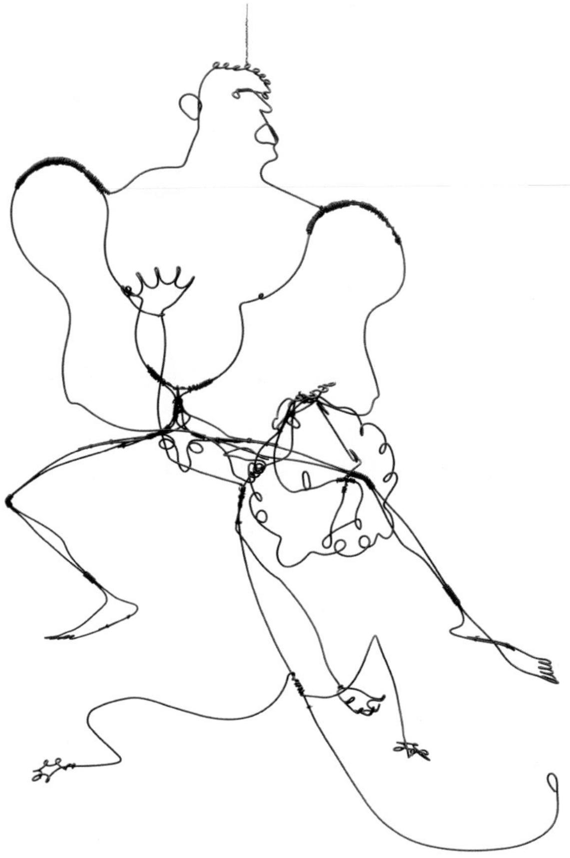

Hercules and Lion 1928, wire, 152.4 × 121.9 × 61, Calder Foundation, New York

Contemporary observers certainly understood Calder's early art to challenge artistic norms, through motion. 'He makes a mockery of the old-fashioned frozen-stone school of sculpture', wrote one critic in the *New Yorker* of Calder's wire figures.[19] In this context, motion itself serves satirical ends. Consider *Medusa* c.1930, for instance, whose surging serpentine locks appear electrically charged, yet whose presence threatens to perform her own mythical act – turning the viewer into yet more frozen statuary. In *Hercules and Lion* 1928, the puffed-up torso of the hero jiggles comically on his chicken-like legs in a strongman display that makes even the king of the jungle look limp. Or see *Spring* 1928, in which Calder's signature is rendered in wire, hung from a loop at the junction of the figure's limbs and torso – a twirling doodle that sees the artist's moniker dangle between the legs of a distinctly unclassical figure. Small timber knobs (identified by the artist as doorstops) serve as breasts or nipples; forms whose inherently pull-able form promises, in this context, a mischievously interactive erotic encounter.[20]

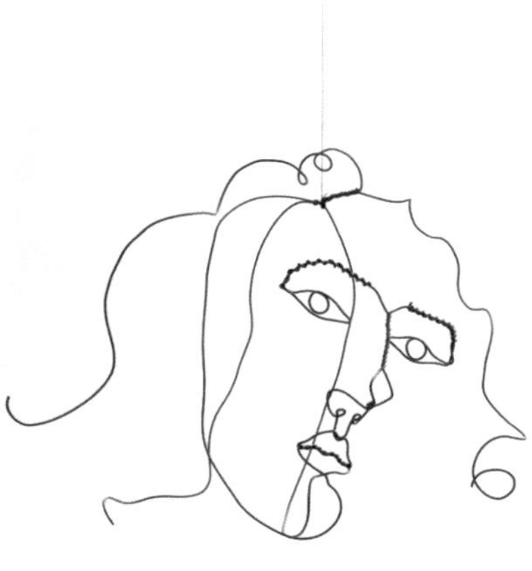

Medusa c.1930, wire, 31 × 43 × 24, Calder Foundation, New York

Calder's wire acrobats pay particular attention to the details of genitalia – features that often flail about rather more wildly than one would expect, even given the artist's depiction of high-flung feats of daring, and are often rendered with at least as much attention as faces or hands. Sometimes the distinctions between the two are comically blurred, or brought into suggestively close proximity. Such details occasionally caused problems for the artist. Calder later recalled that a dealer had 'objected to the size of the breasts of one trapezist'.[21] Such details are, I think, often deliberately subversive. This may seem like a strangely prurient point, but one should not lose sight of the risqué side of Calder's art, the side that can too often be lost amid talk of playfulness and naiveté. To regard Calder's sculpture as 'genteel' and without 'sexual edge', or to claim that it lacks 'menacing overtones of violence or sexual perversity' risks smoothing over Calder's not-infrequent embrace of the lewd, the erotic and, occasionally, the sordid.[22]

This is an artist who, after all, once made a chastity belt with the phrase *ouvert la nuit* (open at night) – a common sight on French café doors – rendered in looping wire;[23] who whipped up a knotty tie-pin for architecture critic Russell Hitchcock that formed a rebus of his surname, or, as one of his friends put it, 'one of the few dirty jokes in the history of jewellery'.[24] Even for an early commercial job, for which he painted ladies on ukuleles, Calder's women apparently 'bulged too much'.[25] The examples could be listed almost indefinitely, especially if one extended to Calder's, often hilariously punning, letters. The point is that Calder frequently revelled in the kind of naughty humour that serious adults – and modernist artists – are ordinarily meant to repress.

Especially in Calder's early drawings and wire sculptures, it is the threat that naïve play might descend into something more aberrant that provides the work with much of its potency. Russian philosopher and critic Mikhail Bakhtin explored how the anarchic humour and grotesque upheavals of the medieval carnival represented an occasion on which the imposed values of officialdom might be temporarily undermined. During carnival, rules and beliefs could be ridiculed and parodied, and, even if hierarchy was restored at its conclusion, the carnival represented 'a second world and a second life outside officialdom' that could clear the way for new ways of thinking about the social order.[26] Bakhtin dubbed the persistence of such traditions in literature the 'carnivalesque', and took the novels of French Renaissance writer François Rabelais as his exemplar, celebrating the transgressions of their comic violence, foul language and descriptions of bodily excess.

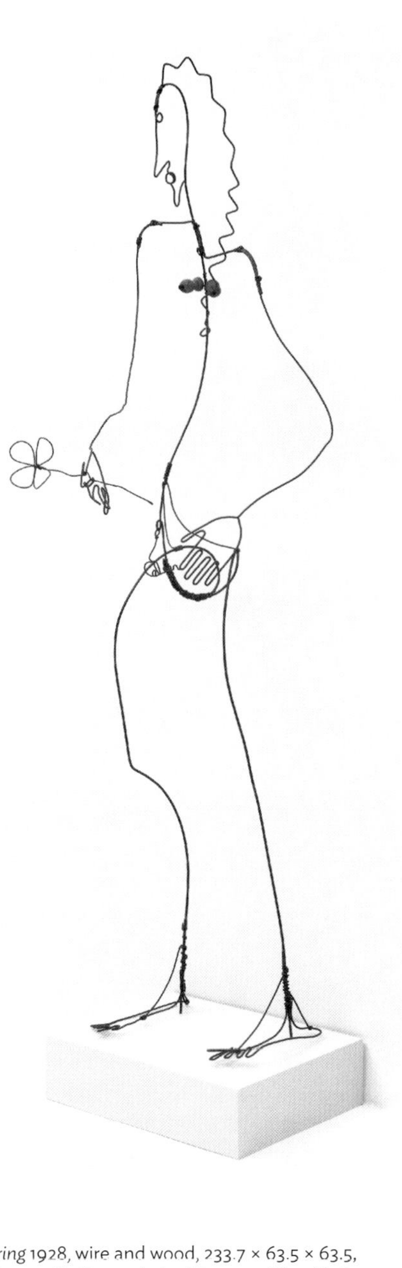

Spring 1928, wire and wood, 233.7 × 63.5 × 63.5, Solomon R. Guggenheim Museum, New York. Gift of the artist, 1965

The bawdy and sometimes puerile attention to the bodily, the erotic and the animalistic in Calder's early work connects his art to the kind of subversive entertainments within which Bakhtin located such power, or at least their modern commercial heirs.[27] Baker had certainly disrupted social norms through the manifold transgressions of her performances. It is possible to locate Calder within an even wider field of carnivalesque traditions. Art historian Joy Sperling has connected Calder's interest in the circus not only to the unpredictable violence of surrealism, but also to the wild slapstick of Buster Keaton, and the macabre rituals of Punch and Judy puppet shows.[28] Calder's sketches of a 'bearded lady' at the circus, or a Coney Island freak show, certainly evidence a taste for the bizarre and grotesque that is attentive to the fringes of social acceptability.[29] Such preoccupations might also explain the images of inebriation, cannibalism and worm-eaten cadavers in Calder's *Three Young Rats and Other Rhymes* (New York, 1944) – ostensibly a children's book – or the image of high-kicking debauchery that the artist managed to sneak into *Fables of Aesop* (1931).[30] It is little wonder that Calder once named Hieronymus Bosch as one of the artists he most admired.[31]

Calder's own suggestion that one of his sculptures was more 'Sewer-realist' than surrealist, provides a pun that suitably captures the artist's embrace of the low and vulgar.[32] Among Calder's earliest illustrations were drawings for Elmer E. Scott's, only recently published, book *The P-culiar Dog or The Piddling Pup*, in which the artist represented a veritable cavalcade of pissing pooches – their airborne loop-the-loops of urine pointing the way to the wire doodles yet to come.[33] Calder later recalled his efforts to chase a Dalmatian until he caught it in 'a good urinating attitude'.[34] When visiting the studio of a friend in 1927, Calder attached a wire dog to the faucet such that it appeared to relieve itself as the water was turned on.[35] In Calder's *Vache (cow)* c.1929, the artist's characteristic spiral form is turned into a curlicue of cow manure, which can be dropped from beneath the animal's tail at will. In *Cirque Calder*, the artist used the same gag. Right before a performing horse left his miniature arena, Calder would deposit its droppings centre-stage, before returning almost immediately with a tin dustpan and brush to sweep up its mess. In Jean Painlevé's 1955 film of the show, the clean-up occurs against the sound of riotous applause, and the strains of nothing less triumphantly inappropriate than John Philip Sousa's march, *El Capitan*.

The traces of such ribaldry remain present in the haywire antics of Calder's later abstract mobiles too. The artist understood the earthy pleasures of his favoured, curvilinear forms in opposition to the rectangle preferred by Mondrian – a shape he thought tended to 'constipate movement'.[36] On another occasion, searching for a metaphor for the unpredictability of the mobile, it was the comedy of the dog chase that came to the artist's mind: 'Like the pound clerk, who catches stray dogs,' Calder explained, as though he envisaged his creations running about like a crazed Harpo Marx, 'the mobile catches any stray wind.'[37] When Calder's mobiles 'dance', their sheer unpredictability and the impending – though rarely consummated – possibility of entanglement, owes something to the lessons he learnt in observing the complexities of a modern world in ever-faster motion, whether the teeming crowds of New York City or the volatile performances of Josephine Baker. These were the pleasures but also the perils of modernity, captured by his art.

Calder's art can easily seem merely playful, like the children's mobiles that his sculpture inspired, but one should not lose sight of the more subversive kinds of play that his art enacted.[38] When the artist joked to interviewer Selden Rodman in the 1950s that he had been known in his Paris years as a 'playboy', the moniker not only pointed to the toys and games that the artist said he had 'always liked', but also to the more disreputable ends to which adult play could be put.[39] Rather than repressing the more vulgar aspects of twentieth-century popular taste, Calder's incorporation of the low and the bawdy into his art imagined a modernism that transgressed the borders between high and low, elite and popular, classical and primitive; an ambitious art in which the arch seriousness of officialdom was not the aspiration. Like the dance hall and the darkened cinema, and before them the carnival, Calder created a world in which the prohibitions of ordinary life could be suspended, and less restrained possibilities imagined.

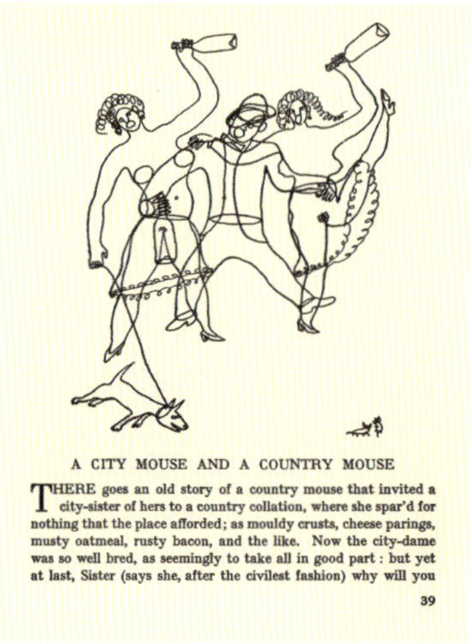

A CITY MOUSE AND A COUNTRY MOUSE

THERE goes an old story of a country mouse that invited a city-sister of hers to a country collation, where she spar'd for nothing that the place afforded; as mouldy crusts, cheese parings, musty oatmeal, rusty bacon, and the like. Now the city-dame was so well bred, as seemingly to take all in good part : but yet at last, Sister (says she, after the civilest fashion) why will you

39

'A city mouse and a country mouse', *Fables of Aesop, According to Sir Roger L'Estrange*, Paris 1931, p.39

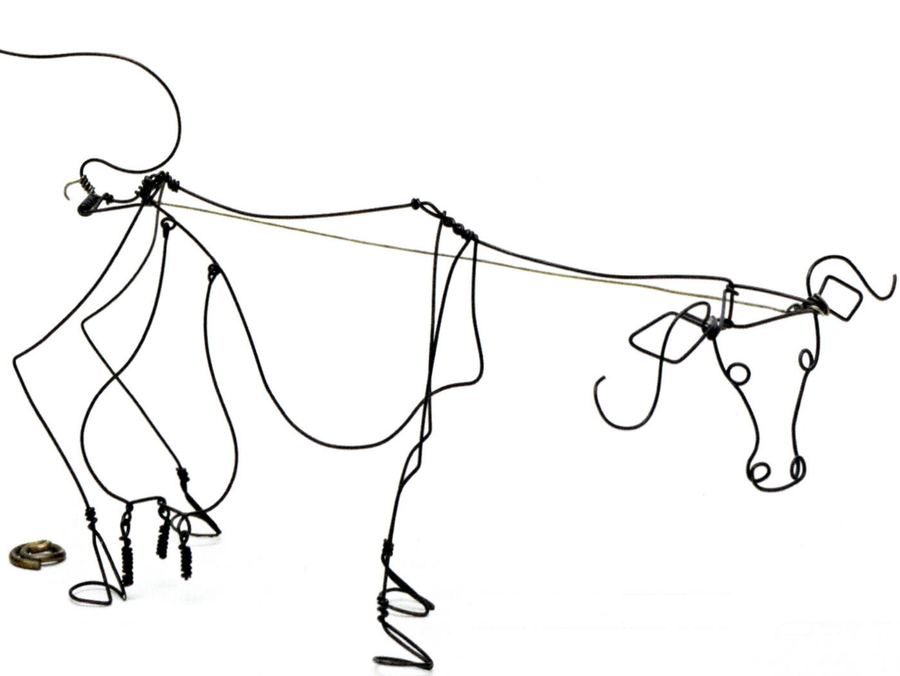

Cow c.1929, wire, 16.5 × 40.7 × 10.5, The Museum of Modern Art, New York. Gift of Edward M.M. Warburg

Notes

1 Jane Adlin, 'Calder and Adornment', in Alexander S. C. Rower and Holton Rower (eds.), *Calder Jewelry*, New York 2007, p.197.

2 Calder quoted in Eleanor Early, 'Made Famous by His Cuckoo Art', *Miami Daily News-Record*, 8 May 1930, p.13; Giovanni Carandente, *Calder*, Milan 1983, p.14.

3 Sieglinde Lemke, *Primitivist Modernism: Black Culture and the Origins of Transatlantic Modernism*, Oxford 1998, p.110.

4 Alexander Calder, *Calder: An Autobiography with Pictures*, London 1967, p.67.

5 Alexander Calder, *Animal Sketching*, Pelham, NY 1926, p.46

6 'Ned Weyburn [*sic*], 68, Dance Director' [Obituary], *New York Times*, 3 September 1942, p.19.

7 'A Spanish Beauty Rehearses her Dances,' *National Police Gazette*, 21 March 1925, p.14.

8 'Wonders of Our Age: Portraits by Wire!', *American Sketch*, April 1928, p.36.

9 Joan Simon and Brigitte Léal, *Alexander Calder: The Paris Years, 1926–1933*, exh. cat., Whitney Museum of American Art, New Haven 2008, p.40.

10 Calder 1967, p.98. Calder had sketched scenes from Chaplin's *The Gold Rush* for the *National Police Gazette* in 1925.

11 For these contemporary stories, see 'Rockefeller Dances Jig', *New York Times*, 27 January 1927, p.10; and J. Brooks Anderson, 'The Play: Behind the Scenes with Ziegfeld', *New York Times*, 3 July 1929, p.25.

12 Thomas Messer [introduction], *Alexander Calder: A Retrospective Exhibition*, exh. cat., Solomon R. Guggenheim Museum, New York 1964, p.13.

13 Alexander Calder, 'No One Thinks of Me When They Have to Make a Horse', in G. Di San Lazzaro (ed.), *Homage to Alexander Calder, Special Issue of the XXe Siecle Review*, New York 1972, p.98.

14 Ibid., p.98. The latter quote is directed at Rodin; see Calder 1967, p.79.

15 For a fascinating indication of the reception of Calder's work in relation to classical prototypes, see Jules Pascin's drawing of Calder, in which the artist is shown (on horseback!) making *the Laocoön* and *Venus de Milo* in an orgy of wire. Calder 1967, p.95.

16 Harry Kessler, *In the Twenties: The Diaries of Harry Kessler*, New York 1971, p.284. This incident is cited as an example of the transgressive power of parodic mimicry in Michael Taussig, *Mimesis and Alterity: A Particular History of the Senses*, New York and London 1993, pp.68–9.

17 James Johnson Sweeney, *Alexander Calder*, exh. cat., Museum of Modern Art, New York 1951, p.9.

18 Alexander Calder, 'What Abstract Art Means to Me', *The Bulletin of The Museum of Modern Art*, vol.18, no.3, Spring 1951, p.8.

19 Pemberton Murdock, 'The Art Galleries: Pigment and Tea Leaves', *New Yorker*, 23 February 1929, pp.76–7.

20 The knobs appear also in Calder's rendering of *Romulus and Remus* 1928, serving equally well as the teats of the she-wolf and the penises of Ancient Rome's famous twins.

21 In the same source, Calder recalls that even a fellow artist could not help but notice the prominence of 'the asshole of the horse'. See Calder 1967, p.118.

22 Joan Marter, *Alexander Calder*, revised edn, Cambridge 1997, pp.181, 197; Mark Rosenthal, *The Surreal Calder*, New Haven 2005, p.25.

23 Simon and Léal 2008, p.272.

24 Ernestine Carter, *With Tongue in Chic*, London 1974, p.37.

25 Calder 1967, p.76.

26 Mikhail Bakhtin, *Rabelais and His World*, trans. by Hélène Iswolsky, Bloomington, IN 1984, p.6.

27 In Bakhtin's view, however, 'the carnival is far distant from the negative and formal parody of modern times'. Ibid., p.11.

28 Joy Sperling, 'Calder in Paris: The Circus and Surrealism', *Archives of American Art Journal*, vol. 28, no. 2, 1988, p.26.

29 See 'Seeing the Circus with "Sandy" Calder', *National Police Gazette*, 23 March 1925, p.14; and 'Sandy Calder Goes a-Sketching at Coney Island', *National Police Gazette*, 1 August 1925, p.14.

30 See his high-kicking illustration for 'A City Mouse and Country Mouse', in *Fables of Æsop according to Sir Roger L'Estrange. With Fifty Drawings by Alexander Calder*, Paris 1931, p.39.

31 Katharine Kuh, *The Artist's Voice: Talks with Seventeen Artists*, New York 1962, p.50.

32 Quoted in Rosenthal 2005, p.12.

33 Although completed in 1925, this work remained unpublished until 2001. See Elmer E. Scott, *The P-culiar Dog, or, The Piddling Pup*, New York 2001.

34 Quoted in Jean Lipman, *Calder's Universe*, London 1977, p.81.

35 Stanley William Hayter, 'Alexander Calder at Paris', in Lazzaro 1972, p.8.

36 Kuh 1962, p.39.

37 Calder 1972, p.98.

38 On Calder's relationship to the visual culture of childhood, see Alex J. Taylor, 'The Calder Problem: Mobiles, Modern Taste, and Mass Culture', *Oxford Art Journal*, vol. 37, issue 1, March 2014, pp.15–17.

39 Selden Rodman, *Conversations with Artists*, 4th edn, New York 1961, p.140; Alexander Calder, 'The Evolution', 1955–6, manuscript, Calder Foundation archives, quoted in Jed Perl, 'Play Theory', in Alexander S.C. Rower and Tae Hyun-sun (eds.), *Calder*, exh. cat., Leeum Samsung Museum of Art, Seoul 2013, p.53.

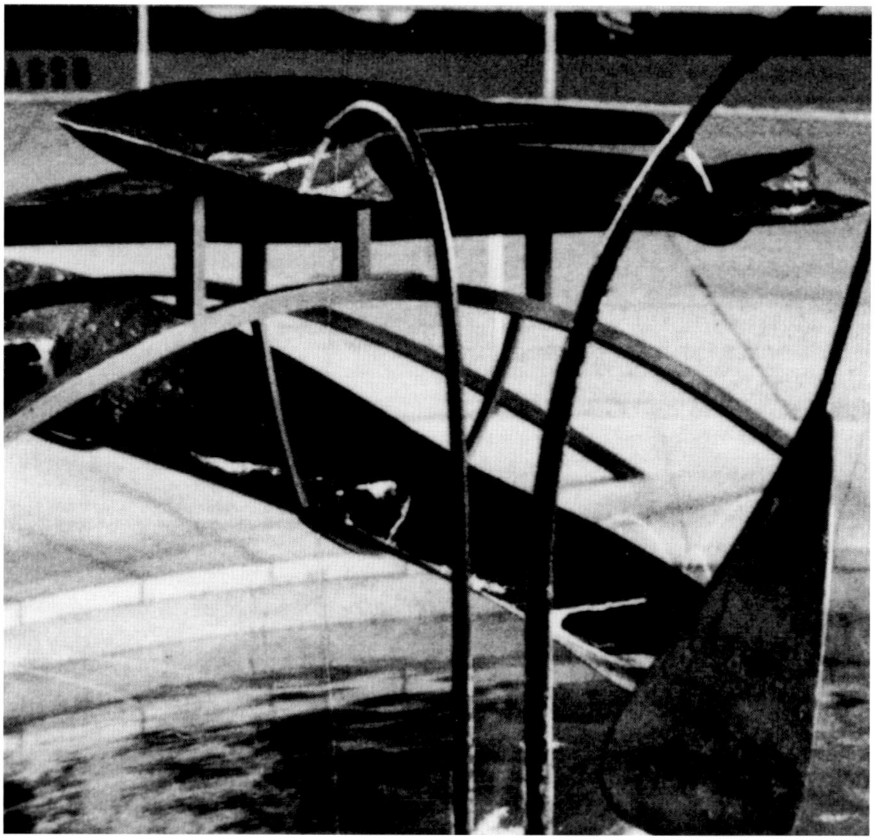

Between Paris and New York: Fountains, Fluidity, Politics

Marko Daniel

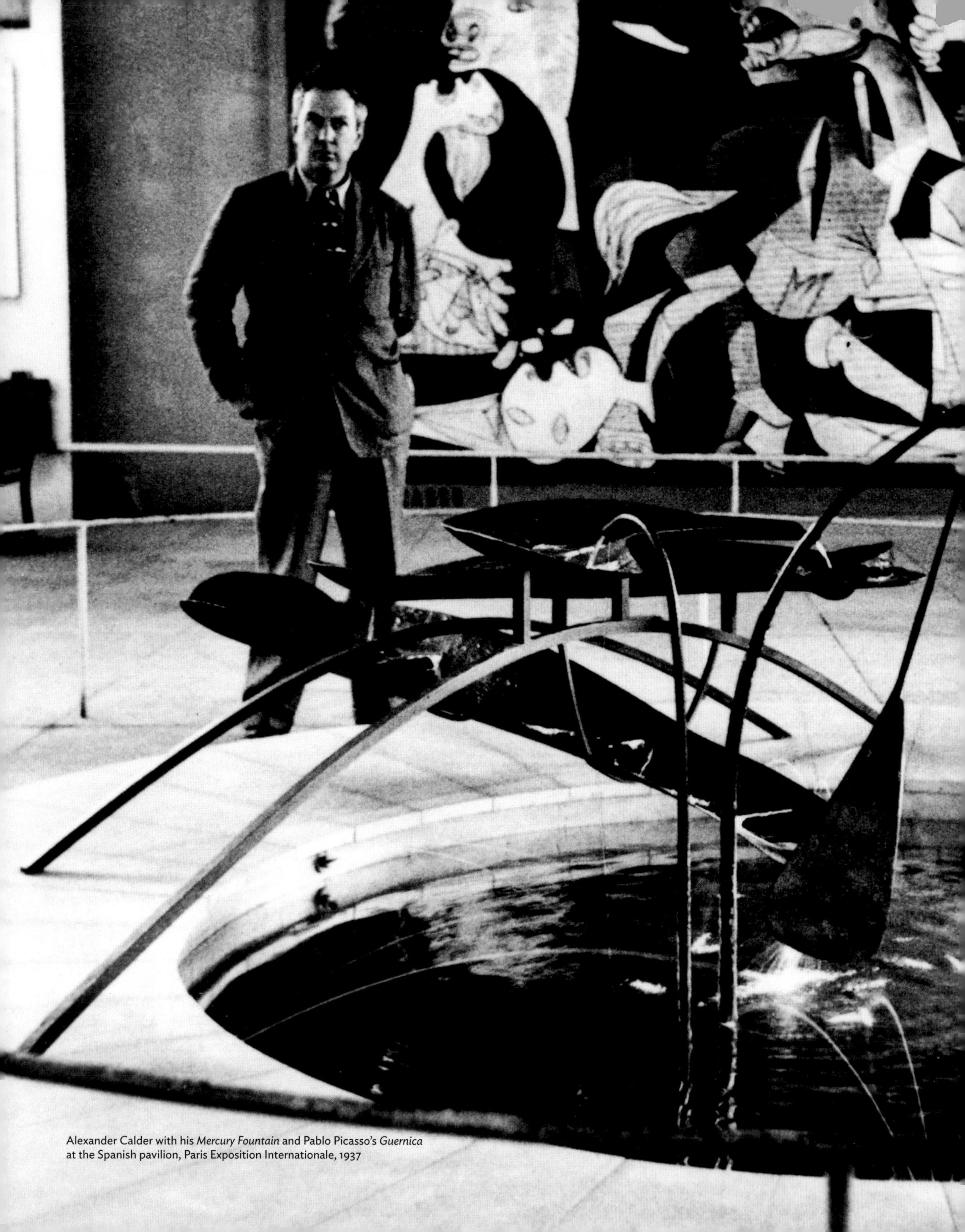

Alexander Calder with his *Mercury Fountain* and Pablo Picasso's *Guernica* at the Spanish pavilion, Paris Exposition Internationale, 1937

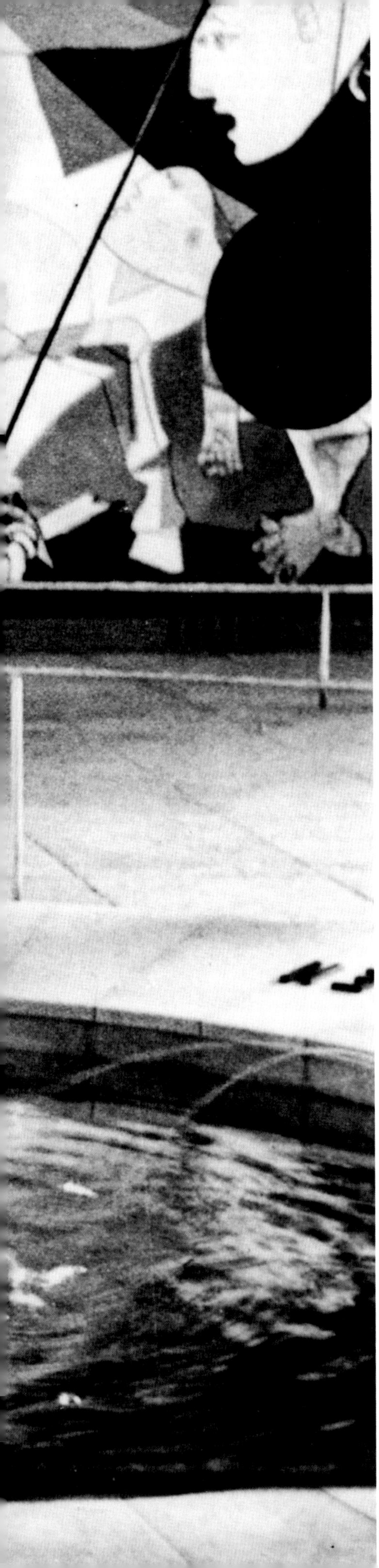

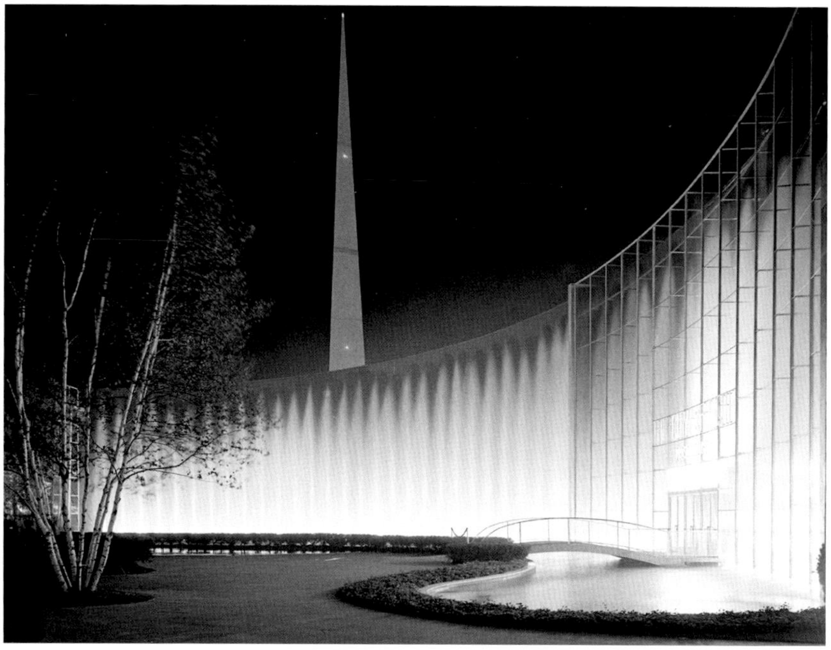

A World's Fair night view of Consolidated Edison's fountains on 24 June 1939

A strip of metal rises vertically in a spiral behind a horizontally elongated trapezoid. Two waves are formed from alternating coloured semicircles of different diameters. These four elements are mounted on horizontal pulley wheels that are connected by string. The string, when tugged, sets the components in rotary motion. Together, these elements make up one of the models that Alexander Calder designed for the New York World's Fair of 1939. The Fair's slogan, 'Dawn of a New Day', indicated the degree to which it sought to provide a purposefully optimistic response to the continued economic depression that had characterised so much of the 1930s. In marked difference to its predecessor – the 1937 Exposition Internationale des Arts et Techniques dans la Vie Moderne in Paris – the New York World's Fair was intent on privileging business interests over ideology, a manoeuvre rendered all the more poignant by the fact that the event overlapped with the outbreak of the Second World War (the Fair lasted from 30 April 1939 until the end of October 1940).

As one of the foremost artists of the US, with prominent links to the European avant-garde, Calder was commissioned by the architects Wallace K. Harrison and Jacques André Fouilhoux to produce a new work for the fountain outside of the Consolidated Edison pavilion, in the Commerce section of the fair. A pool ran along the side of this building, while jets of water formed a spectacular screen covering its façade (described by Calder as a 'concave quadrant') – this was especially effective at night, when the illuminated plumes of water formed what looked like a single, continuous smooth skin.[1] Calder's *A Water Ballet* was to consist of a programme lasting five minutes that would include 'jets of water from 14 nozzles which are designed to spurt, oscillate or rotate in fixed manners and at times as carefully predetermined as the movements of living dancers'. These movements were to be interspersed with 'bombs' of water, and a 'cannonade' or 'large detached mass of water which gives off a considerable report when it falls back onto the surface of the lagoon'.[2]

Technical difficulties meant that the project, hugely ambitious and energetic, was not fully realised in its intended form.[3] Calder's friend, the curator and writer James Johnson Sweeney, commented that, 'Unfortunately, he did not receive the same sympathetic cooperation from the New York engineers in charge that he had in Paris.'[4] Whether this criticism was justified or not, it was a pointed reference to Calder's contribution to the Exposition of two years previous, for which he had also made a fountain.

The very different history of Calder's 1937 project, and of the critical conversation surrounding it, strikingly illuminates the complex relationship that his seemingly autonomous sculptures sustained, through the quality of movement, not only with their architectural environment but also their wider social and political context. It also serves as an example of how, as Europe fell under the yoke of totalitarianism and war, a formal vocabulary initially aligned with the utopian ideals of early modernism found refuge in, and then was absorbed by, corporate culture in the US, only to resurface once again in the post-war period as a visual idiom of societies conceiving themselves anew.

> *We arrived in Paris about the middle of April, last year [1937], and at once proceeded to look up our old friends. Among these was Joan Miró, Spanish painter, often listed as a surrealist, but who, to my mind, has been in a class all by himself for quite a number of years. He and Picasso were to do paintings to be placed on the walls of the Spanish pavilion at the Paris 1937 Exposition. So one Sunday I went with him, and the architect, [Josep Lluís] Sert, to see what sort of space he was to work on. At that time there was little but a few girders and columns to indicate where the wall would eventually be.* [5]

The question of which wall Miró was to work on was moot. None were ready and the pavilion of the Spanish Republic was running behind schedule. Perhaps the biggest surprise was that the Paris Exposition was happening at all. An initial plan to host an exposition celebrating agriculture and industry was considered in the aftermath of the stock market crash of 1929 and the ensuing worldwide economic downturn. In early 1934, the French government cancelled the exposition, only for it to be revived under political pressure from trade unions in July of the same year, with a new emphasis on art and technology in modern life. [6] Despite a climate of political uncertainty, under the sign of the conflict between the dominant ideologies of fascism and communism, virtually all industrialised nations grasped the opportunity to take part in the fair. Yet, at the time of the official opening on 25 May 1937, only two of the pavilions were complete: those of Germany and the USSR, facing off in the Trocadéro, across the river from the Eiffel Tower. The forwards and upwards sweep of Vera Mukhina's giant, shining, stainless-steel sculpture *Industrial Worker and Collective Farm Worker* on the Soviet building was seemingly stopped in its tracks by the static tower of Albert Speer's German pavilion, with a large bronze eagle holding a swastika in its claws on the top. [7]

In this symbolically charged atmosphere, the cool lines of the understated Spanish pavilion, a mere fifty metres or so from the Soviet-German confrontation, were a striking example of rational modernism. The Spanish Republic's participation in the Exposition was daring, and fragile, given that an uprising of Nationalist rebels led by Francisco Franco on 17 July 1936 had started a civil war that would last until 1 April 1939, and eventually tear the Republic apart.

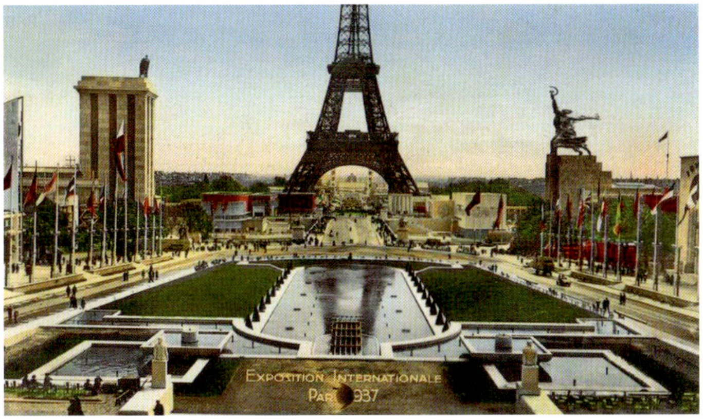

Exposition Internationale, Paris, 1937. View of the German and Soviet pavilions

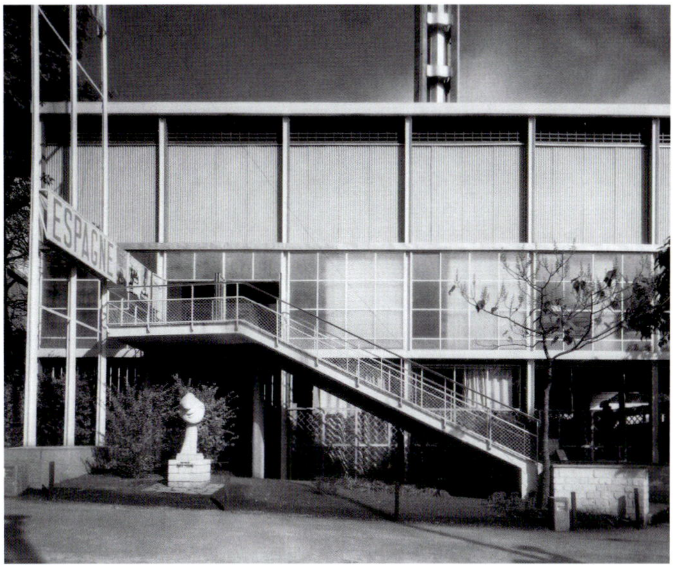

Exterior view of the Spanish pavilion at the Exposition Internationale, Paris, 1937

A combination of factors contributed to the Republic's decision to dedicate scarce resources to an enterprise that might, under the circumstances, have been considered frivolous. First of all, the Spanish Embassy in Paris had played a key role in promoting the new Republic's cause, via diplomatic negotiations with France and other European and international friends. Luis Araquistáin, the ambassador appointed shortly after the outbreak of the Civil War in 1936, was instrumental in 'normalising' the underground flow of much-needed arms into his home country – an endeavour that was all the more difficult following the signing of a multinational non-intervention pact that banned third parties from selling weapons to Spain.

In this specific context, the propaganda potential of taking part in the Paris Exposition was seized upon by Araquistáin. It provided the opportunity to send a strong message to the world about the reality of Spain – at war yet sufficiently normal and stable for successful participation in the fair – and, at the same time, to showcase the advances in the social, economic and cultural realms that had been achieved since the establishment of the Second Republic in 1931.

> *It would seem expedient to participate in the Exhibition, and we should immediately take all necessary steps to give an impression of security [by showing] that our government continues to pursue such matters. In the worst case, if the participation of private, commercial and industrial exhibitors etc. proved difficult ... it would always be possible to make a cheap but decorative pavilion and to exhibit works of art, propaganda etc.* [8]

In the end, given the serious impact of the Civil War on commerce, the Republic represented itself almost entirely through art and culture. The fortuitous presence of Spanish and Catalan avant-garde artists in Paris; the close ties between the architects of the pavilion – Luis Lacasa for the Republic, and especially Josep Lluís Sert for the Generalitat de Catalunya – with these artists; and the involvement on site of artist Josep Renau, head of the Spanish government department responsible for art and culture, all set the scene for what turned out to be a powerful conjunction of art and politics.

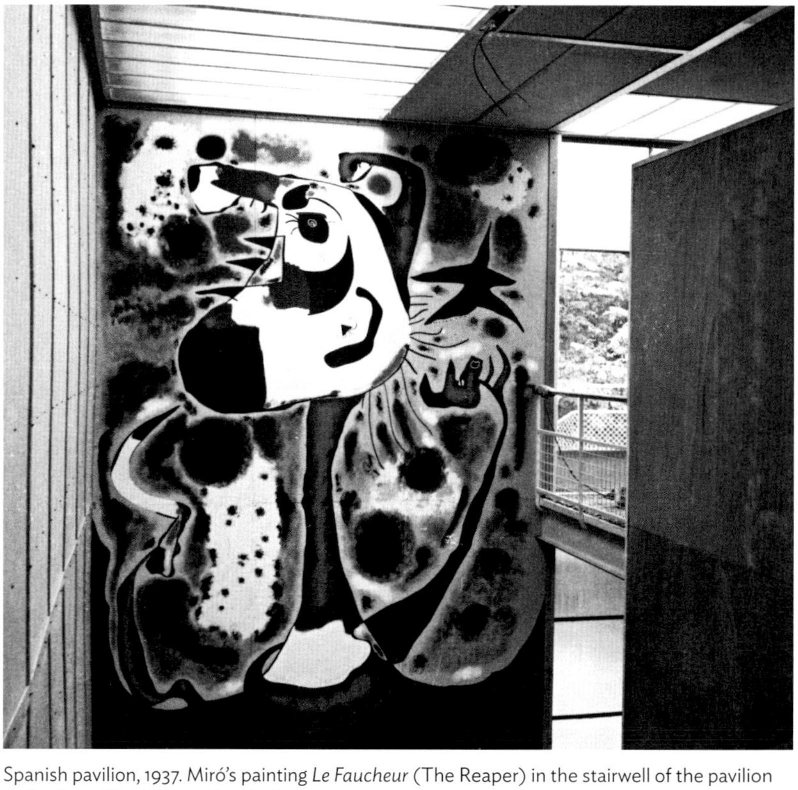

Spanish pavilion, 1937. Miró's painting *Le Faucheur* (The Reaper) in the stairwell of the pavilion at the Exposition Internationale, Paris, 1937

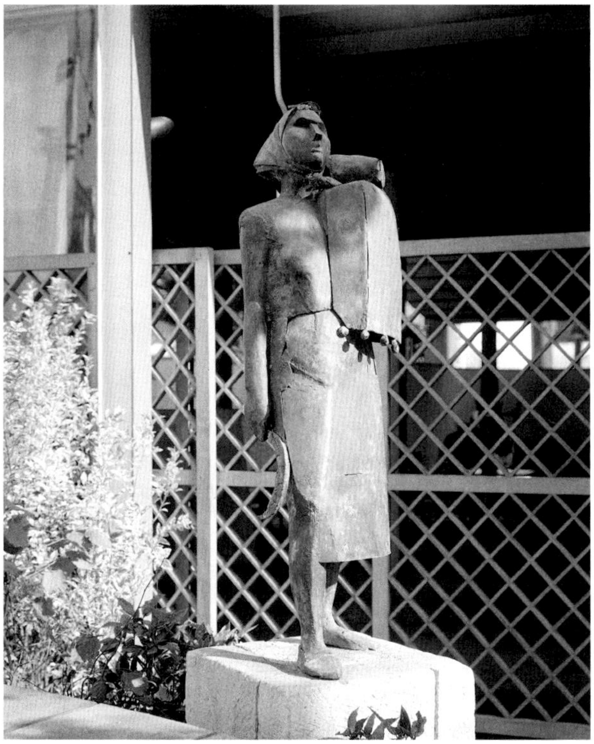

Julio González's *La Montserrat* 1935 in the Spanish pavilion, Exposition Internationale, Paris, 1937

Renau, himself the author of the photomontages – representations of contemporary life in Spain – that made up the pavilion's other element of visual communication, commissioned Picasso for the pavilion in January, though it was only after the bombing of the Basque town of Gernika in April 1937 that the artist settled on the topic for his large painting *Guernica*, which was installed on the main wall of the open ground-floor space, under the raised pavilion. Joan Miró's mural *The Reaper*, an allegorical work showing a Catalan peasant wearing the traditional red *barretina*, with a raised left fist and holding a sickle in the other hand, was painted directly onto the wall panels of the staircase leading from the second floor down to the first floor of the building. Miró was unusually outspoken about the obvious symbolism: 'Of course I intended it as a protest. The Catalan peasant is a symbol of the strong, the independent, the resistant. The sickle is not a communist symbol. It is the reaper's symbol, the tool of his work, and, when his freedom is threatened, his weapon.'[9] Miró's strategic resistance to overly literal interpretations of his work – combined perhaps with the moment in which he made this statement, in New York at the height of the Cold War – explains his coyness about communism, but the message to all visitors to the pavilion was clear. It was brought home by the inclusion at the pavilion's entrance of Alberto Sánchez Pérez's twelve-and-a-half-metre-tall sculpture *The Spanish People Have a Path that Leads to a Star* (*El pueblo español tiene un camino que conduce a una estrella*) and Julio González's *La Montserrat* 1935, the latter a life-size sculpture of a woman holding a sickle in one hand, while clutching an infant, shield-like, against her chest with the other.

While none of these artworks were installed when Alexander Calder visited the site, he immediately thought that there were plenty of spaces in the unfinished building that 'might well be embellished by something of my own – "MOBILE" – ie an abstract sculpture which moves, propelled by wind, motor, jet of water, or some other means'.[10] At the time, irrespective of the self-deprecating tone of these comments, his willingness to participate was probably based on a profound desire to join a project with which so many of his friends, and artists whose work he admired, were involved. Sert, and most importantly José Gaos, the overall commissioner of the Spanish pavilion, initially rejected Calder's offer, as it seemed inconceivable to have a non-Spaniard working on the project and also contravened the guidelines for foreign pavilions laid down by the French organisers of the Exposition.[11]

All of this changed when a problem arose with one of the exhibits sent from Spain – a mercury fountain due to be installed in a prime position on the ground floor. The presence of this fountain was considered a political necessity, given that the mercury mines at Almadén in southern Spain were responsible for well over half of the global production of mercury at that time. A sunken base, 2.2 metres in diameter, had already been prepared for it, right in front of Picasso's *Guernica*. However, the young assistant architect Antonio Bonet Castellana describes how, halfway through the construction of the pavilion, a Government van arrived from Spain containing the white marble fountain from the Ibero-American Exhibition held in Seville in 1929. It was in bad condition, with overly complicated mechanisms that made mercury look like water.[12] This did not at all fit with the coherent strategy for the pavilion – to use rationalist architecture as a container and structuring principle for avant-garde art and sophisticated social and political messaging about the modernity of the new Spain.

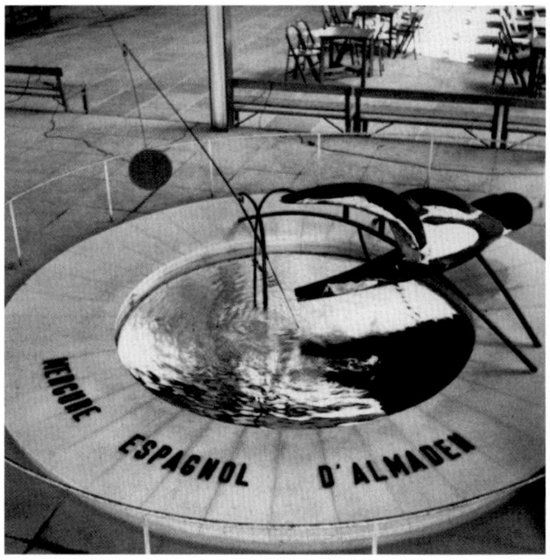

Mercury Fountain 1937 in the Spanish pavilion at the Exposition Internationale, Paris, 1937

Mercury production in Almadén was to feature prominently in the large documentary section of the pavilion, which was based on information sent from Spain and presented almost entirely through photomontages and graphics created by Renau himself. This section included displays on social reform; childcare and social security; international export-import; agriculture (including land reform); university, school and popular education, including the famous 'pedagogic missions' to take art to remote villages;[13] and the protection of works of art during the Civil War. While the presentation of such information always has a propagandistic intent, in the sense of advocating for a nation's achievements, everything here carried a double message: the promotion of the new Spanish Republic and its autonomous regions, and a clear differentiation of this new social order from the forces of conservatism and fascism represented by the Republican government's opponents in the Civil War.

The mercury mines of Almadén were used to communicate this message with great clarity. Data about the international mercury trade and its economic value were juxtaposed with information about the modernisation of the historic mines themselves. In addition to this social dimension, the political significance of the mines, or rather their product – mercury – was also highlighted. Control of the mines was intensely fought over during Spain's Civil War, not just because of the commercial benefit it brought but also because, among the many uses to which mercury was put, it had a key role in military technology – from sensors to trigger switches for bombs. Here was another reference to the inescapability of the War in all aspects of life. The carefully planned visual experience of the pavilion extended to the integration in the mercury display of the stainless steel transport flasks in which the metal for the intended fountain had been delivered. The bar charts showing export statistics were made in the shape of these distinctive bottles, which themselves stood along the bottom of the display. The incongruity between the message of this display and its intended medium (the old-fashioned marble fountain) was clear.

Sert had the task of finding a new solution and he turned to Calder, who was keen to accept this commission. By this time, the Exposition had already opened and work on the Spanish pavilion and its contents was proceeding with great urgency.[14] Calder produced a model in sheet aluminium, with ball bearings as a substitute for mercury, which he gave to Sert for his approval. While Calder's 1938 note about *Mercury Fountain's* construction emphasised, in capital letters, the 'MOBILE' ambitions of his potential contribution, this initial design was entirely static, apart from the movement of the 'liquid' on it.

Once begun, work was undertaken at great speed and Calder worked quickly to develop his sculpture within the limitations determined by the site and medium. It eventually consisted of three, vaguely kidney-shaped, shallow plates mounted on arched supports that rose up from a basin in the ground. Mercury flowed from a simple spout onto the upper plate and then ran down across the other two, collecting in pools and behind small weirs that were designed to break and slow its flow. At the end of its journey, the liquid metal ran against a paddle, connected by a long rod to a small mobile arm; this had a red disc at one end and brass wire bent to form the word ALMADEN at the other. The flow of the mercury falling into the basin activated the paddle in such a way that the disc and letters swayed gently in response.

Given the highly corrosive qualities of mercury, all surfaces of the iron construction were covered in a protective coating of pitch and the rest of the sculpture was painted black to give it a simple visual coherence, with the only note of colour provided by the dancing red disc. Calder noted that the weight of the mercury meant that the sculpture was only allowed to rise to a height of about one metre, with very small drops between levels to minimise spillage. To complicate matters further, delivery of the mercury itself was, like everything about the pavilion, late: it only arrived on the day of the building's inauguration. Thus, 'the construction of the fountain was done without any opportunity to try out the flow on the surfaces, which I made up with careful thought, and a design which would permit of final adjustment of the inclination of the surfaces after the installation.'[15] When the fountain was put into operation, it needed one final adjustment to catch escaping droplets of mercury: small pieces of wire mesh were placed at the lips where the liquid ran from one plate to another.

The success of the fountain, functionally, is quite extraordinary when one takes into consideration the speed of production and the fact that it took place largely without the possibility of preliminary tests under operating conditions. Aesthetically it was also a great success, as a piece that was unmistakably an avant-garde sculpture as much as it was a fountain. The pitch-black elements contrasted with the shiny silvery surfaces of the mercury, which was in constant motion as it flowed from plate to plate and into the rippling pool at the bottom. The simple curves and lines of the sculpture also sat perfectly within the wider visual context of a pavilion that was strongly determined by the ubiquity of avant-garde art. Compared with many of Calder's other sculptures, this work was downright sombre, as was appropriate for its location, opposite *Guernica*, and in the context of the overall message – the defiant battle for survival during the Civil War – that the pavilion's organisers were sending out.

A strange quirk of the fountain was that coins dropped by visitors making wishes floated on top of the mercury rather than sinking down, due to the metal's high density.[16] The etymology of 'mercury' is rich: its old name, hydrargyrum, translates as 'water-silver', while the common name – 'quicksilver' – literally means 'living silver', in reference to the material's tendency to rapid movement. The material itself, as a metal that is liquid at room temperature, elicits in the viewer a cognitive dissonance between the usual, expected hardness and rigidity of metal and the fluidity of the ever-moving quicksilver. In Calder's sculpture, this paradox is expressed by the juxtaposition of metals in these different states, solid and liquid, and is further alluded to by the black surface coating of pitch, itself a highly viscous, slow-moving liquid; a viscoelastic solid polymer is protecting a metal solid from being corroded by a liquid metal.

The Spanish pavilion as a whole represents a coming together of avant-garde aesthetics and left-wing, radical and revolutionary politics, whether one is looking at the architecture, documentary displays or artworks. Calder's *Mercury Fountain* sat comfortably in this environment, at least on formal grounds. Not given to overt political statements, the sculptor was nevertheless perfectly at ease in the company of his fellow artists and collaborators in the pavilion of the Spanish Republic; the question now is to what extent, if any, his work made a contribution to the political ethos of that enterprise.

One approach to this question is to examine the quite uncommon circumstances of the fountain's commission. The fact that the selection of Calder's work was based, in the first instance, on the rejection of the originally proposed, traditional, old-fashioned fountain from Seville, makes the choice seem all the more active and significant. If the rejection of one was based on a clearly perceived aesthetic and political identity (old-fashioned and conservative), then so was the adoption of the alternative (modern and radical). Another possibility would be to take a closer look at the materiality of the liquid in the fountain, whose multiple layers of economic, social and political meaning were reiterated throughout the experience of walking through the pavilion. If the first option was rejected for underplaying the effects of mercury, the second brought full attention to it.

Here, fluidity and movement in the *Mercury Fountain* also need to be examined formally. In traditional fountains, movement tends to be provided mainly by water, as it flows out of an otherwise immobile structure. *Mercury Fountain* not only makes great play of the relationship between static black support and shiny running quicksilver, as discussed above, but also uses the metal's flow as a means of agitating mobile elements of the sculpture (the disc and wire letters). At this point in Calder's career, the inclusion of mobile elements, if not the construction of a mobile *per se*, was very much intrinsic to his way of working and might have been expected at the point of commissioning. This alone does not turn the mobile into a political gesture, but it suggests that the way *Mercury Fountain* operates can be summarised by a startlingly simple premise: fluidity is associated with socially and politically progressive or radical meaning. Is it really as simple as equating movement with progress and stasis with conservatism? On a grand scale, this opposition was certainly staged by the confrontation between the German and Soviet pavilions, discussed above. It was not only, let us say, an innocent eruption of political beliefs made form – a coincidence that happened to manifest in this spectacular form – but the outcome of a call-and-response dialogue between artists, architects and ideologies.

Calder's incorporation of movement in sculpture is, in this context, not just potentially, but always political. He follows in the footsteps of painter and sculptor Umberto Boccioni, who asserted in 1910 that 'movement and light destroy the materiality of bodies',[17] and in those of Naum Gabo and Antoine Pevsner, who renounced, in 1920, 'the thousand-year-old delusion in art that held the static rhythms as the only elements of the plastic and pictorial arts', and affirmed 'the kinetic rhythms as the basic forms of our perception of real time'.[18] These steps by different artists towards a new understanding of movement are crucial not so much in terms of providing art-historical antecedents but in so far as they draw attention to a fundamental desire to make art political by making it analyse more profoundly the realities of contemporary life – doing so through its dynamic and kinetic aspects.

One might see Calder as a pioneer of kinetic art. I would like to emphasise in his work the notion of experimentation itself – a way of trying out new things and seeking change. This approach allows for a radical reading of work whose appearance is gentle but which proposes fundamental readjustments not just to art but to our interaction with it and to our subsequent reflections on society and our place in it. Herbert Matter's striking strobe-light photographs of Calder's 'mobiles in movement' 1936 are exemplary in drawing out the simultaneous complexity and simplicity of these sculptures and the changing configurations of form they produce. The political quality that is communicated through fluidity and movement is performed through dialectical relationships (material, experiential, affective and linguistic) that actively bring into opposition the notions of change and sameness; of rupture and torpor; progress and stagnation, enjoyment and boredom; being alive and being dead.

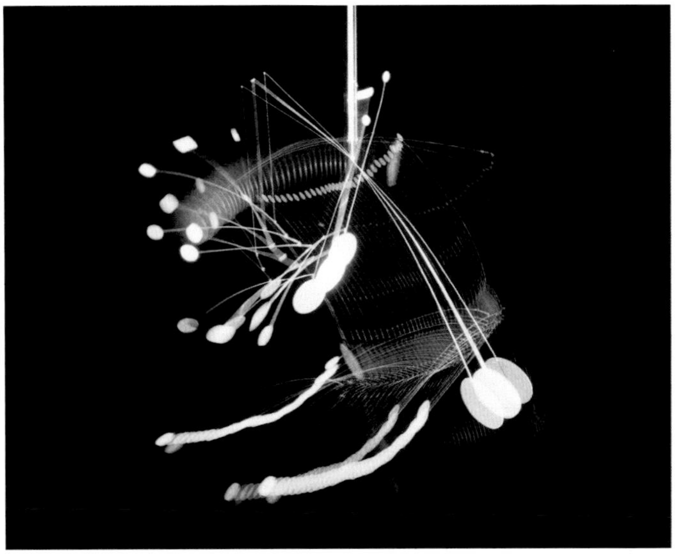
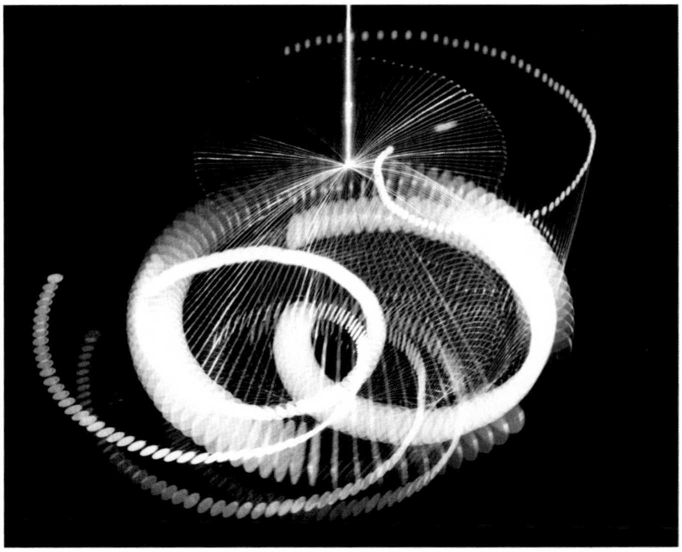

Untitled 1936, in motion, from the catalogue for the exhibition *Alexander Calder: Sculptures and Constructions*, The Museum of Modern Art, New York, 1943

Notes

1 Alexander Calder, 'A Water Ballet', *Theatre Arts Monthly*, vol.23, no.8, August 1939, pp.578–9.

2 Ibid.

3 Although the project itself served as the basis for a 1956 commission for the General Motors Technical Center in Detroit, MI. See Thomas Messer, *Alexander Calder: A Retrospective Exhibition*, exh. cat., Solomon R. Guggenheim Museum, New York 1964, p.52.

4 James Johnson Sweeney, *Alexander Calder:* Museum of Modern Art, New York 1951, pp.51–2.

5 Alexander Calder, 'Mercury Fountain', *Stevens Indicator*, vol.55, no.3, May 1938, p.3.

6 Patrick Weiser, 'Arts plàstiques, tècniques i societat a l'Exposició Internacional de París, 1937', in *Art contra la Guerra: Entorn del Pavelló Espanyol a l'Exposició Internacional de París de 1937*, exh. cat., Palau de la Virreina, Barcelona 1986, p.29.

7 See Albert Speer, *Inside the Third Reich*, London 1970, p.81, where Speer claims to have created his building as visual full stop to the striding forms of the Soviet design: 'The Soviet Russian and German pavilions were to be placed directly opposite one another on the fairgrounds; the French directors of the fair had deliberately arranged this confrontation. While looking over the site in Paris, I by chance stumbled into a room containing the secret sketch of the Soviet pavilion. A sculpted pair of figures thirty-three feet [sic] tall, on a high platform, were striding triumphantly towards the German pavilion. I therefore designed a cubic mass, also elevated on stout pillars, which seemed to be checking this onslaught, while from the cornice of my tower an eagle with a swastika in its claws looked down on the Russian sculptures. I received a gold medal for the building; so did my Soviet colleague.'

8 Luis Araquistáin, letter to to Álvarez del Vayo, quoted in Josefina Alix Trueba, *Pabellón español: Exposición Internacional de París, 1937*, exh. cat., Centro de Arte Reina Sofía, Madrid 1987, p.25.

9 Aline B. Saarinen, 'A Talk with Miró about his Art', *New York Times*, section 2, 24 May 1959, p.17.

10 Calder 1938, p.3.

11 Alix Trueba 1987, p.96 (see n.8 above).

12 Fernando Martín Martín, *El pabellón español en la Exposición Universal de París en 1937*, Seville 1982, p.108.

13 See Eugenio Otero Urtaza and María García Alonso, *Las Misiones pedagógicas, 1931–1936*, Madrid 2006.

14 Martín Martín 1982, p.151, refers to invoices for *Mercury Fountain* that show work starting on 9 June 1937, two weeks after the official opening.

15 Calder 1938, p.3.

16 Edmond Labbé, *Exposition internationale des arts et techniques dans la vie moderne. Rapport general*, Paris 1938–40, vol.9, p.175, reports that these coins were removed nightly and a total of 15,000 F was collected in this way.

17 Umberto Boccioni et. al., 'Futurist Painting: Technical Manifesto' [1910], in Charles Harrison and Paul Wood (eds.), *Art in Theory 1900–2000: An Anthology of Changing Ideas*, revised edn, Oxford 2003, p.152.

18 Naum Gabo and Anton Pevsner, 'The Realistic Manifesto' [1920], in Harrison and Wood (eds.) 2003, p.300.

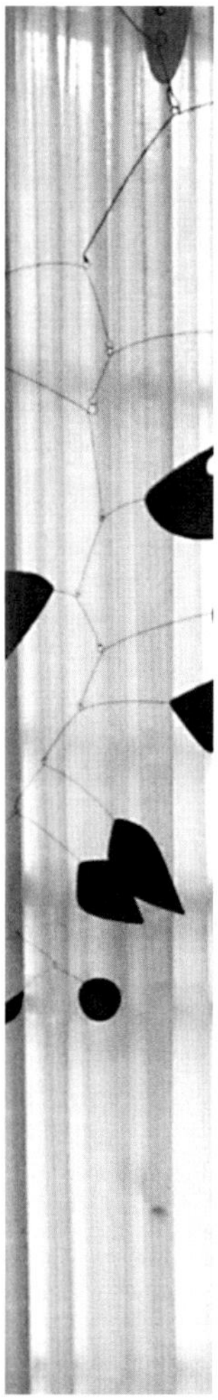

Wind Chimes of Modernity: Calder's 1948 Trip to Brazil

Sérgio B. Martins

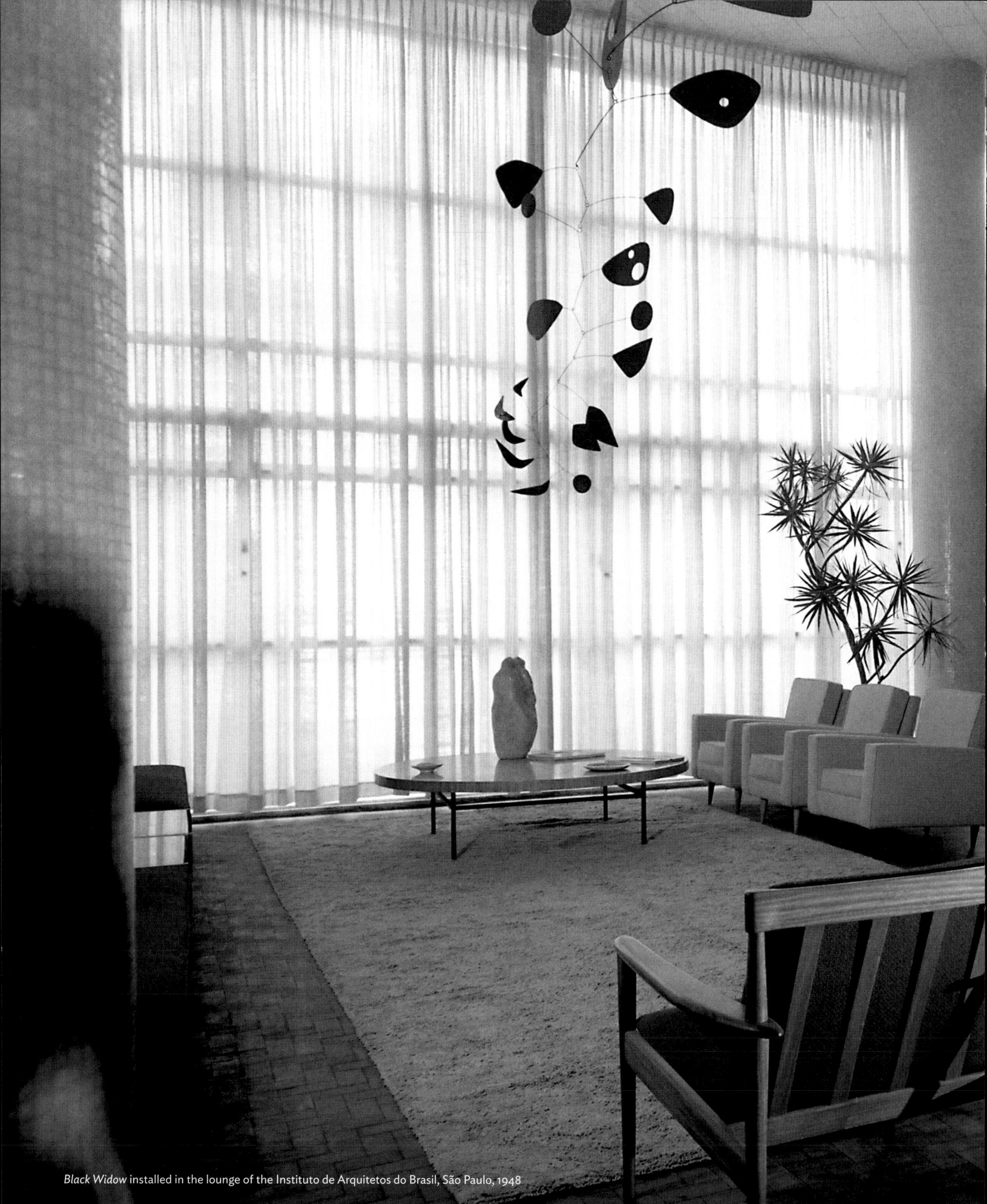

Black Widow installed in the lounge of the Instituto de Arquitetos do Brasil, São Paulo, 1948

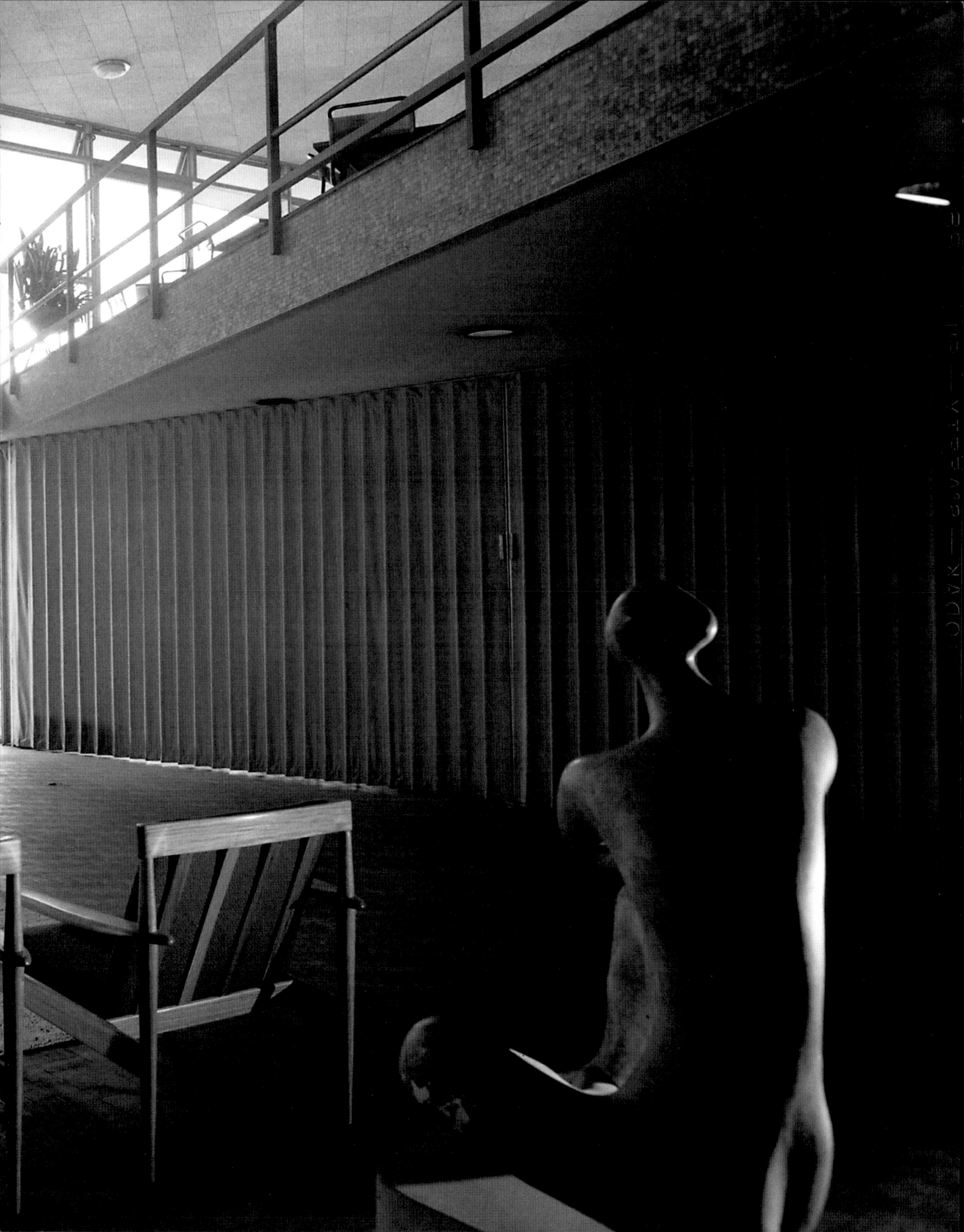

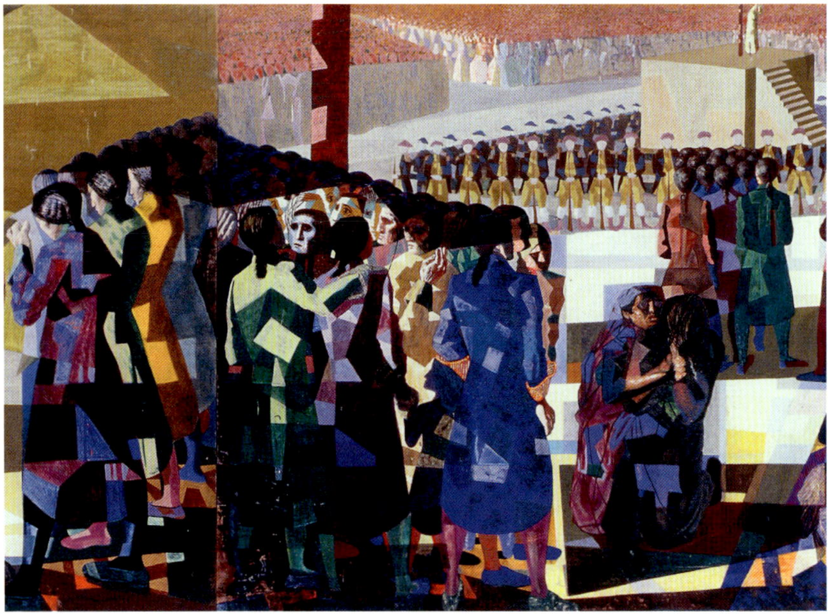

Candido Portinari, *Tiradentes* 1948, egg tempera on canvas, 309 × 1767 (detail), originally commissioned for the Colégio Cataguases, designed by Oscar Niemeyer

Due to its properties, wire is a material that lies in the threshold of the specific field of sculpture.

(Mário Pedrosa, 'Calder, escultor de cata-ventos')[1]

While accounts of Brazilian post-war artistic modernism focus mostly on the 1950s – ranging from the creation of the Bienal de São Paulo in 1951, to the country's concrete and neo-concrete artistic movements – it was the ebullient atmosphere of the late 1940s that laid the foundations of much of what was to come. In the years leading up to the end of President Getúlio Vargas's dictatorship, in 1945, modernist architecture began to shift out of the orbit of state voluntarism – though not radically, as the construction of the capital, Brasília, would attest – and gained traction among progressive sectors of the urban bourgeoisie in São Paulo and, to a lesser extent, in Rio de Janeiro. The creation of new museums in both cities, some modelled after the Museum of Modern Art (MoMA) in New York, and supported by none other than North-American businessman and philanthropist Nelson Rockefeller, attracted the backing of press moguls. Those new institutions were instrumental in shifting the ideological thrust of modernism towards the envisioning of a modern democratic society, in keeping with Rockefeller's role, securing good relations between the United States and Latin American countries through commercial and cultural politics during the Cold War. In the meantime, local newspapers chronicled the fiery critical debates that inevitably followed – abstraction was still regarded with suspicion by many established artists and critics, including major representatives of the modernist movement of the 1920s and 1930s.

Alexander Calder's 1948 visit to the country was both a symptom of, and a catalyst for, this state of affairs. Calder did not simply parachute into an unknown context: the ground for his arrival had been enthusiastically laid by Brazilian intellectuals he had befriended, who were all too happy to champion his work – most notably architect Henrique Mindlin and critic Mário Pedrosa (himself a political exile during the Vargas years). The highlights of the trip were solo shows in the Ministério da Educação e Saúde (MES) building in Rio de Janeiro and in the Museu de Arte de São Paulo (MASP), both of which generated a great deal of media interest. Calder also left several works behind, as gifts to supportive individuals and institutions, including the large mobile *Black Widow* 1948, donated to the Instituto de Arquitetos do Brasil (IAB) and hung in the lobby of its São Paulo headquarters following its completion a few years later. For both Mindlin and Pedrosa, mobiles like this were akin to wind chimes, heralding an eagerly expected gust of modernisation, their sound intensified, no doubt, both by Calder's nationality and by his international profile.[2] The images that the two evoke in their writings are unequivocal in this respect. The architect muses on the difficulty of describing the mobiles' effect in writing and regrets that 'we do not yet have recourse to the television', thus associating a much-anticipated modernising technology with the epochal sensibility the proper apprehension of these works supposedly required.[3] For the critic, in turn, Calder reconciled nature and spontaneity with a machine-oriented historical tendency that originated with 'the promotion of the Eiffel Tower to a work of art' – a quintessentially North American synthesis that led to the Parisian acclamation of the Pennsylvania-born artist as 'le roi du fil de fer' (the king of wire).[4]

These authors have set the terms in which Calder's enduring influence in Brazil can be re-evaluated, terms that cannot be entirely reduced to a matter of Cold War cultural imperialism. In the first instance, Calder's work clearly seemed to provide the missing link that would integrate the country's new architectural, institutional and artistic landscape. This is particularly remarkable given that most artistic contributions to Brazilian modernist buildings were made precisely by artists such as Emiliano Di Cavalcanti and Candido Portinari – the early, anti-abstraction modernists I mentioned above (both of whom reportedly scorned Calder[5]), whose stereotypical or monumental representations of 'Brazilianness' were well suited to the ideological tenor of the Vargas years. The engagement with Calder was also crucial for Pedrosa specifically – alongside the critic's studies of Gestalt theory and his experience in the painting workshop of the Engenho de Dentro psychiatric hospital – as he forged the critical backbone of his enduring influence over the Brazilian avant-garde in the following decades. I will discuss each claim in turn.

'Touched by the breeze'

Needless to say, no sympathetic critic failed to single out motion as one of Calder's chief sculptural achievements. However, a closer look at the arguments and designs of supportive architects reveals that the integration of his sculptures into modern architectural environments – both actually and in imagination – was also staked on their spatial novelty, and specifically on the fact that they hung from above. So, for example, both at the IAB headquarters in São Paulo – built soon after the donation of *Black Widow*, by a team that included Calder's friends and enthusiasts, architects Rino Levi and Jacob Ruchti – and in an award-winning country house Mindlin designed for George Hime, Calder's mobiles were installed so as to anchor the visitor's perception of an integrated vertical space as he or she moved from ground floor to mezzanine and back again. Mindlin went so far as to praise them as a means of 'establishing a kind of "psychological" connection' between different floors.[6]

The 3.5-metre-high *Black Widow* is a powerful case in point: viewed from the entrance of the IAB's second-floor lounge, the mobile lures one's attention upwards, towards what was originally the bar area, and subsequently diffuses it, framing the richly textured background of the white brick wall and the vast windows that open onto an outside terrace. The mobile is actually visible from outside, drawing attention to the lively interior; conversely, the circular perforations in some of its deep-black panels channel the bright daylight from the windows, thus highlighting the room's visual and symbolic openness, both to the street and to the city as a whole. *Black Widow* can feel massive and daunting to anyone standing right below it, and yet its gentle motion, far more pronounced in the work's 'tail' than in its higher and larger 'petals', eases this very feeling by suggesting a gradual and ordered – albeit playful – transition from bodily lightness to architectural mass. Viewed from above, on the other hand, the mobile cascades towards the ground, restoring a sense of gravity that is nevertheless devoid of sculptural weight, and punctuating one's commanding view of the lounge, the courtyard and the street. Such weightless evocation of both the kinetic and the kinaesthetic certainly contributed to the fascination Calder's mobiles exerted on many modernist architects.

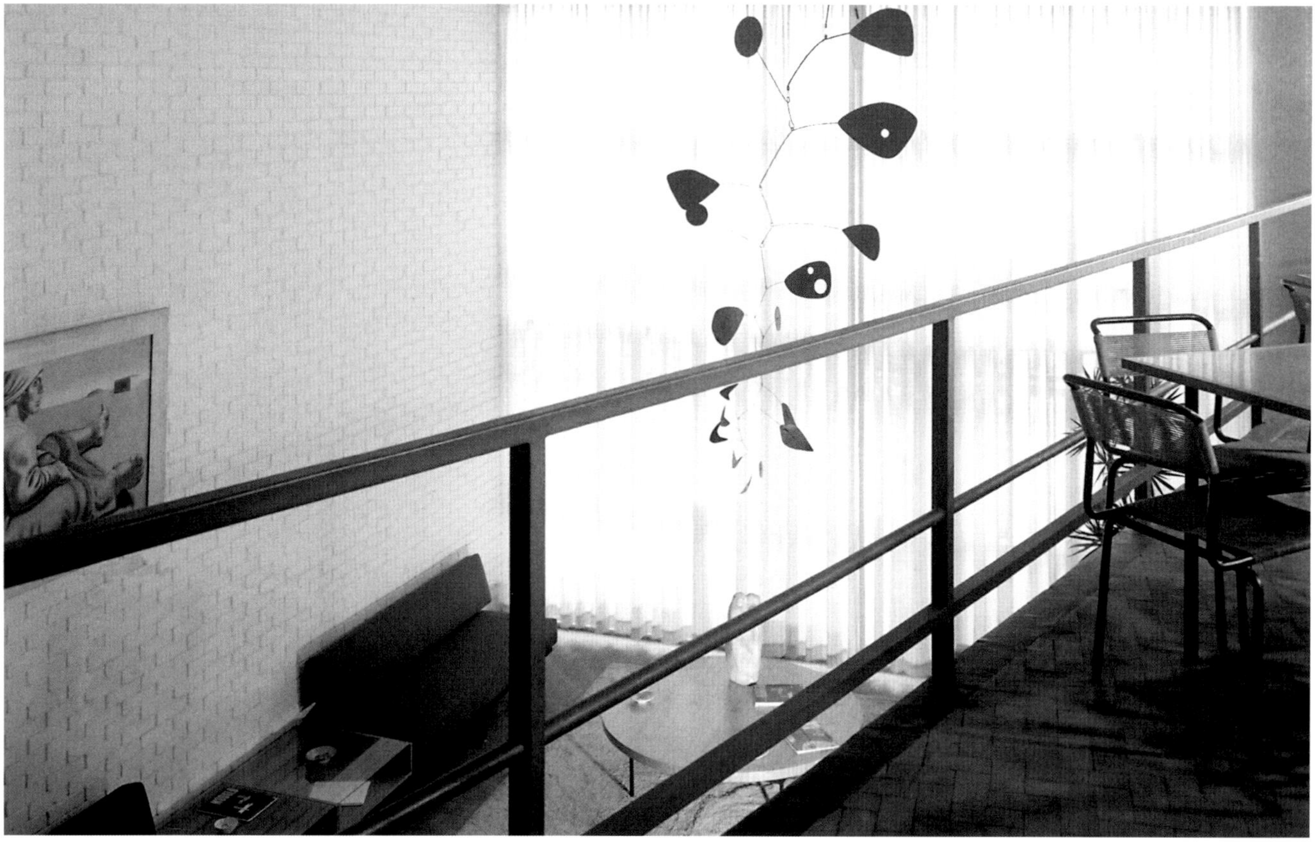

Black Widow viewed from the mezzanine of the IAB headquarters, São Paulo

The mobiles established not only a psychological connection between different architectural spaces, but also an ideological rapport between architecture itself and the utopian allure of modernisation. In 1945, in preparation for the campaign that would bring Calder to Brazil three years later, Mindlin celebrated the artist's oeuvre for its potential to 'integrat[e] sculpture into the new architecture of today', and urged the reader to picture a mobile hanging from the MES building: 'One needs only imagine it touched by the breeze, filling the clear space with its ever-new rhythms, in order to realize not only the importance of Calder's contributions to architecture, but specifically to the solar architecture of open spaces that Brazil is currently making.'[7] This lively picture of Calder's willowy works actually 'filling' an open space rather than simply residing in it resonates with the high expectations modernist architecture evoked in 1940s Brazil.

The MES building is a rather unorthodox example of Le Corbusier's famous 'five points': the Brazilian team in charge of constructing the building modified the Swiss architect's sketches, making it far more monumental than anything he ever envisaged. Whereas Le Corbusier's balanced proportions suggested a grounded mass that could potentially set an example to be replicated throughout the urban plan, the building ended up as a towering emblem of modernism. In other words, the MES was intended to be aesthetically effective as a singular construction rather than as a blueprint for urbanism. While odd as regards Le Corbusier's practice, these changes were largely responsible for solidifying the ideological status of the building. As mentioned above, state voluntarism was a major factor in the success of modernist architecture in a nation without a vibrant industrial sector (especially outside São Paulo) – meaning that the cultural and economic conditions for a widespread assimilation of modernist architecture within existing urban settings were lacking – and all the more so in the Vargas years, when the MES was built. Indeed, key modernist projects in Brazil were often carried out in newly developed areas (e.g. the Oscar Niemeyer-designed Pampulha complex in a suburb of Belo Horizonte) or *ex nihilo*, as in the later case of the Aterro do Flamengo – a park area created by reclaiming a large portion of the sea near (but still outside) downtown Rio. On its own, a building like MES could establish no meaningful links, either actual or prospective, with the surrounding urban area; monumentality was a solution – contradictory, unorthodox, but no less brilliant – that lent cultural traction to a building that might have otherwise remained displaced and eccentric.[8]

The building is particularly striking to visitors emerging from landscape architect Roberto Burle Marx's ground-floor garden plaza, as the uncharacteristic height of the pilotis – an example of Corbusian aesthetics, once again – thrusts it upwards. The structure unfolds *in the air* rather than on the ground, thus casting modernist architecture as an ideological sign of creative autonomy – both political and aesthetic. This, in the heart of a country eager to refashion itself from above as a modern society, and no longer toil on the overworked soil of Brazilian-ness in order to assert itself both internally and internationally. Hanging from the suspended construction, the mobile of Mindlin's vision blends into this picture rather neatly. Touched by the sunlight and reacting rhythmically to the breeze, it would not only join the gardens in signalling the organic complementarity between architecture and natural environment, but also affirm the endless wealth of possibilities – formal, but also cultural and social – that this harmonious blend was meant to afford, especially with the dawn of a new democratic period. Coincidentally or not, the mobile Calder chose to donate to the IAB can be read as a fitting emblem of this utopian vision: in this context, *Black Widow* suggests a spider/architect hanging (and working) from above, in collusion with the ungrounded building.

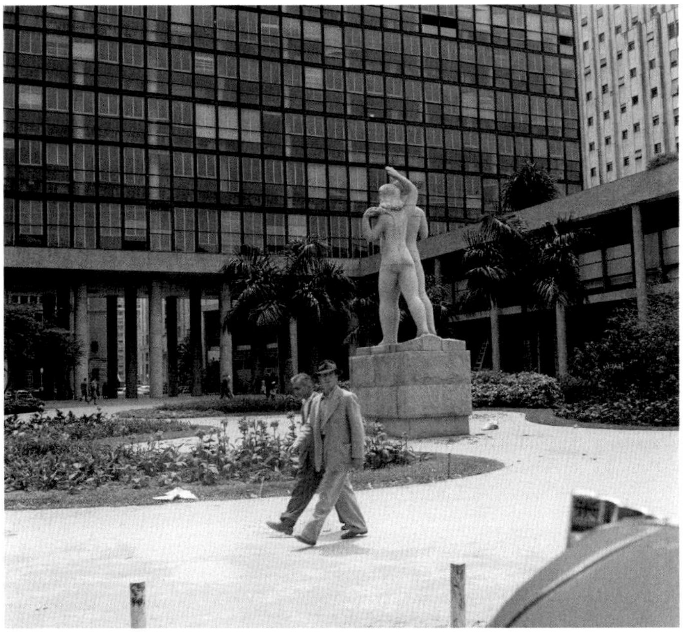

MES building viewed from the ground plaza, with Bruno Giorgi's *Monumento à Juventude Brasileira* in the foreground

The exhibition of Calder's work at the MES building was by no means as impeccable as the scene pictured by Mindlin: Calder's own account and extant photographs indicate that the hanging was hasty and disorganised, resulting in an eclectic array of mobiles and other works mixed in with the chairs, plants and curtains that formed the room's décor.[9] When the show travelled to the Museu de Arte de São Paulo (MASP), however, things were different. MASP's director, Pietro Maria Bardi, and his wife and collaborator, the architect Lina Bo Bardi, carefully designed a setting for the exhibition, with directed lighting, variously coloured panels, and electric fans, to stir the mobiles. In a letter to Mindlin, Pietro Maria Bardi revealed his concern that the mobiles tended to be read lightly, as a kind of visual joke, and maintained that this could be avoided by having them 'inserted in their own atmosphere (form-colour-light)', adding that 'it is necessary that moving colours enter in a relation with inert colours, and that lights go on and off according with the movement'.[10]

This choice – illegible in black-and-white photographs – probably dematerialised the wire sculptures even further, directing the focus of viewers to shifting chromatic iterations of the floating coloured fragments and the backgrounds. In keeping with Lina Bo Bardi's unorthodox take on exhibition design, individual works were given no absolute priority over their surroundings. The museum's aim, as she envisaged it, was to 'form an atmosphere, a disposition [*conduta*] that could endow the visitor with a mental form adapted to the comprehension of the artwork ... Likewise, the artwork ... is presented almost as if to produce a shock that would stir reactions of curiosity and investigation.'[11] Less committed to picturing emblematic modernist ensembles than with rooting the modern in the social, the Bardis ultimately wrested the mobiles away from the pristine abode envisaged by Mindlin and heightened visitors' awareness of their own spatial presence, as chromatic juxtapositions changed with each step taken and animated the room as a whole. This interpretation also ran counter to the sense of 'cyclical fatality' that Pedrosa had detected in some of Calder's works: with the introduction of the viewer's moving body as a variable in the overall environmental effect and the visual blurring of the last remnants of a sculptural axis – the individual wire structure that ultimately pulled each work together – the mobiles arguably ceased to operate as pendulums bridging aerial liveliness and structural balance and became decentred conduits to environmental awareness.[12] Was this a creative misreading of Calder's own intentions? Probably, but it nonetheless revealed a dimension of his work that remained latent under the rhetoric of architectural integration that marked his reception in 1948, and arguably anticipated an environmental concern that would be fully articulated in the Brazilian context almost two decades later, by artist Hélio Oiticica.

Lines in Space

The Bardis' environmental hanging of the mobiles was largely at odds with Mário Pedrosa's critical treatment of them as objects. The fact that Calder's works were able to sustain so much dynamic tension – that their movement opened them up to formal play, that is – was, for the critic, a testament to their extraordinary underlying cohesion. He pointed out, for example, that the 'chaotic multiplicity of positions' the works assumed as they swung was necessarily transient:

> *The whole system hung from a fixed point, so that its parts may drag along the way as they describe their orbits or their different movements, either pendular, circular or elliptic, but they tend to close the cycle, coming back to their point of departure, to the inert object. Therefore, movement is not arbitrary, and has occurred along a predetermined formal path.*[13]

Pedrosa's argument for the mobile as a limit case of aesthetic objectivity proved to be timely; much of the resistance he and other Brazilian advocates of abstraction faced in those years related precisely to charges of its supposedly irrational subjectivism. The critic's allusion to 'Mirovian [after Miró] microbes and germs' playing a role in Calder's development struck the same metaphorical chord as a 1948 article by artist Di Cavalcanti on abstraction in general, except that there was nothing even remotely positive in the latter's indictment of abstract works as 'amoebian residues of sick minds'.[14] Indeed, the objective cohesion of the abstract artwork became a major critical concern for Pedrosa in the late 1940s, and may well have been the thread that connected Calder to the critic's experiences in the Engenho de Dentro psychiatric hospital in the same period. His first encounter with the production of the patients working under the supervision of painter Almir Mavignier in the hospital's newly opened painting studio happened in 1947, the year before the exhibition in Rio, when their works were exhibited at the MES building. Pedrosa would soon engage in a staunch defence of both abstraction and the art of the mentally ill, with Gestalt theory – emphasising the spontaneous rather than intellectually mediated nature of perception – as his weapon of choice.[15] His contact with Gestalt certainly predates his systematic study of it in the late 1940s and, while I don't want to overemphasise its theoretical influence over the 1944 essays on Calder, it may not be too far-fetched to argue that the critic's insistence on the wire works' detachment from their surroundings – as in his definition of the mobile as a 'total unity in sharp contrast with the surrounding space' – suggests a dynamic comprehension of perception. This understanding may well be indebted to early contact with German psychological debates and certainly resonates with Pedrosa's future arguments about perception and form.

Given this context, it is surprising that Pedrosa's writings on Abraham Palatnik – a young Brazilian who also frequented the Engenho de Dentro workshop and experimented with 'kinechromatic' devices – largely ignore Calder. I credit this to an art-historical distinction: Pedrosa aligned Palatnik with Hungarian artist László Moholy-Nagy's technologically inflected transition from colour to light, and treated it as a painterly problem.[16] Conversely, for the critic, Calder not only demystified the typically modern (and European) 'fetish' of the machine by virtue of his rather casual (and North American) assimilation of it, but also belonged to an eminently sculptural lineage. Pedrosa acknowledges the deep impact Piet Mondrian's studio environment had on Calder, but nevertheless stresses that the latter's resulting decision to turn to painting was short-lived; the effect of his epiphanic encounter with the Dutch artist, Pedrosa maintained, was that it aligned Calder's sculptural vocabulary with the language of abstraction and, more specifically, of geometric abstraction.[17] This prompts the critic to praise Calder for trumping cubist sculptor Jacques Lipchitz, arguing that bronze was a medium ill-suited to achieving 'transparency of volume'. Whereas Lipchitz's 'decadent' sculptures only 'lost their structural solidity' without 'gaining spatial projection', due to the 'abstract but formless [*informes*]' quality of their twisting bronze contours, Calder's recourse to wire rejected the materiality (and the history) of casting altogether, thus allowing him to construct transparent volumes with clear contours that bore no trace of shadow or mass.[18] In short, the line was the crucial element that allowed Calder's work to re-found the relationship between sculpture and space, both in constructive terms and in keeping with the widespread critical characterisation of his wire sculptures as 'drawings in space'.

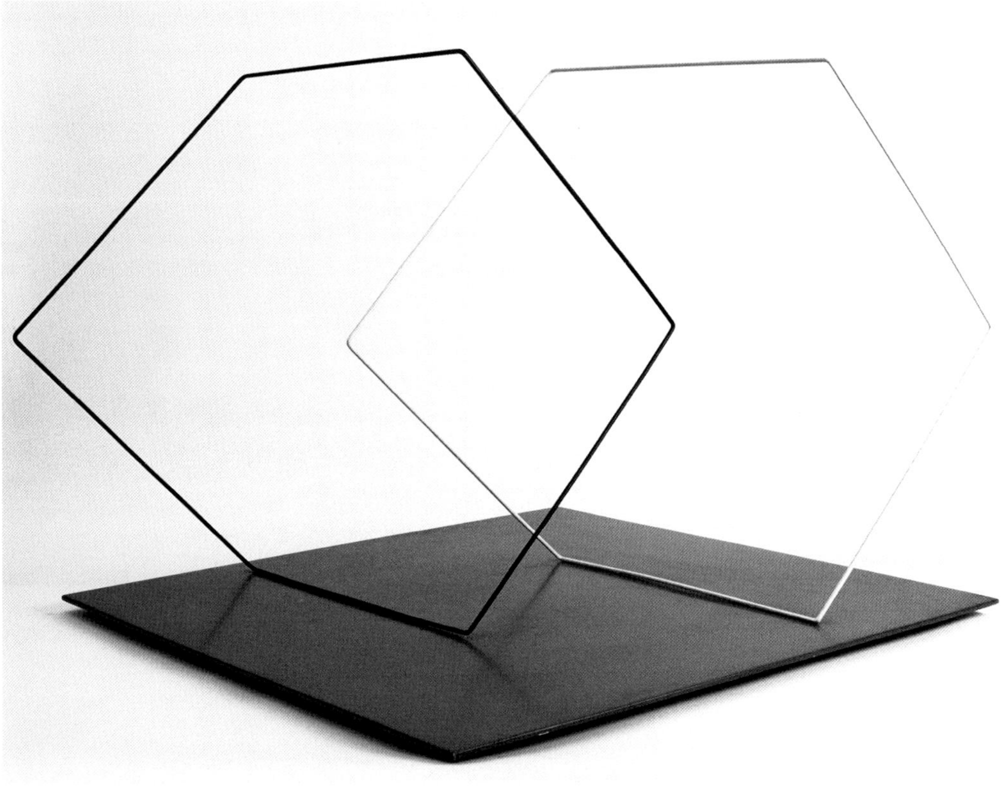

Franz Weissmann, *Dois Cubos Lineares Virtuais (Estrutura Linear)* [Two Virtual Linear Cubes (Linear Structure)] 1954, painted iron, 52 × 77 × 65

In the following decade, key artists in Brazil took up the line as the cornerstone of their radically renewed aesthetic language. Calder is not often cited as their predecessor (although they shared his admiration for Mondrian), but one should not underestimate his impact, either direct or indirect – which is to say, via Pedrosa. The critic argued in 1952 that Franz Weissmann, a sculptor who would go on to identify with the neo-concrete movement, would take up 'the main challenge of modern sculpture', which was 'to represent spatially and not volumetrically', with his attempts to 'substitute filling [*os cheios*] for emptiness [*pelos vãos*]', and later classified his work as a sculpture of 'lines in space'.[19] The line was also the thread that Lygia Clark followed in order to challenge the metaphysical primacy of the picture plane.[20] Pedrosa opens a 1960 article on her work by stressing the 'decadence of [recent] sculpture' and salvaging only those who followed the path of Russian sculptor Antoine Pevsner's 'return to constructivity', or employed the inventiveness brought about by the 'Calderian revolution'.[21] Clark was meant to lie precisely at this juncture.

Instead of arguing that Clark remained a painter, as he had argued that Calder remained a sculptor, Pedrosa now regarded both as agents of a historical crisis that increasingly blurred distinctions between painting and sculpture (even Moholy-Nagy now appeared as an experimental predecessor of this crisis rather than as a 'light painter'). The fact that Pedrosa lacked – or rather resisted – conceptual solutions, such as neo-concrete poet Ferreira Gullar's theory of the non-object, hindered his discussion of this crisis.[22] Gullar's theory itself, however, was indebted to Pedrosa's defence of a sculpture that sought to re-found rather than occupy space (which is precisely what justified joining Calder and Clark in the same historical lineage). Both critics expected a new spectator to be born out of such experiences and often stressed the bodily involvement they solicited. Pedrosa's jest upon seeing Clark's *Trepantes* in the mid-1960s – 'Finally a work of art one can kick!' – may have become famous, but it was not truly unprecedented: in 1944, his younger self had marvelled at the fact that whoever approached Calder's mobiles at MoMA could 'touch them, move them and even push them with the foot'.[23]

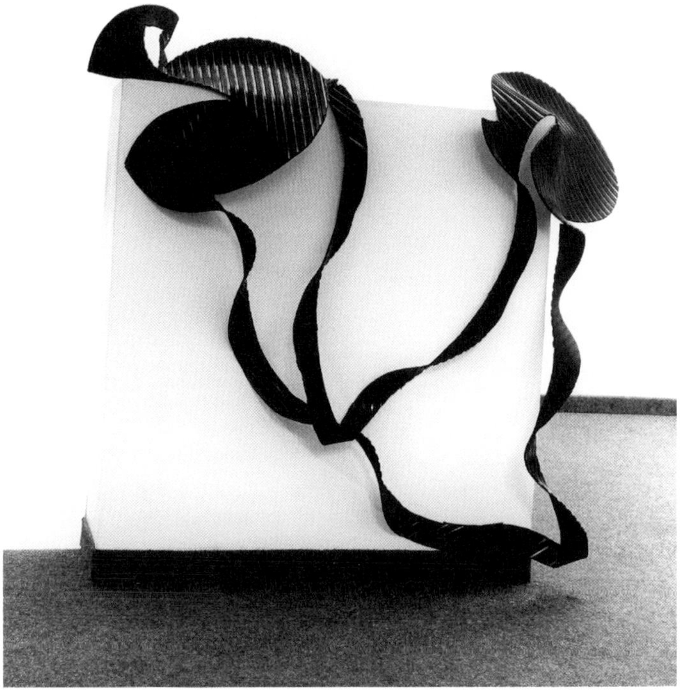

Lygia Clark, *Obra Mole (Trepante)* [Soft Work (Grubs)] 1965, rubber, dimensions variable, courtesy 'The world of Lygia Clark' Cultural Association

Notes

1 Mário Pedrosa, 'Calder, escultor de cata-ventos' [author's translation], in Roberta Saraiva (ed.), *Calder no Brasil*, São Paulo 2006, p.121. Saraiva's excellent book is the best resource available on Calder's relationship with Brazil.

2 Aleca LeBlanc goes so far as to characterise Calder's trips to Brazil as an early sign of an increasingly internationalised art world. Her account of Calder is thoughtful and addresses some of the same issues I do, although my closer analytical focus on Mindlin's and Pedrosa's arguments differs from her broader reconstruction of Calder's dealings with Brazilian individuals and institutions. See Aleca LeBlanc, 'Travelling through Time and Space: Calder in Brazil', in Stephanie Barron and Lisa Gabrielle Mark (eds.), *Calder and Abstraction: From Avant-Garde to Iconic*, exh. cat., Los Angeles County Museum of Art (LACMA), New York and London 2013, pp.120–35.

3. Henrique Mindlin, 'Calder, ferreiro e escultor' [author's translation], in Saraiva (ed.) 2006, p.121.

4 Mário Pedrosa, 'Tensão e coesão na obra de Calder' [author's translation], in Saraiva (ed.) 2006, pp.124–7.

5 See Saraiva (ed.) 2006, pp.72–3.

6 Henrique Mindlin [author's translation], as quoted in Saraiva (ed.) 2006, p.88.

7 Henrique Mindlin, 'Alexander Calder' [author's translation], in Saraiva (ed.) 2006, p.58.

8 My brief account of the MES building specifically, and the relative lack of integration as regards most modernist projects in Brazilian cities, is indebted to Luiz Recaman's excellent article 'High-Speed Urbanisation', in Elisabetta Andreoli and Adrian Forty (eds.), *Brazil's Modern Architecture*, London 2004, pp.106–39.

9 See Alexander Calder, *Calder: An Autobiography with Pictures*, New York 1966, pp.200–1.

10 Pietro Maria Bardi, letter to Henrique Mindlin [author's translation], cited in Saraiva (ed.) 2006, p.74.

11 Lina Bo Bardi, 'O Museu de Arte de São Paulo – função social dos museus', *Habitat*, no.1, October–December 1950, p.17.

12 Mário Pedrosa, 'Tensão e coesão na obra de Calder', in Saraiva (ed.) 2006, p.130.

13 Ibid., pp.128–9.

14 Mário Pedrosa, 'Calder, escultor de cata-ventos' [author's translation], in Saraiva (ed.) 2006, p.47; Emiliano Di Cavalcanti, 'Realismo e abstracionismo', *Revista Fundamentos*, no.3, 1948.

15 For an excellent discussion of Pedrosa's approach to Gestalt theory in the context of his involvement with the Engenho de Dentro workshop, see Kaira Cabañas, '*O dentro é o fora*: Art, Madness and Physiognomic Gestalt in Rio de Janeiro', *October*, no.154, Fall 2015. I discuss the role of Pedrosa's engagement with Gestalt as a key precedent for Ferreira Gullar's theory of the non-object in chapter 1 of Sérgio B. Martins, *Constructing an Avant-Garde: Art in Brazil, 1949–1979*, Cambridge, MA 2013.

16 Mário Pedrosa, *Panorama da pintura moderna*, Rio de Janeiro 1952, pp.47–8.

17 Mário Pedrosa, 'Calder, escultor de cata-ventos', in Saraiva (ed.) 2006, pp.44–5.

18 Ibid. [author's translation], p.41.

19 Mário Pedrosa, 'Experiência e arte', *Tribuna da Imprensa*, 31 May 1952; Mário Pedrosa, 'A escultura do salão', *Jornal do Brasil*, 17 July 1958. Both texts at http://www.franzweissmann.com.br/est50.htm, accessed 24 April 2015.

20 See Sérgio B. Martins, 'Eye and Line', in *Lygia Clark: a Retrospective*, exh. cat., Itaú Cultural, São Paulo [2014].

21 Mário Pedrosa, *Dos murais de Portinari aos espaços de Brasília*, São Paulo 1981, pp.195–203.

22 See note 14, above. I delve deeper into the genesis of Gullar's *Theory of the Non-Object* (1959) in Sérgio B. Martins, '"The Pulp of Color": Toward a Notion of Expenditure in Ferreira Gullar's Neoconcrete Writings', *October*, no.152, Spring 2015, pp.103–20.

23 Lygia Clark, interview with Fernando Cochiarale and Anna Bella Geiger, in Fernando Cochiarale and Anna Bella Geiger (eds.), *Abstracionismo geométrico e informal: a vanguarda brasileira nos anos 1950*, Rio de Janeiro 2004, p.150; Mário Pedrosa, 'Calder, escultor de cata-ventos', in Saraiva (ed.) 2006, p.48.

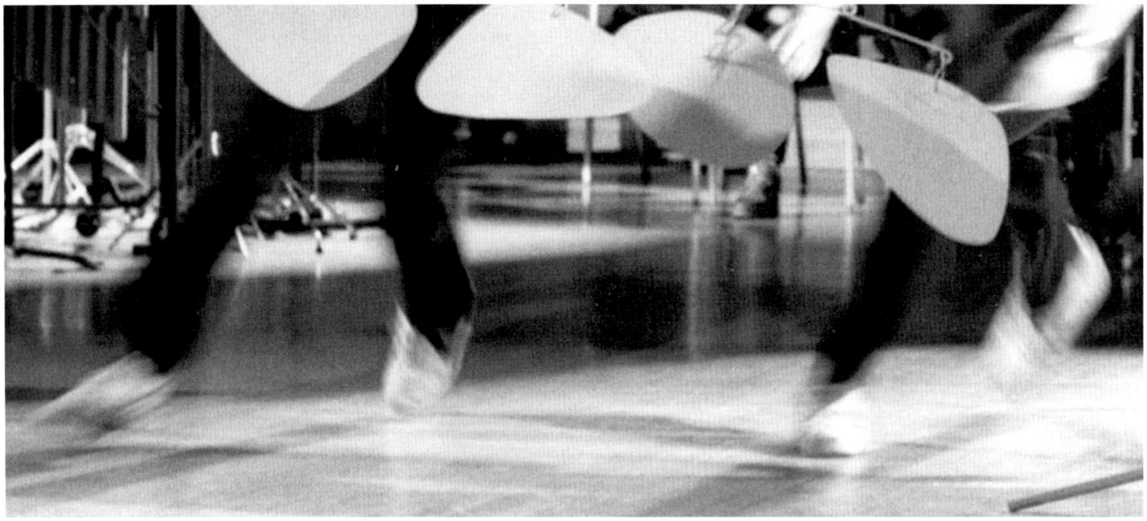

Earle Brown's *Calder Piece* and Alexander Calder's *Chef d'orchestre*

Thomas Fichter

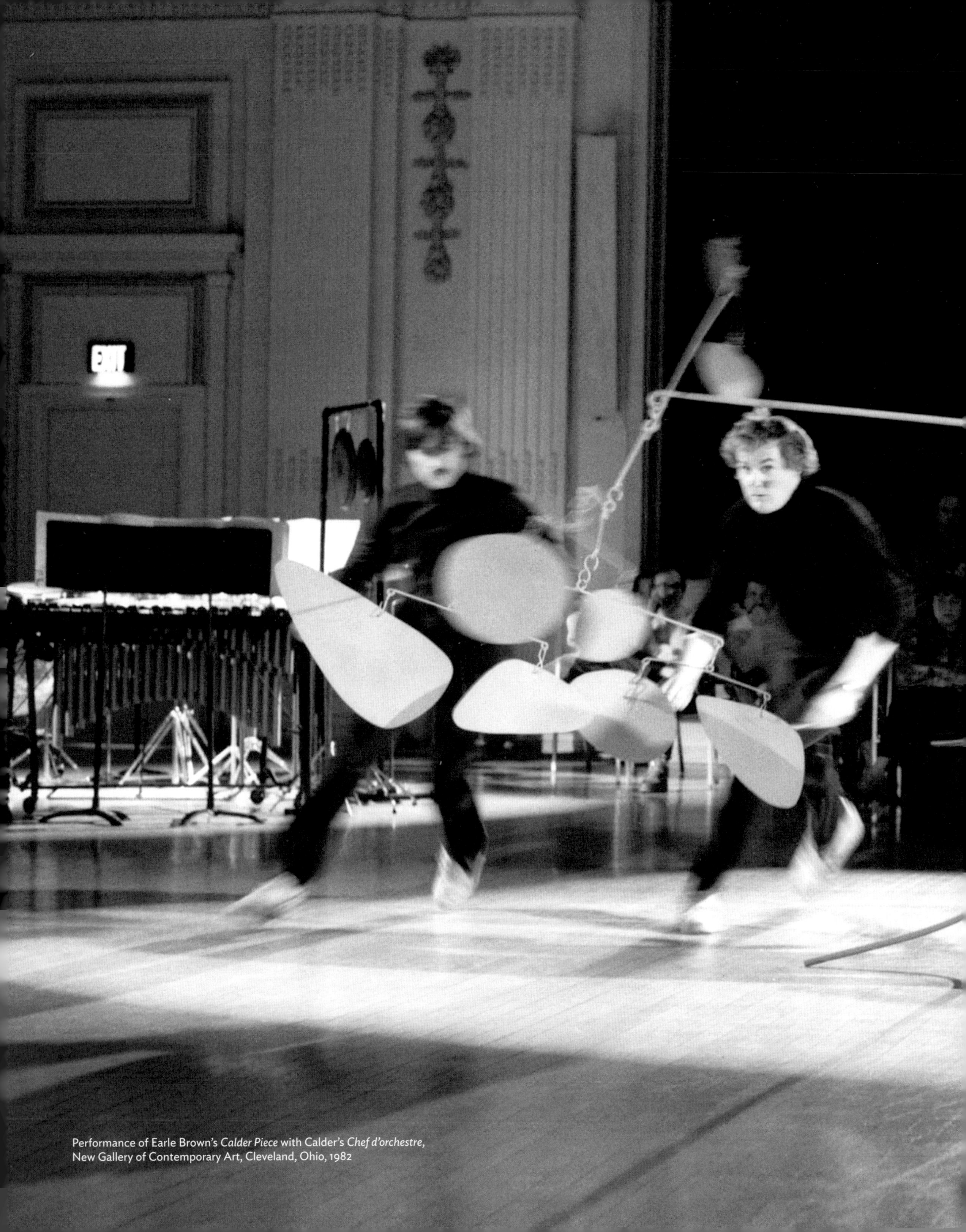

Performance of Earle Brown's *Calder Piece* with Calder's *Chef d'orchestre*,
New Gallery of Contemporary Art, Cleveland, Ohio, 1982

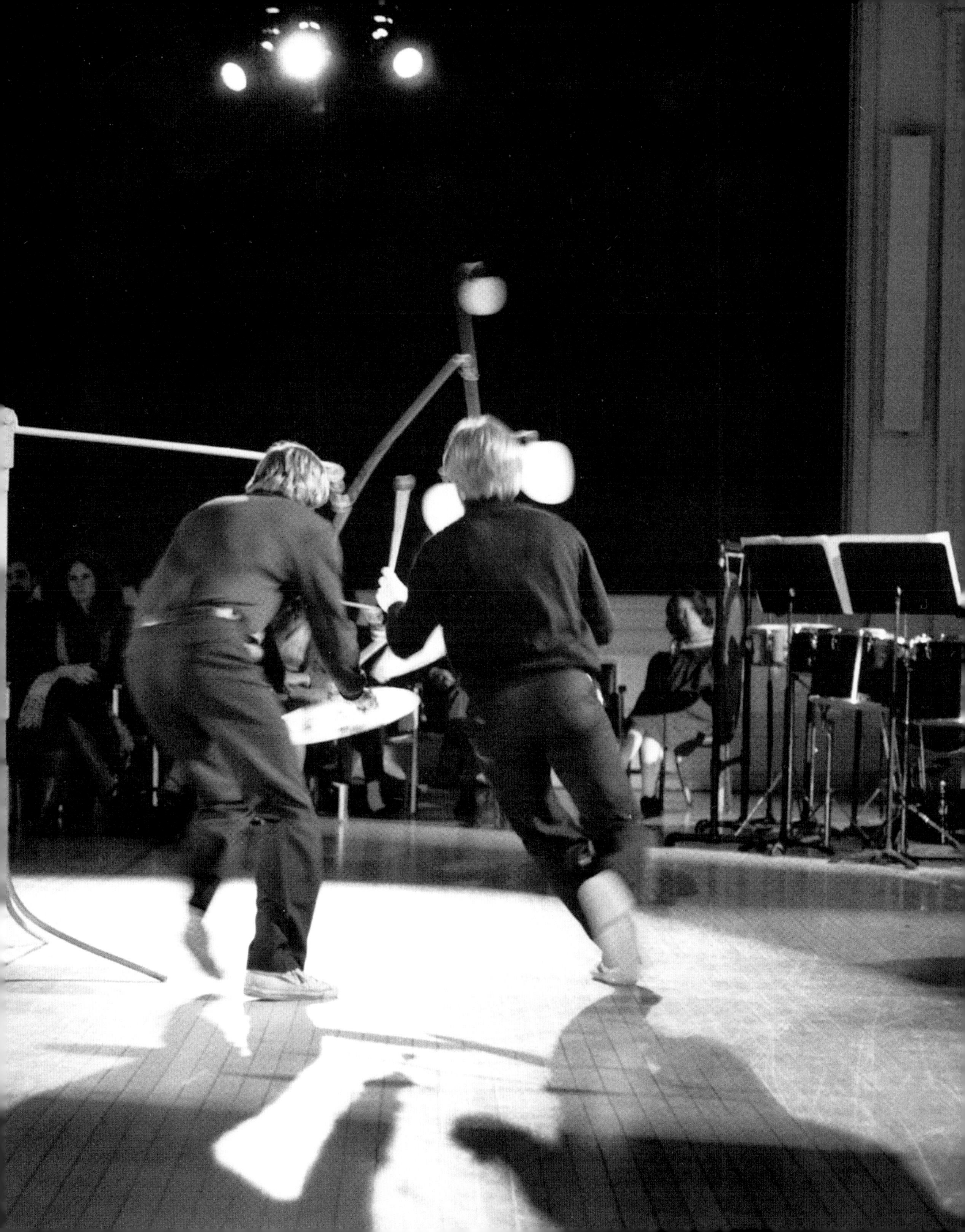

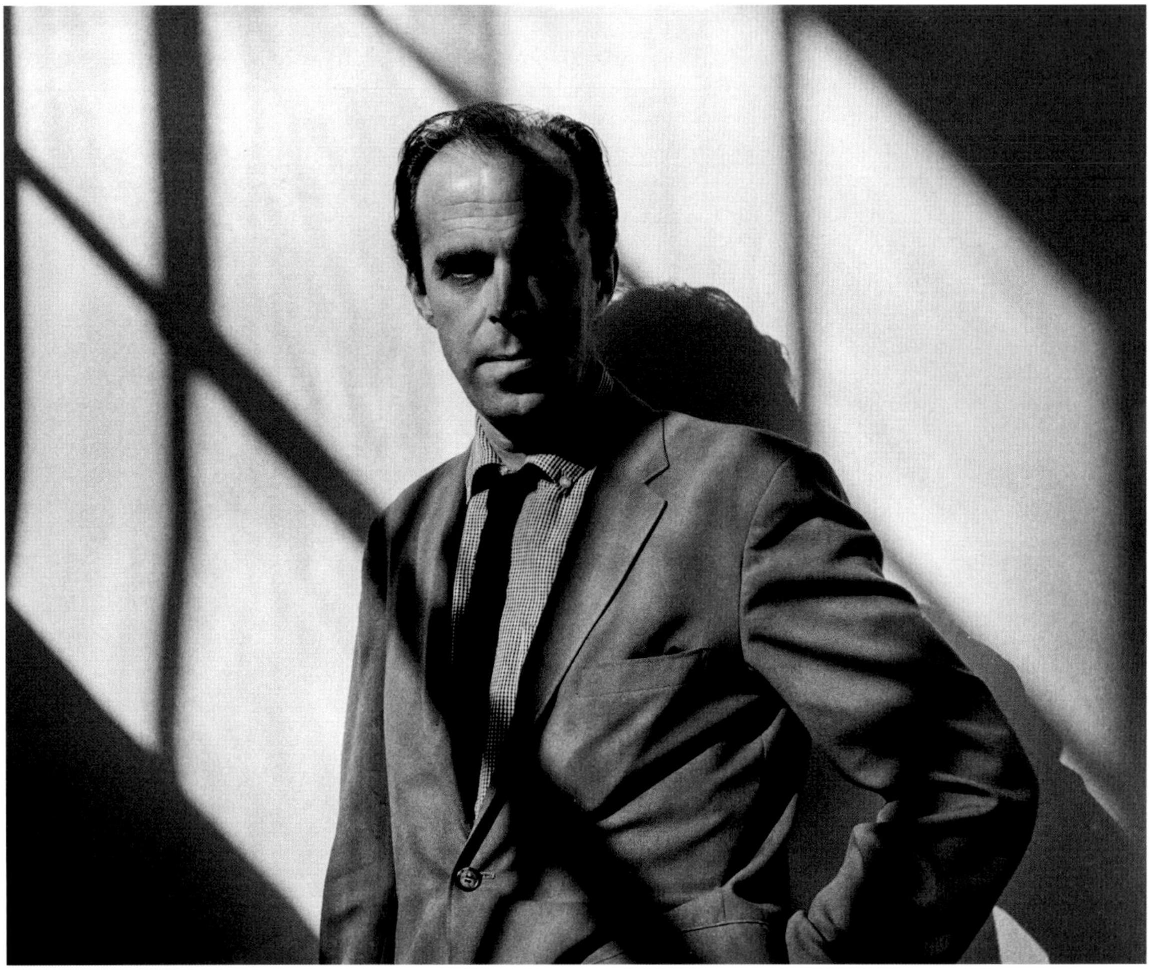

Earle Brown, photographed by Hiro, c.1963

The American composer Earle Appleton Brown was a major figure in the European musical avant-garde of the 1960s, along with Karlheinz Stockhausen, Pierre Boulez, Luigi Nono and Bruno Maderna. As an American, however, he was also affiliated with his New York peers John Cage, Morton Feldman and Christian Wolff. That group later became known as the New York School. During his composition studies in Boston, as a young man, Brown came across a small booklet about Alexander Calder, issued by MoMA in New York.[1] Brown would have his first opportunity to meet Calder in person just a few years later, at the sculptor's home in Roxbury, Connecticut, but the influence of Calder's art would be felt across Brown's entire career.[2]

From 1951 to the spring of 1953, Brown had worked with Cage on the now legendary Project for Music for Magnetic Tape in New York. When the French composer Pierre Boulez came to visit Cage in Manhattan in 1952, Cage arranged for him to see Calder, who lived about ninety miles further north. Brown, who happened to have a car, drove Boulez to Connecticut. Thus, Brown met Calder and had the opportunity to discuss the ways in which he was applying Calder's concepts for mobile sculptures to his own musical thinking.[3]

Ten years later, Earle Brown was highly regarded as a composer, mainly in Europe – although not without a significant detour. Between 1955 and 1960 he had worked as a recording engineer for Capitol Records in Manhattan, in recording sessions with top jazz musicians of the day, including Gerry Mulligan, John Lewis and the Modern Jazz Quartet, Count Basie, Ray Charles, Sarah Vaughan and Dizzy Gillespie. Brown had been a jazz trumpeter himself, and had an excellent understanding of improvisation and of the interactions between individual musicians in jazz. This, along with his background in engineering (Brown studied engineering and mathematics at Northeastern University, Boston), as well as the time he had spent with Cage, cutting and splicing tape, provided him with skills perfectly suited to work in the recording industry. For the first time in his life he earned a significant income, which allowed him to take time off from his job (in 1956, and then again in 1958) and to travel to Europe for several months, in order to pursue his calling as a composer and to visit his European musician and composer friends.

With an intense workload as a recording engineer, Brown came to realise that he needed more time for writing music. He also needed to develop contacts in the music world, in order to find commissions and opportunities for performances. It was Boulez who wrote several letters of recommendation to important European presenters and conductors for him. This introduction helped tremendously in jump-starting Brown's European career, and he decided to leave Capitol Records in 1960. Three years later he was in demand in Europe: as a composer, as a conductor of his own music, and as a lecturer.

The idea Calder's work had inspired in Brown was that of creating music that would specify an immeasurable continuum similar to those of the sculptor's mobiles: movable elements of a composition would provide a situation that allowed for different versions in every performance, while the work would also have a single identity through its fully composed elements. Initially Brown called this concept in music 'mobile form', later naming it 'open form'.

Between 1959 and 1962, Brown had written four important open-form pieces. Three of these had premiered at well-established music festivals in Germany and Italy.[4] Now, he would once again meet Calder, whose art and thinking had inspired his, now fully developed, concept of open form. Much later, looking back on his life and career, Brown said, 'It was way back in '47, '48, '49 that I really became conscious of the fact that I had something to do in music, which was to do a mobile composition, a composition which could be different every time it was played.'[5]

> *I was a jazz musician … and you can understand the idea of spontaneity and flexibility and mobility in some of that … the idea of the floating relationship of elements, never the same twice … always just the same object but … in different perspectives and relationships to one another. That was the key of my entire life as a composer, for better or for worse, and I developed out of that a kind of work called open form, the form of which is open but the materials of which are prescribed and written by me.*[6]

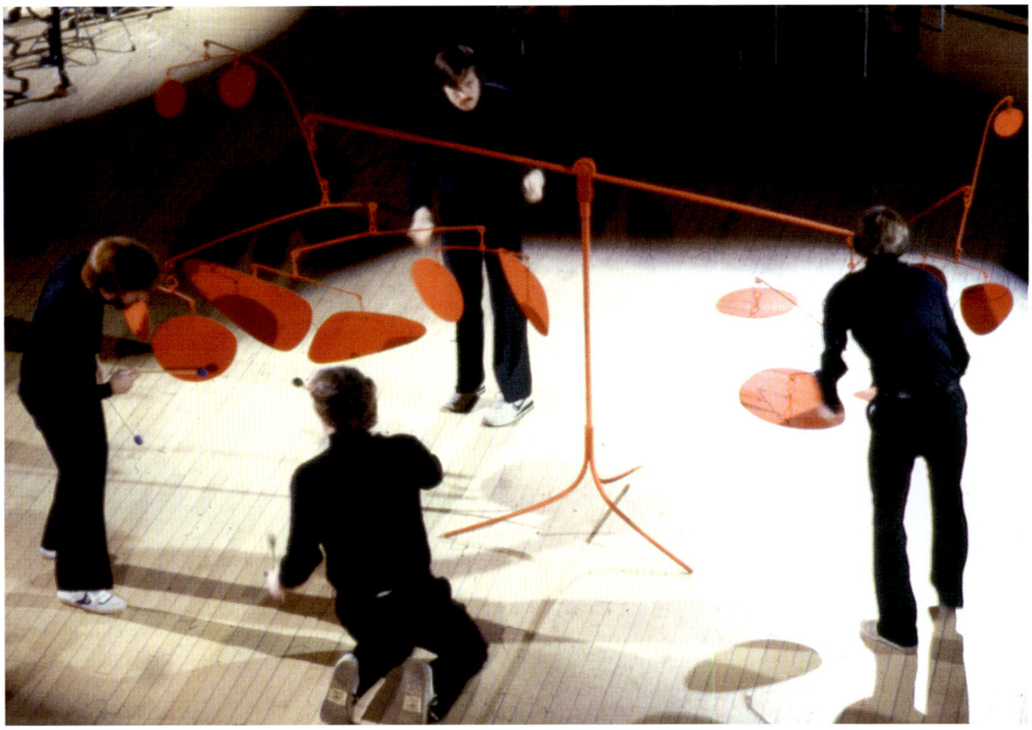

Earle Brown's *Calder Piece* being performed, New Gallery of Contemporary Art, Cleveland, Ohio, 1982

In the spring of 1963, Brown was working on his latest commission, *Times Five*, a piece for five instruments and four pre-recorded channels of tape, for the Service de la Recherche de l'ORTF (the French radio and television service) in Paris.[7] The leader of the Quatuor à percussion de Paris (Paris Percussion Quartet), Diego Masson, offered Brown his next commission. Brown wanted to include a Calder mobile in the instrumentation for the piece. In programme notes for the resulting work, *Calder Piece*, written in 1980, Brown wrote, 'In Paris I began the work for the quartet with the idea that it would be conducted by a mobile in the center of the performance space with the four percussionists placed equidistantly around it, the varying configurations of the elements of the mobile being read by the performers and the evolving open form of each performance different, and changing perspectives in relation to it.'[8]

Masson and Brown drove from Paris to Calder's studio in the town of Saché and presented the idea; Calder's response was positive. Brown later described that afternoon: 'Calder was immediately intrigued and excited by the idea and after a marvelous lunch [prepared] by Louisa, much wine, a few games of billiards, and after fixing a flat on Calder's Citroen, everything was happily agreed to.'[9] Calder promised to create a mobile specifically for the piece Brown was going to write. Based on Brown's description of what the composition would become, Calder named his mobile *Chef d'orchestre*.

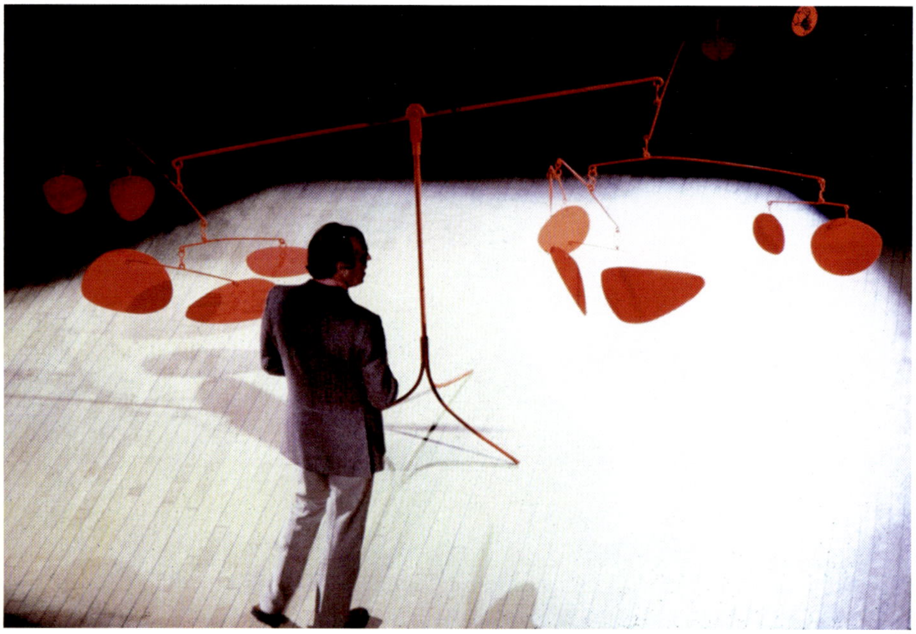

Earle Brown with Calder's *Chef d'orchestre*, New Gallery of Contemporary Art, Cleveland, Ohio, 1982

Brown's idea for having the Calder mobile 'conduct' the four percussionists can be traced back to *December 1952*, a seminal and radical concept piece that he had written in 1952. A set of solid black lines and rectangles on a single page gave the performer(s) a two-dimensional map of musical 'events' that they were to spontaneously invent. The instructions for performance suggest turning the map into a three-dimensional space – in the musicians' minds. The performers were to imagine moving musically in this space in any direction, using the score as a visual stimulus to find the pitch, volume and duration of the next event to be played.

Brown applied a similar concept in some sections of *Calder Piece*, although the musical events were now fully written out (not invented by the musicians, as in *December 1952*). He instructed the percussionists to look at the moving mobile, take a mental snapshot of the outline of its petals, imagine superimposing that outline on the written score, and choose to play the music that was encircled by the imaginary petals on that page.[10] The result would obviously be different every time and for every player, depending on his or her view of the moving mobile in the moment of performance.

Earle Brown's score for *December 1952*

DECEMBER 1952

for one or more instruments and/or sound-producing media

The following note and sketch appear on a notebook page dated Oct. & Nov. '52, but they are the basis of the composition "December 1952" as well as being particularly relevant to "Four Systems".

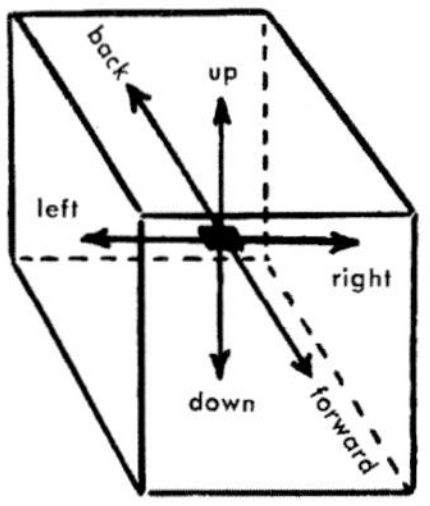

space relative to conceptual mobility and transformation of events in arbitrary, unstable time

". . . to have elements exist in space . . . space as an infinitude of directions from an infinitude of points in space . . . to work (compositionally and in performance) to right, left, back, forward, up, down, and all points between . . . the score [being] a picture of this space at one instant, which must always be considered as unreal and/or transitory . . . a performer must set this all in motion (time), which is to say, realize that it is in motion and step into it . . . either sit and let it move or move through it at all speeds."

"[coefficient of] intensity and duration [is] space forward and back."

Earle Brown's notes for *December 1952*

Calder Piece premiered on 27 February 1967, at Théâtre de l'Atelier, Paris. After several more concerts in France, the last of which was in Saint-Paul de Vence on 8 September 1967, Brown recorded notes on tape about his own impressions of the performances. Calder's standing mobile, *Chef d'orchestre*, was meant not only to be the conductor of the piece, but to be played on as an instrument. Brown noted that audience members had told him how surprised they were to see a Calder mobile being hit. He was worried that some might feel that the precious artwork was being attacked. Calder himself did not seem to mind. He had imagined that the players would hit it much harder, and even offered to make new petals out of brass, as he thought it might sound better. Brown objected, because it was the unique sound of those petals that made it special to him.[11] He also wondered if the impression of aggression towards the mobile did not stem so much from the way it was hit, but from the fact that the performers, who had been instructed to set the mobile in motion by simply playing sounds on it with mallets, were in fact sometimes 'chasing' it to achieve the desired result. Brown felt strongly that the performers, in future performances, should 'stay very much in the same position, each one of them, and merely by striking the mobile, no overt pushing of it, merely by the striking,' it would start being in motion. 'It must be done,' he said, 'in some kind of an elegant, almost choreographic way, where it doesn't communicate that feeling of aggression.'[12]

Performances continued during the ensuing decades in Europe, and in the United States in the early 1980s. The last performances were scheduled in Paris at Centre Pompidou in December 1983 in the context of the museum's exhibition of its extensive Calder collection. In about 1989 Diego Masson sold the mobile, making it impossible, unfortunately, for the piece to be performed or heard again in public. *Chef d'orchestre* later went up for auction incorrectly titled as *Musique Vivante*, which was also the name of Masson's ensemble for contemporary music.[13]

In his performance instructions for *Calder Piece*, Brown had written that 'the piece is one of a kind, and the music must never be independent of that particular mobile. It is my very deeply felt homage to one-of-a-kind Sandy Calder and to his life and work.'[14] After the 1983 performance in Paris, Earle Brown never saw *Chef d'orchestre*, or a performance of *Calder Piece* incorporating the mobile, again, though he and his wife, Susan Sollins-Brown, kept two large empty wooden crates – custom made for *Chef d'orchestre* – in the garage of their house in Rye, New York.[15] Brown died in 2002; Sollins-Brown died in 2014. The crates remain where they left them, reminding us that the mobile might once again travel between concert venues one day.

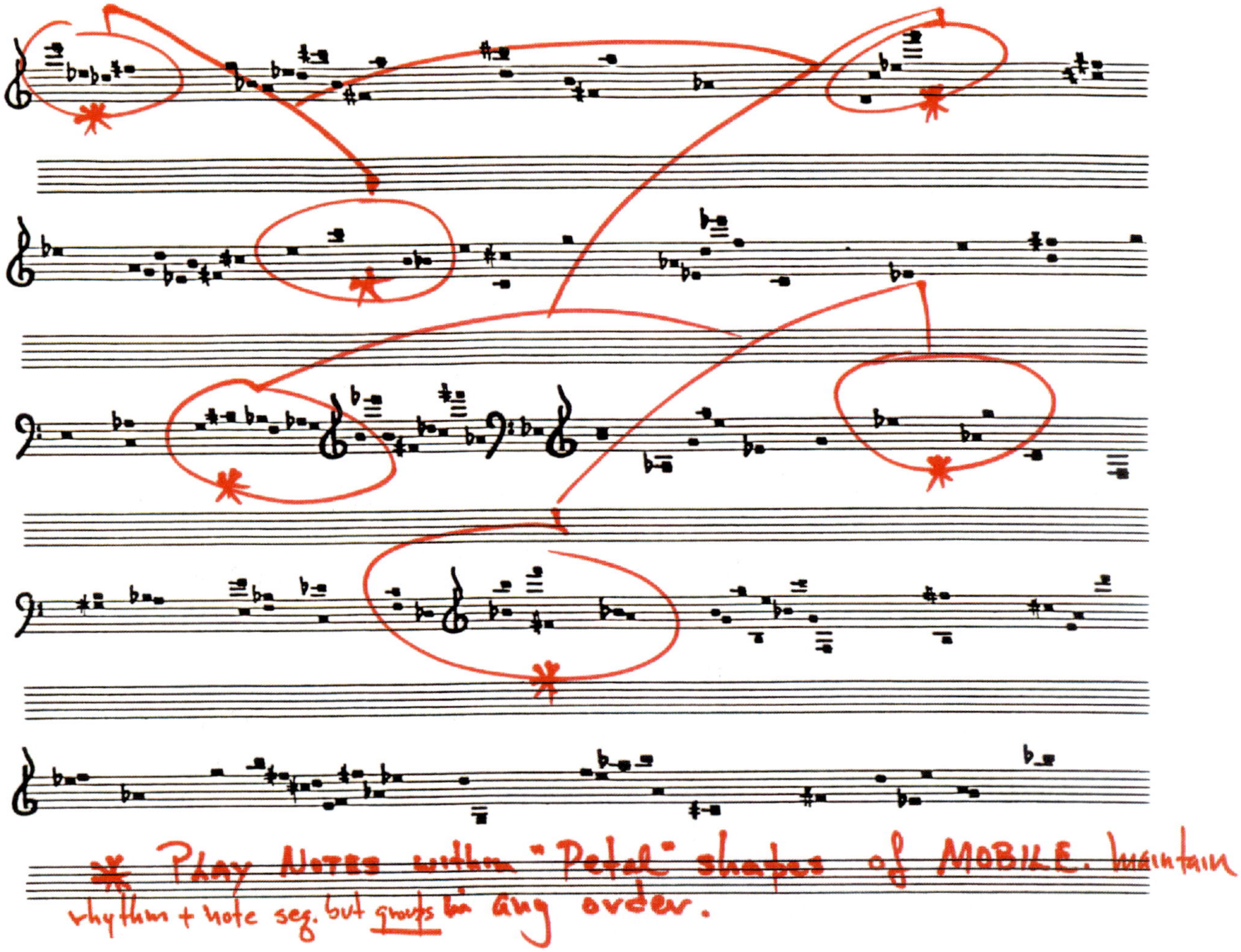

Earle Brown's notes for performers of *Calder Piece*

Notes

1 MoMA presented a major retrospective of Calder's work in 1943 and this was most likely the accompanying publication. See the revised version of this publication, James Johnson Sweeney, Alexander Calder, exh. cat., Museum of Modern Art, New York 1951.

2 Earle Brown: 'Well, Calder influenced my entire way of thinking about music and art in general.' Interviewer: 'How did he do that?' Earle Brown: 'Very early in my life. How did he? Well, I remember when I was still in Boston before I went to Denver [1950] ... I came across the Museum of Modern Art small booklet on Calder ... Some of the statements ... were on a kind of flexibility and the philosophy behind his creating of the mobiles and it just knocked me out. I mean it was just terrific, the philosophy, the aesthetic of a transformable work of art.' Audio interview with Therese Kiene, 18 November 1982, Earle Brown Music Foundation archive, inventory no.MD03 [0:21:04–10]. Earle Brown and Calder are also discussed in Gryphon Rue Rower-Upjohn, 'Calder and Sound', in Susanne Meyer-Büser (ed.), *Alexander Calder: Avant-Garde in Motion*, exh. cat., Kunstsammlungen Nordrhein-Westfalen, Munich 2013, pp.99–111.

3 'I later met Calder at his home in Connecticut (in 1953) [sic] and he therefore knew of my work and my indebtedness to his concept and work.' Earle Brown, Calder Piece programme notes, 1980, http://earle-brown.org/works/view/33, accessed 1 May 2015.

4 *Hodograph I* 1959, for chamber ensemble, and *Available Forms I* 1961, for chamber orchestra, were both commissioned by the City of Darmstadt for the Darmstädter Ferienkurse; *Available Forms II* 1962, for two orchestras, commissioned by the radio orchestra of Rome, premiered in April at the Venice Biennale, conducted by Earle Brown and Bruno Maderna; and *Novara* 1962, for chamber ensemble, premiered at the Tanglewood Music Festival, Lenox, MA.

5 Earle Brown, transcript of a taped interview with Ev Grimes, 21 January 1987, for Oral History of American Music (OHAM) at Yale University Library, Major Figures in American Music 189 a–h, p.18.

6 Audio interview, Earle Brown Music Foundation archive, inventory no.MD025.

7 *Times Five* 1963, for chamber ensemble and four pre-recorded channels of tape, commissioned by Service de la recherche, L'Office de radiodiffusion-télévision Française (ORTF), Paris.

8 Earle Brown, draft for *Calder Piece* performance notes, 1980. Earle Brown Music Foundation archive, drawer 72.

9 Earle Brown, *Calder Piece*, programme notes, 1980, http://earle-brown.org/works/view/33, accessed 1 May 2015.

10 Earle Brown, *Calder Piece*, handwritten instructions for performance, n.d., http://earle-brown.org/works/view/33, accessed 1 May 2015.

11 Brown recorded his thoughts about *Calder Piece* in Autumn 1967. Earle Brown Music Foundation archive, inventory no. MD49.

12 Ibid.

13 *Chef d'orchestre* was sold at Sotheby's, New York, on 8 November 1989. It was again listed for sale in April 1991 (see Contemporary Art, Part I, auction catalogue, Sotheby's, New York, 30 April 1991, lot 4).

14 *Calder Piece* was performed without the mobile on 5 April 1992 at the Albright-Knox Art Gallery in Buffalo, NY. Brown attended the event. After that concert, according to Brown's wife, Susan Sollins-Brown, who had organised the US tour of the piece and mobile during the 1980s, Brown decided not to allow further performances.

15 The house is now home to the Earle Brown Music Foundation.

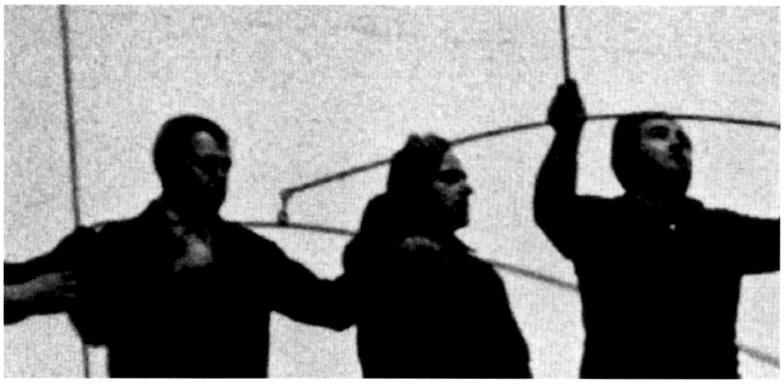

Work in Progress or 'My Life in Nineteen Minutes'

Vassilis Oikonomopoulos

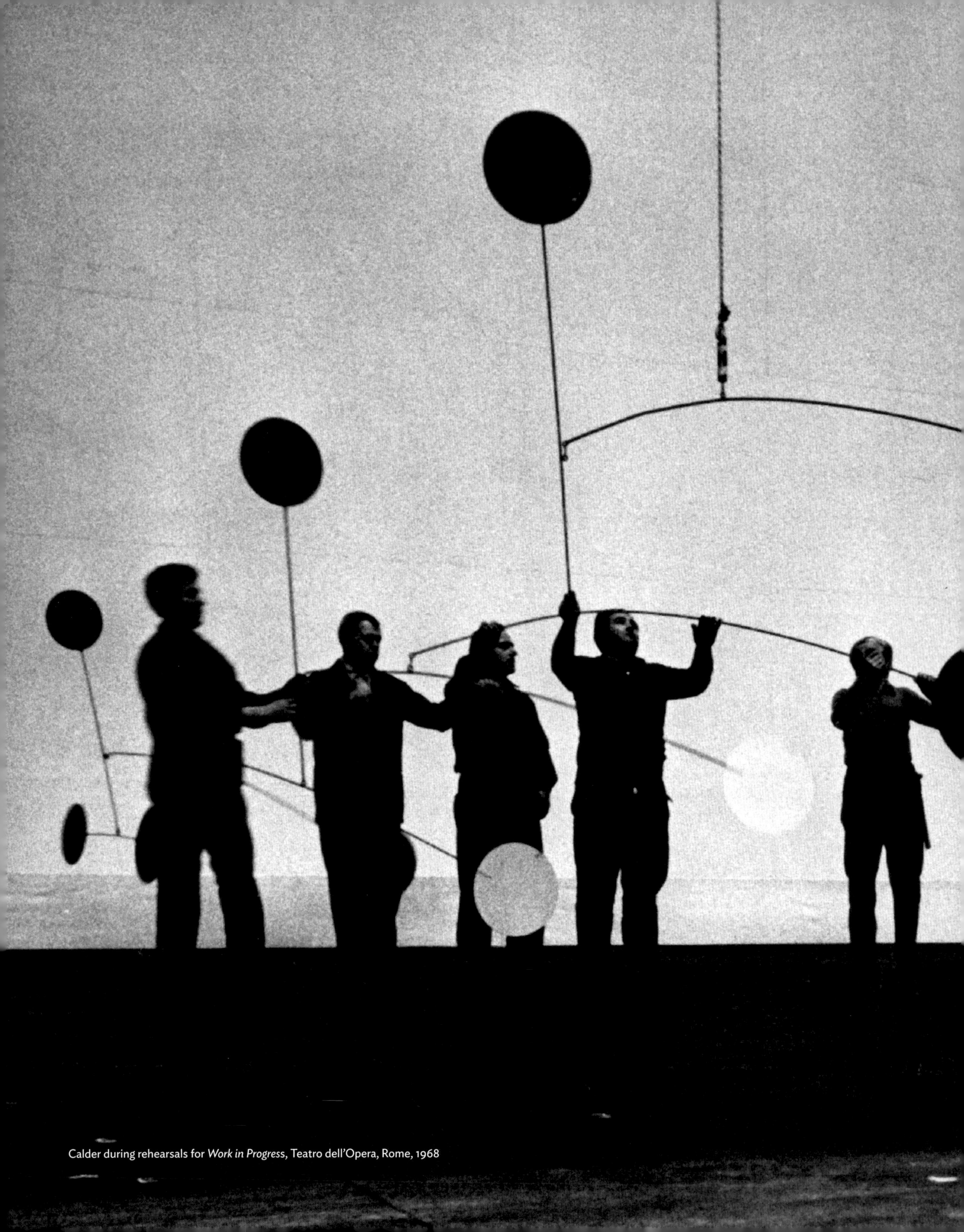

Calder during rehearsals for *Work in Progress*, Teatro dell'Opera, Rome, 1968

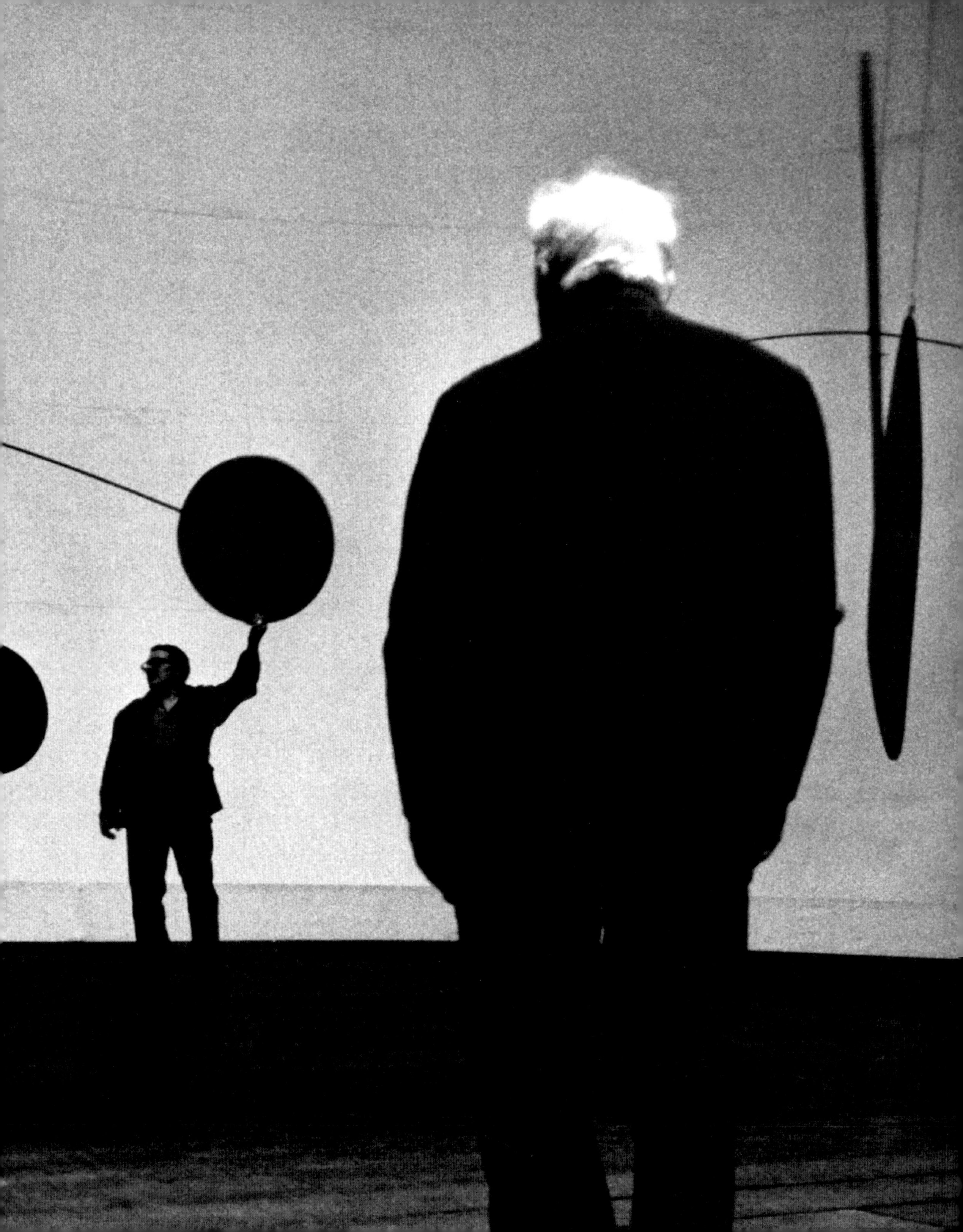

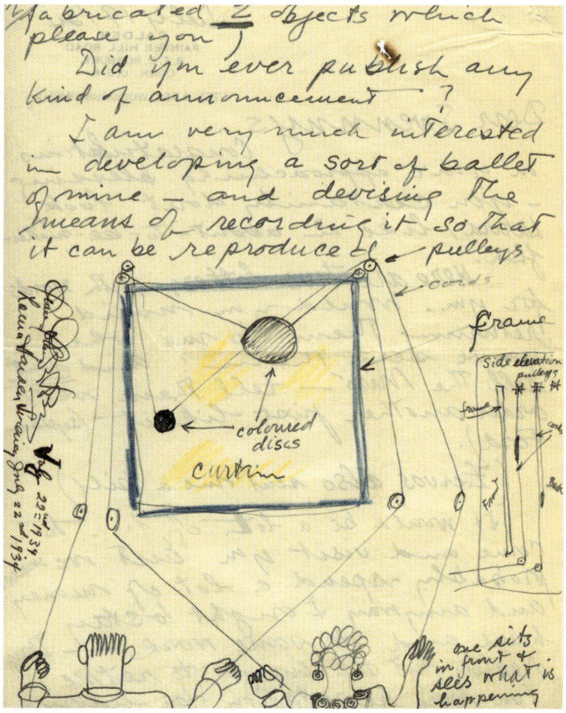

Letter from Calder to James Johnson Sweeney, 19 July 1934, illustrating *A Merry Can Ballet* 1933

Less well known among Calder's works are his collaborations and commissions for the stage, which were equally as radical as his sculptural output. One of his most significant productions was *Work in Progress,* a performance realised (at the Teatro dell'Opera di Roma, in Italy) in 1968. *Work in Progress* presented, for the first time, a 'ballet without dancers' – a performative concept, which Calder had envisaged many decades before, at an earlier stage in his international career. The conceptual underpinnings of the 'ballet without dancers' originate in the idea of the 'ballet-object', which had occupied a central position in Calder's thinking since the 1930s and which, as a sculptural device, was adopted in many examples of Calder's output.

The term 'ballet-object' first appears in Calder's writings in 1937. However, the concept is already evident in his earlier personal correspondence.[1] In a letter to James Johnson Sweeney, curator at the Museum of Modern Art, New York, and, later, director of the Solomon R. Guggenheim Museum, dated 19 July 1934, Calder referred to one of his drawings, which presented an almost square frame, explaining his interest in developing it into a sort of ballet. Inside the frame, two coloured discs could be moved using strings and pulleys.

> *The discs can move anywhere within the limits of the frame, at any speed. Each disc and its supporting pulleys is in a separate vertical plane parallel to the frame [underlining in original]. The number of discs can be increased indefinitely – depending on the necessary clearances. In addition to discs there are coloured pennants (of cloth), with weights on them, which fly at high speed – and various solid objects, bits of hose, springs etc.*[2]

Calder wrote that 'the backgrounds can be changed – and the lighting varied'. In a note included with the drawing, Calder described the experience of a potential performance, in which he specified that 'one sits in front and sees what is happening'. Elsewhere in the letter, Calder noted 'Of course, the real problem [is] to magnify the movement to a full sized proscenium – but I can see various [ways] of obtaining it.'[3]

While Calder certainly experimented extensively with the idea of the 'ballet-object' specifically, a number of other works could be read as driven by the concept of choreographed movement. A series of works, which could be broadly characterised as 'open frames' or 'panels', emerged in Calder's practice between the years 1931 and 1938.

These unique sculptural objects arguably exemplify his desire to combine the concept of the 'ballet-object' with elaborate sculptural construction, explicitly infusing a three-dimensional composition with performative elements. His experimentations at this time could be analysed in terms of three, at times coexisting, components, described as motorised movement, free movement and background, or support.

The use of motorised movement in this period of Calder's development is instantiated by *Black Frame* 1934 (p.161) – a wooden, square frame, which hosts within it a combination of a helix, a disc and a sphere, set against a background made of curved metal sheets. In *Black Frame*, Calder combines the motorised movement of the helix, which turns, with the rotational movement of a disc that flips back and forth and a sphere describing an arching motion. The elaborate design testifies to his distinct take on sculpture; when activated, the work foreshadows the idea of a theatrical scene – a mechanical choreography of sculptural moments that takes place within the space of a black box. Two years later, Calder created another important work, *Snake and the Cross* (p.168), in which he explored the logic of an open frame and free motion by employing highly abstract, sheet-metal shapes, suspended in the centre of a white frame. The striking, three-dimensional and brightly coloured elements of this sculpture could be set in motion using a set of hand cranks. Without the control of a motor, the suspended elements could also be activated by 'natural' means, such as draughts of air.

Snake and the Cross can be seen as a work characterised by its time-based quality as much as by its abstract materiality. A photograph by Herbert Matter captures a moment in Calder's studio when the entire frame of this work was suspended mid-air. Inside the frame, Calder has positioned sets of strings and wires, in an attempt to understand the forces that affect the structure and that will inform his final composition – the complexity of the movements that Calder was aiming to harness becomes explicit. The dramatic composition of this photograph, with all its tension, reflects Calder's desire to orchestrate and commandeer in his work the unseen forces that define the relationships of forms in space.

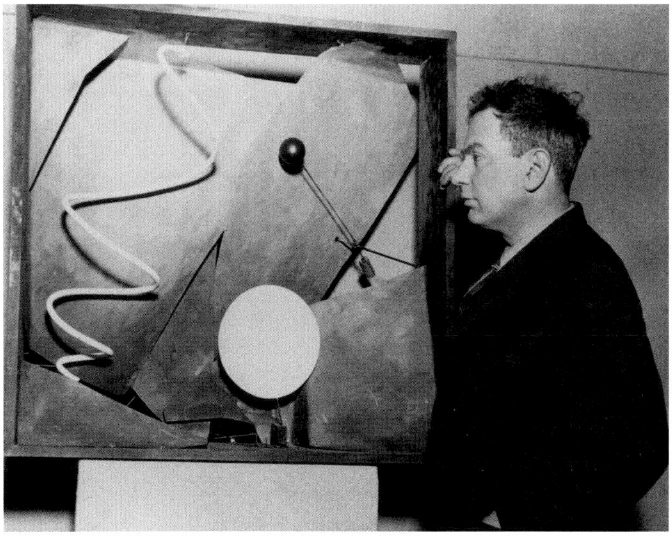

Calder with *Black Frame* 1934 at the Renaissance Society of The University of Chicago, 1935

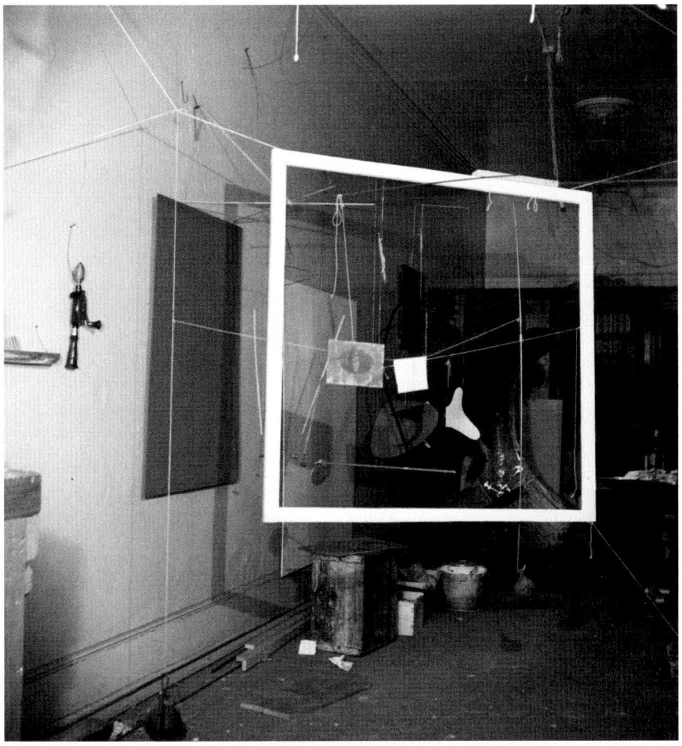

Frame for *Snake and the Cross*, New York City storefront studio, in an earlier configuration, 1936

Calder made his stage debut in 1935, when he constructed mobile sets for Martha Graham's dance piece *Panorama*. In 1936, Calder created the mobile decor for Erik Satie's symphonic drama *Socrate* (1919–20), as commissioned by Virgil Thomson and Arthur Everett 'Chick' Austin, Jr, for the Wadsworth Atheneum in Hartford, Connecticut. This commission was an opportunity to test some of his ideas for performing sculpture in a theatre setting. Calder devised the set, which featured three geometrical objects positioned on stage: a rectangle, a disc and a sphere executed a series of movements in space. Their actions can be interpreted as representing the transition from day to night and from life to death, signifying on stage the death of the Greek philosopher. In relation to *Socrate*, Calder mentioned that 'It serves as an indication of a good deal of my subsequent work.'[4] The simplicity of its geometrical elements; the combination of concurrent motions; and the principle of co-existence for three-dimensional objects in space – all of these motifs and techniques were introduced and have been studied extensively in Calder's most innovative works.

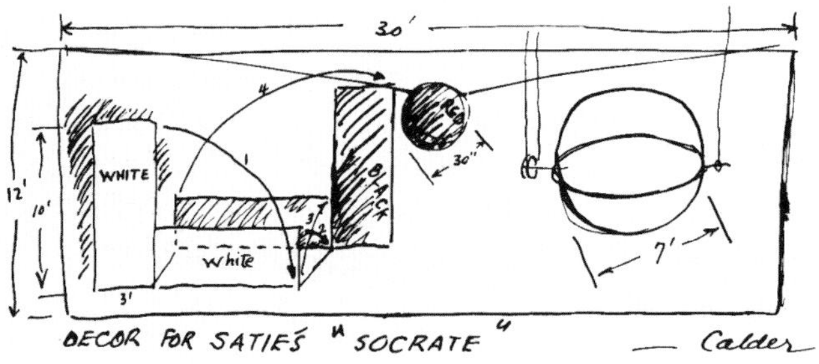

Calder's stage design for Erik Satie's *Socrate* 1936

Work in Progress was realised more than thirty years later. Having gained international recognition for his pioneering role in rethinking modern sculpture, Calder embarked on this remarkable theatrical production for it to become something of the culmination of a career that, by then, spanned the better part of half a century. As the art historian Arnauld Pierre put it: 'Calder had to wait until the end of his life to realise the most ambitious of his goals concerning the staging of movement.' Pierre noted that 'his *Work in Progress*, performed in 1968 [...] arose from frustration. Although the thirty years following *Socrate* had been punctuated by about a dozen theatre collaborations, his role had never gone beyond contributing what amounted to a stage prop in productions in which he did not control all the elements.'[5]

The point of departure for *Work in Progress* was Calder's introduction to the celebrated pianist and artistic director of Teatro dell'Opera, Massimo Bogianckino, through the Italian art historian Giovanni Carandente. Carandente and Calder had become friends in the mid-1950s and, in 1962, the two had collaborated for the Festival dei Due Mondi in Spoleto, near Rome, which Carandente directed. Their collaboration resulted in the creation of the impressive *Teodelapio*, widely regarded as one of Calder's most significant outdoor, steel sculptures.

In 1966, at the suggestion of Carandente, Bogianckino spearheaded a plan to have Calder work on the production of sets for one of the ballets or operas due to be staged at the Teatro dell'Opera. Calder initially refused to work on such a project. The reason may be that, as Arnaud Pierre argued, Calder had felt, in all his previous collaborations for the stage, that the final result compromised his vision for his sculpture and that his output had always been considered secondary in relation to the actions performed by dancers or actors on stage. However, during a subsequent visit that Calder made to Rome, and in the company of artists Max Ernst, Dorothea Tanning, Renato Guttuso and novelist Alberto Moravia, Bogianckino took a remarkable decision and offered the artist the freedom to conceive and realise a performance entirely his own, offering him full control of the final result, without any conceptual or practical limitations. In a letter to Carandente, Calder reflected on this new proposition:

> *For thirty years I have been thinking about a production that would be entirely mine, form and music working together. I long ago discussed this with [choreographer, Léonide] Massine, but he insisted on having dancers. I later made stage sets, but this is not exactly what I wanted to do ... for Satie's* Socrate, *[playwright, Henri] Pichette's* Nucléa, *[choreographer] John Butler's* The Glory Folk *in Spoleto, for [dancer and choreographer] Joe Lazzini in Marseille. The idea of a production that was totally mine had already come to me in spirit in 1926 when I finished the Cirque* [Cirque Calder]*, and when I tried to frame it in a stage opening, amusing myself by thinking it an actual theatre.*[6]

The project itself began with Calder having to choose the music and, as the programme for the Teatro dell'Opera had to be announced in advance, coming up with a title for the work. In the course of finding a suitable soundtrack, Calder and Bogianckino explored a number of recordings of classical music, including works by baroque composers Antonio Vivaldi, Giuseppe Tartini and Tomaso Albinoni, alongside contemporary, twentieth-century composers such as Arnold Schoenberg, Anton Webern, Alban Berg and Alfredo Casella. The final selection of music consisted of three pieces that Calder had heard on a record called *Electron*: Niccolò Castiglioni's *Divertimento* 1961, Aldo Clementi's *Collage* 1960 and Bruno Maderna's *Musica su due dimensioni* 1951. In a letter to Carandente, Calder mentioned: 'I decided to call my part *Work in Progress*, which is old hat but noncommittal.'[7]

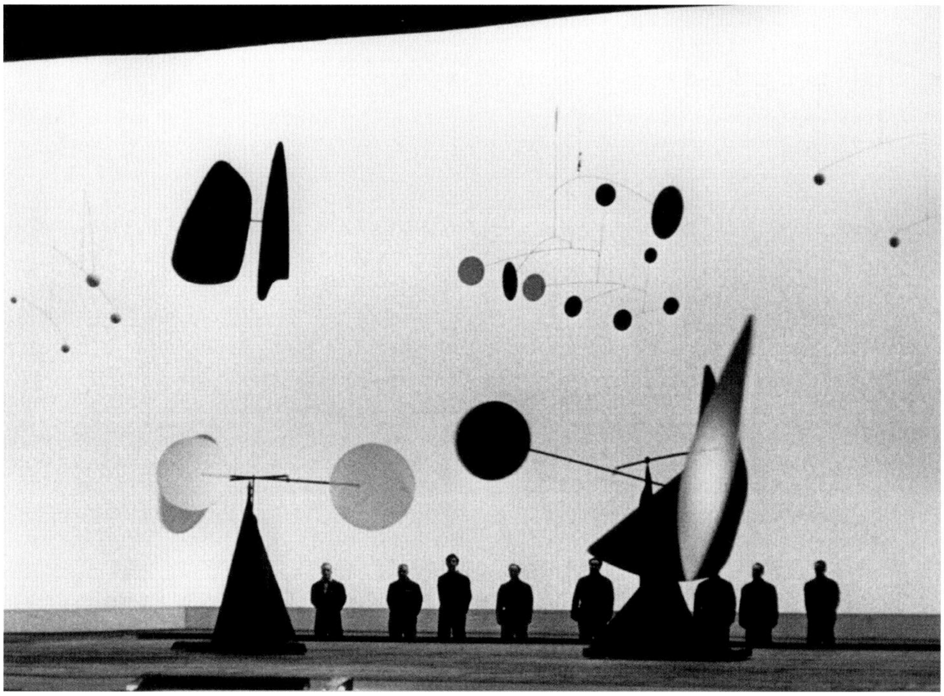

Work in Progress, Teatro dell'Opera, Rome, 1968

Calder arrived in Rome at the end of 1967 to begin work on the project in earnest, bringing with him scale models of sculptures, and diagrams. The scale models consisted of a group of four, small, standing mobiles. The resulting mobiles were meant to be included in the final scene of the performance. According to Carandente, he, Bogianckino and Calder discussed Calder's ideas, focusing on the way in which the mobiles would move and how their rotating elements could function on stage.[8] Calder also referred at this time to his concept for a scene of action during which a group of cyclists would storm the stage. He left his diagrams and notes with Carandente, who then composed the first sequence of scenes for Calder's approval.

Following many months of intense preparation, the first performance of *Work in Progress* was held at the Teatro dell'Opera on 11 March 1968. From surviving footage and historical images we can put together the sequence of this extraordinary and visually exciting production. The action on stage reflected the ingenuity and diversity of Calder's sculptural language: the stage itself was alive and vibrating with motion, turned into a landscape in which large-scale standing mobiles, hanging mobiles and other geometrical forms were juxtaposed, with coloured elements rotating and moving at different speeds. One might distinguish vibrantly coloured discs and other, more abstract, forms spinning vertically on top of stable bases. The expansive tentacles of the hanging mobiles and the large, bold, rotating forms seemed to dwarf their surroundings. They stood in stark contrast with their simple background – a screen on which changing, softly coloured lights were projected. In the 1967–8 programme for the Teatro dell'Opera, we find a description for *Work in Progress*:

> Work in Progress*, therefore, has no plot, even if the audience will easily be able to understand that it is an abstract conjuring up of natural elements and that it seeks to represent the infinite mystery of the Universe. The spectacle is not based on any narrative, but a theme there is, and it is full of unexpected surprise. In the end, the whole big game does include the vital, active participation of the vicissitudes of the modern world, the yearning for freedom and peace felt by all free men.*[9]

Referring to the sheet of directions, we can establish the structure of the performance, which was divided into four acts.[10] The first act opened with a series of light effects on a cyclorama and the shadows on it of three hanging mobiles that were hidden high above the stage. A large mobile, central among them, was based on one of the models that Calder had presented to Bogianckino when he first explained his ideas to him the previous year. The other two mobiles were similar to a work called *Black Clouds* – a mobile consisting of two large sheets of metal painted black, both suspended on string from a metal rod – which Calder had created in around 1939.

After a few moments, the light changed to a strong violet shade, which made the shadows of the mobiles disappear. That change signalled the beginning of a light show, consisting of an, apparently slow-motion, projection of coloured discs. The changing projection gradually revealed two images – 'sun' and 'tête nègre' – on the cyclorama. (Both images are characteristic among Calder's painted motifs and exemplify his experiments in this medium.) Soon after, the large mobile, which was centrally positioned among the three above the stage, was slowly lowered. At the same time, the stage floor opened up and a group of scene-shifters were raised up from underneath. They re-assembled the large mobile under a blue iridescent light. As the mobile moved upwards once again, the scene-shifters stood still, looking up. Two standing mobiles, *Object with Red Discs* and *Spider*, which were stage reproductions of works from 1931 and 1939, then entered from either side of the stage.

The second act opened with a seascape projected onto the cyclorama. As soon as the tulle curtain went up, the light changed, and a stage reproduction of *The Orange Panel* 1936 (p.164), a seminal work in Calder's earlier practice, came down slowly, with its moving, motorised parts running at full speed. The backdrop changed, with a bright-red sky now projected onto the cyclorama. Two standing mobiles then entered the stage and, as a tulle curtain came down, left again. *The Orange Panel* moved upwards, with clouds projected onto its surface as it slowly disappeared from view. With the 'sky' now projected onto the cyclorama, a mobile with birds entered, before the stage was flooded with a blinding light, signalling the end of the second act.

The third act began with the group of cyclists storming the stage, describing a double figure-of eight. When the last cyclist had left the stage, a black pyramid slowly appeared from stage right. The sun came down again over the pyramid, while the 'tête nègre' approached from stage right. Light effects described the transition from day to night and then back to day again. As the sun and 'tête nègre' disappeared, a man standing on top of the pyramid began fluttering a red flag.

The fourth and final act began with the large mobile returning to the stage again, with the other two hanging mobiles. Four standing mobiles were moved onto the stage from the wings. Their elements moved and rotated in a dynamic way for an extended period of time before the curtain signalling the end of the performance came down.

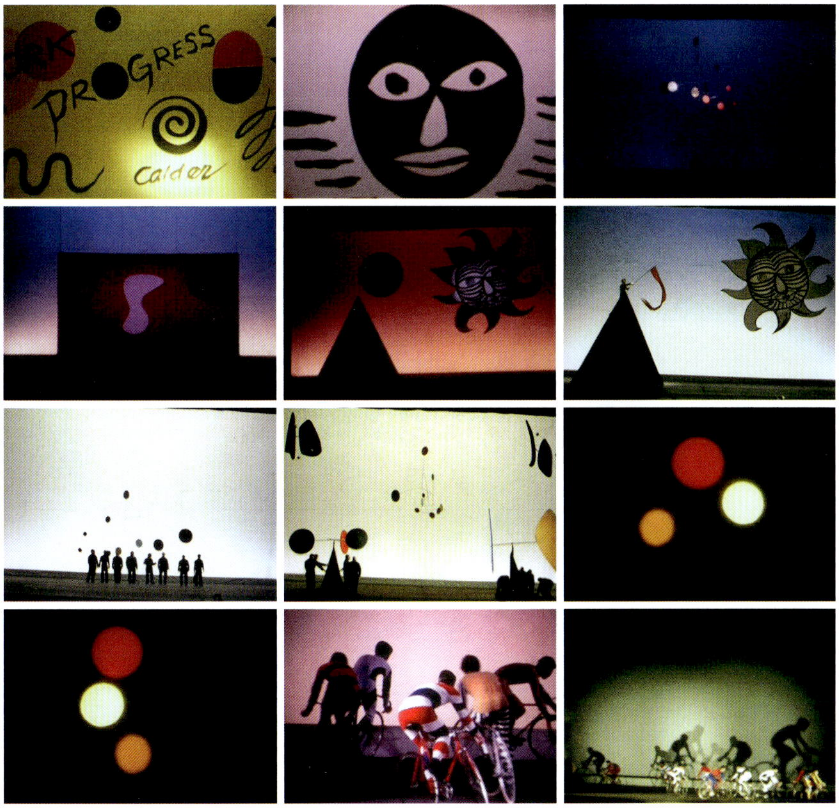

Film stills from the performance of *Work in Progress*, Teatro dell'Opera, Rome, 1968

Central to comprehending the importance of *Work in Progress* is an understanding of the division that has historically existed between the disciplines of sculpture and theatre. There has always been a tendency to approach sculpture on stage as the backdrop or set – the scene in front of which action is taking place. However, with the production of *Work in Progress,* Calder brought sculpture into the foreground, making it the active element of an event. Size and scale had always fascinated Calder, and the delicate movement of great forms, which was central to his thinking, can be seen in this work, connected with the idea of the mechanical ballet – a ballet produced and existing independent of dancers. Elements of controlled and free movement coexisted during the performance. Mobiles and 'stabiles' – two of Calder's greatest contributions to modern art – were repurposed for the stage. Balance, motion and rhythm, which were central principles of his work, were introduced as performative devices on stage. These rhythms were combined in a positive way – superimposed – as a variety of movements, one acting upon another. For an artist whose entire life and career were devoted to transgressing boundaries and exploring motion in its infinite possibilities, this can be seen as the moment where the ideas of infinite motions and infinite combinations of motions were actualised.

In combining sculpture and performance, Calder produced a hybrid form, which challenged the evolution of sculpture and the possibilities of performance alike. The convolution of the two disciplines amplified their strong connections and indicated that Calder's vision was not only reassessed but also finally reached a place he could easily call his own.

Reflecting on the performance, Carandente later wrote:

> *The performance itself is difficult to define in theatrical terms: it is not a 'ballet' as Calder often liked to call it, yet it is accompanied by excellent contemporary music; nor is it an opera, essentially because it has no singing or recitative and the performance is in no way conditioned by the musical score. The painted, three-dimensional stage design is neither a backdrop nor simply a place where the action takes place: it is the action, albeit of an abstract kind.*[11]

Carandente's recollections offer further insight into the innovative nature of the work, confirming that *Work in Progress* captured Calder's career-long celebration of movement and performance as conceptual tools. Calder's vision for a sculpture that performed, and the development of his ideas regarding the 'ballet-object' on a theatre stage; the vivacity of the production and its dazzling array of forms, colours and movement – these sum up the exuberance that characterises the artist's entire practice.

Carandente remarked, on the artist's reaction to the performance of *Work in Progress*:

> *Calder and his wife Louisa were present at the public dress rehearsal: the theatre was filled with artists and friends, the atmosphere was electric, while from outside the theatre the first signs of student unrest could be heard. Louisa was sitting in one of the last seats and it was the one and only time I saw tears in her proud eyes. Calder and I were sitting together just opposite the stage. When the curtain finally fell he looked intensely at me and said 'I should have called it "My life in nineteen minutes."'* [12]

Work in Progress was never performed outside of the Teatro dell'Opera. Over the years, there have been a number of attempts to restage it. According to Carandente:

> *The Centre Pompidou, the Whitney Museum [of American Art] in New York, George Balanchine, the Metropolitan Opera House, the Paris Opéra, the National Theatre of Stockholm, a British ballet company, and Covent Garden all wanted to stage it and made numerous requests to do so. But* Work in Progress *never left the Teatro dell'Opera after the three seasons that it played in Rome. Because it is a very complex production, a work of this kind cannot always be performed on the traditional opera set.* [13]

The last time *Work in Progress* was performed in Rome was on 10 May 1977, six months after Calder's death. Following its last performance, Carandente wrote to Louisa Calder:

> *The Ballet last night has had a great success, greater than in 1968. Loud cheers at the end and three times during the performance. All our friends were in the theatre and [the]* Work in Progress *revival has had the meaning of an Italian Hommage [sic] to Sandy's Memory. I was so glad that everything went on perfectly and [am] deeply touched.* [14]

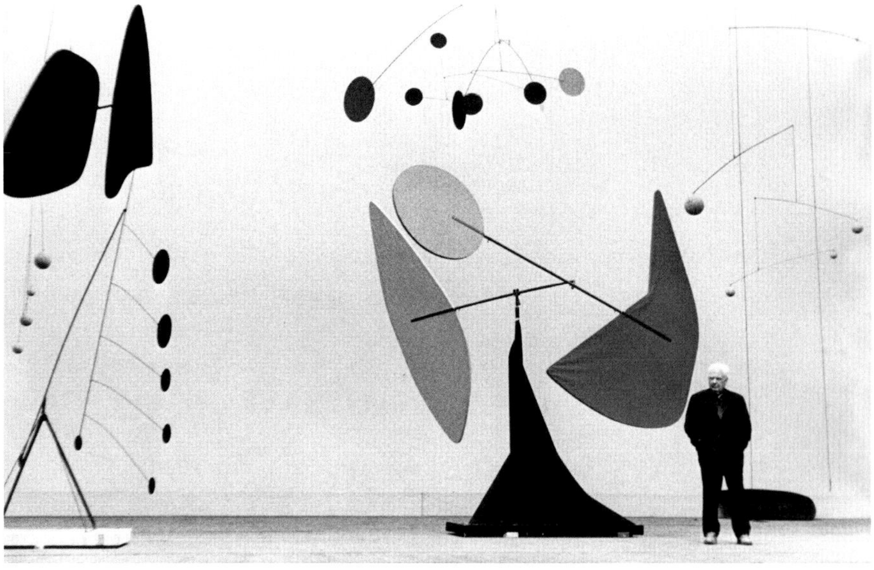

Calder on the set for *Work in Progress*, Teatro dell'Opera, Rome, 1968

Notes

1 In an autobiographical text of 1937, Calder mentions: 'For a couple of years in Paris I had a small ballet-object, built on a table with pulleys at the top of the frame. It was possible to move coloured discs across the rectangle, or fluttering pennants, or cones; to make them dance, or even have battles between them.' Alexander Calder, 'Mobiles', in Myfanwy Evans (ed.), *The Painters' Object*, London 1937, p. 64.

2 Alexander Calder, letter to James Johnson Sweeney, 19 July 1934, Calder Foundation archives.

3 Ibid.

4 Alexander Calder, 'Mobiles', in Myfanwy Evans (ed.) 1937, p.64.

5 Arnauld Pierre, 'Staging Movement', in Marla Prather and Arnauld Pierre, *Alexander Calder: 1898–1976*, exh. cat., National Gallery of Art, Washington DC, London and New Haven 1998, p.345.

6 Alexander Calder, quoted in Giovanni Carandente, *Calder*, Milan 1983, p.231.

7 Alexander Calder, letter to Giovanni Carandente, 20 October 1967, location unknown, reproduced in Alexander S.C. Rower (ed.), *Calder: Sculptor of Air*, exh. cat., Palazzo delle Esposizioni, Milan 2009.

8 Giovanni Caradente reflects on his conversation with Calder: '"I'll bring a few objects and diagrams in order to explain my idea" [Calder] said. At the airport, Calder had a suitcase and a box with him: the latter contained four small standing mobiles, the maquettes for the final scene. He also had sketches and notes on small pieces of paper, the orbits for the discs, and the circular tracks for the cyclists, which he had already conceived of as including an oval, a figure eight, and a double "S".' Giovanni Carandente, 'Work in Progress', in Alexander S.C. Rower (ed.) 2009, p.234.

9 Teatro dell'Opera di Roma, programme, 'Teatro dell'Opera, Roma, Stagione 1967–68'. Calder Foundation archives.

10 Giovanni Carandente, 'Work in Progress by A. Calder: Sequence of the Ballet', 14 April 1975. Calder Foundation archives.

11 Alexander S.C. Rower (ed.) 2009, p.234.

12 Alexander S.C. Rower (ed.) 2009, p.235.

13 Ibid.

14 Giovanni Carandente, letter to Louisa Calder, 11 May 1977, Calder Foundation archives.

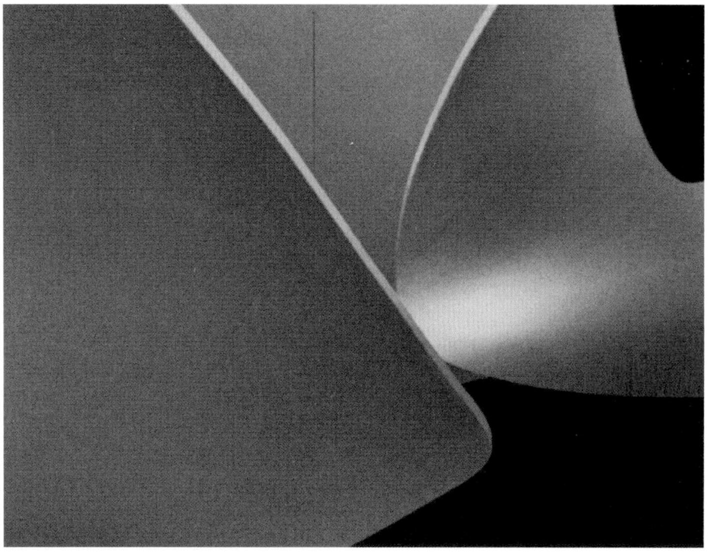

Plates

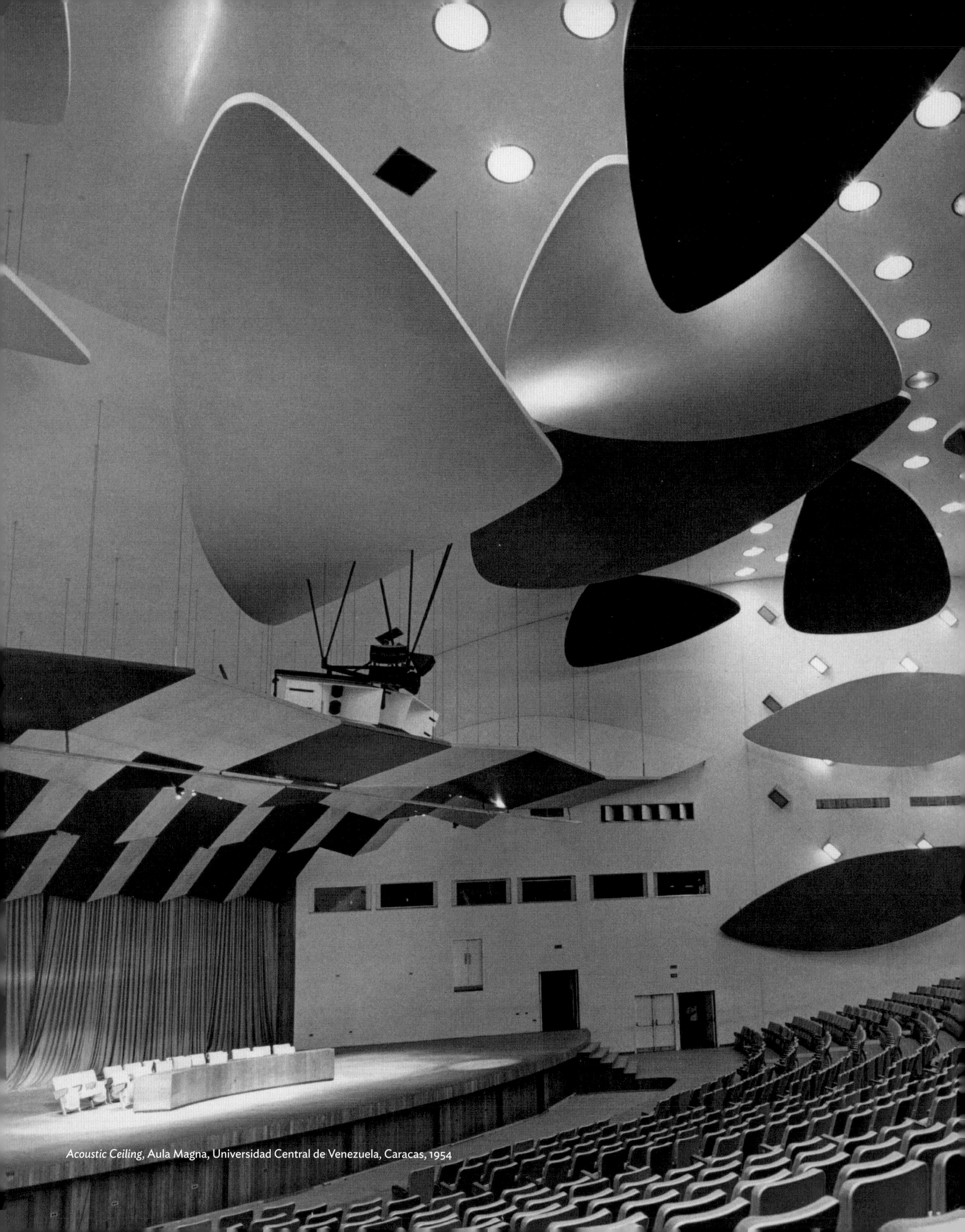

Acoustic Ceiling, Aula Magna, Universidad Central de Venezuela, Caracas, 1954

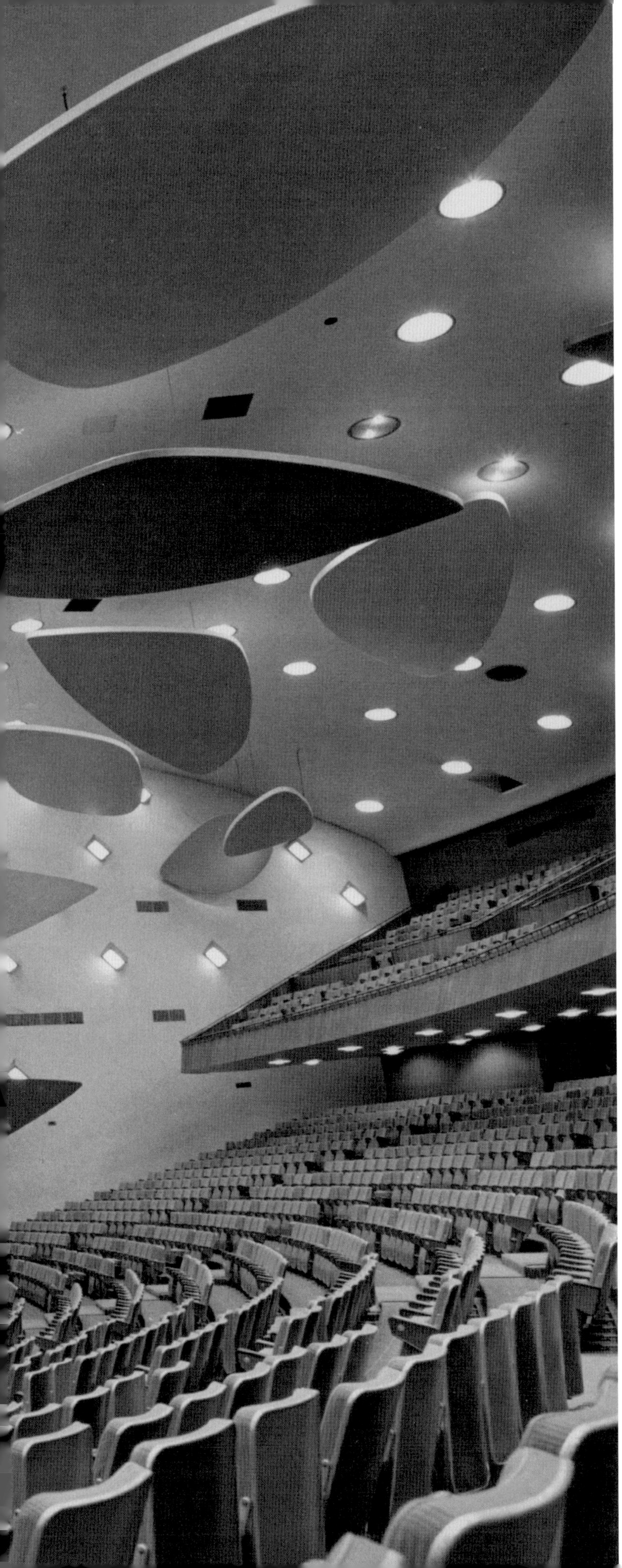

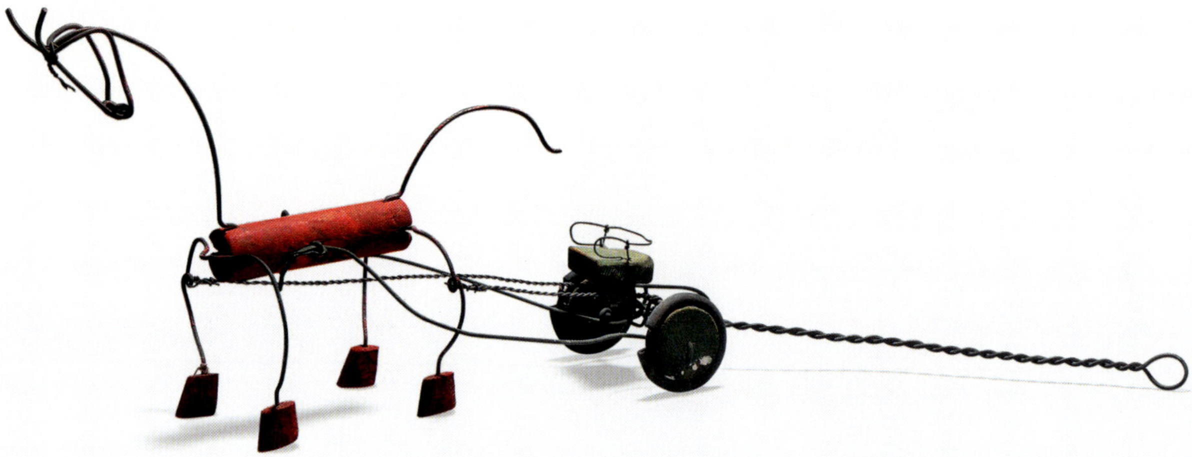

Red Horse and Green Sulky 1926

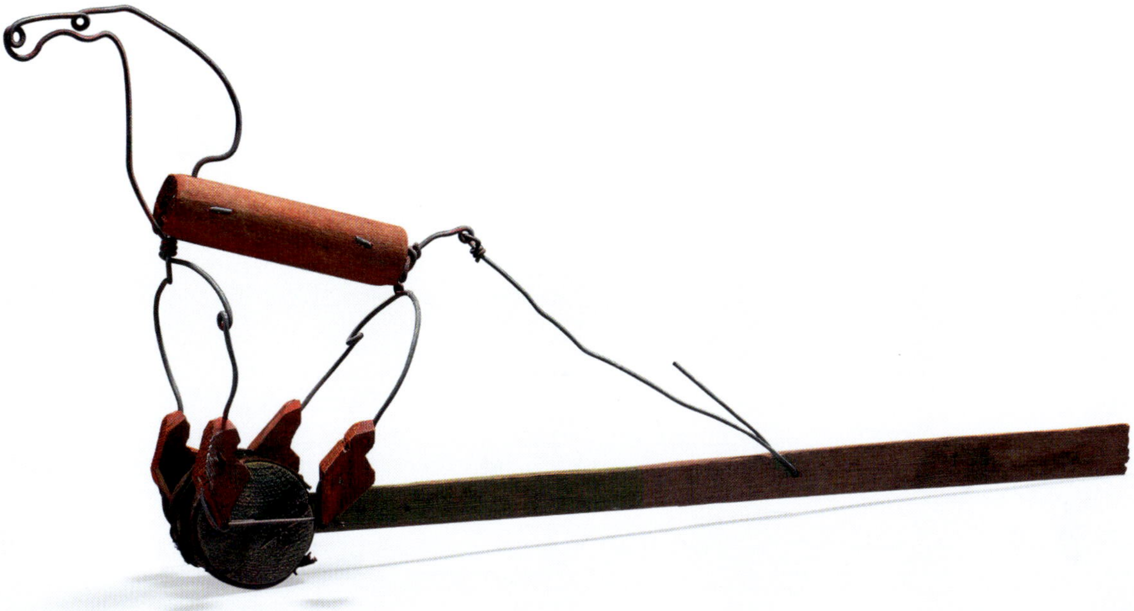

Galloping Horse 1926

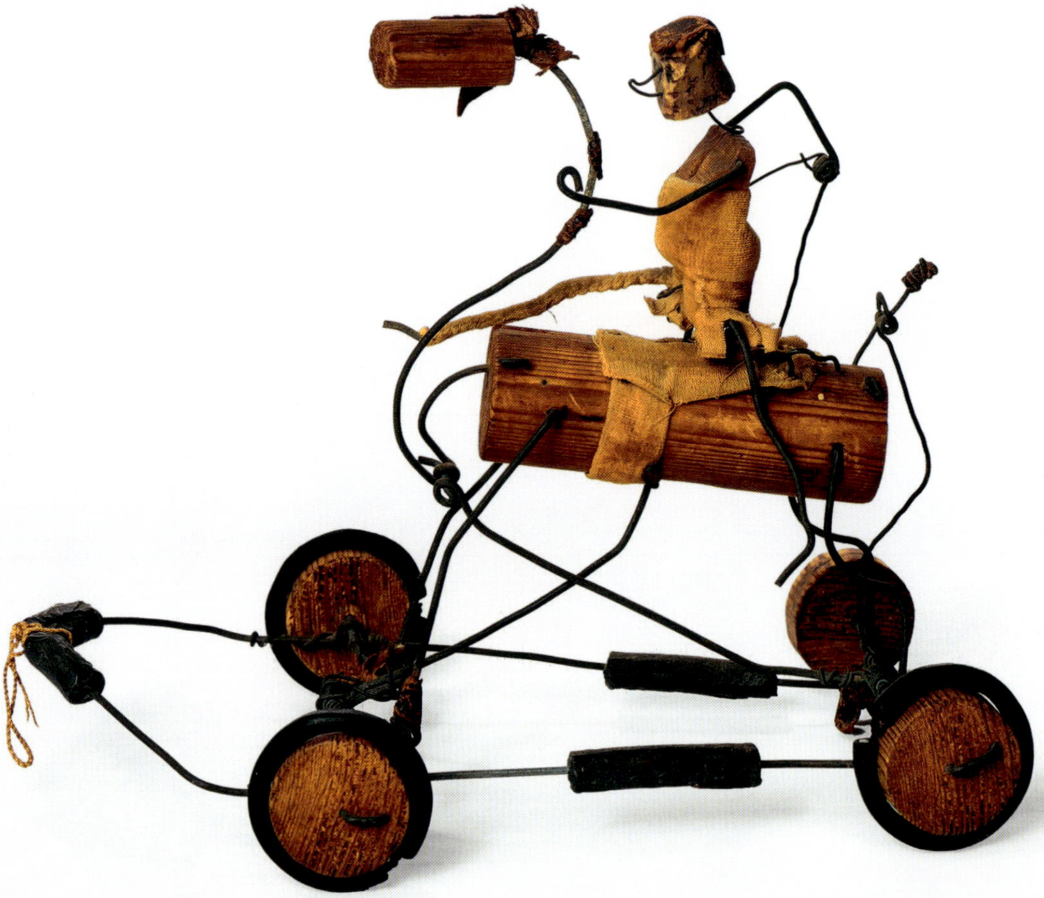

Horse and Rider 1926–31

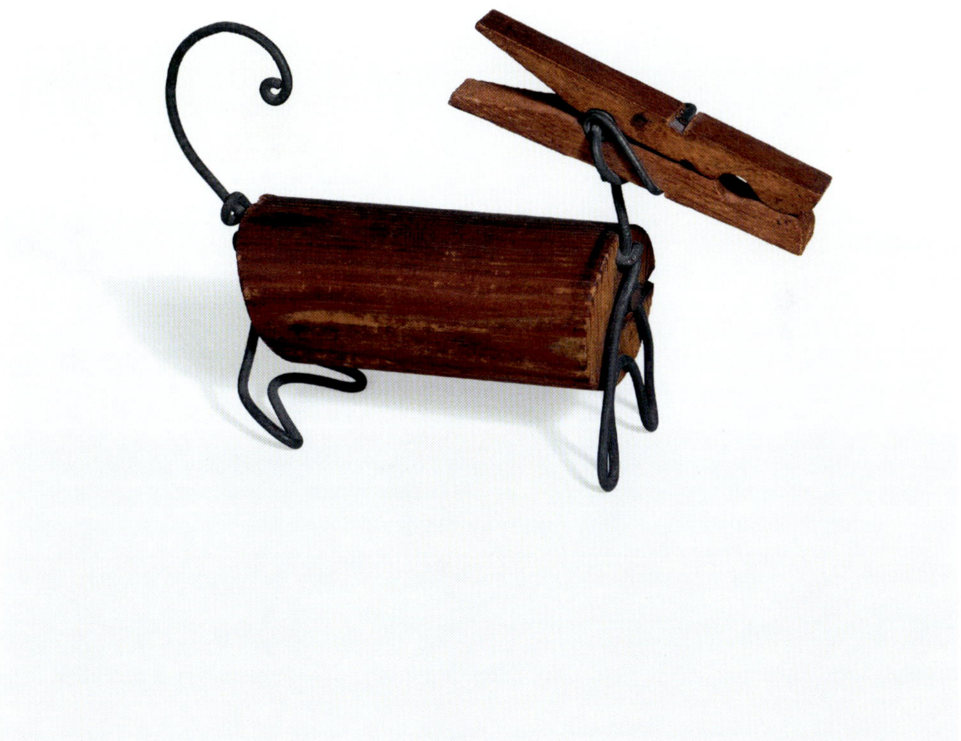

Dog 1926–31

Torrero c.1927

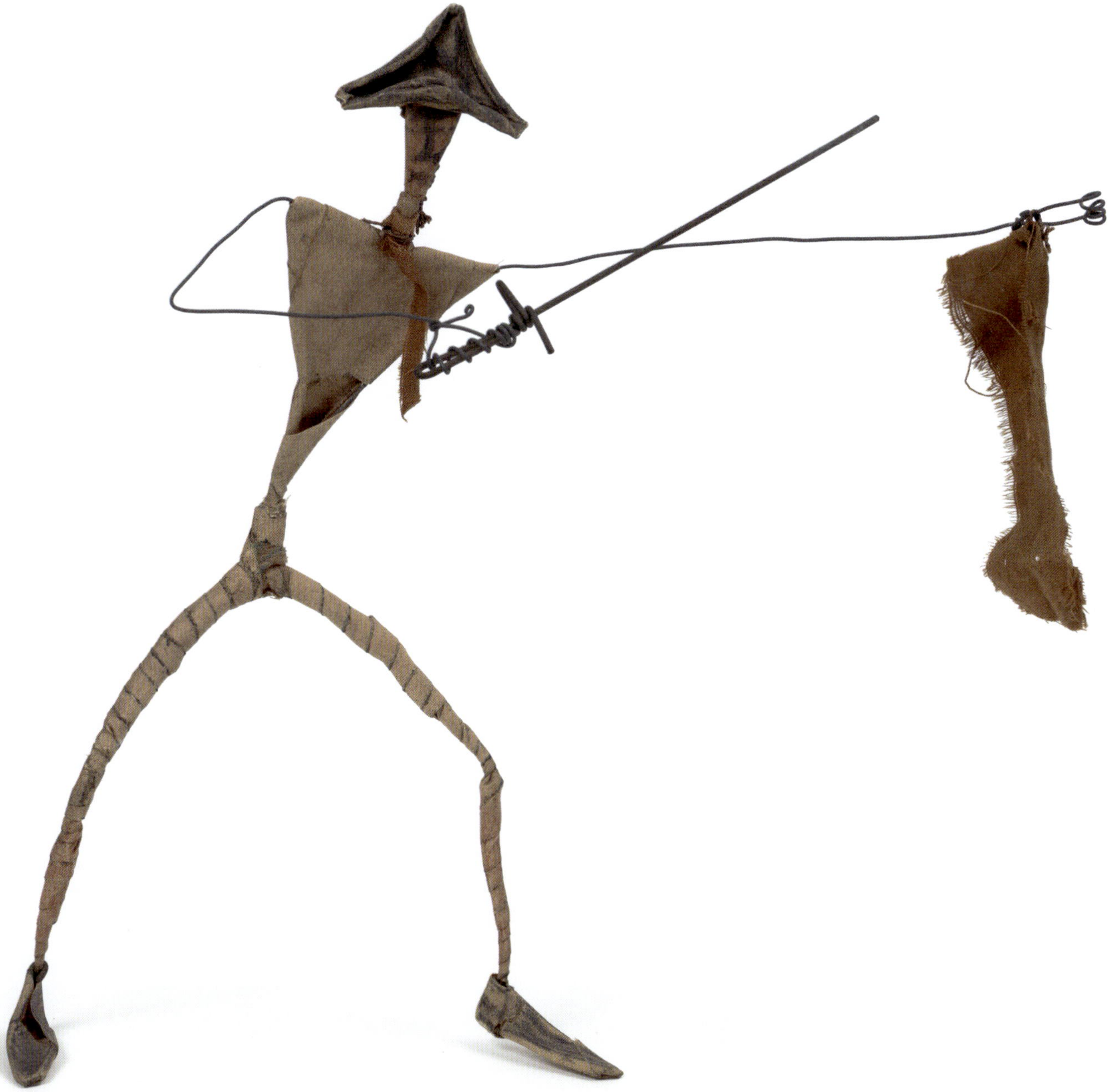

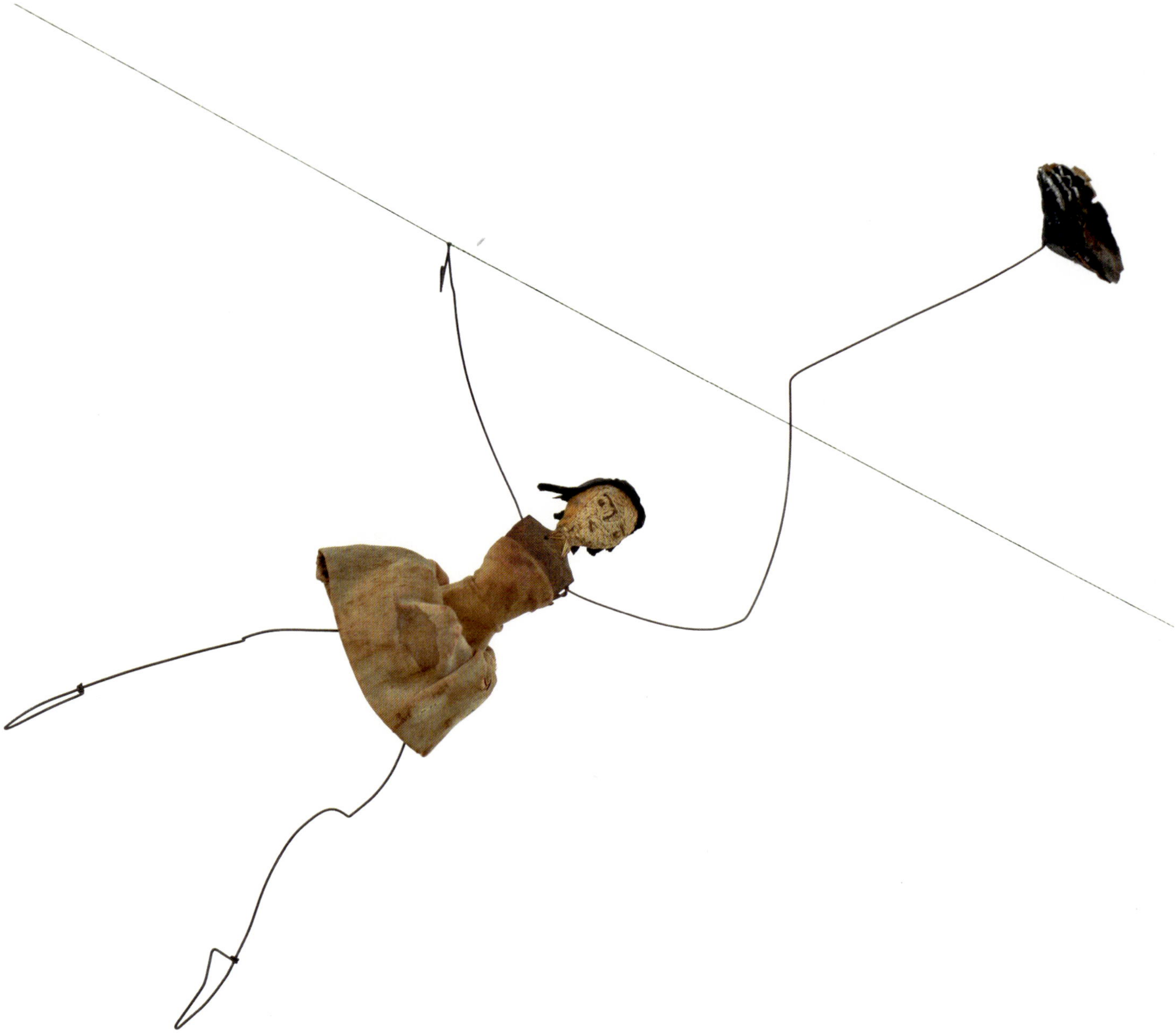

Aerialist c.1926–31

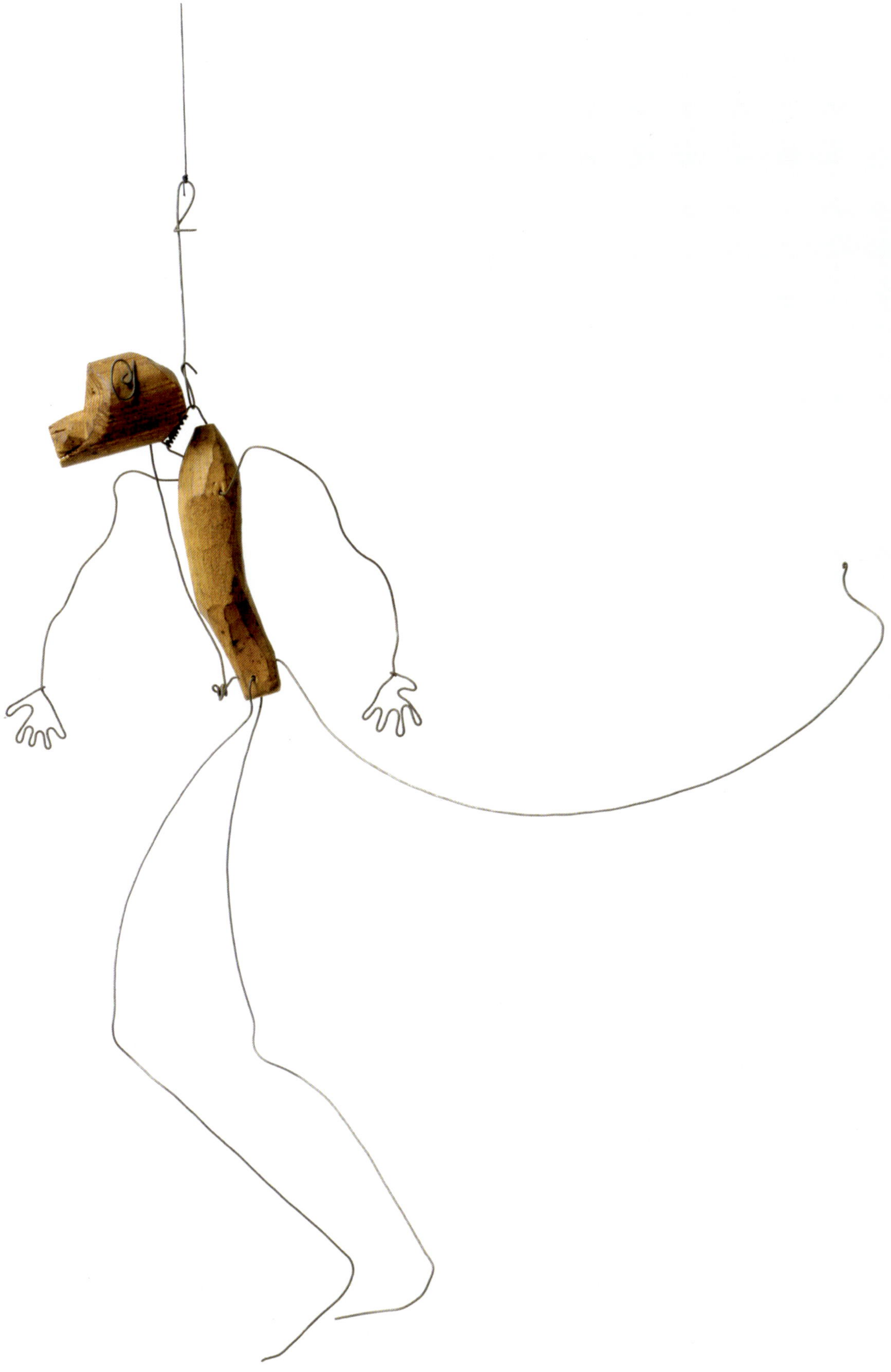

Singe c.1928

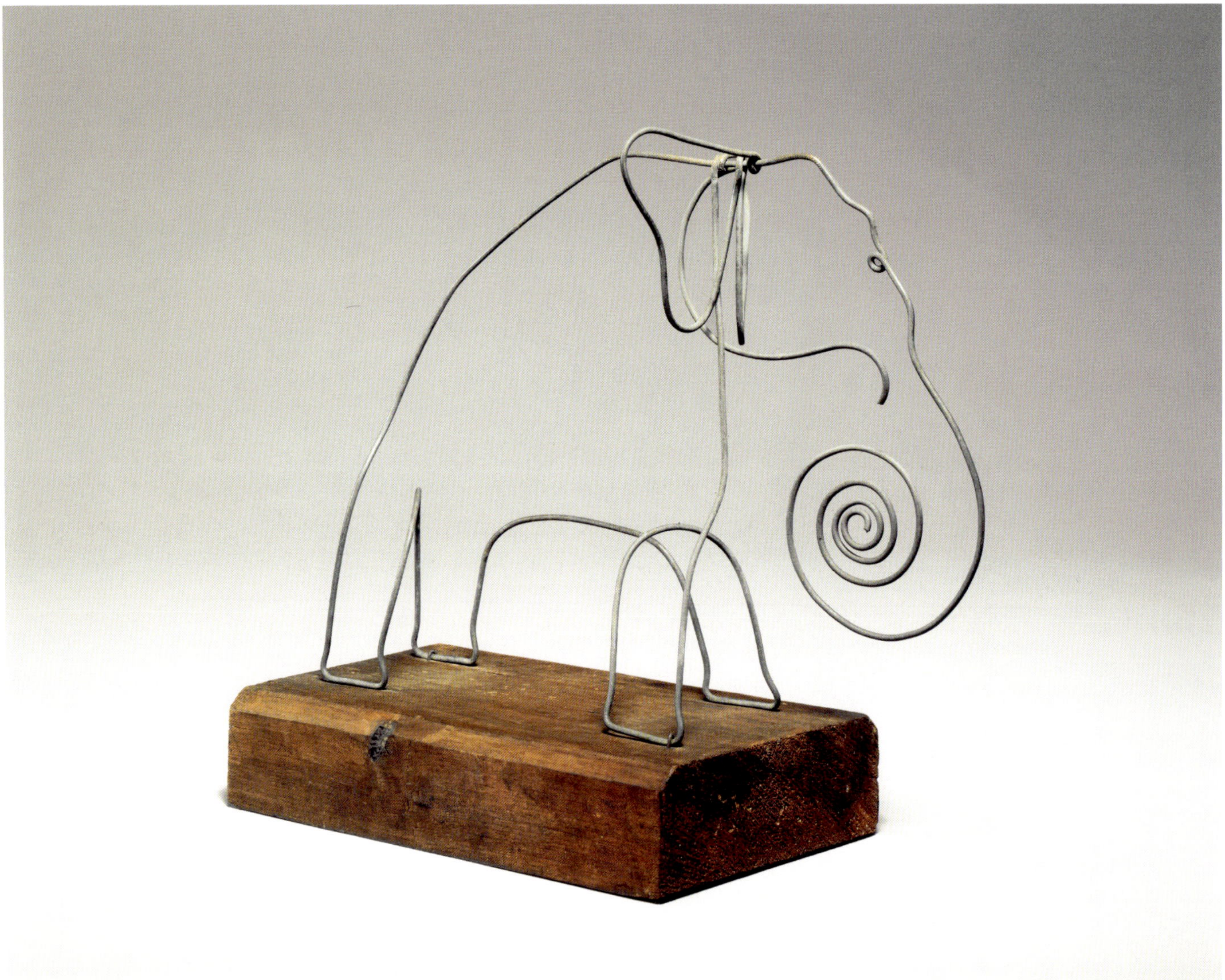

Elephant c.1927

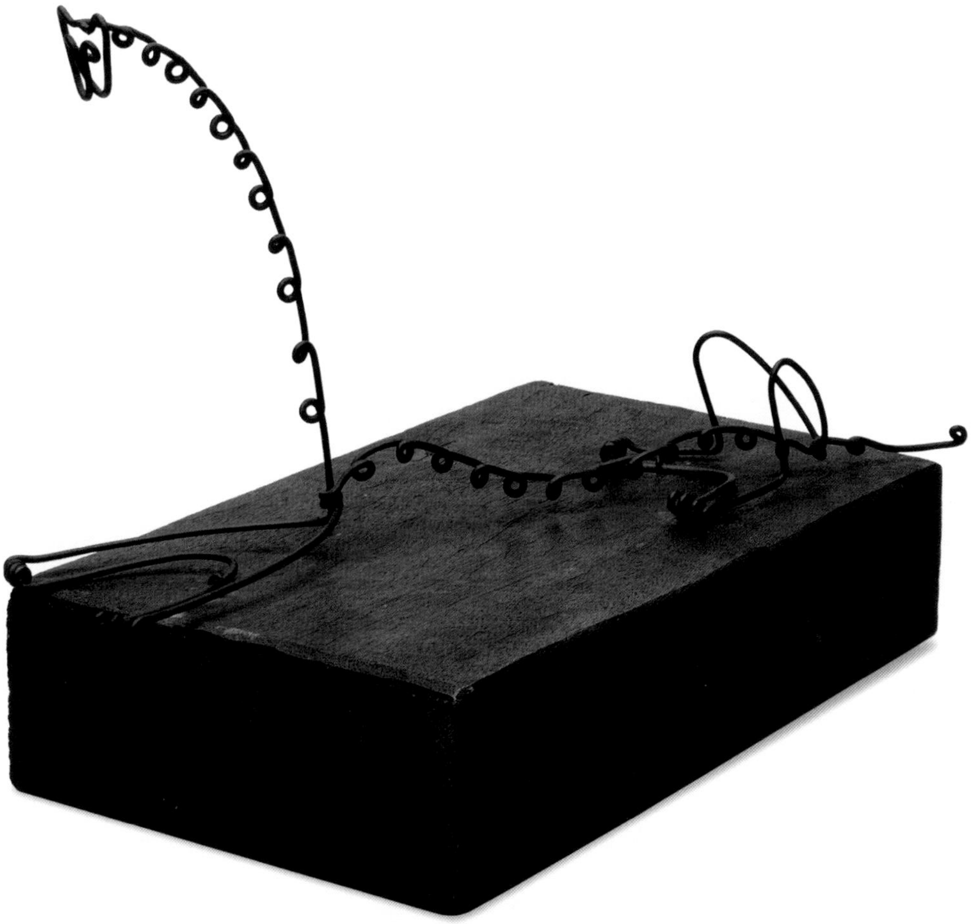

Leopard c.1927

Goldfish Bowl 1929

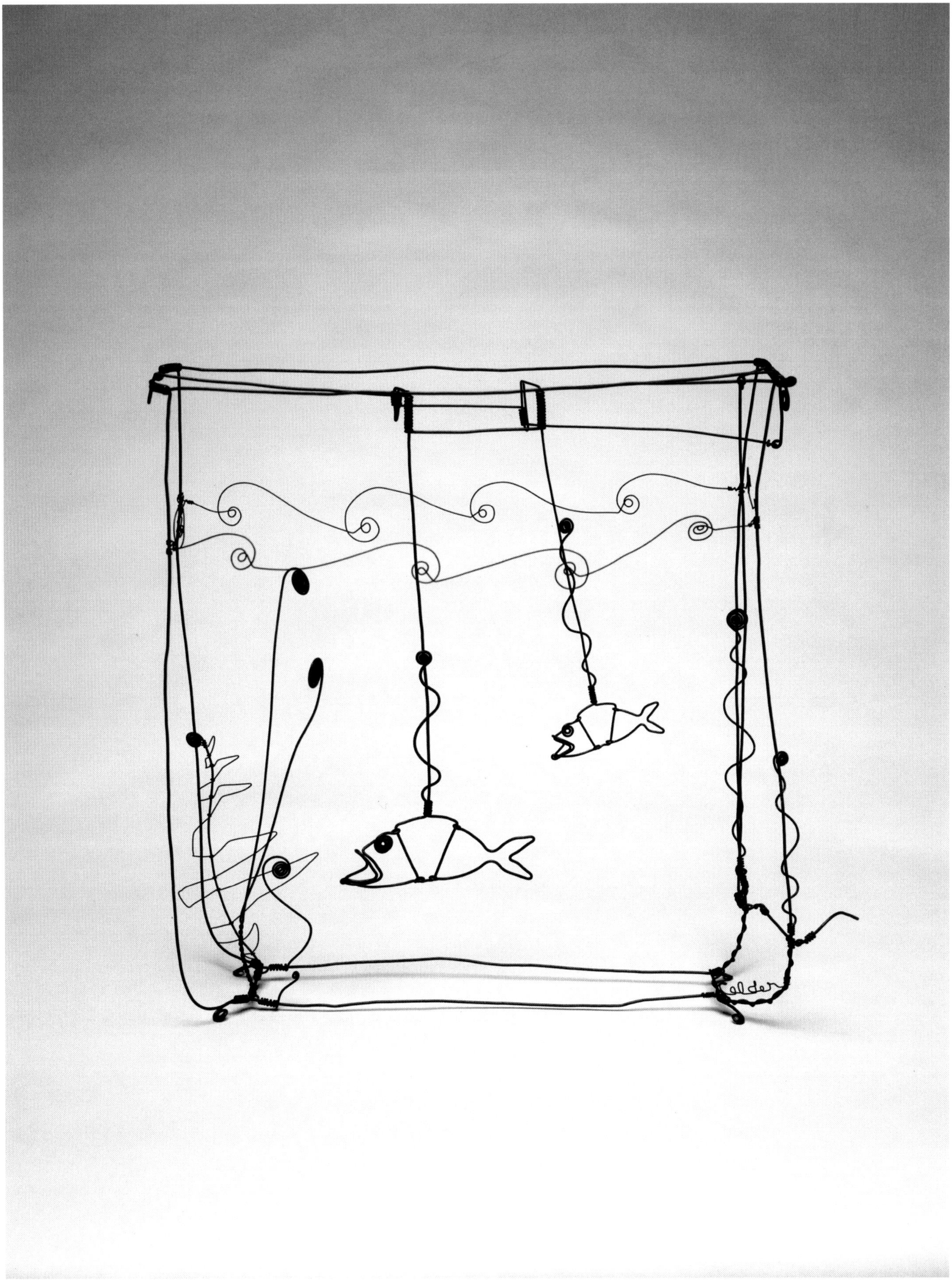
Calder

Hercules and Lion 1928

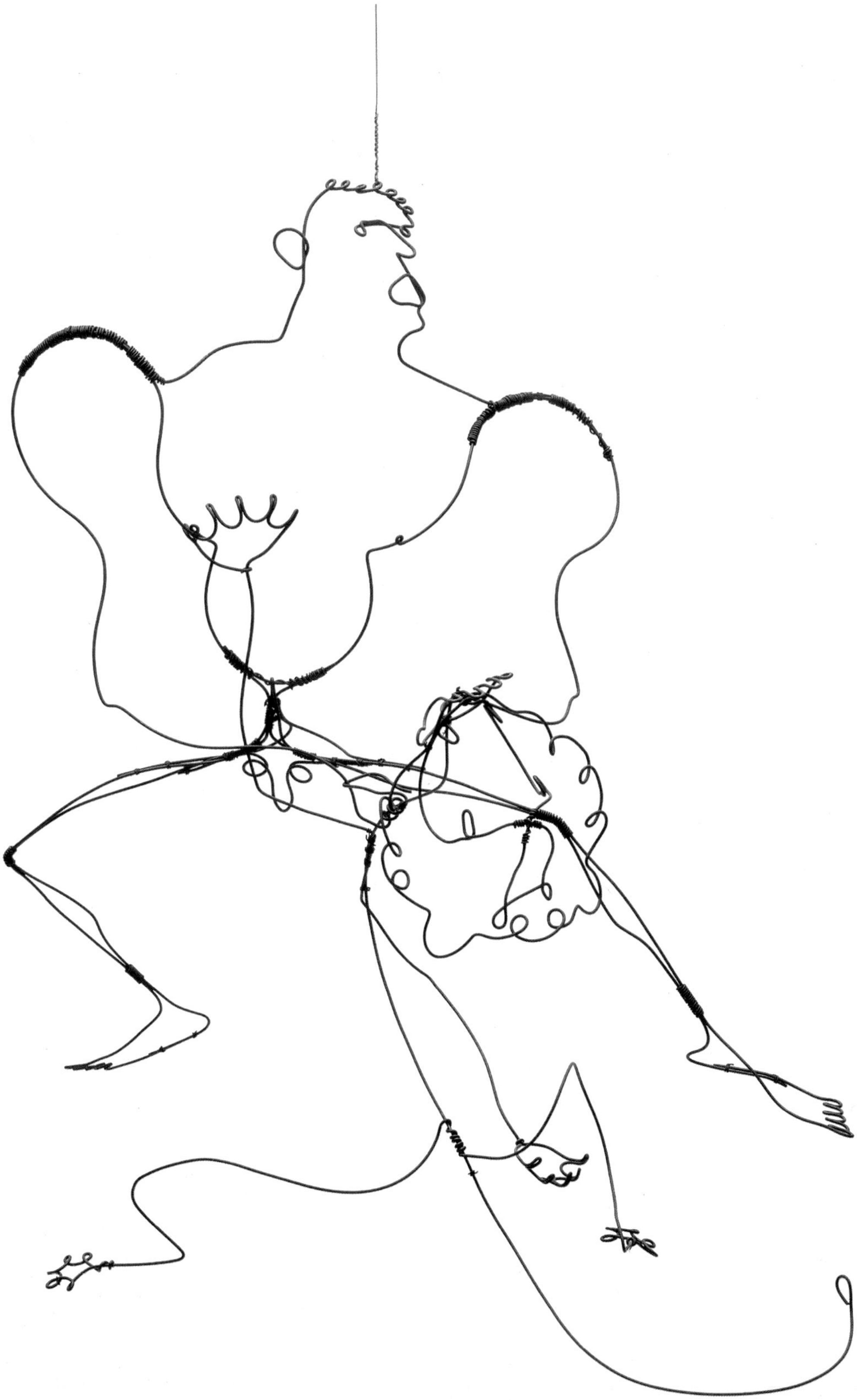

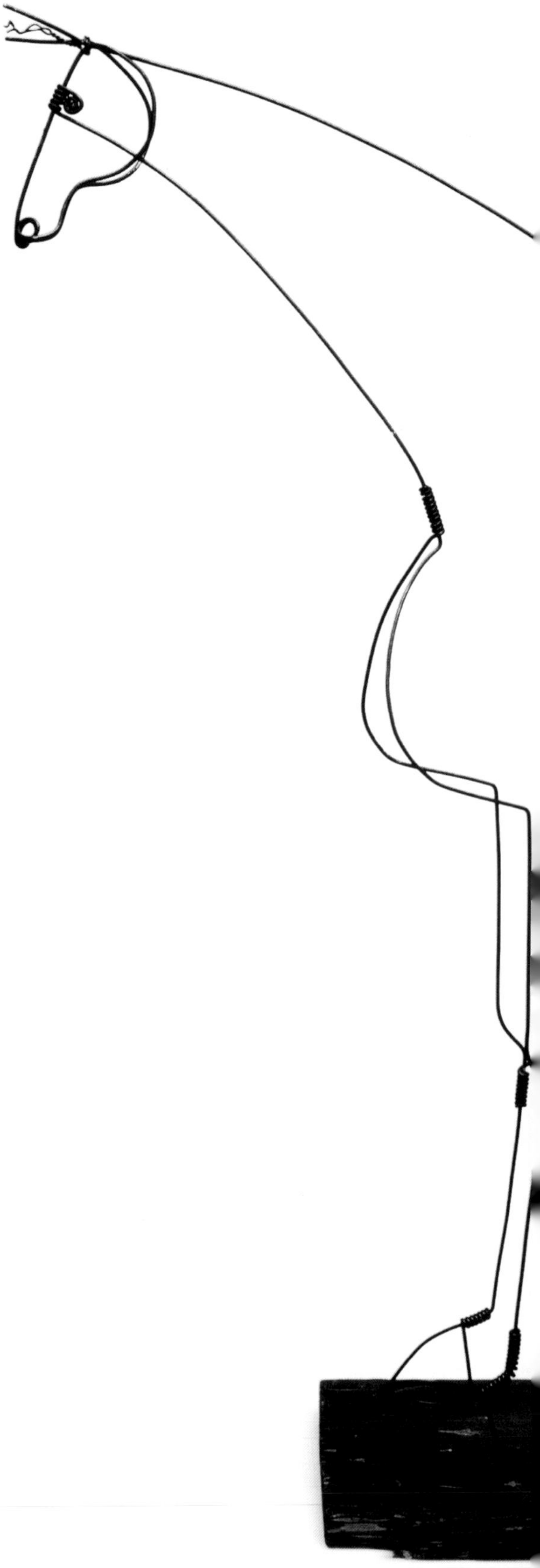

Horse c.1928

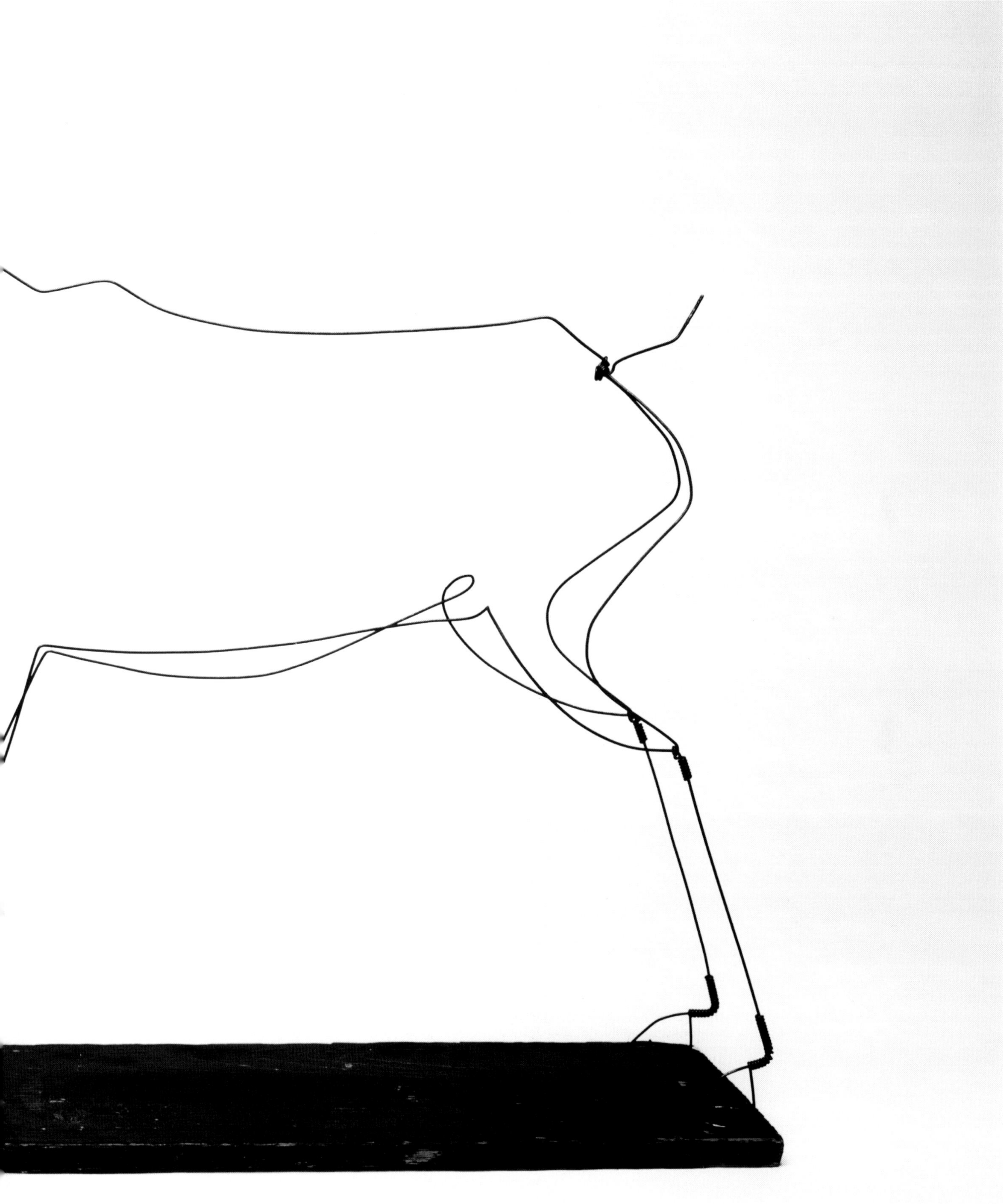

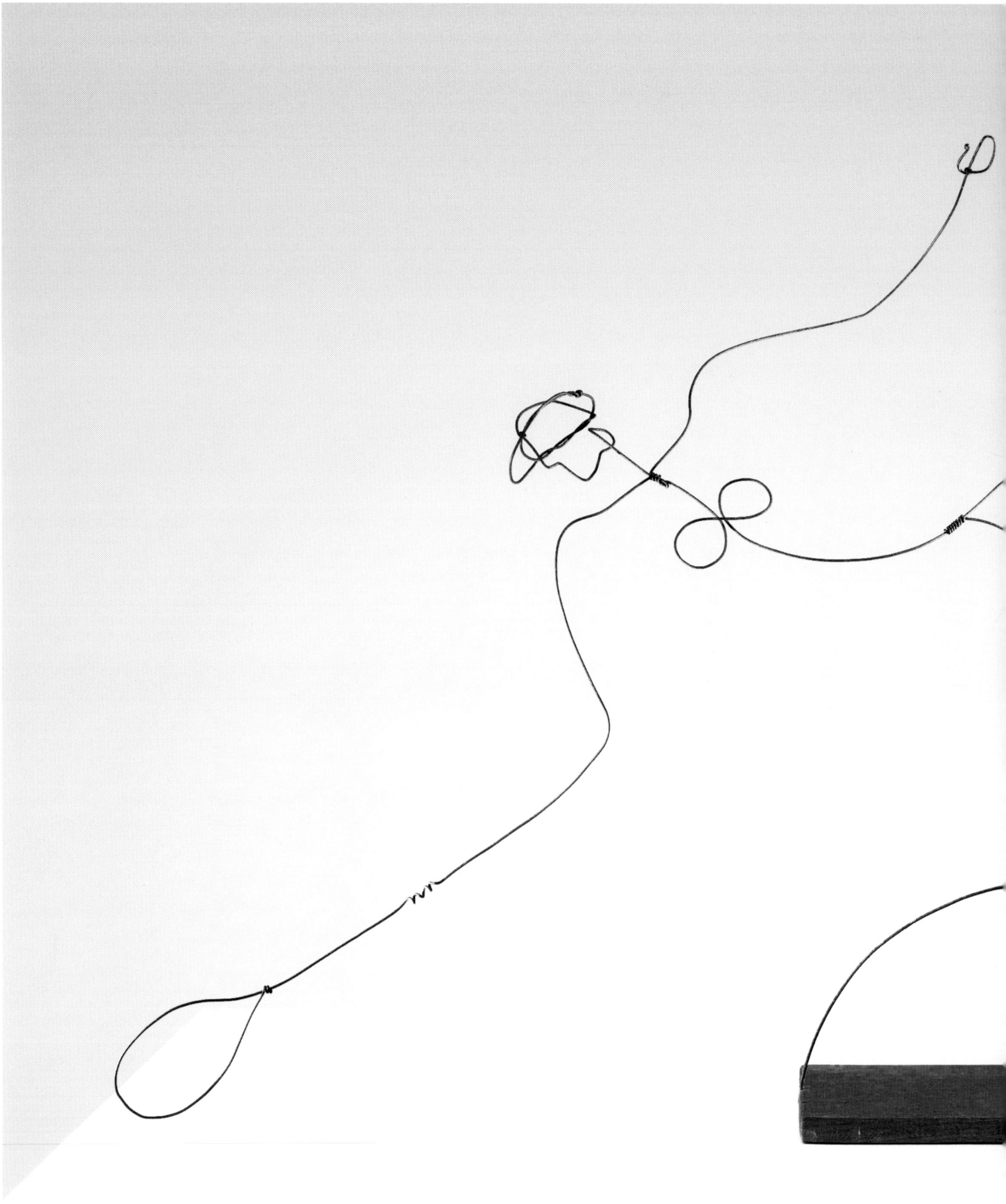

Helen Wills II 1928

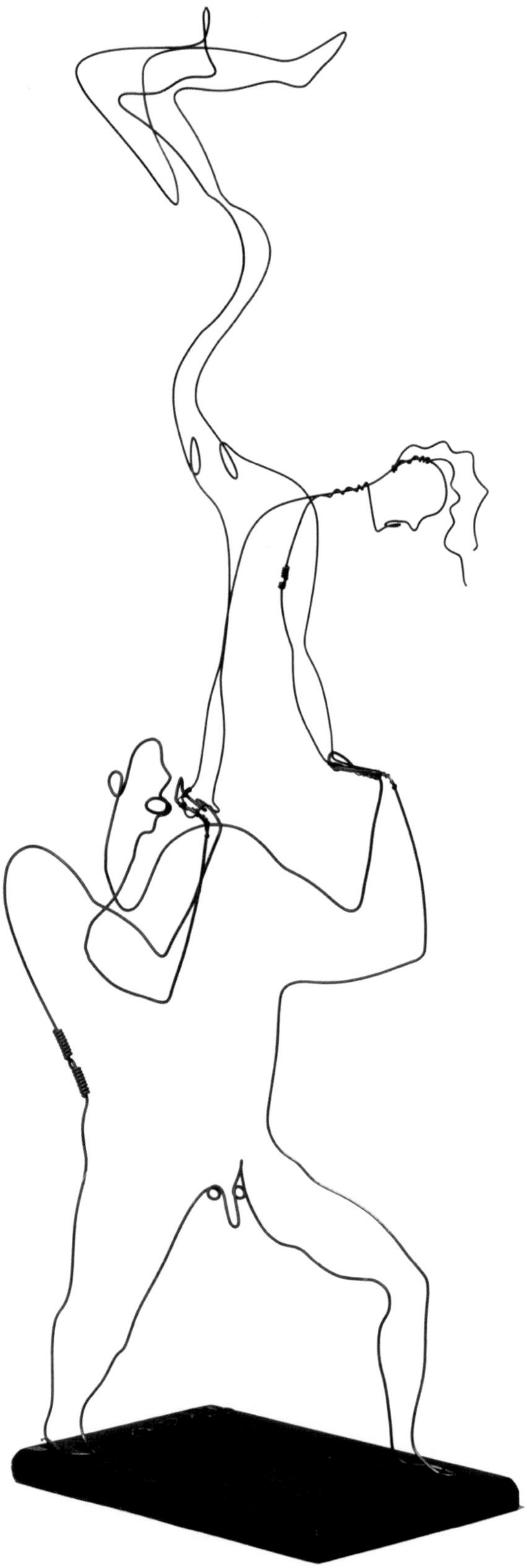

Acrobats c.1927

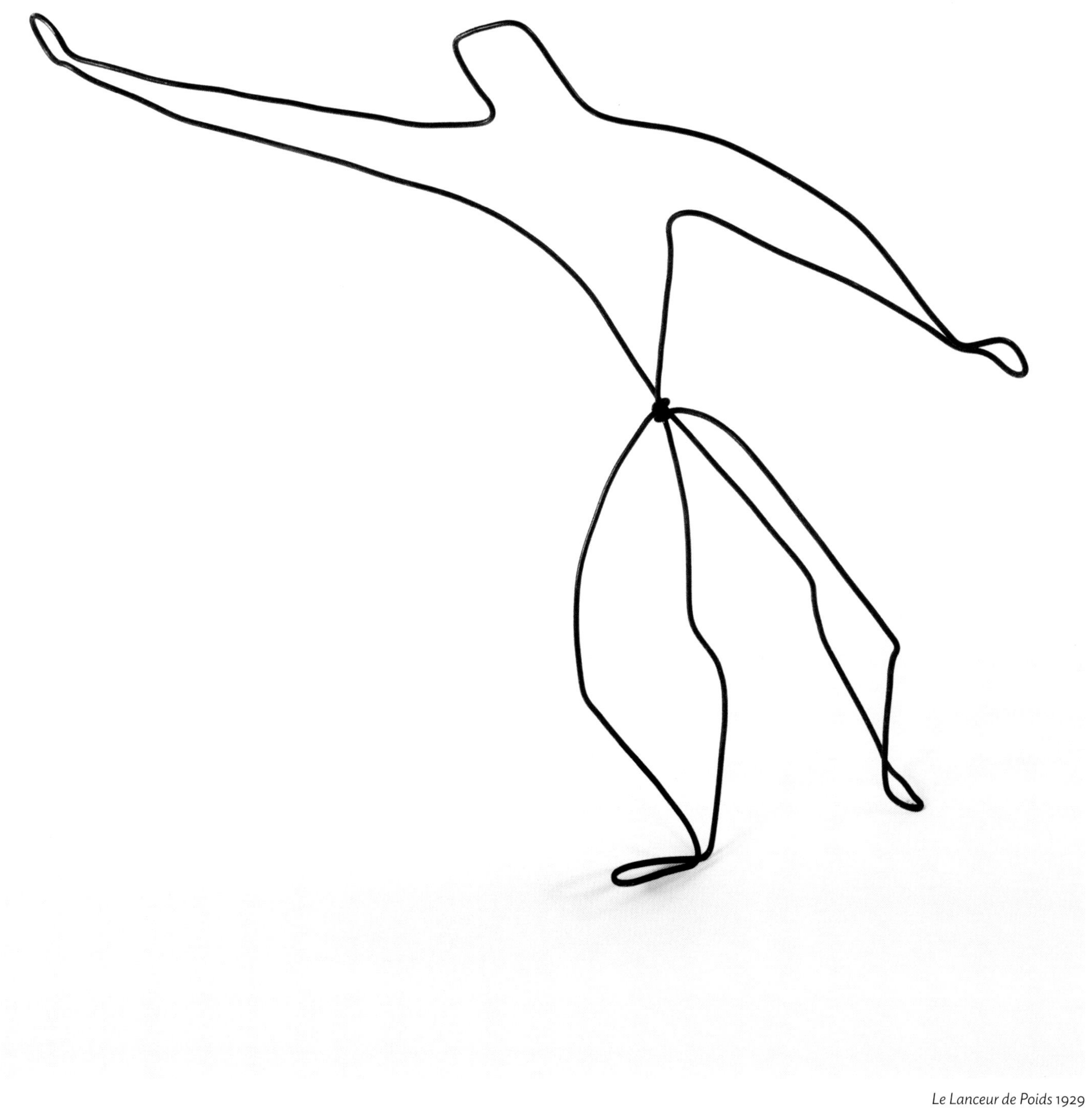

Le Lanceur de Poids 1929

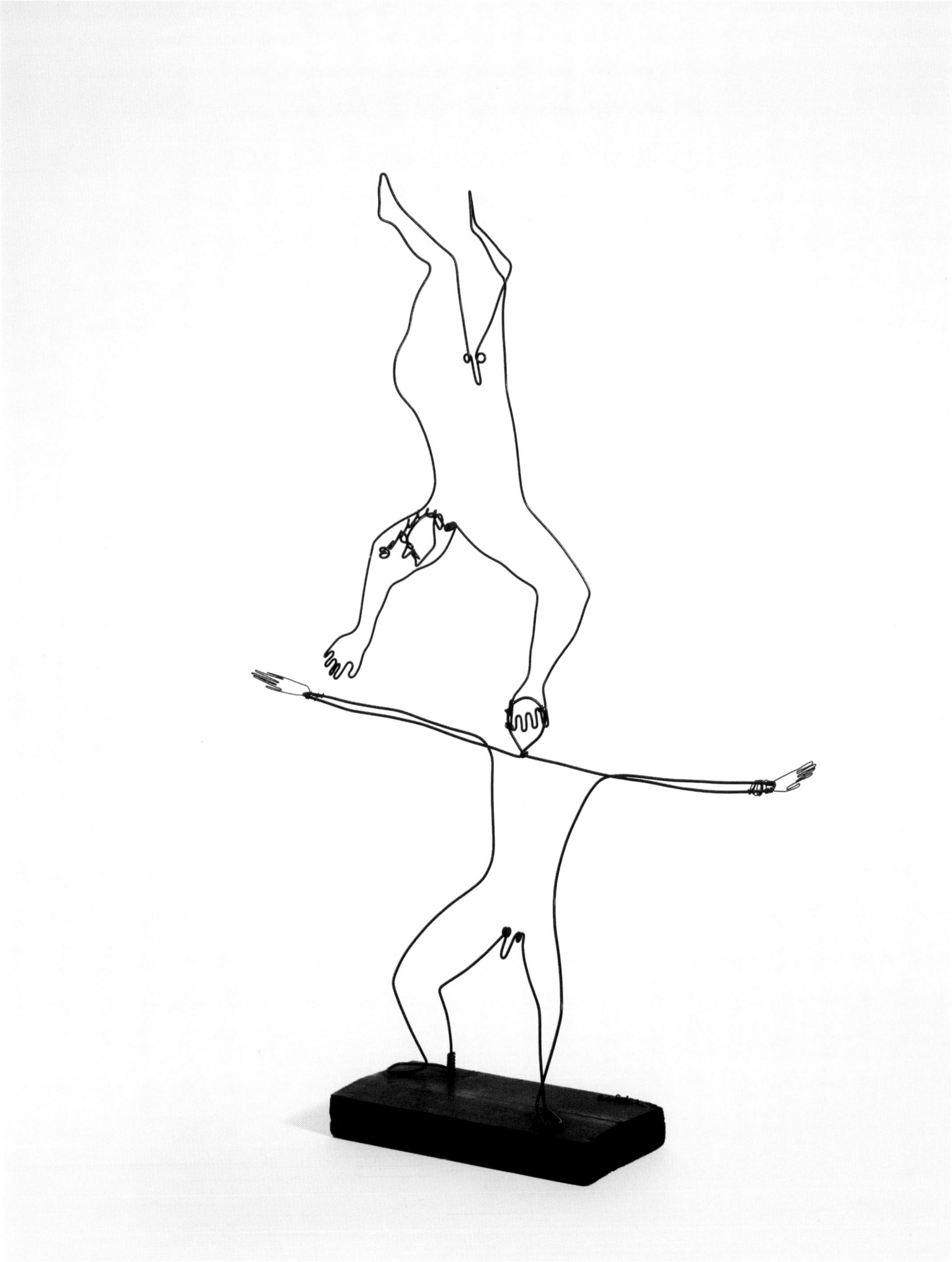

Two Acrobats 1929

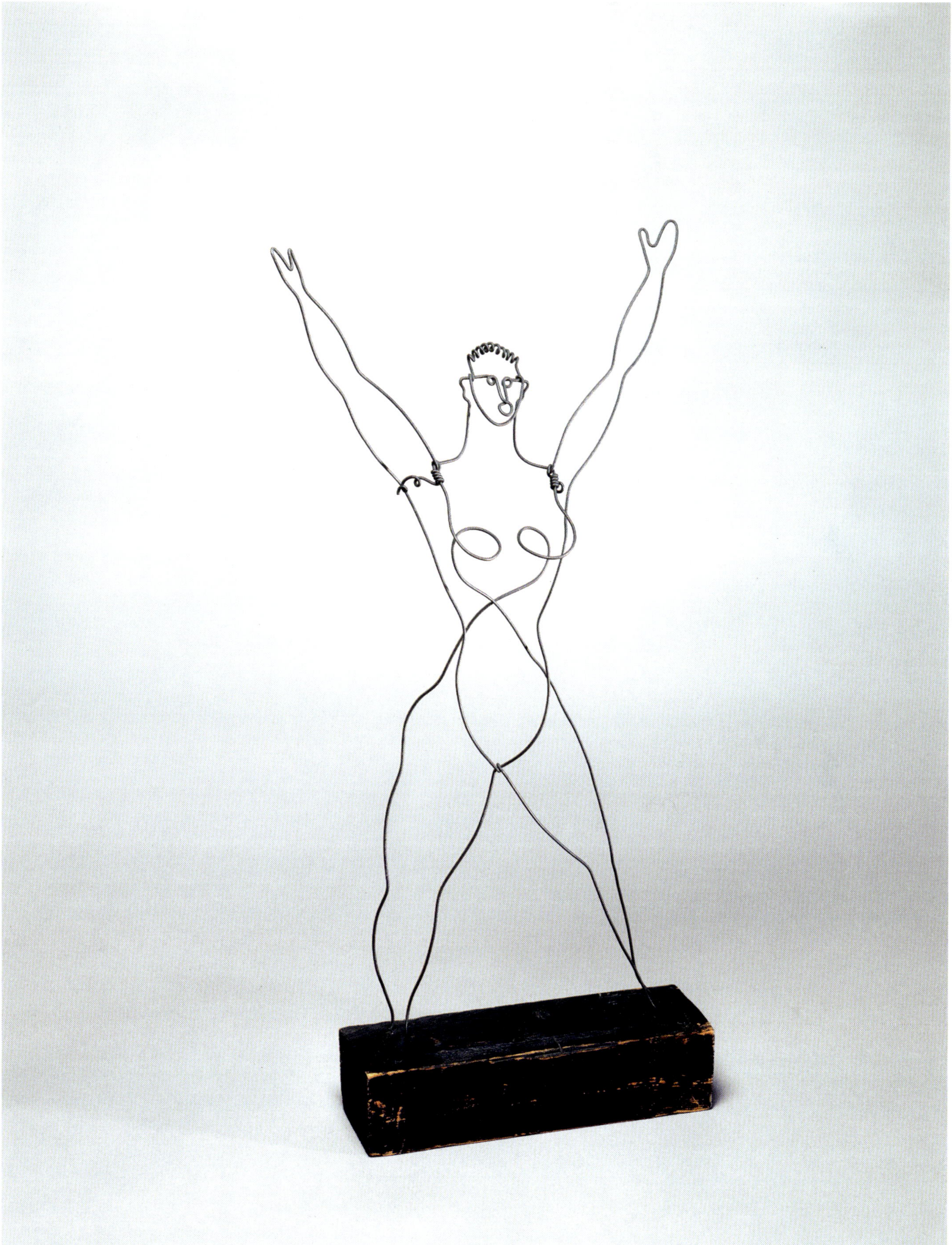

Acrobat 1929

The Brass Family 1929

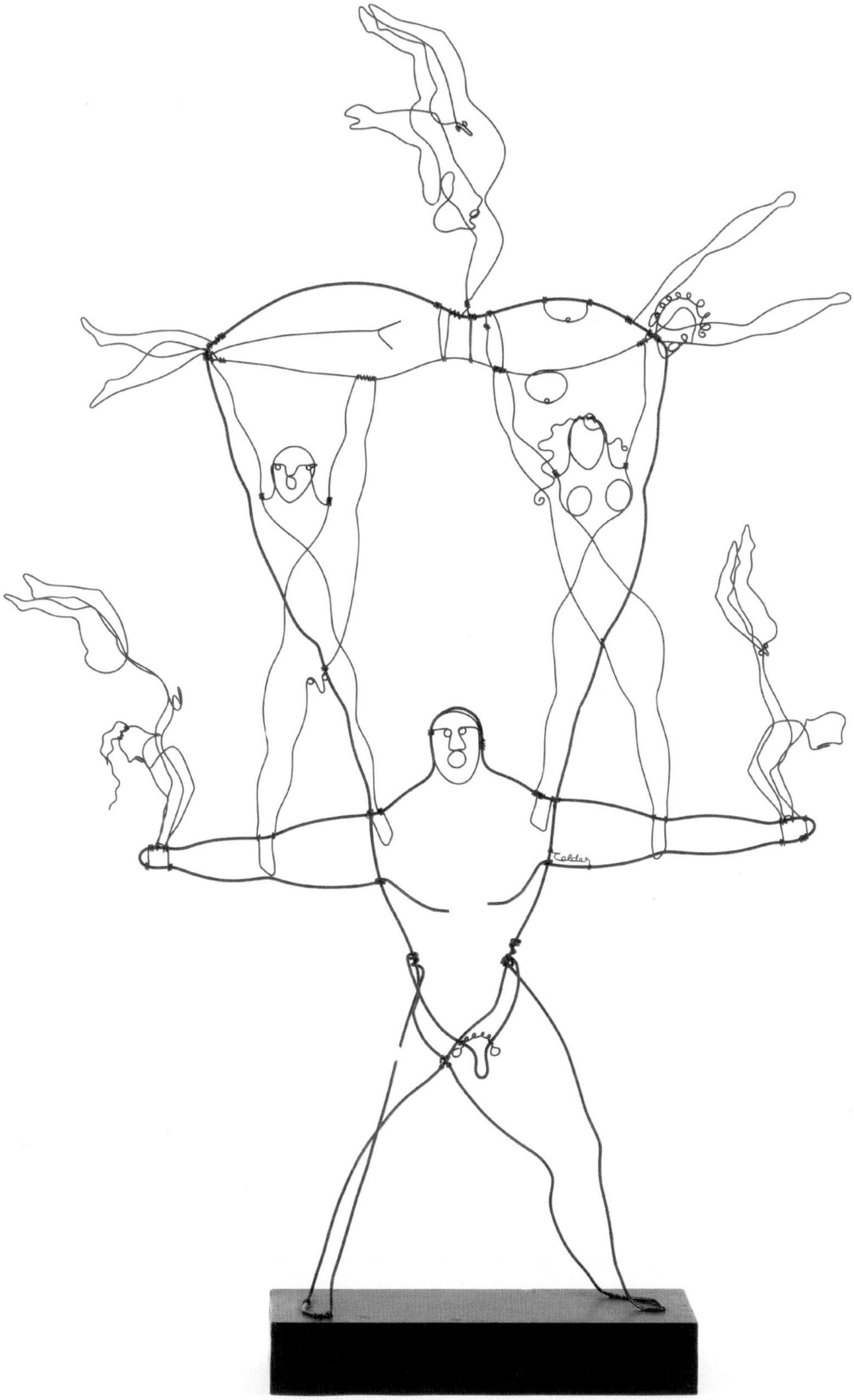
Calder

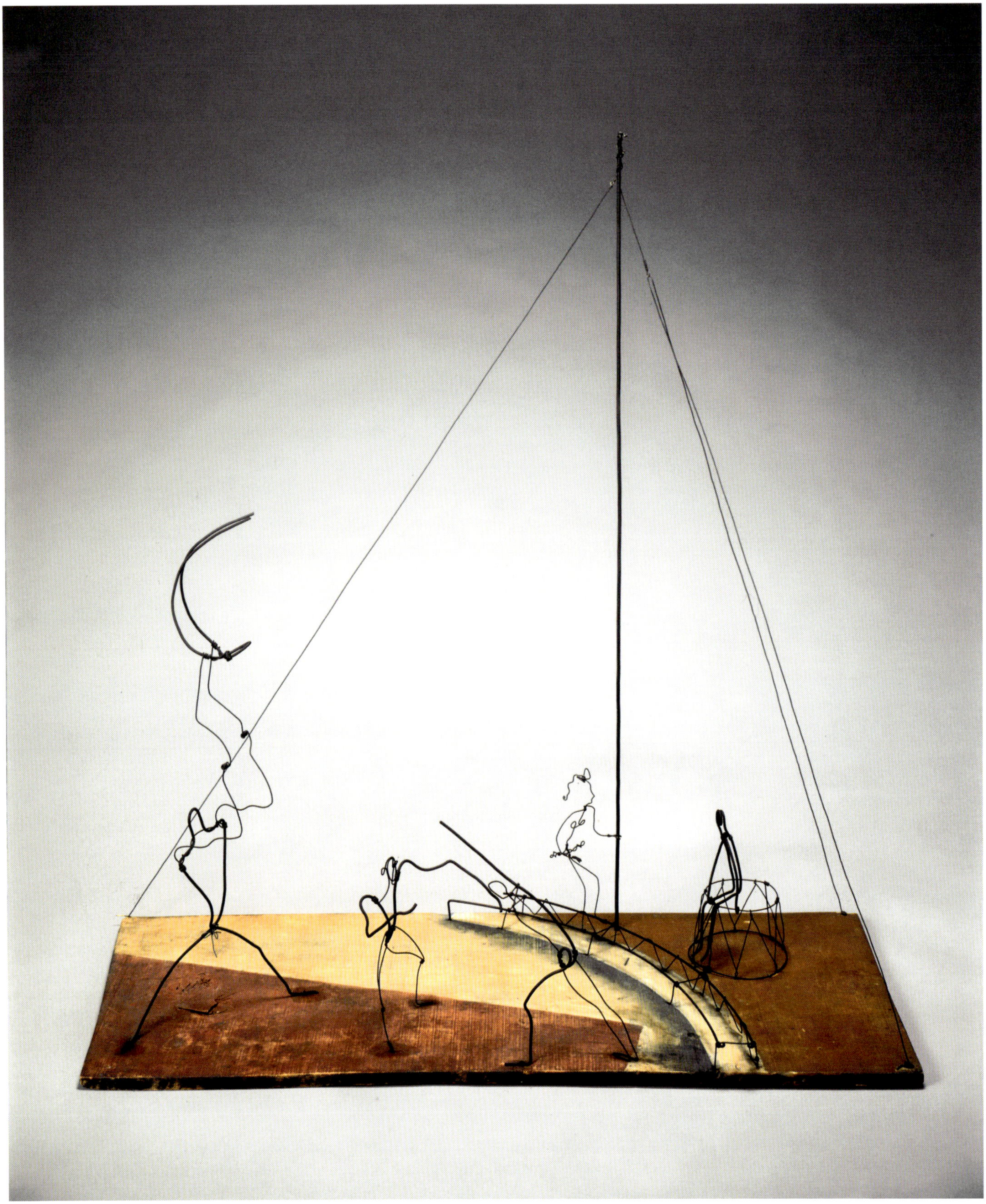

Circus Scene 1929

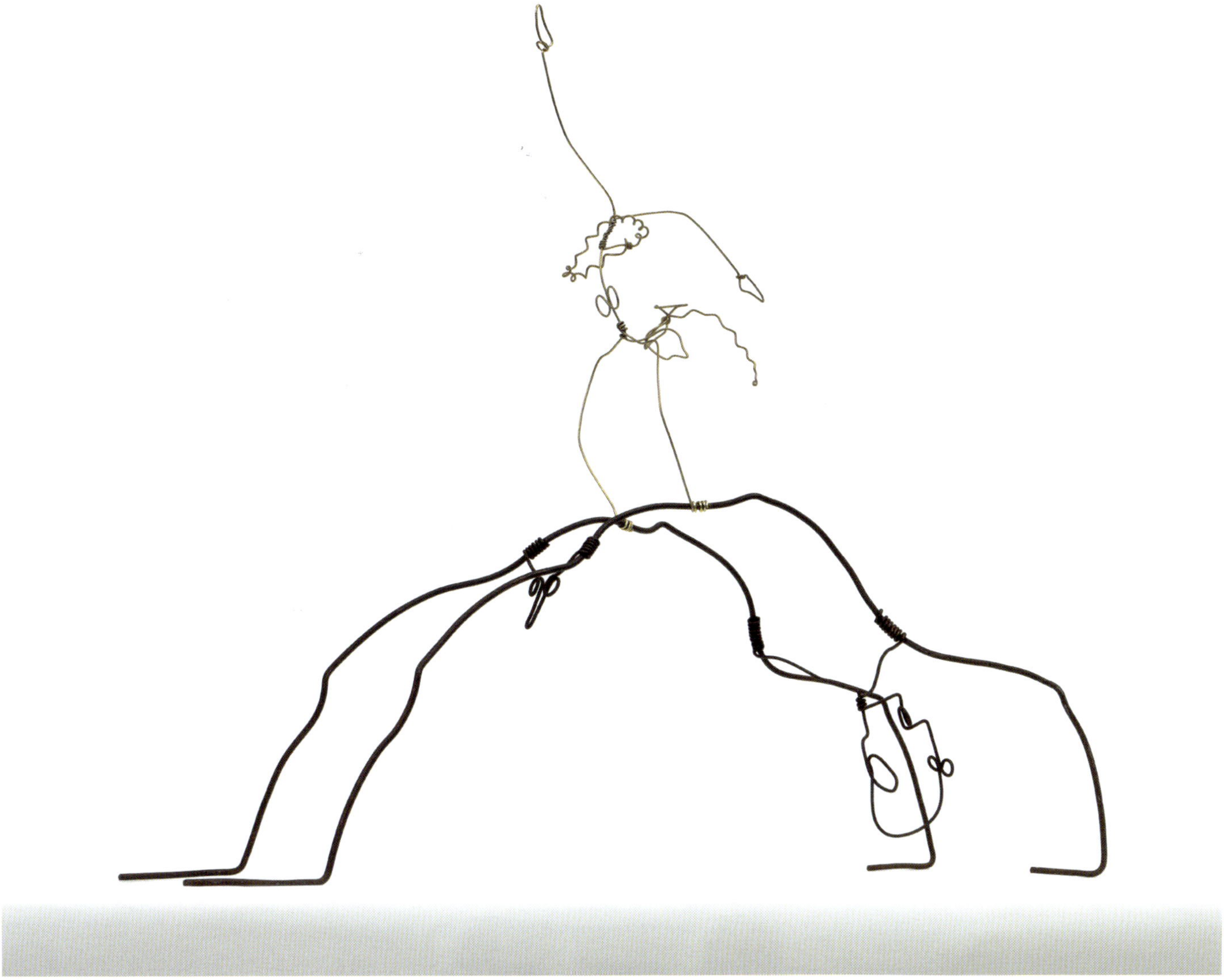

Acrobats 1929

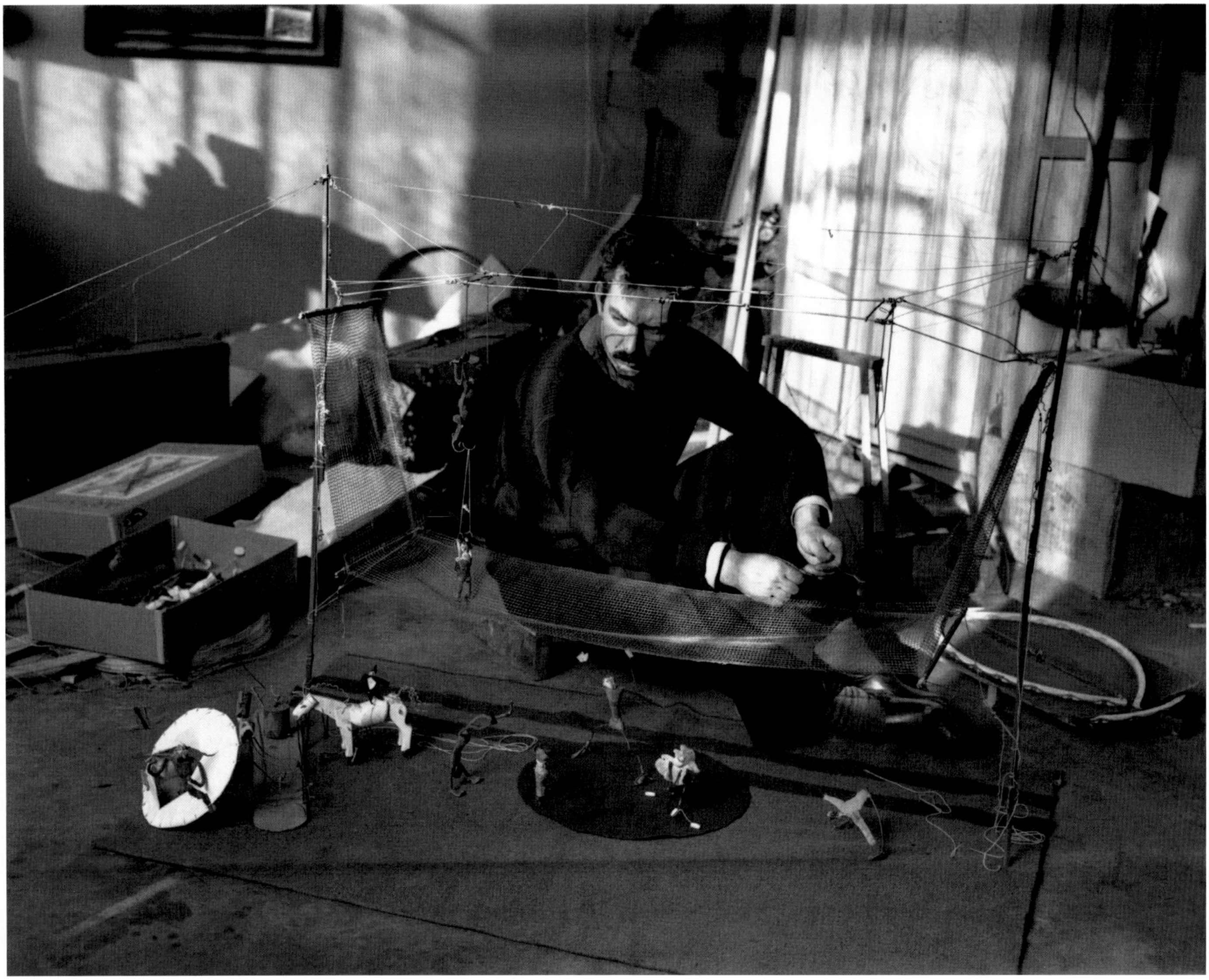

Calder presenting *Cirque Calder* 1926–31 in his studio at 7 rue Cels, Paris, 1929

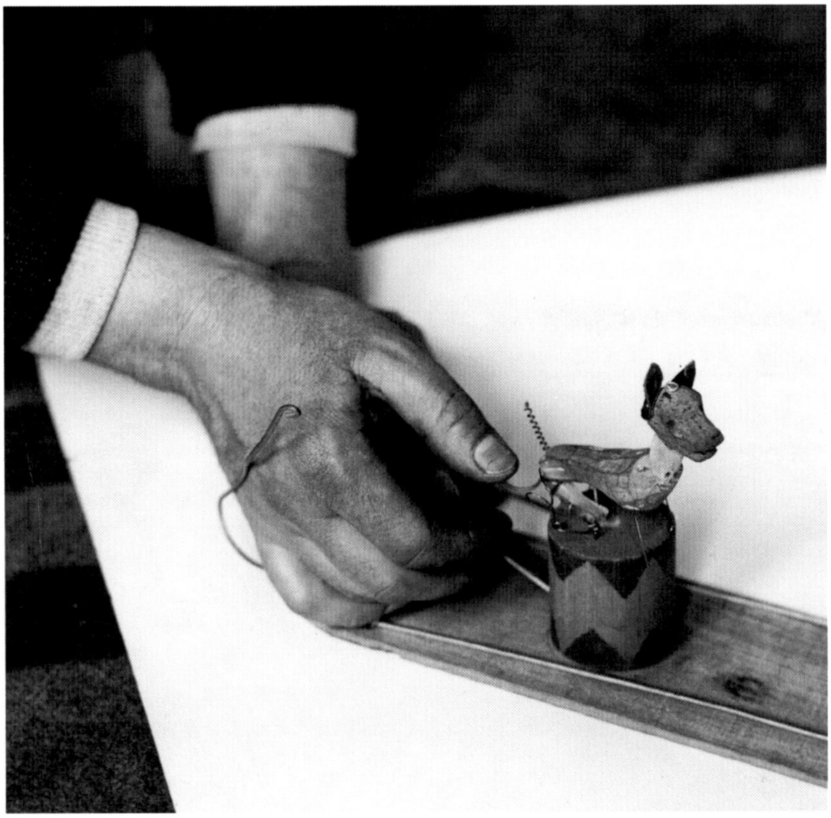

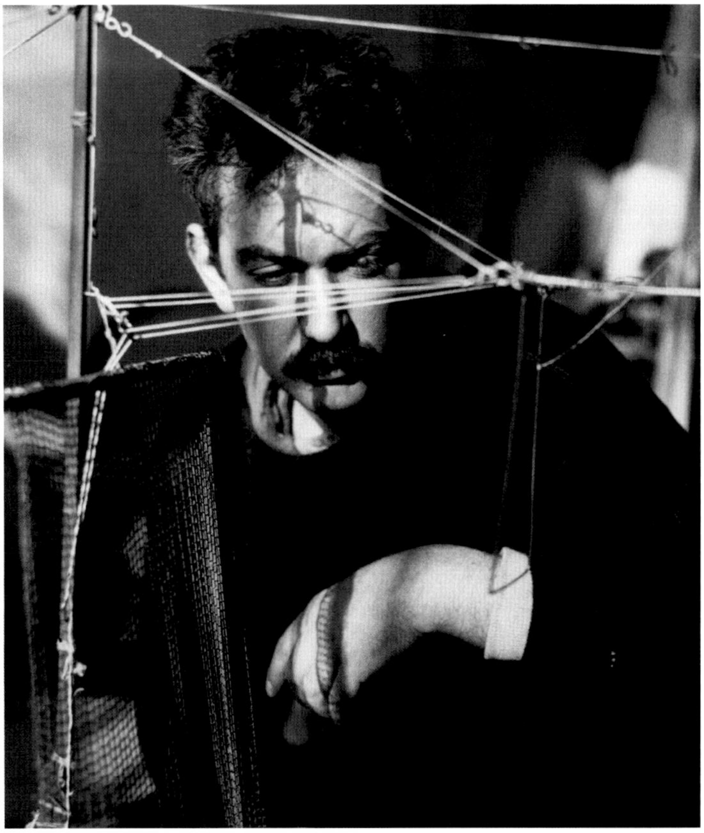

Above: Calder with the Dog Trainer act, part of *Cirque Calder* 1926–31, 1929; Below: Calder with *Cirque Calder*, 1929

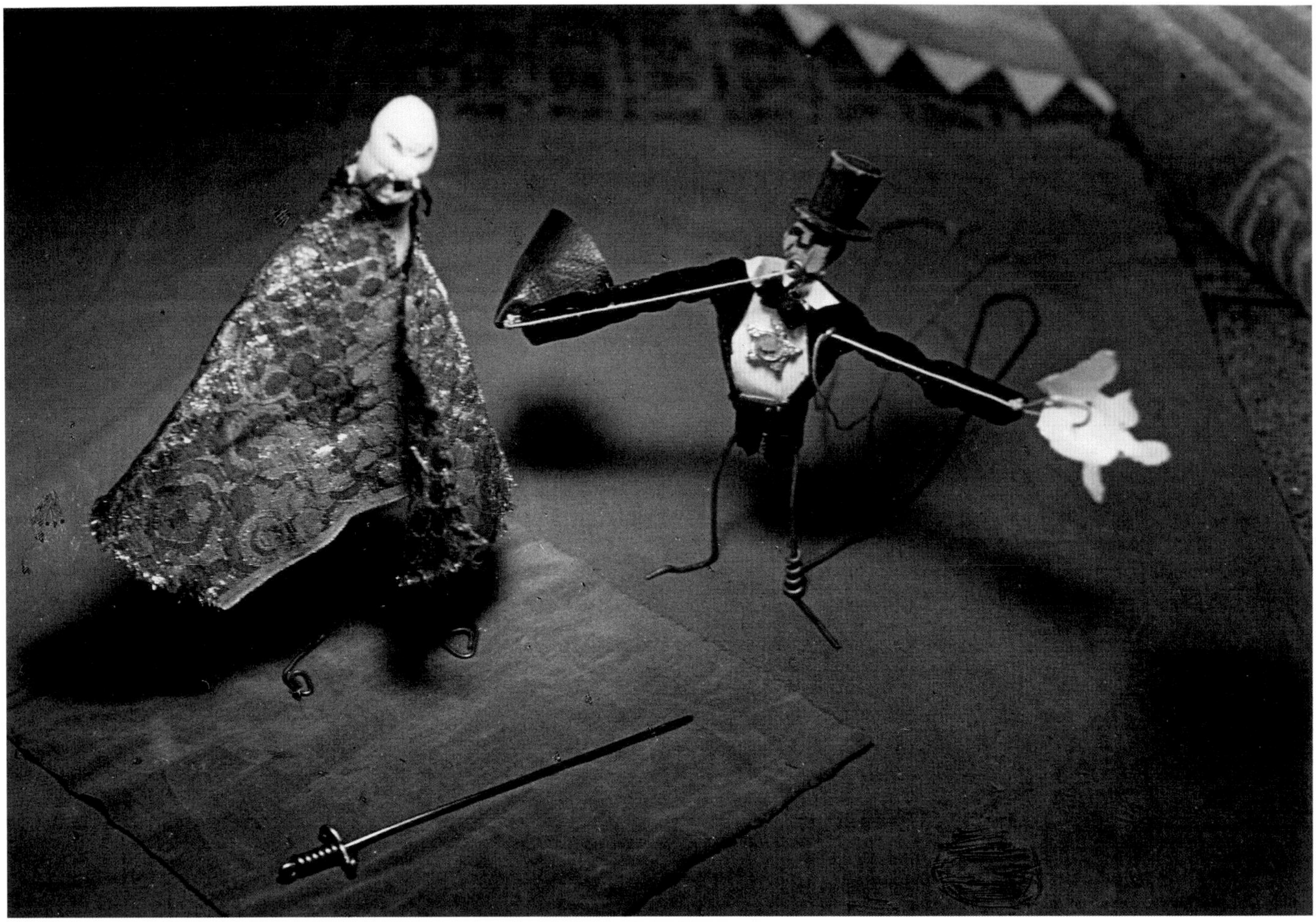

Monsieur Loyal and Sword Swallower act, part of *Cirque Calder* 1926–31, Paris c.1931

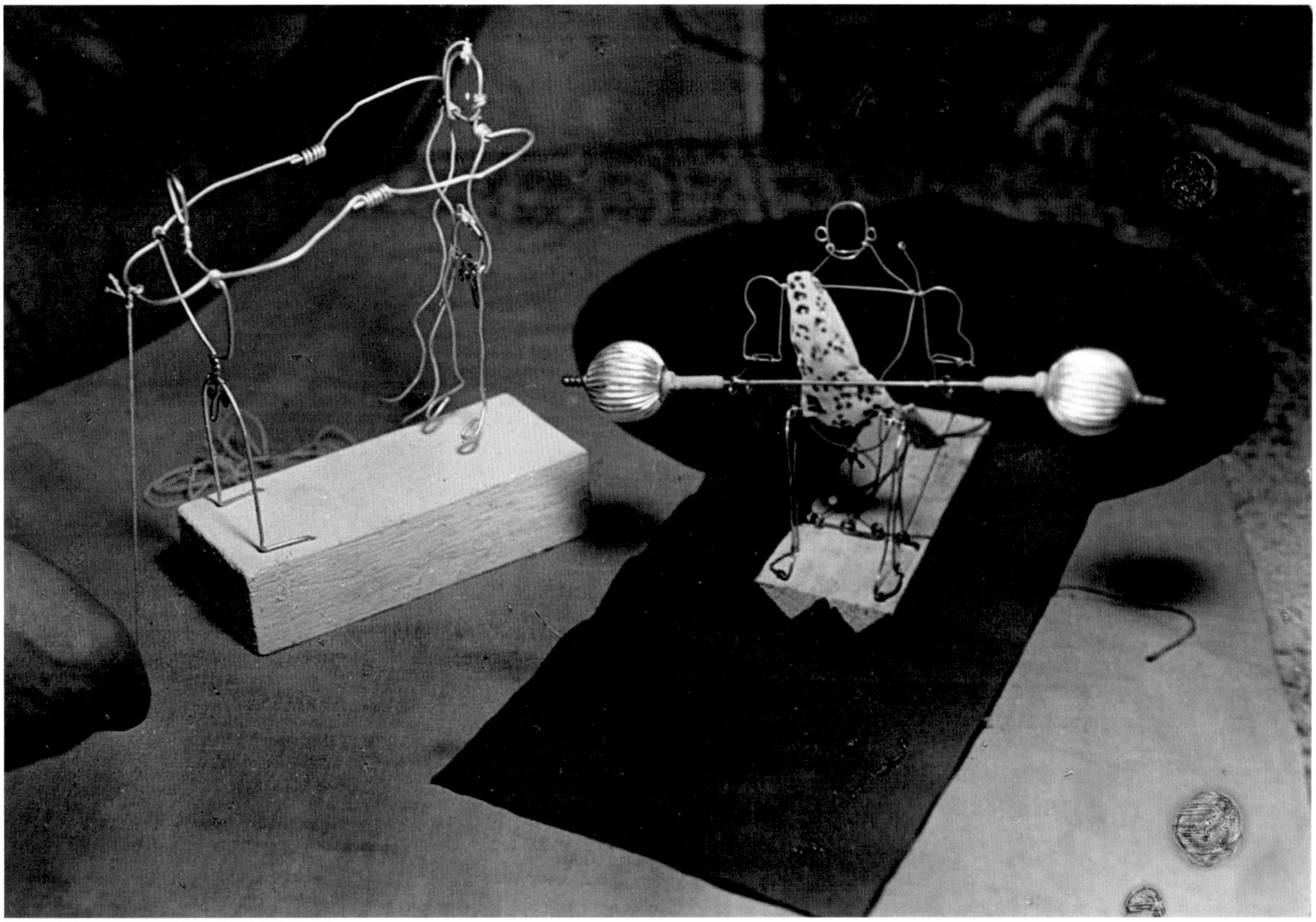

Two Acrobats and Weight Lifter act, part of *Cirque Calder* 1926–31, Paris c.1931

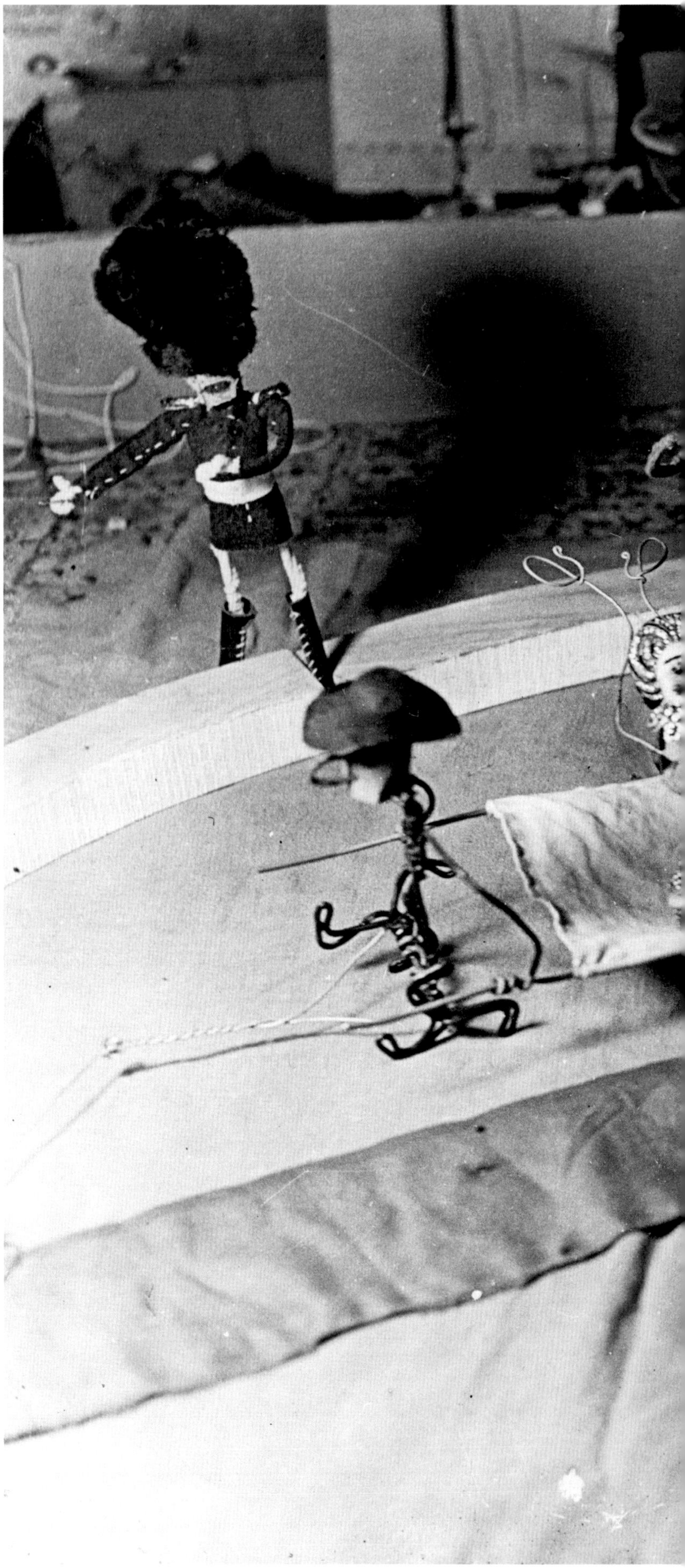

Spear Thrower act and Cowboy act, part of *Cirque Calder* 1926–31, Paris c.1931

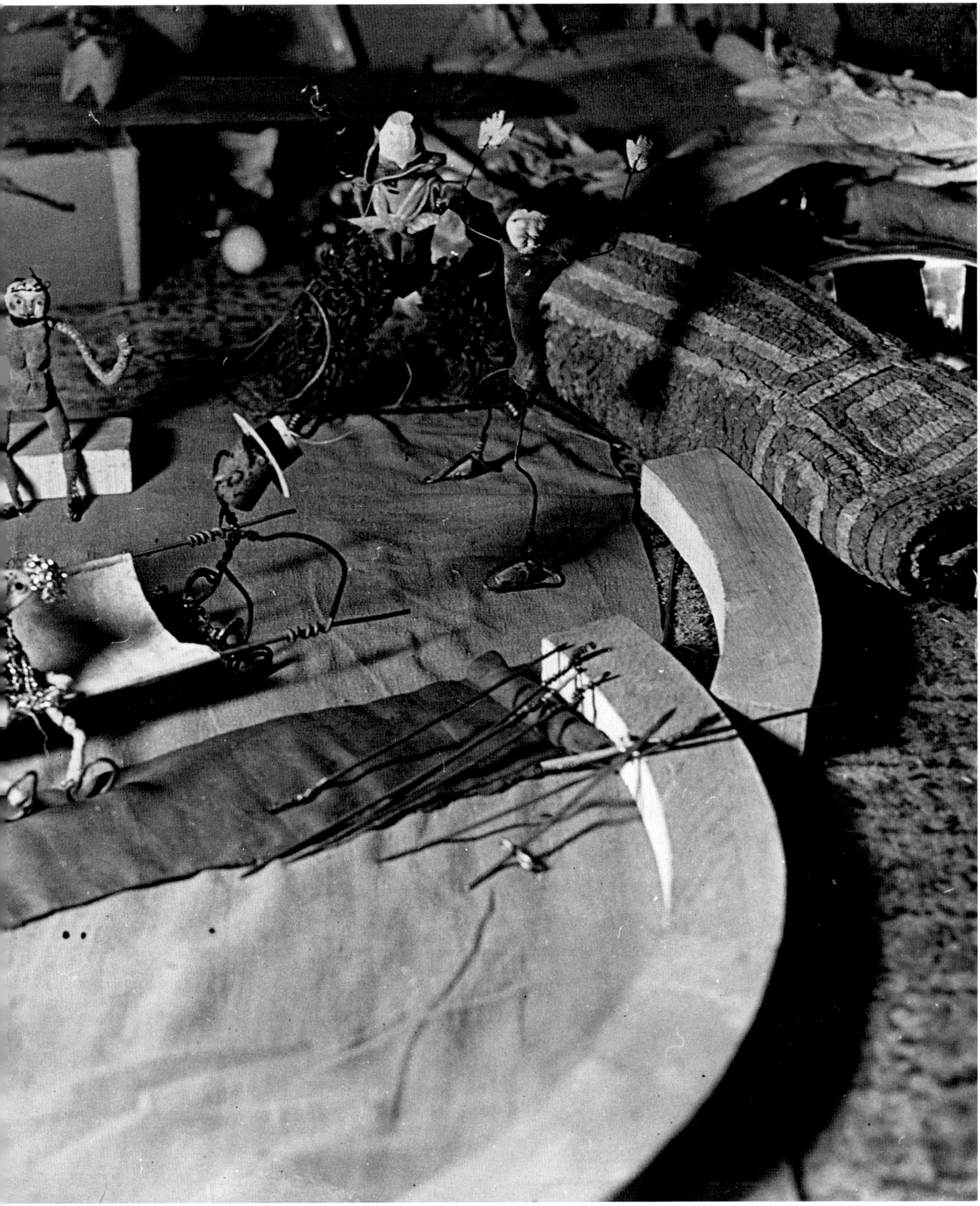

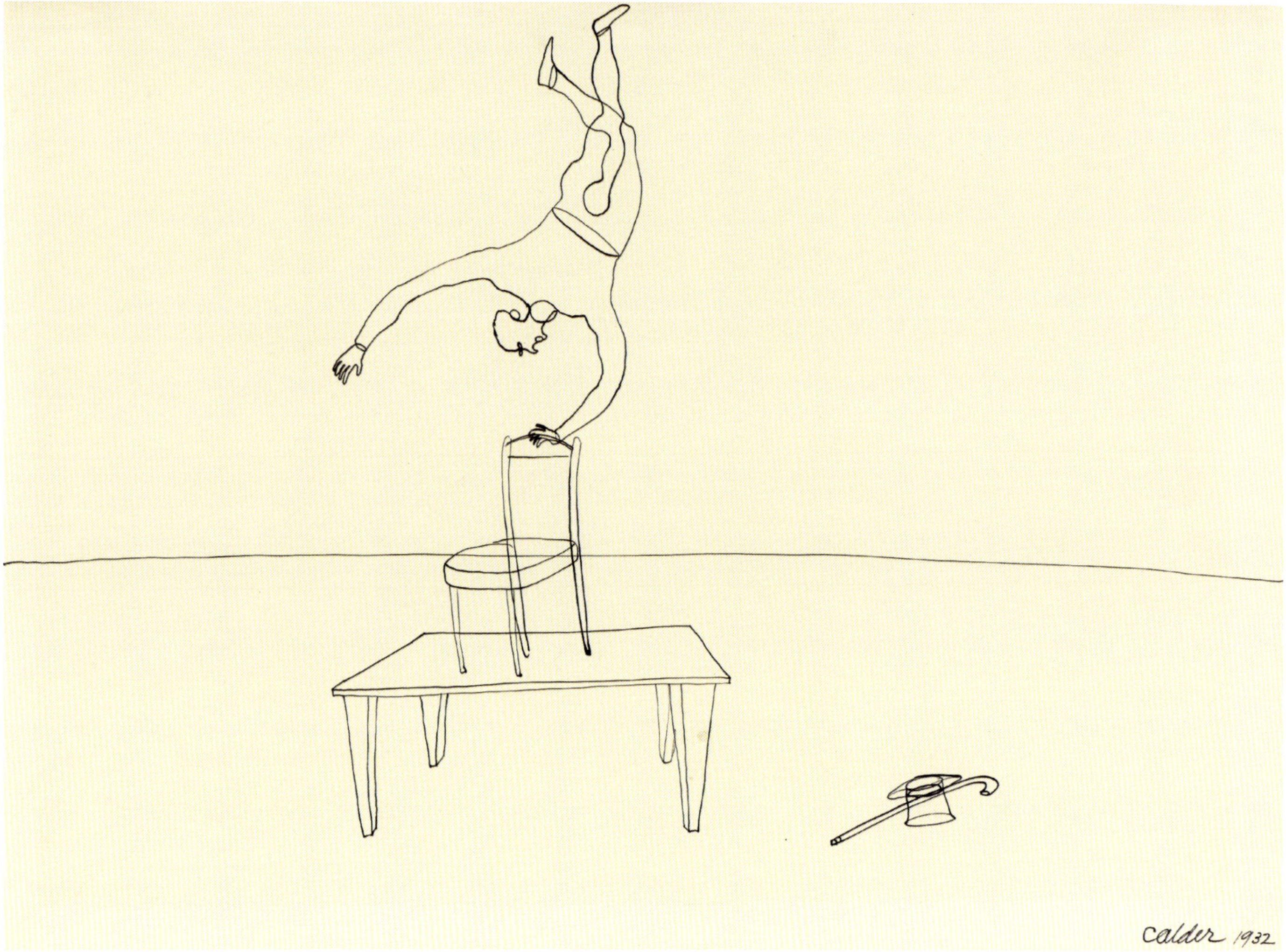

Acrobat 1932

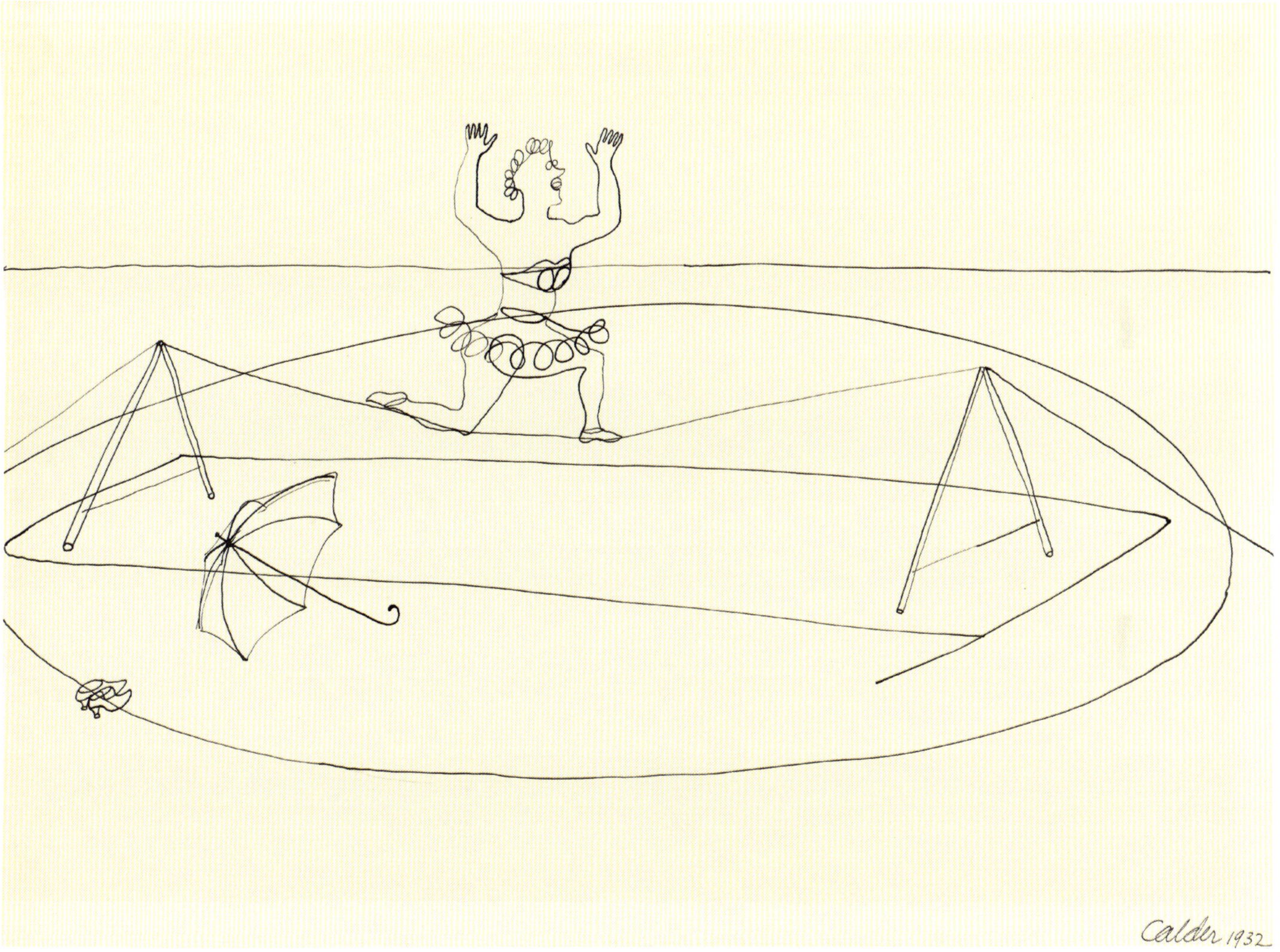

Tightrope Artist 1932

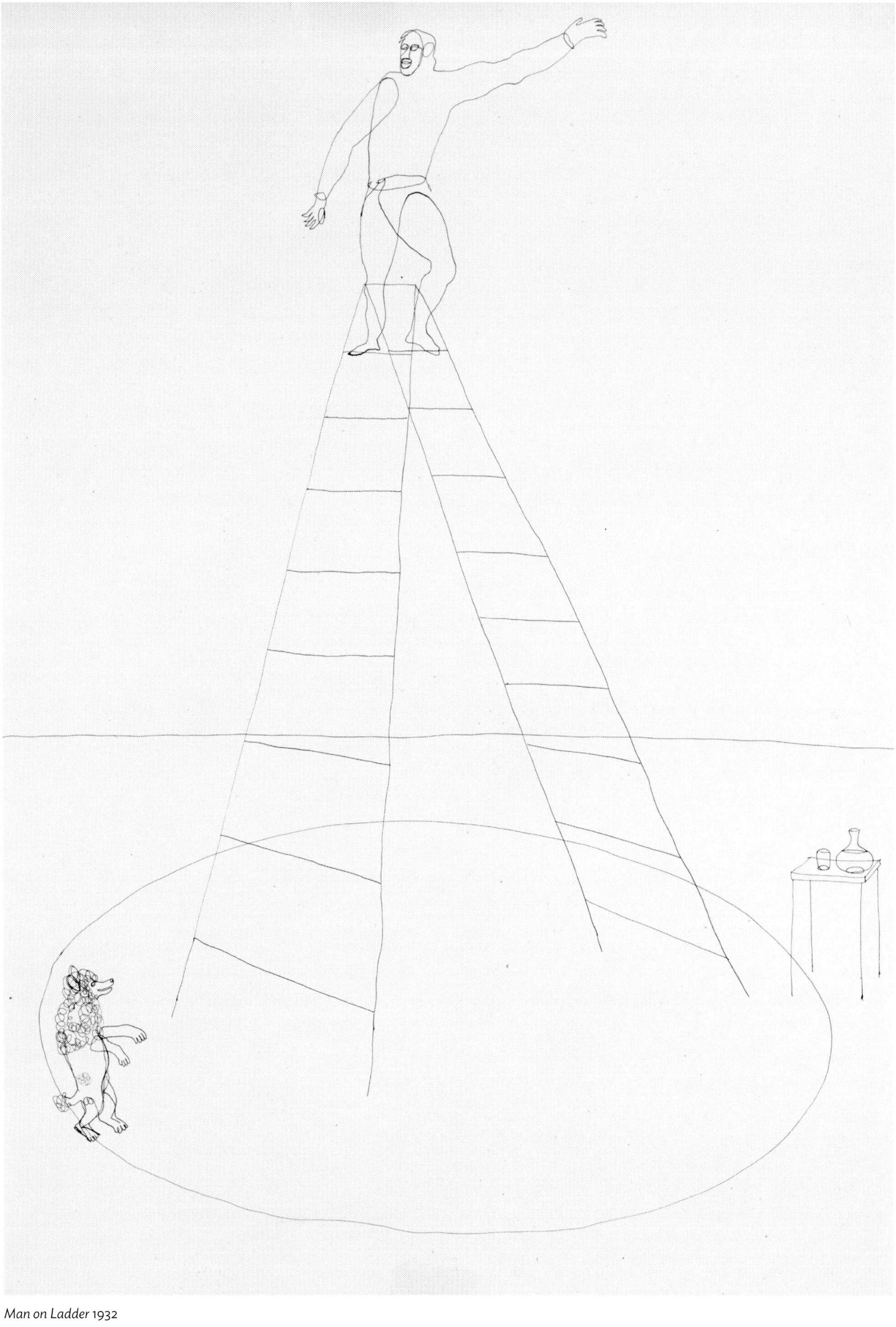

Man on Ladder 1932

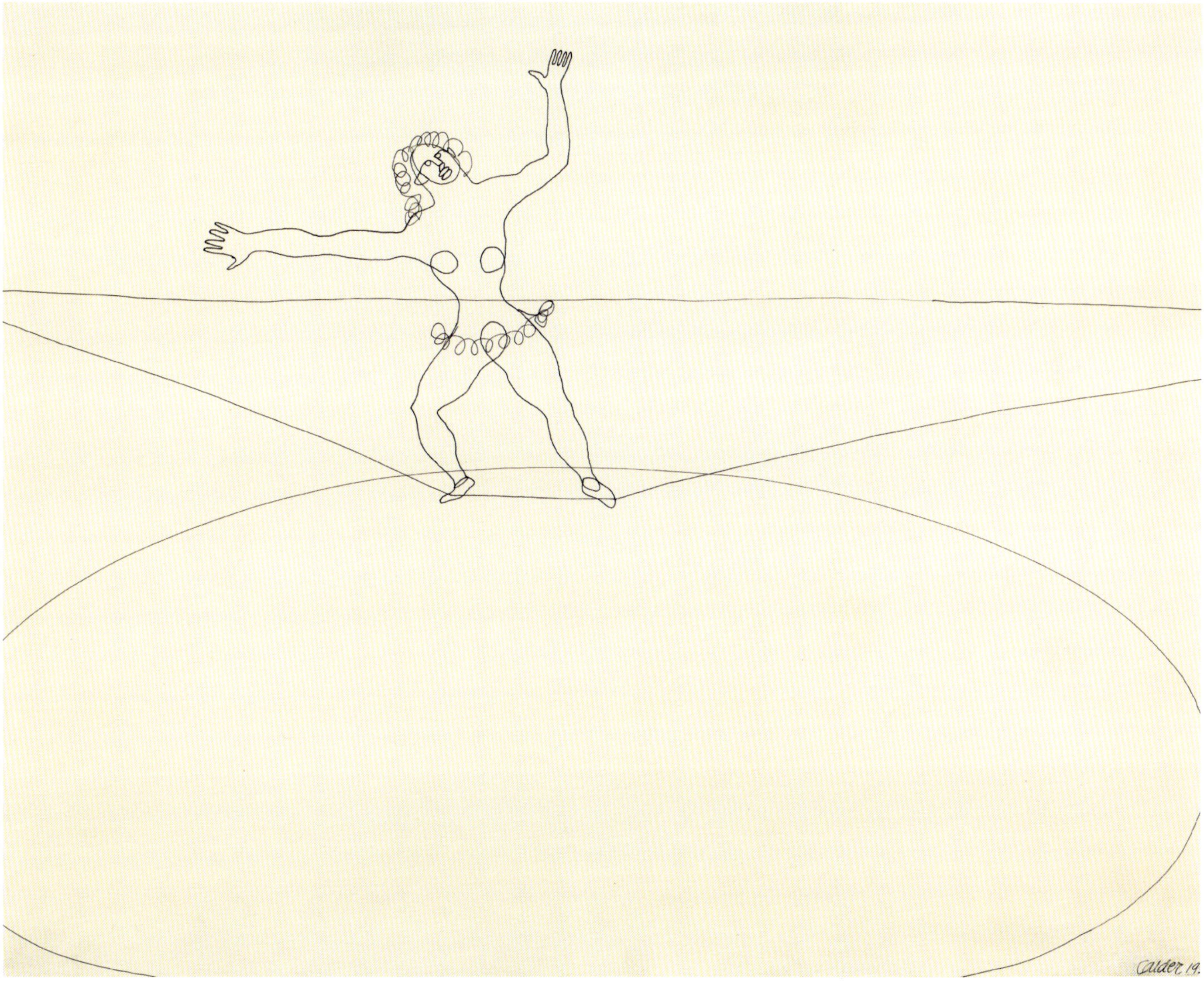

On the High Wire 1932

Aztec Josephine Baker 1930

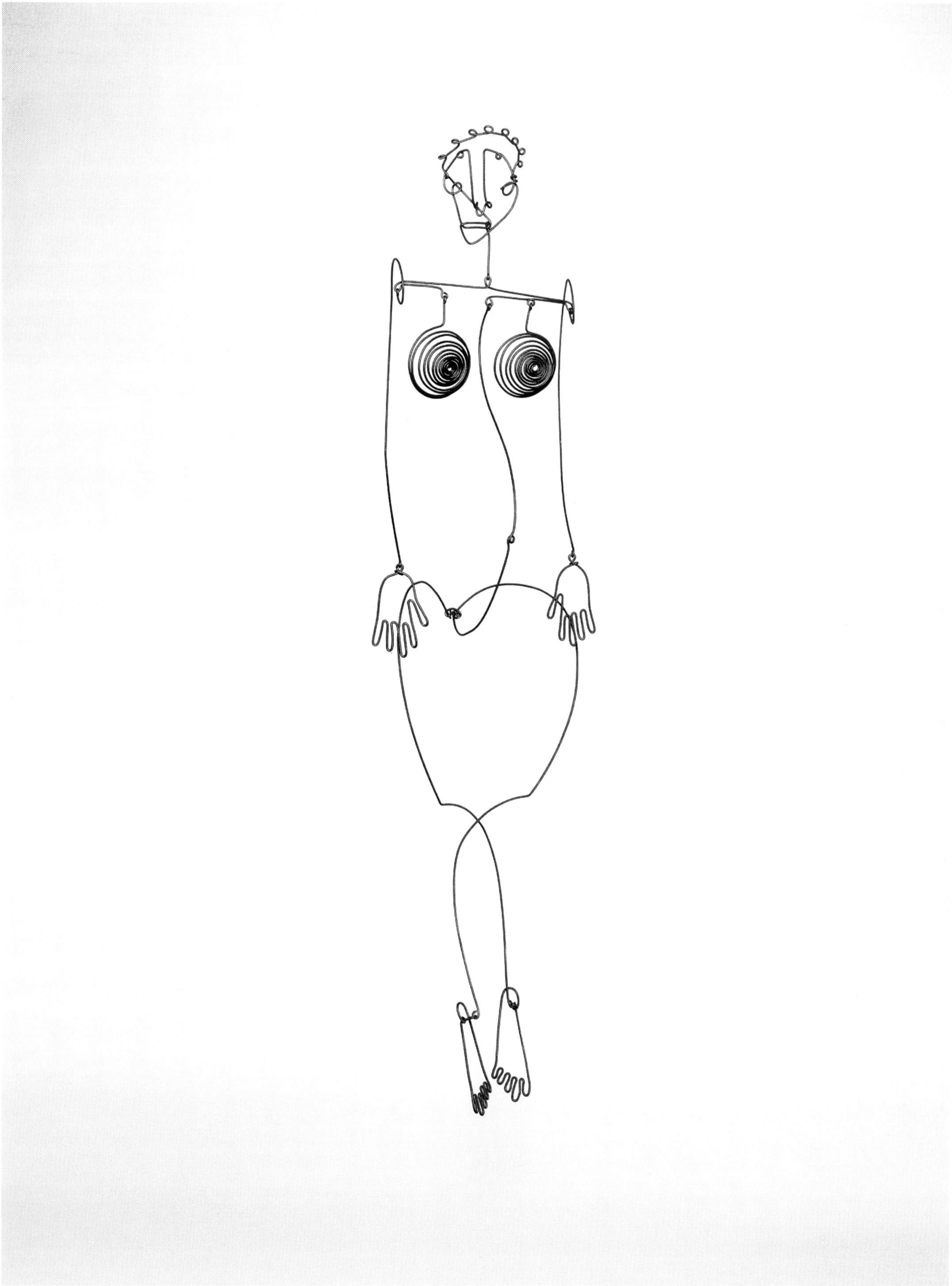

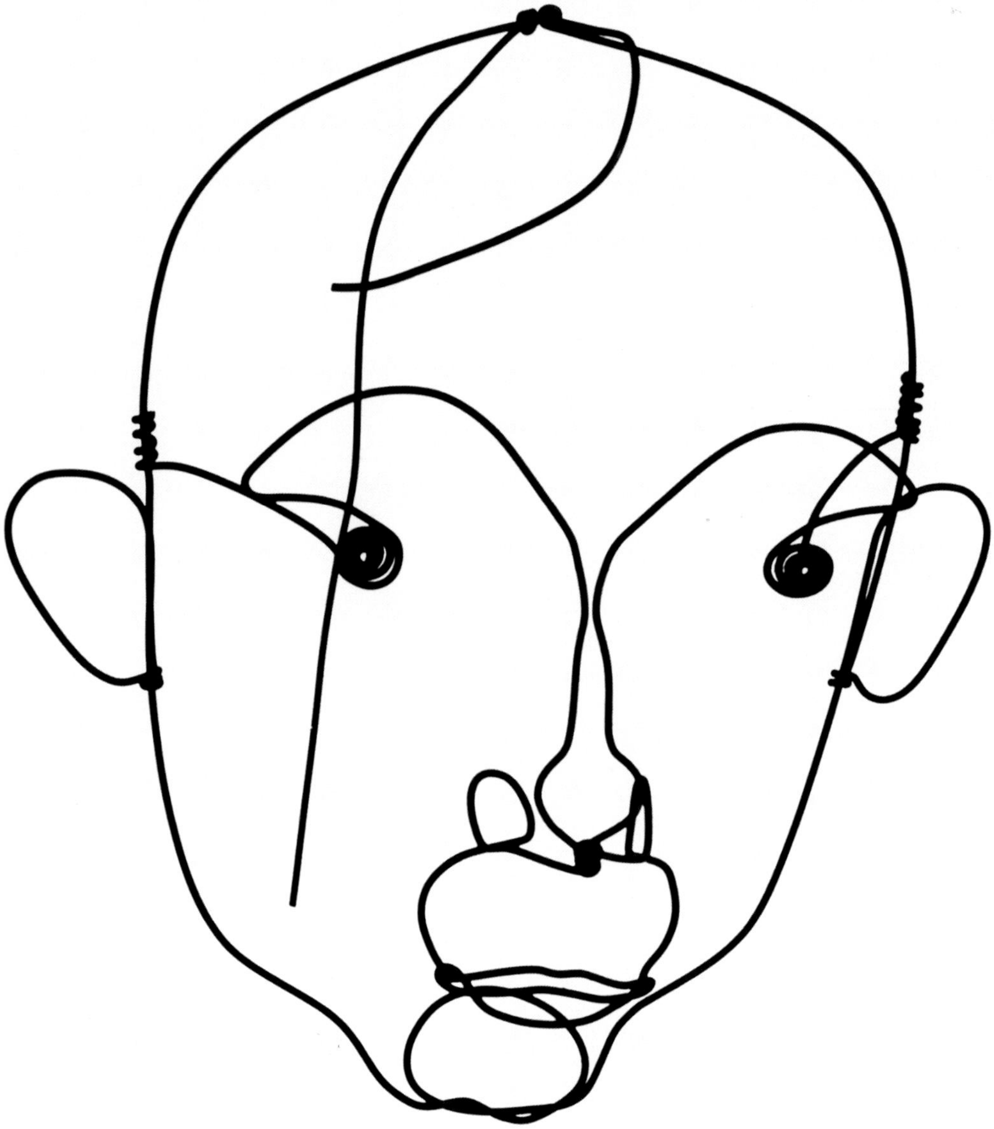

Joan Miró c.1930

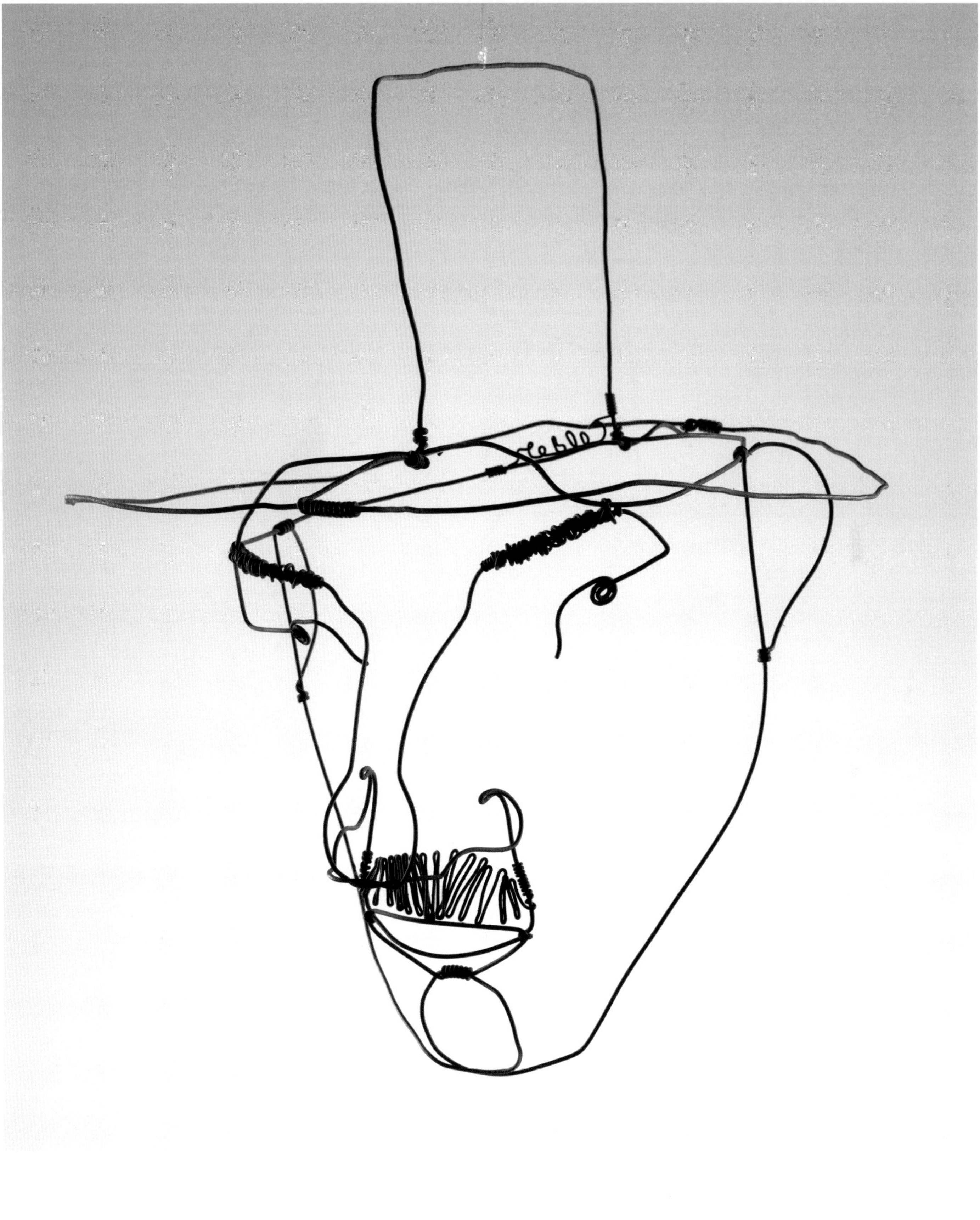

Fernand Léger c.1930

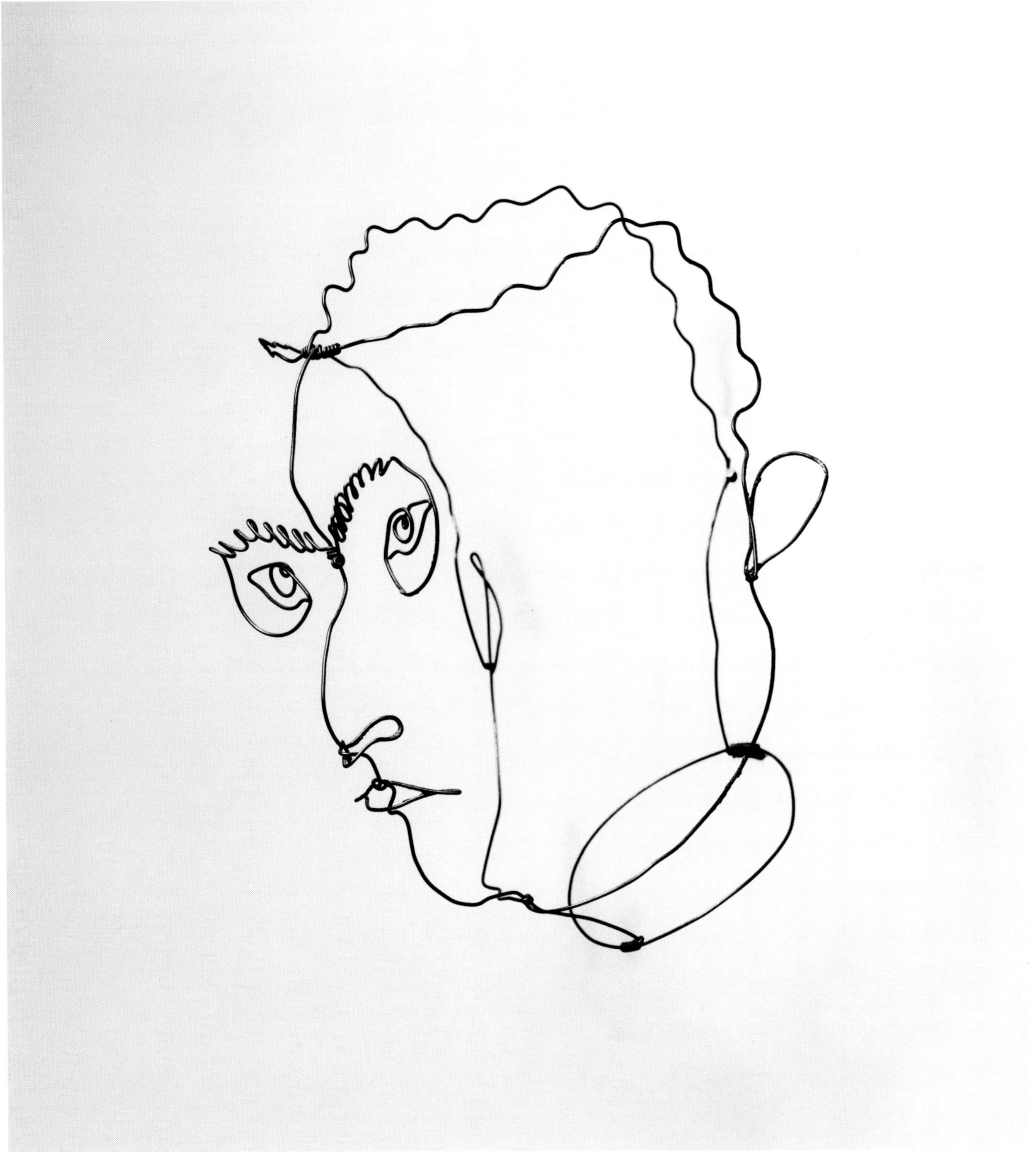

Varèse c.1930

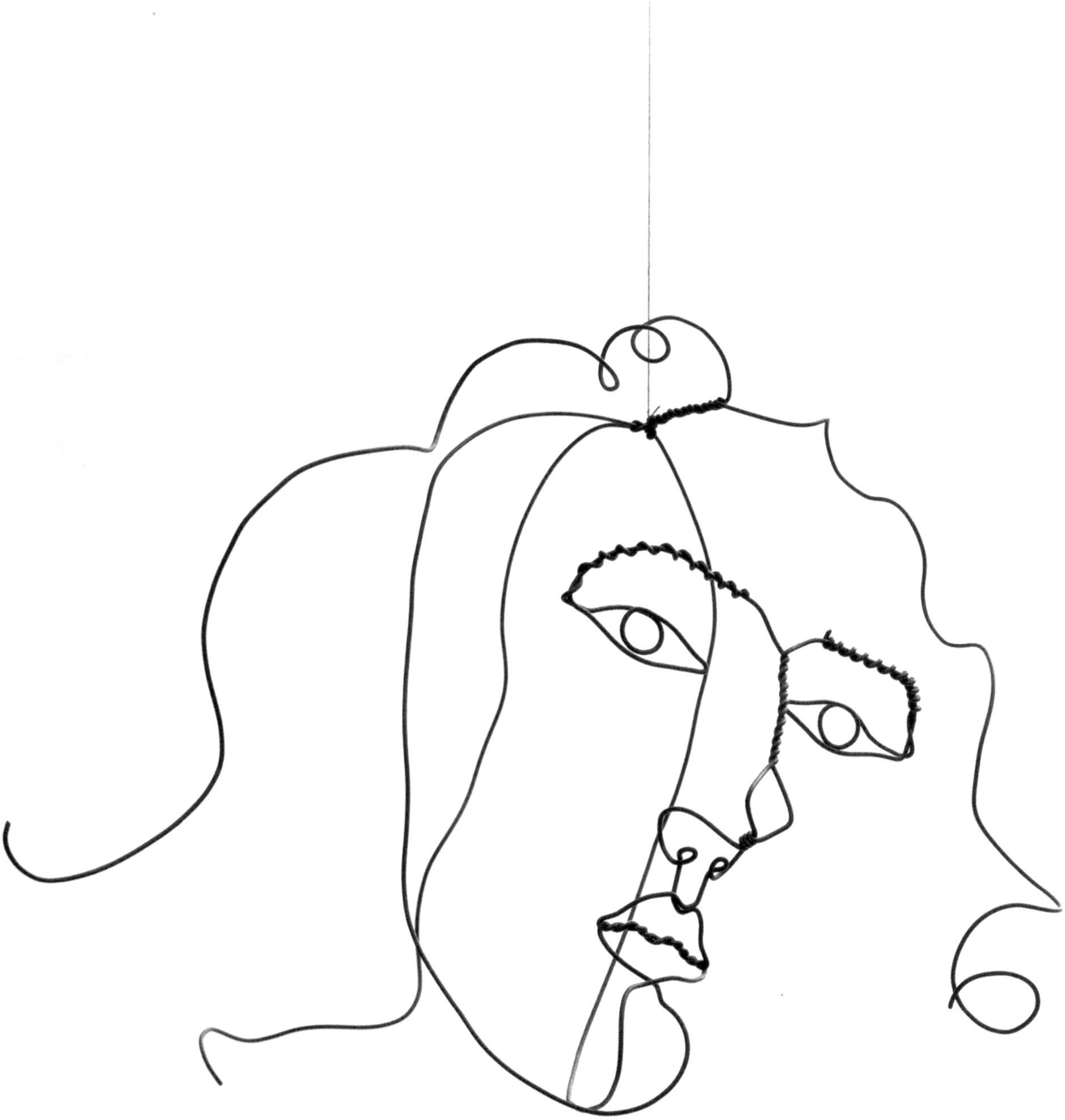

Medusa c.1930

Amédée Ozenfant c.1930

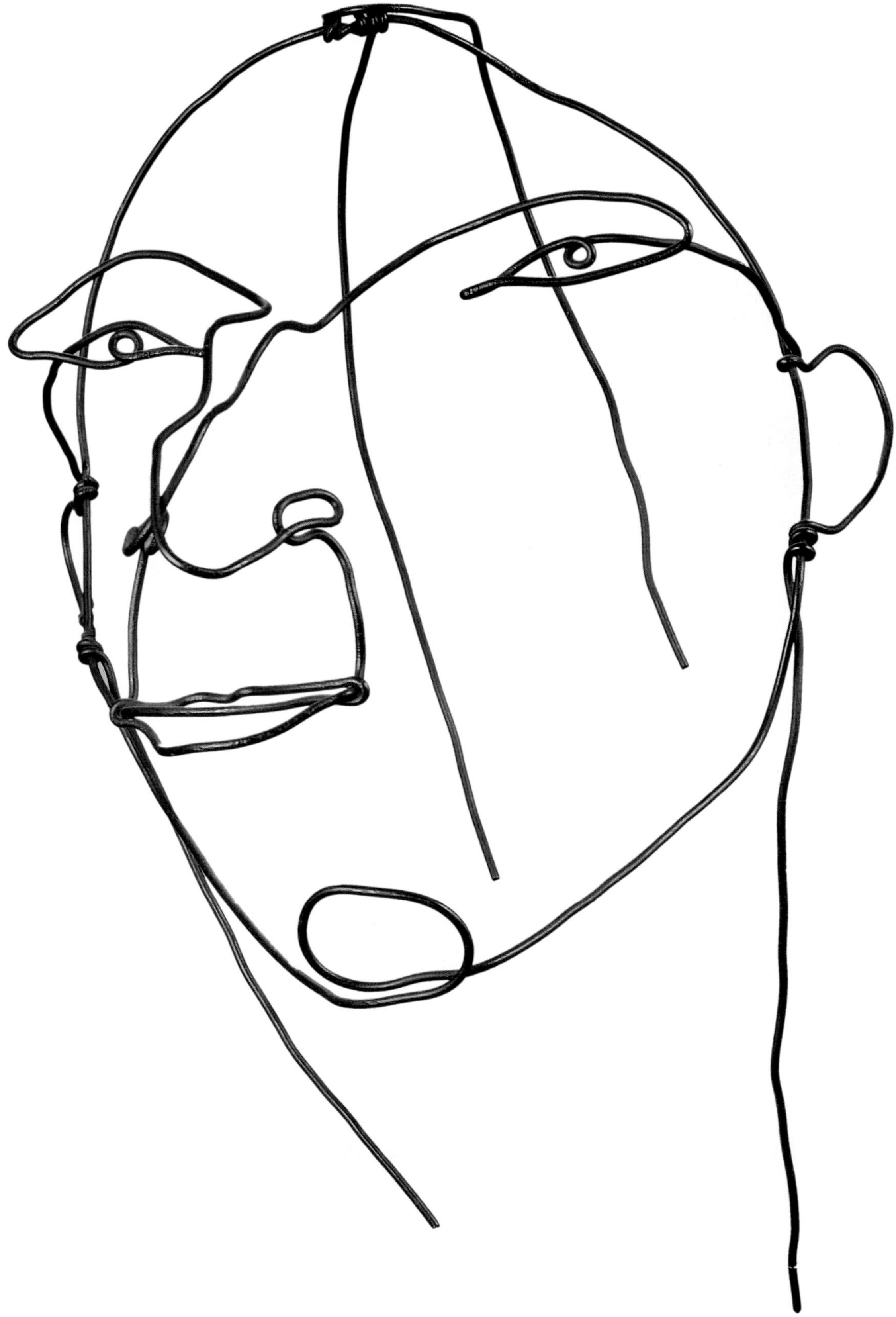

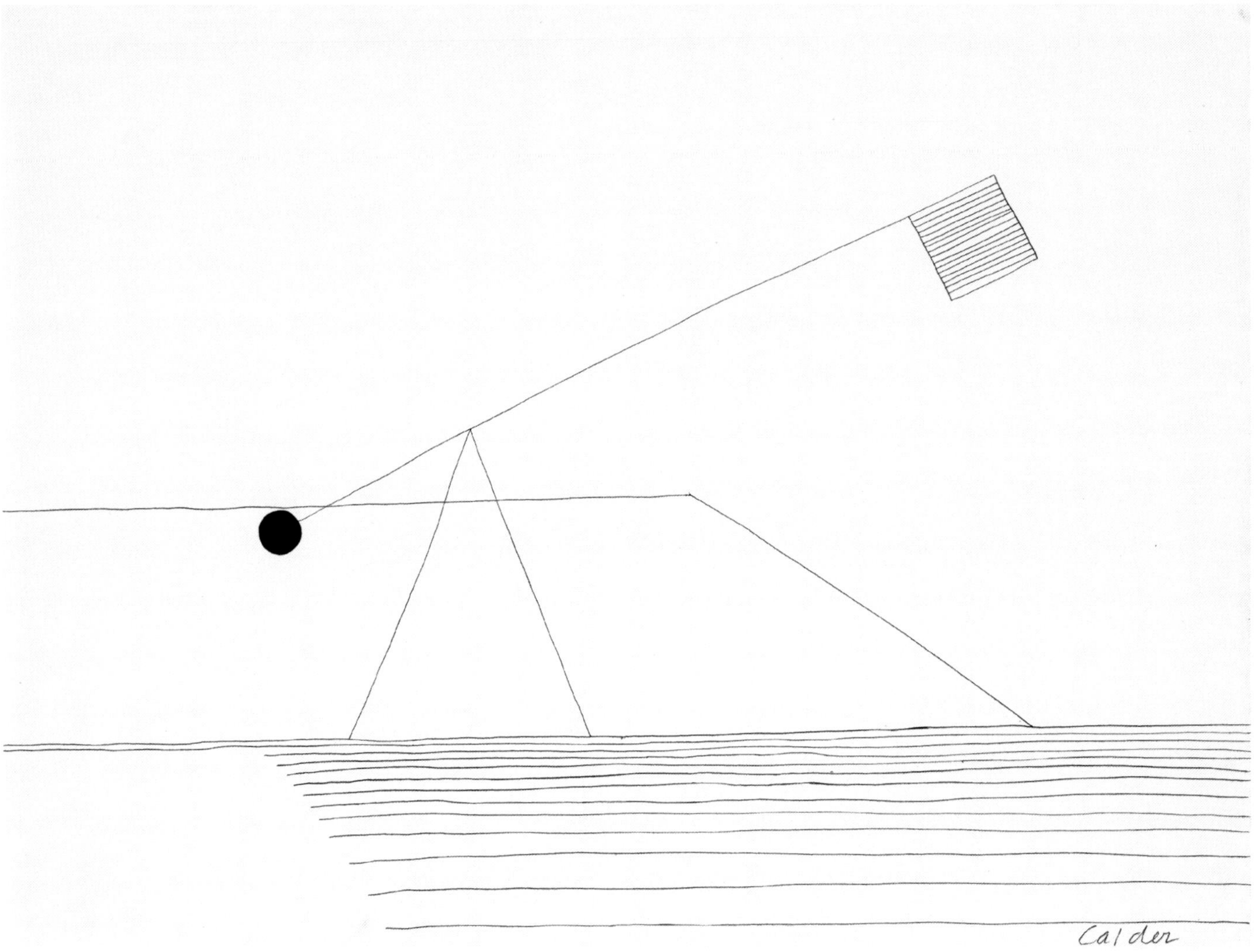

Study for a Mobile c.1931

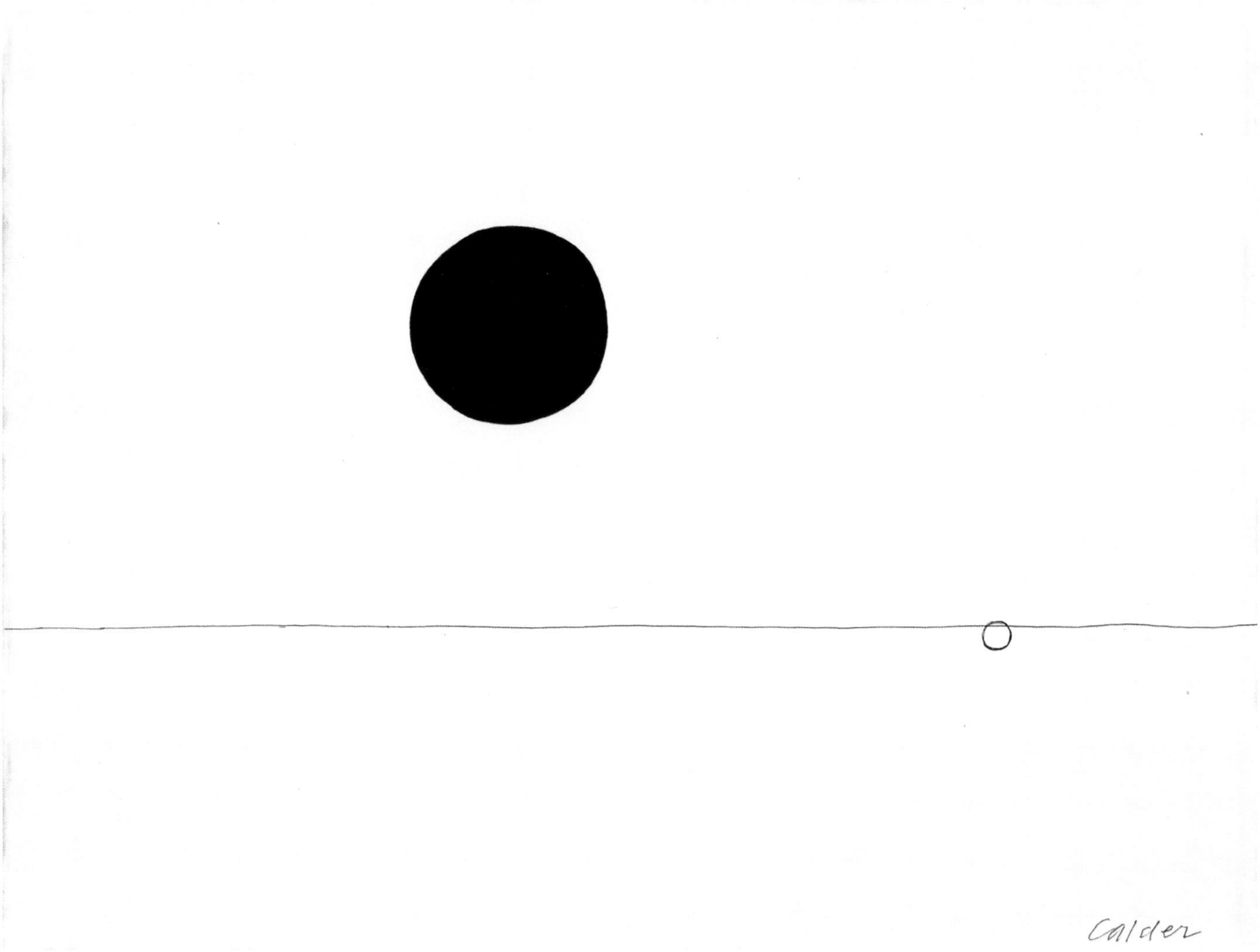

Big Black Disc c.1931

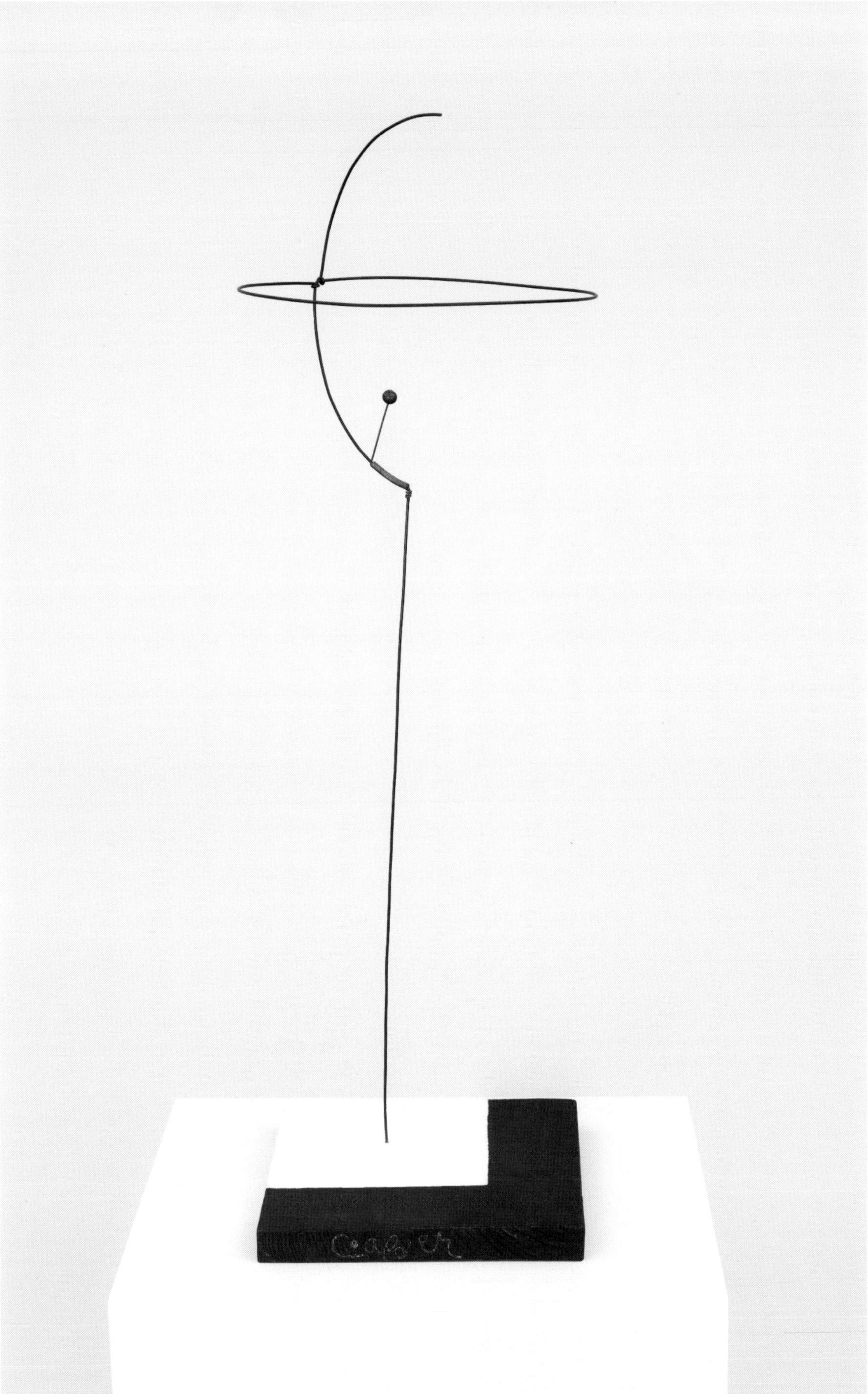

Sphérique I 1931

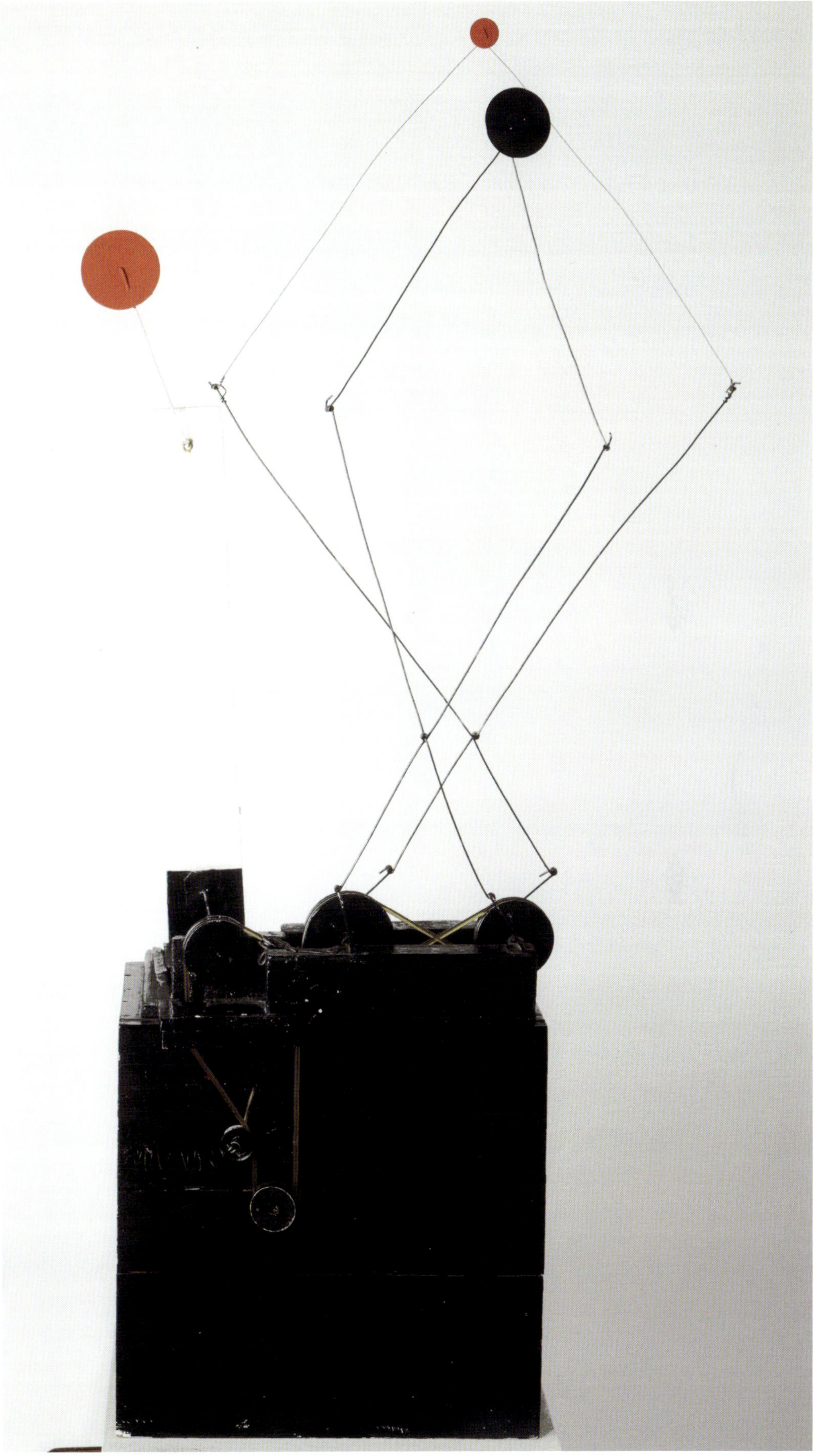

Pantograph 1931

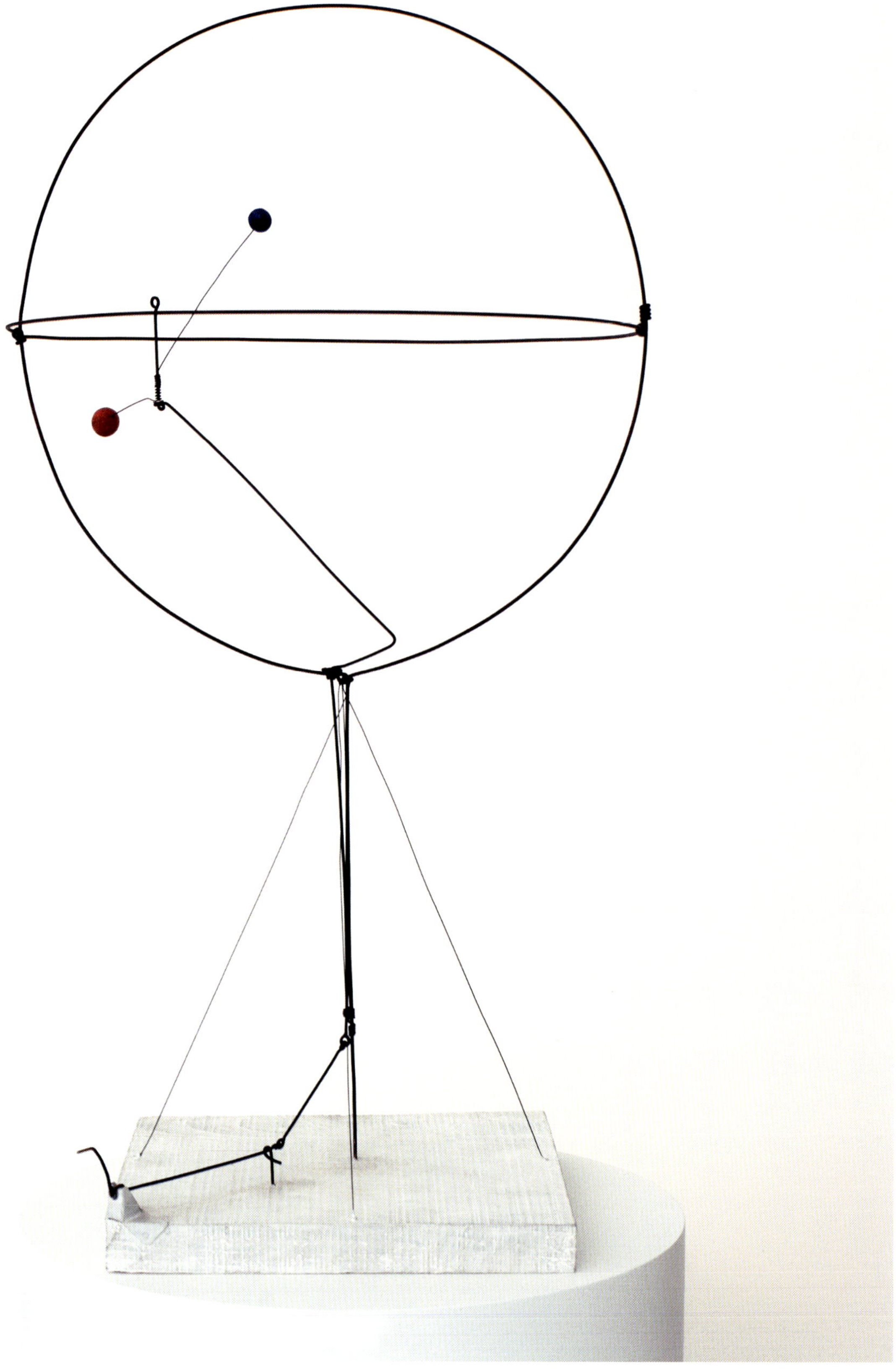

Two Spheres Within a Sphere 1931

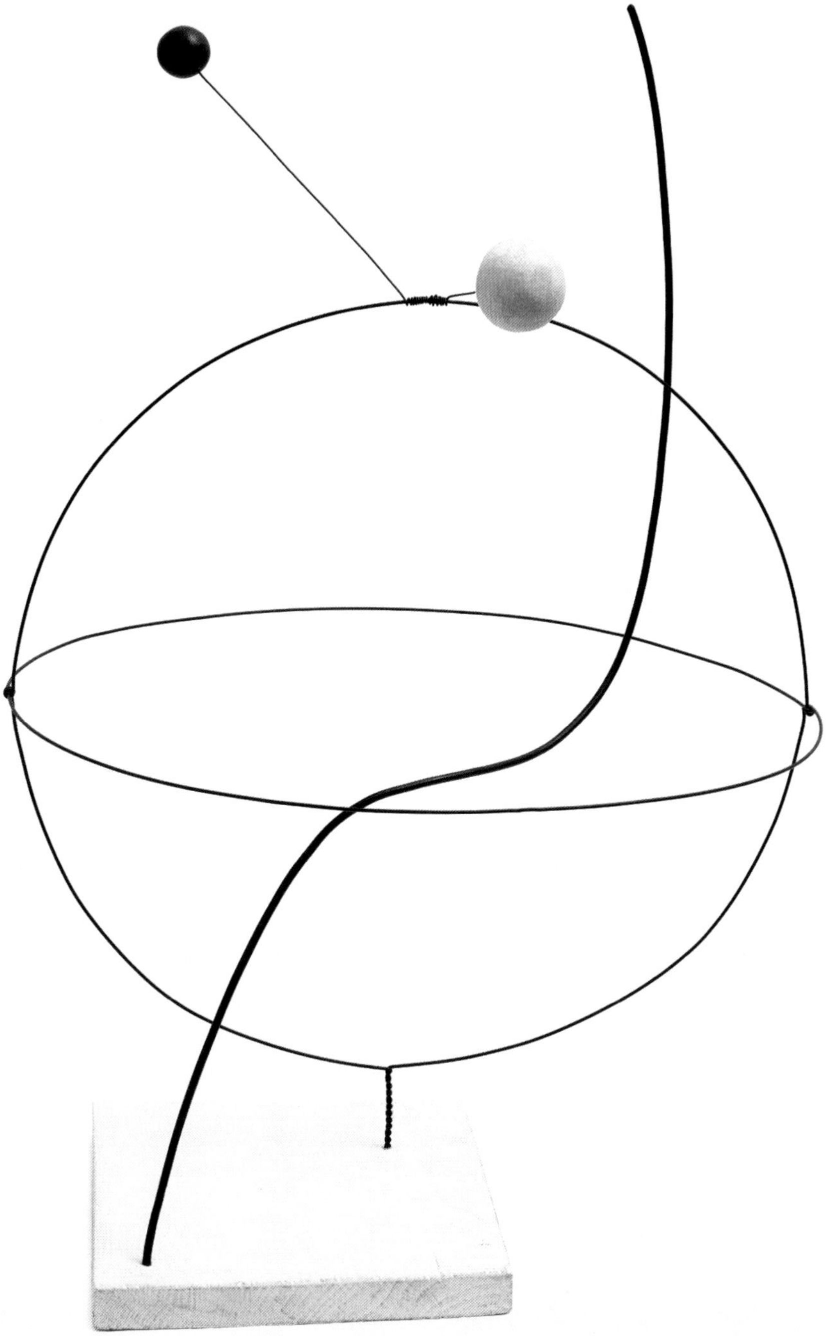

Croisière 1931

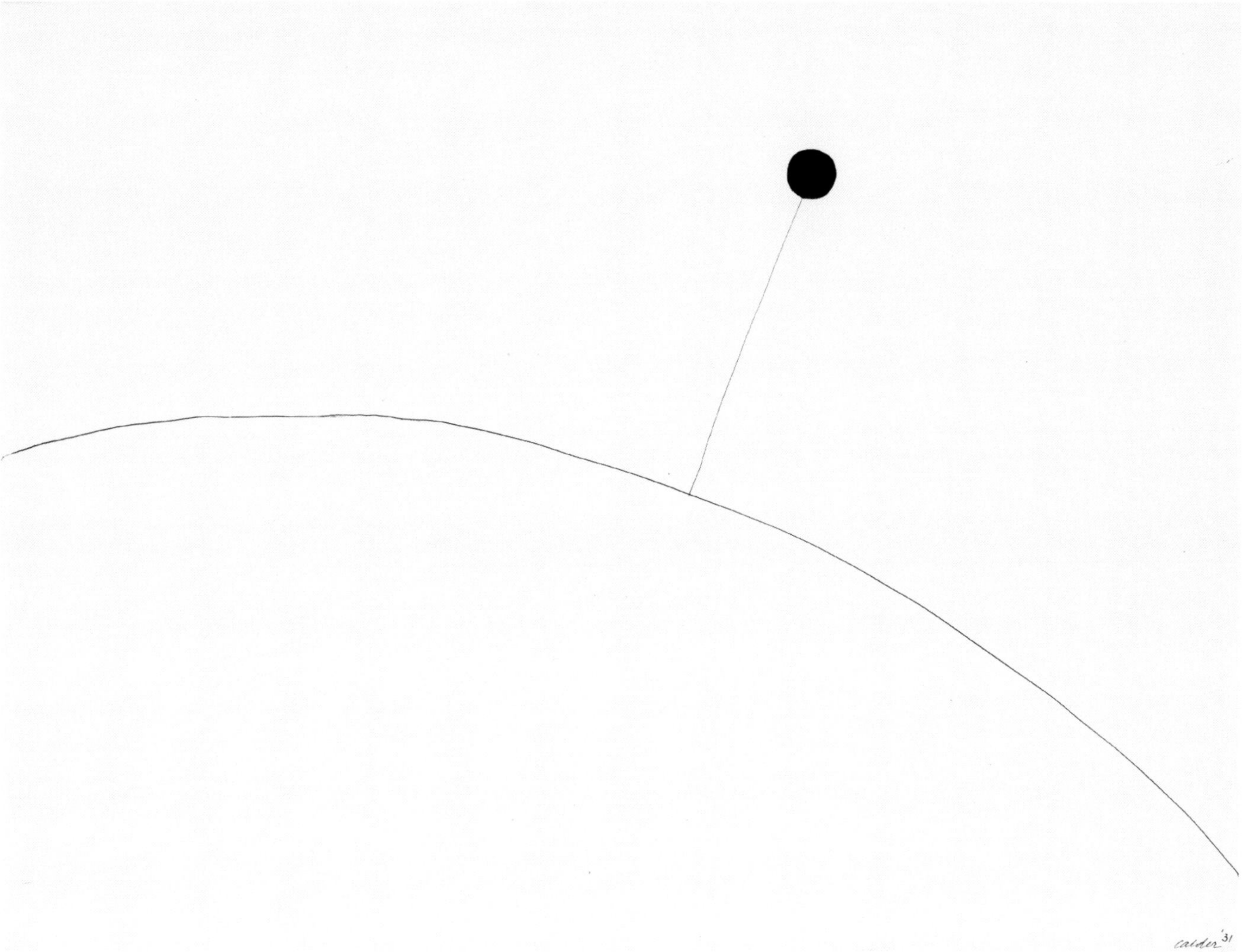

Up, Over the Horizon 1931

Many 1931

Two Spheres 1931

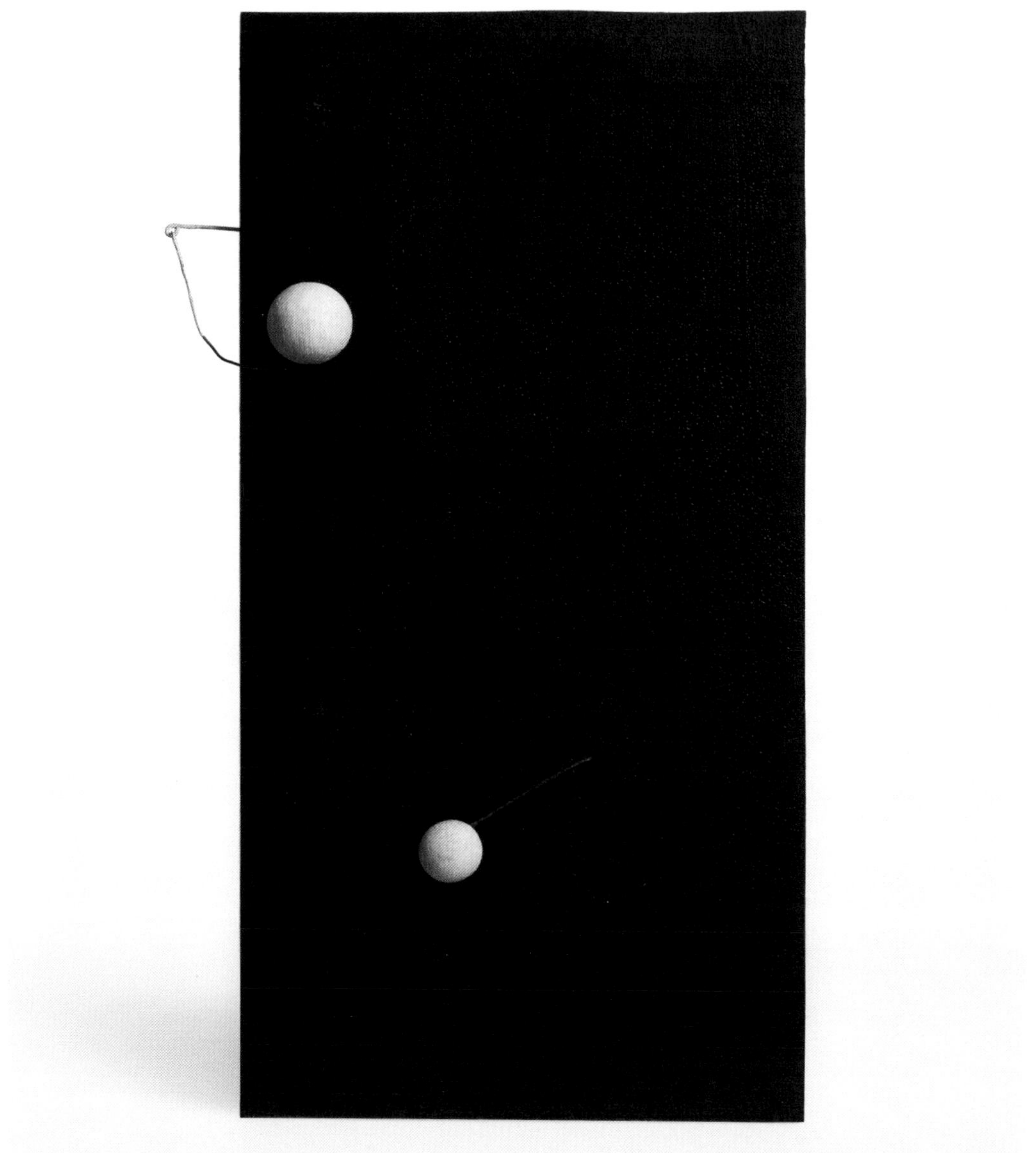

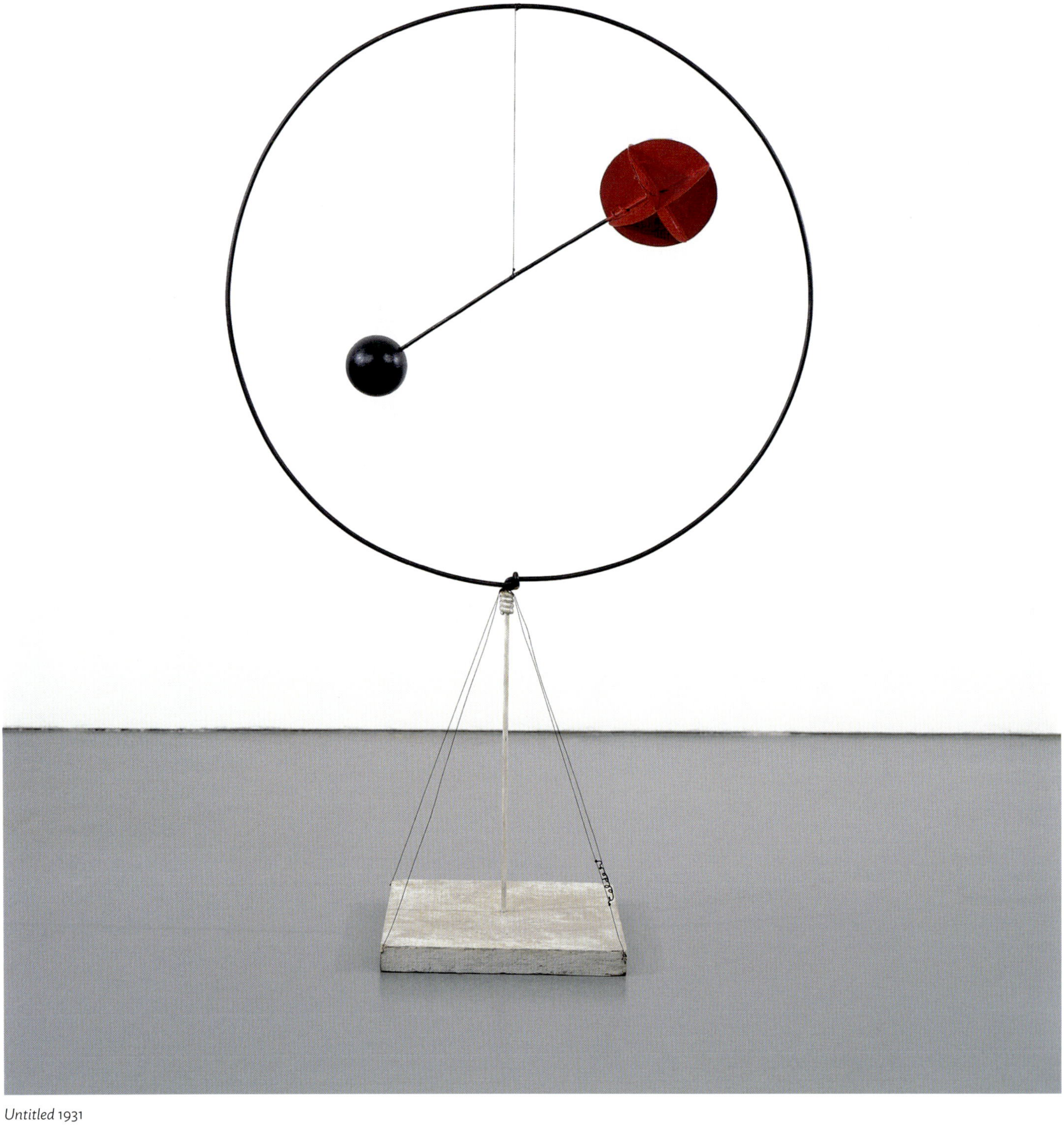

Untitled 1931

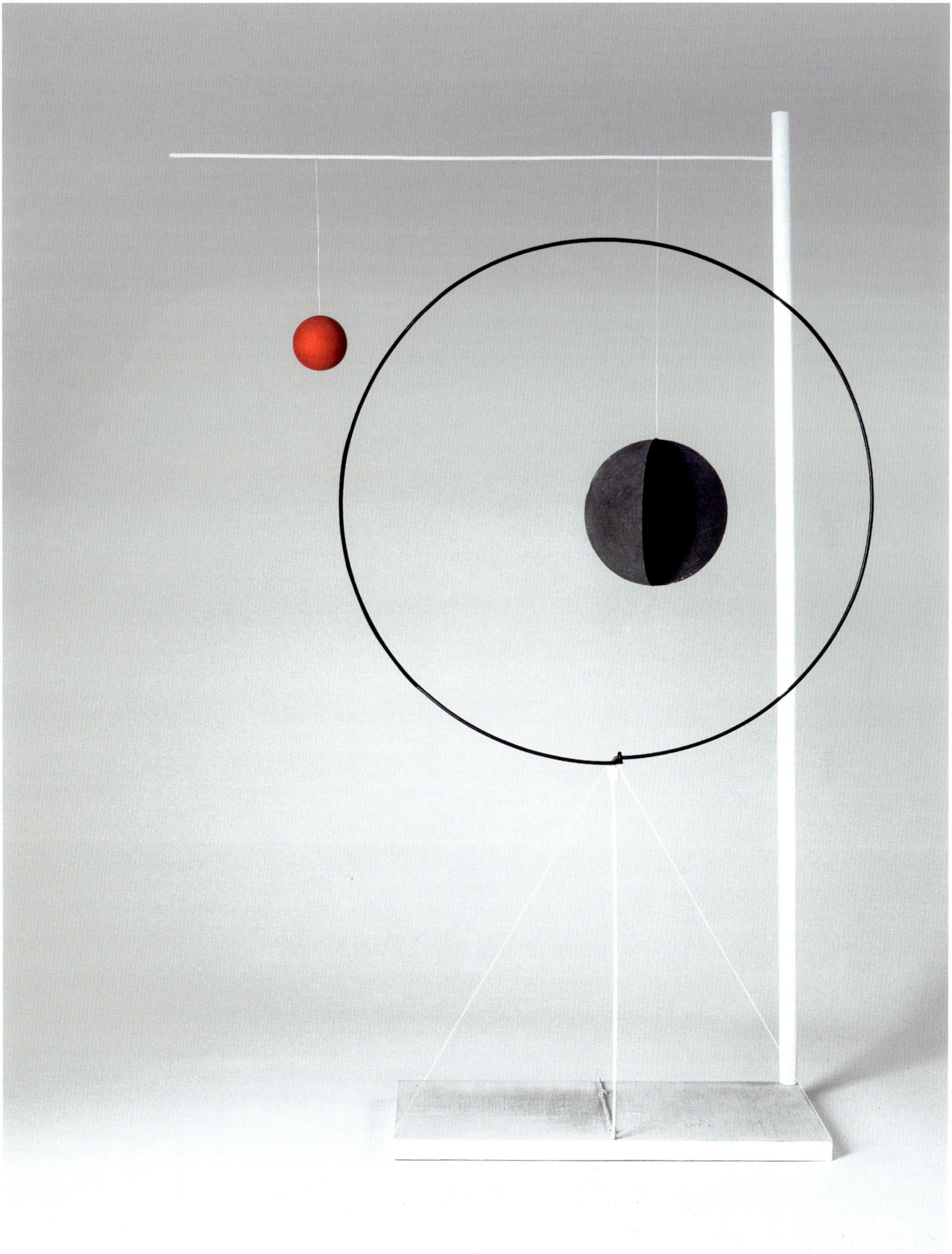

Object with Red Ball 1931

Small Feathers 1931

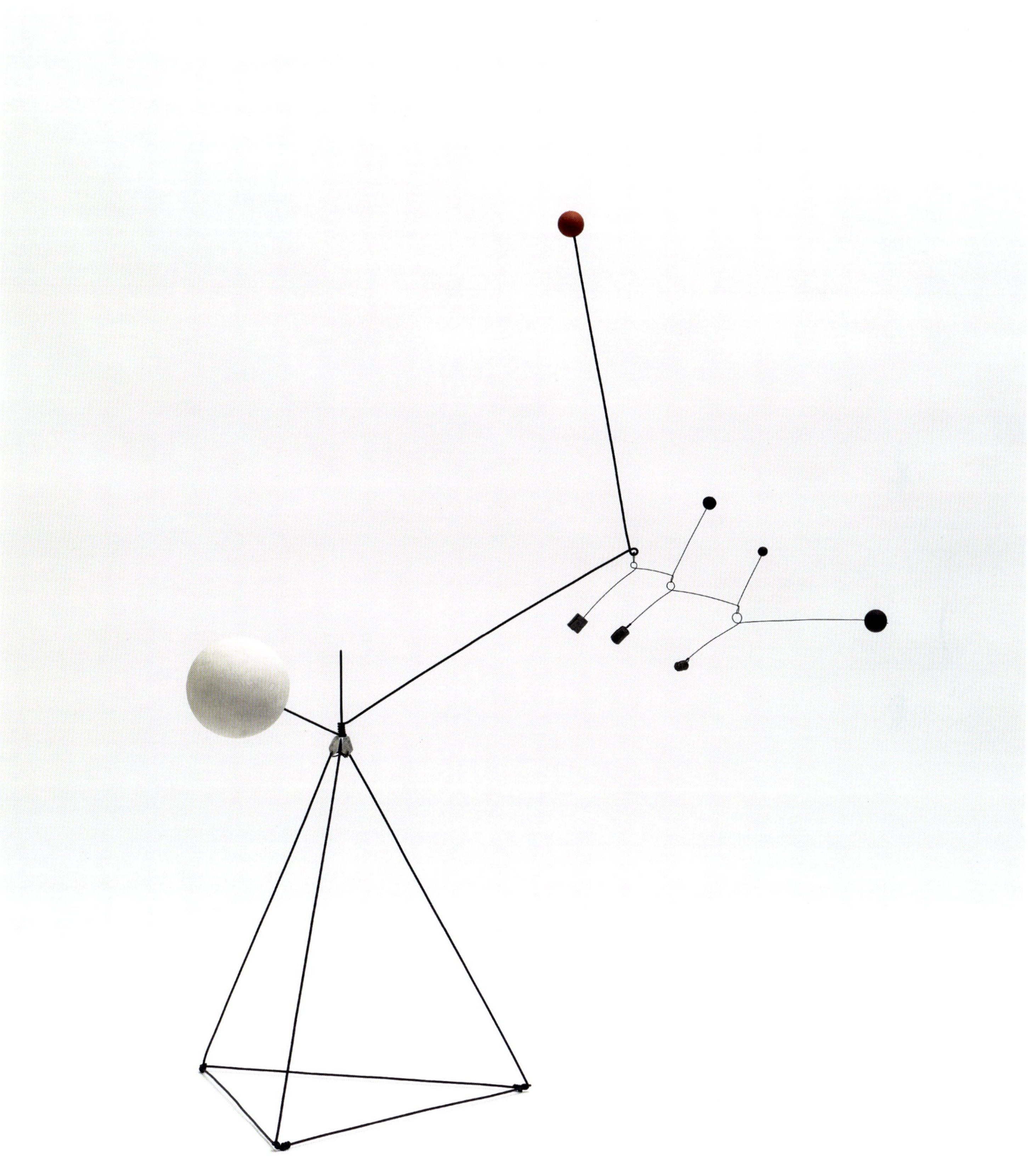

Small Sphere and Heavy Sphere 1932/3

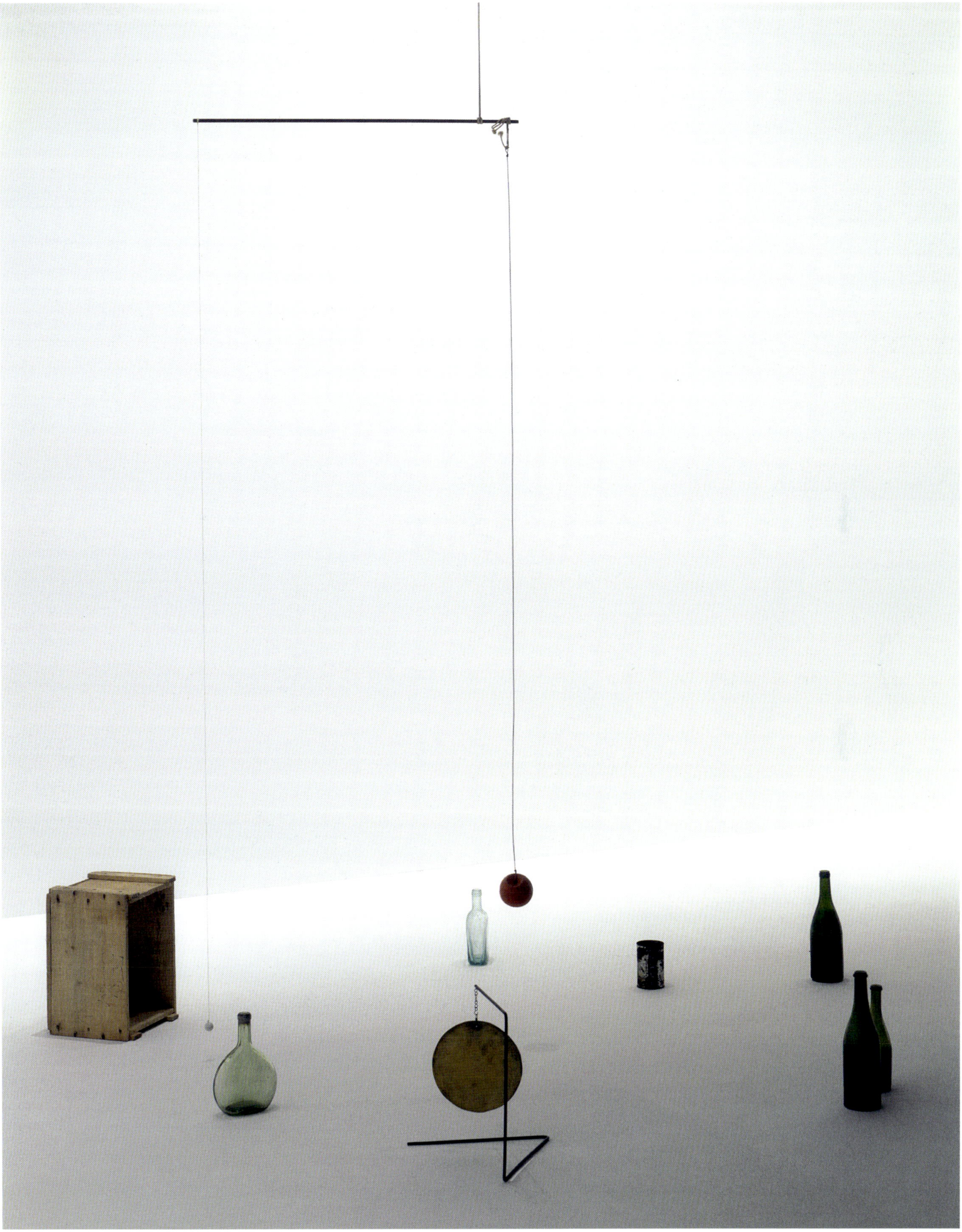

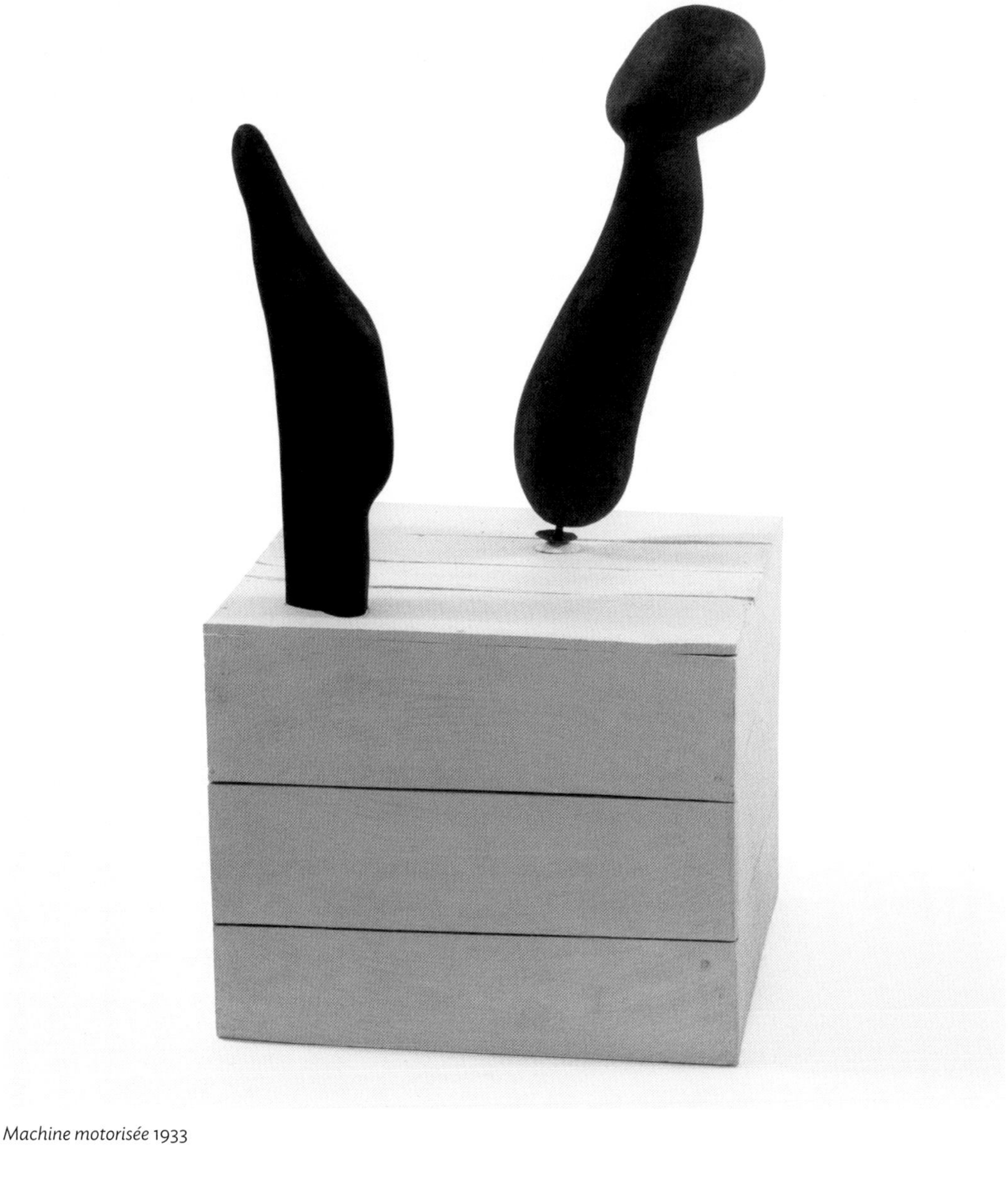

Machine motorisée 1933

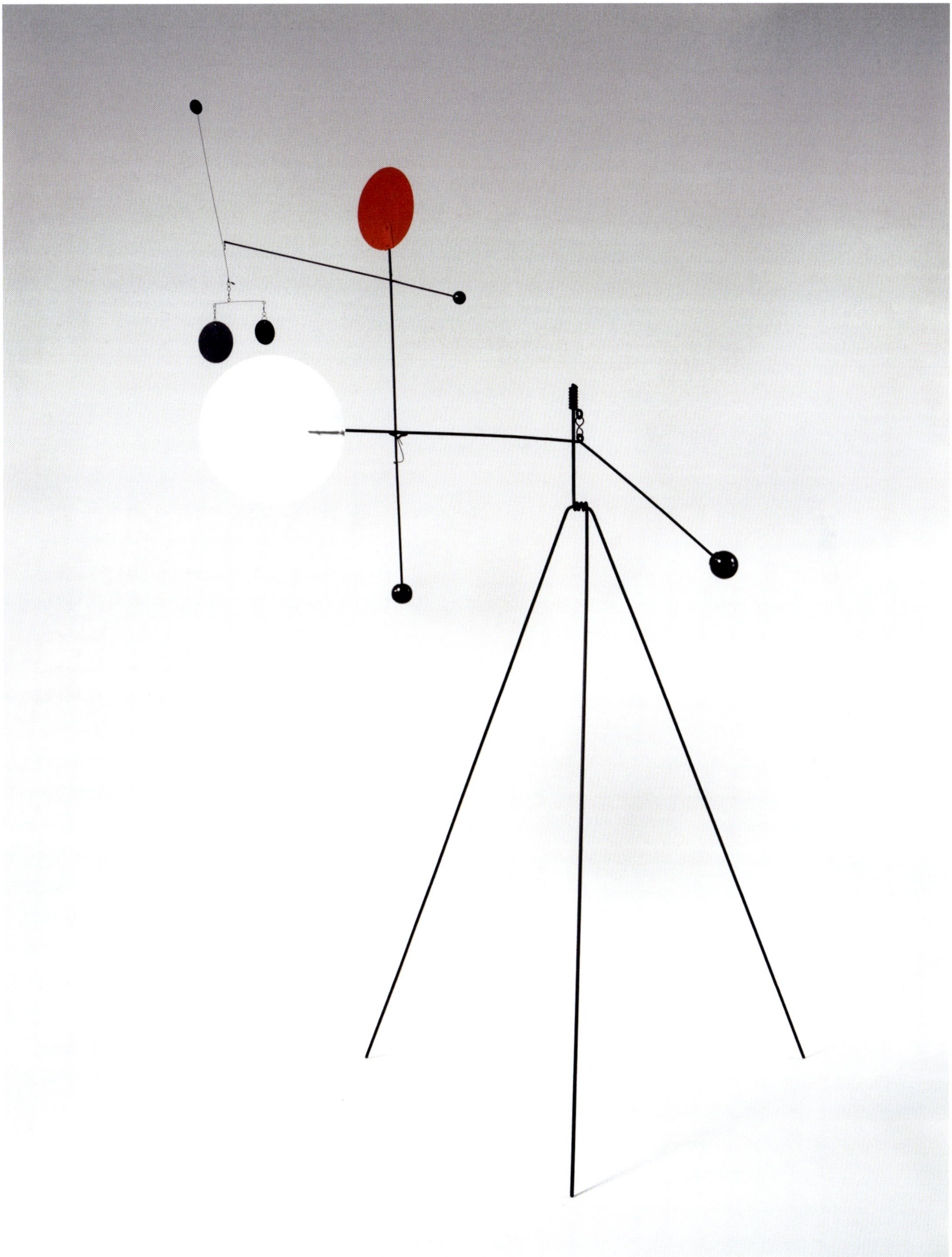

Red, White, Black and Brass 1934

Red and Yellow Vane 1934

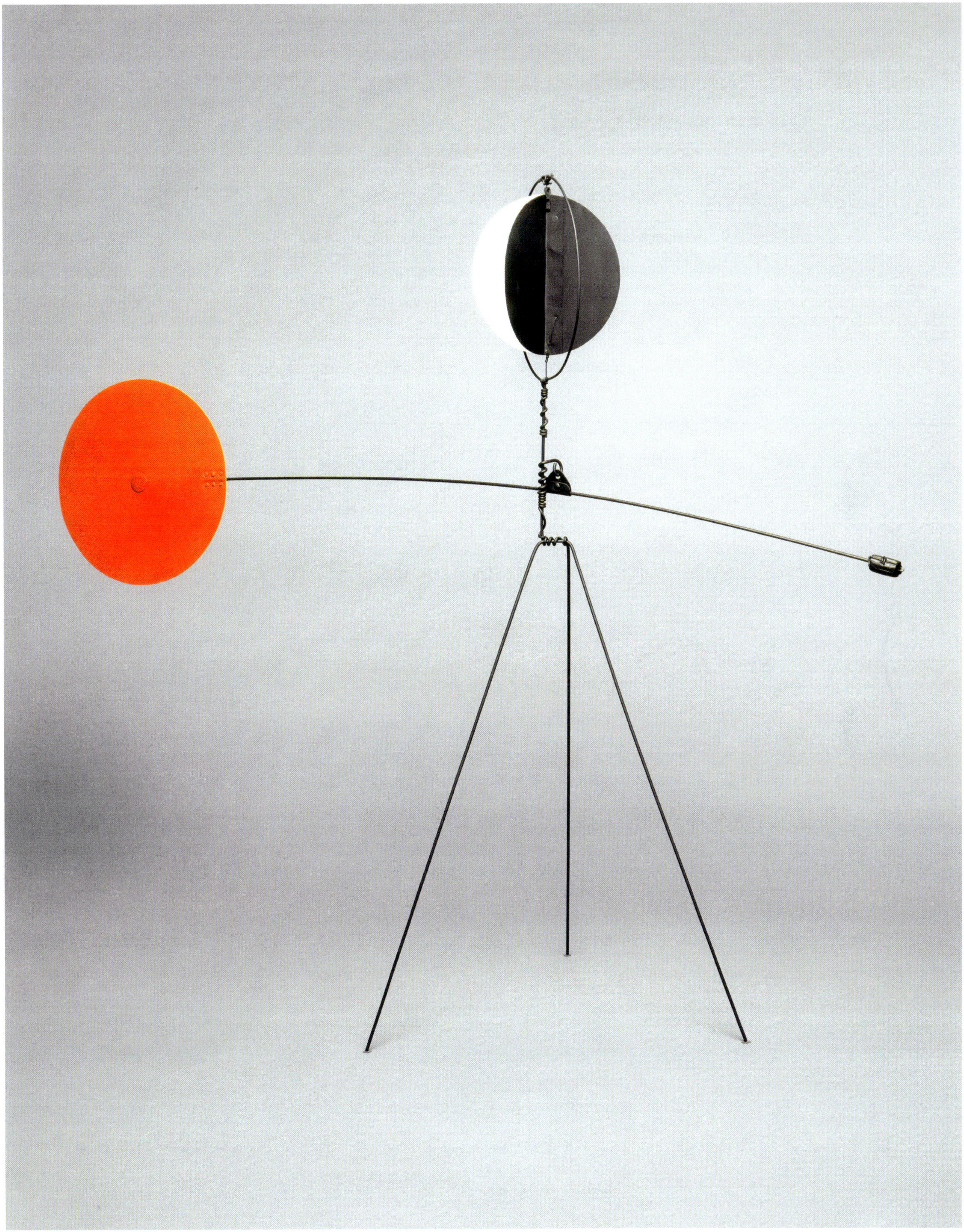

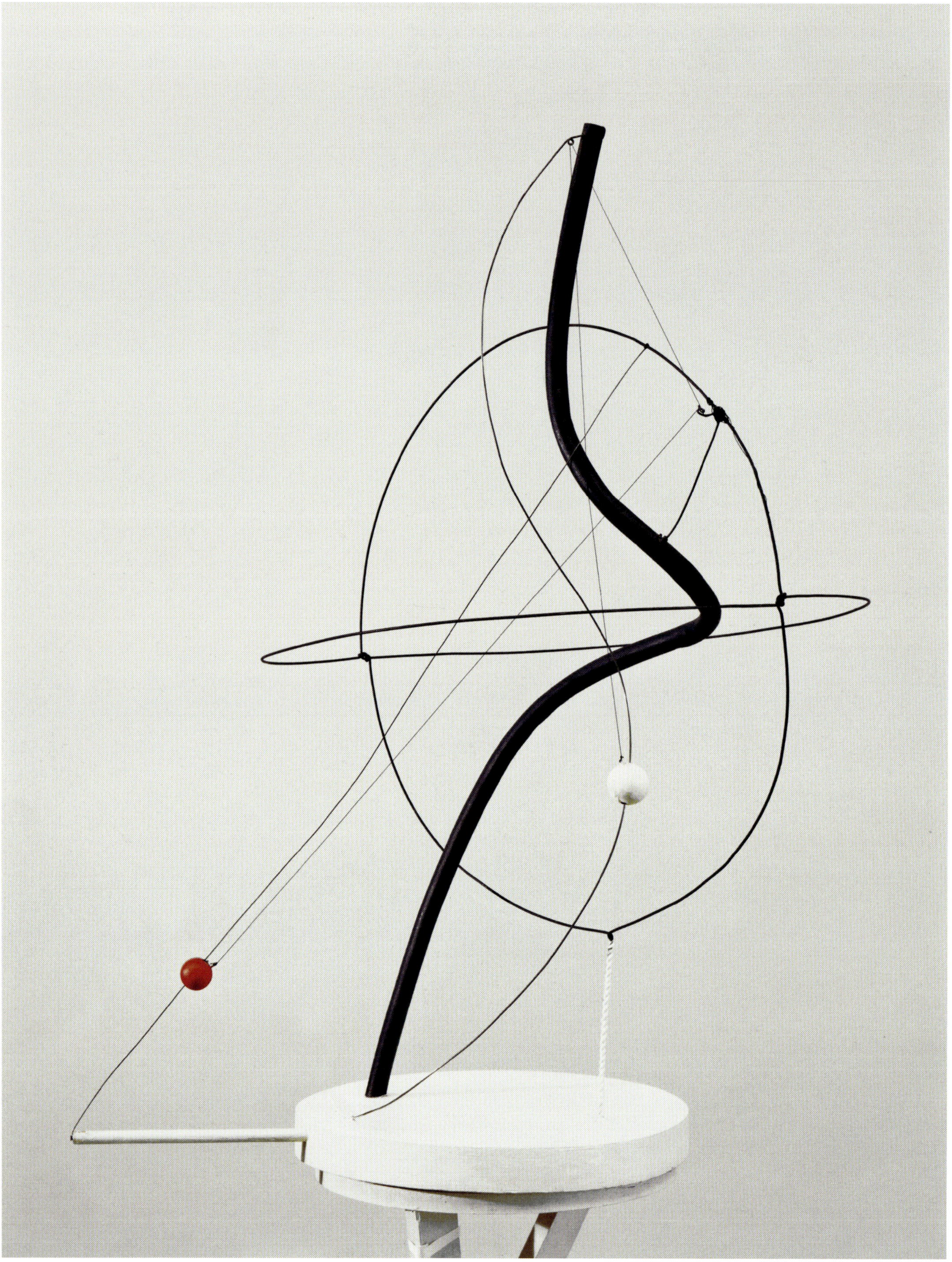

A Universe 1934

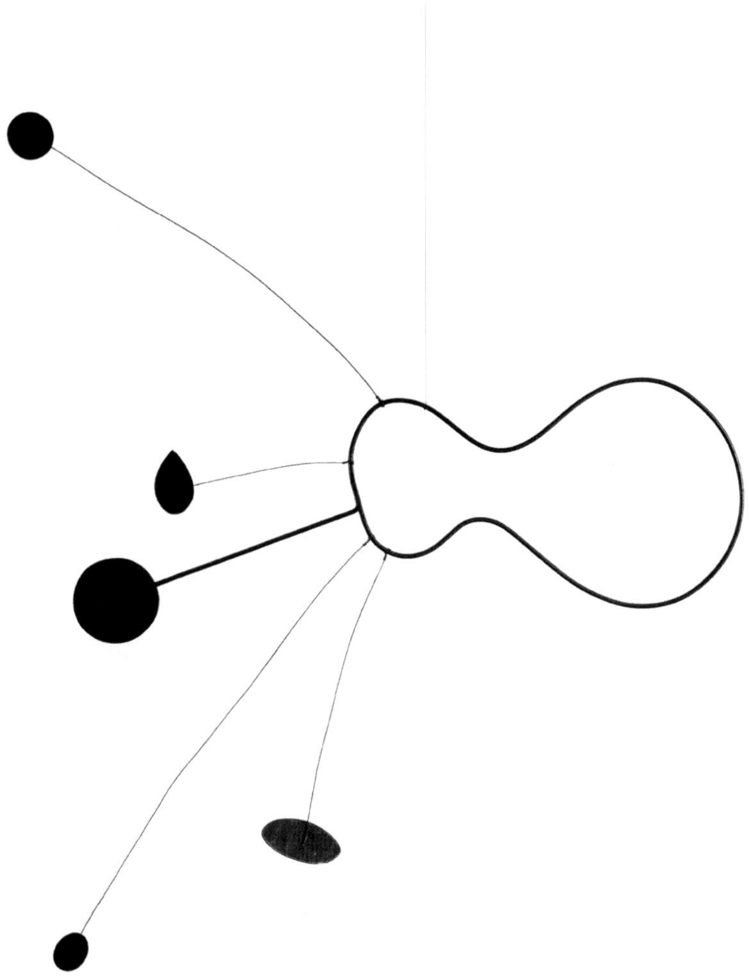

The Spider c.1935–7

Untitled c.1934

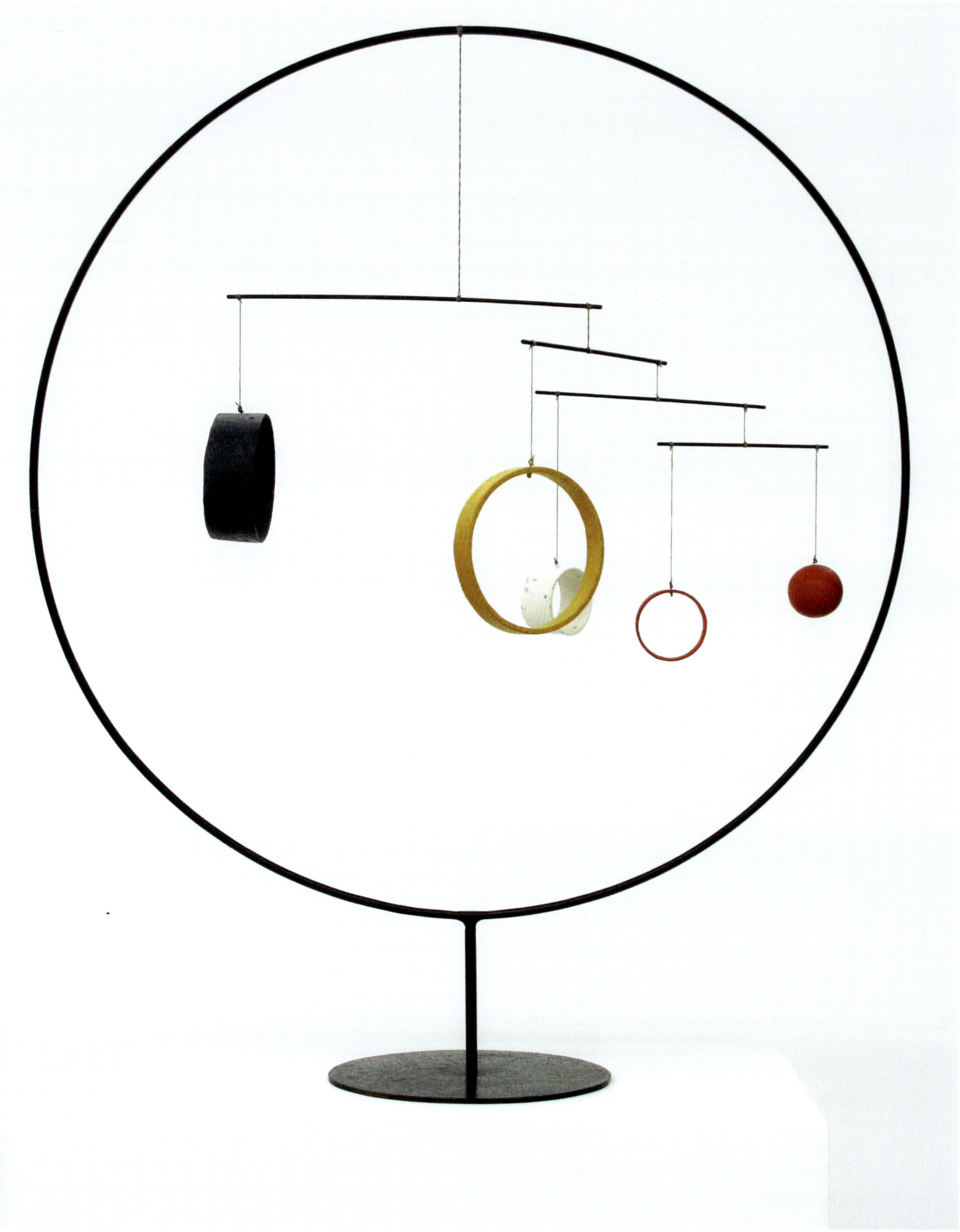

Black Frame 1934

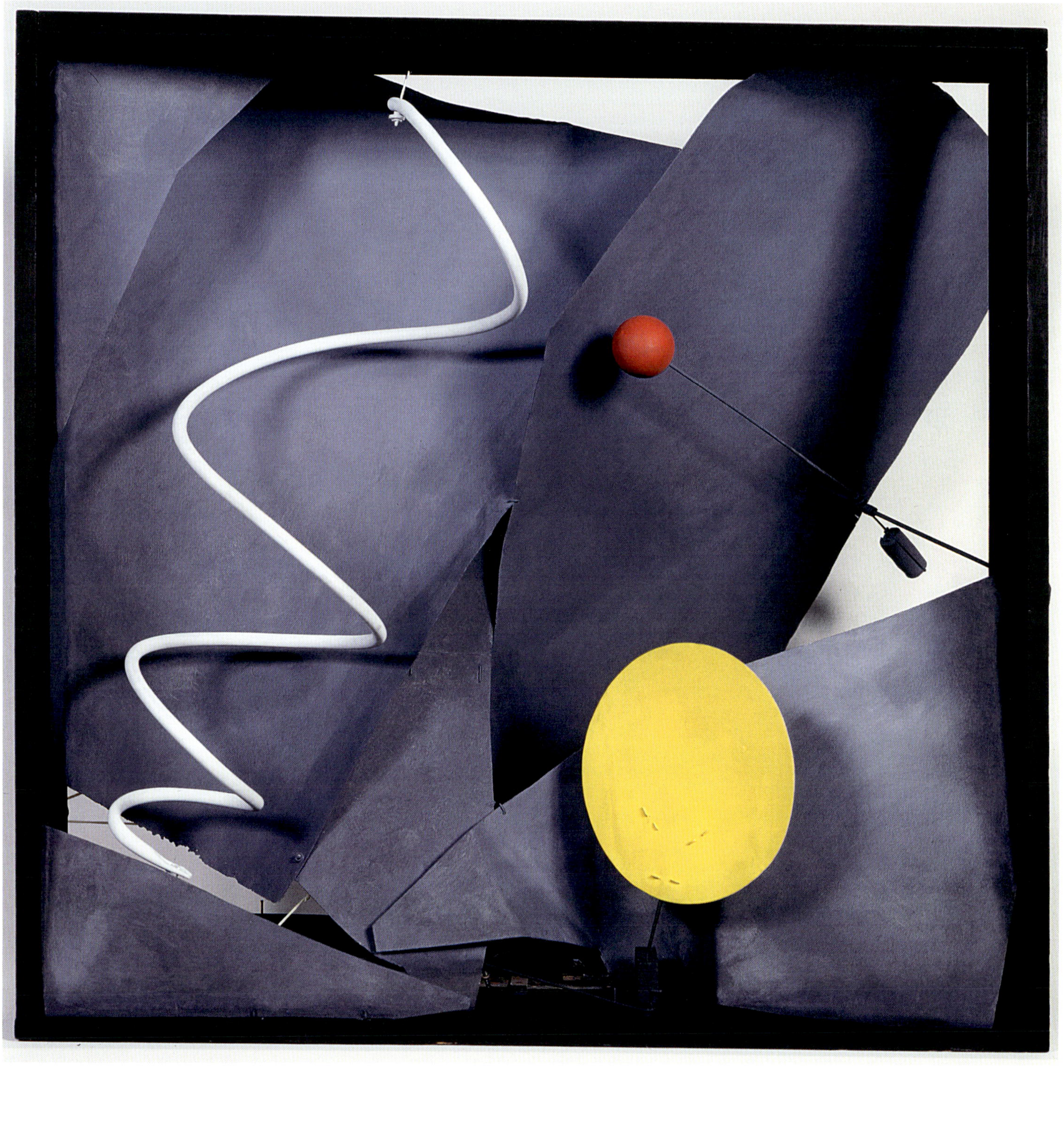

Little Blue Panel 1934

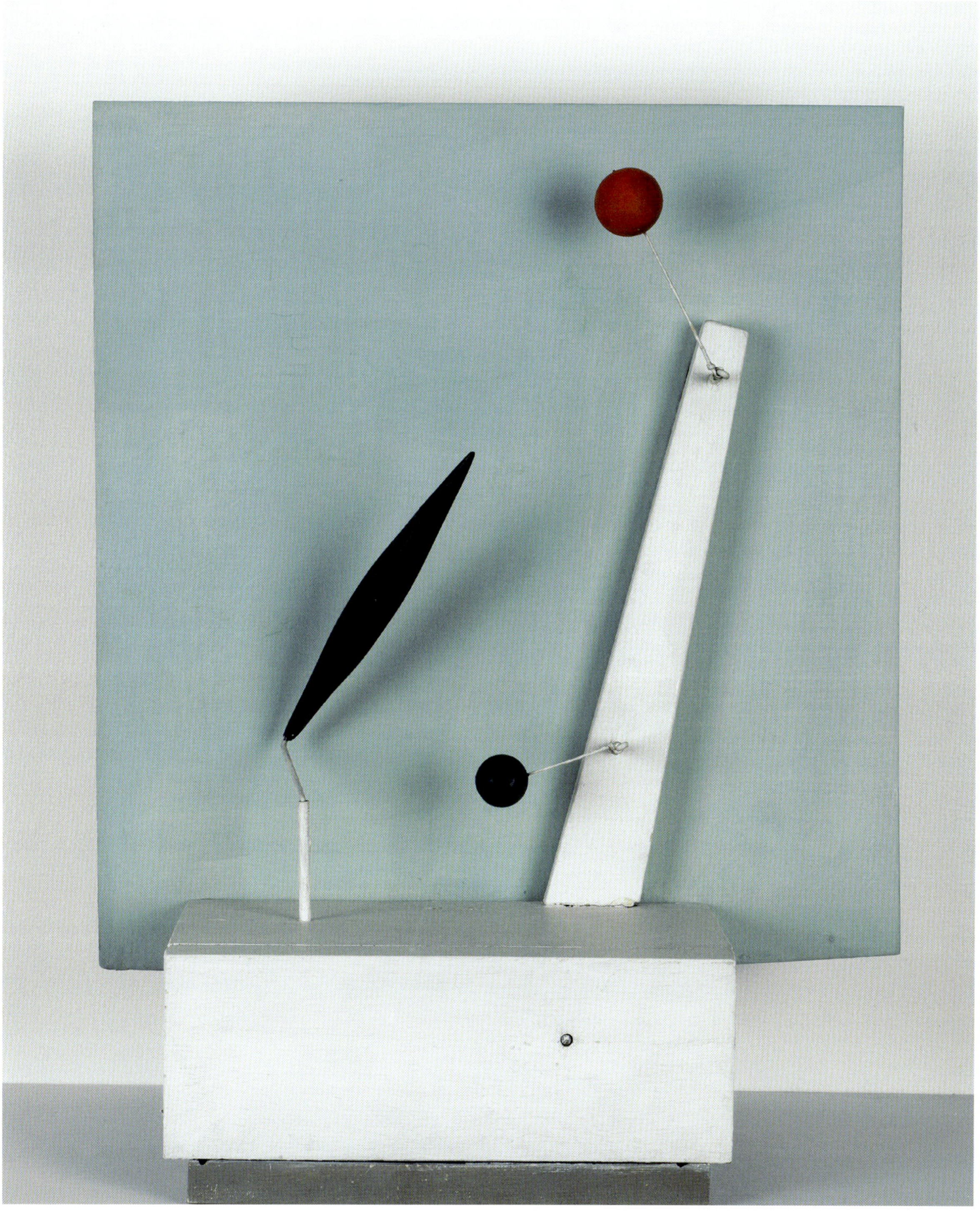

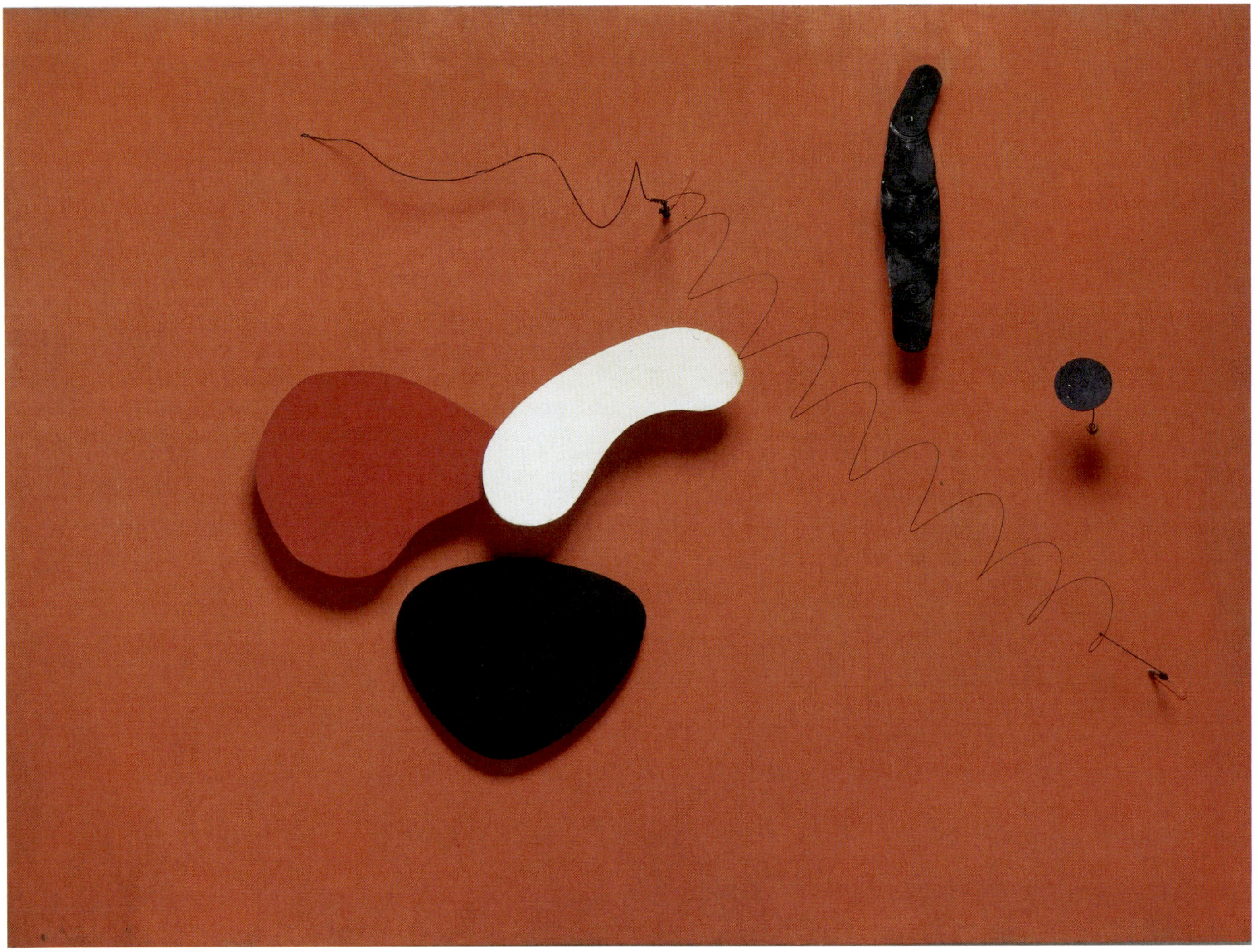

The Orange Panel 1936

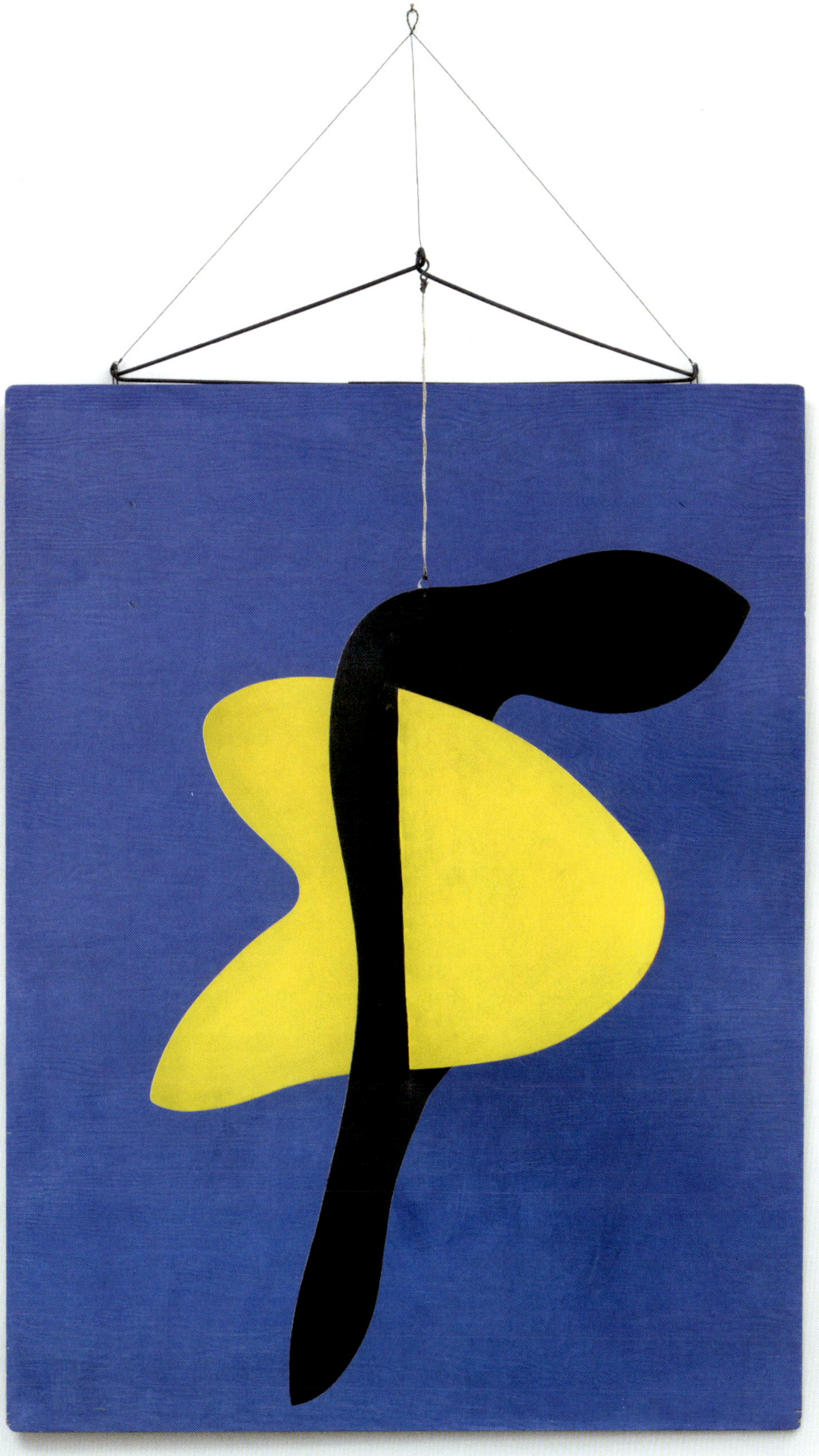

Blue Panel 1936

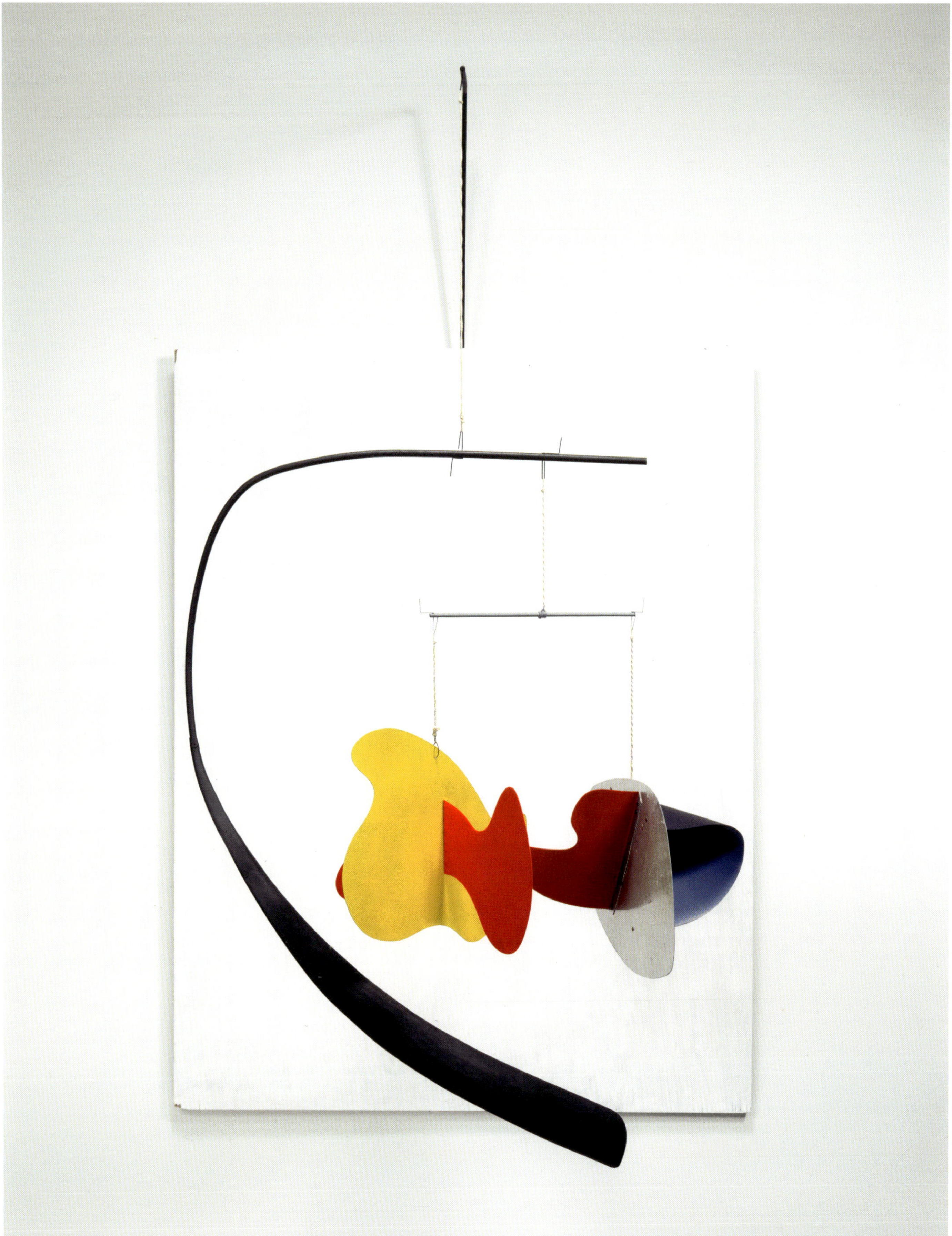

White Panel 1936

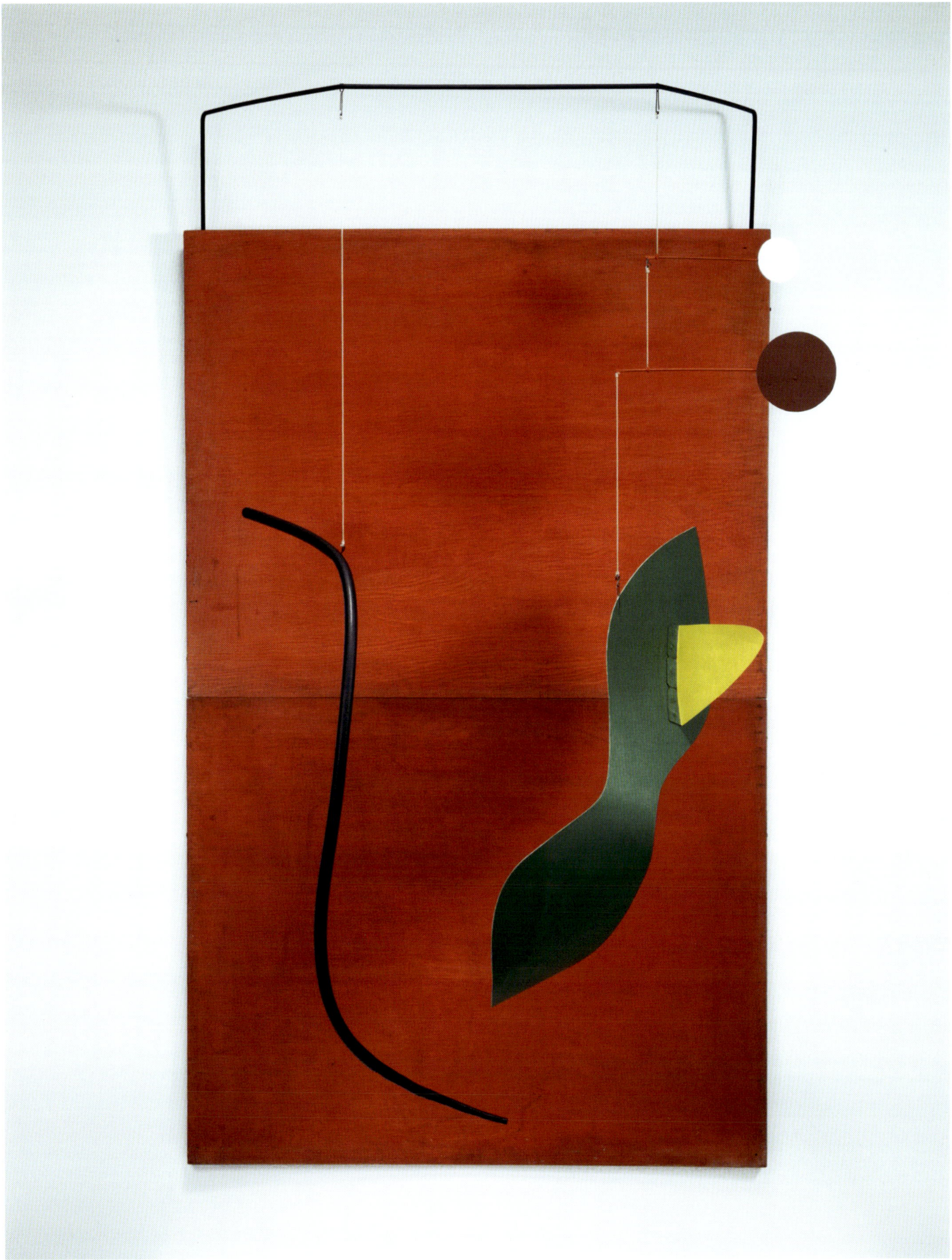

Red Panel 1936

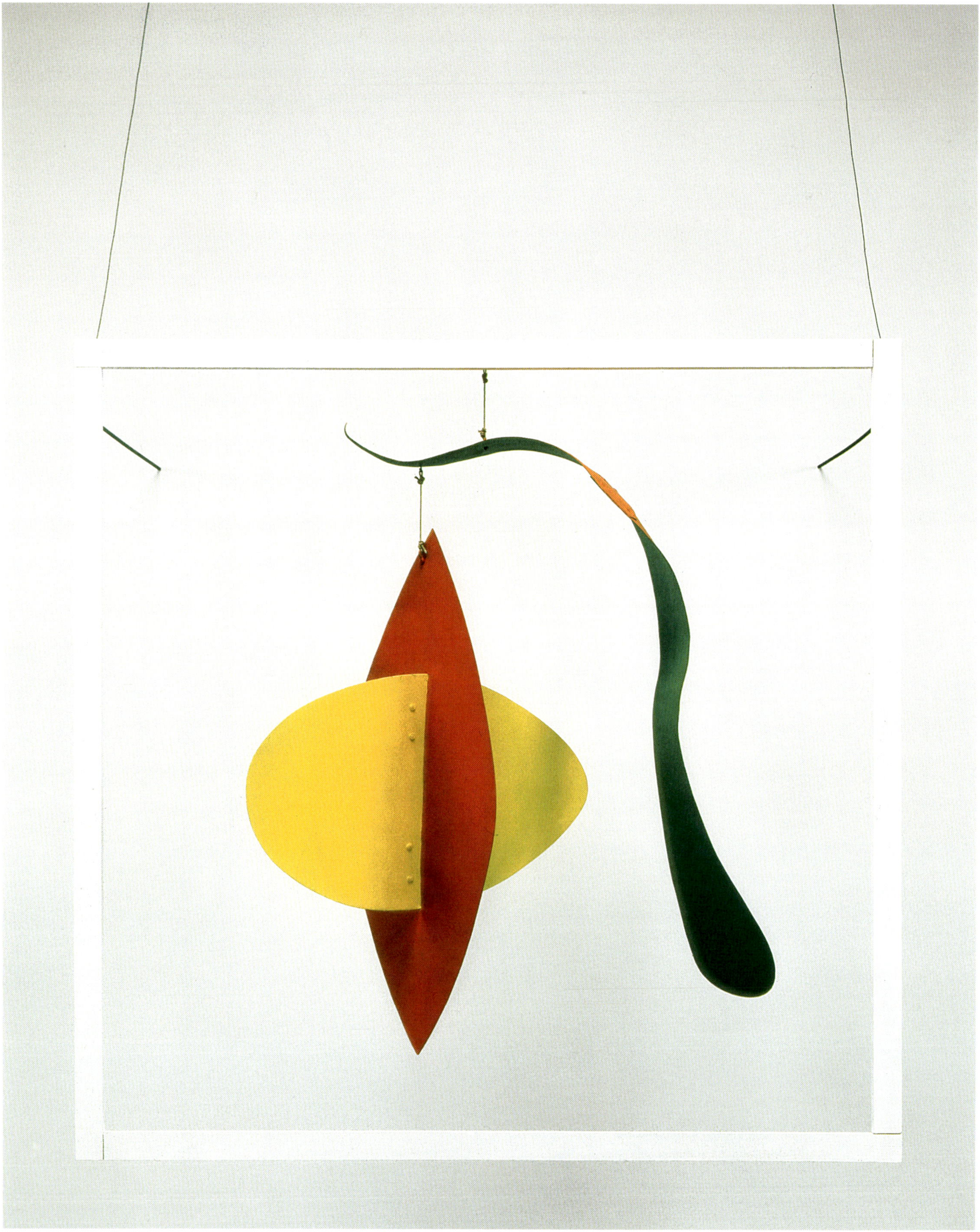

Snake and the Cross 1936

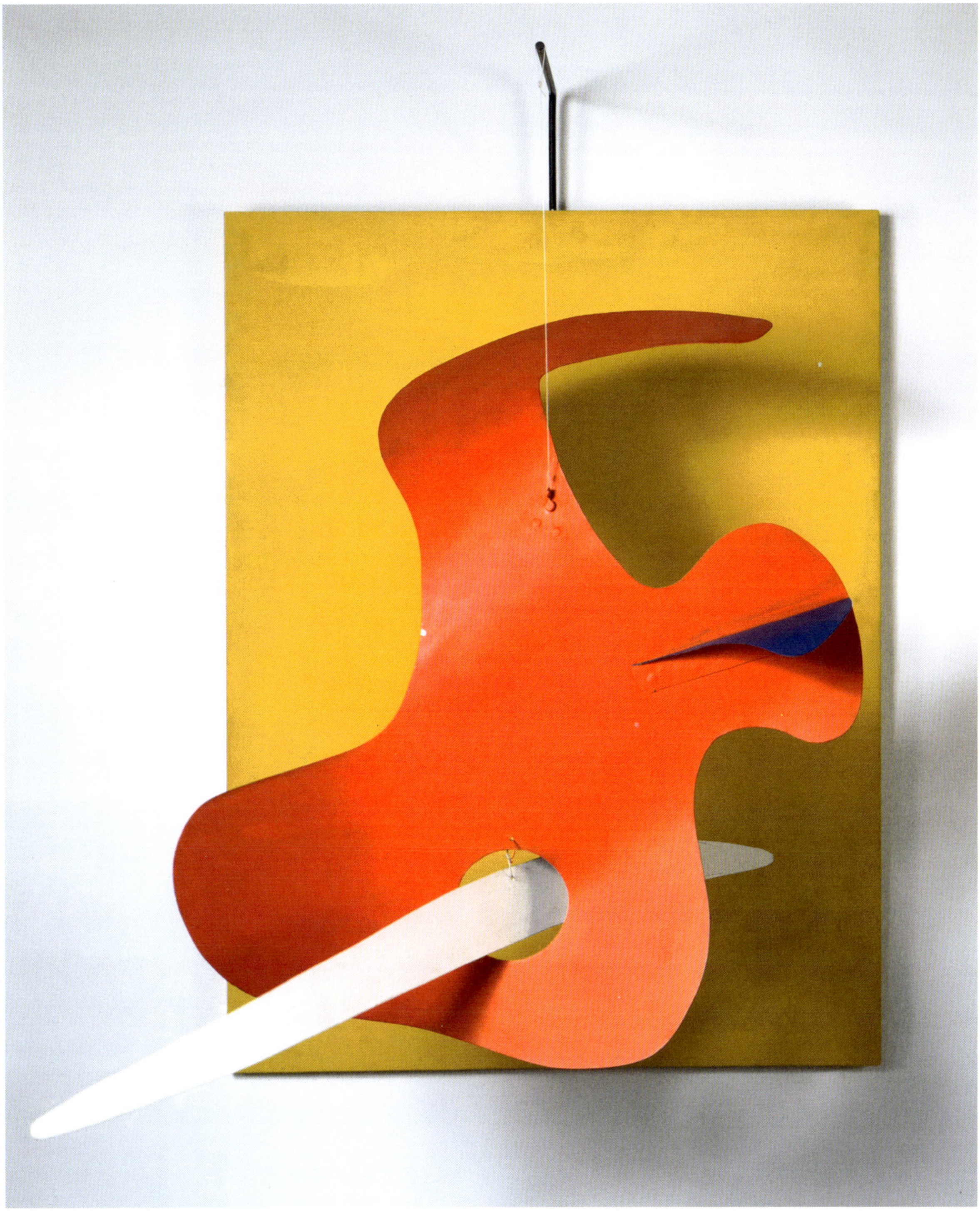

Form Against Yellow 1936

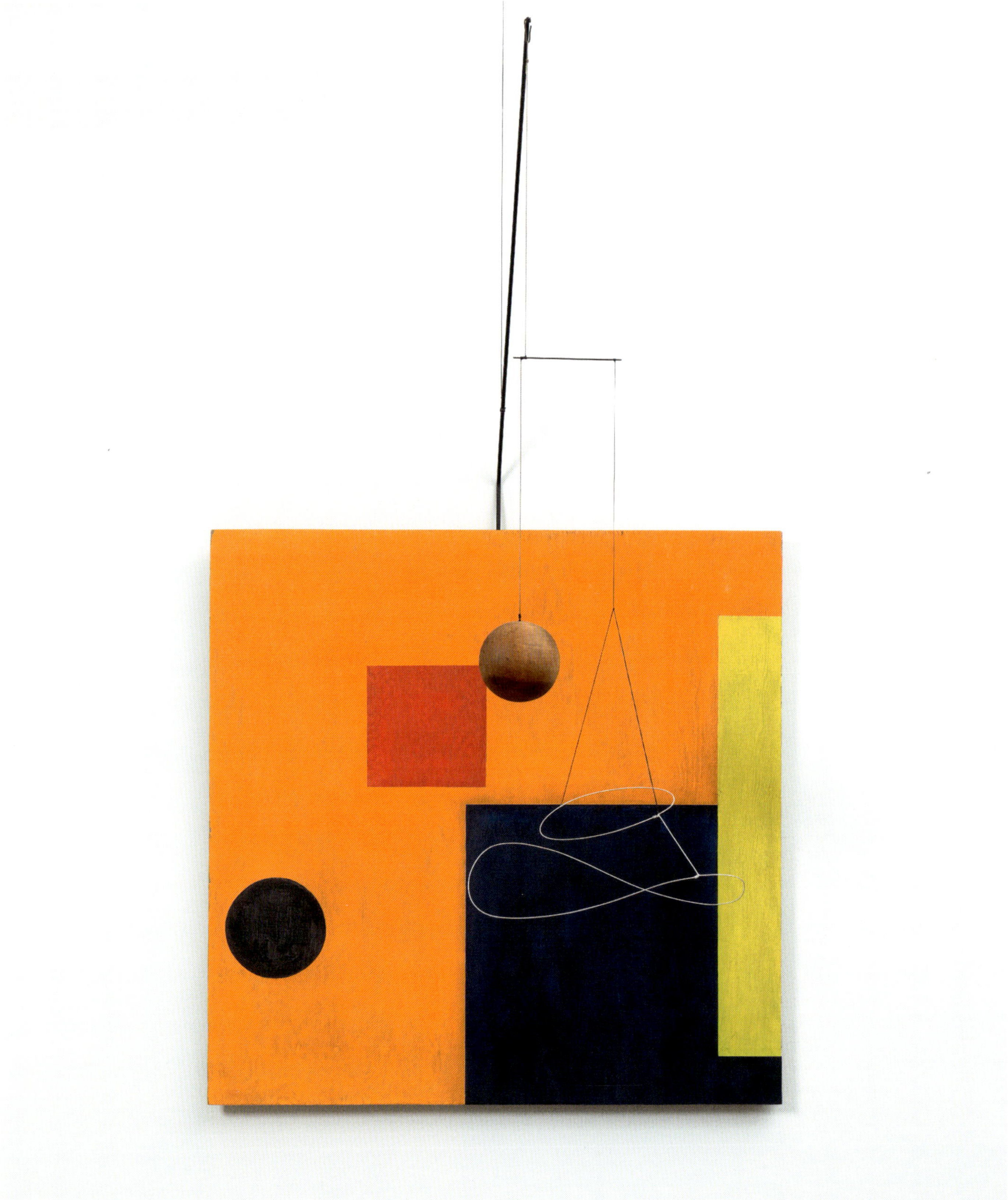

Untitled 1937

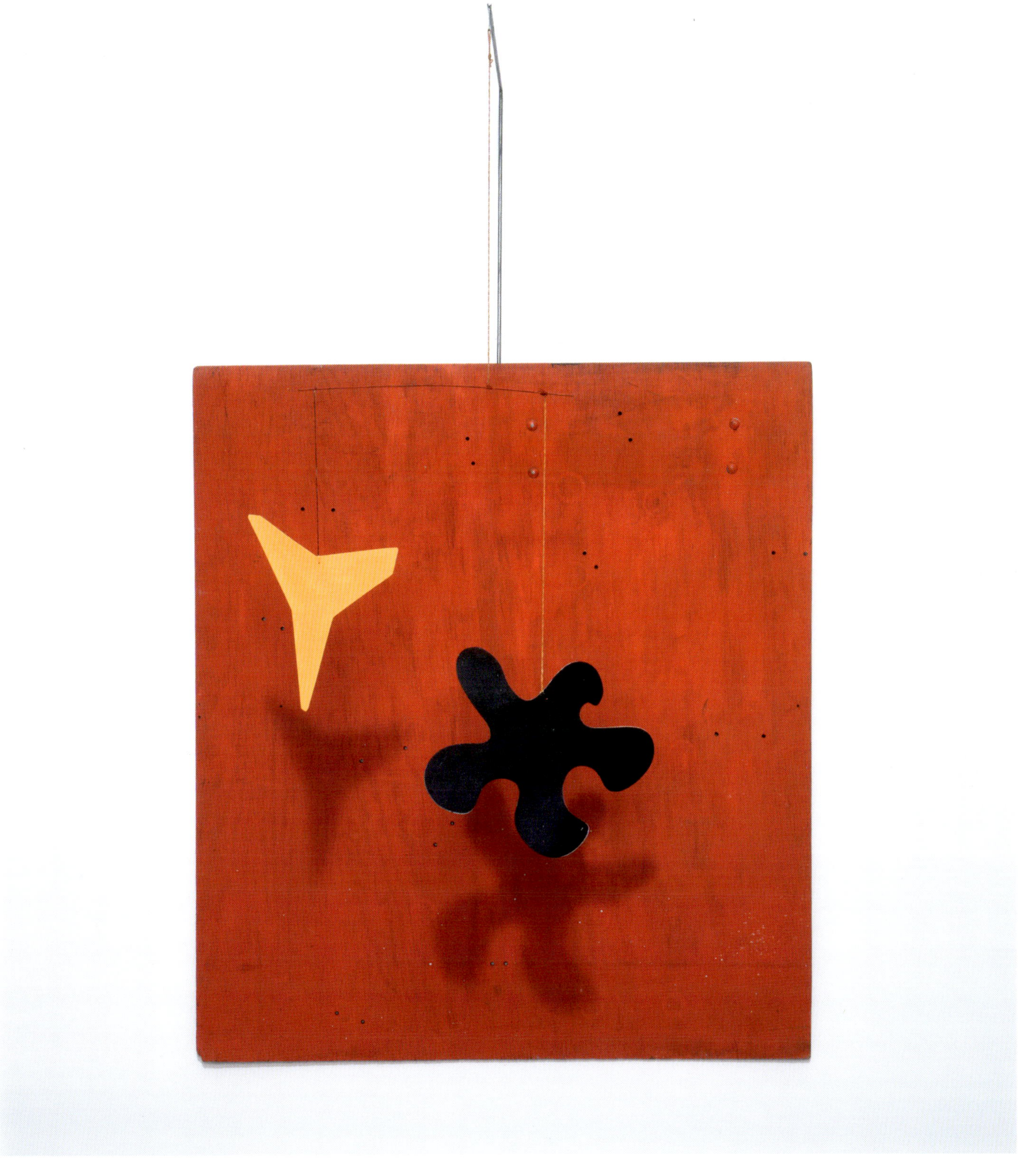

Red Panel 1936

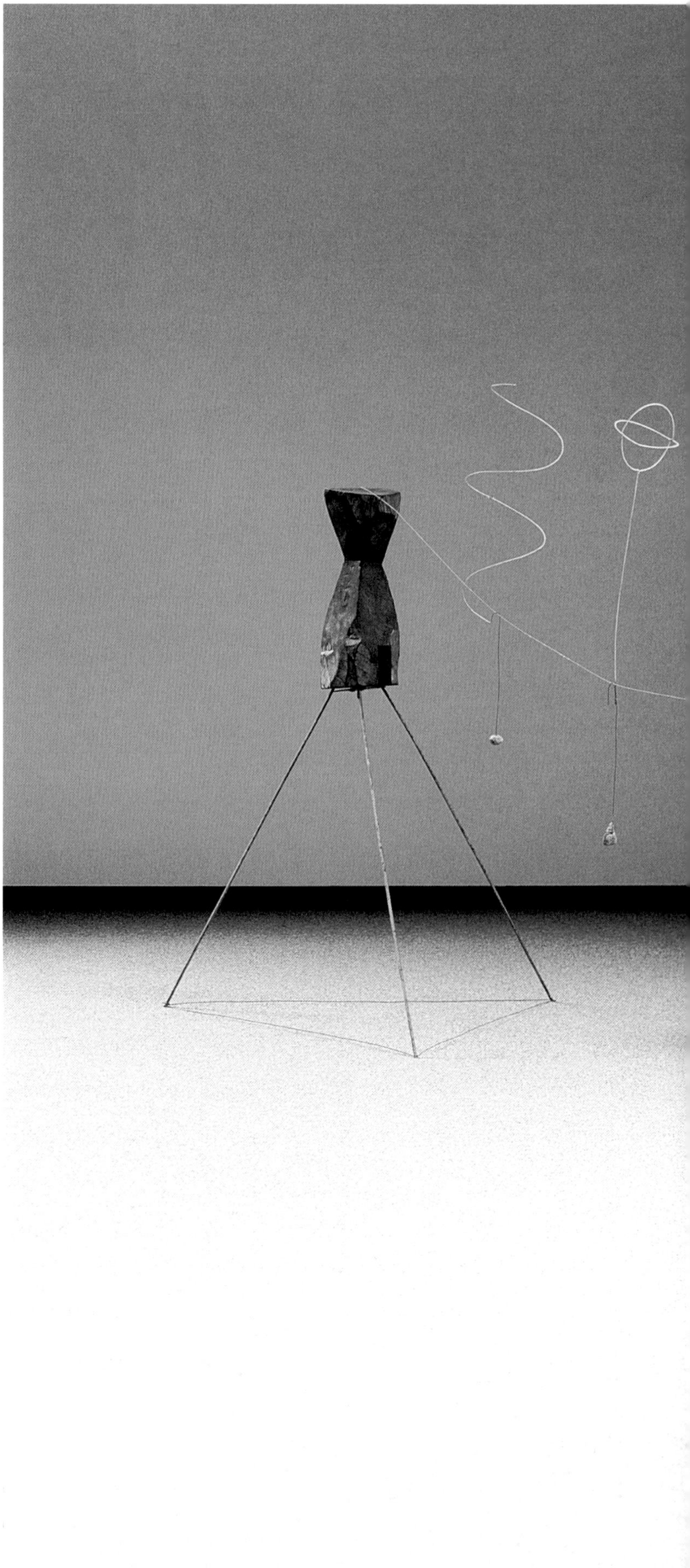

Tightrope 1936

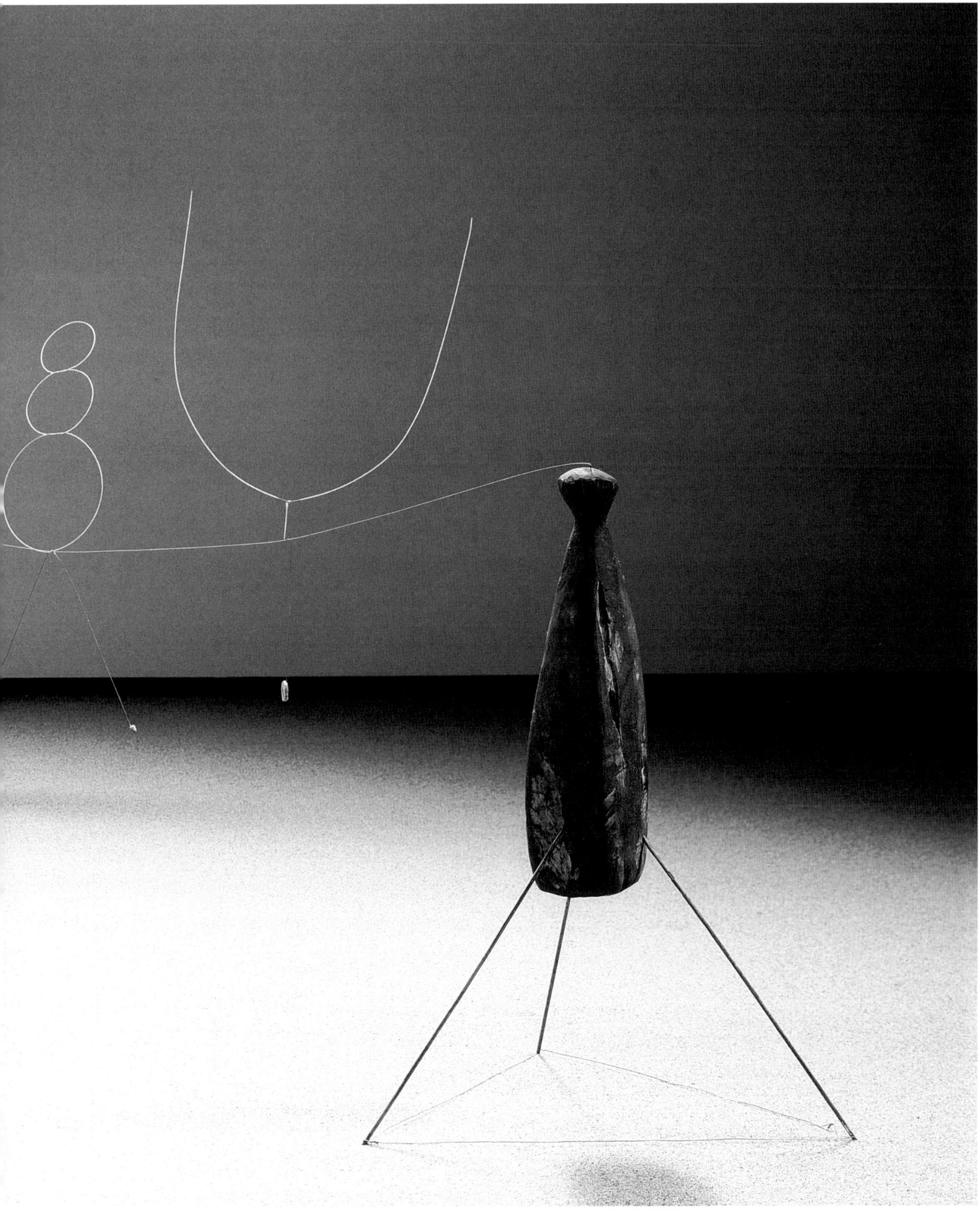

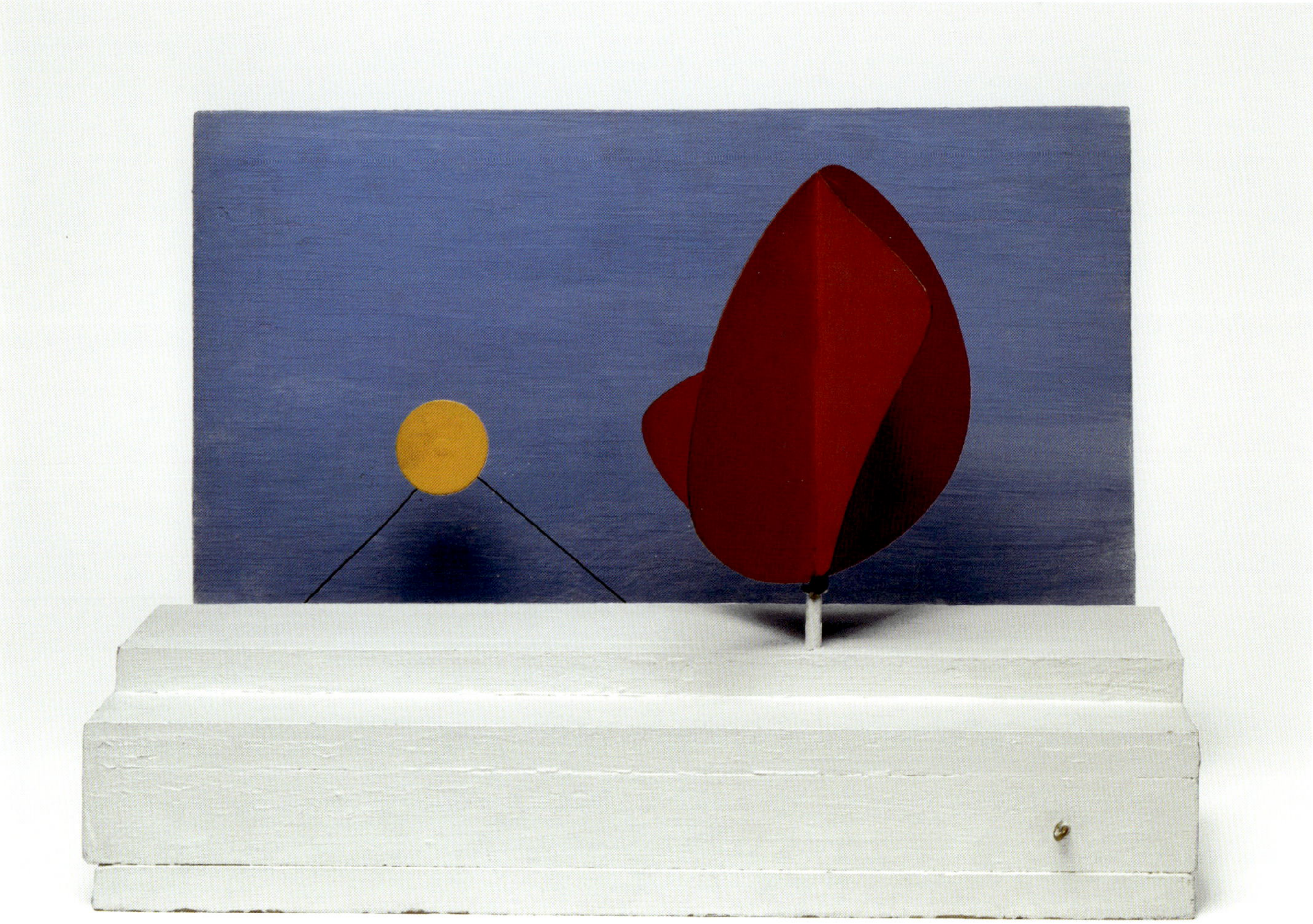

Petit Panneau Bleu c.1936

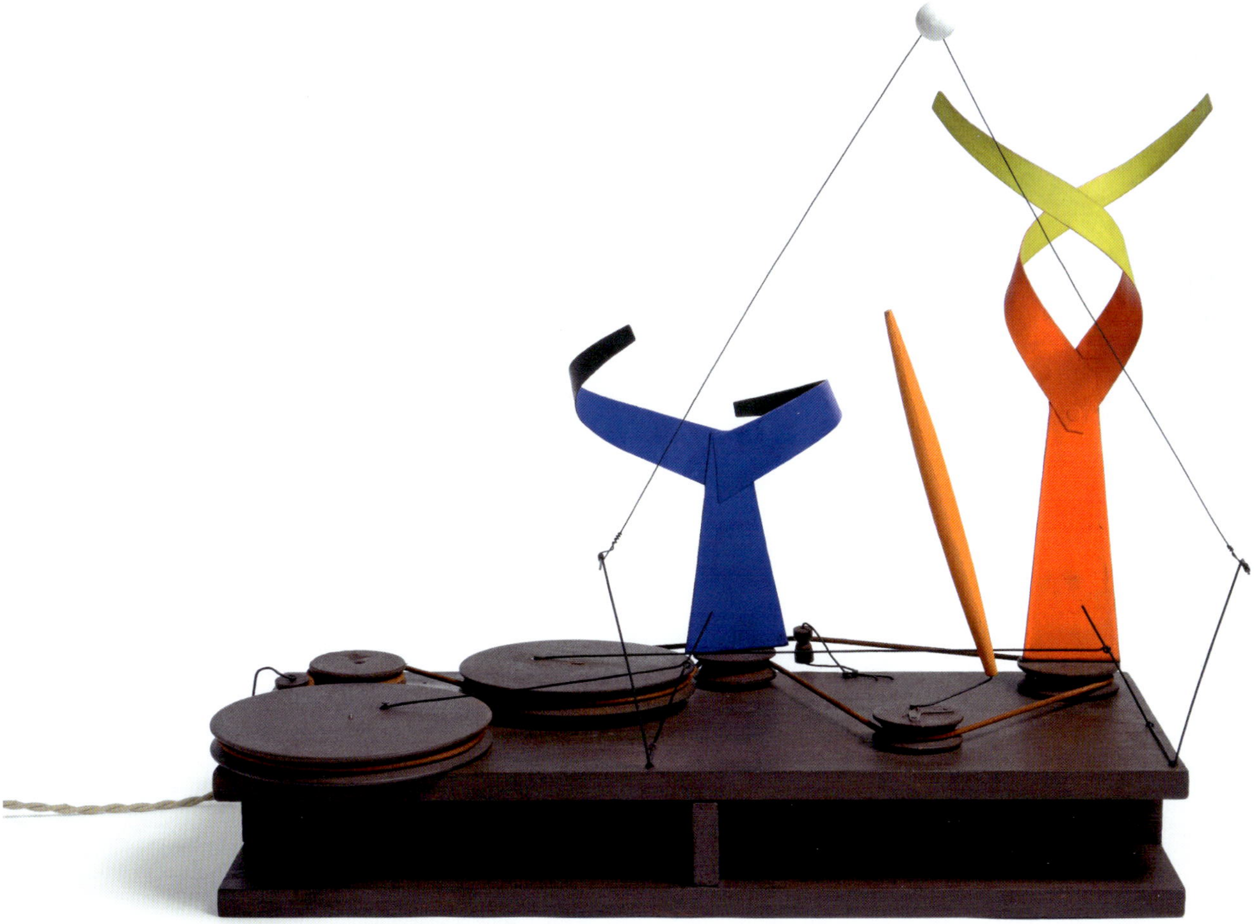

Dancers and Sphere 1938
[New York World's Fair 1939, maquette]

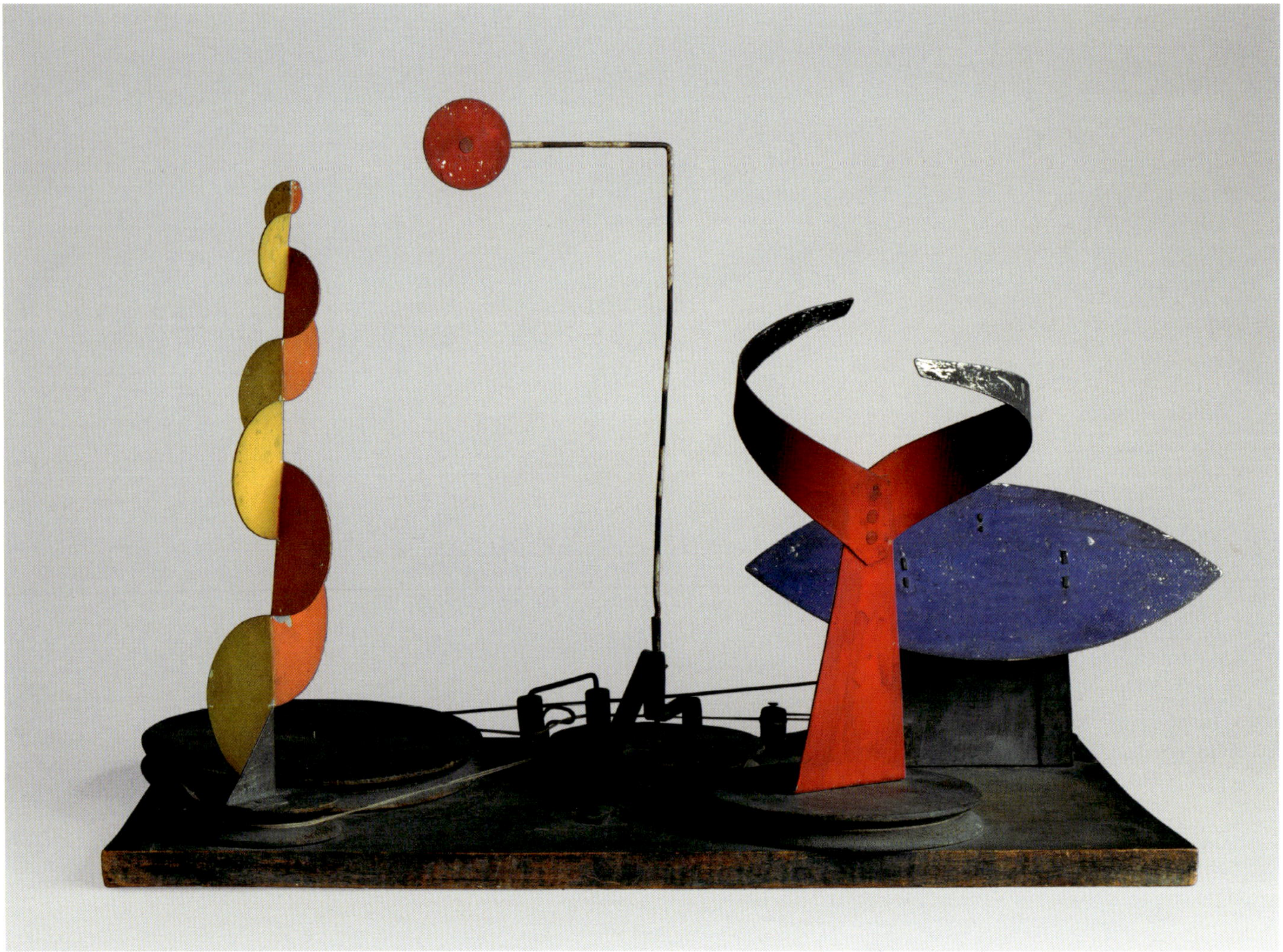

Four Elements 1938
Maquette for 1939 New York World's Fair

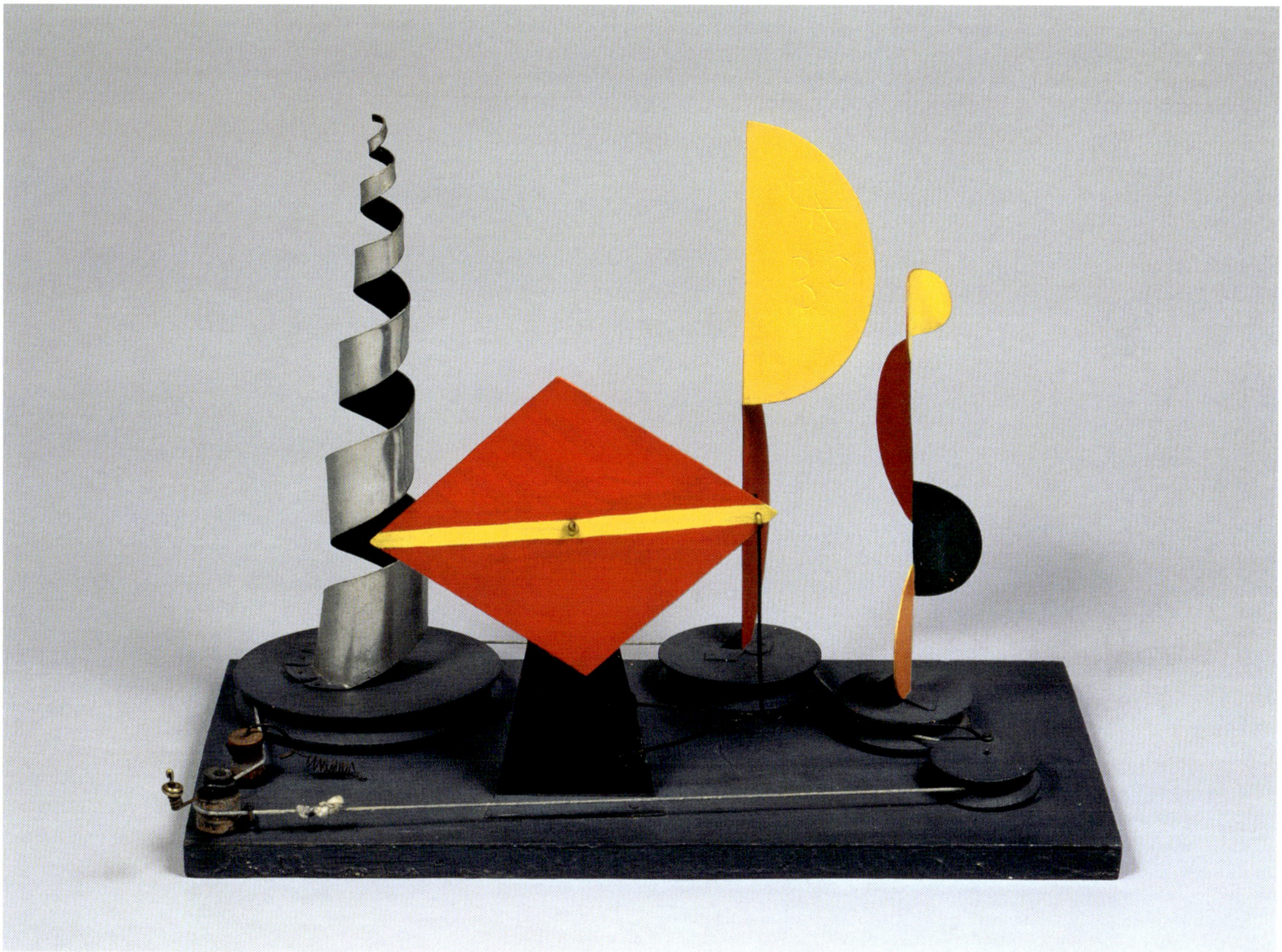

Untitled 1938
Maquette for 1939 New York World's Fair

Untitled 1937

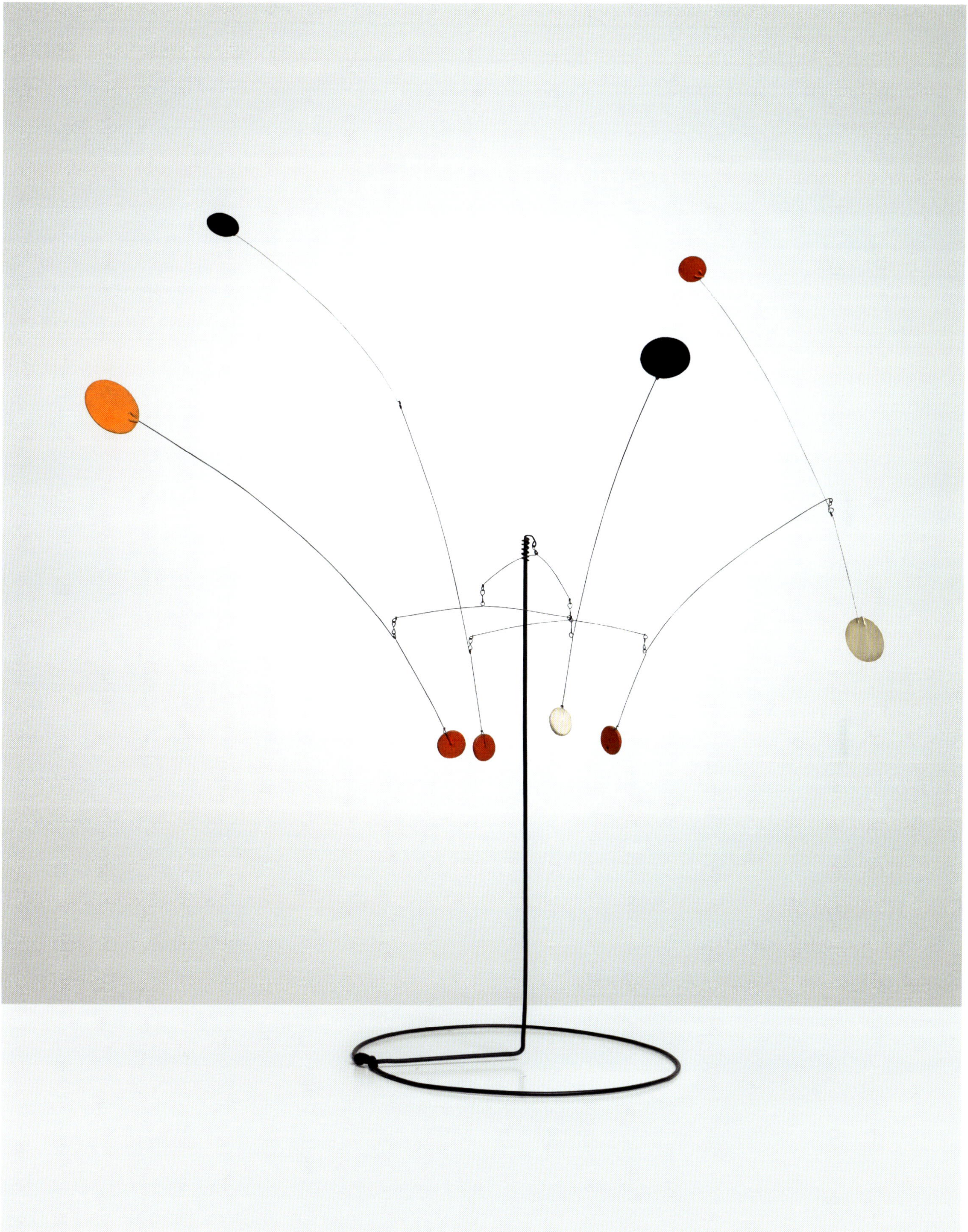

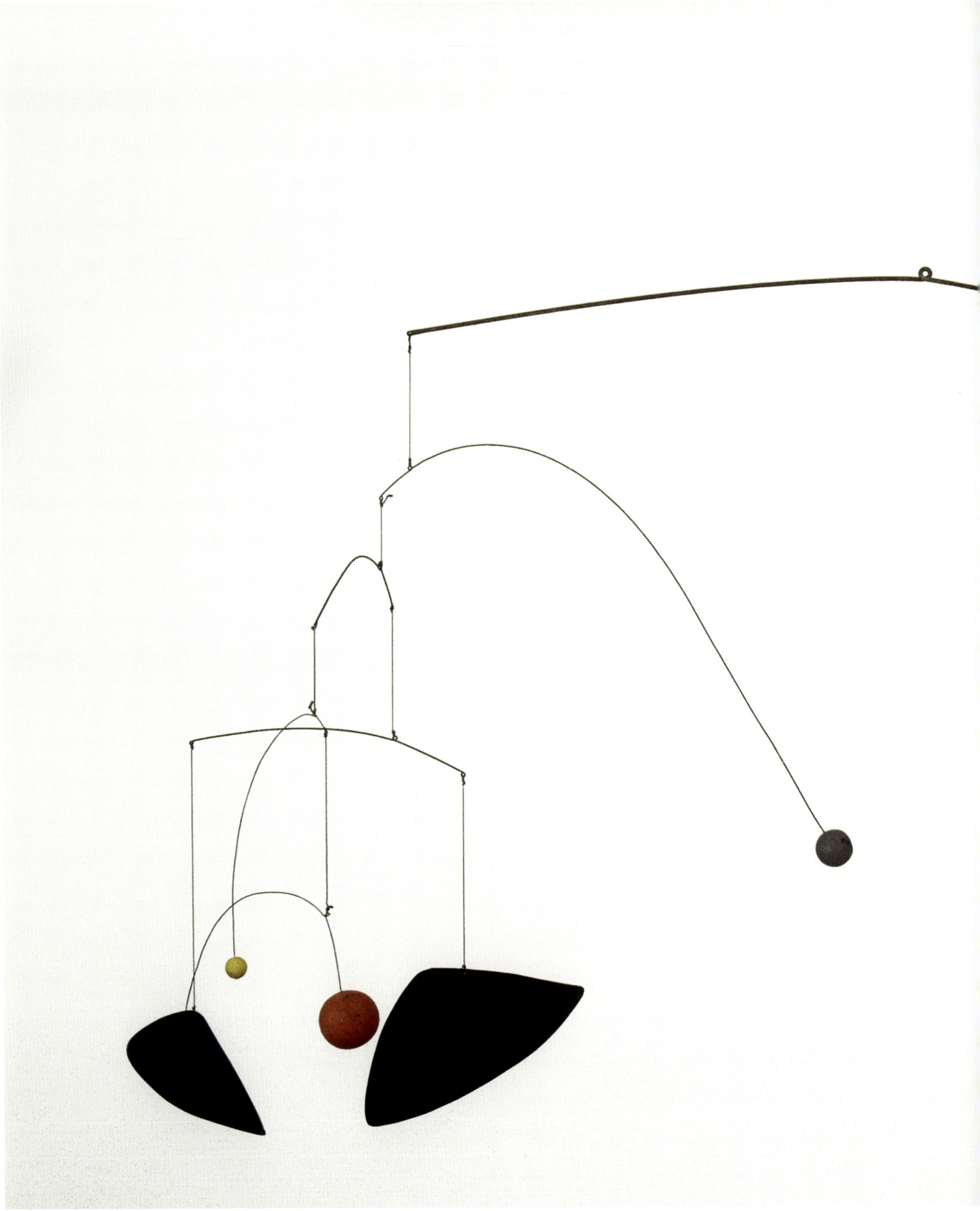

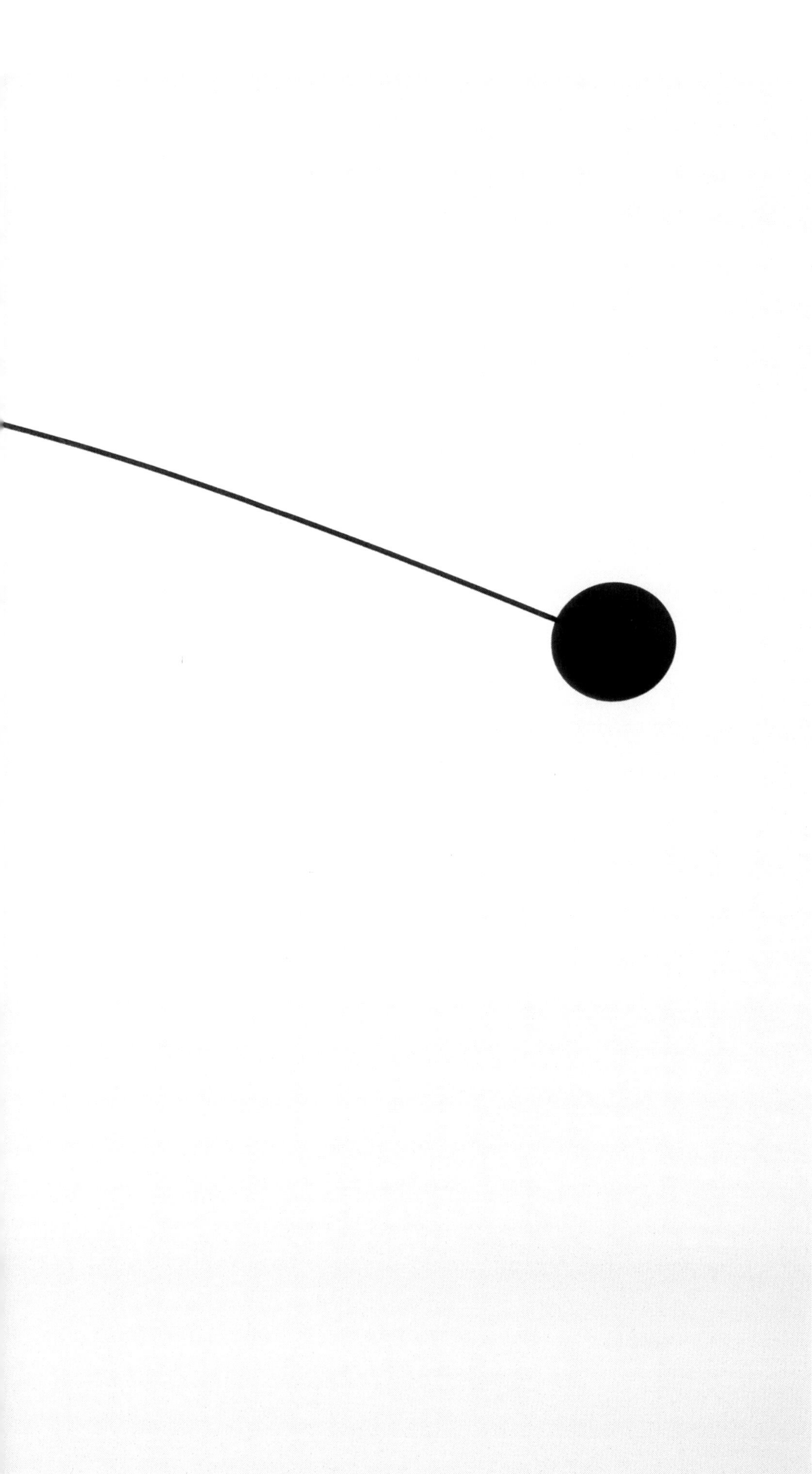

Mobile mid-1930s

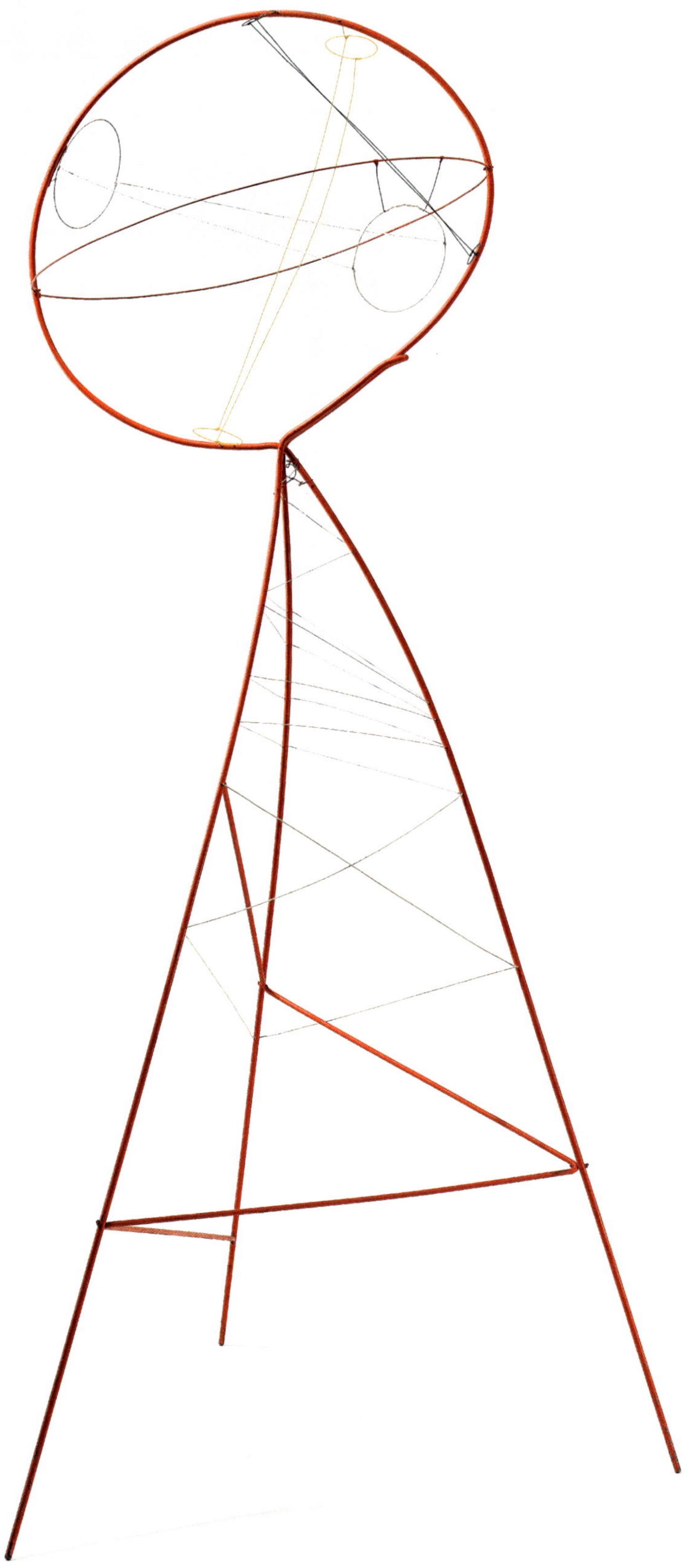

Sphere Pierced by Cylinders 1939

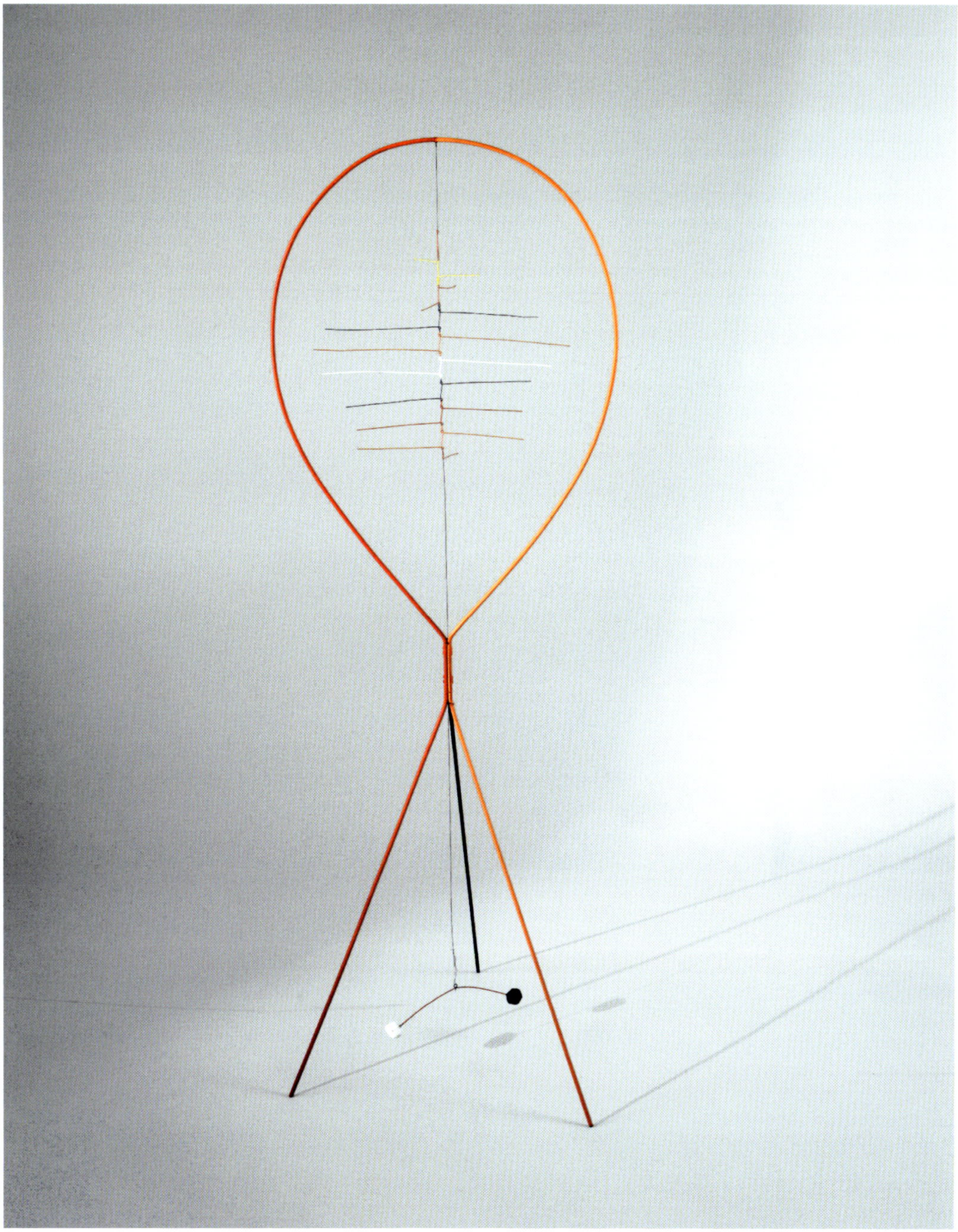

Hourglass 1941

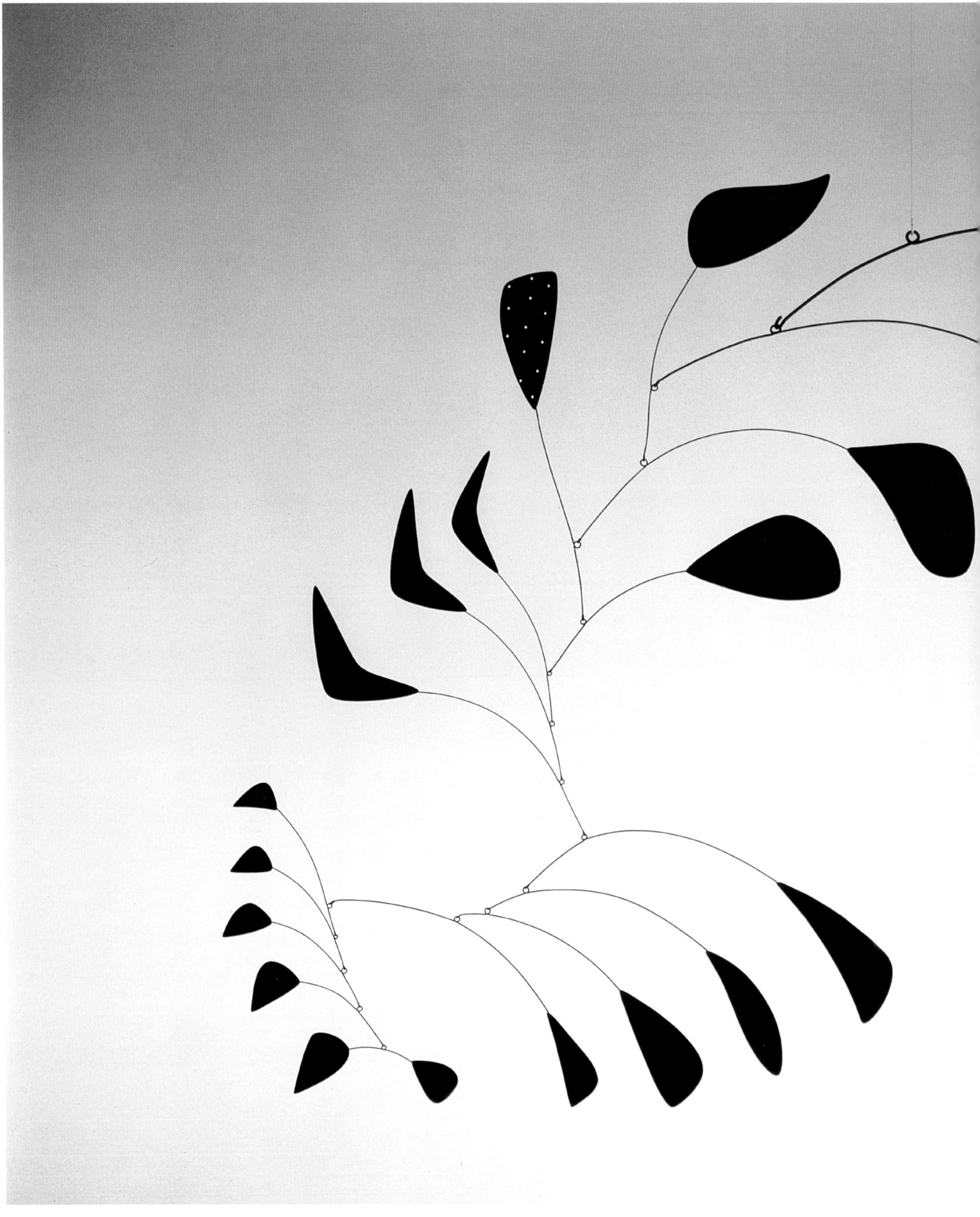

Vertical Foliage 1941

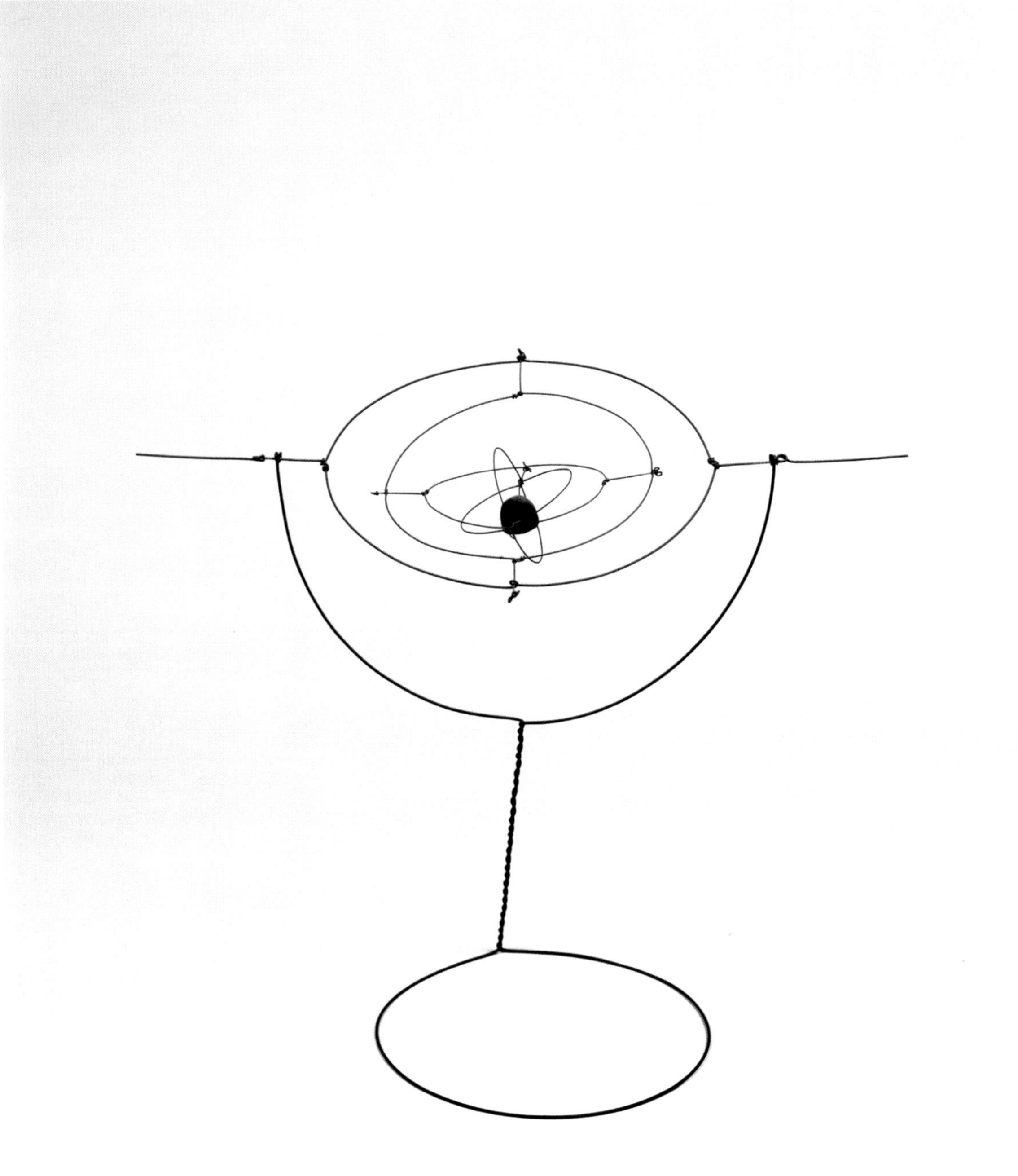

Black Spot on Gimbals 1942

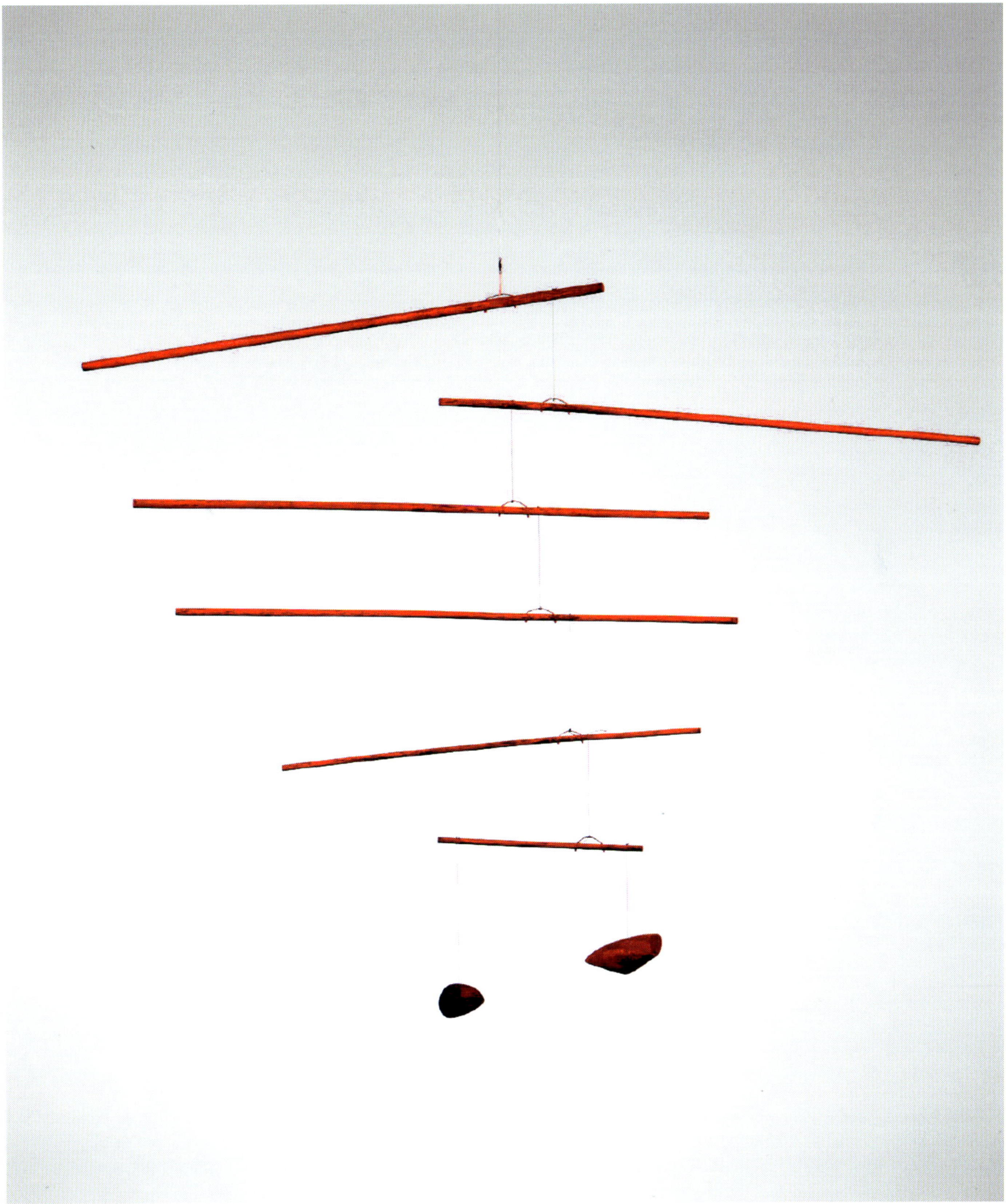

Red Sticks c.1942

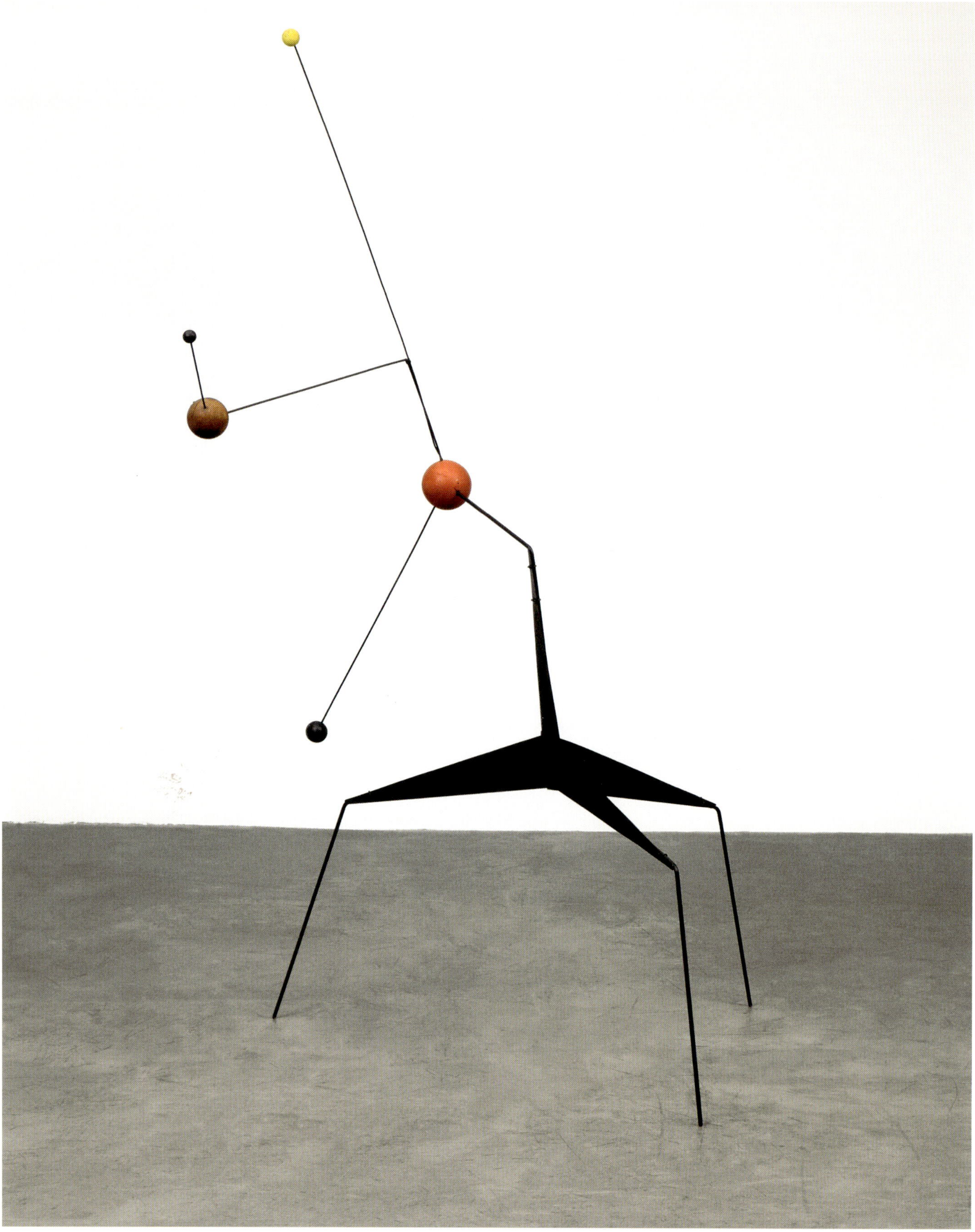

Morning Star 1943

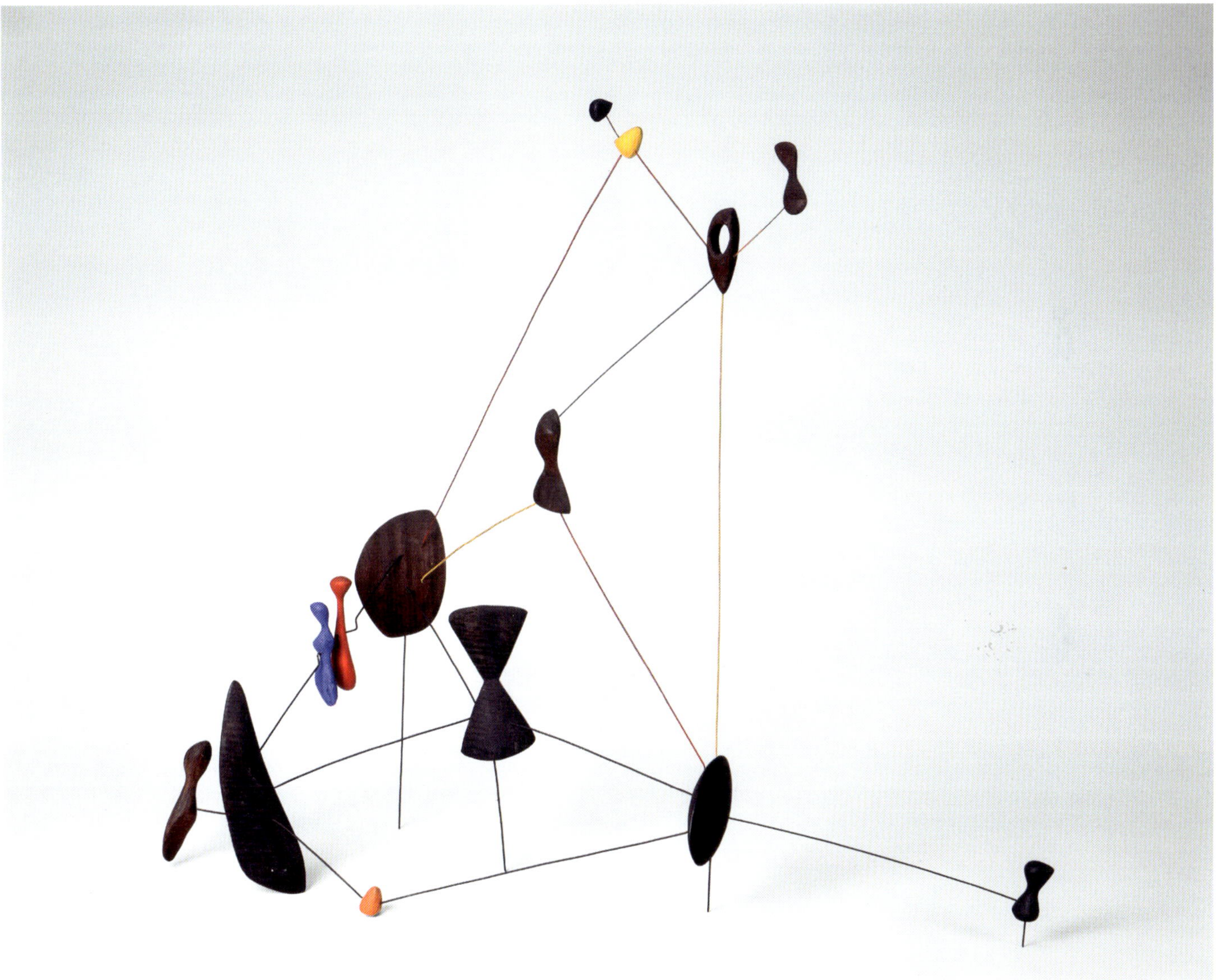

Constellation 1943

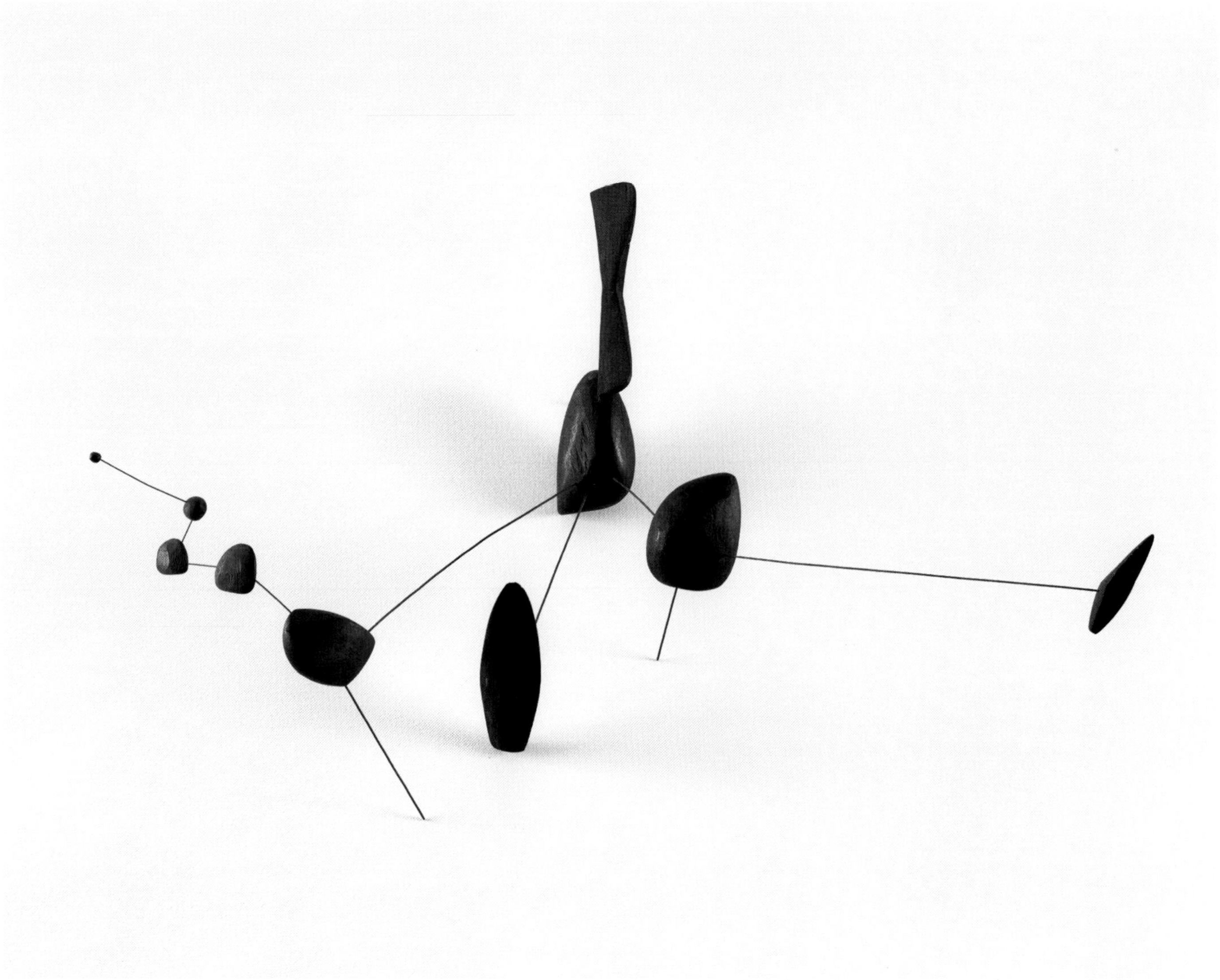

Black Constellation 1943

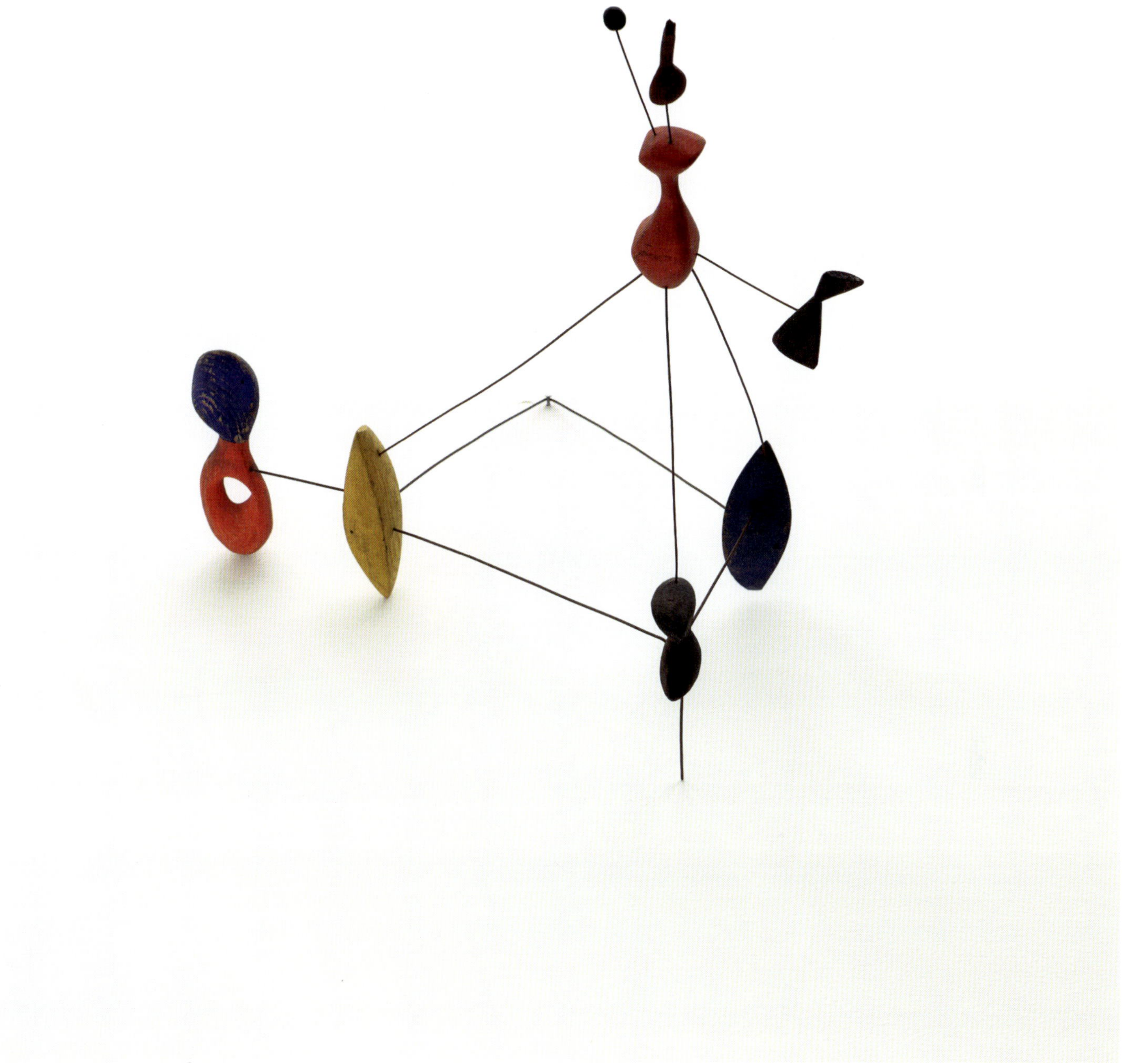

Constellation with Two Pins 1943

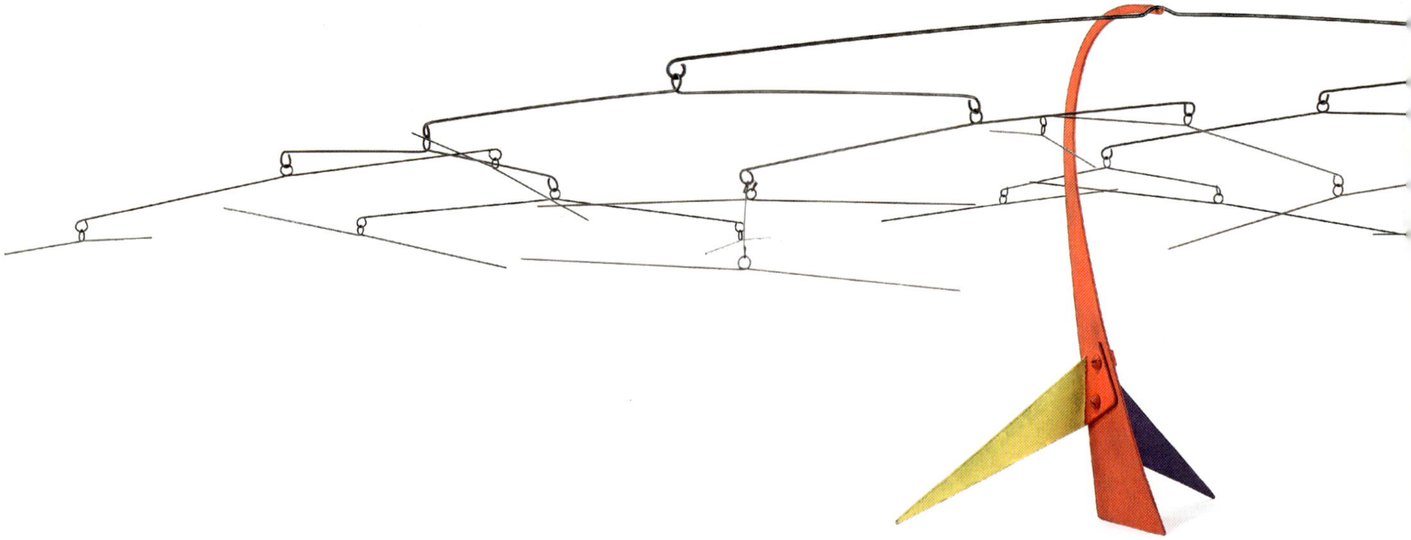

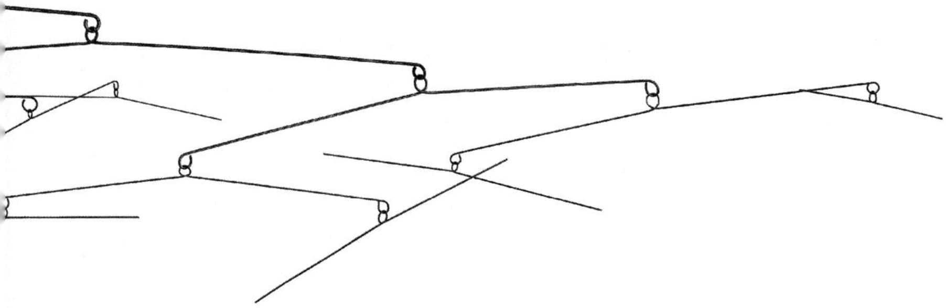

Untitled (Mobile with N Degrees of Freedom) 1946

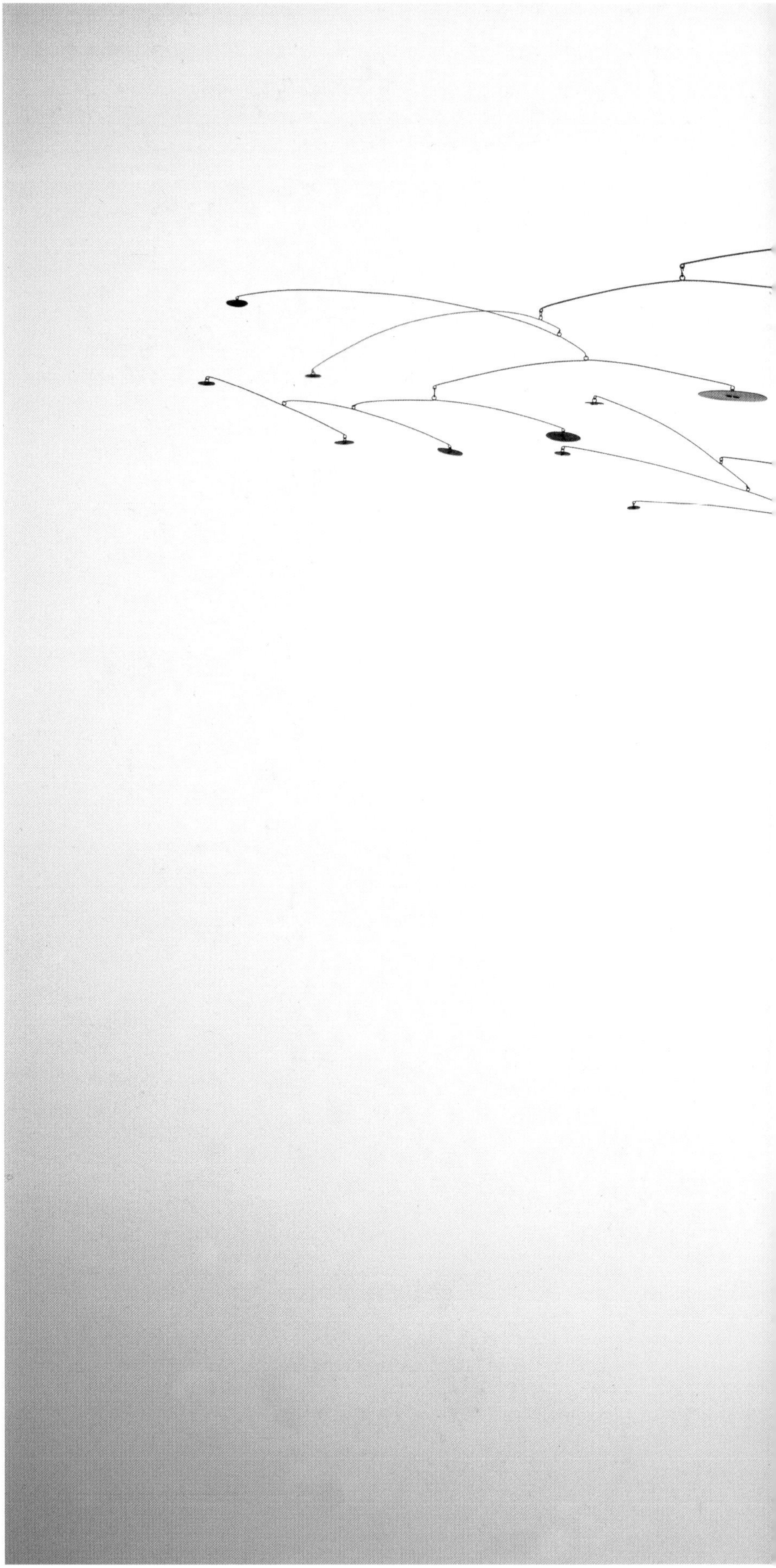

Gamma 1947

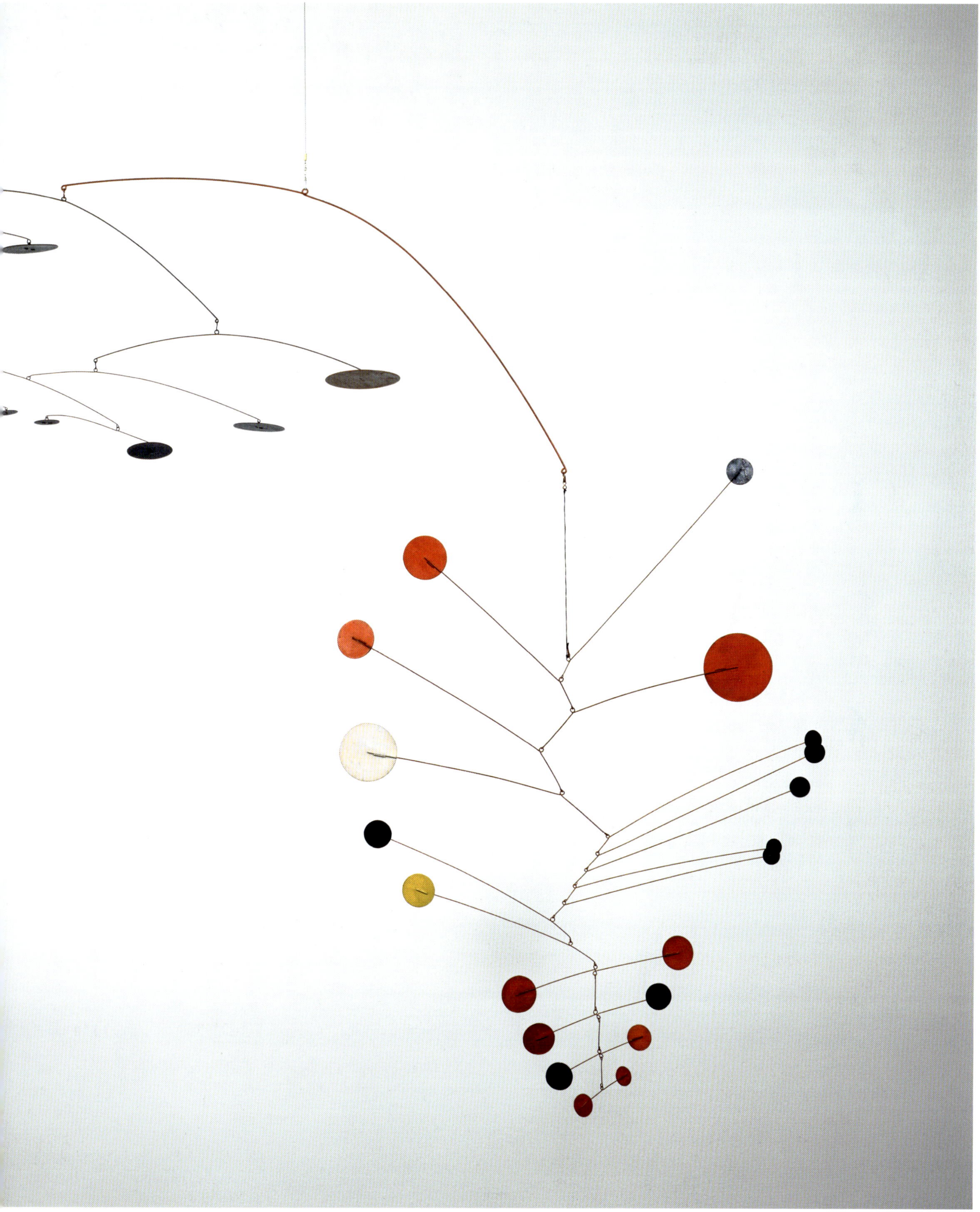

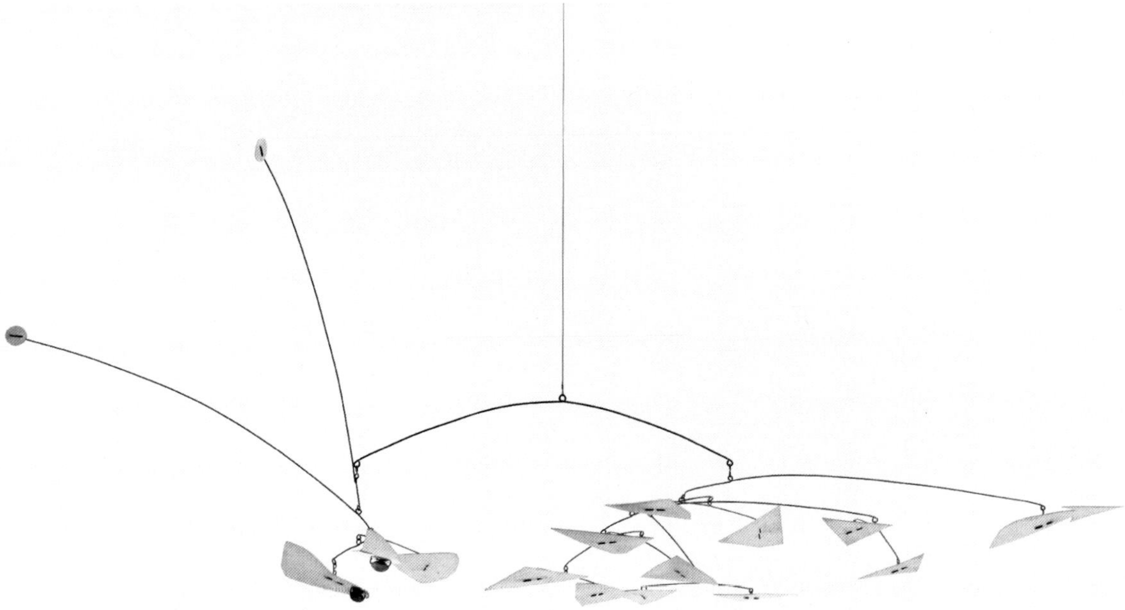

Untitled 1948

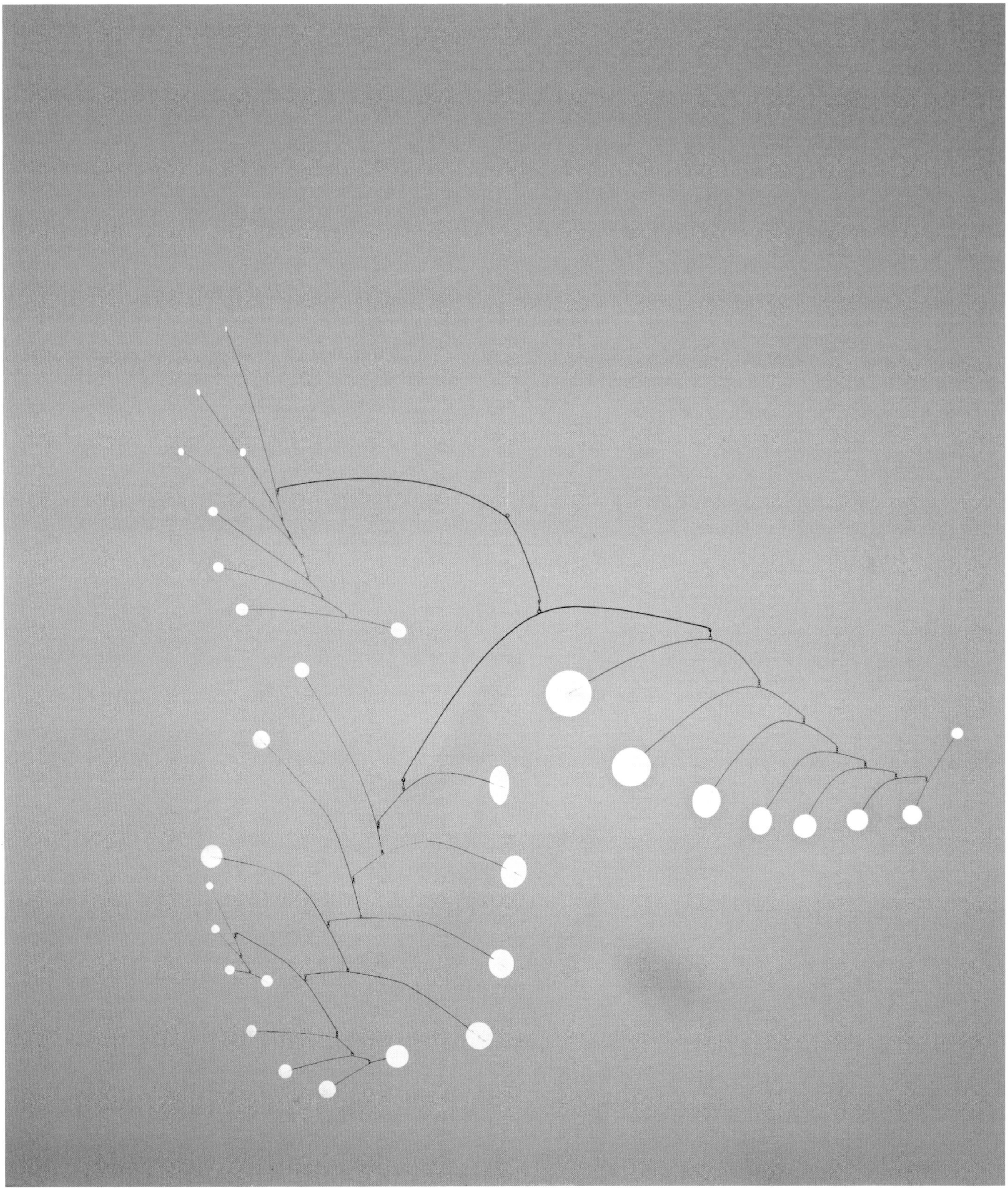

Snow Flurry I 1948

Black Widow 1948

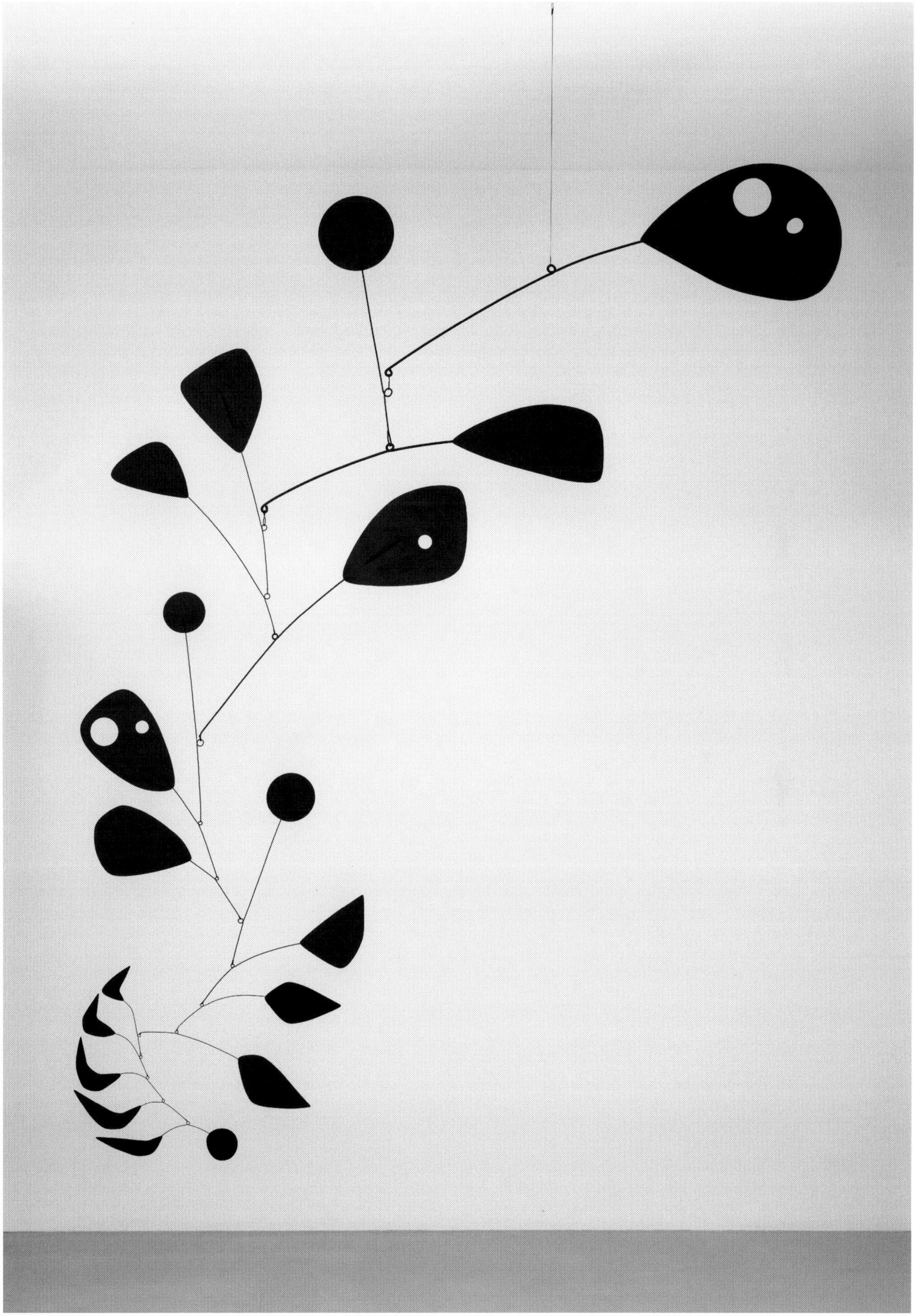

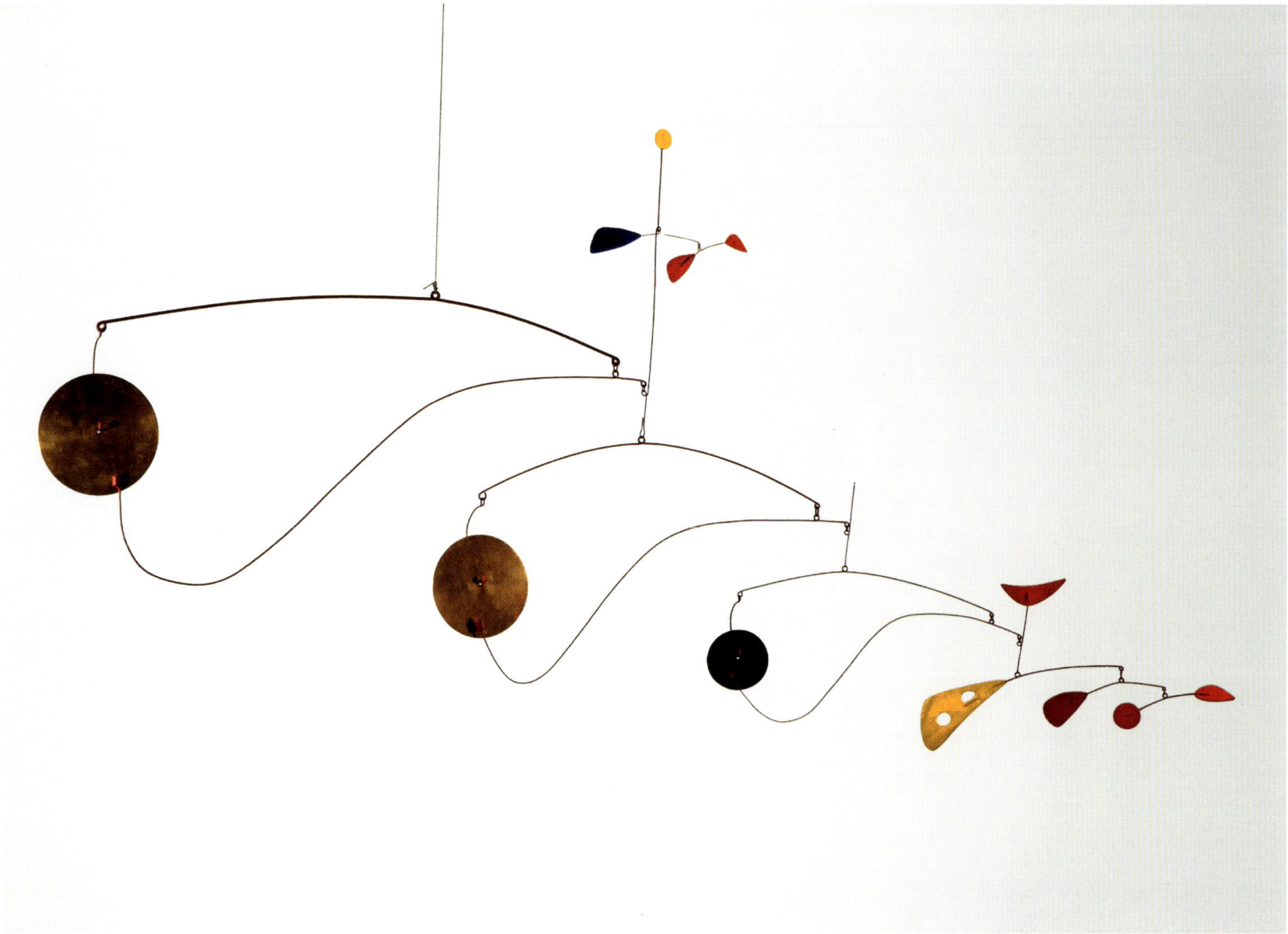

Triple Gong c.1948

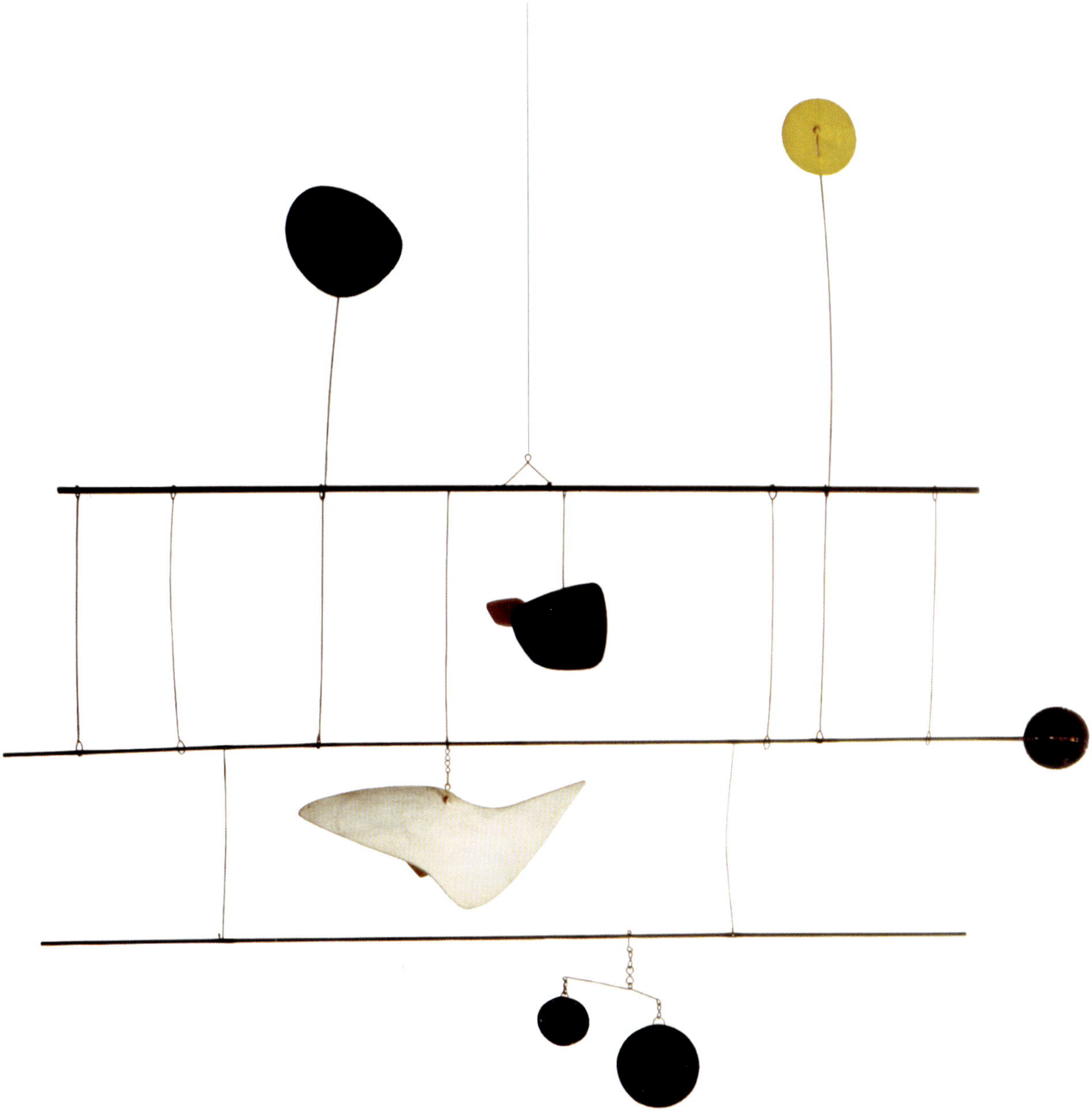

Blériot 1949

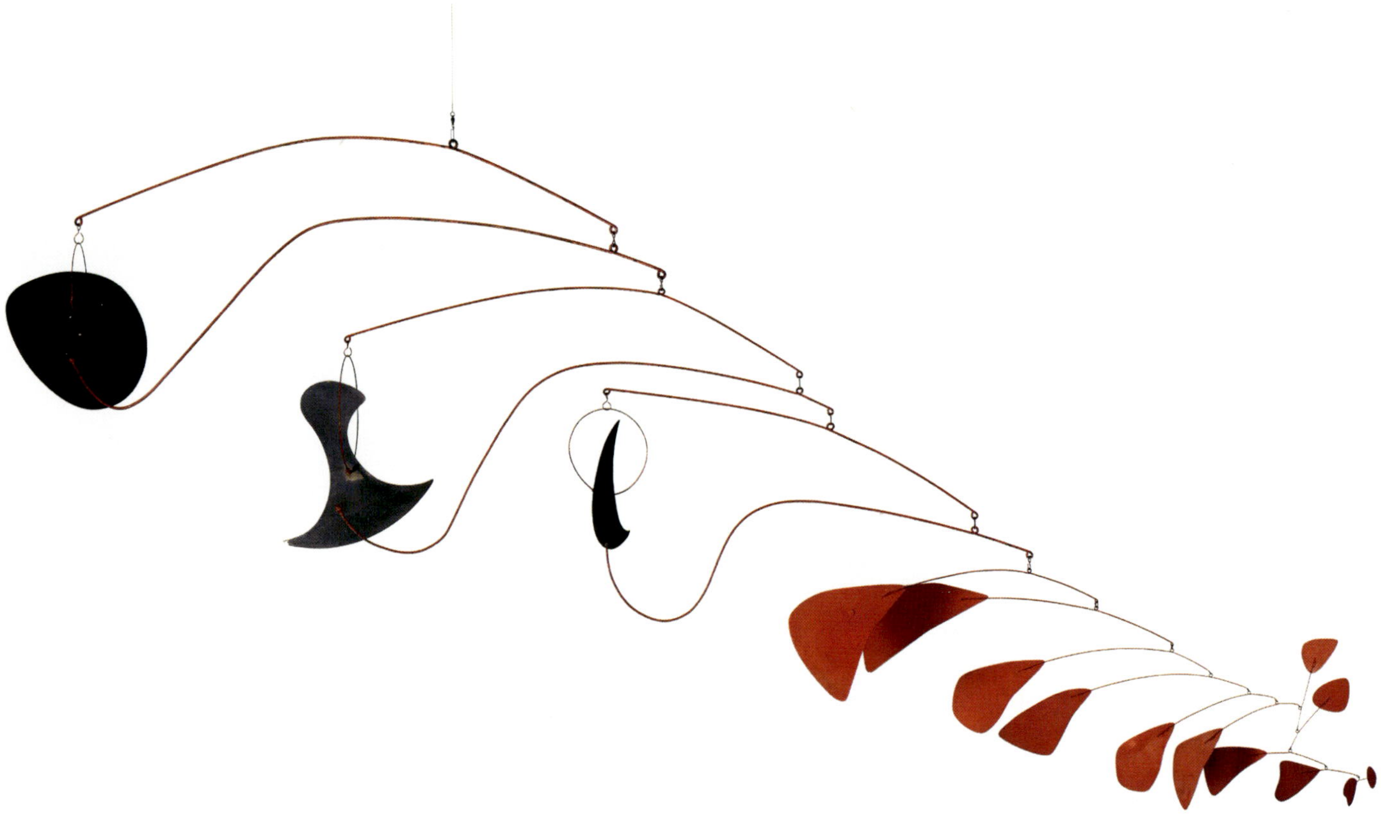

Red Gongs 1950

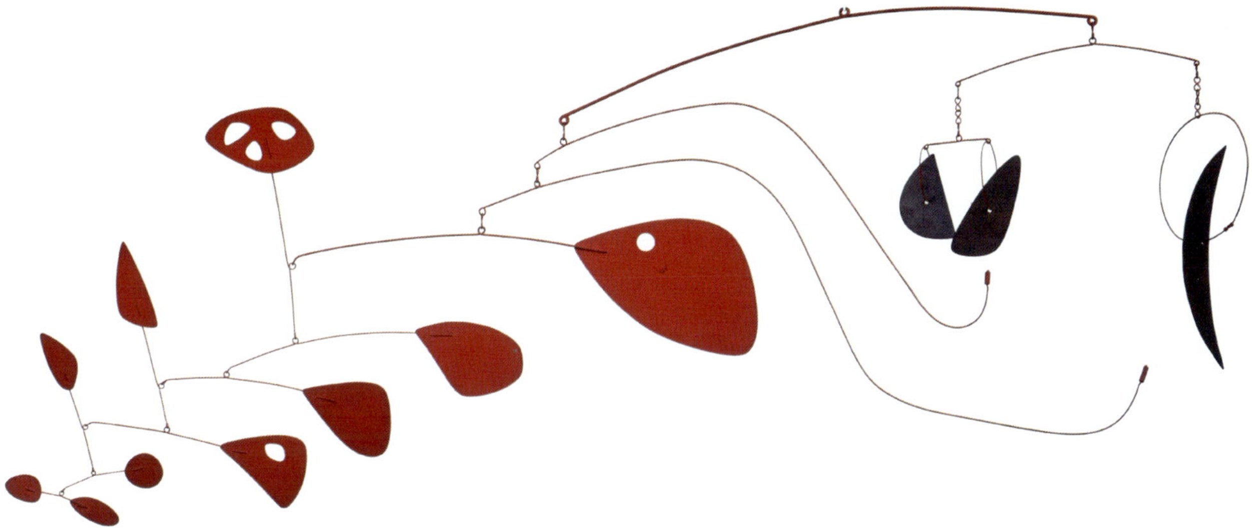

Triple Gong 1951

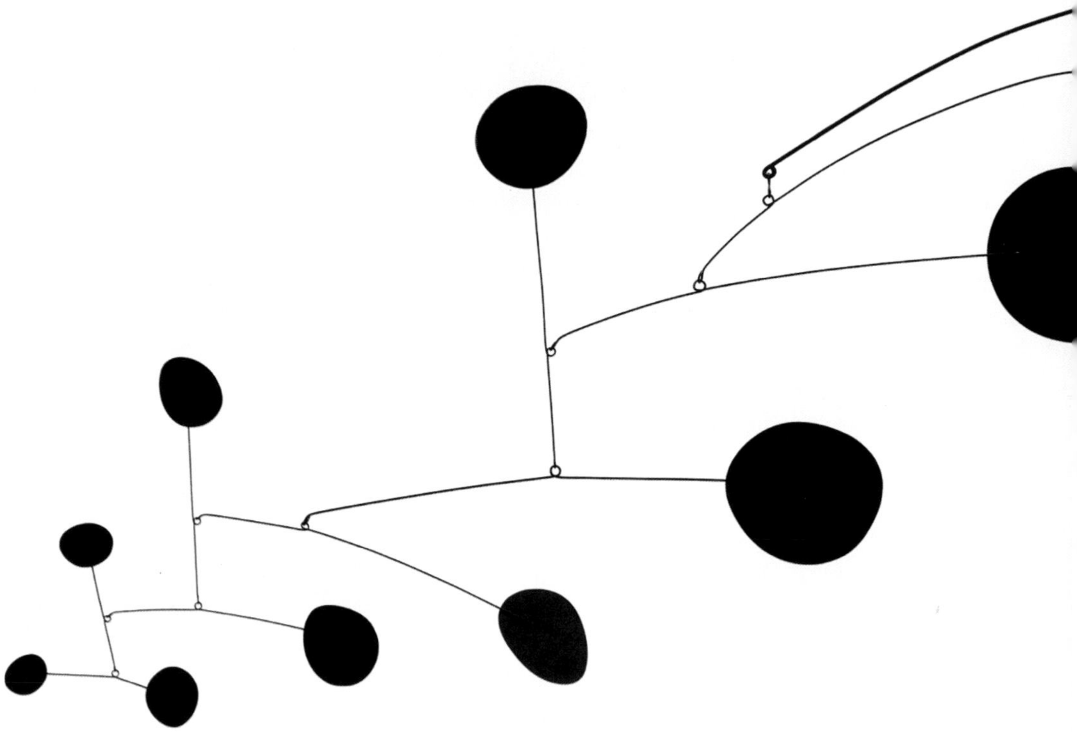

Streetcar 1951

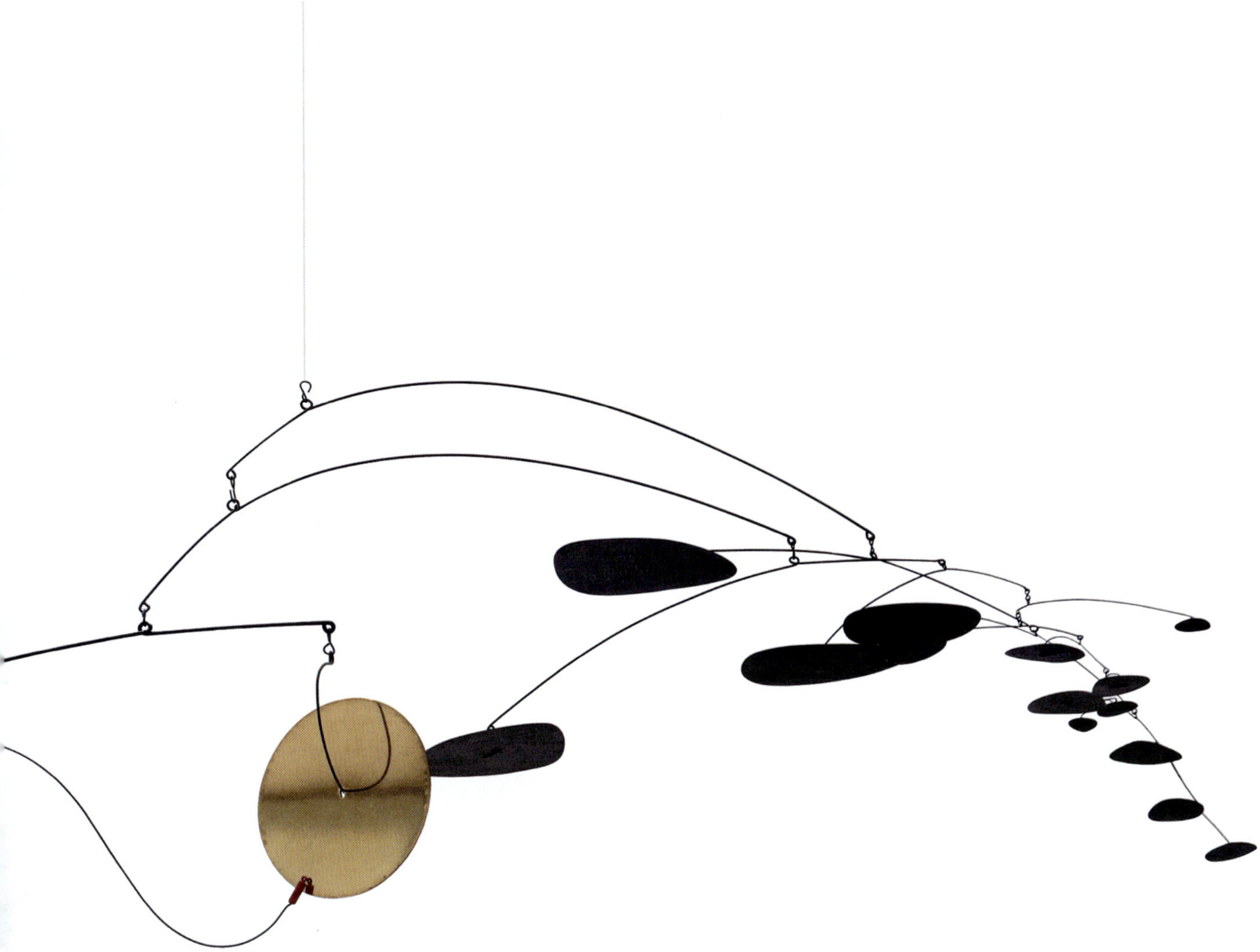

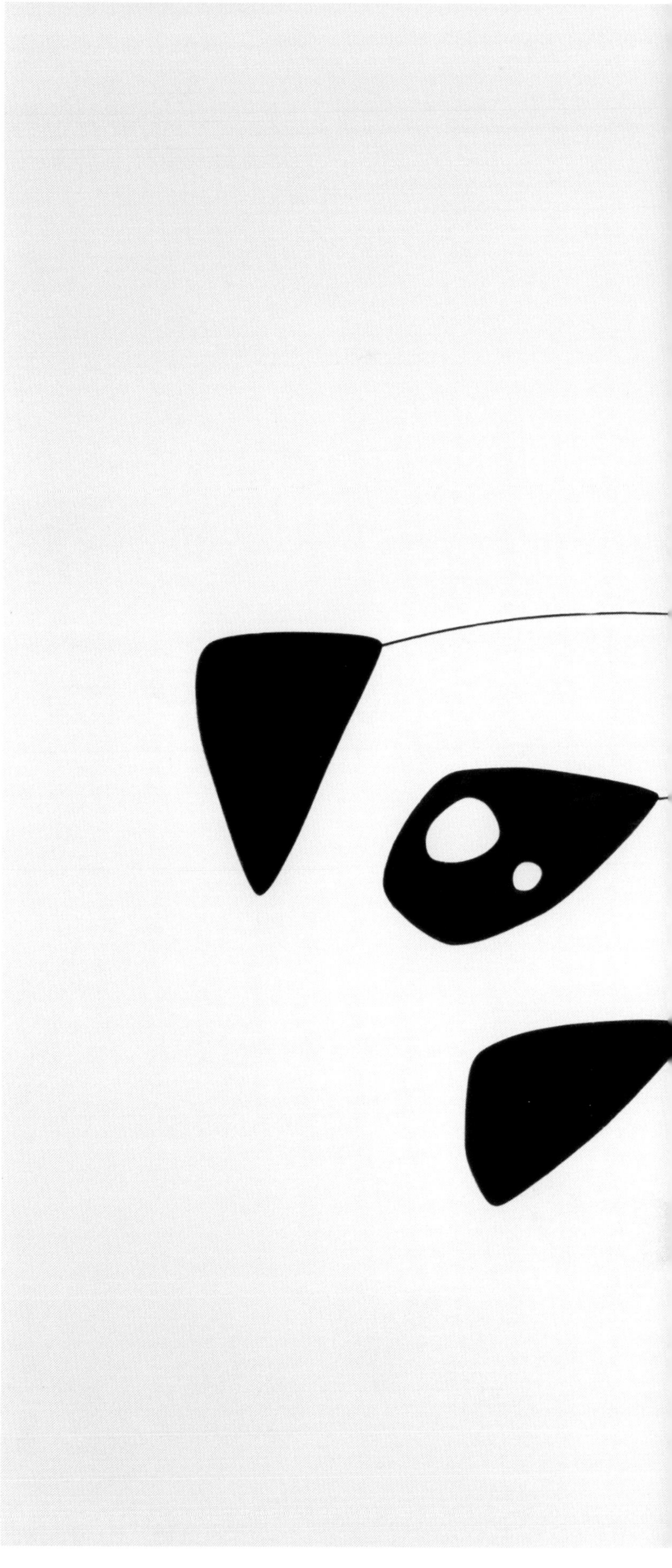

Antennae with Red and Blue Dots c.1953

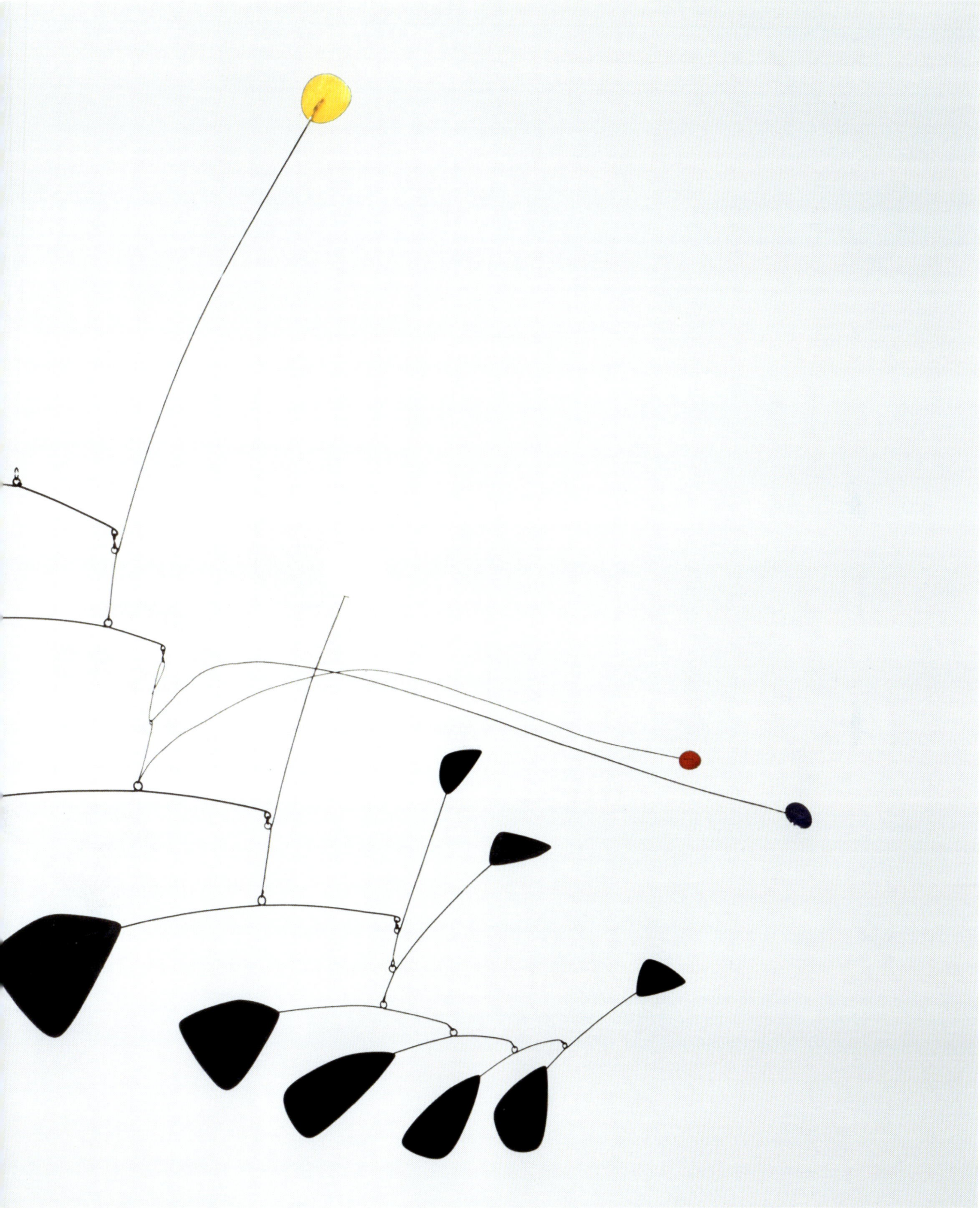

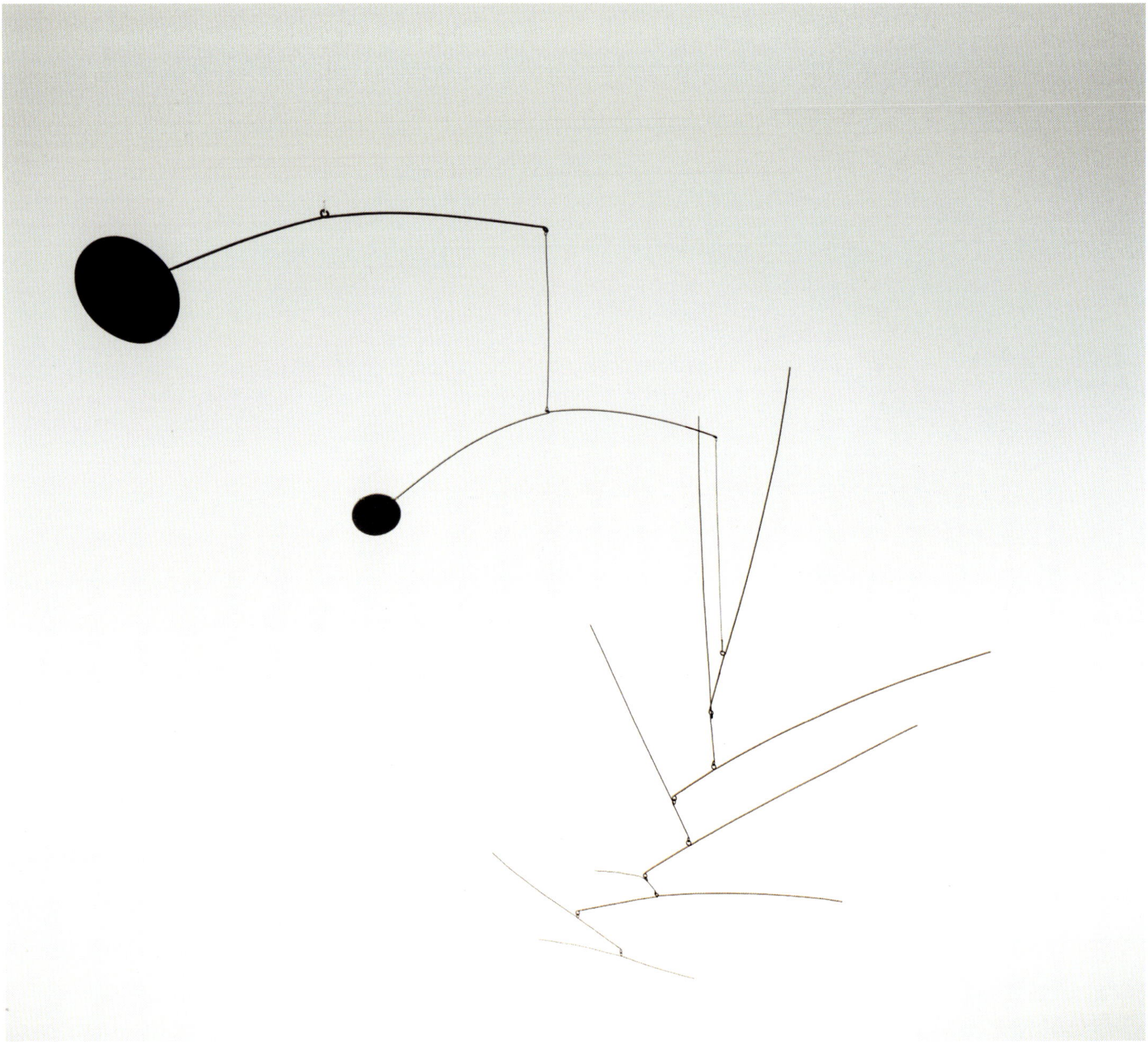

Descending Spines 1956

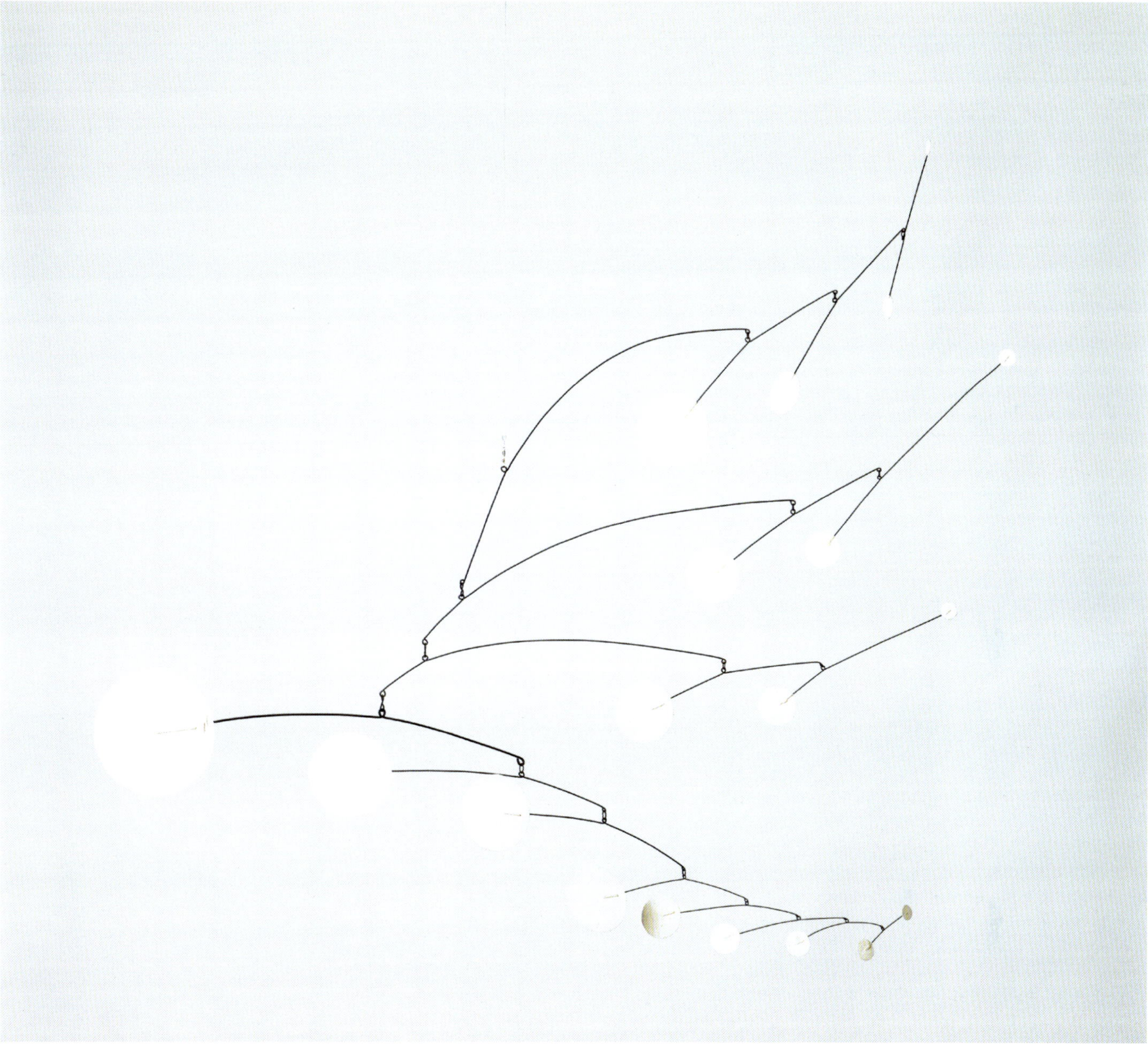

Nineteen White Discs 1961

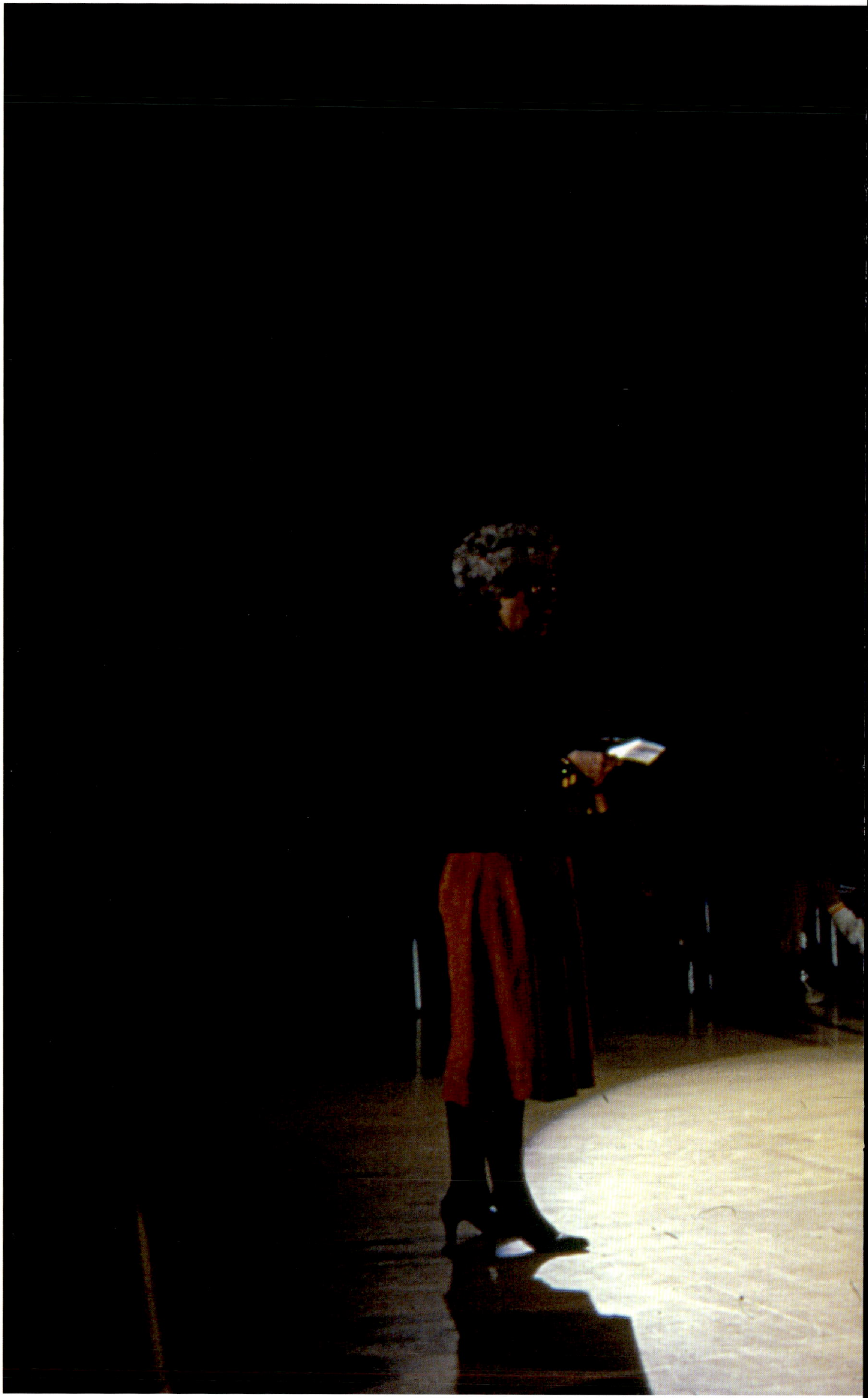

Chef d'orchestre 1966

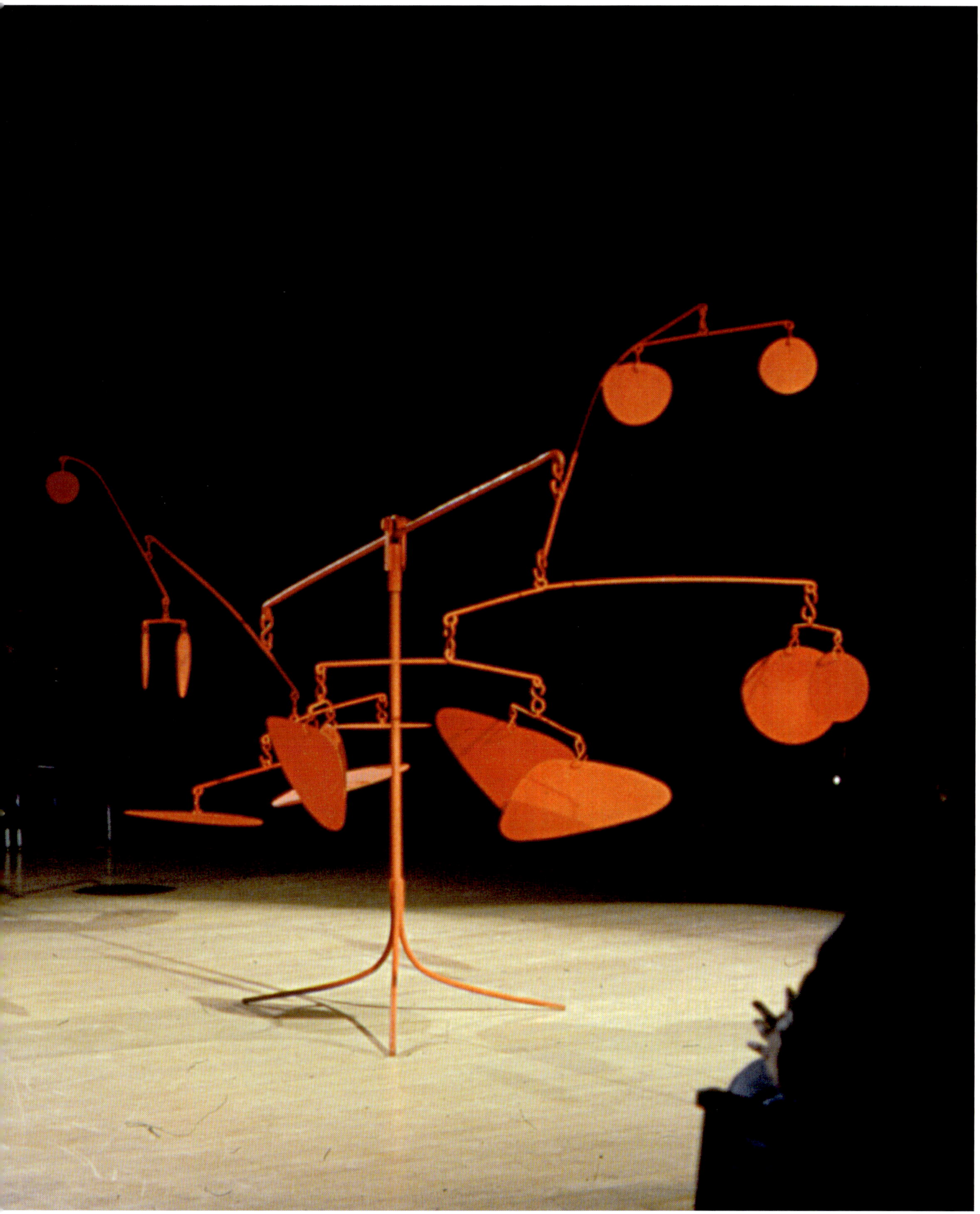

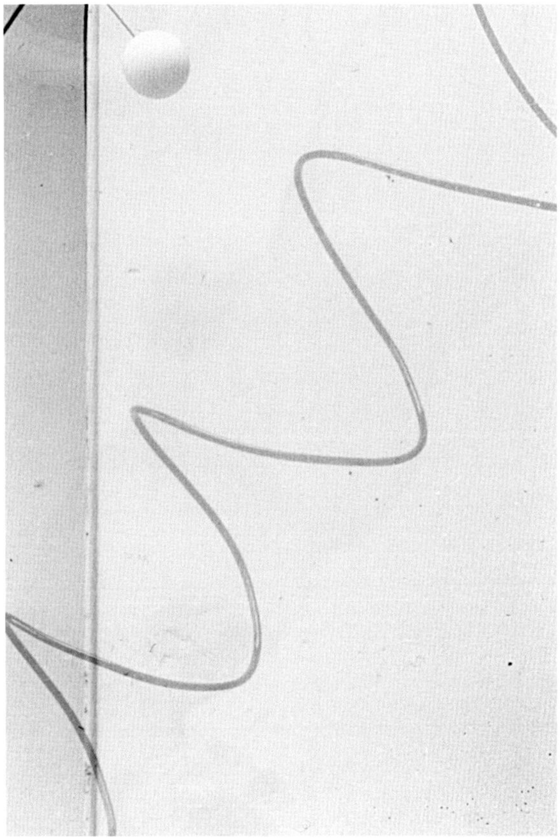

Select Chronology

Alexander S.C. Rower

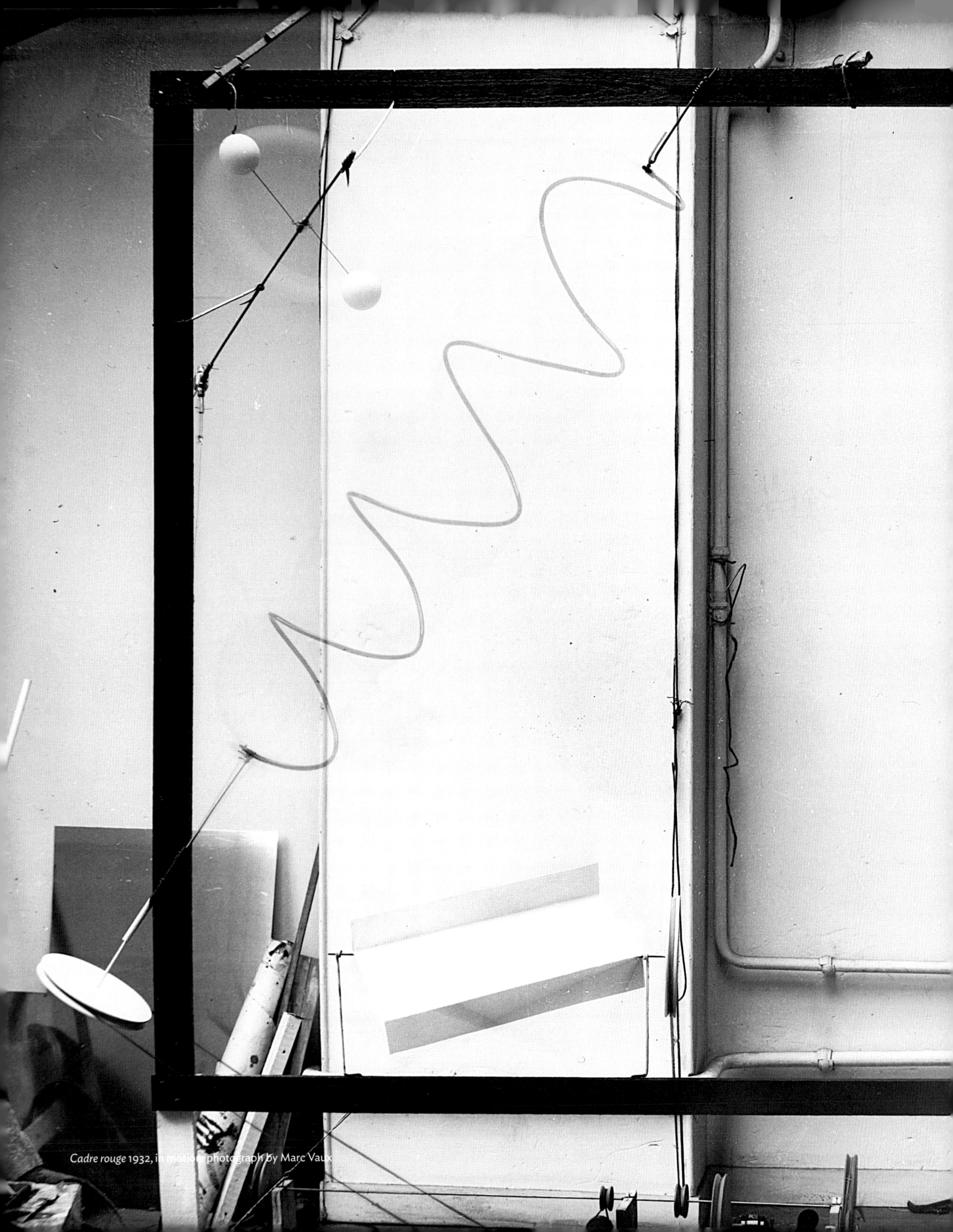

Cadre rouge 1932, in motion: photograph by Marc Vaux

For a comprehensive chronology, please visit http://www.calder.org

Abbreviations and archival sources

AAA: (Archives of American Art, Smithsonian Institution, Washington, DC, Alexander Calder papers) includes artist-donated letters, photographs, press clippings, exhibition announcements and a scrapbook containing hundreds of clippings and memorabilia from the years 1926 to 1932.
ASCR: Alexander S.C. Rower
ASL: Art Students League
CF: (Calder Foundation, New York) consists of over 130,000 documents (including correspondence and unpublished manuscripts), 26,000 photographs and thousands of press clippings, articles, books and films. In addition, the Foundation itself maintains a database listing over 22,000 works of art by Calder (with photography, physical data, provenance, and publication and exhibition history for each piece).
FJM: (Fundació Pilar i Joan Miró a Mallorca)
JJS: (James Johnson Sweeney Archive [private collection])
SM: (Stedelijk Museum Amsterdam)

1898

22 August: Calder is born in Lawnton, Pennsylvania, to Nanette Lederer Calder, a painter, and Alexander Stirling Calder, a sculptor. His sister Peggy is two years old (Calder 1966, 11).

1902

Before 20 January: Calder poses for his father's sculpture, *Man Cub*, in Philadelphia. Calder sculpts his own clay elephant (Calder 1966, 13).

1906

Autumn: The Calders move to Pasadena, California.

> *At that time, on Euclid Avenue in Pasadena, I got my first tools and was given the cellar with its window as a workshop. Mother and father were all for my efforts to build things myself – they approved of the homemade … My workshop became some sort of a center of attention; everybody came in* (Calder 1966, 21).

1907

1 January: Calder attends Pasadena's Tournament of Roses, where he experiences the four-horse chariot races (Calder 1966, 22).

1913

September: Calder begins his studies at Stevens Institute of Technology, Hoboken, New Jersey, where he takes courses that include chemistry, mechanical drawing, shop practice, and surveying, among others (Calder 1966, 39).

1918

Autumn: Calder joins the Student Army Training Corps, Naval Section, at Stevens, where he is made guide of the battalion (Calder 1966, 48).

1919

17 June: Calder graduates from Stevens with a degree in mechanical engineering (CF, certificate of graduation; Lipman 1976, 329).

1922

Spring: Calder attends night classes in drawing with Clinton Balmer at the New York Public School on 42nd Street (Calder 1966, 51).
9 June: Serving on the *H.F. Alexander* as a fireman in the boiler room, Calder sails from New York to San Francisco via the Panama Canal.

> *It was early one morning on a calm sea, off Guatemala, when over my couch – a coil of rope – I saw the beginning of a fiery red sunrise on one side and the moon looking like a silver coin on the other. Of the whole trip this impressed me most of all; it left me with a lasting sensation of the solar system* (Calder 1966, 53–5; CF, Patterson to ASCR, 26 April 2010).

1923

October–December: Calder begins classes at the Art Students League of New York, studying life and pictorial composition with John Sloan and portrait painting with George Luks (Calder 1966, 59–61, 66–7; ASL, registration records).

1924

January–April: Calder enrols again at the League, where he continues to study until 1925, taking classes in portrait painting with Luks, head and figure with Guy Pène du Bois, a drawing class with Boardman Robinson, and an etching class (ASL, registration records).

1925

Before 23 May: Calder spends two weeks illustrating the Ringling Bros. and Barnum & Bailey Circus for the *National Police Gazette*.

> *I could tell by the music what act was getting on and used to rush to some vantage point. Some acts were better seen from above and others from below* (Calder 1966, 73; *Gazette*, 23 May).

Winter: Calder travels to Florida. First he visits Miami, then Sarasota, where he sketches at the winter grounds of the Ringling Bros. and Barnum & Bailey Circus.

> *I was very fond of the spatial relations. I love the space of the circus. I made some drawings of nothing but the tent. The whole thing of – the vast space – I've always loved it* (Gray 1964, 23).

1926

Autumn: In Paris, Calder begins creating *Cirque Calder*, a complex and unique body of art. Fashioned from wire, fabric, leather, rubber, cork, and other materials, *Cirque Calder* is designed to be performed for an audience by Calder. It develops into a multi-act articulated series of mechanised sculpture in miniature scale, a distillation of the natural circus. Calder is able to travel with his easily transportable circus and hold performances on both continents. Over the next five years, Calder continues to develop and expand this work of performance art to fill five large suitcases (CF, project file).
Autumn: Calder performs *Cirque Calder* for Mrs Frances C.L. Robbins, a patron of young artists. On her recommendation, English novelist Mary Butts comes to see it and in turn sends Jean Cocteau to a performance (CF, Calder 1955–6, 68; Hawes 1928).

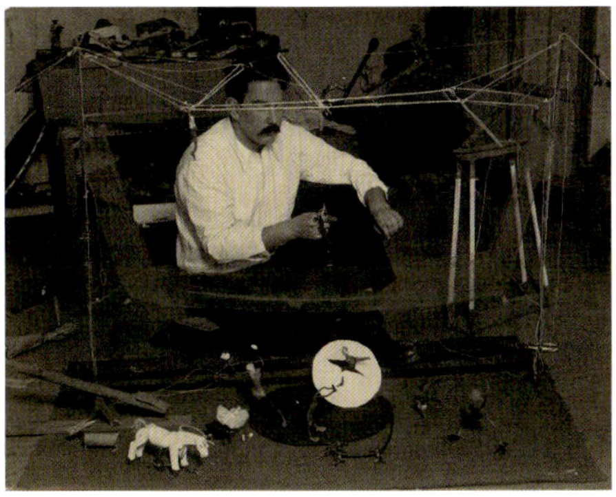

Calder with *Cirque Calder* 1926–31, 1929: photograph by Sasha Stone

1927

1 May: Marc Réal, artistic advisor at *Le Boulevardier*, brings Guy Selz and the circus critic Legrand-Chabrier to see Calder perform *Cirque Calder*. Legrand-Chabrier admires Calder's work and writes several articles on the *Cirque*.

> *Oh, these are stylized silhouettes, but astonishing in their miniature resemblance, obtained by means of luck, iron wire, spools, corks, elastics … A stroke of the brush, a stroke of the knife, of this, of that; these are the skillful marks that reconstruct the individuals that we see at the circus. Here is a dog who seems like a prehistoric cave drawing with a body of iron wire. He will jump through a paper hoop. Yes, but he may miss his mark or not. This is not a mechanical toy … All of this is arranged and balanced according to the laws of physics in action so that it allows for the miracles of circus acrobatics* (Calder 1966, 83; CF, Calder 1955–6, 149–50; *Candide*, 23 June).

Winter: In New York, Calder rents a room at 46 Charles Street where he gives *Cirque Calder* performances (Calder 1966, 87; CF, Calder 1955–6, 46).

1928

After 9 April: ACME Film Company produces *Sculptor Discards Clay to Ply his Art in Wire*, a film of Calder's wire sculpture that includes footage of Calder creating a wire portrait of Elizabeth 'Babe' Hawes, a reporter and aspiring fashion designer whom he had met in Paris (CF, project file).

1929

April: In Berlin, Dr Hans Cürlis directs a short film of Calder creating *Two Acrobats* as part of the series *Artists at Work*. Calder makes a wire portrait of Cürlis (CF, Calder to parents, before 8 May).

> Before 8 May:
> *I have had 2 large circus parties since coming back to Paris. At one of them we had Paul Fratellini, one of the famous clowns at the Cirque d'Hiver. It was quite a swell party – and I am making one of the toys in a size large enough for him to use in the Cirque d'Hiver* (CF, Calder to parents, before 8 May).

Before 21 May: Pathé Cinema, Paris, produces a short film of Calder at work in his rue Cels studio. Calder invites Kiki de Montparnasse to model for a wire portrait during the filming (Calder 1966, 99; *New York Herald* [Paris edition], 21 May).
Before 22 June: Calder performs *Cirque Calder* in the studio of Tsuguharu Foujita, a painter and well-known denizen of Montparnasse. Foujita plays a drum to accompany Calder's performance. Man Ray and Kiki are among the guests in attendance (*Illustrirte Zeitung*, 29 August).
22 June: Calder embarks for New York on the *De Grasse*, bringing *Cirque Calder* with him. During the voyage, he meets Edward Holton James and his daughter Louisa.

> *So once on board the De Grasse, I started walking the deck. I overtook an elderly man and a young lady. I could only see them from the back, so I reversed my steps the better to see them face on. Upon coming abreast of them the next time around, I said, 'Good evening!' And the man said to his daughter, 'There is one of them already!' He was Edward Holton James, my future father-in-law. She was Louisa. Her father had just taken her to Europe to mix with the young intellectual elite. All she met were concierges, doormen, cab drivers – and finally me* (AAA, passport; Calder 1966, 101).

28 August: Calder performs *Cirque Calder* at Hawes's couture house, 8 West 56th Street, New York (AAA, circus poster).
29 October: Calder performs *Cirque Calder* at art patron Mildred Harbeck's apartment, 306 Lexington Avenue, New York (AAA, circus poster).
November–December: Calder stays with his friend, book designer Robert Josephy, at Beekman Place and 50th Street.

> *Josephy was very enthusiastic over my circus. This encouraged me and while at his house, I worked on it very hard. He helped me. We made the chariot race and the lion tamer, and it got to be quite a full blown circus, growing from two suitcases into five* (Calder 1966, 103).

30 November: After the *New Yorker* announces that performances of *Cirque Calder* can be arranged through the Junior League Entertainment Center at Saks Fifth Avenue, Calder is hired by Newbold Morris to perform in his Babylon, Long Island, home; Isamu Noguchi operates a phonograph providing the music ('Sudden Brain Waves', *New Yorker* 1929; CF, Calder 1955–6, 142).
25 December: Calder performs *Cirque Calder* in the home of Aline Bernstein on Park Avenue. Noguchi is present, as is Thomas Wolfe, who later incorporates a wry fictionalised account of the event into his novel, *You Can't Go Home Again* (Calder 1966, 106–7; Hayes 1977, 226).
31 December: Calder performs *Cirque Calder* on New Year's Eve at the home of Jack and Edith Straus on West 57th Street, New York (CF, Calder 1955–6, 142).

1930

Before 27 January: Calder stays in the apartment of his friend Paul Nitze at 112 East 40th Street. At Nitze's request, he performs *Cirque Calder* (Calder 1966, 107; CF, Calder 1955–6, 110).
27 January–4 February: Harvard Society for Contemporary Art, Cambridge, Massachusetts, exhibits 'Wire Sculpture by Alexander Calder'. Calder performs *Cirque Calder* for the faculty and students on 31 January (CF, exhibition file).
10 September: Calder performs *Cirque Calder* in his Paris studio, 7 Villa Brune. For seating, he invites spectators to bring their own boxes (CF, project file).
October: In need of money to pay rent, Calder charges admission to performances of *Cirque Calder*.

I bought planks, pinched some boxes, and made bleachers. I handled thirty people an evening on, I believe, four evenings. At the end of my professional run, the concierge came and said the proprietor who lived in the front could not get to sleep on account of the cymbals (Calder 1966, 113–14).

14 October: On the advice of Frederick Kiesler, a Viennese architect, Calder invites Le Corbusier, Karl Einstein, Fernand Léger, Piet Mondrian, and Théo van Doesburg to a presentation of *Cirque Calder* at 7 Villa Brune. To avoid conflicts, Kiesler insists that Calder send a telegram inviting van Doesburg for the following night (Calder 1966, 112–13; AAA, circus poster).
15 October: Van Doesburg and his wife, Pétronella [Nelly], attend a performance of *Cirque Calder*.

I got more of a reaction from Doesburg than I had from the whole gang the night before (Calder 1966, 112–13; AAA, circus poster).

Autumn: Kiesler introduces Calder to composer Edgard Varèse and Calder makes a wire portrait of him. Varèse, who feels that his own compositions resonate with Calder's new abstract sculpture, becomes a frequent visitor to Calder's studio (Calder 1966, 125; CF, Calder 1955–6, 78).
October: Accompanied by another American artist, William 'Binks' Einstein, Calder visits Mondrian's studio at 26 rue de Départ. Already familiar with Mondrian's geometric abstractions, Calder is deeply impressed by the studio environment.

It was a very exciting room. Light came in from the left and from the right, and on the solid wall between the windows there were experimental stunts with colored rectangles of cardboard tacked on. Even the victrola, which had been some muddy color, was painted red. I suggested to Mondrian that perhaps it would be fun to make these rectangles oscillate. And he, with a very serious countenance, said: 'No, it is not necessary, my painting is already very fast.' This one visit gave me a shock that started things. Though I had heard the word 'modern' before, I did not consciously know or feel the term 'abstract.' So now, at thirty-two, I wanted to paint and work in the abstract. And for two weeks or so, I painted very modest abstractions. At the end of this, I reverted to plastic work which was still abstract (Calder 1966, 113; CF, Calder 1955–6, 78).

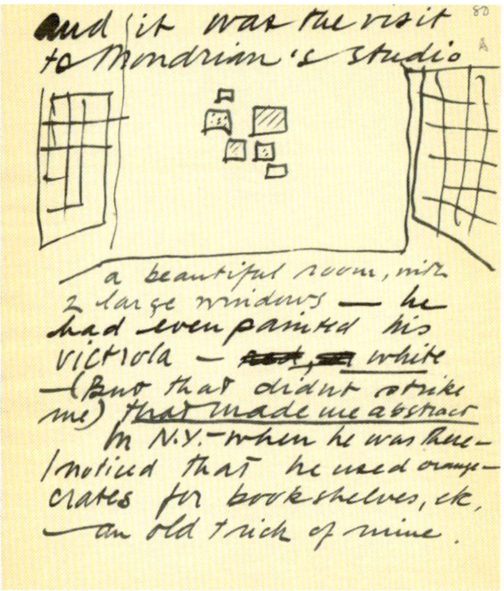

Sketch of Piet Mondrian's 1930 Paris studio from Calder's manuscript 'The Evolution', 1955–6, p.80

1931

Before 16 January: Calder prints postcards to announce performances of *Cirque Calder* at 903 7th Avenue, New York. Five performances are given; each audience includes about thirty spectators (AAA, circus announcement; *The World*, 18 January).
16 January: Calder performs *Cirque Calder* at the James's home in Concord, Massachusetts (Calder 1966, 115).
17 January: Calder and Louisa James are married.

The reverend who married us apologized for having missed the circus the night before. So I said: 'But you are here for the circus today' (Calder 1966, 115).

27 April–9 May: Calder's abstract work is presented for the first time in the exhibition *Alexandre Calder: Volumes–Vecteurs–Densités / Dessins–Portraits* at Galerie Percier, Paris. Léger writes in the introduction to the catalogue:

Eric Satie illustrated by Calder.
Why not?
'It's serious without seeming to be.'
Neoplastician from the start, he believed in the absolute of two colored rectangles …
Looking at these new works – transparent, objective, exact – I think of Satie, Mondrian, Marcel Duchamp, Brancusi, Arp – these unchallenged masters of unexpressed and silent beauty. Calder is in the same family.
He is 100-percent American.
Satie and Duchamp are 100-percent French.
And yet, we meet?
(CF, exhibition file).

Before 12 July: Calder continues to expand the use of motion in his abstract sculpture.

I felt that perhaps I was exactly a perfectionist: i.e. that who was I to decide that a thing should be just this way, or just that way – so I made one or 2 objects articulated, so that they could be in a number of positions (CF, Calder 1955–6, 108).

12 July: Calder writes to his parents of his new work:

I have been making a few new abstractions which have certain movements combined with their other features. I think there is something in it that may be good (CF, Calder to parents, 12 July).

29–30 October: Calder performs *Cirque Calder* in his studio, 14 rue de la Colonie (FJM, Calder to Miró, 1931).
Autumn: Using cranks and small electric motors, Calder concentrates on making mechanised abstract sculptures (Calder 1966, 126).
Autumn: Marcel Duchamp visits the studio at 14 rue de la Colonie again and sees Calder's latest works.

There was one motor-driven thing, with three elements. The thing had just been painted and was not quite dry yet. When he put his hands on it, the object seemed to please him, so he arranged for me to show in Marie Cuttoli's Galerie Vignon, close to the Madeleine. I asked him what sort of a name I could give these things and he at once pro-

duced Mobile. In addition to something that moves, in French it also means motive. Duchamp also suggested that on my invitation card I make a drawing of the motor-driven object and print: CALDER / SES MOBILES (Calder 1966, 127).

1932

Calder publishes 'Comment réaliser l'art?' for the first issue of *Abstraction-Création, Art Non Figuratif*.

> *Out of volumes, motion, spaces bounded by the great space, the universe.*
> *Out of different masses, light, heavy, middling – indicated by variations of size or color – directional line – vectors which represent speeds, velocities, accelerations, forces, etc.*
> *... these directions making between them meaningful angles, and senses, together defining one big conclusion or many.*
> *Spaces, volumes, suggested by the smallest means in contrast to their mass, or even including them, juxtaposed, pierced by vectors, crossed by speeds.*
> *Nothing at all of this is fixed.*
> *Each element able to move, to stir, to oscillate, to come and go in its relationships with the other elements in its universe.*
> *It must not be just a fleeting moment but a physical bond between the varying events in life.*
> *Not extractions,*
> *But abstractions*
> *Abstractions that are like nothing in life except in their manner of reacting* (Calder 1932).

Before 12 February: Calder makes *Cadre rouge*, the first in a series of 'frames' and 'panels' that consist of moving abstract forms set in front of coloured plywood panels or within boxlike frames. These works relate to the idea of three-dimensional paintings in motion that Calder proposed to Mondrian during his 1930 visit (Sweeney 1951, 38; CF, object file).
20–2 February: Calder performs *Cirque Calder* in his studio, 14 rue de la Colonie (AAA, circus poster).

Spring:
Joan Miró, the Spanish painter who lives now in Barcelona, is in Monte Carlo, doing the decors for a Ballet Russe. He knows my stuff, so I wrote him, and sent him photos and perhaps I will be able to arrange for myself to do a ballet next year. The Russian who used to do them, Daglieff (?) [sic], died 2 years ago, but one of the McCormacks has put up some money for their continuance (CF, Calder to parents; Hayes 1977, 264).

Before 16 June: The Calders visit Louisa's parents in Concord. Calder performs *Cirque Calder* at the James's home (CF, Calder 1955–6, 146; *Concord Herald*, 16 June).
11 July: While visiting Calder's parents in Richmond, Massachusetts, Calder performs *Cirque Calder* in an old barn that Stirling uses as a studio. Invitees include Nitze, Josephy, and Bill Drew, Calder's fraternity brother from Stevens (CF, Calder to Nitze, 11 July; CF, Calder 1955–6, 146).
12 September: The Calders arrive at the Miró farm in Montroig, Spain, for an eight- to ten-day visit. During their stay, Calder performs *Cirque Calder* for the Mirós, their farmhands, and their neighbours. Miró recalls the event:

> *He came to Montroig and brought the circus figures; he never stopped working on them. We organized a presentation for the local farmers who were very pleased with the spectacle of the wire performers. Later the Cirque was presented in galleries, but there in Montroig it was really a performance for the people* (Calder 1966, 139; Lanchner 1993, 330; Raillard 1977, 114–15).

Before 29 September: The Calders travel to Barcelona and visit Gaudí's basilica. Invited by the Amics de l'Art Nou, Calder performs *Cirque Calder* in the hall of the Grup d'Arquitectes i Tècnics Catalans per al Progrés de l'Arquitectura Contemporània (GATCPAC). Shortly thereafter, the Calders return to Paris (Calder 1966, 140–1; Gasch 1932).

1933

Calder publishes 'Un Mobile' for the second issue of *Abstraction-Création, Art Non Figuratif*.

> *A 'Mobile.'*
> *Dimensions: 2 meters by 2 meters 50.*
> *Frame: 8 centimeters, neutral red.*
> *The 2 white balls turn very rapidly.*
> *The black helix turns less rapidly and seems to always climb.*
> *The iron plate turns still less quickly, the two black lines seeming always to climb.*
> *The black pendulum, 40 centimeters in diameter, climbs by 45° on each side, passing in front of the frame, at the rate of 25 turns a minute* (Calder 1933).

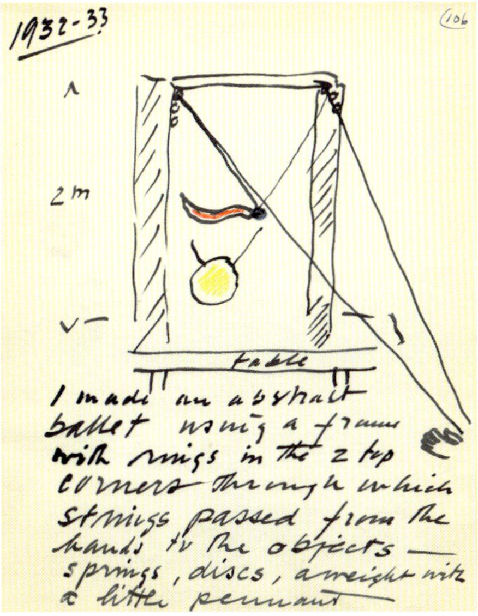

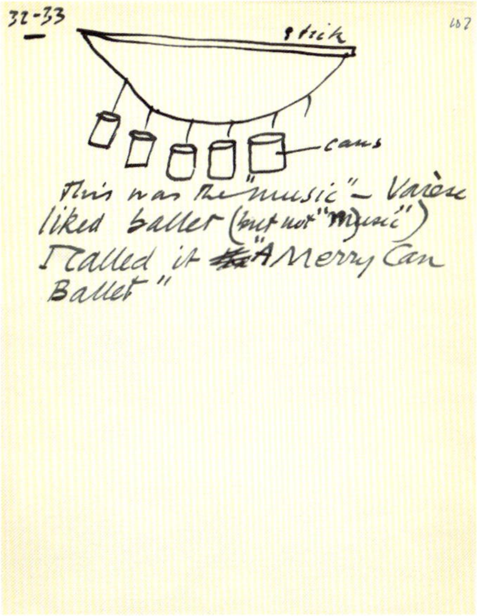

Sketch illustrating *A Merry Can Ballet* 1933 from Calder's manuscript 'The Evolution', 1955–6, p.106

1–2 February: Works by Calder are presented at the Sociedad de Cursos y Conferencias, Residencia de Estudiantes de la Universidad de Madrid. Calder also performs *Cirque Calder* for the students (AAA, Circus program; CF, Louisa to mother, 11 February).
11–12 February: Calder performs *Cirque Calder* in Barcelona (CF, Louisa to mother, 11 February).
Spring: Back in Paris, Calder constructs an interactive 'performance' sculpture.

> *I had a small ballet-object, built on a table with pulleys at the top of a frame. It was possible to move coloured discs across the rectangle, or fluttering pennants, or cones; to make them dance, or even have battles between them. Some of them had large, simple, majestic movements; others were small and agitated* (Calder 1937, 64).

Spring: Marc Vaux photographs *A Merry Can Ballet* and *The Gong* in Calder's studio, 14 rue de la Colonie (CF, photography file).

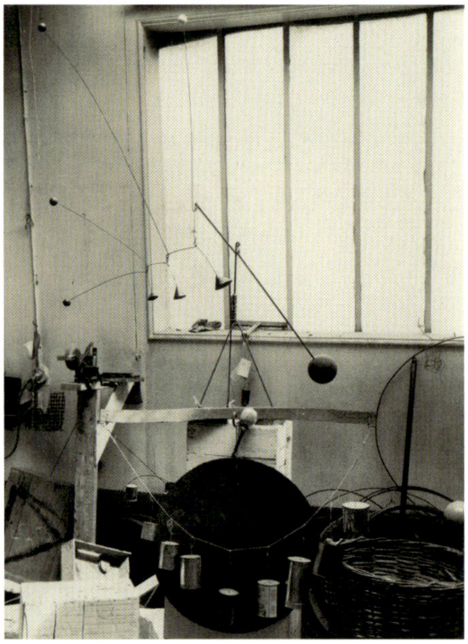

Calder's studio at 14 rue de la Colonie, Paris, 1933. From top: View of *Untitled* 1932, *A Merry Can Ballet* 1933, and *The Gong* c.1933: photograph by Marc Vaux

16–18 May: Galerie Pierre Colle, Paris, exhibits *Présentation des œuvres récentes de Calder*, including an untitled standing mobile and *Small Sphere and Heavy Sphere*. Paul Recht reviews the show:

> *The liberty of some of the ensembles is absolutely disconcerting: we see two balls, one little and one big, in turn fixed to wires of very different lengths that are themselves fixed to the two extremities of a balancing arm hung above the ground. The big ball is animated by a pendular and rotary movement; it leads the little one on unexpected evolutions that multiply by impact upon surrounding objects. They are extraordinary visual variations on the theme of calamity, by the means of gravity and centrifugal force* (CF, exhibition file; Recht 1933).

1934

30 January: Calder performs *Cirque Calder* at the Park Avenue home of Mr & Mrs Huntington Sheldon (JJS, Calder to Sweeney, c. January 1934).
Winter: At his studio in Roxbury, Connecticut, Calder makes *Project for Mechanical Ballet* for the American composer Harrison Kerr (CF, object file).

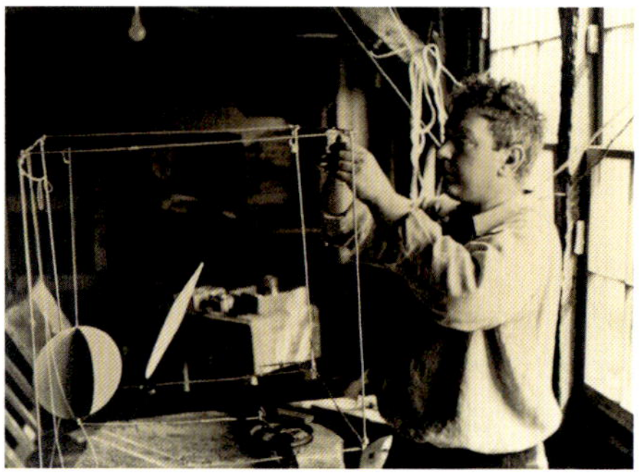

Calder at work on *Project for Mechanical Ballet* for Harrison Kerr in his Roxbury icehouse studio, 1934

> 23 March:
> *I thought for a moment that I was going to London last December. The Ballets Russes de Monte Carlo wired me to come to London to work on a ballet (but at my expense). They have been here for 3 months now and I am supposed to go to Monte Carlo with them when they return, but that may fall thru, too. In the meantime I am having one of my funny expositions – at the Pierre Matisse Gallery in New York* (CF, Calder to Thomson, 23 March).

Before 6 April: Calder creates *Black Frame*.

> *One I like very much myself is a black wooden frame, with sheets of metal within it, warped into various planes, and having certain moving elements, which are the brilliant spots in an otherwise sombre setting* (CF, object file; CF, Calder to Gallatin, 13 September 1935).

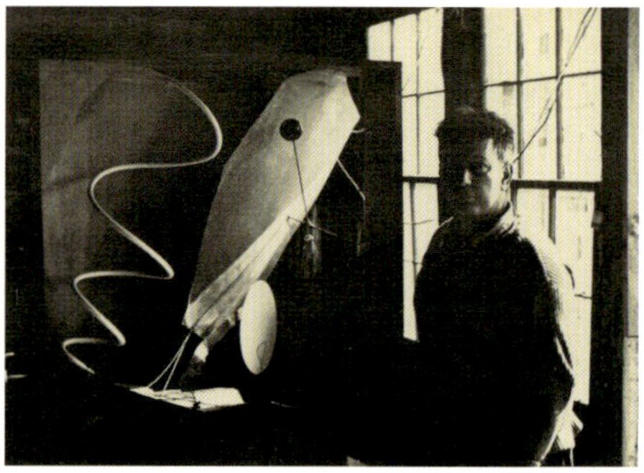

Calder with *Black Frame* in his Roxbury icehouse studio, 1934

> 26 May:
> *Massine had wired me to come to London (at my expense) last November, and in January decided to pay my fare to and from Monte Carlo, and I had decided to go (at about this time) – but as it was only to bolster up a ballet which had been very badly done sometime previous I finally declined to have anything to do with it, preferring to wait till I was given carte blanche. It's very annoying, for I am positive that I could do something excellent for them – but the other fellow's 'work' would have been too hampering* (CF, Calder to Nicholson, 26 May).

Summer: In Roxbury, Calder works prolifically on 'panels' and 'frames' (Sweeney 1951, 38).

> 19 July:
> *I am very much interested in developing a sort of ballet of mine – and devising the means of recording it so that it can be reproduced. The backgrounds can be changed – and the lighting varied. The discs can move anywhere within the limits of the frame, at any speed. Each disc and its supporting pulleys is in a separate vertical plane parallel to the frame. The number of discs can be increased indefinitely – depending on the necessary clearances. In addition to discs there are coloured pennants (of cloth), with weights on them, which fly at high speed – and various solid objects, bits of hose, springs, etc. ... I had this in Paris the spring of 1933 and showed it to Massine

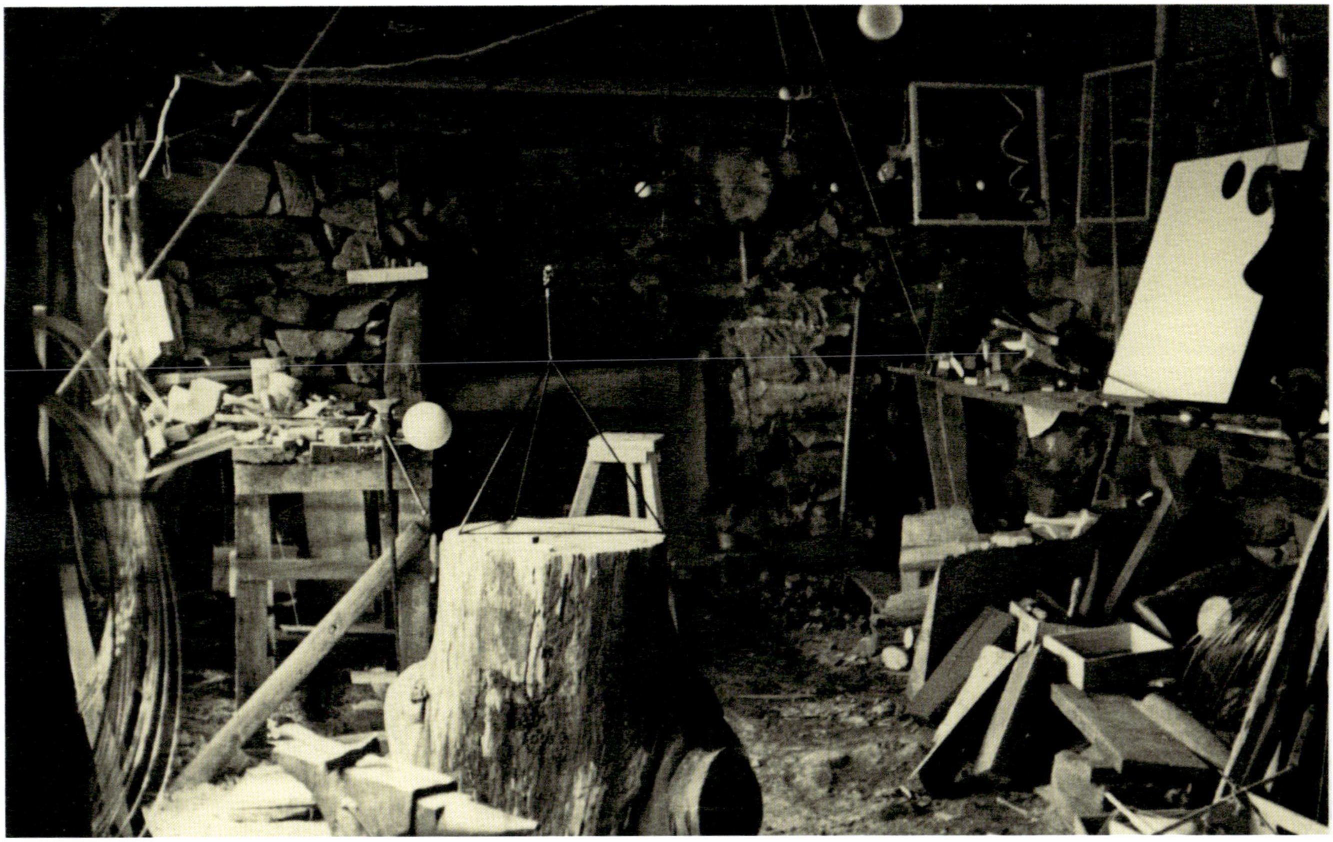

Roxbury icehouse studio, 1934

along with many other things, and it's what I wanted to do for the Ballets Russes. Of course the real problem [is] to magnify the movement to a full sized proscenium – but I can see various ways of obtaining it (CF, Calder to the Sweeneys, 19 July).

28 July:
As to the ballet – I hear from Zervos that they have no cash – and can't even put on the ballets which have been done for them. I hope to do something with Martha Graham – the American dancer – whom I saw dance this spring – and whom I think excellent (CF, Calder to Nicholson, 28 July).

11 August:
Martha Graham, the dancer, whose performances you may have seen last April in New York, and whom I consider very fine, was here last night – and we are going to try to do something together – my part being based on the idea of the ballet I worked by hand (with discs, bits of cloth, etc.) when you came to the house in Paris (CF, Calder to Gallatin, 11 August).

1935

14–31 January: *Mobiles by Alexander Calder* is held at the Renaissance Society at the University of Chicago; Sweeney writes the preface for the catalogue. On the 16th and 19th of January, Calder gives performances of *Cirque Calder* in the University of Chicago's Wieboldt Hall for the Renaissance Society. He also performs at the home of Walter S. Brewster, a trustee of the Art Institute of Chicago, on 20 January (Calder 1966, 153; CF, exhibition file; *Chicago Tribune*, 10 January).

Summer: Calder constructs mobile sets for Martha Graham's dance *Panorama*. On 5–6 August, Calder and Louisa visit Graham in Bennington, Vermont, to preview *Panorama* before its premiere at the Vermont State Armory, Bennington, on 14 August (CF, project file).

After 27 September: Calder and Louisa visit Charlotte Whitney Allen in Rochester, New York. While there, Calder constructs the large standing mobile she had commissioned for her garden and he gives a performance of *Cirque Calder* (CF, Calder to Allen, 24 September).

5 December: Thomas H. Fisher, husband of choreographer Ruth Page, writes to Calder:

> *Ruth and I have the novel idea that you should construct for her a large scale 'mobile' to be used alone on the stage, with music and lights between her ballets. The idea would be to enlarge such a mobile as the one I saw in the Museum of Modern Art to stage proportions using different colored objects in motion and then playing lights on the mobile from the wings and elsewhere in the theatre. The music would, perhaps, be something like Varèse or something else which would be suitable to the particular mobile being displayed* (CF, Fisher to Calder, 5 December).

Winter: Calder again collaborates with Graham, making a group of six mobiles – 'visual preludes' – for her dance *Horizons* (CF, project file; 'Martha Graham and Dance Group', 1936).

> 24 December:
> *The large 'overhead' mobile should be in its box in your basement (awaiting my pleasure). Do you think you would care*

to put it up anywhere during la semaine folle – only a suggestive question – because Ruth Page wishes me to do an object which she can use, here, and in Chicago, to pinch-hit for one of her solo dances – and I thought of that one. (CF, Calder to Austin, 24 December).

1936

Page writes to Calder:

> *I have been experimenting with my brass mobile which you sent here and have decided that it is much more beautiful without me than with me. Any movements of mine just spoil it. However, we tried it just in the room here with lights and music and it is a thrilling dance all by itself and we would love to produce it just by itself with lights and music. Blow an electric fan on it so that it moves very slightly. But it seems to me there should be a little group of 2 or 3 to make an impression – like 3 short dances* (CF, Page to Calder).

15 February: First Hartford Music Festival, Wadsworth Atheneum, presents Erik Satie's symphonic drama *Socrate*. Virgil Thomson and A. Everett 'Chick' Austin, Jr, have commissioned Calder to create the mobile decor for the performance. As the singers stand still at either end of the stage, Calder's simple geometric objects in space enact a series of movements. Later that night the festival continues with *Paper Ball: Le Cirque des Chiffoniers*, designed by Pavel Tchelitchew and featuring thirteen processions of paper costumes created especially for the event. For James Thrall Soby's procession, Calder contributes *A Nightmare Side Show*, a suite of animal costumes designed to wear over evening clothes (CF, project file).
23 February: Graham premieres *Horizons* at the Guild Theatre in New York City. The program note reads:

> *The 'Mobiles,' designed by Alexander Calder, are a new conscious use of space. They are employed in* Horizons *as visual preludes to the dances in this suite. The dances do not interpret the 'Mobiles,' nor do the 'Mobiles' interpret the dances. They are employed to enlarge the sense of horizon* (CF, project file; 'Martha Graham and Dance Group', 1936).

2 April: Calder performs *Cirque Calder* in New York at the Pierre Matisse Gallery (AAA, Calder to Bunce, 26 March).
24–25 April: Satie's *Socrate* with Calder's mobile decor is performed at the Colorado Springs Fine Arts Center (CF, project file).
15 December: Calder performs *Cirque Calder* in his apartment at 244 East 86th Street and 2nd Avenue, New York (AAA, Calder to Bunce, 9 December).

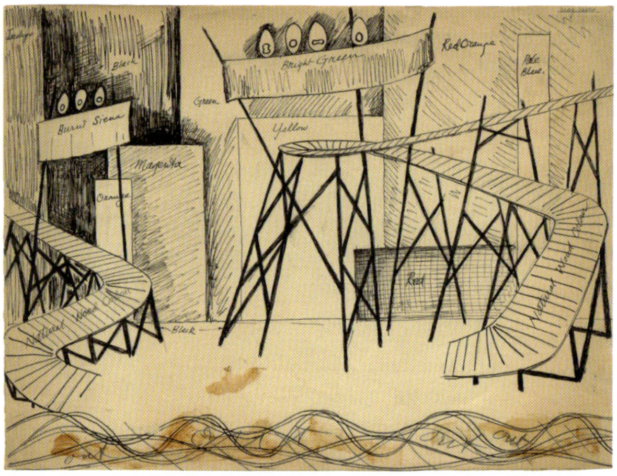

OO to AH (scene I), 1937

1937

Calder designs scenery and costumes for *OO to AH*, a playlet in two scenes written by Charles Tracy but never performed (CF, project file; Tracy 1937).

May: Calder and Miró visit the Spanish pavilion under construction at the 1937 World's Fair site in Paris. Calder meets the pavilion's architects, Josep Lluís Sert and Luis Lacasa. Sert eventually commissions Calder to make *Mercury Fountain* for the Spanish pavilion. Mined in Almadén in Spain, the mercury symbolises Republican resistance to fascism (Calder 1966, 158; Freedberg 1986, 504–5).
3 June: Calder performs *Cirque Calder* at 80 boulevard Arago, Paris (Bruguière Collection, Paris, circus invitation).
12 July: The Spanish pavilion, featuring Picasso's *Guernica*, Miró's *Le Faucheur*, and Calder's *Mercury Fountain*, opens at the Paris World's Fair (CF, exhibition file).
21 October: The Calders arrive in Folkstone, England, later renting an apartment at Belsize Park, London. Calder establishes a studio in Camden Town and gives *Cirque Calder* performances (CF, passport; Calder 1966, 164–5).

1939

After 1 March: Calder is commissioned by Wallace K. Harrison and André Fouilhoux, architects of Consolidated Edison's pavilion at the 1939 New York World's Fair, to design a 'water ballet' for the building's fountain. Although water jets are installed around the pavilion, this ballet is never executed (Calder 1966, 176).

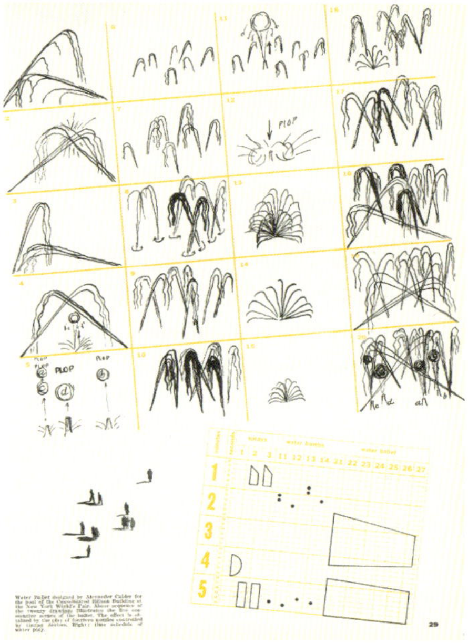

Drawings for *A Water Ballet* 1939

1941

9 August: Calder performs *Cirque Calder* in Roxbury. Yves Tanguy assists (CF, family photographs).

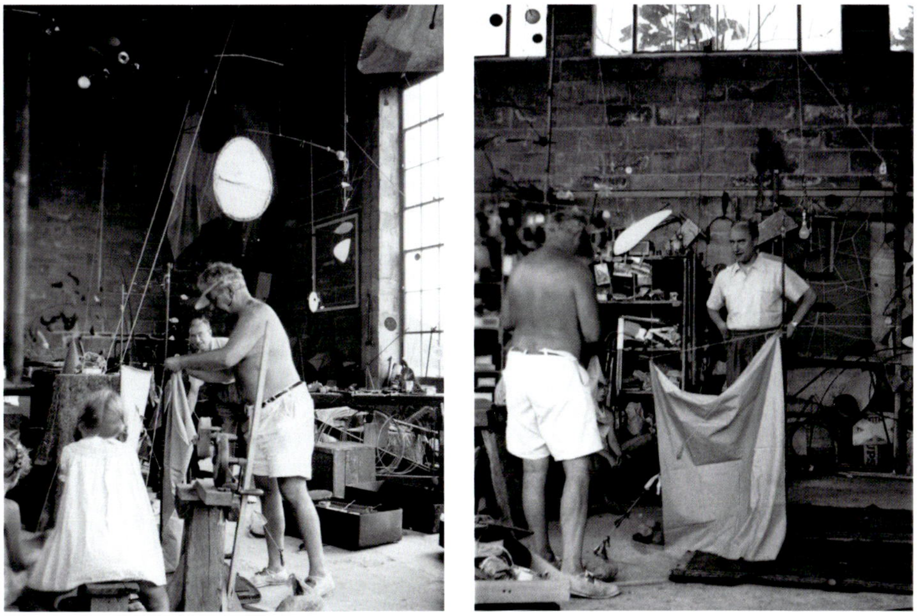

Calder and Yves Tanguy preparing a performance of *Cirque Calder* 1926–31 in his Roxbury studio, 1941

1942

20 May: Calder performs *Cirque Calder* at Herbert and Mercedes Matter's apartment, 328 East 42nd Street, New York (CF, Calder to de Creeft, 18 May).

1943

28 August: Calder writes to Sweeney about his forthcoming retrospective at the Museum of Modern Art, New York.

> *I forgot to show you this object. One swings the red (iron) ball in a small circle – this movement and the inertia of the rod and the length of thread develops a very complicated pattern of movement. The impedimenta – boxes, cymbal, bottles, cans etc. add to the complication, and also add sounds of thuds, crashes, etc. – This is a reconstruction of one I had in Paris in '33. I will bring it down and set it up for you to see. I call it the 'Small Sphere and Heavy Sphere'* (CF, Calder to Sweeney, 28 August).

20–1 October: Calder gives two performances of *Cirque Calder* in the Members Room of the Museum of Modern Art, New York, for friends and staff (CF, exhibition file).

1944

Agnes Rindge Claflin writes and narrates *Alexander Calder: Sculpture and Constructions*, a film based on the retrospective at the Museum of Modern Art, New York. Cinematography is by Matter (CF, project file).
27 March–9 April: Calder's *Black Flower* is loaned by the Russian Embassy in Washington, DC, to *Calder: Paintings, Mobiles, Stabiles and Jewelry*, held at the local gallery France Forever. Calder performs *Cirque Calder* twice during the exhibition (CF, exhibition file; Calder 1966, 184–5).

1945

14 March: Calder receives a contract from composer Remi Gassmann on behalf of the University of Chicago for the design of costumes and scenery for the dance project *Billy Sunday* (CF, Gassmann to Calder, 14 March; AAA, Calder to Warner, 6 March, 2 April).

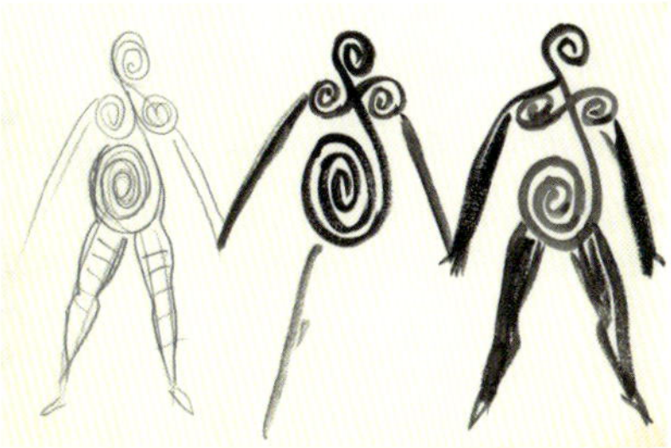

Costume design for *Billy Sunday*, 1945

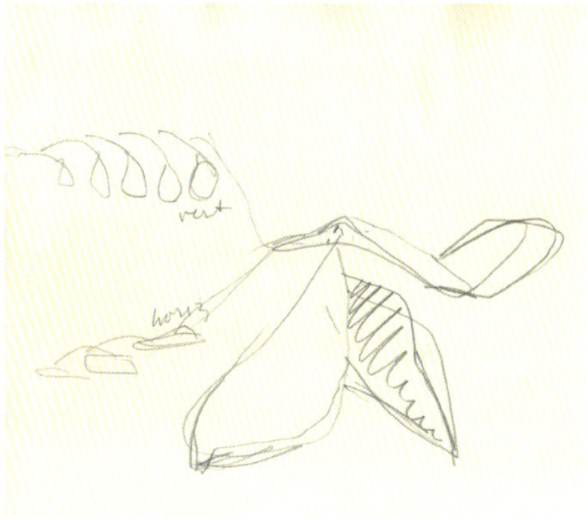

Preliminary drawing for set design of *Billy Sunday* c.1945

1946

12 August: Calder and Louisa attend the premiere of Padraic Colum's play *Balloon* with mobile sets by Calder, performed at the Ogunquit Playhouse, Maine (AAA, Calder to Warner, July).
7 September: Calder holds a performance of *Cirque Calder* in the family's Roxbury studio for his daughters.

> *I have to show the children how to run it so that they can carry on* (AAA, Calder to Warner, 30 August).

1947

Before 7 March: Calder performs *Cirque Calder* at his home in Roxbury for the Mirós; Henri Seyrig, Director of the Institut Français d'Archéologie; and Brazilian architect Henrique Mindlin and his wife Helena (SM, Miró to Sandberg, 7 March; CF, Calder 1955–6, 155).

1948

Hans Richter's film, *Dreams that Money Can Buy*, is finally released after being in production since 1945. Two sequences are made with Calder's collaboration: 'Ballet', the fifth dream, and 'Circus', the sixth dream (CF, project file).

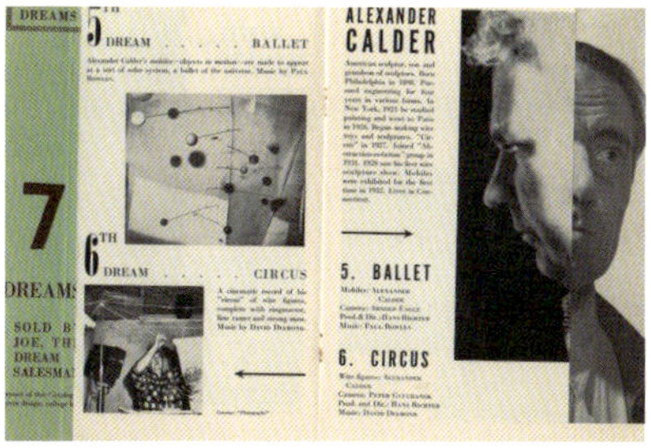

Interior of programme for *Dreams That Money Can Buy*, 1948

1949

Calder creates mobiles for *Symphonic Variations*, choreographed by Tatiana Leskova with music by César Franck. The dance is performed in Rio de Janeiro (CF, object file).

1950

6 January: *Happy as Larry*, a play written by Donagh MacDonagh and directed by Burgess Meredith with sets by Calder, opens in New York at the Coronet Theatre (CF, project file).

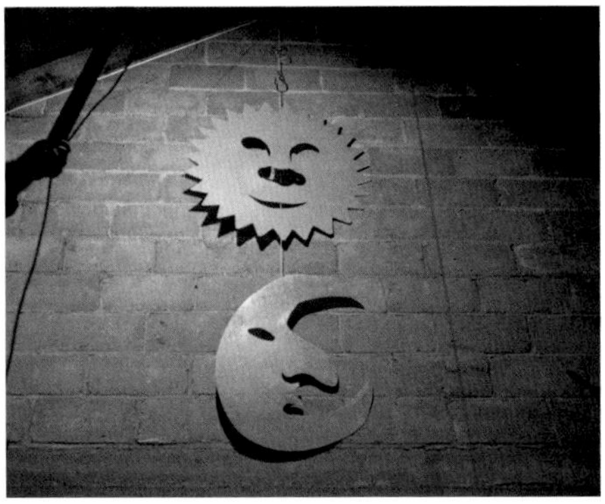

Sun and moon from *Happy as Larry* (1949), Roxbury studio, 1950: photograph by Herbert Matter

1951

24 January: After two years of production, *Works of Calder* previews at the Museum of Modern Art, New York. The film was directed by Matter and produced and narrated by Burgess Meredith, with music by John Cage (CF, project file).

1952

April: Calder designs the sets and costumes for *Nucléa*, written by Henri Pichette. The costumes include two large silver necklaces and a silver bracelet (CF, project file; Calder 1966, 209–10).

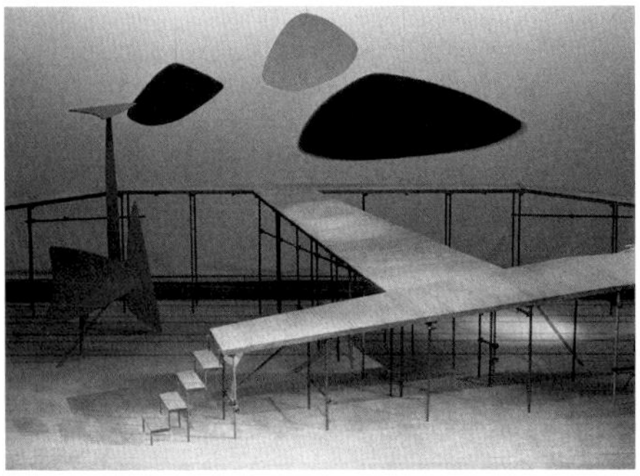

Set for *Nucléa*, 1952: photograph by Agnès Varda

3 May: Calder and Louisa attend the opening of *Nucléa* at the Théâtre du Palais de Chaillot, Paris. Directed by Jean Vilar with music by Maurice Jarre, the play is performed by Théâtre national populaire (CF, project file; Calder 1966, 210).
28 June: Calder accepts the commission from Carlos Raúl Villanueva, whom he met through Sert in 1951, to design an acoustic ceiling for Aula Magna, the auditorium of the Universidad Central de Venezuela. He collaborates with the engineering firm Bolt, Beranek, and Newman, Cambridge, Massachusetts (Calder 1966, 240; CF, Calder to Villanueva, 28 June).
5–6 September: Calder performs *Cirque Calder* in Roxbury (CF, Calder to Rockefeller; CF, Osborn to Calder, 8 September).
Winter: Calder presents *Cirque Calder* in Washington, DC; Jean invites 'what seemed half of Washington, DC, to see it' (Calder 1966, 213).

1953

3 September: Calder performs *Cirque Calder* at Galerie Maeght, Paris (CF, photography file).
7 November: Calder leaves Aix for Paris to begin filming *Cirque de Calder*, directed by Jean Painlevé, with André Bac as cameraman (CF, Calder to mother and the Sterns, 16 November).

1954

28 August–15 November: Belgiojoso, Peressutti & Rogers of Milan build a labyrinth for the X Triennale di Milano at the Uffici Palazzo dell'Arte al Parco. Calder's *Le Cagoulard* is installed in the centre, and Saul Steinberg's drawings are on the walls (CF, project file).

1955

15 August: Calder arrives in Caracas. He sets up a studio at the metal shop of the Universidad Central de Venezuela and sees *Acoustic Ceiling* installed in Aula Magna for the first time (CF, passport; Calder 1966, 242).

1956

May: Calder completes his fountain commission *Water Ballet* for the General Motors Technical Center, Warren, Michigan. There is a dedication on 15 May (CF, Saarinen to Calder, 27 April; CF, Dinkeloo to Calder, 17 May).

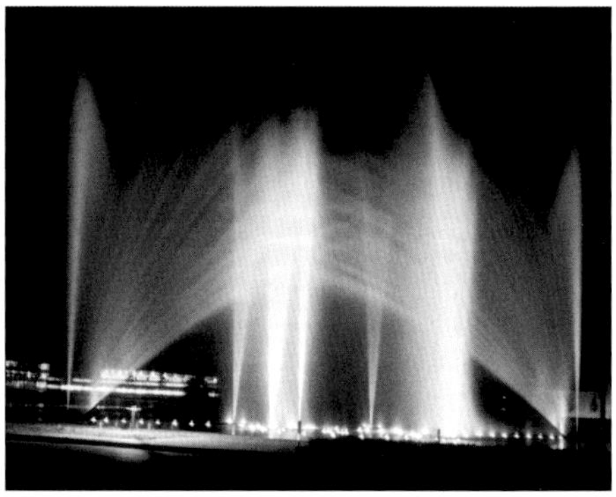

Water Ballet, General Motors Complex, Michigan, 1956

1957

Hans Richter brings together Arp, Paul Bowles, Calder, Cocteau, Duchamp, Sert, and Tanguy in a film entitled *8 x 8: A Chess Sonata in 8 Movements* (CF, project file).

1958

January: Calder completes the motorised, monumental sculpture *The Whirling Ear*, a commission made for the pool in front of the United States Pavilion at the Brussels Universal and International Exhibition. The sculpture was made by Calder at Gowans-Knight in Watertown, Connecticut (CF, project file; Calder 1966, 258, 260).
5–29 June: *The Glory Folk*, a ballet choreographed by John Butler with sets by Calder, is performed during the 'Festival of Two Worlds', Spoleto, Italy. Calder flies to Spoleto to oversee the construction of his sets (CF, project file).

1961

26 March: Calder performs *Cirque Calder* in Saché, France (CF, Calder to Piper, 30 March).
Before 3 August: Carlos Vilardebó directs *Le Cirque Calder*, a film with narration by Calder (CF, project file; CF, Calder to the Pipers, 3 August).

1963

Hans Richter directs and films *Alexander Calder: From the Circus to the Moon* (CF, project file).

24 December: La Comédie de Bourges performs *La Provocation*, with sets and costumes designed by Calder and choreography by Pierre Halet. The play opens in Bourges and is performed the following year in Tours (10 May 1964) and Paris (4 November 1964) (CF, project file).

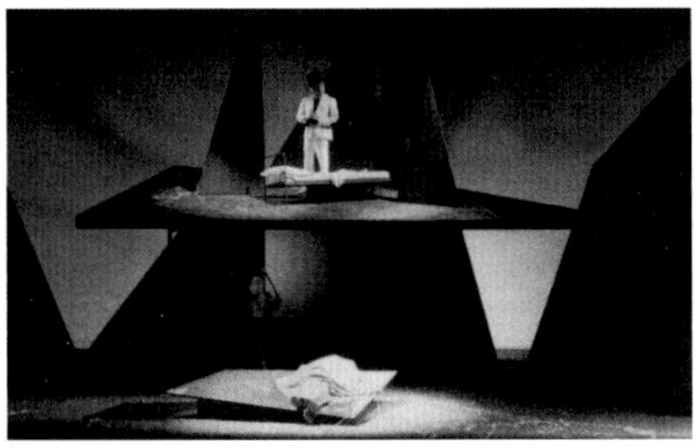

La Provocation 1963

1965

Calder designs sets for *Eppur si muove*, a ballet choreographed by Joseph Lazzini and performed at the Marseilles Opera (CF, project file).

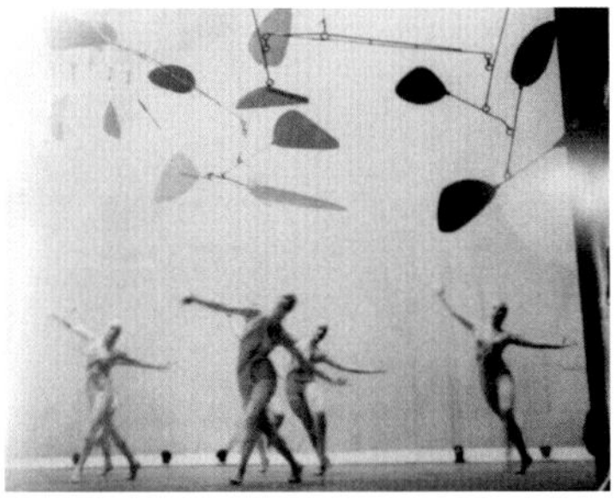

Eppur si muove 1965

1966

Carlos Vilardebó films *Mobiles*, narrated by Calder and produced by Pathé Cinema, Paris (CF, project file).

Calder completes the monumental standing mobile *Chef d'orchestre* for composer Earle Brown's *Calder Piece*, which was commissioned by Diego Masson in spring 1963. The mobile functions both as a 'conductor', determining the sequence and speed of the music, and as one of the instruments whereupon the elements are struck or 'played'. On 27 February 1967, *Calder Piece* is performed by Masson and the Percussion Quartet of Paris at the Théâtre de l'Atelier (CF, project file; CF, Sollins-Brown to ASCR, 23 November 1993).

1967

Autumn: The Calders travel to Italy. At the suggestion of Carandente, Massimo Bogianckino, Artistic Director of the Teatro dell'Opera, Rome, commissions Calder to develop a work for the stage. Calder begins *Work in Progress* in December 1967 (Carandente 1983, 231).

1968

11 March: Calder's *Work in Progress* is performed by the Teatro dell'Opera, Rome.

> *For thirty years I have been thinking about a production that would be entirely mine, form and music working together. I long ago discussed this with Massine, but he insisted on having dancers. I later made stage sets, but this is not exactly what I wanted to do… for Satie's* Socrate, *Pichette's* Nucléa, *John Butler's* The Glory Folk *in Spoleto, for Joe Lazzini in Marseille. The idea of a production that was totally mine had already come to me in spirit in 1926 when I finished the* Cirque, *and when I tried to frame it in a stage opening, amusing myself by thinking it an actual theatre* (CF, project file; Carandente 1983, 231).

1969

Calder designs sets and costumes for *Métaboles*, choreographed by Joseph Lazzini, scored by Henri Dutilleux, and produced by Théâtre français de la danse (CF, project file).

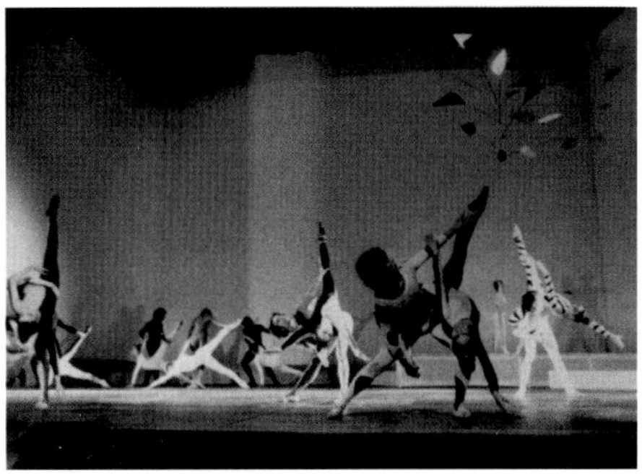

Métaboles 1969

Spring: *Janey Waney*, commissioned by the N.K. Winston Corporation, is installed at the Smith Haven Mall in the Long Island village of Lake Grove. The force behind the site-specific project is the developer's wife, Jane Holzer – or 'Baby Jane', a star of Andy Warhol's films – for whom the sculpture was named (CF, project file).

1971

Calder designs sets and costumes for the ballet *Amériques*, choreographed by Norbert Schmuki, scored by Edgard Varèse, and performed by the Ballet-théâtre Contemporain in Amiens, France (CF, object file).

1974

The film *Gouaches de Calder*, directed by Carlos Vilardebó, is released (CF, project file).

25 October: The festival Alexander Calder Day in Chicago includes a circus parade with the Schlitz forty-horse hitch and the dedications of the motorised *Universe* at the Sears Tower and the monumental stabile *Flamingo* at the Federal Center Plaza. *Flamingo* is the first work of art commissioned by the General Services Administration (GSA) under the new federal program wherein 0.5 percent of the budget for new construction goes toward commissioning art (CF, exhibition file).

1976

11 November: Calder dies in New York City at the home of his daughter Mary (*New York Times*, 12 November).

1977

10–11 November: *The National Tribute to Alexander Calder* at the Beacon Theater, New York City, celebrates the artist with a program that includes a revival of the 1936 presentation of Satie's symphonic drama *Socrate* with mobile decor recreated from Calder's designs, funded by a grant from the National Endowment for the Arts; and *Four Saints in Three Acts* by Gertrude Stein with music by Virgil Thomson (CF, project file).

Select Bibliography

For an extended chronological bibliography – including a list of primary archival holdings and film appearances featuring Calder and his work – see Alexander S.C. Rower (ed.), *Calder: Sculptor of Air*, exh. cat., Palazzo delle Esposizioni, Milan 2009, pp.249–62, or the updated listings on the website of the Calder Foundation: http://www.calder.org

Alexander Calder: Sculpture, Mobiles, exh. cat., Tate Gallery, London 1962. Introduction by James Johnson Sweeney.

Alexandre Calder: Volumes–Vecteurs–Densités/ Dessins–Portraits, exh. cat., Galerie Percier, Paris 1931. Preface by Fernand Léger.

H. Harvard Arnason, *Calder*, London and Princeton, NJ 1966. Photographs by Pedro E. Guerrero.

H. Harvard Arnason, *Calder*, London 1971. Photographs and design by Ugo Mulas.

Stephen Bann and John Russell, *Calder*, exh. cat., Royal Academy of Arts, London 1992.

Stephanie Barron and Lisa Gabrielle Mark (eds.), *Calder and Abstraction: From Avant-Garde to Iconic*, exh. cat., Los Angeles County Museum of Art (LACMA), New York and London 2013. Texts by Stephanie Barron, Ilene Susan Fort, Aleca Le Blanc, Lisa Gabrielle Mark, Jed Perl and Harriet Senie.

Peter Bellew, *Calder*, Barcelona 1969.

David Bourdon, *Calder: Mobilist/Ringmaster/ Innovator*, New York 1980.

Maurice Bruzeau, *Calder à Saché*, Paris 1975.

Alexander Calder, *Animal Sketching*, Pelham, NY 1926.

Alexander Calder, 'A Water Ballet', *Theatre Arts Monthly*, vol.23, no.8, August 1939, pp.578–9.

Alexander Calder, *Calder: An Autobiography with Pictures*, New York 1966. Introduction by Jean Davidson.

Alexander Calder, 'Comment réaliser l'art?', *Abstraction-Création, Art Non Figuratif*, no.1, 1932, p.6.

Alexander Calder, 'Mobiles', in Myfanwy Evans (ed.), *The Painter's Object*, London 1937, pp.62–7.

Alexander Calder, 'Un 'Mobile', *Abstraction-Création, Art Non Figuratif, no.2*, 1933, p.7.

Alexander Calder, 'Voici une petite histoire de mon cirque', *Permanence du Cirque*, Paris 1952.

Alexander Calder, 'What Abstract Art Means to Me', *Bulletin of the Museum of Modern Art*, vol.18, no.3, Spring 1951, pp.8–9.

Calder: After the War, exh. cat., Pace London, London 2013. Texts by Norman Foster and Barbara Rose. Chronology by Alexander S.C. Rower.

Calder: Mobiles & Stabiles, exh. cat., Galerie Maeght, Paris 1950. Texts by Henri Hoppenot, Henri Laugier, Fernand Léger and James Johnson Sweeney.

John Canaday, 'The Alexander Calder Problem', *New York Times*, 8 November 1964, X21.

Giovanni Carandente, *Calder*, Milan 1983.

Giovanni Carandente, *Teodelapio: Alexander Calder*, Milan 1996.

Judith Cass, 'Calder to Give His Circus at Dinner Party', *The Chicago Tribune*, 10 January 1935.

Samuel Taylor Coleridge, *The Rime of the Ancient Mariner*, New York 1946. Illustrated by Alexander Calder.

'Copper Wire Wins Place in Art Show', *New York Times*, 9 March 1928, p.11.

Jean Davidson, 'Four Calders', *Art in America*, vol.50, no.4, Winter 1962, pp.68–73.

Gualtieri di San Lazzaro (ed.), *Homage to Alexander Calder*, special issue of *XXe siècle Review*, Paris 1972. Texts by Giovanni Carandente, Charles Chabound, Jean Davidson, Pierre Descargues, Jacques Dupin, Pierre Gueguen, Stanley William Hayter, Alain Jouffroy, Gilbert Lascault, Charles Daniel Lelong, Yvon Taillandier and Patrick Waldberg.

Albert E. Elsen, *Alexander Calder: A Retrospective Exhibition – Works from 1925–1974*, exh. cat., Museum of Contemporary Art Chicago, Chicago 1974. Foreword by Stephen Prokopoff.

Fables of Aesop According to Sir Roger L'Estrange. With Fifty Drawings by Alexander Calder, Paris 1931. Illustrated by Alexander Calder.

Catherine Blanton Freedberg, *The Spanish Pavillion at the Paris World's Fair*, New York 1986.

Sebastiá Gasch, 'El circ d'un escultor', *Mirador*, no.191, 29 September 1932.

Michael Gibson, *Calder*, London 1988.

Siegfried Giedion, 'The Hammock and Alexander Calder', *Interiors*, vol.106, no.10, May 1947, pp.100–104.

Carola Giedon-Welcker, *Alexander Calder: Retrospektive*, exh. cat., Galerie Maeght, Zürich 1973.

Carmen Giménez and Alexander S.C. Rower (eds.), *Calder: Gravity and Grace*, exh. cat., Fundación del Museo Guggenheim, Bilbao 2003. Text by Francisco Calvo Serraller.

Amy Goldin, 'Alexander Calder, 1898–1976', *Art in America*, vol.65, no.2, March–April 1977, pp.70–73.

Dorothy Grafly, 'Alexander Calder: Creator of Moving Forms in Space', *American Artist*, vol.15, no.8, October 1951, pp.36–9, 69–70.

Cleve Gray, 'Calder's Circus', *Art in America*, vol.72, no.5, October 1964, pp.20–48.

Clement Greenberg, 'Alexander Calder: Sculpture, Constructions, Jewelry, Toys, and Drawings', *The Nation*, no.157, 23 October 1943, p.480.

Howard Greenfeld, *The Essential Alexander Calder*, New York 2003.

Pedro E. Guerrero, *Calder at Home: The Joyous Environment of Alexander Calder*, New York 1998.

Nicholas Guppy, *Calder*, exh. cat., Kettle's Yard, Cambridge 1980.

Margaret Calder Hayes, *Three Alexander Calders: A Family Memoir*, Middlebury VT 1977.

Elizabeth Hawes, 'More than Modern—Wiry Art', *Charm*, vol.9, no.3, April 1928., pp.47, 68.

Geoffrey T. Hellman, 'Calder Revisited', *New Yorker*, 1 November 1976, pp.163–78.

Geoffrey T. Hellman, 'Everything is Mobile', *New Yorker*, 4 October 1941, pp.25–33.

'International Artist Pays Visit to Concord', *The Concord Herald*, vol.3, no.24, 16 June 1932.

Katharine Kuh, *The Artist's Voice: Talks with Seventeen Artists*, New York 1962.

Carolyn Lanchner, *Joan Miró*, exh. cat., Museum of Modern Art, New York 1993.

Harald Lechenperg, 'Atelierfest am Montparnasse', *Illustrierte Zeitung* [Liepzig], 29 August 1929.

Legrand-Chabrier, 'Un petit cirque a domicile', *Candide*, no.171, 23 June 1927, p.7.

Jean Lipman, *Calder's Universe*, exh. cat., Whitney Museum of American Art, New York 1976.

Jean Lipman and Nancy Foote (eds.), *Calder's Circus*, New York 1972.

Bernice Winslow Mancewicz, *Alexander Calder: A Pictorial Essay*, Grand Rapids, MI 1969.

Joan M. Marter, *Alexander Calder*, Cambridge 1991.

Joan M. Marter, 'Alexander Calder at the Art Students League', *American Art Review*, vol.4, no.5, May 1978, pp.54–61, 117–18.

Joan M. Marter, 'Alexander Calder: Cosmic Imagery and the Use of Scientific Instruments', *Arts Magazine*, vol.53, no.2, October 1978, pp.108–13.

Joan M. Marter, 'Alexander Calder's Stabiles: Monumental Public Sculpture in America', *American Art Journal*, vol.11, no.3, July 1979, pp.75–85.

Joan M. Marter, 'The Engineer behind Calder's art', *Mechanical Engineering*, vol.120, no.12, December 1998, pp.52–7.

Joan M. Marter, 'The Legacy of Alexander Calder', *Sculpture*, vol.17, no.6, July–August 1998, pp.30–35.

'Martha Graham and Dance Group', *Dance Observer*, April 1936.

André Masson, 'L'atelier de Calder', *Cahiers d'Art*, vol.24, no.2, 1949, pp.274–80.

Thomas M. Messer, *Alexander Calder: A Retrospective Exhibition*, exh. cat., Solomon R. Guggenheim Museum, New York 1964.

Susanne Meyer-Büser (ed.), *Alexander Calder: Avant-Garde in Motion*, exh. cat., Kunstsammlungen Nordrhein-Westfalen, Munich 2013. Texts by Marion Ackermann, Daniela Hahn, Susanne Meyer-Büser, Alexander S.C. Rower and Gryphon Rue Rower-Upjohn.

New York Herald [Paris], 21 May 1929.

Eric Newton, 'A Critic Wiretaps Alexander Calder', *New York Times Magazine*, 10 August 1952, pp.16–18.

Robert Osborn, 'A Conversation with Alexander Calder', *Art in America*, vol.57, July–August 1969, p.31.

Robert Osborn, 'Calder's International Monuments', *Art in America*, vol.57, no.2, March–April 1969, pp.32–49.

Murdock Pemberton, 'Calder's Circus', *New Yorker*, 7 December 1929, pp.24–5.

Murdock Pemberton, 'The Art Galleries', *New Yorker*, 3 March 1928, p.91.

Arnauld Pierre, *Calder: La sculpture en movement*, Paris 1996.

Arnauld Pierre, *Calder: Mouvement et Réalité*, Paris 2009.

Hickman Powell, 'His Elephants Don't Drink', *The World*, 18 January 1931.

Marla Prather and Arnauld Pierre, *Alexander Calder: 1898–1976*, exh. cat., National Gallery of Art, Washington D.C., London and New Haven 1998. Chronology by Alexander S.C. Rower.

Georges Raillard, *Miró: Ceci est la couleur de mes rêves: entretiens avec Georges Raillard*, Paris 1977.

Paul Recht, 'Dans le mouvement, les sculptures mouvantes', *Mouvement*, no.1, June 1933, p.49.

Pierre Restany, 'L'autre Calder', *Art International*, vol.3, nos.5–6, 1959, pp.46–7.

George Rickey, 'Calder in London', *Arts Magazine*, vol.36, no.10, September 1962, pp.22–7.

Selden Rodman, *Conversations with Artists*, New York 1957.

Mark Rosenthal, *The Surreal Calder*, exh. cat., The Menil Collection, Houston TX, London and New Haven 2005. Chronology by Alexander S.C. Rower.

Alexander S.C. Rower, 'Calder and Lipman: A Friendship', *Art in America*, March 2013, pp.55–9.

Alexander S.C. Rower (ed.), *Calder by Matter*, Paris 2013. Texts by Jed Perl and John T. Hill.

Alexander S.C. Rower (ed.), *Calder: Sculptor of Air*, exh. cat., Palazzo delle Esposizioni, Milan 2009. Texts by Giovanni Carandente, Daniela Lancioni, Jed Perl, Terry Erskine Roth, Alexander S.C. Rower and Judith Farley Upjohn.

Alexander S.C. Rower, *Calder Sculpture*, New York 1998.

Alexander S.C. Rower and Holton Rower (eds.), *Calder Jewelry*, New York 2007. Texts by Jane Adlin and Mark Rosenthal. Photographs by Maria Robledo.

John Russell, 'Alexander Calder, Leading U.S. Artist, Dies', *New York Times*, 12 November 1976, A1, D14.

Jean-Paul Sartre, 'Les Mobiles de Calder' [French], in *Alexander Calder: Mobiles, Stabiles, Constellations*, exh. cat., Galerie Louis Carré, Paris 1946, pp.9–19.

Elmer E. Scott, *The P-culiar Dog or, The Piddling Pup*, New York 2001. Illustrated by Alexander Calder.

'Seeing the Circus with "Sandy" Calder', *National Police Gazette*, 23 May 1925, p.14.

Dorothy Seiberling, 'Calder, his Gyrating "Mobile" Art Wins International Fame and Prizes', *Life*, vol.33, no.8, 25 August 1952, pp.83–90.

Joan Simon and Brigette Léal, *Alexander Calder: The Paris Years*, 1926–1933, exh. cat., Whitney Museum of American Art and Centre George Pompidou, London and New Haven 2008. Texts by Quentin Bajac, Annie Cohen-Solal, Pepe Karmel, Carol Mancusi-Ungaro, Eleonora Nagy, Henry Petroski, Arnauld Pierre and Alexander S. C. Rower.

'Speaking of Pictures', *Life*, vol.17, no.14, 2 October 1944, pp.12–14.

L. Joy Sperling, 'Calder in Paris: The Circus and Surrealism', *Journal of the Archives of American Art*, vol.28, no.2, 1988, pp.16–29.

L. Joy Sperling, 'The Popular Sources of Calder's Circus: The Humpty Dumpty Circus, Ringling Brothers and Barnum and Bailey, and the Cirque Medrano', *Journal of American Culture*, vol.17, no.4, Winter 1994, pp.1–14.

Sudden Brain Waves', *New Yorker*, 30 November 1929.

James Johnson Sweeney, *Alexander Calder*, exh. cat., Museum of Modern Art, New York 1943. Revised, enlarged, and issued as a monograph in 1951.

James Johnson Sweeney, 'Alexander Calder: Work and Play', Art in America, vol.44, no.4, Winter 1956–7, pp.8–13.

James Johnson Sweeney, *Mobiles by Alexander Calder*, exh. cat., Pierre Matisse Gallery, New York 1934.

James Johnson Sweeney, 'The Position of Alexander Calder', *Magazine of Art*, vol.37, no.5, May 1944, pp.180–3.

James Johnson Sweeney (ed.), *Three Young Rats, and Other Rhymes*, New York 1944. Illustrated by Alexander Calder.

David Sylvester, 'Mobiles and Stabiles by Alexander Calder', *Art News and Review*, vol.2, no.26, 27 January 1951, p.4.

Alex J. Taylor, 'Unstable Motives: Propaganda, Politics, and the Late Work of Alexander Calder', *American Art*, vol.26, no.1, Spring 2012, pp.24–47.

Alex J. Taylor, 'The Calder Problem: Mobiles, Modern Taste, and Mass Culture', *Oxford Art Journal*, vol.37, no.1, 2014, pp.27–45.

'The Art Galleries: One Man and Some Wire', *New Yorker*, 14 December 1929, pp.44–6.

'The Wonders of Our Age: Portraits by Wire!' *American Sketch*, April 1928, p.36.

Charles Tracy, 'HO to AA, A Stage Playlet in Two Scenes', *Transition*, no.26, Winter 1937.

Lynne Warren, *Alexander Calder and Contemporary Art: Form, Balance, Joy*, exh. cat., Museum of Contemporary Art Chicago, London 2010. Texts by George Baker, Bryan Granger, Dominic Molon, Diana Nawi, Brooke Kamin Rapaport and Julie Rodrigues Wildholm.

Richard Wilbur (ed.), *A Bestiary*, New York 1955. Illustrated by Alexander Calder.

Barbara Zabel, *Calder's Portraits: A New Language*, exh. cat., National Portrait Gallery, Smithsonian Institution, Washington DC 2011.

Eric M. Zafran with Elizabeth Mankin Kornhauser and Cynthia Roman, *Calder in Connecticut*, exh. cat., Wadsworth Atheneum, Hartford 2000. Introduction by Alexander S.C. Rower. Afterword by Arthur Miller.

Exhibited works

The number in bold at the end of each entry refers to the page on which the work is illustrated.

Measurements are in centimetres, height before width and depth.

Galloping Horse
1926
Wire, wood and leather
22.9 × 48.3 × 12.7
Calder Foundation, New York. Mary Calder Rower Bequest, 2011
93

Red Horse and Green Sulky
1926
Wood, wire and paint
20.3 × 66 × 15.2
Calder Foundation, New York
92

Dog
1926–31
Wood, clothespin and wire
9.6 × 14.3 × 3.8
Calder Foundation, New York
95

Horse and Rider
1926–31
Wire, wood, cork, leather, velvet, string, rubber tube and lead
19.3 × 25.4 × 15.2
Calder Foundation, New York
94

Aerialist
c.1926–31
Wood, wire, leather, cloth, lead and string
35.6 × 14.3 × 3.8
Courtesy Jonathan O'Hara Gallery, New York
98

Acrobats
c.1927
Wire and wood
87.6 × 22.8 × 30.4
Calder Foundation, New York. Gift of Katherine Merle Smith Thomas in memory of Van Santvoord Merle Smith, Jr., 2010
110

Elephant
c.1927
Wire and wood
29.2 × 14.6 × 29.2
Calder Foundation, New York
100

Leopard
c.1927
Wire and wood
22.8 × 29.2 × 13.2
Calder Foundation, New York
101

Torrero
c.1927
Cloth, paper, wire, leather and pencil
38.1 × 39.4 × 15.2
Calder Foundation, New York
96–7

Helen Wills II
1928
Wire and wood
52.7 × 73.7 × 21.6
Calder Foundation, New York
108–9

Hercules and Lion
1928
Wire
152.4 × 121.9 × 61
Calder Foundation, New York
104–5

Horse
c.1928
Wire on wood base
70 × 80 × 18
Calder Foundation, New York
106–7

Singe
c.1928
Wood and wire
43.2 × 20.3 × 20.3
Calder Foundation, New York. Gift of Sandra Calder Davidson, 2010
99

Acrobat
1929
Wire and wood
73 × 40 × 10.8
Calder Foundation, New York
113

The Brass Family
1929
Brass wire and painted wood
170.2 × 104.5 × 22.5
Whitney Museum of American Art, New York. Gift of the artist. 69.255
114–15

Circus Scene
1929
Wire, wood and paint
127 × 118.7 × 46
Calder Foundation, New York
116

Goldfish Bowl
1929
Wire
40.6 × 38.1 × 15.2
Calder Foundation, New York
102–3

Le Lanceur de Poids
1929
Wire
82 × 73 × 13.3
Centre Pompidou, Paris, Musée national d'art moderne / Centre de création industrielle. Gift of the artist, 1966
111

Two Acrobats
1929
Wire on wood base
87.8 × 55 × 16.5
The Menil Collection, Houston
112

Acrobats
c.1929
Wire and rod
80.8 × 90.2 × 29.8
Calder Foundation, New York. Gift of Shawn Davidson, 2014
117

Aztec Josephine Baker
1930
Wire
134.6 × 25.4 × 22.9
Calder Foundation, New York
128–9

Amédée Ozenfant
c.1930
Wire
60 × 40 × 37
Larock Granoff Collection, Paris
134–5

Fernand Léger
c.1930
Wire
42 × 38
Private collection
131

Medusa
c.1930
Wire
31 × 43 × 24
Calder Foundation, New York
133

Joan Miró
c.1930
Wire
29 × 27
Private collection
130

Varèse
c.1930
Wire
38.1 × 29.8 × 31.8
Whitney Museum of American Art, New York. 50th Anniversary Gift of Mrs Louise Varèse in honor of Gertrude Vanderbilt Whitney. 80.25
132

Croisière
1931
Wire, wood and paint
94 × 58.4 × 58.4
Calder Foundation, New York
141

Many
1931
Ink on paper
49.7 × 64.8
The Museum of Modern Art, New York. Gift of Mr and Mrs Klaus G. Perls, 1968
143

Object with Red Ball
1931
Wood, sheet metal, rod, wire and paint
155.6 × 97.8 × 31.1
Calder Foundation, New York
147

Pantograph
1931
Wood, wire, sheet metal and motor
132 × 137 × 36
Moderna Museet, Stockholm. Donation 1961 from Louisa and Alexander Calder
139

Small Feathers
1931
Wire, wood, lead and paint
97.8 × 81.3 × 40.6
Calder Foundation, New York
148–9

Sphérique I
1931
Steel wire and brass with painted wood base
100.5 × 32.4 × 31.8
Whitney Museum of American Art, New York. Purchase, with funds from the Howard and Jean Lipman Foundation, Inc. 70.12
138

Two Spheres
1931
Wood, wire and paint, with motor
54.6 × 27.9
Calder Foundation, New York
144–5

Two Spheres Within a Sphere
1931
Wire, wood and paint
80 × 43.2 × 43.2
Calder Foundation, New York. Mary Calder Rower Bequest, 2011
140

Untitled
1931
Wood, iron, wire, aluminium, thread and paint
120 × 74.3 × 30
MACBA Collection. MACBA Foundation
146

Up, Over the Horizon
1931
Ink on paper
50 × 65.2
Hirshhorn Museum and Sculpture Garden, Smithsonian Institution, Washington, DC. The Joseph H. Hirshhorn Bequest, 1981
142

Big Black Disc
c.1931
Ink on paper
48.4 × 63.3
Hirshhorn Museum and Sculpture Garden, Smithsonian Institution, Washington, DC. The Joseph H. Hirshhorn Bequest, 1981
137

Study for a Mobile
c.1931
Ink on paper
48.3 × 63.4
Hirshhorn Museum and Sculpture Garden, Smithsonian Institution, Washington, DC. The Joseph H. Hirshhorn Bequest, 1981
136

Acrobat
1932
Pen and black ink on cream wove paper
35.6 × 48.3
Philadelphia Museum of Art. Purchased with the Thomas Skelton Harrison Fund, 1941
124

Man on Ladder
1932
Ink on paper
76 × 55.8
Calder Foundation, New York
126

On the High Wire
1932
Pen and ink on paper
51 × 62.9
Whitney Museum of American Art, New York. Gift of Howard and Jean Lipman, 81.23.3
127

Tightrope Artist
1932
Pen and black ink on cream wove paper
35.7 × 48.1
Philadelphia Museum of Art. Purchased with the Thomas Skelton Harrison Fund, 1941
125

Small Sphere and Heavy Sphere
1932/3
Iron, wood, cord, thread, rod, paint and impedimenta
317.5 high; dimensions variable
Calder Foundation, New York. Mary Calder Rower Bequest, 2011
150–1

Machine motorisée
1933
Wood, wire and paint, with motor
95.3 × 50 × 48.9
Calder Foundation, New York
152

Black Frame
1934
Wood, sheet metal, tubing, rod, wire and paint, with motor
94 × 94 × 61
Calder Foundation, New York
160–1

Red, White, Black and Brass
1934
Sheet metal, rod, wire, brass, lead and paint
287 × 172.7 × 134.6
Calder Foundation, New York
153

Red and Yellow Vane
1934
Sheet metal, rod, wire, lead and paint
175.3 × 203.2 × 71.1
Calder Foundation, New York
154–5

Little Blue Panel
1934
Wood, wire and paint, with motor
48.2 × 38.1 × 24.7
Wadsworth Atheneum Museum of Art, Hartford, CT. Purchased through the gift of Henry and Walter Keney
162–3

A Universe
1934
Painted iron pipe, steel wire, motor and wood with string
102.9 × 76.2
The Museum of Modern Art, New York. Gift of Abby Aldrich Rockefeller (by exchange), 1934. Accession number: 163.1934
156

Untitled
c.1934
Pipe, rod, wood, wire, paint and string
114.5 × 94
Calder Foundation, New York
158–9

The Spider
c.1935–7
Metal and paint
104 × 89 × .7
Scottish National Gallery of Modern Art, Edinburgh
157

Mobile
Mid-1930s
Metal, wood, wire and string
150 × 200 × 200
Tate. Lent from a private collection 1992
180–1

Blue Panel
1936
Plywood, sheet metal, rod, wire, string and paint
167.1 × 92.1 × 94
Calder Foundation, New York
165

The Orange Panel
1936
Sheet metal, wire, wood paint and motor
91.4 × 121.9 × 22.9
Private collection
164

Red Panel
1936
Plywood, sheet metal, tubing, rod, wood, wire, string and paint
274.3 × 152.4 × 111.8
Calder Foundation, New York
167

Red Panel
1936
Plywood, sheet metal, rod, wood, string and paint
121.9 × 76.2 × 61
Calder Foundation, New York
171

Snake and the Cross
1936
Sheet metal, wood, rod, wire, string and paint
205.7 × 129.5 × 111.8
Calder Foundation, New York
168

Tightrope
1936
Wood, wire, rod, lead and paint
115.6 × 69.9 × 351.8
Calder Foundation, New York
172–3

Form Against Yellow
1936
Painted sheet metal, painted wood, steel rod and wire
123.2 × 82.6 × 77.5
Hirshhorn Museum and Sculpture Garden, Smithsonian Institution, Washington, DC. Gift of Joseph H. Hirshhorn, 1972
169

White Panel
1936
Plywood, sheet metal, tubing, wood, rod, wire, string and paint
214.6 × 119.4 × 129.5
Calder Foundation, New York. Mary Calder Rower Bequest, 2011
166

Petit Panneau Bleu
c.1936
Wood, painted sheet metal, steel wire and motor
33.5 × 49 × 43
Centre Pompidou, Paris, Musée national d'art moderne / Centre de création industrielle. Dation of the Estate of the Artist, 1983
174

Untitled
1937
Plywood, wood, rod, wire, string and paint
163.8 × 91.4 × 73.7
Calder Foundation, New York
170

Untitled
1937
Painted metal, steel rods and wire
91.5 h
The Mayor Gallery, London
178–9

Dancers and Sphere
1938
[New York World's Fair 1939, maquette]
Painted wood, sheet metal, wire, with motor
55 × 66 × 35
Galerie Natalie Seroussi
175

Four Elements, also known as 'Model for the Four Elements'
1938
Maquette for 1939 New York World's Fair
Metal plate, string and steel wire
42 × 64 × 30
Moderna Museet, Stockholm
176

Untitled
1938
Maquette for 1939 New York World's Fair
Sheet metal, wood, wire, string and paint
35.5 × 49.5 × 23.5
Calder Foundation, New York
177

Sphere Pierced by Cylinders
1939
Wire and paint
210.8 × 86.4 × 109.2
Calder Foundation, New York
182

Hourglass
1941
Wire, lead and paint
152.4 × 55.9 × 41.9
The Lipman Family Foundation
183

Vertical Foliage
1941
Sheet metal, wire and paint
135.9 × 167.6
Calder Foundation, New York
184–5

Black Spot on Gimbals
1942
Wire, wood and paint
40.6 × 48.3 × 21.6
Calder Foundation, New York
186

Red Sticks
c.1942
Wood, wire, string and paint
120 × 157
Calder Foundation, New York
187

Black Constellation
1943
Ebony and wire
43 × 105.5 × 20.3
Calder Foundation, New York. Gift of Sandra Calder Davidson in memory of Jean Davidson, 2014
190

Constellation
1943
Wood, wire and paint
83.8 × 91.4 × 35.6
Calder Foundation, New York
189

Constellation with Two Pins
1943
Wood, wire and paint
60 × 44.5 × 43.2
Calder Foundation, New York
191

Morning Star
1943
Painted sheet steel, steel wire, wood and paint
194.8 × 122.8 × 116
The Museum of Modern Art, New York. Gift of the artist, 1966. Accession number: 848.1966
188

Untitled (Mobile with N Degrees of Freedom)
1946
Sheet metal, wire and paint
28.6 × 124.5 × 94
Calder Foundation, New York. Purchase, 2009
192–3

Gamma
1947
Painted sheet metal and steel wire
147.3 × 213.3 × 91.4
Collection of Jon A. Shirley
194–5

Black Widow
1948
Wire and painted metal
325.1 × 251.5
Instituto de Arquitetos do Brasil – Departamento de São Paulo. Gift of the artist, 1948
198–9

Snow Flurry I
1948
Painted steel sheet and steel wire
238.7 × 208.8
The Museum of Modern Art, New York. Gift of the artist, 1966. Accession number: 390.1966.a c
197

Untitled
1948
Sheet metal and wire
44.4 × 172.7 × 10.4
Calder Foundation, New York
196

Triple Gong
c.1948
Brass, sheet metal, wire and paint
99.1 × 190.5 × 7
Calder Foundation, New York
200

Blériot
1949
Sheet metal, wire and iron rod
101 × 80
Private collection
201

Red Gongs
1950
Painted aluminium, brass, steel rod and wire
152.4 × 365.8
The Metropolitan Museum of Art. Fletcher Fund, 1955 (55.181.1a f)
202

Streetcar
1951
Sheet steel, brass, wire and paint
106.7 × 294.6
The Art Institute of Chicago. Gift of Florence May Marx and Samuel A. Marx
204–5

Triple Gong
1951
Painted steel, painted wire and brass
78.7 × 172.7
National Gallery of Art, Washington. Gift of Mr. and Mrs. Klaus G. Perls, 1966. 1966.120.27
203

Antennae with Red and Blue Dots
c.1953
Aluminium and steel wire
111.1 × 128.3 × 128.3
Tate. Purchased 1962
206–7

Descending Spines
1956
Sheet metal, wire and paint
147.3 × 182.9 × 121.9
Calder Foundation, New York
208

Nineteen White Discs
1961
Sheet metal, paint and steel wire
114.3 × 134.6 × 134.6
Collection Museum of Contemporary Art Chicago. Gift of Ruth Horwich, 1991.91
209

Chef d'orchestre
1966
Painted steel
Dimensions variable
Nancy E. and Peter C. Meinig, Courtesy of Edward Tyler Nahem Fine Art, New York
210–11

Copyright Credits

All works by and likenesses of Alexander Calder © 2015 Calder Foundation, New York/DACS, London.

© Earle Brown Music Foundation pp.73 (both), 74

© Gerard Byrne p.16 (top)

© 2015 Calder Foundation, New York/DACS, London/© Estate of Brassaï – RMN-Grand Palais pp.120, 121, 122–3

© 2015 Calder Foundation, New York/DACS, London/© Paolo Gasparini pp.88 (detail) 90–1

© 2015 Calder Foundation, New York/DACS, London pp.24 (both), 25 (top), 52 (both), 81 (left) 224 (top left)

© 2015 Calder Foundation, New York/DACS, London/© Ugo Mulas Heirs p.83

© 2015 Calder Foundation, New York/DACS, London/© Succession Picasso/DACS, London 2015/ © Christian & Klaus Herdeg, Zürich/New York pp.44–5

© 2015 Calder Foundation, New York/DACS, London/© RMN-Grand Palais – Gestion droit d'auteur André Kertész pp.118, 119 (both)

© 2015 Calder Foundation, New York/DACS, London/© Estate of John G. Ross pp.76 (detail), 78–9

© 2015 Calder Foundation, New York/DACS, London/© Estate of Ezra Stoller pp.20 (detail) 22–3

© 2015 Calder Foundation, New York/DACS, London/Courtesy Robert Storr hardback endpapers and inside paperback cover

© 2015 Calder Foundation, New York/DACS, London/© Estate of Soichi Sunami pp.26 (bottom), 27 (top)

© 2015 Calder Foundation, New York/DACS, London/© Agnès Varda pp.6, 224 (bottom left) frontispiece

© 2015 Calder Foundation, New York/DACS, London/© Marc Vaux pp.212 (detail) 214–15, 220 (far left)

© Asta Gröting p.16 (bottom left)

© Hiro p.70

© Successió Miró/ADAGP, Paris and DACS, London 2015 p.48

© Tony Oursler p.17

© Succession Picasso/DACS, London 2015/© RMN – Gestion droit d'auteur François Kollar p.47 (right)

Portinari, Candido/© DACS 2015 p.58

© RMN – Gestion droit d'auteur François Kollar p.49

© Estate of Franz Weissmann p.63

© 'The World of Lygia Clark' Cultural Association p.64

Photo Credits

All images courtesy Calder Foundation, New York/Art Resource, New York, unless stated otherwise below.

Archives of American Art, Smithsonian Institution, Washington DC p.27 (bottom)

The Art Archive/The Solomon R. Guggenheim Foundation/Art Resource, New York p.39

Courtesy the artist p.17

Courtesy the artist and carlier | gebauer p.16 (bottom left)

Mark Babushkin p.98

Courtesy Earle Brown Music Foundation pp.73 (both), 74

Courtesy Earle Brown Music Foundation. Photo: Hiro p.70

Courtesy Earle Brown Music Foundation. Photo: Bruce Kiefer pp.66 (detail), 68–9, 71, 72, 210–11

Christopher Burke Studios p.131

Courtesy Calder Foundation, New York/Art Resource, New York. Photo: Paolo Gasparini pp.88 (detail), 90–1

Courtesy Calder Foundation, New York/Art Resource, New York. Photo: Hugo P. Herdeg pp.42 (detail), 44–5

Courtesy Calder Foundation, New York/Art Resource, New York. Photo: Herbert Matter pp.24 (both), 25 (top), 52 (both), 81 (left), 224 (top left)

Courtesy Calder Foundation, New York/Art Resource, New York. Photo: Ugo Mulas p.83

Courtesy Calder Foundation, New York/Art Resource, New York © Centre Pompidou, MNAM-Bibliothèque Kandinsky – Fonds Marc Vaux p.220 (far left)

Courtesy Calder Foundation, New York/Art Resource, New York. Photo: John G. Ross pp.76 (detail), 78–9

Courtesy Calder Foundation, New York/Art Resource, New York. Photo: Ezra Stoller pp.20 (detail), 22–3

Courtesy Calder Foundation, New York/Art Resource, New York. Photo: Sasha Stone p.217

Courtesy Calder Foundation, New York © The Museum of Modern Art, New York. Photo: Soichi Sunami p.27 (top)

Courtesy Calder Foundation, New York/Art Resource, New York. Photo: Agnès Varda pp.6, 224 (bottom left), frontispiece

© The Art Institute of Chicago pp.204–5

© Museum of Contemporary Art Chicago. Photo: Nathan Keay p.209

Sheldan C. Collins p.183

Library of Congress, Prints & Photographs Division, Gottscho-Schleisner Collection [LC-G613- 35354] p.46

Aldo Durazzi for Dufoto Agency, courtesy Fondazione Teatro dell'Opera di Roma, Archivio Storico p.86

Hirshhorn Museum and Sculpture Garden, Smithsonian Institution, Washington, DC. Photo: Cathy Carver pp.136, 137, 142

Hirshhorn Museum and Sculpture Garden, Smithsonian Institution, Washington, DC. Photo: Lee Stalsworth p.169

Courtesy Galerie Larock-Granoff p.135

Courtesy Lisson Gallery. Photo: Ken Adlard p.16 (top)

Sabine Lubenow/LOOK-foto p.14

MACBA. Museu d'Art Contemporani de Barcelona p.146

Courtesy The Mayor Gallery p.179

Courtesy Menil Collection, Houston. Photo: Paul Hester p.112

© 2015 The Metropolitan Museum of Art/Art Resource/Scala, Florence p.202

© Ministère de la Culture – Médiathèque du Patrimoine, Dist. RMN-Grand Palais/François Kollar pp.47 (right), 49

Successió Miró archive pp.48, 130

José Moscardi pp.54 (detail), 56–7, 60

© 2015 The Museum of Modern Art, New York/Scala, Florence pp.40 (bottom), 143, 156, 188, 197

© 2015 The Museum of Modern Art, New York/Scala, Florence. Photo: Soichi Sunami p.26 (bottom)

Courtesy galerie natalie seroussi p.175

Halley Pacheco de Oliveira p.61

Courtesy Philadelphia Museum of Art pp.124, 125

© Centre Pompidou, MNAM-Bibliothèque Kandinsky – Fonds Marc Vaux pp.212 (detail), 214–15

© Centre Pompidou, MNAM-CCI, Dist. RMN-Grand Palais/Georges Meguerditchian p.34 (top)

© Centre Pompidou, MNAM-CCI, Dist. RMN-Grand Palais/Adam Rzepka p.174

Courtesy João Candido Portinari p.58

Jonathan Rome p.16 (bottom right)

© 2015 Scala, Florence p.18

© 2015 Scala, Florence – courtesy the Ministero Beni e Att. Culturali p.15 (bottom)

Moderna Museet, Stockholm pp.139, 176

© 2015 Tate pp.180–1, 206–7, cover

Wadsworth Atheneum. Photo: Allen Phillips p.163

Courtesy National Gallery of Art, Washington DC p.203

Courtesy Waltraud Weissmann p.63

© Dean and Chapter of Westminster p.15 (top)

© Whitney Museum, New York pp.37, 127, 138

© Whitney Museum, New York. Photo: Sheldan C. Collins p.132

© Whitney Museum, New York. Photo: Jerry L. Thompson p.115

Courtesy 'The World of Lygia Clark' Cultural Association p.64

Index

Page numbers in *italic* type refer to illustrations.

Supporting Tate

Tate relies on a large number of supporters – individuals, foundations, companies and public sector sources – to enable it to deliver its programme of activities, both on and off its gallery sites. This support is essential in order for Tate to acquire works of art for the Collection, run education, outreach and exhibition programmes, care for the Collection in storage and enable art to be displayed, both digitally and physically, inside and outside Tate. Donations make a real difference and enable others to enjoy Tate and its Collection both now and in the future. There are a variety of ways in which you can help support Tate and also benefit as a UK or US taxpayer. Please contact us at:

Development Office
Tate
Millbank
London SWIP 4RG
Tel: +44 (0)20 7887 4900
Fax: +44 (0)20 7887 8098

Tate Americas Foundation
520 West 27 Street Unit 404
New York, NY 10001
USA

Tel: 001 212 643 2818
Fax: 001 212 643 1001

Tate Trustees
Lionel Barber
Tom Bloxham, MBE
The Lord Browne of Madingley, FRS, FREng (Chairman)
Mala Gaonkar
Maja Hoffmann
Lisa Milroy
Elisabeth Murdoch
Franck Petitgas
Dame Seona Reid, DBE
Hannah Rothschild
Monisha Shah
Gareth Thomas

Tate Foundation Trustees and Honorary Members
Abigail Baratta
Joseph P Baratta II*
Victoria Barnsley, OBE
John Botts, CBE*
Mrs James Brice
The Lord Browne of Madingley, FRS, FREng
Susan Burns
Christina Chandris
Melanie Clore
Sir Howard Davies
Dame Vivien Duffield
George Economou
Edward Eisler*
Maryam Eisler
Sasan Ghandehari
Noam Gottesman
Oliver Haarmann
Peter Kellner
The Hon Mrs Rita McAulay
Ronald McAulay
Scott Mead*
Mandy Moross
Elisabeth Murdoch
Lord Myners of Truro, CBE
Marilyn Ofer
Franck Petitgas (Chairman)*
Simon Palley*
John Porter
Lady Ritblat
Sir John Ritblat
Emmanuel Roman*
Dame Theresa Sackler, DBE
The Rt Hon Sir Timothy Sainsbury
Sir Anthony Salz*
Sir Nicholas Serota*
Peter Simon
Jon Snow
Lord Stevenson of Coddenham, CBE*
Mercedes Stoutzker
John Studzinski, CBE
Ian Taylor
Lance Uggla
Viktor Vekselberg
Sir David Verey, CBE
Anita Zabludowicz

* Executive Committee

Tate Members Council
Brian Chadwick
Chris Chinaloy
Hannah Collins
Dominic Harris
Suwin Lee
Rachel Lloyd
Amanda Pinto
Miranda Sawyer
Neil Scott
Jon Snow (Chair)
Simon Wilson
Alan Yates

Tate Americas Foundation Trustees
Frances Bowes
Estrellita Brodsky
James Chanos
Henry Christensen III
Tiqui Atencio Demirdjian (Ex-officio)
Jeanne Donovan Fisher (Chair)
Ella Fontanals-Cisneros
Glenn Fuhrman
Noam Gottesman
Robert Rennie (Ex-officio)
John Studzinski, CBE
Marjorie Susman
Juan Carlos Verme

Donors to The Tate Modern Project
Abigail and Joesph Baratta
Blavatnik Family Foundation
Lauren and Mark Booth
The Deborah Loeb Brice Foundation
The Lord Browne of Madingley, FRS, FREng
John and Christina Chandris
James Chanos
Paul Cooke
The Roger De Haan Charitable Trust
Ago Demirdjian and Tiqui Atencio Demirdjian
Department for Culture, Media and Sport
George Economou
Edward and Maryam Eisler
English Partnerships
Mrs Donald B. Fisher
Jeanne Donovan Fisher
Mala Gaonkar
The Ghandehari Foundation
Thomas Gibson in memory of Anthea Gibson
Lydia and Manfred Gorvy
Noam Gottesman
The Hayden Family Foundation
Maja Hoffmann/LUMA Foundation
Peter and Maria Kellner
Madeleine Kleinwort
Catherine Lagrange
Pierre Lagrange
London Development Agency
Allison and Howard W. Lutnick
Donald B. Marron
Anthony and Deirdre Montagu
Elisabeth Murdoch
Eyal Ofer Family Foundation
Maureen Paley
Midge and Simon Palley
Daniel and Elizabeth Peltz
Catherine and Franck Petitgas
Barrie and Emmanuel Roman
The Dr Mortimer and Theresa Sackler Foundation
The Sackler Trust
John J Studzinski, CBE
Tate Americas Foundation
Tate Members
The Uggla Family
Viktor Vekselberg
Nina and Graham Williams
The Wolfson Foundation
and those who wish to remain anonymous

Tate Modern Benefactors and Major Donors
We would like to acknowledge and thank the following benefactors who have supported Tate Modern prior to June 2015.

Sirine and Ahmad Abu Ghazaleh
Ghazwa and Walid Abu-Suud
Carolyn Alexander
Basil and Raghida Al-Rahim Art Fund
Abdullah Al Turki
Fernando Luis Alvarez
The Ampersand Foundation
Gregory Annenberg Weingarten and the Annenberg Foundation
The Fagus Anstruther Memorial Trust
Art Fund
Art Mentor Foundation Lucerne
Arts and Humanities Research Council
Arts Council England
Artworkers Retirement Society
Charles Asprey
Marwan T Assaf
The Estate of Mr Edgar Astaire
averda
Gillian Ayres
John Baldessari
Lionel Barber
The Estate of Peter and Caroline Barker-Mill
The Barker-Mill Foundation
The Barns-Graham Charitable Trust
Corinne Bellow Charity
Rosamond Bernier
Dorothy Berwin and Dominique Levy
Big Lottery Fund
Blavatnik Family Foundation
Pontus Bonnier
John C Botts, CBE
Louise Bourgeois
Frances Bowes
Frank Bowling, Rachel Scott, Benjamin and Sacha Bowling, Marcia and Iona Scott
Sir Alan and Lady Bowness
Pierre Brahm
Ivor Braka
The Estate of Dr Marcella Louis Brenner
British Council
Rory and Elizabeth Brooks Foundation
The Estate of Mrs Rachel Caro
Mr and Mrs Nicolas Cattelain
Roger Cazalet
The Trustees of the Chantrey Bequest
Henry Christensen III
Clore Duffield Foundation
The Clothworkers' Foundation
Borja Coca
Robert T. Coffland
R and S Cohen Foundation
Steven Cohen
Sadie Coles Gallery
Contemporary Art Society
Isabelle and John Corbani
Corvi-Mora
Douglas S Cramer
Thomas Dane Gallery
Thomas Dane Ltd
Dimitris Daskalopoulos
Tiqui Atencio Demirdjian and Ago Demirdjian
Department for Business, Innovation and Skills
Department for Culture, Media and Sport
Paul Dodds
Anthony and Anne d'Offay
Peter Doig
Joe and Marie Donnelly
Jeanne Donovan Fisher
Jytte Dresing, The Merla Art Foundation, Dresing Collection
Stephen Edge
Stefan Edlis and Gael Neeson
EDP - Energias de Portugal, S.A.
Tony Edwards
The John Ellerman Foundation
Ibrahim El-Salahi
Carla Emil and Rich Silverstein
Tracey Emin
European Union
Eykyn Maclean
Esmée Fairbairn Collections Fund
The Estate of Maurice Farquharson
Ronald and Frayda Feldman
HRH Princess Firyal of Jordan
Wendy Fisher
The Fischinger Trust, Long Beach, CA
Dr Kira and Neil Flanzraich
Eric and Louise Franck
Jay Franke and David Herro
The Estate of Lucian Freud
Erica and Alex Friedman
Frith Street Gallery
Froehlich Foundation, Stuttgart
Anna Fudge and Matthew Fudge
Glenn and Amanda Fuhrman
Gagosian Gallery
Mala Gaonkar
Garcia Family Foundation
Johanna and Leslie J. Garfield
Victoria Gelfand Magalhães and Pedro Magalhães
The Getty Foundation
The Hon HMT Gibson's Charity Trust
Thomas Gibson
Liam Gillick

Milly and Arne Glimcher
Goethe-Institut
Nicholas and Judith Goodison
Marian Goodman Gallery
Douglas Gordon and Artangel
Lydia and Manfred Gorvy
Noam Gottesman
The Granville-Grossman Bequest
Sarah and Gerard Griffin
Guaranty Trust Bank Plc
Calouste Gulbenkian Foundation
Agnes Gund
The Estate of Mr John Haggart
Nigel Hall
Paul Hamlyn Foundation
Mark Hannam
Noriyuki Haraguchi
Hauser & Wirth
Bowness, Hepworth Estate
Heritage Lottery Fund
Mauro Herlizka
The Estate of Miss Grace Patricia Hills
Roger Hiorns
Damien Hirst
David Hockney
The Estate of Mrs Mimi Hodgkin
Karin und Uwe Hollweg Stiftung
Michael Hue-Williams
Vicky Hughes and John A Smith
Huo Family Foundation (UK)
Leili Huth and Reza Asfar Kharaghan
Institut Françias
Iran Heritage Foundation
Amrita Jhaveri
Karpidas Family
Dr Martin Kenig
J. Patrick Kennedy and
Patricia A. Kennedy
Anne Simone Kleinman and
Thomas Wong
Leon Kossoff
Tomio Koyama Gallery
The Kreitman Foundation
Samuel H. Kress Foundation,
administered by the Foundation
of the American Institute for
Conservation
Andreas Kurtz
Kirby Laing Foundation
The Estate of Jay and Fran Landesman
The Leathersellers' Company
Charitable Fund
Agnès and Edward Lee
Legacy Trust UK
The Leverhulme Trust
Ruben Levi
Gemma Levine
Harris Lieberman
Timothy Llewellyn
London Organising Committee of the
Olympic Games and Paralympic
Games
The Loveday Charitable Trust
The Henry Luce Foundation
Luhring Augustine
LUMA Foundation
The Estate of Sir Edwin Manton
The Manton Foundation
Lord McAlpine of West Green
Fergus McCaffrey
The Andrew W Mellon Foundation
The Paul Mellon Centre for Studies in
British Art
Sir Geoffroy Millais
Mondriaan Fund, Amsterdam
The Henry Moore Foundation
Simon and Catriona Mordant
Daido Moriyama
Elisabeth Murdoch
The Estate of Mrs Jenifer Ann Murray
National Heritage Memorial Fund
The Embassy of the Netherlands
The Obayashi Foundation
Massimo Prelz Oltramonti
Oppenheimer Family
Matthew Orr and Sybill Robson Orr
Outset Contemporary Art Fund
Pace Gallery
Desmond Page
Irene Panagopoulos
The Paolozzi Foundation
Stephen and Yana Peel
Catherine Petitgas
Stanley Picker Trust
The Porter Foundation
Gilberto Pozzi
Alan Proudfoot
Mr Robert Randall
Laura Rapp and Jay Smith
Susan and Dennis Richard
Sir John Richardson
Craig Robins and Jackie Soffer
Nick and Alma Robson Foundation
Barrie and Emmanuel Roman
Keith and Kathy Sachs
The Dr Mortimer and Theresa Sackler
Foundation
Elchin Safarov and Dilyara
Allakhverdova
The Estate of Simon Sainsbury
Julião Sarmento
Matt Saunders
Schwab Charitable Fund
James Scott
Robert Scott
The Search Foundation
Stuart Shave / Modern Art, London
Edward Siskind
Candida and Rebecca Smith
Clive K Smith, OBE
The Estate of Mrs Freda Mary Snadow
The Donald R. Sobey Family
Zsolt Somlói and Kati Spengler
George Soros
Keren Souza Kohn,
Francesca Souza and Anya Souza
Sperone Westwater
Nicholas and Elodie Stanley
Mercedes and Ian Stoutzker
Swiss Arts Council Pro Helvetia
Tate 1897 Circle
Tate Africa Acquisitions Committee
Tate Americas Foundation
Tate Asia-Pacific Acquisitions
Committee
Tate International Council
Tate Latin American Acquisitions
Committee
Tate Members
Tate Middle East and North Africa
Acquisitions Committee
Tate North American Acquisitions
Committee
Tate Patrons
Tate Photography Acquisitions
Committee
Tate Russia and Eastern Europe
Acquisitions Committee
Tate South Asia Acquisitions
Committee
The Taylor Family Foundation
Terra Foundation for American Art
Textile Arts, Santa Fe
The Estate of Mr Nicholas Themans
Luis Tomasello
The Tretyakov Family Collection
V-A-C Foundation
Marie-Louise von Motesiczky
Charitable Trust
Andrew Walker
Wellcome Trust
James Welling
The Estate of Fred Williams
Jane and Michael Wilson
Samuel and Nina Wisnia
The Lord Leonard and Lady Estelle
Wolfson Foundation
Rosemary and Tony Yablon
Poju and Anita Zabludowicz
and those who wish to remain anonymous

Platinum Patrons

Mr Alireza Abrishamchi
Ghazwa Mayassi Abu-Suud
Mr Shane Akeroyd
Basil Alkazzi
Ryan Allen and Caleb Kramer
Mr and Mrs Edward Atkin, CBE
Raphael Auerbach and Suzanei
Archer, Palmarium Art AG
Rhona Beck
Beecroft Charitable Trust
Rory and Elizabeth Brooks
The Lord Browne of Madingley,
FRS, FREng
Karen Cawthorn Argenio
Beth and Michele Colocci
Mr Stephane Custot
Pascale Decaux
Elizabeth Esteve
Mr David Fitzsimons
The Flow Foundation
Edwin Fox Foundation
Mrs Lisa Garrison
David Giampaolo, Pi Capital
Hugh Gibson
Alexis and Anne-Marie Habib
Mr and Mrs Yan Huo
Mr Phillip Hylander
Yukiko Ito Pajot
Mrs Gabrielle Jungels-Winkler
Maria and Peter Kellner
Mr and Mrs Eskandar Maleki
Luigi Mazzoleni
Scott and Suling Mead
Pierre Tollis and Alexandra Mollof
Mr Donald Moore
Mary Moore
Jacqueline and Anthony Orsatelli
Simon and Midge Palley (Chair)
Damian and Maria Perl
Mr and Mrs Paul Phillips
Jill and Russell Platt
Mr Gilberto and Mrs Daniela Pozzi
Frances Reynolds
Simon and Virginia Robertson
Mr and Mrs Richard Rose
Mr and Mrs J Shafran
Mrs Andrée Shore
Maria and Malek Sukkar
Michael and Jane Wilson
Lady Wolfson of Marylebone
Chizuko Yoshida
Poju and Anita Zabludowicz
and those who wish to remain anonymous

Gold Patrons

Eric Abraham
Maria Adonyeva
Elena Bowes
Louise and Charlie Bracken
Nicolò Cardi
Matt Carey-Williams and
Donnie Roark
Melanie Clore
Mr Dónall Curtin
Harry G. David
Ms Miel de Botton
Mr Frank Destribats
Mrs Maryam Eisler
Kate Groes
Ms Nathalie Guiot
Nazli Hariri
Philipp Humm
Ms Natascha Jakobs
Tiina Lee
Fiona Mactaggart
Paul and Alison Myners
Reem Nassar
Mr Francis Outred
Marie-Laure Prevost
Mathew Prichard
Valerie Rademacher
Almine Ruiz-Picasso
Ralph Segreti
Carol Sellars
Mr and Mrs Stanley S. Tollman
Victoria Tollman O'Hana
Manuela and Iwan Wirth
Barbara Yerolemou
and those who wish to remain anonymous

Silver Patrons

Allahyar Afshar
Sharis Alexandrian
Mrs Malgosia Alterman
The Anson Charitable Trust
Toby and Kate Anstruther
Mr and Mrs Zeev Aram
Mrs Charlotte Artus
Ms Alexandra Aslaksen
Tim Attias
Trevor Barden
Peter Barham
Mrs Jane Barker
Oliver Barker
Mr Edward Barlow
Victoria Barnsley, OBE
Jim Bartos
Mr Harold Berg
Jody and Brian Berger
Lady Angela Bernstein
Madeleine Bessborough
Ms Karen Bizon
Janice Blackburn
Shoshana Bloch
David Blood and Beth Bisso
Mrs Sofia Bogolyubov
Mr Brian Boylan
Ivor Braka
Viscountess Bridgeman
The Broere Charitable Foundation
Mr Dan Brooke
Ben and Louisa Brown
Beverley Buckingham
Michael Burrell
Mrs Marlene Burston
Scott Button
Mrs Aisha Caan
Timothy and Elizabeth Capon
Mr Francis Carnwath and
Ms Caroline Wiseman
Countess Castle Stewart
Roger Cazalet
Lord and Lady Charles Cecil
Dr Peter Chocian
Frank Cohen
Mrs Jane Collins

Dr Judith Collins
Terrence Collis
Mr and Mrs Oliver Colman
Carole and Neville Conrad
Giles and Sonia Coode-Adams
Alastair Cookson
Cynthia Corbett
Mark and Cathy Corbett
Tommaso Corvi-Mora
Mr and Mrs Bertrand Coste
Kathleen Crook and James Penturn
James Curtis
Michael Cutting
Sir Howard Davies
Sir Roger and Lady De Haan
Giles de la Mare
Mr Damon and
The Hon Mrs de Laszlo
Maria de Madariaga
Anne Chantal Defay Sheridan
Marco di Cesaria
Simon C Dickinson Ltd
Liz and Simon Dingemans
Shari Dusansky
Joan Edlis
Lord and Lady Egremont
Sara Ellis
John Erle-Drax
Dr Nigel Evans
Stuart and Margaret Evans
Mrs Heather Farrar
David Fawkes
Mrs Margy Fenwick
Mr Bryan Ferry, CBE
The Sylvie Fleming Collection
Lt Commander Paul Fletcher
Katherine Francey Stables
Stephen Friedman
Mala Gaonkar
Mrs Joanna Gemes
Geoffrey and Julian Charitable Trust
Mr Mark Glatman
Ms Emily Goldner and
Mr Michael Humphries
Kate Gordon
Dimitri Goulandris
Penelope Govett
Judith and Richard Greer
Martyn Gregory
Mrs Kate Grimond
Richard and Odile Grogan
Mrs Helene Guerin-Llamas
Louise Hallett
Arthur Hanna
Mark Harris
Michael and Morven Heller
James Holland-Hibbert
Lady Hollick, OBE
Holtermann Fine Art
Jeff Horne
John Huntingford
Maxine Isaacs
Helen Janecek
Sarah Jennings
Mr Haydn John
Mr Michael Johnson
Mike Jones
Jay Jopling
Mrs Brenda Josephs
Tracey Josephs
Mr Joseph Kaempfer
Andrew Kalman
Ghislaine Kane
Ivan Katzen
Dr Martin Kenig
Mr David Ker
Nicola Kerr
Mr and Mrs Simon Keswick
Richard and Helen Keys
Sadru Kheraj
Mrs Mae Khouri
David Killick
Mr and Mrs James Kirkman
Brian and Lesley Knox
Tatiana Kovylina
Kowitz Trust
Mr and Mrs Herbert Kretzmer
Linda Lakhdhir
Ms Anna Lapshina
Simon Lee
Mr Gerald Levin
Leonard Lewis
Sophia and Mark Lewisohn
Mr Gilbert Lloyd
George Loudon
Mrs Elizabeth Louis
Mark and Liza Loveday
Catherine Lovell
Jeff Lowe
Alison Loyd
Daniella Luxembourg Art
Mrs Ailsa Macalister
Kate MacGarry
Anthony Mackintosh
Eykyn Maclean LLC
The Mactaggart Third Fund
Mrs Jane Maitland Hudson
Lord and Lady Marks
Marsh Christian Trust
Ms Fiona Mellish
Mrs R W P Mellish
Professor Rob Melville
Mr Alfred Mignano
Victoria Miro
Jan Mol
Lulette Monbiot
Mrs Bona Montagu
Mrs William Morrison
Ms Deborah Norton
Julian Opie
Pilar Ordovás
Desmond Page
Maureen Paley
Dominic Palfreyman
Michael Palin
Mrs Adelaida Palm
Stephen and Clare Pardy
Mrs Véronique Parke
Frans Pettinga
Trevor Pickett
Mr Alexander Platon
Mr Oliver Prenn
Susan Prevezer QC
Mr and Mrs Ryan Prince
James Pyner
Ivetta Rabinovich
Patricia Ranken
Bernadette Rankine
Mrs Phyllis Rapp
Dr Laurence Reed
The Reuben Foundation
Lady Ritblat
Ms Chao Roberts
David Rocklin
Frankie Rossi
Mr David V Rouch
Mr James Roundell
Mr Charles Roxburgh
Naomi Russell
Mr Alex Sainsbury and Ms Elinor Jansz
Mr Richard Saltoun
Mrs Cecilia Scarpa
Cherrill and Ian Scheer
Sylvia Scheuer
Mrs Cara Schulze
Hakon Runer and
Ulrike Schwarz-Runer
Ellen Shaprio
The Hon Richard Sharp
Neville Shulman, CBE
Ms Julia Simmonds
Paul and Marcia Soldatos
Mr Vagn Sørensen
Louise Spence
Mr Nicos Steratzias
Stacie Styles and Ken McCracken
Ayse Suleyman
Mrs Patricia Swannell
Mr James Swartz
The Lady Juliet Tadgell
Elaine Thomas
Anthony Thornton
Mr Henry Tinsley
Ian Tollett
Karen Townshend
Monica Tross
Andrew Tseng
Melissa Ulfane
Mrs and Mrs Petri Vainio
Mrs Cecilia Versteegh
Gisela von Sanden
Michelle Wafa
Audrey Wallrock
Sam Walsh AO
Stephen and Linda Waterhouse
Offer Waterman
Miss Cheyenne Westphal
Mr David Wood
Mr Douglas Woolf
and those who wish to remain anonymous

Young Patrons
Miss Noor Al-Rahim
Fahad Alrashid
HRH Princess Alia Al-Senussi
(Chair, Young Patrons
Ambassador Group)
Miss Katharine Arnold
Ms Mila Askarova
Miss Olivia Aubry
Daniel Axmer
Katrina Beechey
Sarah Bejerano
Athena Bersimis
William Bertagna
Roberto Boghossian
Georgina Borthwick
Johan Bryssinck
Miss Verena Butt
Sarah Calodney
The Hon Nicholas Campbell
Miss Livia Carpeggiani
Francesca Castelli
Cecile Champy
Alexandra and Kabir Chhatwani
Yoojin Choi
Arthur Chow
Aidan Christofferson
Bianca Chu
Adam Clay
Niamh Coghlan
Caroline Cole
Thamara Corm
Tara Wilson Craig
Sadrine Currimjee Debacker
Mr Theo Danjuma
Henry Danowski
Mr Joshua Davis
Ms Lora de Felice
Countess Charlotte de la
Rochefoucauld
Agnes de Royere
Federico Martin Castro Debernardi
Carine Decroi
Suzana Diamond
Mira Dimitrova
Ms Michelle D'Souza
Guillaume Duval
Indira Dyussebayeva
Alexandra Economou
Miss Roxanna Farboud
Anaïs Ferrier
Ottavia Fontana
Jane and Richard Found
Laurie Frey
Magdalena Gabriel
Mr Andreas Gegner
Benedetta Ghione
Nicolas Gitton
David Green
Lise Grendene
Judith Greve
Antonella Grevers
Georgia Griffiths
Alex Haidas
Angus Haldane
Ms Michelle Harari
Sara Harrison
Andrew Honan
Simona Houldsworth
Hus Gallery
Kamel Jaber
Scott Jacobson
Ms Melek Huma Kabakci
Sophie Kainradl
Miss Meruyert Kaliyeva
Mrs Vasilisa Kameneva
Miss Tamila Kerimova
Ms Chloe Kinsman
Sadie Kirshman
Daniel Klier
Berrak Kocaoglu
Ellie Konstantilieri
Anastasia Koreleva
Maria Korolevskaya
Stephen Kovalcik
Mr Jimmy Lahoud
Isabella Lauder-Frost
Miss MC Llamas
Wei-Lyn Loh
Lindsey Love
Ms Sonia Mak
Dr Christina Makris
Mr Jean-David Malat
Kamiar Maleki
Daria Manganelli
Zoe Marden
Krzysztof Maruszewski
Dr. F. Mattison Thompson
Charles-Henri McDermott
Fiona McGovern
Amanda Mead
Miss Nina Moaddel
Mr Fernando Moncho Lobo
Erin Morris
Nina Neuhaus
Heline Odqvist
Erendira Old
Berkay Oncel
Andrew Paradis
Christine Chungwon Park
William Pelham
Anna Pennink
Sonata Persson
Alexander V. Petalas
The Piper Gallery
Courtney Plummer
Victoria Poniatowski

Asta Ramonaite
Mr Eugenio Re Rebaudengo
Jordana Reuben
Elise Roberts
Louisa Robertson
Katharina Sailer
Mr Simon Sakhai
Miss Tatiana Sapegina
Paola Saracino Fendi
Natasha Maria Sareen
Franz Schwarz
Alex Seddon
Count Indoo Sella Di Monteluce
Jelena Seng
Robert Sheffield
Henrietta Shields
Ms Marie-Anya Shriro
Jag Singh
Tammy Smulders
Dominic Stolerman
Dr Kafui Tay
Soren S K Tholstrup
Mr Giancarlo Trinca
Mr Philippos Tsangrides
Ms Navann Ty
Celine Valligny
Alexandra Warder
Mr Neil Wenman
Kim Williams
Ms Seda Yalcinkaya
Reza Yazdi
Daniel Zarchan
Olivia Zarka
and those who wish to remain anonymous

International Council Members
Mr Segun Agbaje
Staffan Ahrenberg, Editions Cahiers d'Art
Mr Geoff Ainsworth AM
Dilyara Allakhverdova
Doris Ammann
Carol and David Appel
Mr Plácido Arango
Gabrielle Bacon
Anne H Bass
Cristina Bechtler
Nicolas Berggruen
Olivier and Desiree Berggruen
Mr Pontus Bonnier
Frances Bowes
Ivor Braka
The Deborah Loeb Brice Foundation
The Broad Art Foundation
Melva Bucksbaum and Raymond Learsy
Andrew Cameron AM
Fondation Cartier pour l'art contemporain
Nicolas and Celia Cattelain
Trudy and Paul Cejas
Mrs Christina Chandris
Richard Chang (Vice Chair)
Pierre TM Chen, Yageo Foundation, Taiwan
Adrian Cheng
Lord Cholmondeley
Mr Kemal Has Cingillioglu
Mr and Mrs Attilio Codognato
Sir Ronald Cohen and Lady Sharon Harel-Cohen
Mr Douglas S Cramer and Mr Hubert S Bush III
Mr Dimitris Daskalopoulos
Mr and Mrs Michel David-Weill
Julia W Dayton
Ms Miel de Botton
Tiqui Atencio Demirdjian and Ago Demirdjian
Joseph and Marie Donnelly
Mrs Olga Dreesmann
Barney A Ebsworth
Füsun and Faruk Eczacibaşi
Stefan Edlis and Gael Neeson
Mr and Mrs Edward Eisler
Carla Emil and Rich Silverstein
Fares and Tania Fares
HRH Princess Firyal of Jordan
Mrs Doris Fisher
Mrs Wendy Fisher
Dr Kira Flanzraich
Dr Corinne M Flick
Amanda and Glenn Fuhrman
Candida and Zak Gertler
Mrs Yassmin Ghandehari
Mr Giancarlo Giammetti
Alan Gibbs
Lydia and Manfred Gorvy
Mr Laurence Graff
Ms Esther Grether
Konstantin Grigorishin
Mr Xavier Guerrand-Hermès
Mimi and Peter Haas Fund
Margrit and Paul Hahnloser
Andy and Christine Hall
Paul Harris
Mrs Susan Hayden
Jorge and Sylvie Helft
Ms Ydessa Hendeles
Marlene Hess and James D. Zirin
André and Rosalie Hoffmann
Ms Maja Hoffmann (Chair)
Vicky Hughes
ITYS, Athens
Dakis and Lietta Joannou
Sir Elton John and Mr David Furnish
Pamela J. Joyner
Mr Chang-Il Kim
Jack Kirkland
C Richard and Pamela Kramlich
Bert Kreuk
Mrs Grażyna Kulczyk
Andreas and Ulrike Kurtz
Catherine Lagrange
Mr Pierre Lagrange
Baroness Lambert
Bernard Lambilliotte
Agnès and Edward Lee
Mme RaHee Hong Lee
Jacqueline and Marc Leland
Mr and Mrs Sylvain Levy
Mrs Fatima Maleki
Panos and Sandra Marinopoulos
Mr and Mrs Donald B Marron
Mr Ronald and The Hon Mrs McAulay
Mark McCain and Caro MacDonald
Angela Westwater and David Meitus
Mr Leonid Mikhelson
Aditya and Megha Mittal
Mr Donald Moore
Simon and Catriona Mordant
Mrs Yoshiko Mori
Mr Guy and The Hon Mrs Naggar
Fayeeza Naqvi
Mr and Mrs Takeo Obayashi
Hideyuki Osawa
Irene Panagopoulos
Young-Ju Park
Ms Lisa Paulsen
Yana and Stephen Peel
Daniel and Elizabeth Peltz
Andrea and José Olympio Pereira
Catherine Petitgas
Sydney Picasso
Mr and Mrs Jürgen Pierburg
Jean Pigozzi
Lekha Poddar
Miss Dee Poon
Ms Miuccia Prada and Mr Patrizio Bertelli
Laura Rapp and Jay Smith
Maya and Ramzy Rasamny
Patrizia Sandretto Re Rebaudengo and Agostino Re Rebaudengo
Robert Rennie and Carey Fouks
Sir John Richardson
Michael Ringier
Lady Ritblat
Ms Hanneli M Rupert
Ms Güler Sabanci
Dame Theresa Sackler, DBE
Mrs Lily Safra
Muriel and Freddy Salem
Rajeeb and Nadia Samdani
Dasha Shenkman, OBE
Uli and Rita Sigg
Norah and Norman Stone
Julia Stoschek
John J Studzinski, CBE
Maria and Malek Sukkar
Mrs Marjorie Susman
Mr Budi Tek, The Yuz Foundation
Mr Robert Tomei
The Hon Robert H Tuttle and Mrs Maria Hummer-Tuttle
Mr and Mrs Guy Ullens
Mrs Ninetta Vafeia
Corinne and Alexandre Van Damme
Paulo A W Vieira
Robert and Felicity Waley-Cohen
Diana Widmaier Picasso
Christen and Derek Wilson
Michael G Wilson
Mrs Sylvie Winckler
The Hon Dame Janet Wolfson de Botton, DBE
Anita and Poju Zabludowicz
Michael Zilkha
and those who wish to remain anonymous

Africa Acquisitions Committee
Kathy Ackerman Robins
Tutu Agyare (Co-Chair)
Anshu Bahanda
Mrs Nwakaego Boyo
Priti Chandaria Shah
Mrs Kavita Chellaram
Colin Coleman
Salim Currimjee
Harry G. David
Mr and Mrs Michel David-Weill
Robert Devereux (Co-Chair)
Hamish Dewar
Robert and Renee Drake
Mrs Wendy Fisher
Andrea Kerzner
Samallie Kiyingi
Matthias and Gervanne Leridon
Caro Macdonald
Dominick Maia-Tanner
Dale Mathias
Professor Oba Nsugbe QC
Pascale Revert Wheeler
Emile Stipp
Ana Luiza and Luiz Augusto Teixeira de Freitas
Mr Varnavas A. Varnava
Burkhard Varnholt
Mercedes Vilardell
and those who wish to remain anonymous

Asia-Pacific Acquisitions Committee
Matthias Arndt
Bonnie and R Derek Bandeen
Andrew Cameron AM
Mr and Mrs John Carrafiell
Richard Chang
Pierre TM Chen, Yageo Foundation, Taiwan
Adrian Cheng
Mr Yan d'Auriol
Katie de Tilly
Mr Hyung-Teh Do
Ms Mareva Grabowski
Reade and Elizabeth Griffith
Cees Hendrikse
Philippa Hornby
Mr Yongsoo Huh
Mrs Natalie Kadoorie González
Shareen Khattar Harrison
Mr Chang-Il Kim
Ms Yung Hee Kim
Alan Lau (Co-Chair)
Woong-Yeul Lee
Mr William Lim
Ms Dina Liu
Juliette Liu
Ms Kai-Yin Lo
Anne Louis-Dreyfus
Elisabetta Marzetti Mallinson
Elaine Forsgate Marden
Marleen Molenaar
John Porter
The Red Mansion Foundation
Dr Gene Sherman AM (Co-Chair)
Leo Shih
Sir David Tang
Mr Budi Tek, The Yuz Foundation
Neil Wenman
Yang Bin
and those who wish to remain anonymous

Latin American Acquisitions Committee
Ghazwa Abu-Soud
Monica and Robert Aguirre
Karen and Leon Amitai
Luis Benshimol
Celia Birbragher
Estrellita and Daniel Brodsky
Carmen Busquets
Trudy and Paul Cejas
David Cohen Sitton
HSH the Prince Pierre d'Arenberg
Tiqui Atencio Demirdjian (Chair)
Andrea Dreesmann
Patricia Druck
Angelica Fuentes de Vergara
Ronald Harrar
Barbara Hemmerle-Gollust
Rocio and Boris Hirmas Said
Marta Regina Fernandez Holman
Julian Iragorri
Anne Marie and Geoffrey Isaac
Nicole Junkermann
José Luis Lorenzo
Milagros Maldonado
Fatima and Eskander Maleki
Francisca Mancini
Fernanda Marques
Denise and Felipe Nahas Mattar
Veronica Nutting
Victoria and Isaac Oberfeld
Paulina and Alfonso Otero-Zamora
Catherine Petitgas
Claudio Federico Porcel
Frances Reynolds
Erica Roberts

Judko Rosenstock and
Oscar Hernandez
Lilly Scarpetta
Norma Smith
Juan Carlos Verme
Tania and Arnoldo Wald
Juan Yarur Torres
and those who wish to remain anonymous

Middle East and North Africa Acquisitions Committee
HRH Princess Alia Al-Senussi
Abdullah Al Turki
Mehves Ariburnu
Sule Arinc
Marwan T Assaf
Niloufar Bakhtiar Clignet
Perihan Bassatne
Foundation Boghossian
Ms Isabelle de la Bruyère
Füsun Eczacıbaşı
Maryam Eisler (Co-Chair)
Shirley Elghanian
Delfina Entrecanales, CBE
Noor Fares
Raghida Ghandour Al Rahim
Taymour Grahne
Maha and Kasim Kutay
Mrs Fatima Maleki
Fayeeza Naqvi
Dina Nasser-Khadivi
Shulamit Nazarian
Ebru Özdemir
Mrs Edwina Özyegin
Mr Moshe Peterburg
Charlotte Philipps
Ramzy and Maya Rasamny (Co-Chair)
Mrs Madhu Ruia
Mrs Karen Ruimy
Dania Debs-Sakka
Shihab Shobokshi
Miss Yassi Sohrabi
Maria and Malek Sukkar
Faisal Tamer
Ana Luiza and
Luiz Augusto Teixeira de Freitas
Tsukanov Family Foundation
Berna Tuglular
Yesim Turanli
Mahdi Yahya
Roxane Zand
and those who wish to remain anonymous

North American Acquisitions Committee
Carol and David Appel
Jacqueline Appel and
Alexander Malmaeus
Abigail Baratta
Dorothy Berwin and
Dominique Levy
Paul Britton
Many Cawthorn Argenio
Dillon Cohen
Matt Cohler
Michael Corman
and Kevin Fink
Theo Danjuma
James Diner
Wendy Fisher
Glenn Fuhrman
Victoria Gelfand-Magalhaes
Amy Gold
Nina and Dan Gross
Pamela Joyner
Monica Kalpakian
Elisabeth and Panos Karpidas
Christian Keese
Anne Simone Kleinman and
Thomas Wong
Rachelli Mishori and Leon Koffler
Marjorie and Michael Levine
James Lindon
Rebecca Marks
Lillian and Billy Mauer
Liza Mauer and
Andrew Sheiner
Nancy McCain
Stavros Merjos
Gregory R. Miller
Megha Mittal
Shabin and Nadir Mohamed
Jenny Mullen
Elisa Nuyten & David Dime
Amy and John Phelan
Nathalie Pratte
Melinda B and Paul Pressler
Liz Gerring Radke and
Kirk Radke
Laura Rapp and Jay Smith
Robert Rennie (Chair) and
Carey Fouks
Kimberly Richter and Jon Shirley
Carolin Scharpff-Striebich
Komal Shah
Dasha Shenkman
Donald R Sobey
Robert Sobey
Beth Swofford
Laurie Thomson and Andy Chisholm
Dr. Diane Vachon
Christen and Derek Wilson
and those who wish to remain anonymous

Photography Acquisitions Committee
Her Highness Sheikha Fatima Bint
Hazza' Bin Zayed Al Nahyan
Ryan Allen
Artworkers Retirement Society
Nicholas Barker
Cynthia Lewis Beck
Marisa Bellani
Pierre Brahm (Co-Chair)
Mrs. William Shaw Broeksmit
Elizabeth and Rory Brooks
Marcel and Gabrielle Cassard
Nicolas (Co-Chair) and
Celia Cattelain
Mr and Mrs Michel David-Weill
Charlie Fellowes and
Jeremy Epstein, Edel Assanti
Nikki Fennell
David Fitzsimons
Lisa Garrison
Ms Emily Goldner and Mr Michael
Humphries
Margot and George Greig
Alexandra Hess
Bernard Huppert
Dede Johnston
Jack Kirkland
David Knaus
Mr Scott Mead
Sebastien Montabonel
Mr Donald Moore
Alexandra Nash
Saadi Soudavar
Nicholas Stanley
Maria and Malek Sukkar
Mrs Caroline Trausch
Michael and Jane Wilson
and those who wish to remain anonymous

Russia Eastern Europe Acquisitions Committee
Dmitry Aksenov
Dilyara Allakhverdova
Maria Baibakova
Razvan BANESCU
David Birnbaum
Maria Bukhtoyarova
Mark Čuček
Elena Evstafieva
Dr Kira Flanzraich (Chair)
Lyuba Galkina
Suad Garayeva
Dr Dr Joana Grevers
Konstantin Grigorishin
Cees Hendrikse
Mr. Vilius Kavaliauskas
Carl Kostyál
Arina Kowner
Mrs Grażyna Kulczyk
Peter Kulloi
Krzysztof Madelski
Eduard Maták
Teresa Mavica
Luba Michailova
Maarja Oviir-Neivelt
Lorenzo Paini
Neil K. Rector
Valeria Rodnyansky
Robert Runták
Maria Rus Bojan
Ovidiu Şandor
Zsolt Somlói
Elena Sudakova
Mrs Elena Todorova
The Tretyakov Family Collection
Miroslav Trnka
Mrs Alina Uspenskaya
Jo Vickery
Georgi Voynov
Veronika Zonabend
Mr Janis Zuzans
and those who wish to remain anonymous

South Asia Acquisitions Committee
Maya Barolo-Rizvi
Krishna Bhupal
Akshay Chudasama
Anjali and Gaurav Grover
Zahida Habib
Dr Amin Jaffer
Aparajita Jain
Yamini Mehta
Mr Rohan Mirchandani
Shalini Misra
Amna and Ali Naqvi
Fayeeza Naqvi
Mrs. Chandrika Pathak
Puja and Uday Patnaik
Lekha Poddar (Co-Chair)
Mr Raj and Mrs Reshma Ruia
Nadia Samdani
Rajeeb Samdani (Co-Chair)
Mrs Tarana Sawhney
Sanjiv Singhal
Osman Khalid Waheed
Manuela and Iwan Wirth
and those who wish to remain anonymous

The 1897 Circle
Marilyn Bild
David and Deborah Botten
Geoff Bradbury
Charles Brett
Eloise and Francis Charlton
Mr and Mrs Cronk
Alex Davids
Professor Martyn Davis
Jonathan Davis
Ronnie Duncan
Lt Cdr Paul Fletcher
Mr and Mrs R.N. and M.C. Fry
Richard S. Hamilton
L.A. Hynes
John Janssen
Dr Martin Kenig
Isa Levy
Jean Medlycott
Martin Owen
Simon Reynolds
Dr Claudia Rosanowski
Ann M Smith
Deborah Stern
Jennifer Toynbee-Holmes
Estate of Paule Vézelay
D. von Bethmann-Hollweg
Audrey Wallrock
Professor Brian Whitton
Simon Casimir Wilson
Andrew Woodd
Mr and Mrs Zilberberg
and those who wish to remain anonymous

Tate Modern Corporate Supporters
Amsterdam Trade Bank
Bank of America Merrill Lynch
Bloomberg
BMW
BP
Christie's
Credit Suisse
Deutsche Bank AG
EY
Hanjin Shipping
Hildon Ltd
Hyundai Card
Hyundai Motor
Laurent Perrier
Markit
Qantas
Solarcentury
Sotheby's
and those who wish to remain anonymous

Tate Modern Corporate Members
AIG
Bank of America Merrill Lynch
BCS Consulting
Citi
Clifford Chance LLP
CREATIVE HEAD
The Cultivist
Deutsche Bank
EY
Finsbury
GAM (UK) Limited
HSBC
Hyundai Card
JATO Dynamics
Kingfisher plc
Linklaters
McGuirewoods London LLP
The Moody's Foundation
Morgan Stanley
Pearson
Saatchi & Saatchi
Siegel + Gale
Slaughter and May
The Brooklyn Brothers
Tishman Speyer
Unilever
Wolff Olins
and those who wish to remain anonymous

CW01653530

STATUETTES
OF THE
ART DECO PERIOD

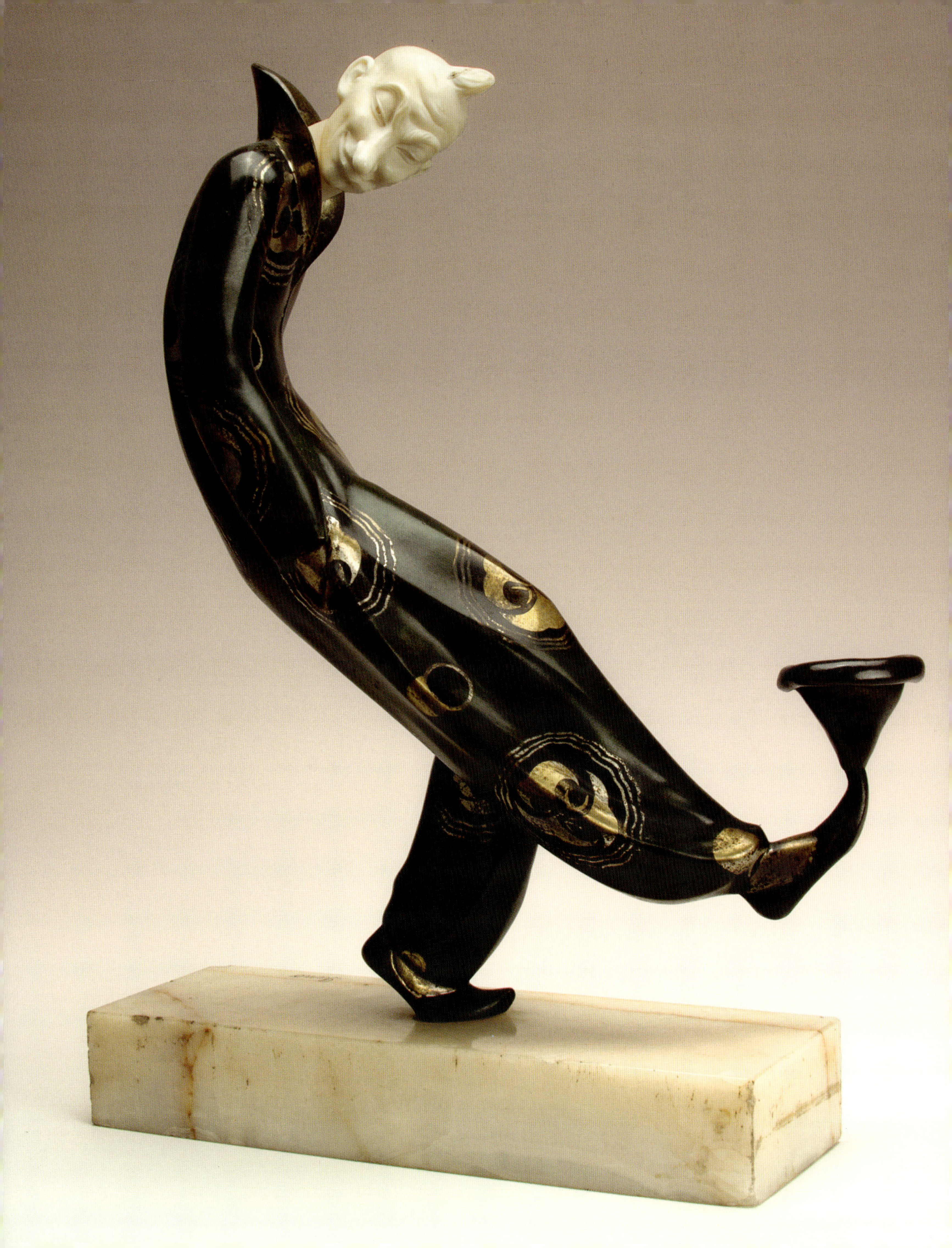

STATUETTES
OF THE
ART DECO PERIOD

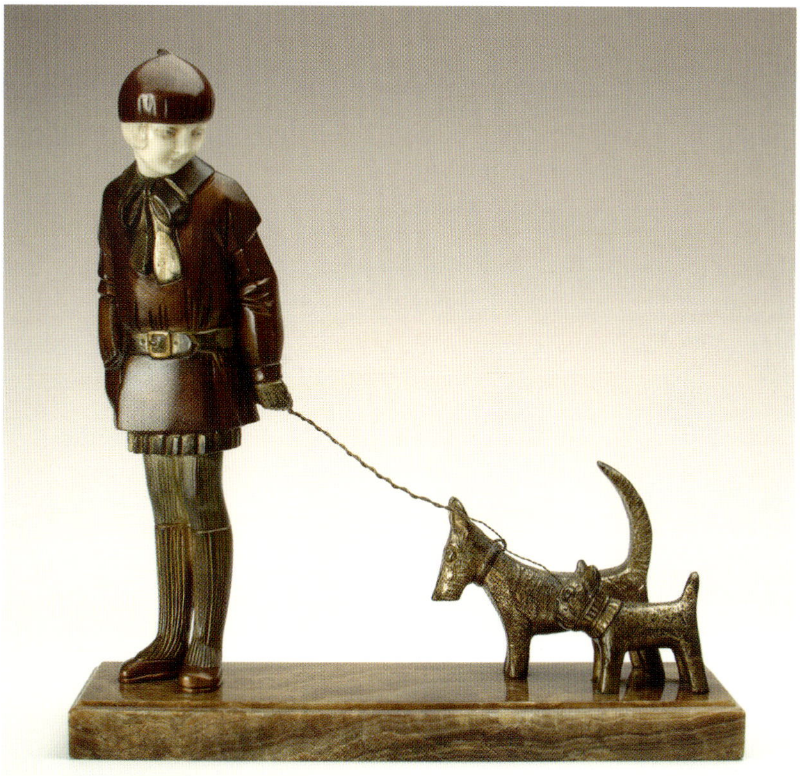

Alberto Shayo

ACC ART BOOKS

© 2016 Alberto Shayo

World copyright reserved

ISBN 978 185149 824 6

The right of Alberto Shayo to be identified as the author of this work has been asserted by him in accordance with the Copyright, Designs and Patents Act 1988

All rights reserved

No part of this publication may be reproduced, stored in a retrieval system, or transmitted in any form or by any means electronic, mechanical, photocopying, recording or otherwise, without the prior permission of the publisher

Every effort has been made to secure permission to reproduce the images contained within this book, and we are grateful to the individuals and institutions who have assisted in this task. Any errors or omissions are entirely unintentional, and the details should be addressed to the publisher.

British Library CIP Data
A catalogue record for this book
is available from the British Library

Frontispiece:
Harlequin by Reno

Title page:
Friendly Walk by André Vincent Becquerel

MIX
Paper from
responsible sources
FSC® C104723
FSC
www.fsc.org

Printed in China
for ACC Art Books Ltd.,
Woodbridge, Suffolk IP12 4SD, U.K.

To

Andy Levy   Sebastian Gordon   Juan Maloney

Craig Schneider   Carlos Morbidelli   Apostolos Mintzis

Christos Chatzivasileiou   David Vaucher   Walter Wolfe

David Gorodisch   Hernan Salazar   Martin Benegas Lynch

Carlo Vogelgesang   Horacio Costa Cordova   David Loring

Scott Barnes

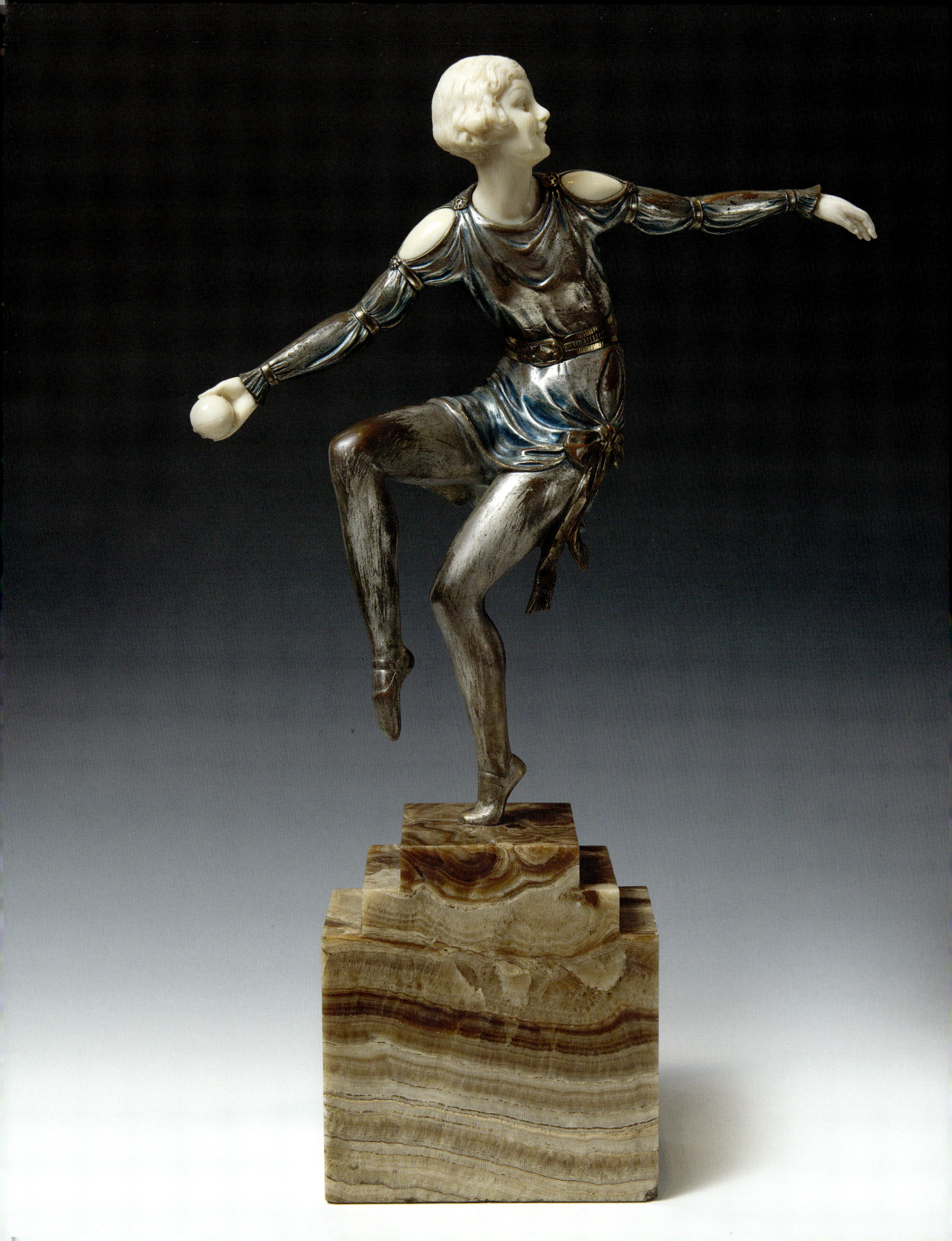

Contents

Throwing the Ball by Joé Descomps

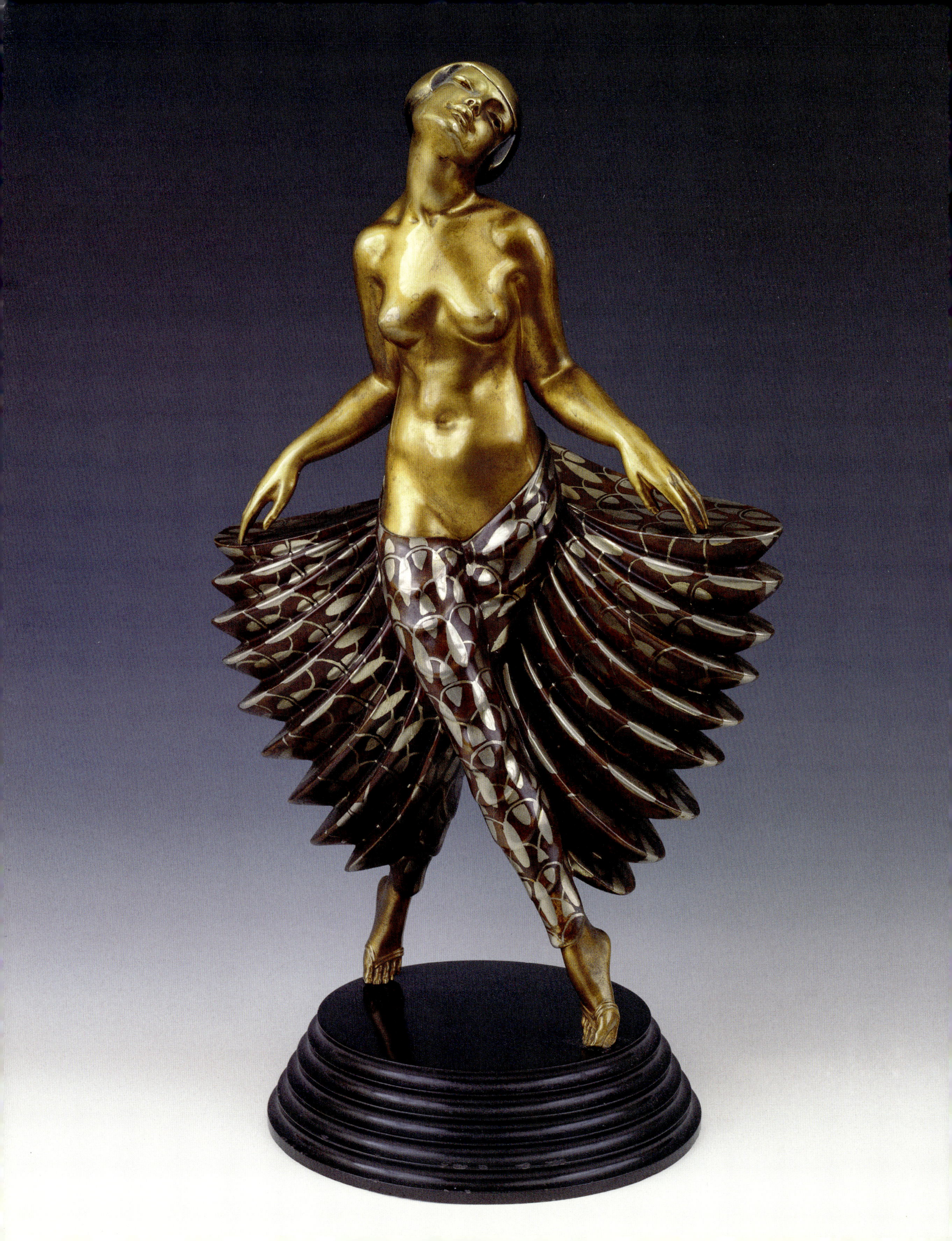

Acknowledgements

If life has a way of balancing itself out in the long run, the same can be said about the creation of this book; things do turn out right in the end. The path that led to that end was full of petals, many vivid fragrances and a few thorns. A rose would not be a rose without them.

I wish to thank Clara Sancovsky, my beacon of light in the dark, for never saying 'no' to me. All my requests have always been promptly answered and her 'yes' is charged with knowledge and the expertise that is acquired over many years. Her goodwill is matched only by her incredible flow of optimism.

Sharon Kerman for putting up with me and discovering 'wonderful things'. She always does.

Tounée, Raimundo, Rita and Joe for constantly supporting me. Please continue to pester me! Hello Arlette!

Alastair Duncan, Art Deco's living legend.

Several artists came to life in this book thanks to memories, invaluable photos and documents supplied by family members. They corrected long-established misconceptions and solved certain puzzles related to pseudonyms. Though they wish to remain individually anonymous I would like to mention the families of Lipchytz, Le Verrier, Le Faguays and Gerdago.

Pedro Tinoco for solving so many of my problems. Never at rest, always searching to expand his insight.

Antonio Amado in Miami for his perseverance.

The collectors, for working with me. They offer me only the best and only the best is accepted. I wish to single out: Dino Menasche, Cornelia and Richard Kastenholz, and Mira and Abdo C.

The relationship with my photographers is paramount: John Dessarzin, Rainer Querfurth, Marcelo Ferrari, Danilo Takano, Federico Adrián Marino, José Dwek, they all know how to interpret me, they all deliver excellence.

Francisco Pinto — 'Francis' — for being my *cultural assistant.*

Exotic Dancer by Alexander Kéléty

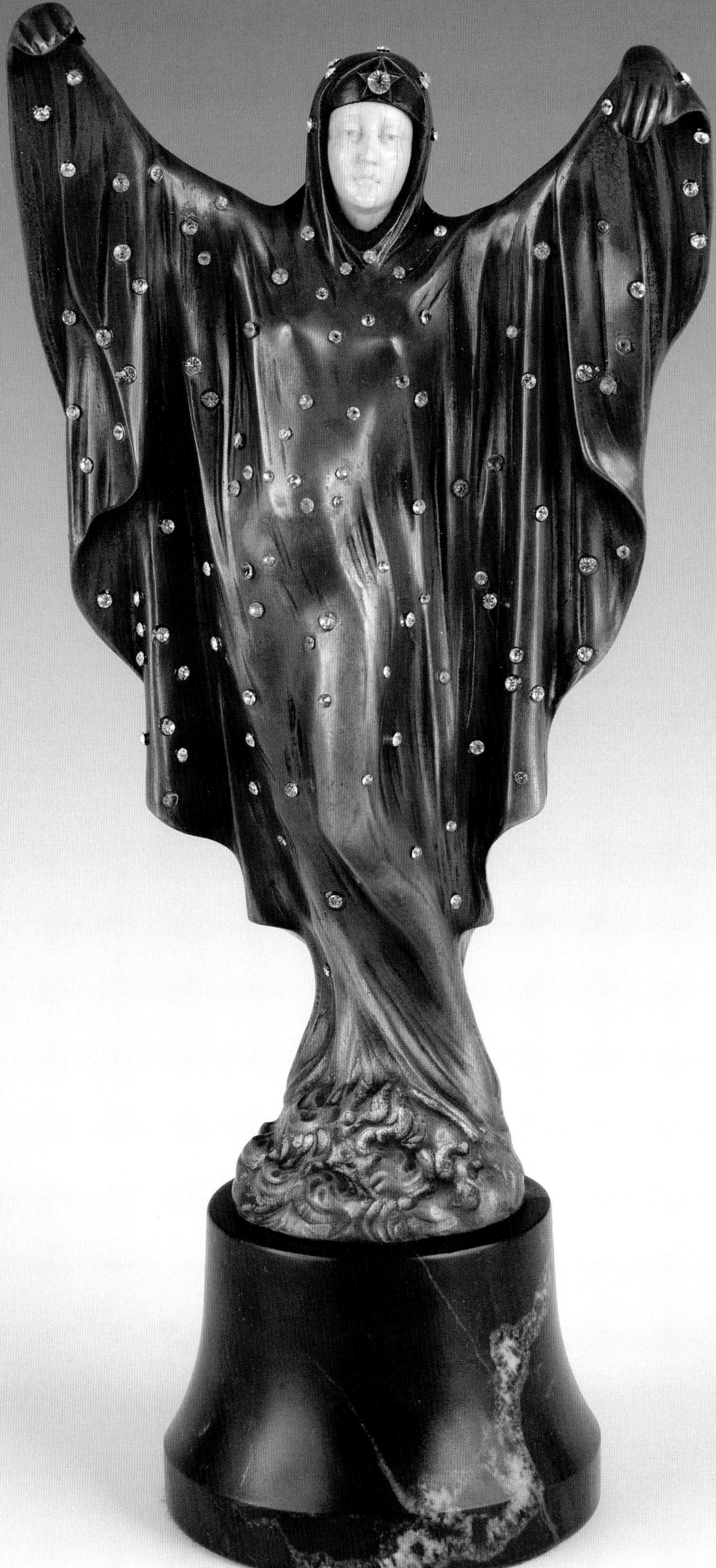

Preface

In my days as a dermatologist, many moons ago, I was taught to have all lesions photographed. They helped in the diagnosis and treatment, and always remained in the archives for future reference.

I left the practice of dermatology decades ago but that teaching remained with me. Favourable winds and tides re-directed me to the world of Art Deco. I developed a passion for it and it has been my driving force ever since.

Travels and research followed, books became a reality and I accumulated images of fabulous figures along the way. An appointment to a museum, collection or gallery, resulted in great images taken of a specific artist and also of whatever I deemed worthy of registering.

The years passed and my archives grew in quality and quantity. A trip to my publisher was decisive. A new book was to be a reality. All the artists whose works I had compiled were to see the light. Many for the first time, and some as a reappearance of past echoes.

This new endeavour shows the ample list of artists and their works. None of them is by any means comprehensive and because when they were created they were considered mere decorative pieces, their cataloguing and archiving has been, at best, superficial. What is not superficial, is the strength with which they mirror the Art Deco period. And although the period ended abruptly with the start of World War II, their commercialisation continued for at least three years. Invoices attest to this fact.

The figures mirror the era with their mood, design, materials chosen and even the names given to them.

Through this book I hope to immortalise these statuettes, their era and, above all, their creators.

Queen of the Night by Richard W. Lange

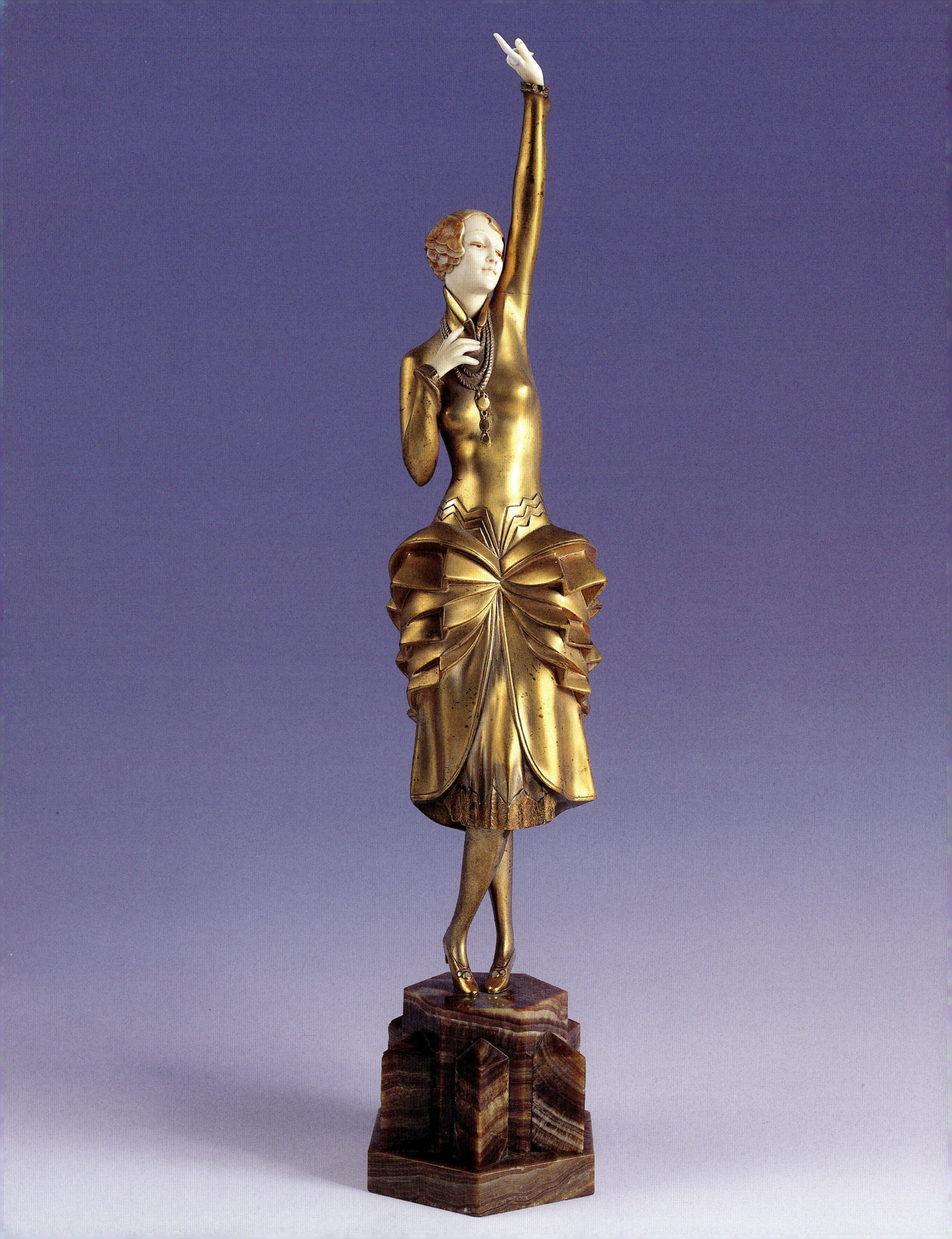

The Allure of Art Deco

The words 'Art Deco' conjure up images of a bygone era, a time of glamour, adventure and excitement. That age seems far-off, yet it is barely 100 years ago.

The statuettes created during the period are its regal ambassadors, disseminated throughout the world. Created as mere decorative objects, they are now collectors' items that are sought-after and treasured.

Most depict dancers poised as if caught in mid-flight. They appear to be frozen in time, about to break loose from their bases. Others depict elegant sportsmen and women, and children engaged in various activities.

These sculptures were never intended to be shown at elite exhibitions nor were they made for the closed circle of a select clientele. Quite the contrary: they were created as ornamental objects and were sold in retail shops, gift shops and department stores. They were ideal gifts for weddings, retirements and special occasions; they were sometimes even used as sports trophies.

Created mainly by French sculptors, but also by German, Austrian and Italian artists, these statuettes were produced during the period between the two World Wars, from 1914 to 1939.

The term 'Art Deco', an abbreviation of the title of the 1925 exhibition in Paris, the 'Exposition International des Arts Décoratifs et Industriels Modernes', was not coined until after the 'World of Art Deco' exhibition held at The Minneapolis Institute of Arts in 1971. Art Deco was a logical reaction to the Art Nouveau style (1880–1914) with its flowing lines, exaggerated curves and excessive ornamentation, yet it was by no means a clean cut from the old. Quite the contrary. It borrowed heavily from the older period but its motifs were given a fresh interpretation. Everything became cleaner and more condensed. The right angle was absolute, and the line was paramount. While flowers, animals and feminine figures continued to be depicted, they were now modernized and streamlined.

The Art Deco era is also known as the '*Années Folles*' (the 'Crazy Years'), the 'Roaring Twenties', the 'Jazz Age', the 'Streamline Period' and the 'Machine Age'. The 'Crazy Years' because after the brutality of World War I, peace had finally come and people were eager to forget the past and its troubles and live life to its fullest. A frenzy of hedonism began.

The 'Jazz Age' because the world discovered the latest American export: jazz. The music was new, catchy and seductive. It invaded the clubs and music halls of Paris, Berlin and London. Jazz singers and musicians were all the rage.

The 'Streamline Period' because all that was superfluous was minimised. Not eliminated, but reduced. Architecture, trains and cars were given geometric shapes. The straight line was sovereign; all manifestations echoed its purity.

The 'Machine Age' because machines, automobiles, household appliances and buildings became affordable to many more people. They improved the quality of life, and gave individuals and families more leisure time.

The three major influences on the artists of this period were Egypt, the Ballets Russes and the Music Hall.

Egyptomania

The fascination for all things Egyptian was one of the most important influences of the time. The public was captivated by the grandiose monumentality and exoticism of Egypt.

Egypt was unknown to most people until the early 18th century. In 1798 Napoleon ventured into Egypt; he sent innumerable treasures back to France. The Rosetta Stone was rediscovered in 1799 by a soldier from Napoleon's expedition. It took another twenty years for Champollion to decipher the stone's hieroglyphics. Suddenly ancient Egypt came alive, and the world fell in love with it.

Obelisks were shipped to London, Paris, New York and Rome — the eternal city alone boasts no fewer than thirteen obelisks. In 1832 the Viceroy of Egypt gave France two obelisks from Luxor, one of which was transported to France. Upon arrival, the base, which featured a frieze of monkeys with their genitals exposed, was deemed too risqué. The base was removed and in 1836 the obelisk was erected in the Place de la Concorde in Paris. The base was sent to the Louvre, where it was exhibited and became an immediate success. The second obelisk was never sent because the French authorities considered it too expensive; in 1986 France 'returned' it by relinquishing its claim on it.

On 25 November 1922 King Tutankhamun's tomb was opened. From it emerged 'wonderful things': jewels, sculptures of gods, sphinxes, furniture, jars and hieroglyphics. They influenced jewellery, fashions, perfume bottles, furniture, paintings and architecture.

The cinema also succumbed to the attraction of Egypt. Many a star appeared on screen as an Egyptian queen or goddess, with glittering robes, elaborate headdresses and fantastic jewellery. Probably the most captivating was Cleopatra, who was depicted as an absolute sovereign. A legendary beauty, she was antiquity's *femme fatale* who exalted in luxury, voluptuousness and cruelty. A seductress able to conquer the most powerful men of her time — Julius Caesar, Mark Anthony and Octavian — she was admired and feared. Even her death was beguiling: she committed suicide by holding a venomous snake to her bosom!

The Ballets Russes

In 1909 Paris experienced an invasion from the east. Unexpected and unforeseeable, it shook and shocked like an icy blast from Siberia: The Ballets Russes, a dance troupe led by Sergei Diaghilev.

Employing the most talented dancers and choreographers, and featuring music that sounded alien to traditional ears, and costumes with vivid and exotic colour combinations, they arrived and conquered the city of Paris as they would later conquer the rest of Europe and the Americas.

Sergei Diaghilev, the impresario of the Ballets Russes, was neither a dancer nor a choreographer, yet he brilliantly orchestrated the talents of many different specialists to create memorable performances.

Suddenly everything Russian was all the rage: decorations, music, clothes and restaurants. The Russian influence was also reflected in the Music Hall, as local stars — and the revues themselves — were given Russian-sounding names.

Music Hall

The period between the two World Wars saw the golden age of the Music Hall in Paris and Berlin.

After the savagery of the war, whilst politicians redrew the map of Europe, people longed for a respite. They wanted to celebrate, and did so with great relish. Paris and Berlin were the centres of the partying. The Music Hall was a revelation of the post-war period. It soon became the grand spectacle, with its gigantic pleasure palaces where performances took place amid smoke and loud chatter.

These shows were called revues, cabaret, music hall; the French called it the *spectacle de variété* (variety show).

The entertainment consisted of light versions of ballets, operas and plays, featuring dance, song, pantomimes and circus acts. Acrobats, gymnasts and, in some cases, animal tamers with lions, horses, dogs and elephants, all amused spectators in pursuit of pleasurable and provocative entertainment rather than intellectual challenges. The pace was frenetic, and audiences found it all wonderfully exciting.

Music Hall could take you on a tour of far-off places: the mysterious Orient, the American Wild West, exotic India. The possibilities were boundless. The sets were dazzling, the colours flamboyant. The audience's imagination went into overdrive. The decors and costumes were created by top designers such as Erté (Romain de Tirtoff), Brunelleschi, Georges Barbier, Max Weldy and Zinowiew.

Events in the inter-war period

1916	**Stainless steel invented**
1921	**Albert Einstein was awarded the Nobel Prize for physics**
1922	**King Tutankhamun's tomb was discovered**
1922	**Insulin was invented**
1926	**First television transmission in London**
1927	**Charles Lindbergh crossed the Atlantic from New York to Paris in 33 ½ hours. He was 25**
1927	**Technicolor invented**
1928	**Alexander Fleming accidentally discovered penicillin**
1928	**Bubble gum was invented**
1930	**The planet Pluto was discovered (now considered a nanoplanet)**
1935	**Nylon was created and in 1939, nylon stockings were introduced**
1938	**Instant coffee was produced**

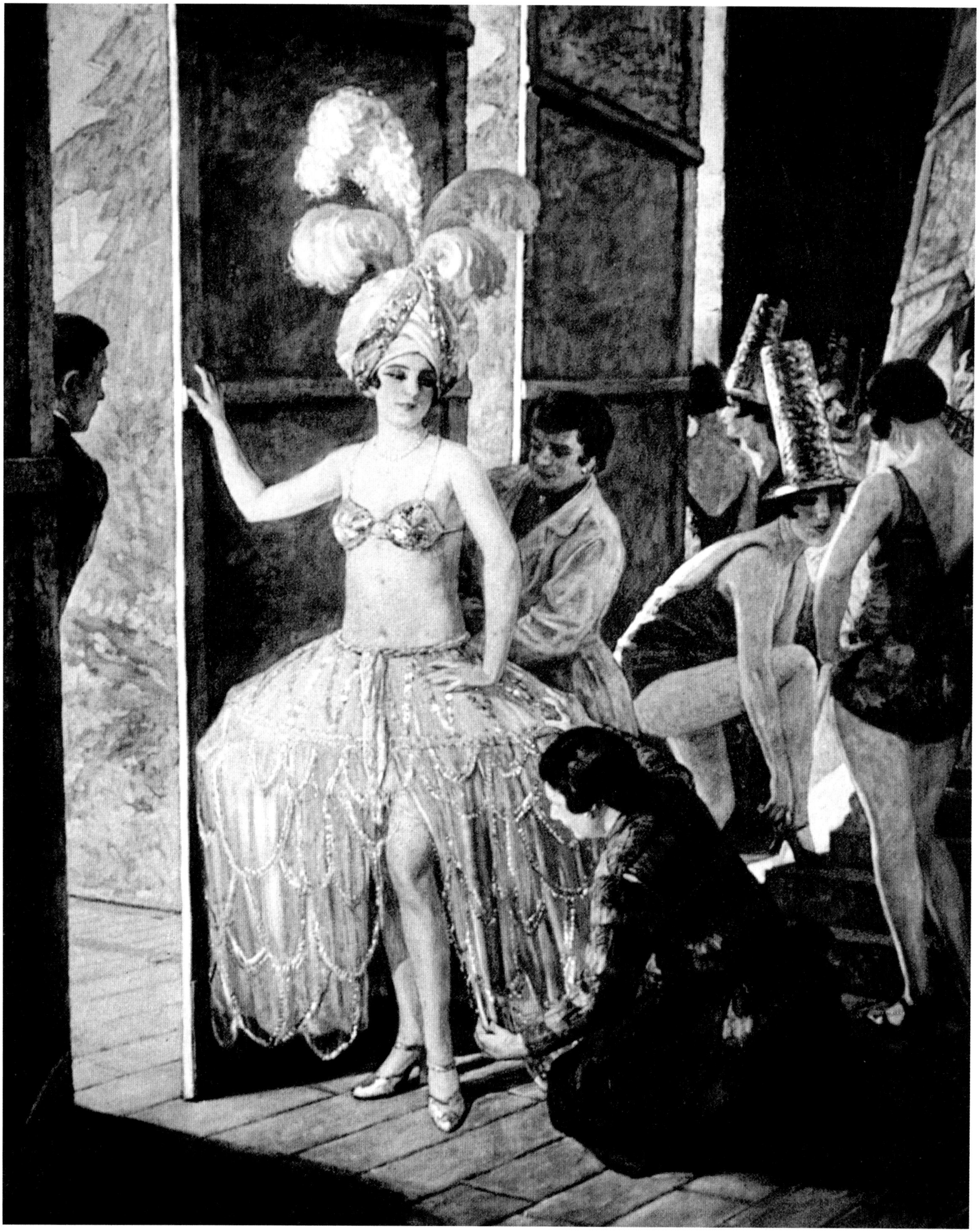

Backstage at the Music Hall. *Oil painting by Henry Zo. Exhibited at a Paris salon in 1929.*

These spectacles were hugely profitable for their impresarios. In 1923 the Folies Bergère alone took in 10 million francs. Music Hall was big business, and performances took place in many venues.

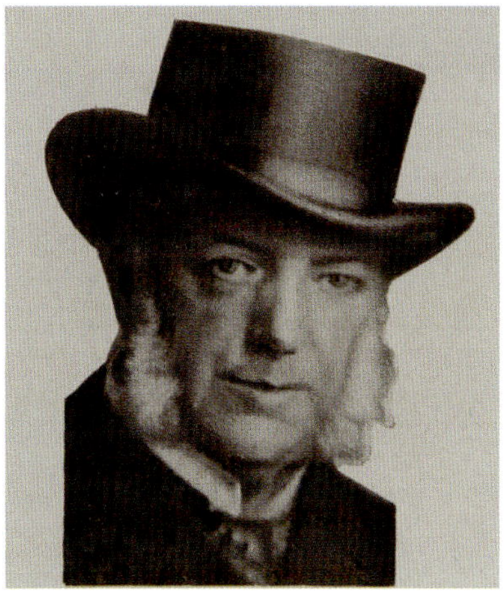

Charles Zidler. *Founder and director of the Moulin Rouge.*

The Moulin Rouge in Montmartre was founded by the entrepreneurs Charles Zidler and Joseph Oller, who created several other attractions in Paris: the Hippodrome, the Nouveau Cirque, the Montagnes Russes and the Jardin de Paris.

The world flocked to the Moulin Rouge. Many came out of curiosity, others only to be able to say they had been there. Some sought a few hours' companionship; others enjoyed the place's perverse charm, or its 'artistic' qualities.

There were wealthy patrons and students, journalists and writers, painters and sculptors, actors and singers. The Moulin Rouge and its performers were depicted by Toulouse-Lautrec, its most famous patron-painter.

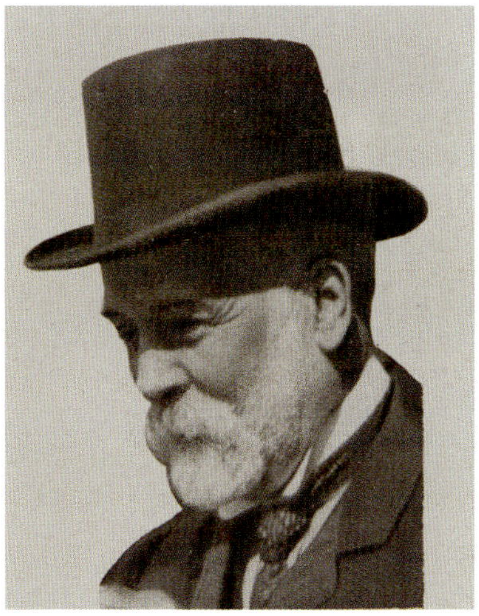

Joseph Oller. First manager of the Moulin Rouge.

Among the other venues were: the Empire (opened in 1924); the Casino de Paris; the Palace (formerly the Eden — the Dolly Sisters, Maurice Chevalier and Carlos Gardel all performed here); the Alcazar de Paris; the Mogador Theatre; the Concert Mayol; the Lido (founded in 1929, it was originally a Turkish bath house; in 1932 its pool was used for music hall revues, and by 1946 it had become a luxurious venue whose converted pool was still used for grandiose effects!); Les Ambassadeurs (where the Cotton Club from Harlem played jazz); the Alhambra (later the Music Hall de Paris; in 1935 Edith Piaf debuted here); the Châtelet; the Jardin de Paris; the Moulin de la Galette; the Elysée-Montmartre; the Divan Japonais; and the Palais de Glace.

The Folies Bergère: founded in 1869, it featured wrestlers, singers, mimes and acrobats. The 'nude' tableau first appeared in 1894. By 1918, the nude girls had become the principal box-office draw and the variety acts secondary.

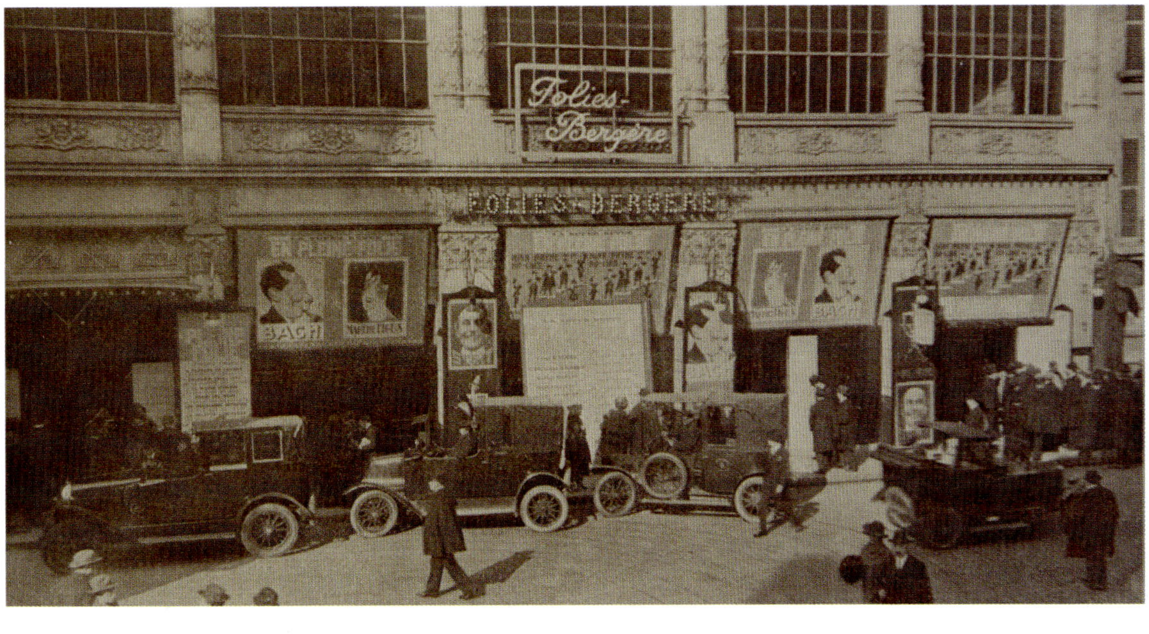

Entrance to the Folies Bergère, 1920s.

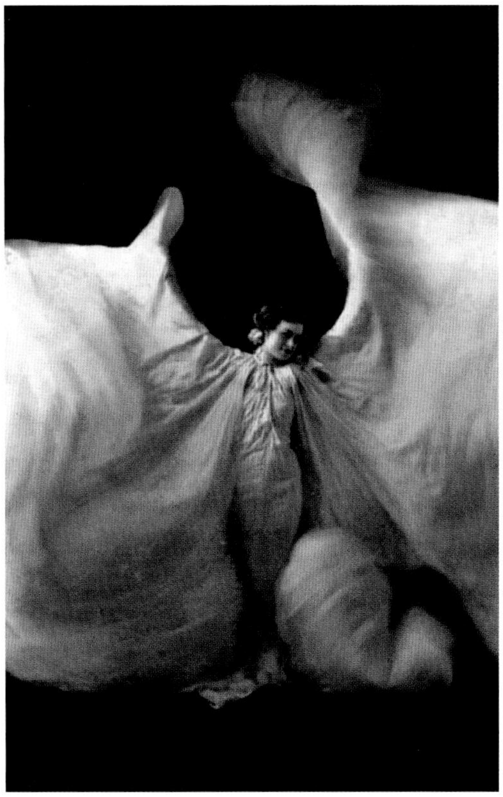

Loïe Fuller performed her 'Fire Dance' at the Folies Bergère in the late 1890s. She claimed to sculpt the light.

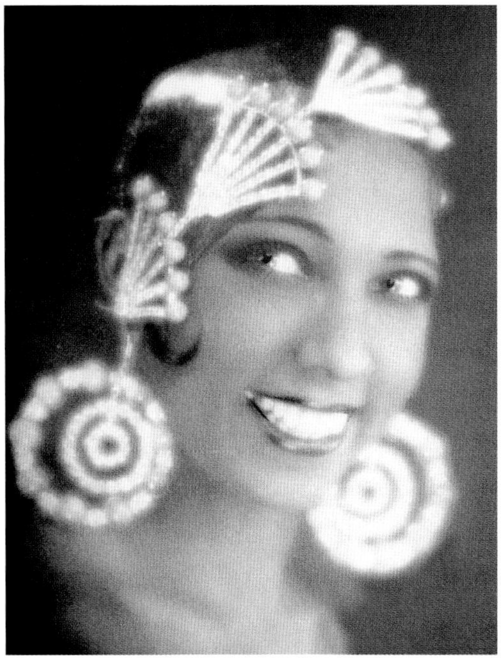

Josephine Baker, Paris, 1920s.

The Olympia: Created in 1893, it stands to this day and is Paris's 'most prestigious venue for performing artists'.

Théâtre des Champs-Elysées: On 2 October 1925 this prestigious theatre was converted into a Music Hall for one season to host a scandalous new American import: 'La Revue Nègre' (The Black Revue). A 19-year-old chorus girl named Josephine Baker was its star. This revue, featuring American jazz music, set Paris on fire.

The popularity of the Music Hall was such that many of its performers attained star status.

The Stars

Many of the dancers — often a euphemism for 'cocotte' or 'cocodette', meaning kept women — had left behind the *demimonde* to enter the world of the Music Hall in search of a rich patron. Young actresses aspired to marry millionaires and many young millionaires wanted to marry beautiful actresses. Crowned heads of state were not immune to the dancers' charm, either.

Both on and off-stage, these priestesses of the Music Hall wore outlandish clothes. Their costumes were decorated with furs and feathers and adorned with jewels. They sometimes sported close-fitting jerseys printed with wave, spider web or sun disc patterns.

On stage they projected sophistication and sensuality, posing and gyrating dizzyingly. The names of the revues had to be as alluring as possible: 'The Sins of Paris', 'The Extravagant Queen', 'Naked Paris'.

Many went on to become international stars, yet they all continued to perform for the Music Hall. Many of their names are still familiar: Maurice Chevalier, the Dolly Sisters, Mistinguett, Carlos Gardel, Josephine Baker, Edith Piaf.

Dance was particularly appreciated, and none more so than the tango. Its accordion music and audacious steps seduced Parisians; when the archbishop of Paris condemned the dance as lascivious, this only added to its appeal.

Equally popular were the *tableaux vivants* ('living pictures'). They were scenes presented on stage by costumed actors who remained silent and motionless as if in a picture. This was an astute way of satisfying customers and 'admirers' of antique sculpture, by exhibiting legs, thighs and bosoms. The actors, however, were not really nude: skin-coloured leotards were *de rigueur*. It was not until 1909 that bare breasts appeared on stage, and total nudity did not occur until 1919. The American dancer, Loïe Fuller was a huge success at the turn of the century, foreshadowing the dance goddesses of the 1920s and '30s. Born in Illinois in

1862, she achieved fame through her costumes that floated in the air thanks to hidden ventilators and were illuminated by coloured lights. As she danced and twirled, she seemed to be drawn irresistibly upwards. She appeared for the first time at the Folies Bergère in November 1892; her Serpentine Dance was a triumph.

Loïe Fuller appeared regularly at the Folies Bergère where she created the 'Fire Dance' (to Richard Wagner's *Ride of the Valkyries*), the 'Dance of the Flowers', and 'The Butterfly', among others. She modelled for sculptors Raoul Larche, Rupert Carabin and Théodore Rivière. Famously saying: "I sculpt the light", she was the precursor of the light effects of the great stage revues in Europe's newly reopened Music Halls.

During the Art Deco period, three stars in particular were emblematic of the Music Hall.

Josephine Baker. On 2 October 1925, the audience of the Théâtre des Champs-Elysées was shocked by the 'Revue Nègre', with its 19-year-old soon-to-be sensation, Josephine Baker.

When Baker was on stage, her hips, stomach and legs went into a frenzied overdrive that seemed almost obscene. Although some members of the audience walked out or booed, many others applauded. Josephine Baker was adulated as the 'Ebony Venus'.

In 1926 she appeared for the first time at the Folies Bergère, wearing her signature costume: a skirt of fake bananas. With it she established herself as the new American star of Europe.

Among Josephine Baker's rivals were the Dolly Sisters and Mistinguett. All had their place on the Paris stage. All were priestesses of the Music Hall.

In 1931, the Paris Colonial Exhibition was organised to celebrate France's Colonial Empire. That same year Josephine Baker appeared at the nearby Casino de Paris as the 'Queen of the Colonies', with costumes and sets designed by Georges Barbier.

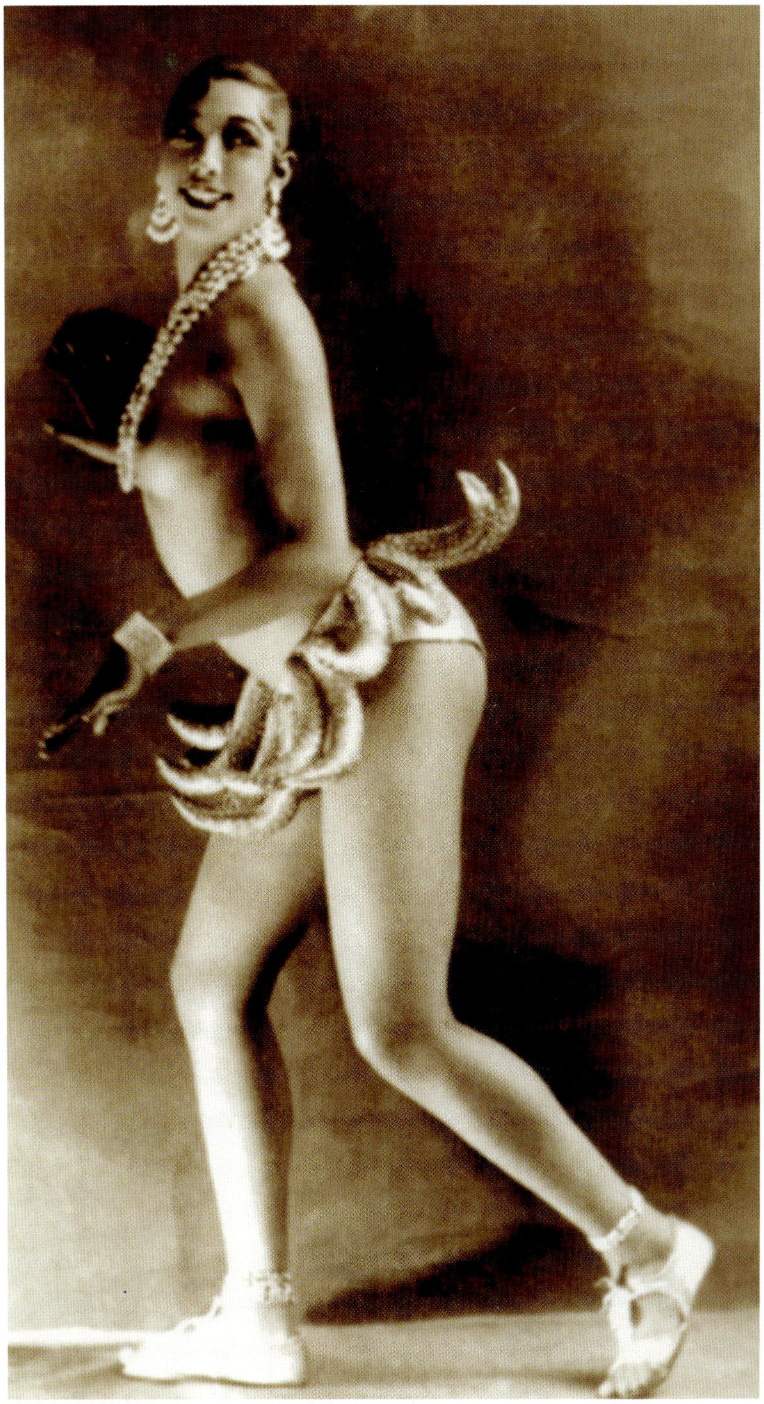

Josephine Baker in the 'Banana Suit'. She starred at the Folies Bergère in 1926.

The Dolly Sisters. Jancsika and Roszika Schwartz, who called themselves Jenny and Rosie, were Hungarian twins who had grown up in New York. Their vaudeville act was popular in Europe. In Paris, they regularly appeared at the Moulin Rouge and the Casino de Paris.

Small and dark, they were not traditionally beautiful, but had an alluringly Oriental air. Known as the Dolly Sisters, they developed their own style, playing up the fact that they were identical twins. They wore identical extravagant costumes, blunt garçonne haircuts and elaborate make-up. They posed and danced as a pair, sometimes side by side, sometimes mirroring each other's movements. Their symmetry was perfect and their costumes became as famous as their performances.

Among their admirers were Edward, Prince of Wales, the Aga Khan and Rudolph Valentino.

In 1927, at the age of 35, they gave their last show in Paris.

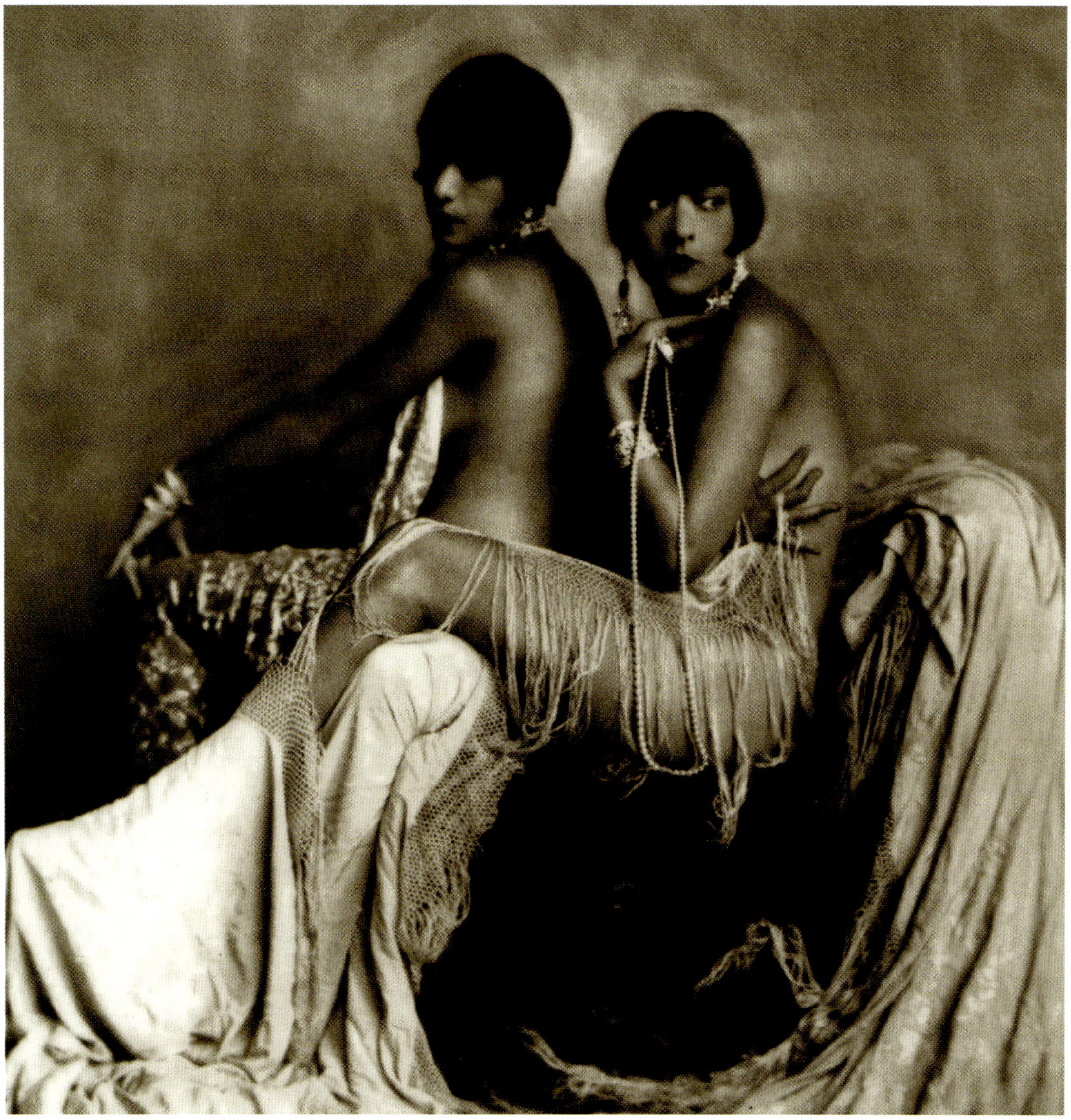

The Dolly Sisters in a photo rehearsal, early 1920s.

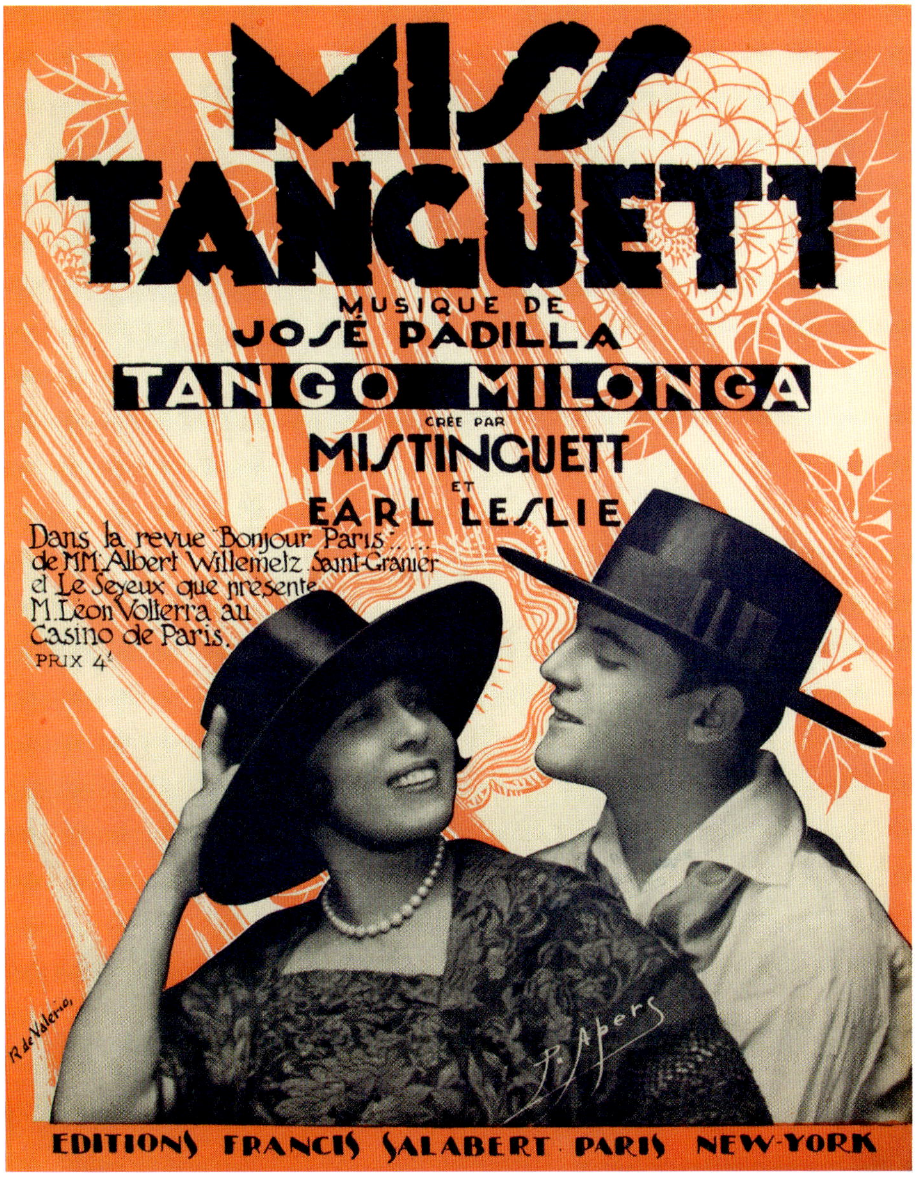

Music score for a Tango featuring Mistinguett and Earl Leslie, 1924. There is a play on words with her name and tango creating 'Miss Tanguett'.

Below: *Mistinguett at the Moulin Rouge, 1927.*

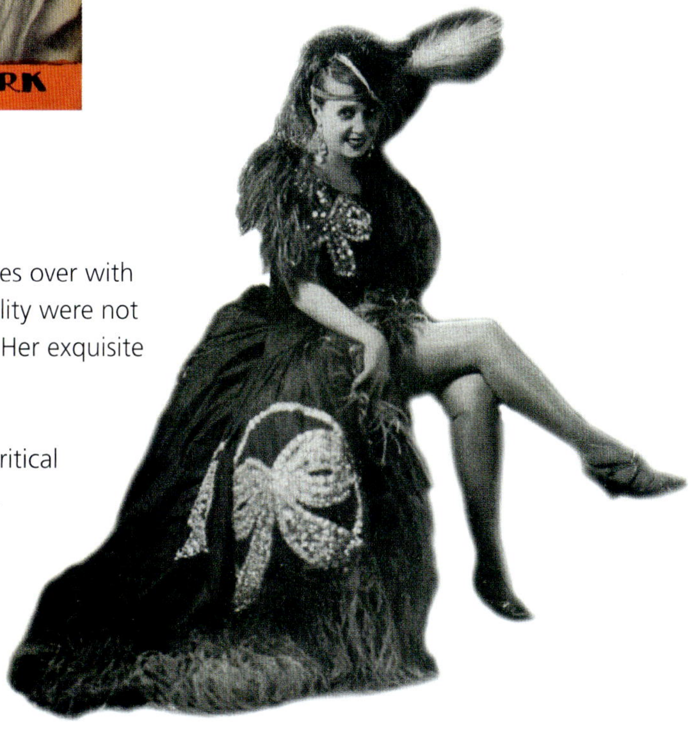

Mistinguett. The darling of the Parisian stage, Mistinguett won audiences over with her wit, charm, versatility and vivacity. Though her voice and dancing ability were not exceptional, she electrified audiences as soon as she appeared on stage. Her exquisite legs remained perfect throughout her long career.

She was relentlessly ambitious and knew what she wanted. Particularly critical toward her fellow performers, she called Josephine Baker "Banana Tits".

Mistinguett performed at all major revues in Paris. In 1938 she famously descended a staircase at the Casino de Paris wearing a headdress weighing 20kg (around 44lb).

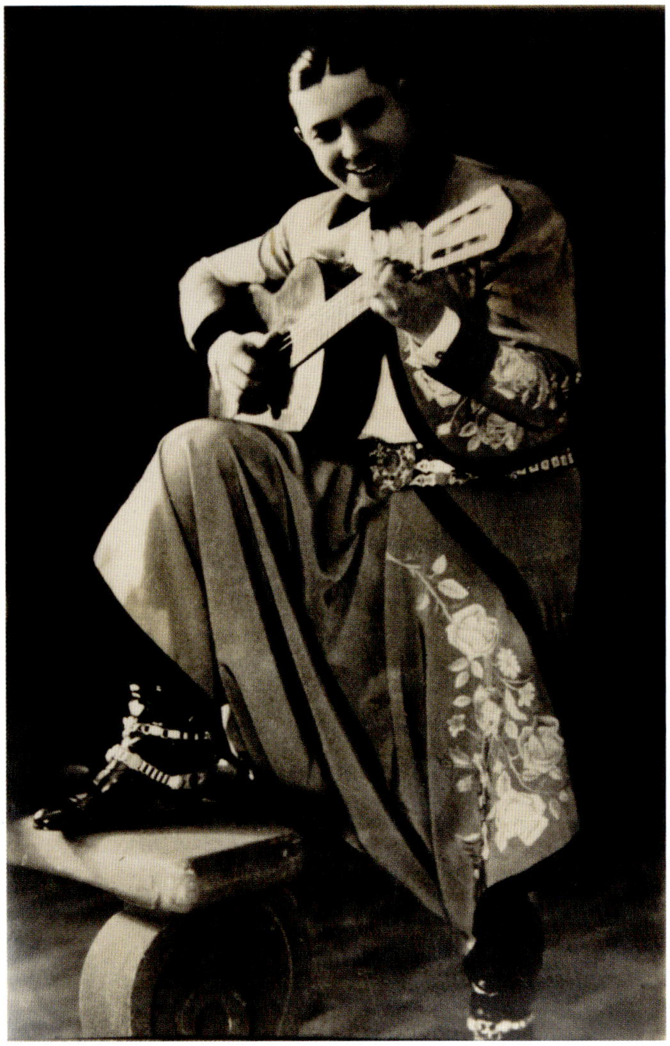

Carlos Gardel

Carlos Gardel. This Argentinean Tango singer was known as *El Zorzal* (The Field Bird), for his vibrant and expressive voice. Born in Toulouse, he emigrated to Argentina. By 1925, he had made several successful European tours. In Paris, he was the talk of the town, performing at the Florida nightclub in the rue de Clichy and at the Empire Music Hall in the avenue Wagram.

Paris

Paris was a magnetic lure to artists, tourists and buyers.

The French capital was the supreme reference for elegance, vibrancy and fine workmanship. Several international fairs were important in the development of the Art Deco style.

The 1889 *Exposition Universelle*, or World's Fair, was held to commemorate the 100th anniversary of the French Revolution. By this time the city had come to epitomise modernity.

Gustave Eiffel built his famous tower for this event; the Eiffel Tower became the tallest man-made structure in the world, surpassing the Pyramid of Cheops in Egypt, which had remained the tallest structure for over 3,800 years. Not intended to be a permanent fixture, it was to be disassembled after the Exhibition. However, despite vociferous critics, its success was such that it still stands today and has become the very symbol of Paris.

By the turn of the century Paris was the centre of the world. It was the haven of liberty, a centre of intellectual life, of sensual pleasures, and of the arts.

In 1900, another *Exposition Universelle* created a flurry of activity in Paris. The first metro line was inaugurated, as was the Alexander III Bridge, named after the Czar Alexandre III, whose son Nicholas II had laid the foundation stone in 1896.

Electric lighting was one of the revelations of the Exhibition. Illuminated by the 'Fairy Electricity' (*la fée électricité*), Paris truly became the City of Light. Indirect lighting was used to illuminate decorative sculptures in an innovative and attractive manner.

By 1913 France had the second largest economy in the world (Great Britain's was the first). The whole world came to Paris, marvelling at everything the city had to offer: elegance, luxury and brilliant lights everywhere.

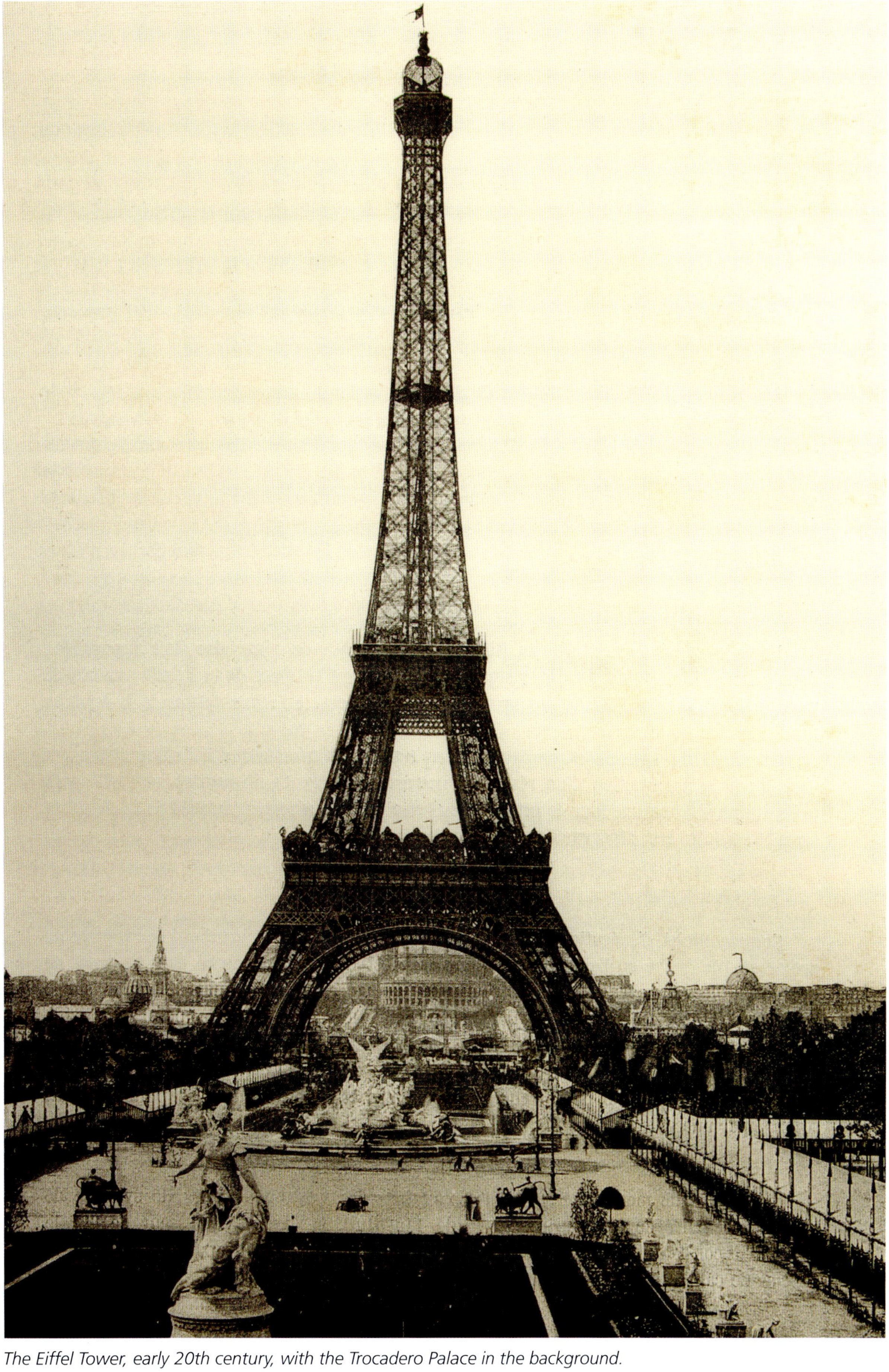

The Eiffel Tower, early 20th century, with the Trocadero Palace in the background.

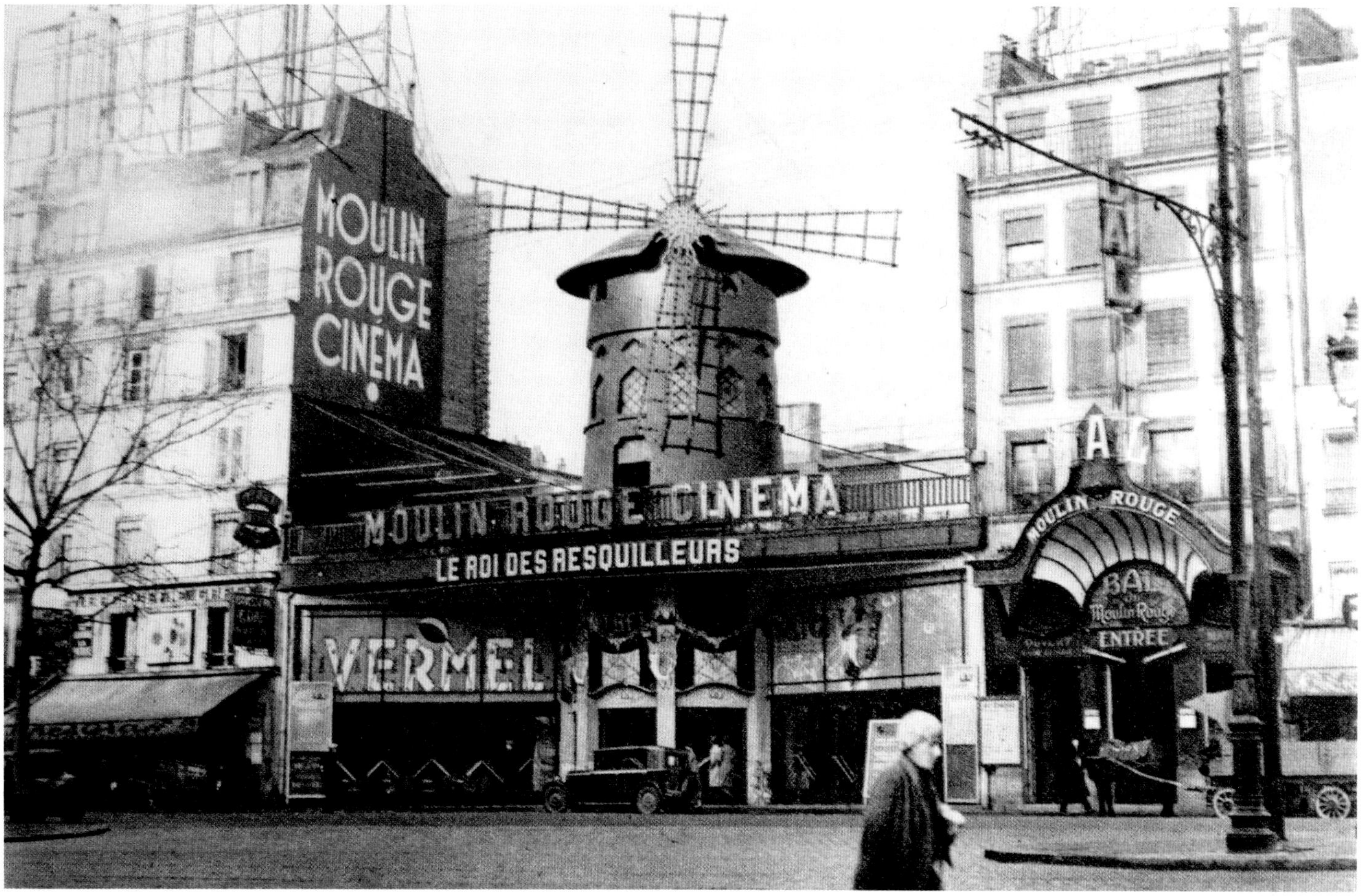

Le Bal du Moulin Rouge with the cinema next door. Paris, 1920s.

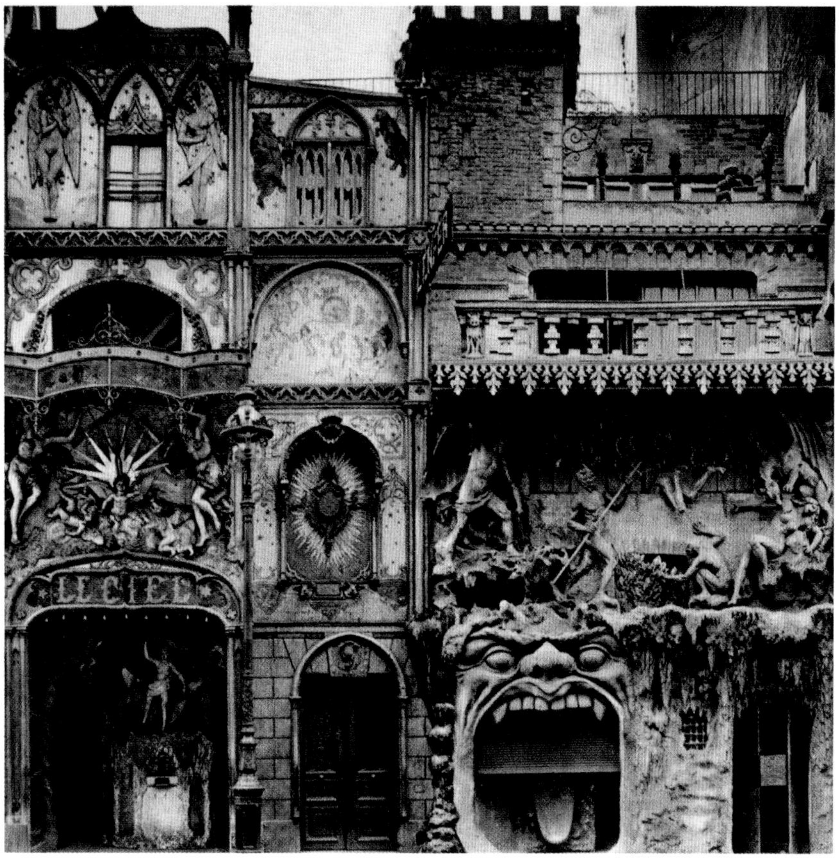

Cabarets. Heaven and Hell, Paris.

Cabarets. The Black Cat, Paris.

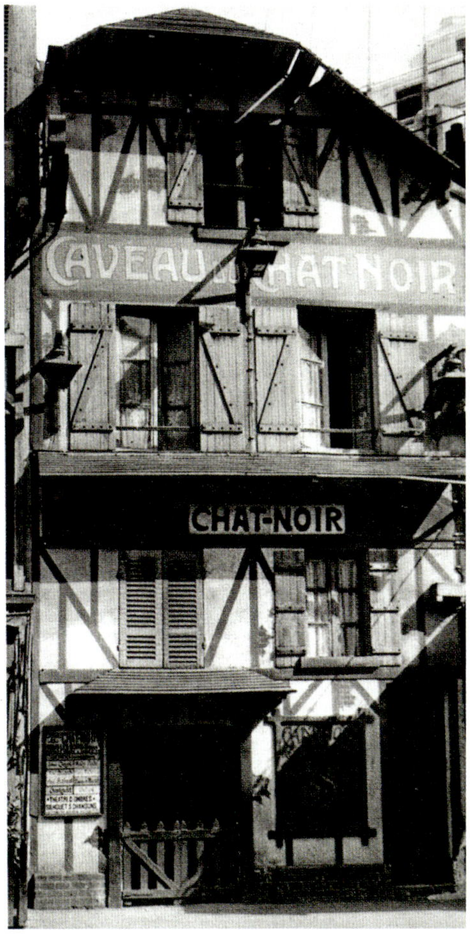

Dancing in public places was popular and smoking had become fashionable. Women who smoked were considered sexy and daring. Patrons came just to ogle this type of woman. In the audience, dandies flirted freely with 'cocodettes', ladies of the night.

Technological innovations such as moving pictures became very popular. In 1907 the city had two cinemas; by 1913 there were 160.

While Paris was the undisputed capital of painting and sculpture, its craftsmanship continued on a small scale, while other cities — London, Berlin, and New York, for example — had become industrial centres. Instead of factory workers, Paris boasted artisans — craftsmen, painters and sculptors — who were proud of their skills. Working for small shops or for a particular clientele, the Parisian artisans were highly respected, by the French and foreigners alike.

The swimming pool at the Lido, Paris. Later transformed into a transparent water tank for revue numbers.

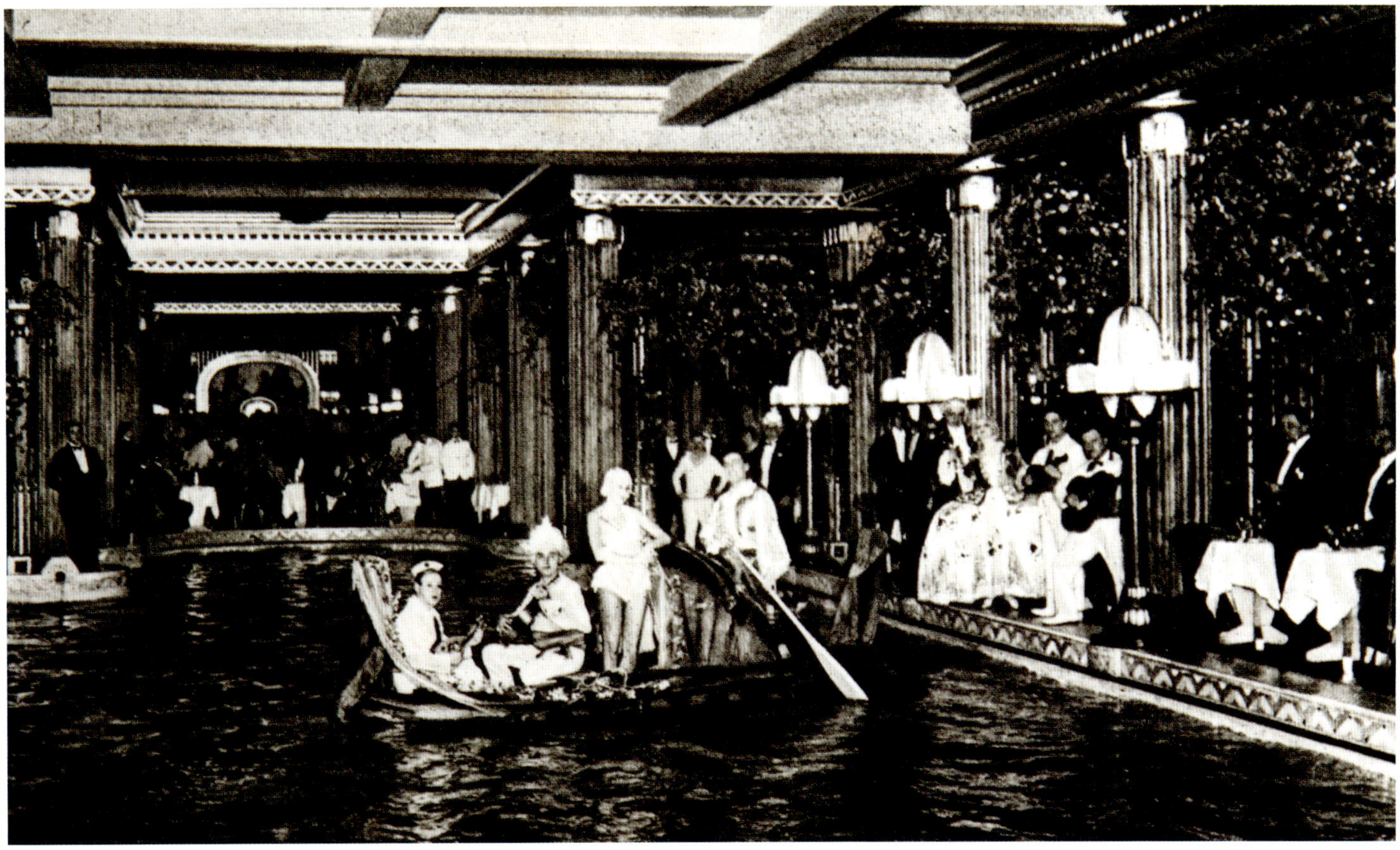

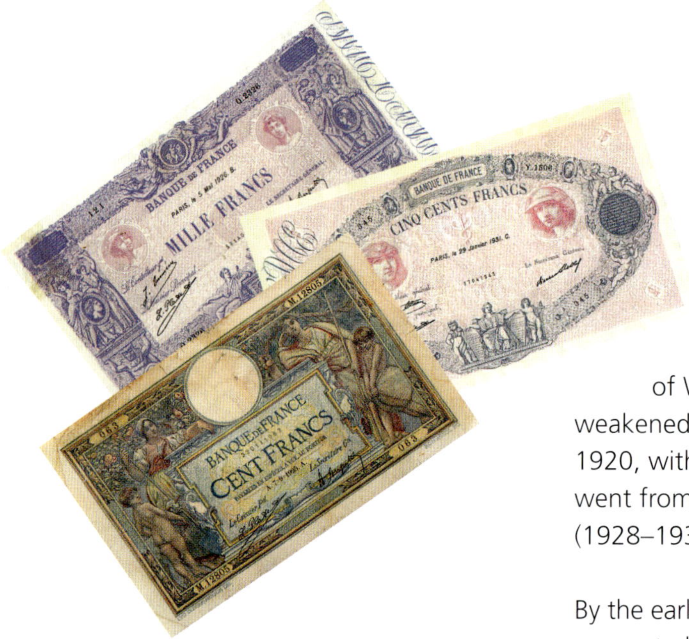

French currency during the 1920s and '30s suffered great devaluations making it all the more attractive for foreign visitors and their shopping extravaganzas.

Artists from all over the world were drawn by the city's distinctive and inimitable charms. In addition, Paris was inexpensive, the cost of living remaining quite low after World War I. With the outbreak of World War I, France had left the gold standard, and the war greatly weakened the franc. Its purchasing power diminished by 70% from 1915 to 1920, with a further 43% drop between 1922 and 1926. In that period the dollar went from 5.50 francs to 50 francs. After a brief return to the gold standard (1928–1936), the currency was again allowed to slide.

By the early 1930s, foreigners represented fewer than 10% of the population, but accounted for 50% of the city's artists. Man Ray, Alexander Calder, Ernest Hemingway, and arts patron Peggy Guggenheim came from the United States; Eugene Ionesco, Constantin Brancusi and Demetre Chiparus arrived from Romania.

The Ecole des Beaux Arts, founded in 1795, was one of the breeding grounds of new talent. Over two thirds of its graduates went on to earn a medal at the salons; this distinction made it easier to obtain state commissions and attract private buyers.

Paris's attraction was twofold: aspiring artists could live there on a limited budget while also gaining exposure to audiences who might be interested in their work.

Wealthy foreign visitors spent lavishly in the city. They attended the art salons and purchased all types of art. They sought out *haute couture* clothes, perfumes and decorative objects for their homes. Fashion shows were scheduled to coincide with the arrival of ocean liners from the United States and South America.

These tourists went on shopping extravaganzas, purchasing Lalique glass, porcelain from Limoges and Sèvres, paintings and small ornamental sculptures. All these items were shipped home.

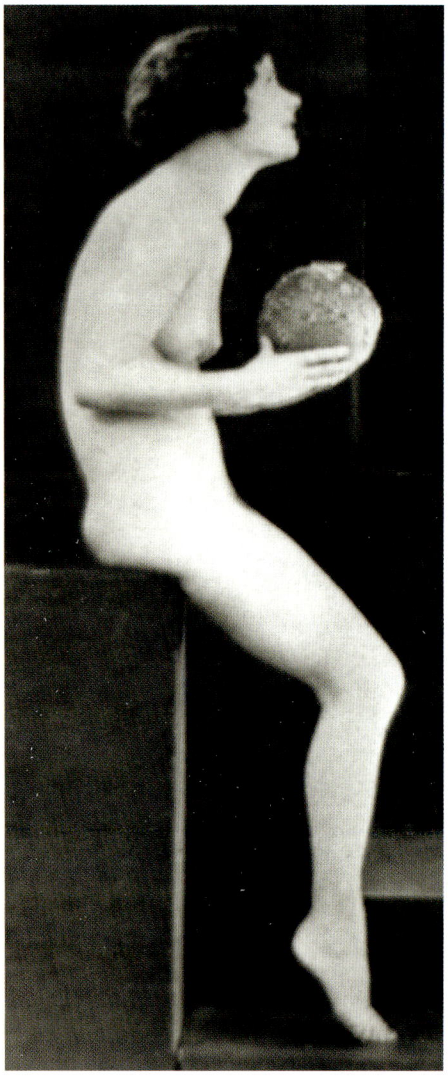

Rosiane at the Casino de Paris holding a Lalique 'Druide' vase, 1920s.

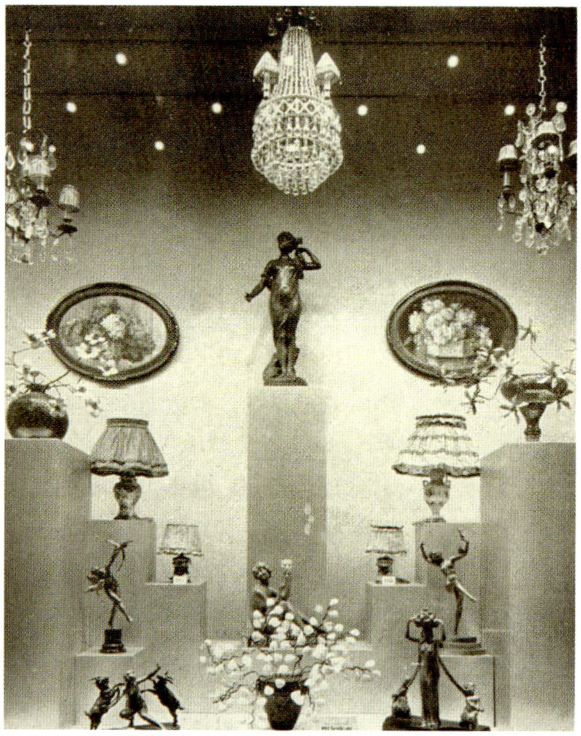

Printemps department store in Paris. Shop window exhibiting home decorations, including sculptures.

In the evening they would dine out and seek amusement and entertainment. The Music Hall particularly appealed to them because one need not understand French to appreciate it.

Paris further enhanced its magnetism by hosting the 1924 Olympic Games.

In 1925 Paris held the International Exposition of Modern Industrial and Decorative Arts (Exposition International des Arts Décoratifs et Industriels Modernes, often called the 'Paris Deco Expo 25').

This long-awaited exhibition (originally planned for 1914, it was postponed due to World War I) was to be the French window to the world. It was intended to showcase elegant and innovative French design, while highlighting novelty and modernity; everything on display had to embody the new stylistic currents.

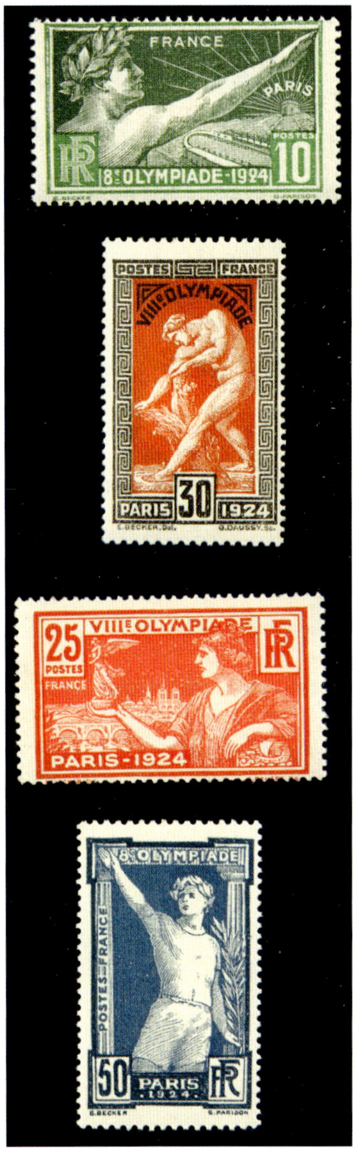

Commemorative postage stamps celebrating the 1924 Olympic Games in Paris.

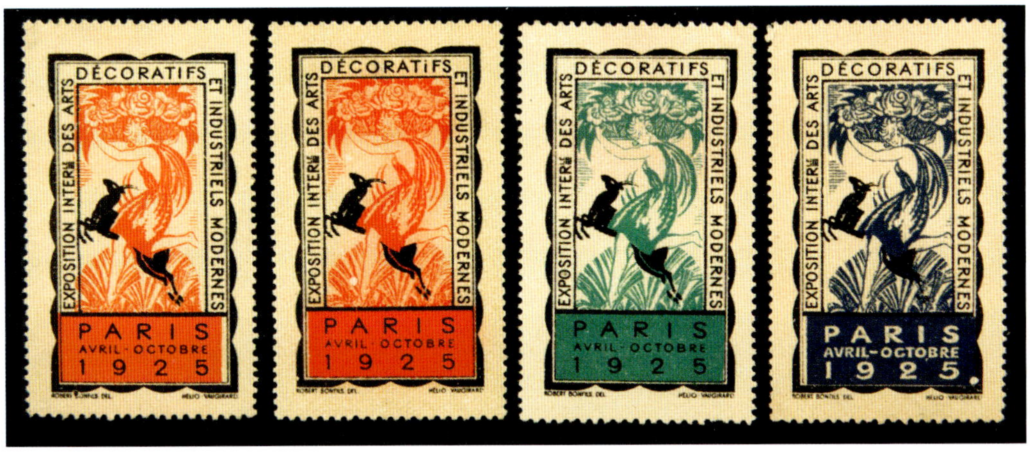

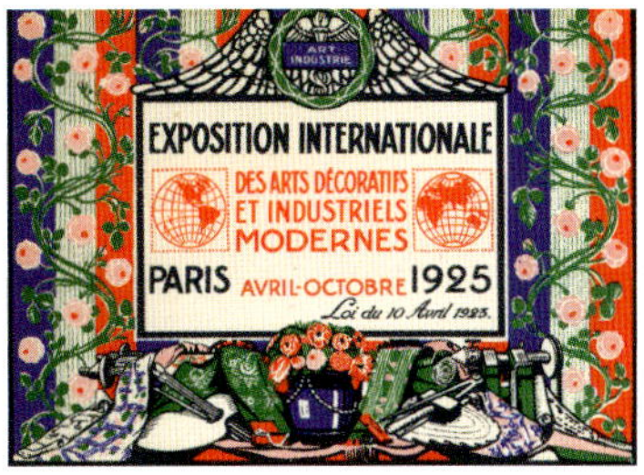

Commemorative souvenir stamps for the 1925 International Exhibition of Decorative and Modern Industrial Arts in Paris.

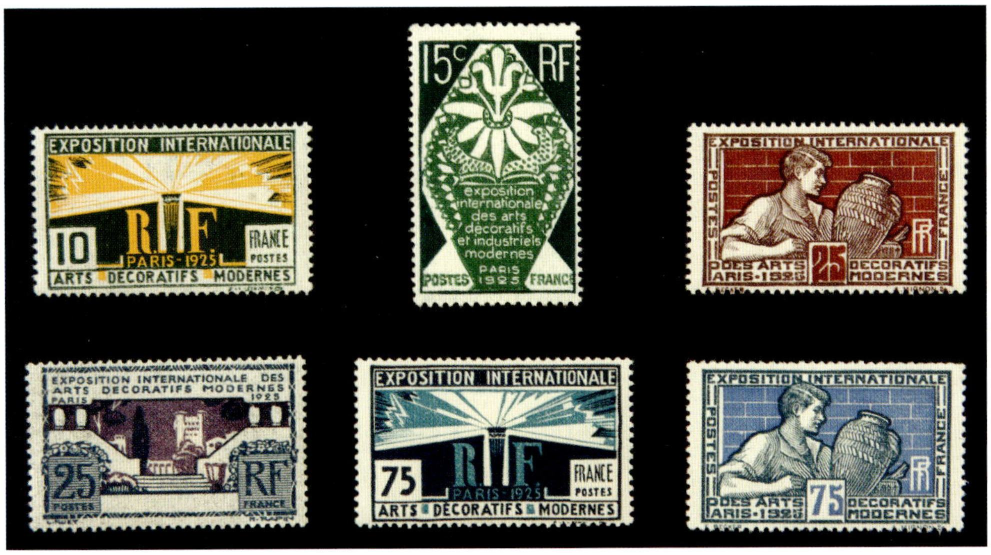

Commemorative postage stamps for the 1925 International Exhibition of Decorative and Modern Industrial Arts in Paris.

Many countries were asked to participate, but the United States declined, claiming there was no modern art in the country! Germany was not invited.

The emerging artistic trends superseded the styles of the past. Shapes were stylised, designs became cleaner and more graphic. New materials appeared: mother-of-pearl, exotic woods, ivory, lacquer and rare leathers. Metal was occasionally used in order to achieve a particular decorative effect.

The style had its detractors, however, among them Le Corbusier, Nikolaus Pevsner and Georges Besson. Some hoped that the Paris Deco Expo 25, its supreme celebration, would also sound its death knell. In fact it turned out to be the triumphant artistic movement of the 20th century, which later named it 'Art Deco'. Glamorous and sophisticated, the style influenced all aspects of life.

Many visitors purchased items at the Exhibition, which re-appeared decades later in far-off places — lost icons of the 'Paris Deco Expo 25'.

In 1937 Paris hosted the International Exposition of Art and Technology in Modern Life (or '*Expo 37'*). Though it hoped to emulate the 1925 exhibition, it attracted fewer exhibitors.

One iconic image of this exhibition shows the Soviet and German pavilions standing face to face. Two buildings erected for this exhibition, the Palais de Chaillot and the Palais de Tokyo, are both still standing and in use today as museums.

The Statuettes

The Art Deco movement brought nature indoors. The concept was not new; the Art Nouveau style had featured vegetal and natural motifs. But in the Art Deco style nature was everywhere, especially in the field of decorative sculpture.

The decoration of modern homes required innovative fabrics, lighting, glass items and sculptures, which epitomised the new trends. The sculptures mirrored contemporary obsessions, among them the follies of the Music Hall, where people went to forget their troubles, hear lively music, see extravagant costumes and vivacious dancing, and — why not? — a glimpse of titillating flesh.

While the great majority of these sculptures depicted scenes from the Music Hall, some showed scenes from everyday life, sportsmen and women, children and even religious themes.

They were not one-of-a-kind pieces; they were produced in series of twenty to thirty pieces, depending on the demand. Some series comprised only four or five examples; in rare instances only one sculpture is known to exist. The more expensive the figure, the less demand there was for it, hence the rarer it is today.

Some statuettes were produced in several sizes — usually two, but occasionally as many as five — depending on the subject matter, the demand and the decorative value.

Even at the time they were made, the sculptures were not inexpensive. Multiple figures on a single base (featuring between two and five figures) were particularly costly. Their high price meant that fewer of them were produced.

Sculptures were also made of wood, marble and alabaster. These materials were sometimes combined with ivory.

A device invented in 1839 by a Parisian engineer named Achille Collas had made it possible to reproduce sculptures in smaller versions. This invention allowed a great number of statuettes to be offered in the small sizes ideally suited to the home.

The Materials

Bronze. Called *airain* in French, bronze is a blend of copper and zinc that takes on a greenish patina over time due to its copper content.

The bodies of the figures were rendered in bronze and in most cases, the faces and limbs in ivory. The contrast of bronze and ivory was subtle, elegant and attractive.

Ivory. Easy to work with, ivory has a soft and elegant look. The combination of bronze and ivory had been used since ancient Greece; it was known as 'chryselephantine' from the Greek word *chrysos* — meaning gold — and *elephantine* — ivory.

Ivory was a raw material that was made available in Europe through its colonies. It was sent from Africa to Europe. Excellent ivory carving schools were created in Erbach, Germany and Dieppe, France. The plentiful supply of ivory made it easy for artists to develop and hone their skills.

Marble. The statuettes had attractive bases that greatly enhanced their appeal, made of marble or onyx and sometimes a combination of the two. High quality pieces of marble were set aside for the pedestals. The figures were anchored to their bases by long screws.

The veins and patterns of the marble and onyx bases contribute to the uniqueness of each statuette. The bronze was cast, but no two pieces of marble are alike.

This was so important that sculptors often dedicated much time and effort to creating elaborate bases. Some of these bases may even be considered elegant sculptures in their own right.

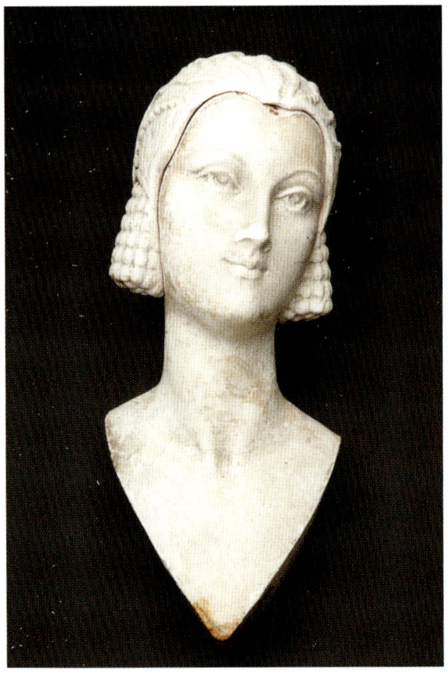

Plaster model for mould and assembly of bronze and ivory.

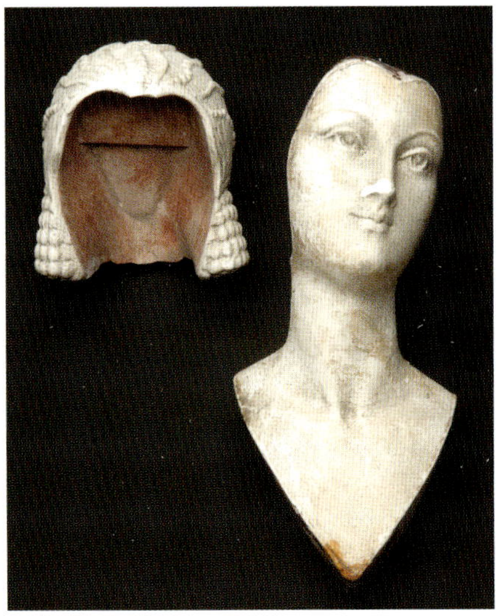

In a few cases the bases are an integral part of the whole. This is the case for Le Faguays's *Signal Man* (p.150), in which the base forms the top of a rampart from which the archer is taking aim, and in Jacquemin's *Skier* (p.129), in which the base is the athlete's jumping board.

Plaster: The hill of Montmartre in the north of Paris, where the Sacred Heart Church stands, is the highest point in the city. It is also a mountain of plaster. By 1860 the city forbade further exploitation of the mineral for fear that the whole hill might collapse. For years afterwards, however, it continued to provide three quarters of all the plaster consumed in Paris.

Plaster has the malleability the artist needs to express his intentions. It was used to make the moulds for the figures, including their bronze, ivory and marble portions.

Terracotta: This is a kind of clay that fires at low temperatures (1,000–1,120° C) — this is what potters call 'bisque firing'. It produces a light brown surface.

The higher the firing temperature, the greater the shrinkage, the stronger the clay body, and the darker the colour of the end product. Terracotta sometimes is glazed for a particular effect.

Wood: Though rarely used in the manufacture of statuettes, it is sometimes added for colour and texture, often for skin tones in particular; it occasionally forms part of the base.

Enamel: This is a vitrified coating, available in many colours and shades, which can either be cold painted or applied to the bronze and then fired for special effects.

White enamel could never replace ivory, though, since its effect when applied to bronze is not as pleasing as that of other colours. Hence limbs and faces are made of either bronze or ivory, or occasionally marble.

Zinc: The zinc metal alloy known as spelter in English (*'régule'* in French) was sometimes used for decorative sculptures. While it was less expensive, more malleable, and lighter than bronze, it does not have that material's nobility.

The Commercial Venues

The founder-merchants who created and sold sculptures in France were known as *'éditeurs'*. They produced sculptures and glass, porcelain and ceramic pieces, selling them through their own retail galleries.

They also offered dinner services, prints, wrought-iron goods and lamps. They had commercial representatives throughout France and in several other cities in Europe, North Africa and South America.

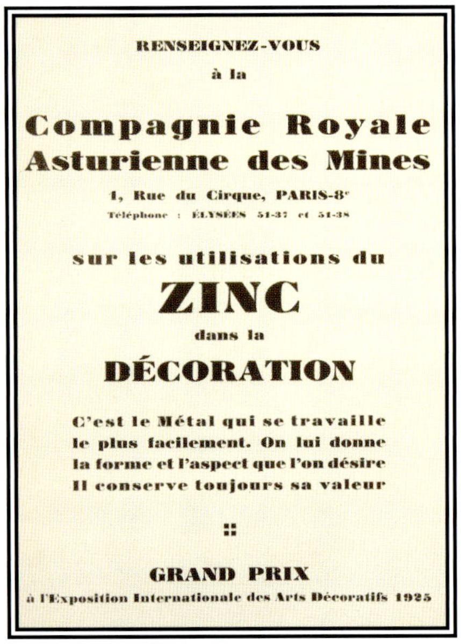

Advertisement for the use of zinc for decorative purposes.

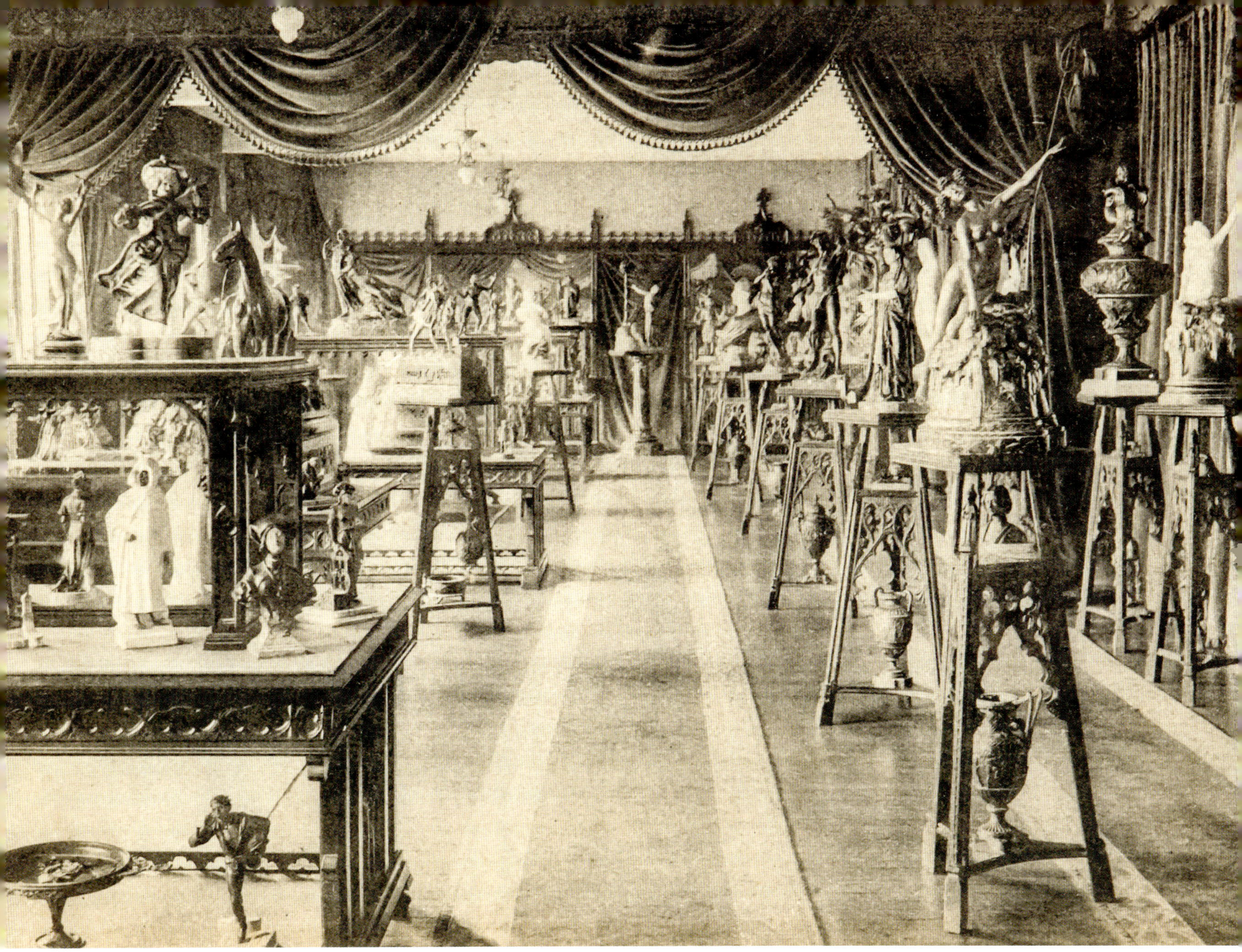

Galerie Béranger — Edmond Etling

Located at 158 rue de Temple in Paris, it specialised in a wide selection of items for home decoration, ranging from furniture, porcelain and glass to various types of lighting: candles, gas and electricity. The Etling Company manufactured and sold many sculptures by such artists as Chiparus, Colinet, Guiraud-Rivière, Bouraine and Fanny Rozet.

The proprietor, Edmond Etling, was awarded a gold medal and a *diplome d'honneur* in Brussels in 1910; the firm was a member of the jury in Frankfurt in 1910; they won the *grand prix* in Turin in 1911 and received a *diplome d'honneur* and a *grand prix* in Paris in 1913.

At the 1925 Paris Exhibition, Etling exhibited in the French Section of the Grand Palais, Hall B, Stand 40.

At the 1937 exhibition the firm showed a salon with lamps by Bonnet, Corchet, Dunaime, Gaillard, Laplanche and Mielot. They also exhibited sculptures by Guiraud-Rivière, Kéléty (*Bust of a Youth with Hat and Vines*) and Bouraine (*Bust of a Young Girl*).

Galerie Béranger in Paris. A vast array of decorations were offered for the home.

L.N.J.L.

Les Neveux de Jules Lehmann was located at 26 rue de Paradis, and at 14 avenue de l'Opéra in Paris. They also had premises in Lyon at 9 rue de la Republique and in Florence at 7 Via Spontini. The proprietor, Jules Levy-Lehmann, knew how to appreciate the talents of sculptors and how to market those sculptors' works. L.N.J.L. represented an impressive list, including: Demetre Chiparus, Guiraud-Rivière, Injalbert, Léonard, Merculiano, Constant Roux, Joé Descomps, Le Faguays, Lamourdedieu, Laurent, J.J. Martel, Hauchecorne, Madeleine Granger, Colinet, Gennarelli, Alfred Pina, George Chauvel and Jean Ortis.

The loose-leaf Lehmann catalogues featured the items for sale; pages could then be added or removed according to availability and demand.

At the 1925 Paris Exhibition Lehmann exhibited in the French Section of the Grand Palais, Hall B, Stand 38.

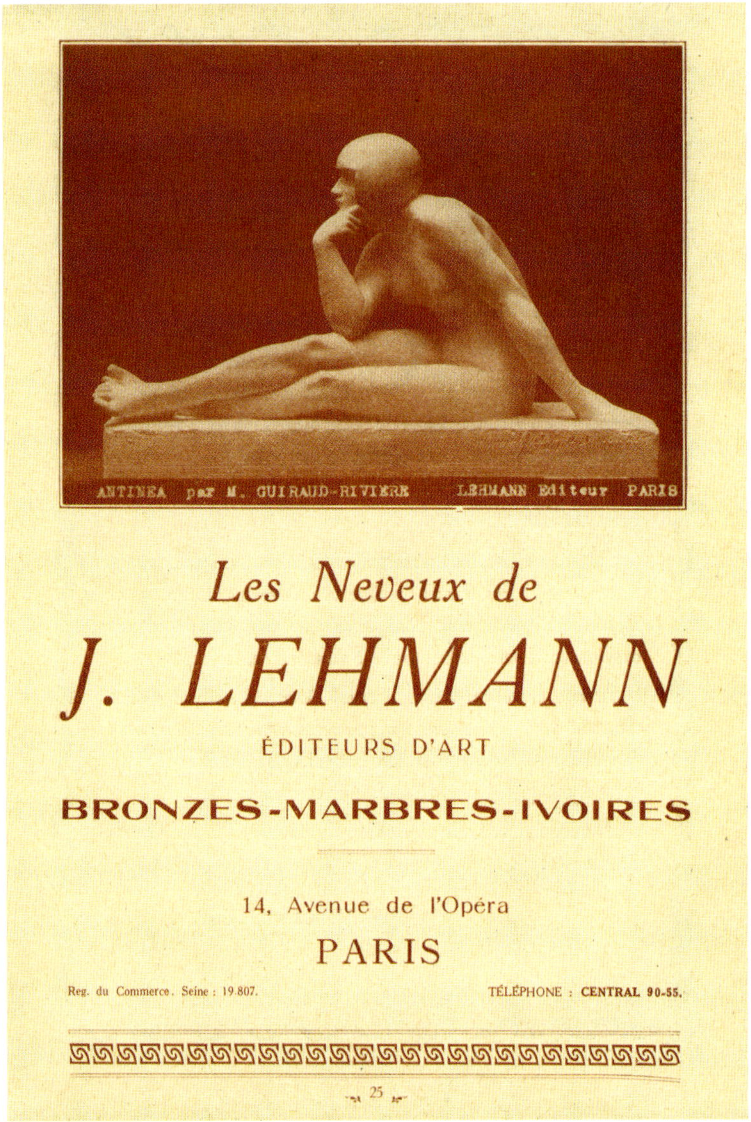

Advertisement for Les Neveux de Jules Lehmann with Guiraud-Rivière's Antinéa.

Arthur Goldscheider

This Viennese firm opened branches in France under the direction of Arthur Goldscheider, which worked with the Goldscheider family's establishments in Europe. The Paris branch had premises at 45 rue de Paradis and 2 avenue de l'Opéra.

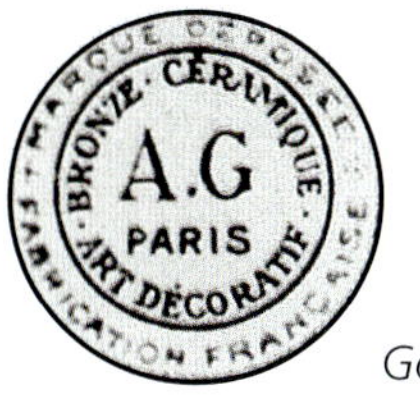

Goldscheider seal

Goldscheider manufactured and sold figures by Lorenzl, Kéléty, Le Faguays, Sarabezolles and Delannoy, among many others.

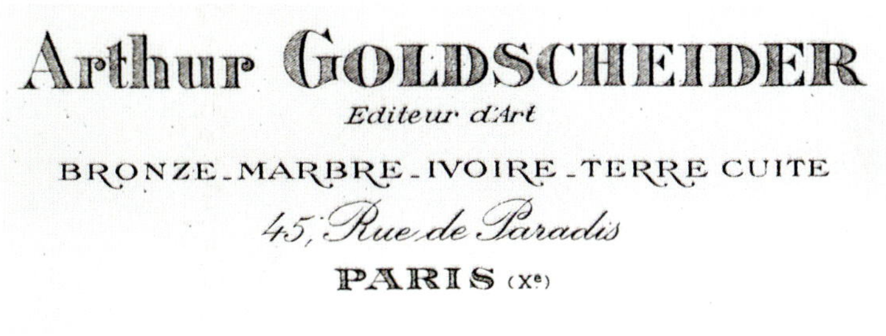

Arthur GOLDSCHEIDER
Editeur d'Art
BRONZE_MARBRE_IVOIRE_TERRE CUITE
45, Rue de Paradis
PARIS (X^e)

Goldscheider Éditeur

Goldscheider advertisement with Le Faguays's Harem Girl.

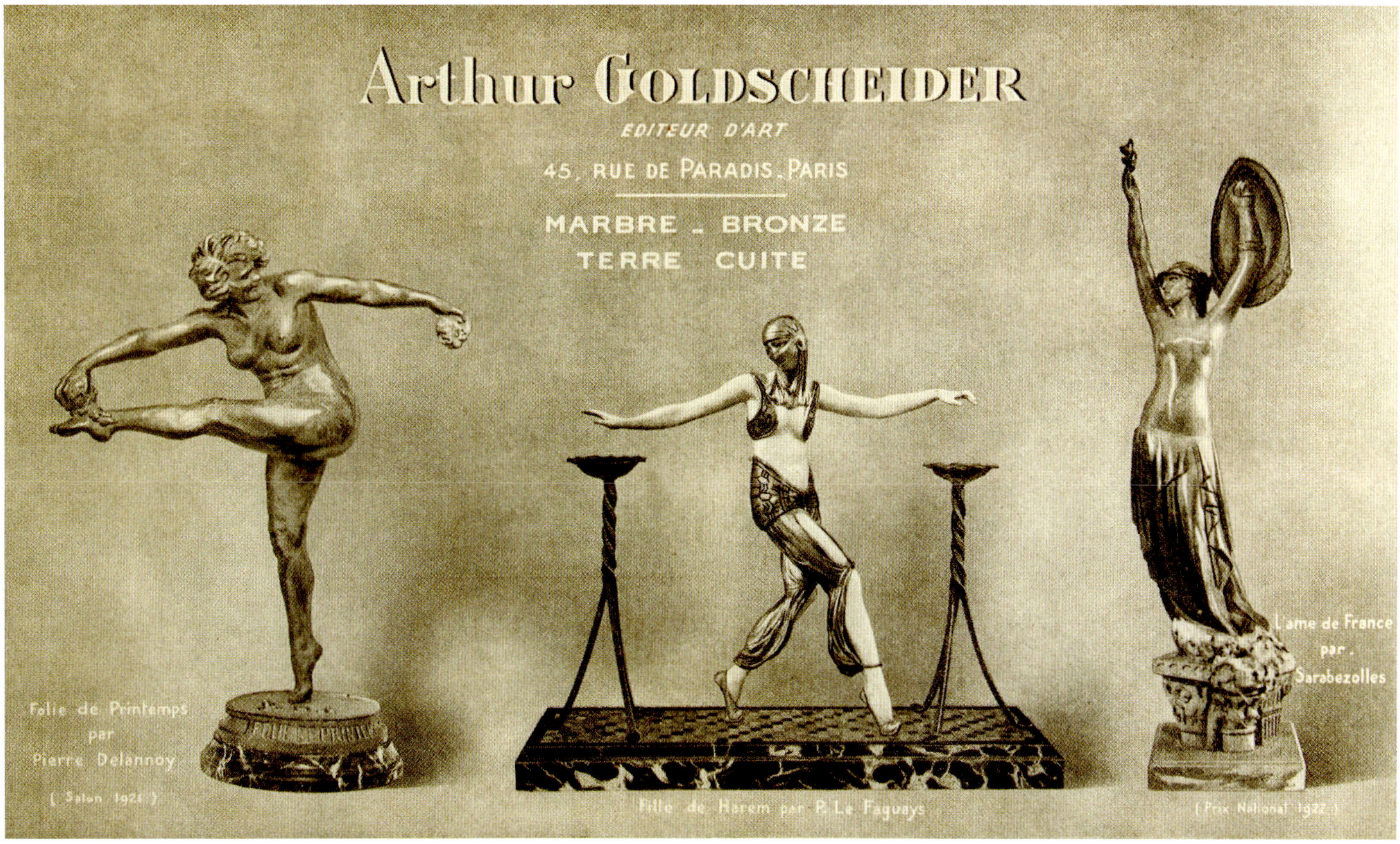

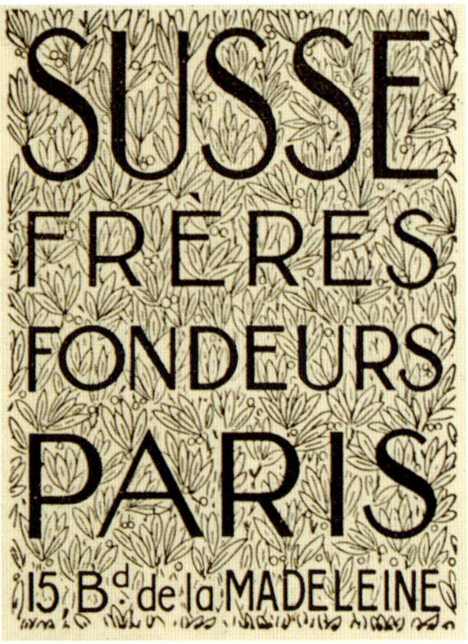

Susse Frères advertisement.

At the 1925 Paris exhibition Goldscheider exhibited in the French Section of the Esplanade des Invalides, Pavilion I–115.

Etling, Lehmann and Goldscheider were among the many Jews who were persecuted by the Nazis and forced to close or 'aryanise' their businesses.

Other enterprises producing Art Deco sculpture were:
Galerie Siot-Decauville 63 av. Victor-Emmanuel III.
André Seligman
V. Félix Cavaroc & Cie (Sociéte française de sculpture d'art) 10 rue de la Paix, Paris.
Georges Bourgeois (Ancienne Maison F. Delarue)
Mansard G. 38 rue de Paradis.
Guillemard E. An atelier of bronze and marble.
Susse Frères In Paris at 15 boulevard de la Madeleine.
Barbedienne F. In Paris at 30 boulevard Poissonnière; worked with Barye, Fremiet, Colinet and Cormier (l'Offrande), among others.
Max Le Verrier 100 rue du Theatre. Edited works by Le Faguays (Fayral), Guerbe, Arthus and Bouraine. Also worked extensively in terracotta and ceramics.
RuM, Rosenthal und Maeder in Berlin. Worked with several artists including Lange, Professor Otto Poertzel, Harders, Philippe and Montini. In 1929 Preiss & Kassler took over this workshop.

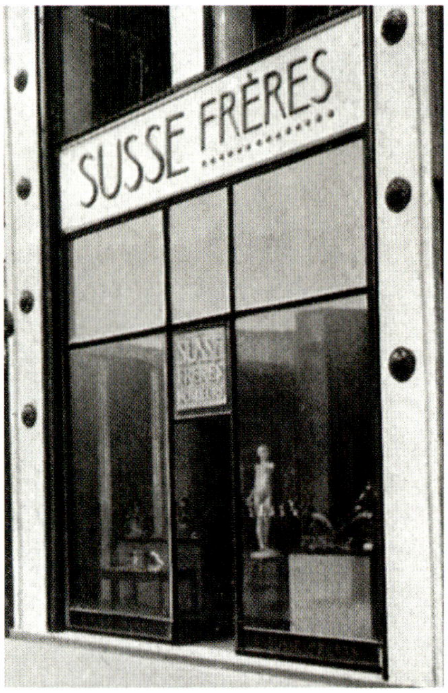

Susse Frères store in Paris. First Offering *by Henri Arnold can be seen in the window.*

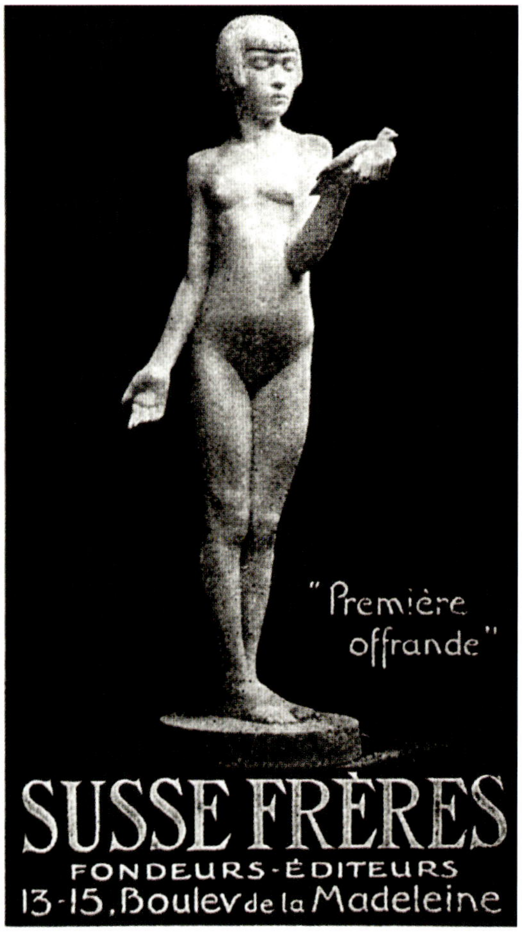

Advertisement for First Offering *by Henri Arnold.*

PK, Preiss & Kassler in Berlin: specialised in figures by Preiss, Philippe, Roland Paris, Professor Otto Poertzel, Schmidt-Cassel, W. Göritz, Eichler, Aichele, Schaeffer, Lorenzl, Horst, Lange, Charol, Professor Wandschneider and Gg. Morin.
Argentor (Viennese) metal figures and glass mounts.
Bergman (Viennese) Oriental themed figures.

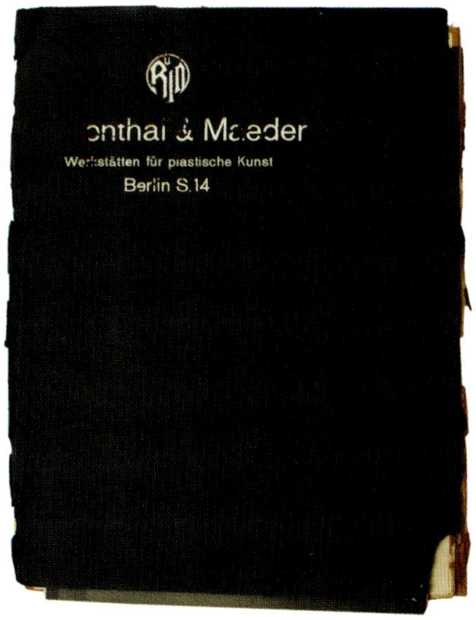

Rosenthal und Maeder catalogue.

Luxury Tax

By 1926 a 12% tax had been levied on luxury items. To avoid it, artists in the field of decorative arts created 'practical' works of art, at prices no higher than those of regular industrial design. However, the French Tax Revenue Service decided the tax would be applied to all authentic artistic expressions, whatever the sales price.

While artists protested (the goal of the 1925 'Deco' exhibition had been to make even the most mundane objects 'artistic' so as to blend in harmoniously in any room), the Tax authorities persisted and the tax was levied.

The Curtain Falls on Les Années Folles

As the 'Années Folles' drew to a close, not everything was glamour and glitter in the City of Lights. Life was no longer one big, endless party; poverty and many other problems were just around the corner. As a result of the sexual freedom, venereal diseases were rampant (it was not until 1928 that penicillin was discovered and the early 1940s before it was used as a medical treatment).

Social discontent was growing on both the extreme right and the left. A mere spark could ignite Europe.

World War II

In 1939 the continent caught fire. The German Nazi regime began invading countries, murdering millions, expropriating properties, raiding bank vaults and confiscating all the artworks they could get their hands on. In 1940, France was invaded and thousands were deported. Hitler visited the city in June 1940, bringing with him Albert Speer and Arno Breker.

Cafés were bustling as usual, restaurants had a new uniformed clientele, some Music Halls closed while others remained open and yet others re-opened in order to entertain their new-found patrons.

Works of decorative art were in great demand. Business boomed at the art galleries patronised by the Germans. During the occupation, approximately seven new galleries opened, while seventy or so advertised their wares in the press. They organised exhibitions and prospered. Auction houses also benefited from the heightened activity, including the long-established ones, which sold over 2 million artworks in 1941 and 1942 alone. The provenance of these artworks was never questioned. Looted art was sold with impunity, and art was a convenient way to launder money made on the black market. It was considered a 'safe' investment that retained its value despite currency fluctuations and inflation. Thus was created a huge bubble, which inevitably burst after France was liberated.

Post-World War II

During the war some sculptures were melted down for their metal, which was used in the war effort; others were destroyed in bombing raids. It is impossible to know how many were lost. Those outside the war zone survived, particularly those in North and South America, Australia, India and the Far East; statuettes have been spotted in nightclubs in Havana and cabarets in Vietnam. They are also sometimes found in unlikely places such as attics or spare rooms, where they were stashed away as unwanted clutter.

After the war they were forgotten. From 1945 to 1965 many Art Deco sculptures lay dormant, abandoned. Their heyday was over. The figures that survived usually did so only because they had become 'invisible'.

As in the fairy tale, they would be gradually rediscovered and come back to life. However, their true 'awakening' came with the retrospective of 1920s and 1930s art held at the Minneapolis Institute of Arts in 1971. This exhibition also popularised the name 'Art Deco'. Some of the visitors had lived through the era, while many others discovered it for the first time.

Certain critics dismissed Art Deco as mere froth and frivolity, nothing more than kitsch. Some commentators even considered it politically tainted. Despite these discordant voices, Art Deco works began to be sought-after and collected.

The Art Deco dealer soon appeared, as pieces began to be bought by show business personalities, patrons of the arts, and other collectors. These people were not interested in the works as investments, but rather as unique depictions of a bygone era. Gradually, due to their scarcity and rising value, statuettes attained the status of highly prized collectors' items.

At the same time, curiosity grew about the artists who had created the sculptures. While their names were often long forgotten, they had been mentioned in contemporary catalogues. Considerable efforts were devoted to rediscovering them.

Although some critics derided the sculptures as icons of vulgarity and bad taste, the works themselves returned to the forefront and gained a following that would no doubt have surprised their creators.

With the changing times, the skills and know-how of the Art Deco artists faded away; their materials disappeared as the use of ivory was restricted, then forbidden. As a result, statuettes became even more rare and desirable. An avid and wealthy clientele began pursuing these icons of a bygone decorative style.

Today museums organise exhibitions of them that attract large and enthusiastic crowds. They have become true emissaries of the Art Deco period.

THE PLATES

ALONZO, Dominique

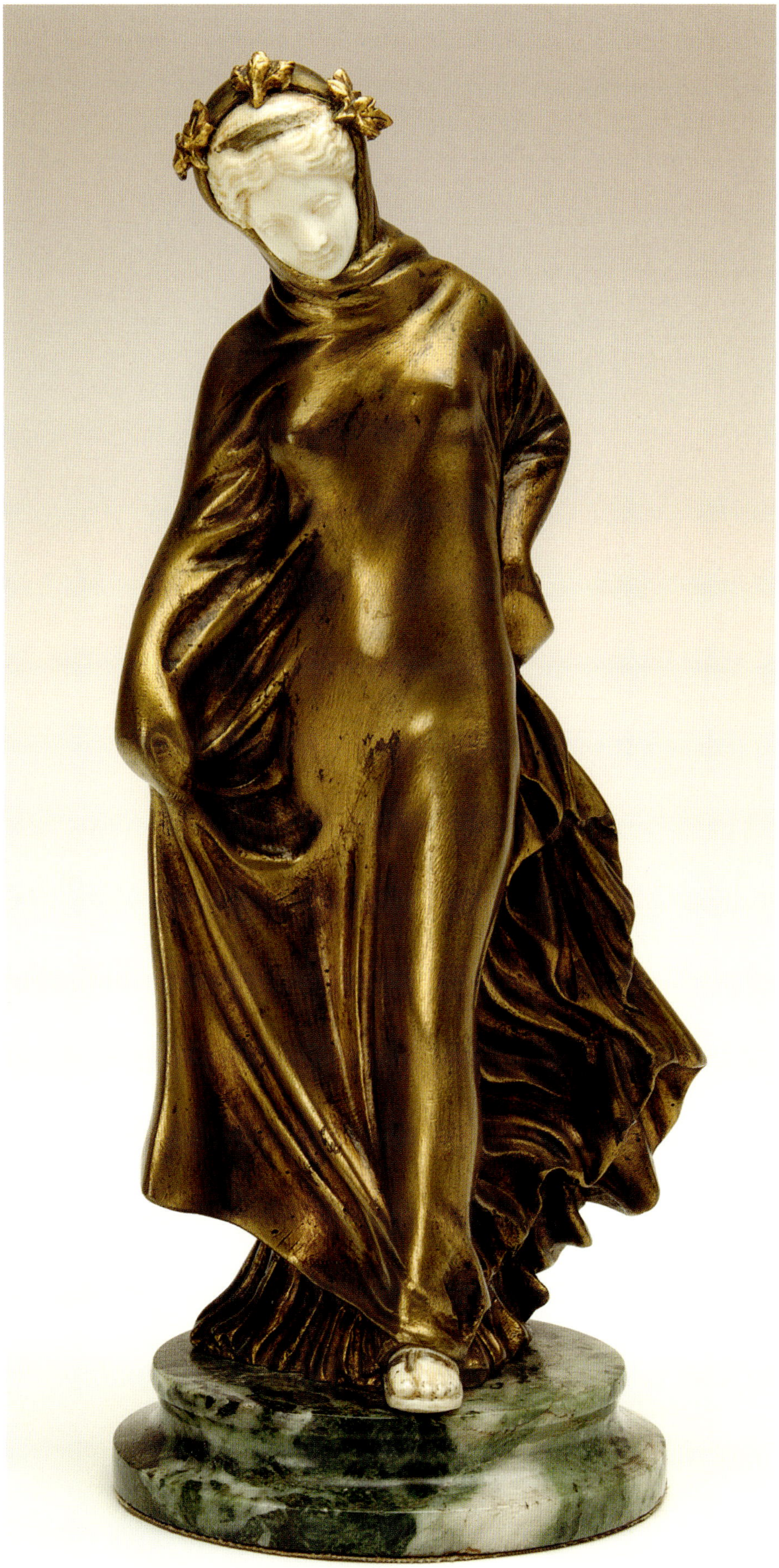

Born in Paris in the late 1900s, she studied with Falguière and took part in the exhibitions at the Salon of the Société des Artistes Français from 1912 to 1926.

At the 1912 Salon she exhibited several small sculptures in a vitrine.

Autumn
Bronze and ivory on marble base
Height: 22cm. (8¾in.)
DINO MENASCHE COLLECTION

Orange Seller
Bronze and ivory on marble base
Height: 23.5cm. (9¼in.)
DINO MENASCHE COLLECTION

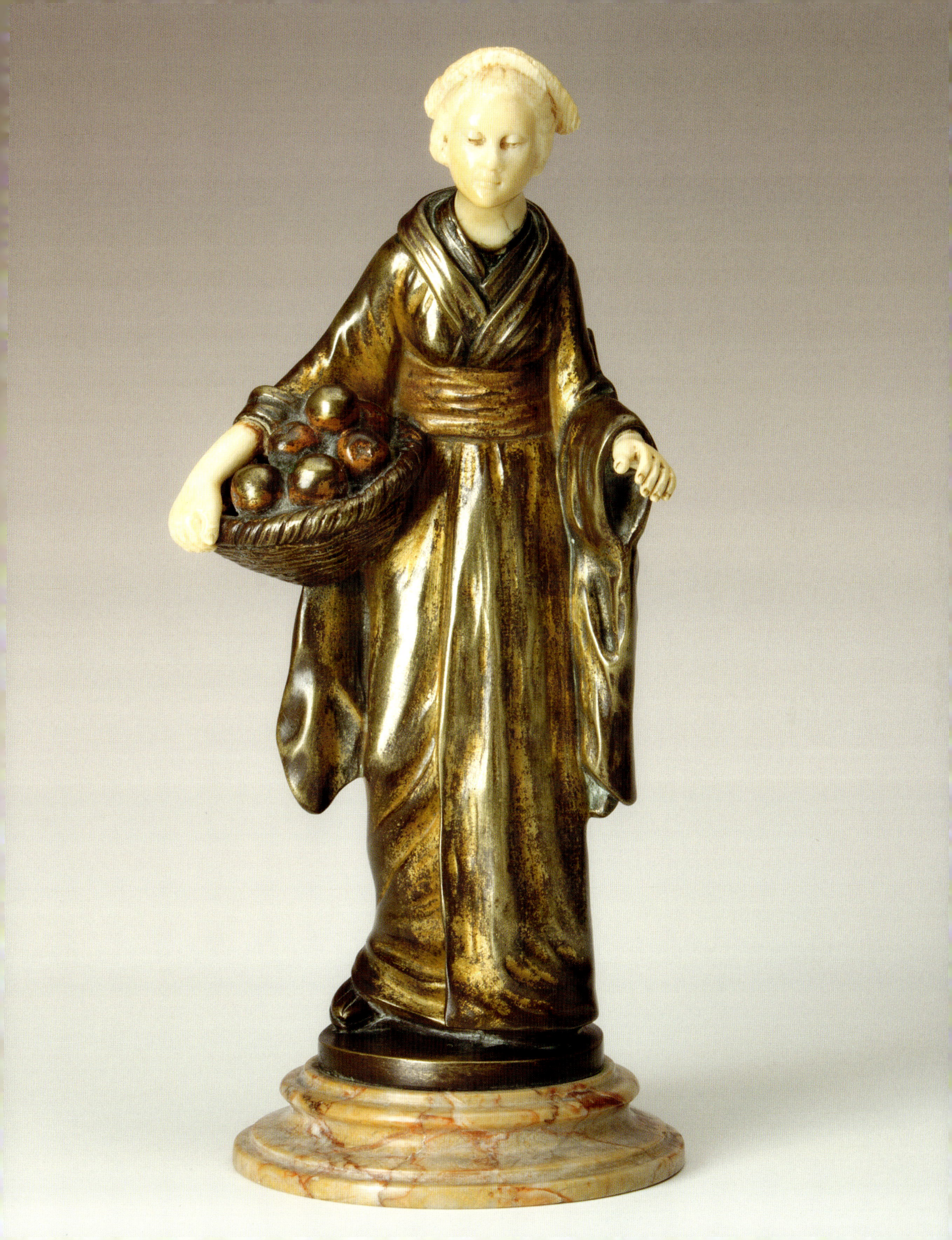

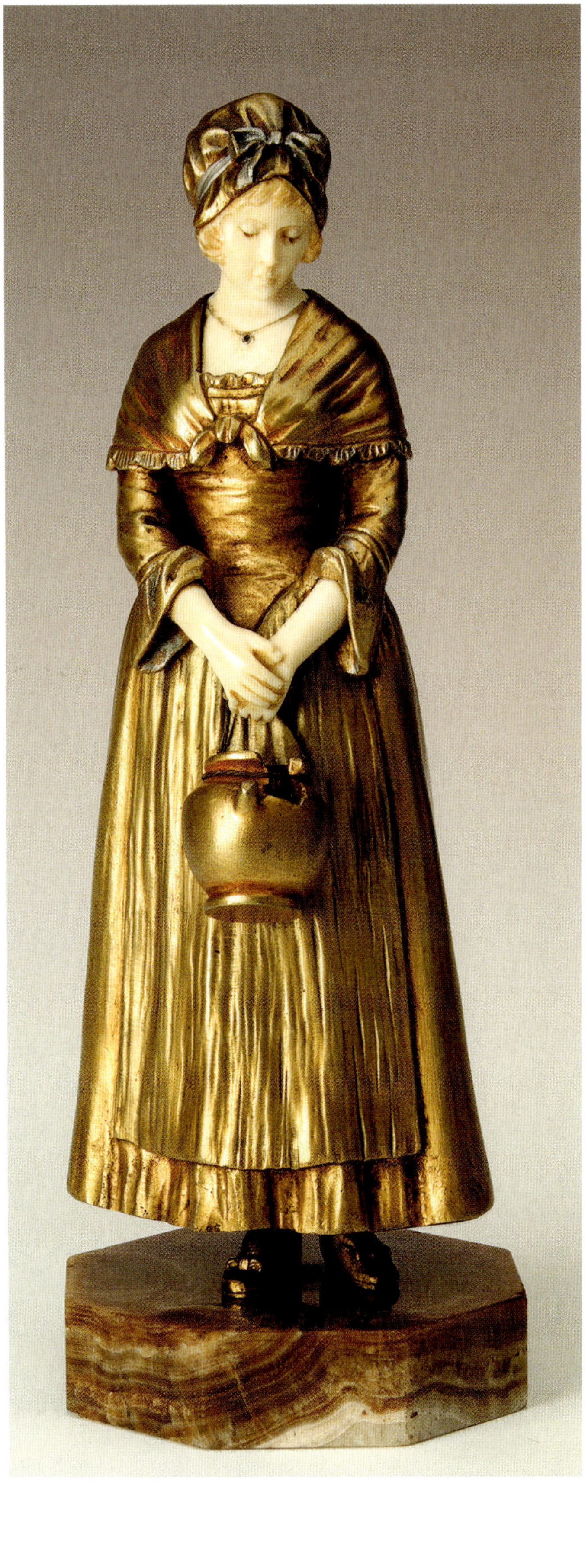

The Broken Jug
Bronze and ivory on onyx base
Height: 23.5cm. (9¼in.)
DINO MENASCHE COLLECTION

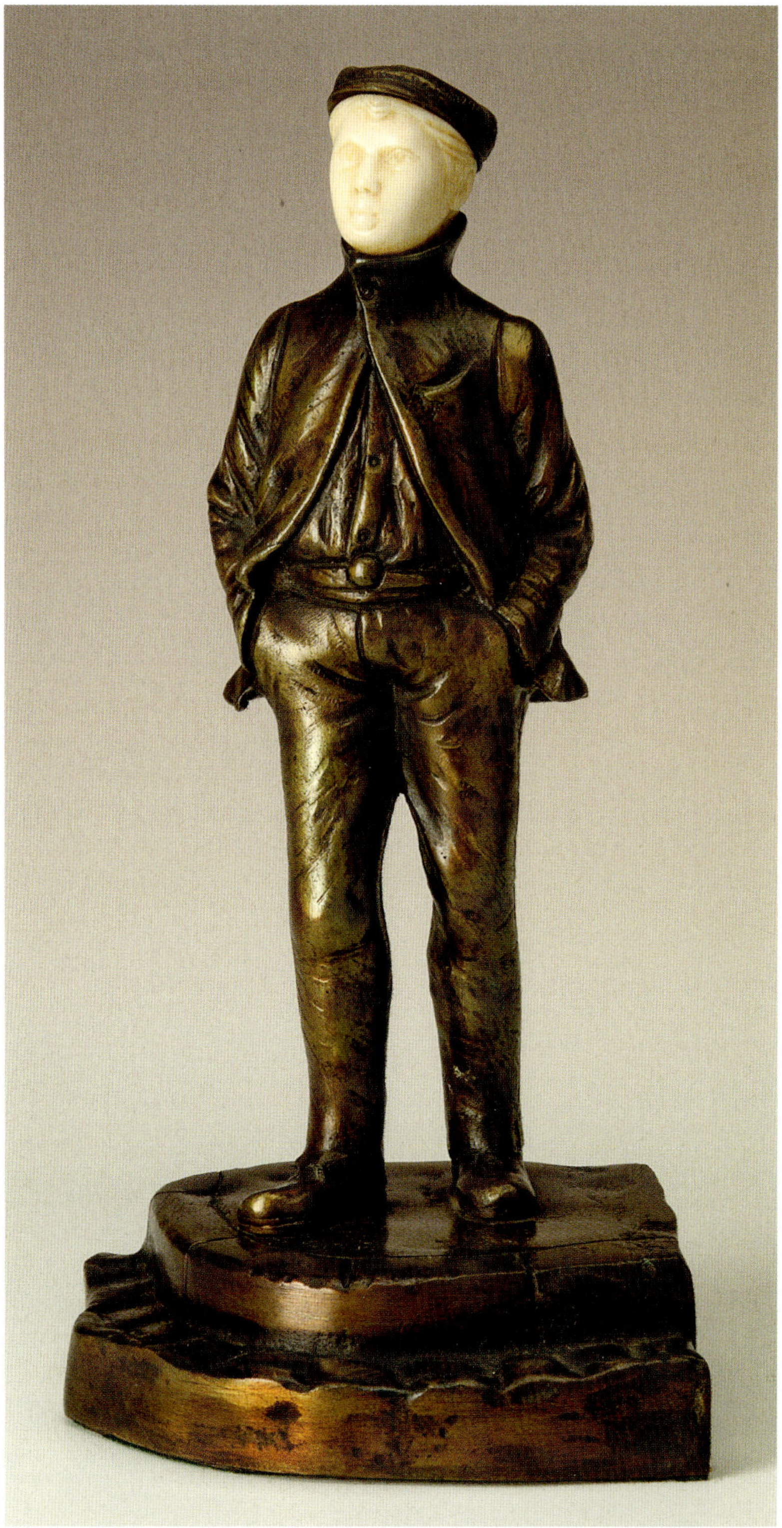

Sailor
Bronze and ivory
Height: 21cm. (8¼in.)
DINO MENASCHE COLLECTION

BAILLY, G.O.

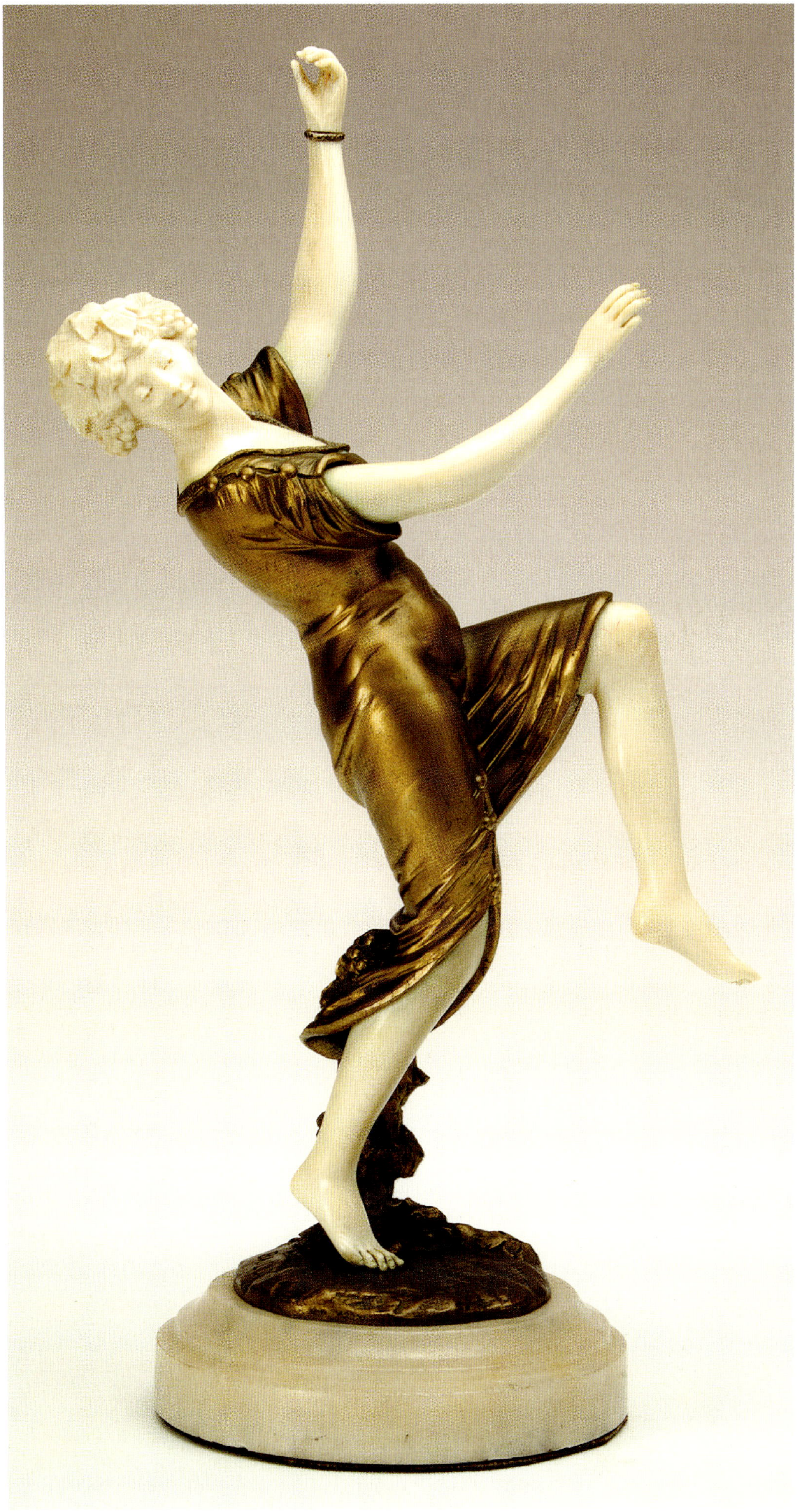

Autumn Dance
Bronze and ivory on marble base
Height: 29cm. (11½in.)
DINO MENASCHE COLLECTION

BARRIAS, Louis-Ernest

(Paris 1841 – 1905)

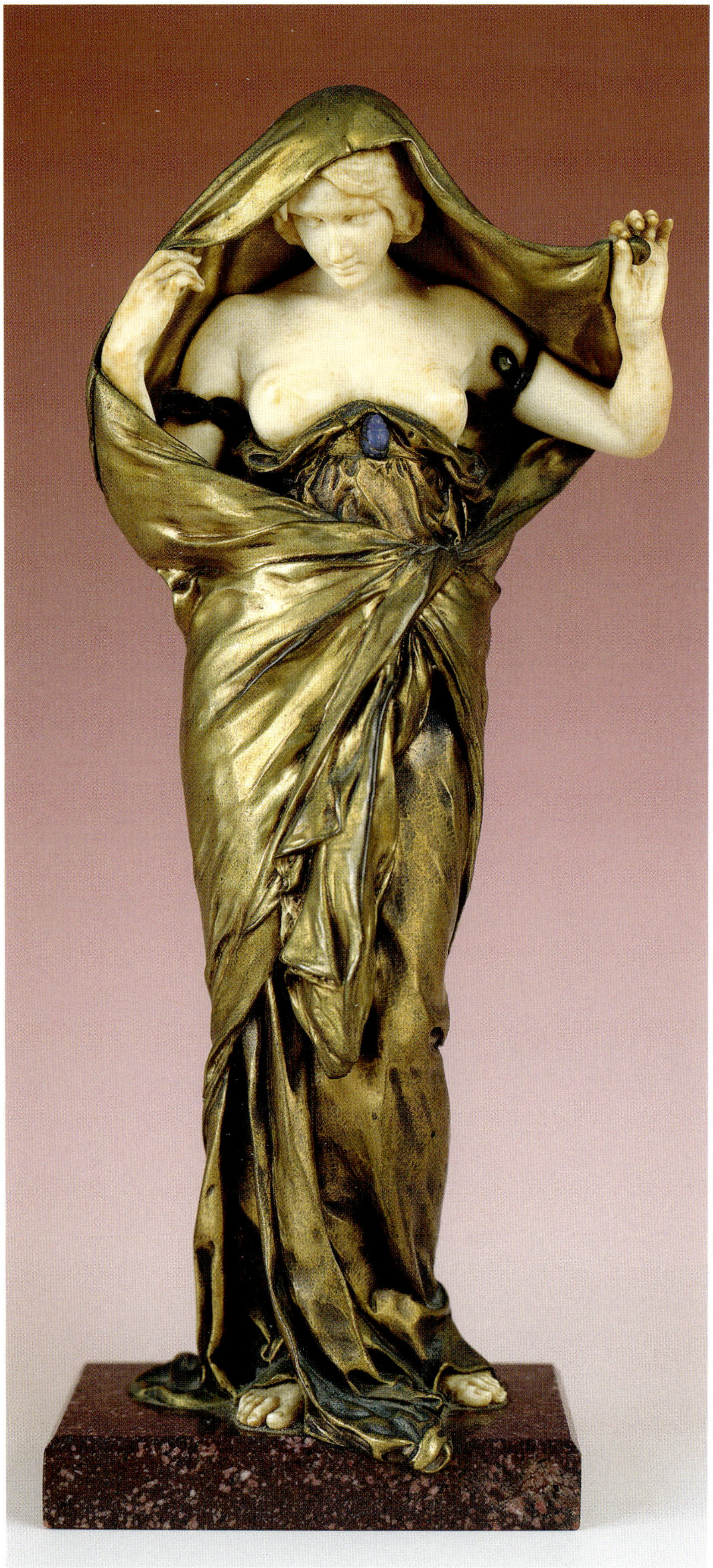

Born in Paris, he was the son of a porcelain painter and the brother of Felix-Joseph Barrias, a well-known 19th-century painter. He studied painting with Léon Cogniet, and sculpture with Jules Cavelier. The latter taught him the techniques of working with stone, marble and bronze. He also learned carpentry and iron forging. He became a student at the Paris Ecole des Beaux Arts in 1858, working under sculptor François Jouffroy.

He won the second *Prix de Rome* in 1861, with a bas-relief entitled *Chryséis Rendue à son Père par Ulysse* (Ulysses Returns Chryseis to her Father), and that same year exhibited portraits of his father and of the engraver Jazet.

In 1865 he won the first *Prix de Rome*, and travelled to that city where he worked and studied at the French Academy.

When the Franco–Prussian War broke out in 1870, Barrias returned to France to become a soldier. It was at this time that he contracted chronic bronchitis, which was to trouble him for the rest of his life.

He exhibited a sculpture called *Le Serment de Spartacus* (The Oath of Spartacus) at the 1872 Salon (the first to be held after the war). The sculpture now stands in the Tuileries gardens in Paris.

Upon the death of his teacher, Cavelier, Barrias took his place as Professor at the Paris Ecole des Beaux Arts. Among his students was the sculptor Ary Bitter.

Nature Revealing Herself to Science
Bronze and ivory on marble base
Height: 24cm. (9½in.)
PRIVATE COLLECTION

Several sizes and combinations are known. This model, in different types of marble and onyx, was exhibited at the Salon of the Société des Artistes Français in 1899. It was later cast in different sizes and materials.

BARTHELEMY, L.

French

Split Dancer
Bronze and ivory on marble base
Height: 26cm. (10¼in.)
DINO MENASCHE COLLECTION

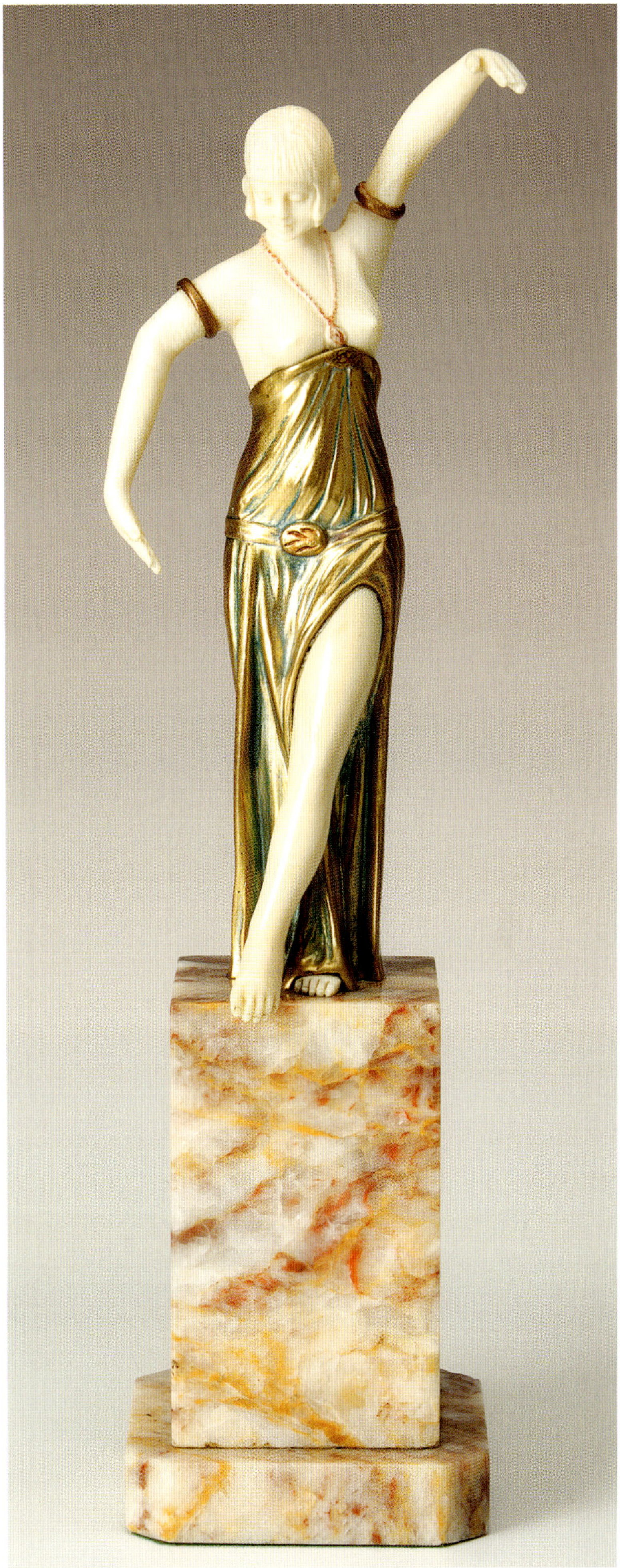

Cupid
Bronze and ivory on marble base
Height: 15.5cm. (6in.)
DINO MENASCHE COLLECTION

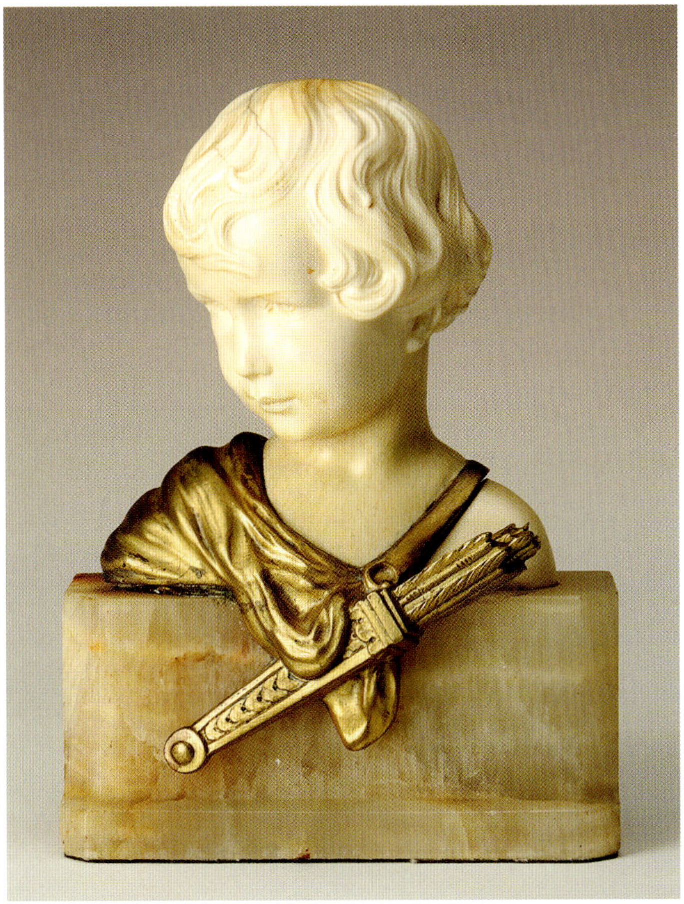

BECQUEREL, André Vincent

(Saint-André-Farivillers 1893 – Paris 1981)

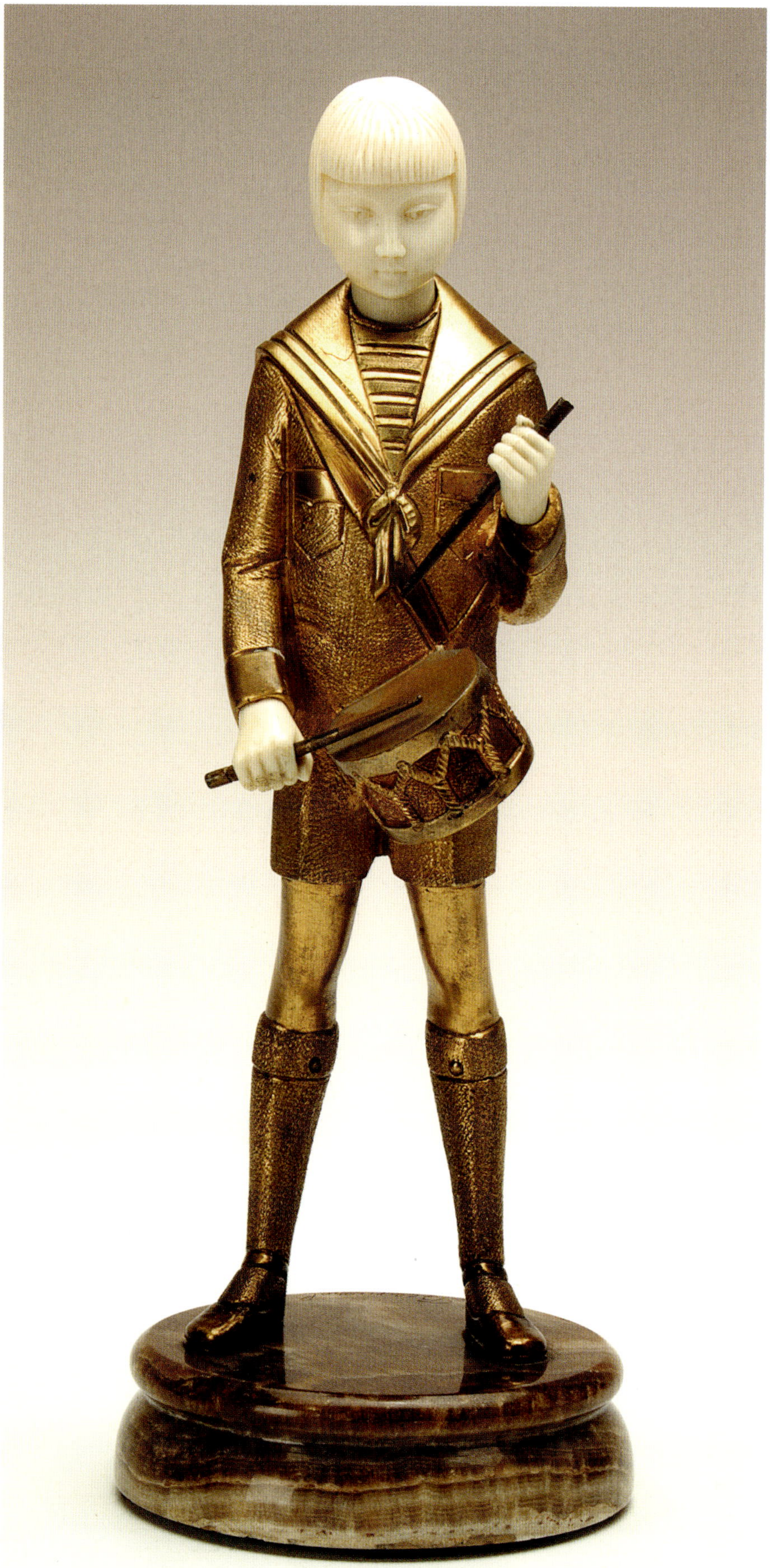

Born in Saint-André-Farivillers in the French Oise region, Becquerel attended the Paris Ecole des Beaux Arts, studying under Hector Lemaire and Prosper Lecourtier. He first exhibited in 1914 at the Salon of the Société des Artistes Français, and was soon elected a member of the group, participating in their exhibitions and other Parisian salons, until at least the early 1920s. He created bronze animal sculptures, and bronze and ivory sculptures, often produced by Etling et Cie.

He executed a monumental patinated plaster statue for the 1937 Exhibition of Arts and Techniques in Paris.

Child with Drum
Bronze and ivory on onyx base
Height: 26cm. (10¼in.)
DINO MENASCHE COLLECTION

Venetian
Bronze and ivory on marble and onyx base
Height: 38.5cm. (15¼in.)
PRIVATE COLLECTION

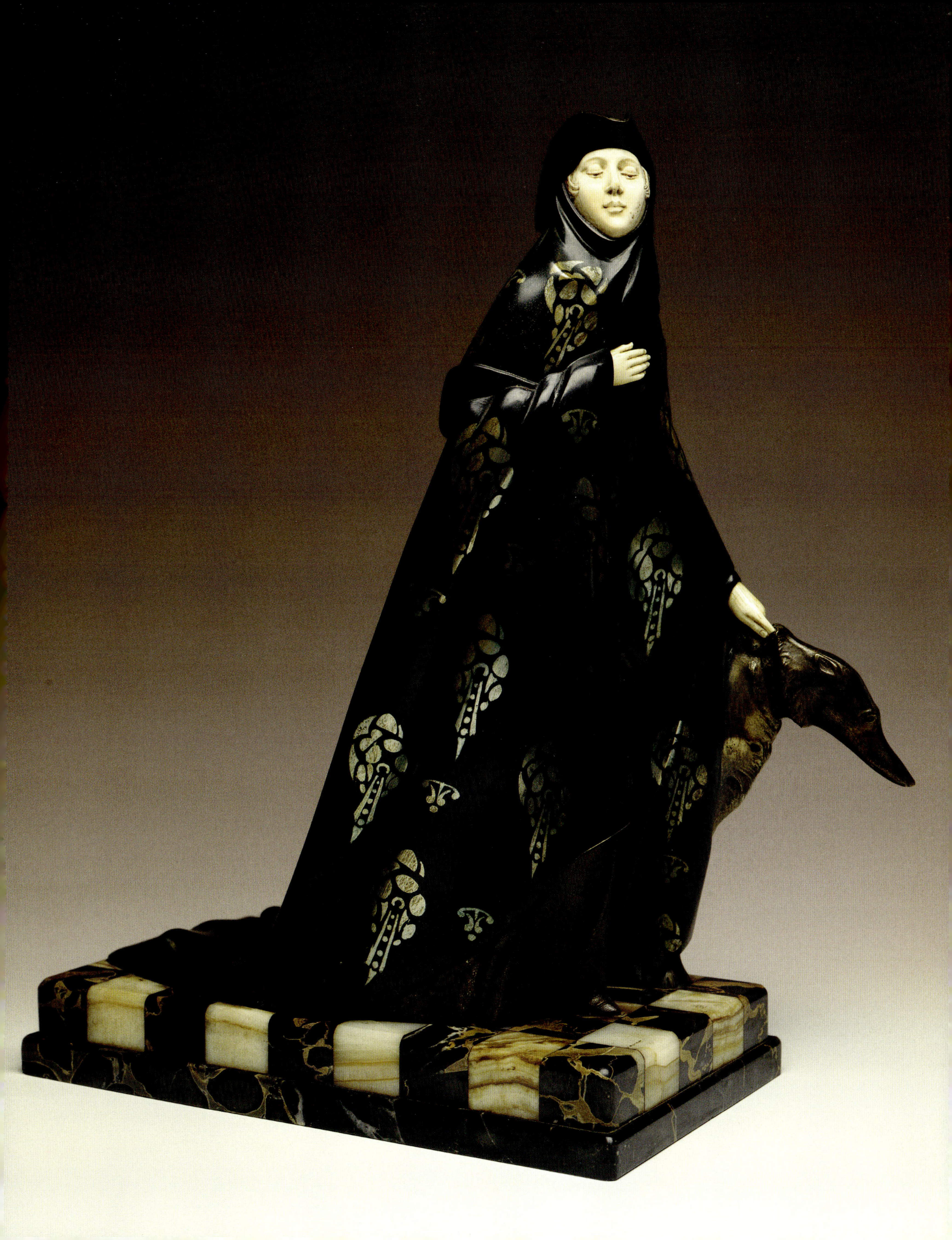

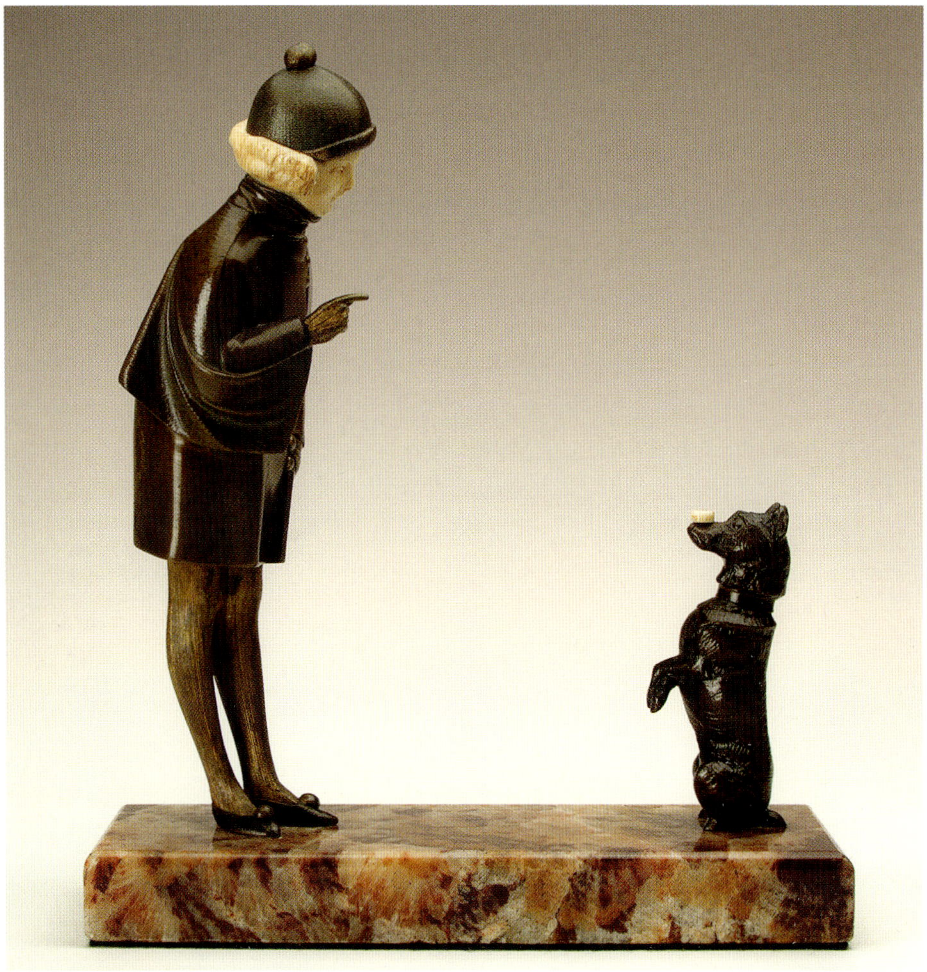

Little Girl with her Dog
Bronze and ivory on marble base
Height: 24cm. (9½in.)
DINO MENASCHE COLLECTION

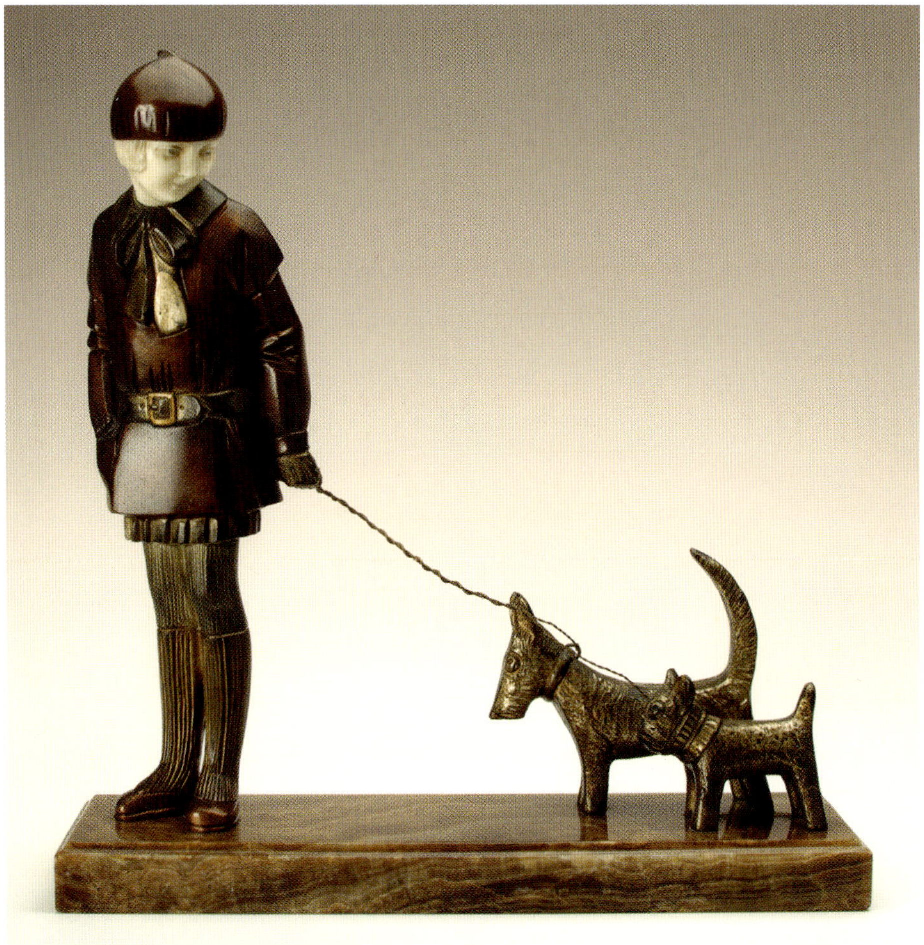

Friendly Walk
Bronze and ivory on marble base
Height: 26cm. (10¼in.)
DINO MENASCHE COLLECTION

The Golden Wedding
Bronze and ivory on marble base
Height: 36cm. (14¼in.)
PRIVATE COLLECTION

Also produced 25cm. (10in.) high

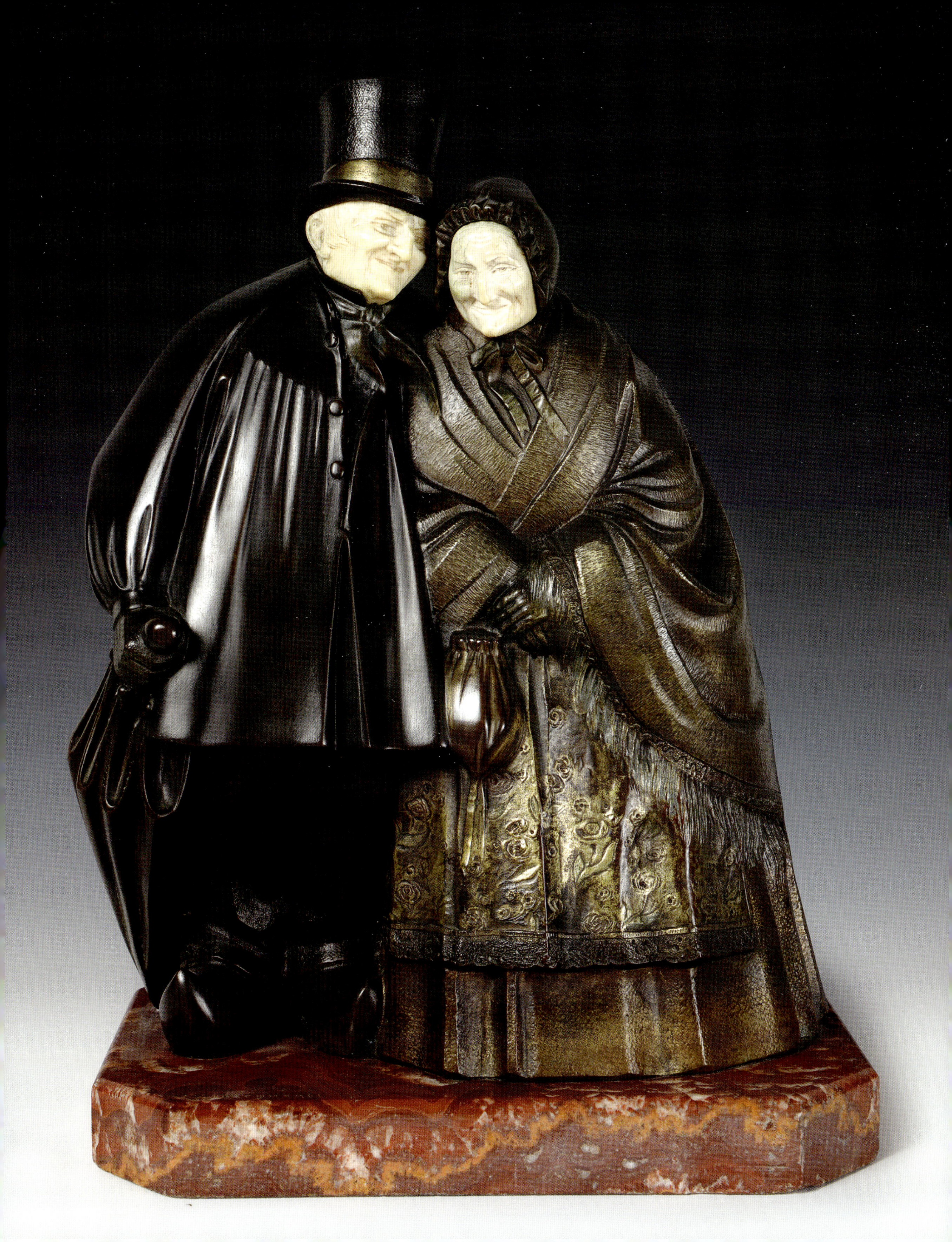

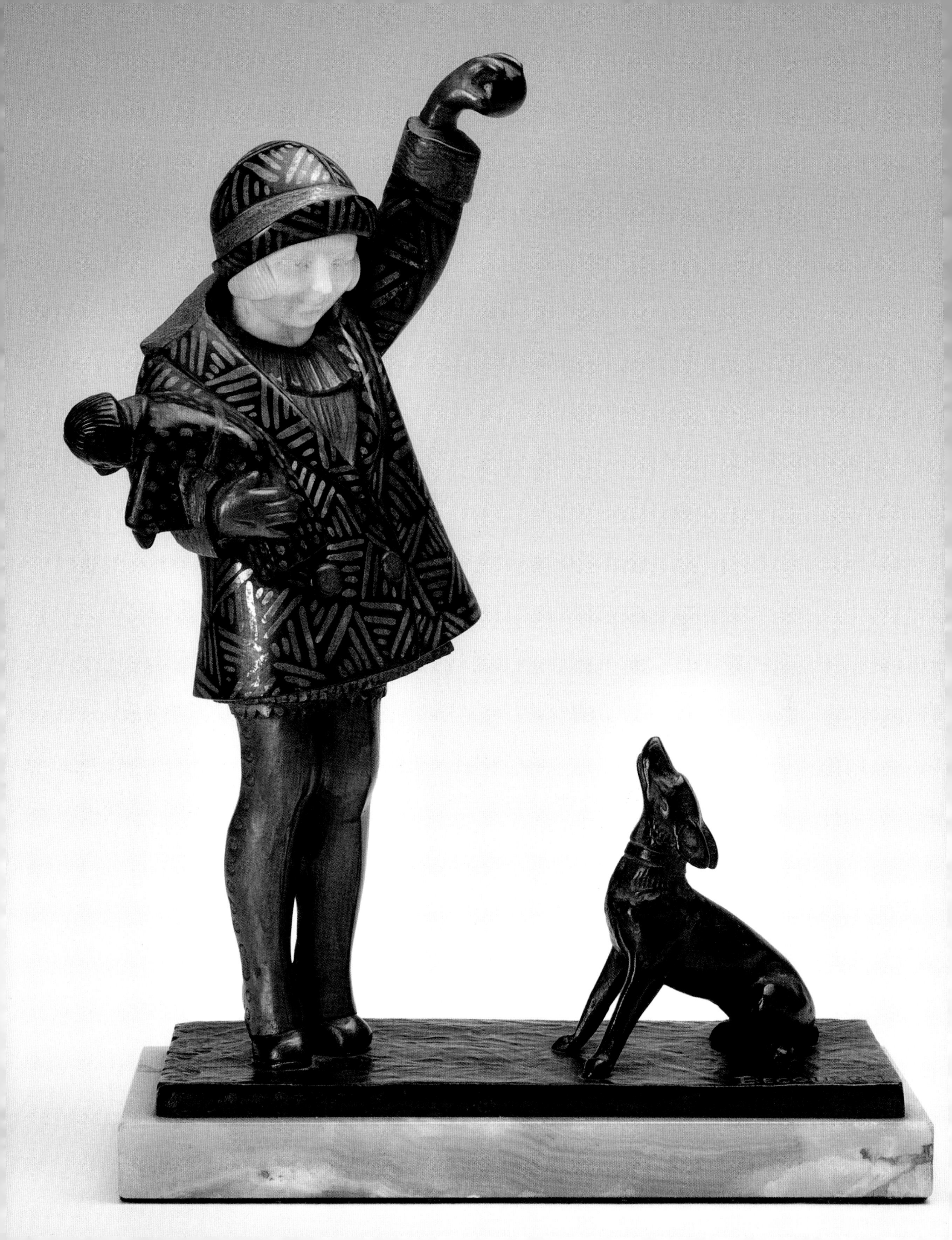

Playful
Bronze and ivory on marble base
Height: 24.5cm. (9¾in.)
DINO MENASCHE COLLECTION

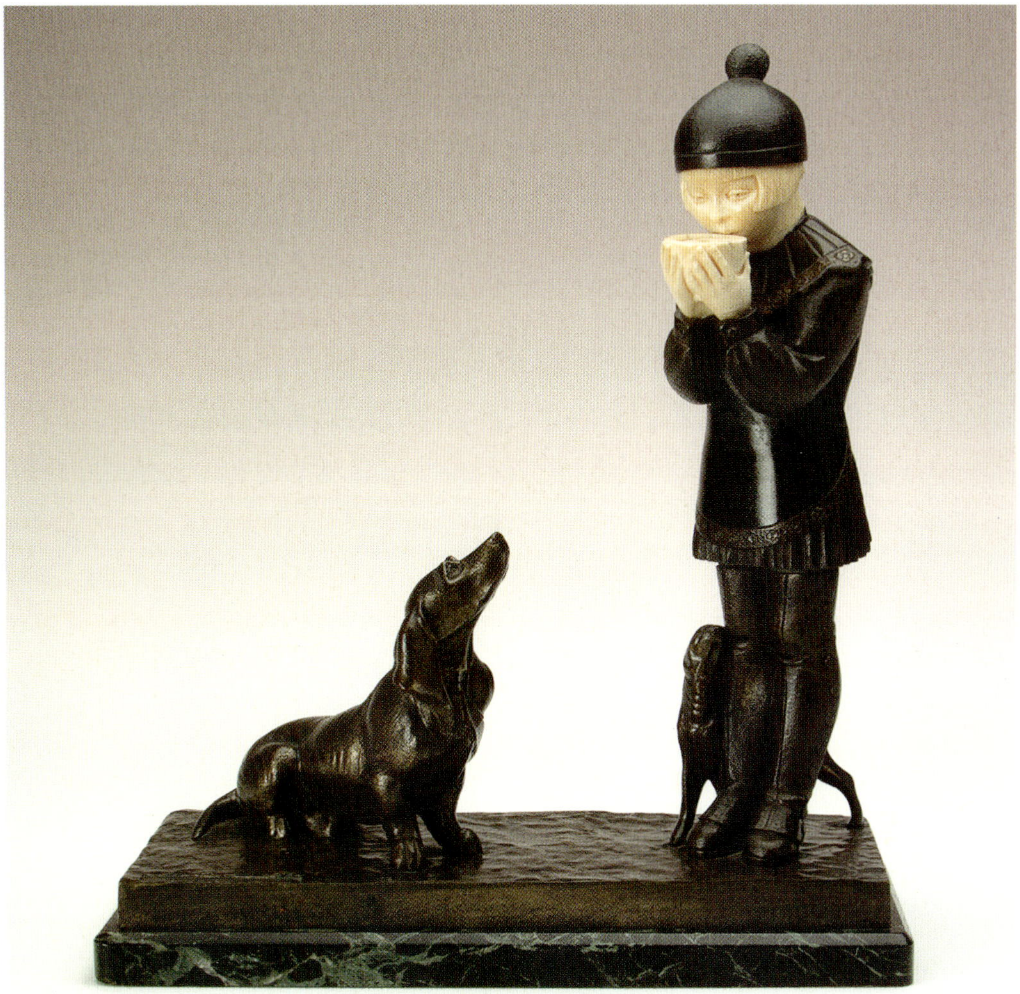

Bowl of Milk
Bronze and ivory on marble base
Height: 24cm. (9½in.)
DINO MENASCHE COLLECTION

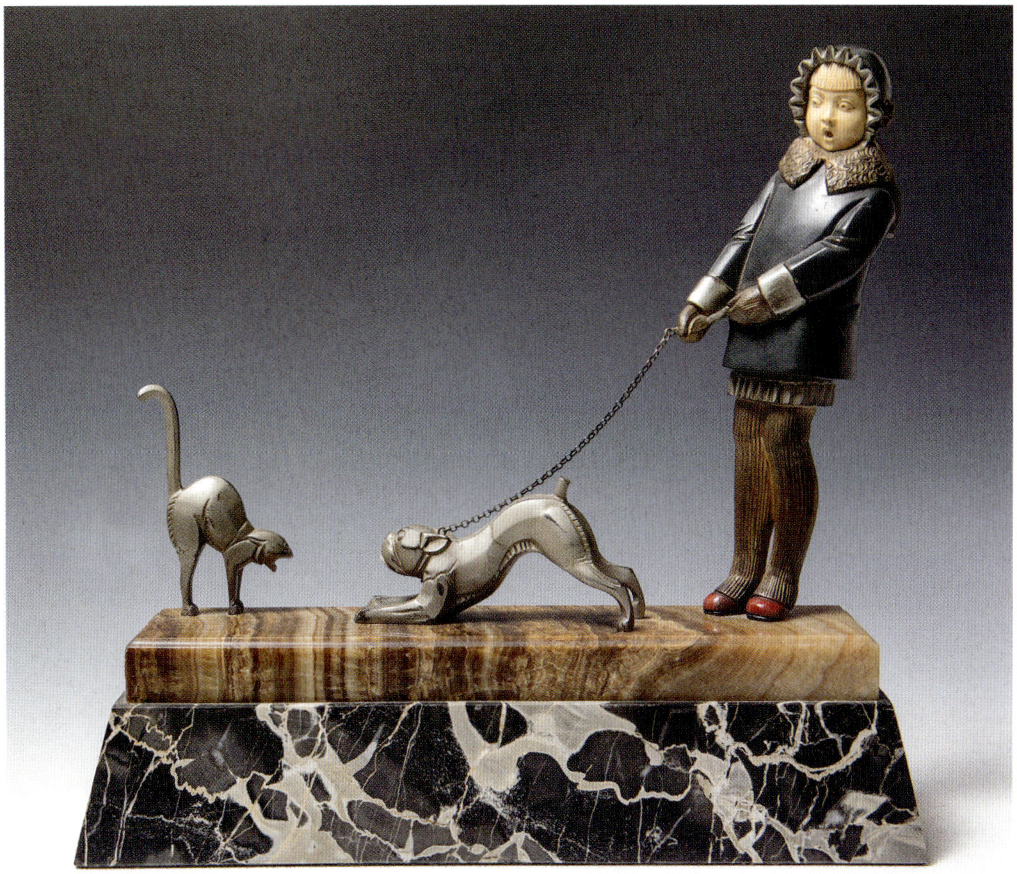

Attack!
Bronze and ivory on marble and onyx base
Height: 31cm. (12¼in.)
PRIVATE COLLECTION

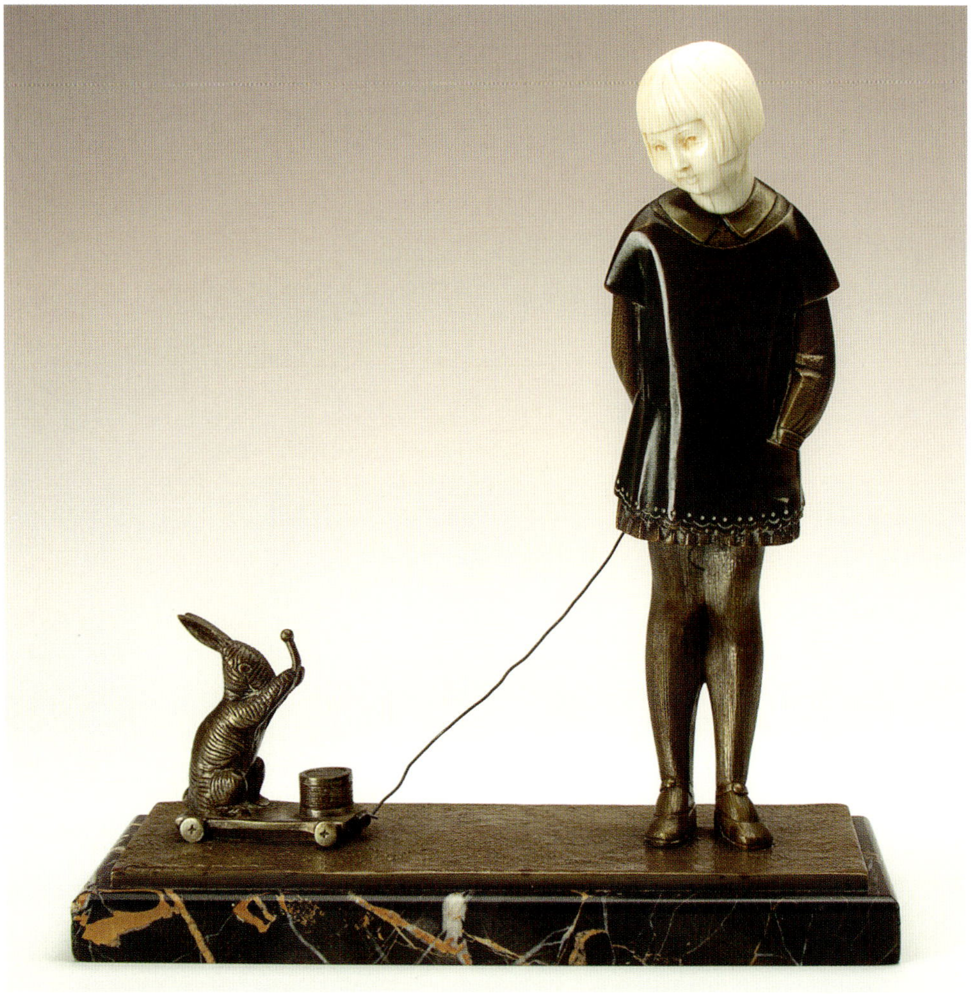

Rabbit on Wheels
Bronze and ivory on marble base
Height: 22cm. (8¾in.)
DINO MENASCHE COLLECTION

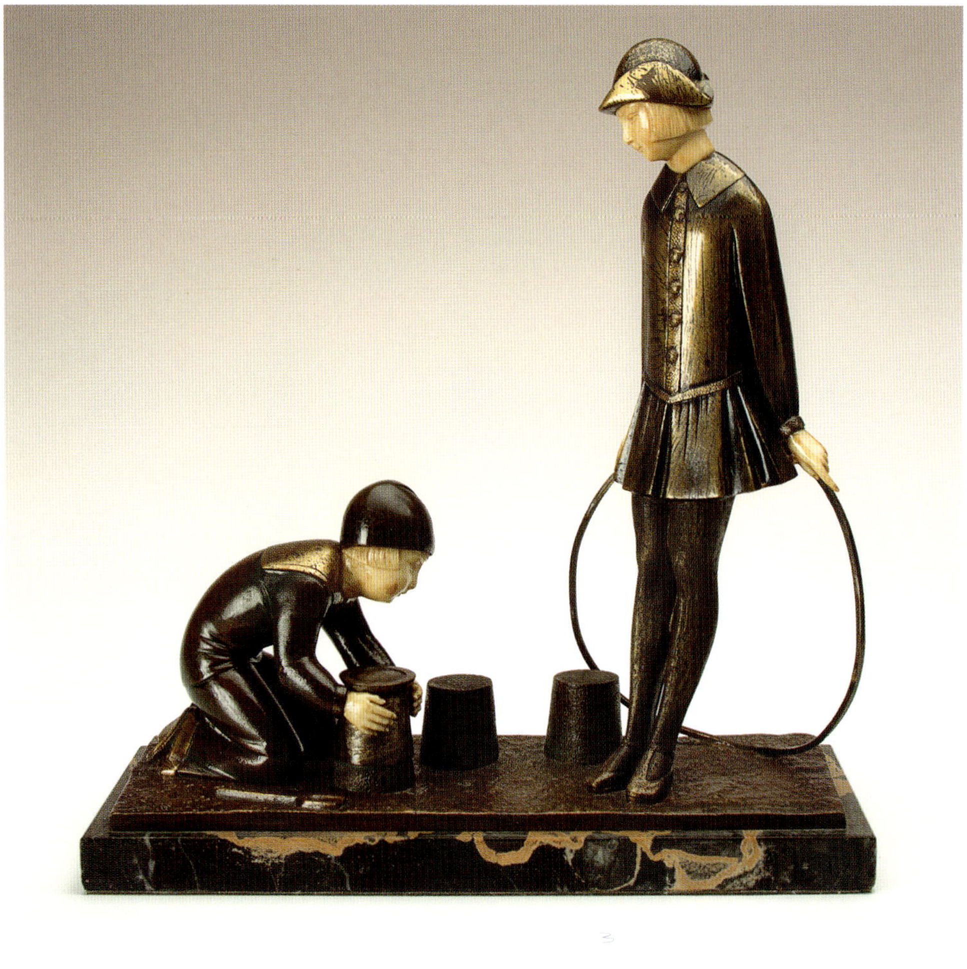

At the Beach
Bronze and ivory on marble base
Height: 24.5cm. (9¾in.)
DINO MENASCHE COLLECTION

Lunch
Bronze and ivory on onyx base
Height: 23cm. (9in.)
DINO MENASCHE COLLECTION

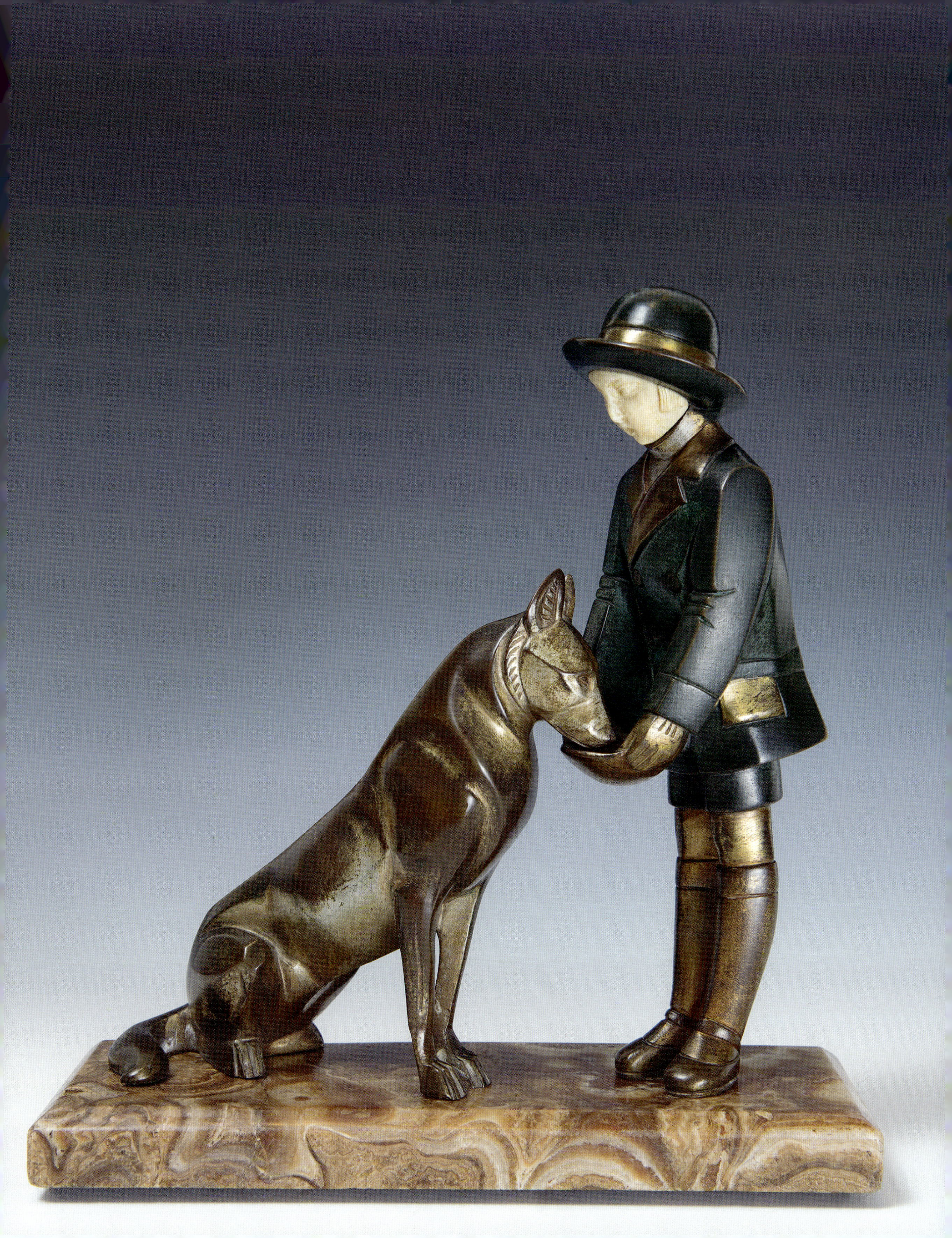

BERGMANN, Franz Xavier

(Austria 1861 – 1936)

Other signatures: 'Nam Greb'; 'B'

Sculptor and owner of his own foundry. His bronzes are mostly small scale and they depict Arab oriental scenes. Sometimes picaresque ones where the sculpture includes a 'hidden' nude. Most are signed with the anagram 'Nam Greb' and some just with the letter 'B'.

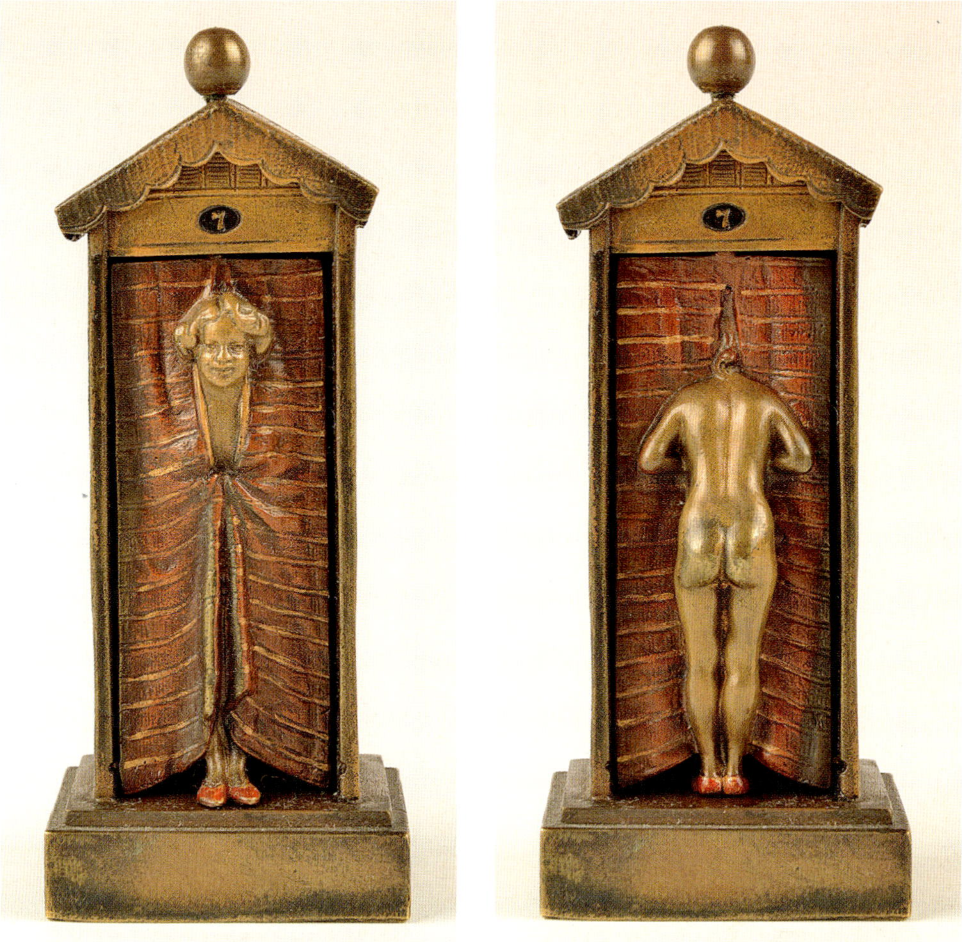

The Beach Cabin
Height: 13cm. (5in.)
MICHAEL AND PESSI JAKOBOV

Erotic pieces are signed 'Nam Greb', 'Bergman' in reverse

BERJEAN, P.

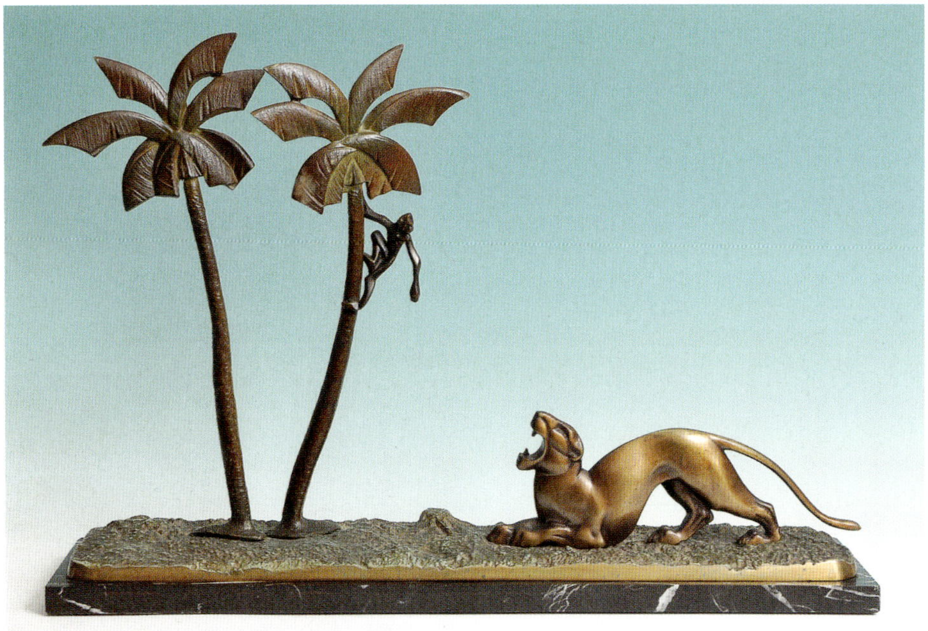

Tropical Chase
Bronze on marble base
Height: 43cm. (17in.)
CLÁUDIO CASTRO COLLECTION

BERTRAND, S.

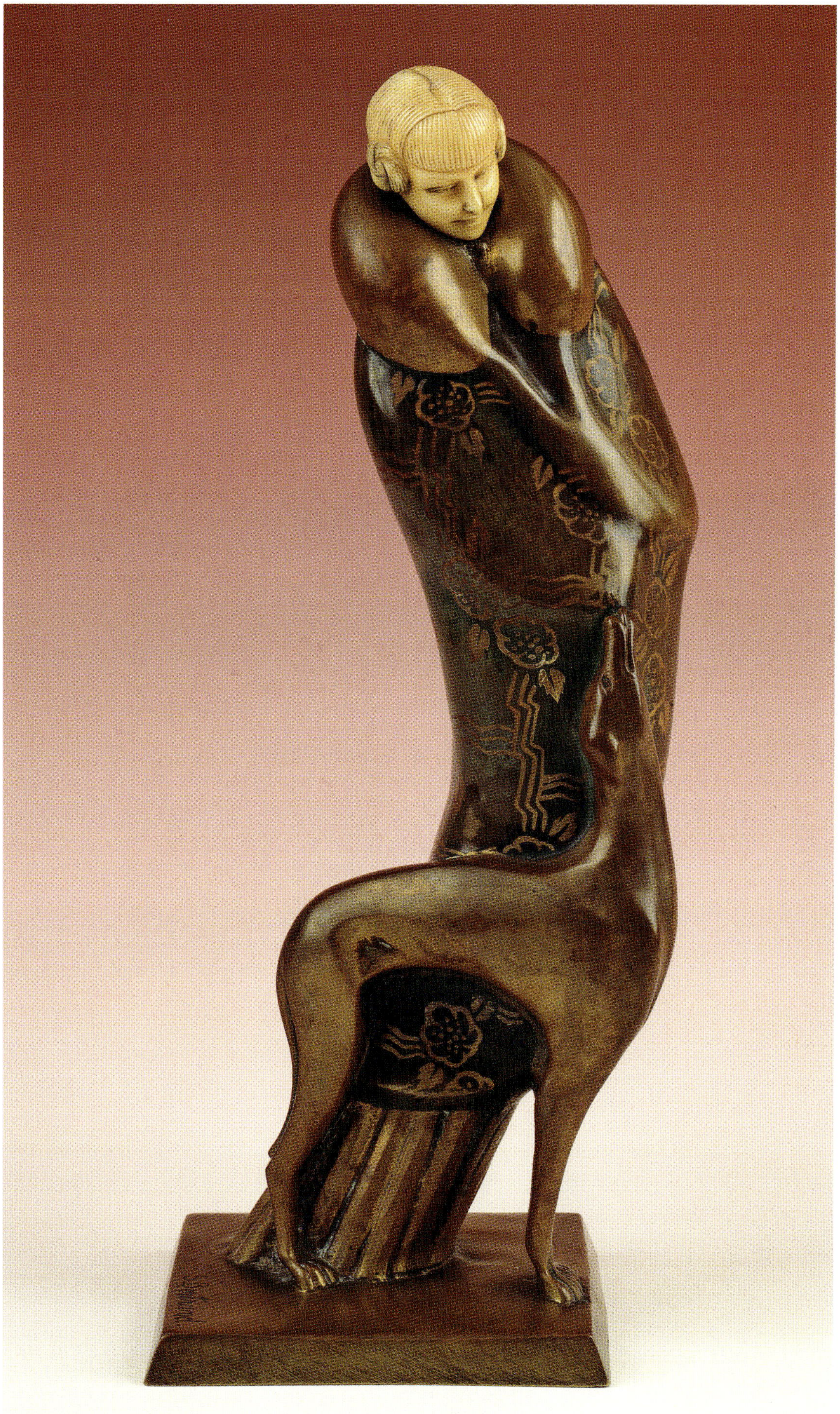

Elégante au Chien
Bronze and ivory
Height: 29.5cm. (11½in.)
PRIVATE COLLECTION

BOURAINE, Marcel André

(Pontoise 1886 – 1948)

Other signatures: 'Derenne'; 'Briand'

Born in Pontoise (Seine-et Oise, France), he was largely self-taught, but also studied for a time with Alexandre Falguière. During World War I he was captured by the Germans and was interned in Switzerland. He exhibited at the 1922 Salon des Tuileries and later at other major Paris salons such as the Salon of the Société des Artistes Français, the Salon des Indépendents and the Salon d'Automne.

Several foundries produced his sculptures: Susse Frères, Edmond Etling et Cie, and Max Le Verrier in France; also Arthur Goldscheider in Paris (originally from Vienna). In the 1920s he took part in exhibitions by Goldscheider's 'La Stèle' and 'L'Evolution' groups.

In 1928 the sculptor and glass artist Gabriel Argy-Rousseau ordered a number of pieces from him, including female nudes, a fountain and an illuminated group in coloured translucent glass. At the 1928 Salon d'Automne, he exhibited three statuettes in *pâte de crystal*: *Baigneuse*, *Danseuse* and *Jeunesse*; they were produced by the Société Anonyme des Pâtes de Verre d'Argy-Rousseau.

For the 1937 Paris International Exhibition of Arts and Techniques he created a large sculpture for the Sèvres pavilion, representing ceramics. He worked in bronze, bronze and ivory, glass, and ceramics; he produced animal sculptures as well as pieces in the Art Deco style. In 1935 the city of Paris purchased a terracotta bust by him.

During World War II his production slowed. Living in Biot, in France's Alpes Maritimes region, he sculpted figural pipe bowls that were sold under the brand 'OPTIM'.

Although his bronze figures are the best known, he also created chryselephantine statuettes, as well as ceramics. He excelled in the depiction of Amazonian athletic women and nudes, as well as Harlequins, Pierrots and clowns.

Bouraine is known to have used the pseudonyms 'Briand' and 'Derenne', often for the non-bronze pieces produced by his friend Max Le Verrier.

Le Verrier, Bouraine and Le Faguays were friends; they had all studied at the Geneva School of Fine Arts.

Bouraine's companion was the artist Aurore Onu (see p.186, Onu).

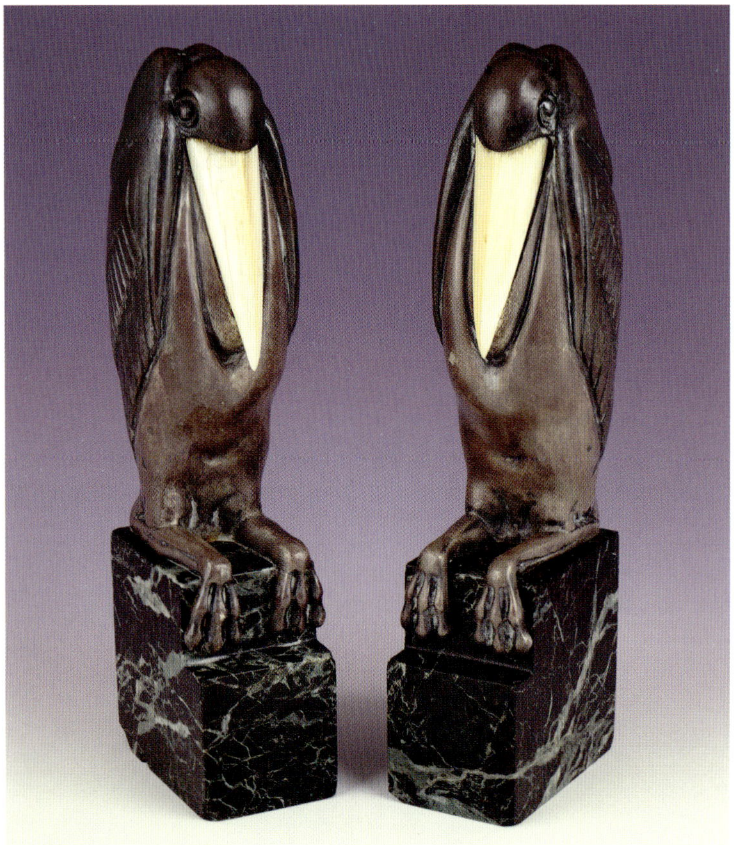

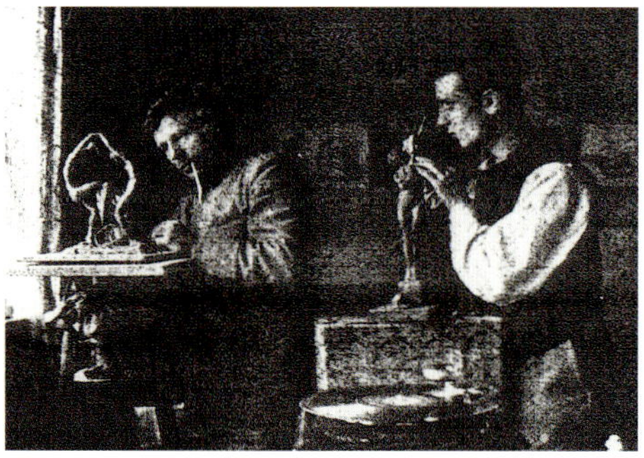

Bouraine (by the window smoking a cigarette) working on a double figure, and Max Le Verrier, Geneva 1918.

Pelicans
Bronze and ivory on marble base
Height: 25.5cm. (10in.)
PRIVATE COLLECTION

Floral
Bronze and marble on onyx base (mounted as a lamp)
Height: 65cm. (25½in.)
PRIVATE COLLECTION

In 1929 a figure like this one sold in Paris at L.N.J.L. (Lehmann Éditeurs) for 4,480 francs

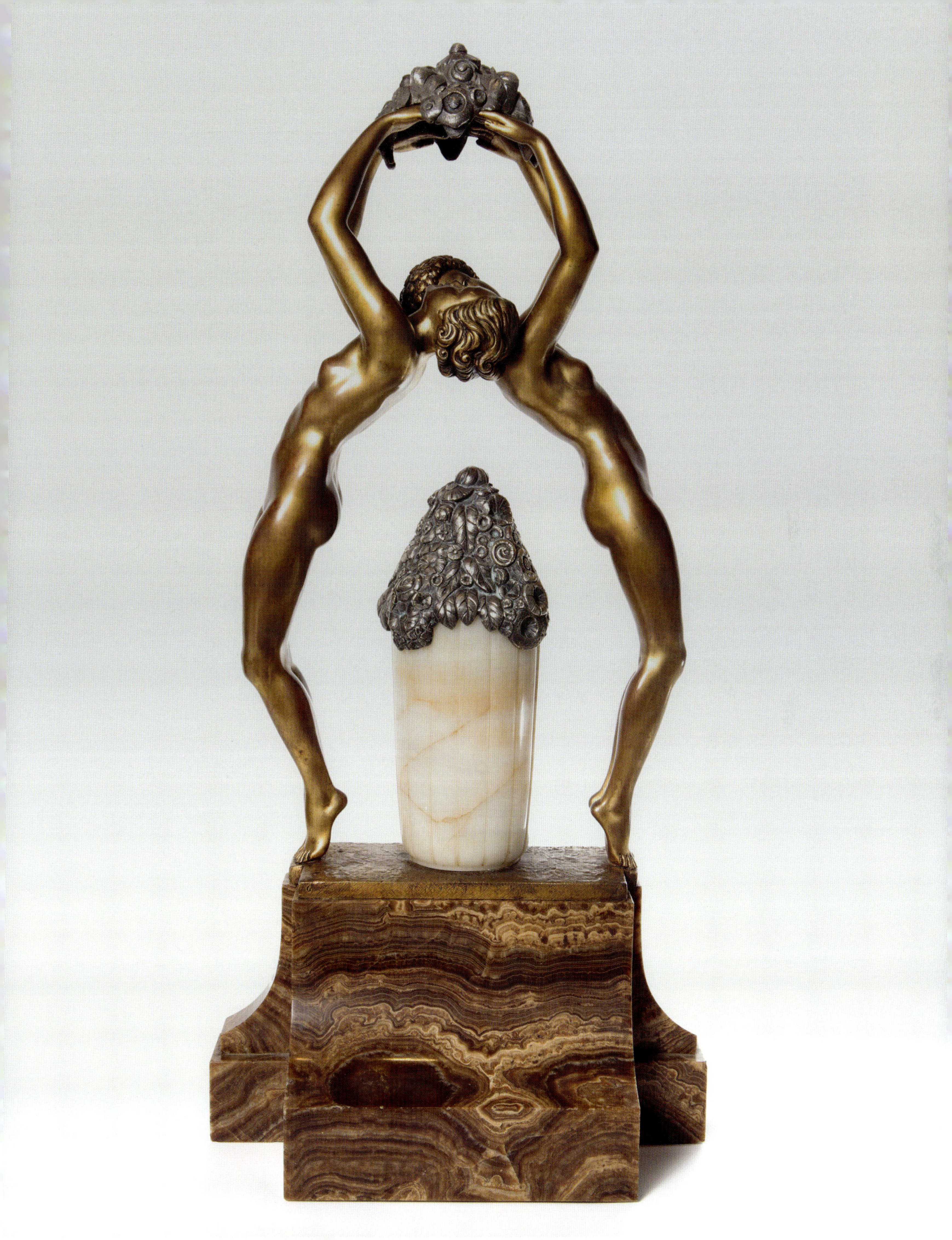

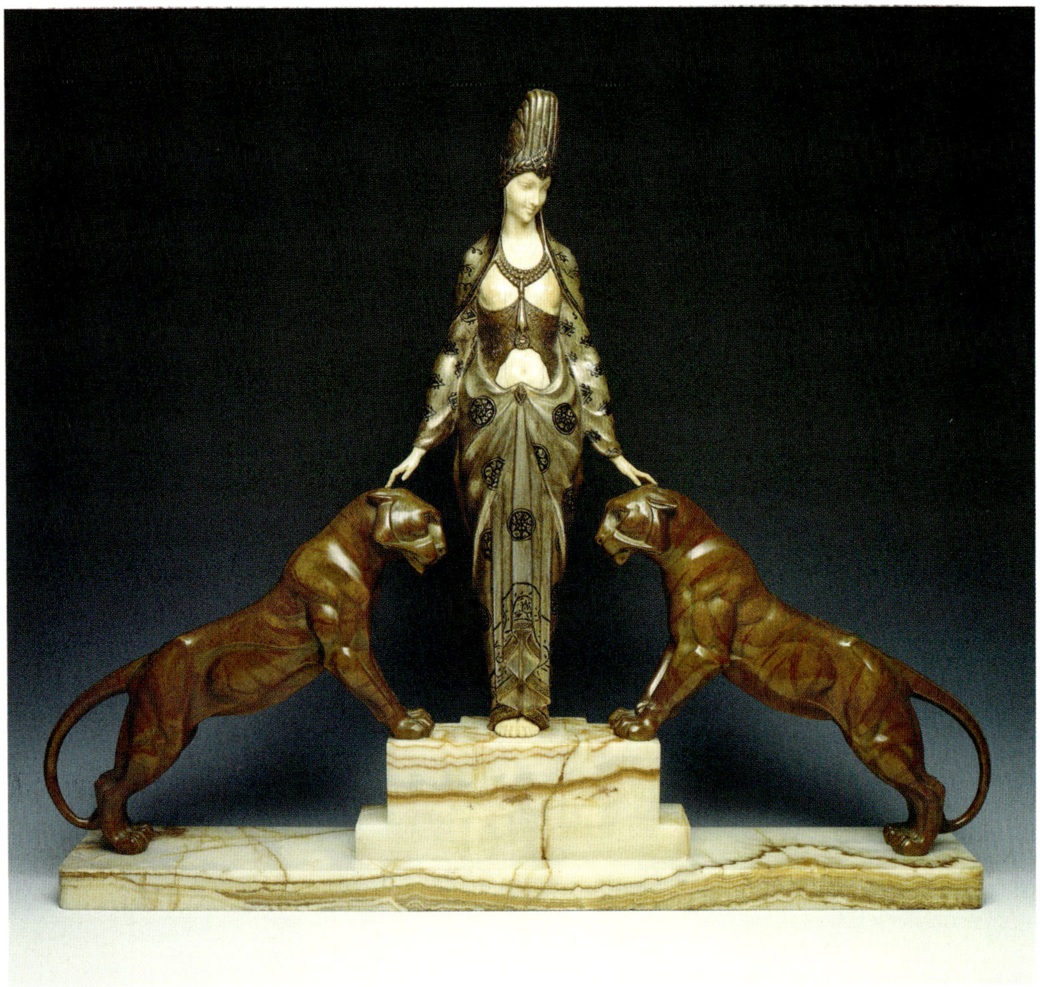

Mistress of the Beasts
Bronze and ivory on marble base
Height: 61.5cm. (24¼in.)
Length: 75cm. (29½in.)
PRIVATE COLLECTION

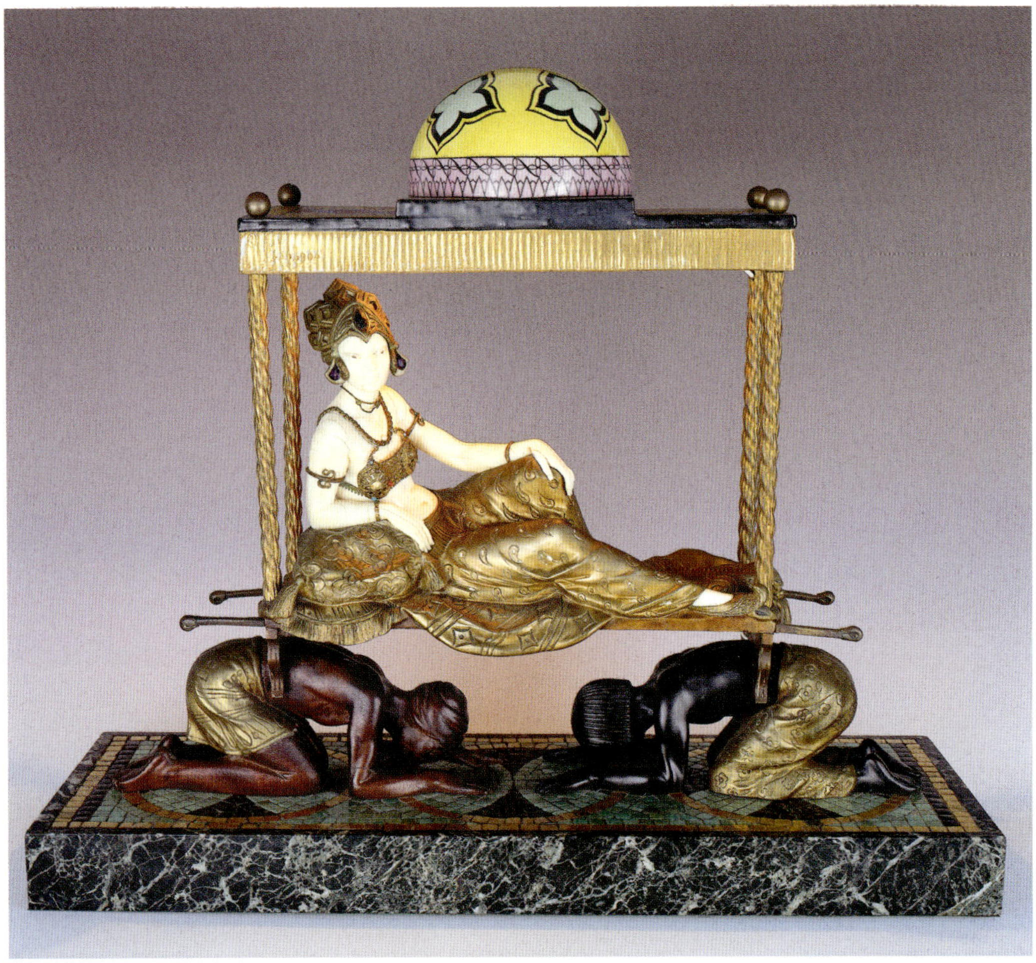

Princess
Bronze, ivory, wood, ceramic and semi-precious stones on marble base
Height: 51.5cm. (20¼in.)
Length: 60.5cm. (23¾in.)
BURR AND MUIR COLLECTION, CAPE TOWN

At Chamonix
Bronze and ivory on marble base
Height: 64cm. (25¼in.)
PRIVATE COLLECTION

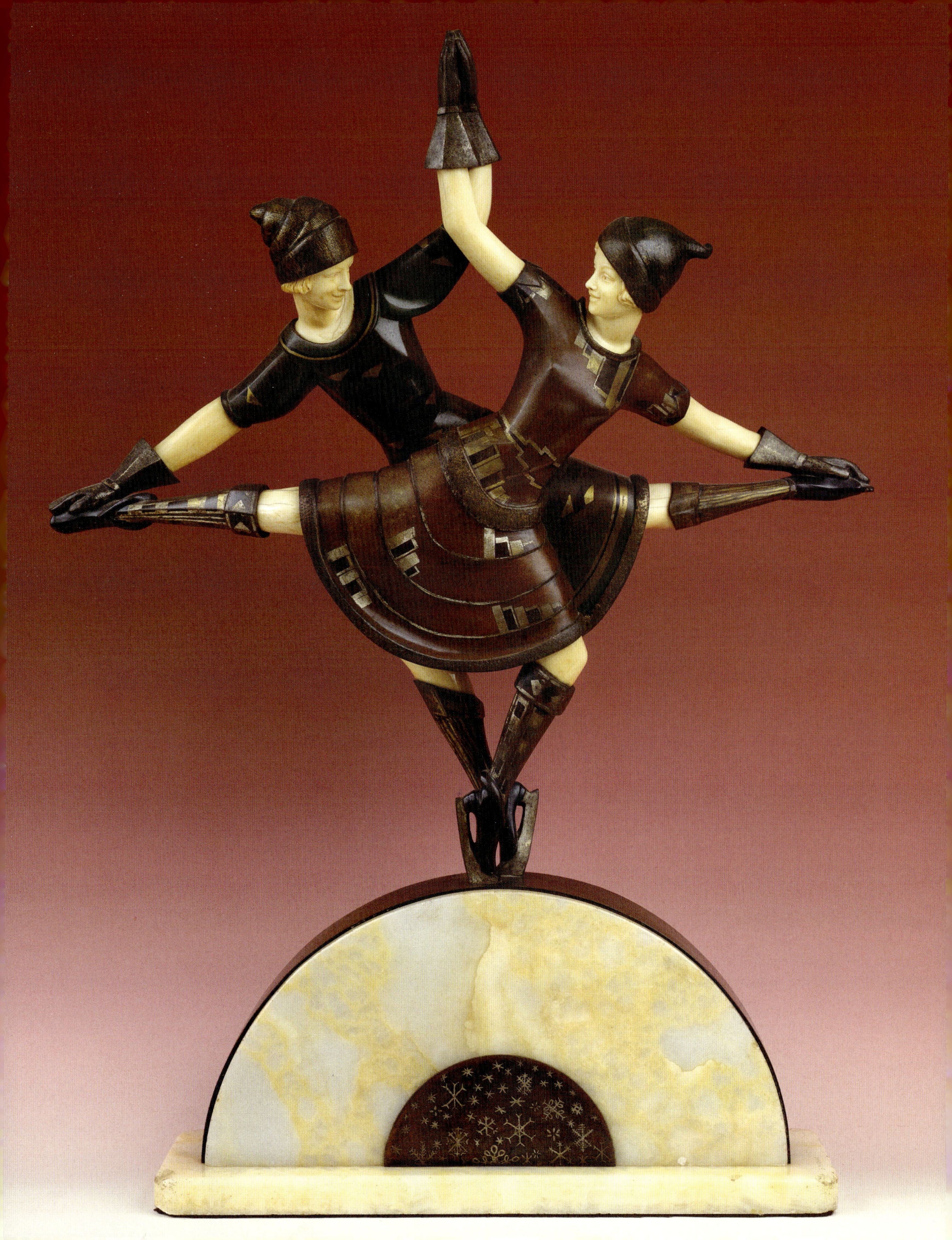

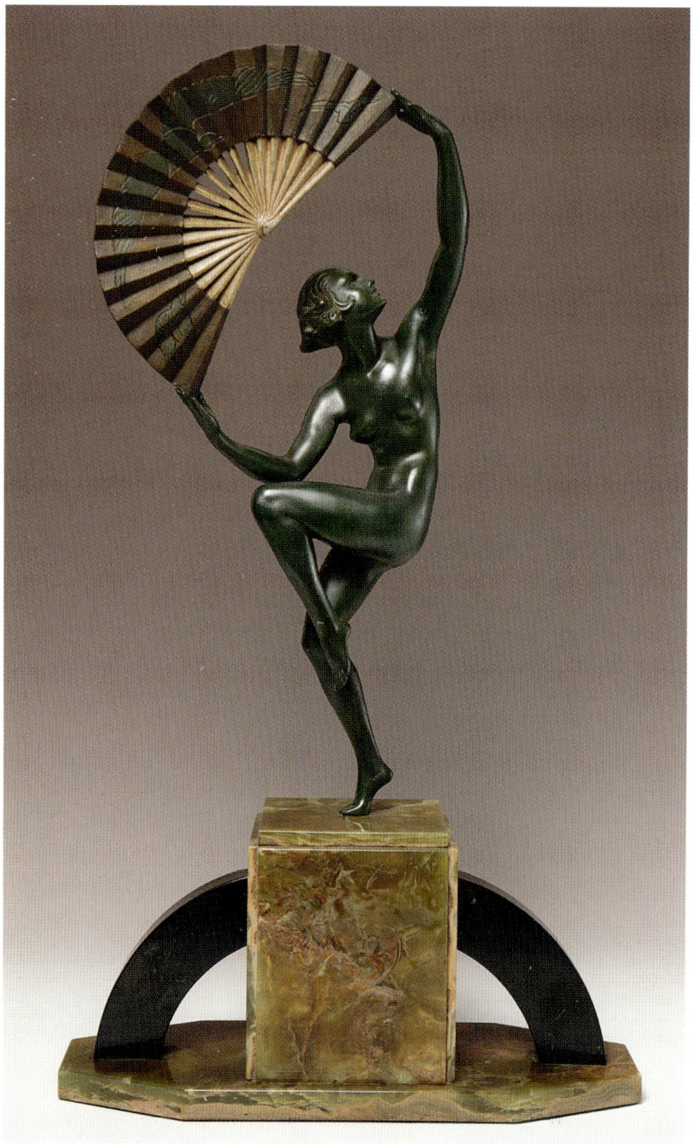

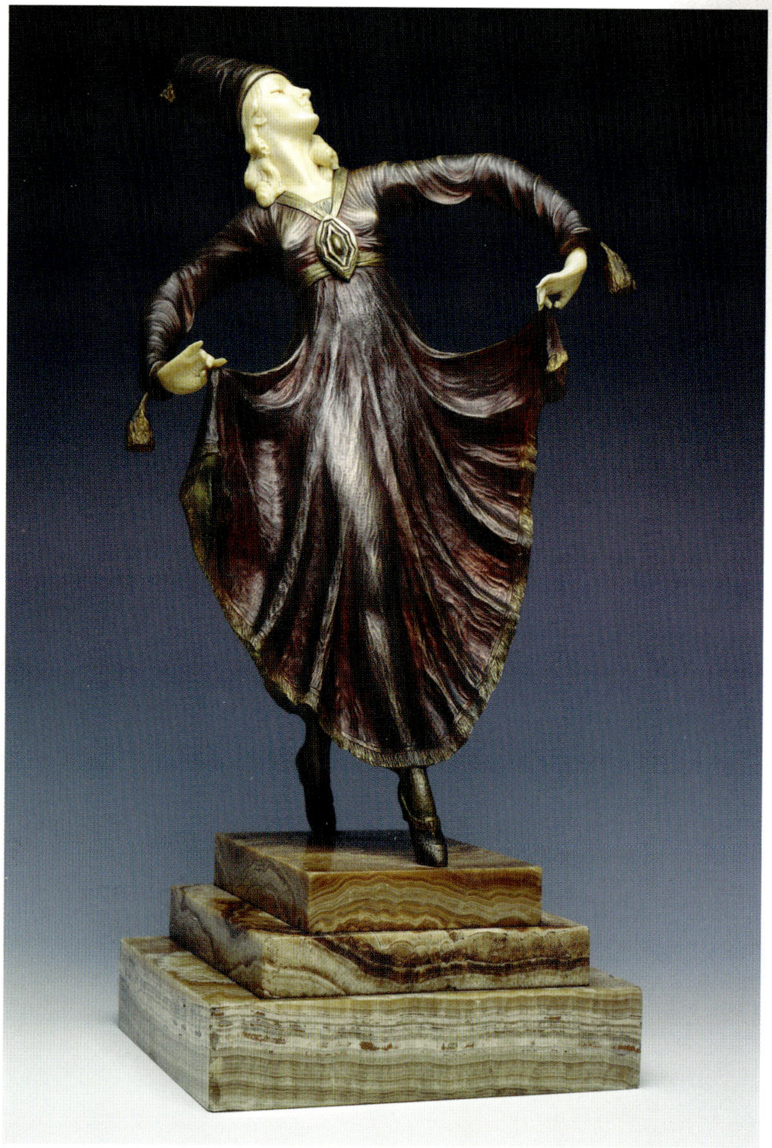

Fan Dancer
Bronze on onyx base
Height: 63cm. (24¾in.)
PRIVATE COLLECTION

Sway
Bronze and ivory on onyx base
Height: 46.5cm. (18¼in.)
PRIVATE COLLECTION

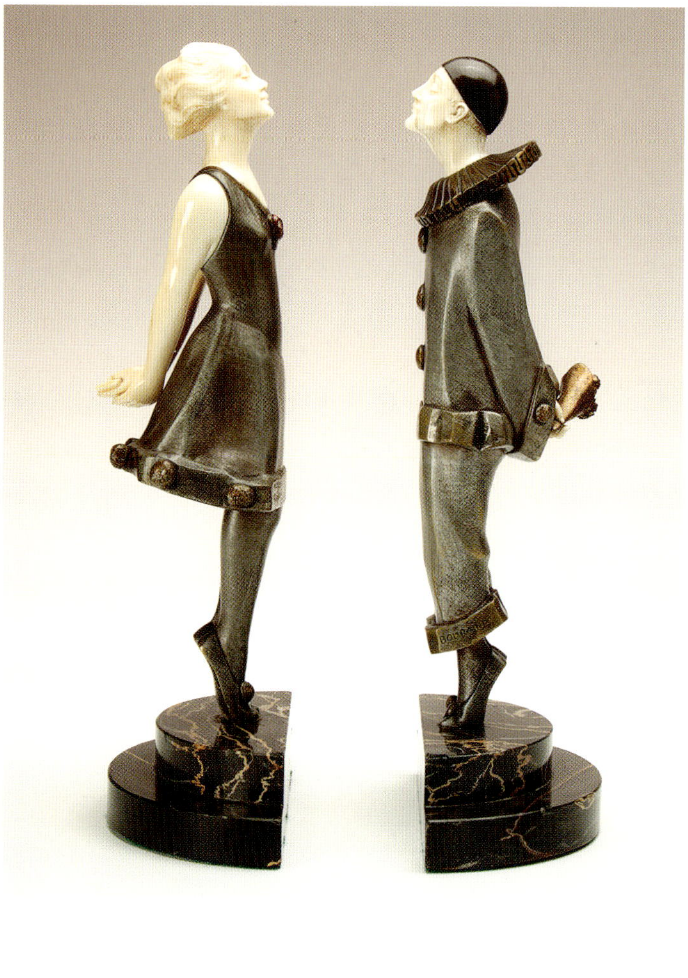

Flirt – Pierrette and Pierrot
Bronze and ivory on marble base (mounted as bookends)
Height: 29 and 28.5cm. (11½ and 11¼in.)
DINO MENASCHE COLLECTION

Harlequin
Bronze and ivory on marble base (mounted as a lamp)
Height: 55cm. (21¾in.)
PRIVATE COLLECTION

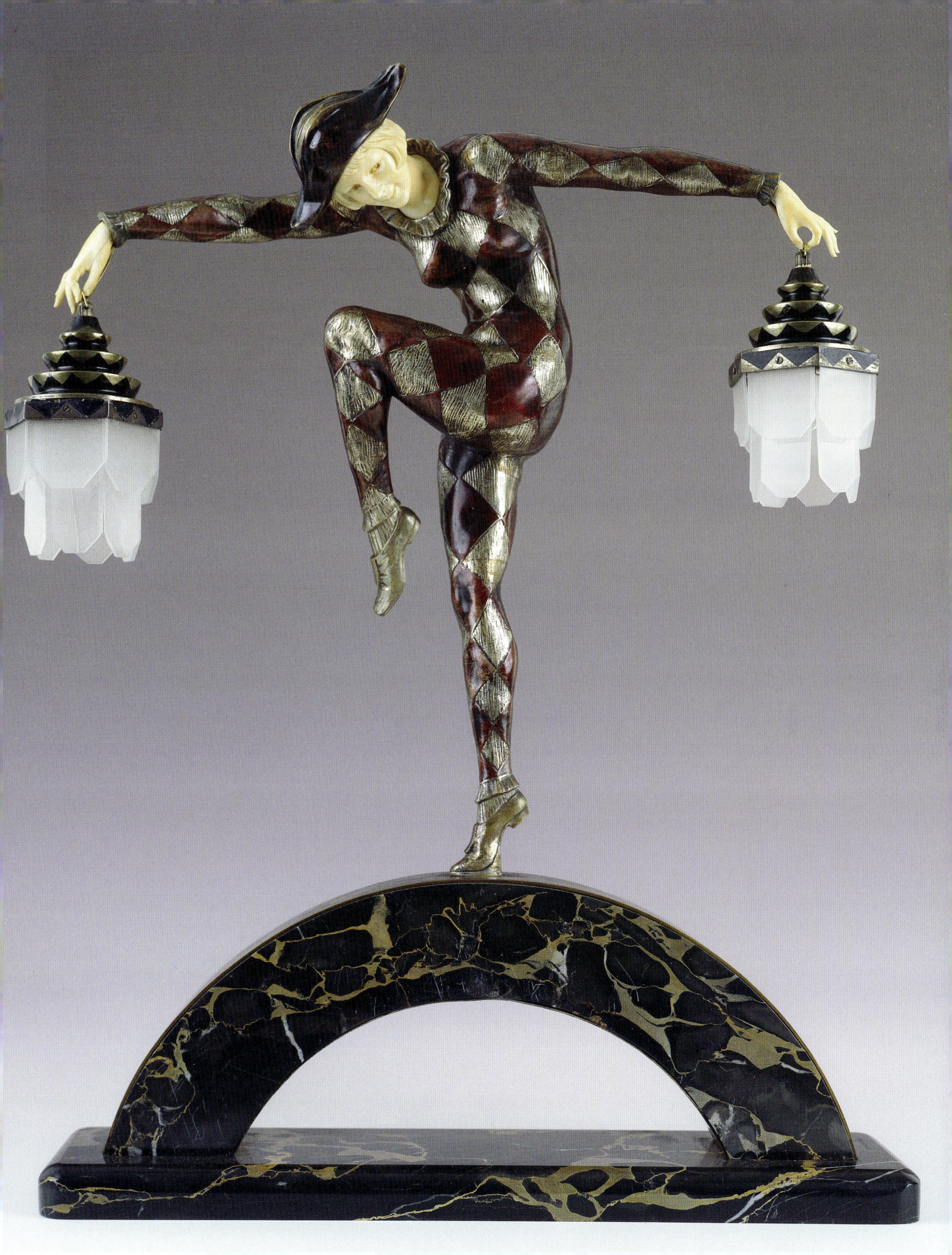

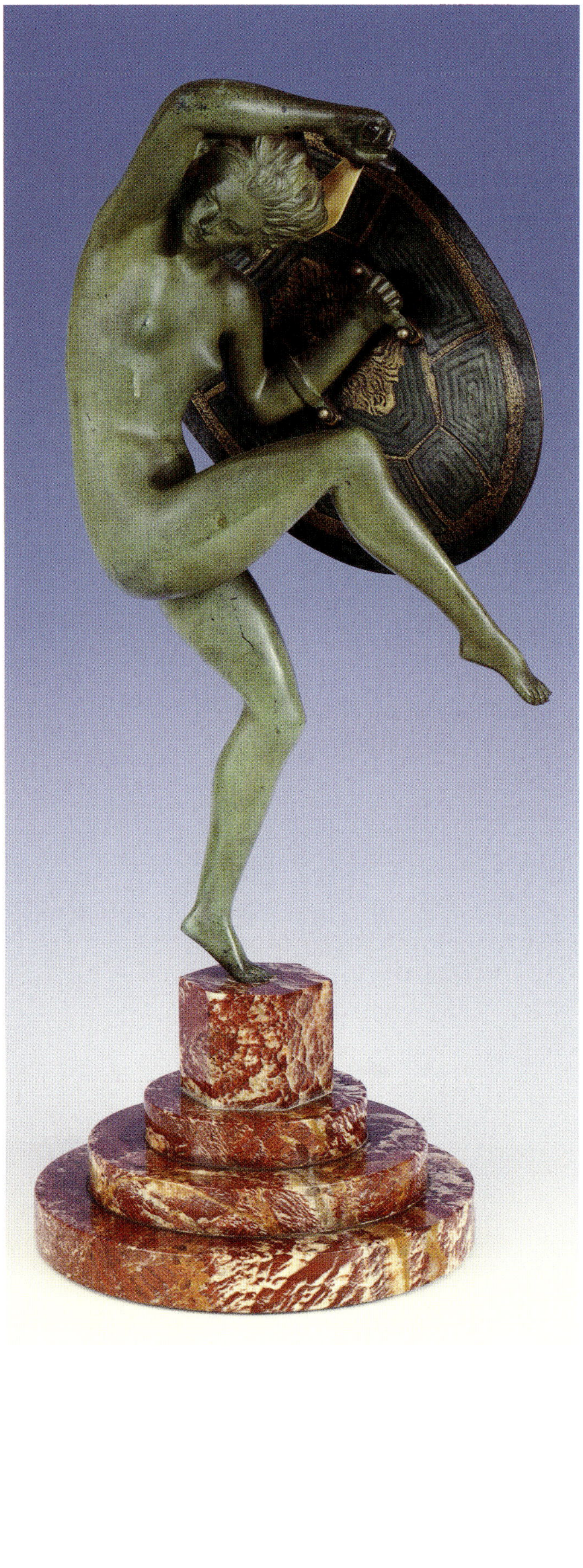

Amazon
Bronze and ivory on marble base
Height: 50cm. (19¾in.)
PRIVATE COLLECTION

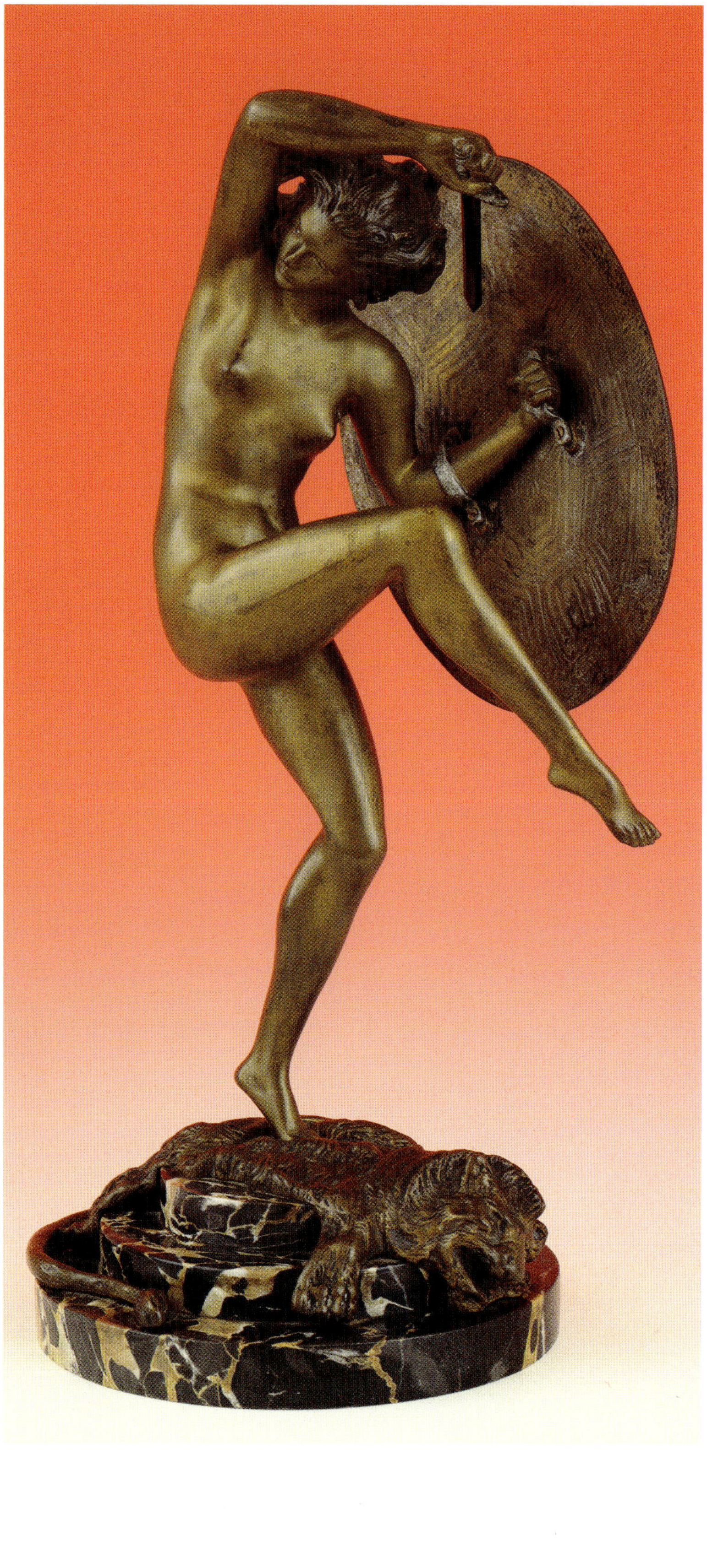

Amazon
Bronze on marble base
Height: 46.5cm. (18¼in.)
PRIVATE COLLECTION

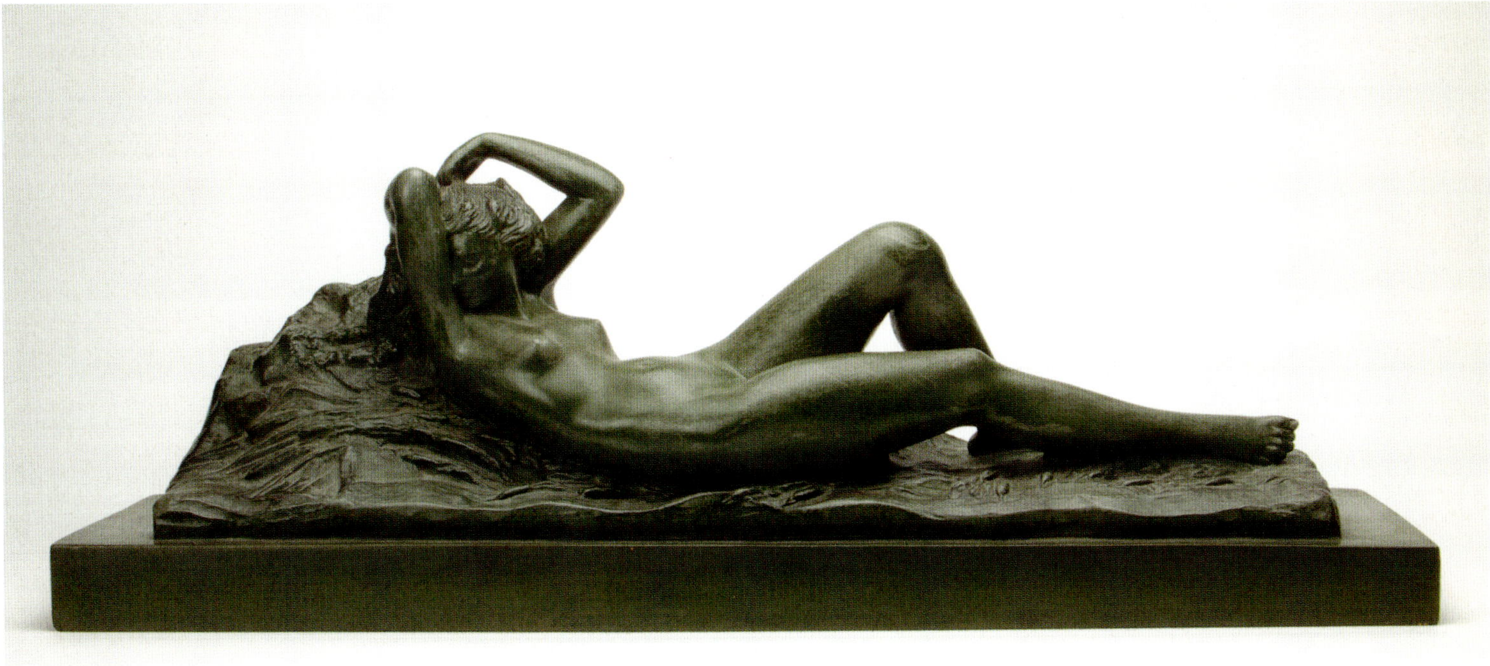

Thoughts
Terracotta
Height: 24cm. (9½in.)
Length: 65.5cm. (25¾in.)
PRIVATE COLLECTION

Playtime
Terracotta
Height: 35cm. (13¾in.)
Length: 54cm. (21¼in.)
PRIVATE COLLECTION

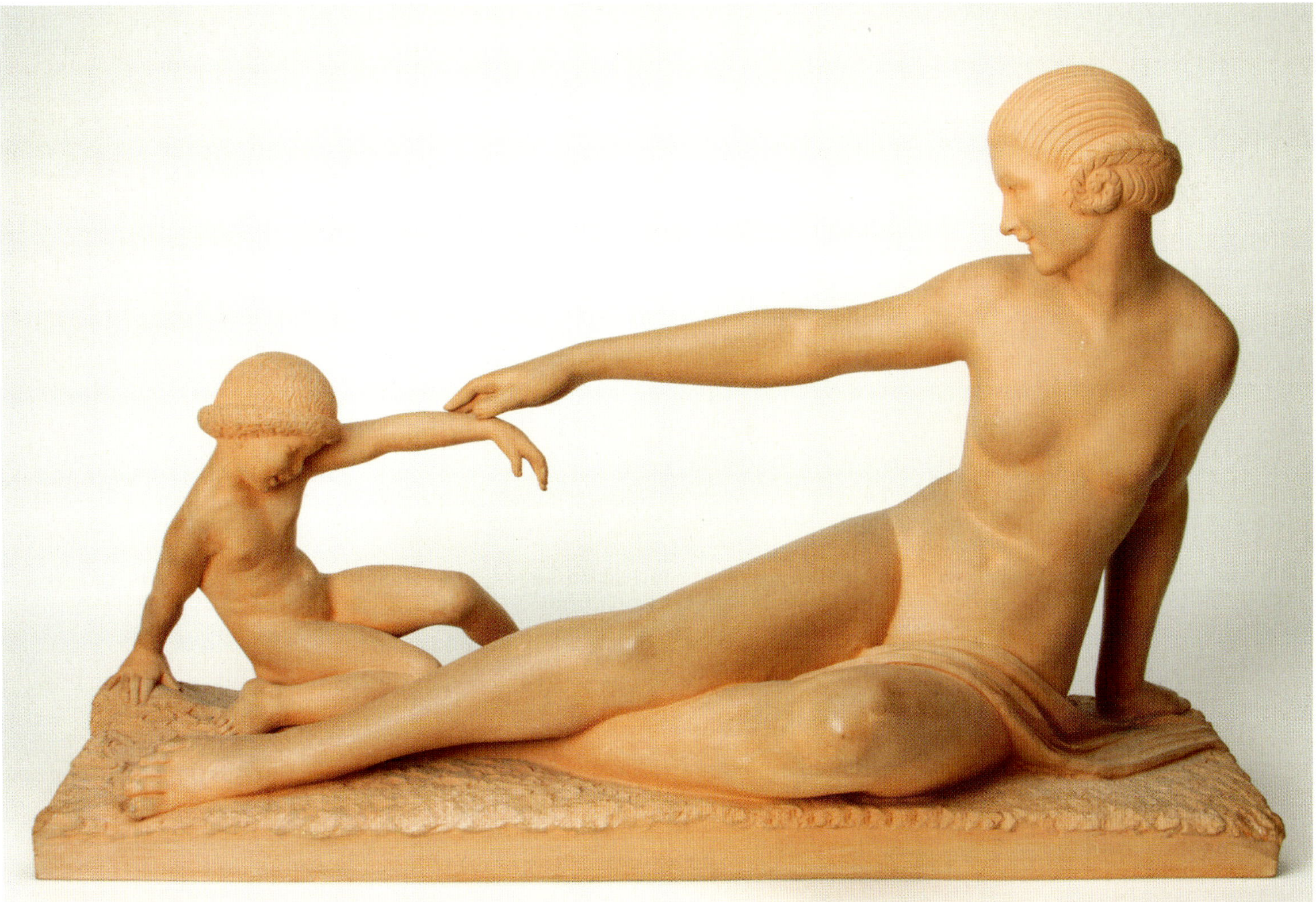

BRIAND (see BOURAINE)

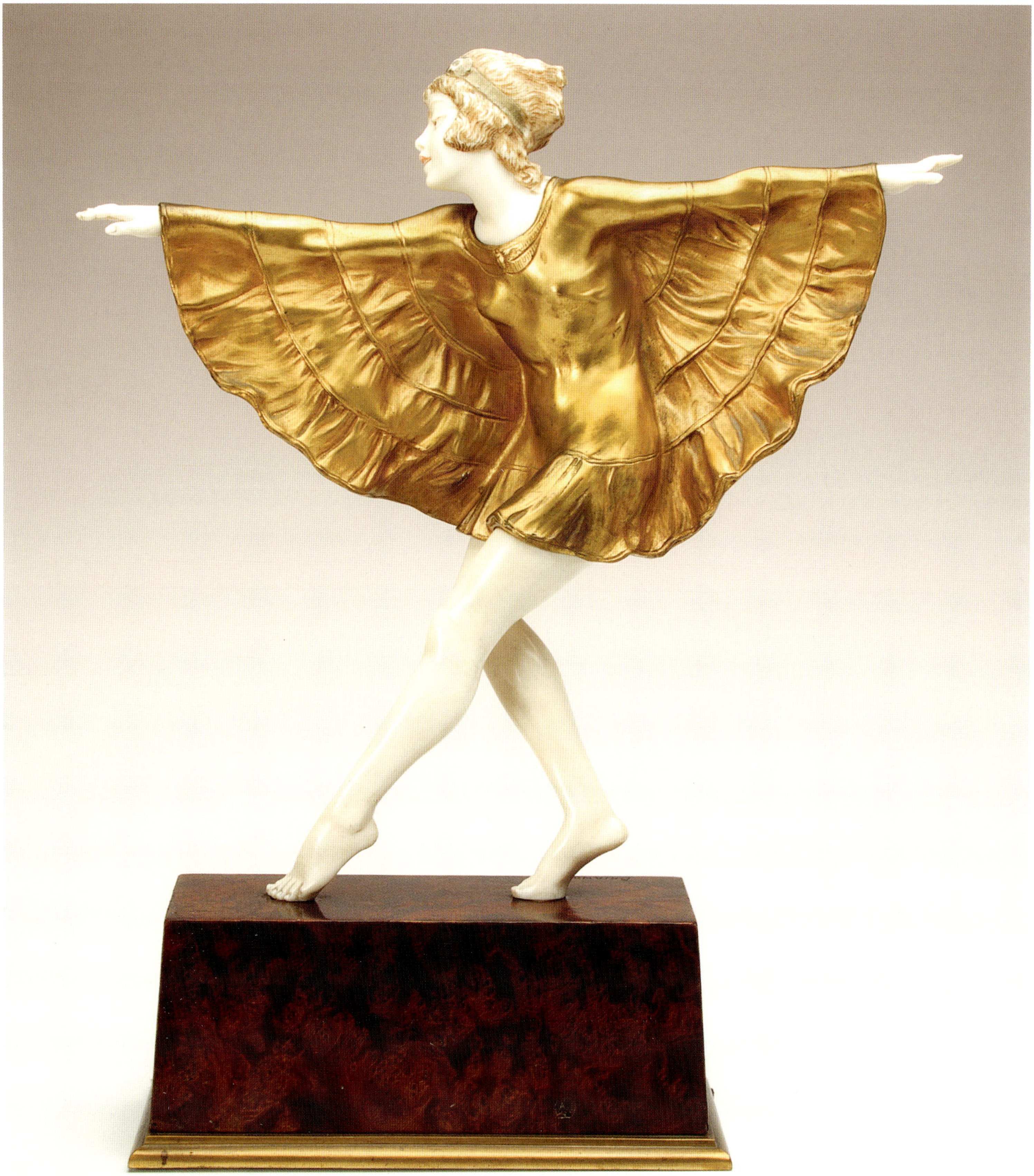

Butterfly Dancer
Bronze and ivory on wood and bronze base
Height: 35cm. (13¾in.)
DINO MENASCHE COLLECTION

CALLENDER, Bessie Stough

(Wichita 1889 – New York 1951)

'. . . she stood in sabots with a huge chisel in her left hand and a heavy mallet in her right, chopping away at a block of marble until there emerged the graceful and animated form of a delicate and sensitive animal.' Harold Callender, Fun Tomorrow: The Story of an Artist and a Way of Life, 1953

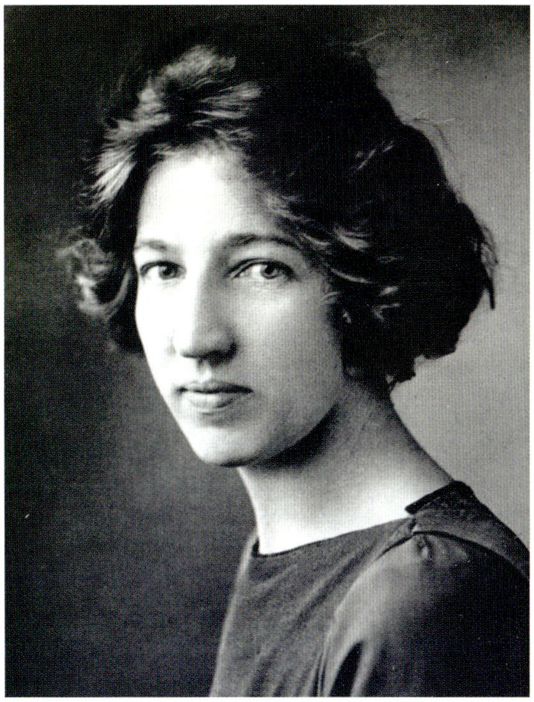

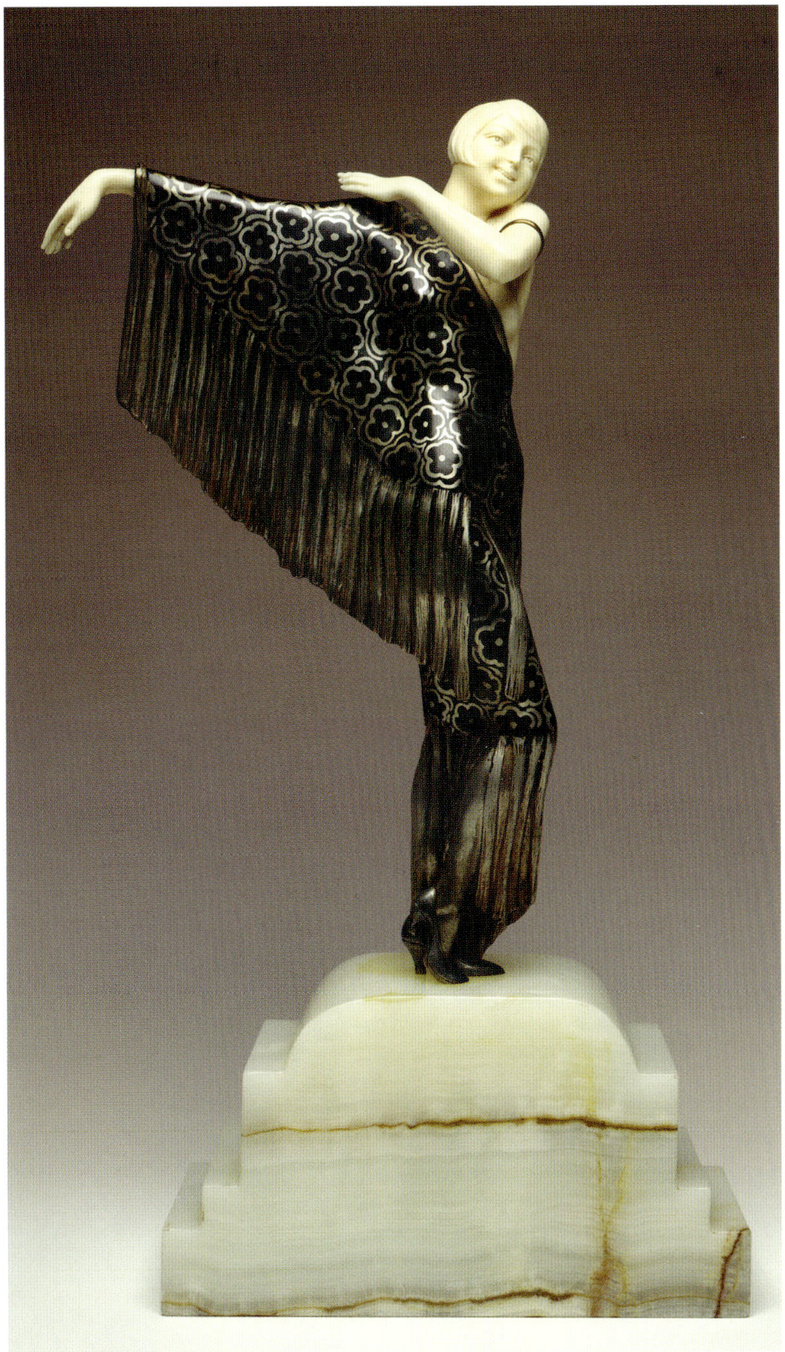

Anita

Bronze and ivory on marble base

Height: 42.5cm. (16¾in.)

PRIVATE COLLECTION

Born near Wichita, Kansas, she was particularly known for her animal sculptures. Her love of animals grew out of her childhood on a farm. She married Harold Callender, a *New York Times* journalist, and in the early 1920s the couple moved to New York. There Bessie took drawing classes with George Bridgman at the Art Students League and modelling from life at the Cooper Union Art School. When Harold was transferred to Paris in 1926, she studied at the Grande Chaumière with sculptor Antoine Bourdelle, and with the animalier Georges Hilbert, who taught her for three years and with whom she learned stone carving.

In Paris she took part in the Salon des Indépendants from 1928 to 1931, and also exhibited at the Salon d'Automne.

In 1930, Bessie and Harold moved to London, where they lived for approximately a decade, exhibiting at the Royal Academy in London, the Walker Gallery in Liverpool, and the Fine Arts Museum in Glasgow.

Callender died of cancer in 1951. After her death, her husband donated several of her pieces to the National Museum of American Art (now the Smithsonian American Art Museum).

At least one of her pieces was produced by Etling et Cie; this was a semi-nude dancer with a cape, called *Anita*, that was offered in both bronze and chryselephantine versions.

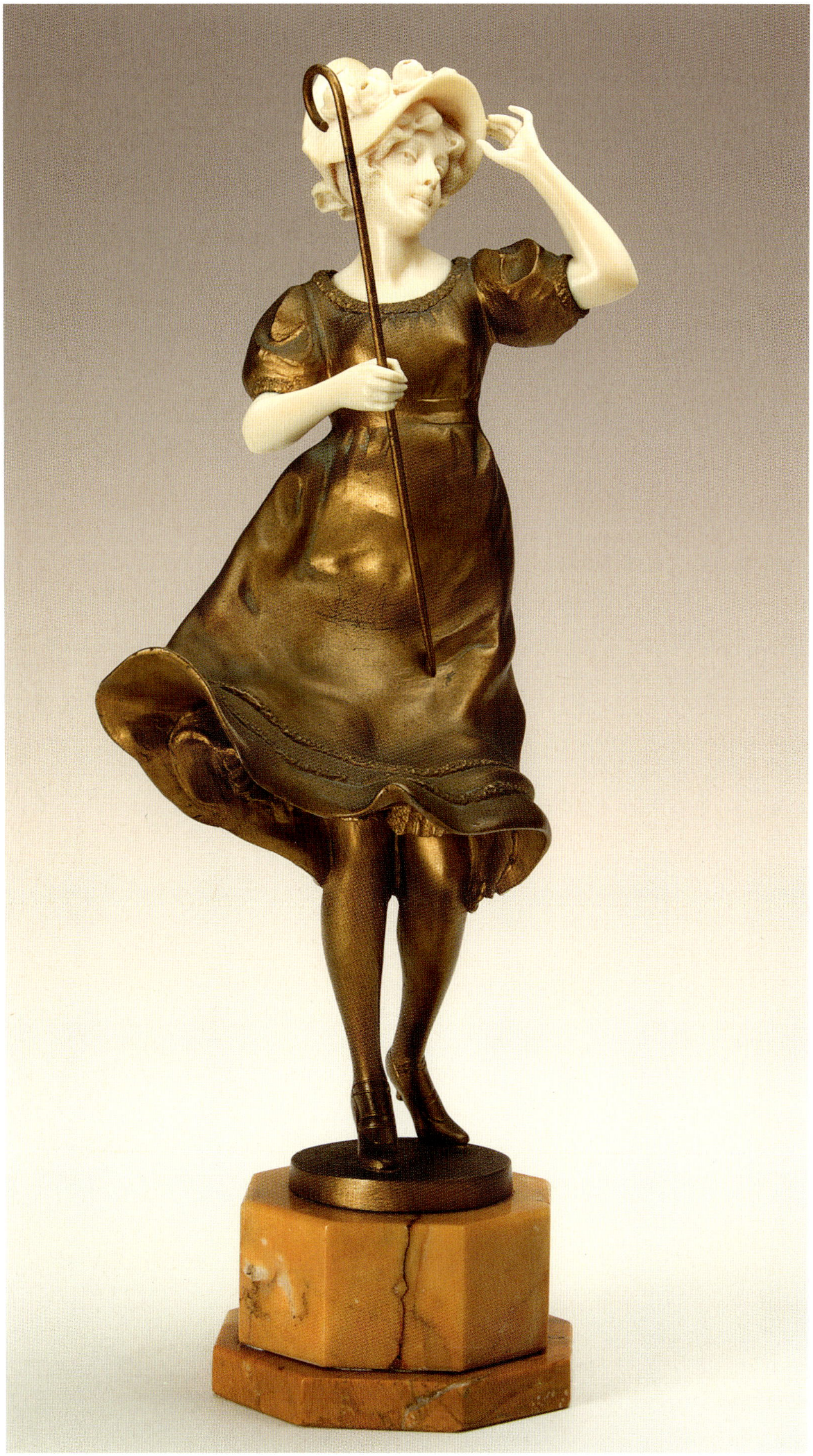

Shepherdess
Bronze and ivory on marble base
Height: 27cm. (10½in.)
DINO MENASCHE COLLECTION

CHAROL, Dorothea

(Odessa 1895 – London 1963)

Born in Odessa, Russia, she attended the Richter Art School in Dresden as well as studying in Brussels, in Munich at the Schwaegerle studio, and in Italy. She also worked in Berlin.

Her work was produced by the Volkstedt Porcelain factory in Thuringia and by the Rosenthal porcelain factory. She died in London in 1963.

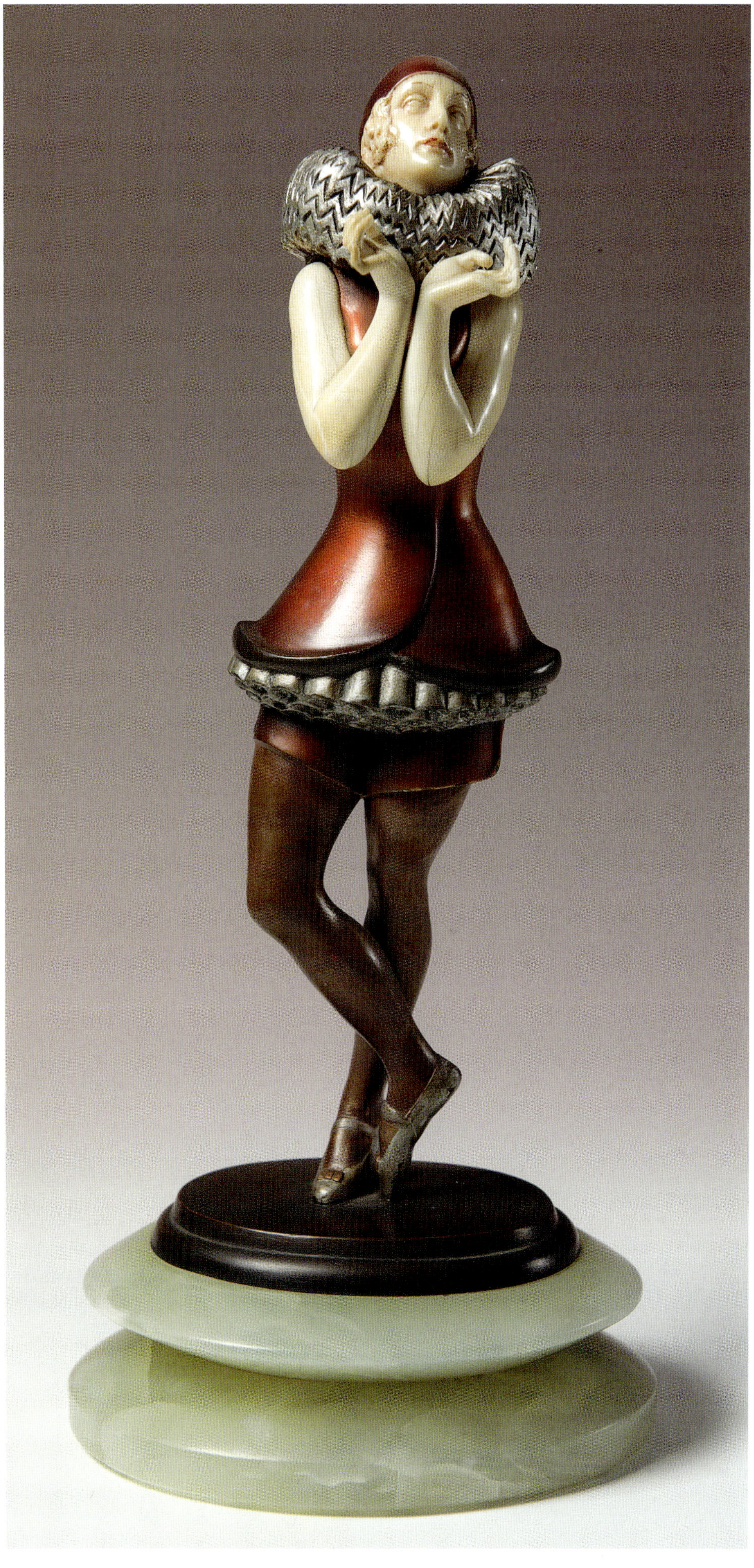

Pierrette
Bronze and ivory on onyx base
Height: 32.5cm. (12¾in.)
PRIVATE COLLECTION

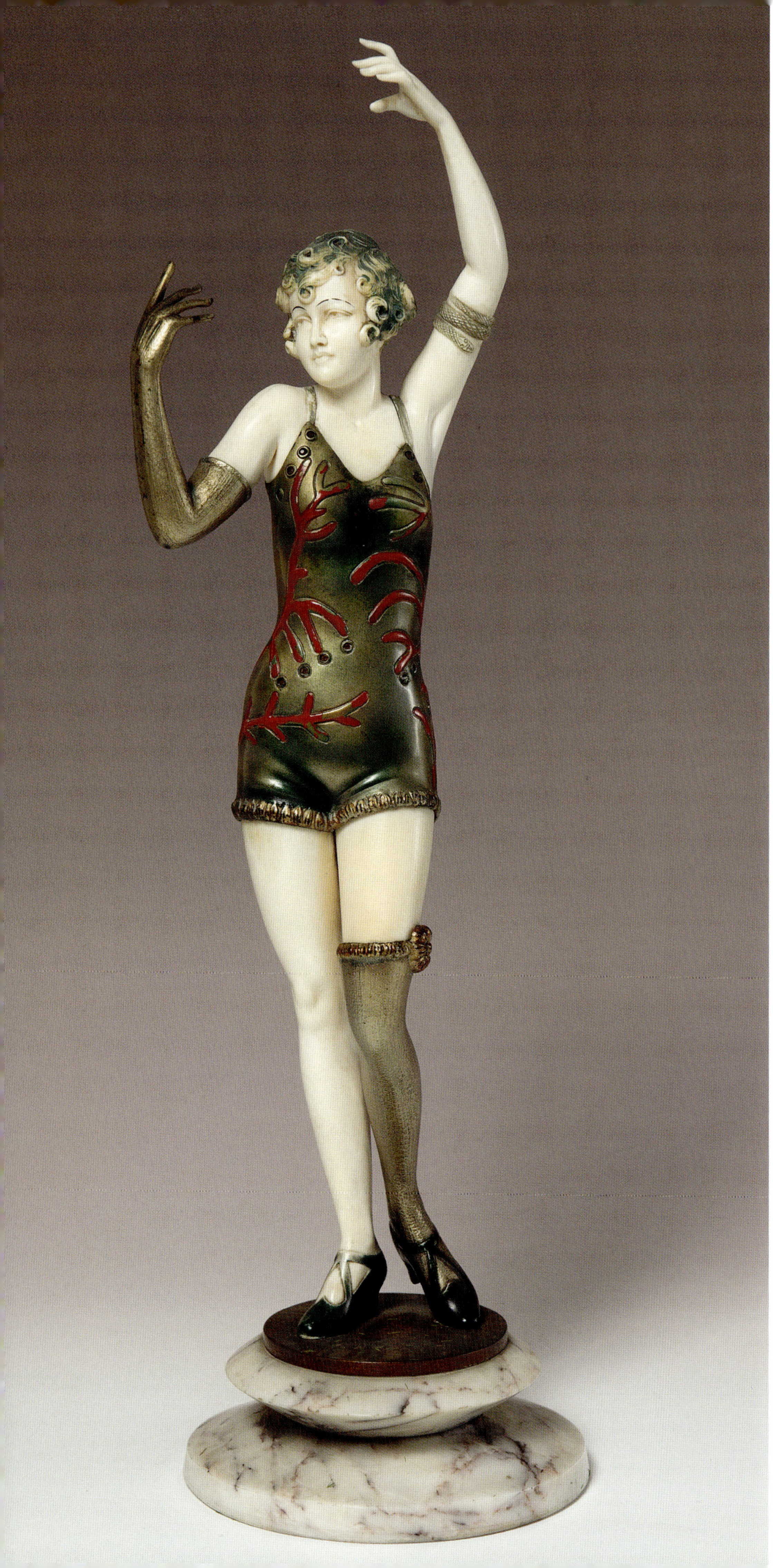

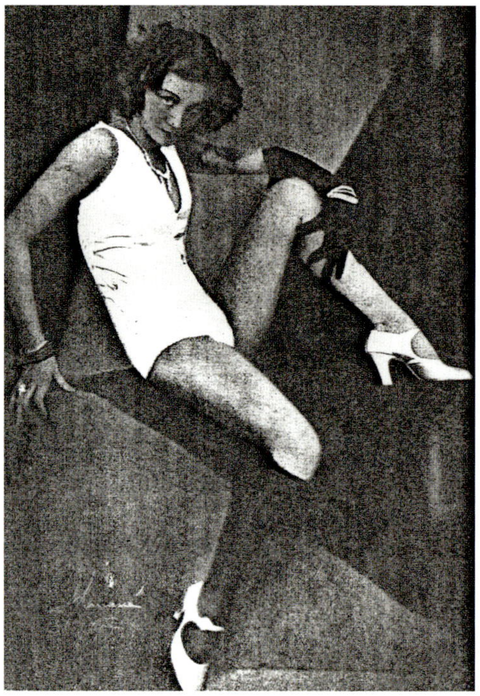

Galina Lazarina performing in a Music Hall

Revue Dancer
Bronze and ivory on marble base
Height: 40cm. (15¾in.)
PRIVATE COLLECTION

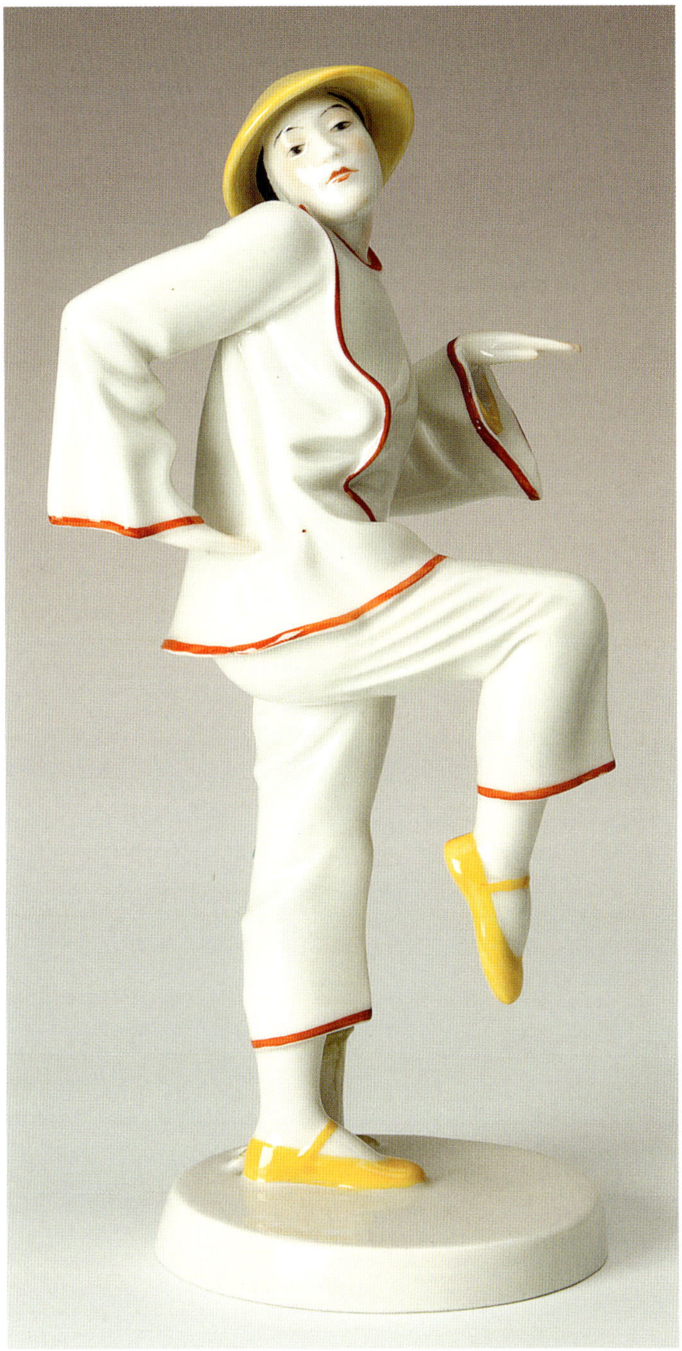

Chinese Dancer
Porcelain, Schwarzburger Werkstätten
Height: 21cm. (8¼in.)
DINO MENASCHE COLLECTION

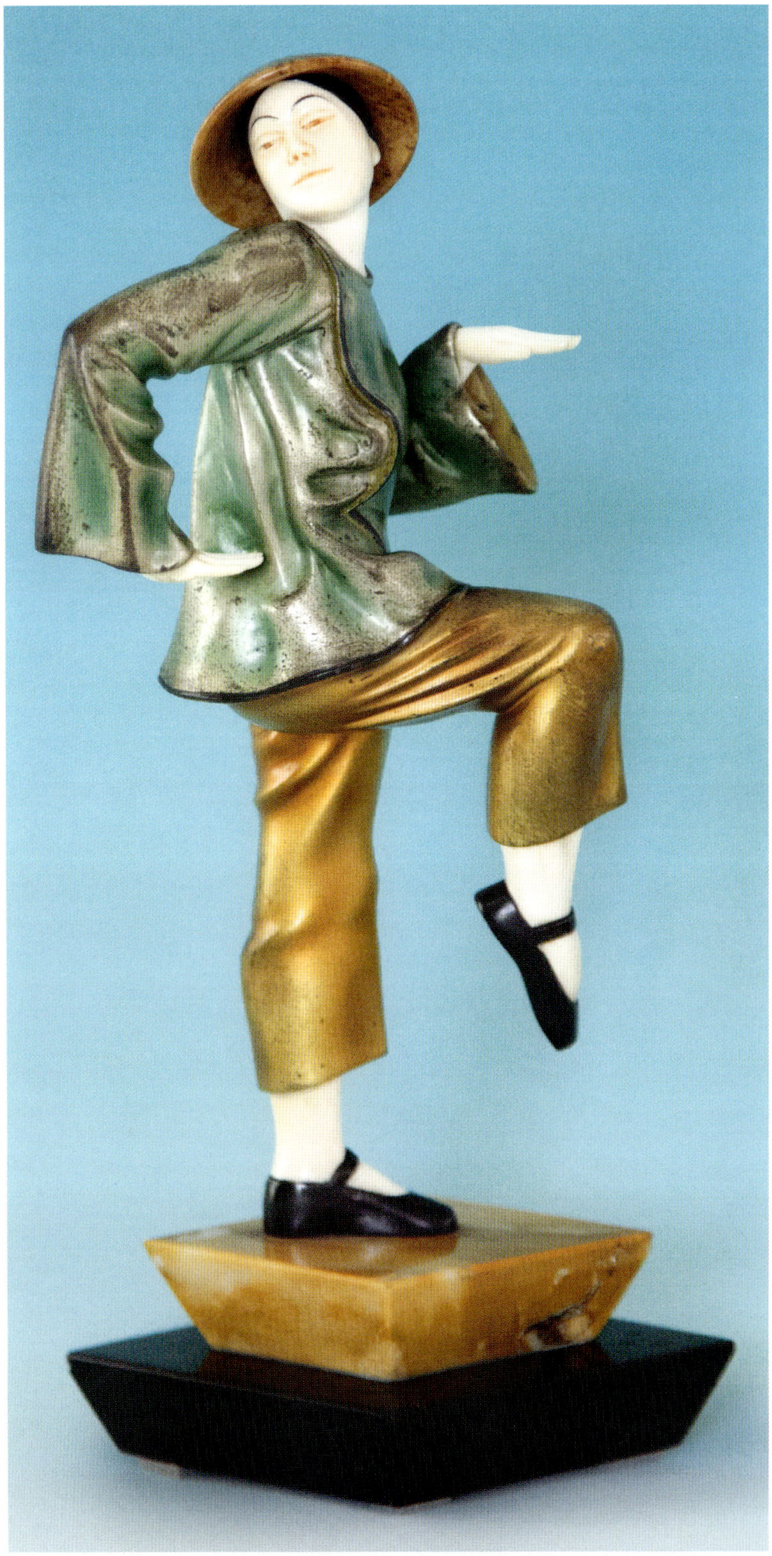

Chinese Dancer
Bronze, ivory and wood on marble base
Height: 28cm. (11in.)
PRIVATE COLLECTION

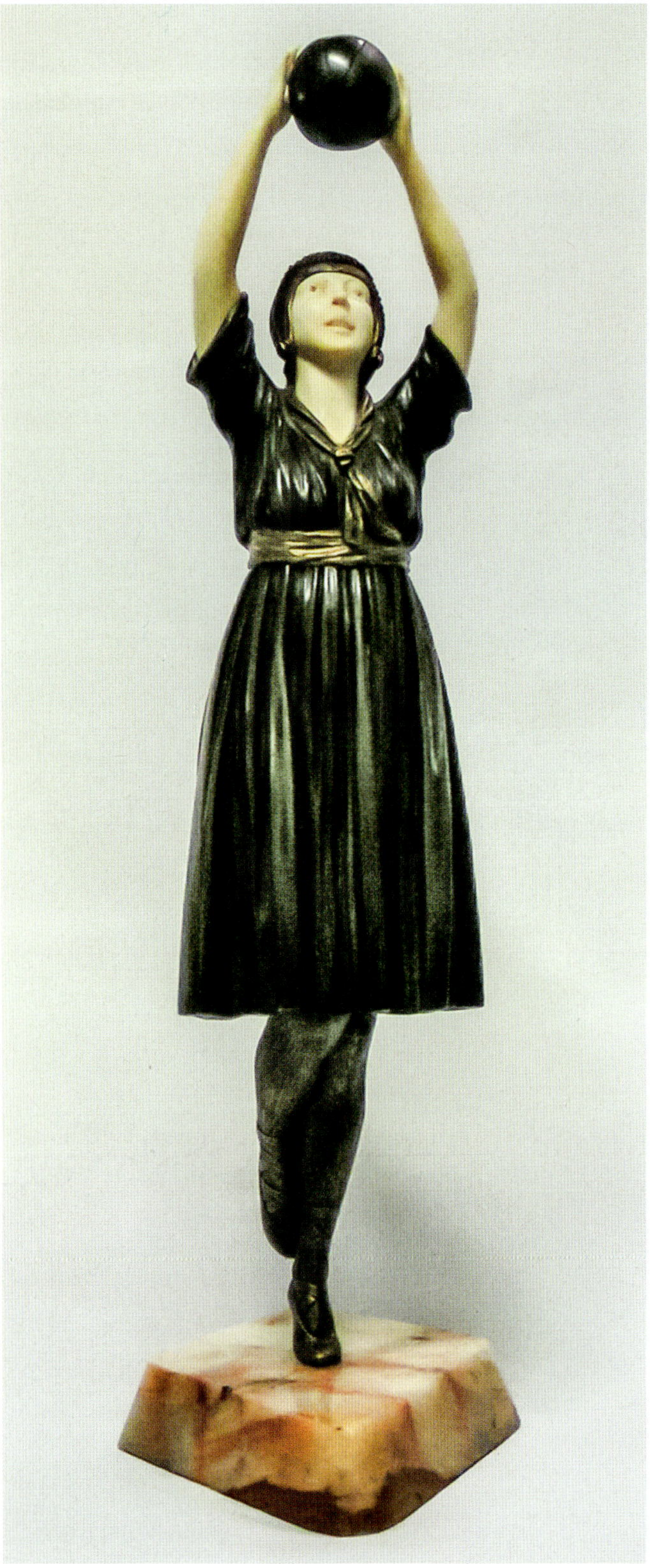

CHIPARUS, Demetre

(Dorohoi 1886 – Paris 1947)

Born in Dorohoi, Romania, he studied in Italy with sculptor Rafaello Romanelli, then went to live in Paris, where he studied under Antonin Mercié and Jean Boucher.

From 1914 to 1928 he exhibited at the Salon of the Société des Artistes Français. In 1914 he received an honourable mention.

Chiparus is best known for his bronze and his chryselephantine sculptures, most of which were produced by L.N.J.L., Etling et Cie and Goldscheider.

Ball Game
Bronze and ivory on marble base
Height: 40cm. (15¾in.)
PRIVATE COLLECTION

Reclining Woman
Bronze on marble base
Height: 33.5cm. (13¼in.)
Length: 57cm. (22½in.)
PRIVATE COLLECTION

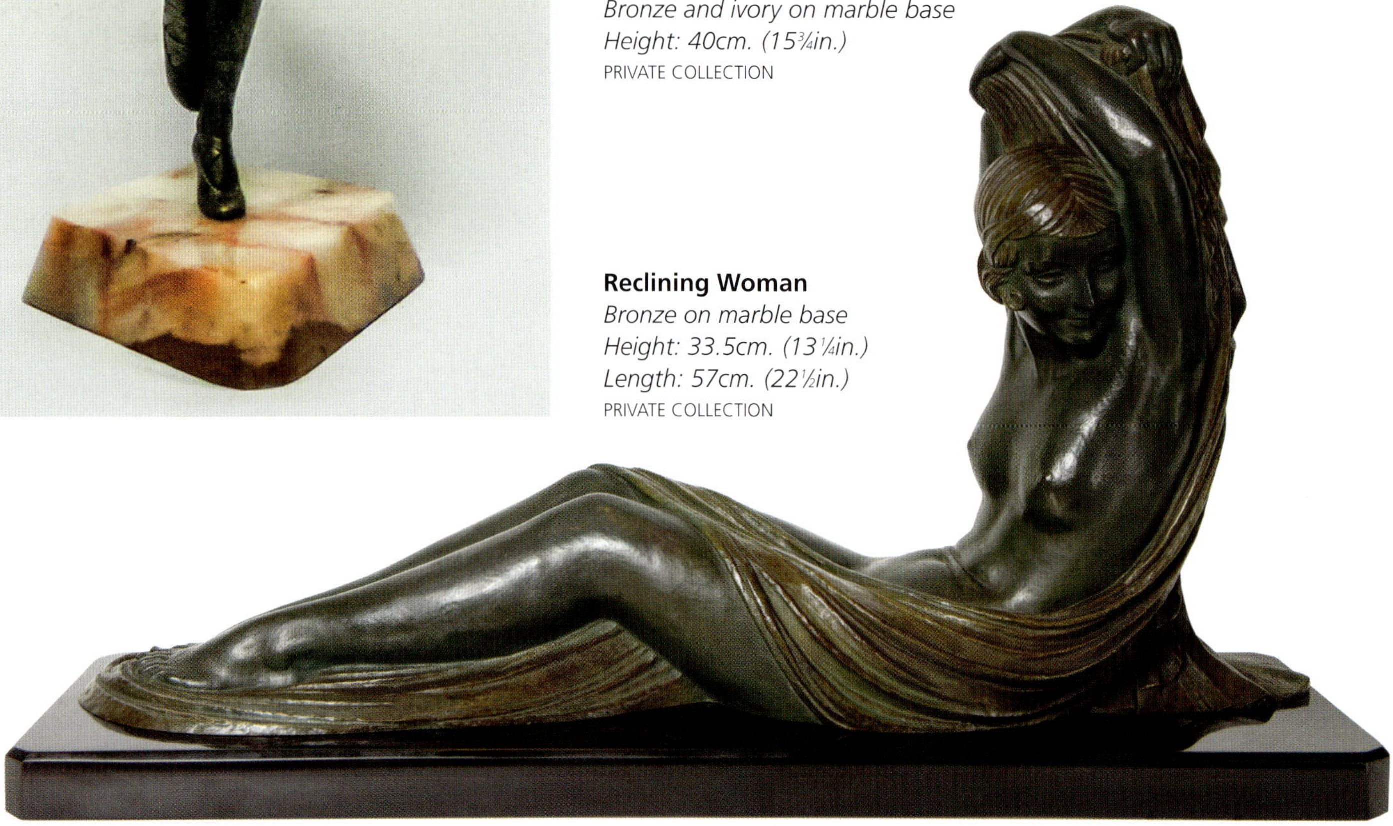

COLINET, Claire

(Brussels 1880 – 1950)

Born in Brussels, Claire Jeanne Roberte Colinet studied there, under Jef Lambeaux. She later settled in Paris, where she began exhibiting at the Salon of the Société des Artistes Français from 1913, receiving an honourable mention in 1914. She became a member of the Société in 1929. In 1935 she exhibited a statue of the young King Albert of Belgium.

From 1937 to 1940 she also exhibited at the Salon des Indépendants and became a member of the Union des Femmes Peintres et Sculpteurs. As an artist she was drawn to exoticism, and worked in a detailed and fluid style.

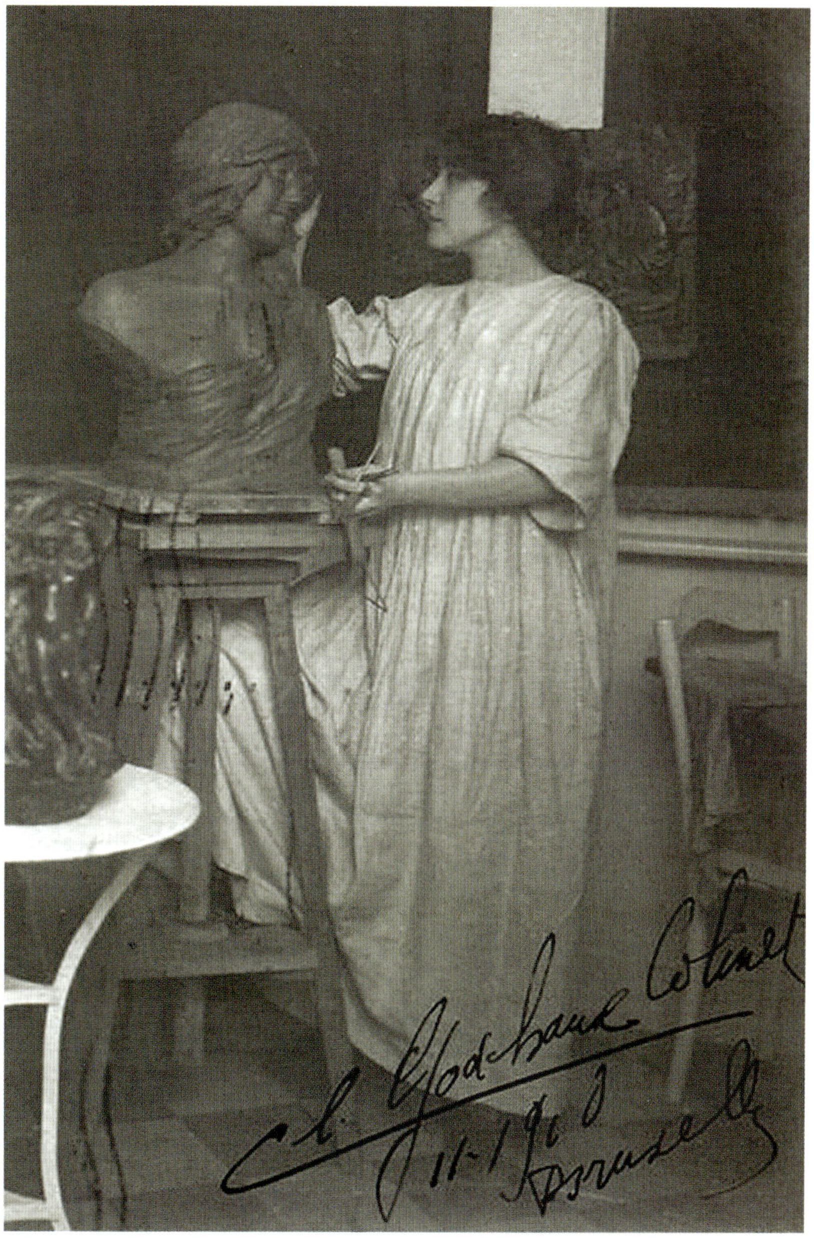

Colinet in her studio, 1910.

Claire Colinet was married twice: the first time, c.1913, to a Mr. Godchaux, who was possibly the painter and animalier sculptor Roger Godchaux. Her second marriage, in March 1929, was to André Marcel Nigron; this marriage enabled her to acquire French nationality.

Colinet's sculptures were produced by Etling et Cie, Arthur Goldscheider, Les Neveux de J. Lehmann and Barbedienne.

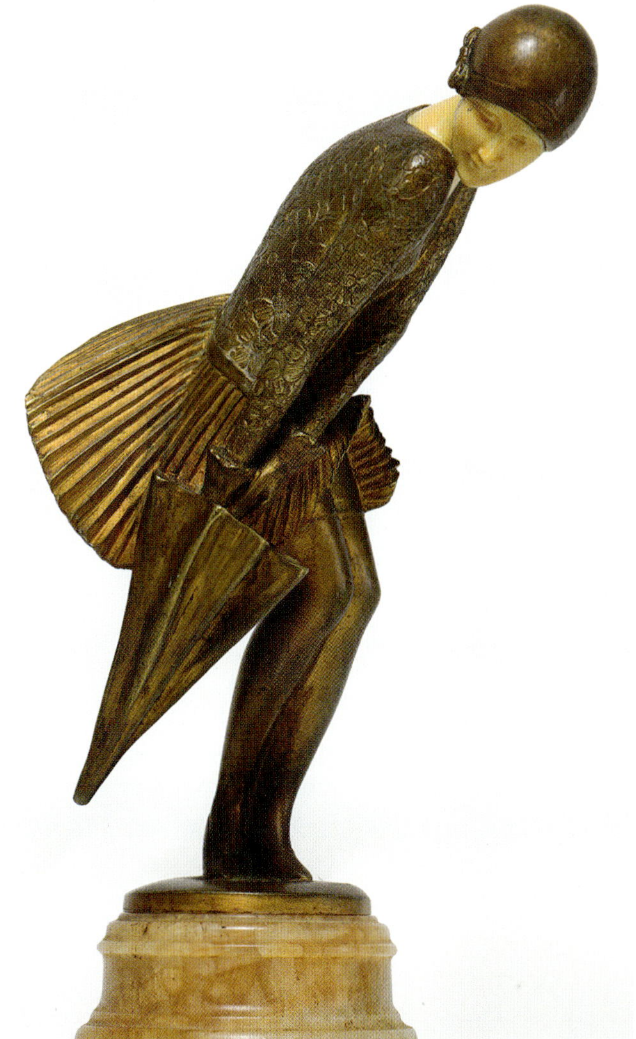

The Squall
Bronze and ivory on marble base
Height: 22cm. (8¾in.)
PRIVATE COLLECTION

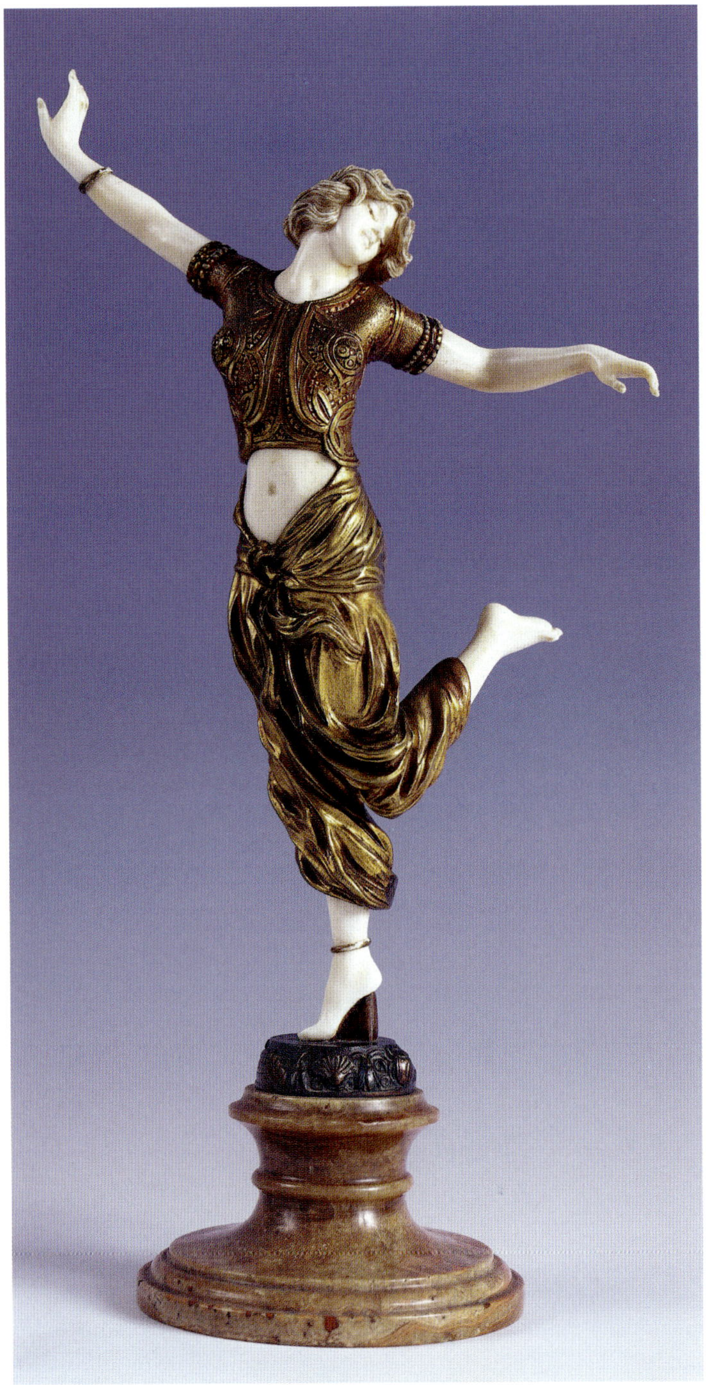

A Dancer
Bronze and ivory on marble base
Height: 35cm. (13¾in.)
BURR AND MUIR COLLECTION, CAPE TOWN

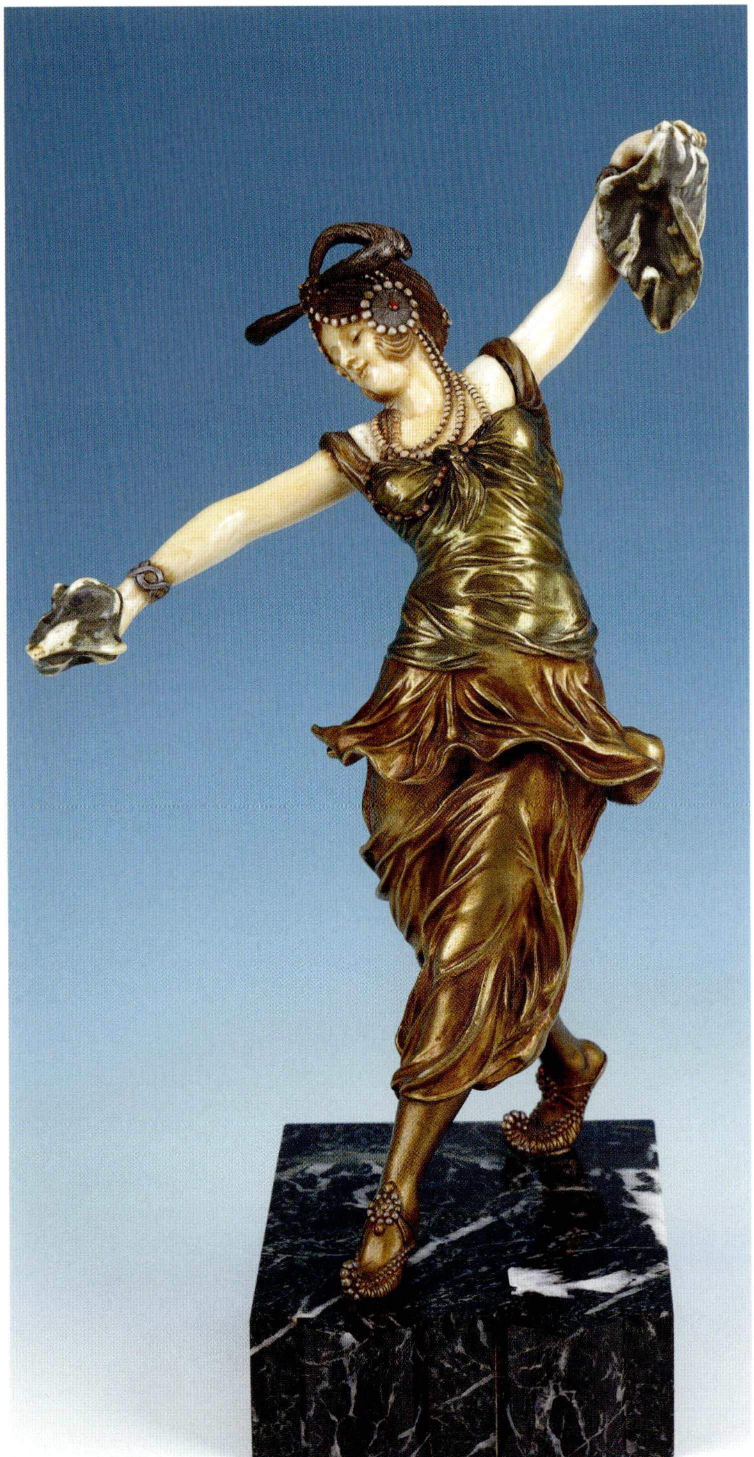

Handkerchief Dance
Bronze and ivory on marble base
Height: 33cm. (13in.)
PRIVATE COLLECTION

Also produced 44cm. (17¼in.) high

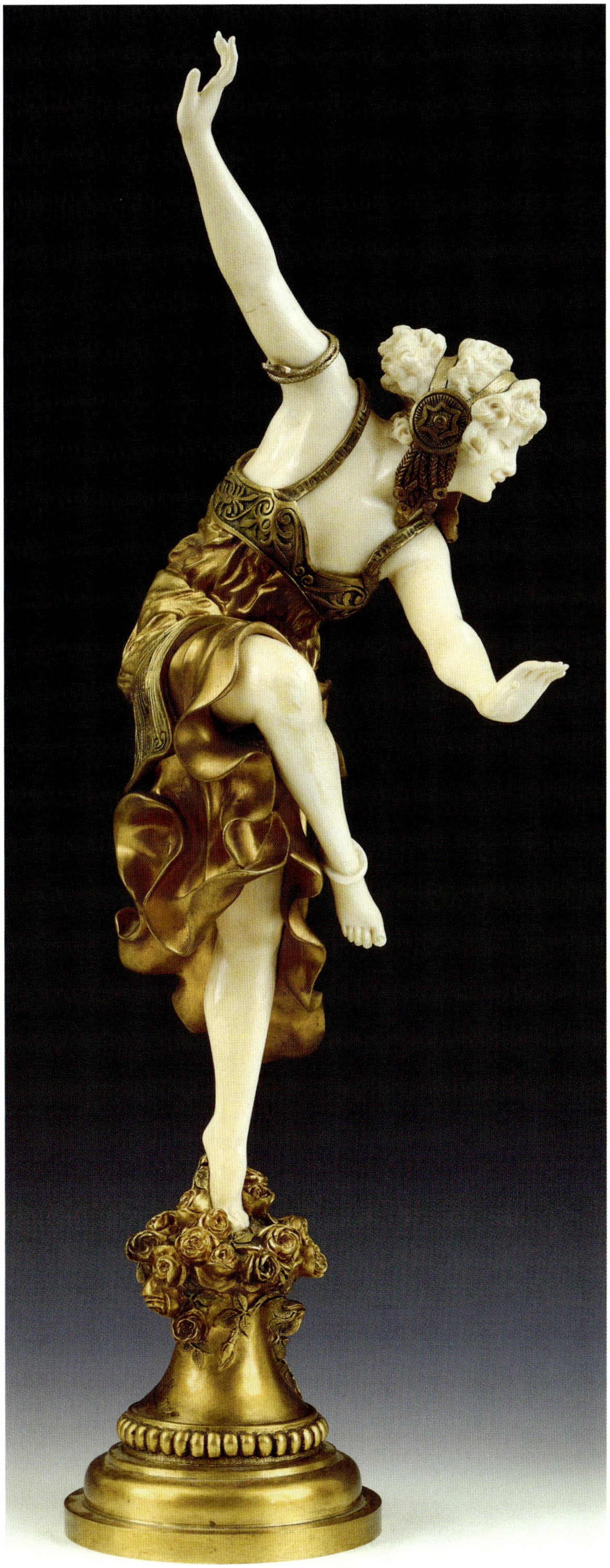

Corinthian Dancer
Bronze and ivory
Height: 42cm. (16½in.)
PRIVATE COLLECTION

Also produced 35cm. (13¾in.) and 25cm. (10in.) high

Hindu Dancer
Bronze and ivory on marble base
Height: 36cm. (14¼in.)
DINO MENASCHE COLLECTION

Also produced 45cm. (17¾in.) high

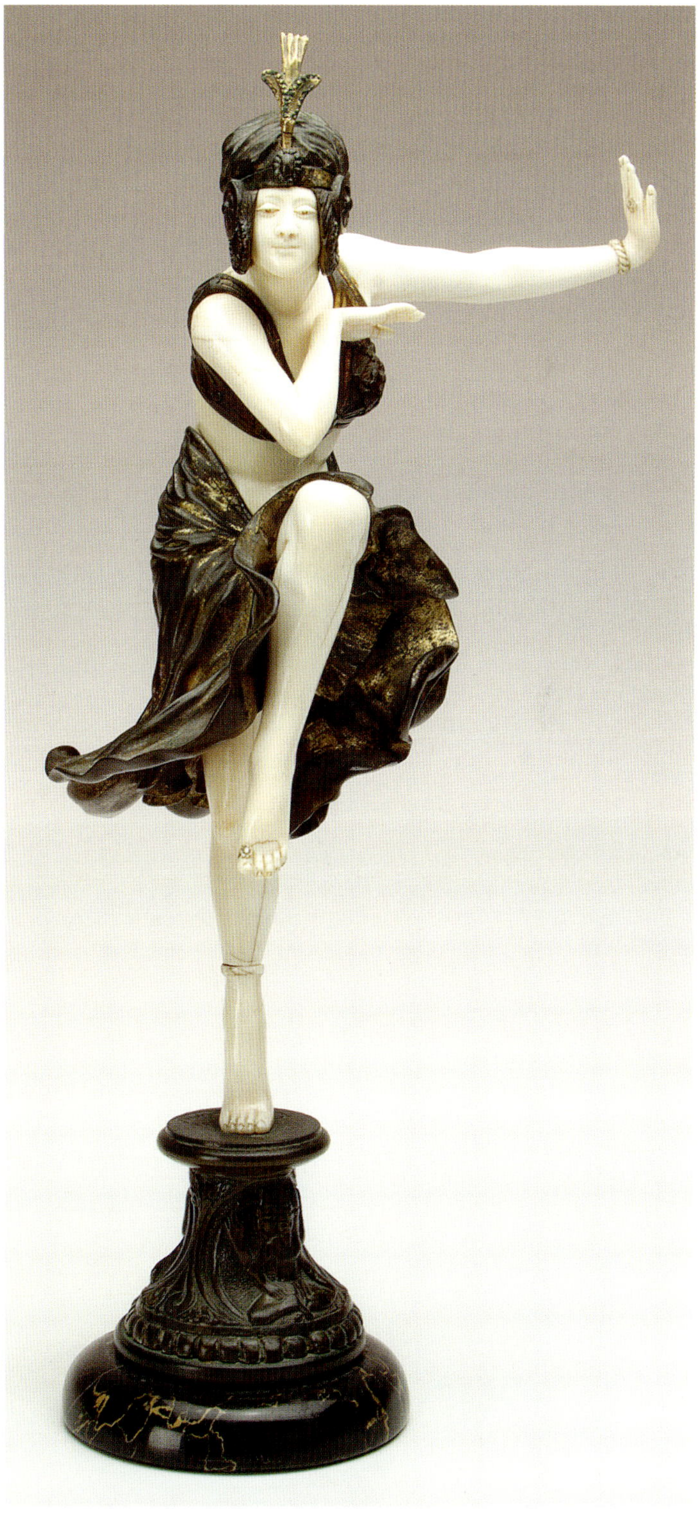

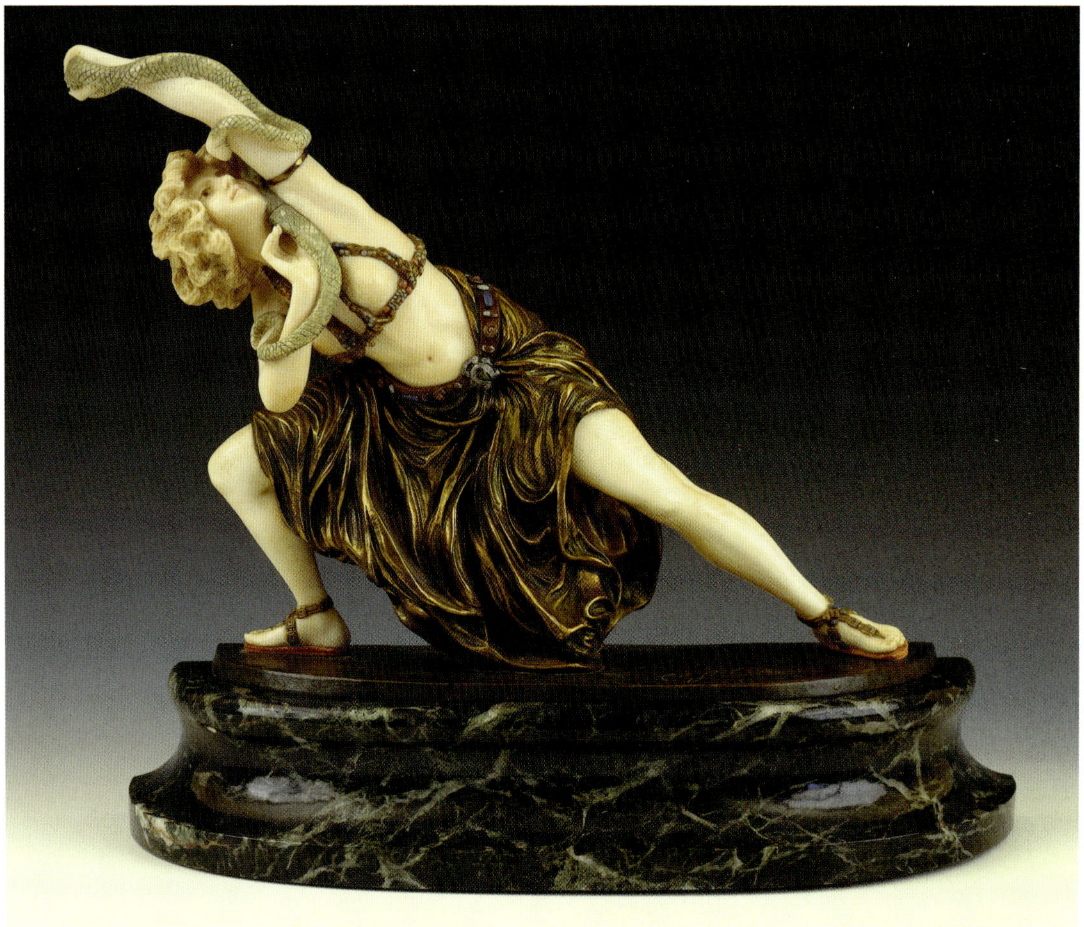

Dancer of Carthage
Bronze and ivory on marble base
Height: 28cm. (11in.)
PRIVATE COLLECTION

Also produced 55cm. (21½in.) high

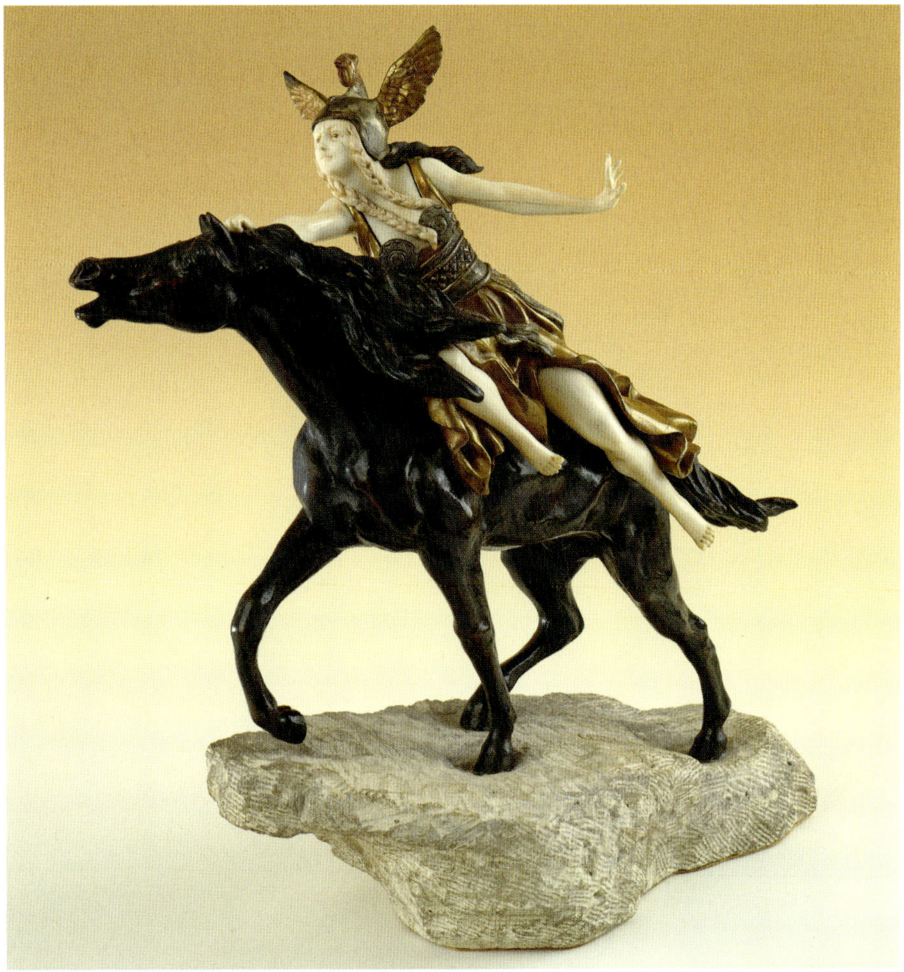

Valkyrie
Bronze and ivory on stone base
Height: 44.5cm. (17½in.)
PRIVATE COLLECTION

Also produced with a bronze base; also 75cm. (29½in.) and 32cm. (12½in.) high

Swirl Dancer
Bronze and ivory on marble base
Height: 59cm. (23¼in.)
PRIVATE COLLECTION

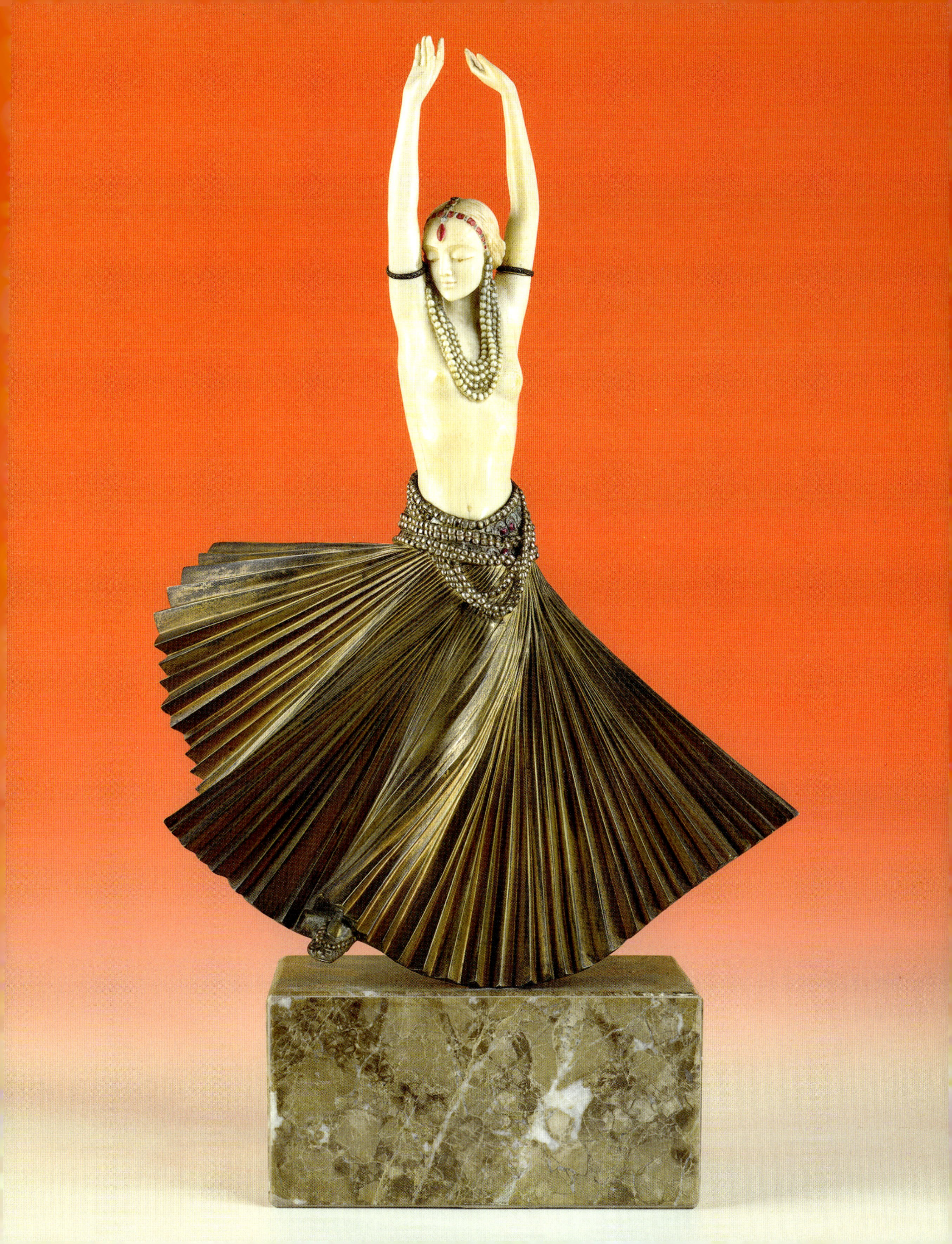

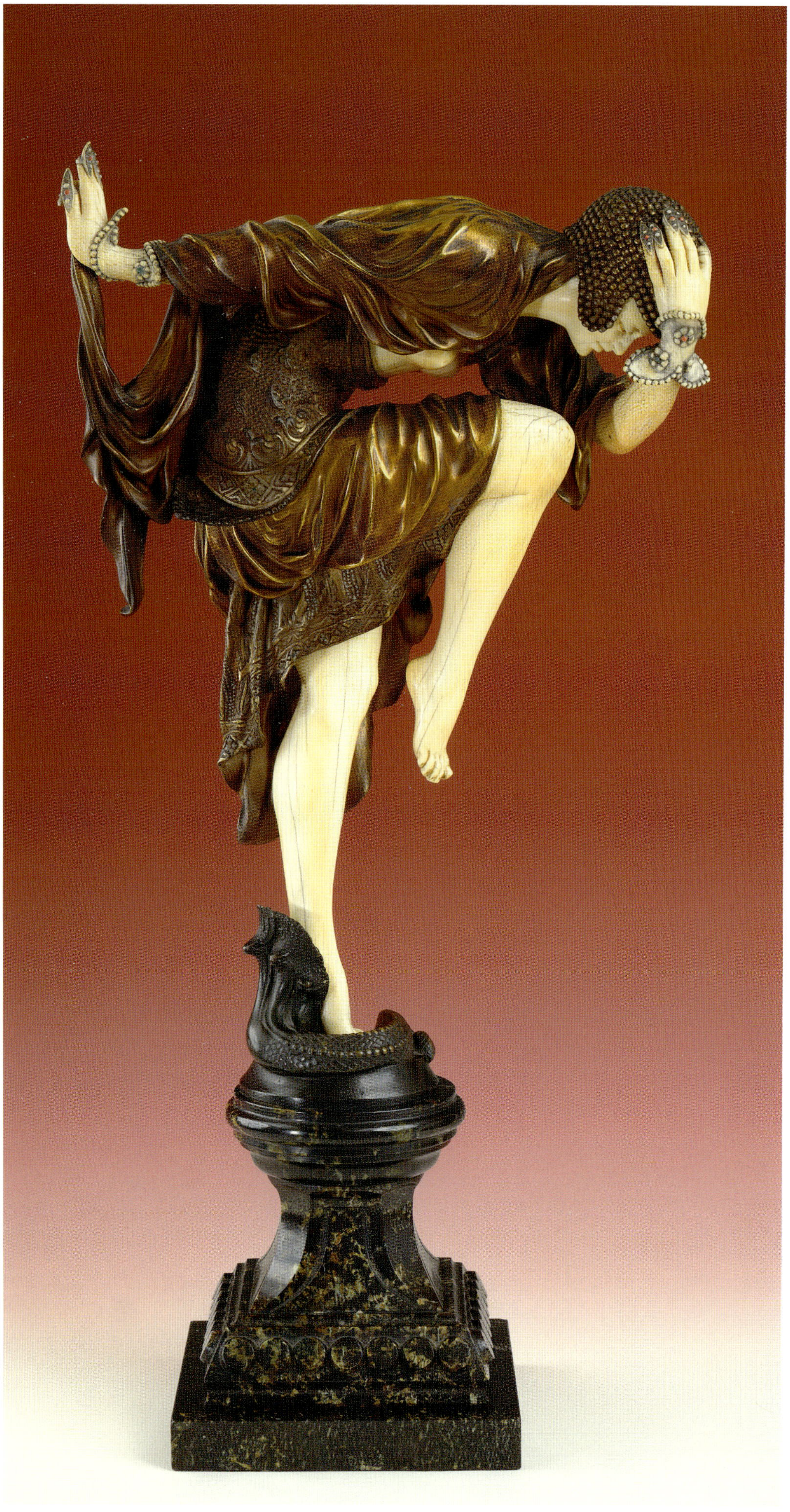

Ankara Dancer
Bronze and ivory on marble base
Height: 62cm. (24½in.)
PRIVATE COLLECTION

Also produced 43.5cm. (17in.) high

Ankara Dancer
Bronze and ivory on marble base
Height: 65cm. (25½in.)
S. AND J.S. COLLECTION

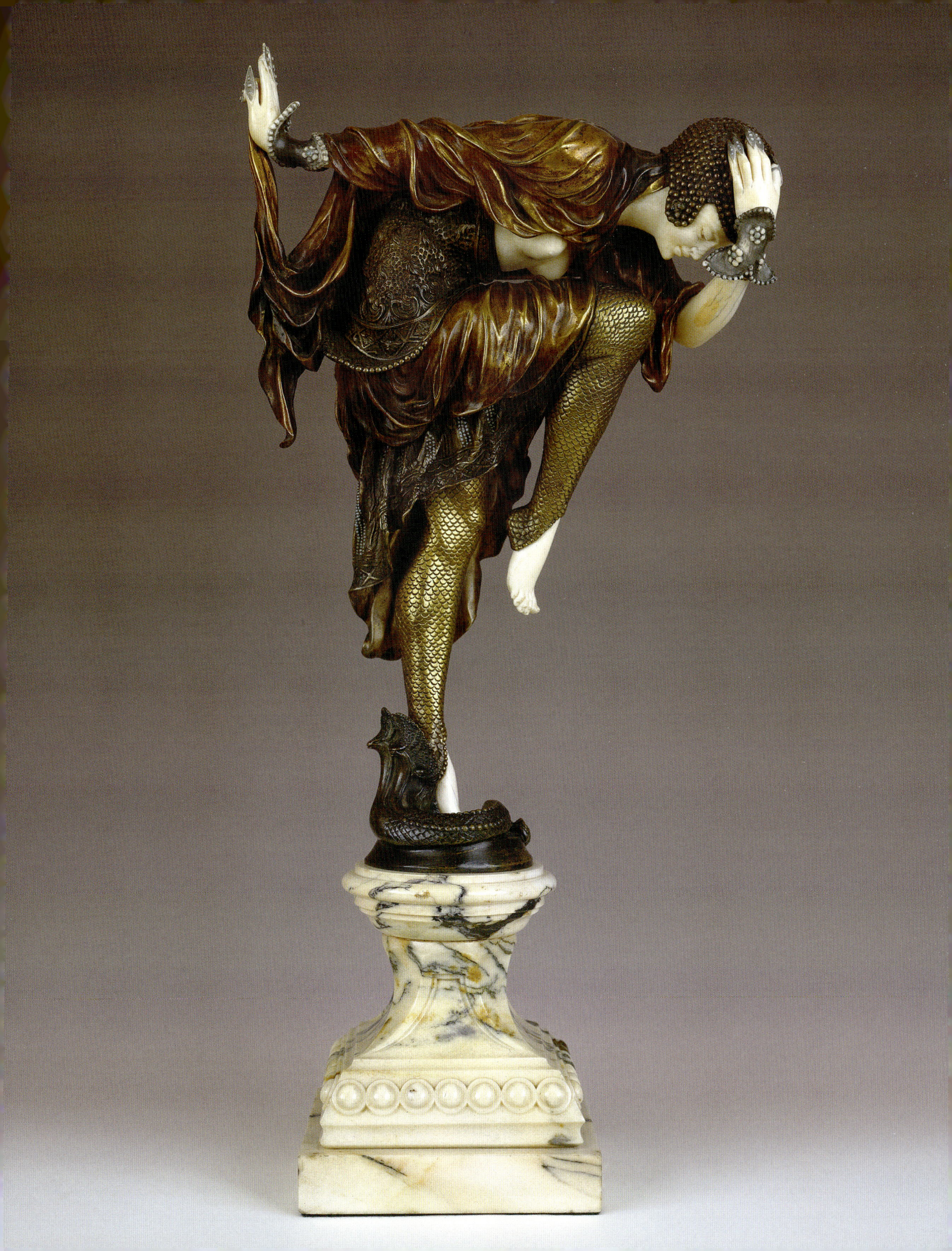

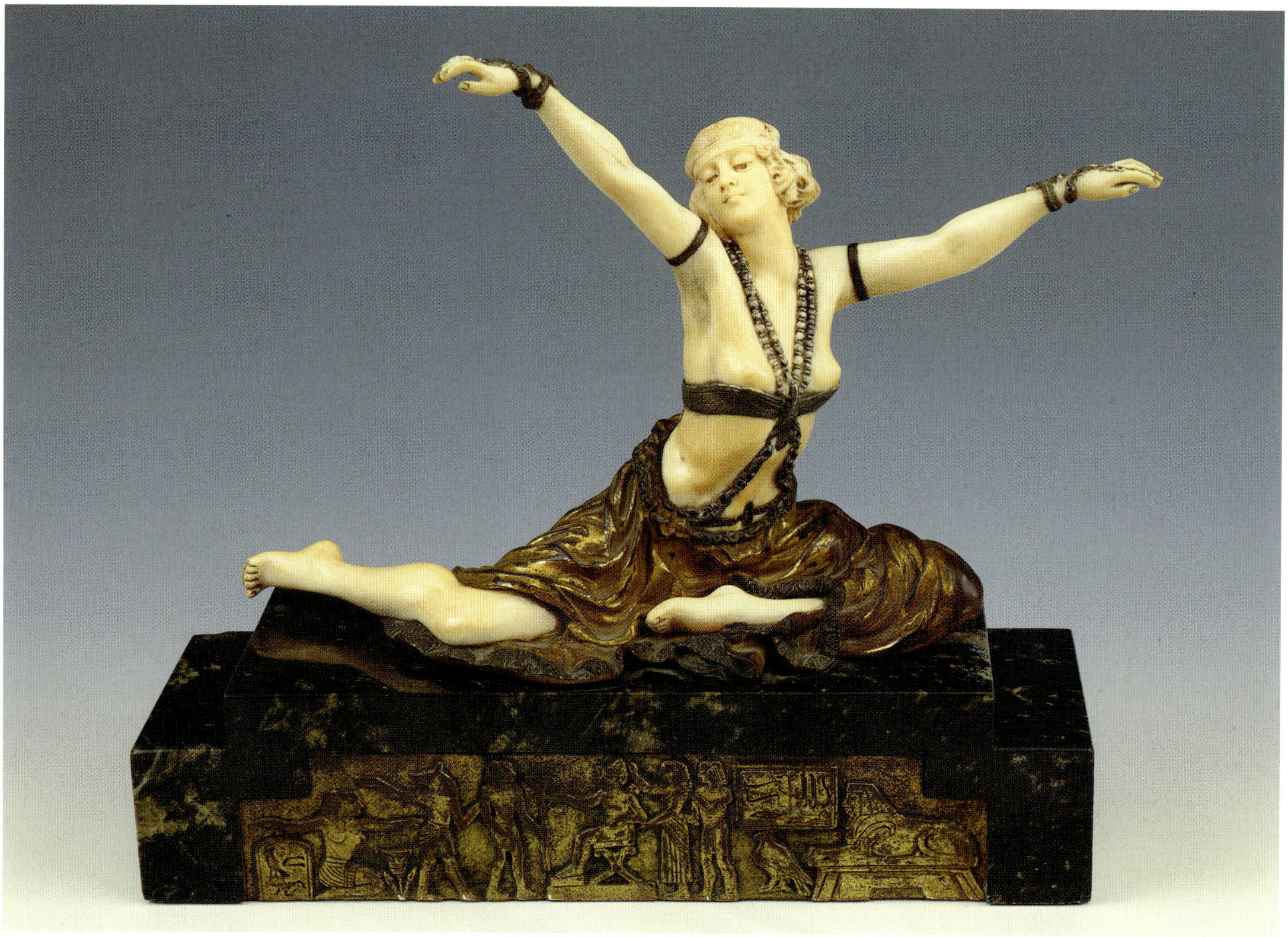

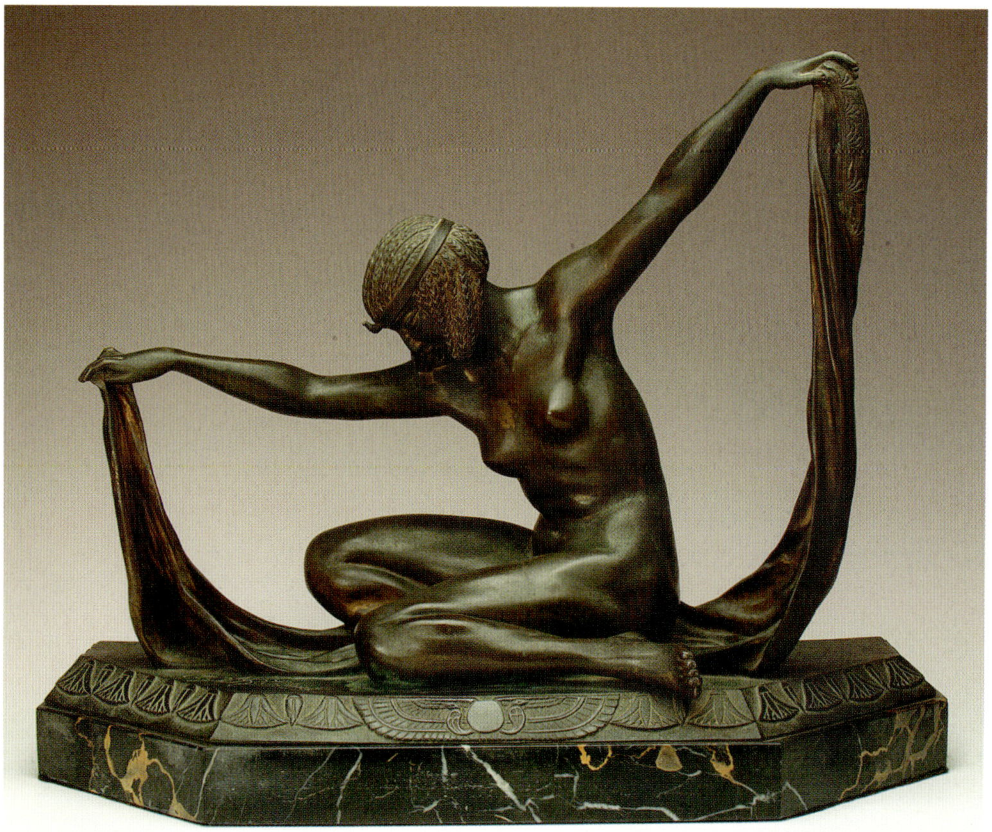

Theban Dancer
Bronze and ivory on marble base
Height: 27cm. (10½in.)
PRIVATE COLLECTION

Also produced 55cm. (21½in.) high

Isis
Bronze on marble base
Height: 42.5cm. (16¾in.)
PAULO SCHERER COLLECTION, RIO DE JANEIRO

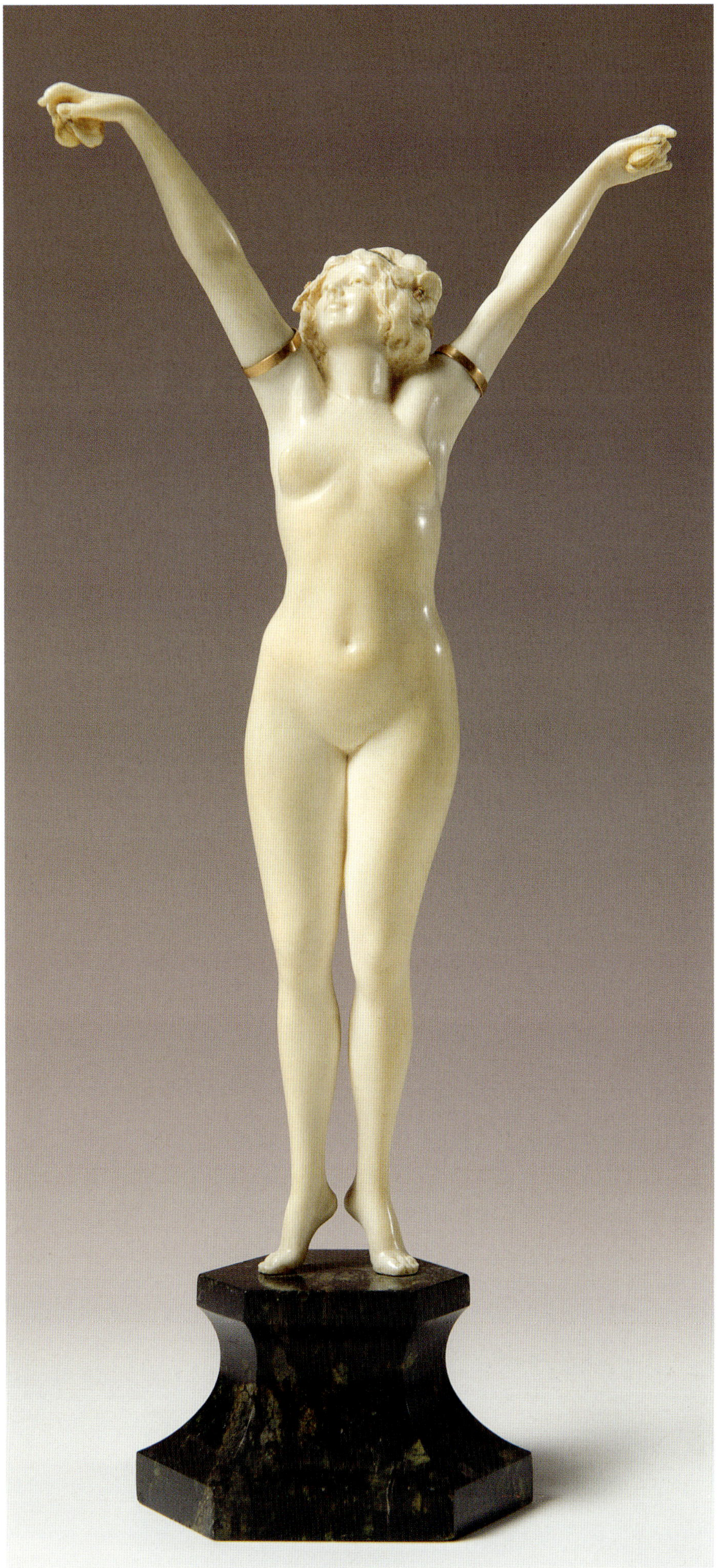

Andalusian
Bronze and ivory on marble
Height: 32.5cm. (12¾in.)
PRIVATE COLLECTION

Five other sizes are known

Darling
Ivory on marble base
Height: 26cm. (10¼in.)
DINO MENASCHE COLLECTION

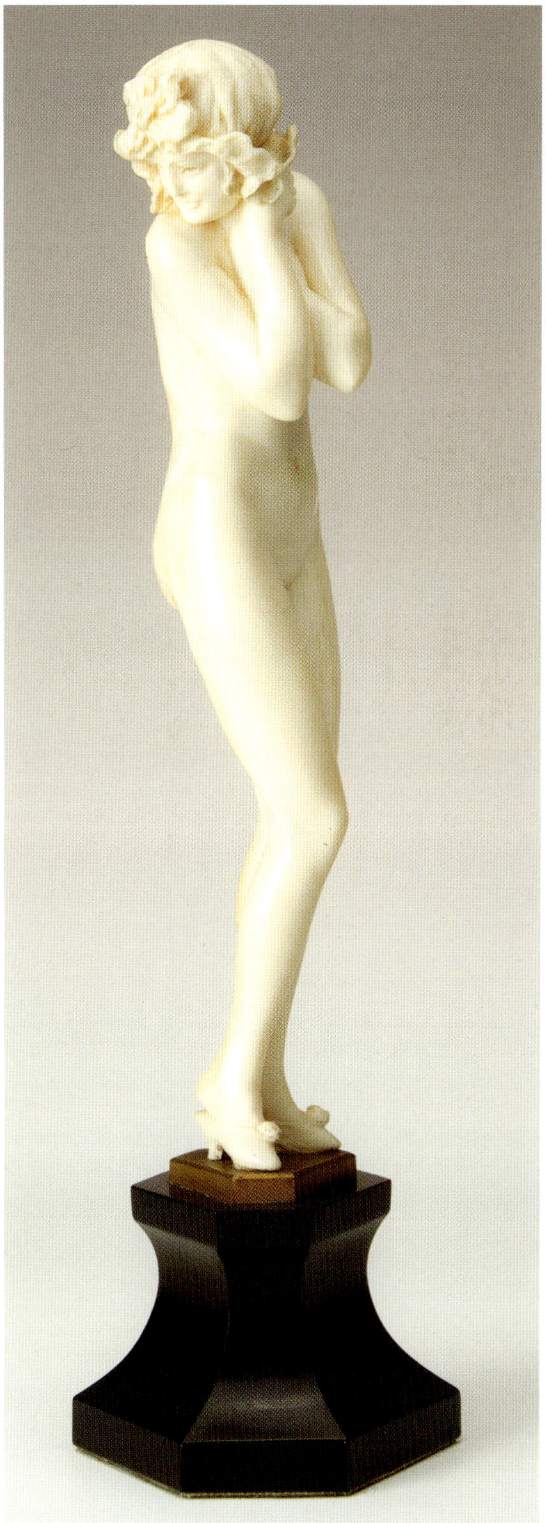

COULON, Noël

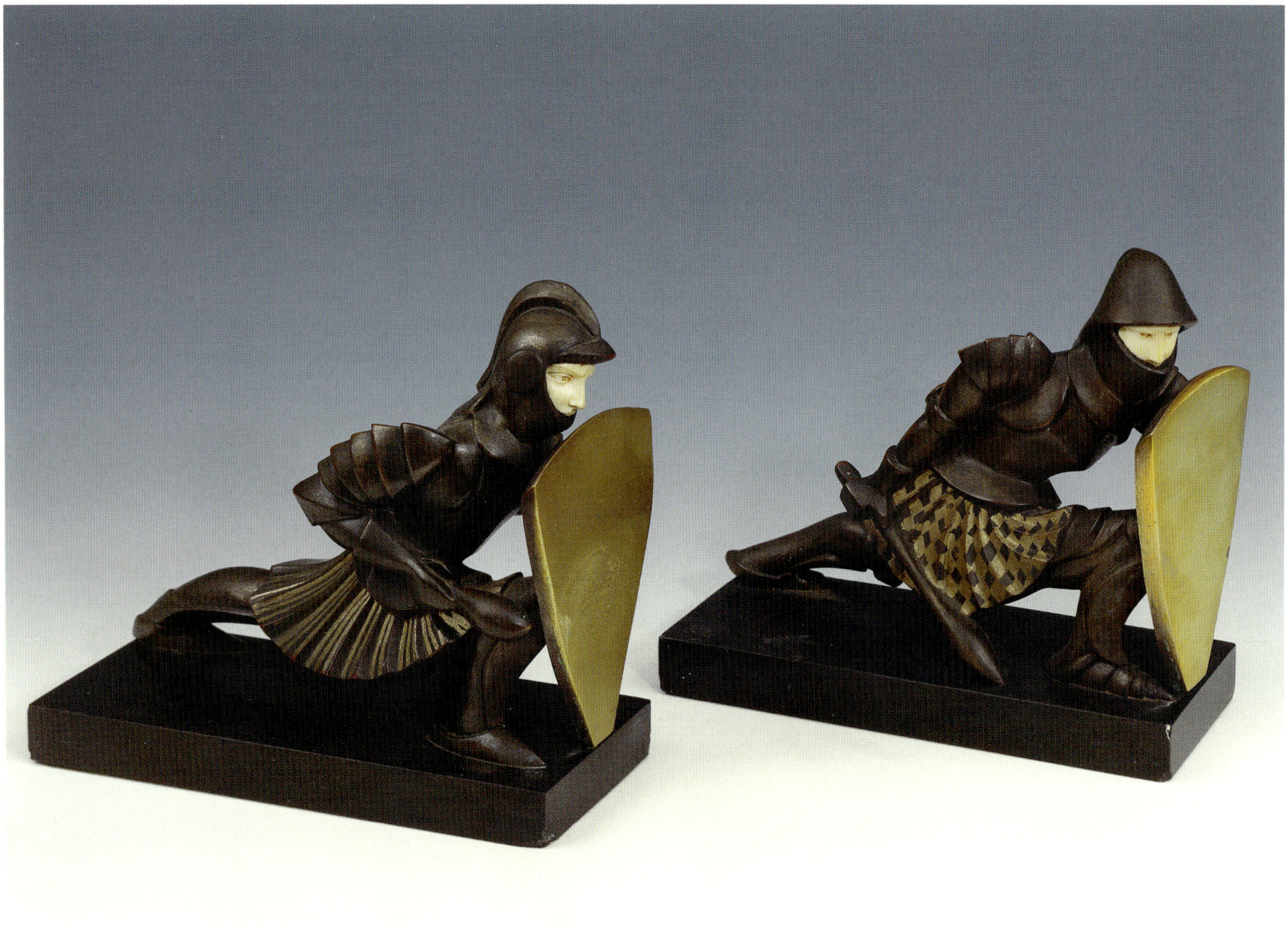

The Knights
Bronze and ivory on marble base
Height: 22cm. (8¾in.)
PRIVATE COLLECTION

Crusaders
Bronze and ivory on marble base
Height: 59.5cm. (23½in.)
PRIVATE COLLECTION

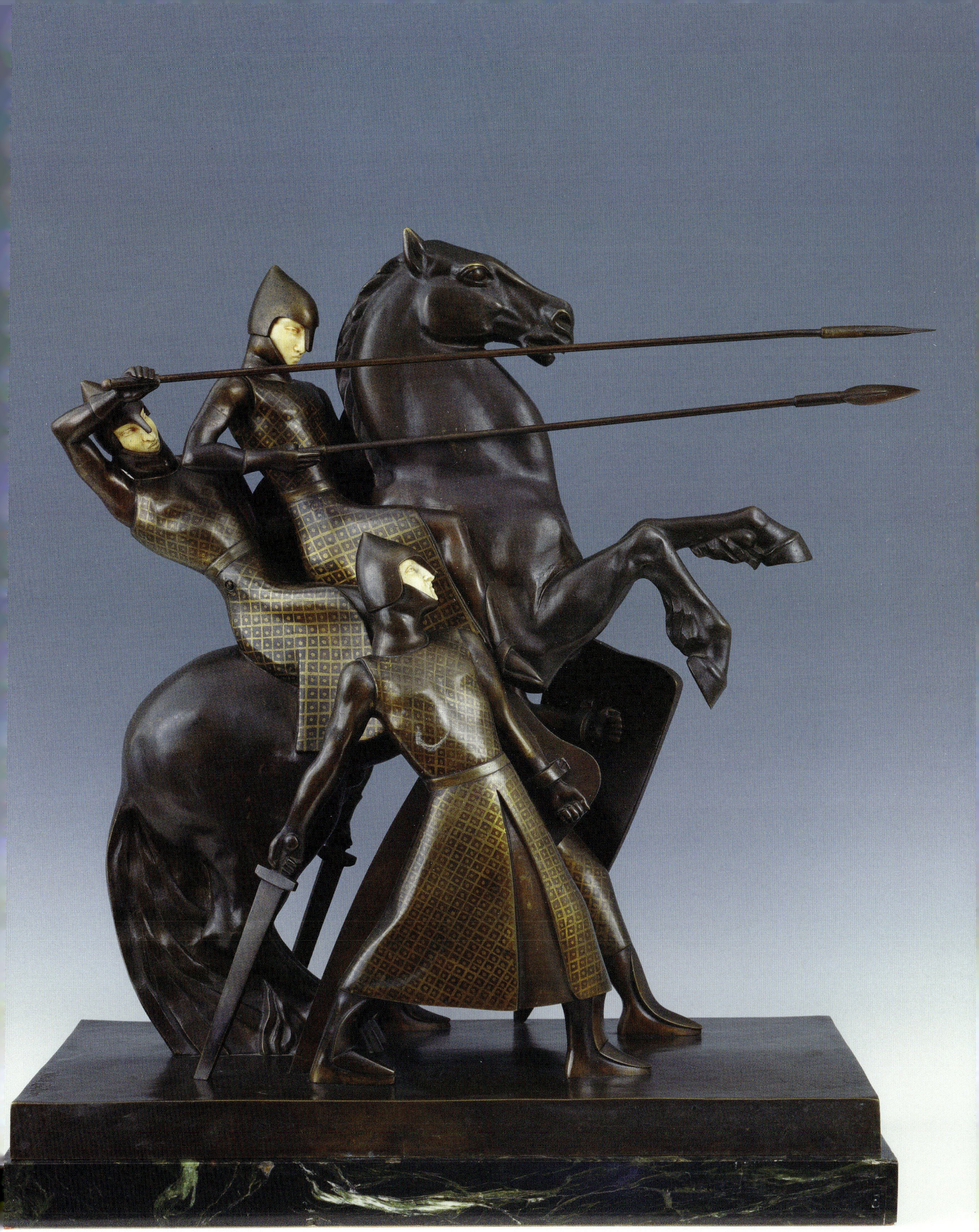

DARCLÈS

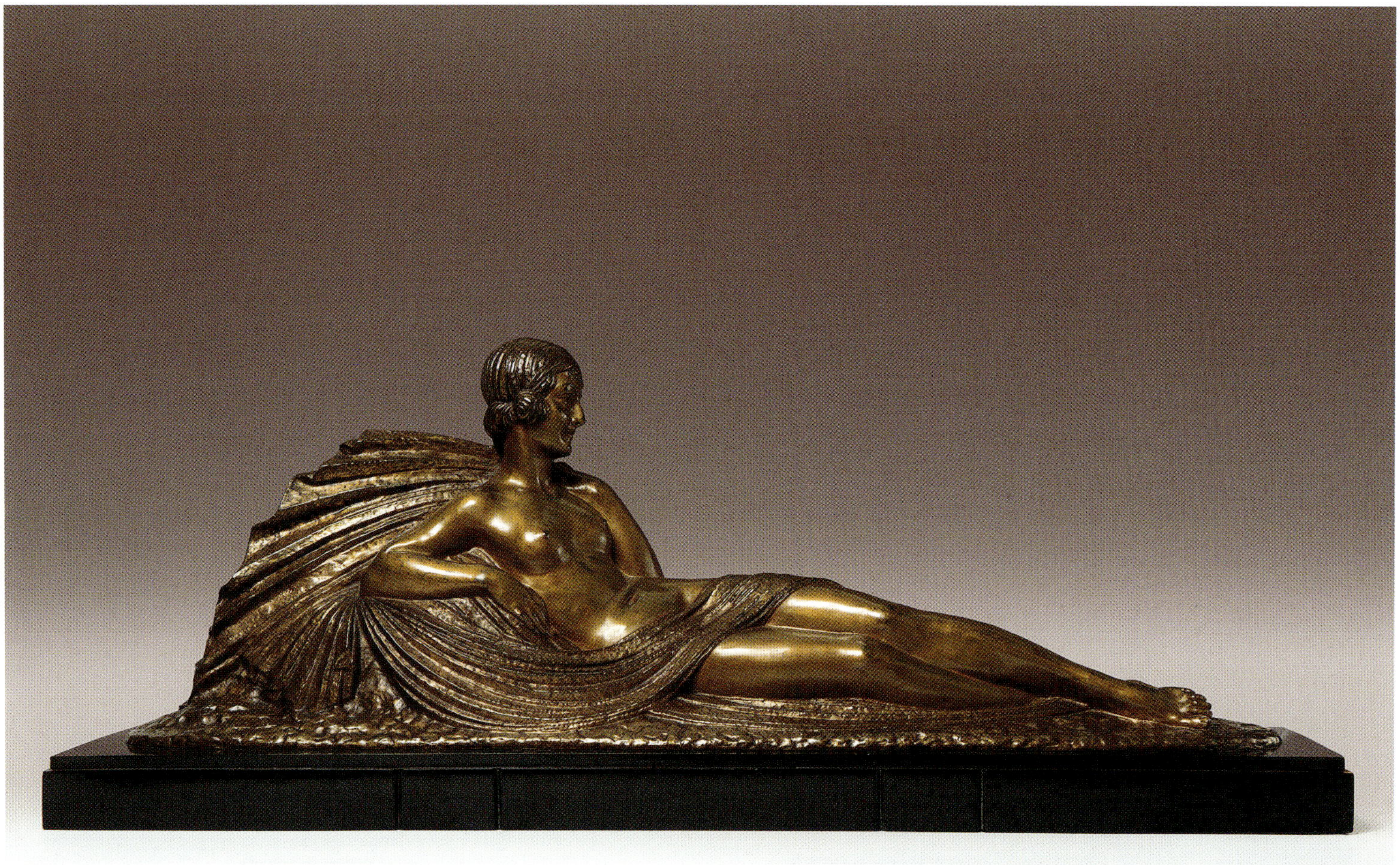

Pleasant Pause
Bronze on marble base
Height: 33.5cm. (13¼in.)
Length: 85cm. (33½in.)
PRIVATE COLLECTION

DELAGRANGE, Léon Noël

(Orléans 1872 – Croix d'Hins 1910)

A French artist. He was a student of Ernest Barrias and Vital-Cornuat at the Ecole des Beaux Arts; he exhibited at the Salon of the Société des Artistes Français from 1894 to 1907.

However, his passion was aviation and by 1907 he had become president of the Aéro-Club de France.

In 1908 he abandoned sculpture altogether to devote himself to aviation.

In 1909 he was decorated with the Legion d'Honneur.

He died in 1910 in an accident in his monoplane *Bleriot* in Croix d'Hins near Bordeaux.

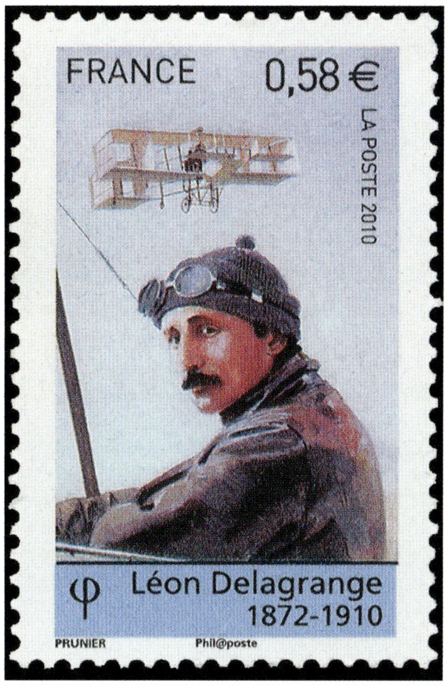

French stamp issued in his honour in 2010 as part of the 'Pioneers of Aviation' series.

Delagrange with his monoplane, Bleriot, *1909.*

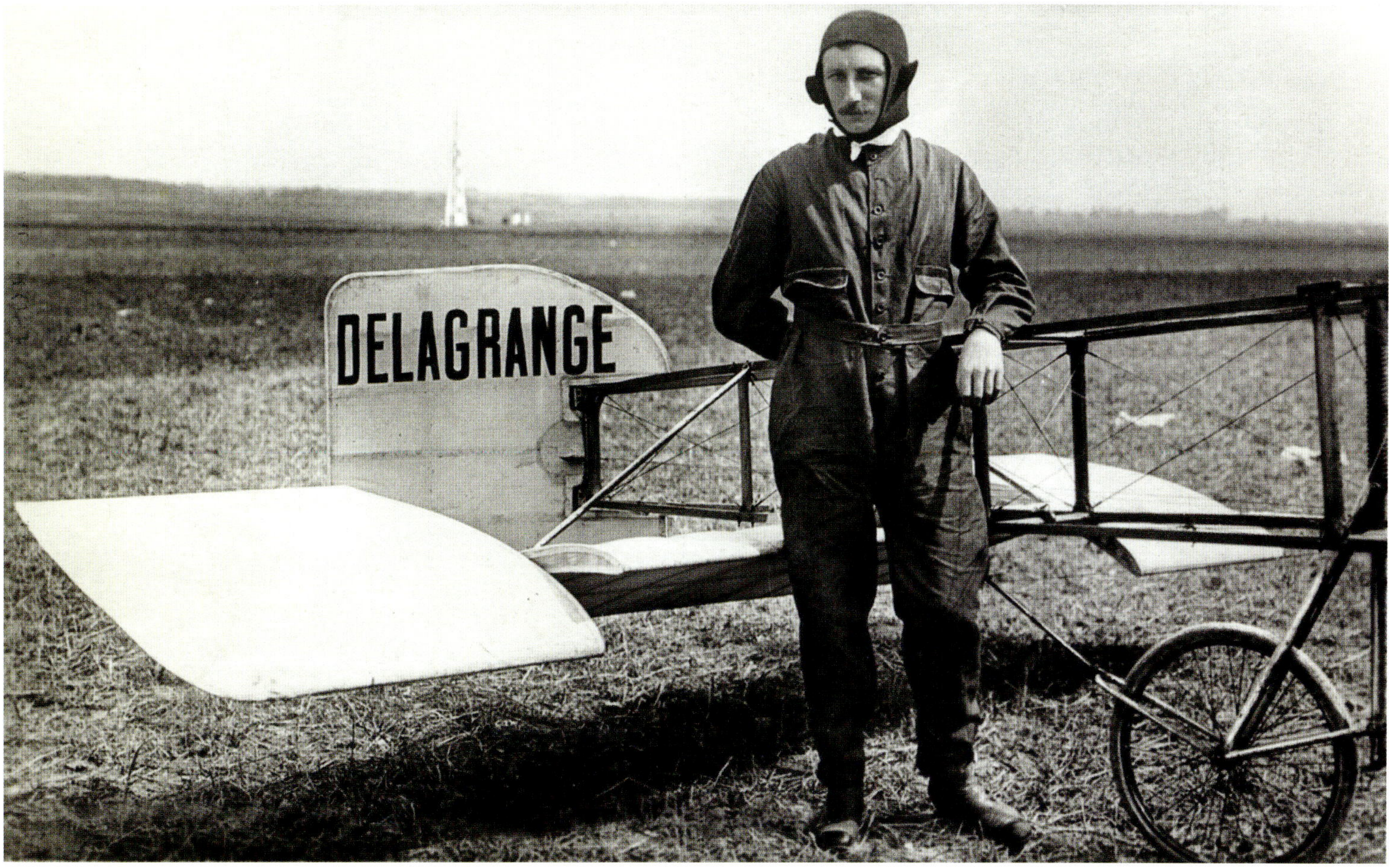

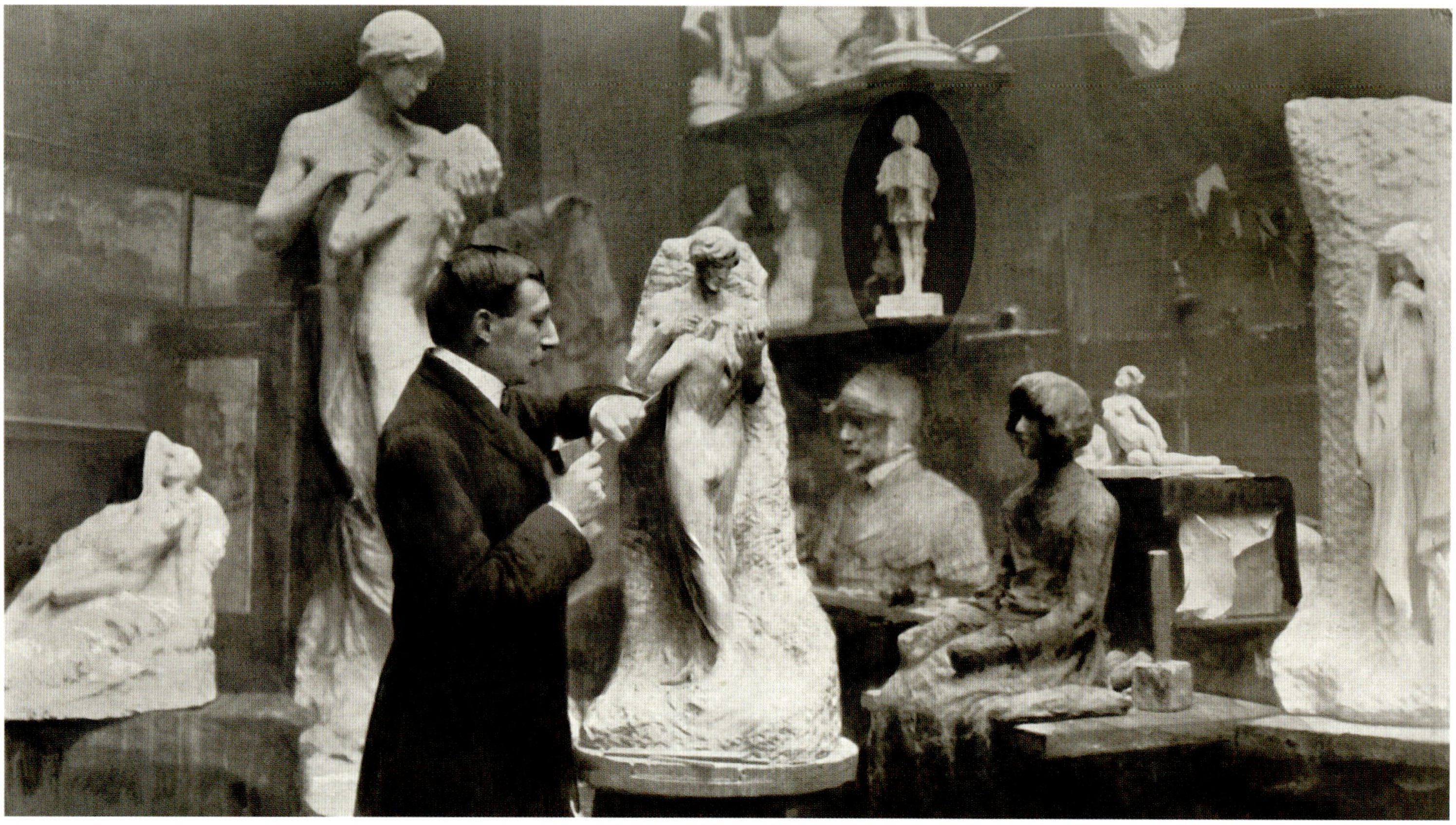

Léon Delagrange in his studio 1908. The maquette for Florentine Pageboy *is highlighted in the background.*

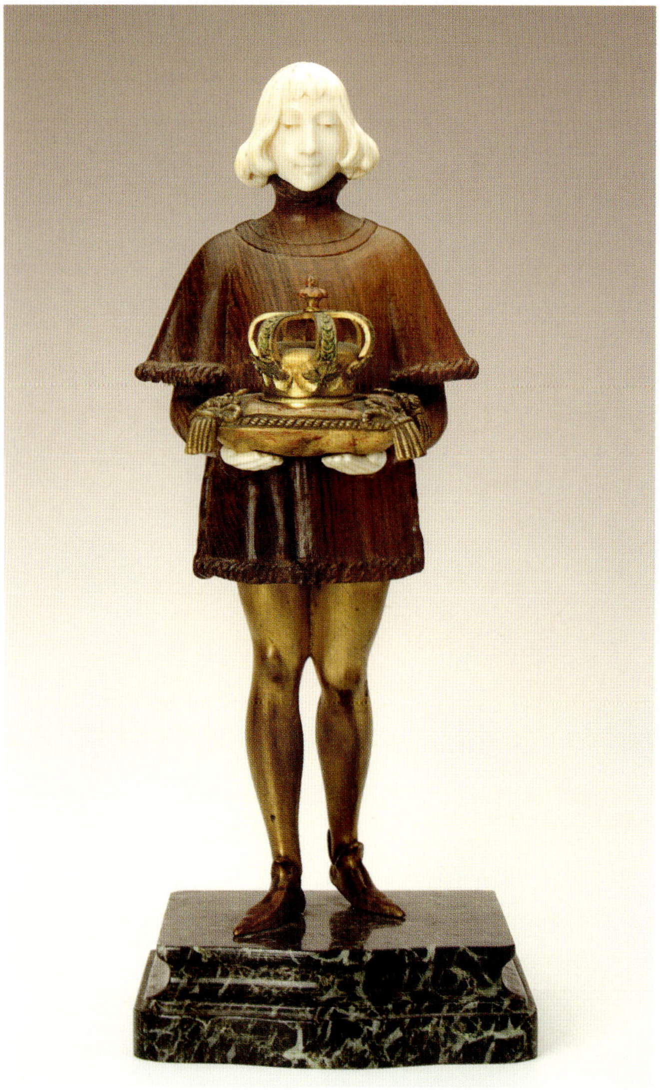

Florentine Pageboy
Bronze, ivory and wood on marble base
Height: 30cm. (11¾in.)
PRIVATE COLLECTION

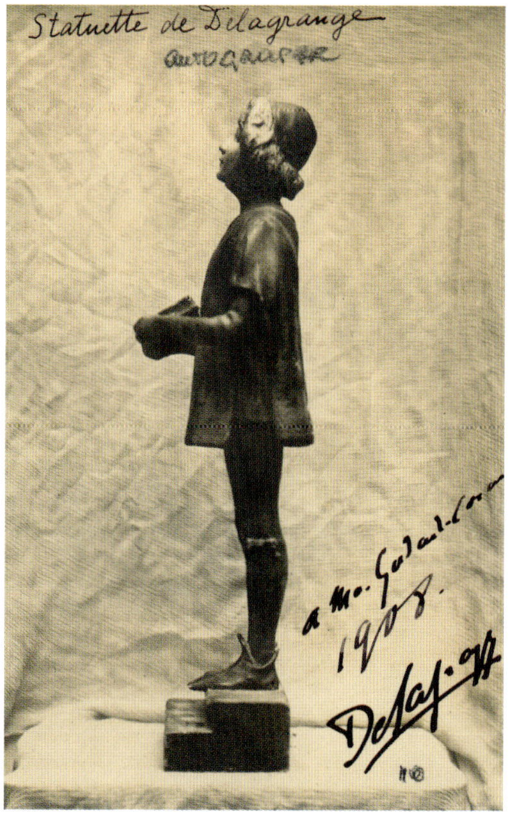

Florentine Pageboy, 1908.

DELAIGUE, Victor Constantin

(Gaujac 1878 – 1968)

A French artist, who became a member of the Société des Artistes Français in 1909 and exhibited there from 1907 until the 1920s.

He worked in bronze, marble, ivory, stone and terracotta.

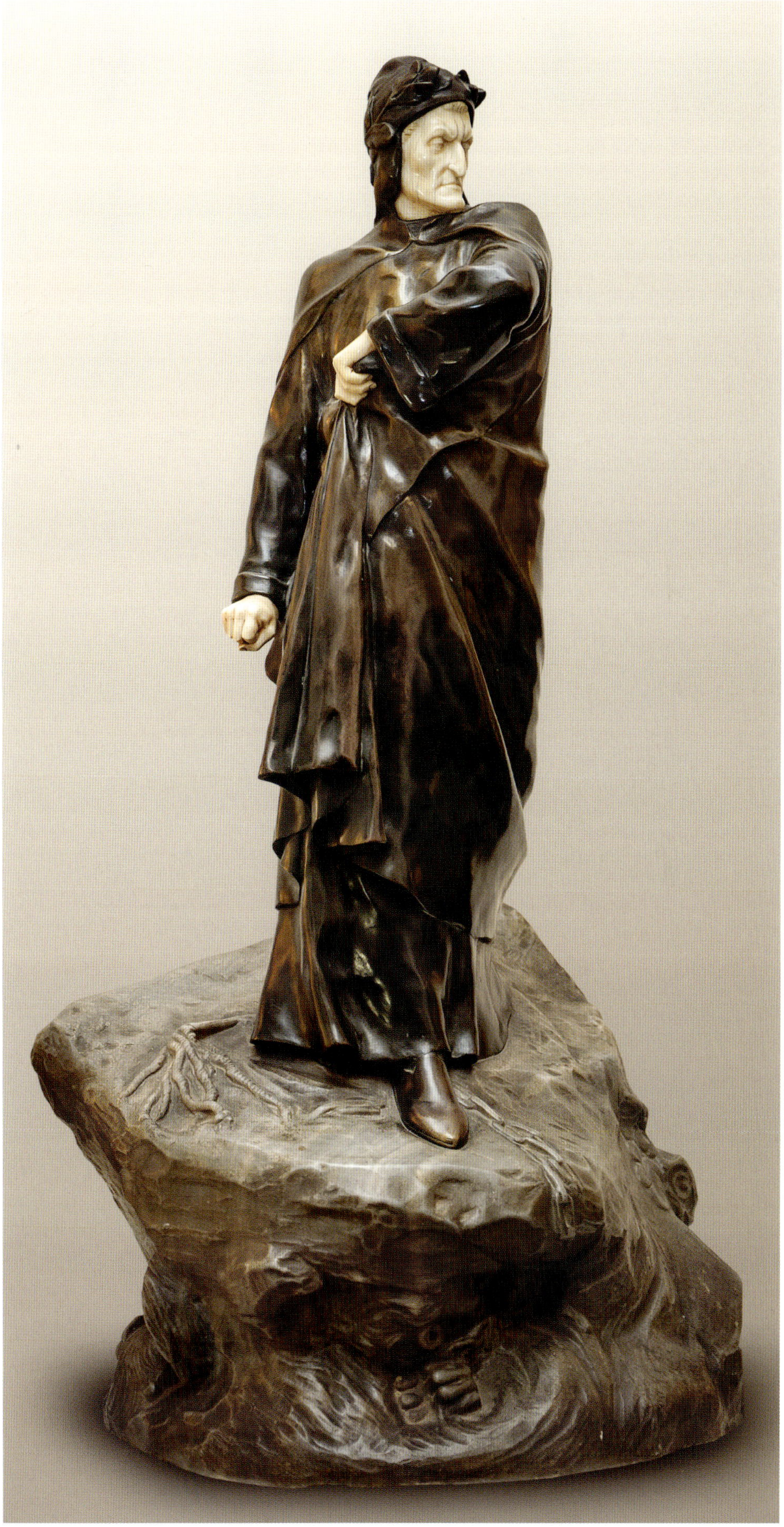

Dante
Bronze and ivory
Height: 76cm. (30in.)
FEDERICO MARINO COLLECTION

Also produced 47cm. (18½in.) high

DESCOMPS, Joé

(Clermont-Ferrand 1869 – Paris 1950)

Other signature: 'Cormier' (after World War I)

Born Joseph Jules Emmanuel Descomps-Cormier in Clermont-Ferrand, he studied under Louis-Auguste Hiolin in Paris. He exhibited at the Salon of the Société des Artistes Français and became a member of the Société in 1883. He won an honourable mention in 1898 and a third class medal in 1900 and 1921; a second class medal in 1925; and a first class medal in 1928; he also exhibited at the Salon d'Automne.

Several of his works were sold to the city of Paris and its museums. Among them, *Pandora* (Galliera Museum); *Danaide* (Luxembourg Museum); *Arthémis* (Musée du Petit Palais); *Le Baiser de Judas* (the French state, 1906); *Nymphe et Satyre* (City of Paris, 1917); and *Enfance de Bacchus* (City of Paris, 1928).

In the 1920s Descomps made ivory, bronze and ivory, and metal statuettes that were produced by Etling et Cie, as well as working for the Barbedienne workshop (éditeur). He also created decorative objects in the Art Nouveau style.

His statue *Femme au Lotus*, a female nude, stood in the vestibule of the French Embassy pavilion at the 1925 Exhibition.

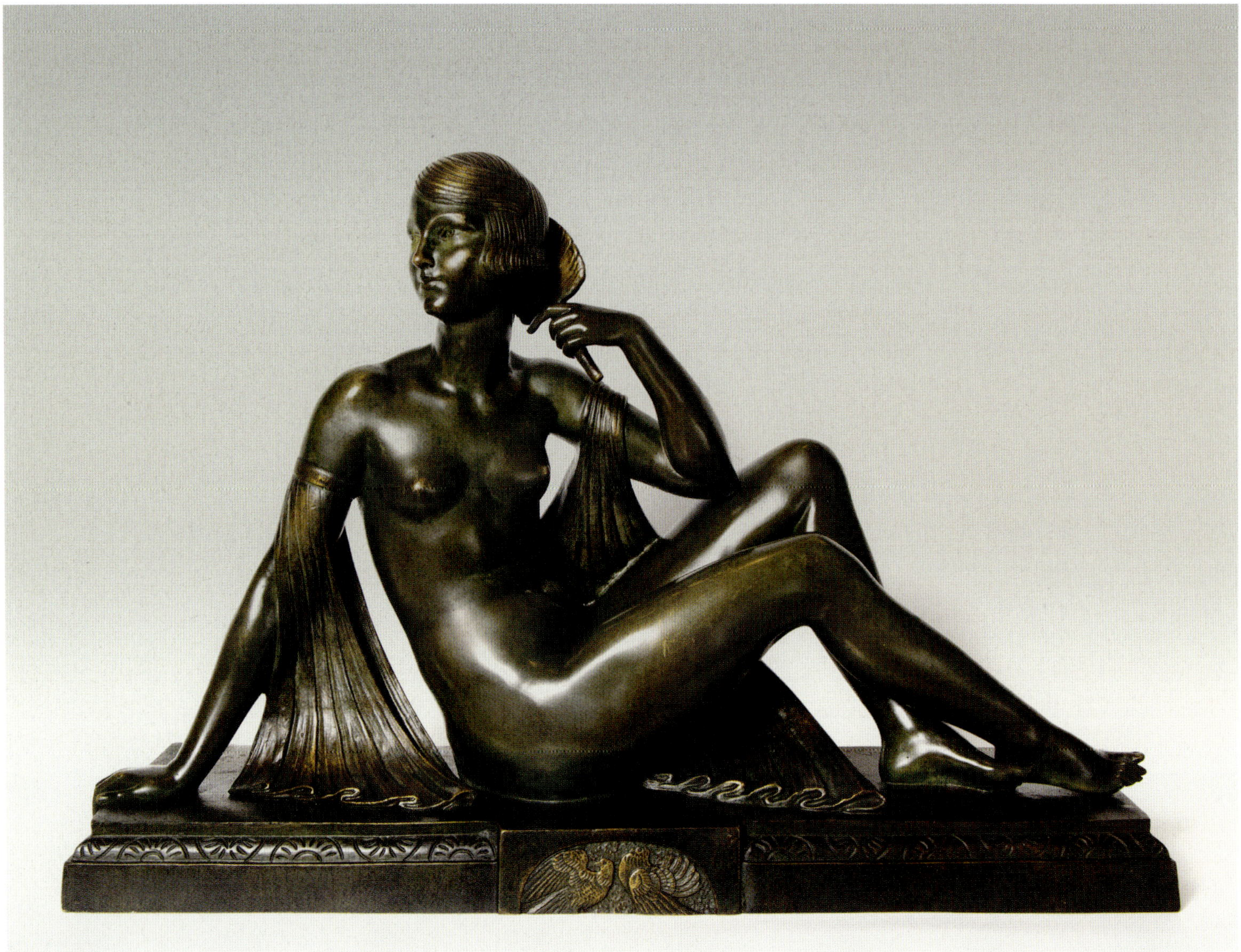

Meditation
Bronze
Height: 42.5cm. (16¾in.)
Length: 61cm. (24in.)
PAULO SCHERER COLLECTION, RIO DE JANEIRO

Throwing the Ball
Bronze and ivory on onyx base
Height: 45cm. (17¾in.)
PRIVATE COLLECTION

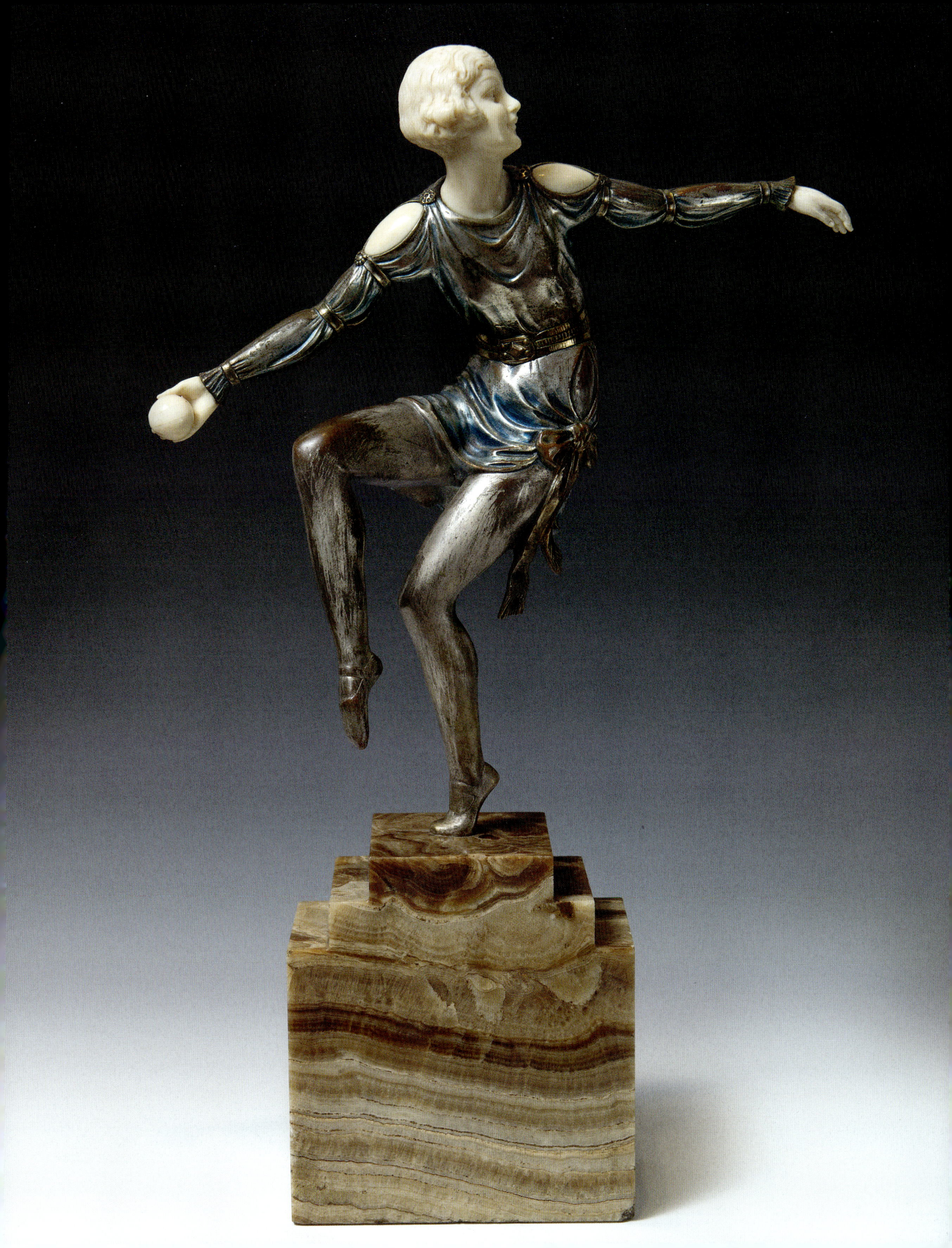

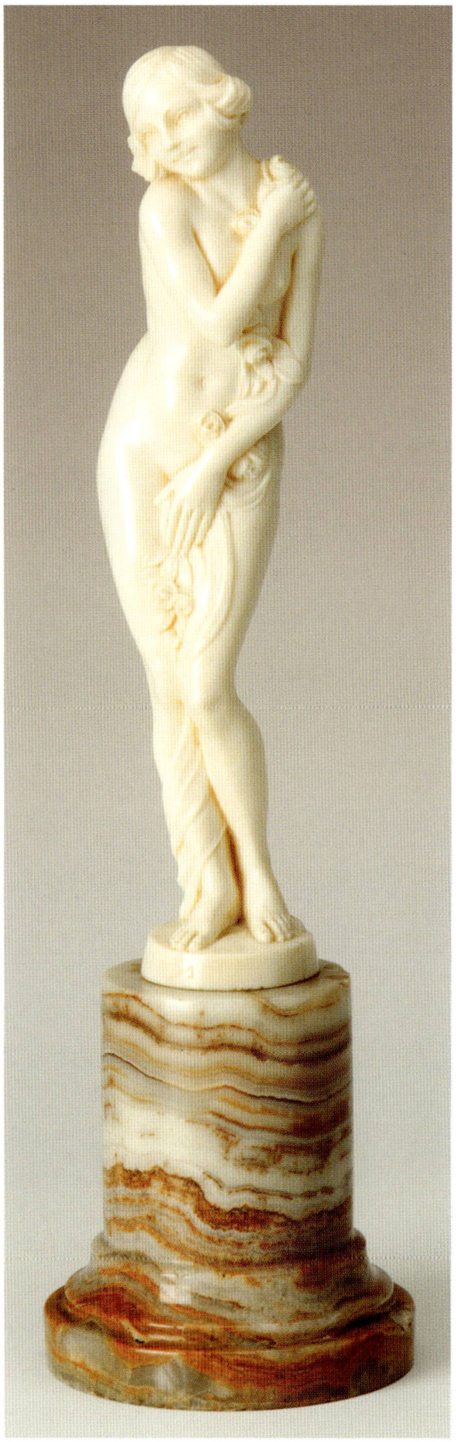

Coy
Ivory on marble base
Height: 21.5cm. (8½in.)
DINO MENASCHE COLLECTION

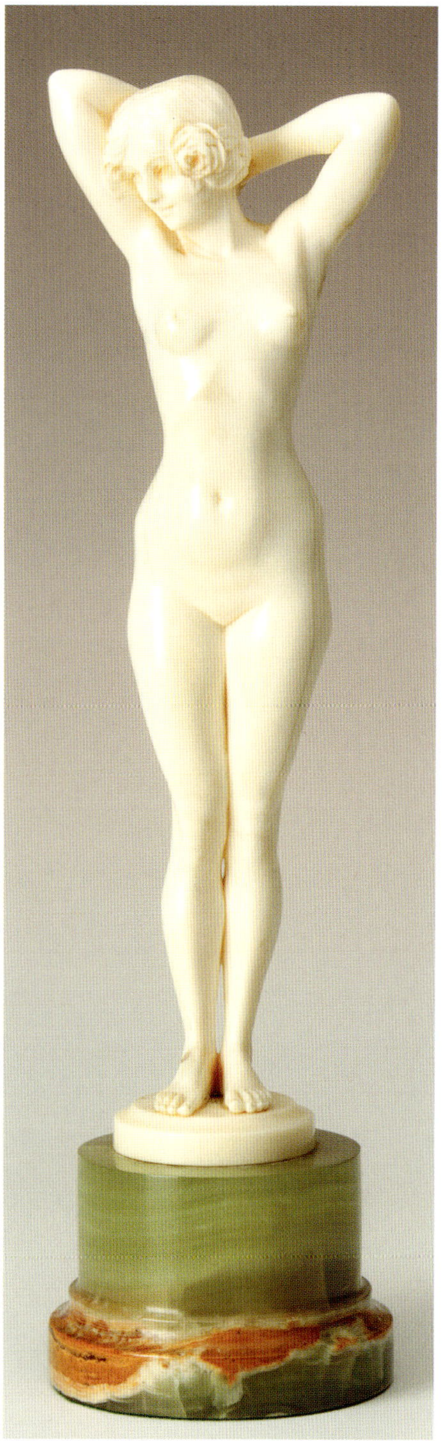

Nude
Ivory on onyx base
Height: 23cm. (9in.)
DINO MENASCHE COLLECTION

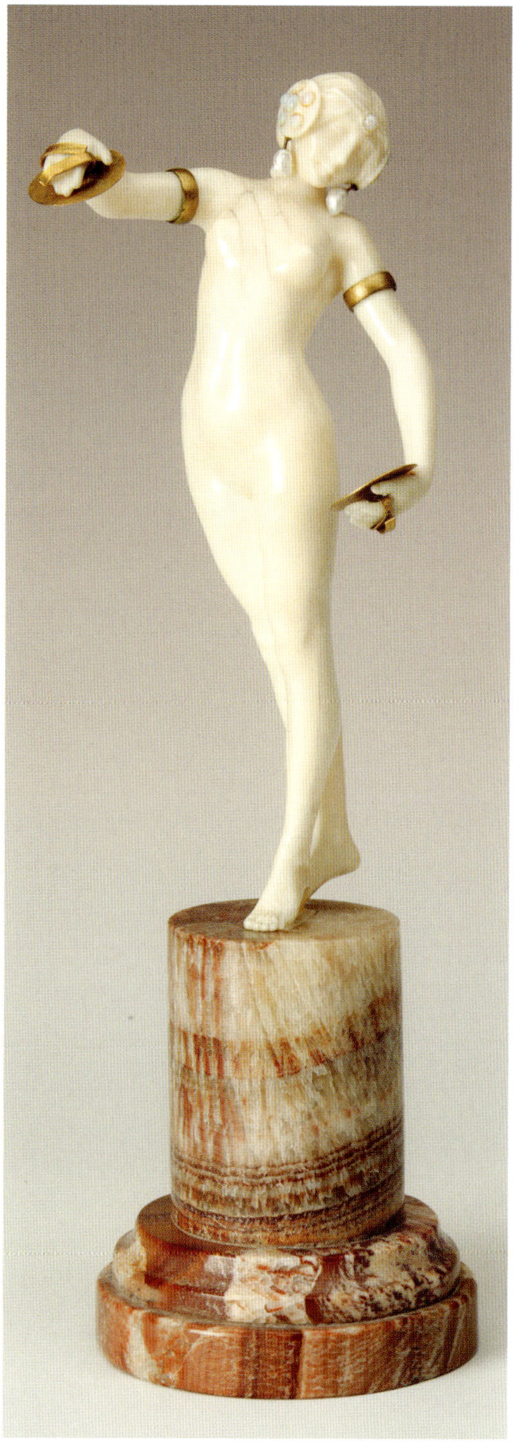

Cymbals Dancer
Ivory, bronze, pearls and opals on marble base
Height: 23cm. (9in.)
DINO MENASCHE COLLECTION

Beauty of Paris
Bronze and ivory on marble and onyx base
Height: 39cm. (15¼in.)
PRIVATE COLLECTION

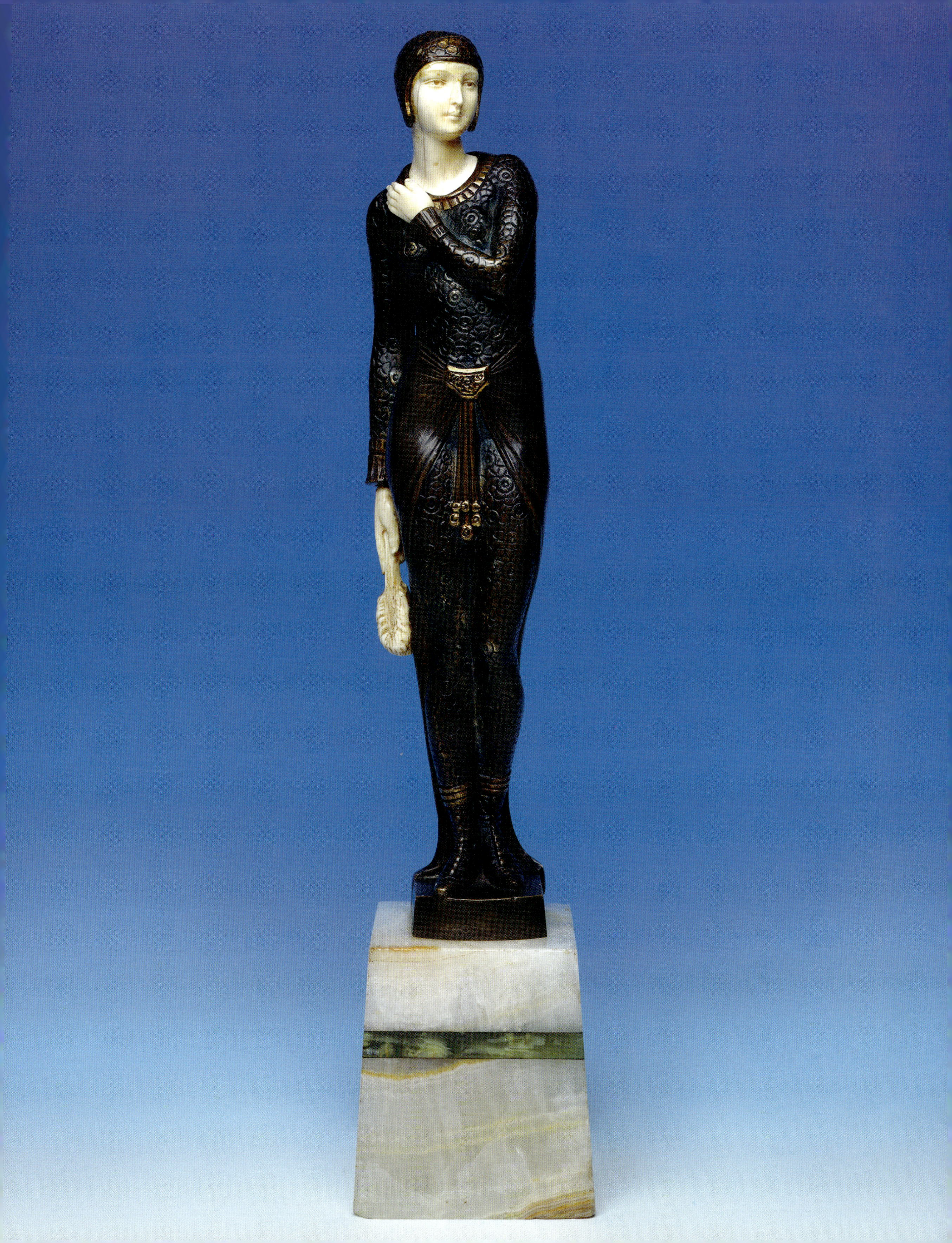

DROUOT, Edouard

(Sommervoire 1859 – 1945)

A prolific French artist, he studied in Paris with Emile Thomas and Mathurin Moreau.

Known for numerous sculptures with different subject matter including animalier works, North African figures and Indians, he is best known for his classical figures.

In 1889 he began exhibiting at the Salon of the Société des Artistes Français. In 1900 he received an honorable mention at the Exposition Universelle in Paris.

His sculptures were produced by several foundries including Thiébaut.

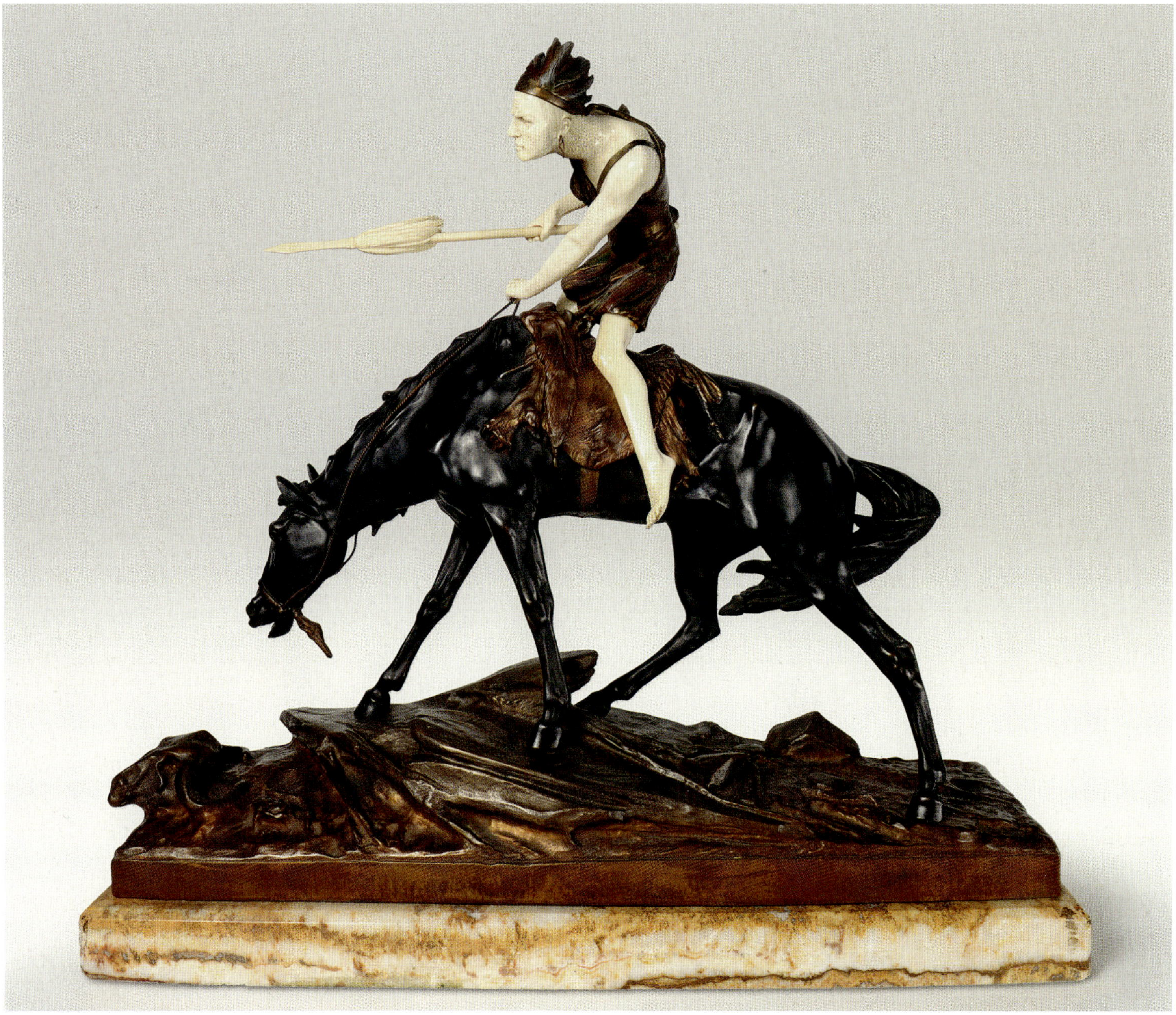

On the Track of Deer
Bronze and ivory on marble base
Height: 57cm. (22½in.)
Length: 62cm. (24½in.)
PRIVATE COLLECTION

DUVERNET, Georges
(1870 – 1955)

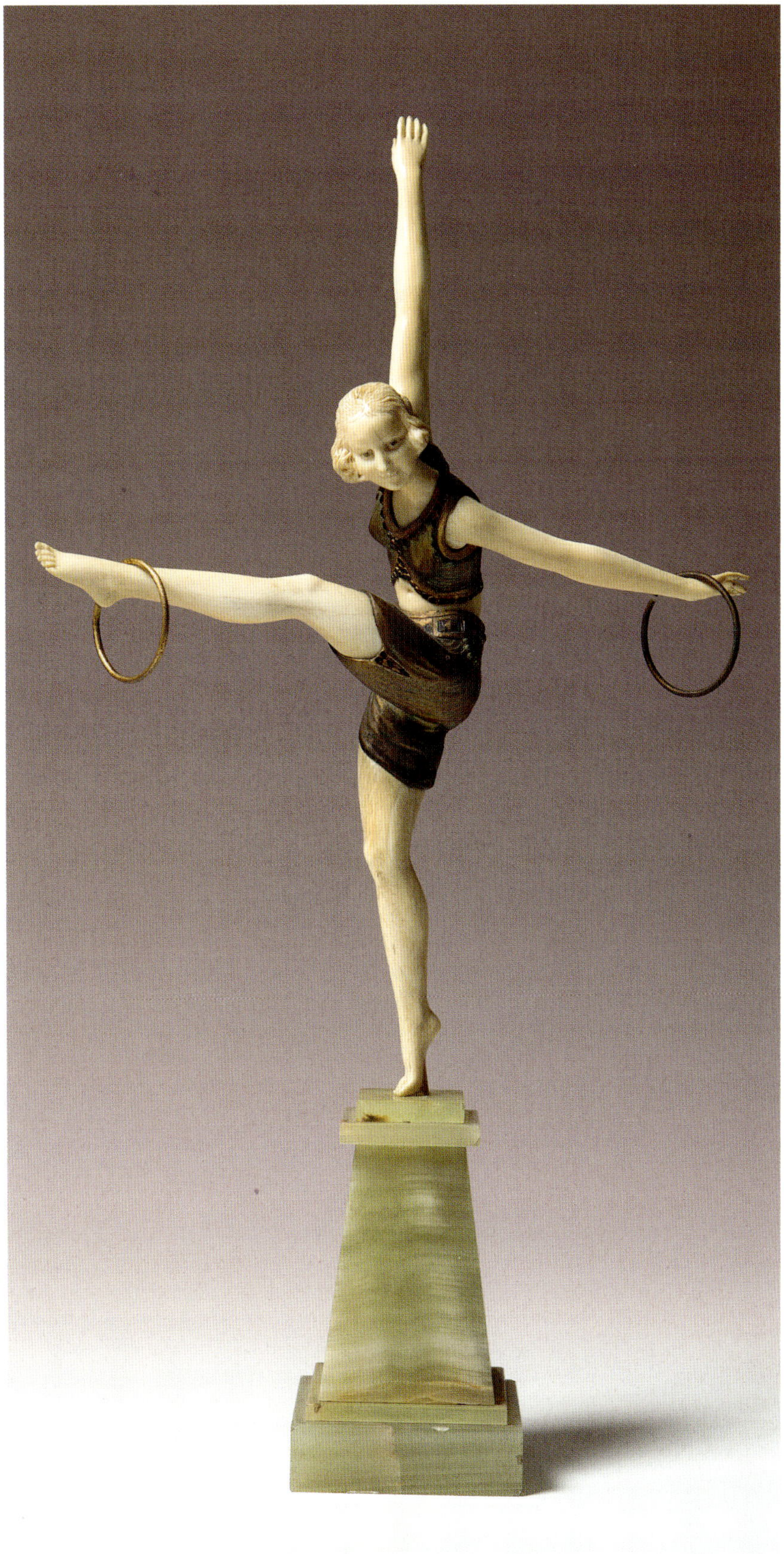

Dancer of the Rings
Bronze and ivory on onyx base
Height: 46cm. (18in.)
PRIVATE COLLECTION

ETLING ET CIE

The Etling foundry and firm was created in 1909 by Edmond Laurent Etling.

After Etling's death, it was run by his nephew Julien Dreyfus.

The company produced fine decorative and ornamental objects and statuettes. They were among the most important creators of excellent quality serially produced pieces, whether in bronze, bronze and ivory, ceramics or glass. Etling's success was due to their keen sense of contemporary taste, as well as working exclusively with a select group of excellent and highly creative artists.

Etling had a shop at 29 rue de Paradis in Paris, where some of the most exclusive art objects of the time were offered.

The Etling firm represented world-famous sculptors and artists such as Demetre Chiparus, Armand Godard, Claire Colinet, Lucile Sevin and her husband Jean Theodore Delabassé, and Maurice Guiraud-Rivière. These artists were all leading representatives of French modern art of the period. Insofar as he helped create a congenial creative climate for them, Etling played a significant role in the style that became known as Art Deco.

FANROSE

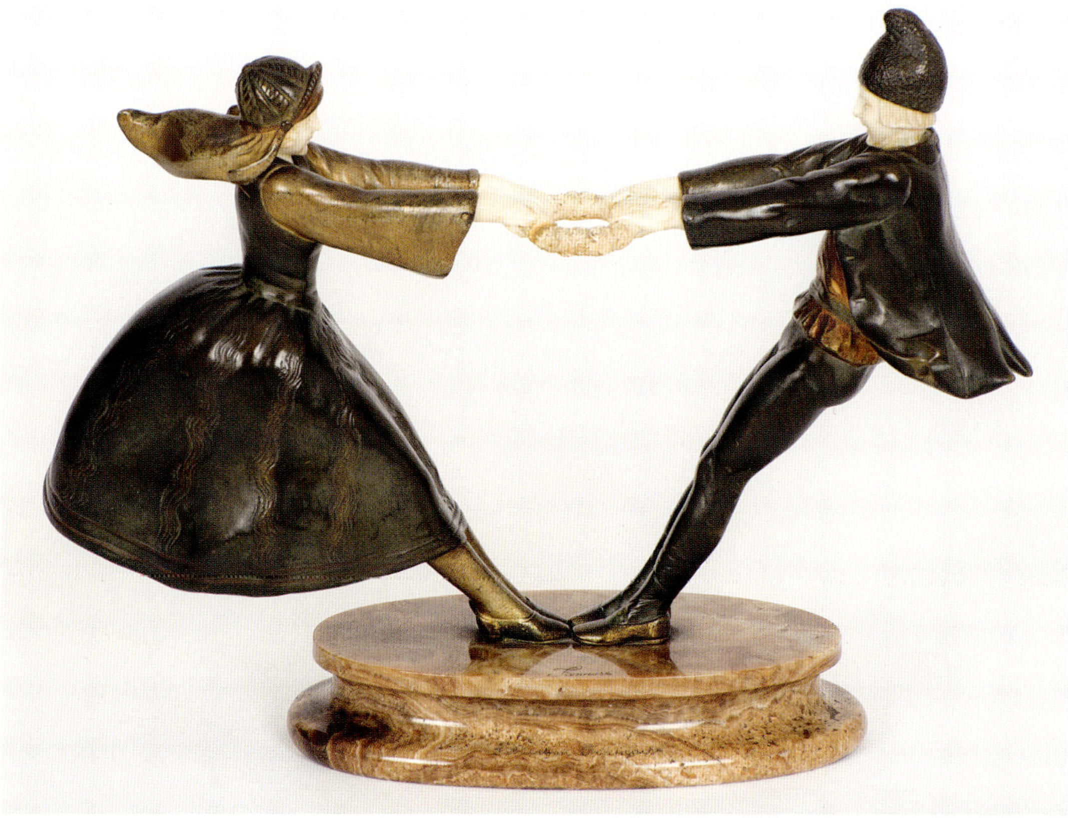

Amorous Twirl (Garland Dance)
Bronze and ivory on marble base
Height: 26cm. (10¼in.)
DINO MENASCHE COLLECTION

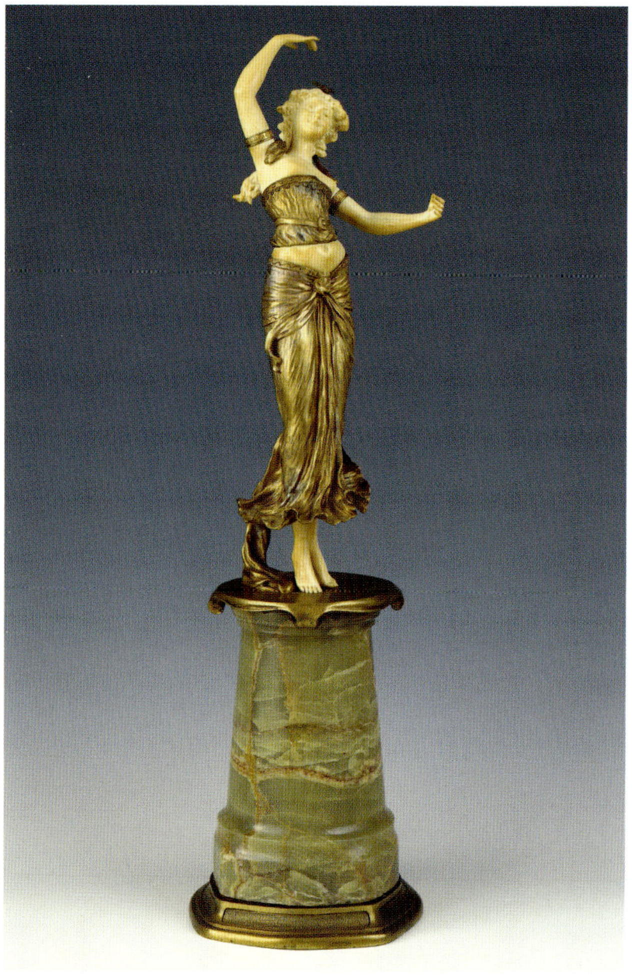

FUGÈRE, Henry

(Saint-Mandé 1872 – Paris 1944)

Born in Saint-Mandé, France, the son of the sulptor Léon Fugère, he attended the Ecole des Beaux Arts in Paris, studying under Jules Cavelier, Louis-Ernest Barrias and Denys Puech.

He worked in bronze, bronze and ivory, and stone. As of 1893, he exhibited regularly at the Salon of the Société des Artistes Français, of which he was eventuallty elected deputy. In 1927 he won an honourable mention.

Dancer
Bronze and ivory on onyx base
Height: 55cm. (21¾in.)
PRIVATE COLLECTION

GALLO, Ignacio

Born in the late 19th century in Valladolid, he worked in Madrid and Paris between the two World Wars. He created sculptures representing female nudes, heroic figures and dancers.

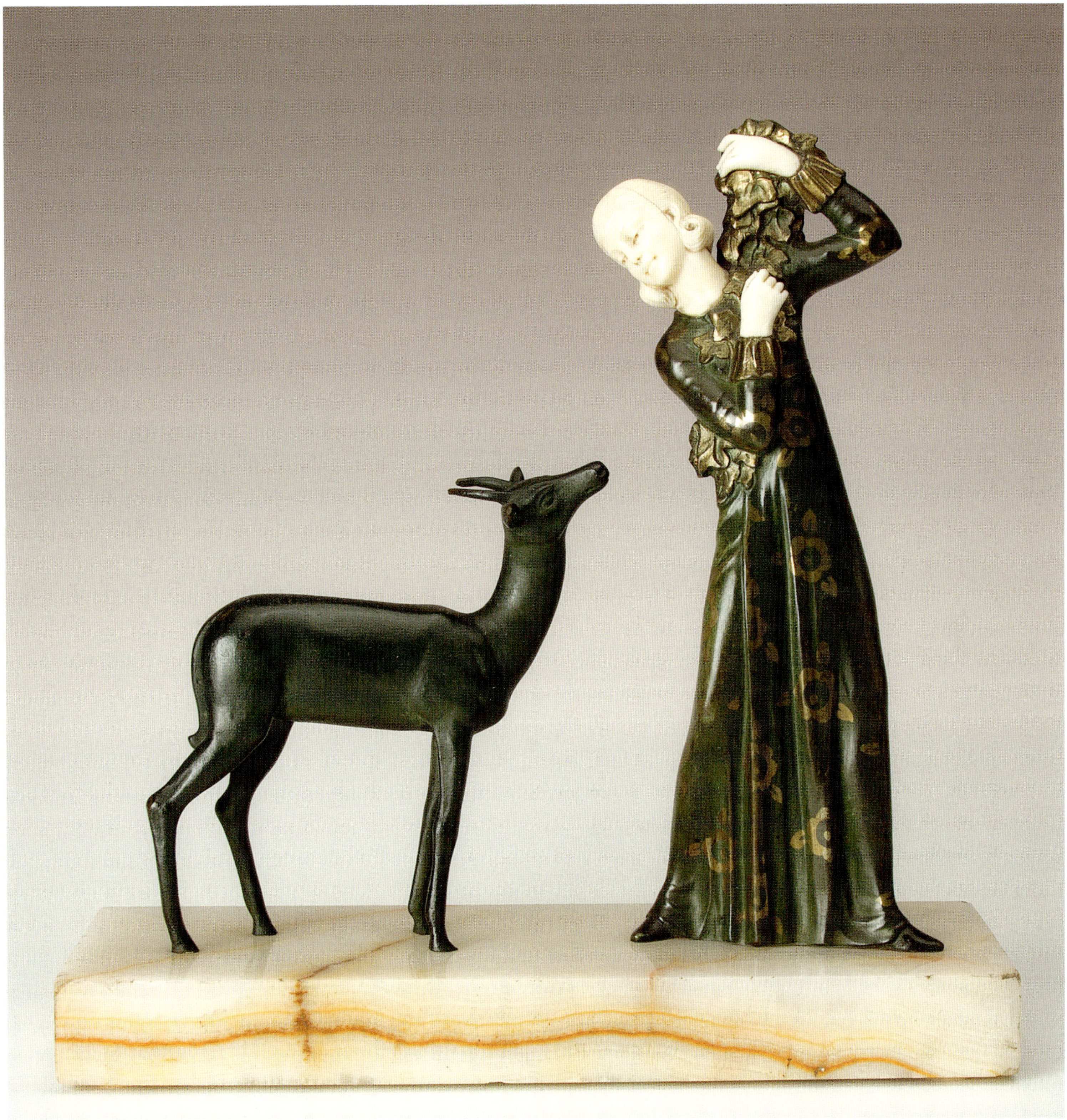

The Offering
Bronze and ivory on marble base
Height: 22cm. (8¾in.)
DINO MENASCHE COLLECTION

GANTCHEFF, Ganu

Born in Kazanlik, Bulgaria, he exhibited at the Paris Salon of the Société des Artistes Français in 1930. His statuette *Pudique* (Modesty) was produced by Arthur Goldscheider.

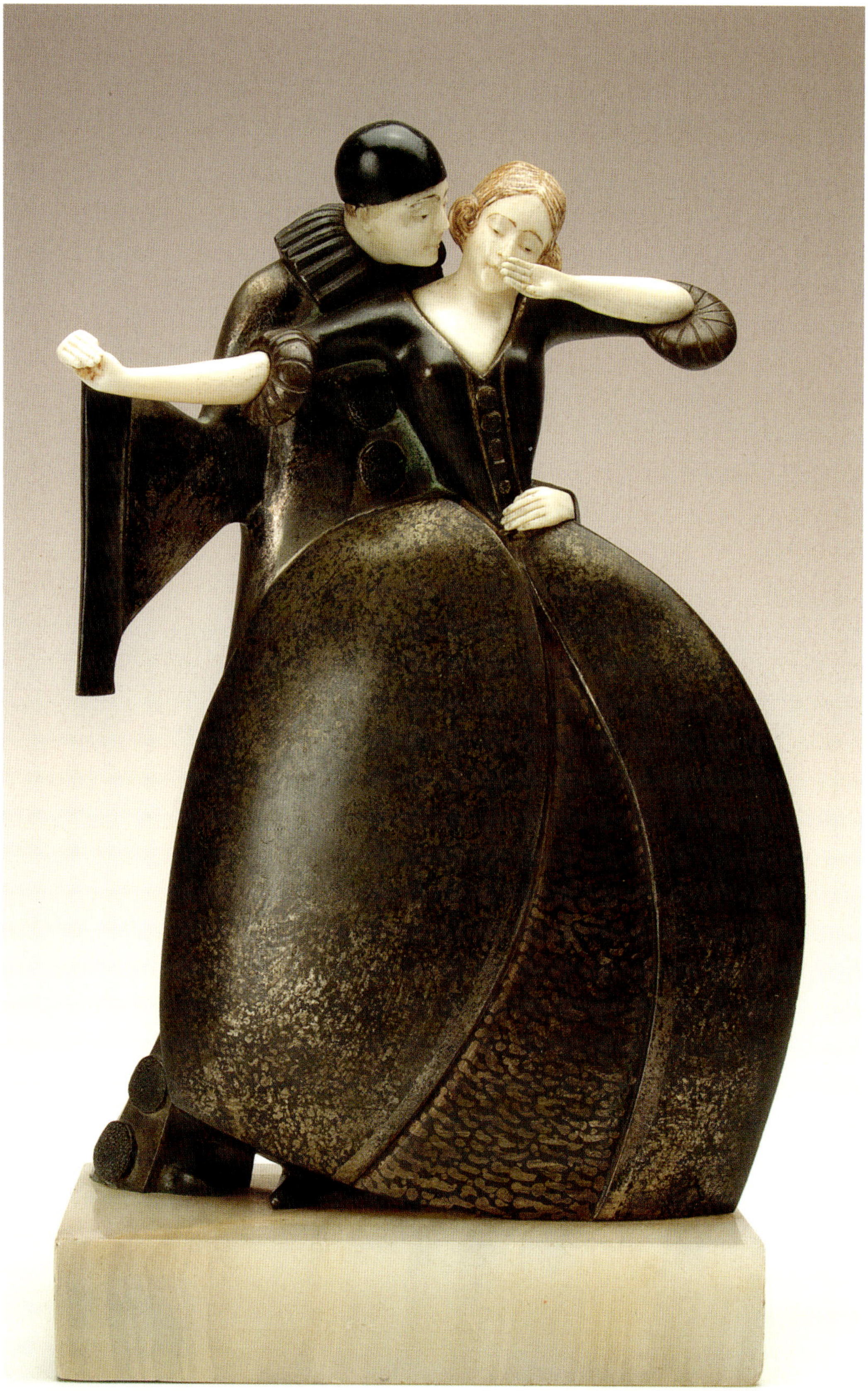

Seduction
Bronze and ivory on marble base
Height: 26.5cm. (10½in.)
DINO MENASCHE COLLECTION

GERDAGO

(Vienna 1906 – 2004)

Born Gerda Gottstein in Vienna, she pursued art studies, first in Berlin in 1927, and then Paris in 1928–29, where she worked as an assistant to architect and stage and film designer Oskar Strnad. The name Gerdago was a professional pseudonym made up from her first name, 'Gerda', and the first two letters of her last name, 'Go'. She was also known as Gerda Gottschlich and Gerda Iro.

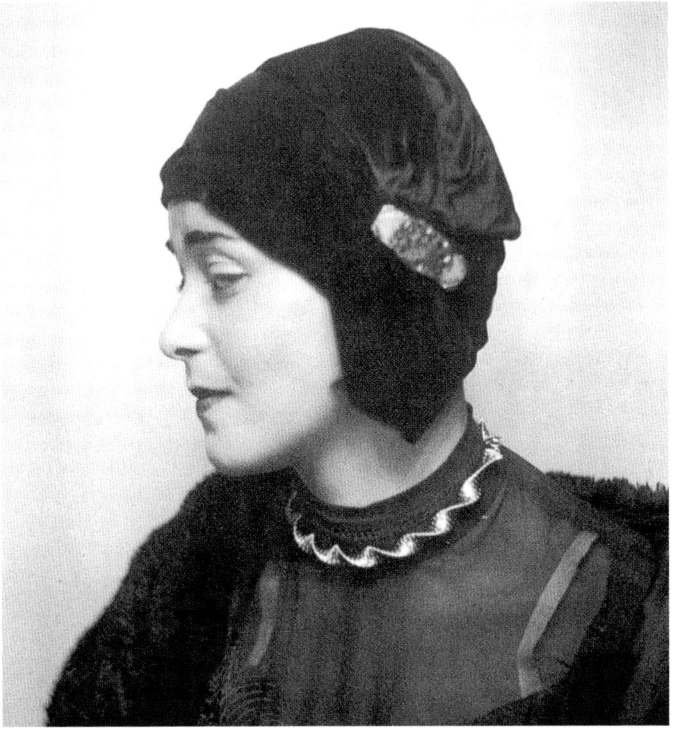

Gerda Gottstein, 1920s.

In the early 1930s she was designing costumes for dance revues, when director Willi Forst discovered her and hired her to design costumes for his films.

During World War II she escaped persecution due to her marriage to a non-Jew, however her parents were deported to Theresienstadt and were gassed in Auschwitz in 1944.

After the war, Gottstein worked for the Vienna Burgtheater and for the cinema, designing the costumes for the *Sissi* trilogy, among other films, in which Romy Schneider played the Empress Elisabeth. From the 1950s to the 1980s, she worked as a theatrical costume designer in Vienna. Famous in her profession, she was sometimes called the 'Austrian Edith Head'. Gerda Gottstein never worked for any fashion enterprise.

Her Art Deco sculptures, which were made in Austria by the Arthur Rubinstein foundry, feature elaborate and exotic costumes. They were created by a sculptor working from her drawings and designs.

To this day the identity of this sculptor remains a mystery. The names of Austrian artists Karl Perl and Theodore Ullmann, who both worked with the Arthur Rubinstein foundry, have been associated with Gerdago sculptures, and the work of both is stylistically similar. However, there is no strong evidence to confirm the identity of the artist who turned Gerda's designs into sculptures.

Gerda Gottstein died in Vienna on 20 January 2004, at the age of 97.

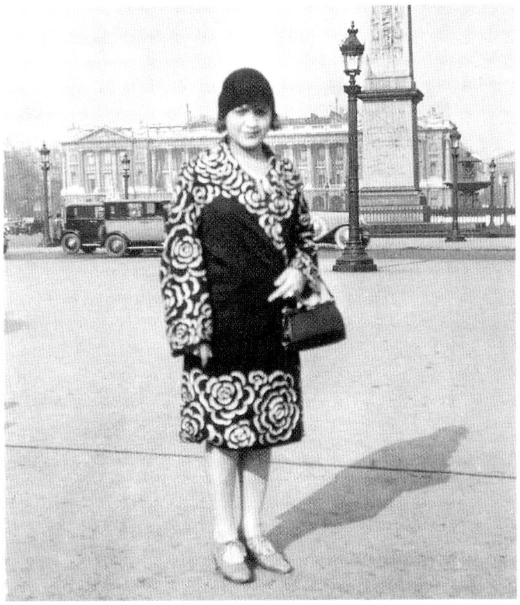

Gerda Gottstein, Paris 1928.

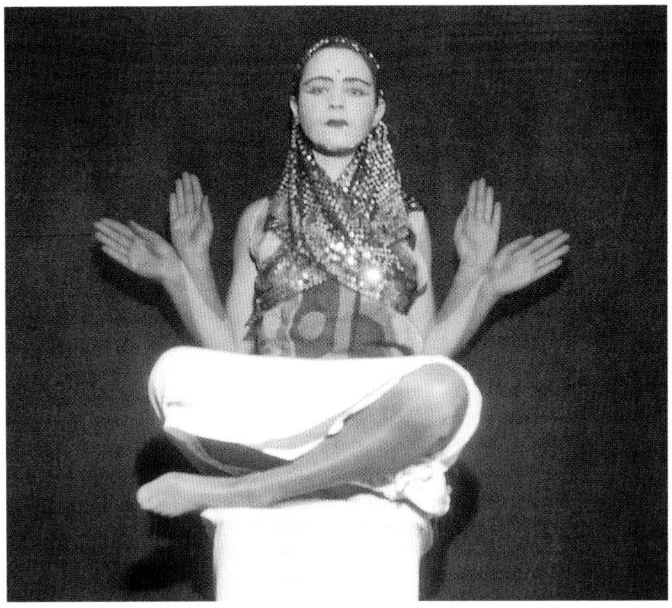

Gerda Gottstein in costume.

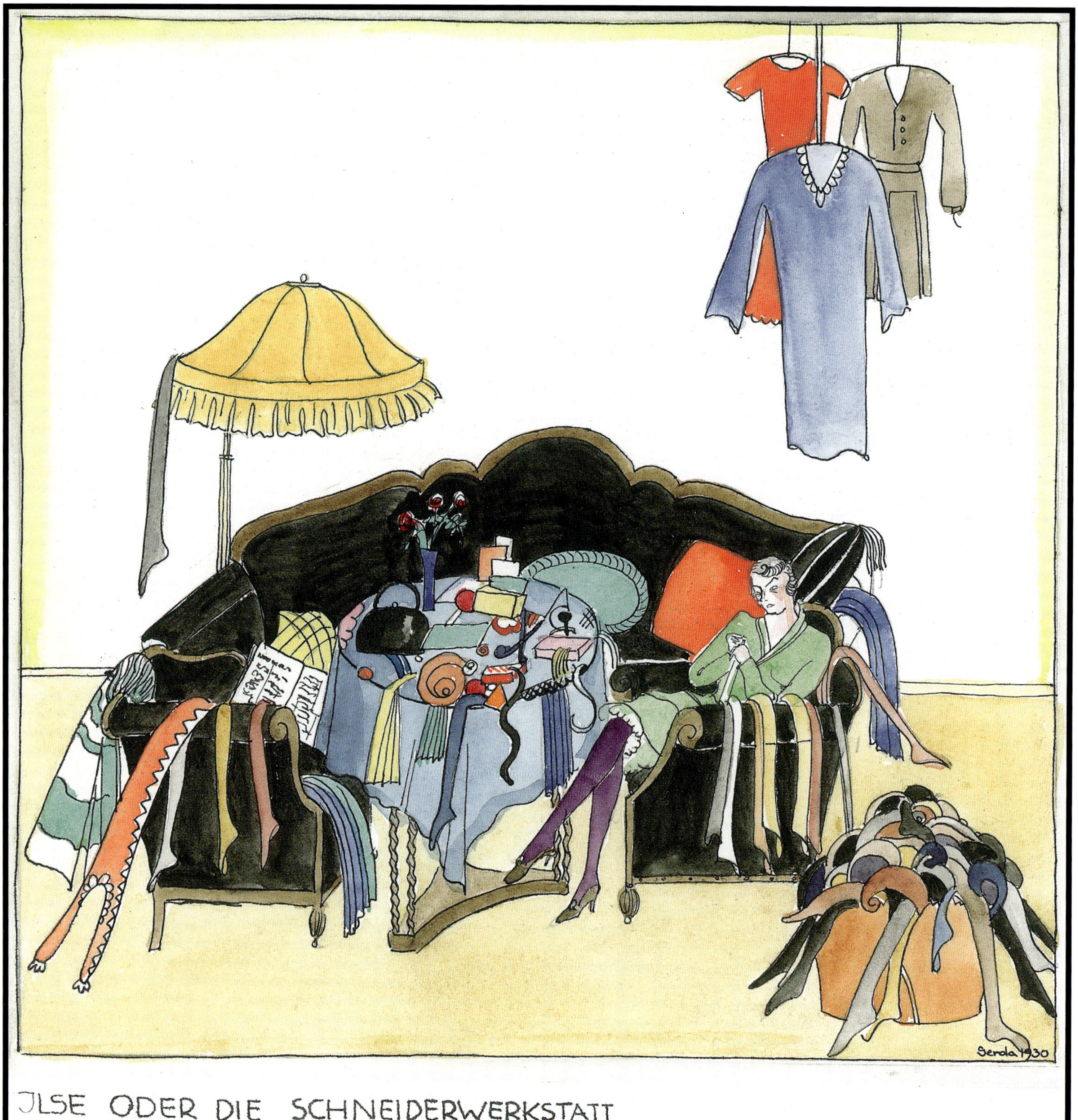

Ilse or The Tailor's Workshop, 1930.

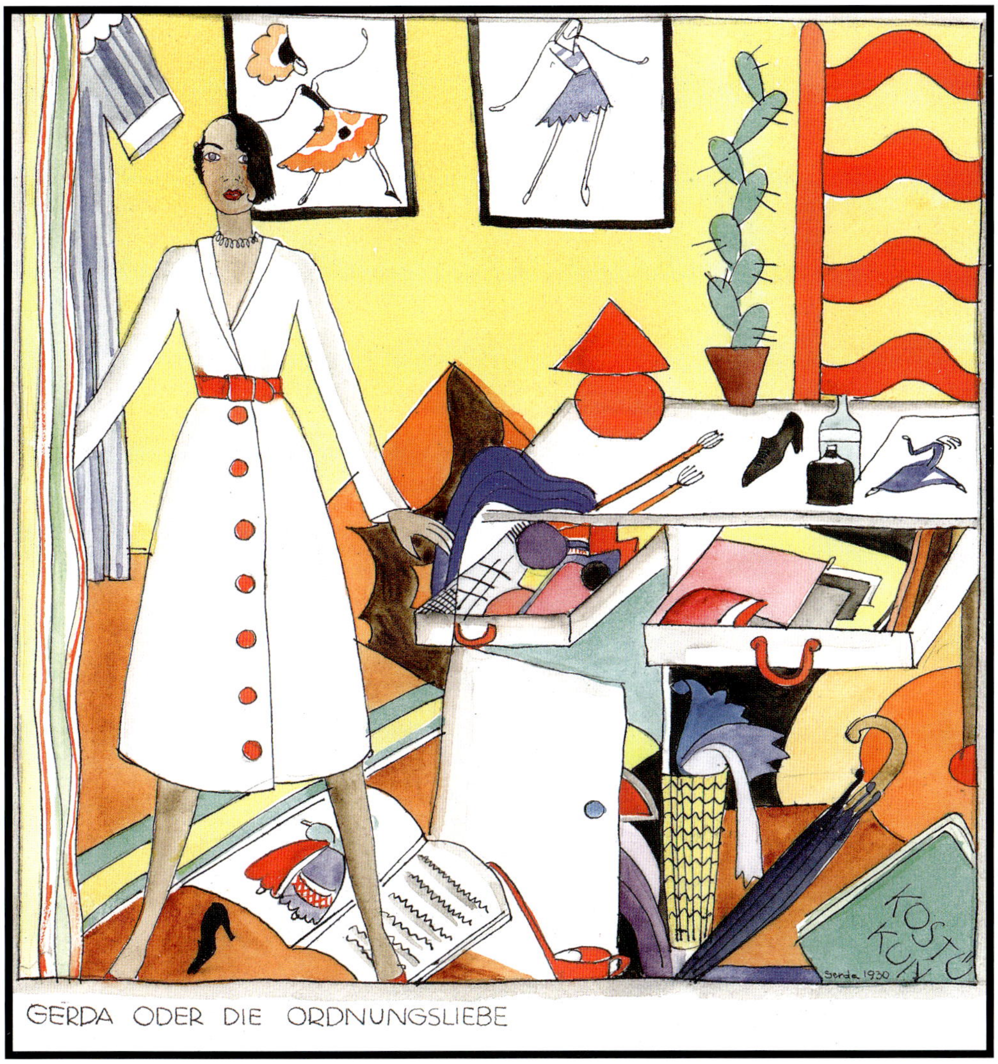

Gerda or The Love of Tidiness, 1930.

Costume design, undated.

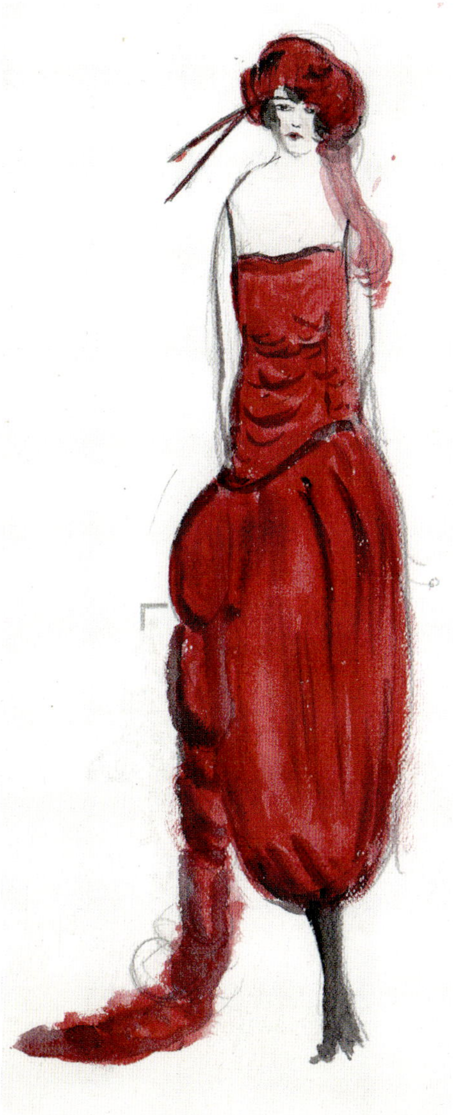

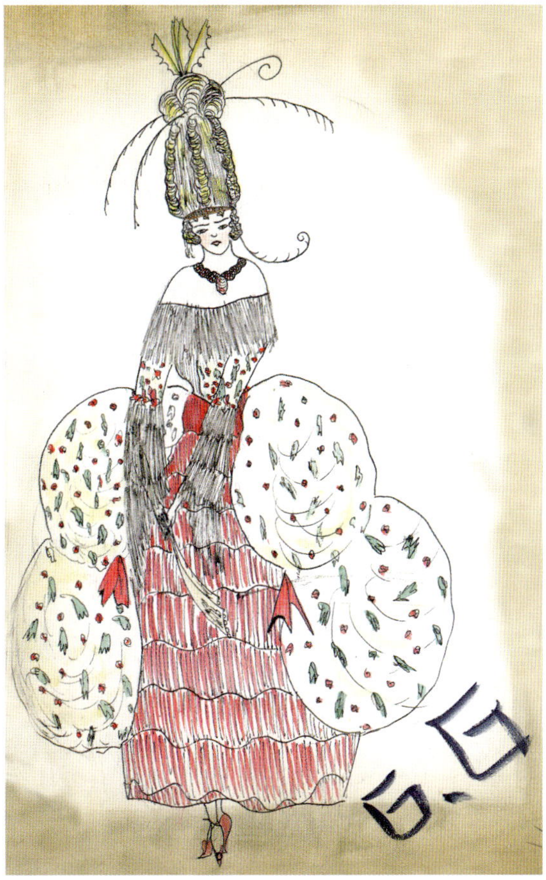

Costume design, signed 'G.G.', 1921.

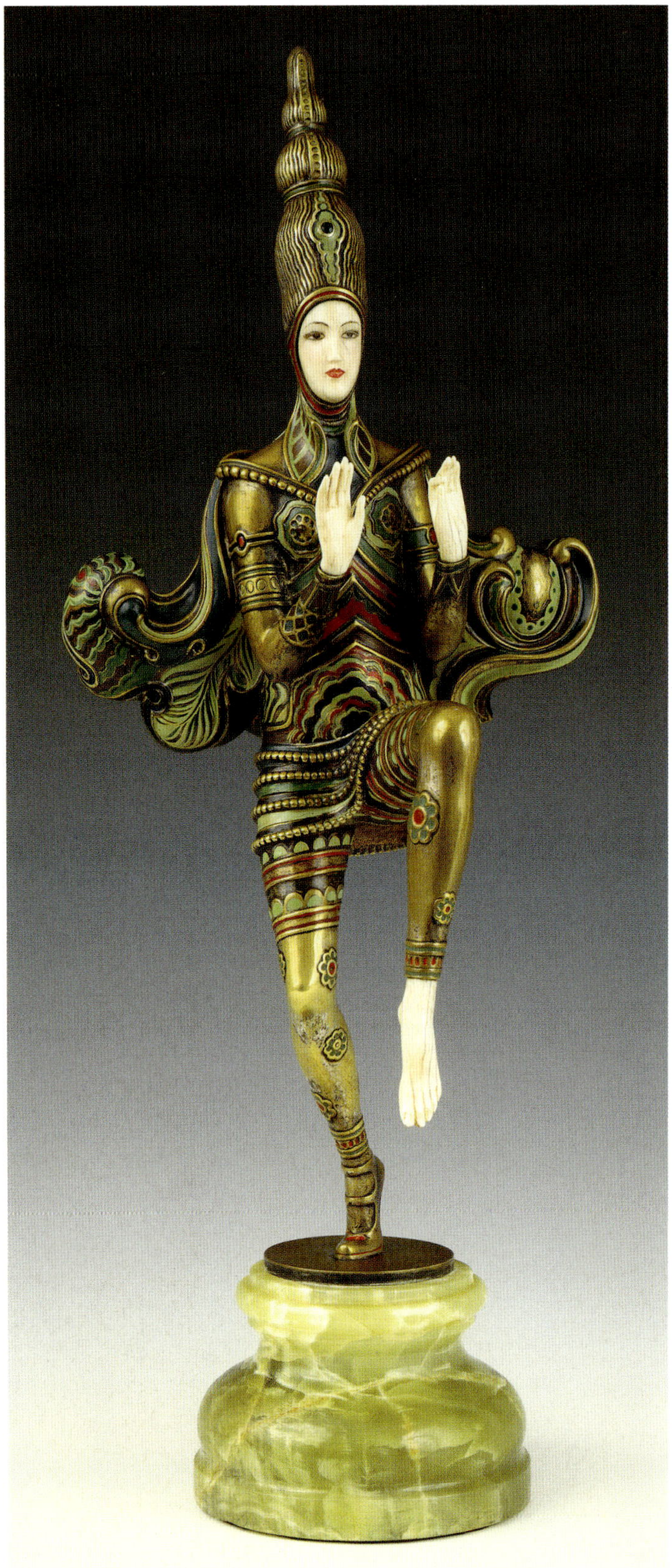

Temple Dancer
Bronze and ivory on onyx base
Height: 47cm. (18½in.)
PRIVATE COLLECTION

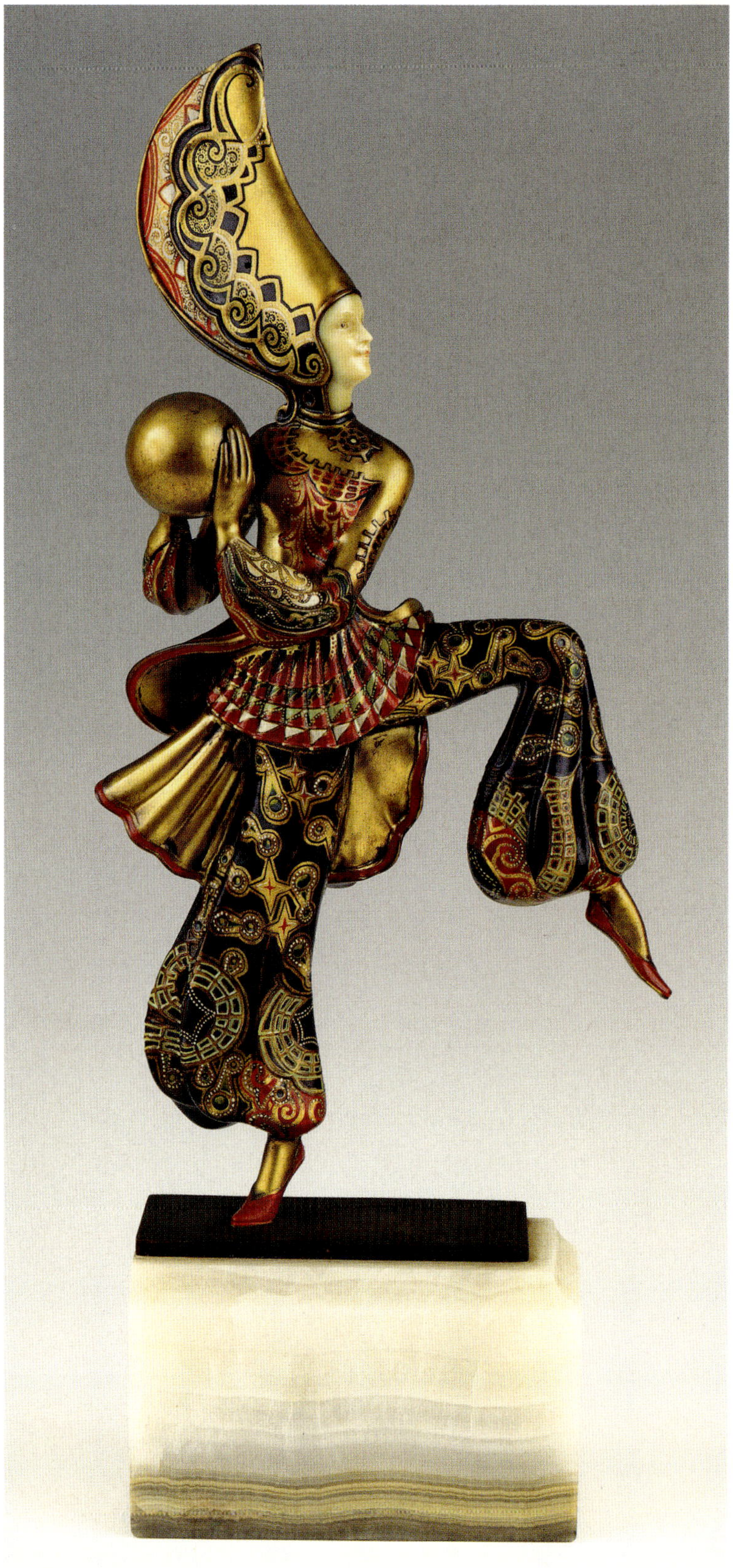

Carnival Dancer
Bronze and ivory on marble base
Height: 40cm. (15¾in.)
PRIVATE COLLECTION

Futuristic Dancer
Bronze and ivory on onyx base
Height: 31cm. (12¼in.)
PRIVATE COLLECTION

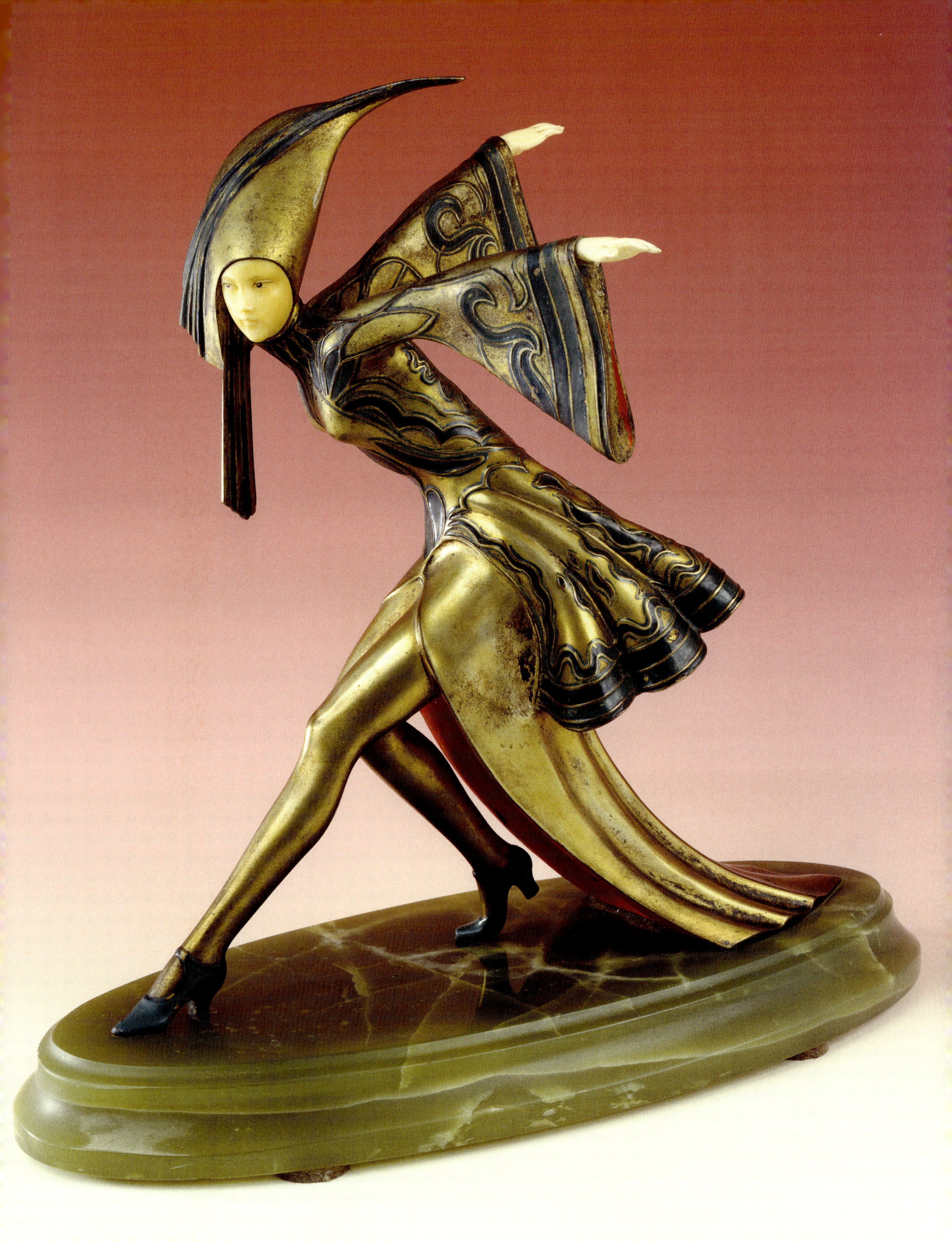

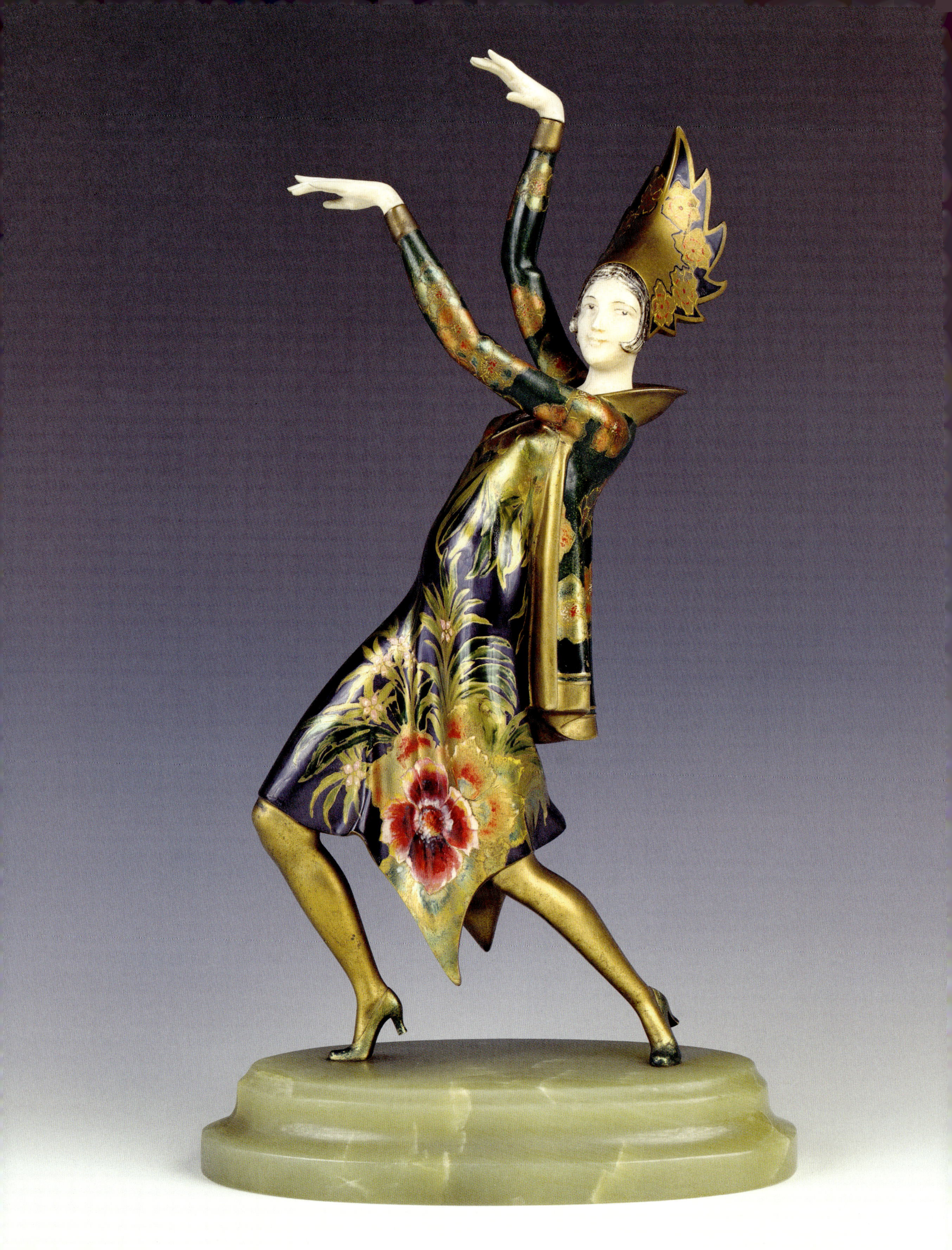

Flower Dress Dancer
Bronze and ivory on onyx base
Height: 31cm. (12¼in.)
VIRGINIA MUSEUM OF FINE ARTS, RICHMOND,
GIFT OF SYDNEY AND FRANCES LEWIS

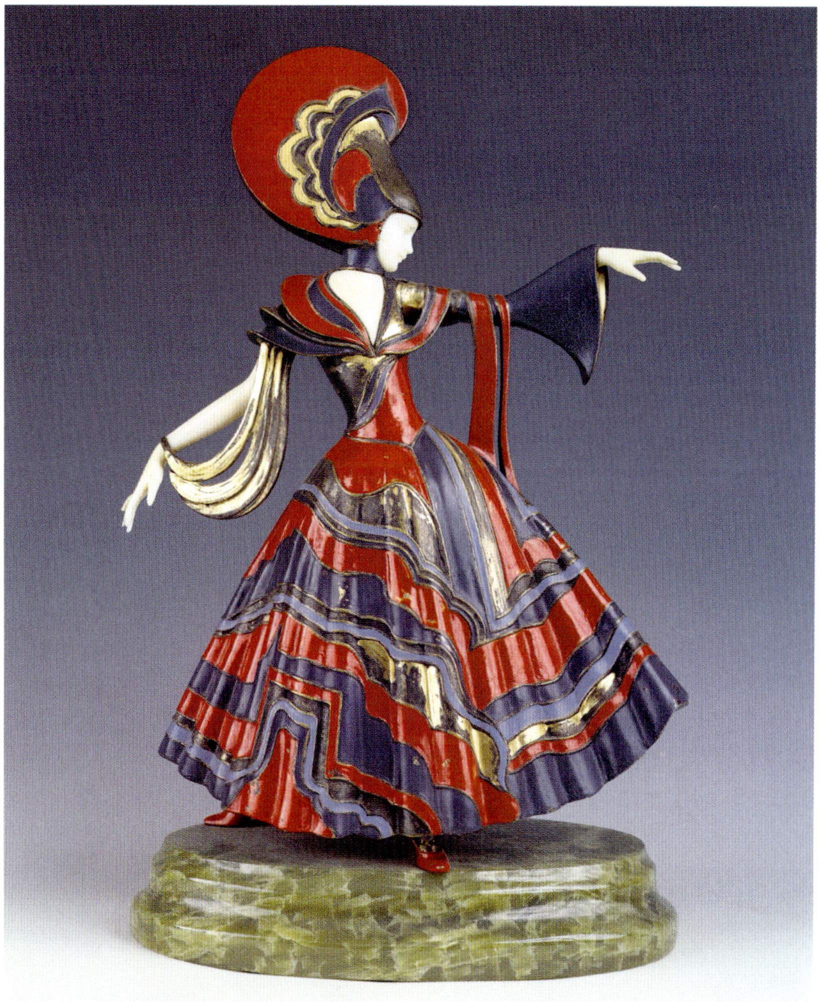

Elegant Dancer
Bronze and ivory on onyx base
Height: 32cm. (12½in.)
PRIVATE COLLECTION

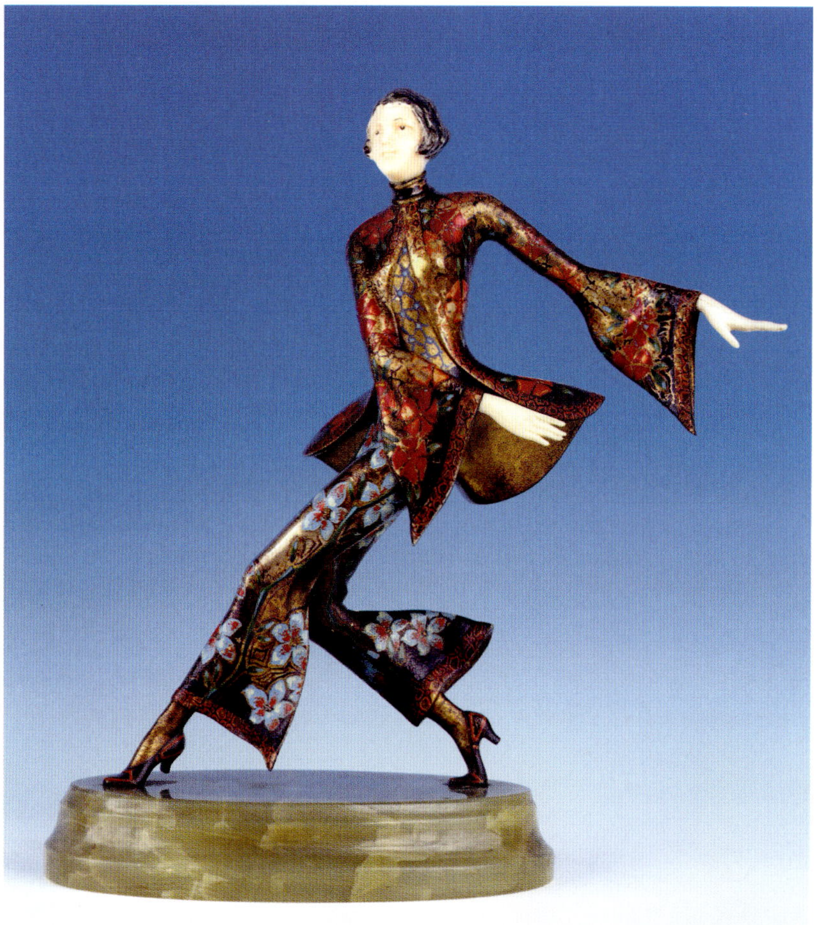

Rhythmic Dancer
Bronze and ivory on onyx base
Height: 26.5cm. (10½in.)
PRIVATE COLLECTION

GÉRÔME, Jean-Léon

(Vesoul 1824 – Paris 1904)

At the age of sixteen he set out for Paris where he studied with Paul Delaroche at the Ecole des Beaux Arts.

He made his debut at the Salon in 1847, with a painting *Combat de Coqs* (Cock Fight), which earned him a third-class medal. During his life he earned multiple honours and participated in many salons and exhibitions. He became professor of the Ecole des Beaux Arts in 1863. In 1878 he was awarded the Legion d'Honneur.

He specialised in historical paintings, Orientalism, erotic subjects and later in sculpture. Various museums have his works.

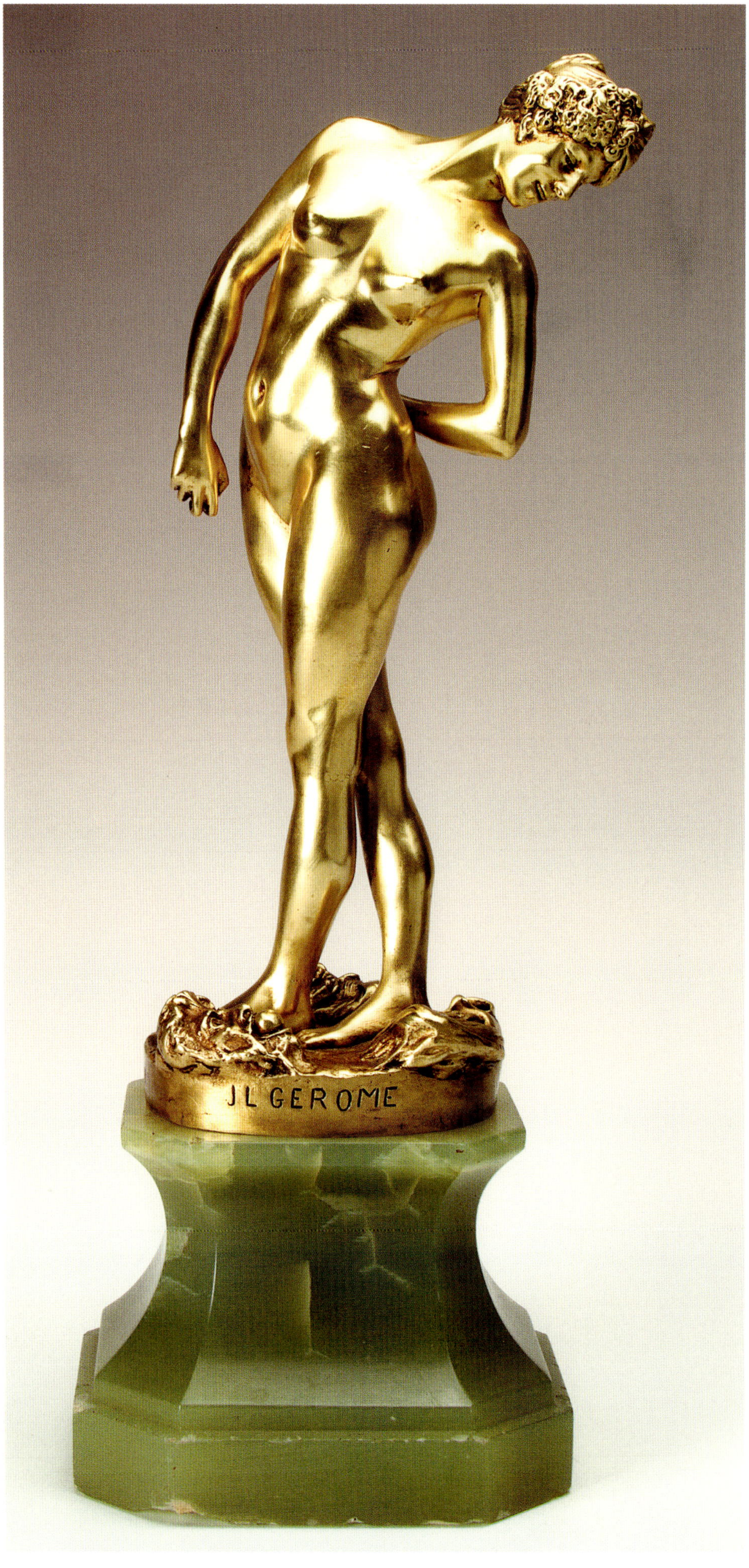

The Ball Player
Bronze and ivory on onyx base
Height: 37cm. (14½in.)
DINO MENASCHE COLLECTION

GILBERT, André

A French artist, born in Pontoise, who created some models for Etling and for L.N. de J. Lehmann. His subjects include Pierrots and Columbines. This artist should not be confused with the British artist Sir Alfred Gilbert, creator of the *Eros* sculpture atop the Piccadilly Circus fountain in London.

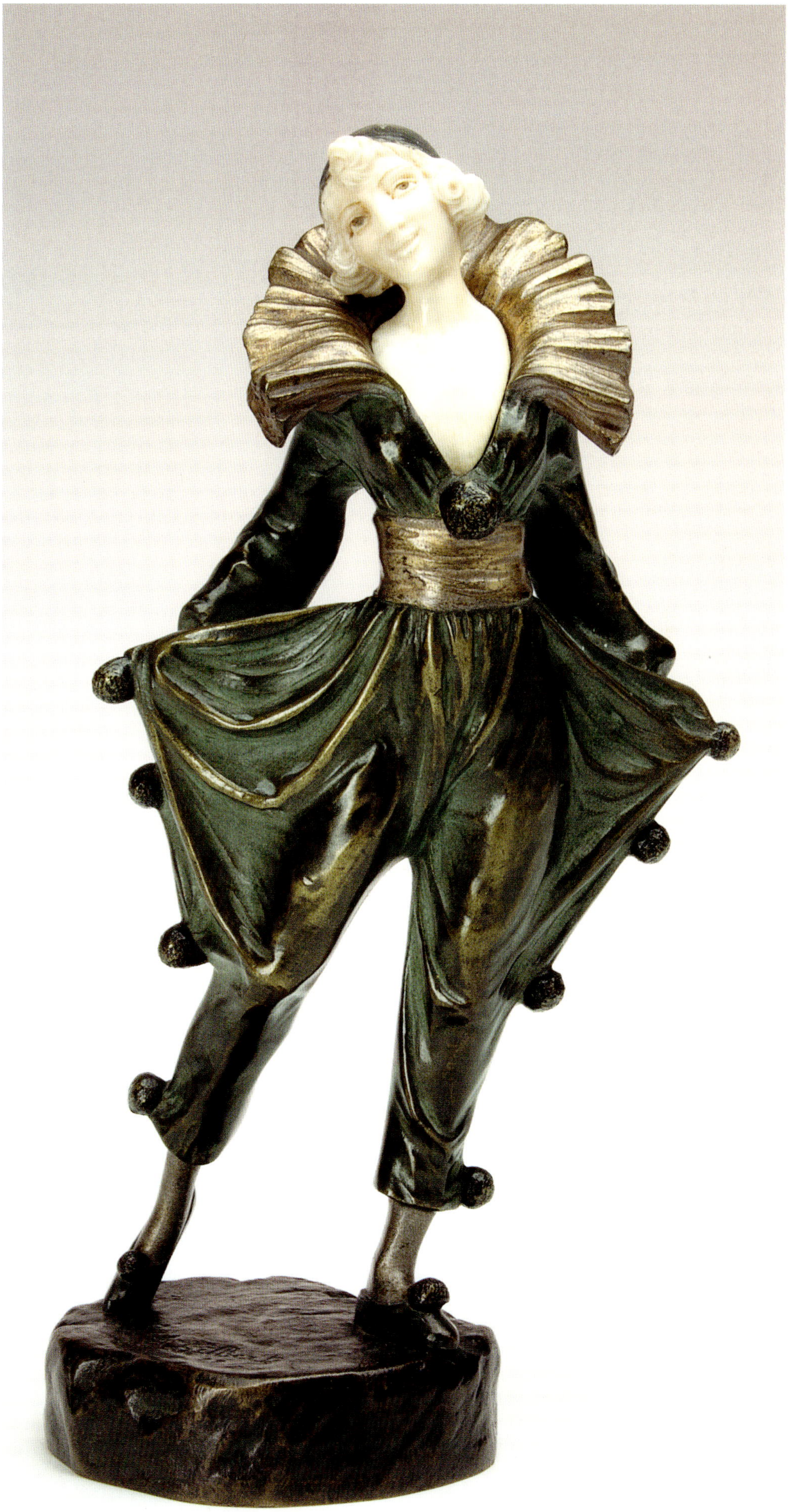

On Parade
Bronze and ivory
Height: 22cm. (8¾in.)
DINO MENASCHE COLLECTION

Also produced 33cm. (13in.) and 58cm. (22¾in.) high

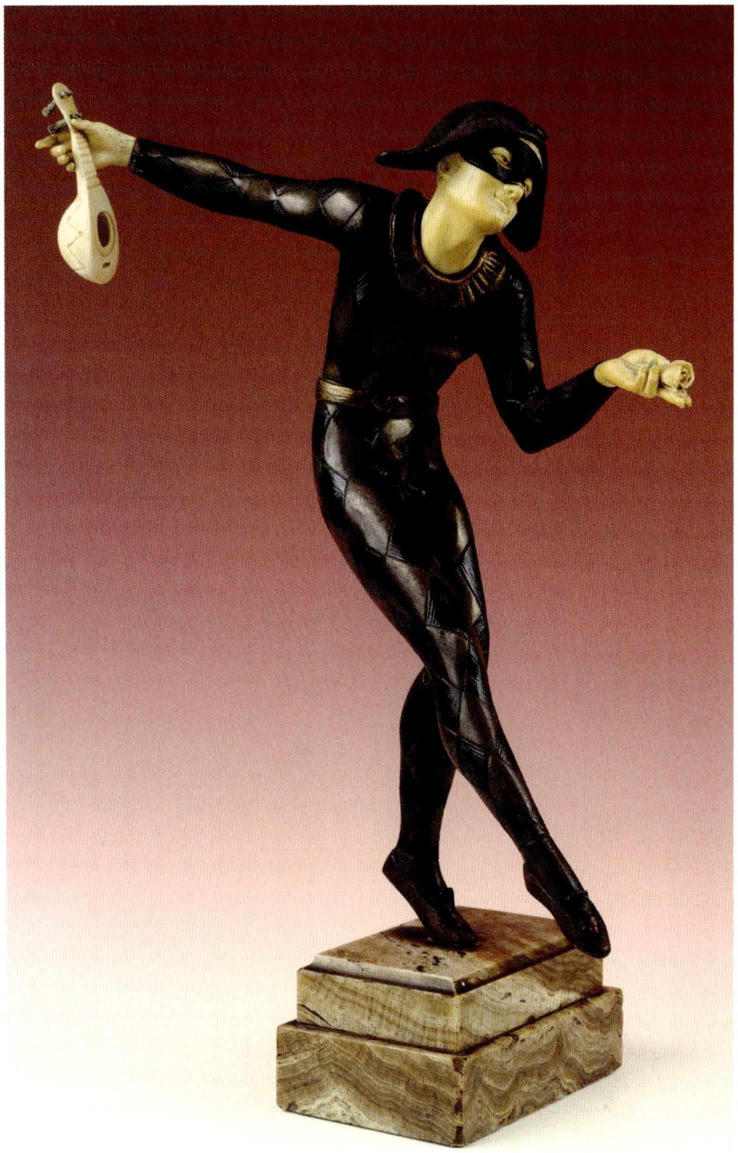

Harlequinade with Rose
Bronze and ivory on onyx base
Height: 44.5cm. (17½in.)
PRIVATE COLLECTION

Seduction
Bronze and ivory on
marble and bronze base
Height: 56cm. (22in.)
ANTONIO AMADO COLLECTION, MIAMI

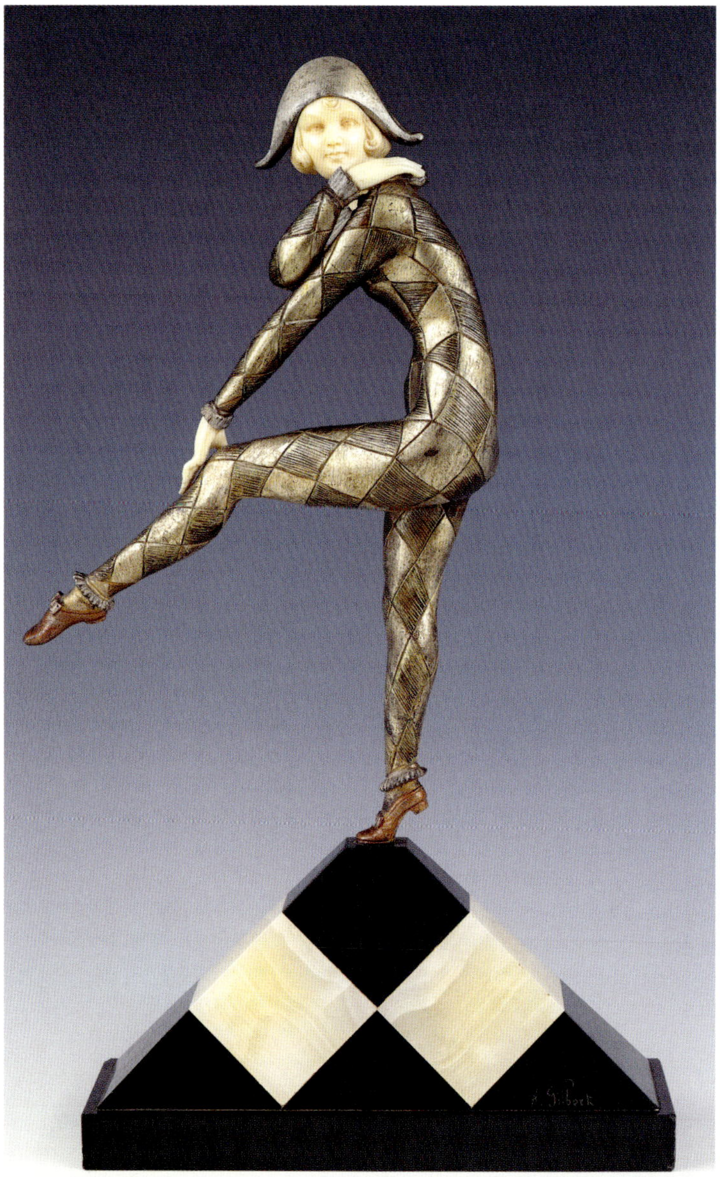

Dance of the Harlequinade
Bronze and ivory on onyx base
Height: 37cm. (14½in.)
PRIVATE COLLECTION

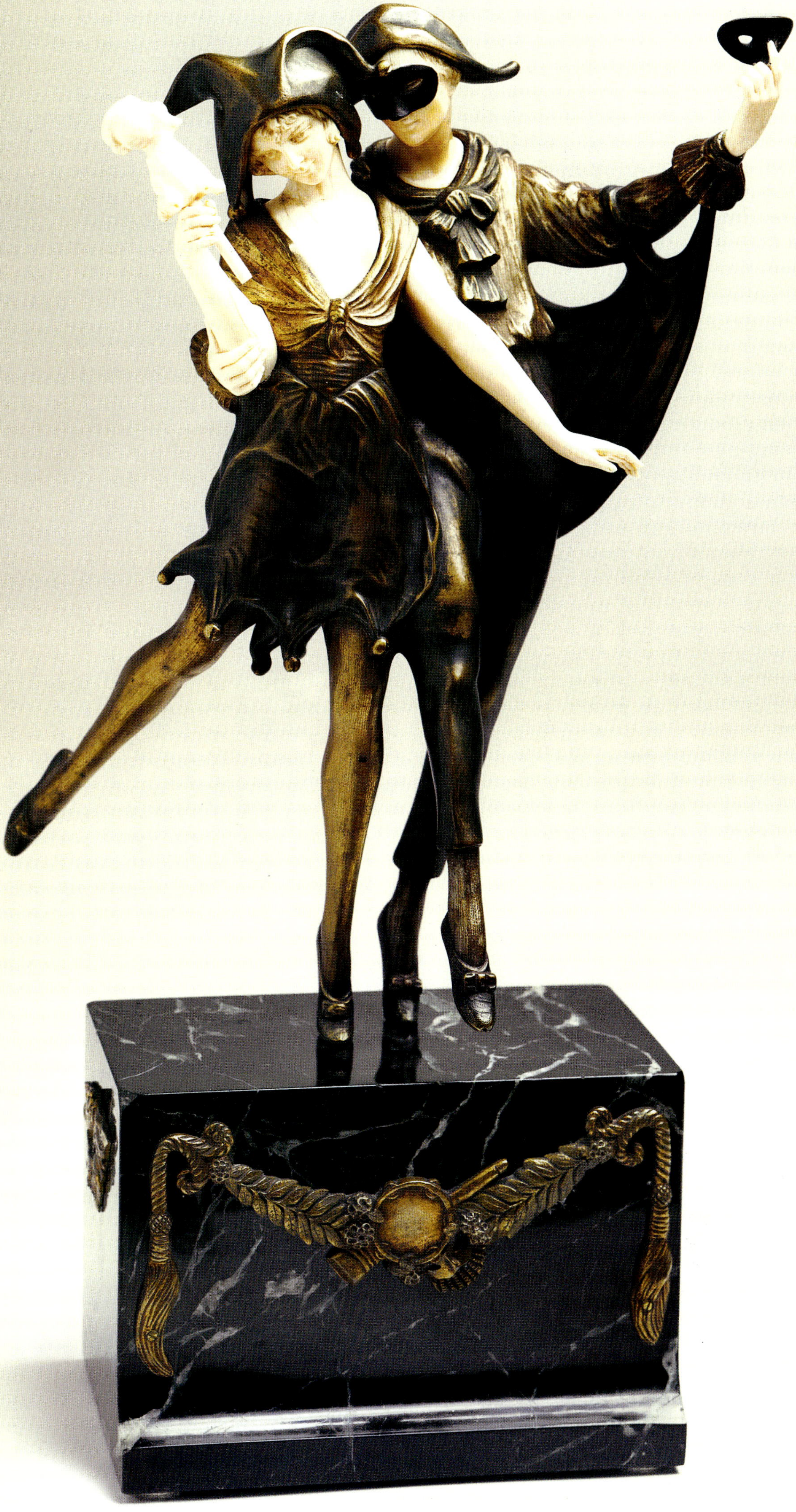

GODARD, Armand

In the 1920s and 1930s, he exhibited at the Salon of the Société des Artistes Français. He produced chryselephantine and bronze sculptures for Edmond Etling.

A monumental statue (4.5m) and a patinated plaster sculpture by him were shown at the 1937 International Exhibition in Paris.

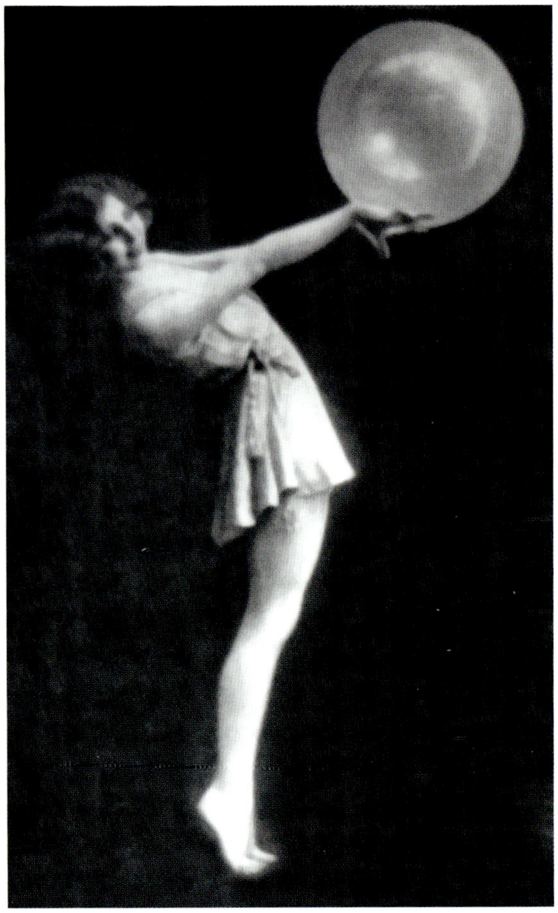

Georgia Graves at the Folies Bergère, 1920s.

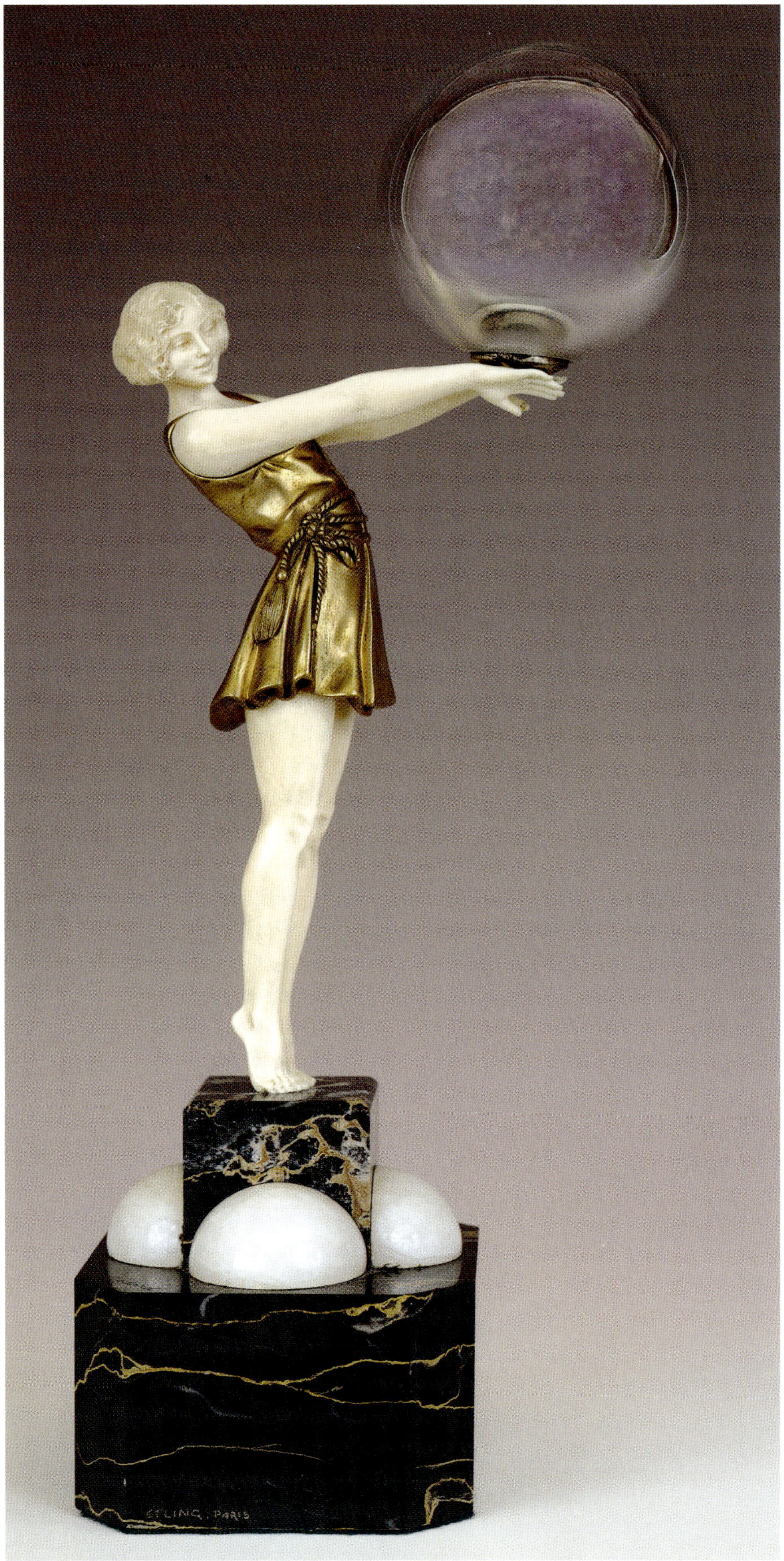

Bubble Dance
Bronze, ivory and glass on marble base
Height: 35cm. (13¾in.)
S. AND J.S. COLLECTION

Also produced 52cm. (20½in.) high

Charm of the Orient
Bronze and ivory on marble base
Height: 49.5cm. (19½in.)
PRIVATE COLLECTION

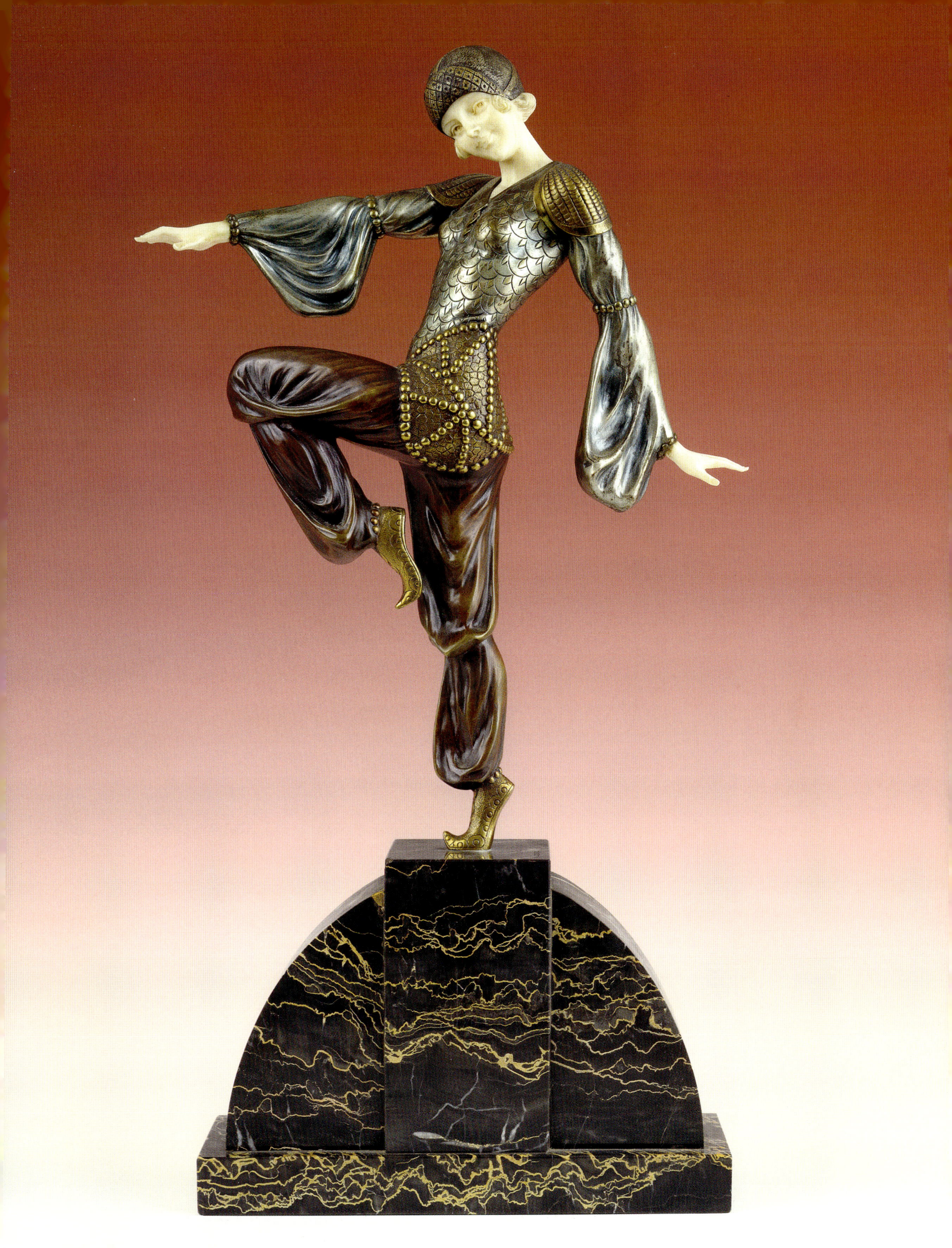

Dutch Tulips
Bronze and ivory on onyx base
Height: 50cm. (19¾in.)
PRIVATE COLLECTION

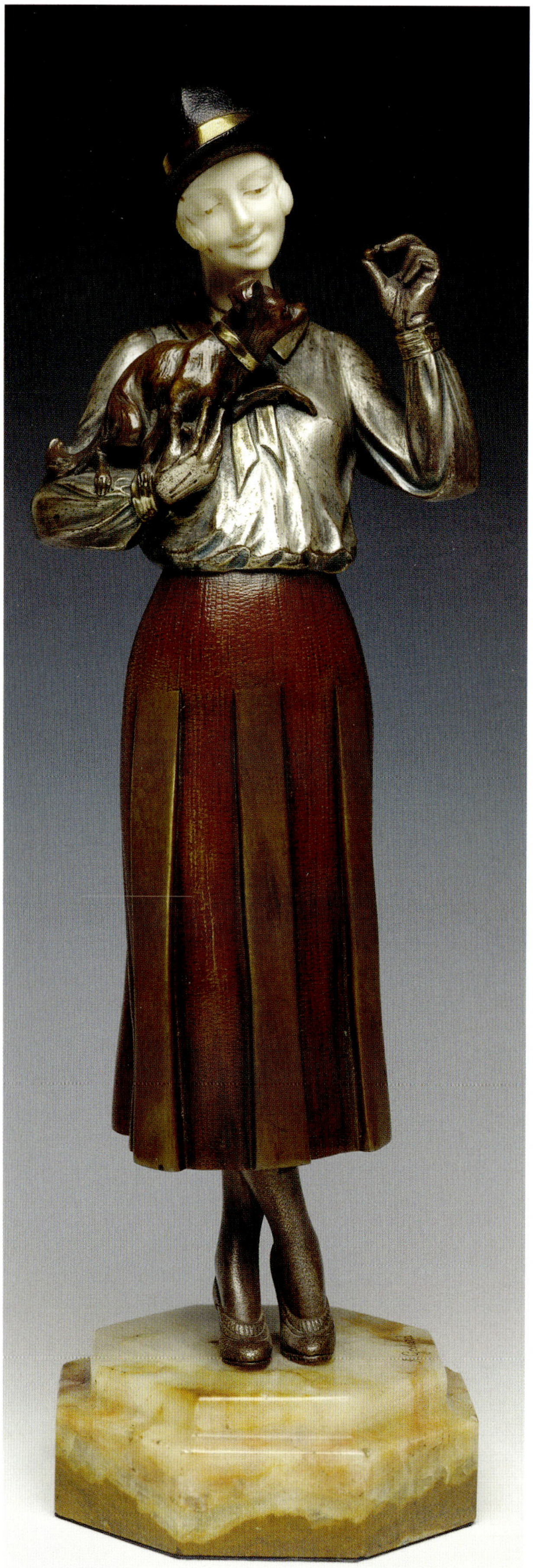

The Treat
Bronze and ivory on marble base
Height: 34cm. (13½in.)
PRIVATE COLLECTION

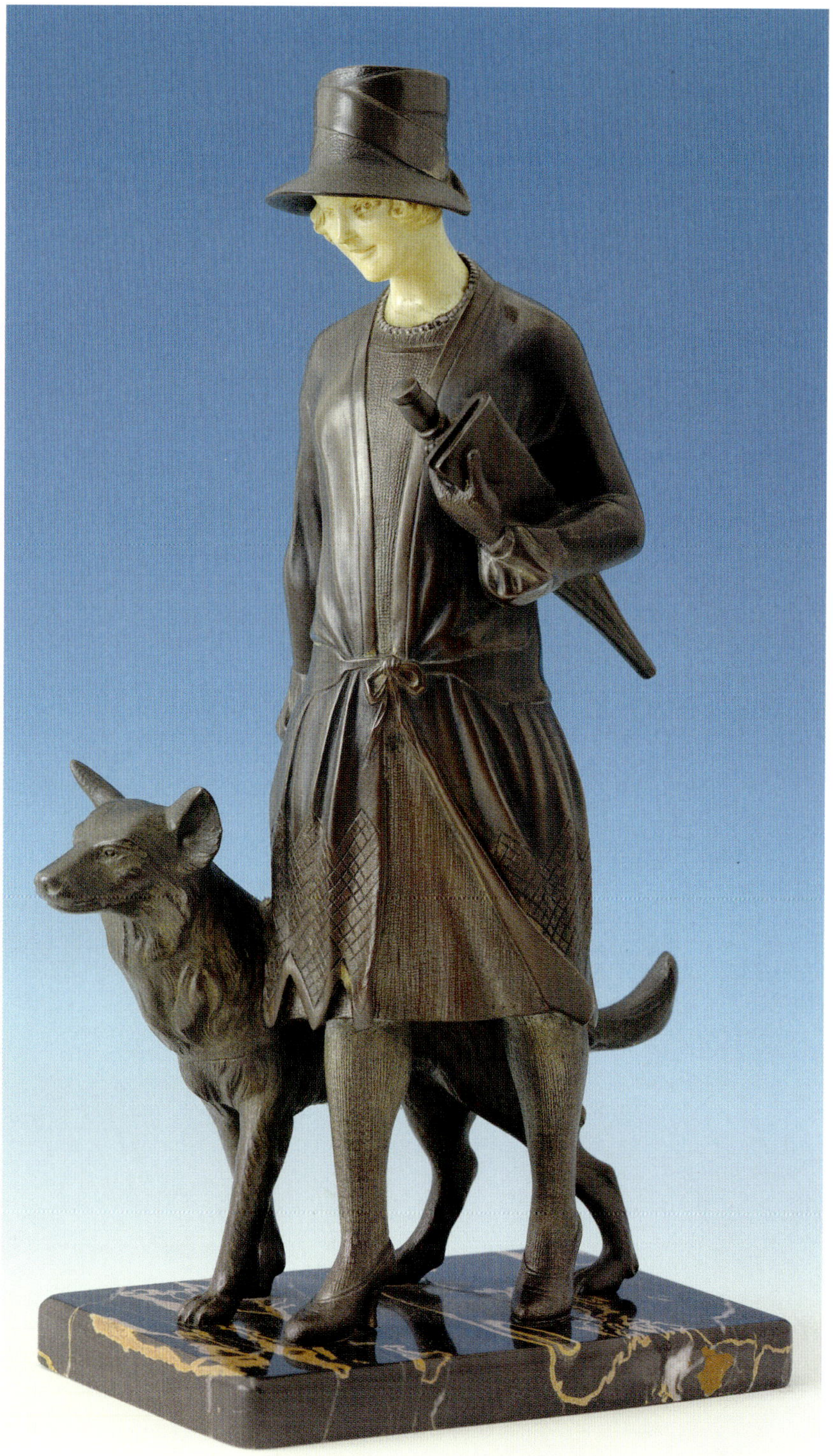

Morning Walk
Bronze and ivory on marble base
Height: 31cm. (12¼in.)
PRIVATE COLLECTION

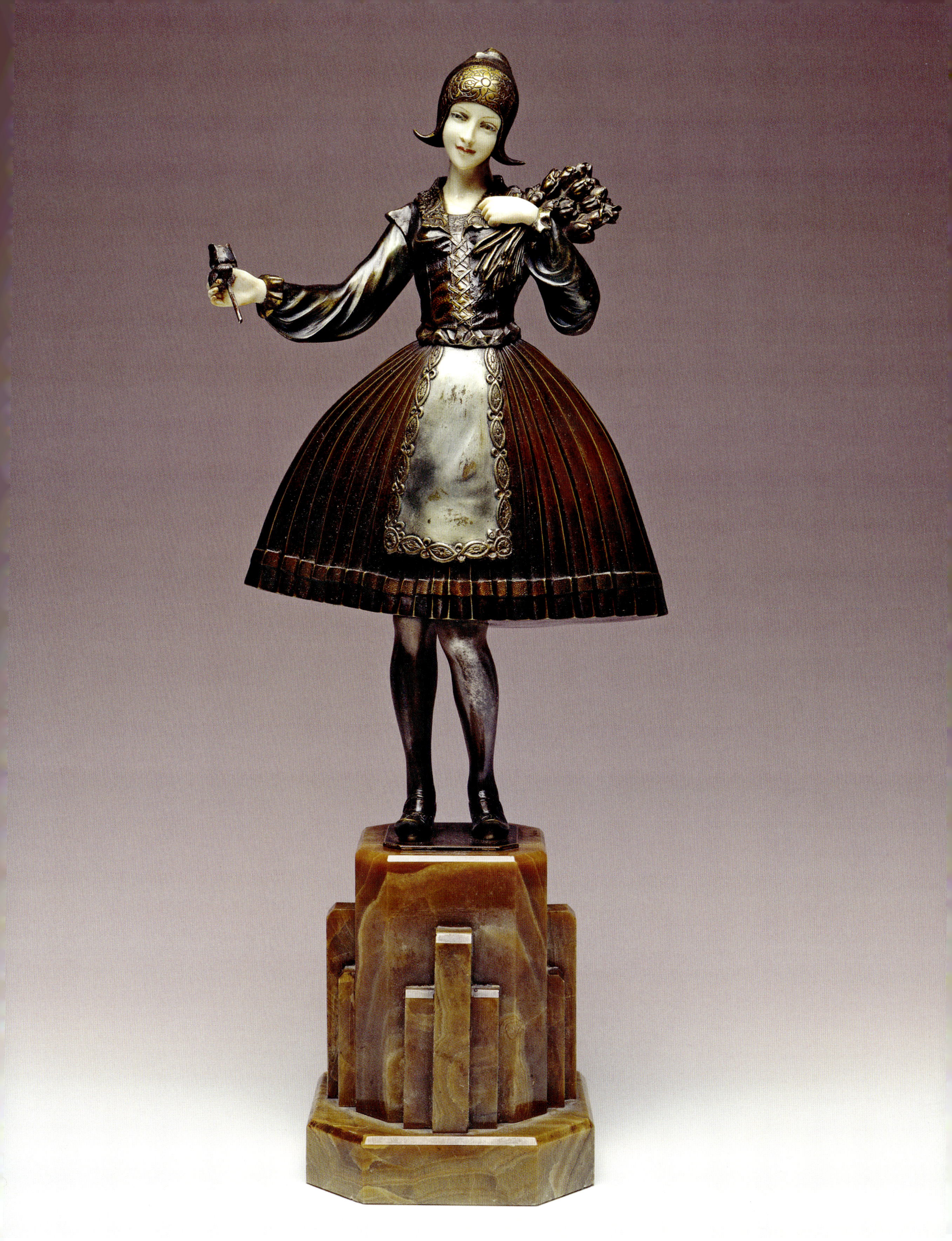

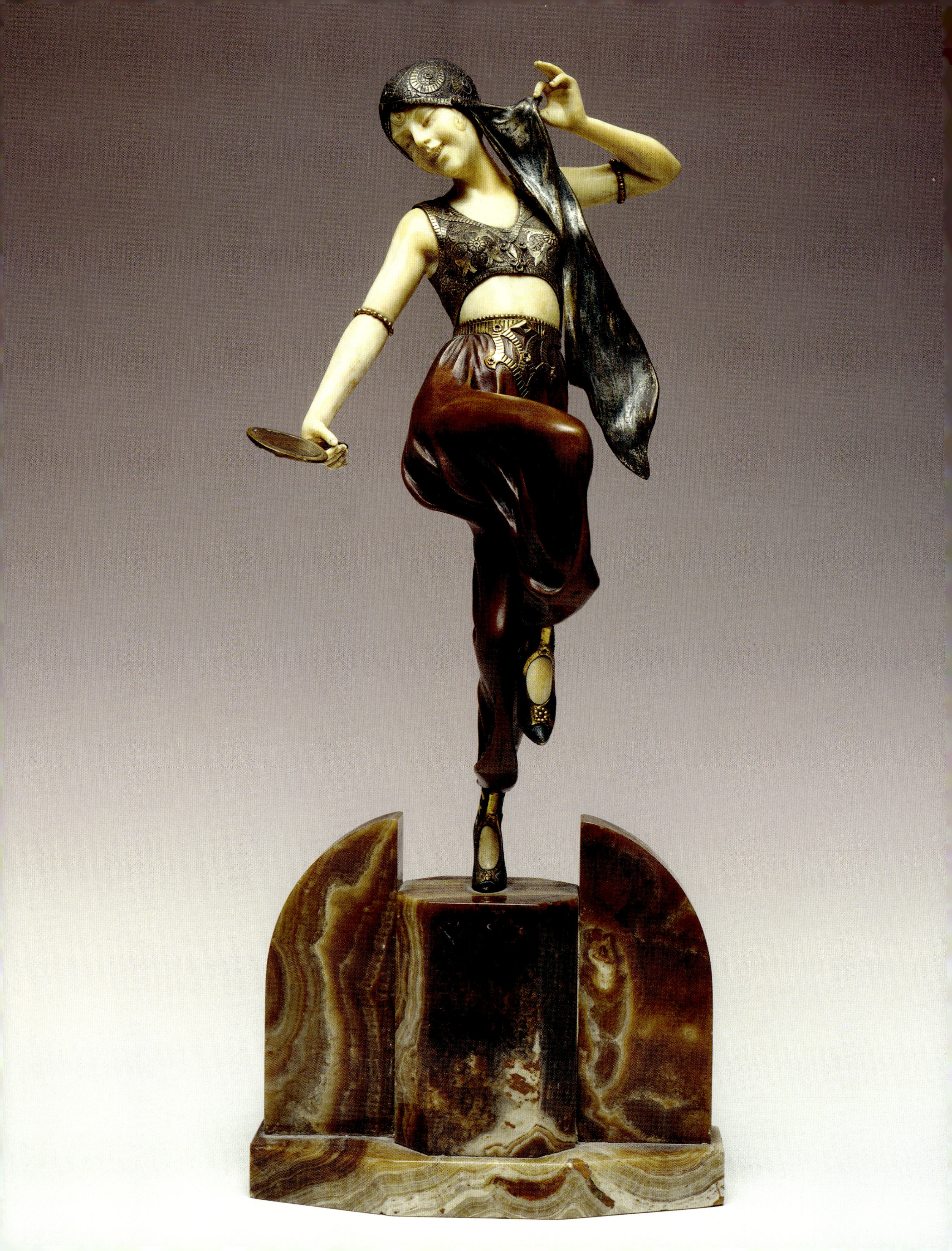

Favourite
Bronze and ivory on marble base
Height: 50cm. (19¾in.)
PRIVATE COLLECTION

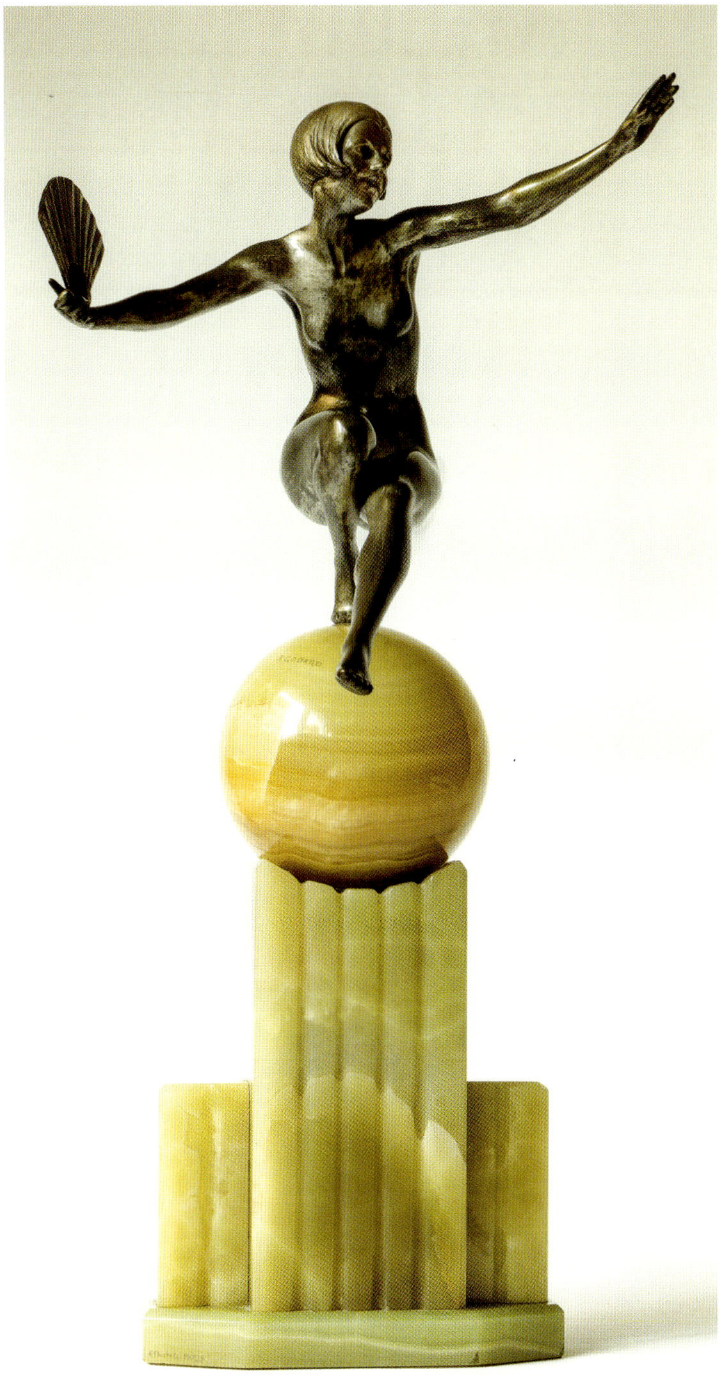

Fan Dancer
Bronze on onyx base
Height: 52.5cm. (20¾in.)
PRIVATE COLLECTION

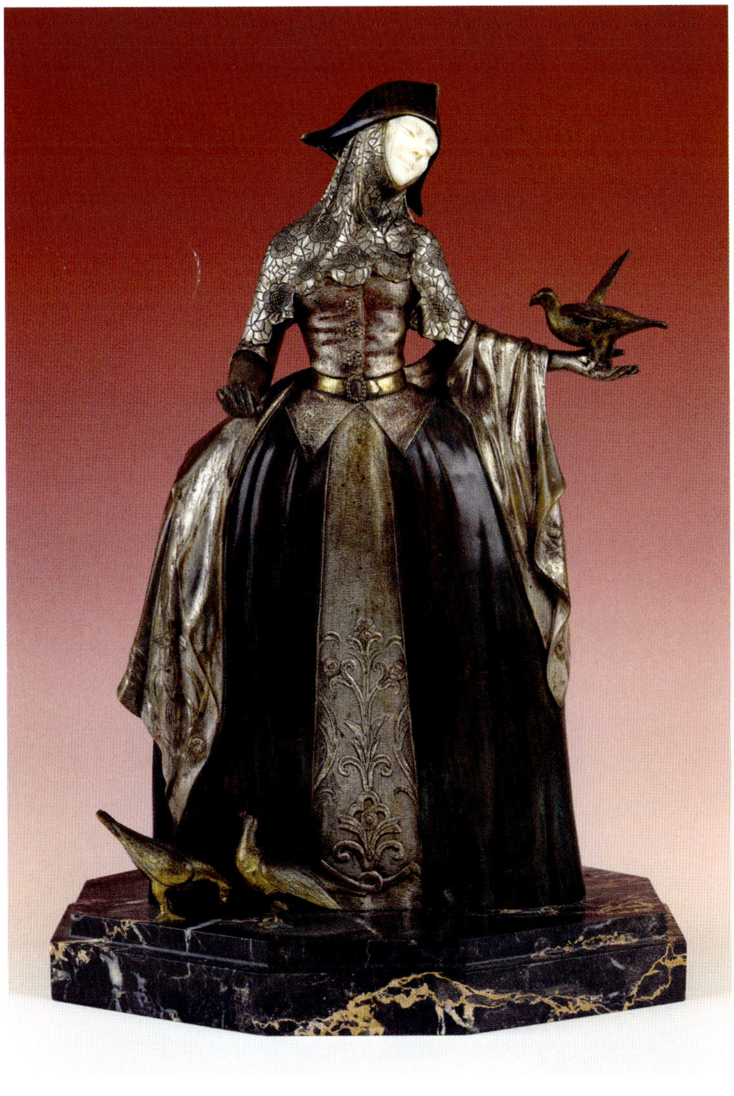

St. Mark's Square
Bronze and ivory on marble base
Height: 40cm. (15¾in.)
PRIVATE COLLECTION

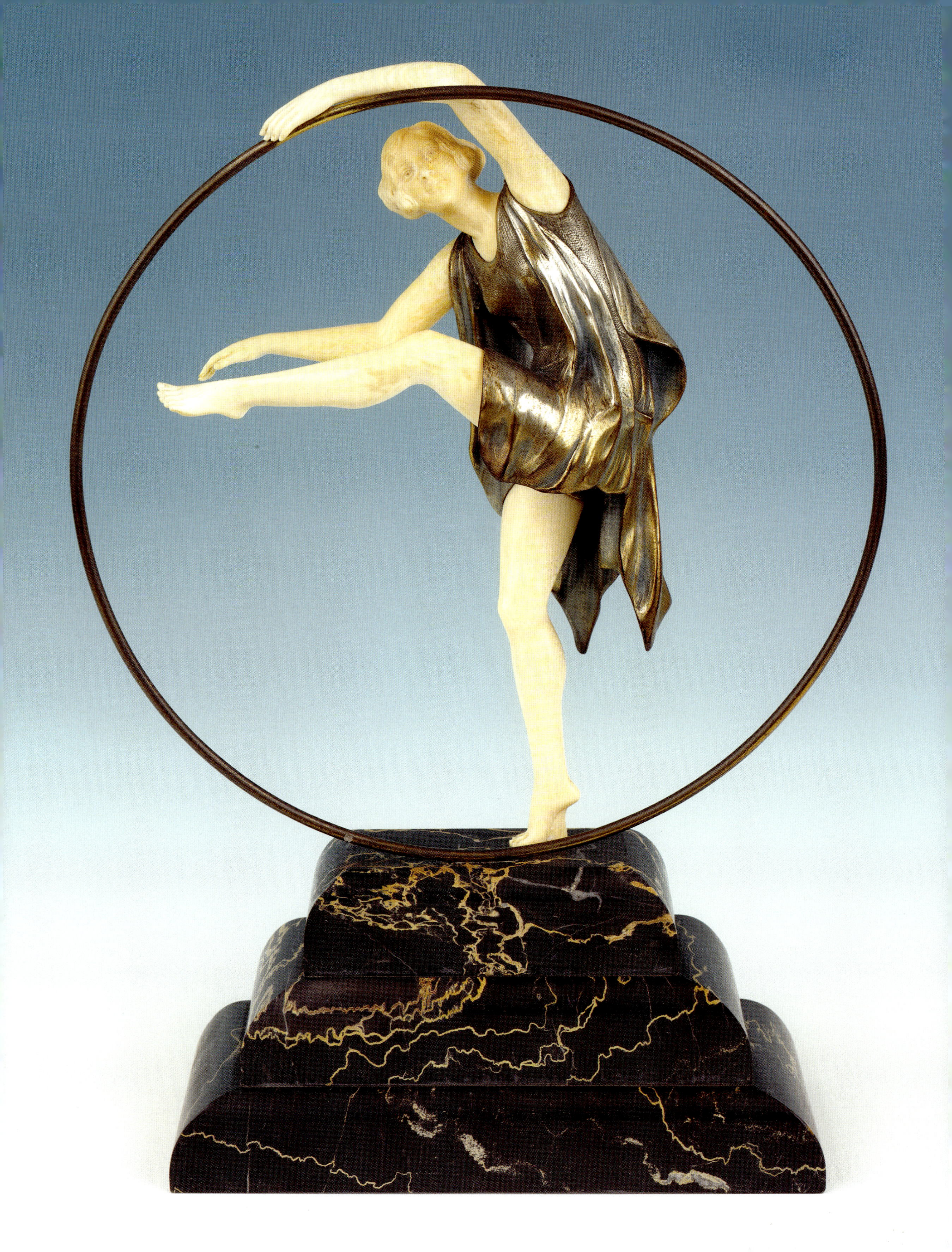

Georgian Dancer
Bronze and ivory on marble base
Height: 43.5cm. (17in.)
MASATOSHI FUKUMARU COLLECTION

Georgia Graves in a Music Hall performance.

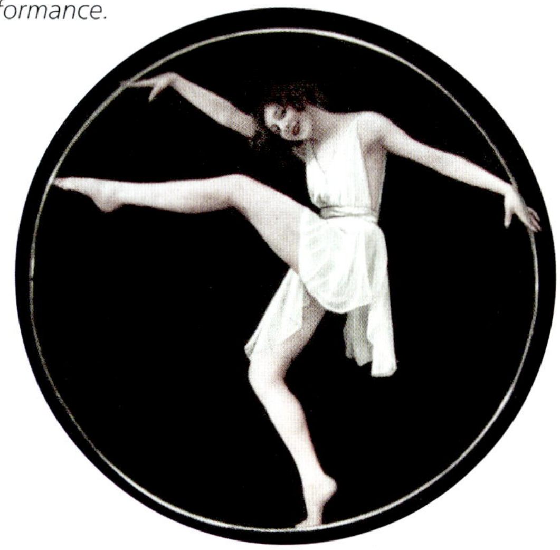

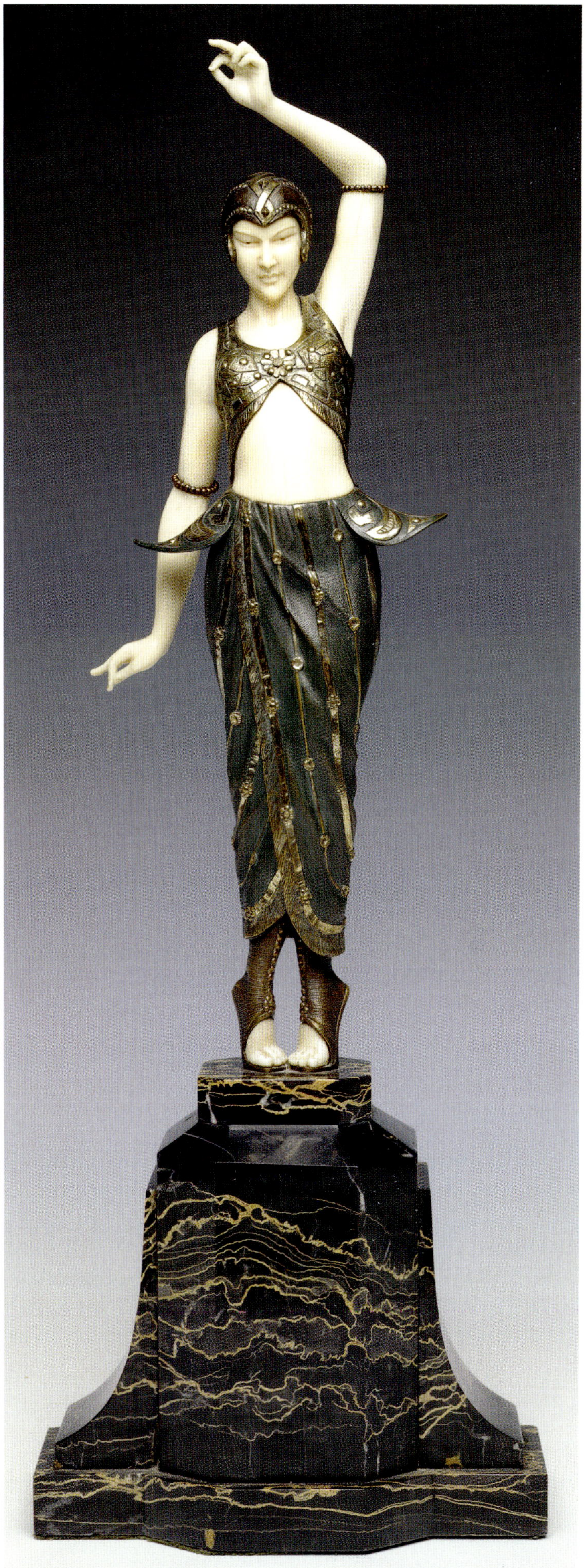

Indian Dancer
Bronze and ivory on marble base
Height: 51cm. (20in.)
PRIVATE COLLECTION

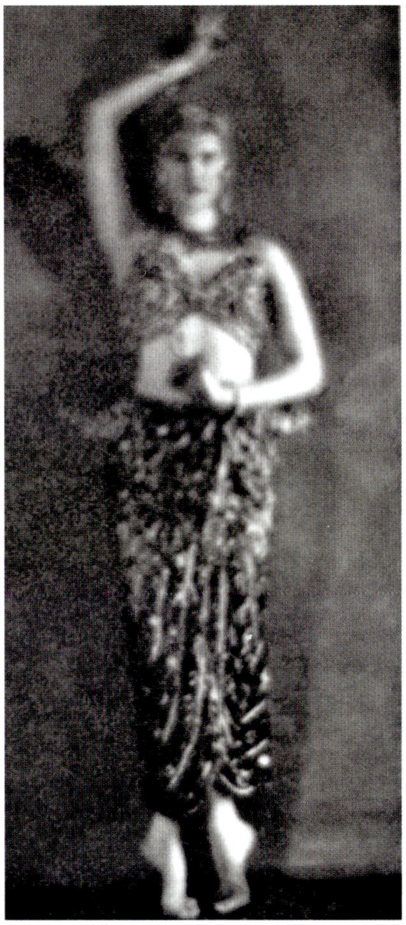

Miss Rhouma-je at the Luxe de Paris revue.

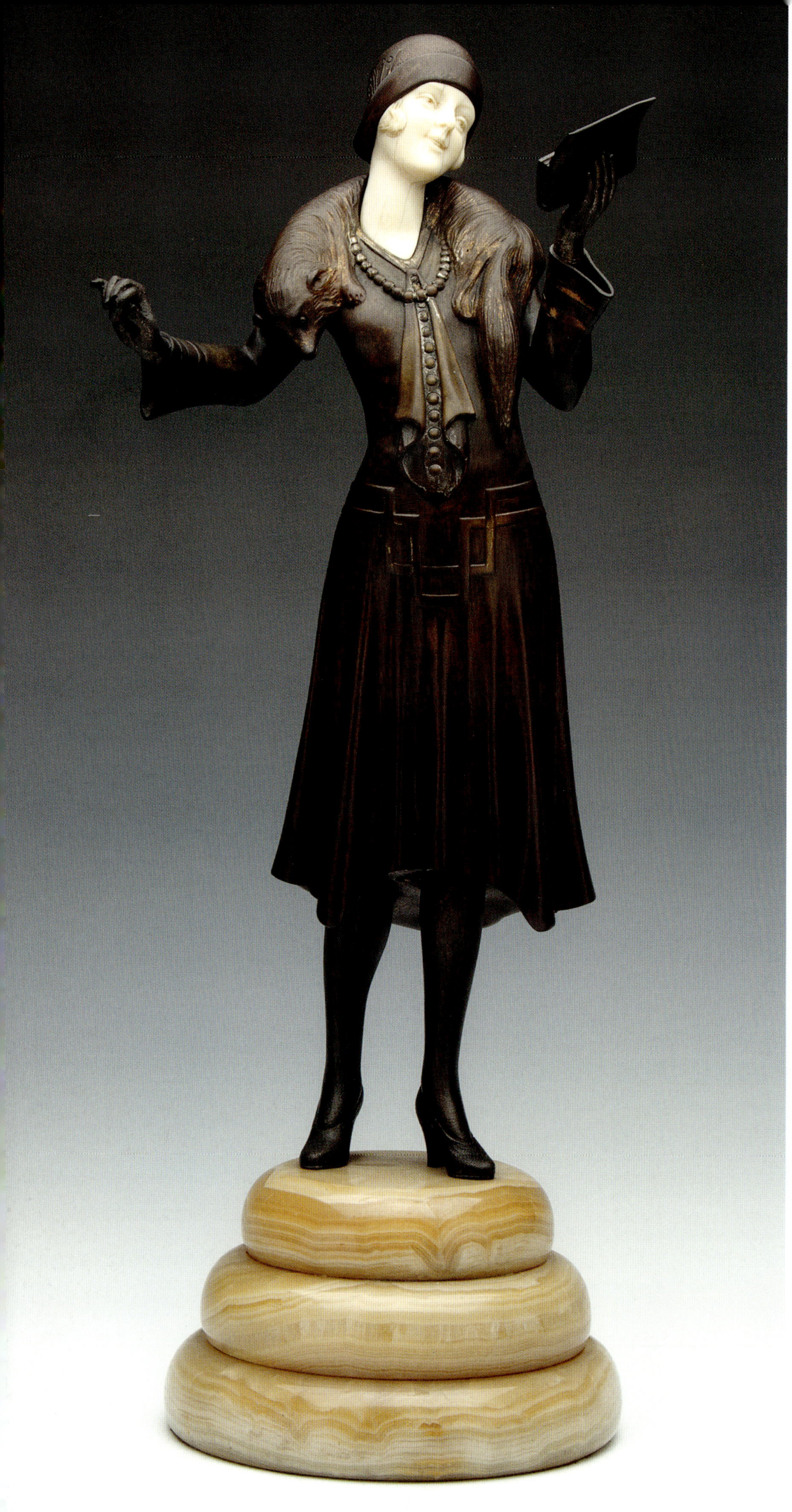

Elegante
Bronze and ivory on marble base
Height: 39.5cm. (15½in.)
PRIVATE COLLECTION

Argentinian Dance
Bronze and ivory on onyx base
Height: 48cm. (19in.)
PRIVATE COLLECTION

Antonia Mercé y Luque, whose stage name was 'La Argentina', was a dancer of neoclassical Spanish Dances. Born in Buenos Aires of Spanish parents, she became a favourite on the Parisian Music Hall circuit, including the Moulin Rouge and the Théâtre des Champs-Elysées.

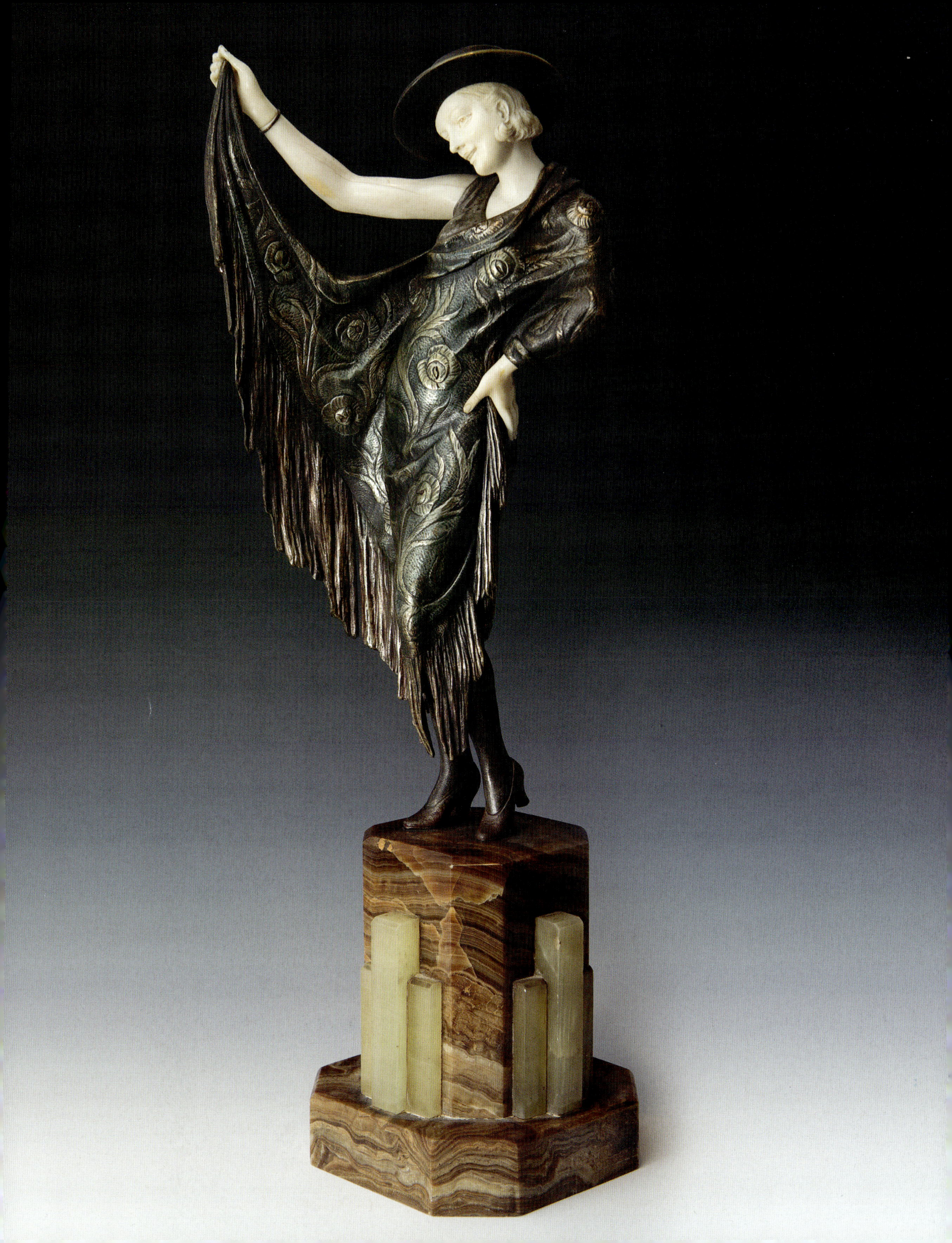

GORI, Georges

Born in Paris around the turn of the century, he studied with Injalbert and Bouchard. As of 1929 he exhibited at the Salon of the Société des Artistes Français; he was a member of the Société des Artistes Français from approximately 1932 to 1939. In 1931 he received a bronze medal.

At the Paris International Exhibition of Arts and Techniques of 1937, his group *La Promenade*, cast by the Champeau foundry, was exhibited.

(This artist should not be confused with Affortunato Gory, see opposite page.)

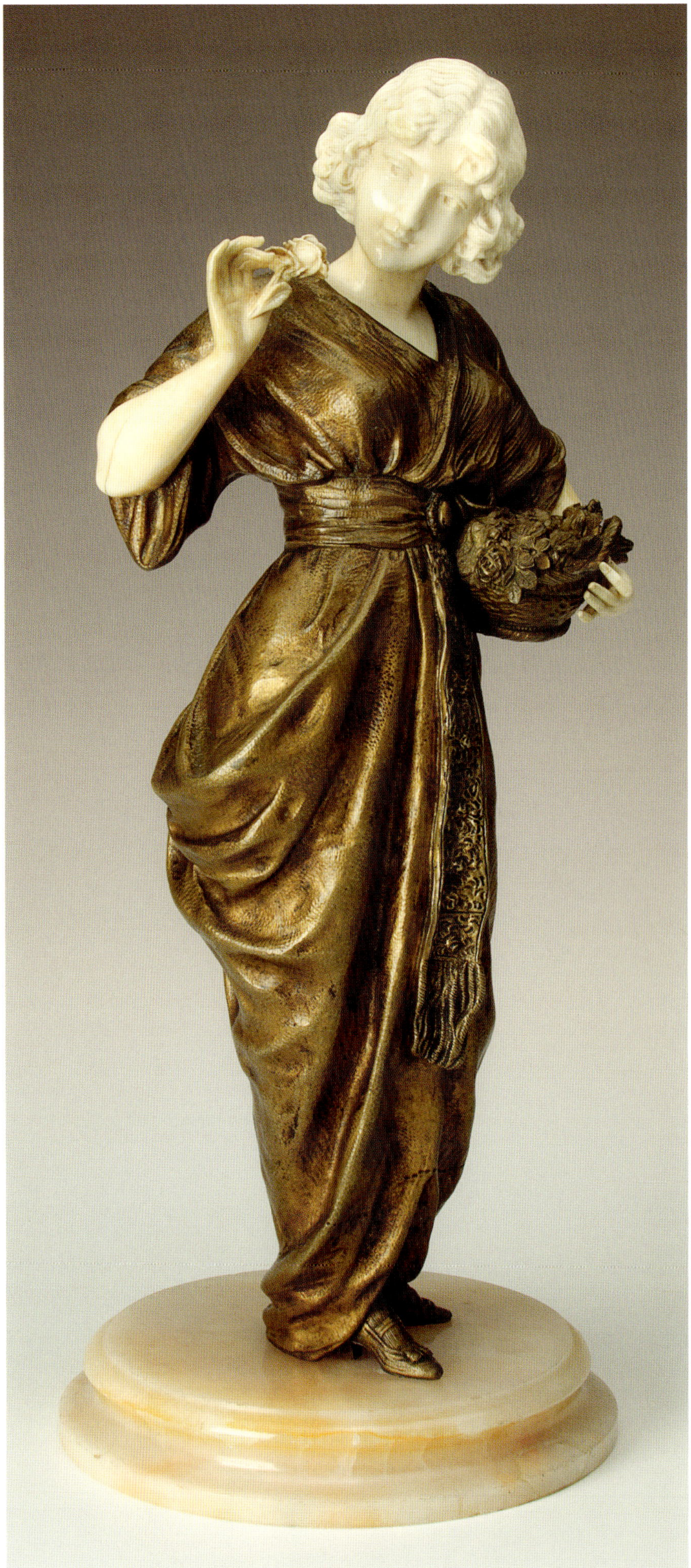

Flower Girl
Bronze and ivory on marble base
Height: 35.5cm. (13½in.)
DINO MENASCHE COLLECTION

GORY, Affortunato ('Fortunato')

Italian sculptor born in Florence. Active between 1895 and 1925.

As of 1904, he exhibited at the Salon of the Société des Artistes Français. He worked in many materials including bronze, marble, ivory and spelter. He continued to exhibit at the Salon of the Société des Artistes Français in Paris up to 1923.

(This artist should not be confused with Georges Gori, see opposite page.)

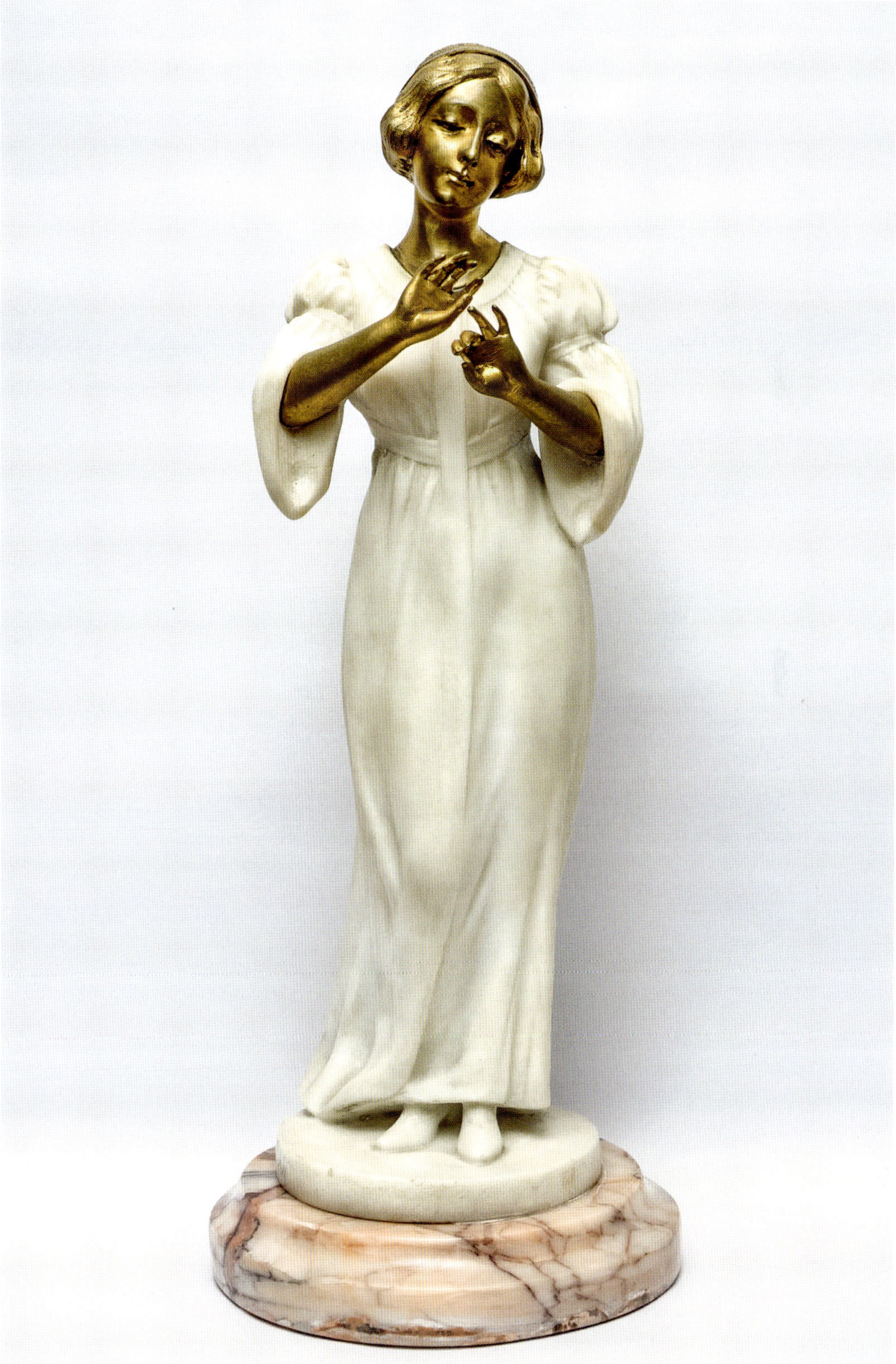

Belle
Marble and bronze
Height: 41cm. (16in.)
FEDERICO MARINO COLLECTION

GUERBE, Raymonde (GUERVAL, Andrée)

(1894 – 1995)

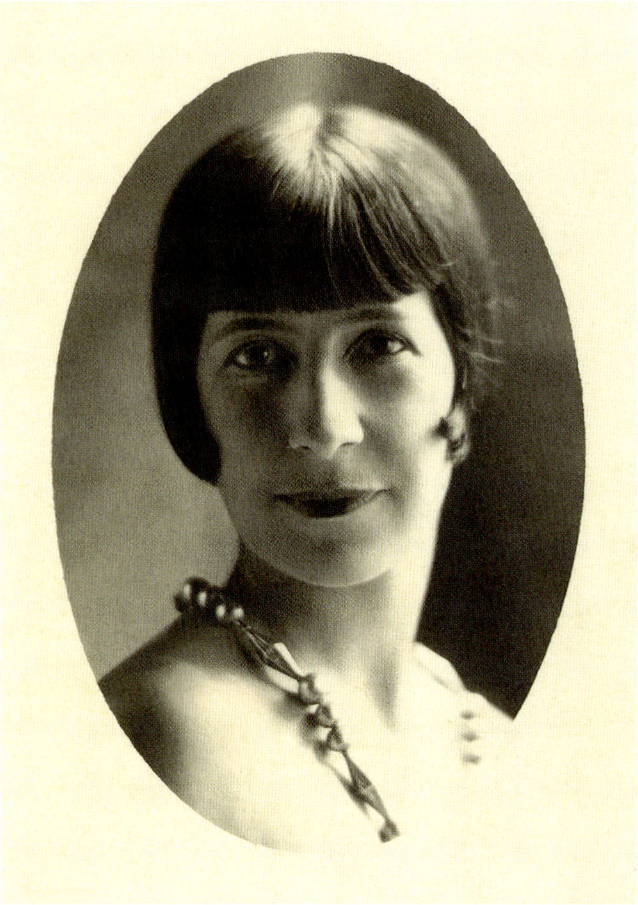

Raymonde Guerbe 1920s.

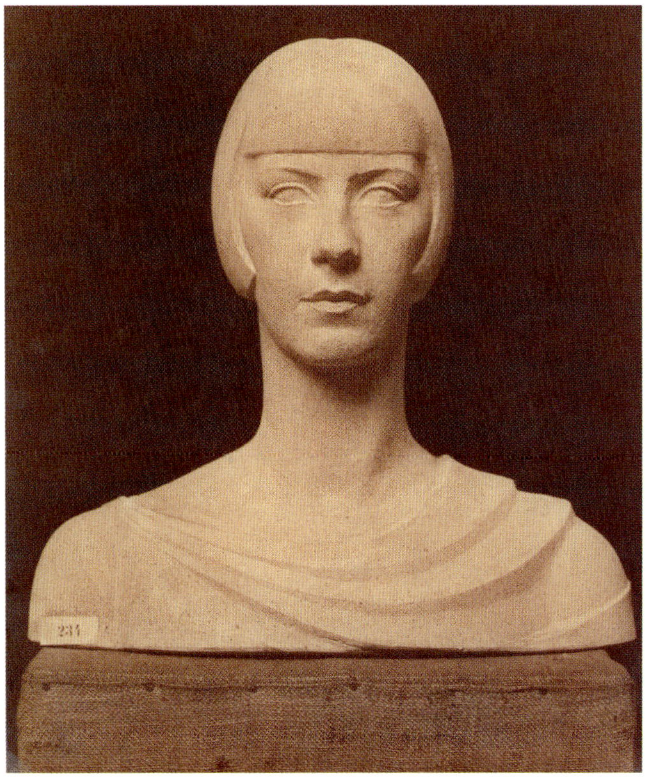

Terracotta bust of Raymonde Guerbe by her husband Pierre Le Faguays exhibited at the Salon d'Automme in 1926.

As an artist she used both her real name, Raymonde Guerbe, and the pseudonym Andrée Guerval. Born in Paris, she was a multi-faceted artist who worked in many media, including bronze, ceramics and terracotta.

Around 1919, Raymonde Guerbe was a student at the dance school in Paris run by Isadora Duncan and her brother Raymond; she took part in many performances.

She exhibited at the Salon d'Automne from 1923 to 1927 and again in 1934, 1936 and 1938. In 1923 she exhibited ebony sculptures of Breton women and a stone sculpture. The following year she presented a portrait bust and the polished copper statuette of a young girl. In 1925 her bas-reliefs *La Roue* (The Wheel) and *Aurore* (Aurora) were presented.

In 1923 Andrée Guerval was living at 5 villa des Camélias. Her husband, Pierre Le Faguays, painted a portrait of her that was exhibited at the Salon d'Automne in 1931. She also modelled for his sculptures.

Many of her bronze and ivory sculptures were made by Les Neveux de J. Lehmann, Etling, Susse Frères and Max Le Verrier.

She was also a painter.

Pieces signed by her have often erroneously been attributed to her husband, Pierre Le Faguays. Although the two artists often worked together, pieces signed 'Guerbe' or 'Guerval' were in fact the work of this talented woman.

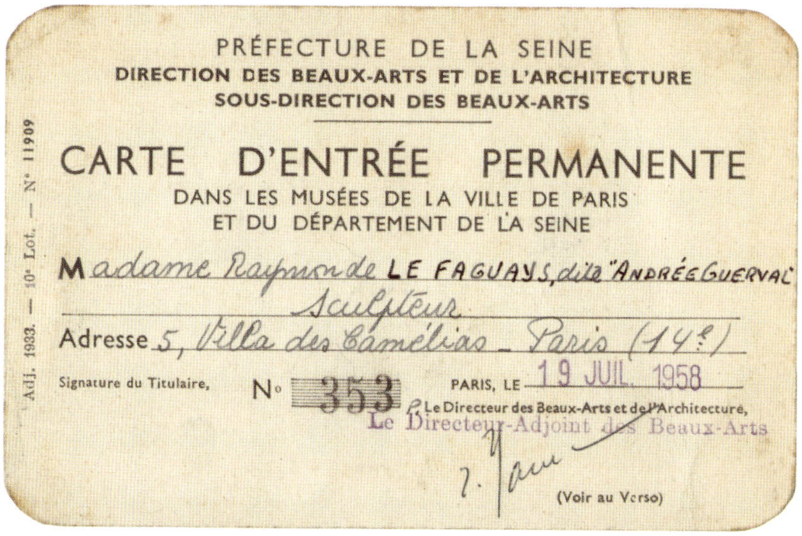

PRÉFECTURE DE LA SEINE
DIRECTION DES BEAUX-ARTS ET DE L'ARCHITECTURE
SOUS-DIRECTION DES BEAUX-ARTS

CARTE D'ENTRÉE PERMANENTE
DANS LES MUSÉES DE LA VILLE DE PARIS
ET DU DÉPARTEMENT DE LA SEINE

Madame Raymonde LE FAGUAYS, dite "ANDRÉE GUERVAL"
Sculpteur
Adresse 5, Villa des Camélias - Paris (14e)
Signature du Titulaire, N° 353 PARIS, LE 19 JUIL. 1958
Le Directeur des Beaux-Arts et de l'Architecture,
Le Directeur-Adjoint des Beaux-Arts
(Voir au Verso)

Adj. 1933. — 10e Lot. — N° 11909

A card issued in 1958 by the Seine Prefecture entitling Raymonde Le Faguays, as a sculptor, to free entrance to all museums in and around Paris. Both her married name, Raymonde Le Faguays, and her pseudonym, Andrée Guerval, are mentioned on the card.

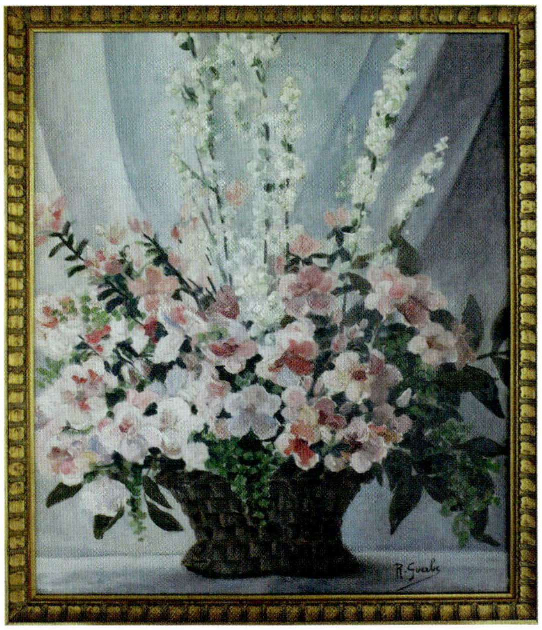

Bouquet of Flowers
Oil on canvas
50 x 60cm. (19¾ x 23½in.)
PRIVATE COLLECTION

Floral Dress
Bronze and ivory on onyx base
Height: 28.5cm. (11¼in.)
PRIVATE COLLECTION

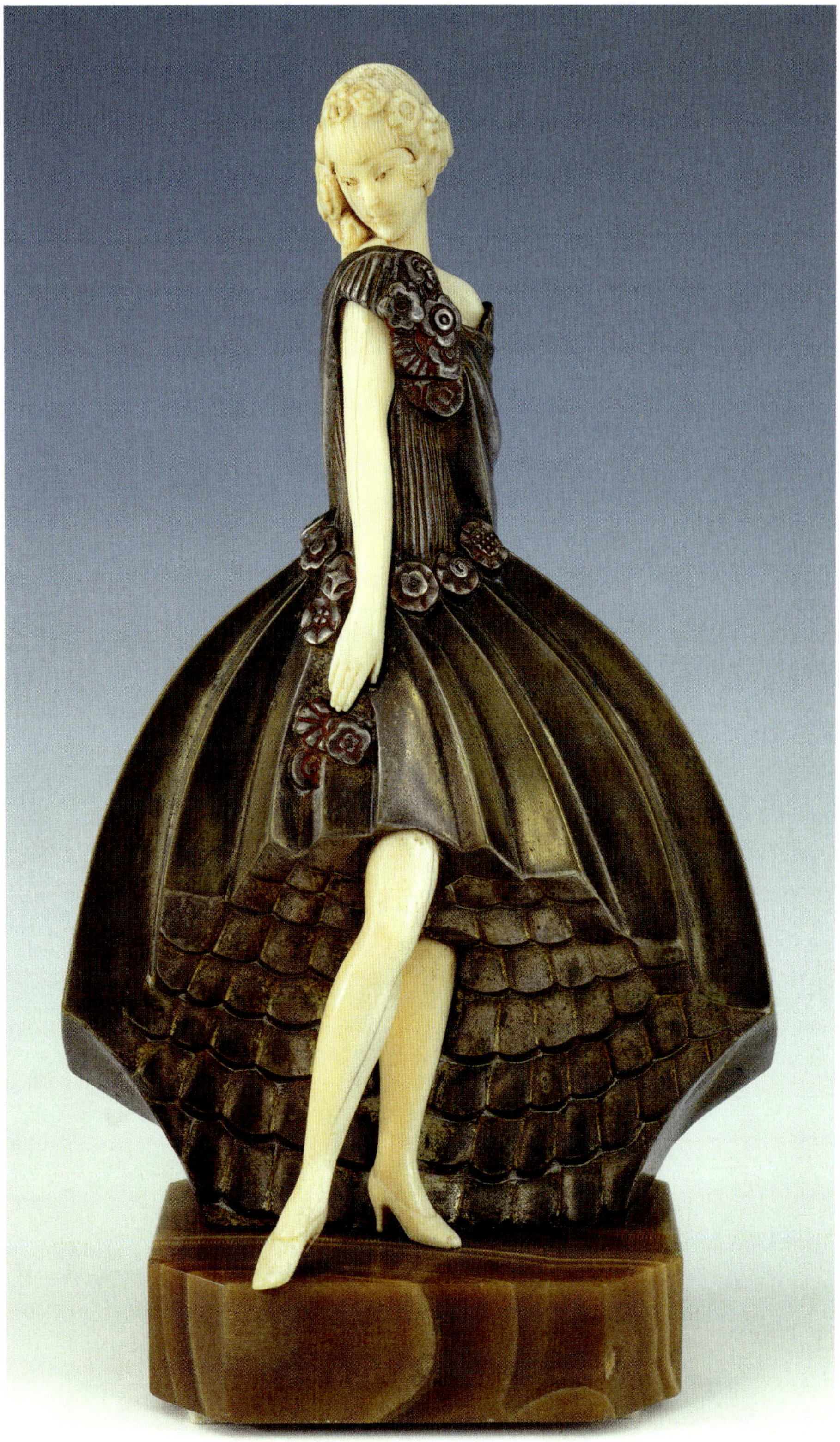

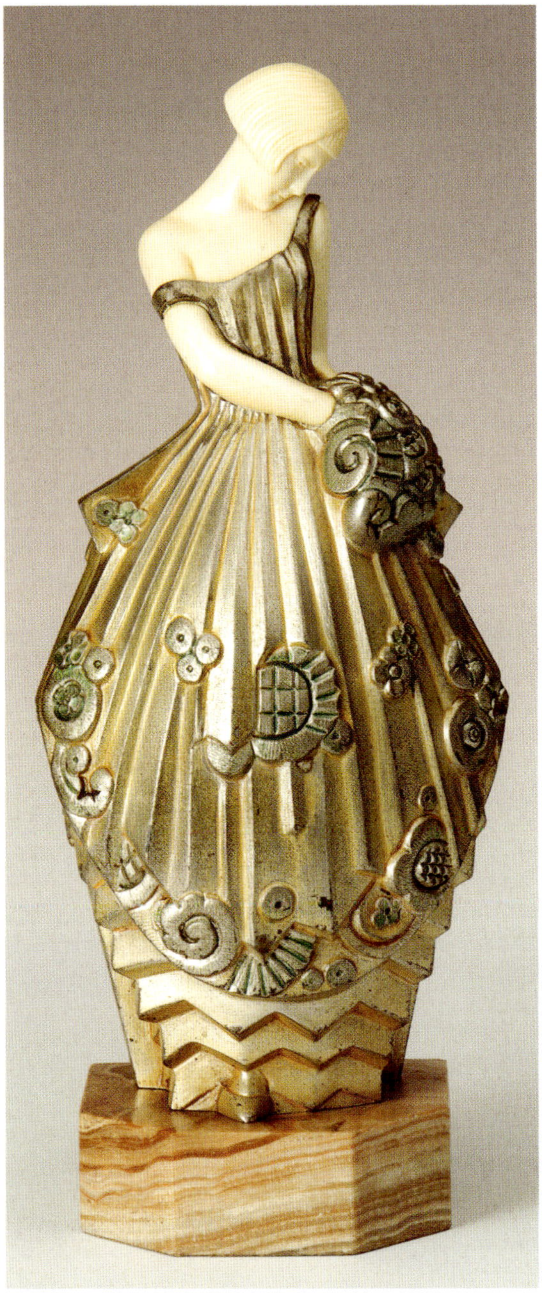

The Bouquet
Bronze and ivory on onyx base
Height: 24cm. (9½in.)
DINO MENASCHE COLLECTION

GUIRAUD-RIVIÈRE, Maurice

(Toulouse 1881 – 1947)

Born in Toulouse, France, Guiraud-Rivière did not immediately choose an artist's life. At 15, he was a sailor and at 20, an actor. His artistic career began at the Paris Ecole Nationale des Beaux Arts, where he studied under Antonin Mercié.

Guiraud-Rivière's fame began in the early years of the 20th century. He became a member of the Société des Artistes Français, where he exhibited at the Salon for the first time in 1907, and where he won an Honourable Mention in 1914. He continued to exhibit at the Salon of the SAF throughout the 1920s and '30s, and took part in the 1937 International Exhibition of Arts and Techniques in Paris. He began exhibiting at the Salon d'Automne in 1906, with *Groupe de Combatants* (Group of Fighters) and *Danseuse Espagnole* (Spanish Dancer). He is also said to have taken part in the Salon des Humoristes, where comical works were shown.

He worked in many media, producing paintings, as well as drawings and illustrations for several magazines. His sculptures — mostly in bronze or bronze and ivory, sometimes cold-painted — were produced by Etling et Cie, Les Neveux de J. Lehmann and André Fau; the ceramic pieces were produced by Sèvres and Robj.

He sold several sculptures to the French state and the city of Paris, including *David Lançant la Fronde* (David with the Slingshot, 1908); and *Enigma* (1926).

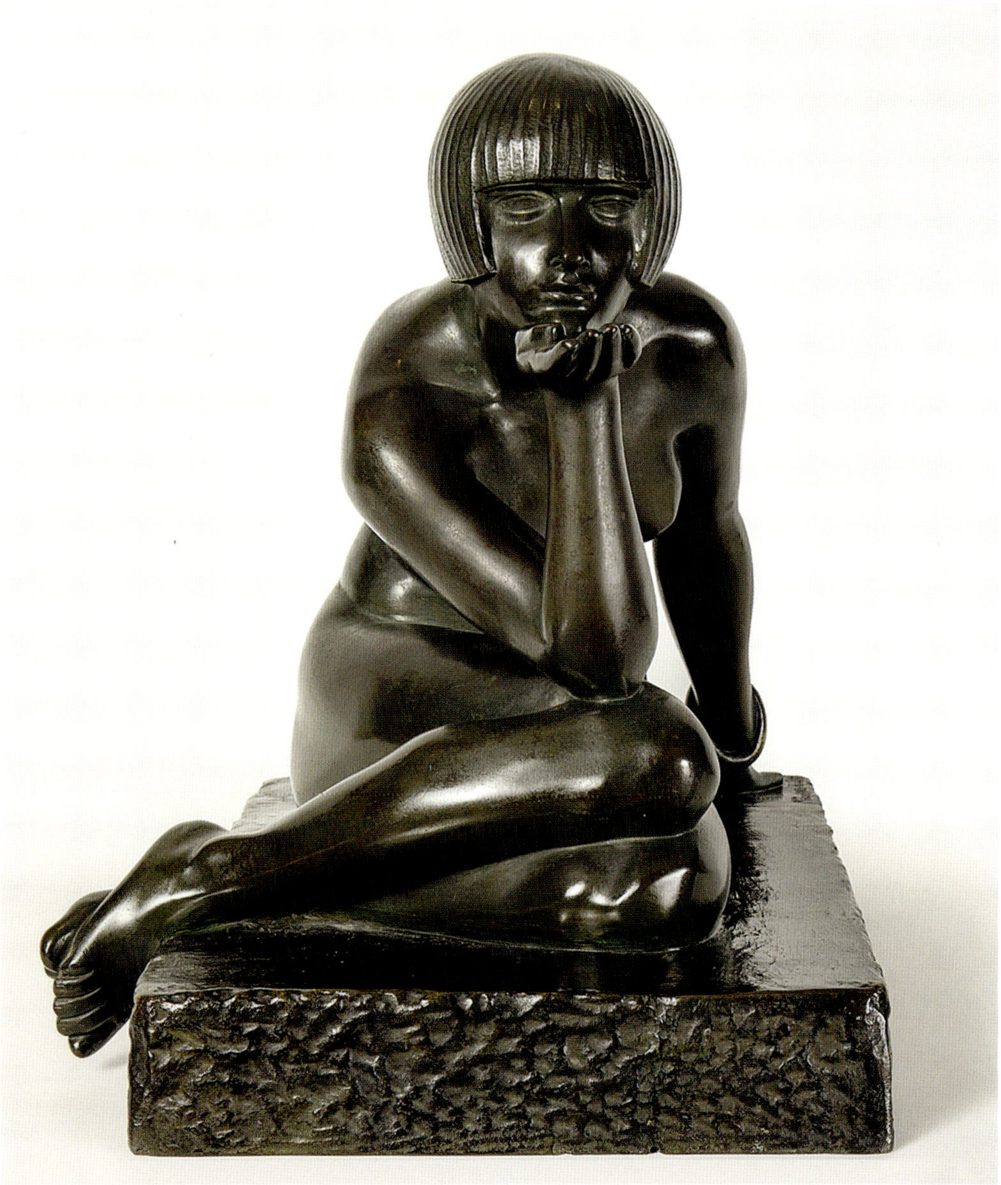

Enigma
Bronze
Height: 37cm. (14½in.)
PRIVATE COLLECTION

Also produced 19cm. (7½in.) high

Nordica
Bronze and ivory on marble base
Height: 73.5cm. (29in.)
PRIVATE COLLECTION

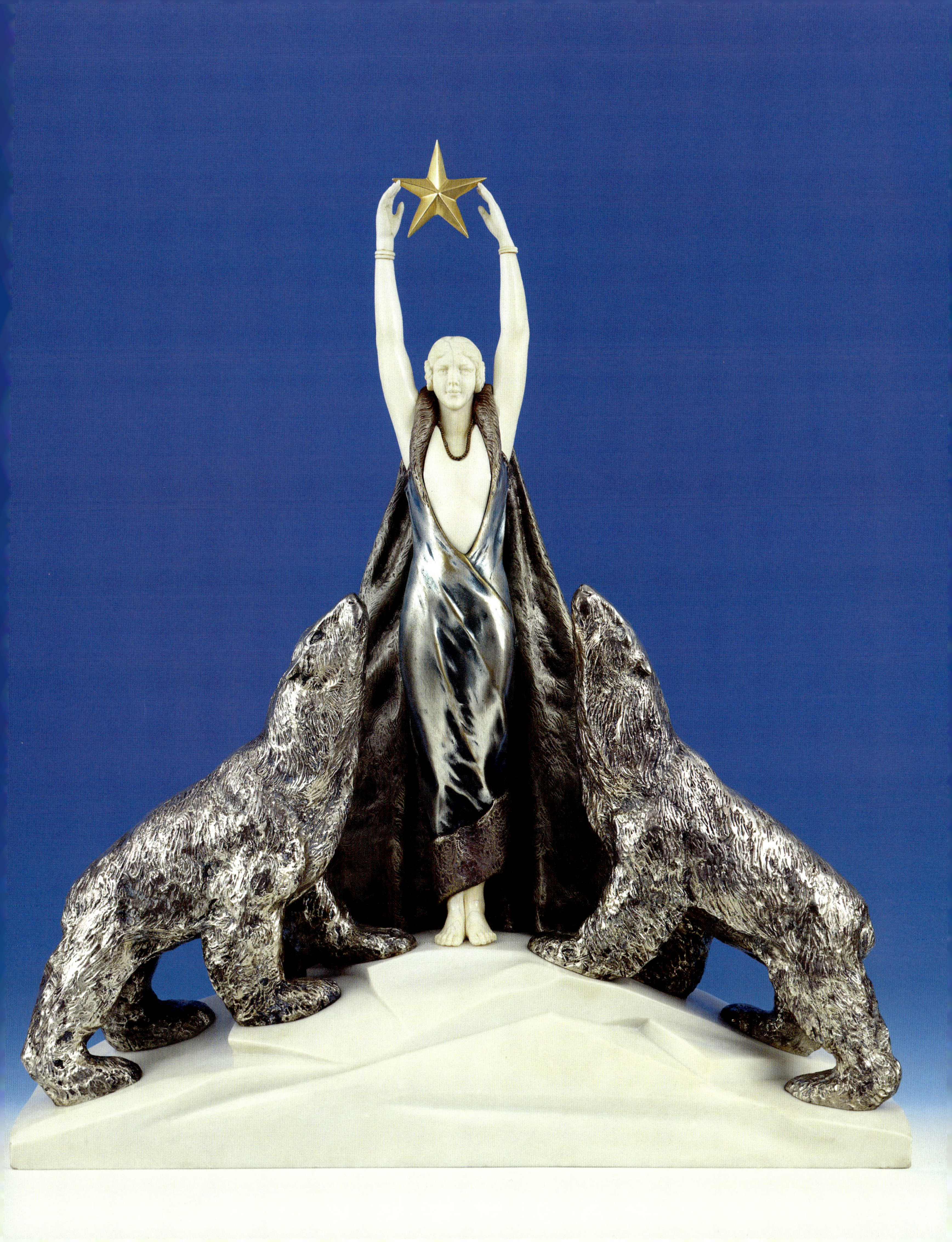

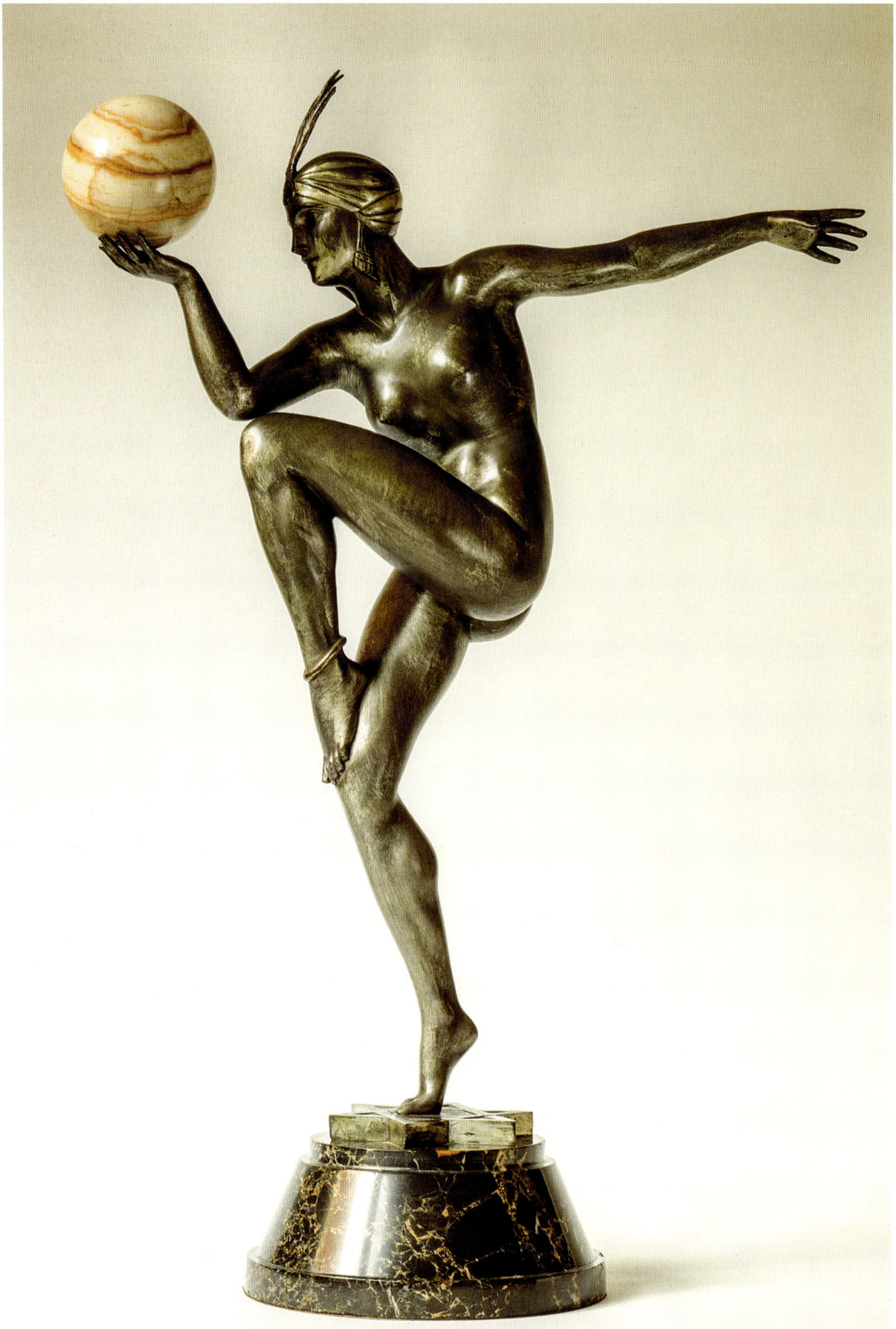

Stella
Bronze and marble on marble base
Height: 66cm. (26in.)
PRIVATE COLLECTION

Etoiles
Bronze on marble base
Height: 63.5cm. (25in.)
PRIVATE COLLECTION

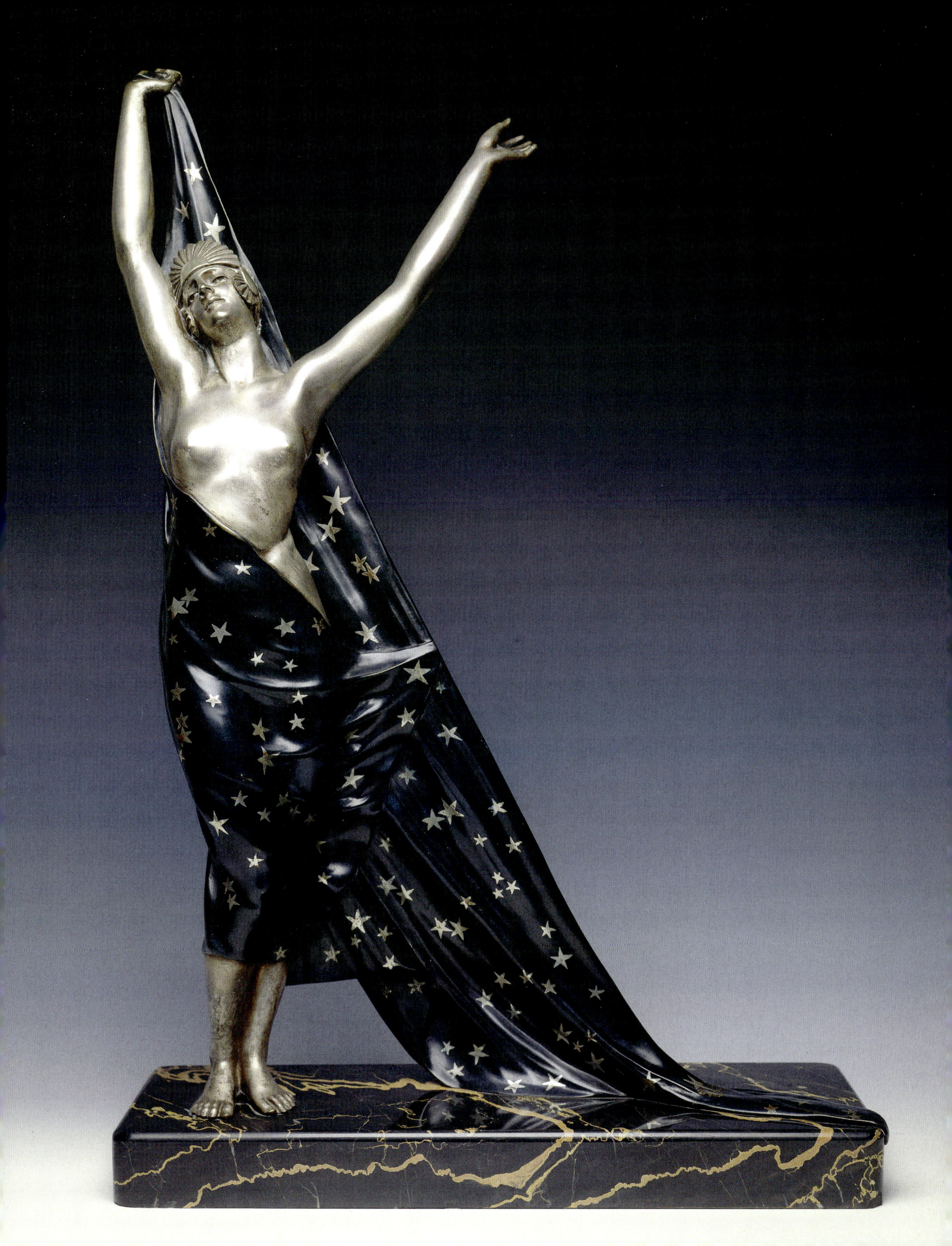

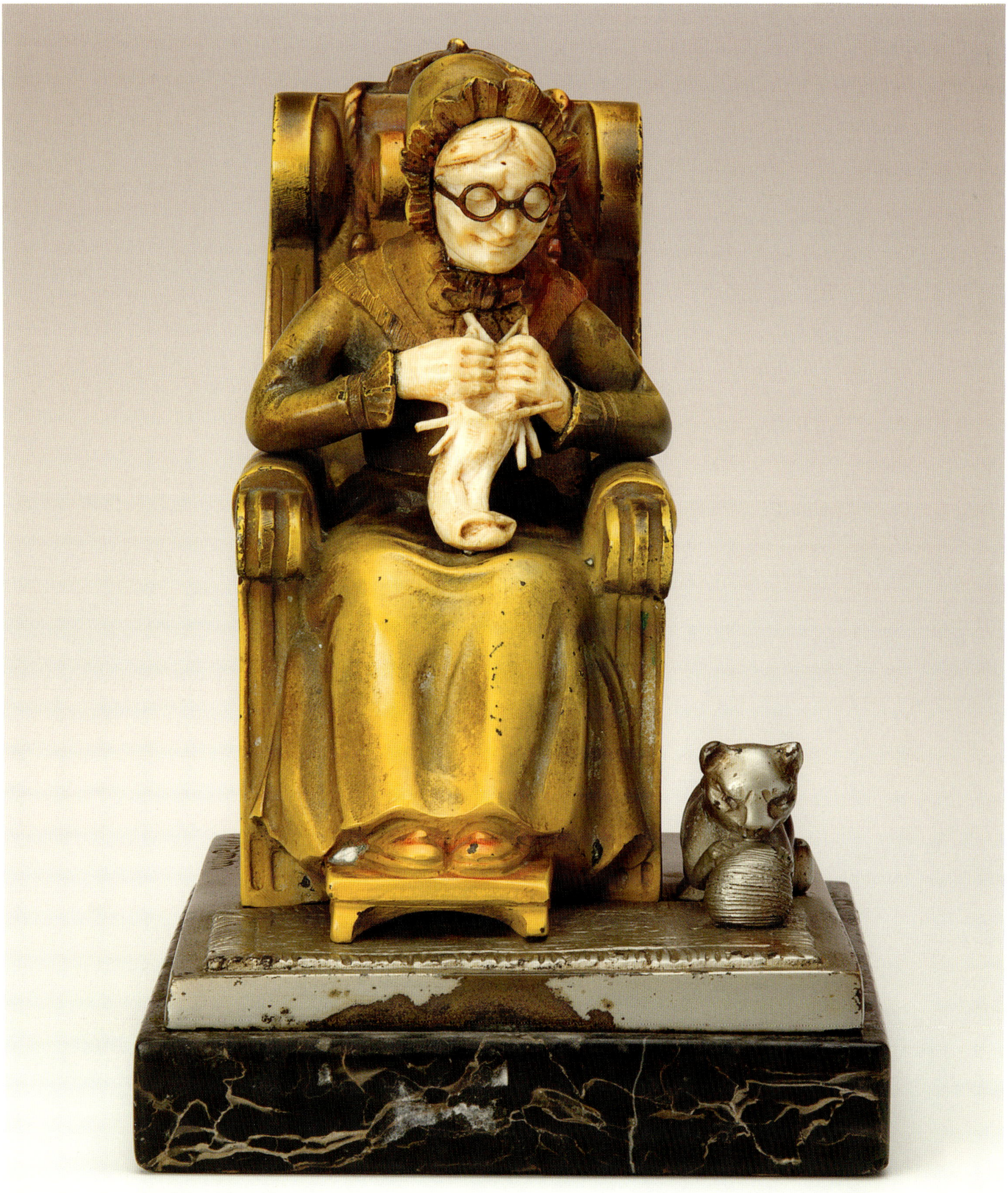

Old Friends
Bronze and ivory on marble base
Height: 15cm. (6in.)
HEBERT GOMES COLLECTION

HARDERS, Hans

(Morelia 1875 – 1955)

German. Studied in Berlin and in Dresden at the Academy of Fine Arts. Worked for Rosenthal und Maeder and later for Preiss & Kassler.

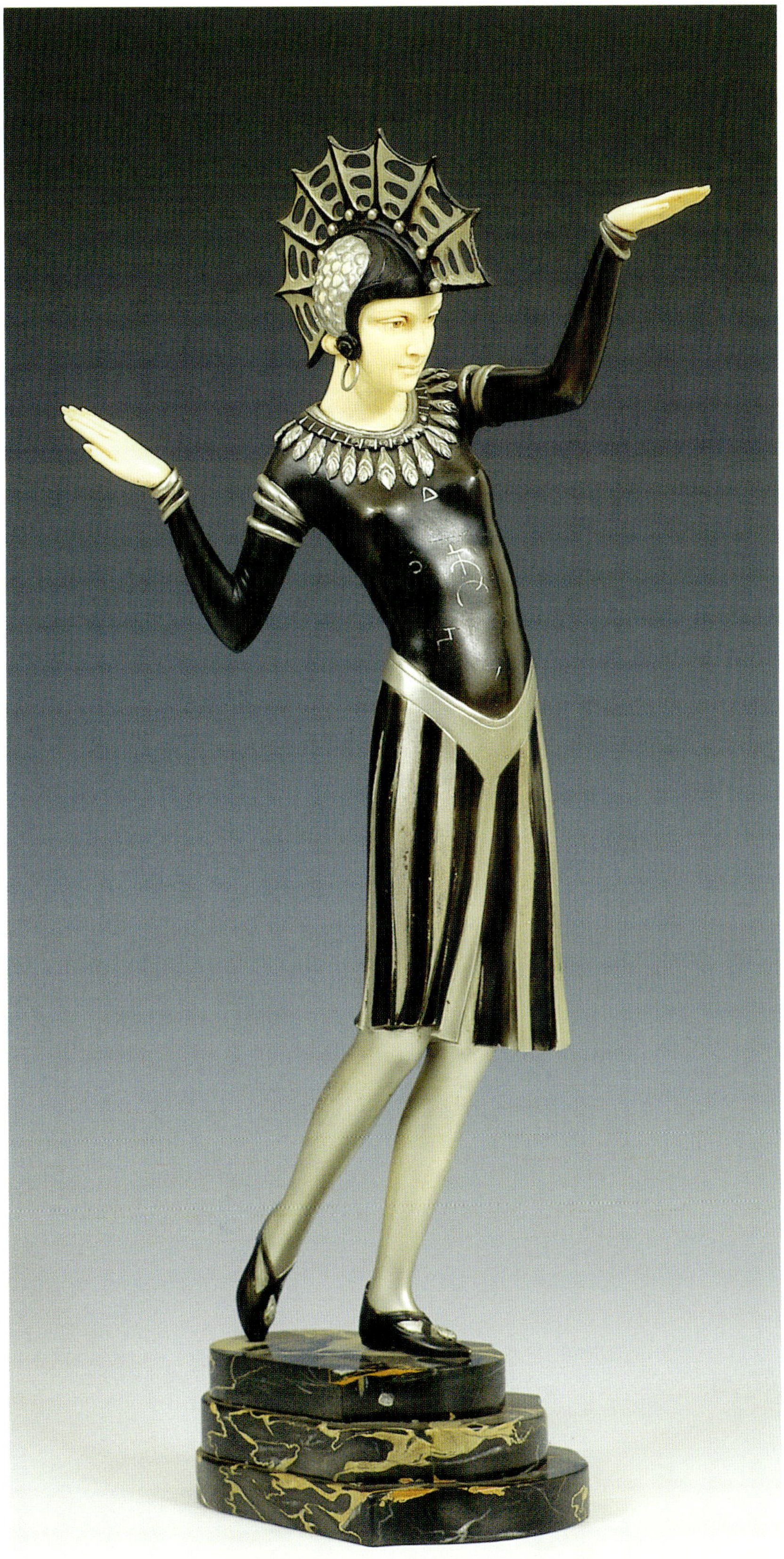

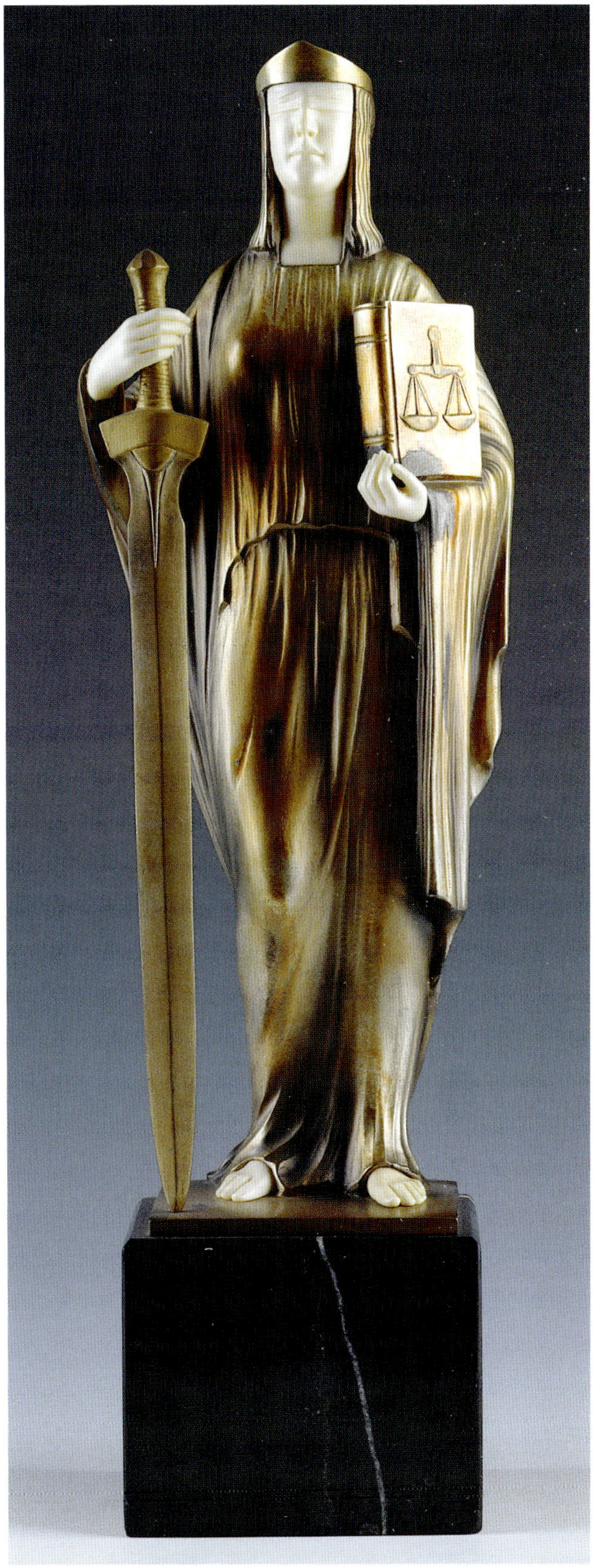

Justice
Bronze and ivory on marble base
Height: 41.5cm. (16¼in.)
RIA KOLLETZKY COLLECTION, GERMANY

Metropolis
Bronze and ivory on marble base
Height: 50cm. (19¾in.)
RONNIE PRICE COLLECTION, SOUTH AFRICA

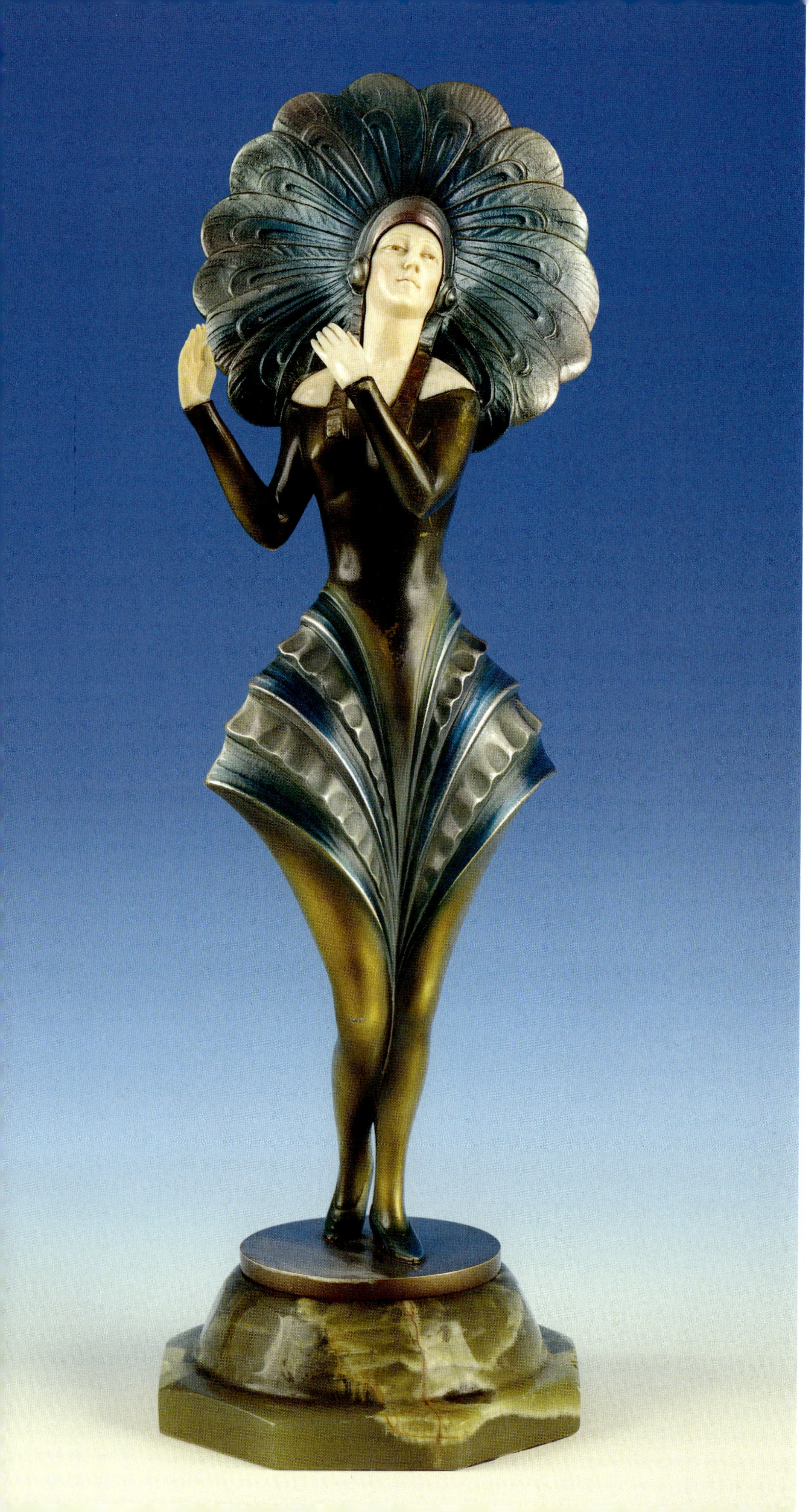

Revue Dancer
Bronze and ivory on onyx base
Height: 35cm. (13¾in.)
PRIVATE COLLECTION

HEUVELMANS, Lucienne Antoinette Adelaide

(Paris 1881 – Saint-Caste 1944)

French. She studied at the Ecole des Beaux Arts with Marqueste, Hannaux and Puech. She exhibited at the Salon de la Société des Artistes Français. In 1911 she became the first woman to win the *Prix de Rome*, which enabled her to study and work in Rome too. She worked for Sèvres. She was awarded the Legion d'Honneur in 1926.

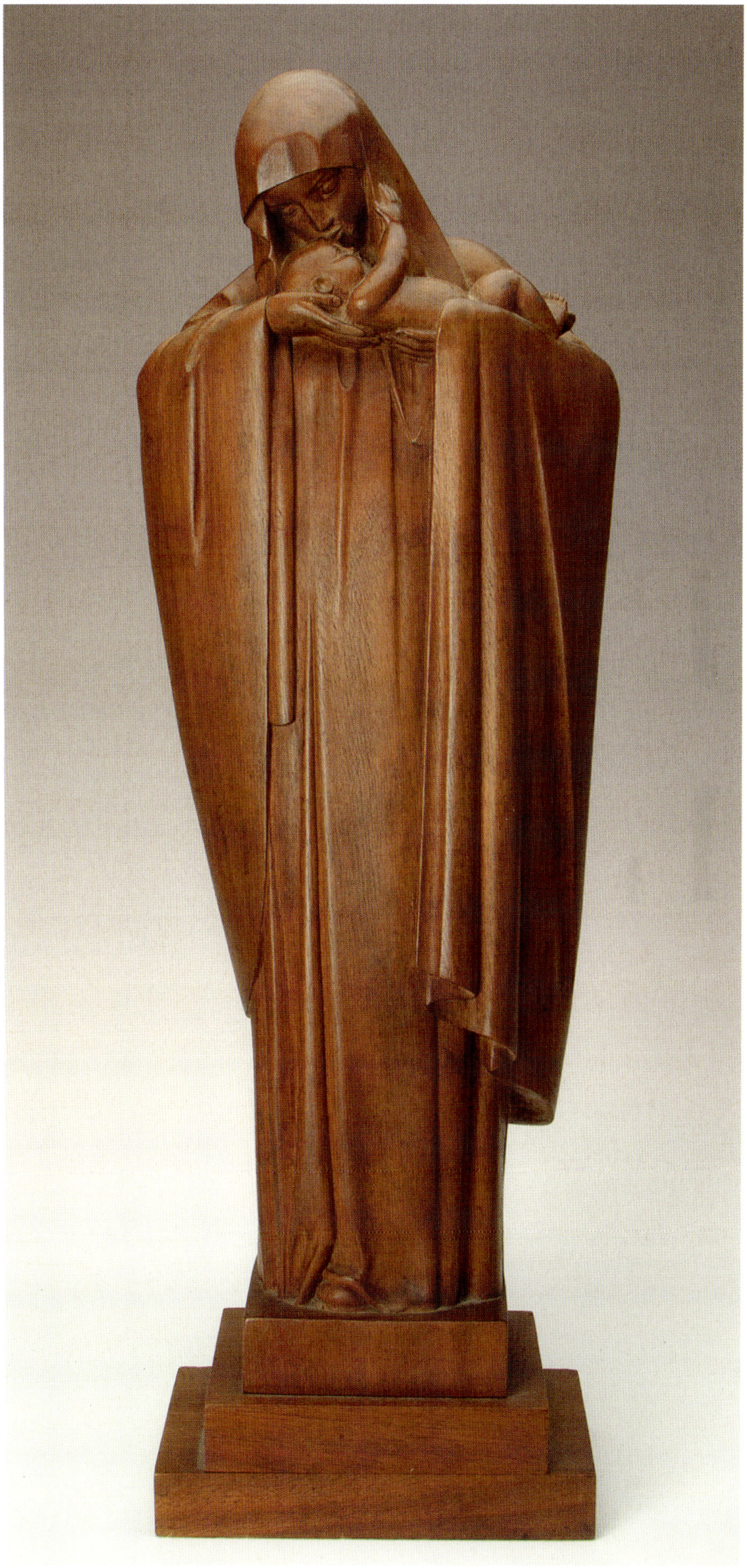

Adoration
Wood
Height: 53.5cm. (21in.)
PRIVATE COLLECTION

HOFFMAN, Alfred

(1879 – ?)

Austrian. A pupil of Anton Brenck. Hoffman travelled extensively in Italy; his subjects were mainly classical.

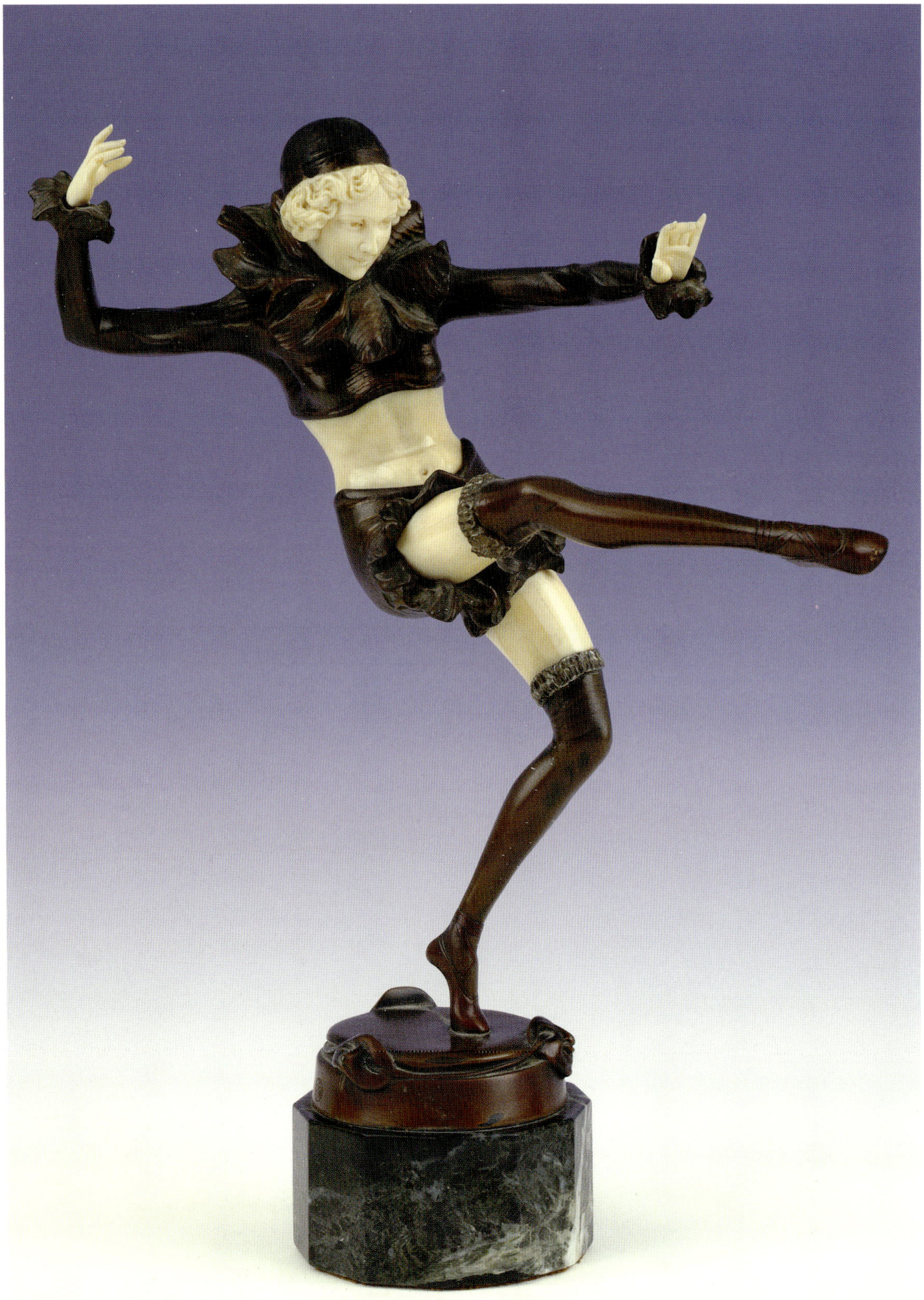

Pierrette
Bronze and ivory on marble base
Height: 32.5cm. (12¾in.)
PRIVATE COLLECTION

Godiva
Bronze and ivory on onyx base
Height: 19cm. (7½in.)
DINO MENASCHE COLLECTION

Also produced 43cm. (17in.) high

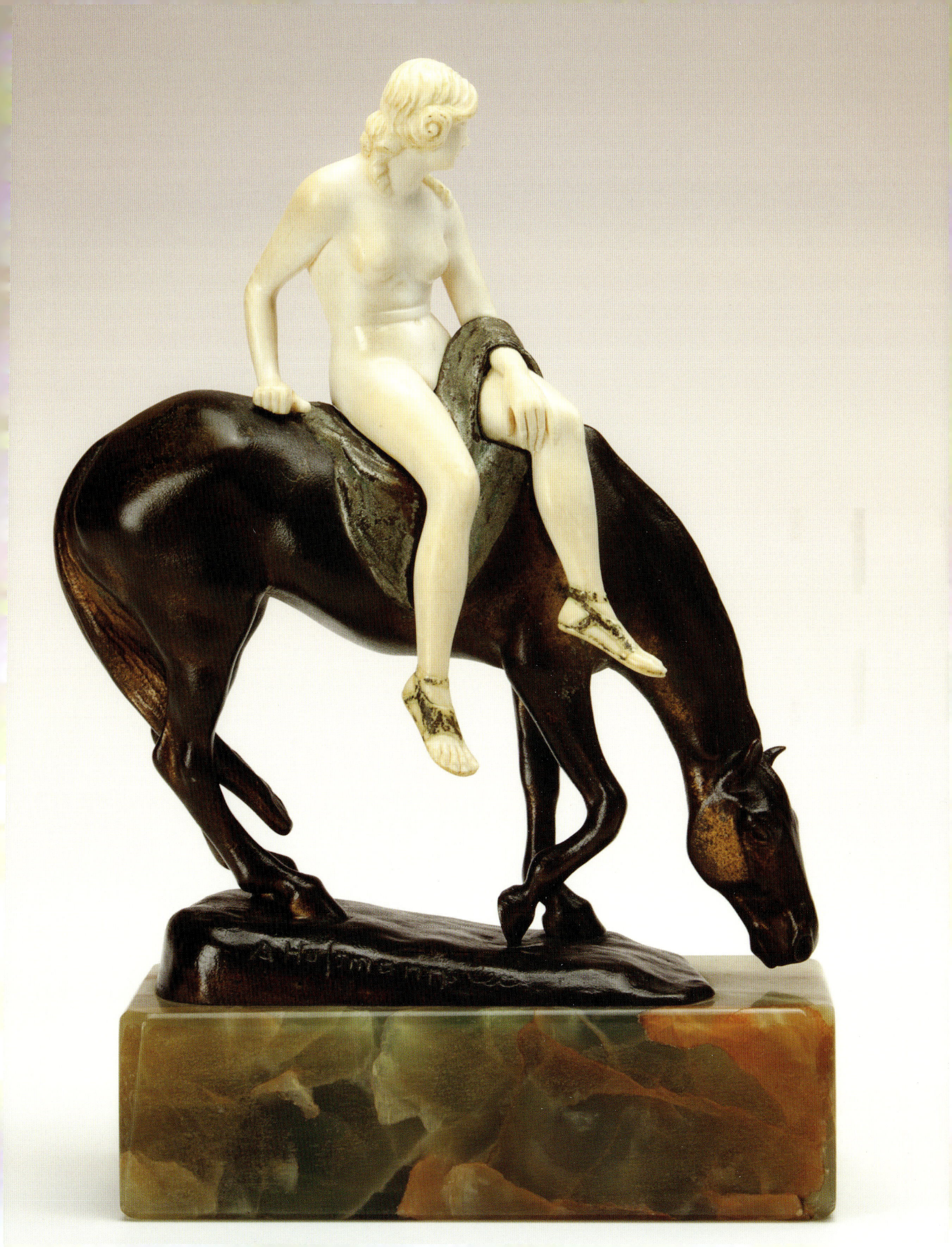

JACQUEMIN, Jean

(1894 – 1941)

A French sculptor, active in the Art Deco period. This *could* be the firm Jacquemin et Blériot, Paris (28 rue Michel Le Comte), which exhibited decorative objects and household objects, including ivory ones, at the 1937 International Exhibition of Arts and Techniques in Paris.

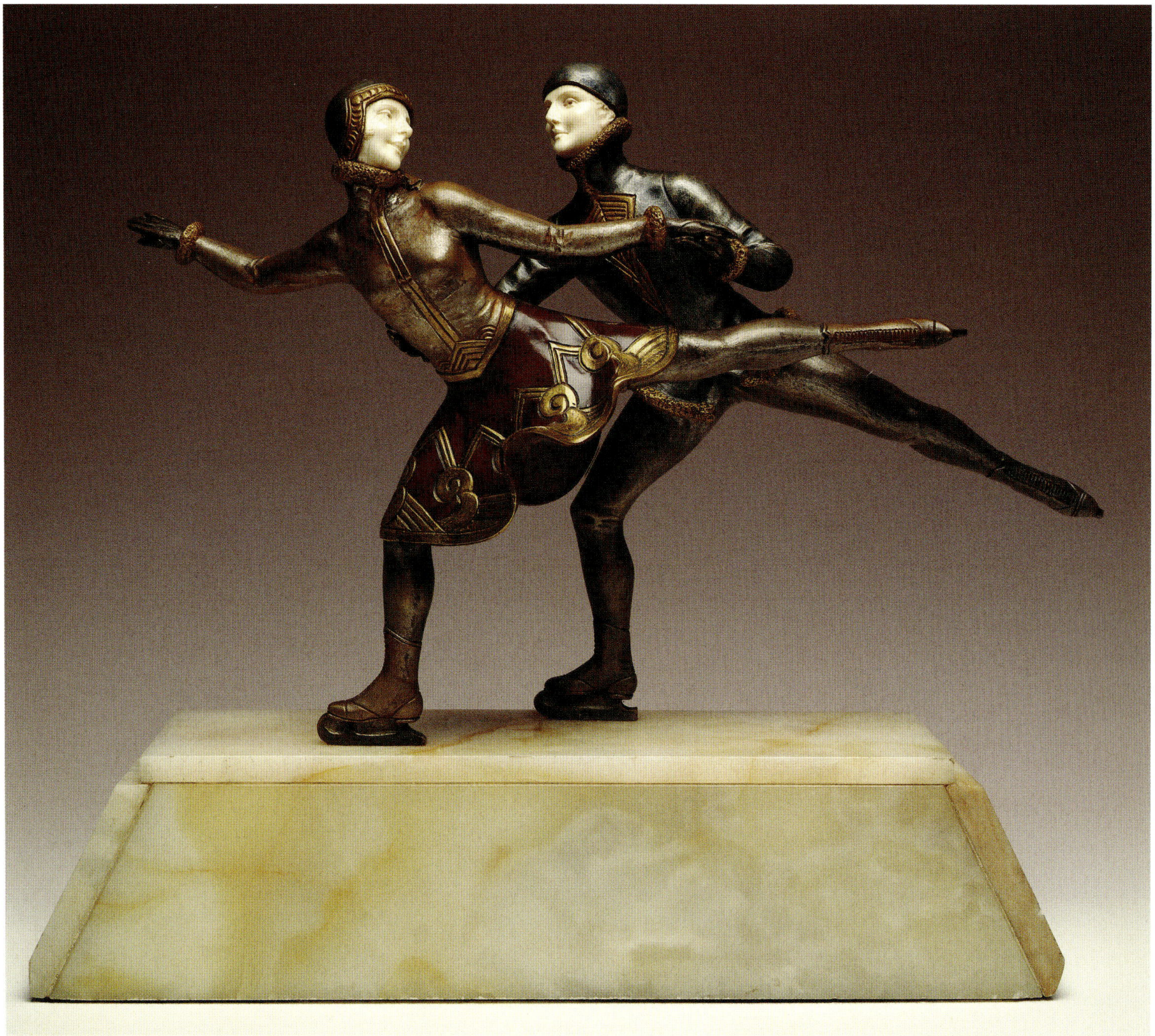

Skaters
Bronze and ivory on marble base
Height: 32.5cm. (12¾in.)
PRIVATE COLLECTION

Skier
Bronze and ivory on marble base
Height: 28cm. (11in.)
PRIVATE COLLECTION

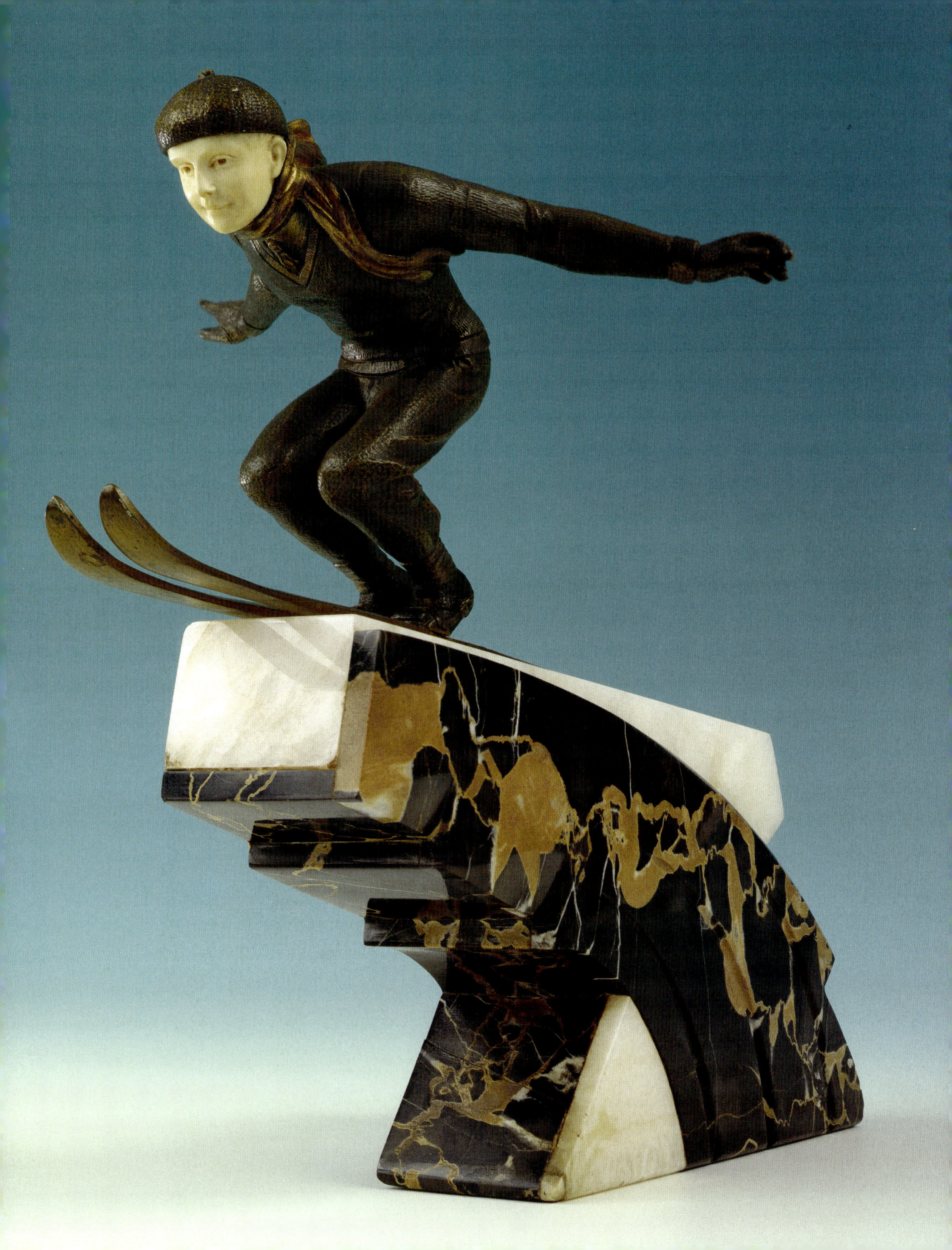

JAEGER, Ernst Gustav

(1880 – ?)

German. Specialised in nudes, animal and Oriental subjects.

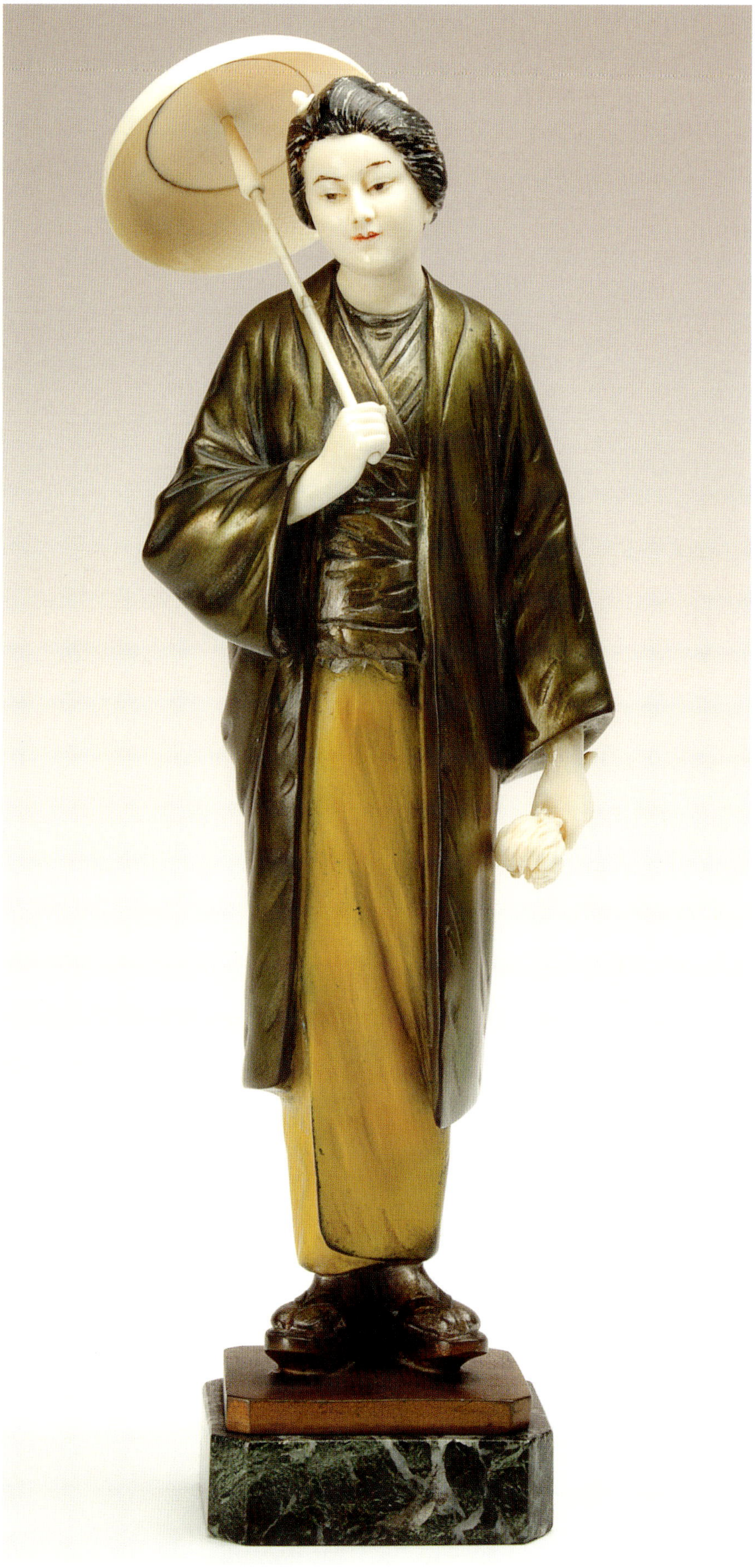

Oriental Beauty
Bronze and ivory on marble base
Height: 27.5cm. (10¾in.)
DINO MENASCHE COLLECTION

Page with Falcon
Bronze and ivory on marble base
Height: 28cm. (11in.)
DINO MENASCHE COLLECTION

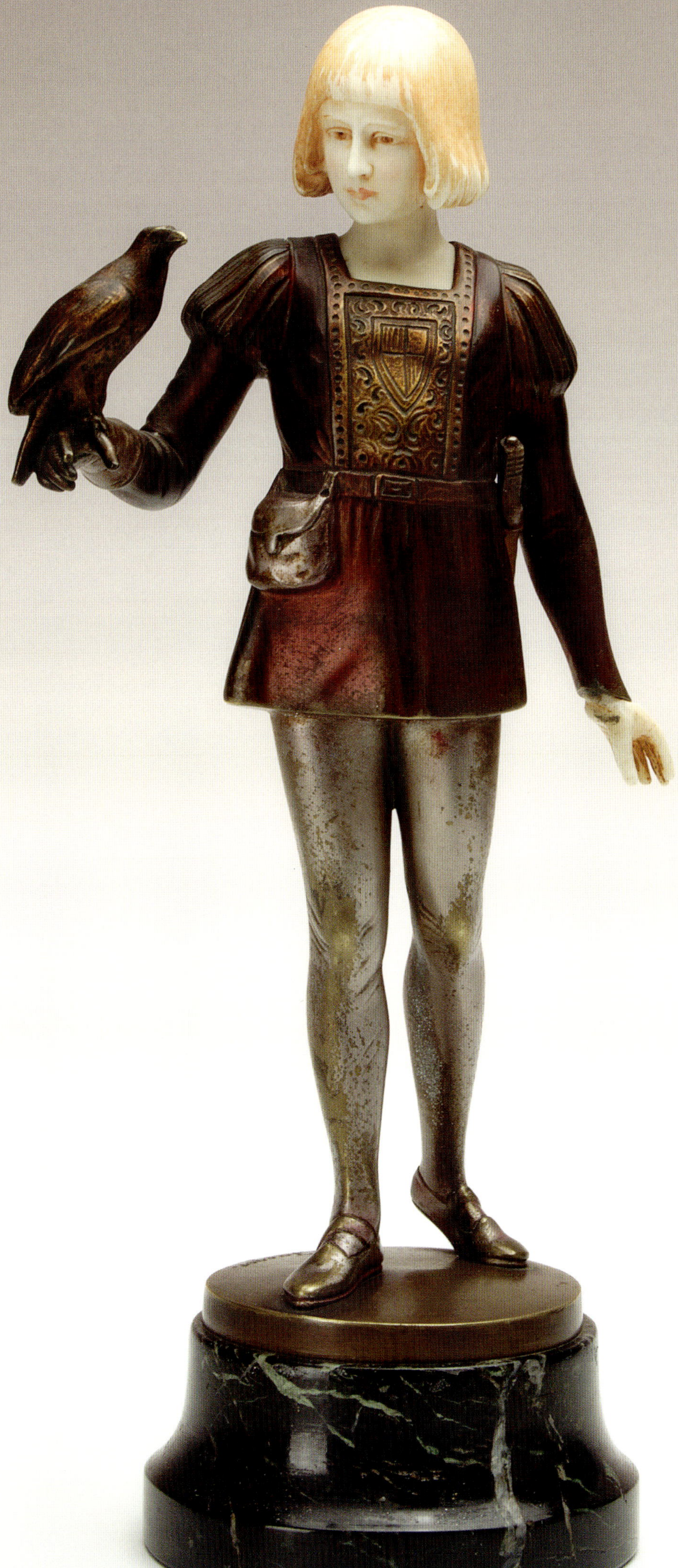

JOREL, Alfred

(c.1860 – Paris 1927)

Born in Paris. A pupil of Carlus.

Jorel created bronze, ivory and chryselephantine sculptures as well as ivory jewellery. His workshop in Paris was at 8 avenue Richerand.

He became a member of the Société des Artistes Français in 1896 and won a medal in 1907.

Many of his figures are of children engaged in everyday activities. They have a certain cuteness and familiarity. He also created works with religious themes.

Workshop continued active after World War II.

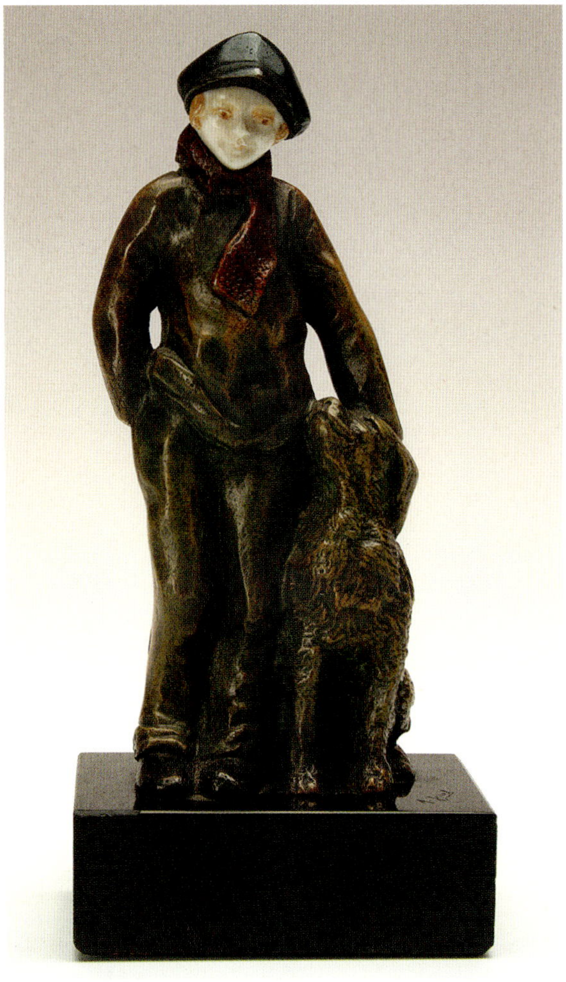

Dog and Friend
Bronze and ivory on marble base
Height: 20.5cm. (8in.)
DINO MENASCHE COLLECTION

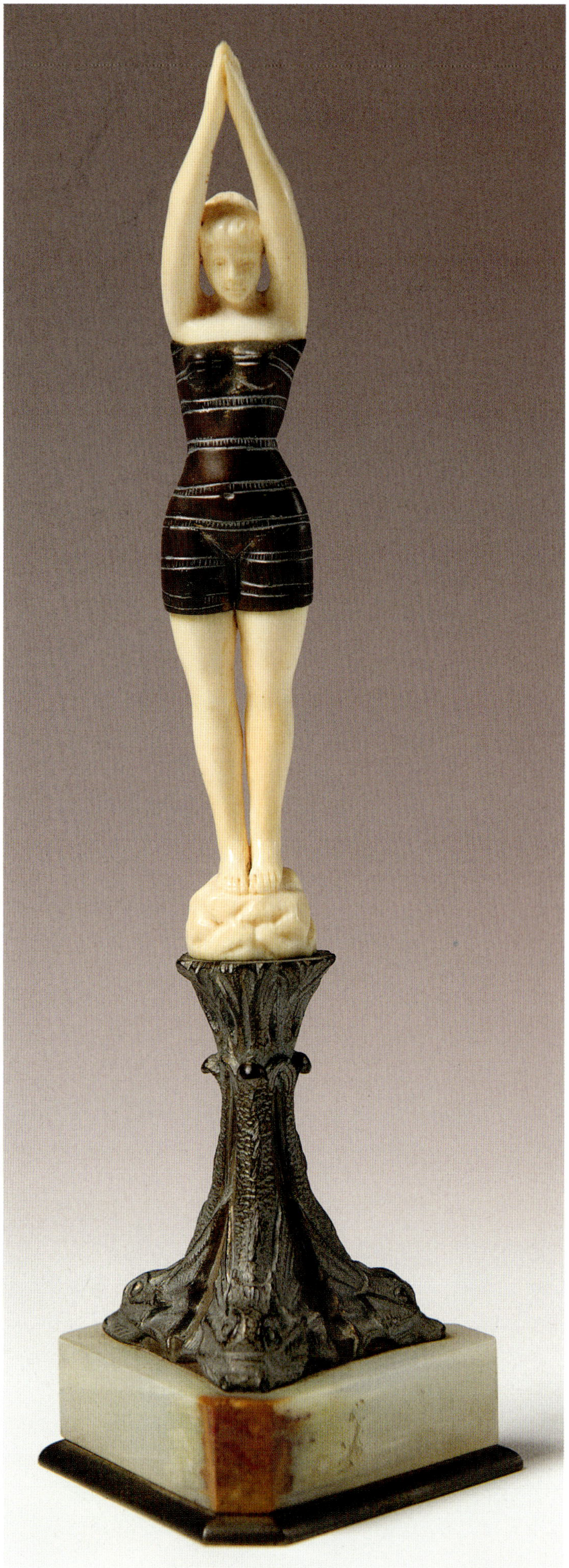

Diver
Bronze and ivory on onyx and bronze base
Height: 21.5cm. (8½in.)
PRIVATE COLLECTION

KECK, Hans

(1875 – 1941)

Born in Austria, he created chryselephantine sculptures that are typical of the transition period between the Art Nouveau and the Art Deco styles.

Keck worked with the Gebrüder Brandel foundry in Berlin.

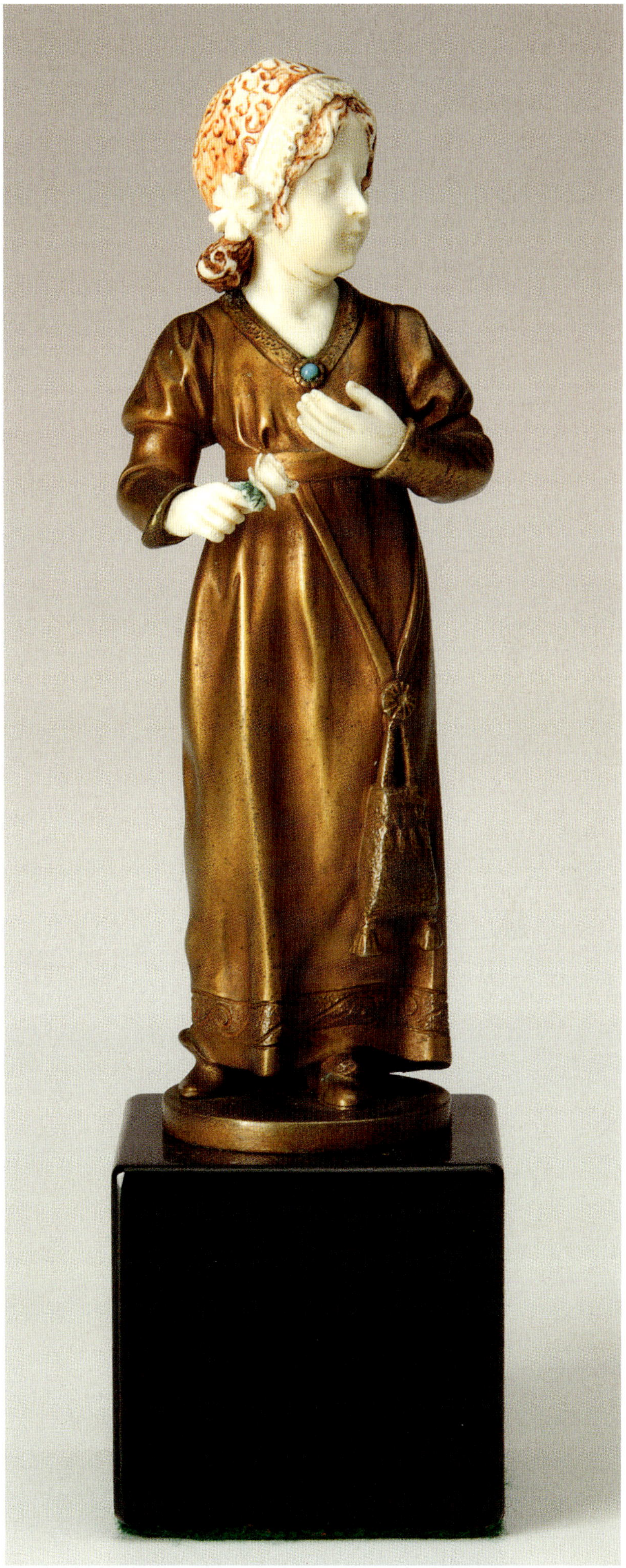

Rose
Bronze and ivory on onyx base
Height: 16cm. (6¼in.)
DINO MENASCHE COLLECTION

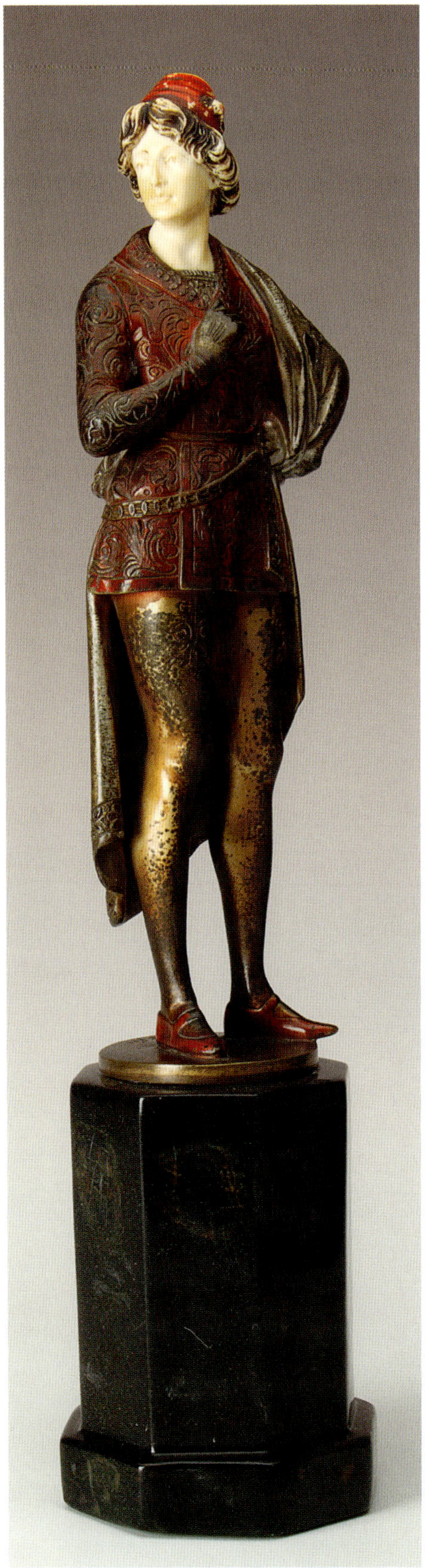

Cavalier
Bronze and ivory on marble base
Height: 32.5cm. (12¾in.)
DINO MENASCHE COLLECTION

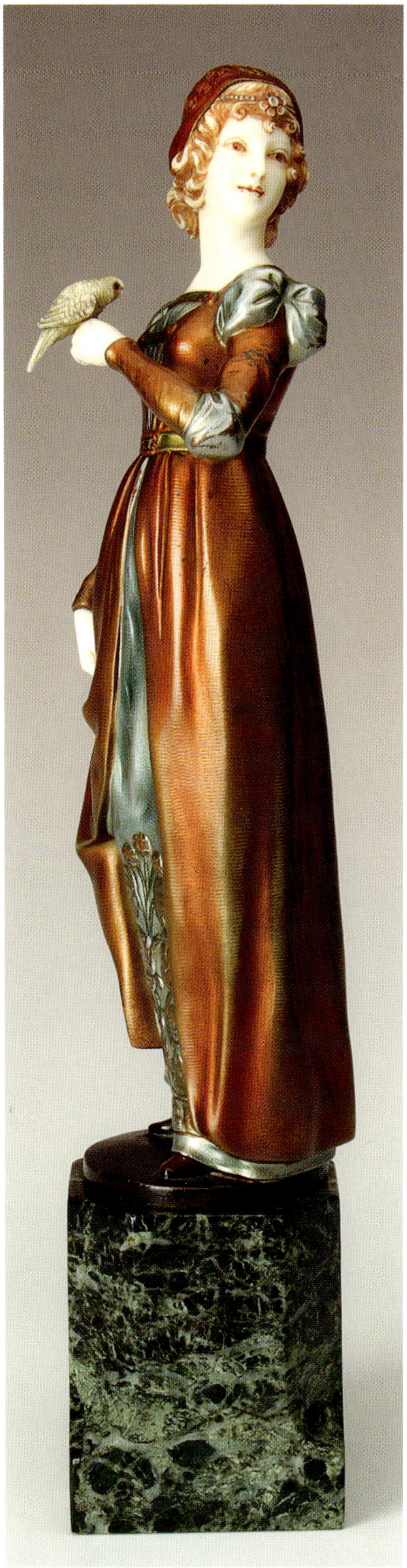

Medieval Lady with Parrot
Bronze and ivory on marble base
Height: 28.5cm. (11¼in.)
DINO MENASCHE COLLECTION

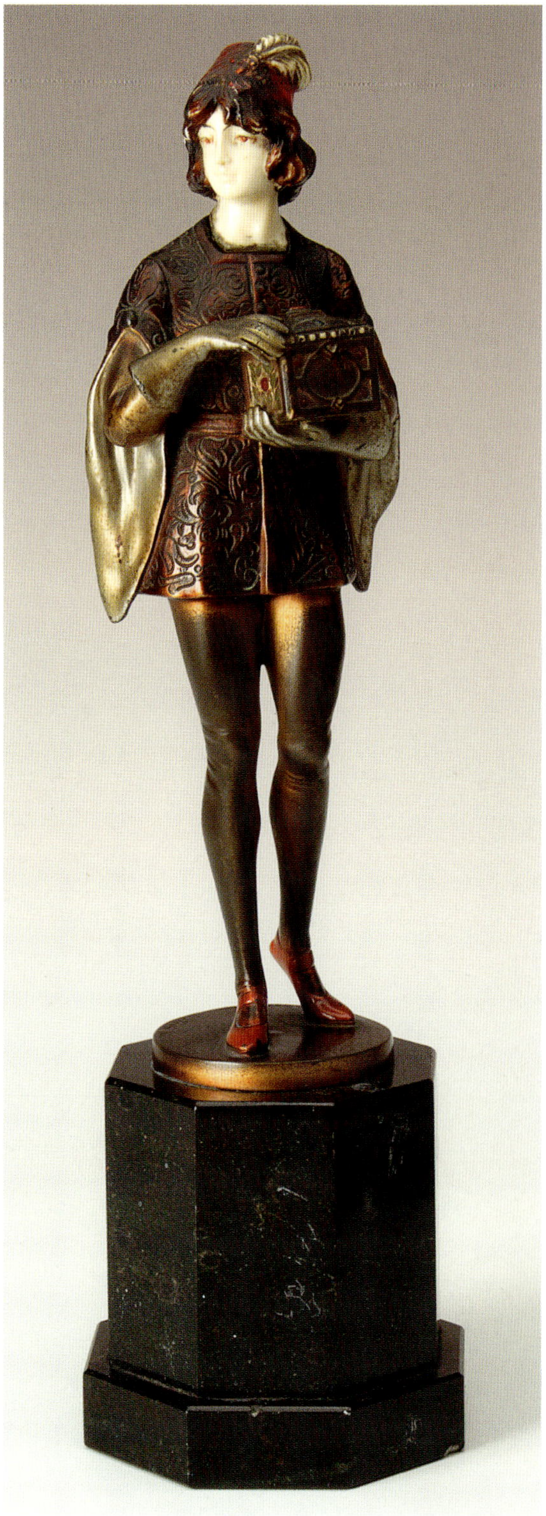

The Offering
Bronze and ivory on onyx base
Height: 26.5cm. (10½in.)
DINO MENASCHE COLLECTION

Indian Dancer
Bronze and ivory on marble base
Height: 33cm. (13in.)
DINO MENASCHE COLLECTION

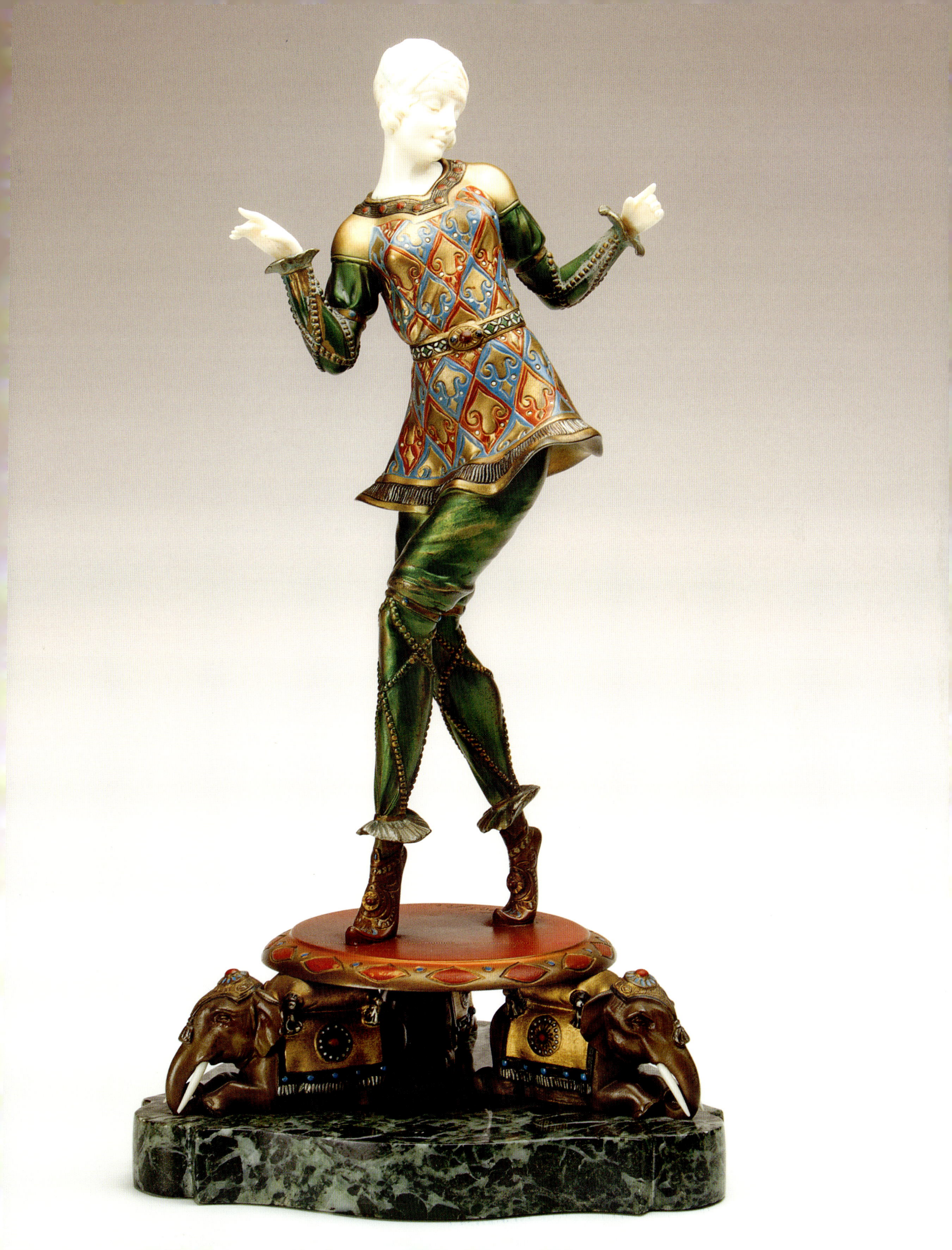

KÉLÉTY, Alexander

(Budapest date unknown – 1940)

Born in Budapest, Hungary, he emigrated to France after World War I studying art in Toulouse under Imre Károly Simay, a well-known Hungarian painter, engraver and animalier sculptor. He later continued his studies in Paris. He exhibited in many salons between the two World Wars.

In 1927 he exhibited a terracotta bust fabricated by Arthur Goldscheider at the Salon of the Société des Artistes Français. In 1928 and 1930 he exhibited more bronze and ivory figures, again by Goldscheider; his work was shown in the Goldscheider and Etling rooms at the 1925 Paris Exhibition. At the International Exhibition of Arts and Techniques in Paris in 1937, he exhibited sculptures produced by Etling and Les Neveux de J. Lehmann, as well as animal sculptures produced by M. Ollier.

A prolific and multi-faceted artist, Kéléty applied the Art Deco style to many decorative objects, such as lamps, incense burners and ashtrays.

His sculpture *The Archer* is particularly well known.

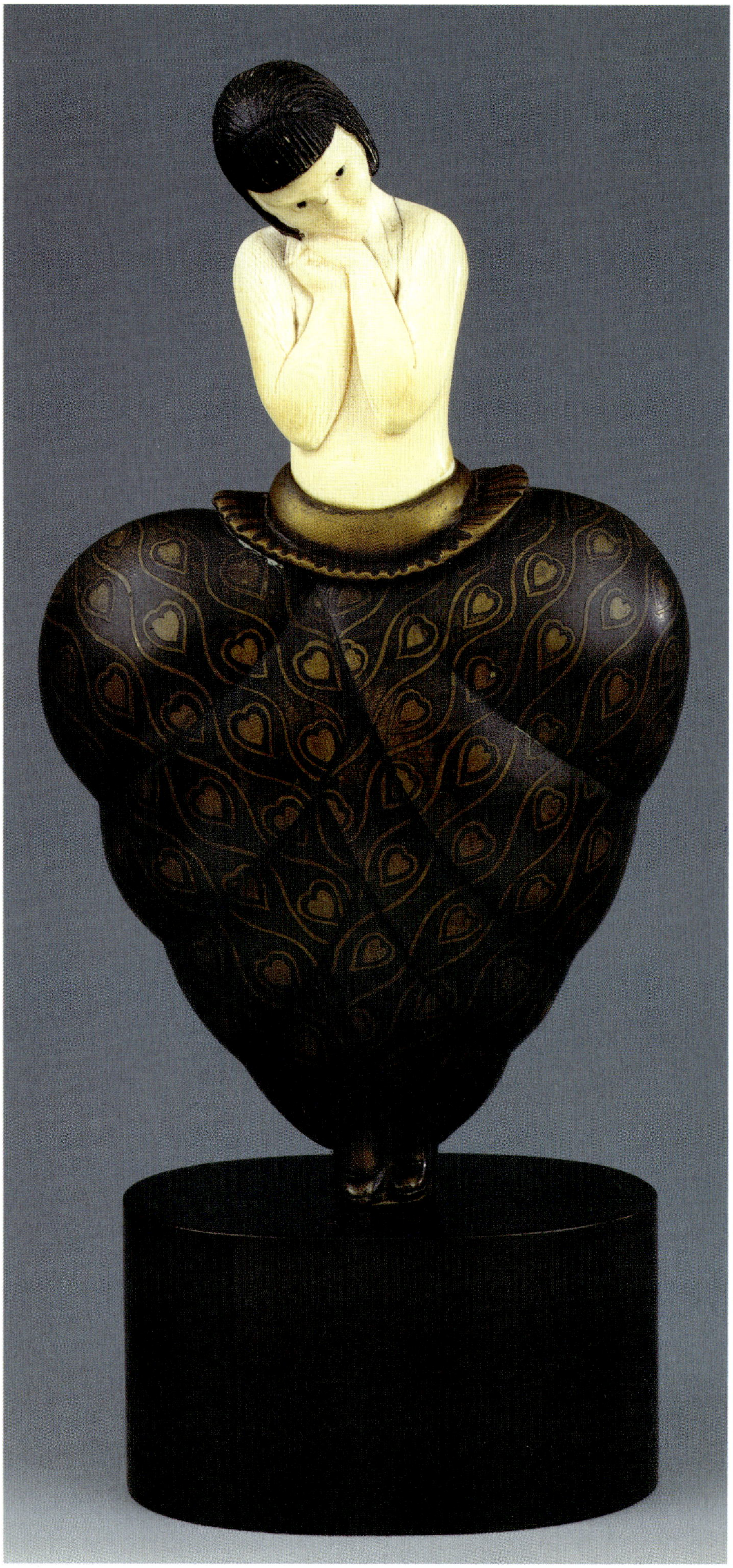

Hearts
Bronze and ivory on marble base
Height: 29.5cm. (11½in.)
PRIVATE COLLECTION

Exotic Dancer
Bronze on marble base
Height: 53cm. (21in.)
PRIVATE COLLECTION

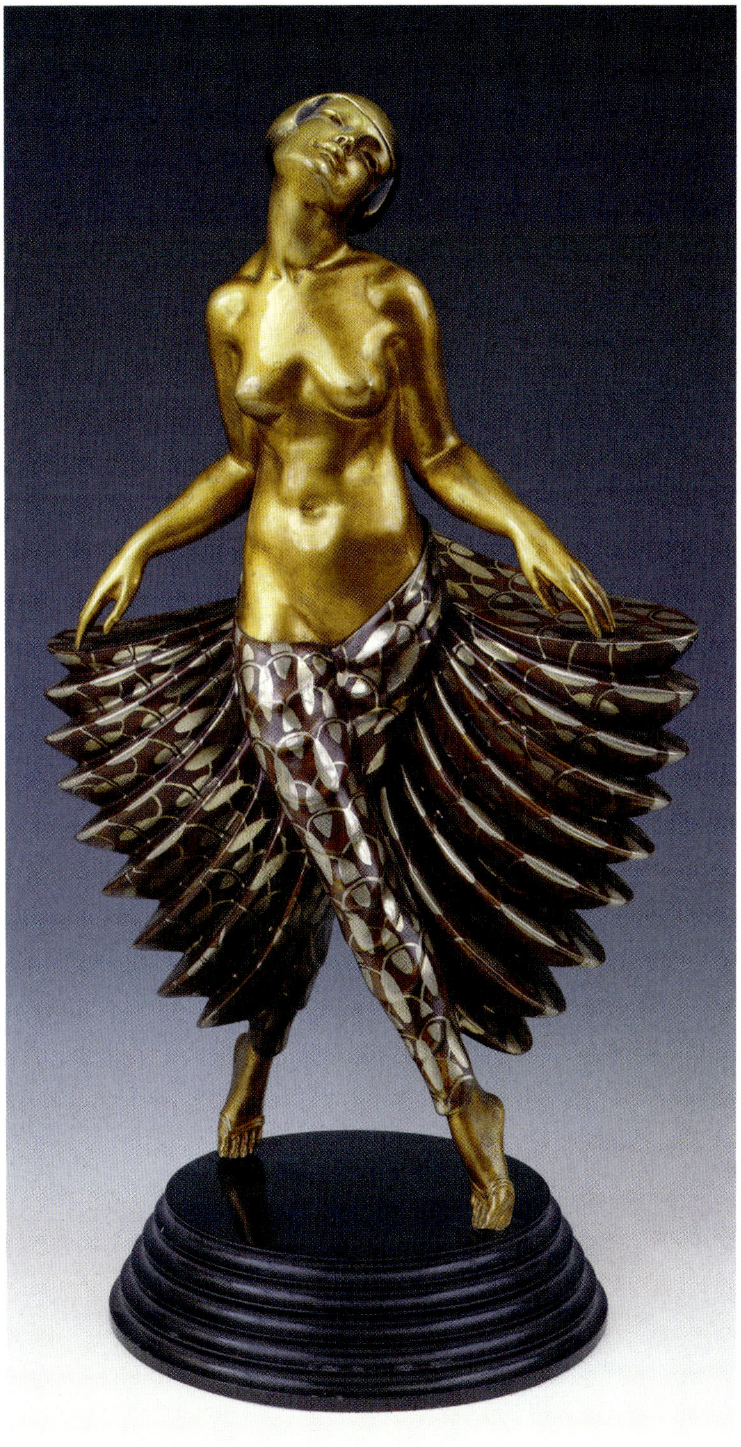

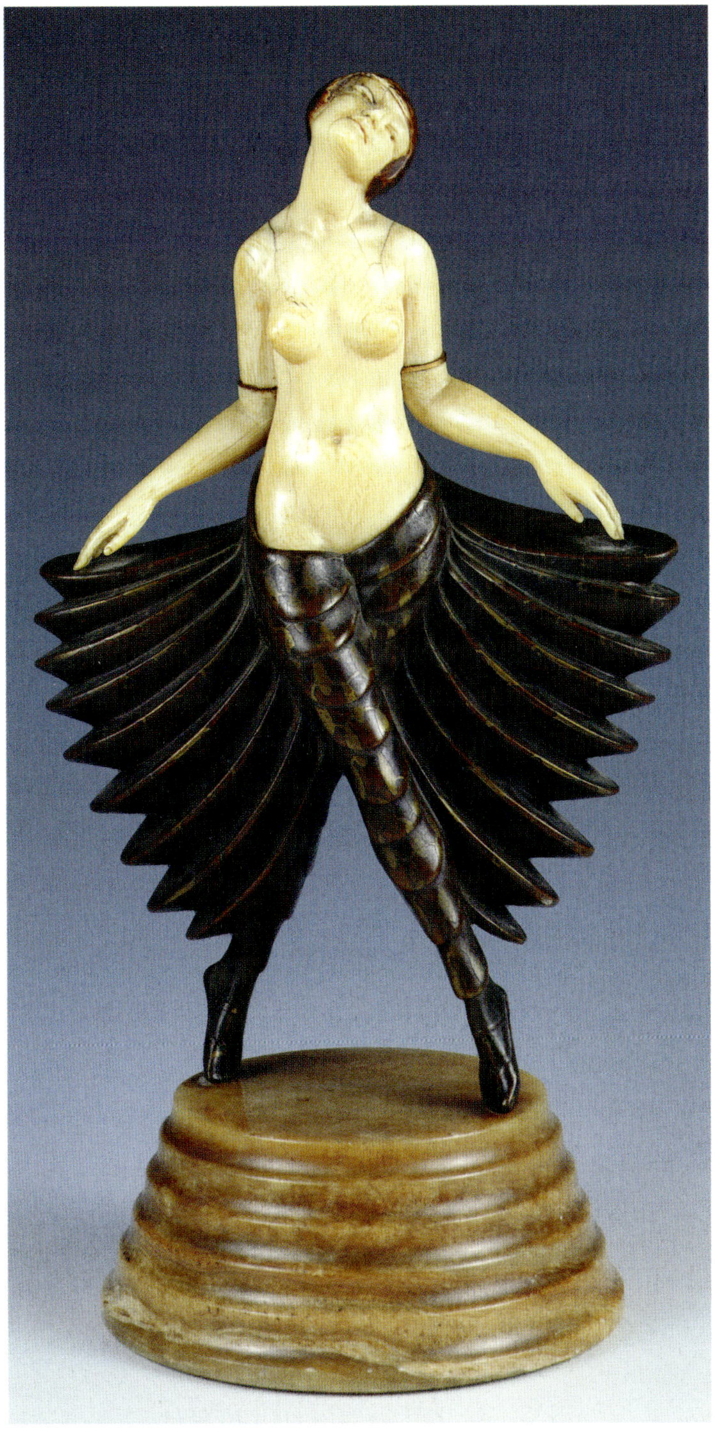

Exotic Dancer
Bronze on onyx base
Height: 28.5cm. (11¼in.)
PRIVATE COLLECTION

Fan Dancer
Bronze and ivory on marble base
Height: 31cm. (12¼in.)
PRIVATE COLLECTION

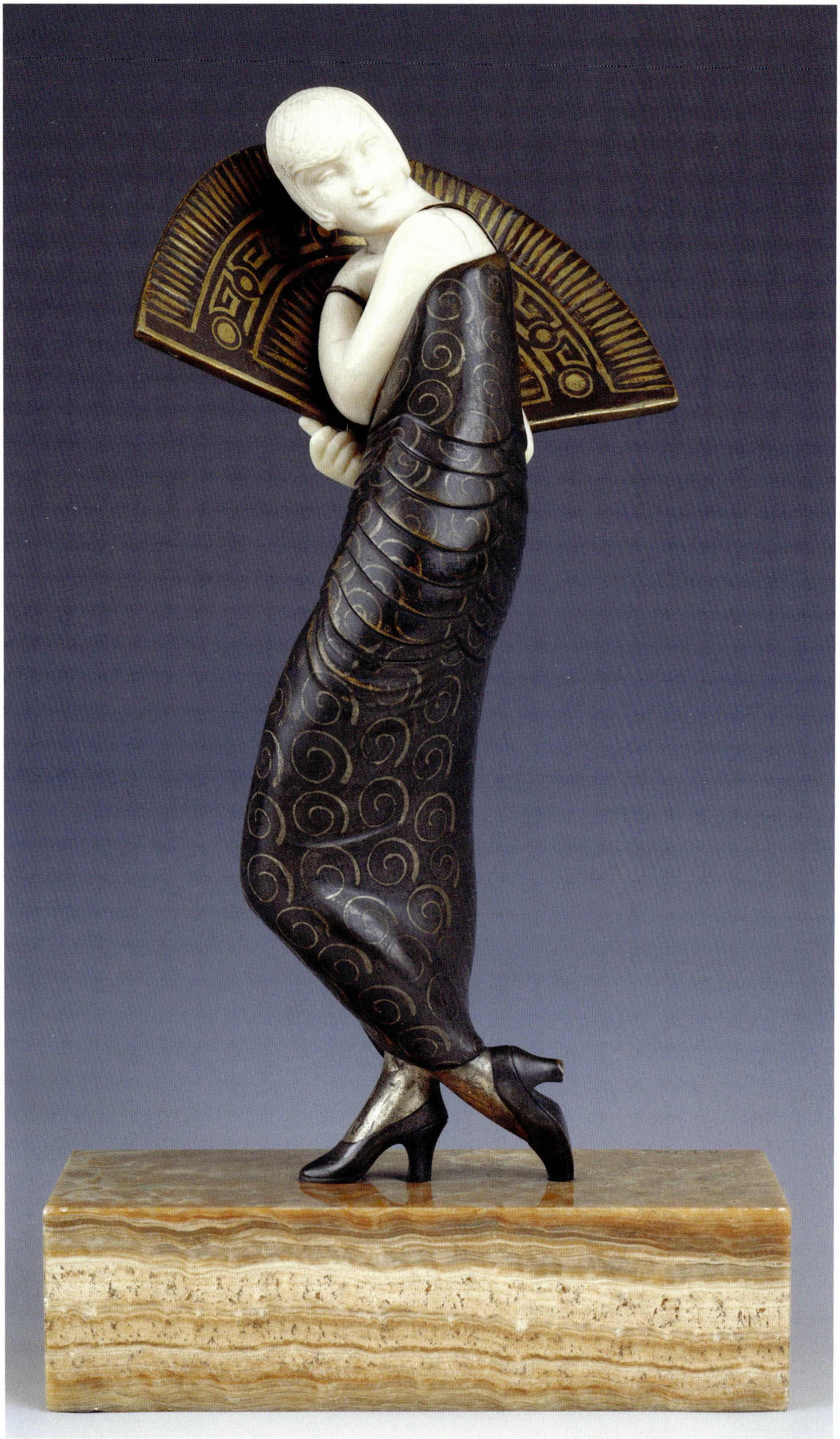

Affection
Bronze and ivory on marble base
Height: 35.5cm. (14in.)
VIRGINIA MUSEUM OF FINE ARTS, RICHMOND, GIFT OF SYDNEY AND FRANCES LEWIS

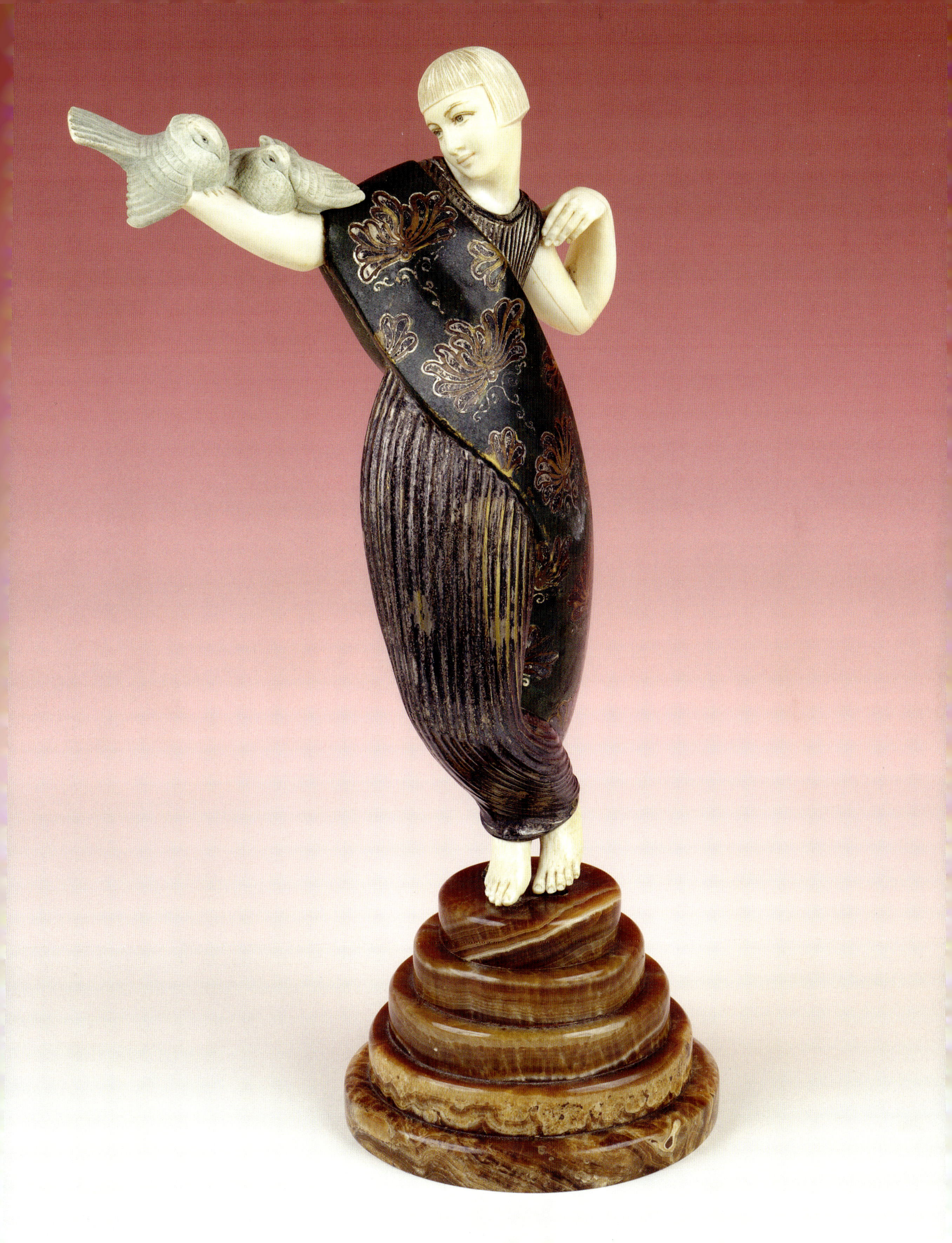

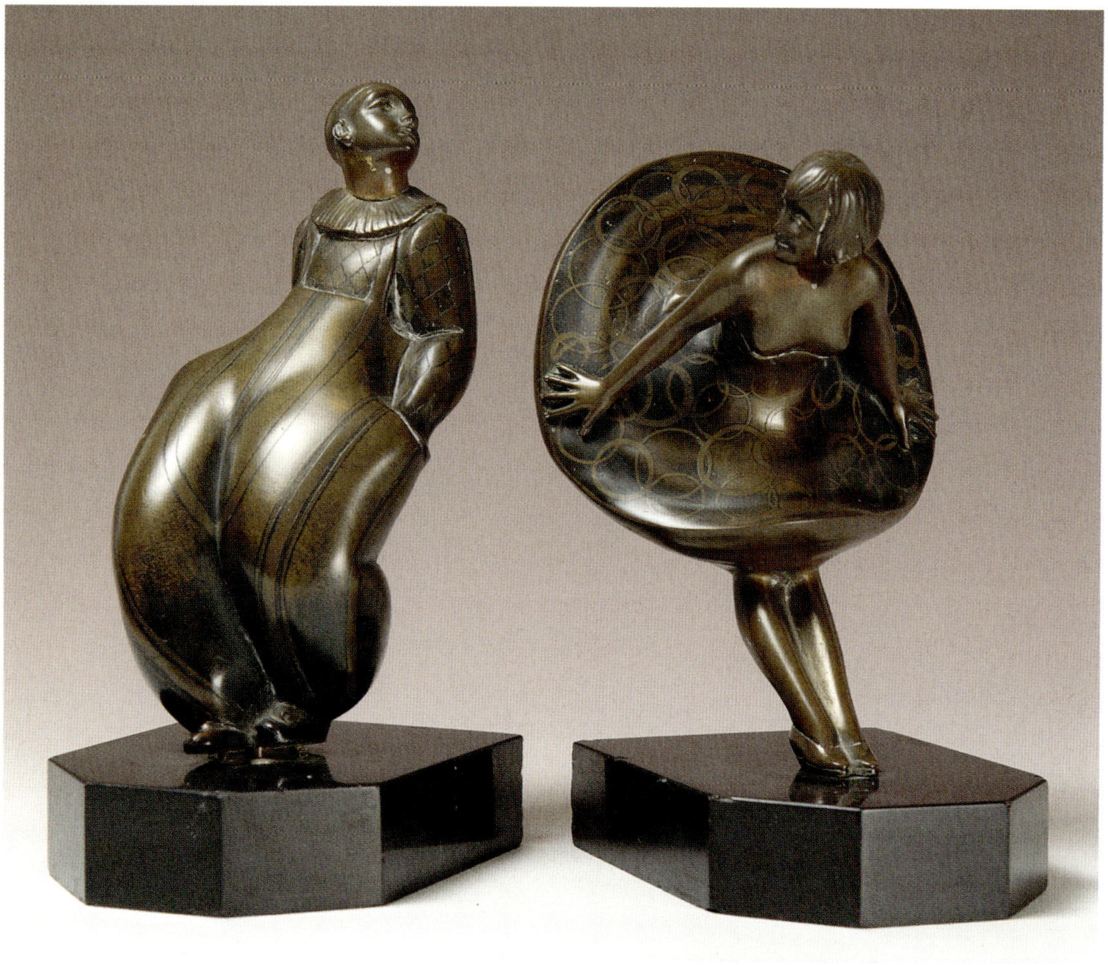

Parrots
Bronze on marble base
Height: 63cm. (24¾in.)
DINO MENASCHE COLLECTION

Pierrot and Columbine
Bronze on marble base
(mounted as bookends)
Height: Pierrot 22cm. (8¾in.);
Columbine 20cm. (8in.)
PRIVATE COLLECTION

Pheasant
Bronze on marble base
Height: 33cm. (13in.)
DINO MENASCHE COLLECTION

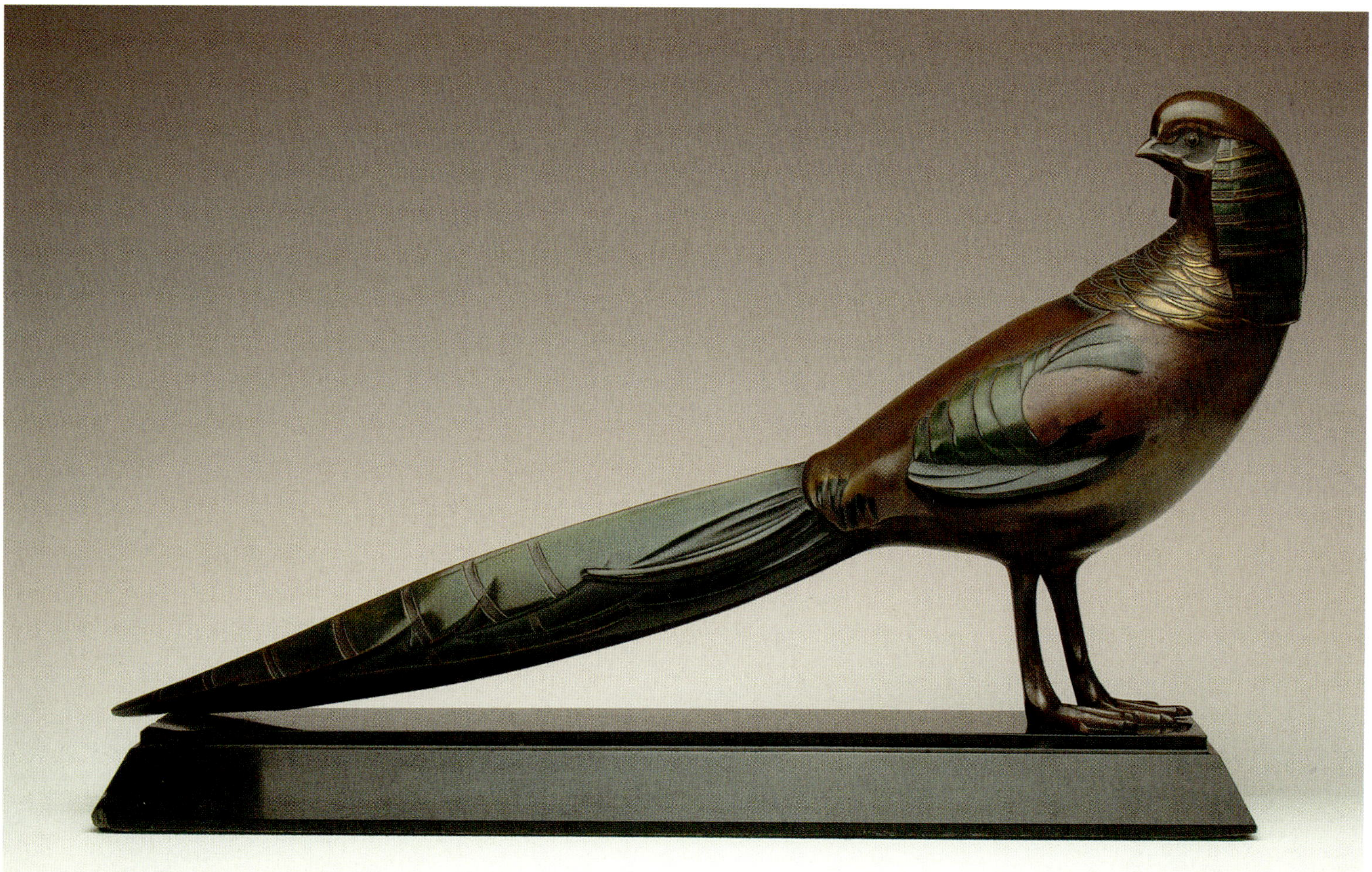

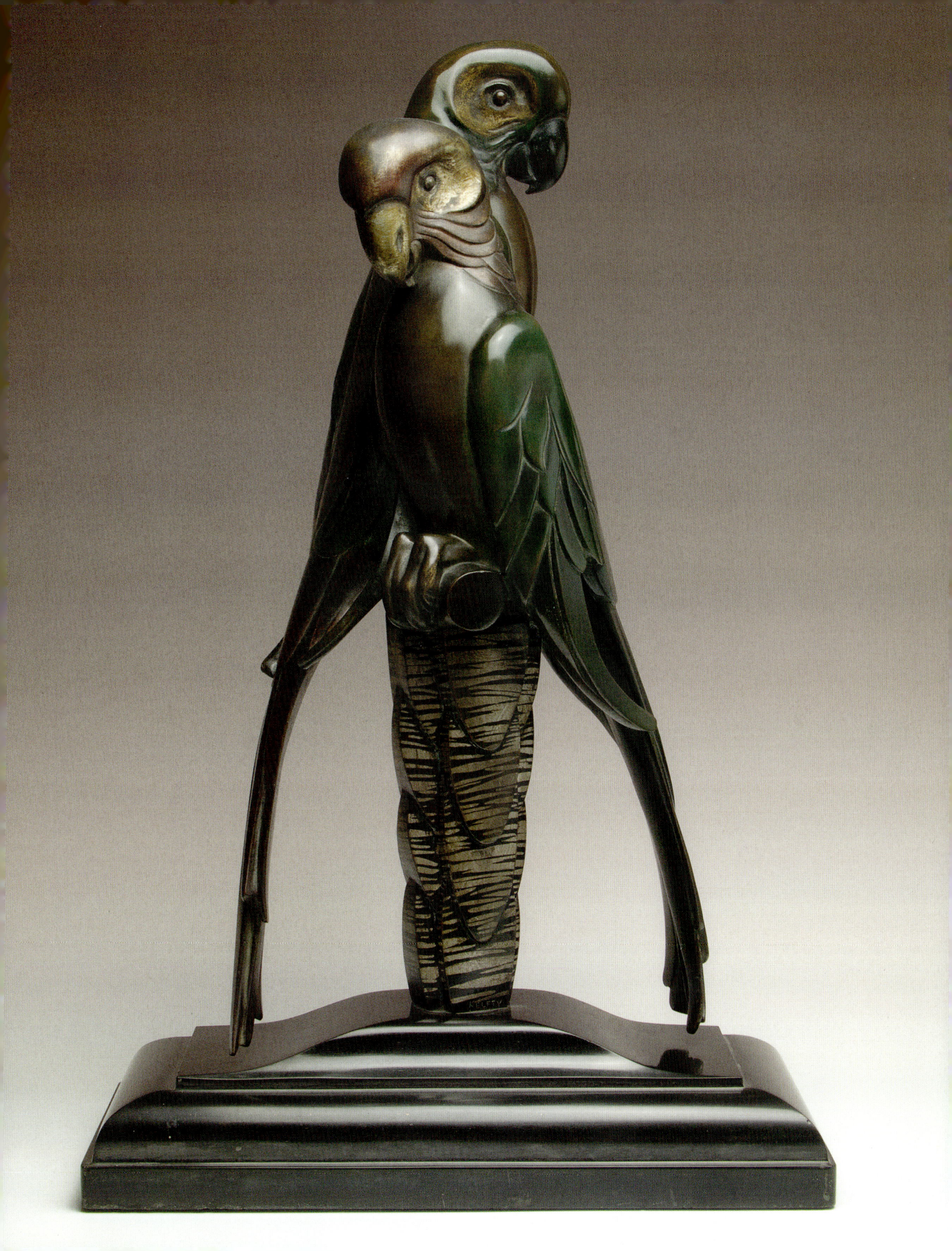

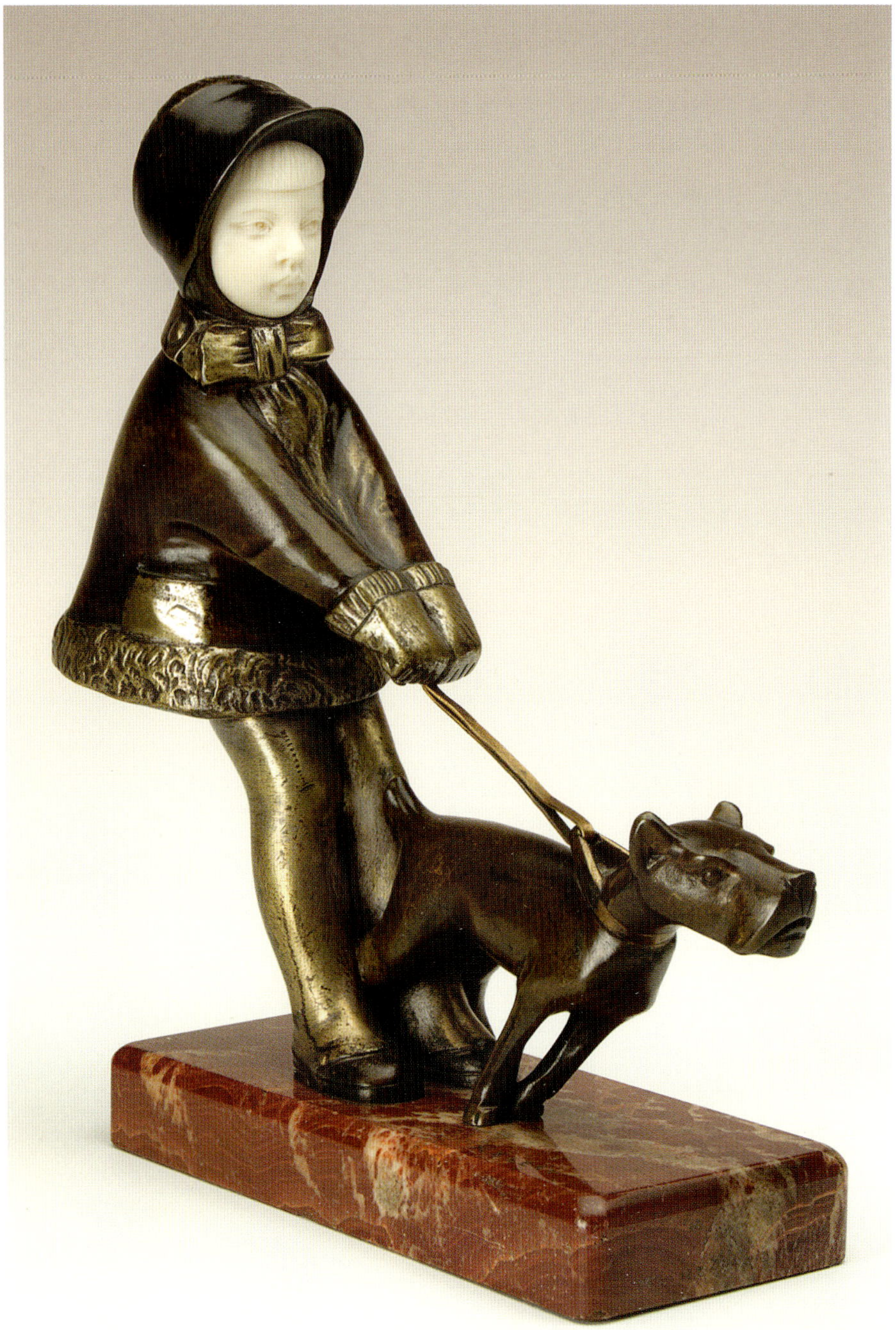

Disobedient
Bronze and ivory on marble base
Height: 19.5cm. (7¾in.)
DINO MENASCHE COLLECTION

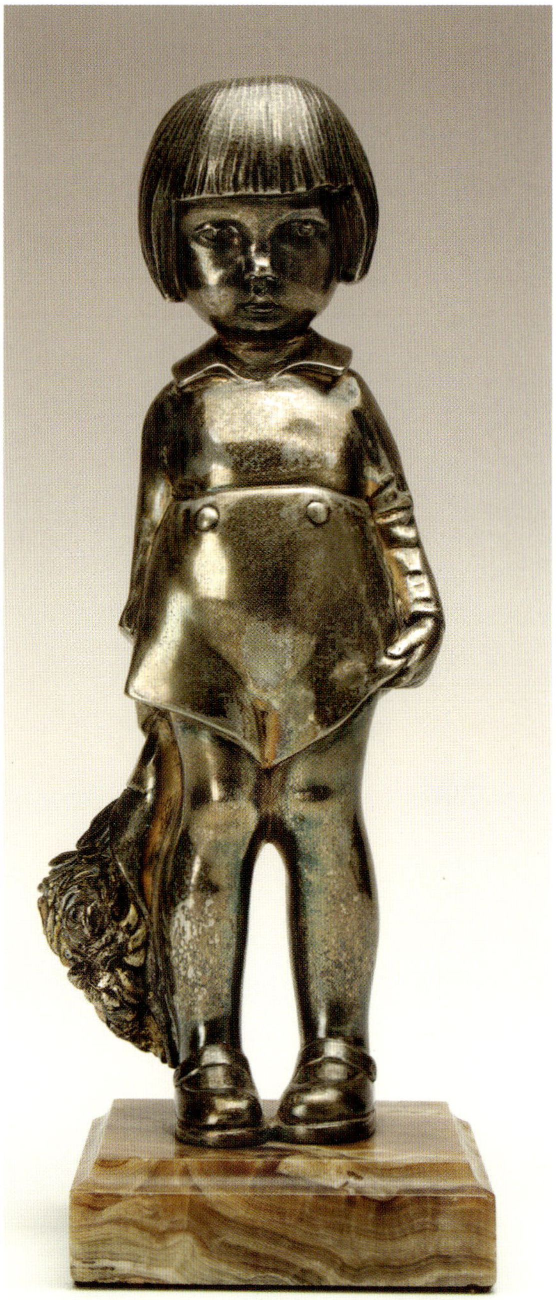

Girl with Bouquet
Bronze on onyx base
Height: 26cm. (10¼in.)
DINO MENASCHE COLLECTION

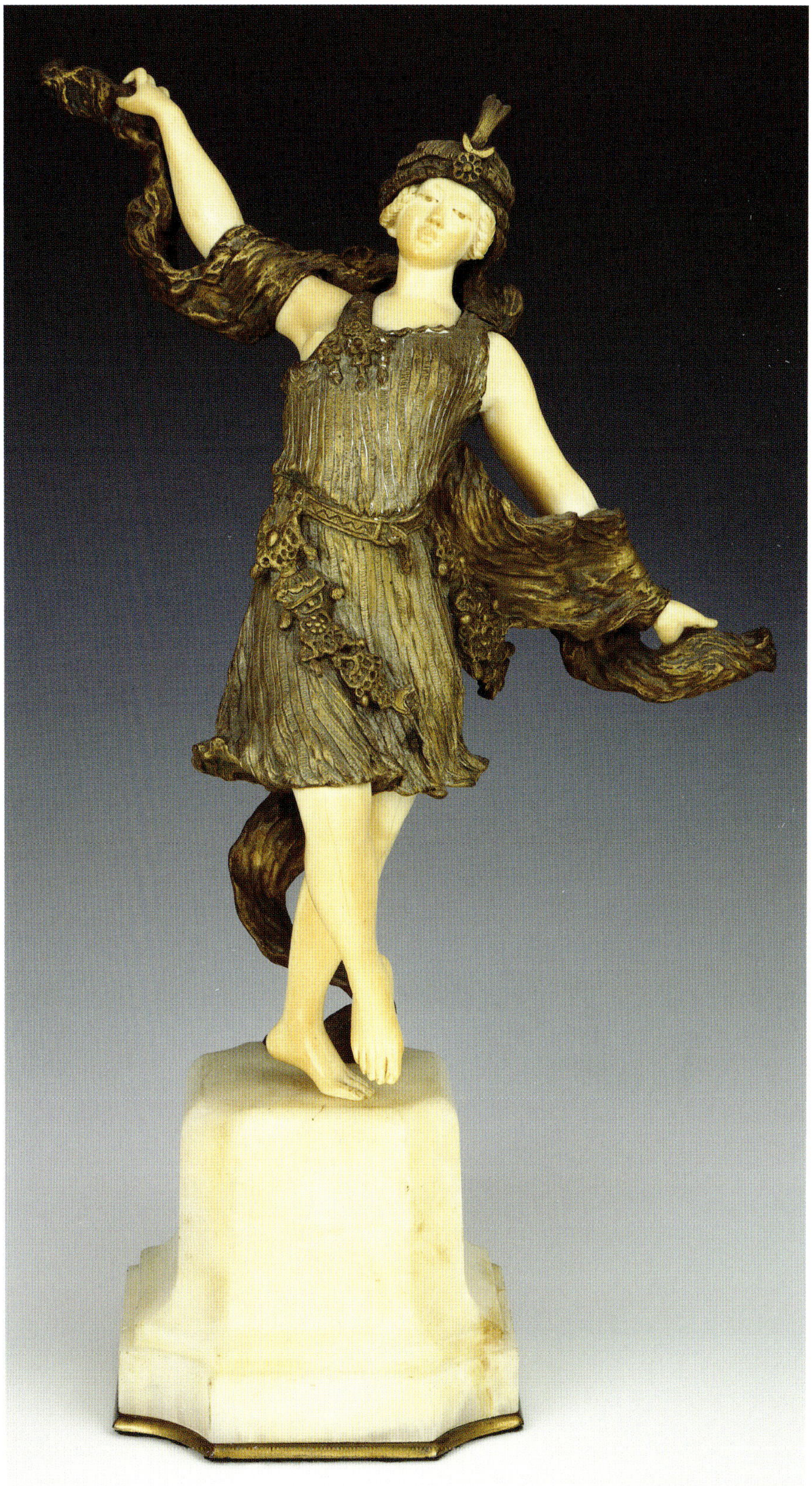

Indian Dancer
Bronze and ivory on marble and bronze base
Height: 37cm. (14½in.)
PRIVATE COLLECTION

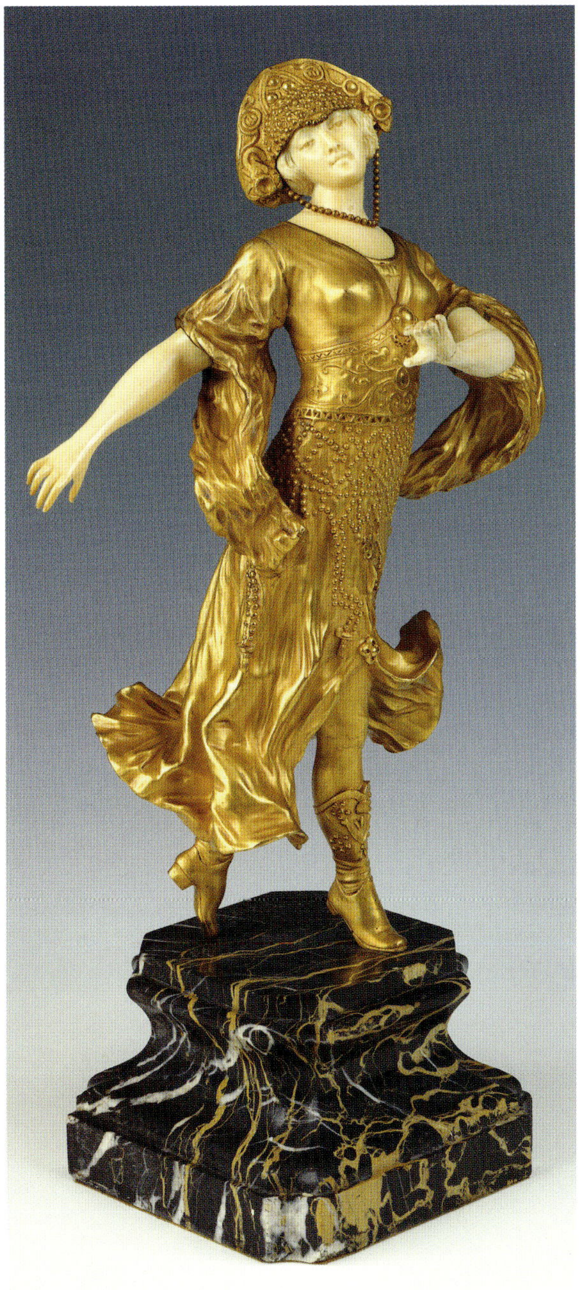

Russian Dancer
Bronze and ivory on marble base
Height: 42cm. (16½in.)
PRIVATE COLLECTION

LANGE, Richard W.

German. Worked for Rosenthal und Maeder.

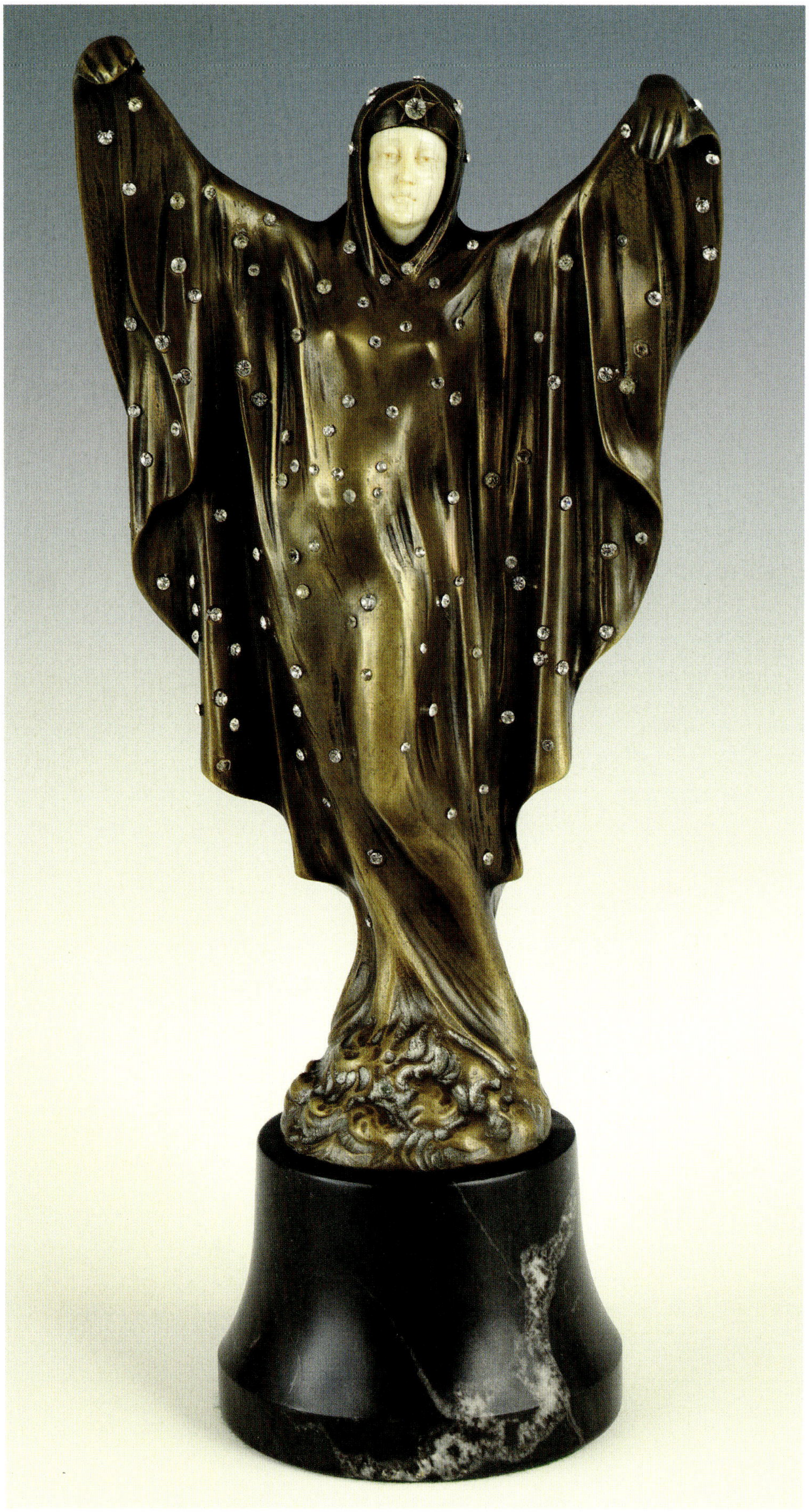

Queen of the Night
Bronze, ivory and rhinestones on marble base
Height: 33cm. (13in.)
PRIVATE COLLECTION

The Parachutist
Bronze and ivory (mounted as a lamp)
Height: 85cm. (33½in.)
PRIVATE COLLECTION

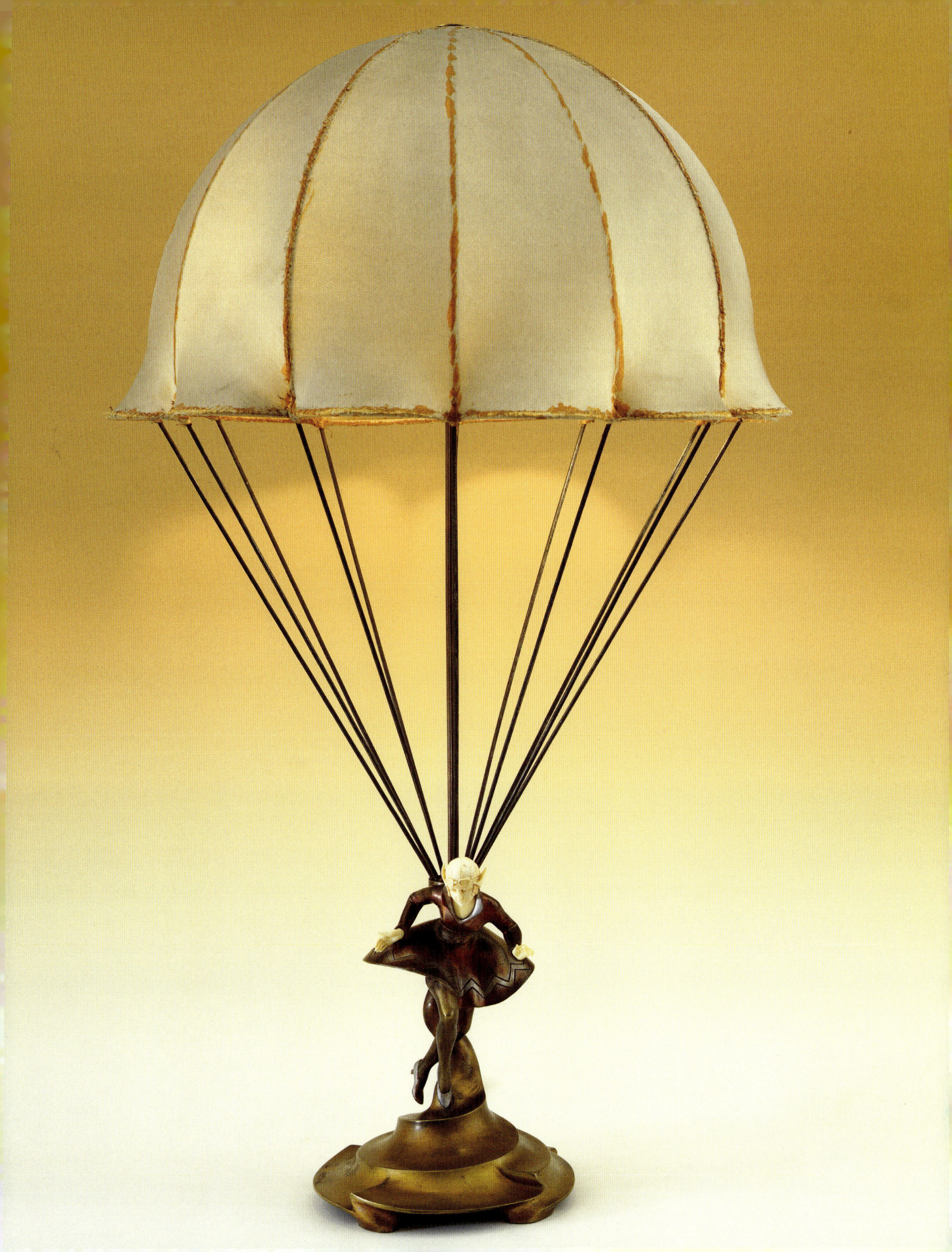

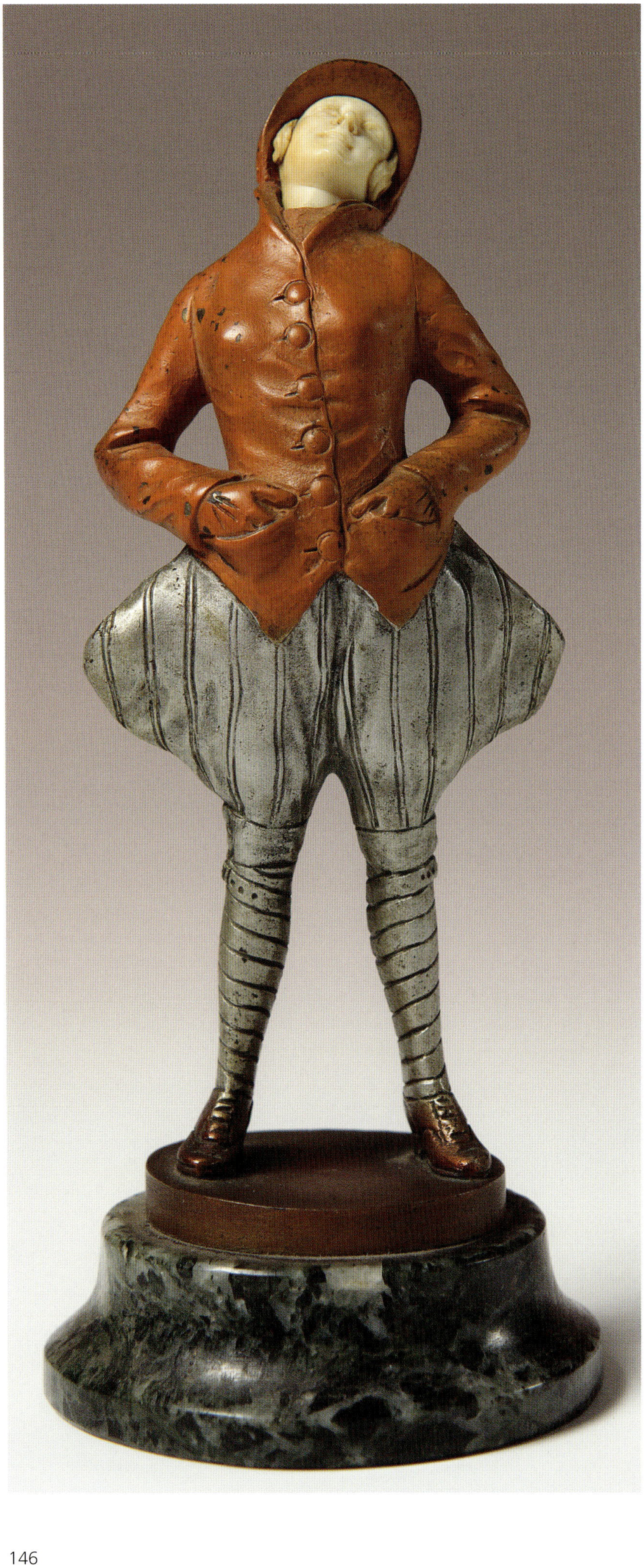

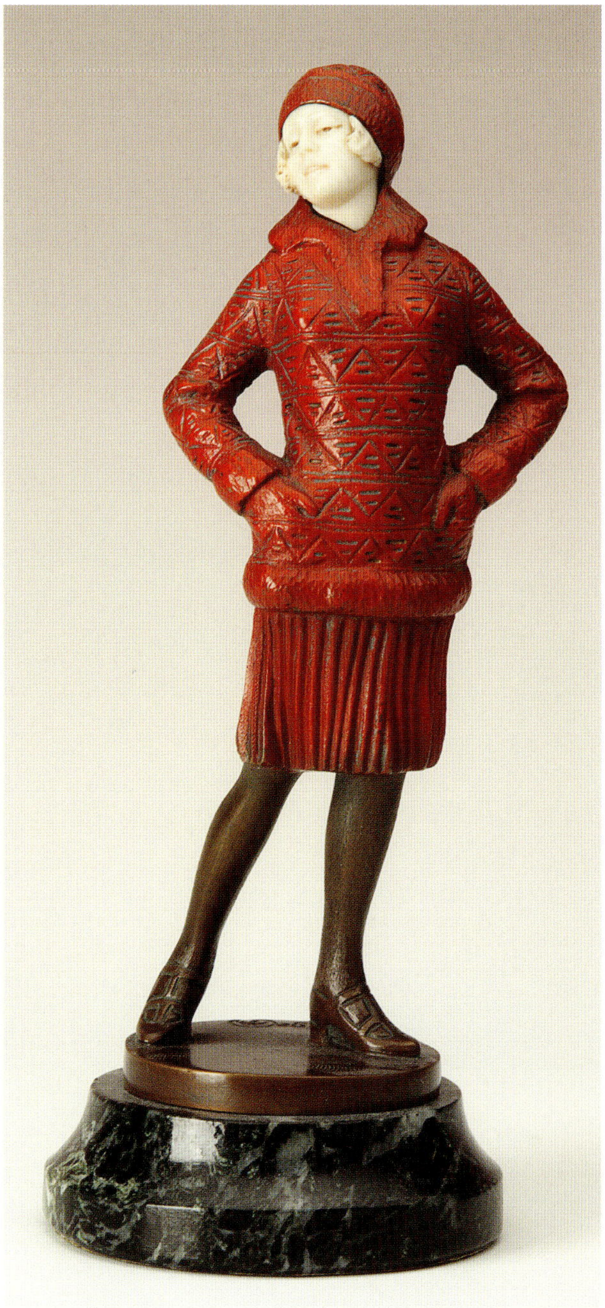

Winter Fashion
Bronze and ivory on marble base
Height: 16cm. (6¼in.)
DINO MENASCHE COLLECTION

Equestrienne
Bronze and ivory on marble base
Height: 15.5cm. (6in.)
PRIVATE COLLECTION

Ballerina
Bronze and ivory on marble base
Height: 22.5cm. (9in.)
HARRY JAROSCH COLLECTION, VIENNA

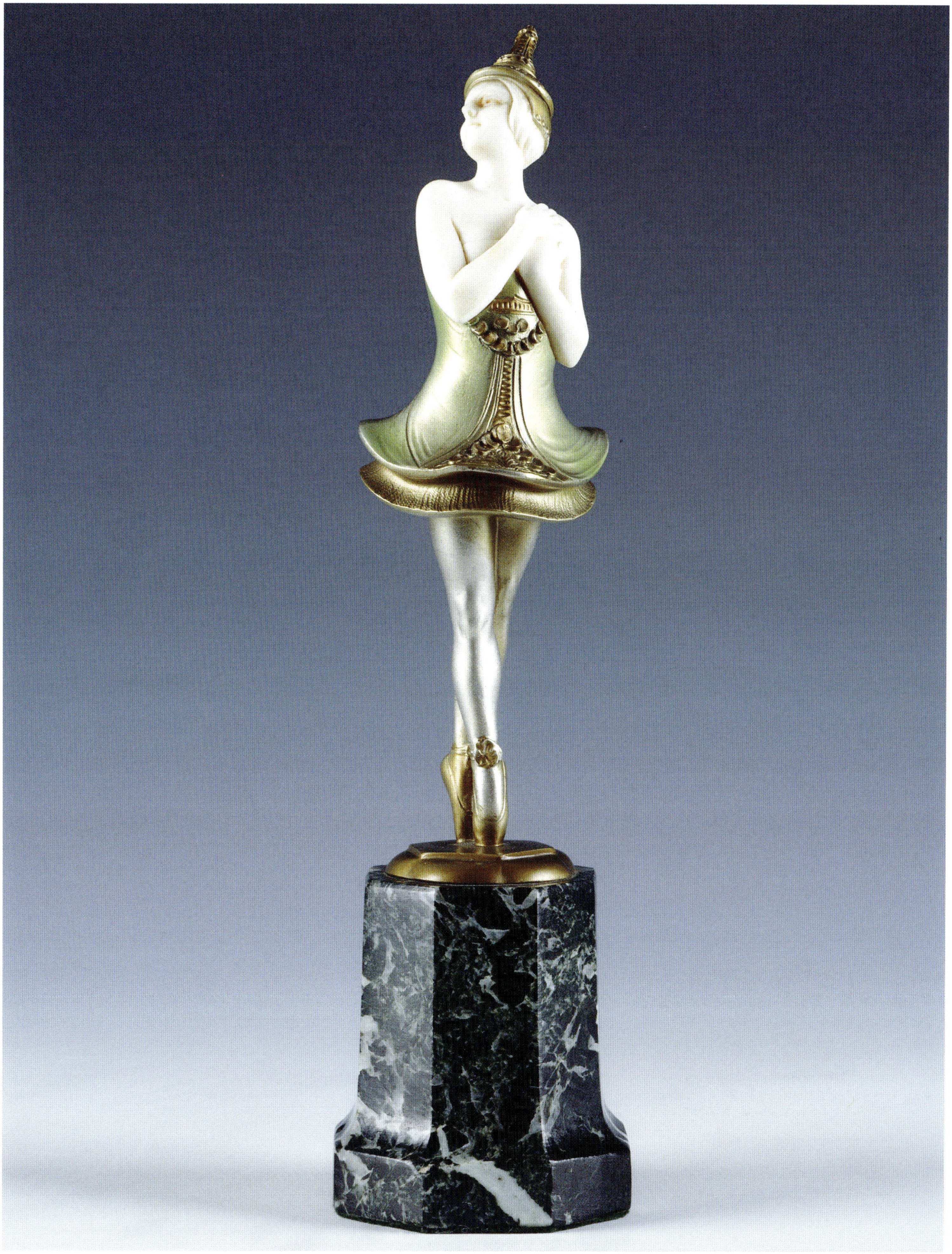

LAVROFF, Georges

(Siberia 1895 – ?)

Studied at the School of Fine Arts in Moscow. He exhibited there until 1927. He moved to Paris and exhibited at the Salon des Indépendants from 1928. His work appears in museums in Russia.

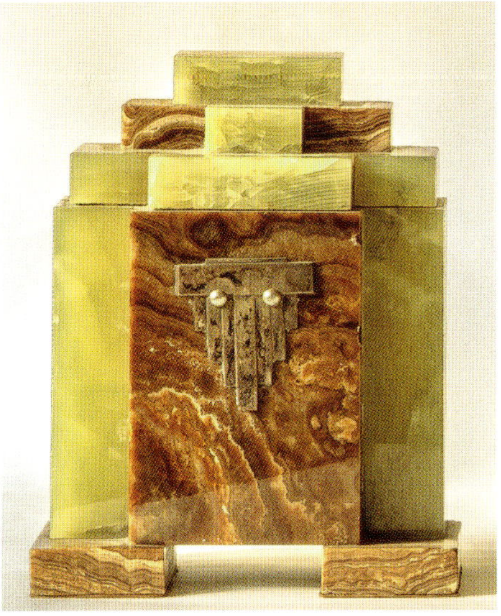

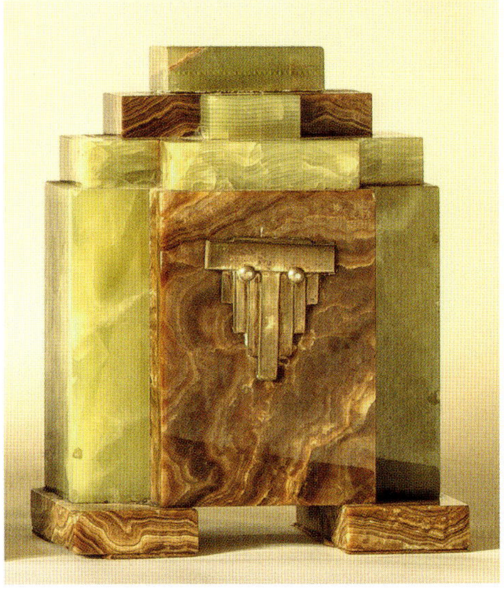

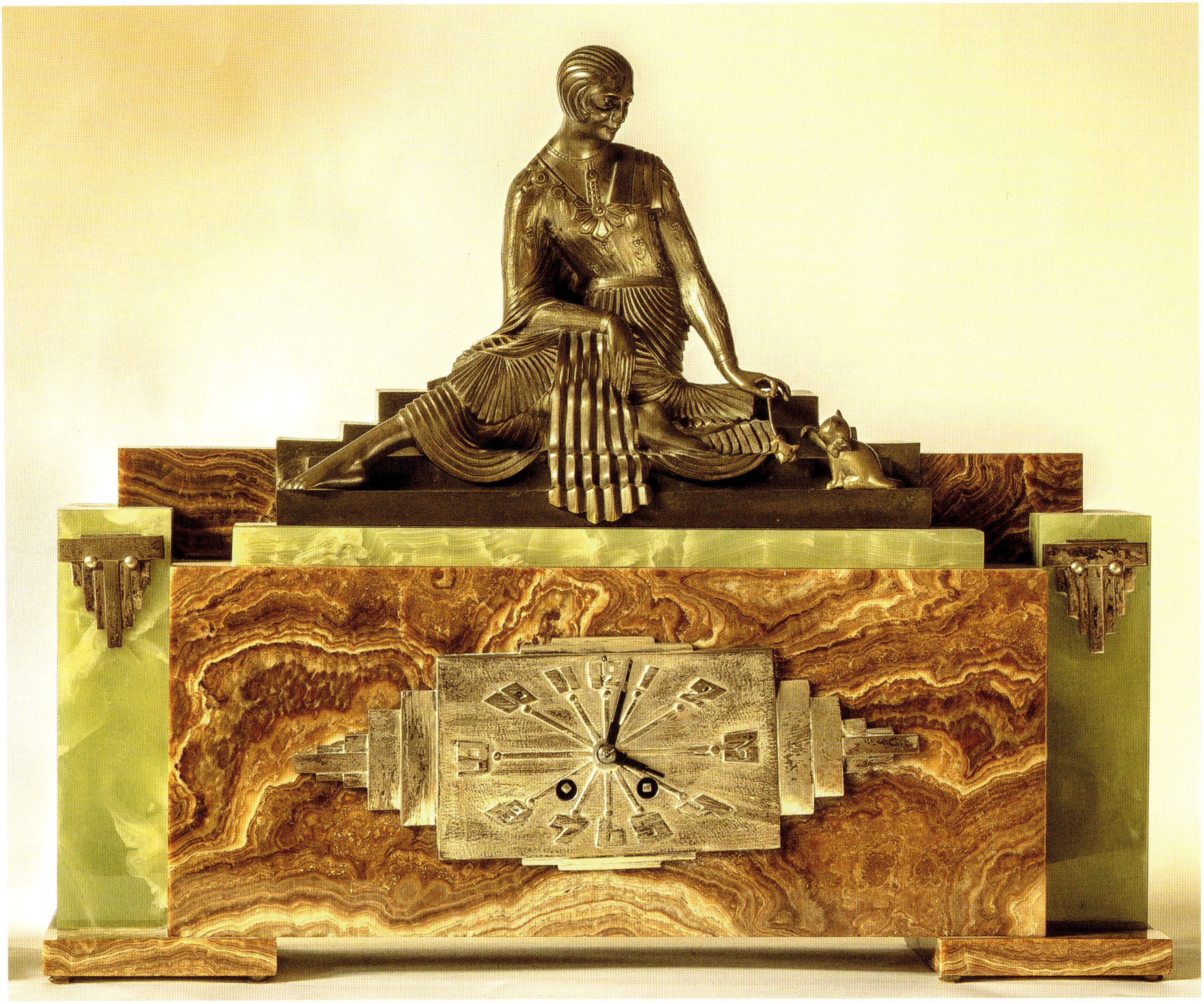

Lady and Cat
Bronze, marble and onyx (mounted as a clock and side ornaments)
Height of centrepiece: 44cm. (17¼in.)
PRIVATE COLLECTION

LE FAGUAYS, Pierre

(Nantes 1892 – Paris 1962)

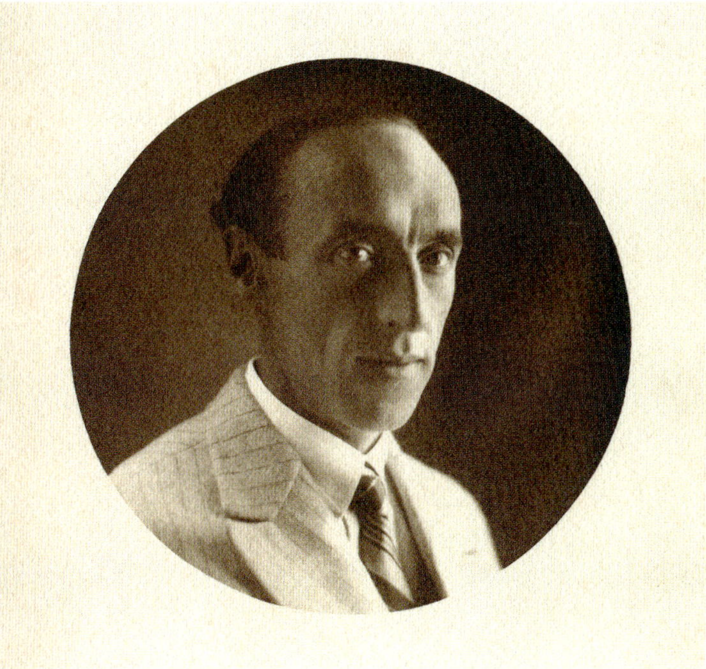

Signatures:
Le Faguays signed bronze pieces with his name. When using other materials he used the pseudonyms 'Fayral', 'Laurel' and 'Pierre Laurel' (his mother's first name, Laure, with the first letter of his last name). The signatures 'Guerbe' and 'Guerval', sometimes attributed to him, are in reality those of his wife Raymonde Guerbe, an artist in her own right.

Born in Nantes, France, he studied with James Vibert at the Geneva Ecole des Beaux Arts.

As of 1920 he exhibited at the Salon d'Automne and, as of 1922, at the Salon of the Société des Artistes Français. His statuettes were produced by Susse, Goldscheider, Les Neveux de J. Lehmann, Etling, Max Le Verrier, and M. Ollier. He was a member of the 'Evolution' and 'La Stèle' groups, and took part in their displays at the Goldscheider pavilion at the 1925 exhibition.

In 1927, at the Salon of the Société des Artistes Français, he received an honourable mention. At the International Exhibition of Paris in 1937, he exhibited a bronze statuette called *Aurore*. That same year he was awarded the Legion of Honour in France and was made a Knight of the Order of the Belgian King Leopold. Le Faguays also produced lamps and decorative objects, working in terracotta, *pâte de verre*, stone, spelter, wood, alabaster, and forged iron as well as bronze, and bronze and ivory.

Several of his works were purchased by the city of Paris: *Pureté* (Purity, 1927); *Danse Rhythmique* (Rythmic Dance, 1931); *Tête d'Enfant* (Child's Bust, 1933).

He was a good friend of the sculptor and founder Max Le Verrier and of the sculptor Marcel Bouraine, whom he met during World War I when they were prisoners of war and then fellow students at the Geneva Ecole des Beaux Arts.

Le Faguays had a daughter with one of his models, Georgette Hayot; he later married artist Raymonde Guerbe (André Guerval); the couple had no children (see p.116 GUERBE, Raymonde).

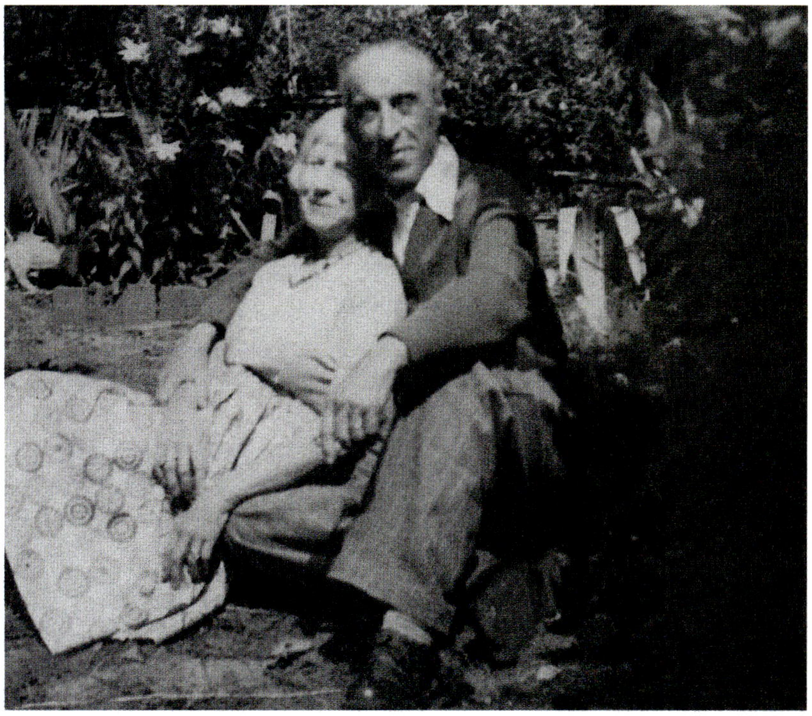

Above:
Pierre Le Faguays.

Left:
Le Faguays with wife Raymonde Guerbe, July 1959.

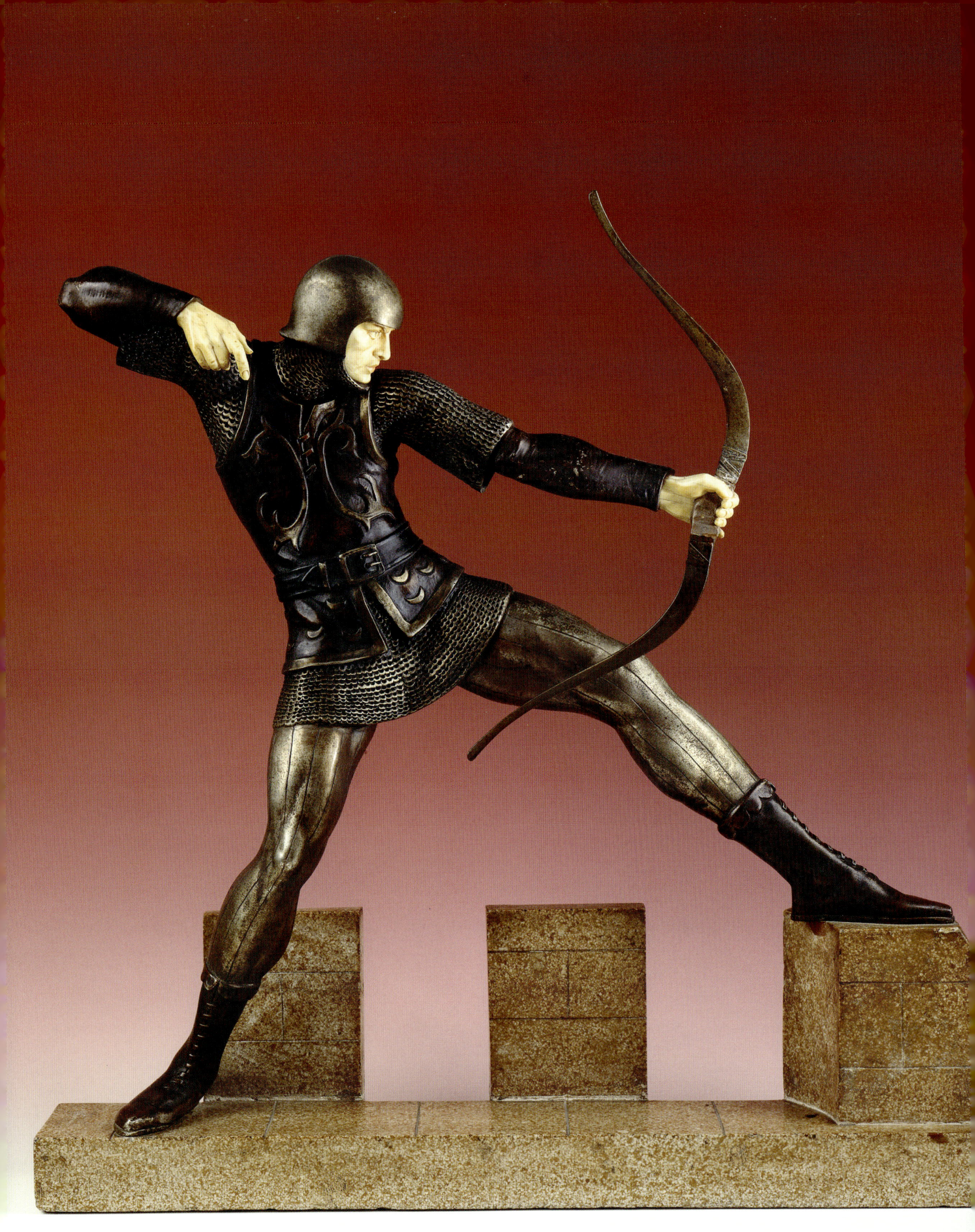

Signal Man
Bronze and ivory on marble base
Height: 38cm. (15in.)
PRIVATE COLLECTION

Also produced 63.5cm. (25in.) high

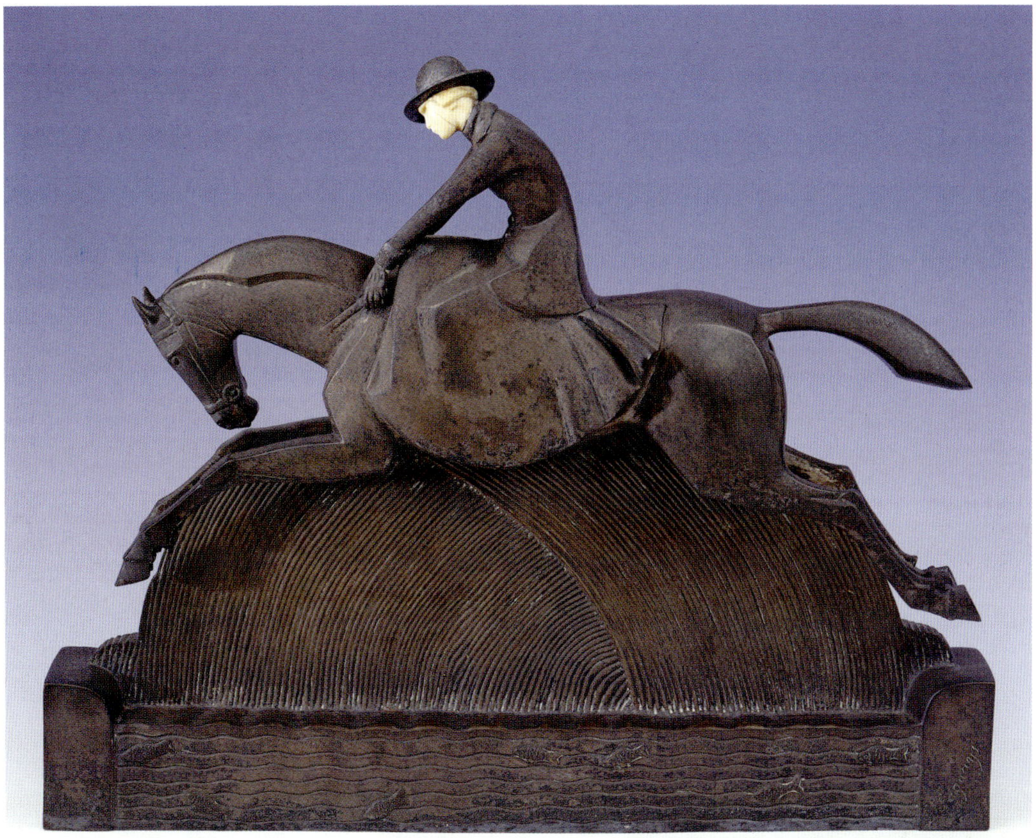

Equestrienne
Bronze and ivory
Height: 36cm. (14¼in.)
PRIVATE COLLECTION

Harem Girl
Bronze and ivory on marble base (mounted as a lamp)
Height: 42.5cm. (16¾in.)
PRIVATE COLLECTION

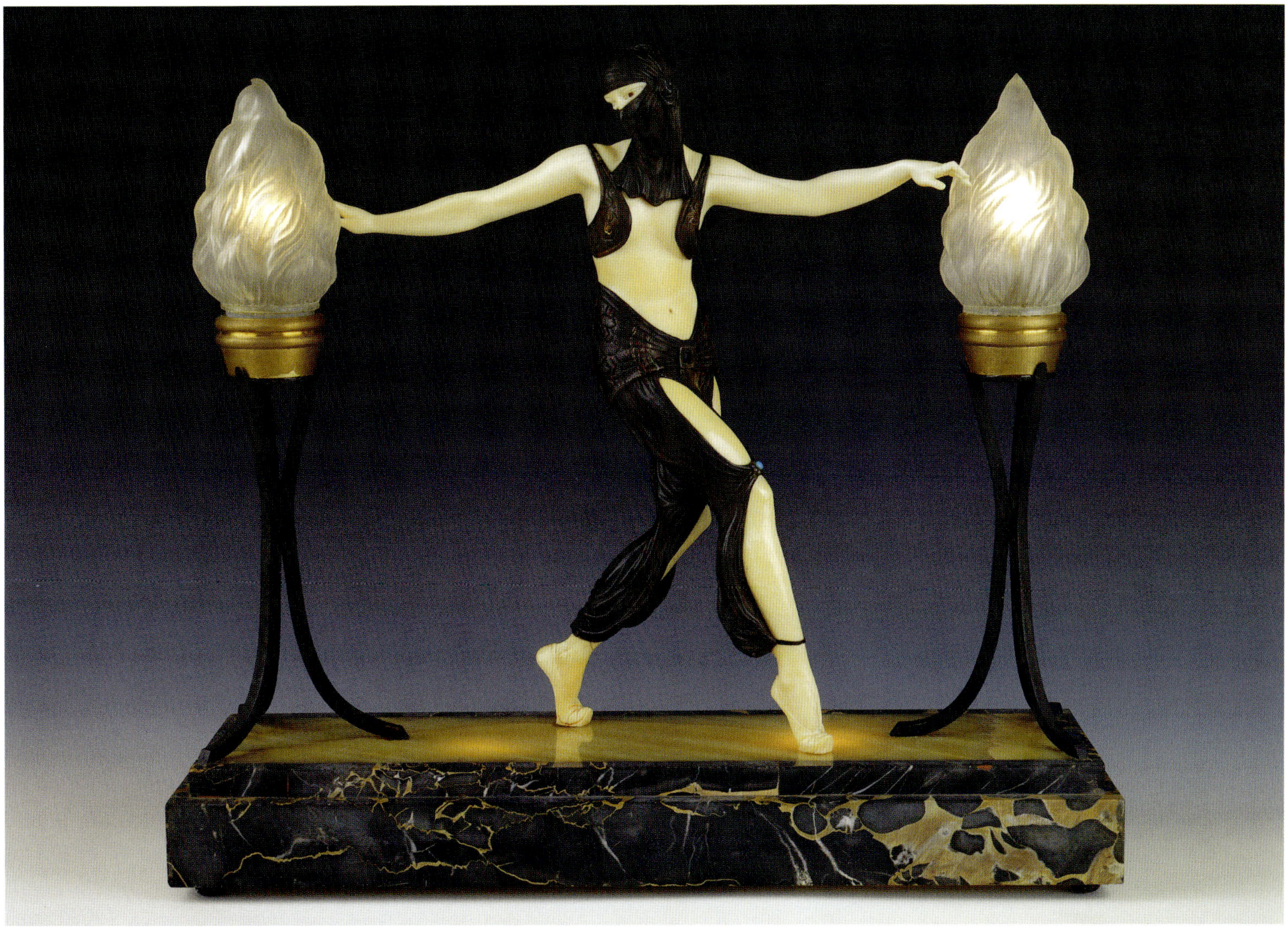

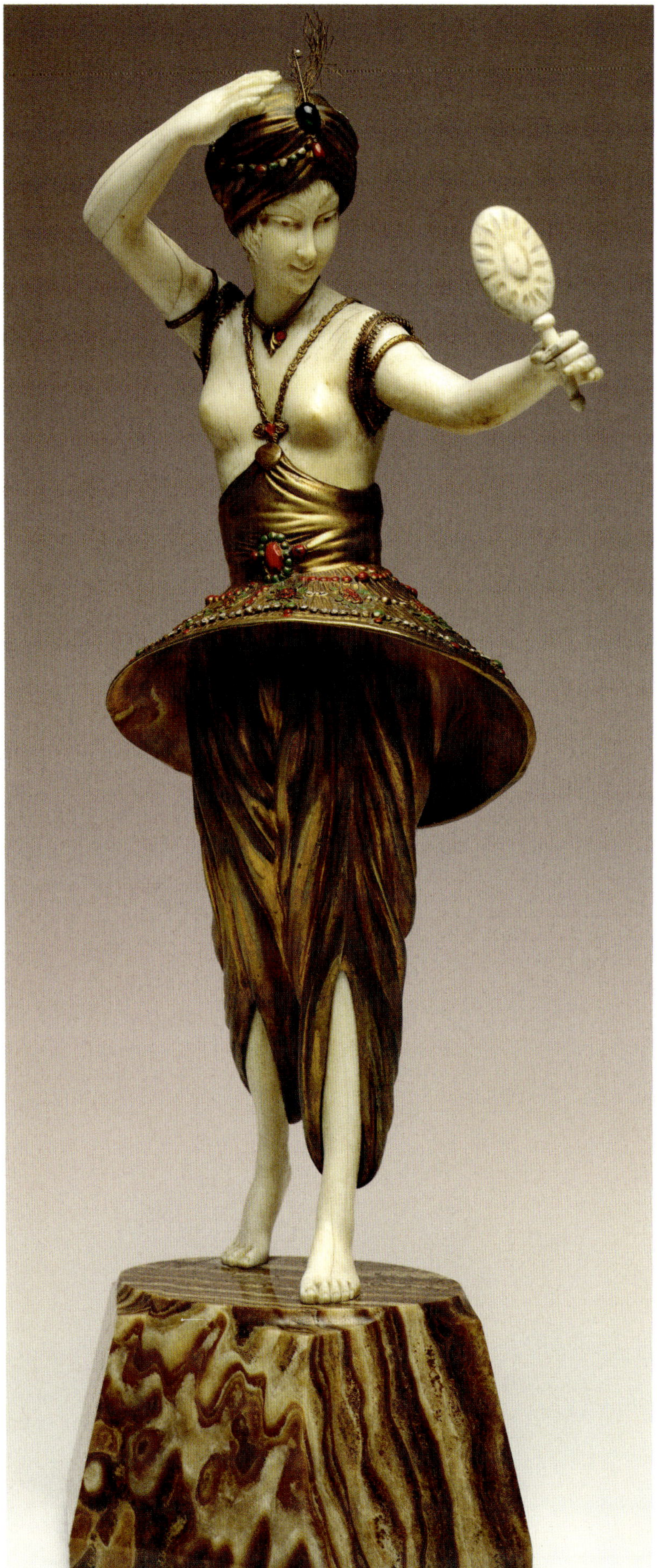

Minaret
Bronze and ivory on onyx base
Height: 46cm. (18in.)
PRIVATE COLLECTION

Dancer with Floral Skirt
Bronze and ivory on marble base
Height: 46cm. (18in.)
PRIVATE COLLECTION

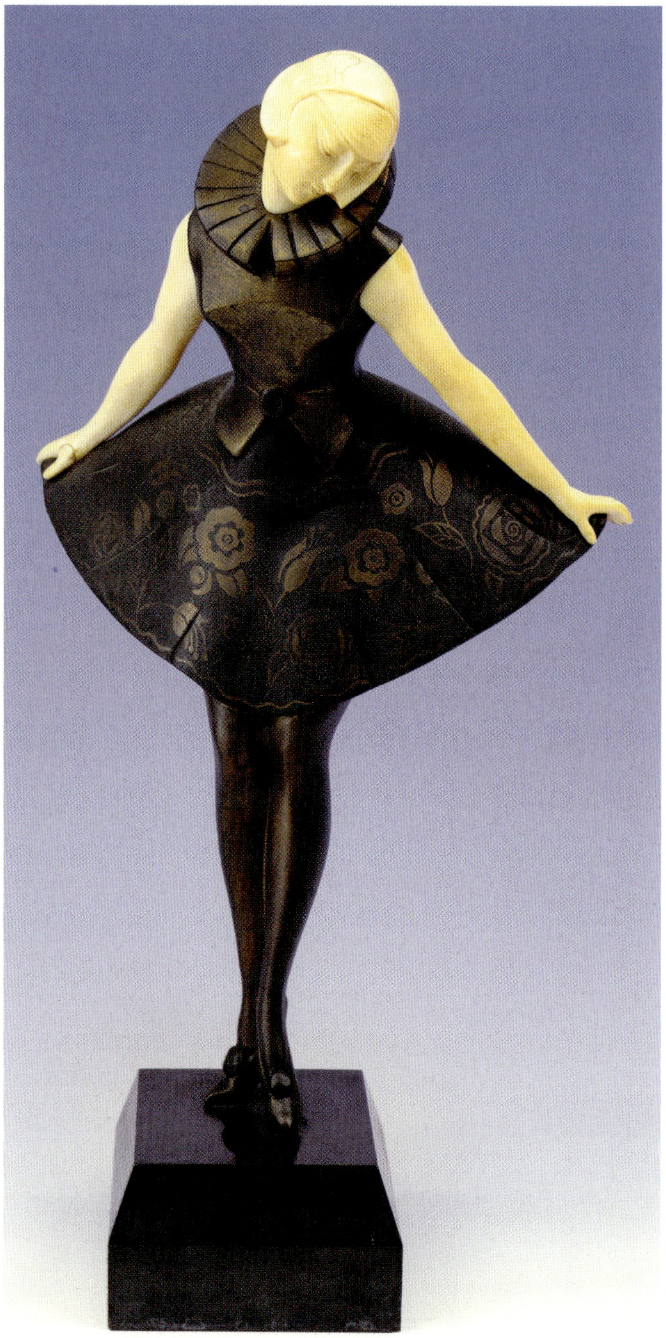

Puppets
Bronze and ivory on onyx base
Height: 48cm. (19in.)
PRIVATE COLLECTION

Also produced as a lamp within a marble niche

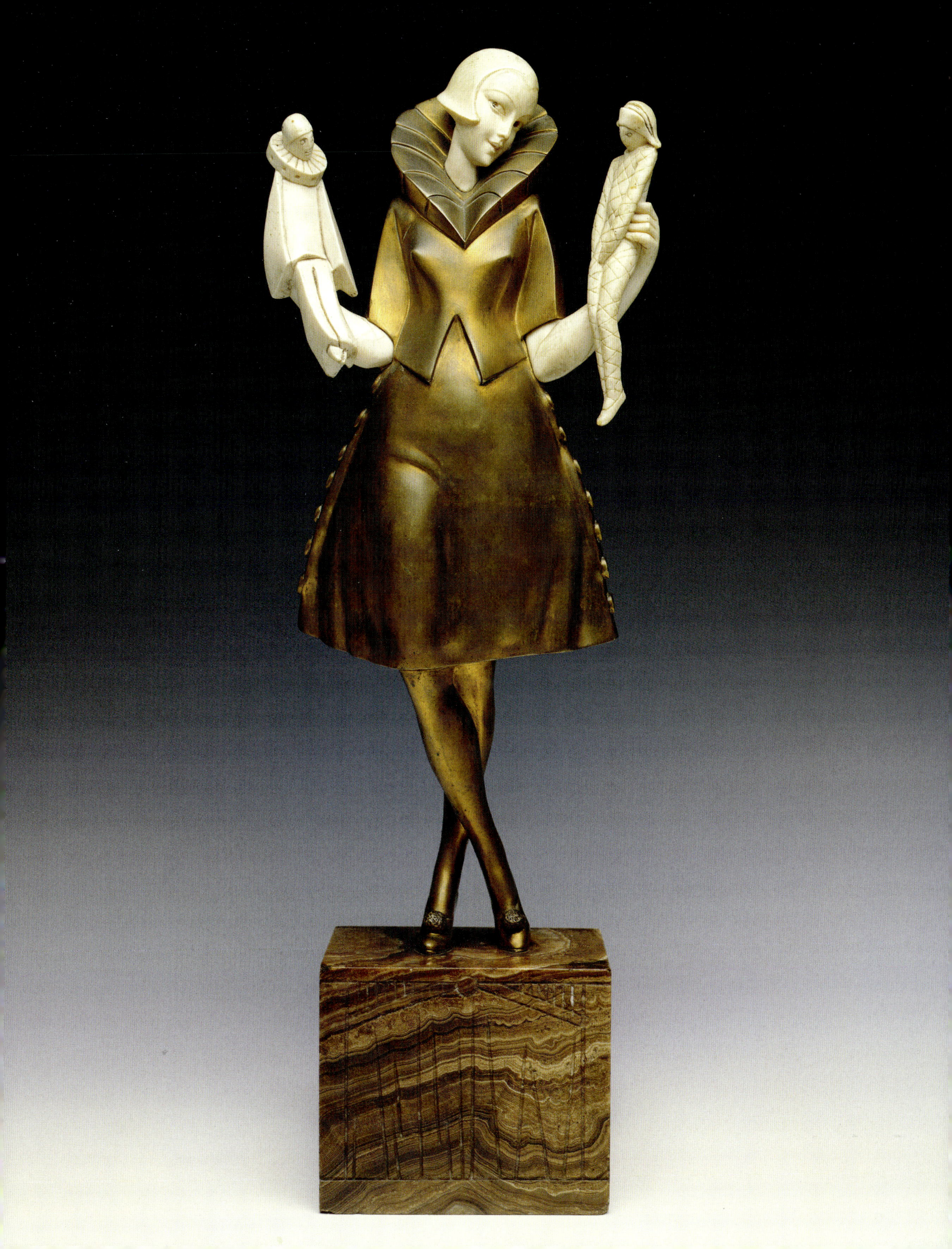

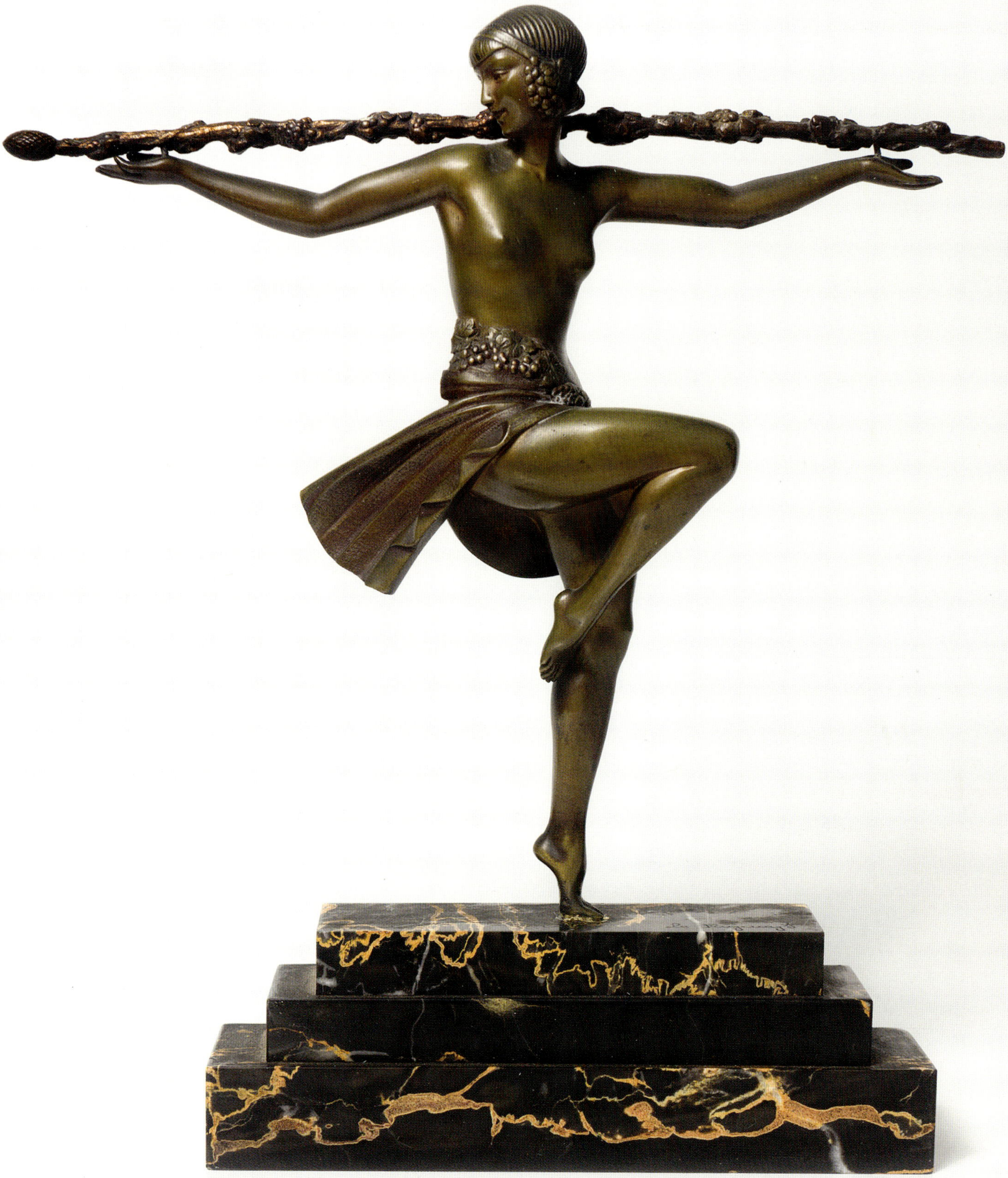

Dancer with Thyrsus
Bronze on marble base
Height: 27.5cm. (10¾in.)
PRIVATE COLLECTION

Also produced 56cm. (22in.) and 19cm. (7½in.) high

Pyrrhic Dancer
Bronze and resin on marble base
Height: 53cm. (21in.)
HARRY JAROSCH COLLECTION, VIENNA

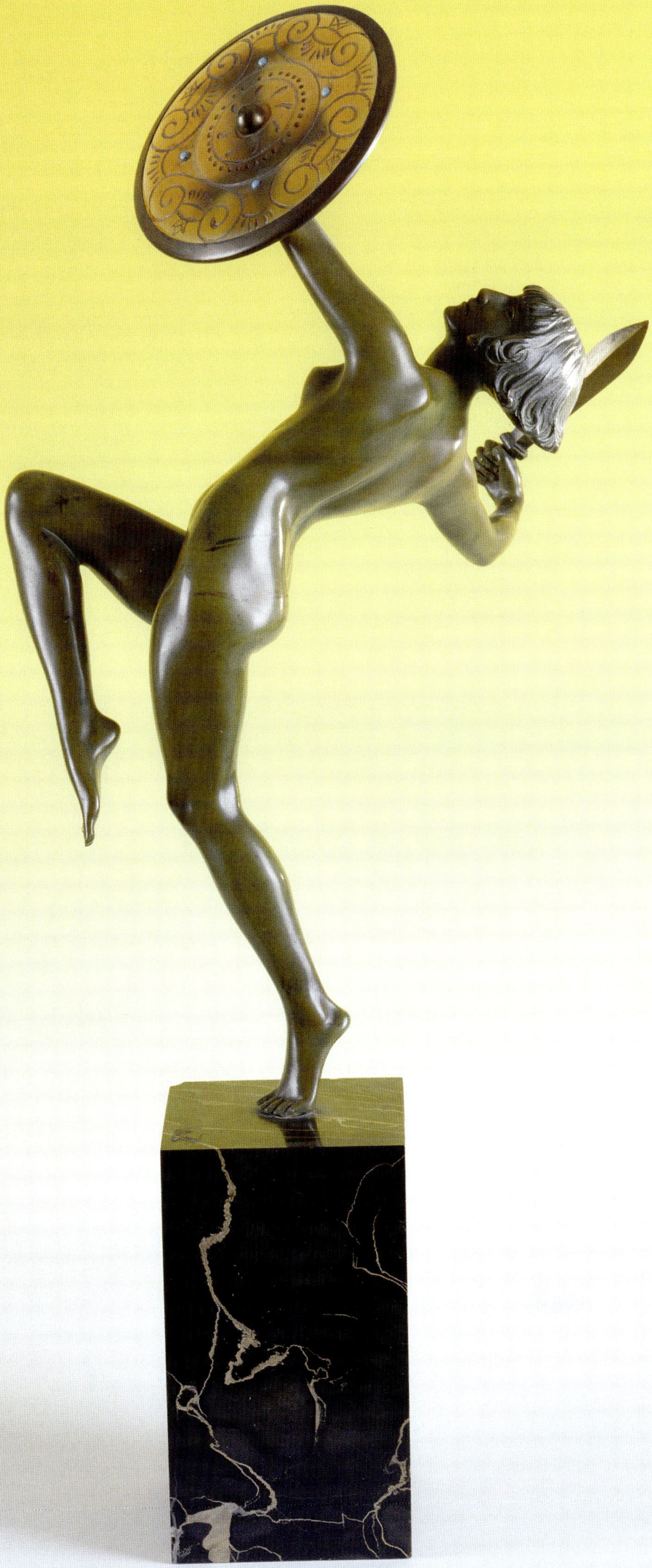

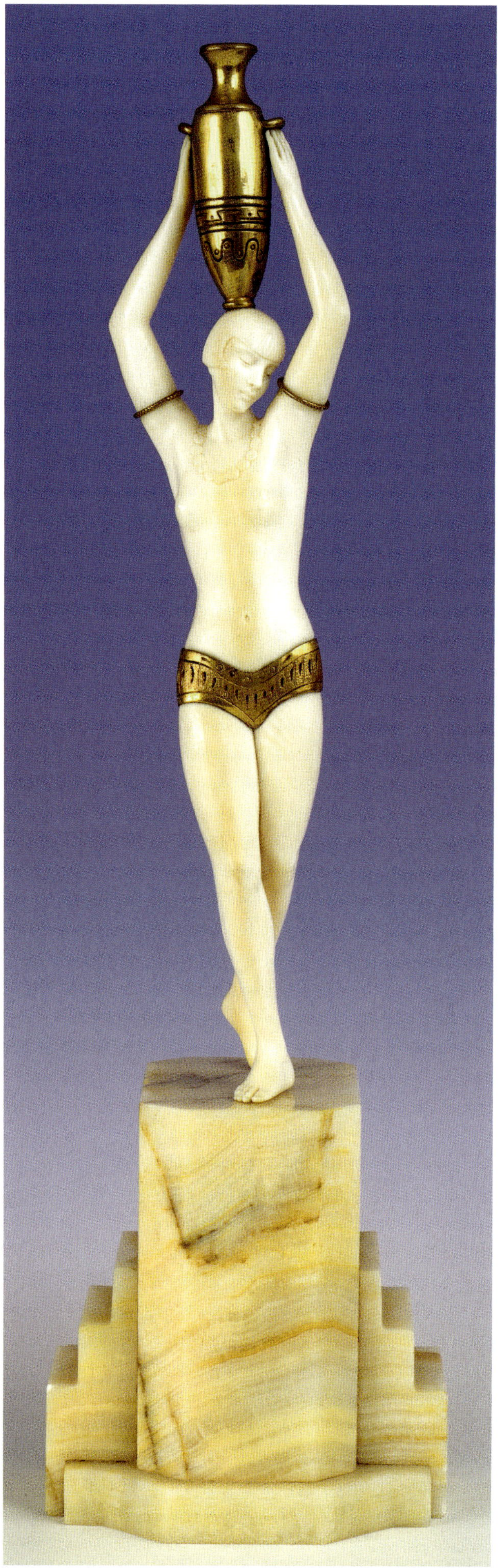

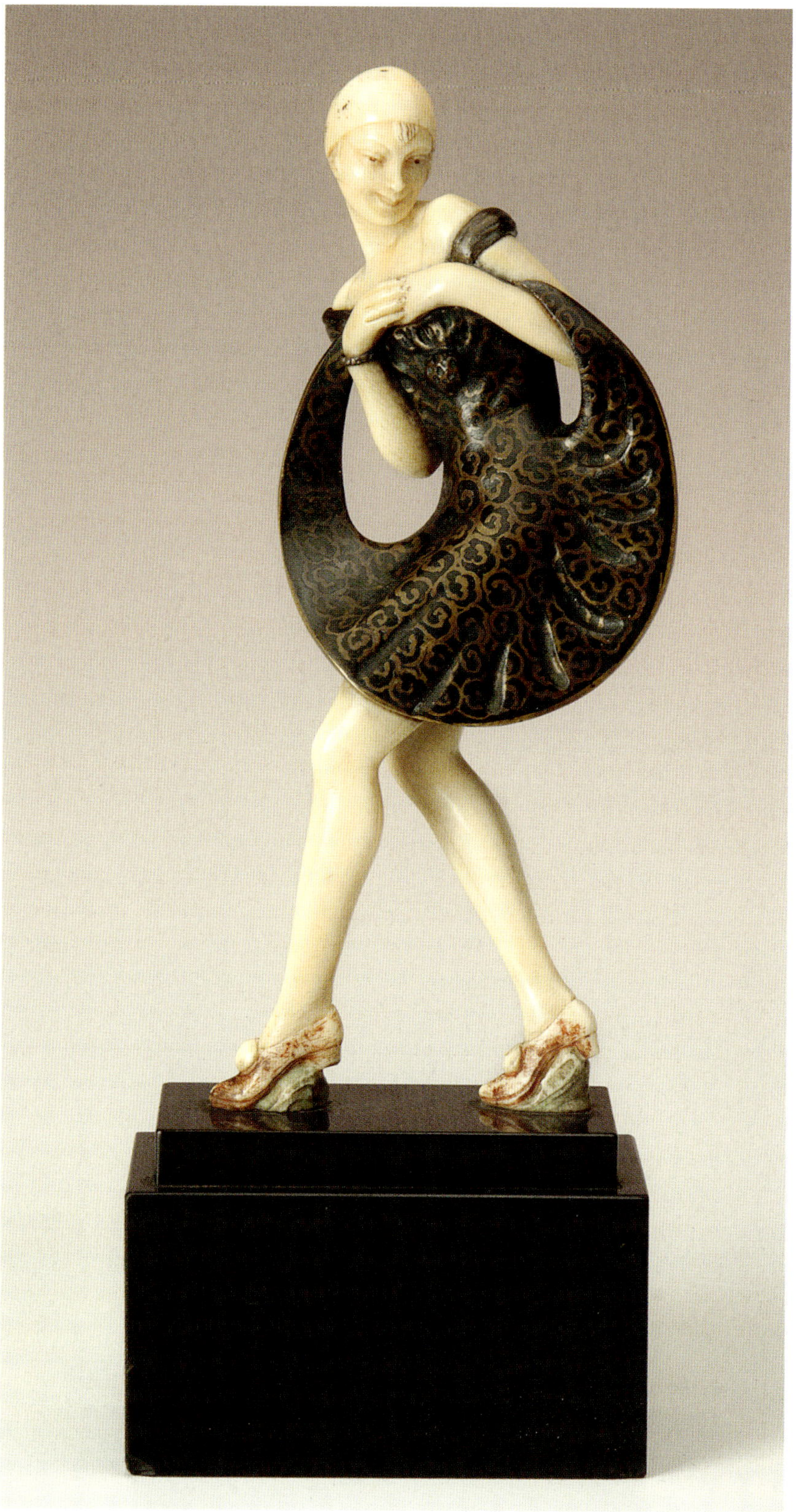

Elegante
Bronze and ivory on onyx base
Height: 24cm. (9½in.)
DINO MENASCHE COLLECTION

Oriental
Bronze and ivory on marble base
Height: 37cm. (14½in.)
PRIVATE COLLECTION

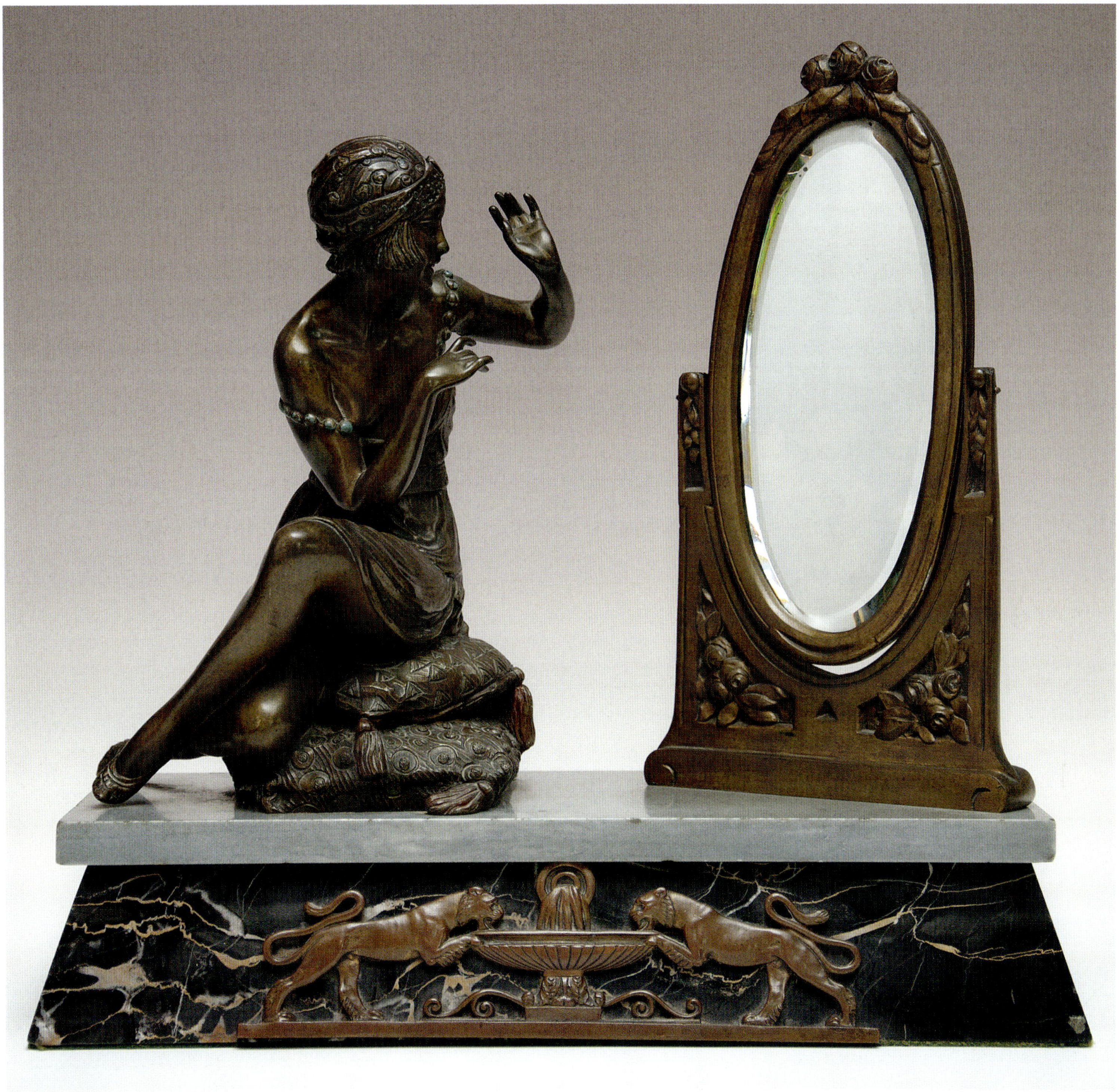

Mirror Mirror
Bronze and glass on marble base
Height: 36cm. (14¼in.)
S. AND J.S. COLLECTION

LE VERRIER, Max

(Neuilly sur Seine 1891 – 1973)

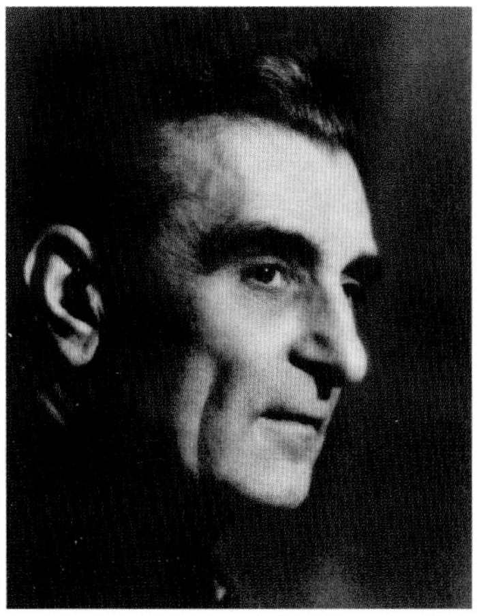

Louis Octave Maxime Le Verrier was born in Neuilly sur Seine to a Belgian mother and a Parisian father who was a goldsmith and jeweller. He enrolled in the Geneva Ecole des Beaux Arts, where he met the artists and fellow students Pierre Le Faguays and Marcel Bouraine; the three artists became life-long friends.

In the early 1920s Le Verrier inherited a small foundry and soon began running it, producing small sculptures and decorative objects, including lamps, ashtrays, bookends and car mascots. Among the artists whose work he cast were the sculptors Pierre Le Faguays, André Vincent Becquerel, Marcel Bouraine and Jules Masson, as well as his own works. These items were sold in a shop at 100 rue du Théâtre in Paris, while the workshop was at 30 rue Deparcieux.

Le Verrier worked in bronze, bronze and ivory, zinc, ceramics and terracotta. His pieces were shown at the Salon of the Société des Artistes Décorateurs, of which he had been elected a member.

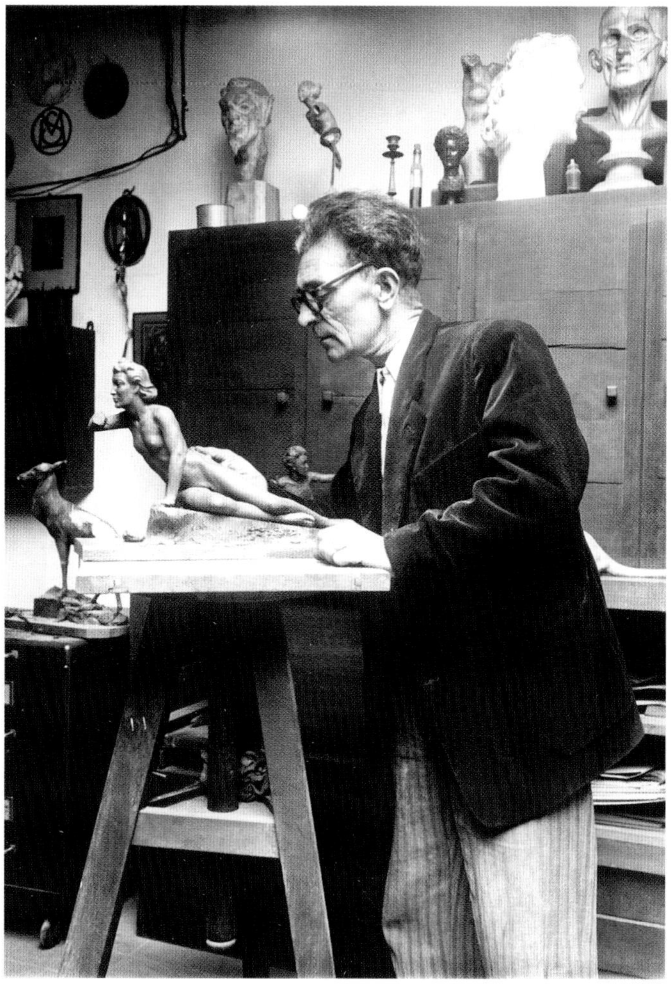

At the 1925 Exhibition, Le Verrier won a gold medal; he also took part in the Paris Exhibition of Arts and Techniques in 1937.

Max Le Verrier's figures continue to be produced by his great-grandson Damien Blanchet.

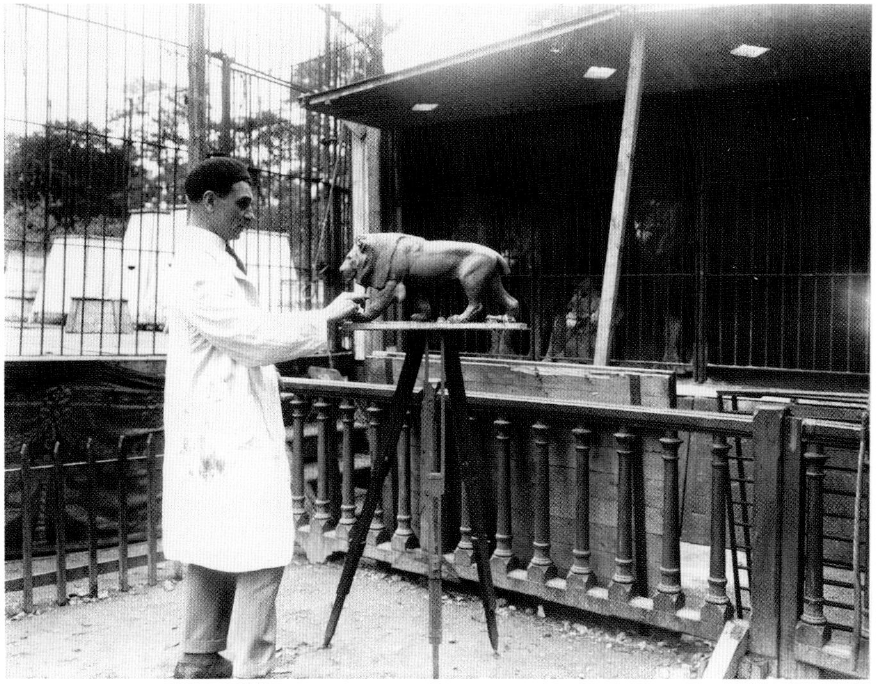

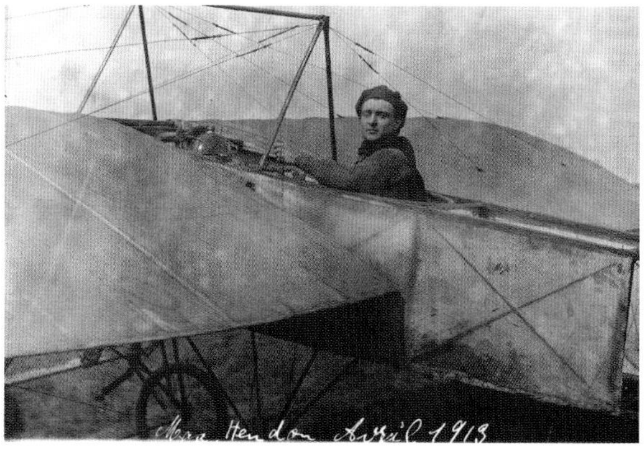

Clockwise from top left:

Max Le Verrier.

Le Verrier in his studio.

Le Verrier in Heudon air field, April 1913.

Le Verrier modelling at the zoo.

LE VERRIER BLANCHET COLLECTION

LEMO

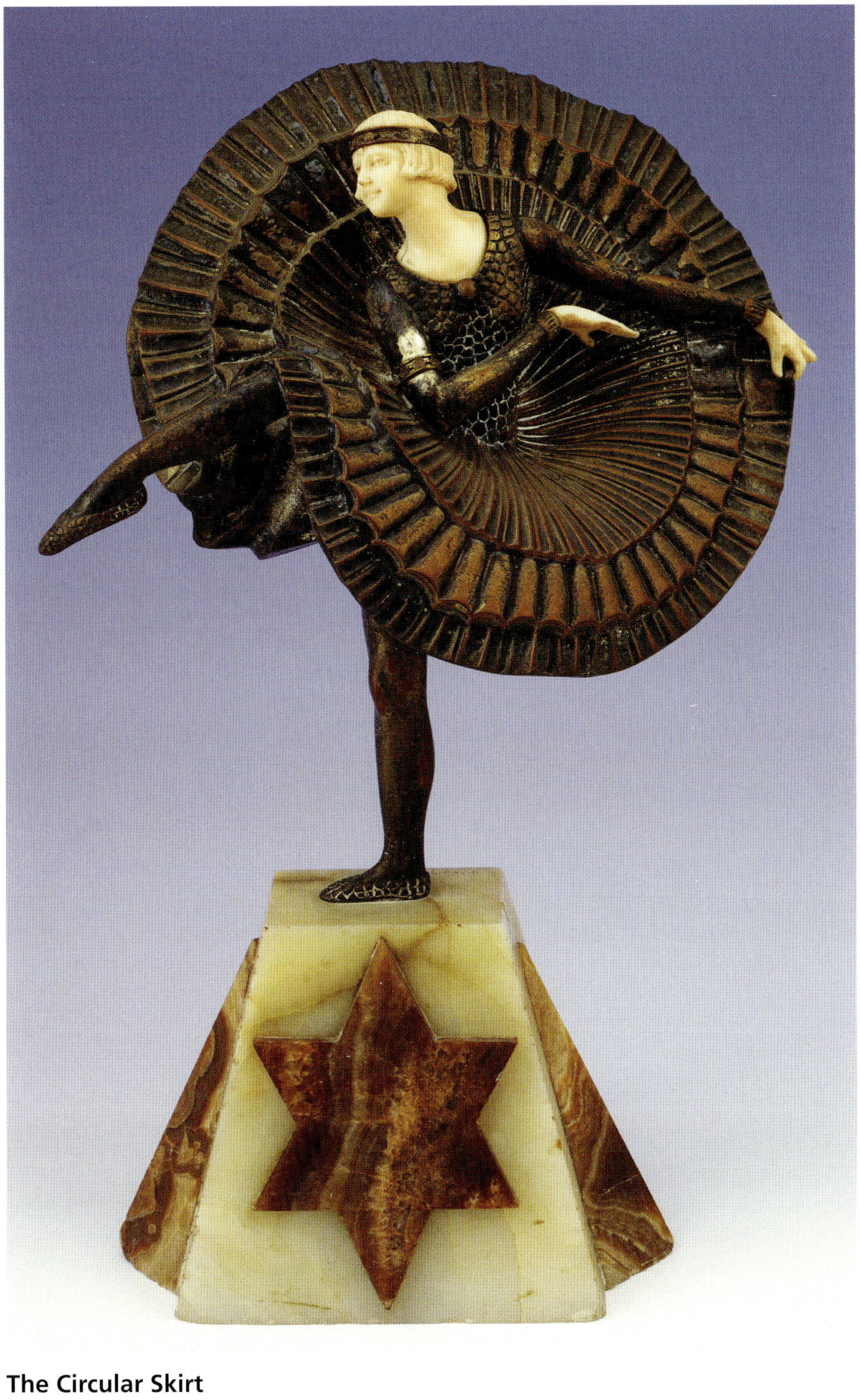

The Circular Skirt
Bronze and ivory on marble and onyx base
Height: 35cm. (13¾in.)
PRIVATE COLLECTION

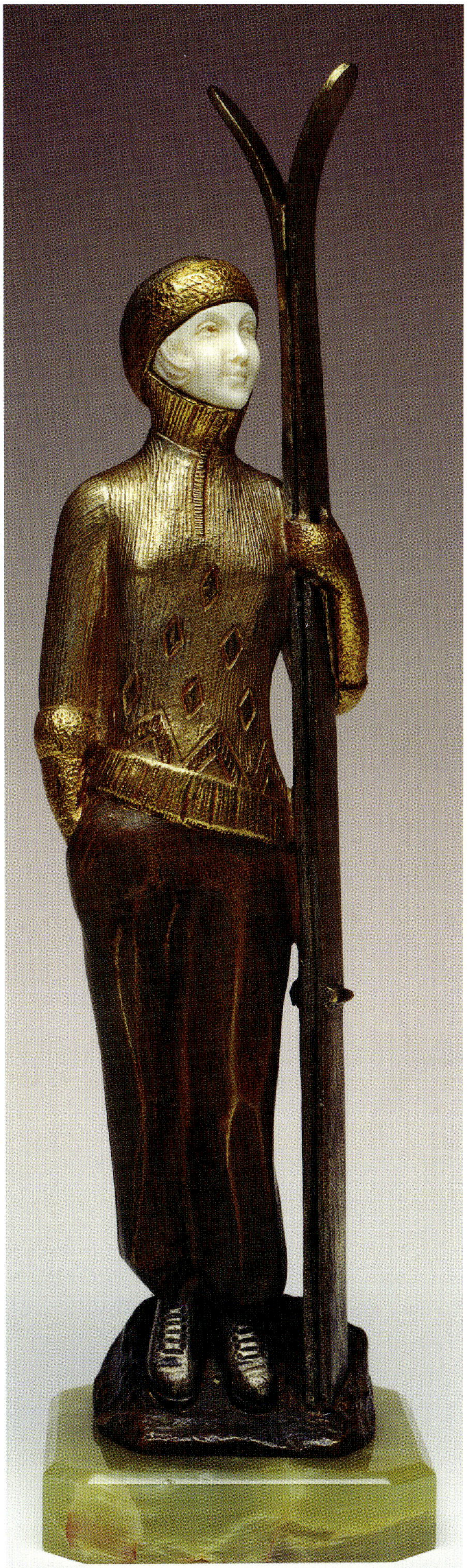

Skier
Bronze and ivory on onyx base
Height: 26.5cm. (10½in.)
PRIVATE COLLECTION

LÉONARD, Agathon

(Lille 1841 – Paris 1923)

An artist of Belgian origin, he was born Agathon Leonard van Weydeveldt in Lille (France). He attended the Lille Ecole des Beaux Arts and went on to study with Eugène Delaplanche at the Paris Ecole des Beaux Arts.

In 1868 he exhibited at the Salon of the Société des Artistes Français, and as of 1887 became a member of that Société. In 1897 he became a member of the Société Nationale des Beaux Arts. At the 1889 International Exhibition he was awarded a silver medal.

Working in the Art Nouveau style, in 1898 he sculpted two bronze figures depicting the dancer Loïe Fuller. They were used by the Royal Manufacture of Sèvres for their group of 15 bisque figures called *Le Jeu de l'Echarpe* (The Scarf Play), which was shown at the 1900 International Exhibition in Paris, where it won a gold medal.

His bronze figures were produced by Susse Frères and Siot-Decauville in Paris, and his porcelain works by Sèvres, Richard Ginori, Sesto Fiorentino, and by Gebrüder Heubach, in Lichte, Germany.

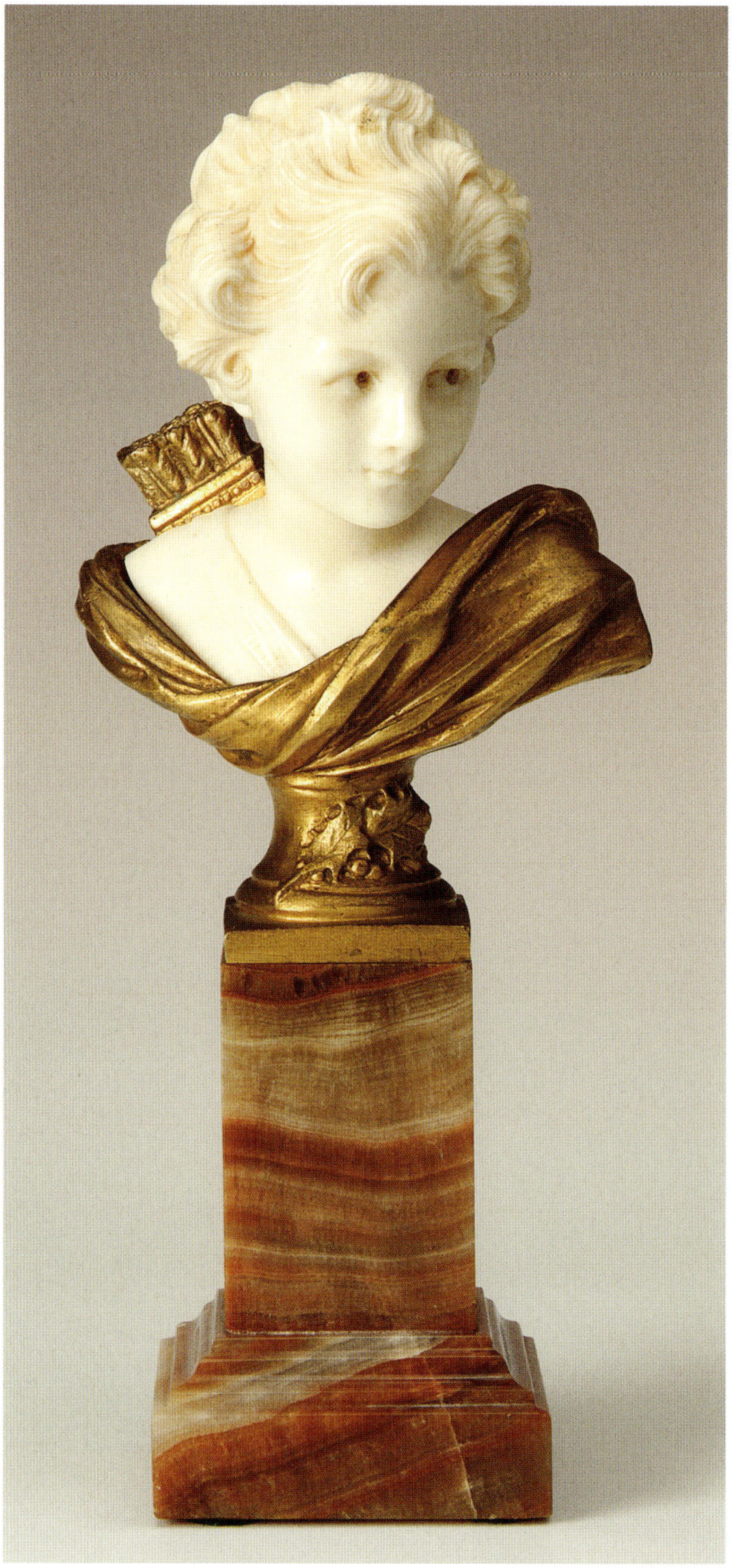

Cruel Love
Bronze and ivory on onyx base
Height: 18cm. (7in.)
DINO MENASCHE COLLECTION

Also produced in several sizes with and without the onyx base

Goddess of Youth
Ivory and bronze on marble base
Height: 34cm. (13½in.)
PRIVATE COLLECTION

Also produced 65cm. (25½in.) high

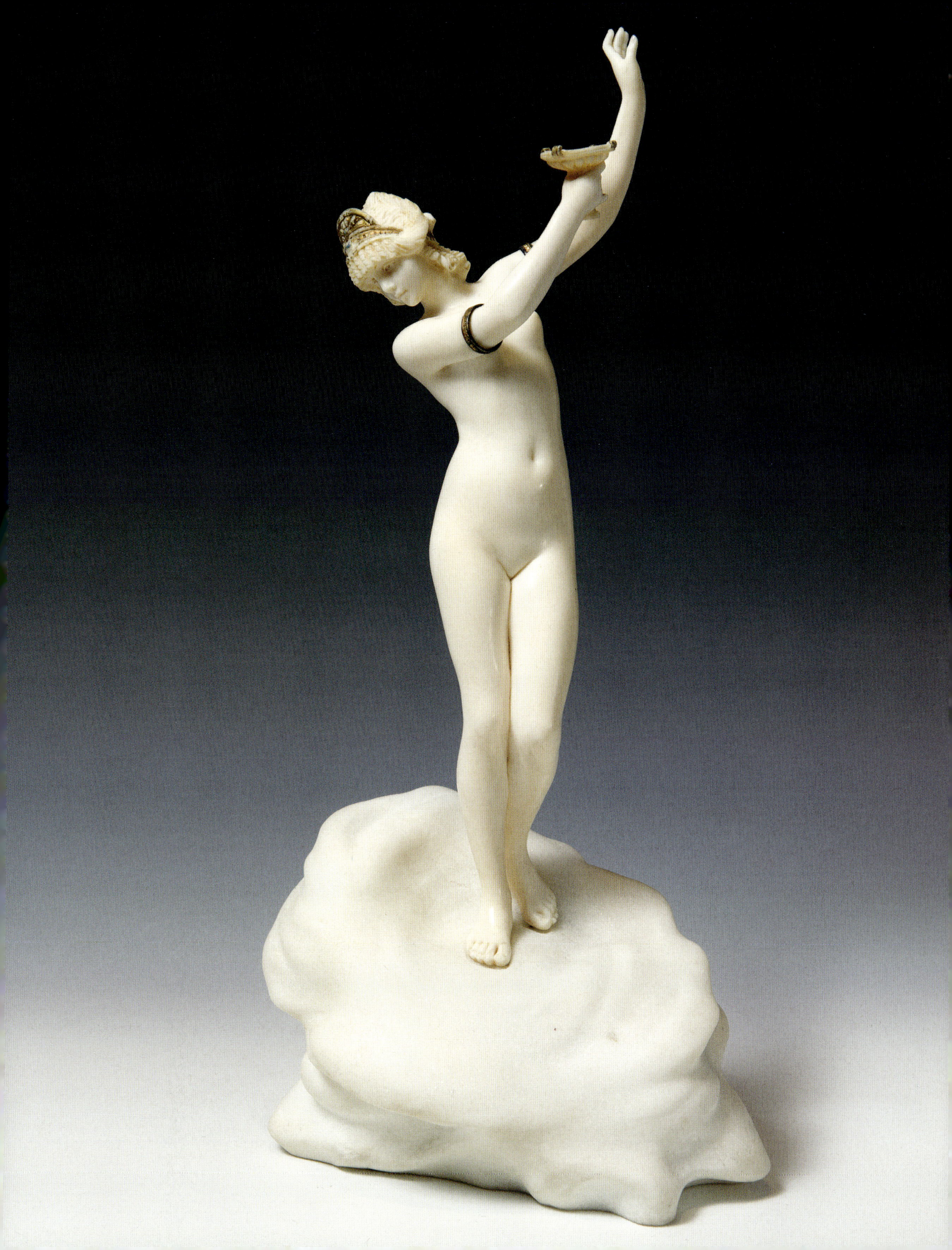

LES NEVEUX DE J. LEHMANN

The bronze foundry was run by the brothers Jules and Hugo Levy in Paris. Their premises were located at 26 rue de Paradis; there was a second shop at 14 avenue de l'Opéra. They also had a shop in Lyon at 9 rue de la République and in Florence at 7 Via Spontini.

Very active in the 1920s and 1930s, the company produced statuettes and decorative objects; at the 1929 Salon of the Société des Artistes Français a bronze vase was exhibited, made by Helene Grun and produced by Lehmann. At the 1937 International Exhibition in Paris, they showed pieces by Genarelli, Kéléty, Pina and Le Faguays.

LIPCHYTZ, Samuel (LIPSZYC)

(Pabianice 1880 – Auschwitz 1943)

Born in what at the time were the Polish provinces of Imperial Russia, Lipchytz grew up in Lodz. He travelled first to Berlin and then to Paris at the turn of the century to finish his studies and practice his art. He lived and worked in La Ruche, the famous artists' studio in Montparnasse, and participated in Paris's vibrant art scene.

He learned to sculpt ivory, which he prized for its delicacy and subtlety, and gained some renown as a sculptor working in both ivory and marble. He taught the art of ivory sculpture to his younger brother Morice, whom he brought to Paris in 1912 to pursue his art studies, at the age of 14. (Morice also lived in La Ruche, and slightly modified his name to Lipsi; he became a well-known abstract sculptor who produced many monumental pieces.) Samuel worked primarily in bronze, ivory, bronze and ivory, onyx and exotic woods. He also created fine pieces of furniture with ivory encrustations.

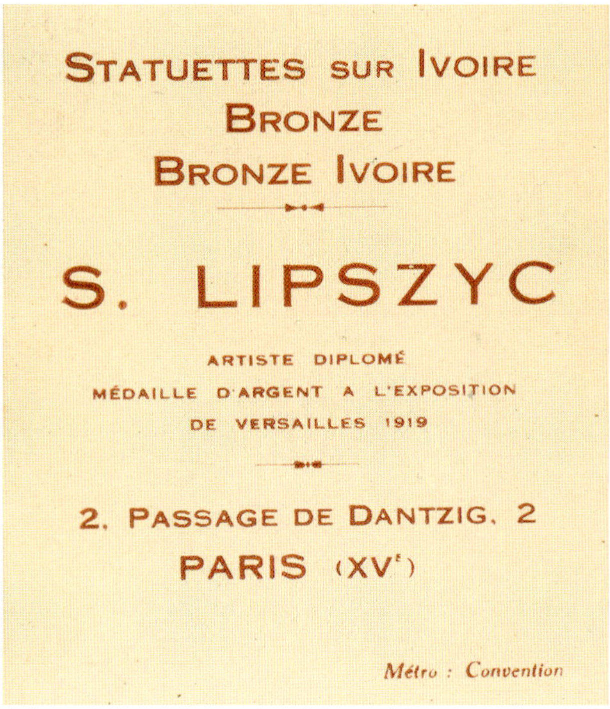
STATUETTES SUR IVOIRE
BRONZE
BRONZE IVOIRE

S. LIPSZYC

ARTISTE DIPLOMÉ
MÉDAILLE D'ARGENT A L'EXPOSITION
DE VERSAILLES 1919

2. PASSAGE DE DANTZIG. 2
PARIS (XVᵉ)

Métro : Convention

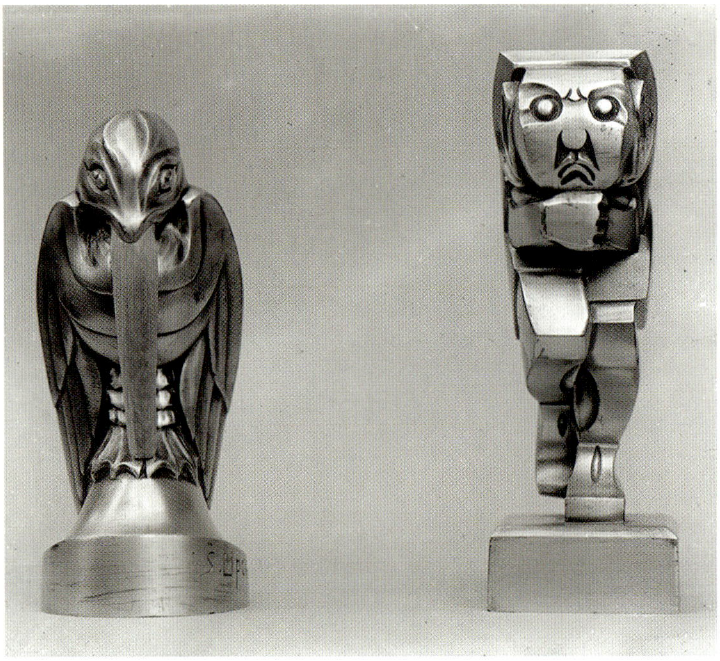

When the Art Deco style came into fashion, Samuel Lipchytz produced chryselephantine statuettes often depicting dancers.

Samuel Lipchytz was deported and died in Auschwitz in 1943, at the age of 63. His brother Morice survived, dying in Switzerland in 1996.

Two modernist bronze sculptures,
Bird *and* Rugby Man.
BECK-LIPSI COLLECTION

Samuel Lipchytz in his studio.
BECK-LIPSI COLLECTION

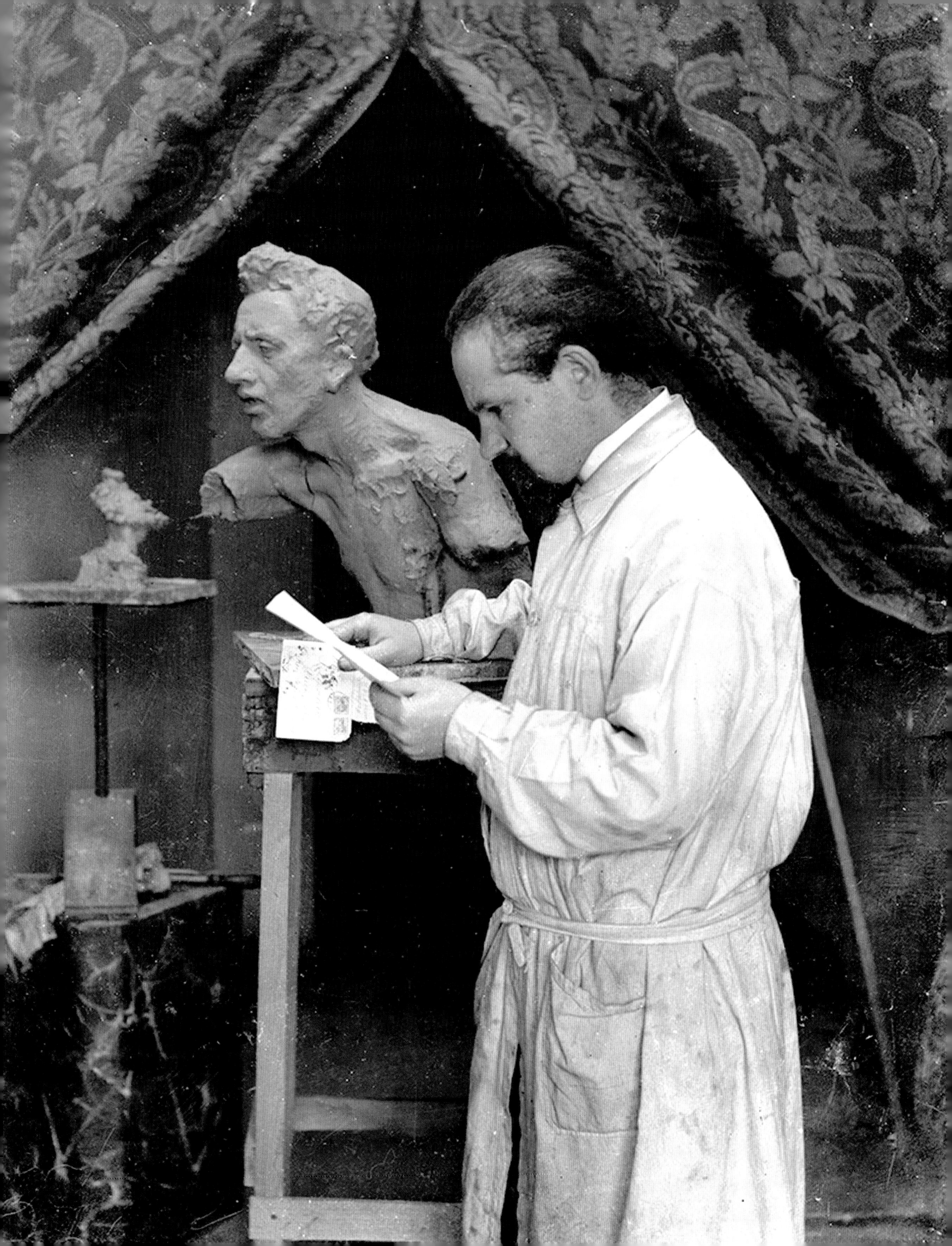

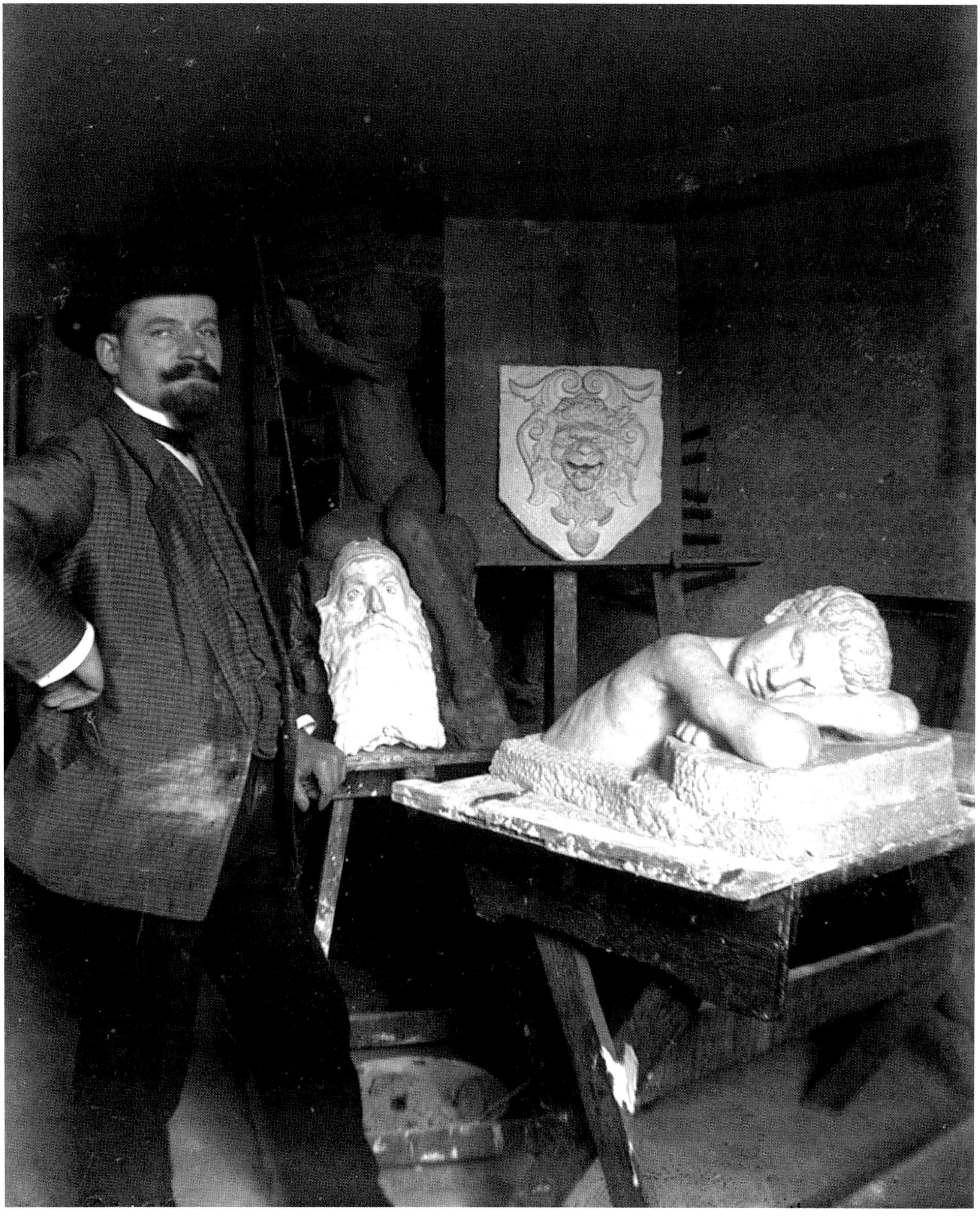

Samuel Lipchytz in his studio.
BECK-LIPSI COLLECTION

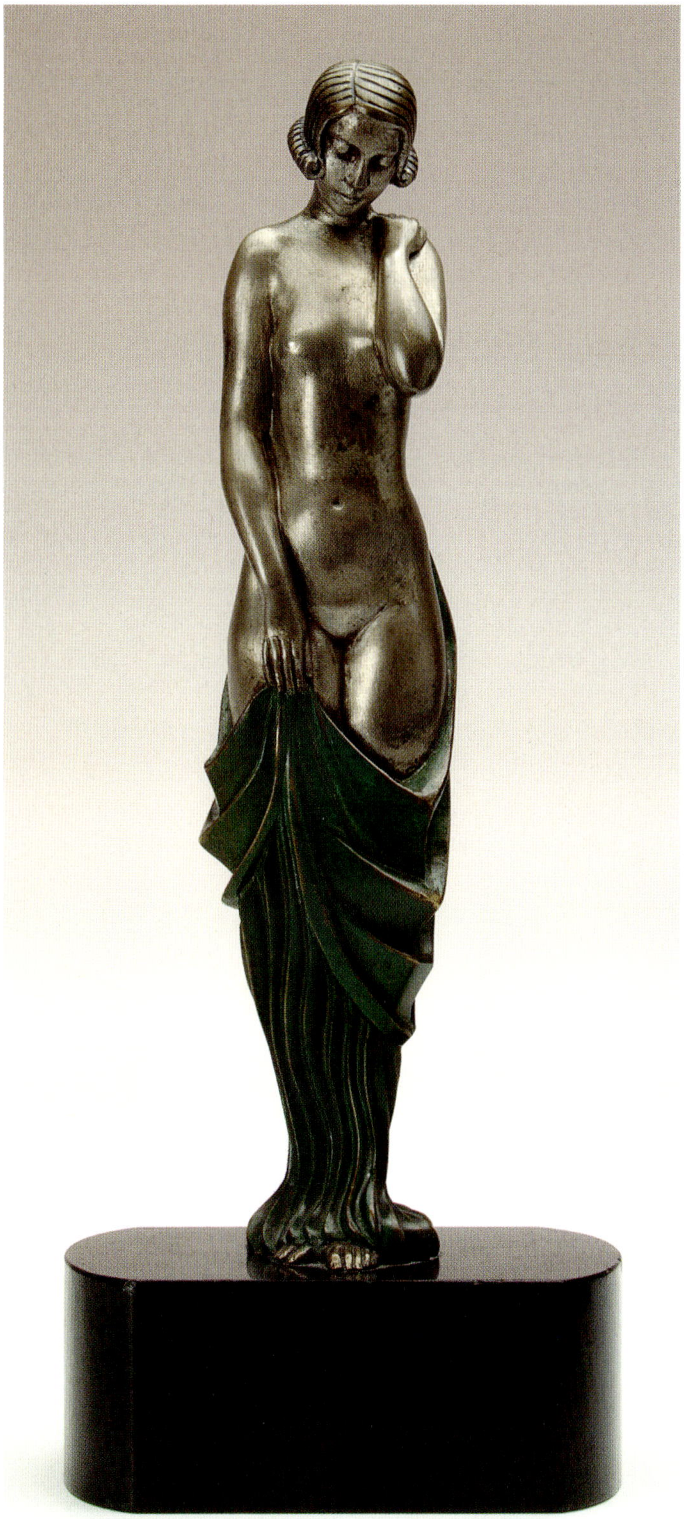

Semi-nude
Bronze on onyx base
Height: 30.5cm. (12in.)
DINO MENASCHE COLLECTION

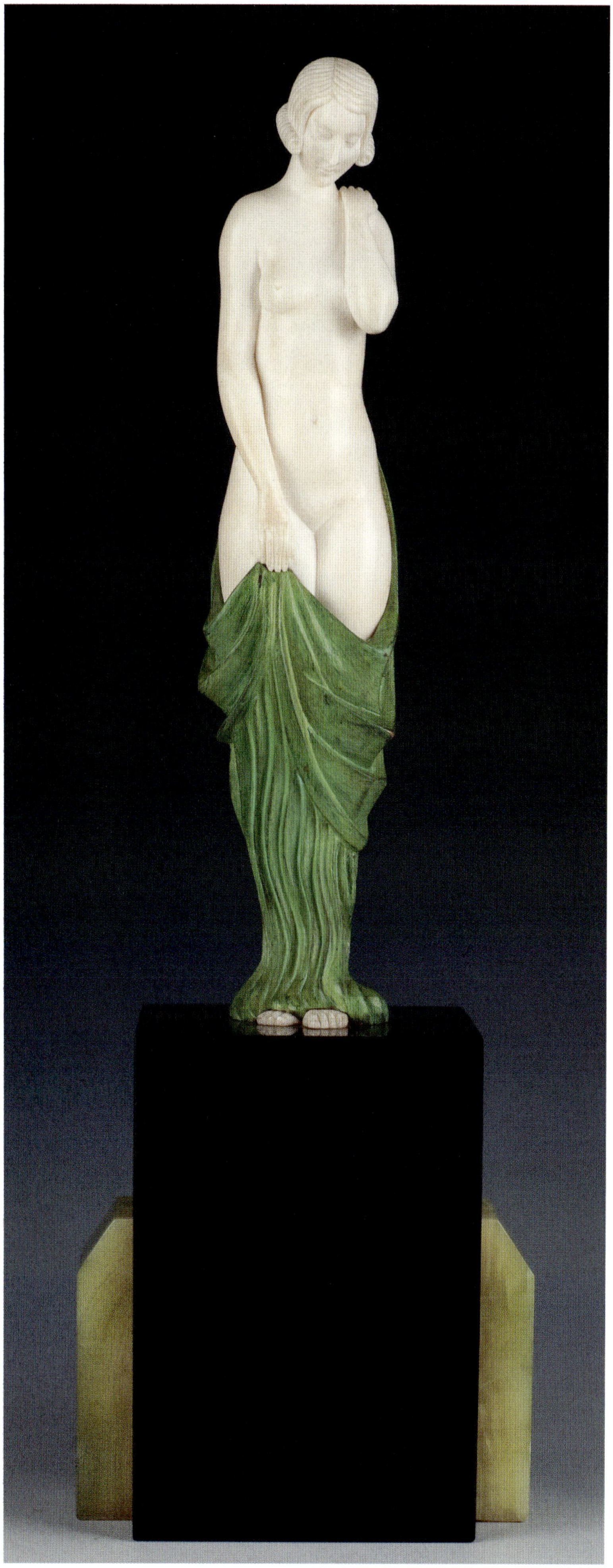

Semi-nude
Bronze and ivory on onyx base
Height: 38cm. (15in.)
CORNELIA AND RICHARD KASTENHOLZ COLLECTION, GERMANY

Highball
Bronze and ivory on marble base
Signed: 'Lip'
Height: 52cm. (20½in.)
PRIVATE COLLECTION

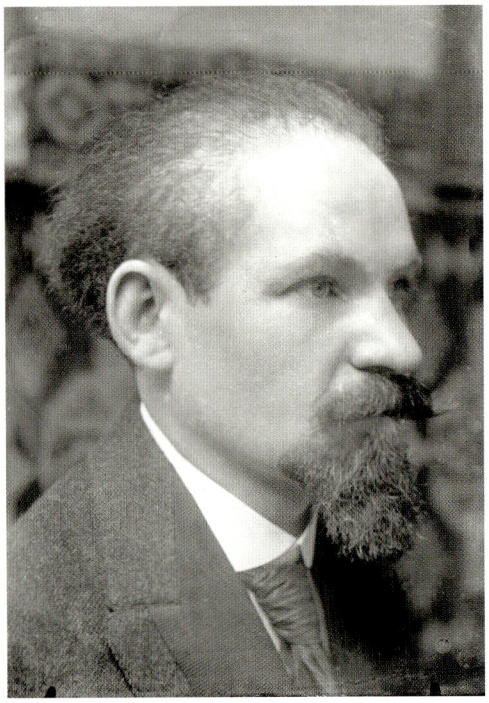

Samuel Lipchytz.
BECK-LIPSI COLLECTION

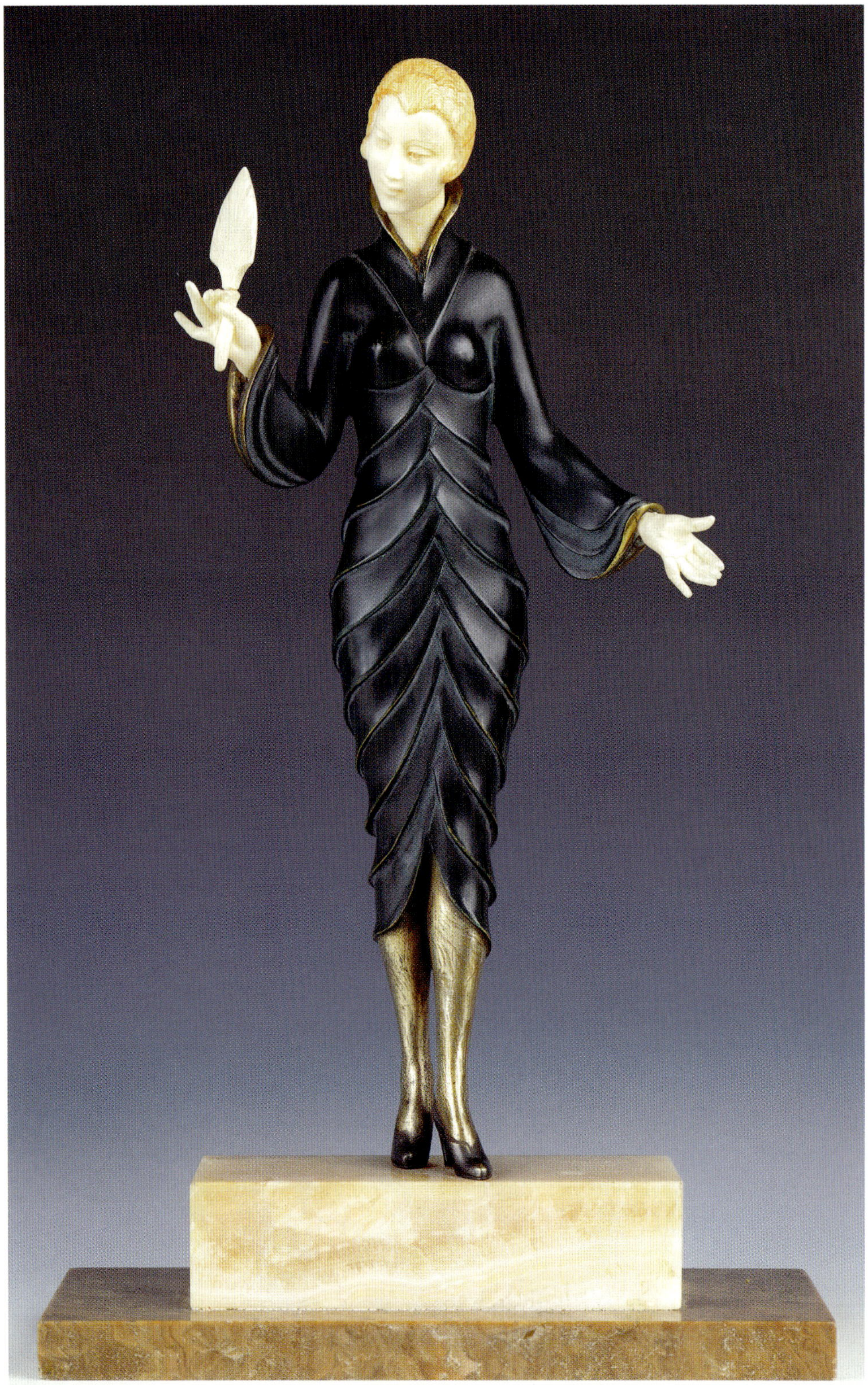

Lady with Mirror
Bronze and ivory on marble base
Height: 39.5cm. (15½in.)
VIRGINIA MUSEUM OF FINE ARTS, RICHMOND,
GIFT OF SYDNEY AND FRANCES LEWIS

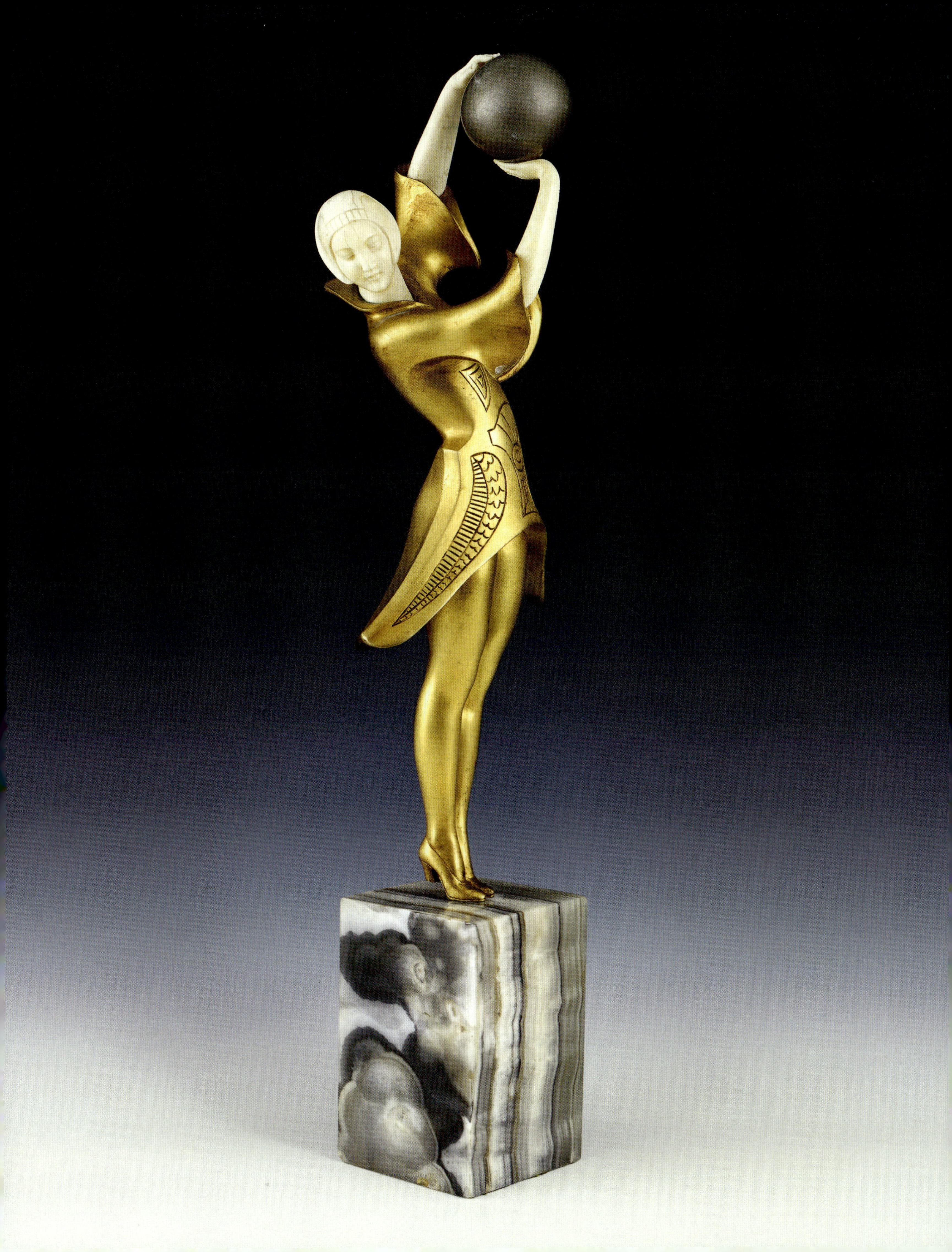

LORENZL, Josef

(Vienna 1892 – Vienna 1950)

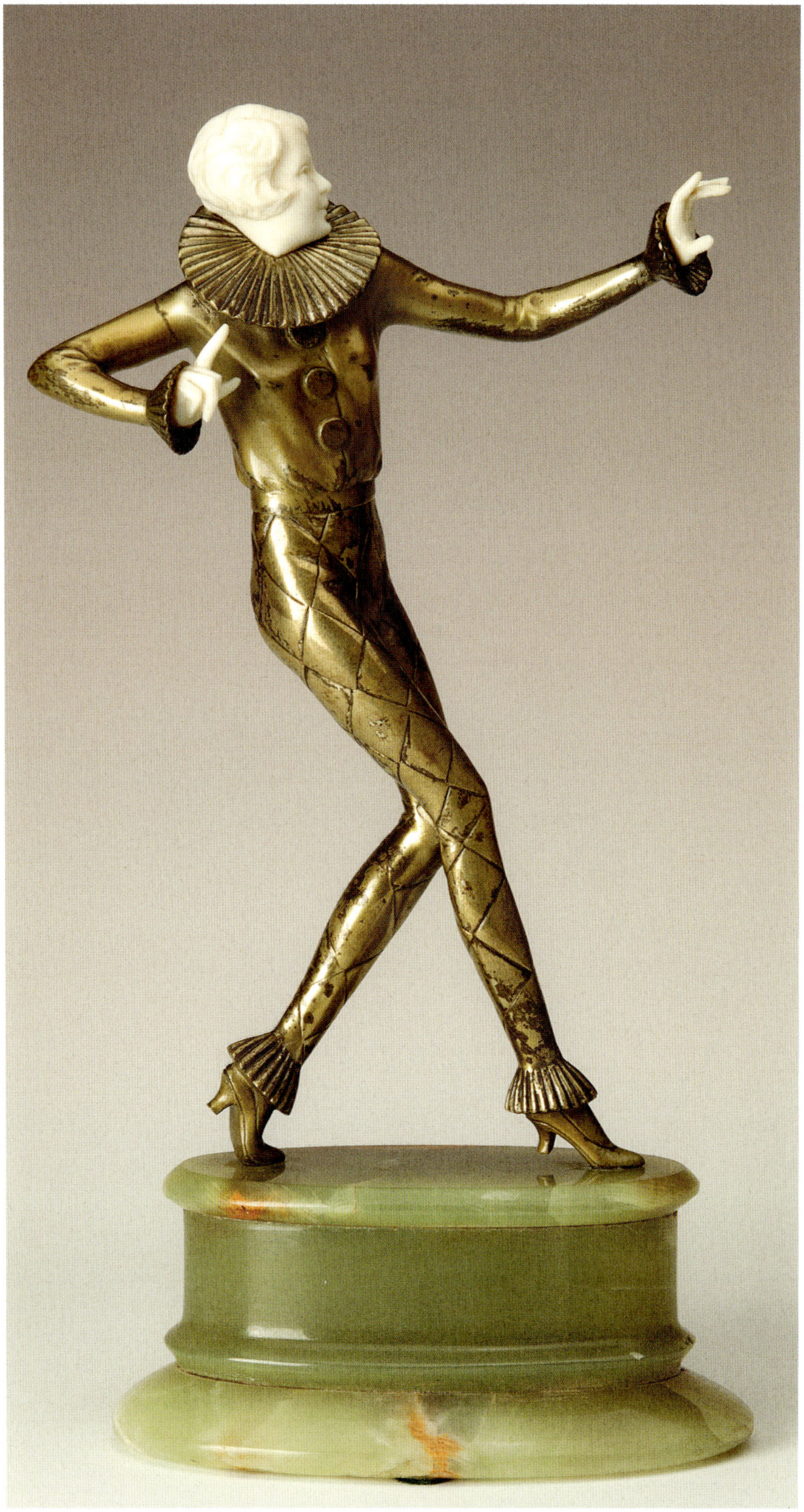

Other signatures: 'Laurenzl'; 'K Lorenzl'; 'K Lor'; 'R Lor'; 'Lor'; 'Renzl'

Born in Vienna, Lorenzl worked in bronze, bronze and ivory, spelter, and ceramics. His pieces were produced by Goldscheider, Keramos, and the Wiener Kunst Keramic und Porzellanmanufaktur AG; he also worked in the bronze factory at the Vienna Arsenal.

Very prolific during the 1920s and 1930s, Lorenzl exhibited at the Salon of the Société des Artistes Français during this period.

Ruffles
Bronze and ivory on onyx base
Height: 24cm. (9½in.)
DINO MENASCHE COLLECTION

Draped Dancer
Bronze and ivory on onyx base
Height: 37cm. (14½in.)
PRIVATE COLLECTION

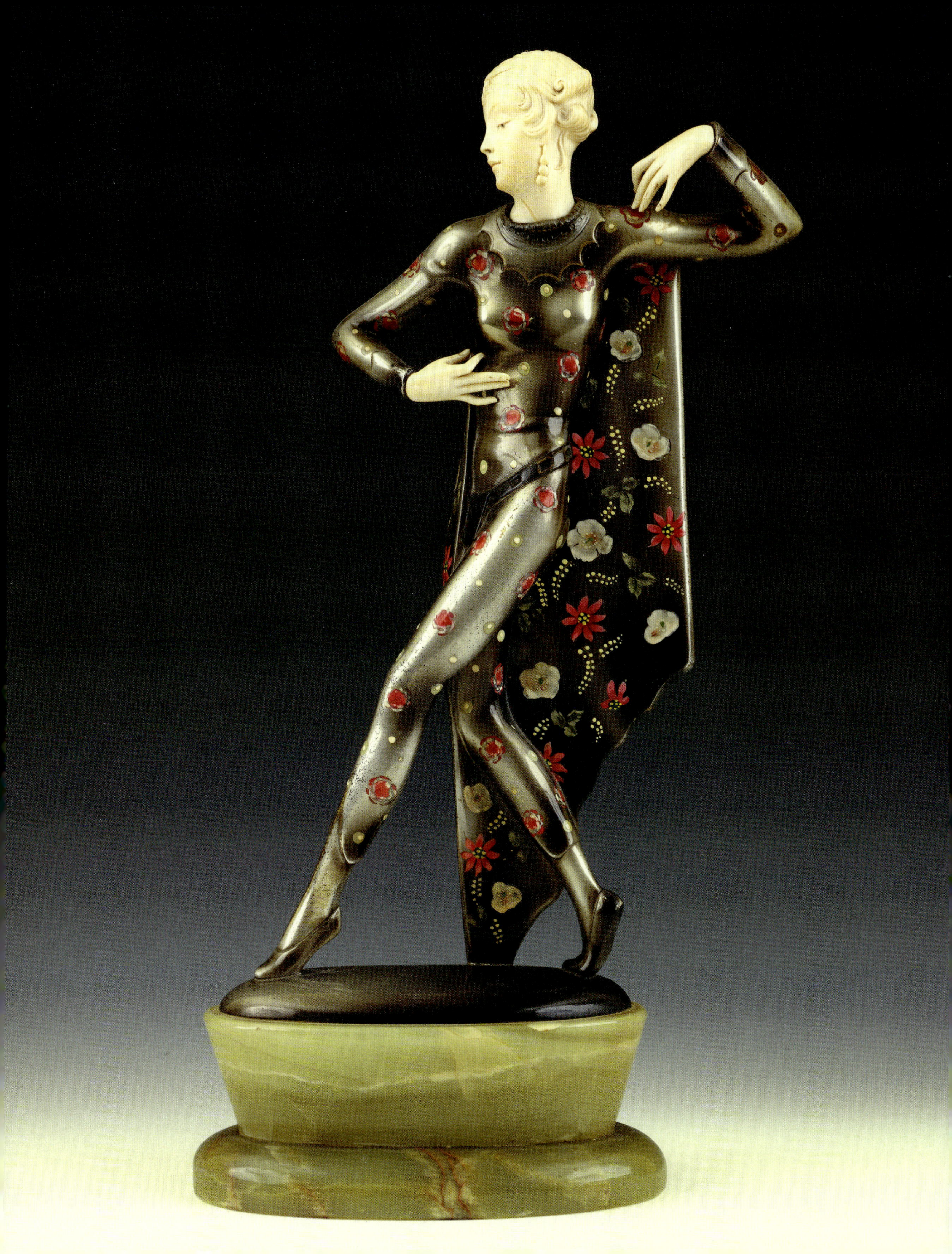

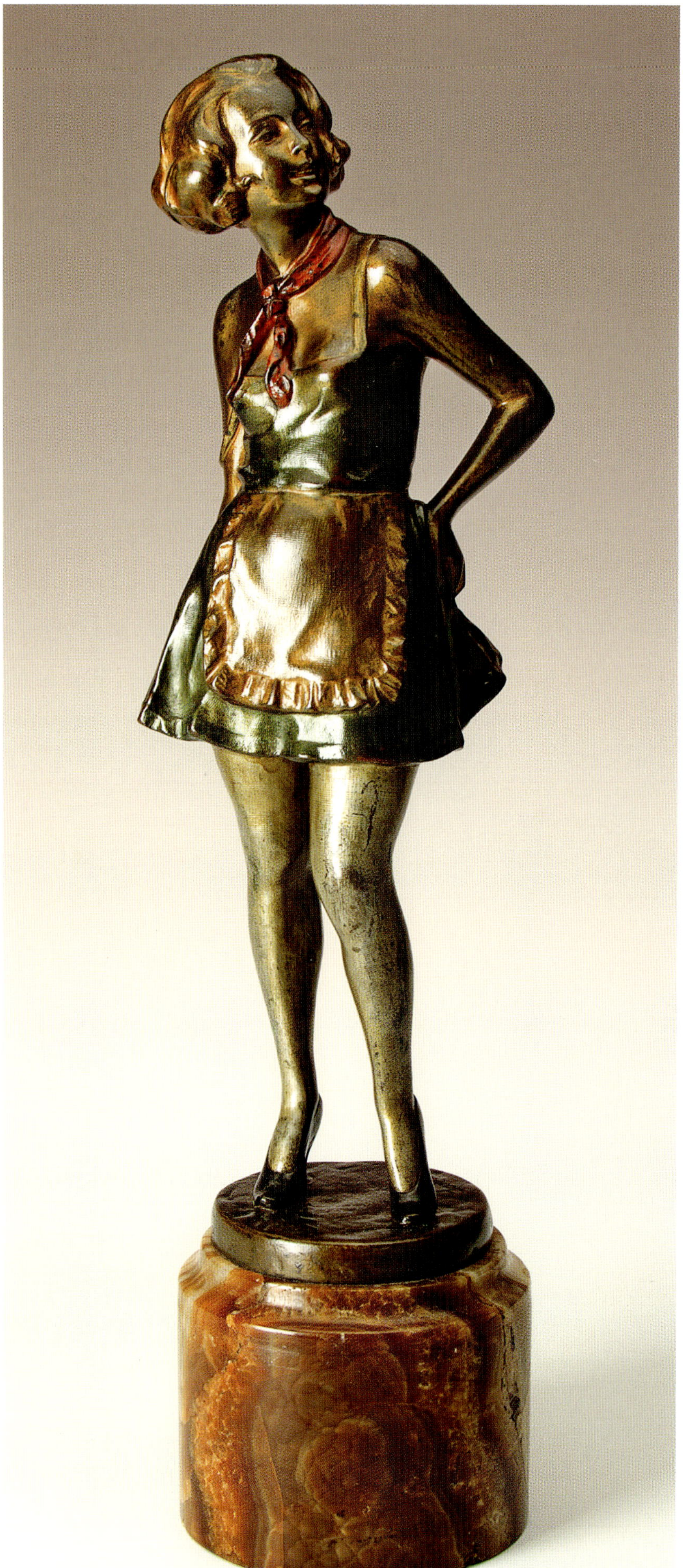

Scarf and Apron
Bronze on marble base
Height: 36.5cm. (14½in.)
DINO MENASCHE COLLECTION

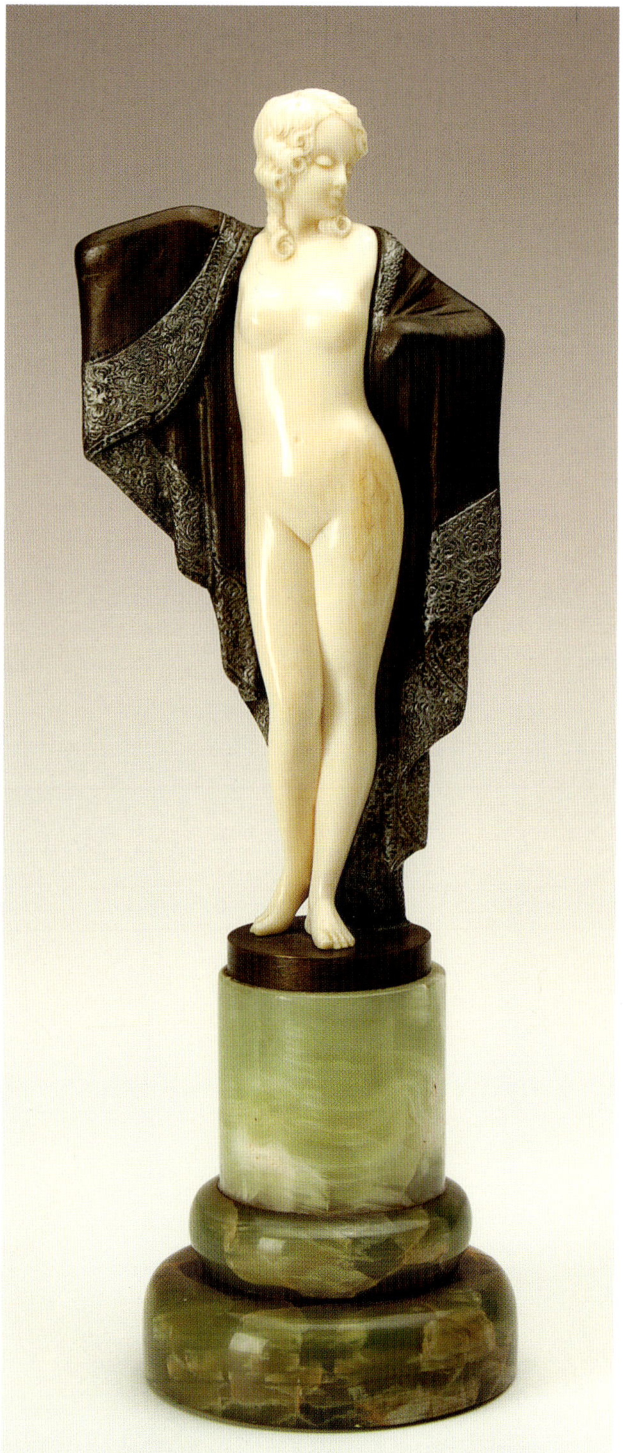

Nude with Shawl
Bronze and ivory on onyx base
Height: 24.5cm. (9¾in.)
DINO MENASCHE COLLECTION

Style Dancer
Bronze and ivory on onyx base
Height: 67.5cm. (26½in.)
PRIVATE COLLECTION

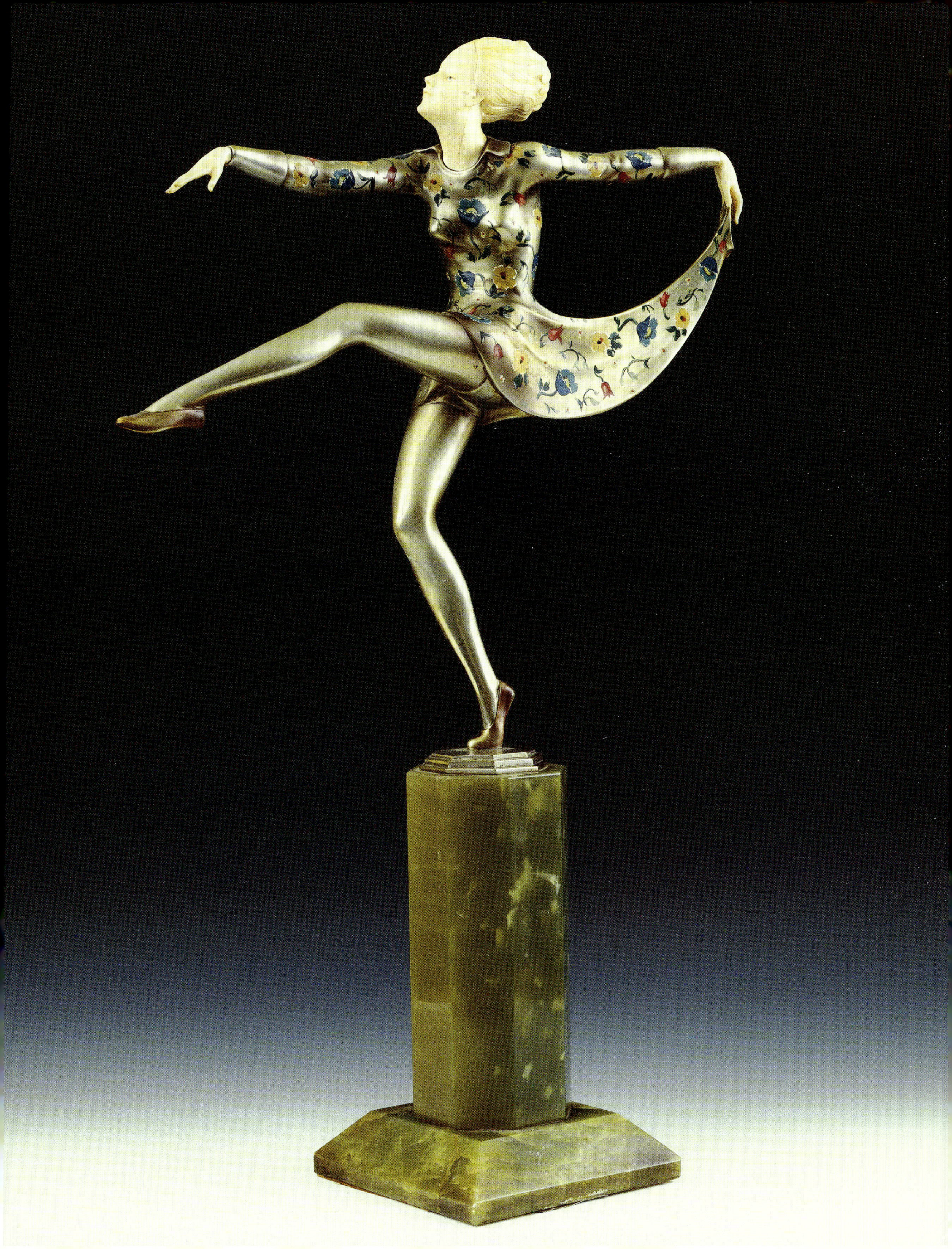

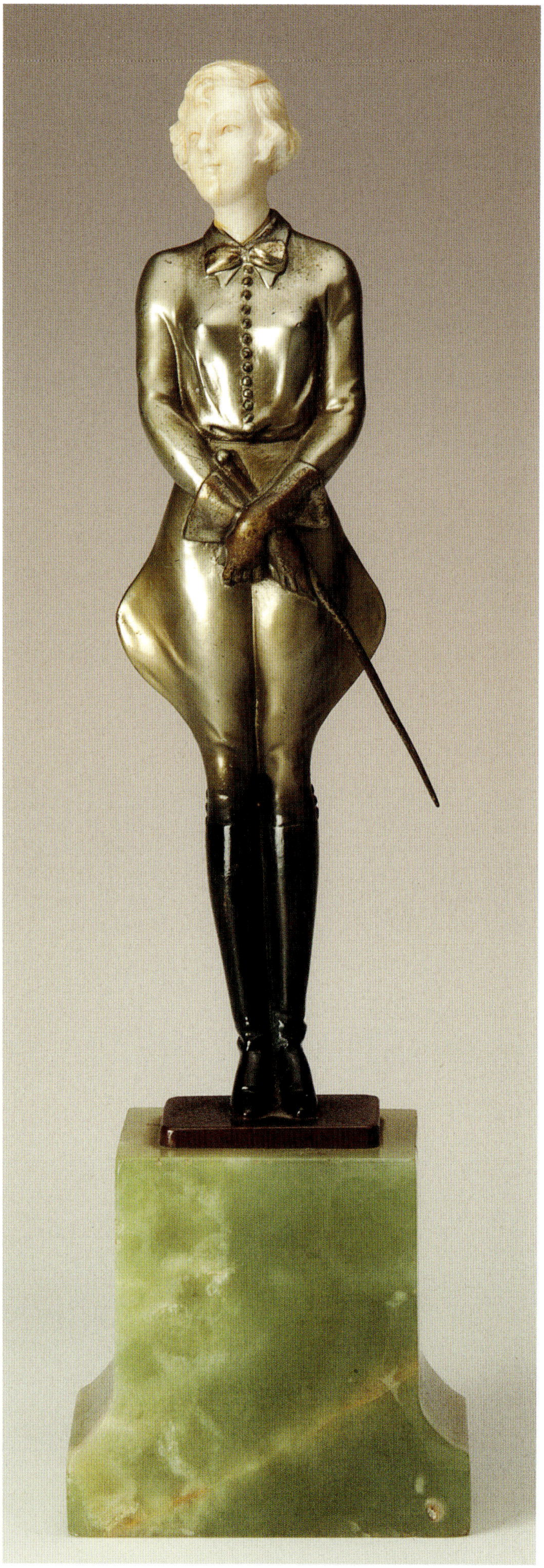

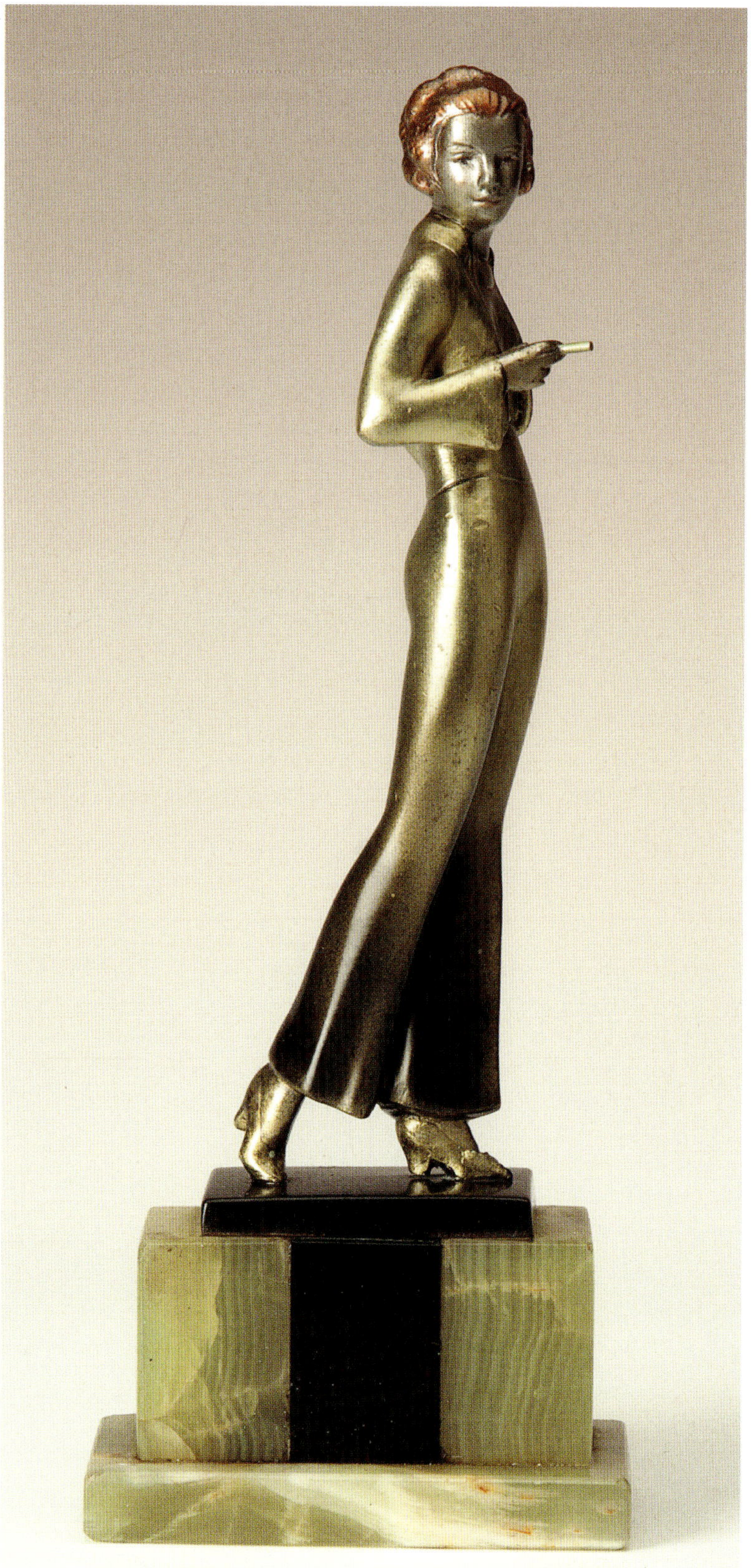

The Cigarette
Bronze and ivory on onyx base
Height: 19.5cm. (7¾in.)
DINO MENASCHE COLLECTION

Whip and Boots
Bronze and ivory on onyx base
Height: 23.5cm. (9¼in.)
DINO MENASCHE COLLECTION

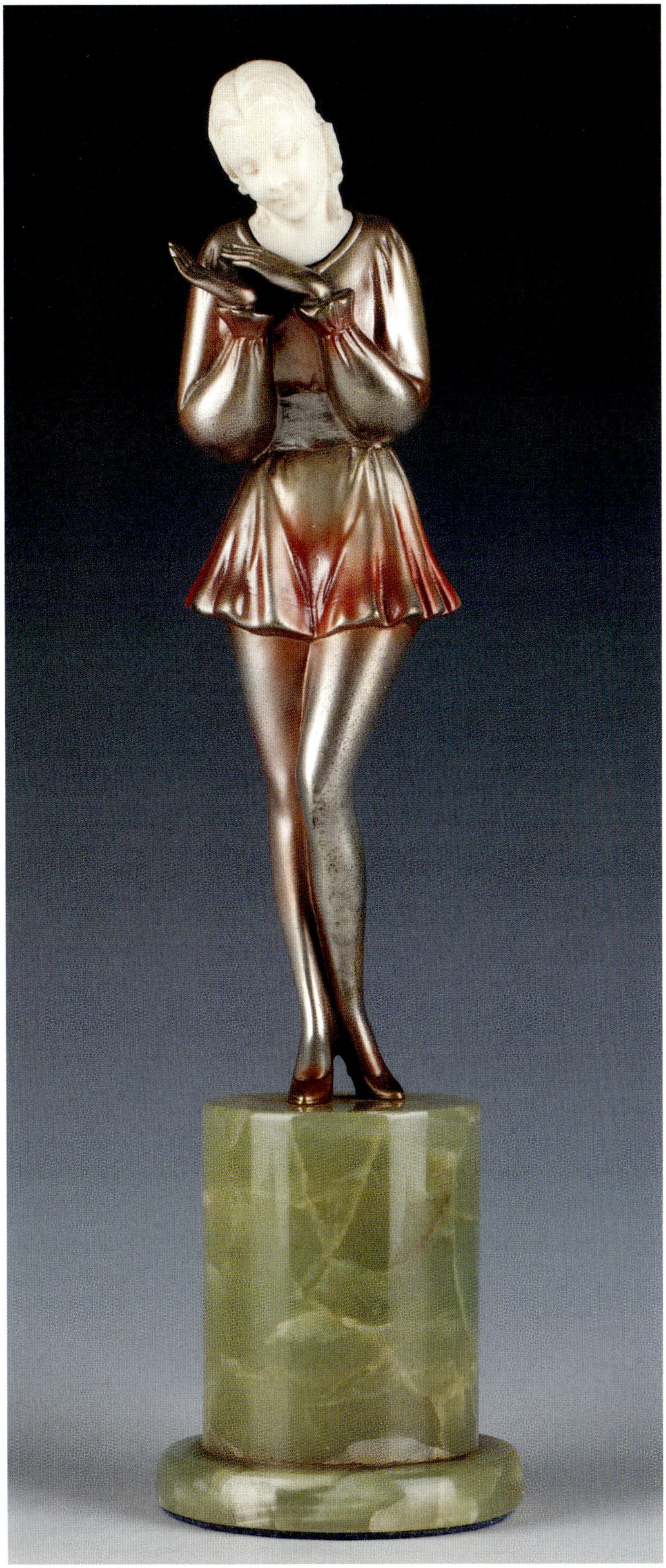

Repose
Bronze and ivory on onyx base
Height: 22.5cm. (9in.)
CORNELIA AND RICHARD KASTENHOLZ COLLECTION, GERMANY

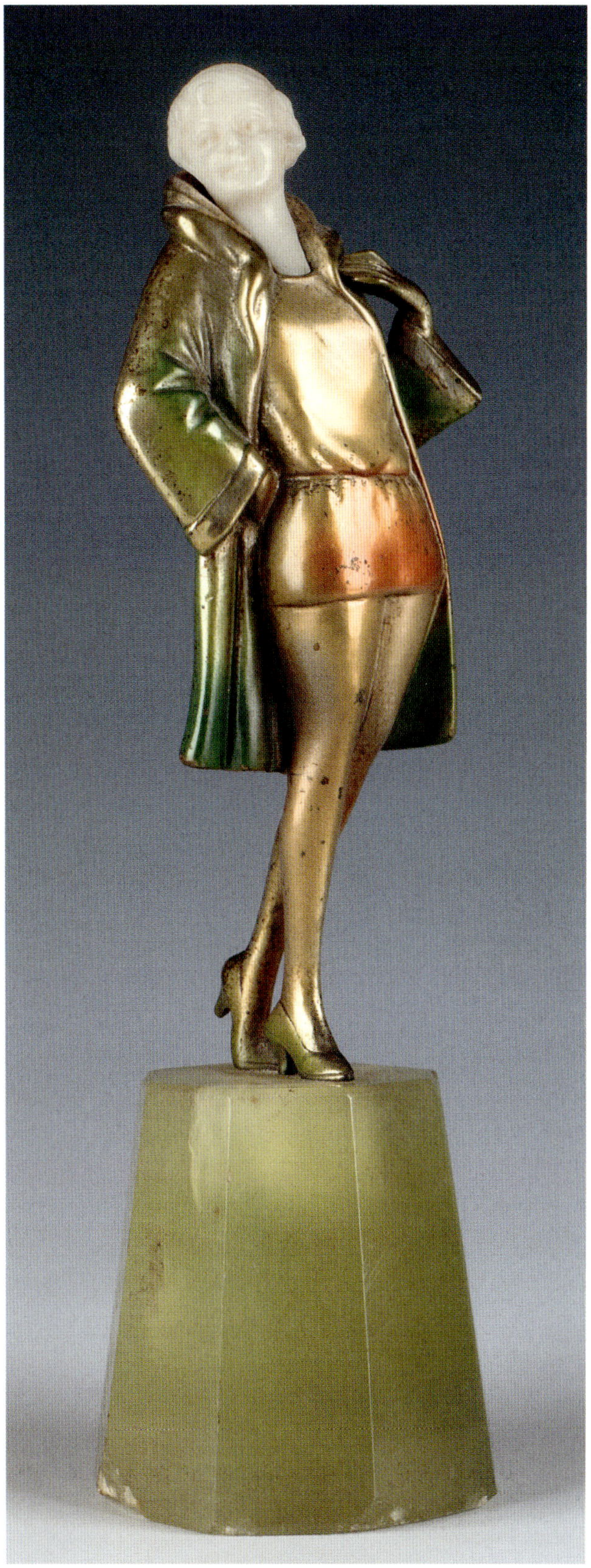

The Overcoat
Bronze and ivory on onyx base
Height: 13.5cm. (5¼in.)
CORNELIA AND RICHARD KASTENHOLZ COLLECTION, GERMANY

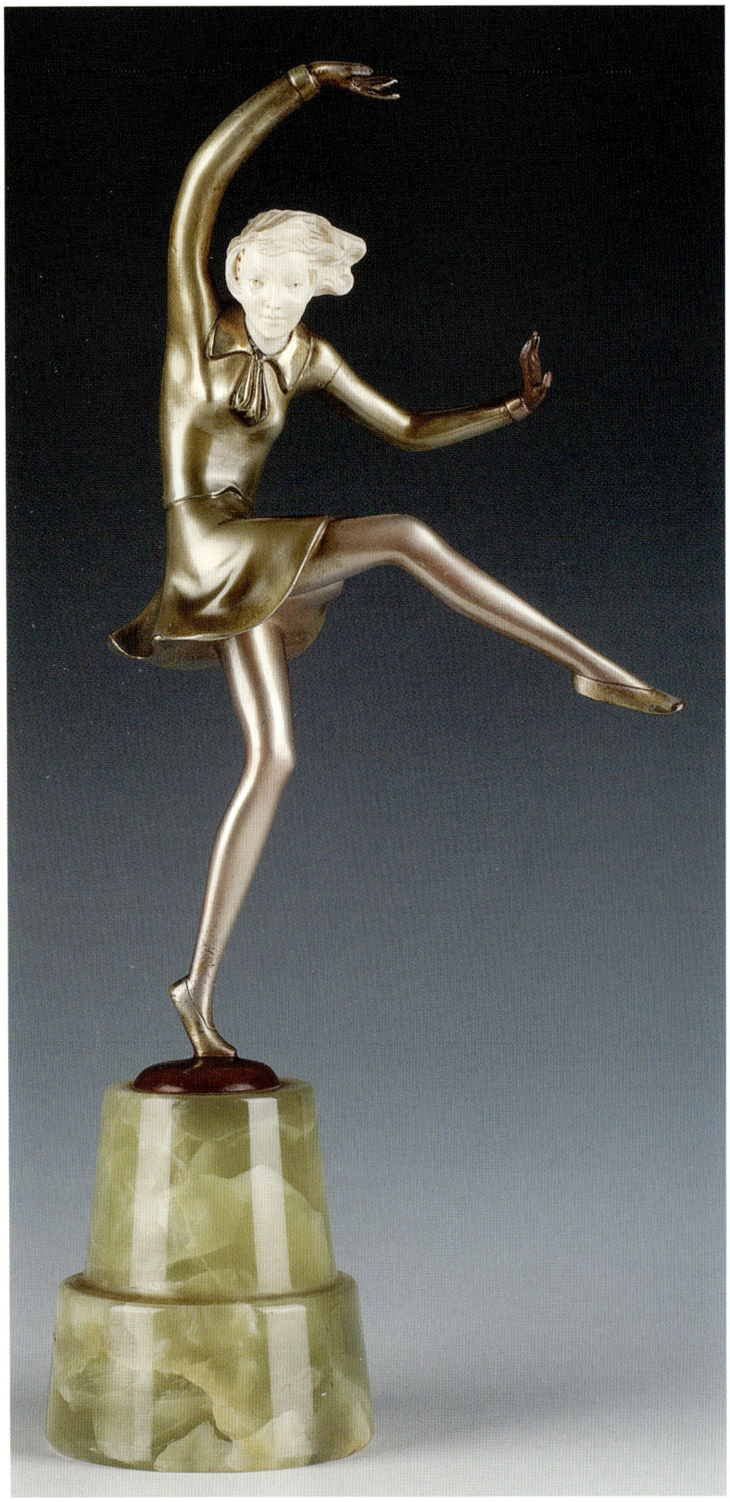

Tiptoed Dancer
Bronze and ivory on onyx base
Height: 26cm. (10¼in.)
CORNELIA AND RICHARD KASTENHOLZ COLLECTION, GERMANY

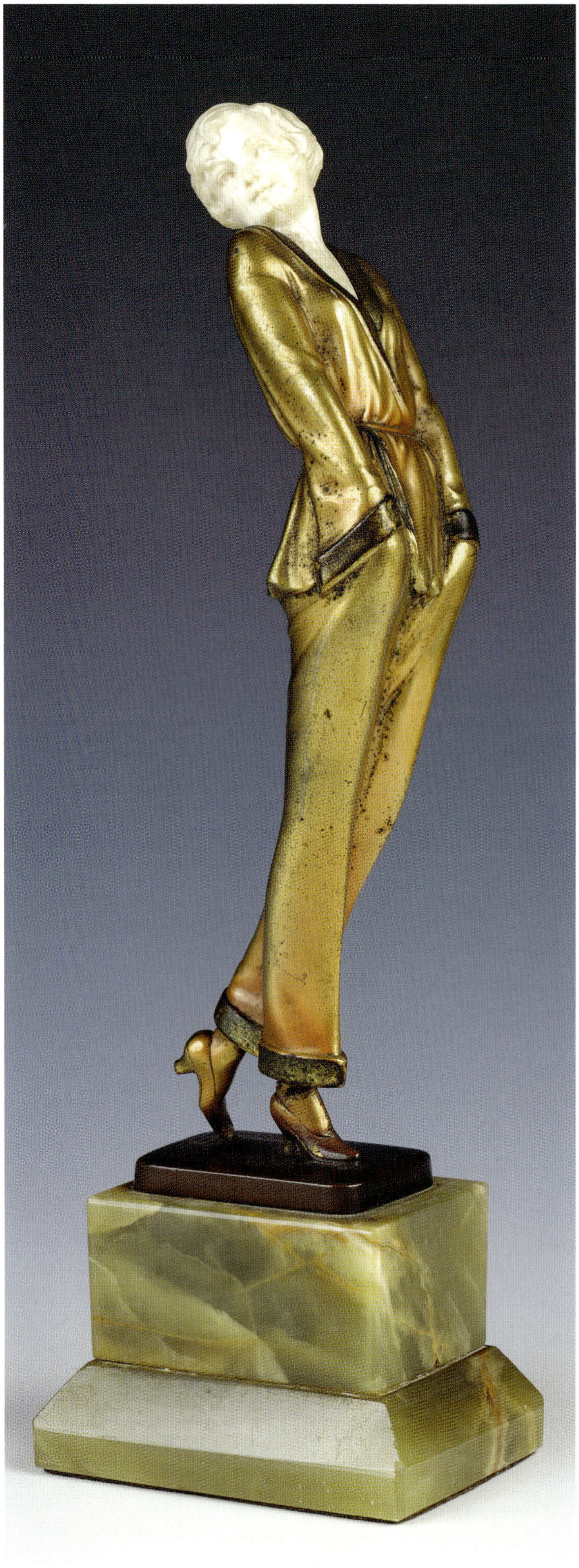

Pyjama Girl
Bronze and ivory on onyx base
Height: 23cm. (9in.)
VIRGINIA MUSEUM OF FINE ARTS, RICHMOND,
GIFT OF SYDNEY AND FRANCES LEWIS

LORMIER, Jean

French

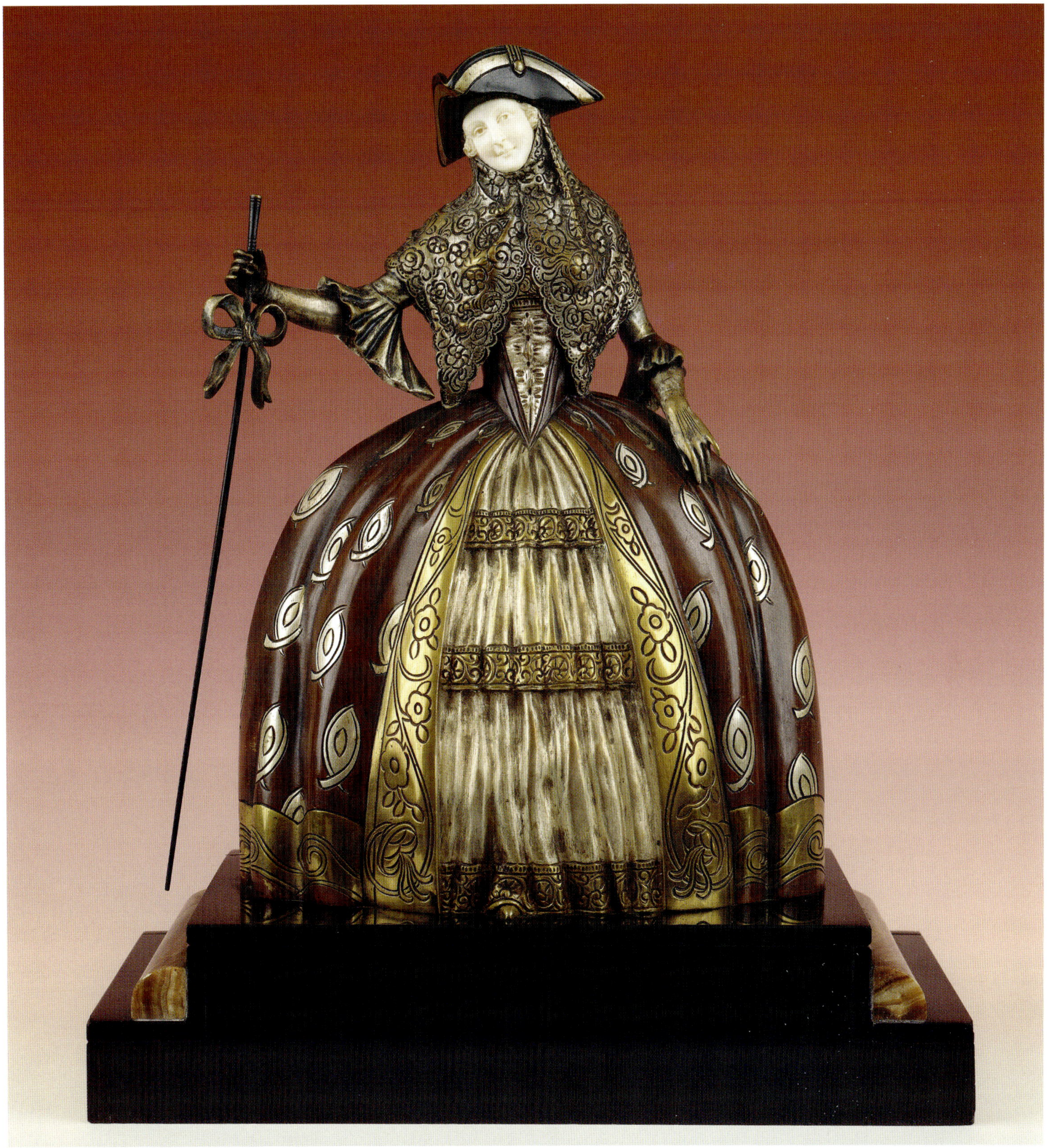

Venetian

Bronze and ivory on onyx base

Height: 42cm. (16½in.)

PRIVATE COLLECTION

MARCUSE, Rudolf (MARKUSE)

(1878 – 1930)

German. Studied at the Berlin Academy. Created monuments in Berlin and Stellingen.

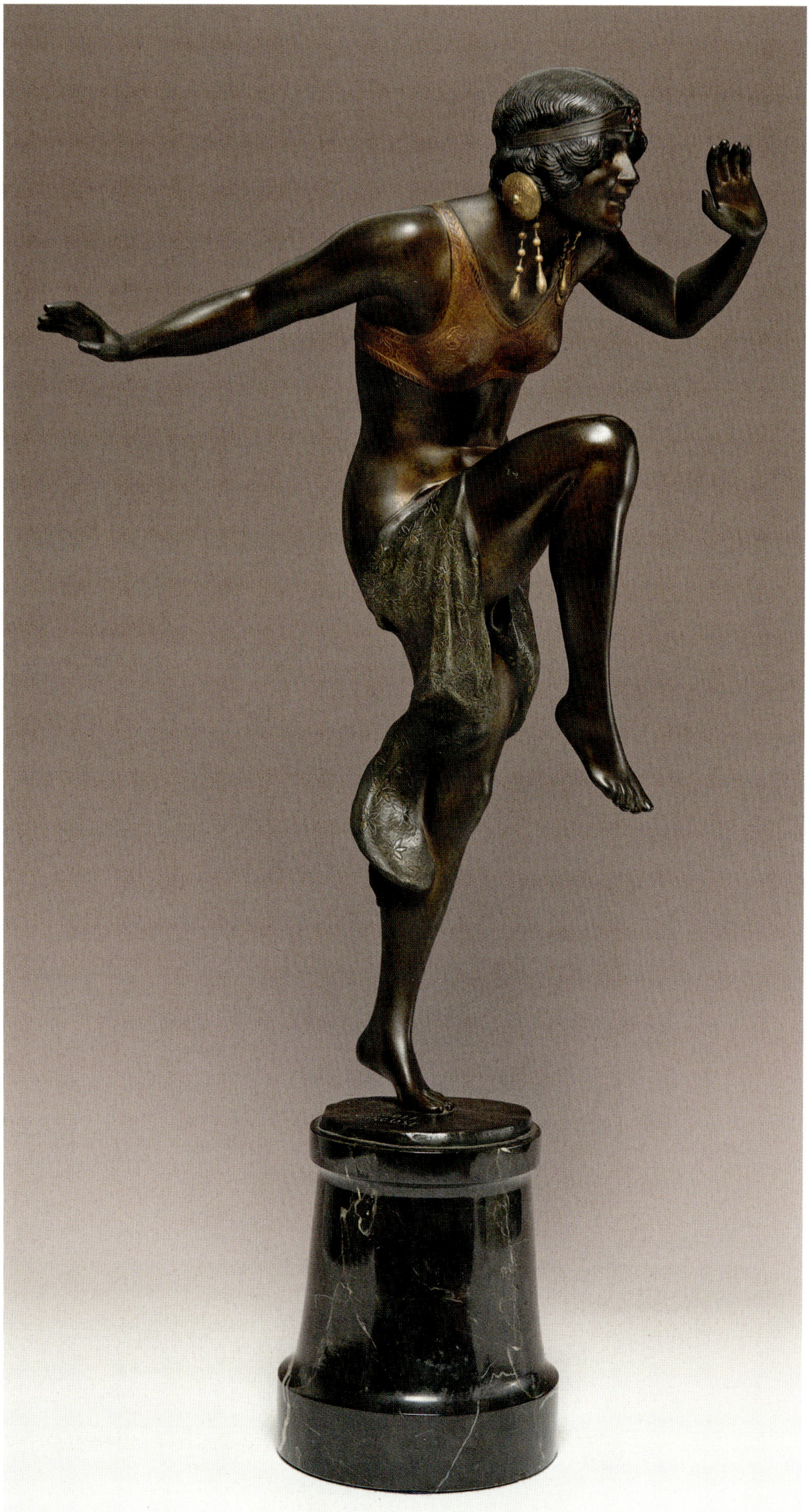

Native dancer
Bronze on marble base
Height: 61.5cm. (24¼in.)
PRIVATE COLLECTION

MARQUET, René-Paul

(Port Louis 1875 – 1939)

René-Paul Marquet studied sculpture at the Ecole Nationale des Beaux Arts in Paris, under Emmanuel Fontaine and Alexandre Falguière.

He exhibited at the Salon of the Société des Artistes Français, winning an honourable mention in 1909.

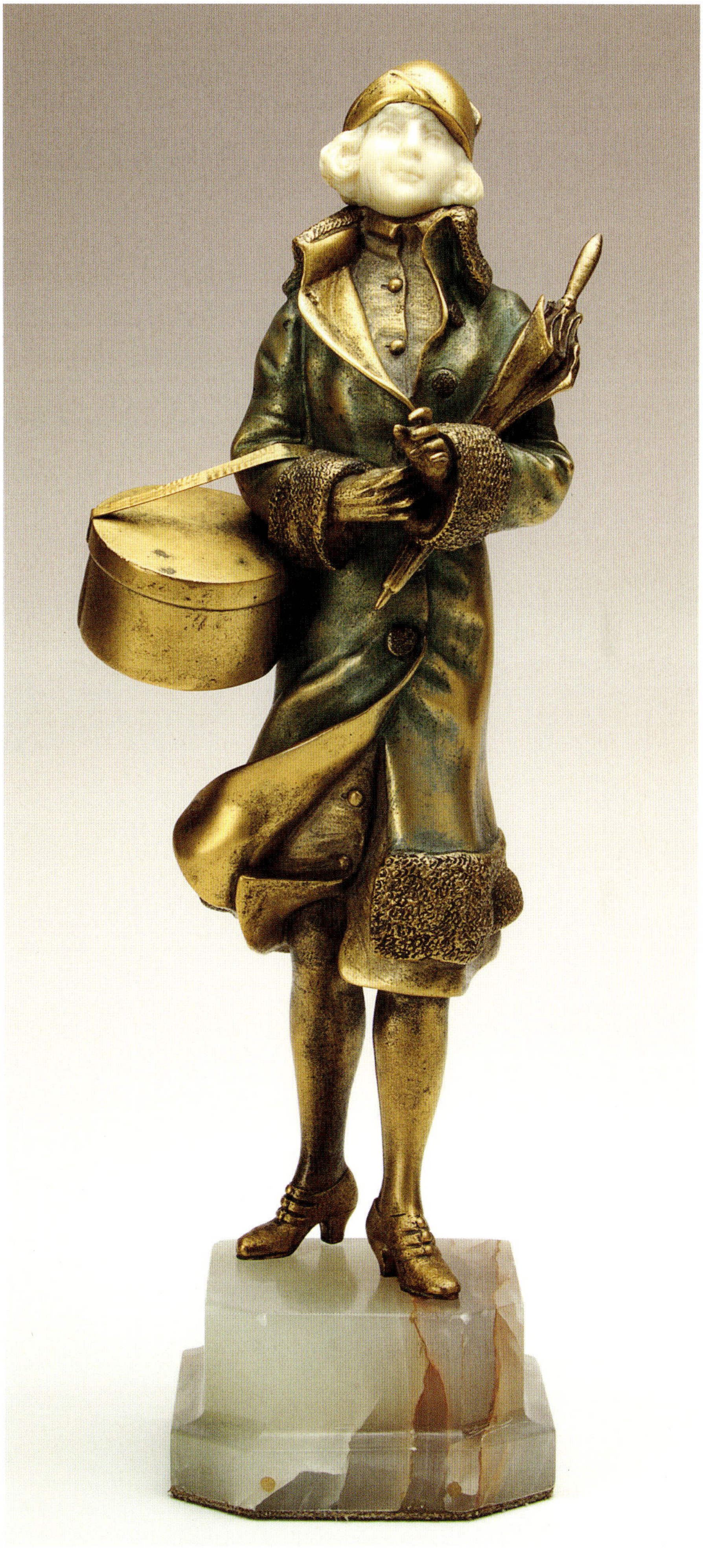

Windy Promenade
Bronze and ivory on marble base
Height: 30cm. (11¾in.)
DINO MENASCHE COLLECTION

MAY, Sibylle

English. She worked in France. Belonged to the La Stèle and Evolution groups. She worked with Pierre Le Faguays and Edouard Cazaux.

Arthur Goldscheider in Paris produced various bronzes and ceramics for her.

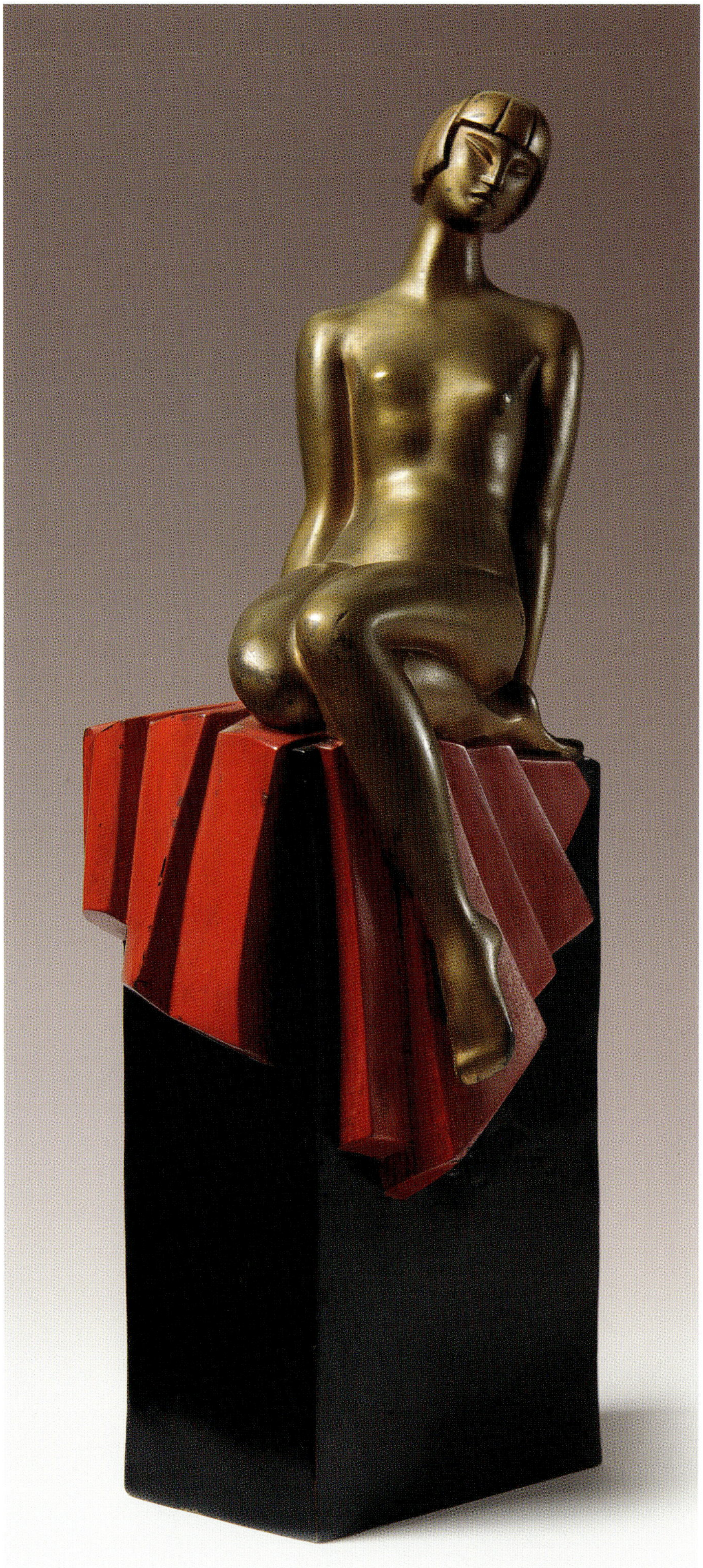

Perched Nude
Bronze
Height: 34.5cm. (13½in.)
PRIVATE COLLECTION

MOLINS-BALLESTE, Enrique

(Barcelona 1893 – 1958)

Other signatures: 'H. Molins' (the initial H. stands for Henri – Enrique in French.); 'Balleste'; 'BAL'; 'GUAL' (part of his wife's name Concepcion Gual-Cuberes)

Born in Barcelona, he later moved to Paris. Known for his dramatic style and figural lighting models, Molins-Balleste also produced wood sculptures.

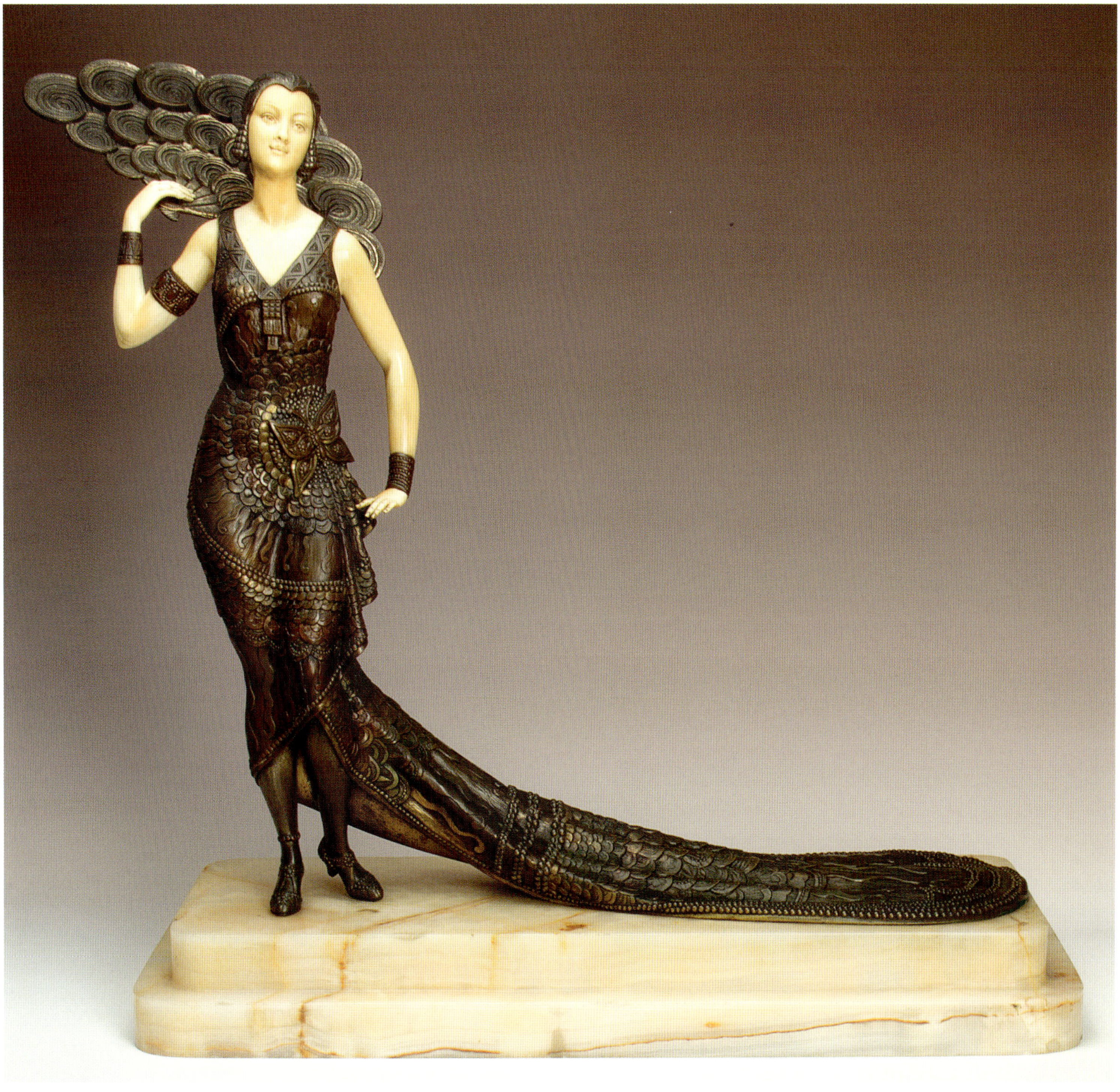

Peacock
Bronze and ivory on marble base
Height: 52.5cm. (20¾in.)
PRIVATE COLLECTION

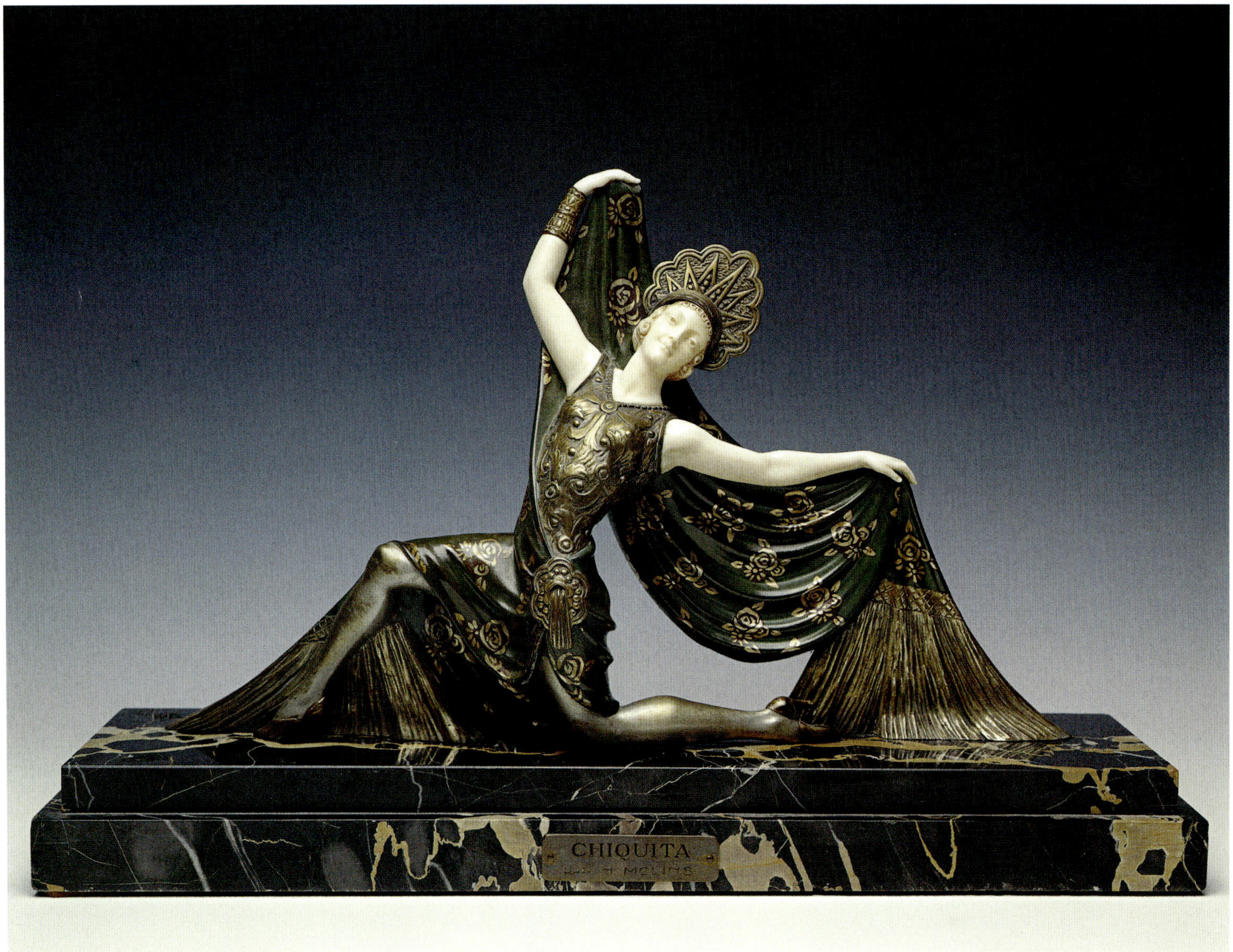

Chiquita
Bronze and ivory on marble base
Height: 30.5cm. (12in.)
PRIVATE COLLECTION

MONTINI

Worked for Rosenthal und Maeder. Identity unknown.

This could be Igino, Italian sculptor born in Rimini in 1874 – d.1954 in Florence. A student of Antonio Garella, he worked mainly in Florence. In 1913 he created a colossal bust of Dante for the University in Lima (present whereabouts unknown).

Igino was director of the Royal School for Ceramic Arts in Sesto Fiorentino. In 1922 he exhibited at the Fiorentina Primaverile. As of 1925 he exhibited at the Belle Arte di Torino.

Or: Roberto. Dates given as 1882–1963.
Or: Tullio. Dates given as 1878–1964.

The *Dante* sculpture bears the 'RuM' stamp of the Berlin foundry Rosenthal und Maeder.

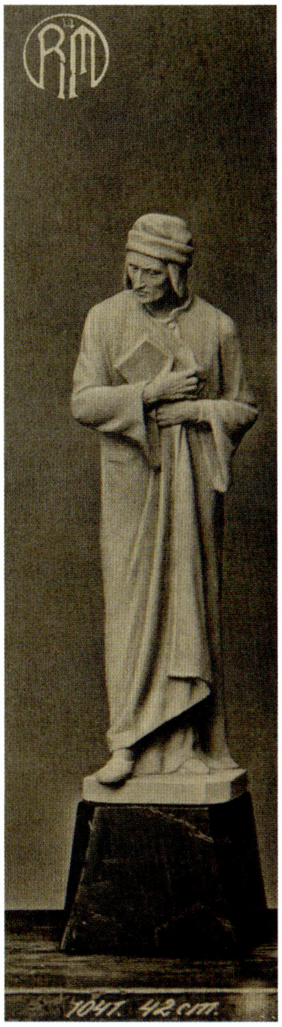

Image of Dante *from the Rosenthal und Maeder catalogue.*

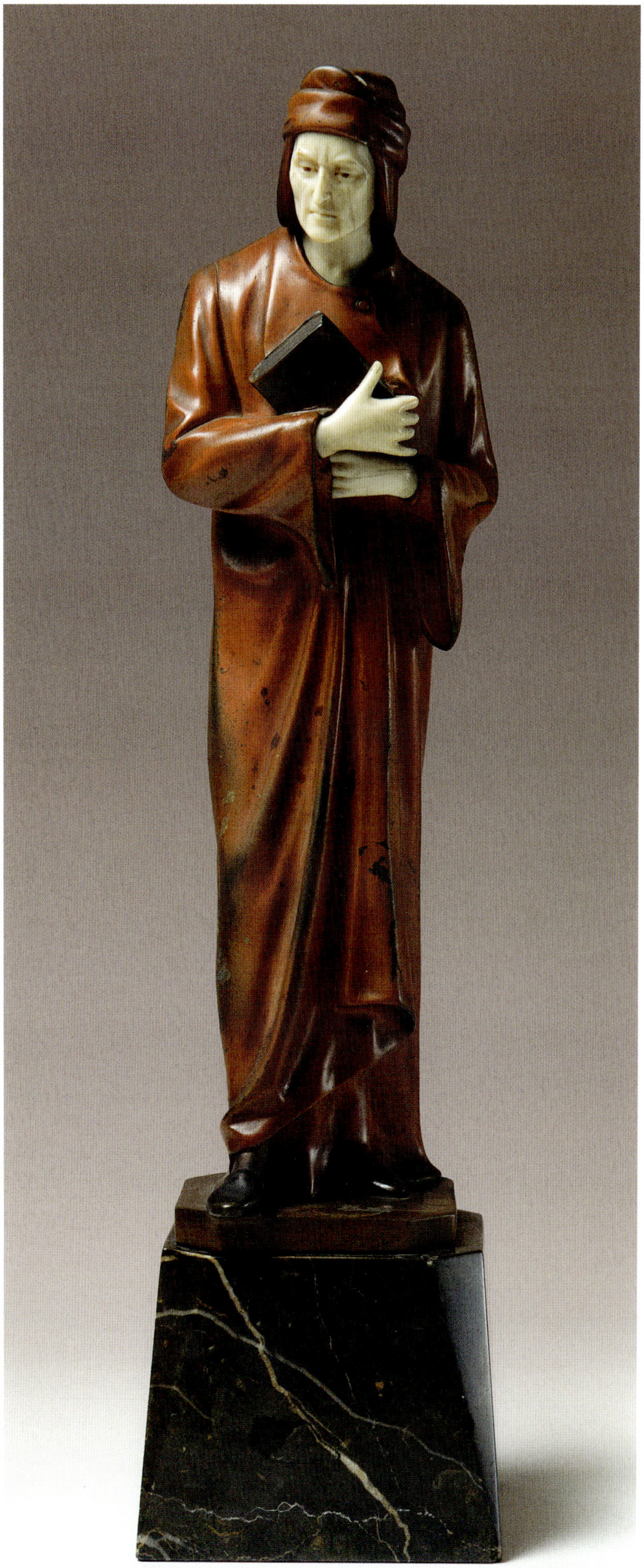

Dante
Bronze and ivory on marble base
Height: 40.5cm. (16in.)
PRIVATE COLLECTION

MULLER, Charles Arthur

(Flavigny-sur-Moselle 1868 – ?)

Born in Flavigny-sur-Moselle (Meurthe-en-Moselle) in 1868, he was a student of Hector Lemaire at the Paris Ecole des Beaux Arts.

Elected a member of the Société des Artistes Français in 1898, he exhibited at the Salons there from 1895 to 1930. He won an honourable mention in 1902 and 1914, a third-class medal in 1907, and a bronze medal in 1924.

He created several bronze figures for the founders Wesley Lapointe and Charles Paillet, as well as bronze and ivory pieces for Edmond Etling. Muller also produced polychrome ceramics for Mougins Frères in Nancy.

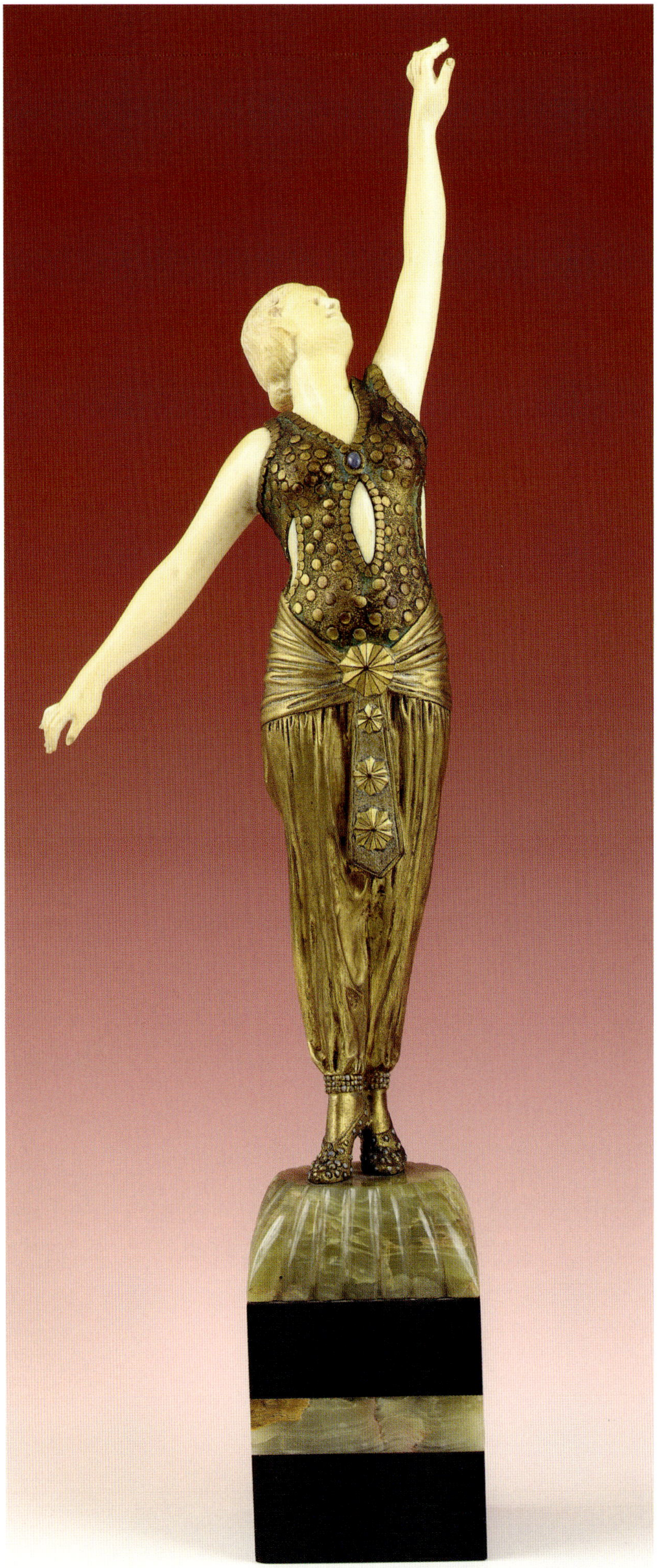

Oriental Dance
Bronze and ivory on onyx base
Height: 50cm. (19¾in.)
PRIVATE COLLECTION

NANNINI, Raphaël

(Florence 1852 – Lastra a Signa 1925)

Born in Florence, Italy, he studied at the Florence Academy of Fine Arts. He worked as a sculptor in Italy, but also lived for a time in Paris in the early 20th century, creating pieces that were produced by French companies such as Les Neveux de J. Lehmann and Edmond Etling in the early 20th century.

He exhibited at Parisian Salons, such as that of the Société des Artistes Français, where, in 1909, he showed a plaster bust entitled *Portrait of Mme Florence Gromier*, and a plaster statuette, *Cimateur*.

His sister Maria, also a sculptor, came to Paris in the early 20th century (she exhibited at the Salon of the Société des Artistes Français in 1909 and 1910); both lived in the artists' house called the *Cité des Fusains*, located at 22 rue Tourlaque, in Montmartre. Well-known sculptors and painters such as Jean Arp, Max Ernst, and Miró also lived there.

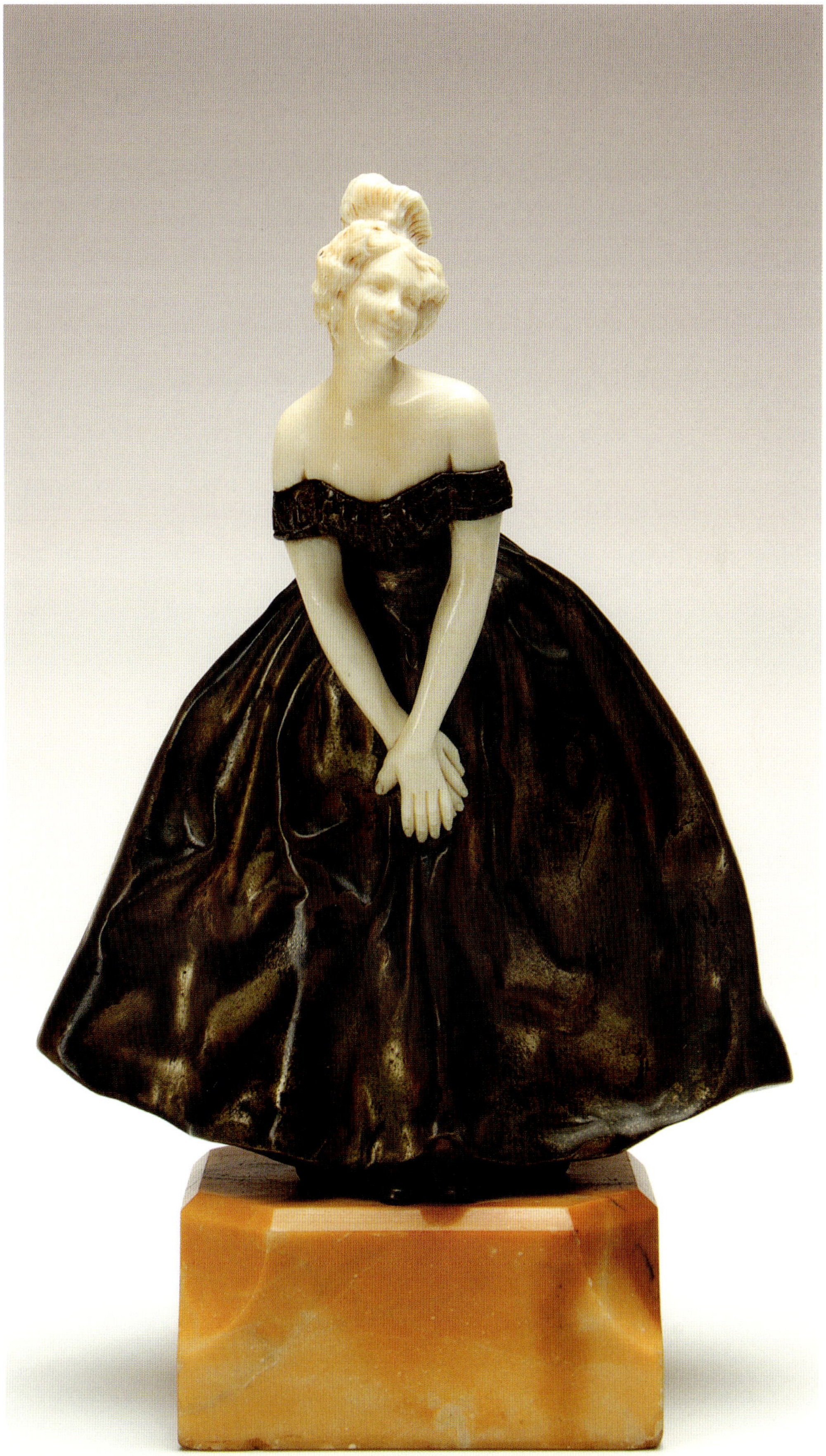

Pleasantries
Bronze and ivory on marble base
Height: 18.5cm. (7¼in.)
DINO MENASCHE COLLECTION

Also produced 31cm. (12¼in.) high

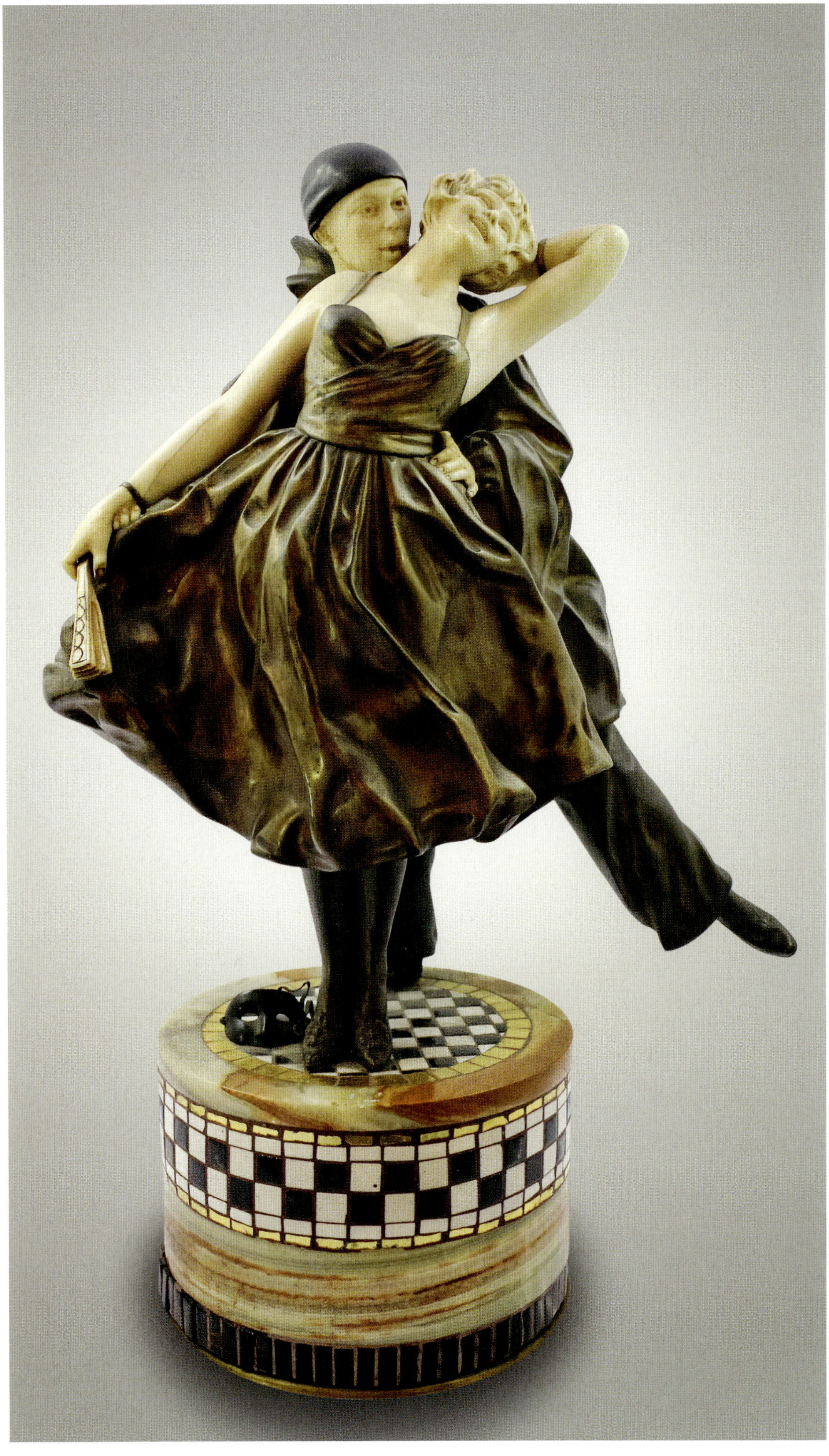

The Vanquished Pierrot
Bronze and ivory on a marble and glass base
Height: 43cm. (17in.)
OSCAR AND MANOLO PICERNO COLLECTION

This figure has been erroneously attributed to Chiparus

OMERTH, Georges

(active 1895 – 1925)

A pupil of Ernst Carrier Belleuse. He appears in the Salon of the Société des Artistes Français.

He was active during the first half of the 20th century, producing many figures in bronze, bronze and ivory, spelter and biscuit porcelain.

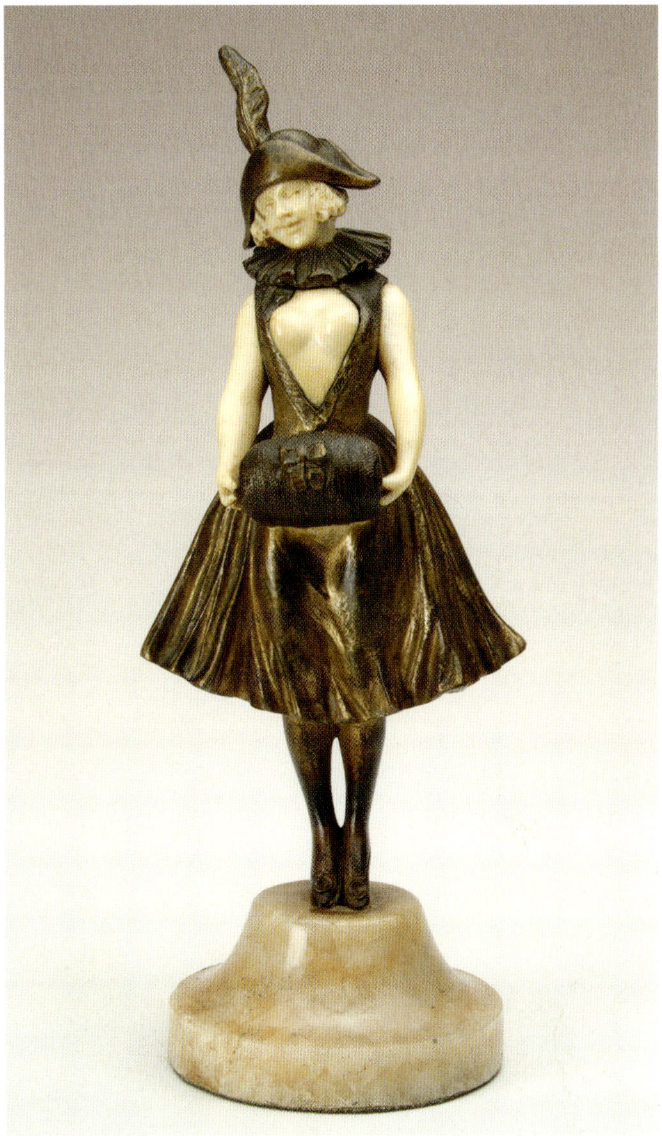

Paradox
Bronze and ivory on marble base
Height: 25cm. (10in.)
DINO MENASCHE COLLECTION

Georges Omerth seated in his studio at Les Lilas, with his assistant standing in the shadows.

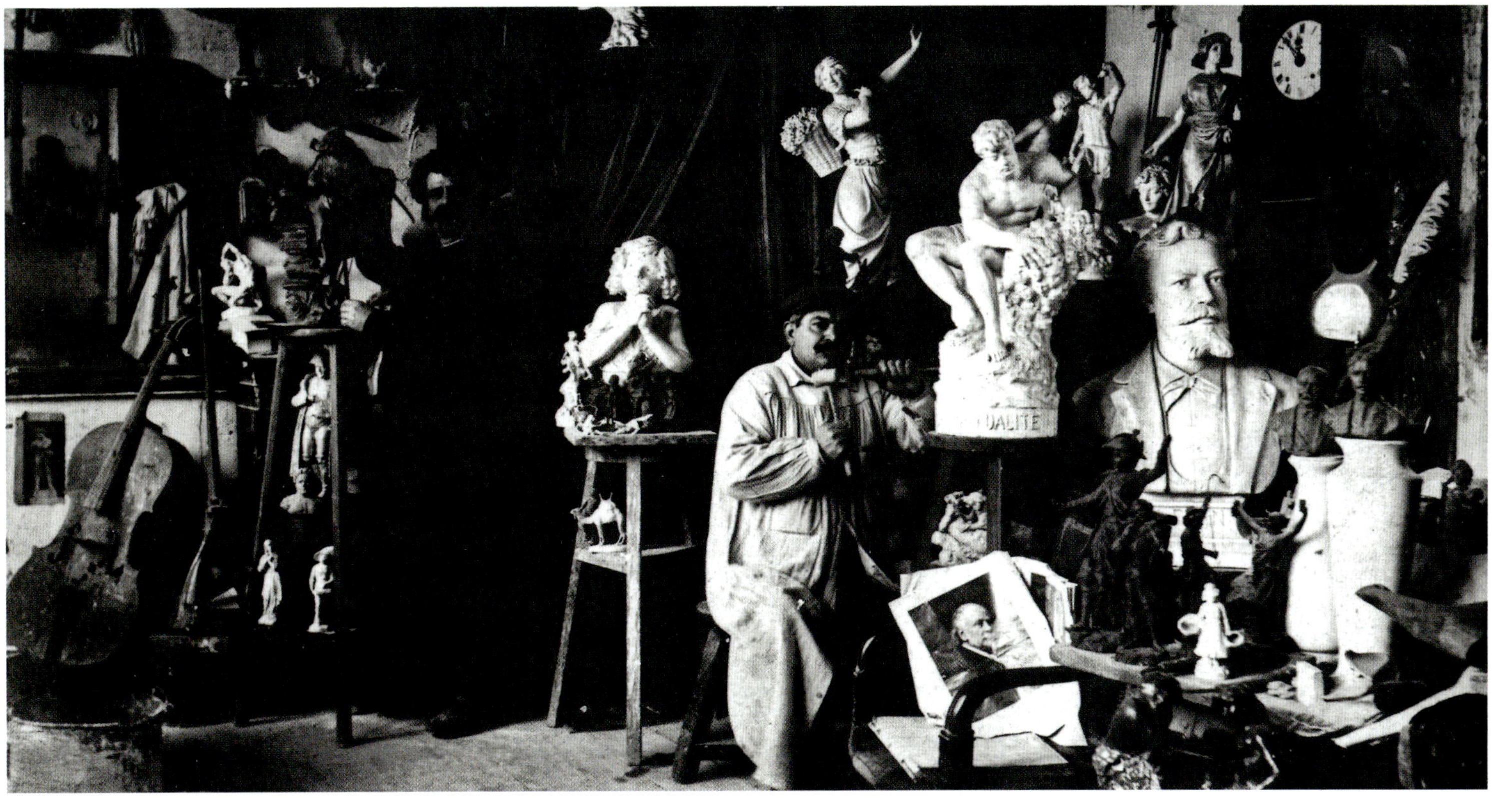

ONU, Aurore

Aurore Onu was born in Bucharest, Romania, and moved to Paris in the 1920s. There she met the artist Marcel André Bouraine, and became his companion. At the time the couple were neighbours of the sculptor Pierre Le Faguays.

Onu made several bronze and chryselephantine sculptures, which were produced by the Les Neveux de J. Lehmann Company; others were cast by the Etling Company. One such piece, the *Bacchante au Thyrse* (Bacchant with Thyrsus), was shown at the Salon of the Société des Artistes Français in 1924; Onu exhibited there several times. The figures Onu created are often elegant and athletic female figures typical of the ideal woman of the period (see p.54, Bouraine).

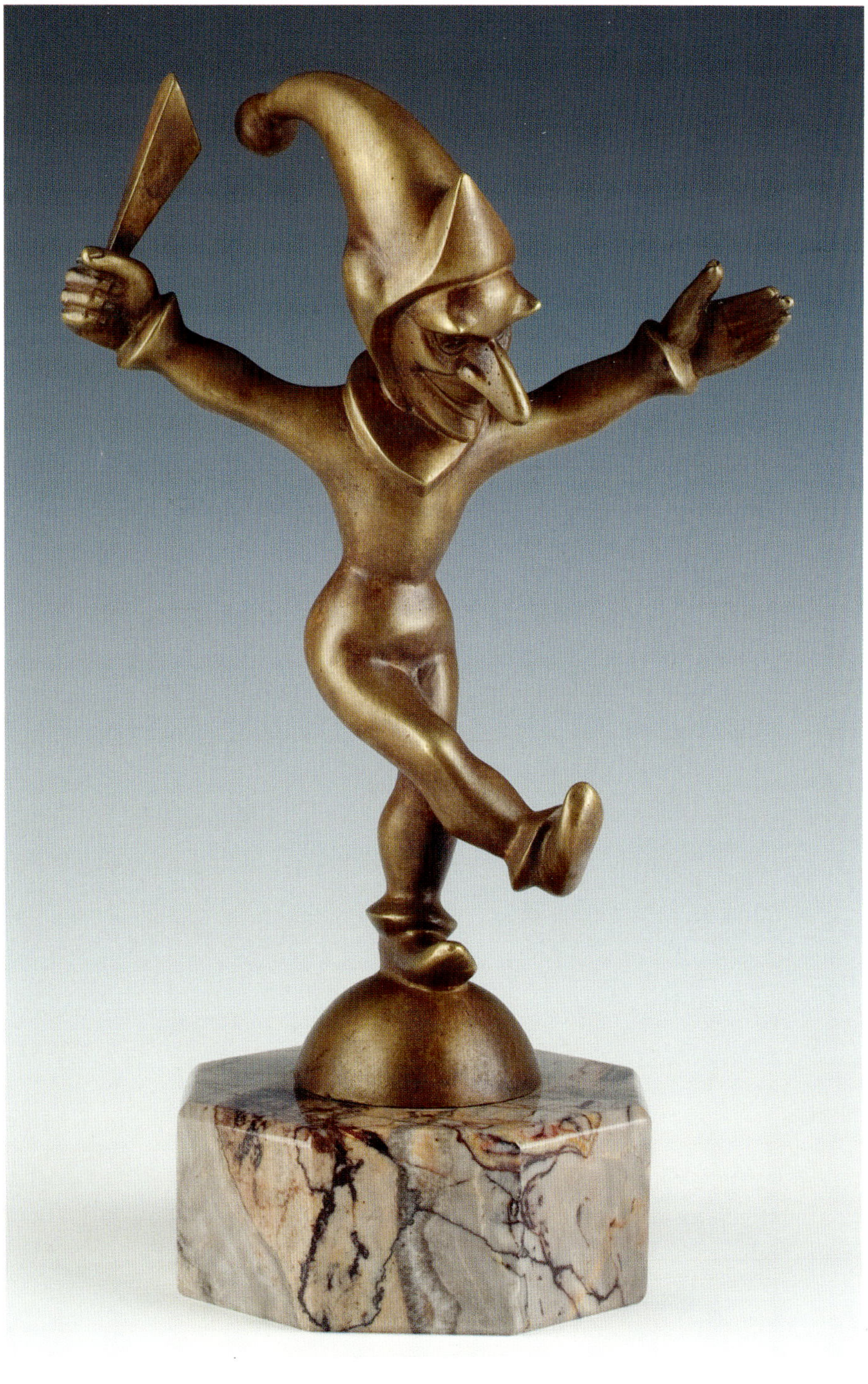

PARIS, Roland

(Vienna 1894 – Swinemünde 1945)

Born in Vienna to German parents, he grew up in an artistic family in Weimar (both his parents were writers, one brother was an actor, and his sister was artistic and married a painter). He was trained at the Weimar Applied Arts School (Weimar Kunstgewerbeschule) under Henry van de Velde, and the School of Sculpture (Weimar Bildhauerschule) under Gottlieb Elster; he also trained under Walther Klemm and spent some time in Munich perfecting his craft.

Paris served in World War I, then moved to Berlin after the war to pursue a career as an artist, working in many media: lithography, woodcuts, painting, bronze, bronze and ivory, wood and ceramics.

He lived and worked in Berlin. Towards the end of World War II he was again called to fight as a wave of conscriptions sought to bolster the failing German war effort, though he was by then nearly 50; he was killed in action at the age of 51.

Paris's figures are very unusual, showing a keen sense of satire and caricature.

Punch
Bronze on marble base
Height: 23.5cm. (9¼in.)
PRIVATE COLLECTION

Free Ride
Bronze and ivory on marble base
Height: 14cm. (5½in.)
PRIVATE COLLECTION

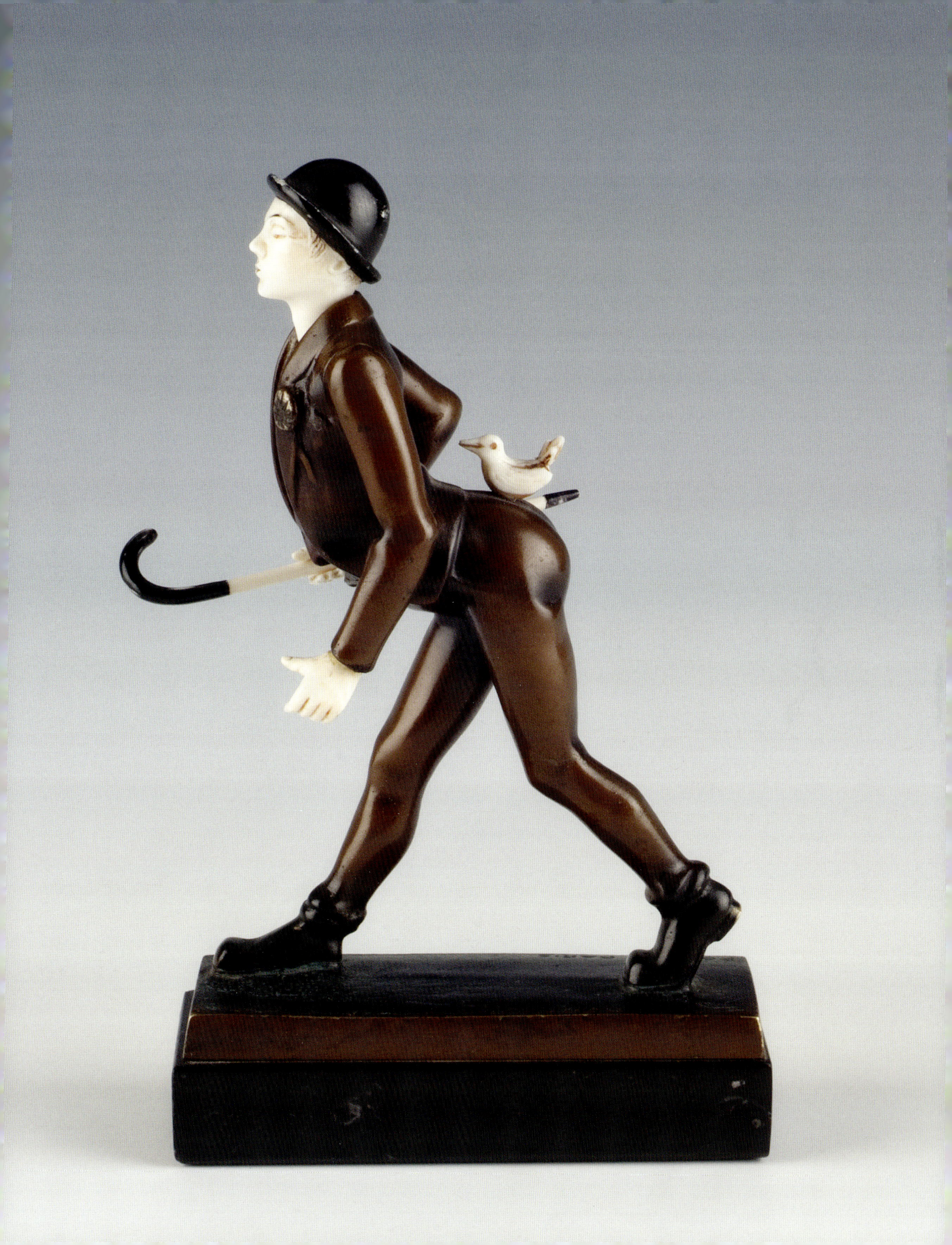

PELESCHKA-LUNARD, Franz (PELESKA-LUNARD)

(Vienna 1873 – ?)

Studied at The Vienna Academy under E. Helmer. He lived and worked in Berlin. He used the Rosenthal und Maeder (RuM) foundry, later taken over by the Preiss & Kassler (PK) workshop, for some of his models.

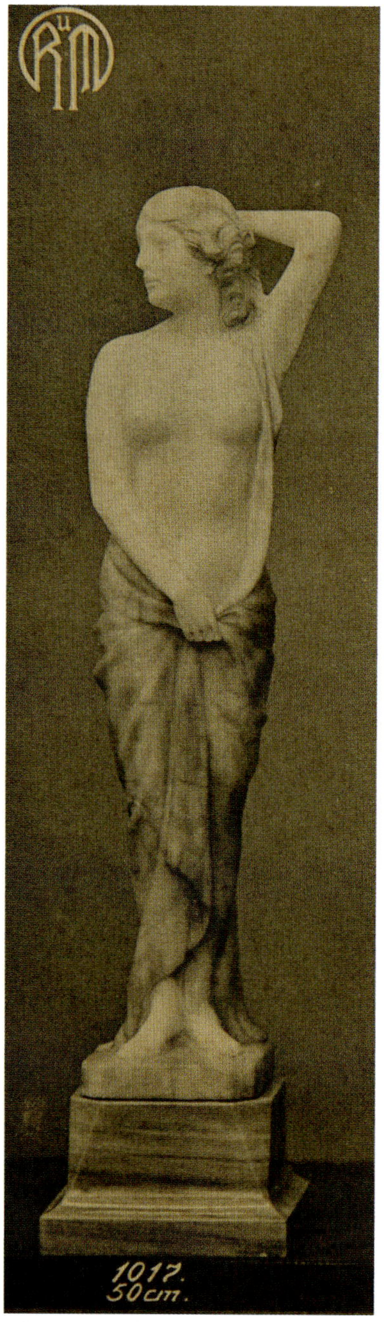

Image of The Pose *from the Rosenthal und Maeder catalogue.*

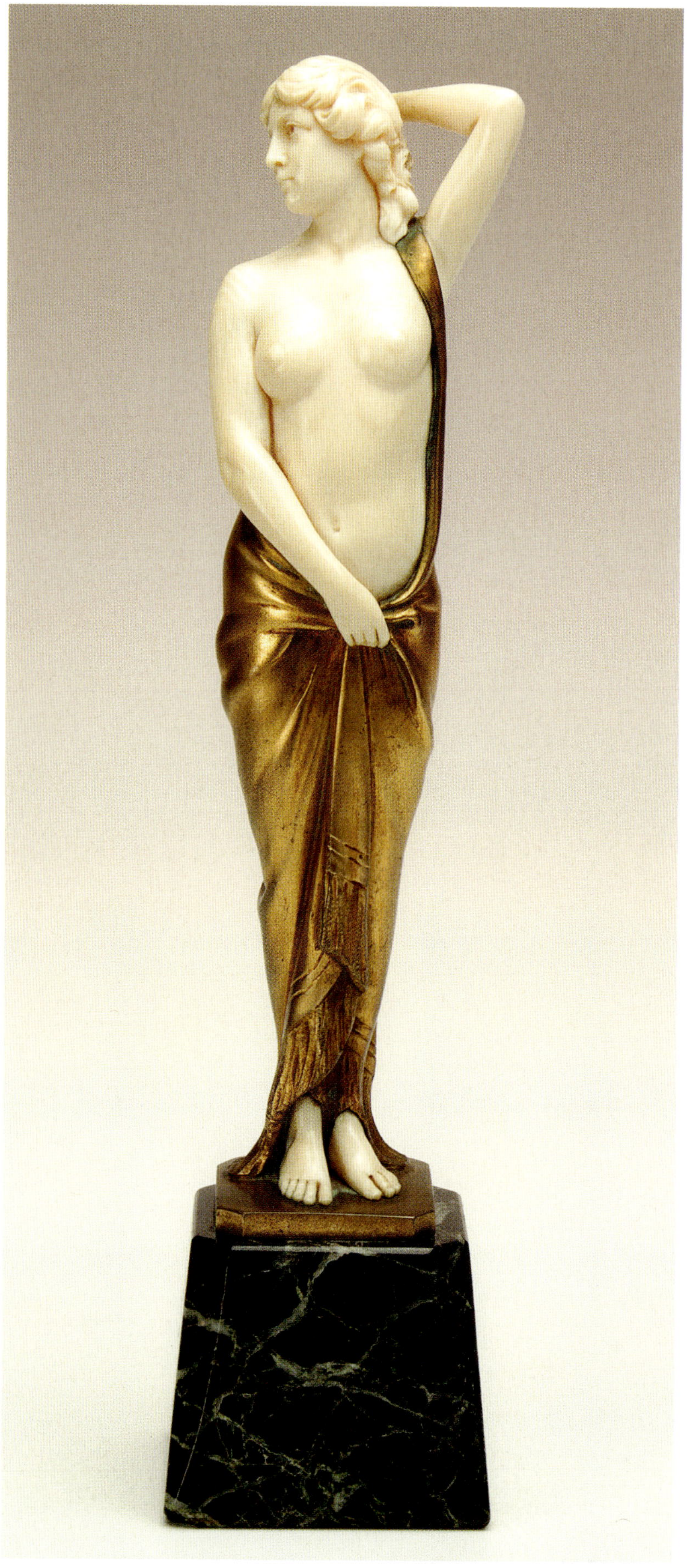

The Pose

Bronze and ivory on marble base

Height: 26cm. (10¼in.)

DINO MENASCHE COLLECTION

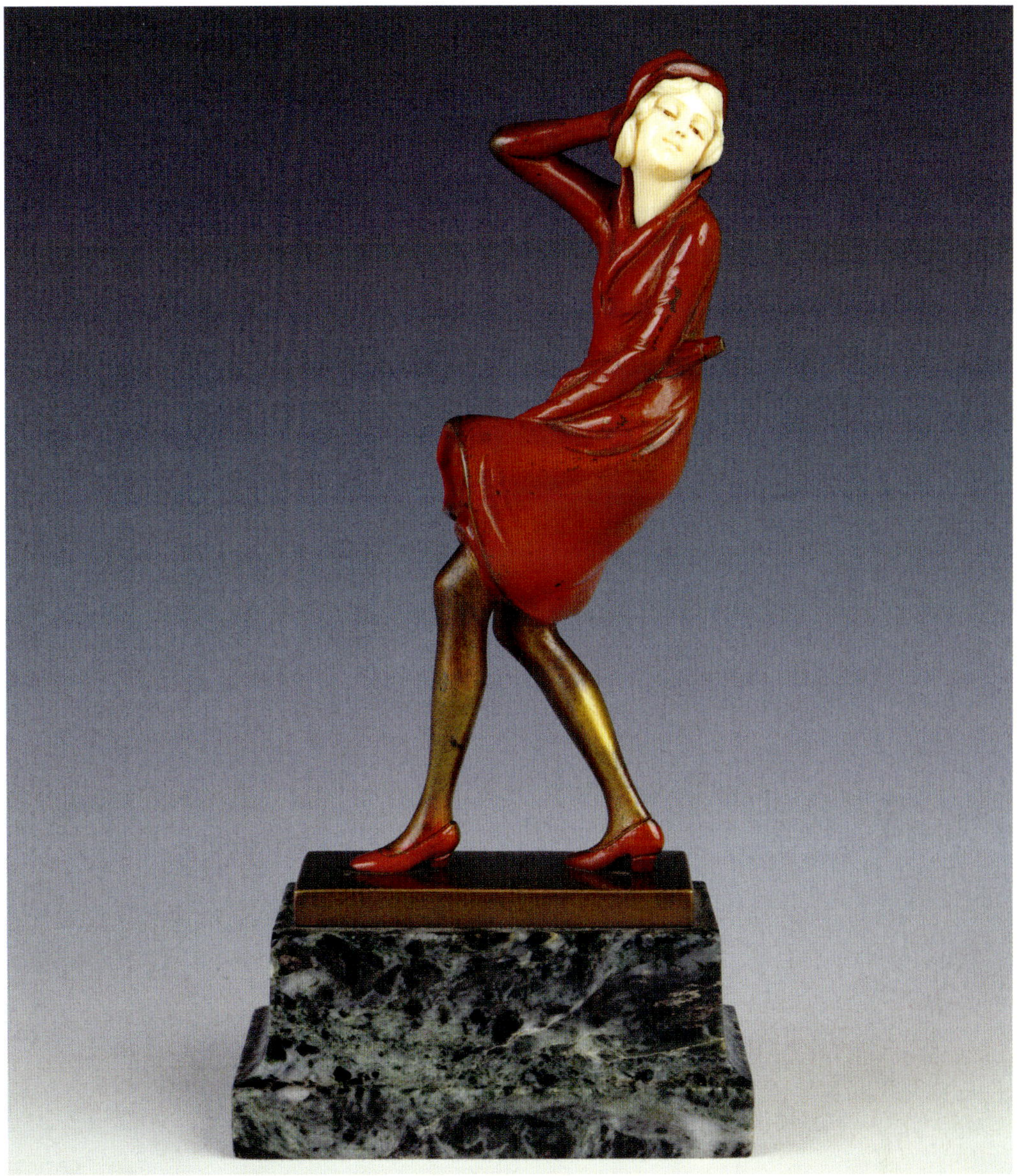

The Gust
Bronze and ivory on marble base
Height: 19cm. (7½in.)
VIRGINIA MUSEUM OF FINE ARTS, RICHMOND, GIFT OF SYDNEY AND FRANCES LEWIS

PFEIFFER

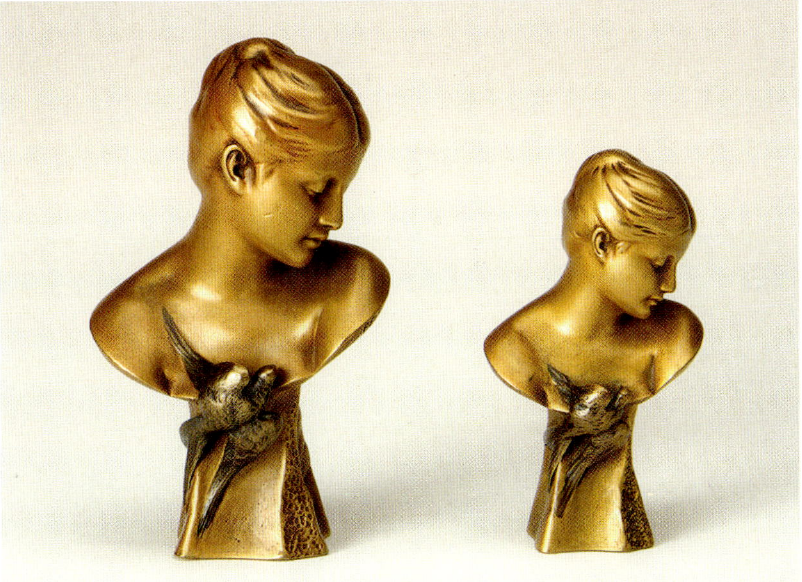

Message of Love
Bronze
Height: 10 and 7.5cm. (4 and 3in.)
DINO MENASCHE COLLECTION

PHILIPPE, Abel René

Born in the final years of the 19th century, he was active during the first part of the 20th century.

A native of Lestiou, a town in the Loir-et-Cher department in the Loire valley, France, Philippe worked for L.N.J.L. (Lehman); his figures were featured in the firm's catalogue pages.

This artist should not be confused with Paul Philippe.

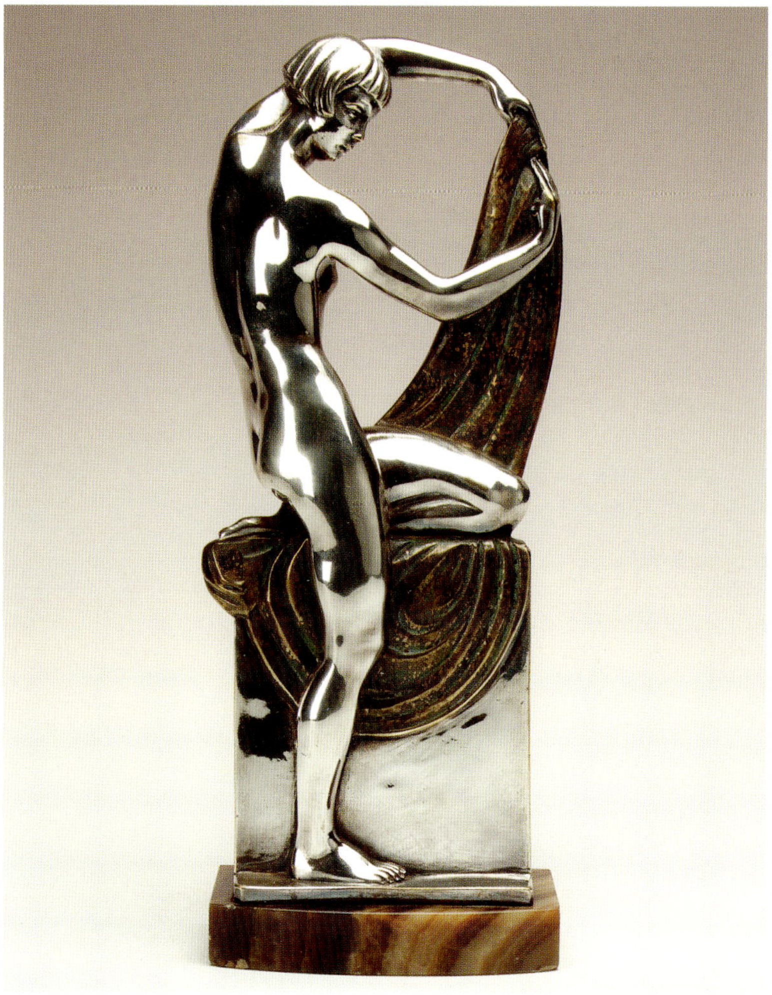

The Bather
Bronze on onyx base
Height: 28.5cm. (11¼in.)
DINO MENASCHE COLLECTION

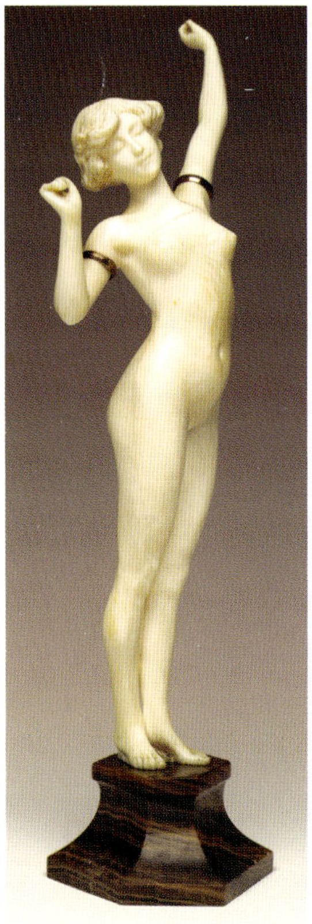

Arising
Ivory and bronze on marble base
Height: 28cm. (11in.)
PRIVATE COLLECTION

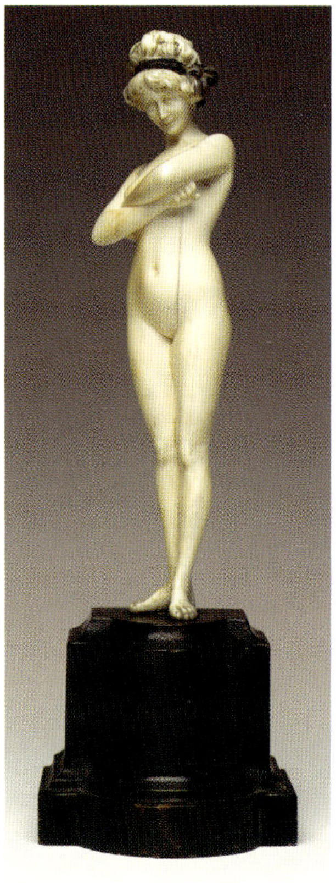

The Challenge
Ivory on marble base
Height: 23cm. (9in.)
PRIVATE COLLECTION

Also produced 68cm. (26¾in.), 48cm. (19in.), 31cm. (12¼in.) and 13cm. (5in.) high

PHILIPPE, Paul

(Thoruń, Poland 1870-1930)

He studied at the Königliche Akademie of Berlin. In 1900 he went to Paris, where he lived at the Cité des Fusains, an artists' residence located at 22 rue Tourlaque in Montmartre, and studied under Antonin Larroux.

From 1902 to 1909 he exhibited at the Salon of the Société des Artistes Français, where in 1909 his bronze, marble and ivory statuette *Farniente*, and his bronze, marble and ivory group *Grâce et Force* (Grace and Strength), both produced by Goldscheider, were shown. In 1907 his sculpture *Le Réveil* (The Awakening) was exhibited. In 1910 his *Girl with Mirror* gained critical acclaim. It was produced in two versions: nude and draped, both in bronze and ivory.

In the 1920s Philippe again worked in Berlin, where he created several figures for Rosenthal und Maeder (RuM), and later for Preiss & Kassler (PK) – when the latter took over the former. In 1930 his figures were exhibited on the Preiss & Kassler stand at the Leipzig fair.

Paul Philippe's ceramics were produced by Friedrich Goldscheider.

This artist should not be confused with Abel René Philippe.

Girl with Mirror
Bronze and ivory on onyx base
Height: 32cm. (12½in.)
PRIVATE COLLECTION

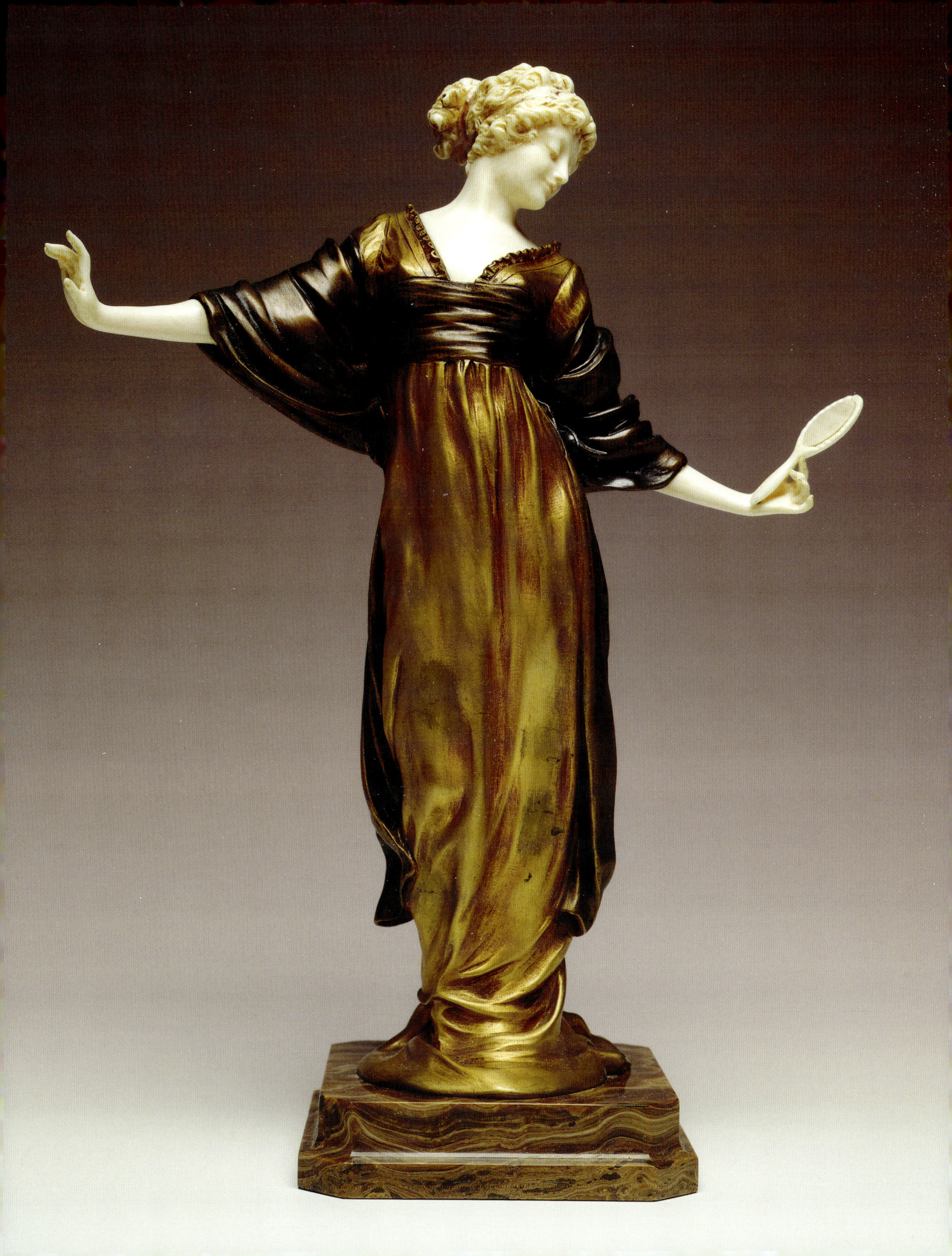

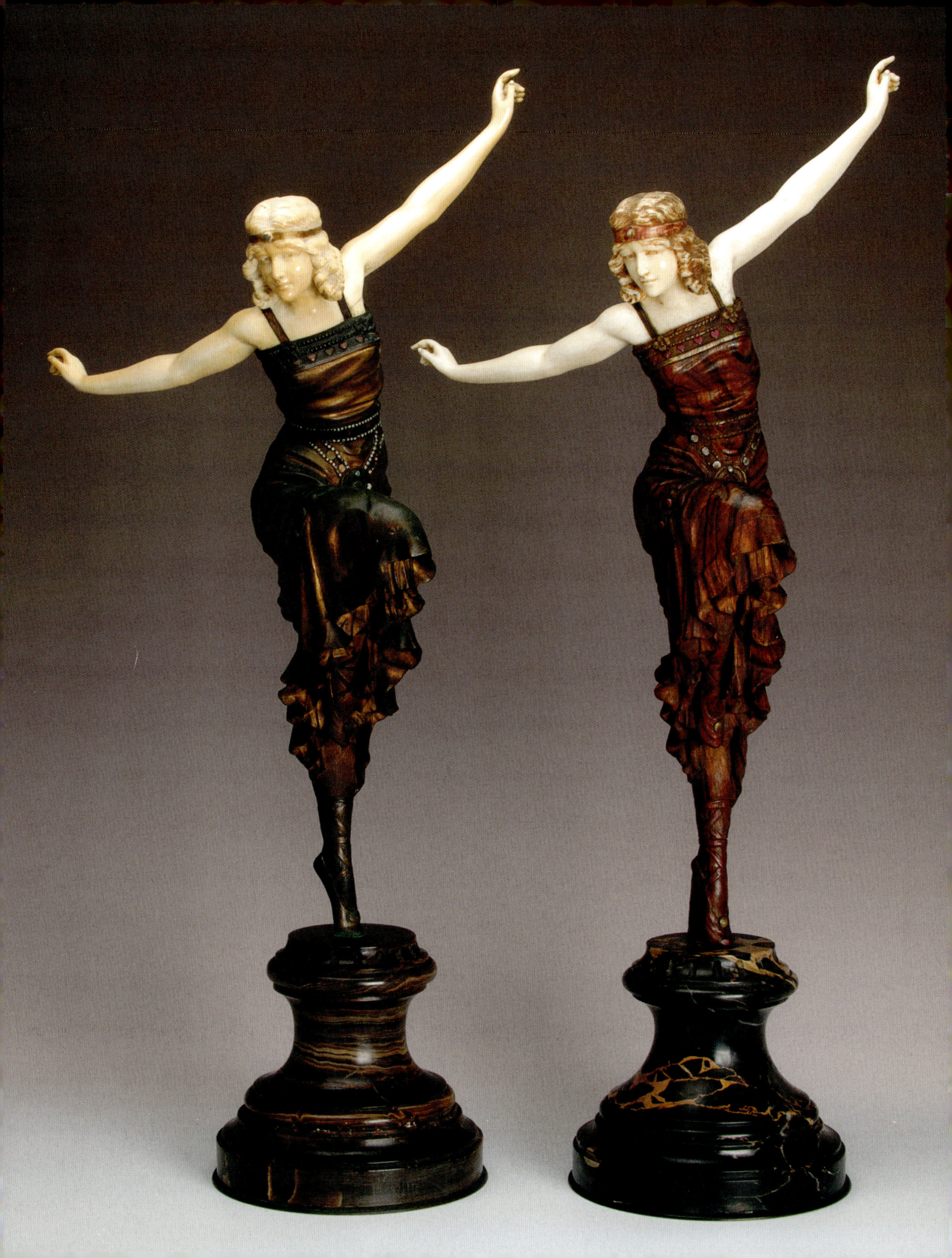

Russian Dancer
Left: bronze and ivory on onyx base
Height: 61cm. (24in.)
Right: wood and ivory on marble base
Height: 61.5cm. (24¼in.)
PRIVATE COLLECTION

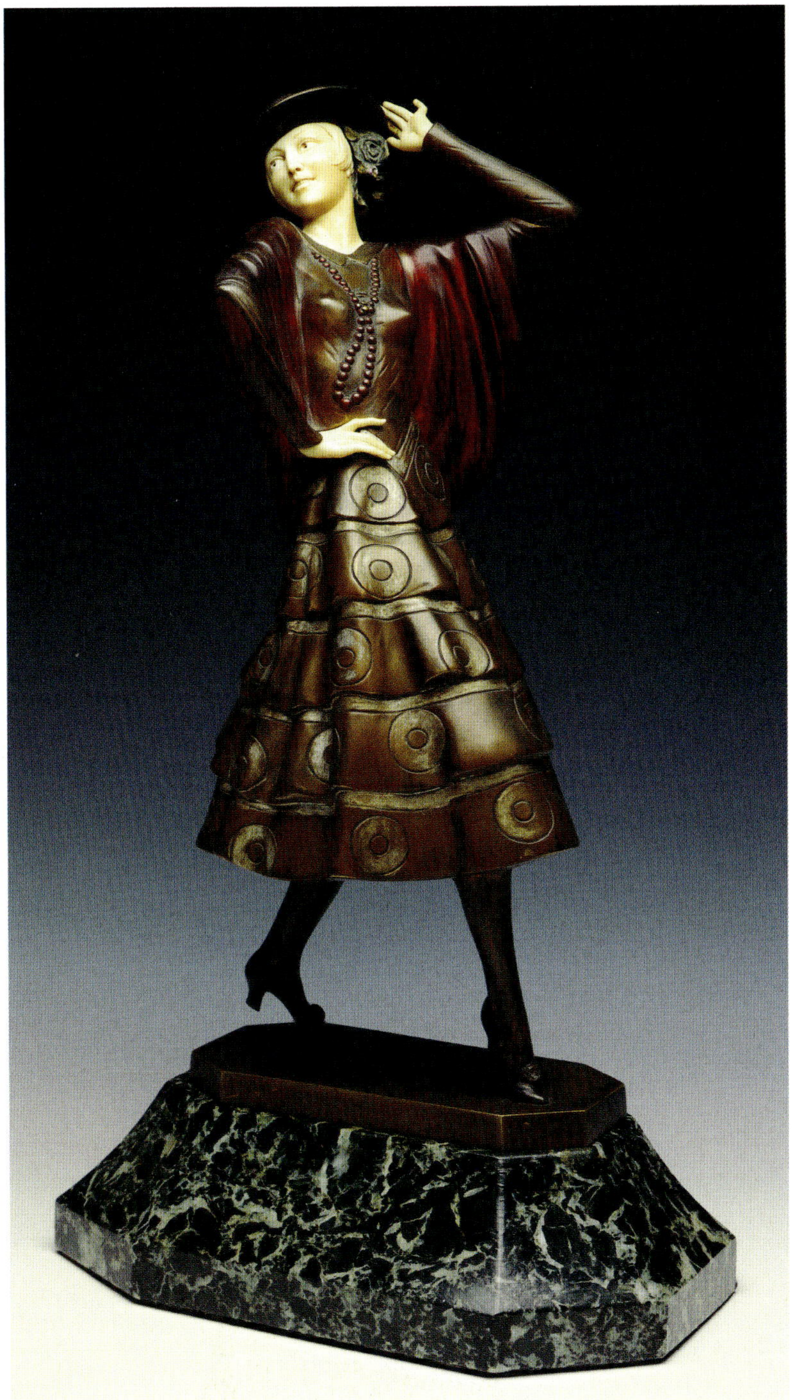

Spanish Dancer
Bronze and ivory on marble base
Height: 43cm. (17in.)
PRIVATE COLLECTION

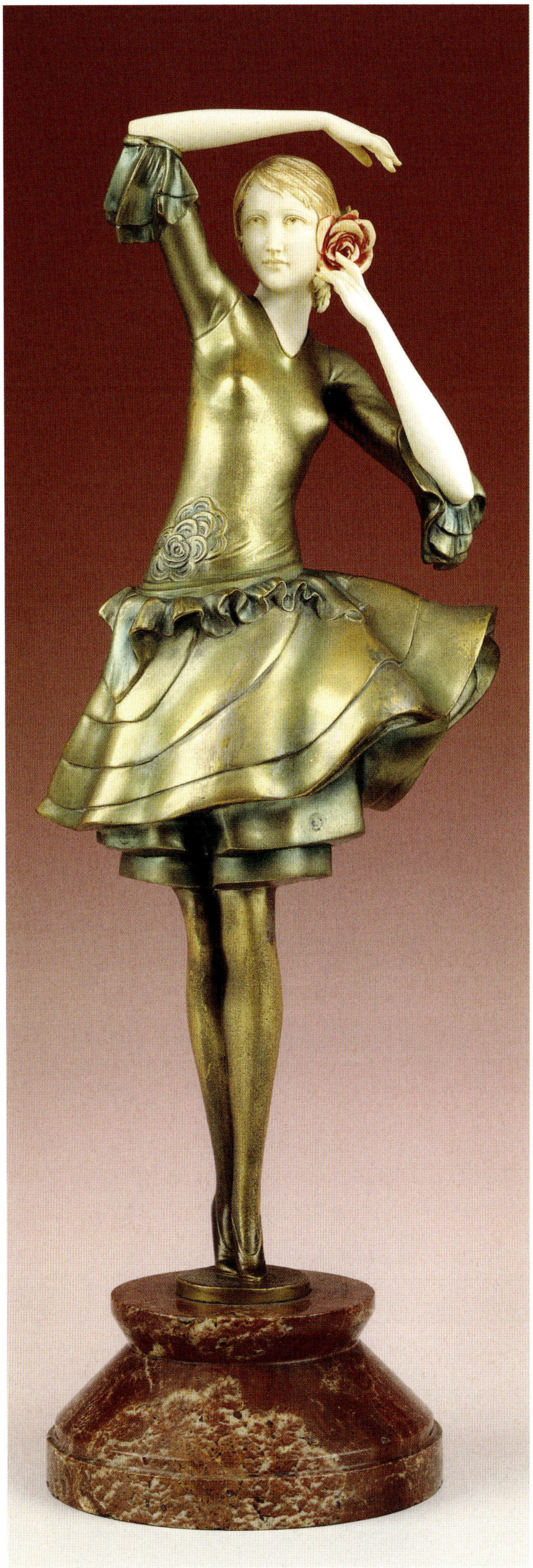

The Rose
Bronze and ivory on marble base
Height: 50cm. (19¾in.)
PRIVATE COLLECTION

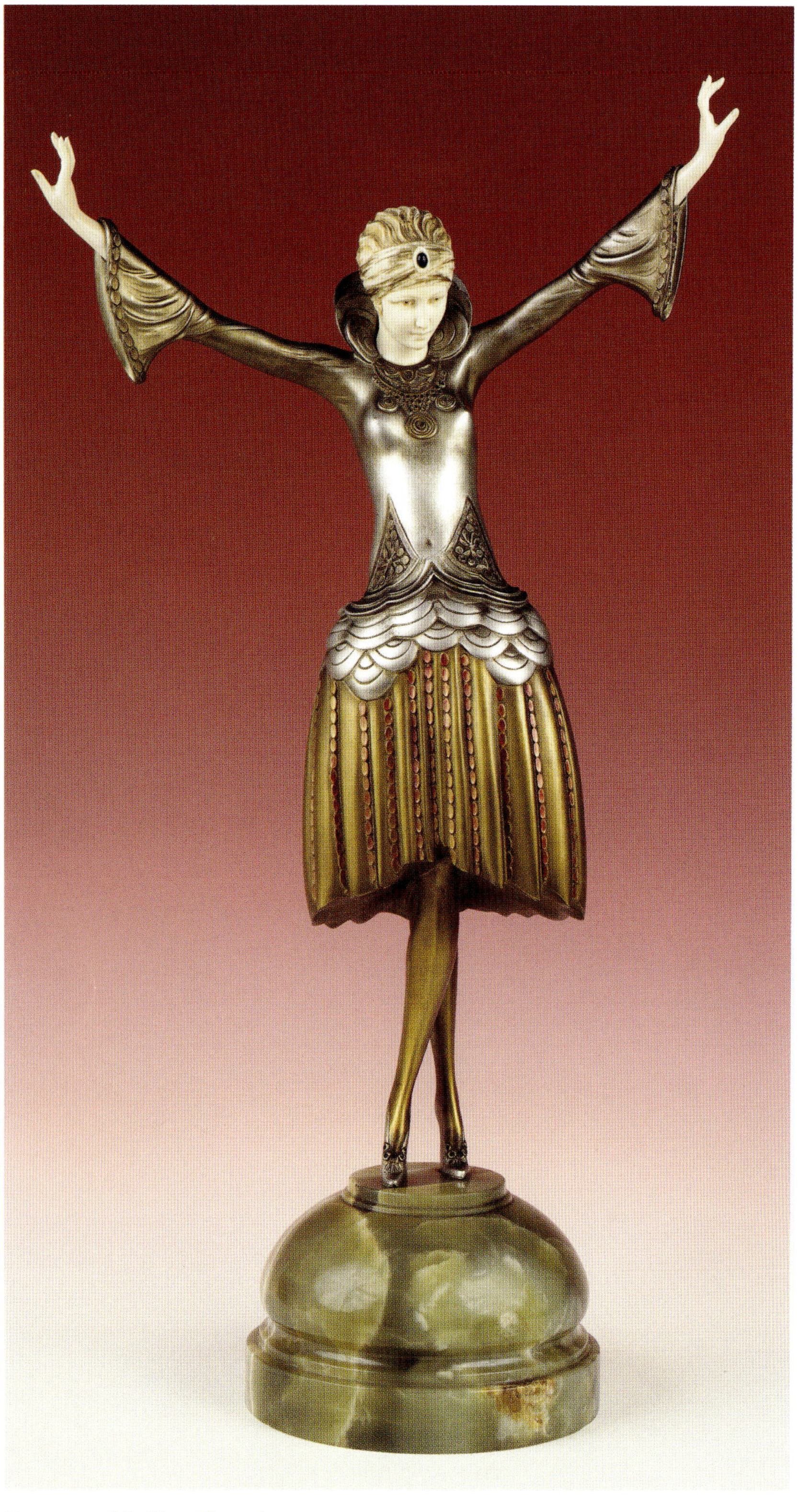

Dancer with Headband
Bronze and ivory on onyx base
Height: 66.5cm. (26¼in.)
VIRGINIA MUSEUM OF FINE ARTS, RICHMOND,
GIFT OF SYDNEY AND FRANCES LEWIS

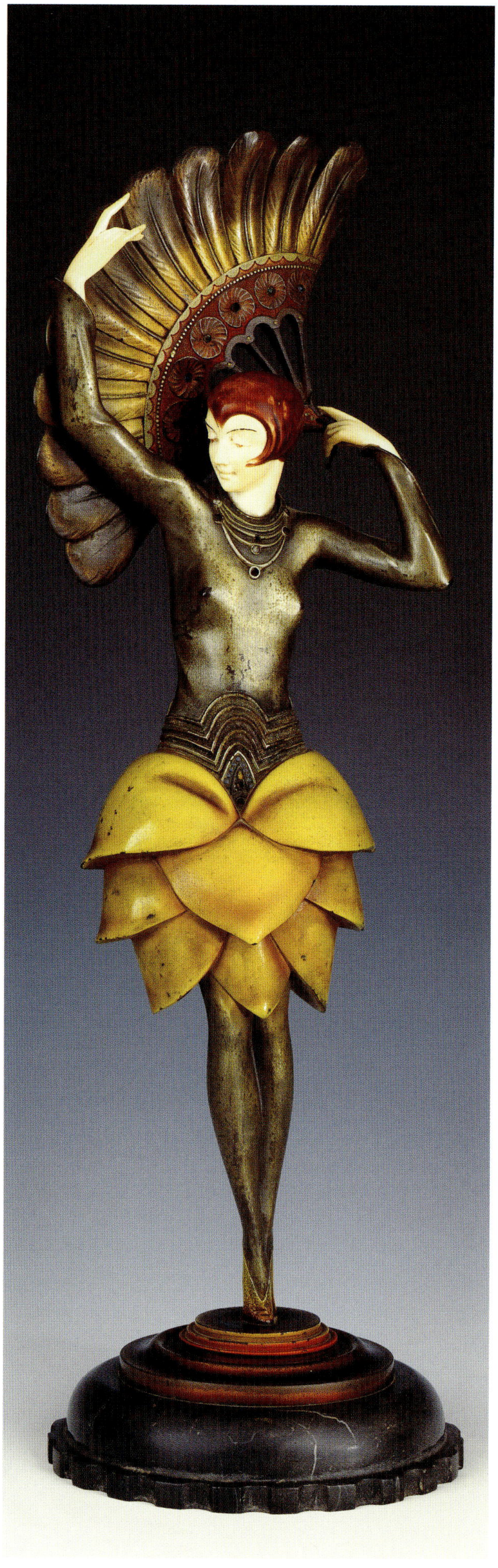

Fan Dancer
Bronze and ivory on marble base
Height: 49cm. (19¼in.)
PRIVATE COLLECTION

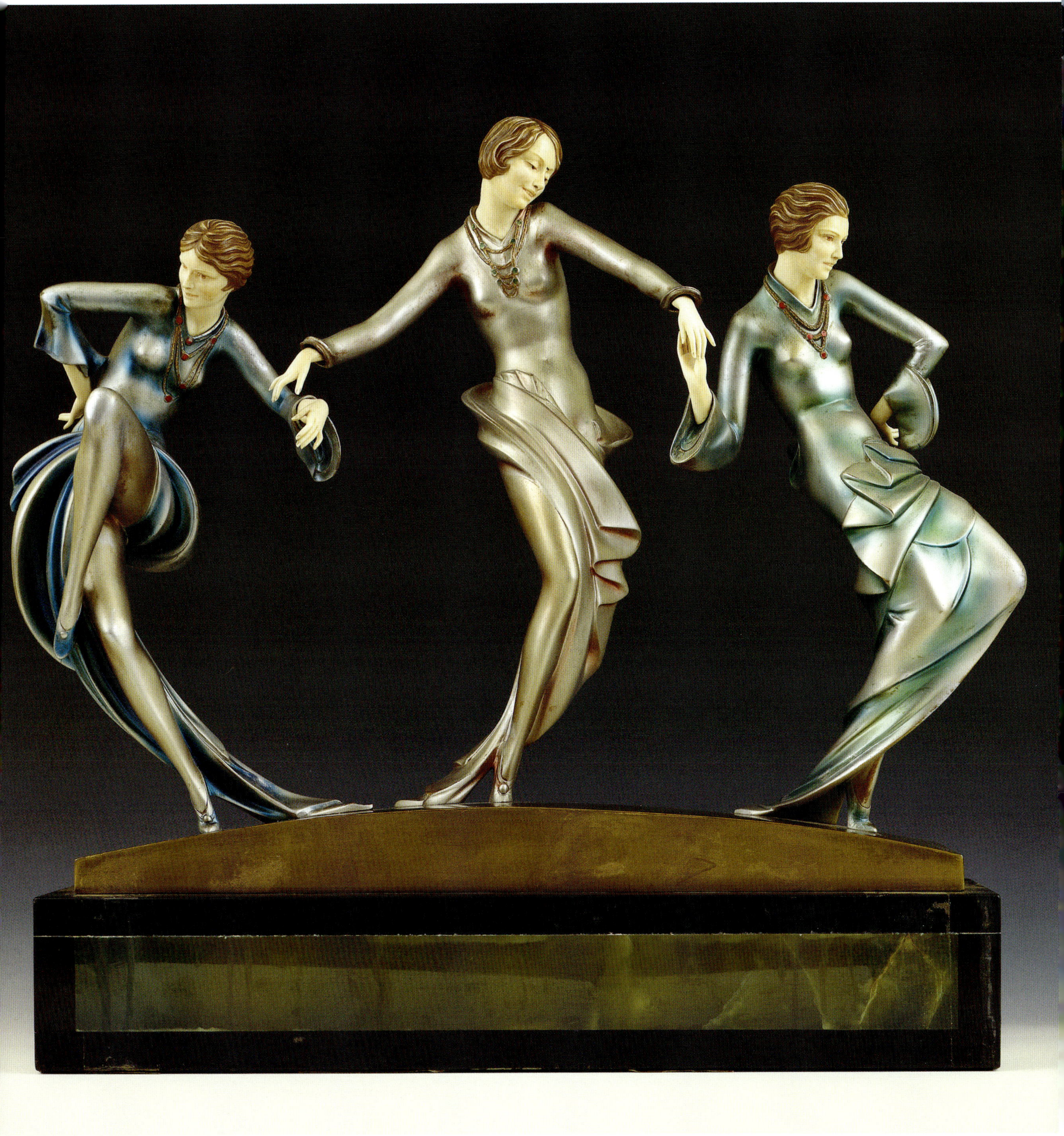

Round Dance
Bronze and ivory on onyx base
Height: 46.5cm. (18¼in.)
PRIVATE COLLECTION

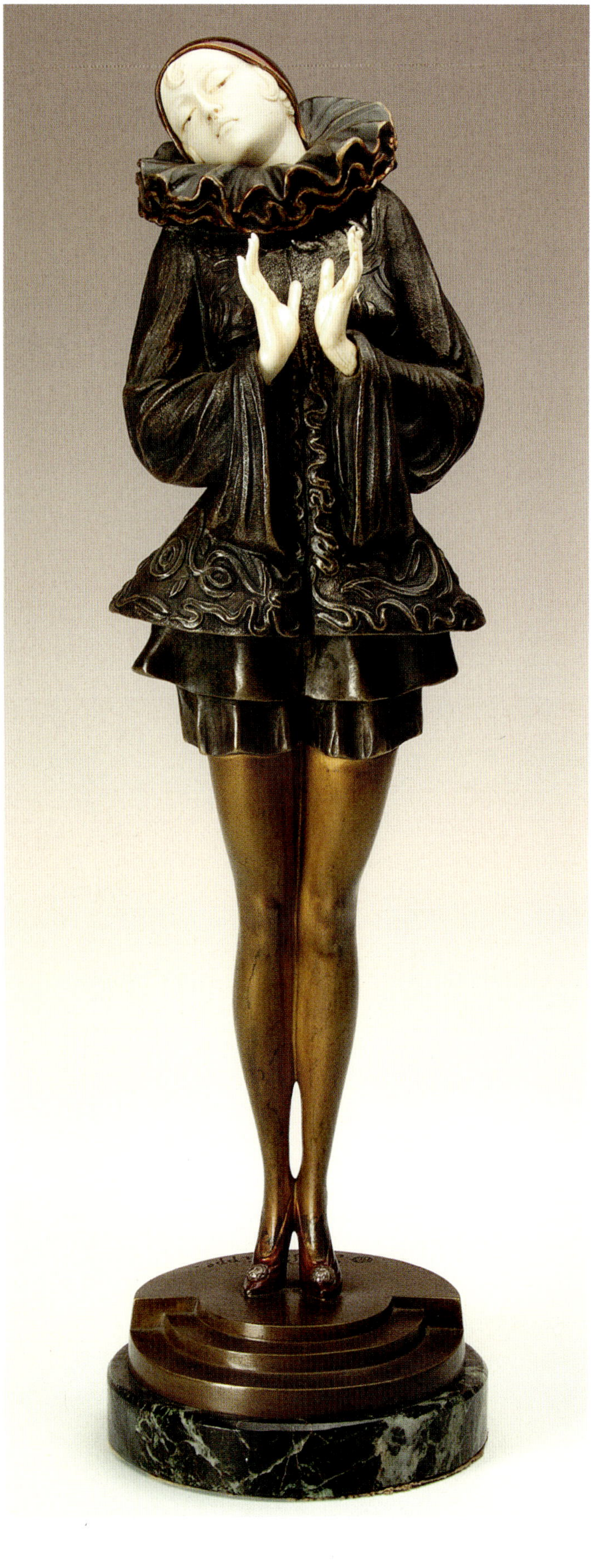

High Style
Bronze and ivory on onyx base
Height: 54.5cm. (21½in.)
BURR AND MUIR COLLECTION, CAPE TOWN

Pierrette
Bronze and ivory on marble base
Height: 38cm. (15in.)
DINO MENASCHE COLLECTION

Also produced 20.5cm. (8in.) high

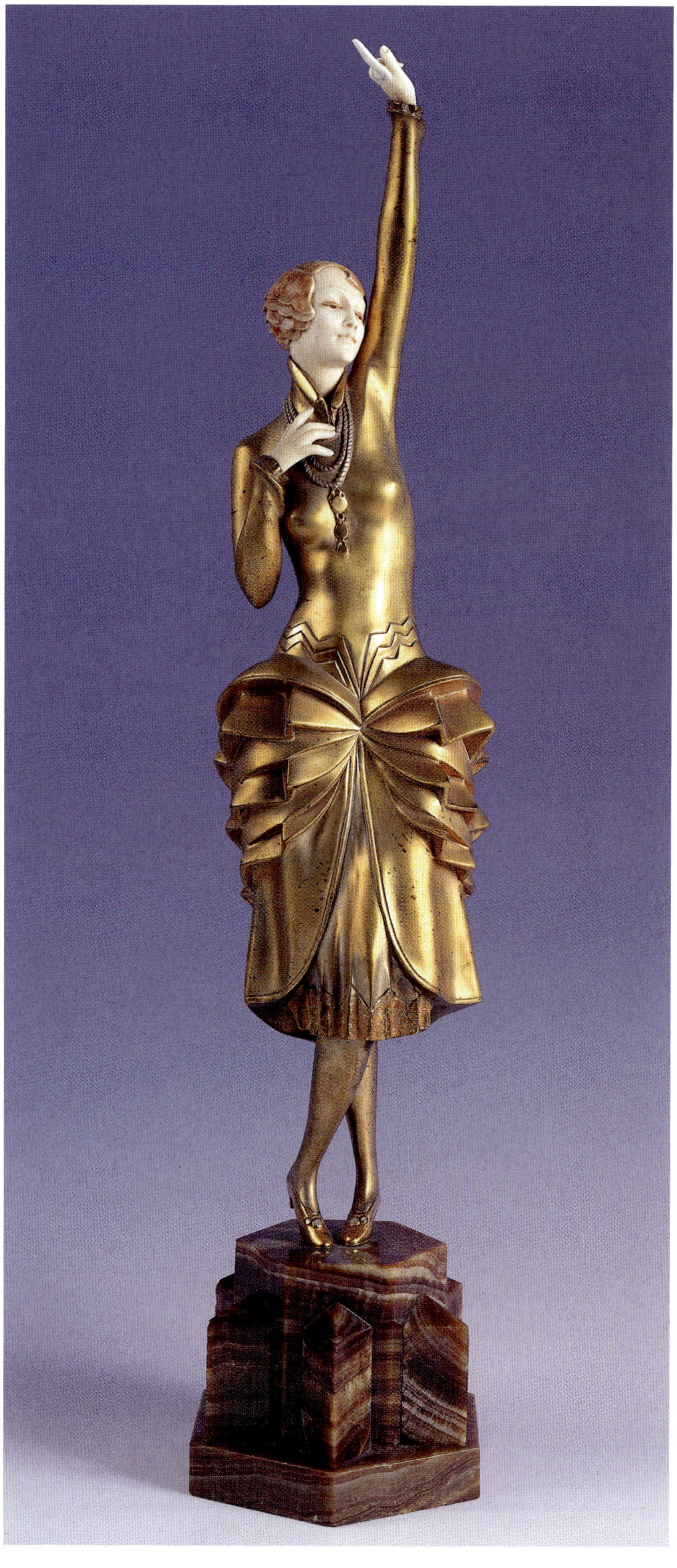

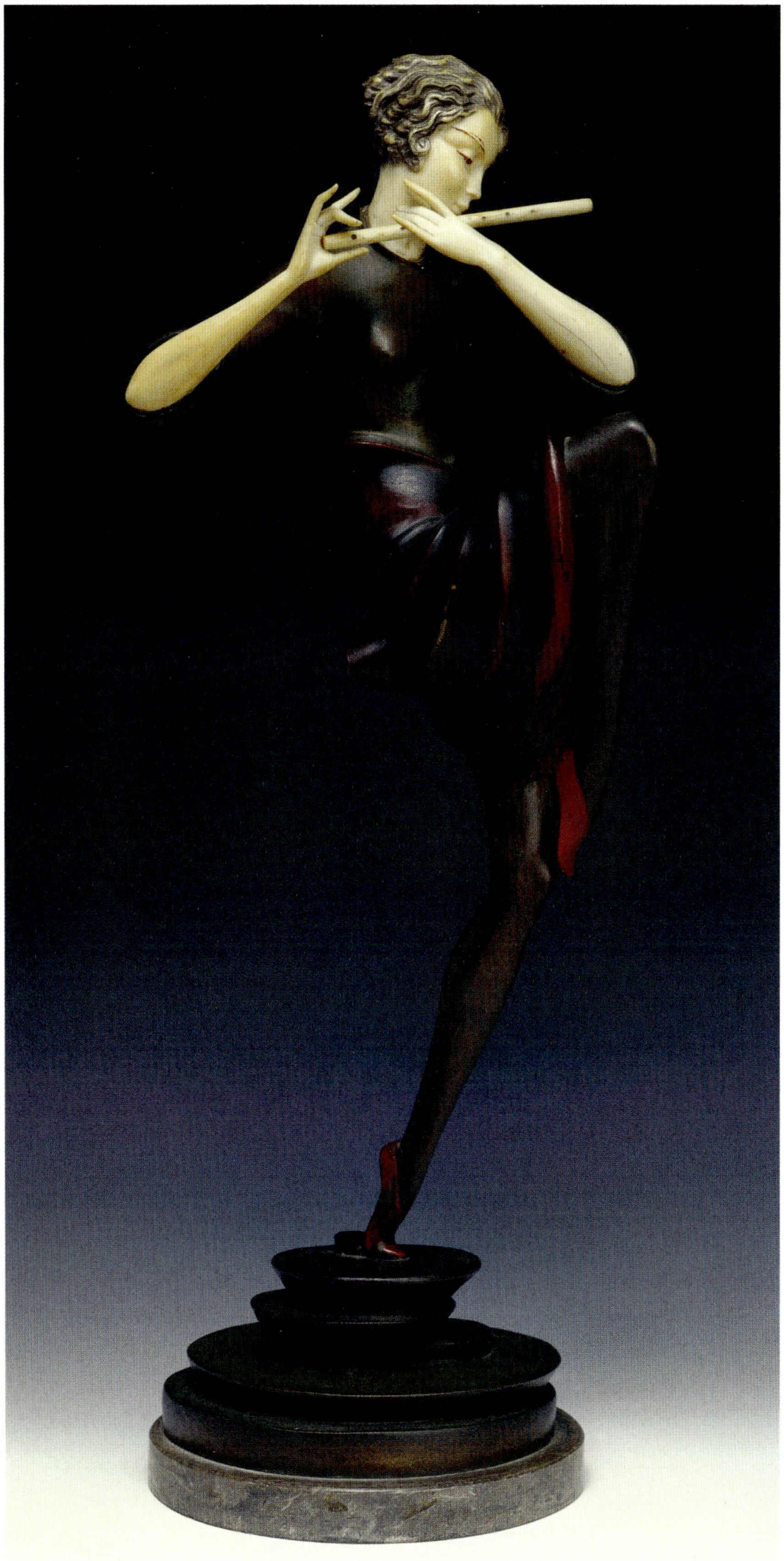

Flute Player
Bronze and ivory on marble base
Height: 56cm. (22in.)
PRIVATE COLLECTION

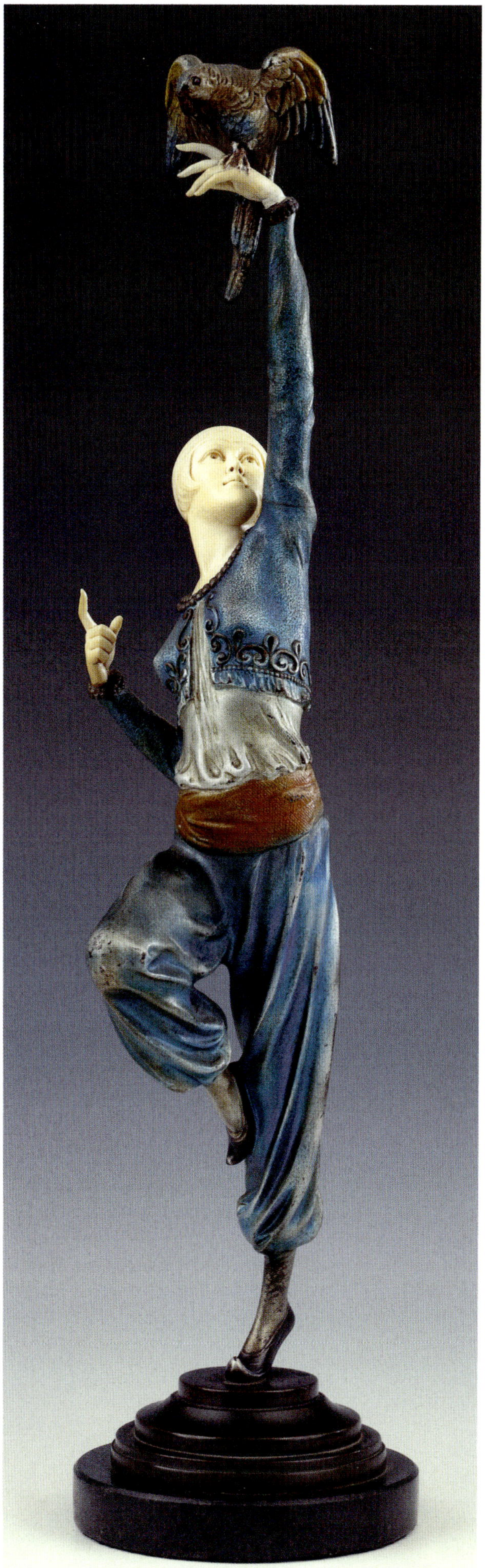

Girl with Parrot
Bronze and ivory on marble base
Height: 49.5cm. (19½in.)
PRIVATE COLLECTION

POERTZEL, Hermann Hugo Otto (POERTZL)

(Scheibe 1876 – Coburg 1963)

Born in Scheibe, Germany, the son of a porcelain designer and decorator, he served an apprenticeship at the A. W. Fr. Kister porcelain factory. In October 1893 he began a 3-year course of studies at the Sonneberg Technical Porcelain Academy (Technischen Akademie für Porzellan), working under Reinhard Möller.

From 1900 Poertzel worked as an independent sculptor in Coburg. In 1908 he moved to Munich, where he had his own workshop and attended classes by Erwin Kurz and Adolf von Hildebrand at the Munich Art Academy.

Otto Poertzel took part in many international exhibitions, including the St. Louis World's Fair (1904) and the Brussels International Art Exhibition (1910).

He is particularly known for his chryselephantine statuettes, representing dancers, circus artists, film stars and elegant young women in graceful poses. His figures were cast by Rosenthal und Maeder and Preiss & Kassler.

The honourary title of Professor was bestowed upon him by the German State; this explains the signature 'Professor Poertzel' on certain pieces.

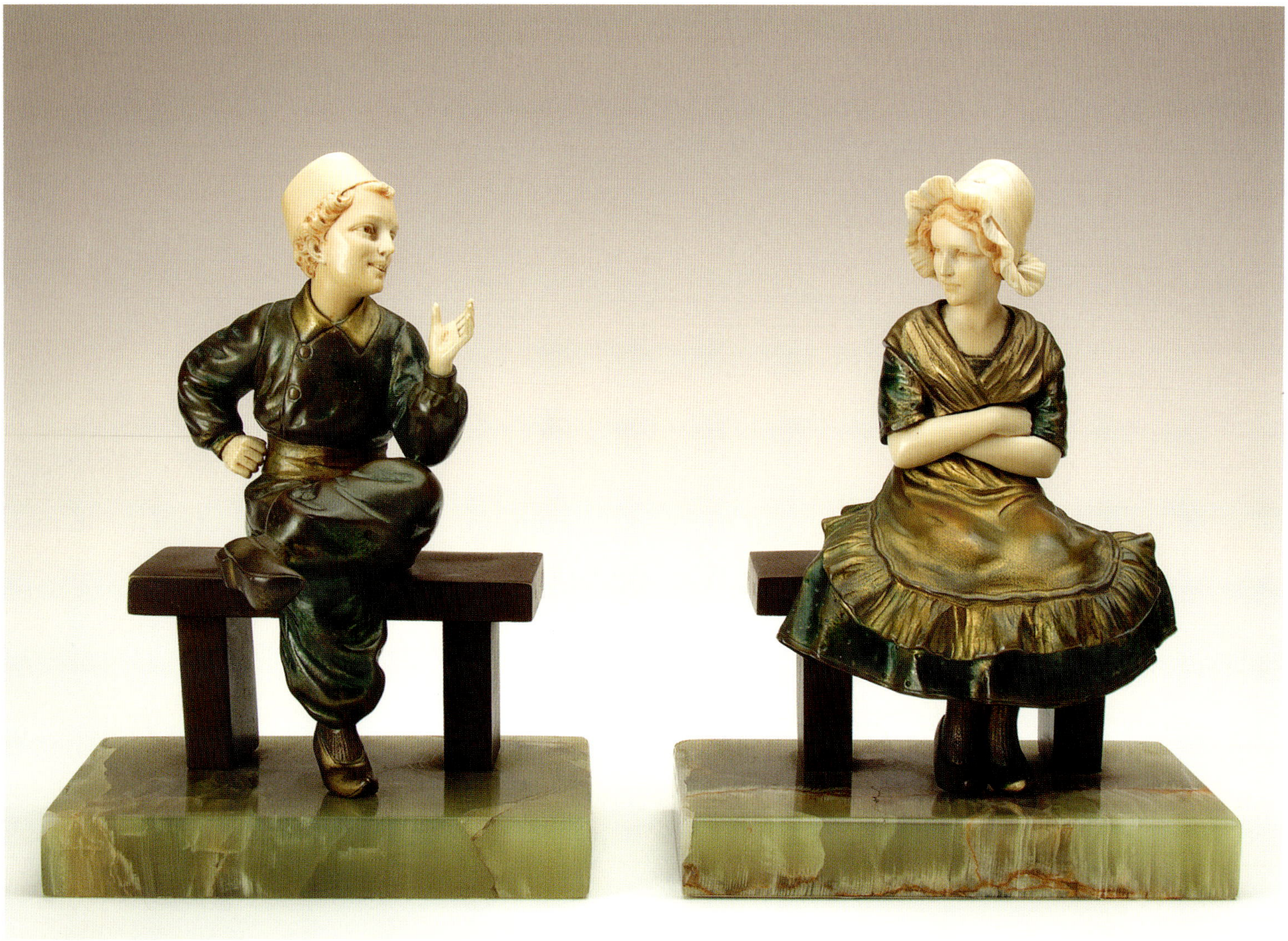

Dutch Boy - Dutch Girl
Bronze and ivory on onyx base
Height: 17.5cm. (7in.) each
DINO MENASCHE COLLECTION

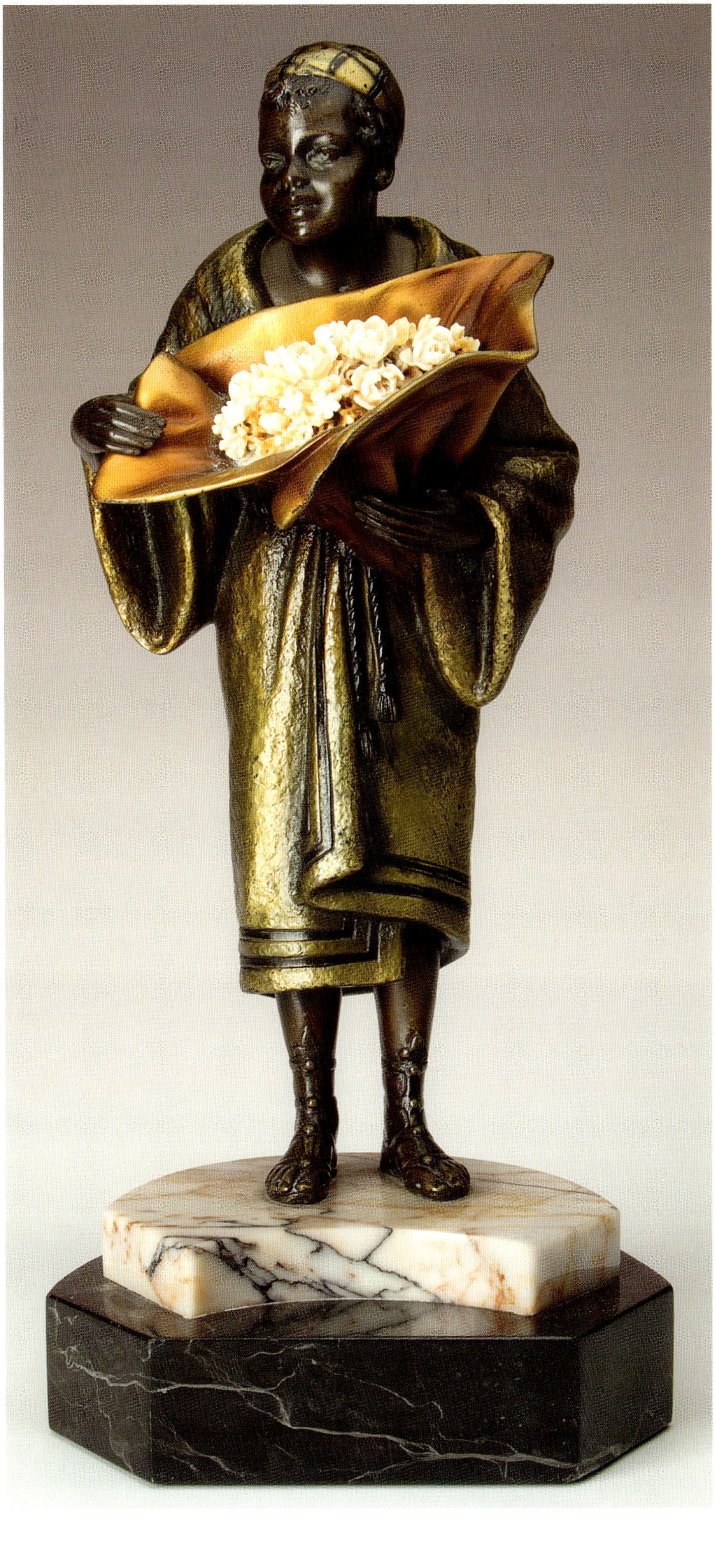

Flower Merchant
Bronze and ivory on marble base
Height: 30.5cm. (12in.)
DINO MENASCHE COLLECTION

Youth
Marble and bronze on marble base
Height: 18.5cm. (7¼in.)
CORNELIA AND RICHARD KASTENHOLZ COLLECTION, GERMANY

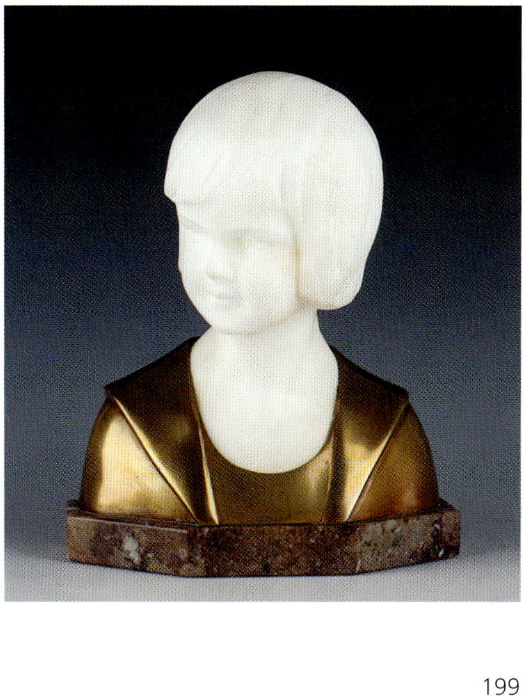

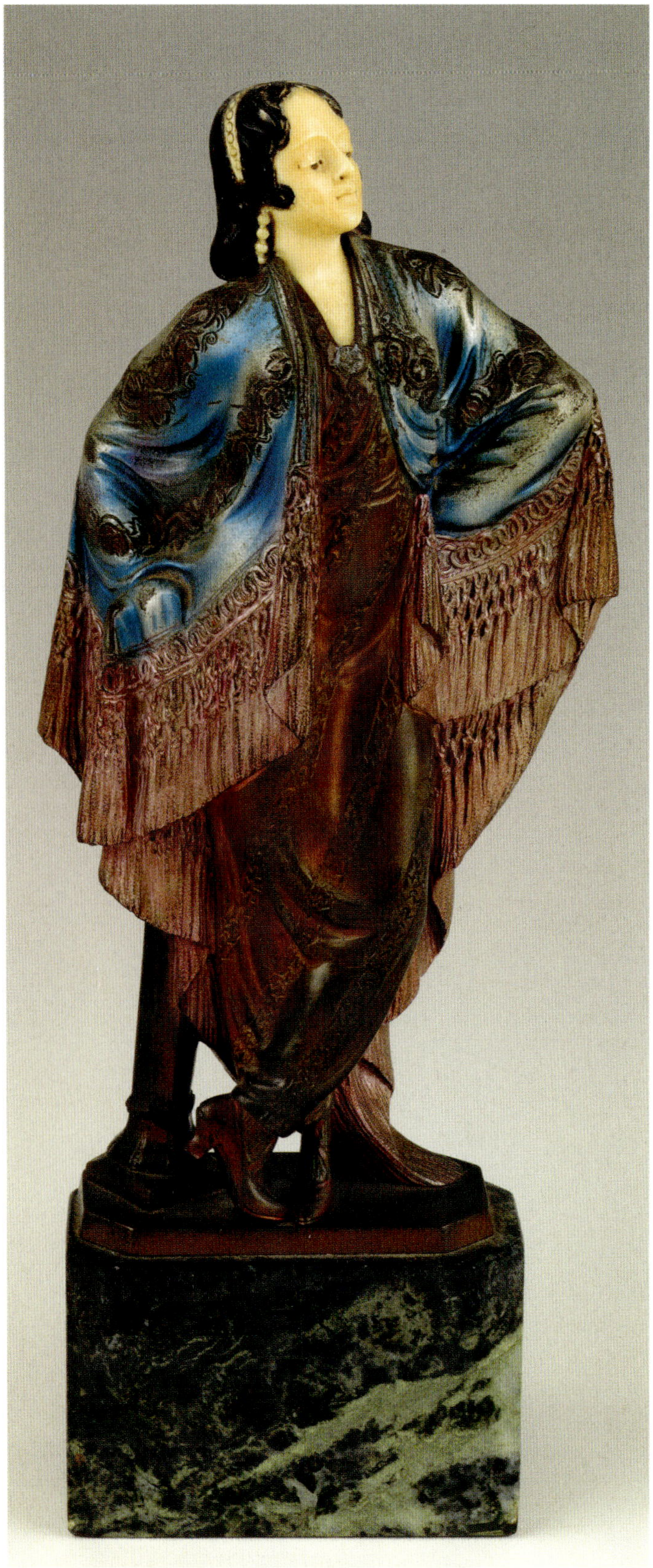

Señorita
Bronze and ivory on marble base
Height: 26cm. (10¼in.)
PRIVATE COLLECTION

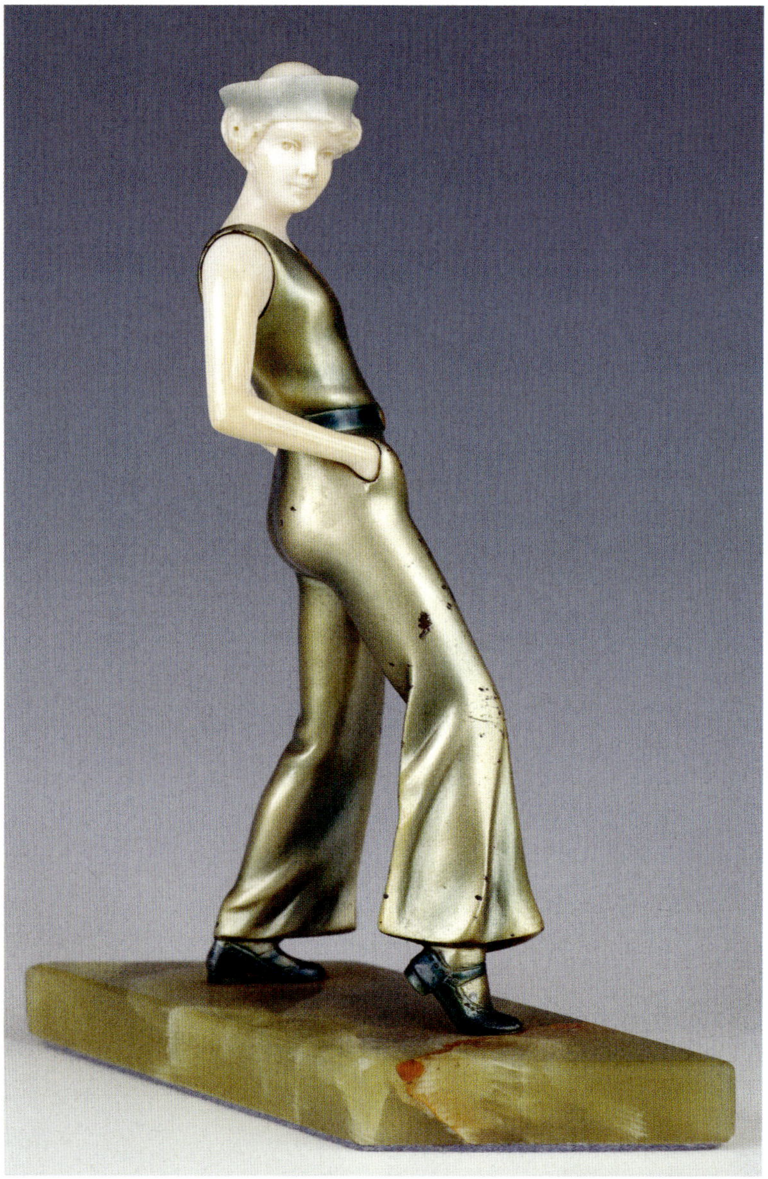

Sailor
Bronze and ivory on onyx base
Height: 17cm. (6¾ in.)
DINO MENASCHE COLLECTION

Also known in multiples of 2 and 3 sailors

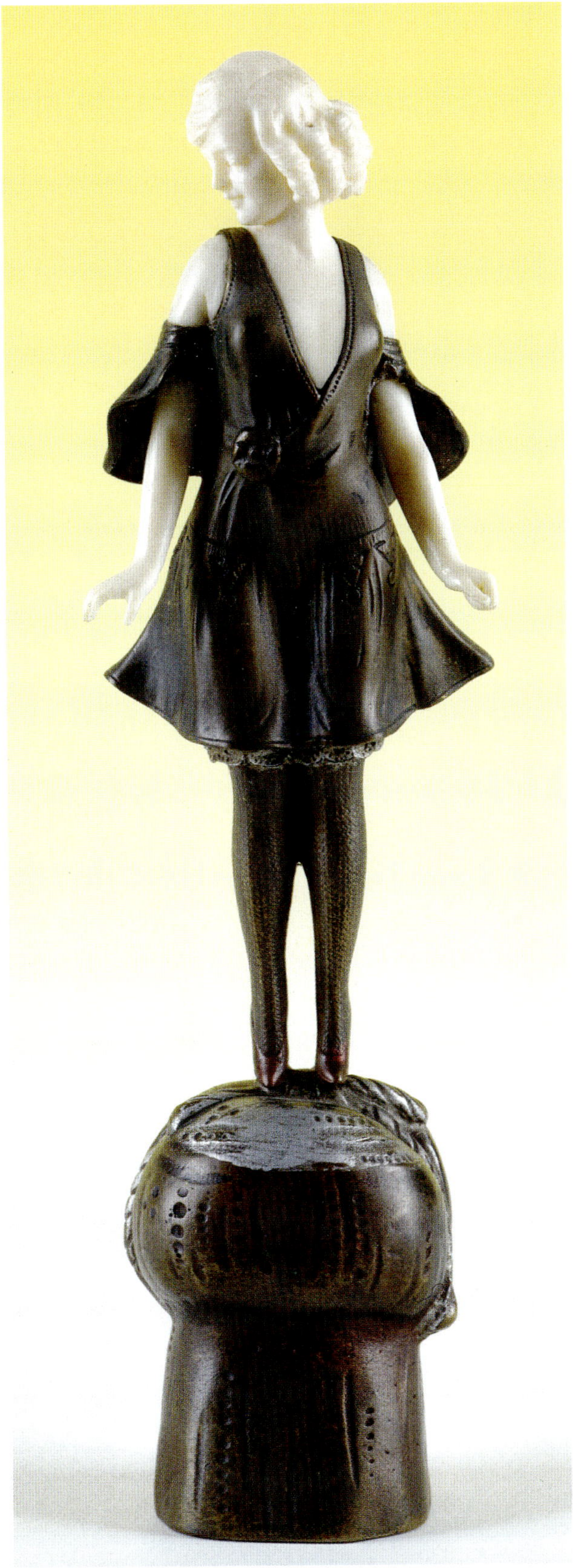

Champagne Girl
Bronze and ivory
Height: 17.5cm. (7in.)
HARRY JAROSCH COLLECTION, VIENNA

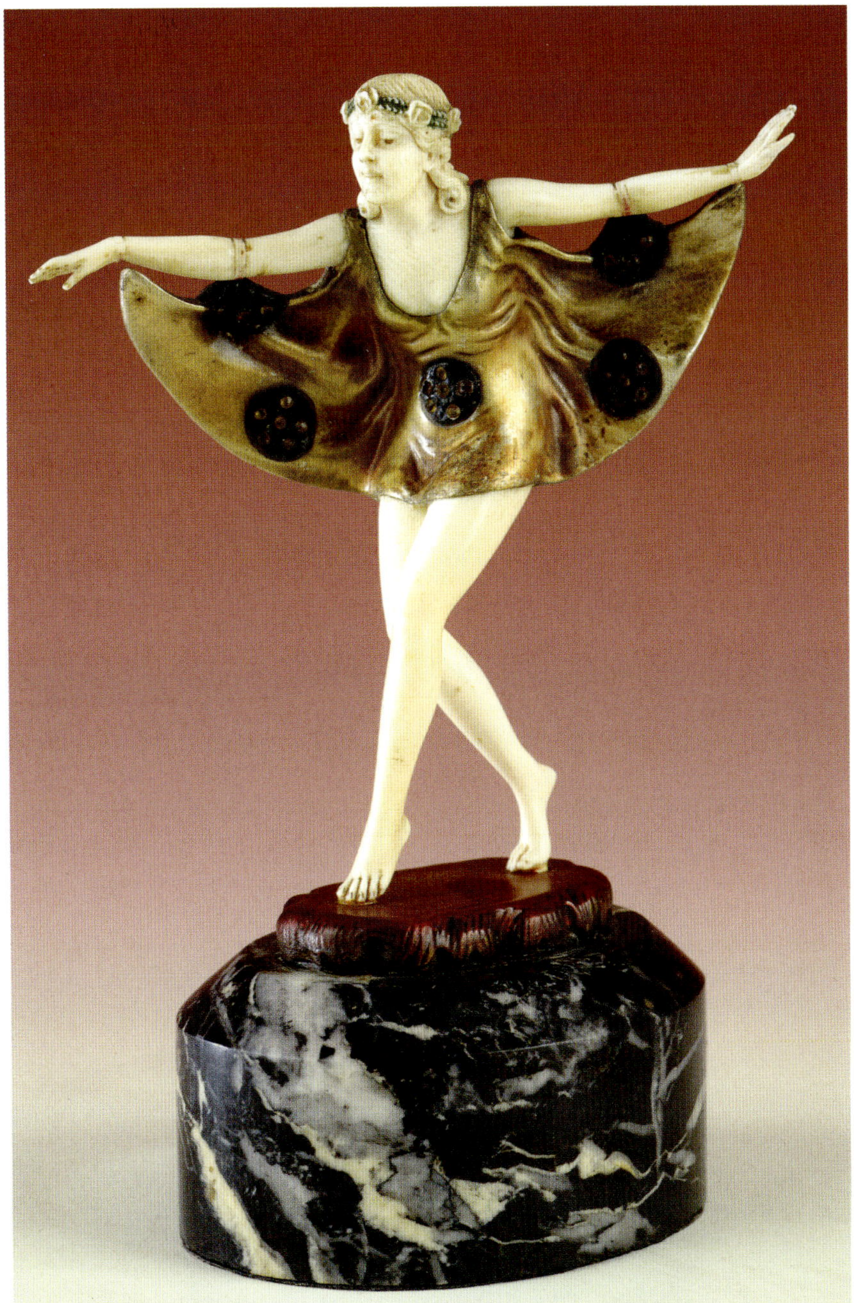

Bat Dancer
Bronze, ivory and rhinestones on marble base
Height: 20cm. (8in.)
PRIVATE COLLECTION

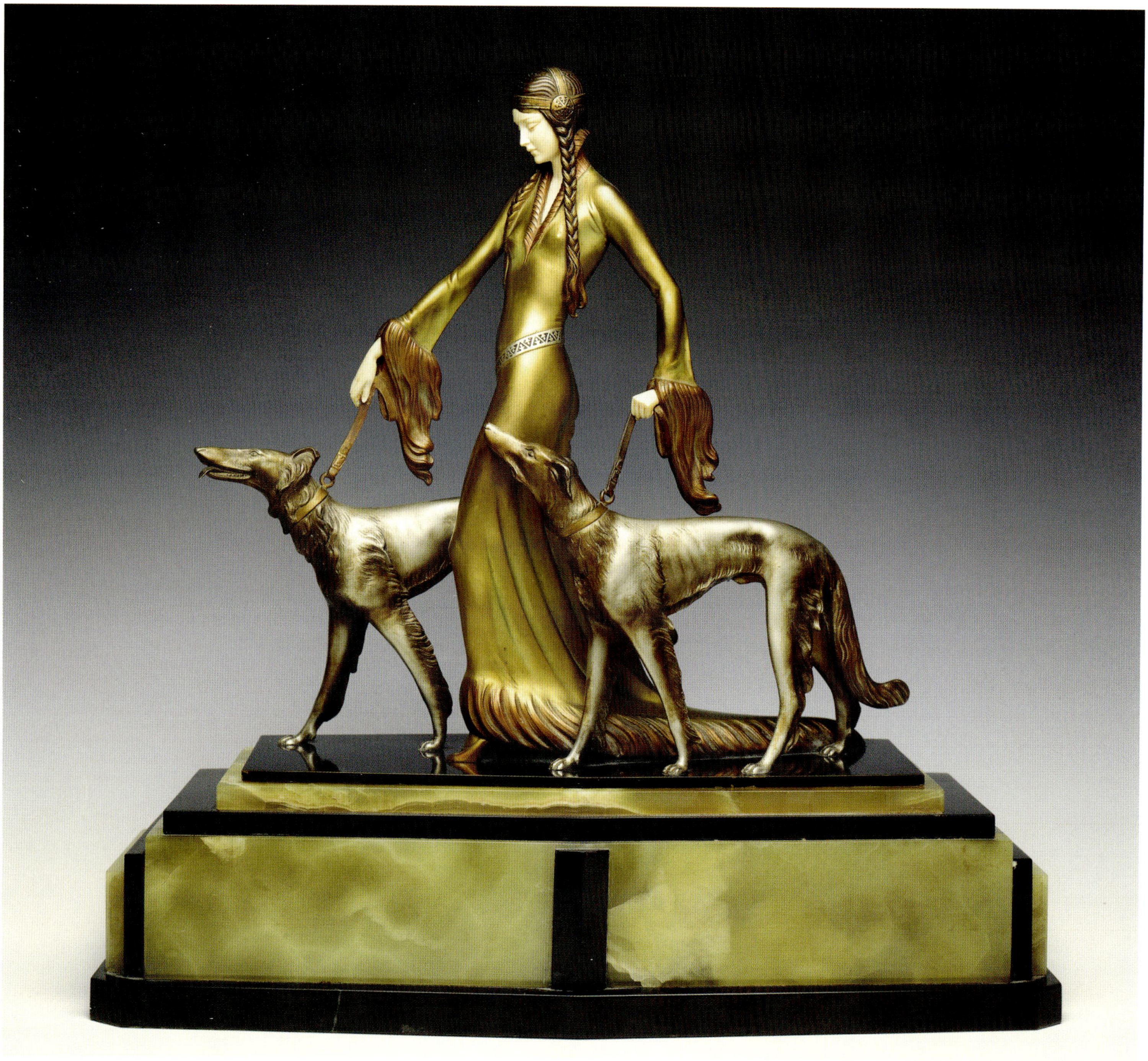

The Aristocrats
Bronze and ivory on onyx base
Height: 49cm. (19¼in.)
PRIVATE COLLECTION

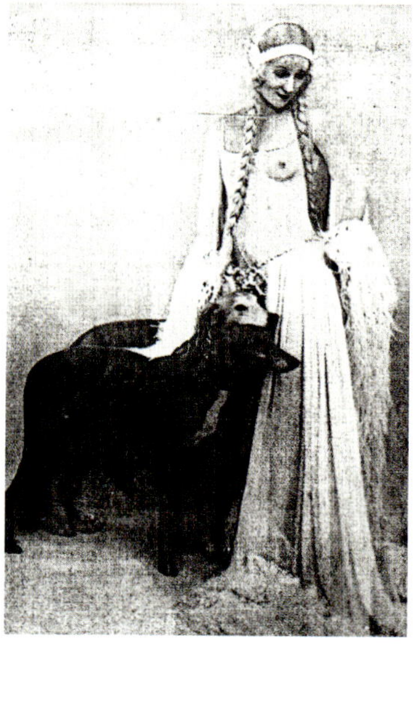

Miss Edmonde Guy at the Casino de Paris Music Hall.

The Top
Bronze and ivory
(mounted as a lamp)
Height: 48cm. (19in.)
PRIVATE COLLECTION

The Top
Bronze and ivory on onyx base
Height: 30.5cm. (12in.)
DINO MENASCHE COLLECTION

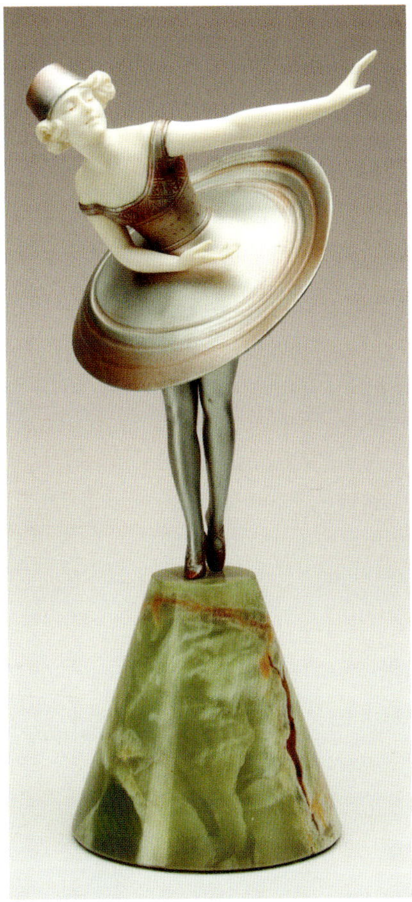

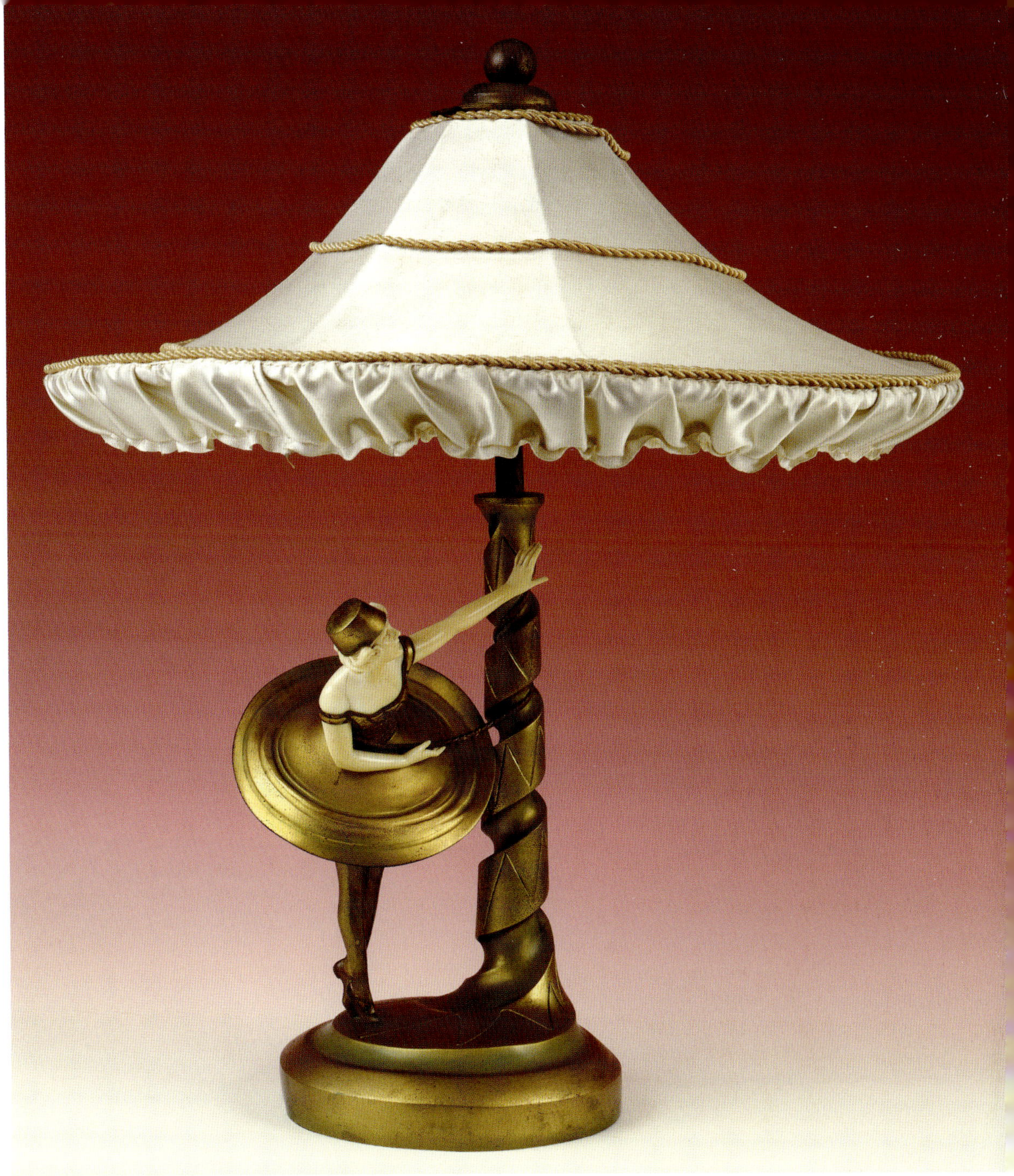

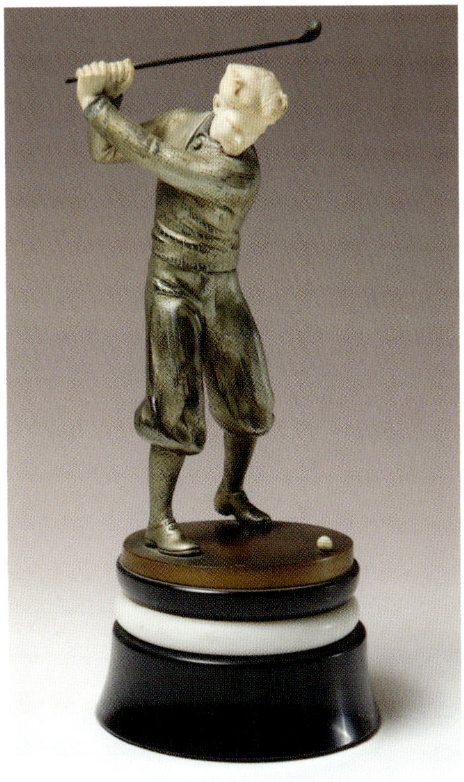

Golfer
Bronze and ivory on marble and onyx base
Height: 30cm. (11¾in.)
PRIVATE COLLECTION

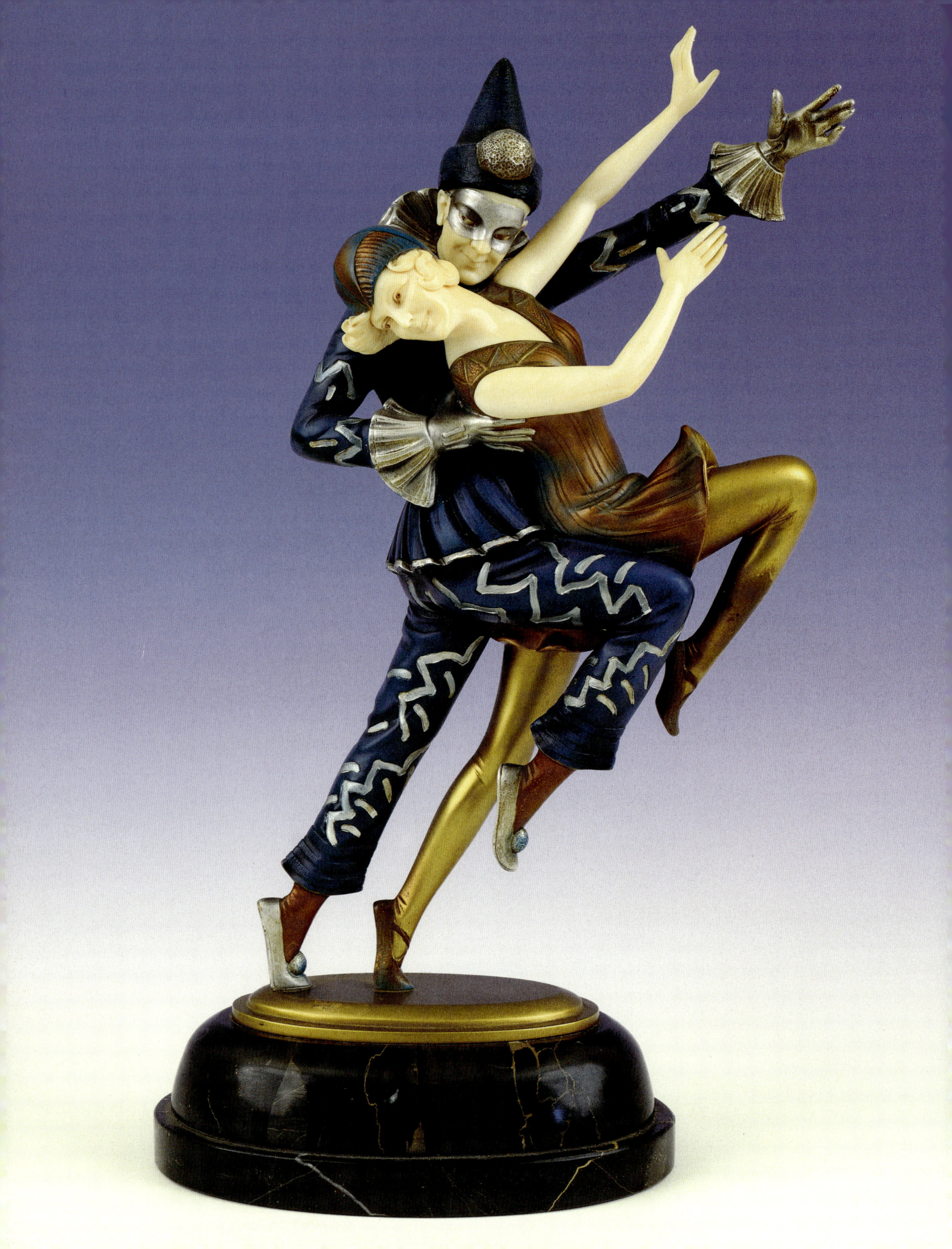

Columbine and Harlequin
Bronze and ivory on marble base
Height: 35.5cm. (14in.)
PRIVATE COLLECTION

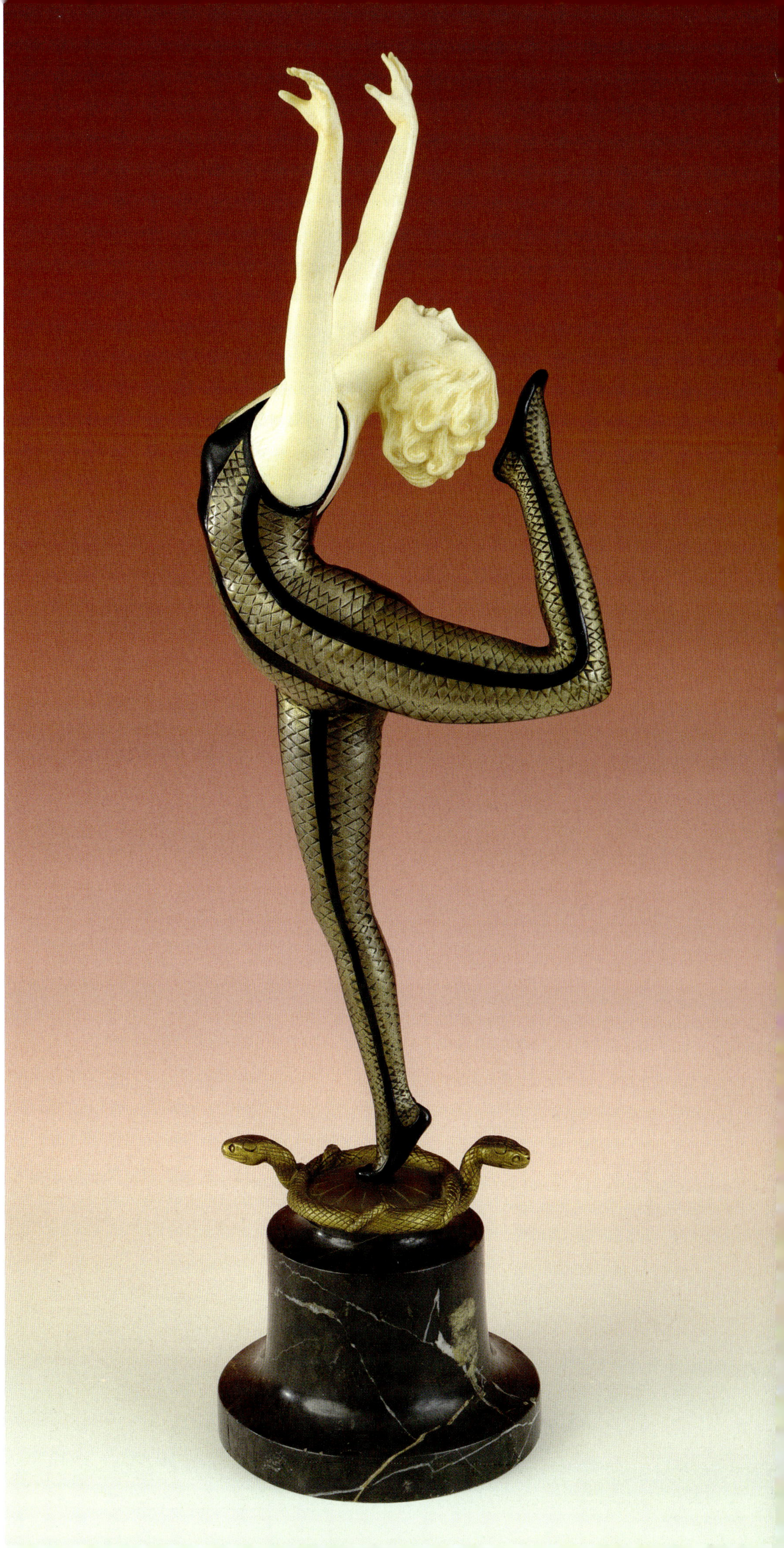

Snake Charmer
Bronze and ivory on marble base
Height: 53cm. (21in.)
PRIVATE COLLECTION

Also produced 27cm. (10½in.) high

PREISS, Ferdinand

(Erbach 1882 – Berlin 1943)

Born in Erbach, Germany, he began his career as an ivory carver, having learned his trade from his uncle, Philip Willmann, and then pursued his studies at the Royal School of Art in Berlin, under ivory carver Michael Kern.

In 1905 he began working at the Karl Haebler firm, where he met fellow sculptor Arthur Kassler. They joined forces in 1906, founding the Preiss & Kassler firm in Berlin; their foundry mark was PK.

In 1929 Preiss & Kassler took over the Rosenthal und Maeder foundry, which worked with such artists as Professor Otto Poertzel, Philippe, Harders and Lange.

Red Dancer
Bronze and ivory on marble base
Height: 37cm. (14½in.)
PRIVATE COLLECTION

Cyclist
Bronze and ivory on onyx base
Height: 19.5cm. (7¾in.)
PRIVATE COLLECTION

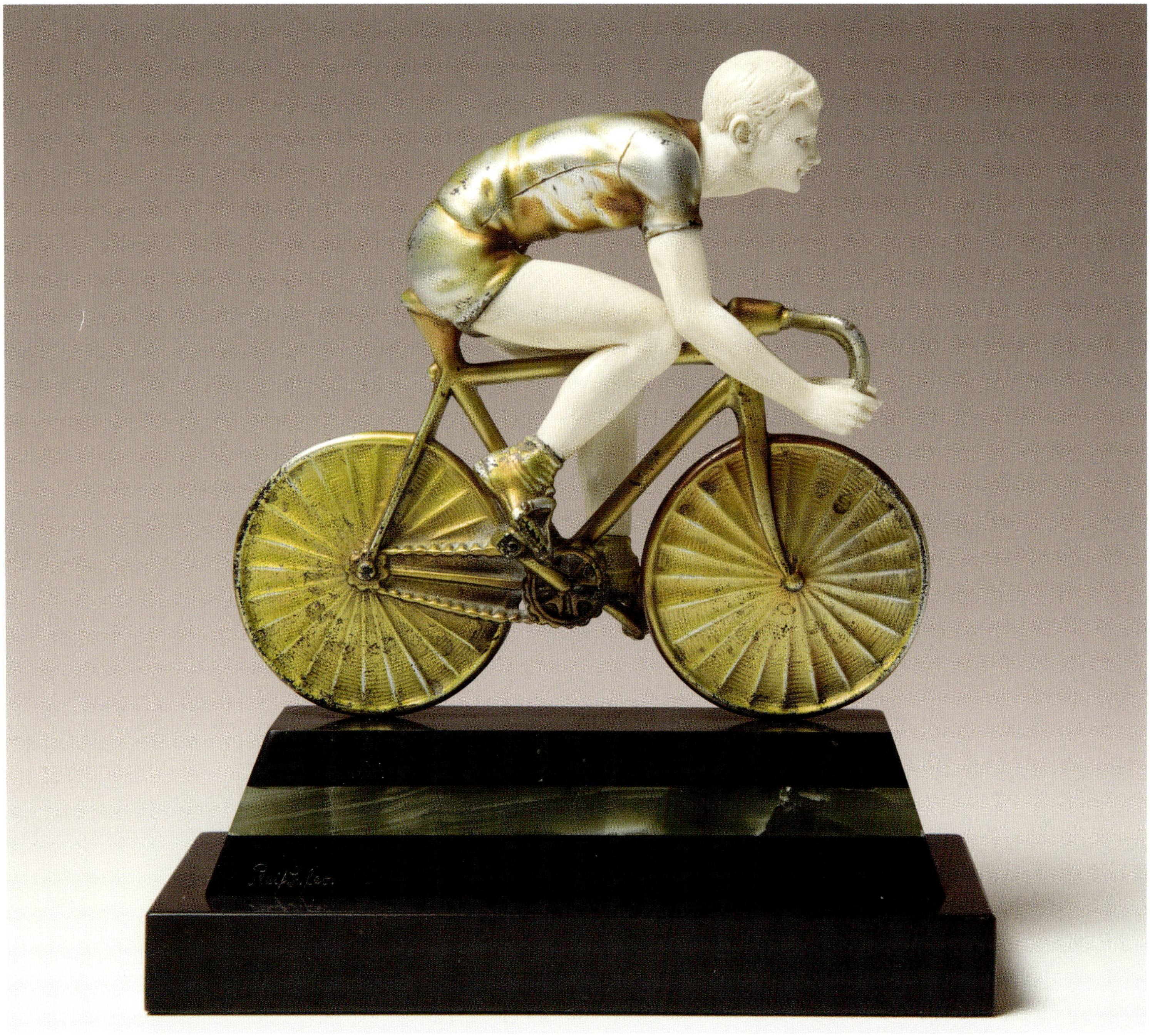

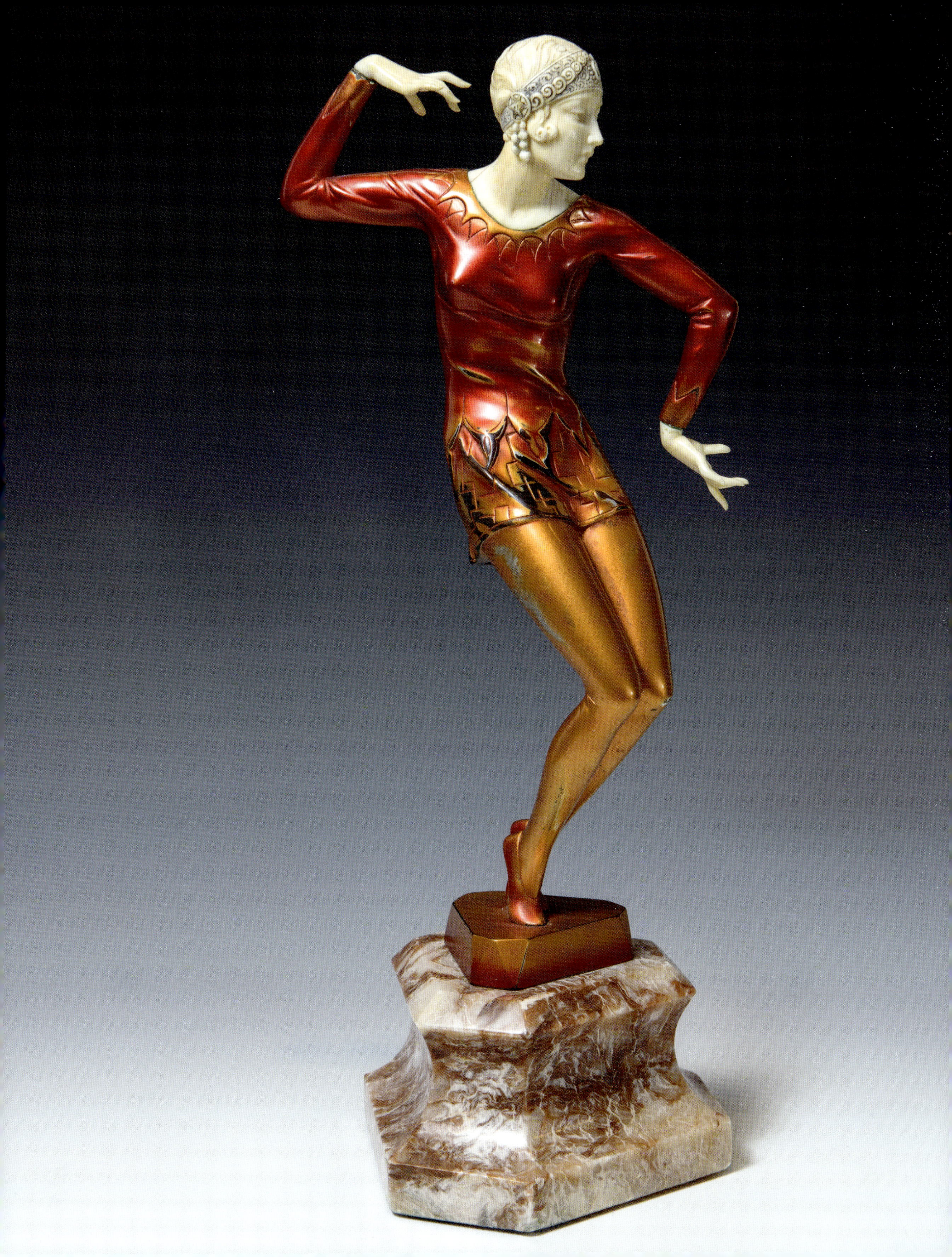

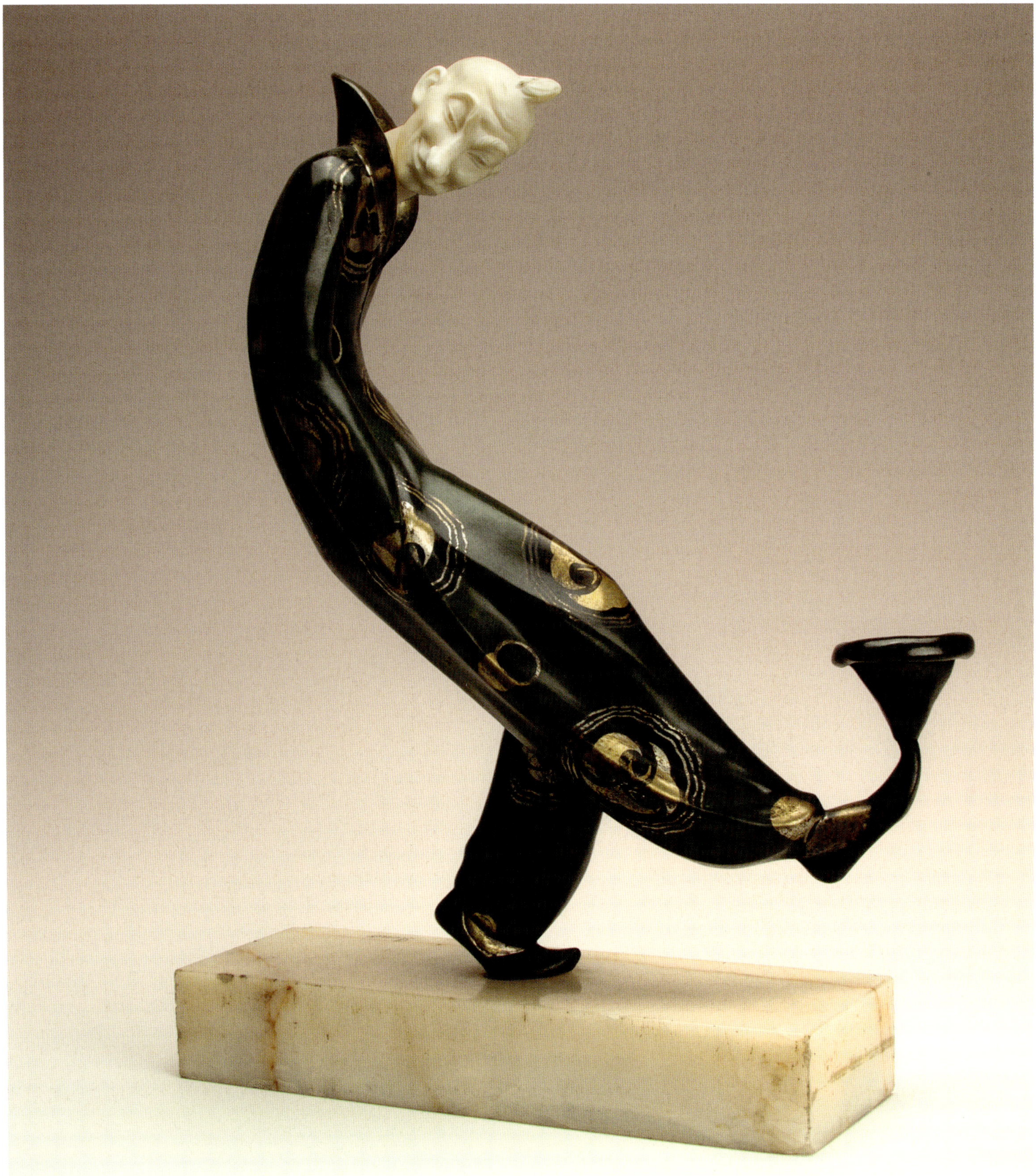

Harlequin
Bronze and ivory on marble base
Height: 35cm. (13¾in.)
PRIVATE COLLECTION

RIGAUD, F.

French

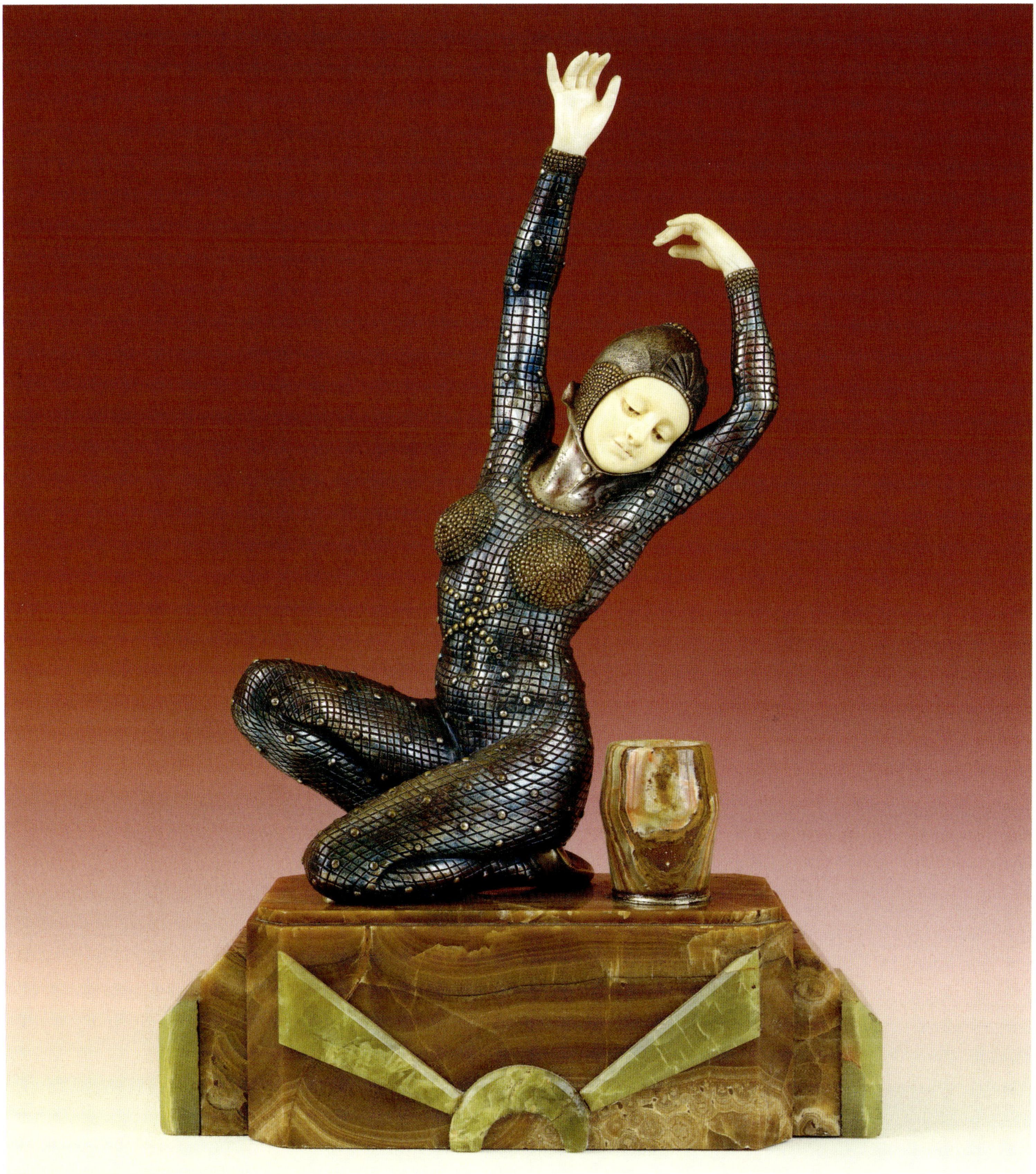

Kneeling Dancer

Bronze and ivory on onyx base

Height: 60cm. (23½in.)

PRIVATE COLLECTION

RIGAULT, C.

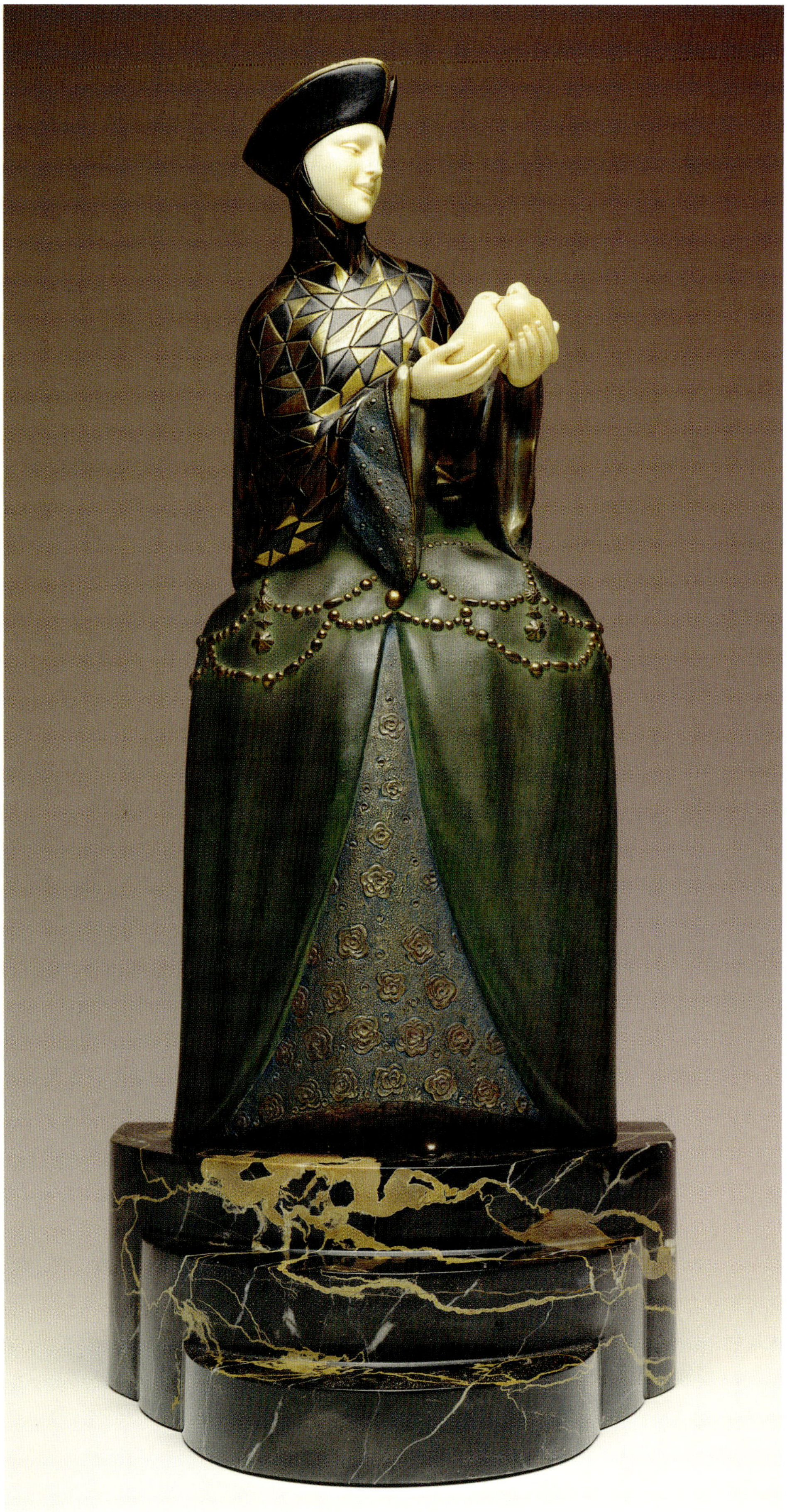

Venetian Love
Bronze and ivory on marble base
Height: 50cm. (19¾in.)
PRIVATE COLLECTION

The Skip
Bronze and ivory on marble base
Height: 51cm. (20in.)
PRIVATE COLLECTION

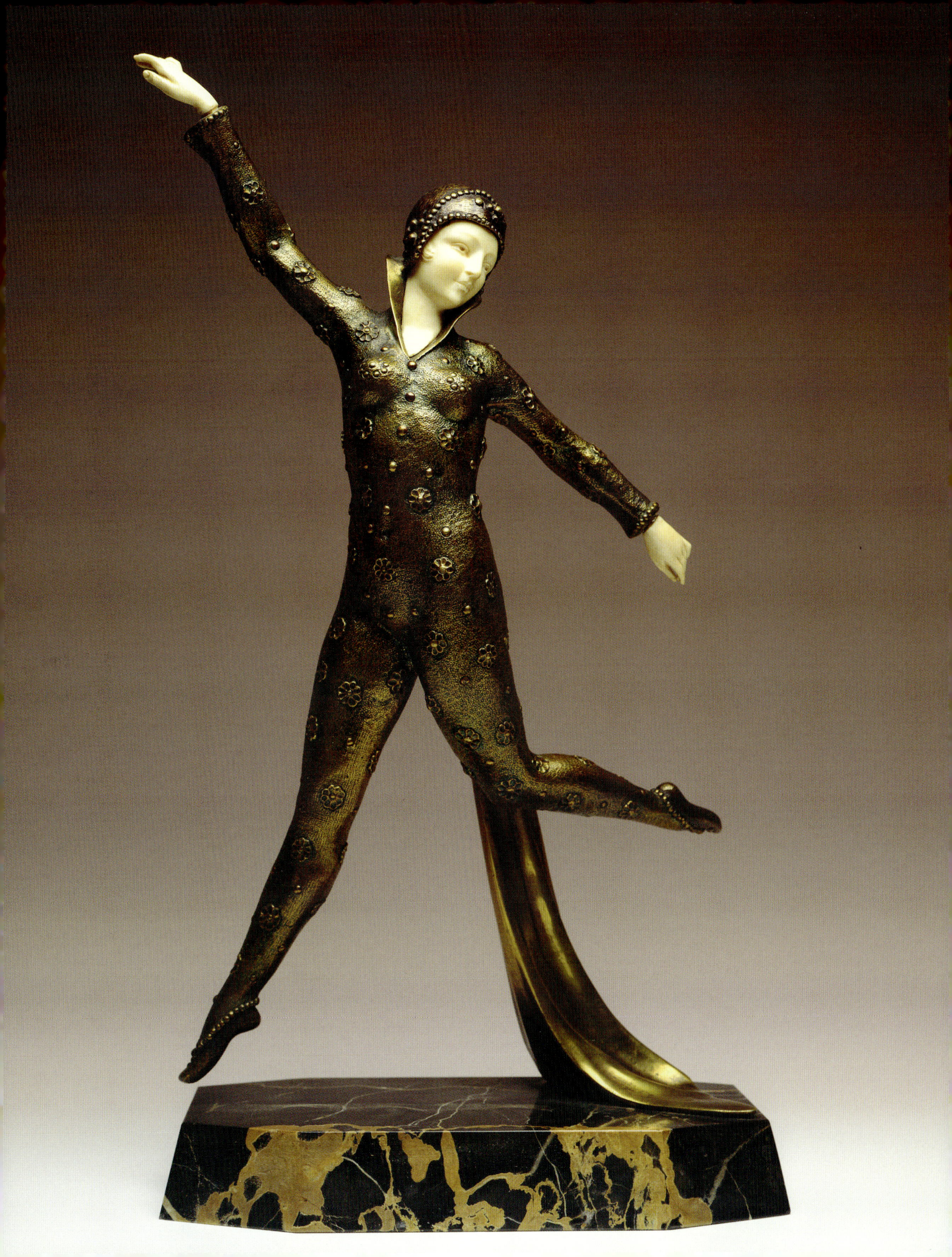

RIGOT, G.

This could be Georges L. Rapaire Rigot (1905–1999) who became a painter later in life (originally a dentist) and lived in Monaco.

Or: Gérard, active in the 1920s.

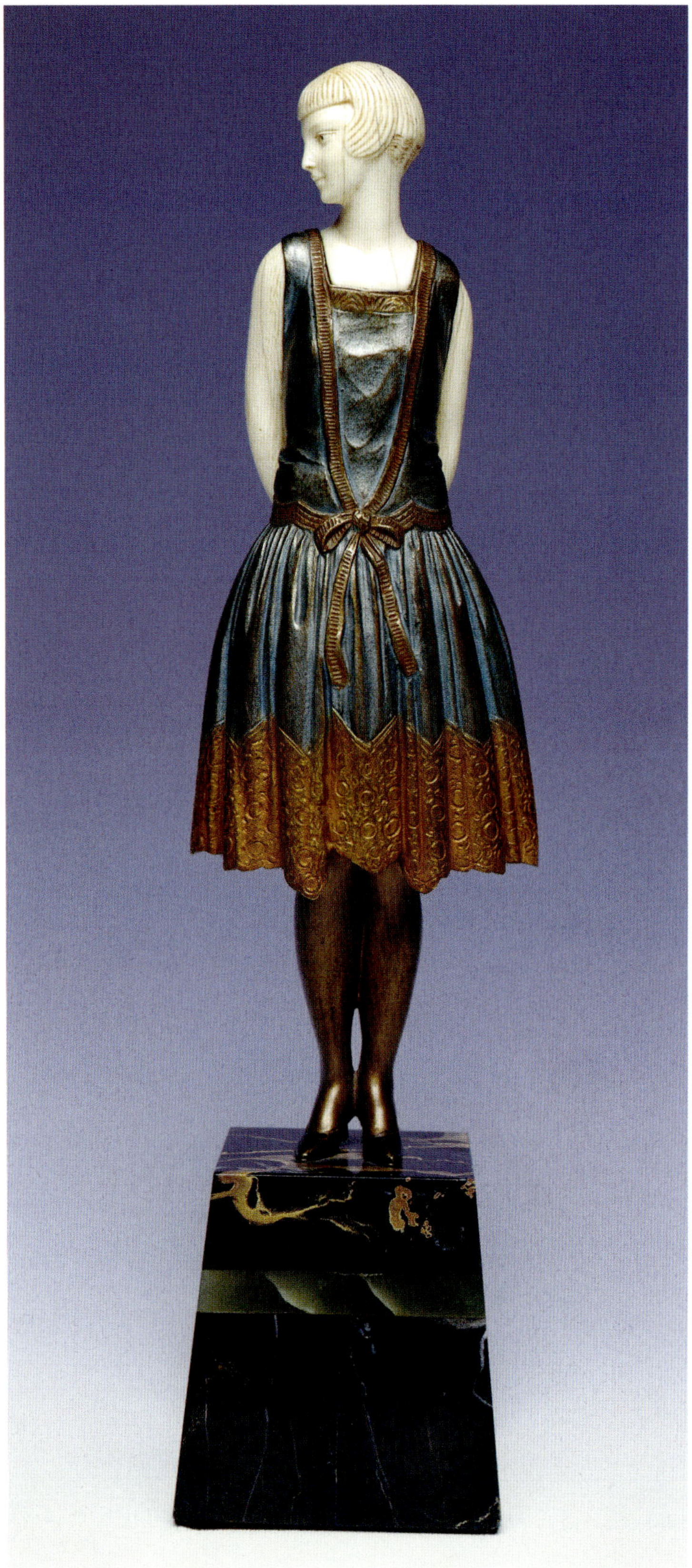

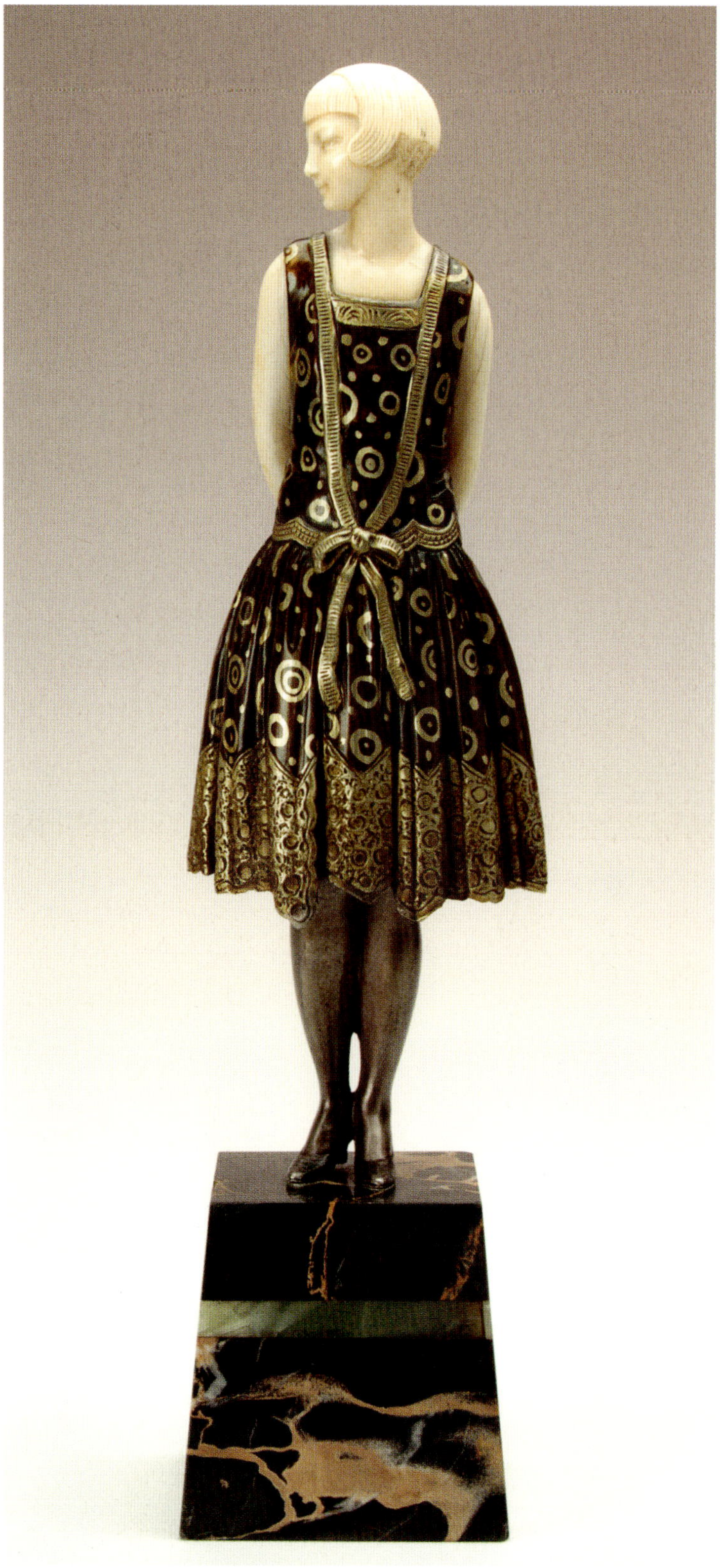

Awaiting
Bronze and ivory on marble and onyx base
Height: 35.5cm. (14in.)
DINO MENASCHE COLLECTION

Awaiting
Bronze and ivory on marble and onyx base
Height: 35.5cm. (14in.)
PRIVATE COLLECTION

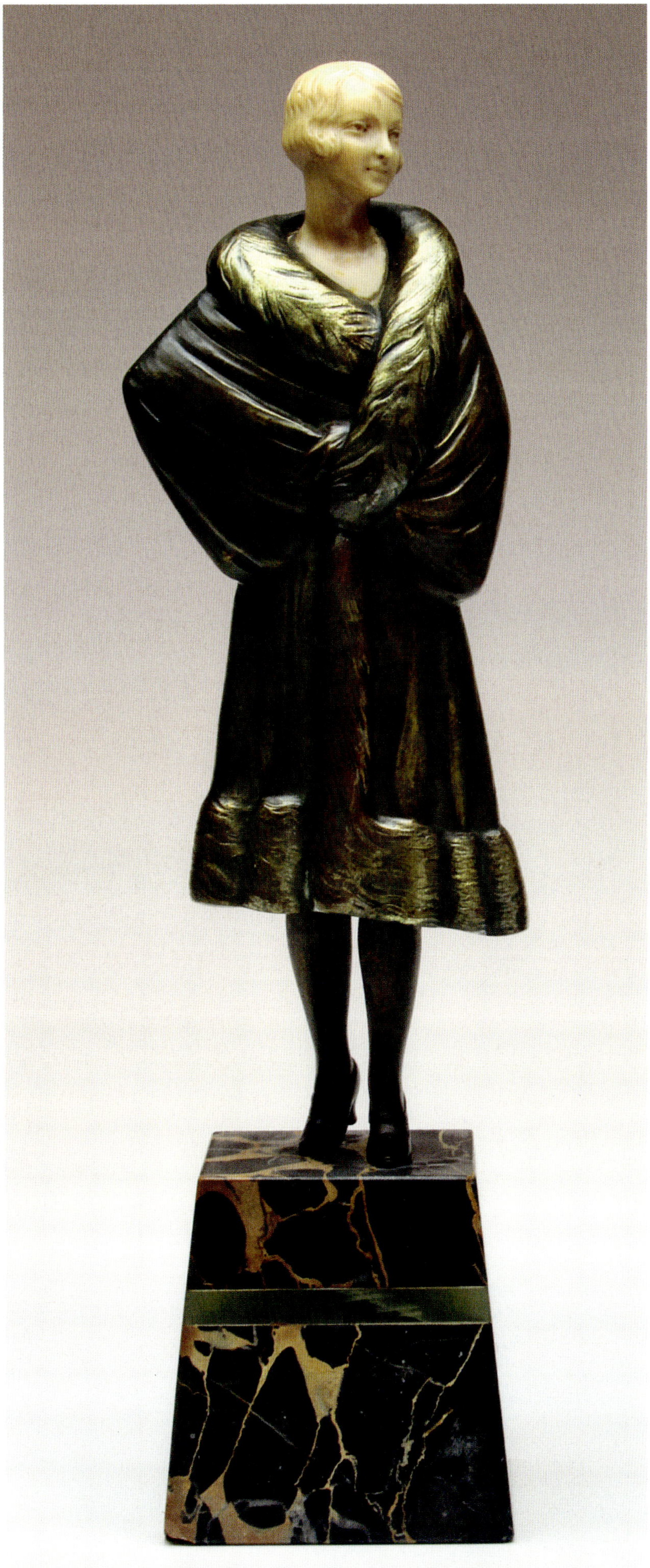

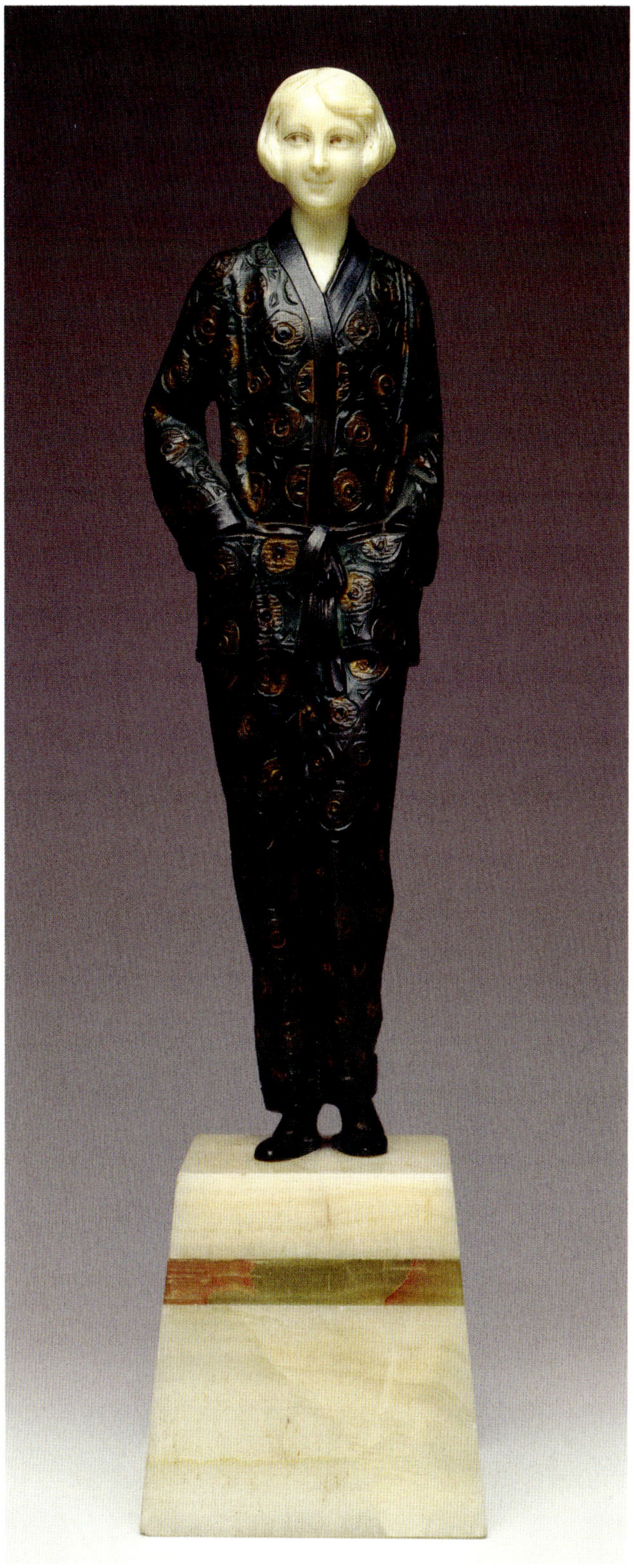

Pyjamas
Bronze and ivory on marble and onyx base
Height: 35cm. (13¾in.)
PRIVATE COLLECTION

Girl in a Fur Coat
Bronze and ivory on marble and onyx base
Height: 35.5cm. (14in.)
PRIVATE COLLECTION

ROUSSEL, Paul

(Paris 1867 – Paris 1928)

He trained at the Paris Ecole des Beaux Arts, a student of Pierre-Jules Cavelier, Louis Ernest Barrias and Jules-Félix Coutan.

Roussel won the *Grand Prix de Rome* in 1895, with the plaster bas-relief *David, Vainqueur de Goliath, Amené en Triomphe à Saül* (David, Having Defeated Goliath, is Brought to Saul in Triumph). He lived and worked at the Villa Medicis in Rome until 1899.

After his return from Rome, Paul Roussel regularly exhibited at the Salon of the Société des Artistes Français, producing many sculptures for the French state or for private collectors. In 1900 he won a silver medal at the Exposition Universelle in Paris.

In July 1920 he was named Chevalier de la Légion d'Honneur.

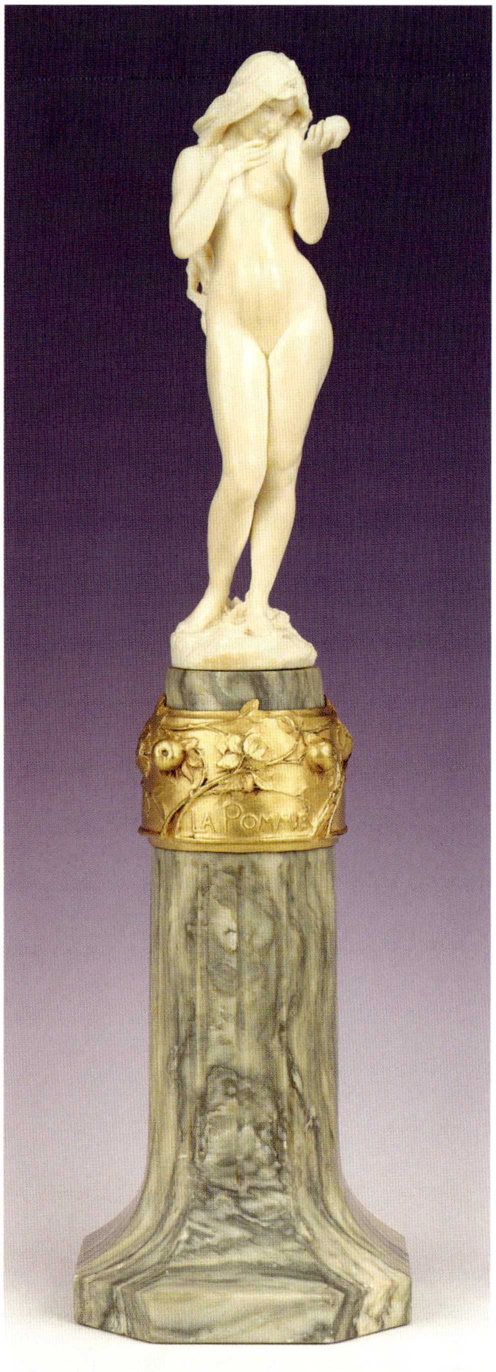

La Pomme
Ivory on marble and bronze base
Height: 45.5cm. (18in.)
PRIVATE COLLECTION

This model was exhibited in 1908 at the Salon of the Société des Artistes Français

---

ROZET, Fanny

(Paris 1881 – ?)

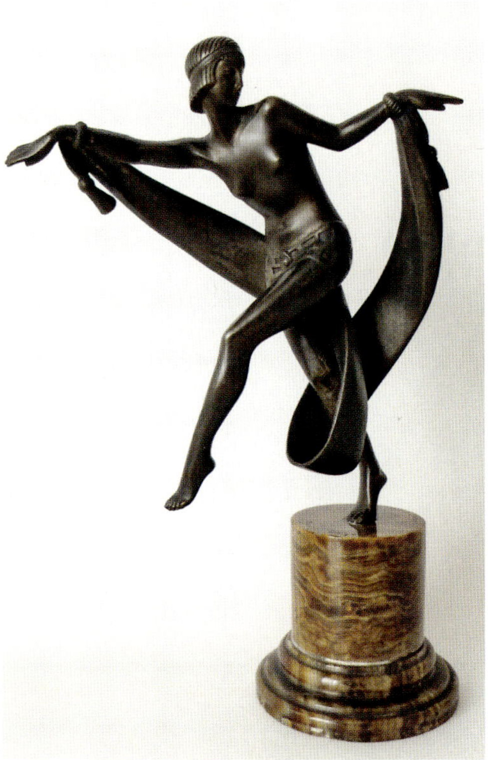

The Scarf Dance
Bronze on onyx base
Height: 30cm. (11¾in.)
PRIVATE COLLECTION

Also produced 47cm. (18½in.) high

Fanny Rozet became a notable member of the Union des Femmes Peintres et Sculpteurs (Union of Female Painters and Sculptors), which demanded entry for women to the Paris Ecole des Beaux Arts. Women were eventually allowed to enter the prestigious institution in 1896. Rozet was the first female sculptor to be admitted. There she studied under Laurent Honoré Marqueste. Rozet exhibited at the Salon of the Société des Artistes Français beginning in 1904. She was awarded an honourable mention in 1904, a bronze medal in 1921, another honourable mention in 1923, and a silver medal in 1926 (in the field of applied arts).

She was elected member of the Société des Artistes Français. Rozet worked in various media, including bronze, ivory, terracotta, ceramics, plaster and wood. Her pieces — including sculptures, decorative objects, and lamps — were produced by Goldscheider, Susse Frères, Eyffinger et Marquet, Etling and Les Neveux de J. Lehmann.

SANDOZ, Edouard Marcel

(Basel 1881 – Lausanne 1971)

Born in Basel, Switzerland, he studied at the Geneva Ecole des Arts Appliqués and at the Paris Ecole des Beaux Arts, where he was a student of Antonin Mercié and Jean Antoine Injalbert.

He worked mainly as an animalier sculptor, his favoured materials being stone, onyx, porcelain, semi-precious stones, bronze and precious metals.

At the 1937 International Exhibition of Arts and Techniques his work was exhibited in the Pavilion of the Société des Artistes Décorateurs.

SCHMIDT-CASSEL, Gustav (SCHMIDT-KASSEL)

(Kassel 1867 – Berlin 1954)

Born in Kassel, Germany, he studied at the Berlin Academy of Fine Arts and then travelled to Italy, Paris and Russia. He studied under Ernst Herter, and later became Herter's assistant and took over his workshop.

He was a member of the Reichsverband bildender Künstler Deutschlands (Imperial Federation of Visual Artists of Germany), the Bildhauer Vereinigung Berlin (Sculptors' Association of Berlin) and the Verein Berliner Künstler (Association of Berlin Artists).

Schmidt-Cassel exhibited his first sculptures at collective exhibitions in Berlin, and received his first commission in 1910, for a monumental equestrian statue of Peter the Great for the city of Riga (destroyed in 1917). He also created a statue of Emperor Frederick for the city of Grätz (now Grodzisk Wielkopolski) in Poland.

In the 1920s Schmidt-Cassel created sculptures of exotic dancers with detailed costumes, in the Art Deco style. He also made a series of bronze and ivory figures for Rosenthal und Maeder and Preiss & Kassler.

At the 1929 Hundert Jahre Berliner Kunst exhibition, he exhibited a plaster statue called *Zusammenbruch* (Collapse).

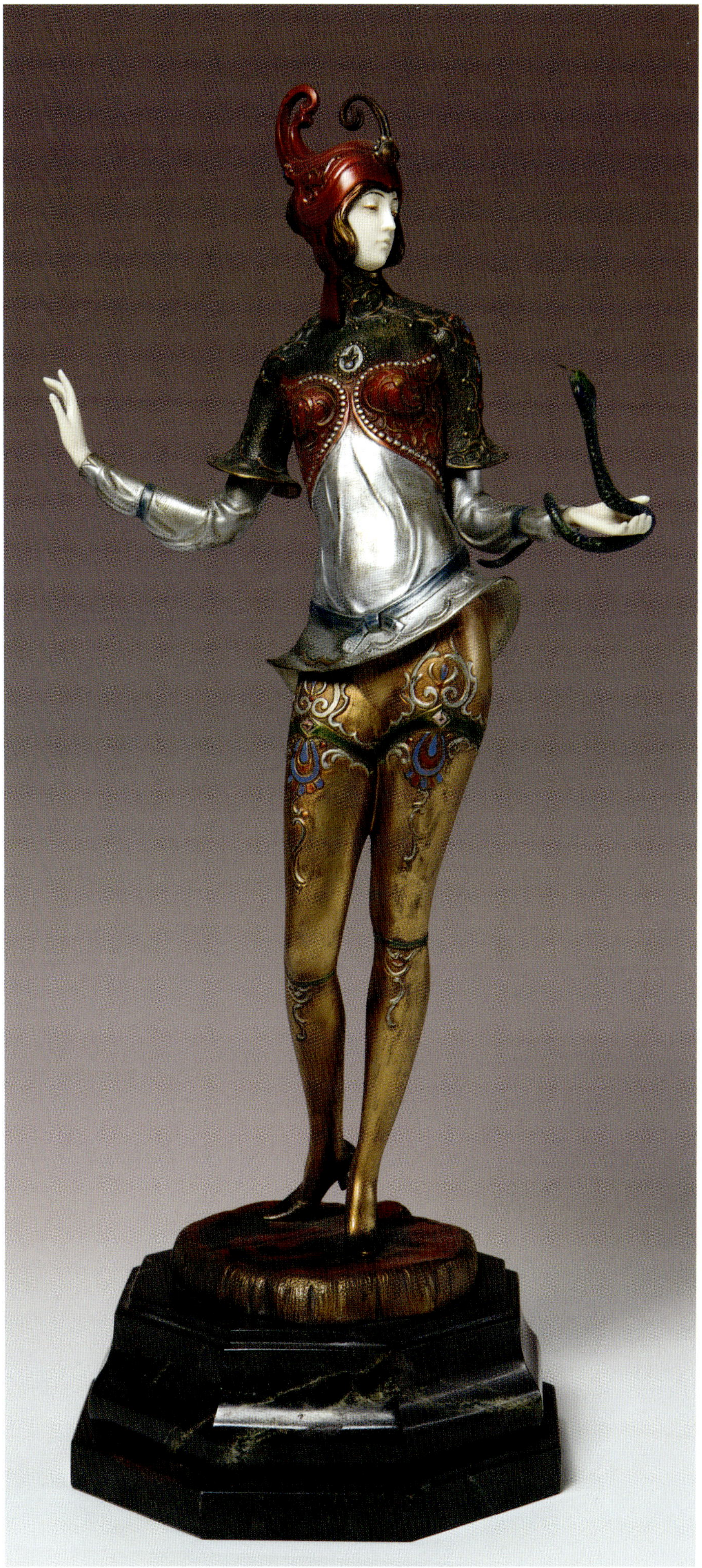

Snake Dancer
Bronze and ivory on marble base
Height: 43cm. (17in.)
PRIVATE COLLECTION

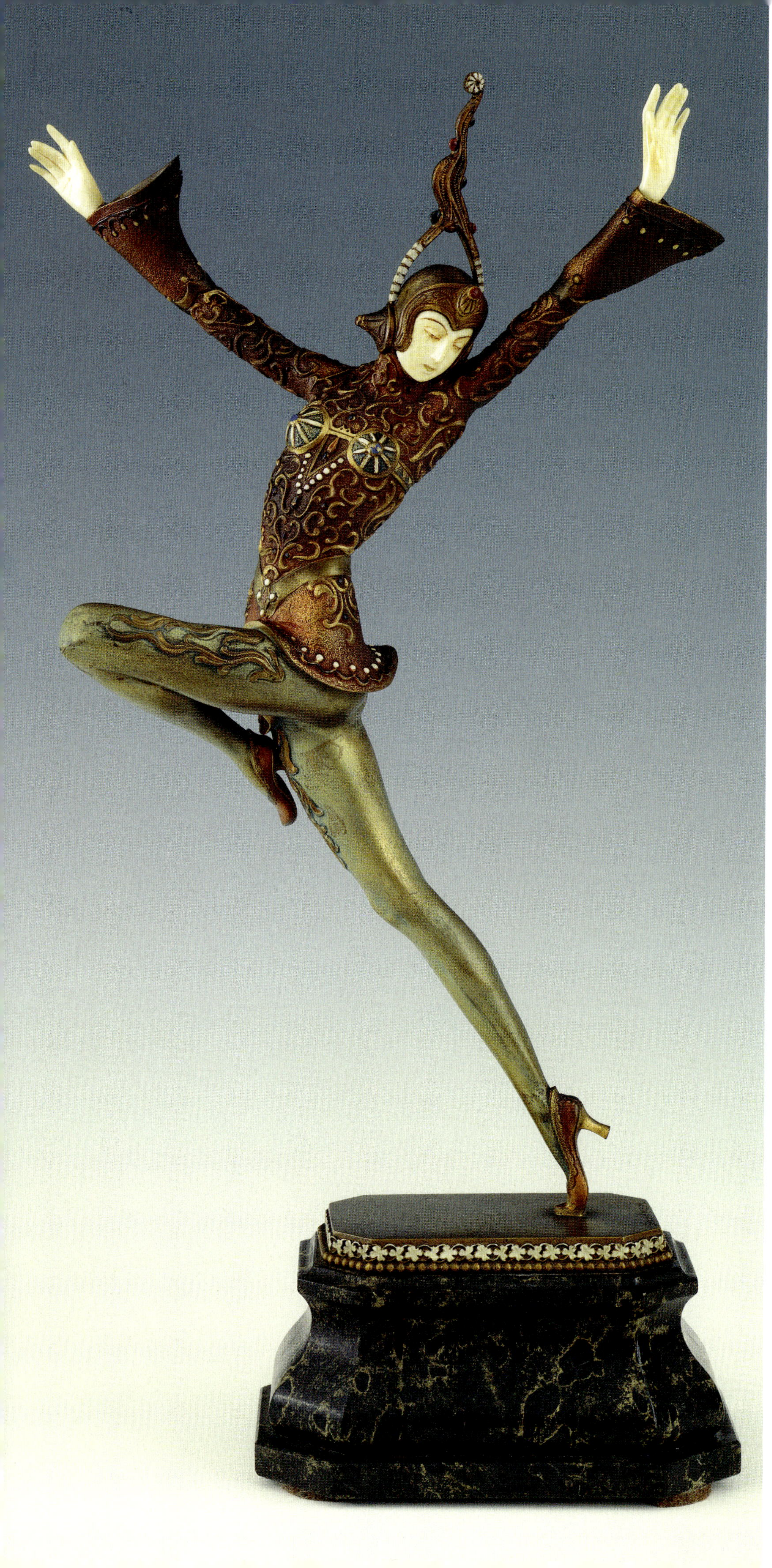

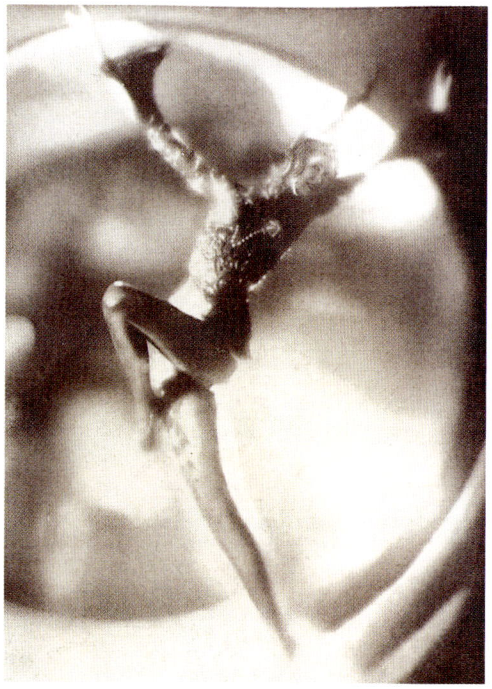

Dancer, 1930.

Eastern Dancer
Bronze and ivory on marble base
Height: 37cm. (14½in.)
PRIVATE COLLECTION

SCHMIDT-FELLING, Julius Paul

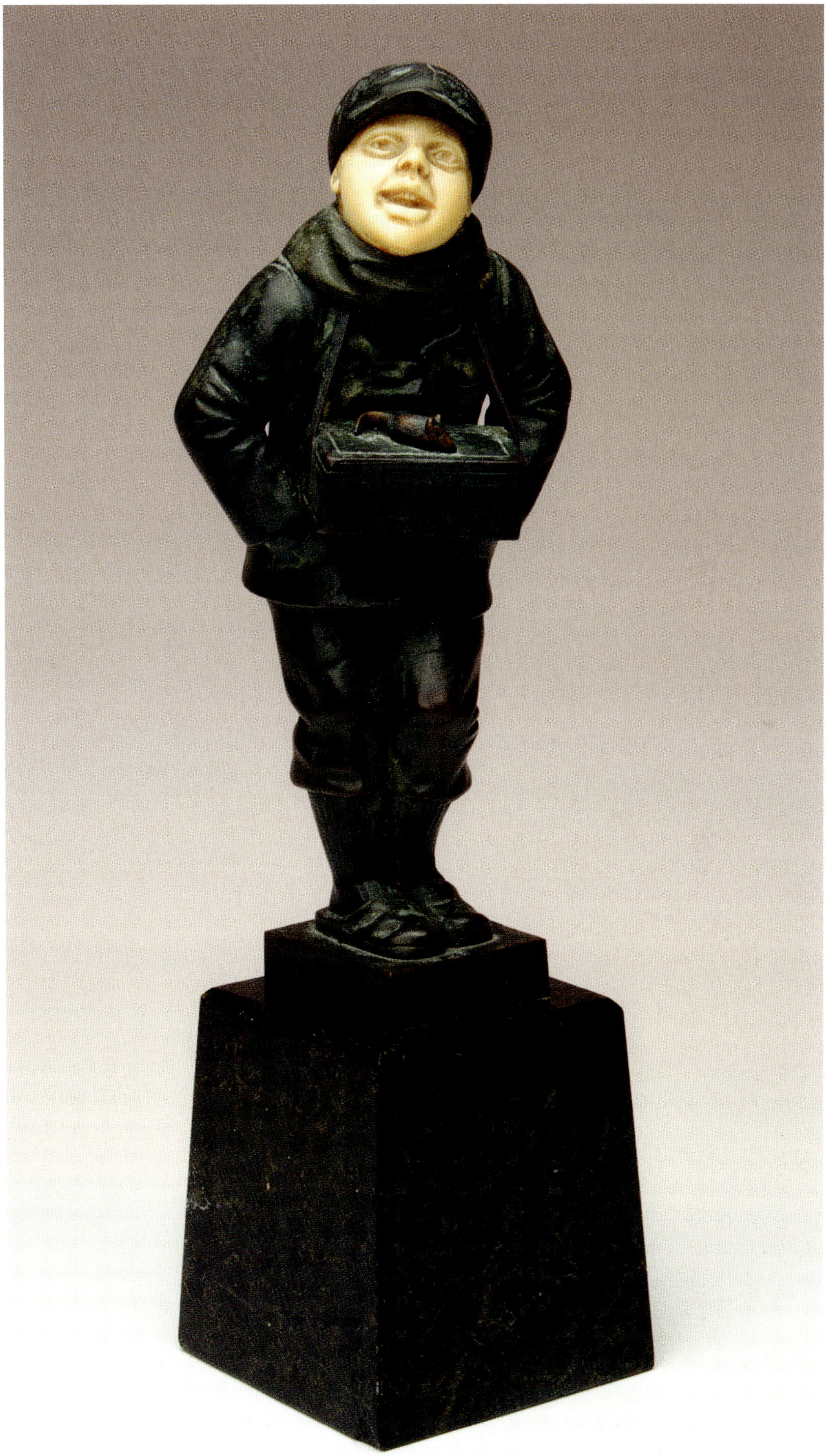

Rascal
Bronze and ivory on marble base
Height: 30cm. (11¾in.)
PRIVATE COLLECTION

SEGER, Ernst

(Neurode 1868 – Berlin 1939)

Born in Neurode, Silesia, his early training was at the Breslau Art School, where his teachers were Robert Härtel and Christian Behrens. He pursued his studies in Auguste Rodin's studio in Paris.

From 1894 he lived and worked in Berlin. He created many monuments in the early years of the 20th century, including those of Eichendorf (1888) and Frederick the Great (1899).

Seger exhibited at the Salon of the Société des Artistes Français, showing a bronze sculpture, *Jeunesse* (Youth) in 1925. His work was produced by Friedrich Goldscheider, KPM, and the State Majolica factory in Karlsruhe.

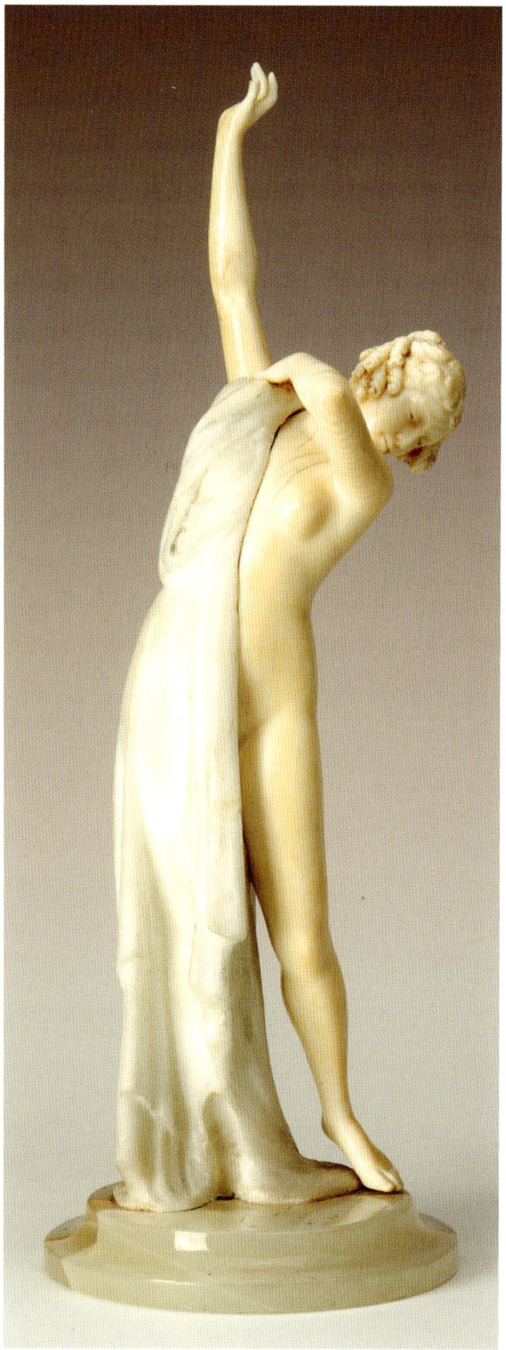

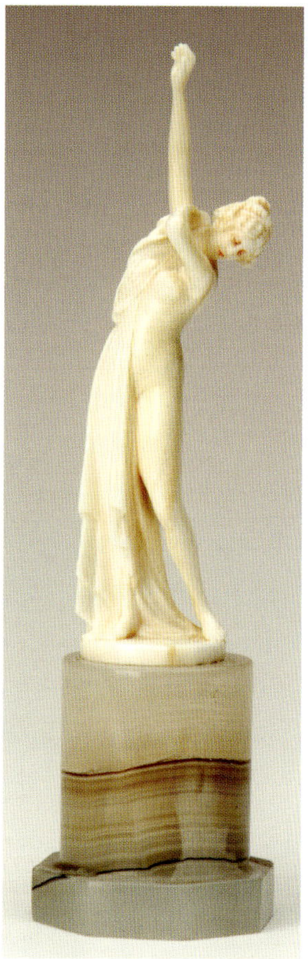

Suzanne
Ivory on onyx base
Height: 12.5cm. (5in.)
PRIVATE COLLECTION

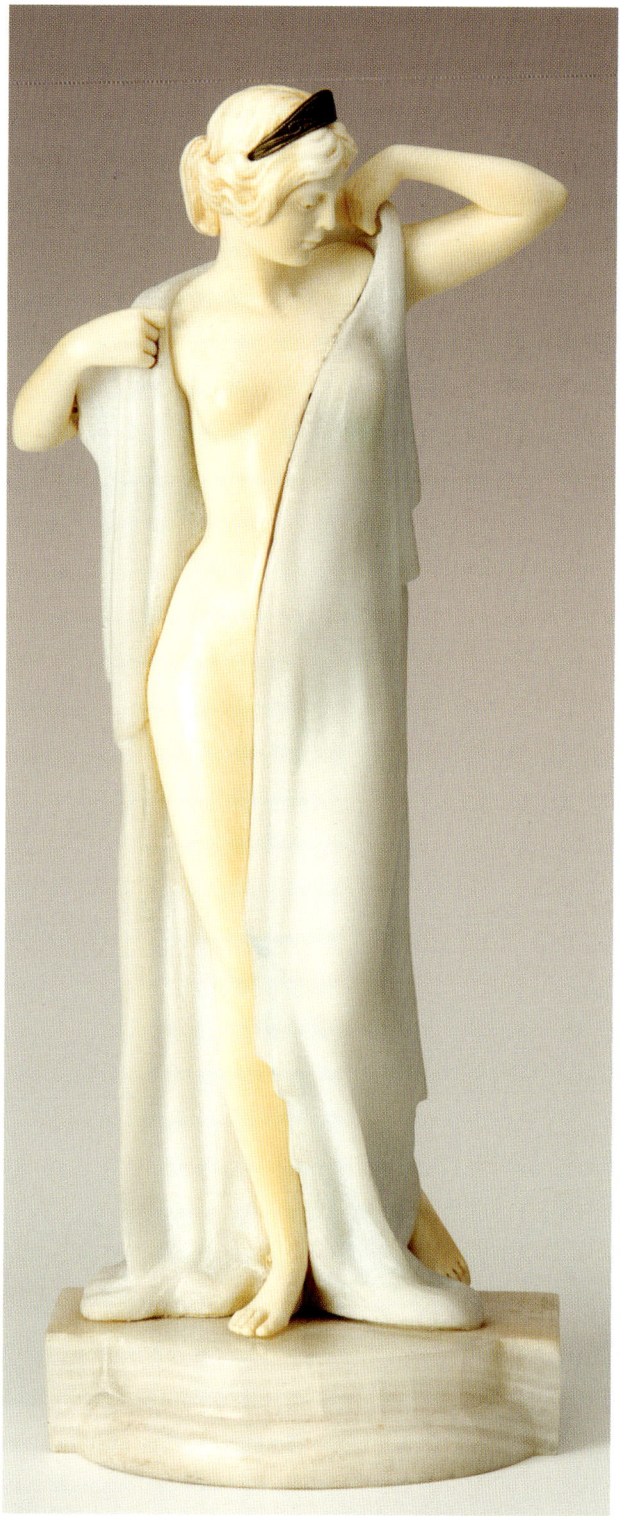

Phryne
Marble and ivory on marble base
Height: 22cm. (8¾in.)
DINO MENASCHE COLLECTION

Suzanne
Marble and ivory on marble base
Height: 26cm. (10¼in.)
DINO MENASCHE COLLECTION

Dancer with Rings
Bronze and ivory on marble base
Height: 20.5cm. (8in.)
CORNELIA AND RICHARD KASTENHOLZ COLLECTION, GERMANY

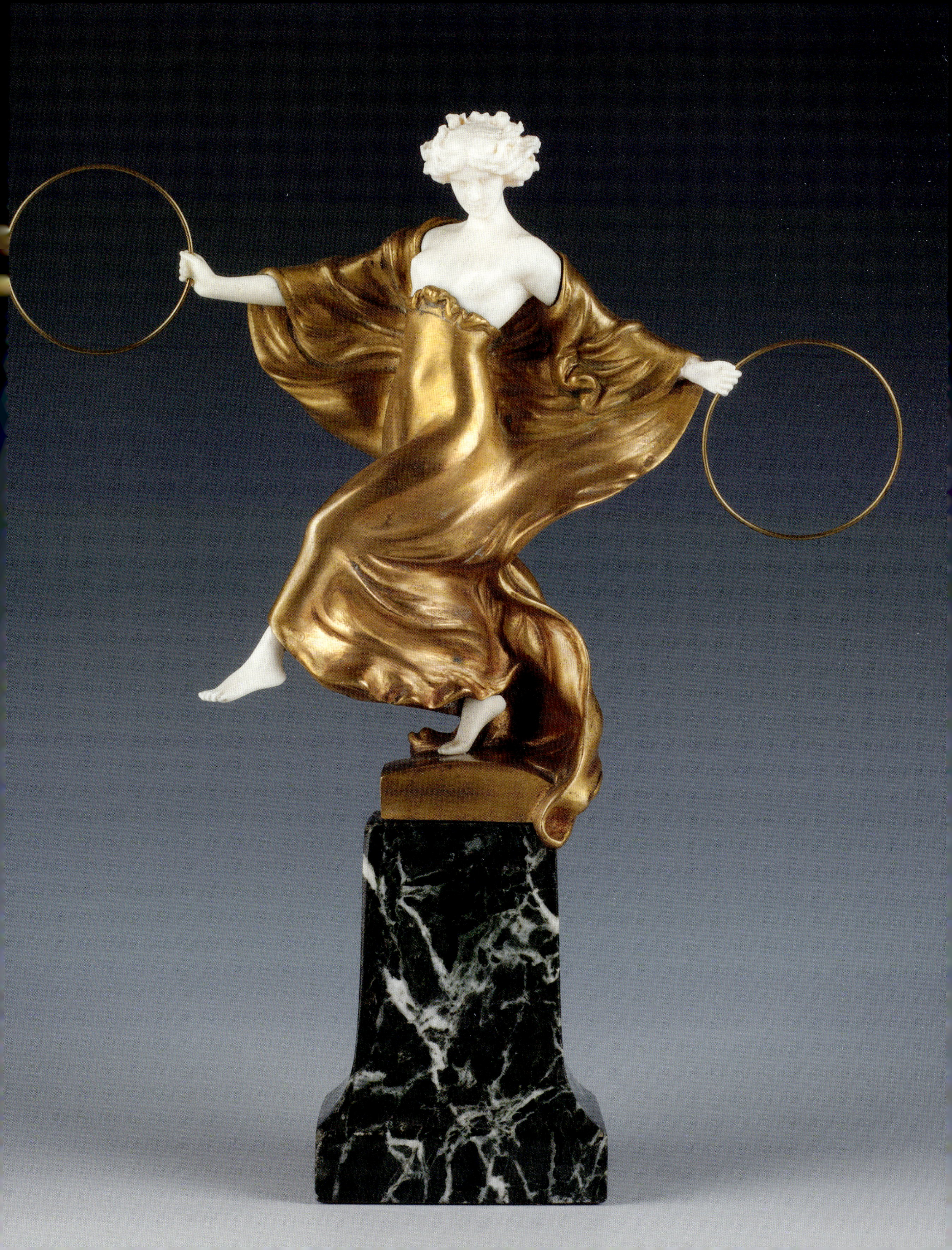

SEVIN, Lucile

(active 1920 – 1940)

Born in Sèvres, near Paris, she studied sculpture with François Léon Sicard. She exhibited at the Salon of the Société des Artistes Français, of which she became a member, winning a bronze medal in 1932, a silver medal in 1937, and a gold medal at the Paris International Exhibition of 1937. She also exhibited at the Salon d'Automne.

Sevin created many sculptures in bronze, silvered or gilt bronze, and bronze and ivory; they were edited by Etling. She also worked in glass, ceramics and porcelain. Her opaline glass sculptures of dancers were produced for Etling by the glass works in Choisy-le-Roi.

Lucile Sevin, whose work was extremely representative of the 'Etling style', became, for a time, artistic director of the firm. Her husband, sculptor Jean Théodore Delabassé, also worked with Etling.

SOSSON, L.

Two names are attributed to this artist:

Louis. Active between 1905 and 1930, he worked with Edmond Etling.

Lucien. Born in Paris, he exhibited at the Salon of the Société des Artistes Français. In 1910 he had a showcase there containing an ivory bust of a child.

Whether it is one person using both names or two different people remains to be discovered. He was prolific. His ivories of dancing maidens are well known.

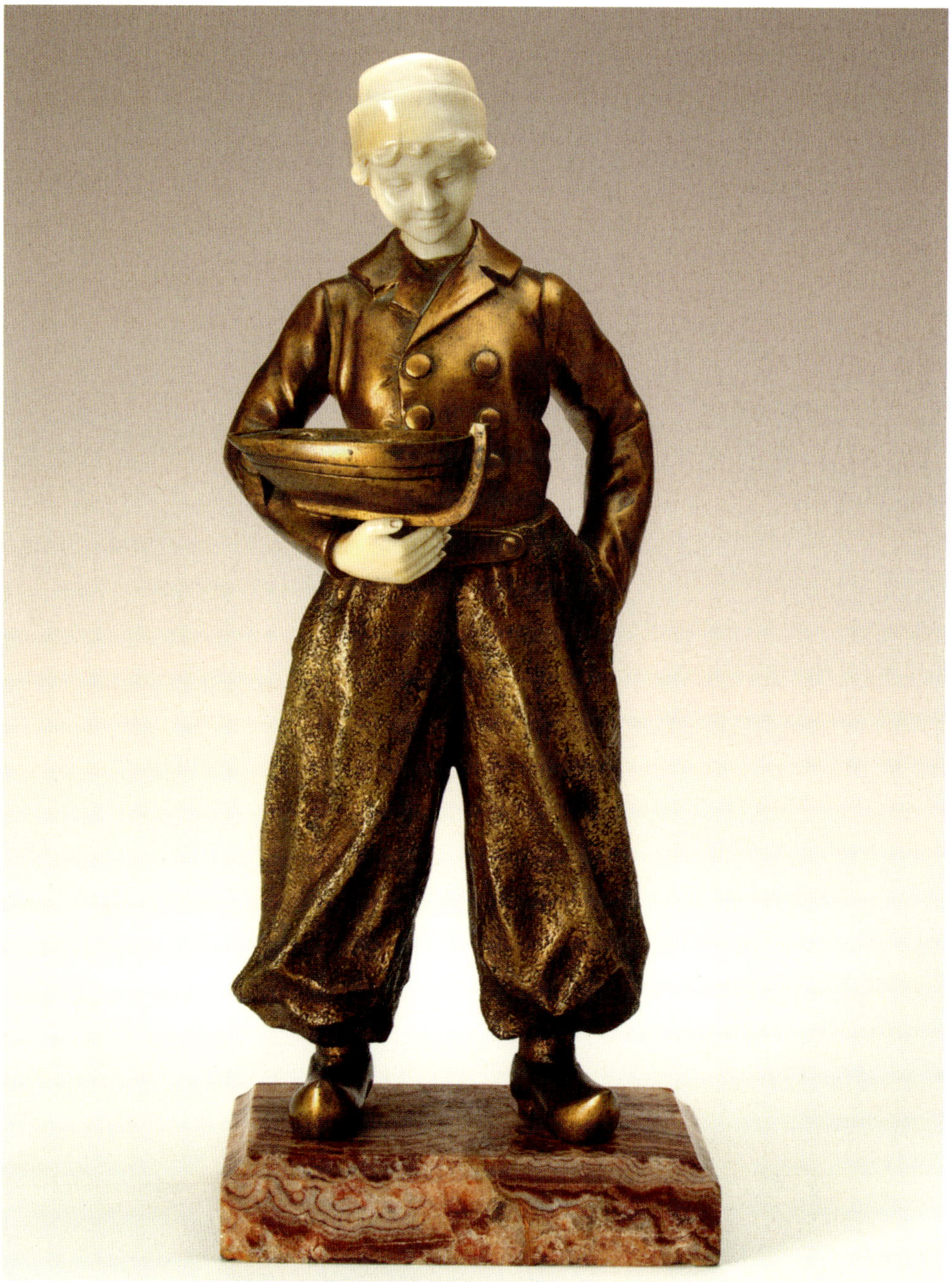

Dutch Boy
Bronze and ivory on marble base
Height: 29cm. (11½in.)
DINO MENASCHE COLLECTION

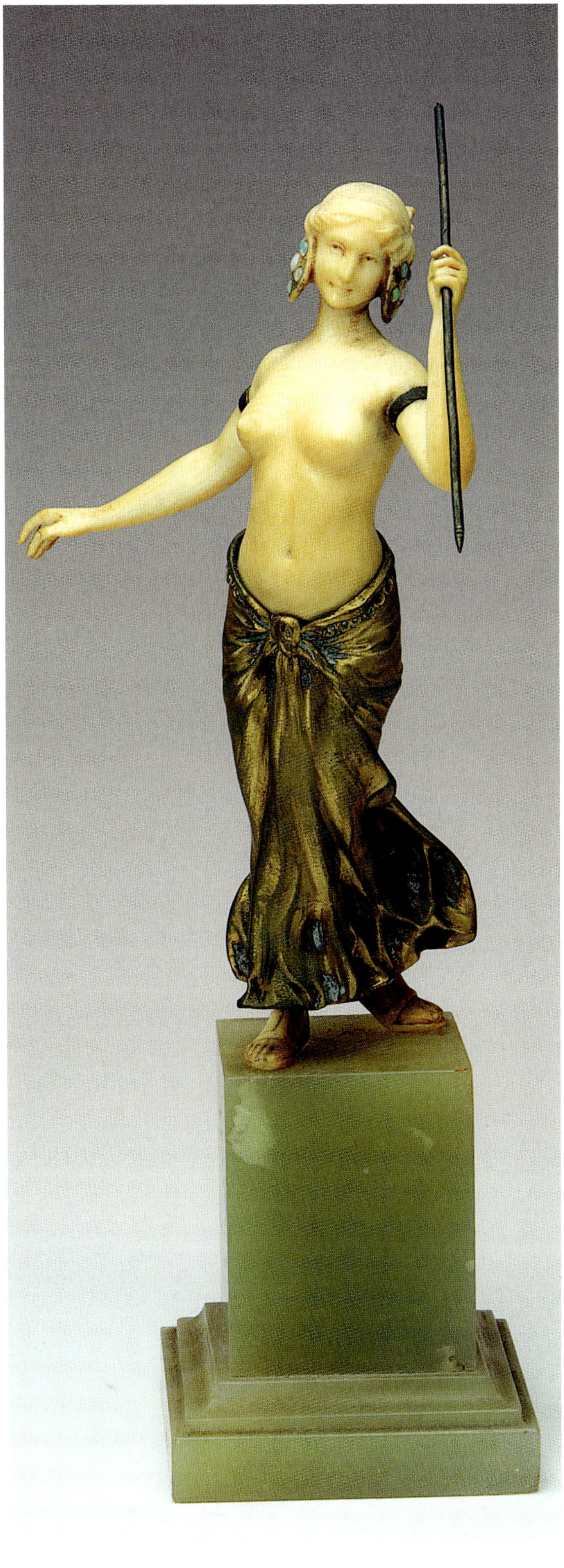

Amazon
Bronze, ivory and opals on onyx base
Height (to top of head): 25.5cm. (10in.)
PRIVATE COLLECTION

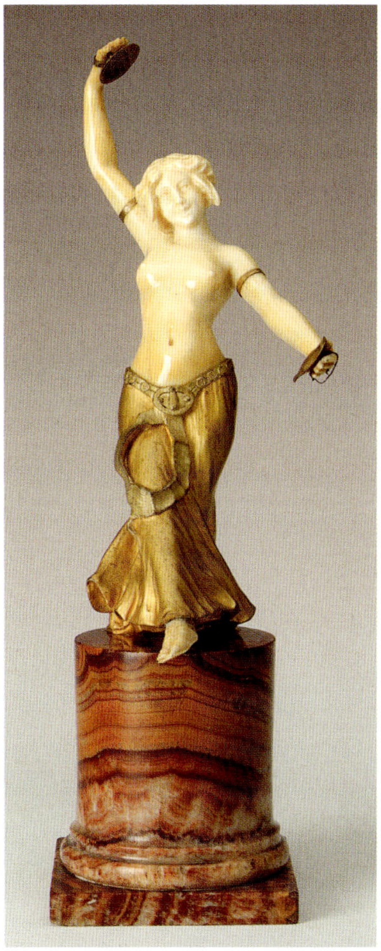

Cymbal Dancer
Bronze and ivory on marble base
Height: 28cm. (11in.)
DINO MENASCHE COLLECTION

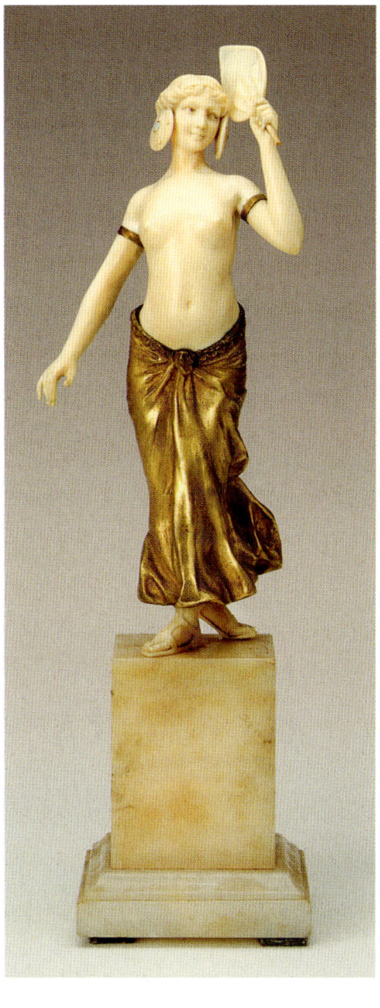

Fan Dancer
Bronze and ivory on marble base
Height: 26.5cm. (10½in.)
HEBERT GOMES COLLECTION

TERESZCZUK, Peter

(Wybudow 1875 – Vienna 1963)

Born in 1875 in the Ukrainian city of Wybudow, he lived and worked mainly in Vienna. Tereszczuk's sculptures were in bronze, bronze and ivory, and glass. He also made decorative objects such as inkwells, card trays, lamps and other items.

His pieces were produced by Arthur Rubinstein.

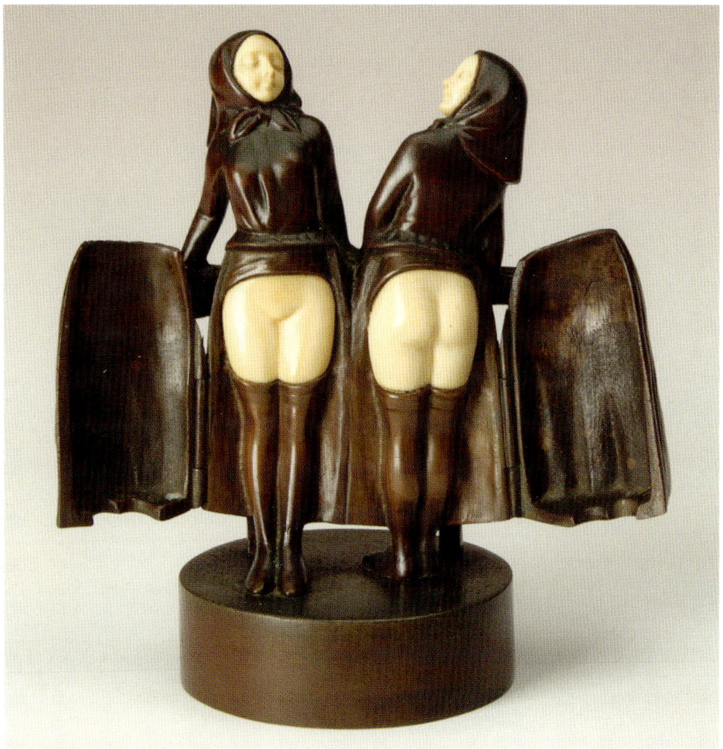

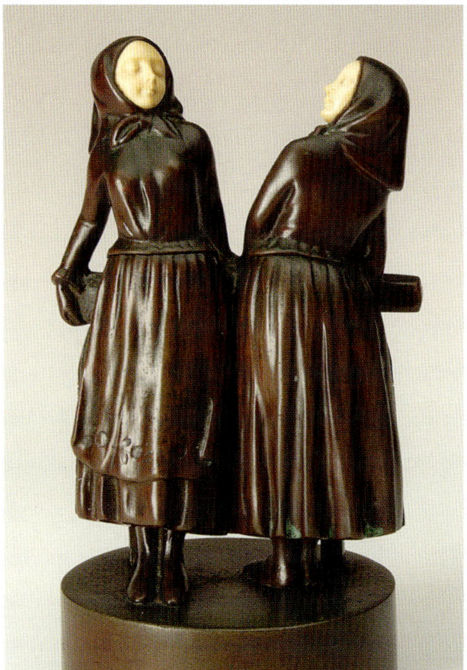

Appearances
Bronze and ivory
Height: 14cm. (5½in.)
DINO MENASCHE COLLECTION

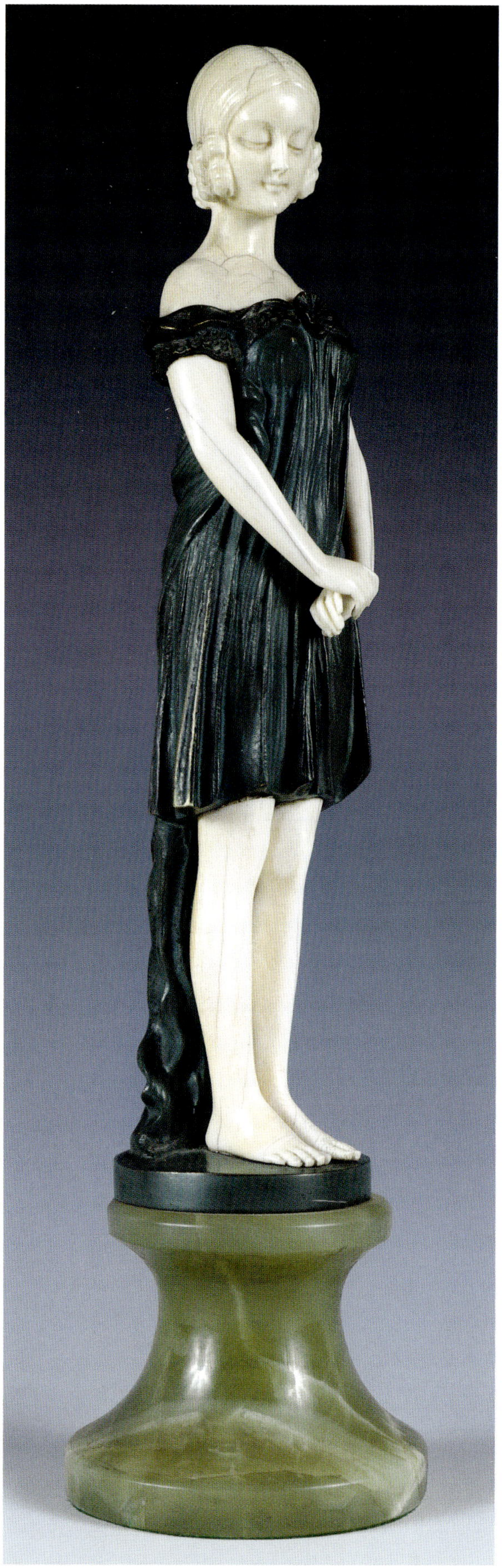

Innocence
Bronze and ivory
on onyx base
Height: 38.5cm. (15¼in.)
PRIVATE COLLECTION

Tender Love
Bronze and ivory on marble base
Height: 21cm. (8¼in.)
DINO MENASCHE COLLECTION

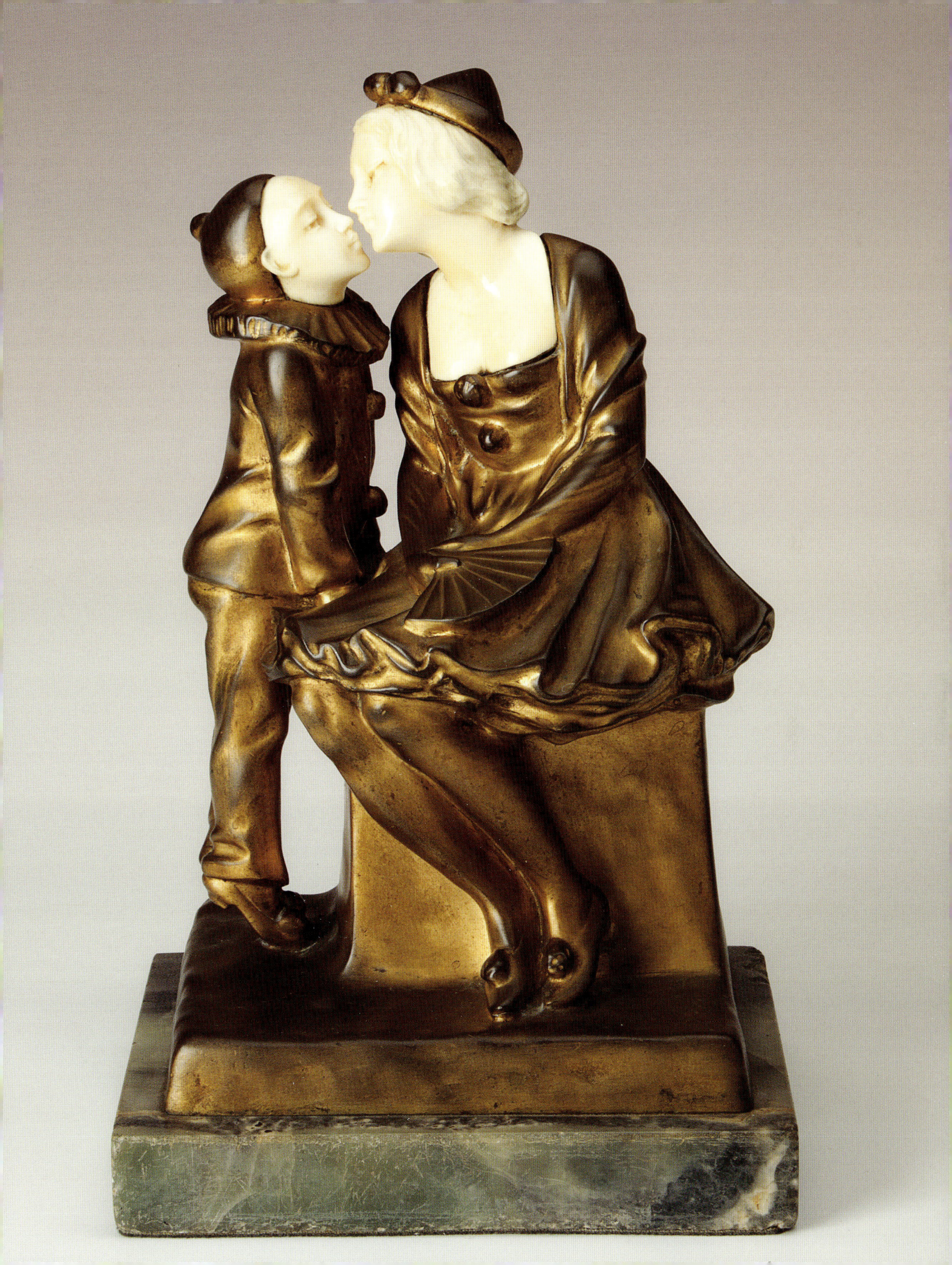

ULRICH, J.

An Austrian sculptor who was active during the early part of the 20th century.

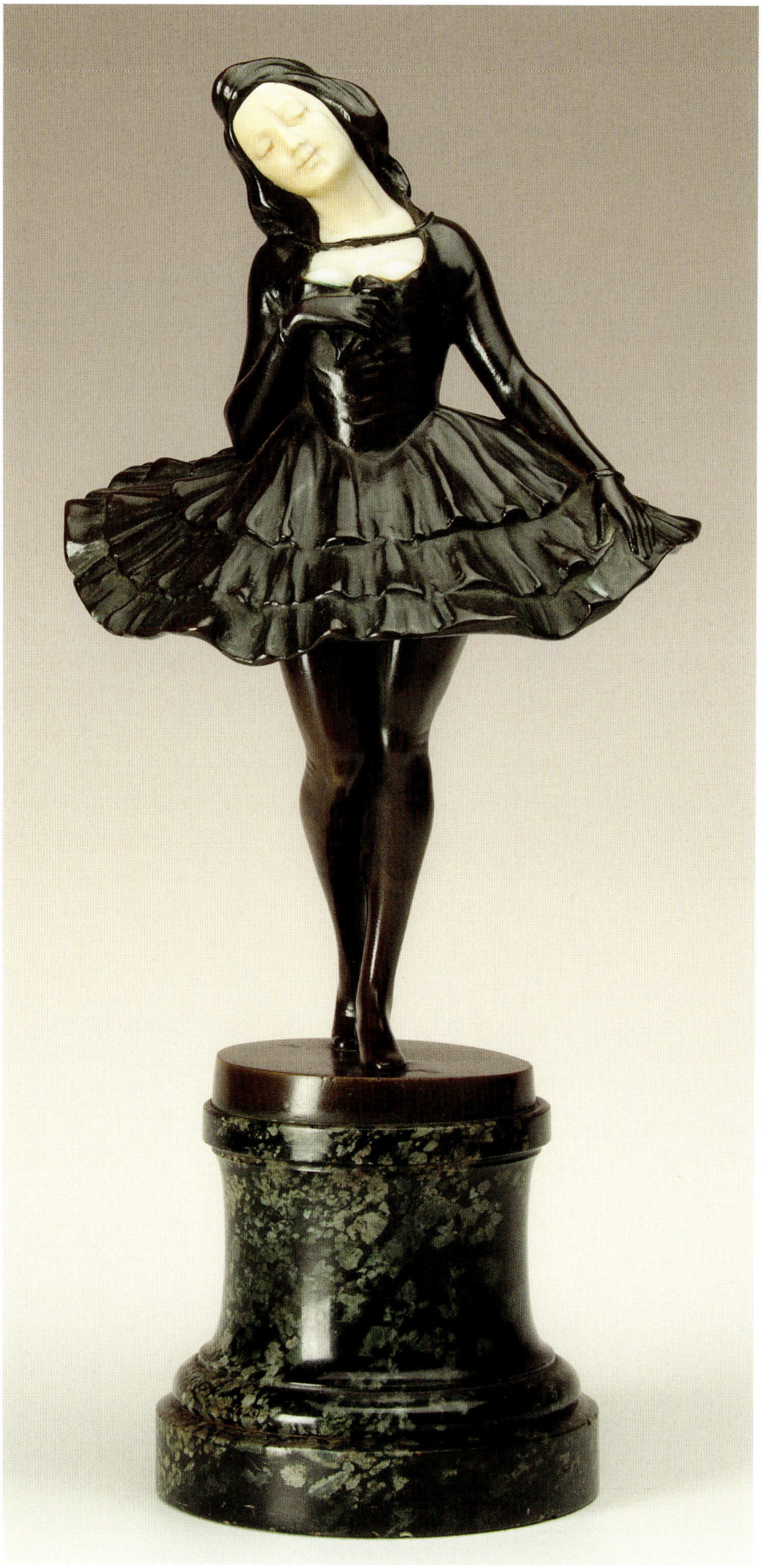

Ballerina
Bronze and ivory on marble base
Height: 29cm. (11½in.)
DINO MENASCHE COLLECTION

VARNIER, R.

French

Designed some striking car mascots.

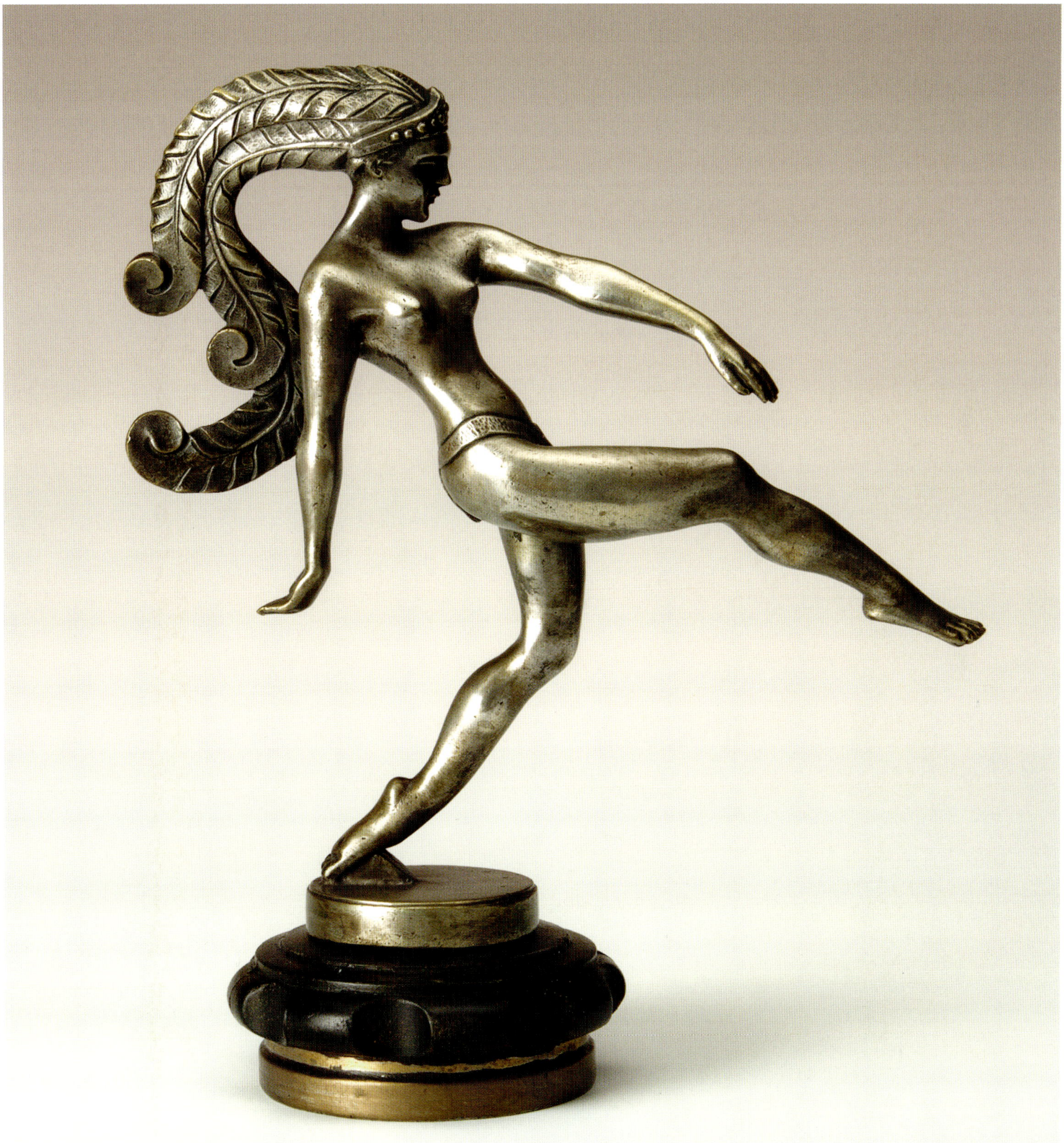

Exotique

Bronze (mounted as a car mascot)

Height: 20cm. (8in.)

DINO MENASCHE COLLECTION

WHITE, Helene Maynard

(Baltimore 1870 – ?)

Studied in the United States and continued her studies in Paris, where she began sculpting. She returned to Philadelphia continuing her statuary work.

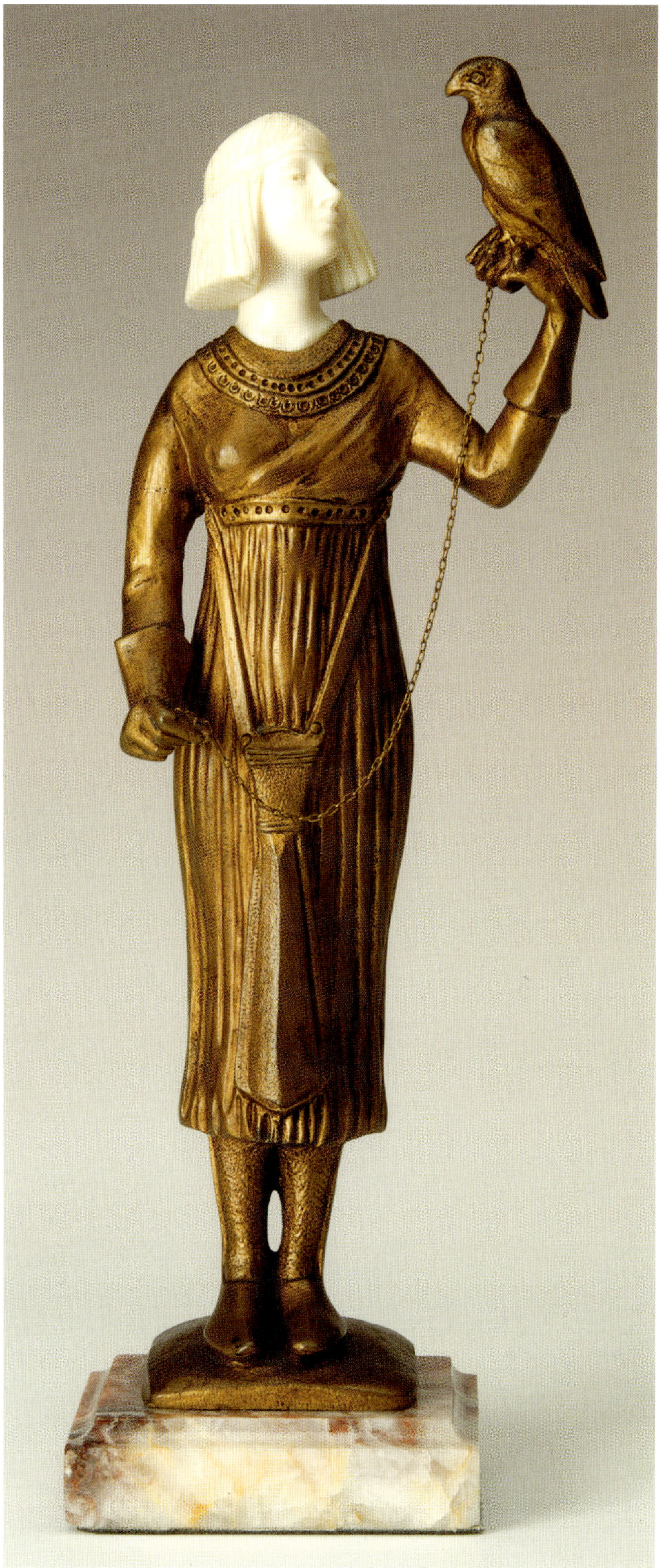

Horus

Bronze and ivory on marble base

Height: 19.5cm. (7¾in.)

DINO MENASCHE COLLECTION

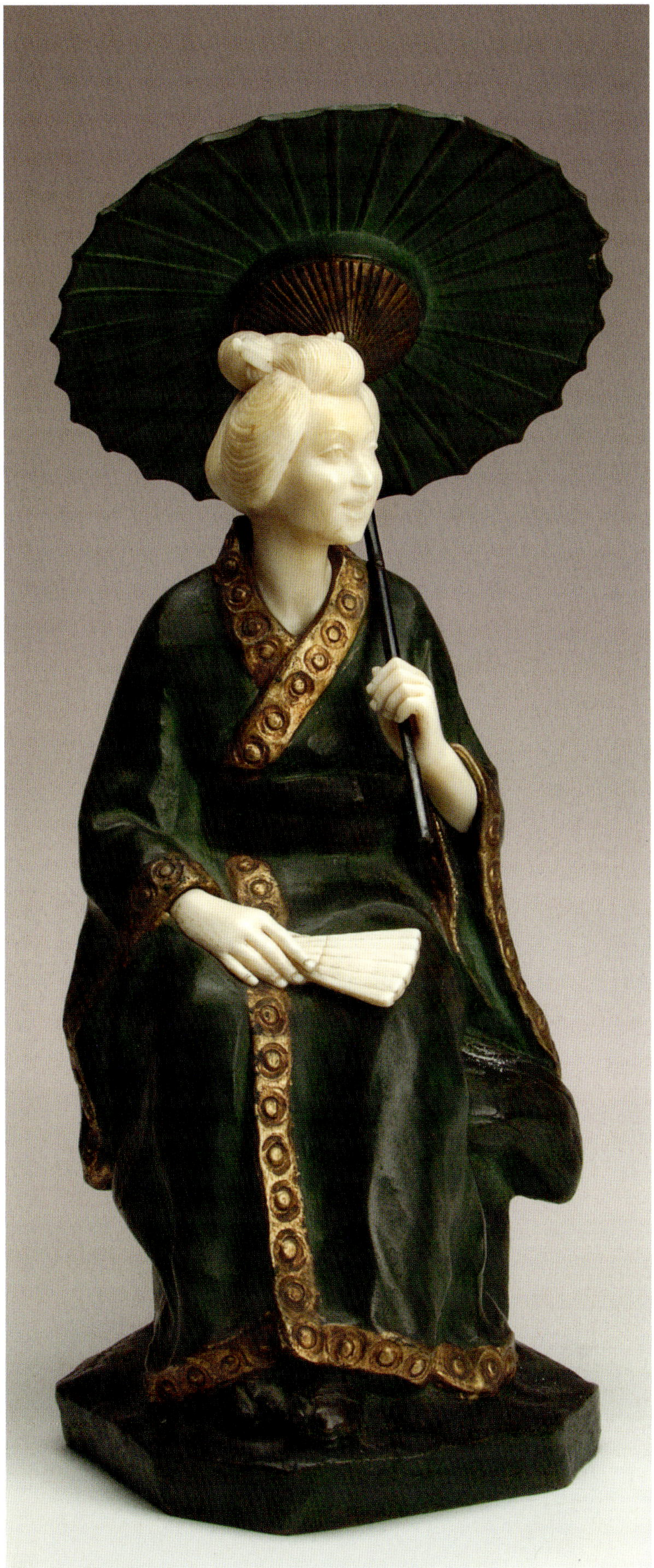

Oriental Lady with Umbrella
Bronze and ivory
Height: 28.5cm. (11¼in.)
DINO MENASCHE COLLECTION

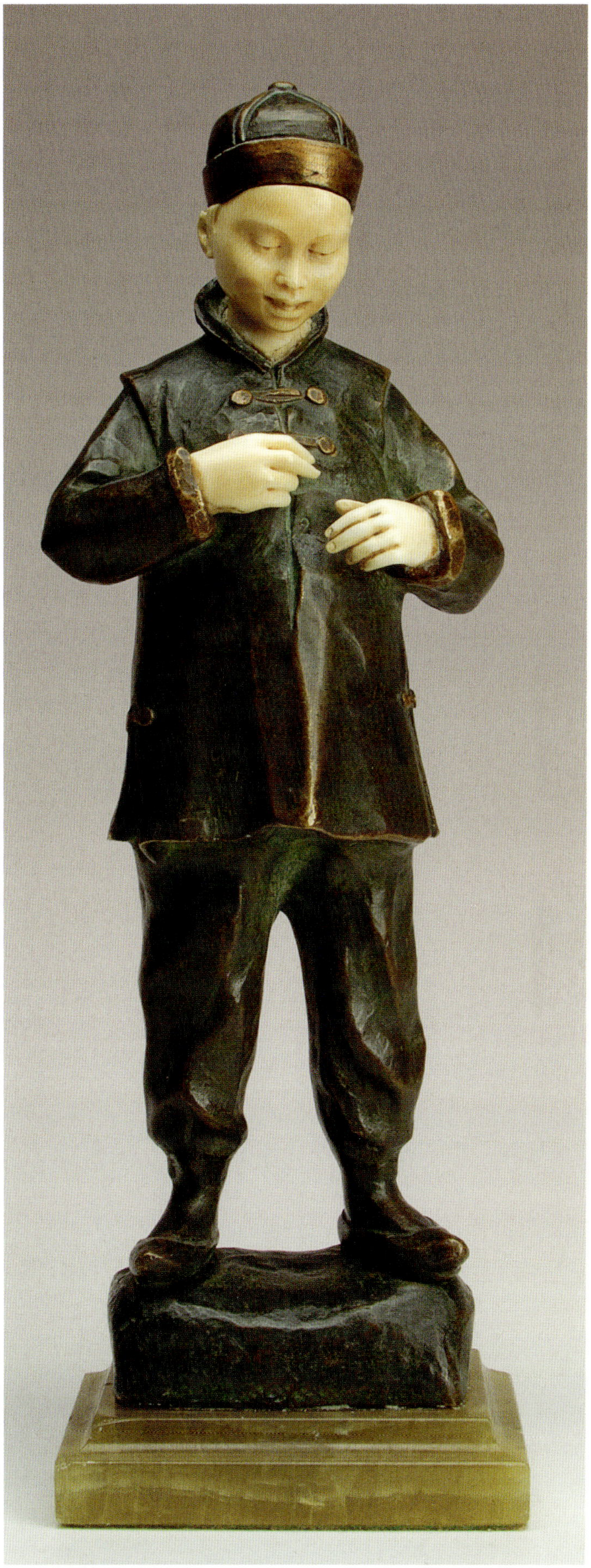

Oriental Man
Bronze and ivory on onyx base
Height: 27.5cm. (10¾in.)
DINO MENASCHE COLLECTION

ZACH, Bruno

(Schitomir 1891 – Vienna 1945)

Other signatures: Tuch

Born in Schitomir, Ukraine. Early in his life he moved to Vienna. He studied at the Vienna Academy of Fine Arts under Hans Bitterlich and Josef Müllner.

He generally worked in bronze, but also produced chryselephantine figures that were often erotically charged, some verging on the sado-masochistic.

They were produced by companies such as Argentor-Werke, Broma, S. Altmann & Co. and Franz Bergmann.

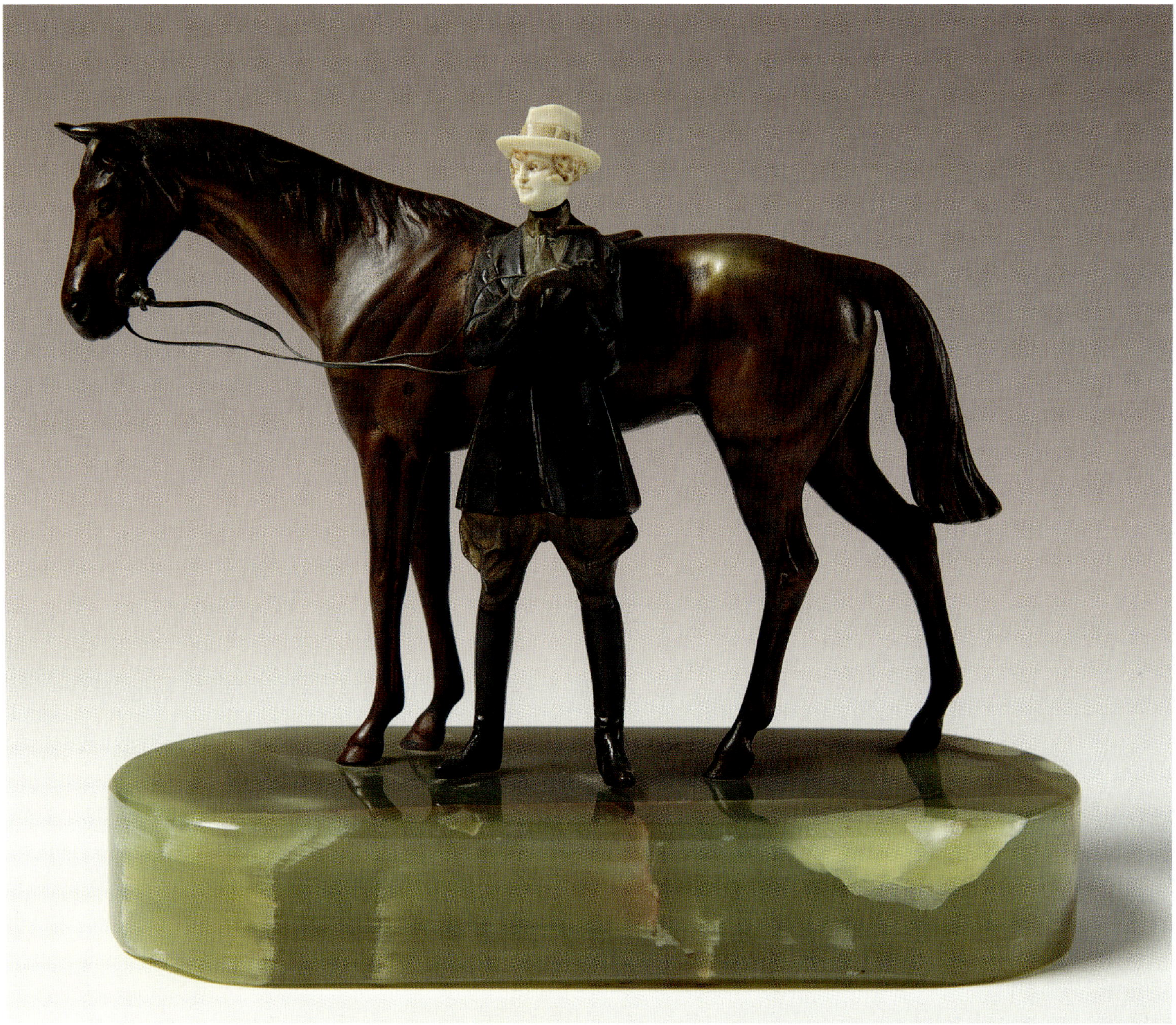

Amazon with Horse
Bronze and ivory on onyx base
Height: 16cm. (6¼in.)
PRIVATE COLLECTION

Amazon
Bronze and ivory on onyx base
Height: 42cm. (16½in.)
PRIVATE COLLECTION

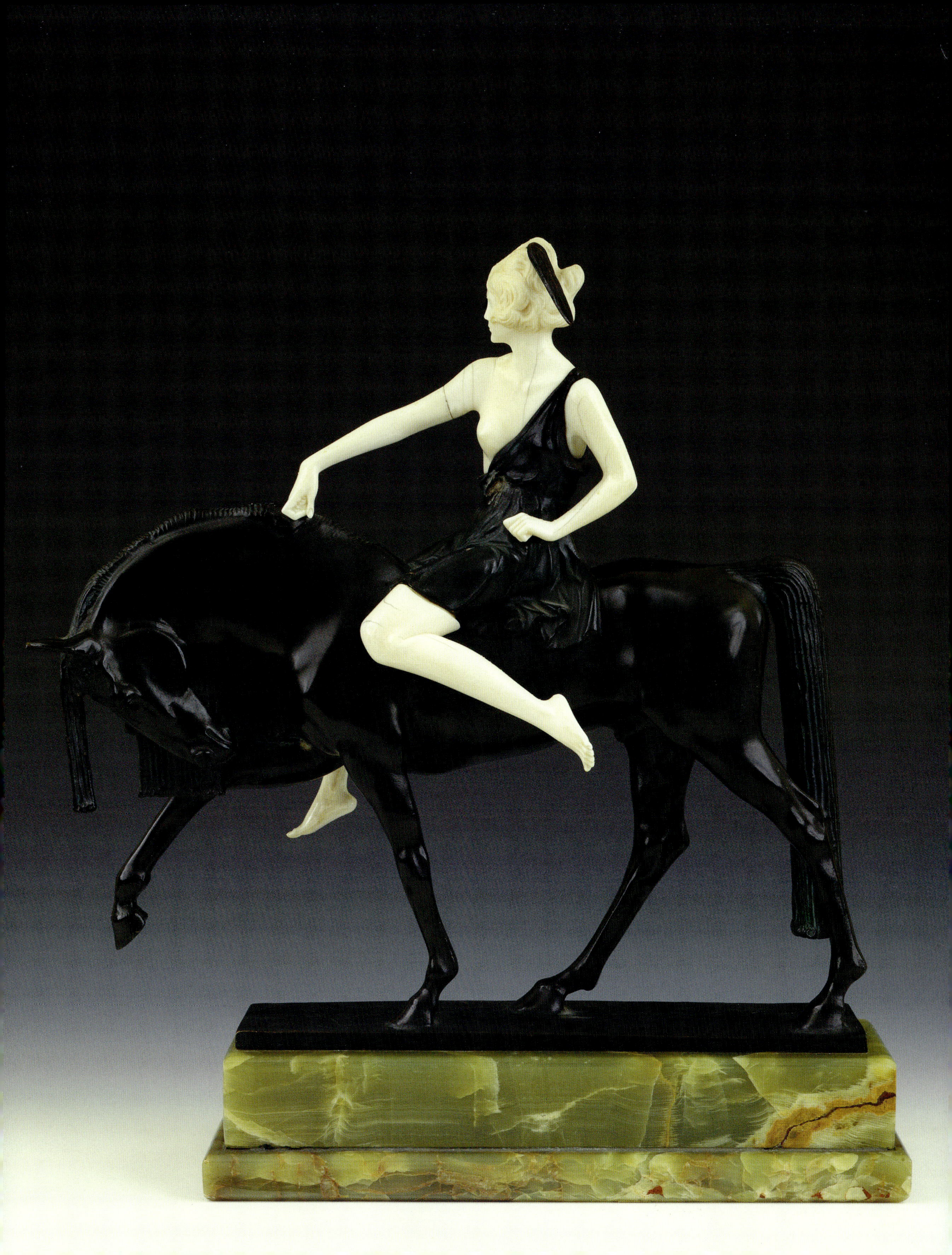

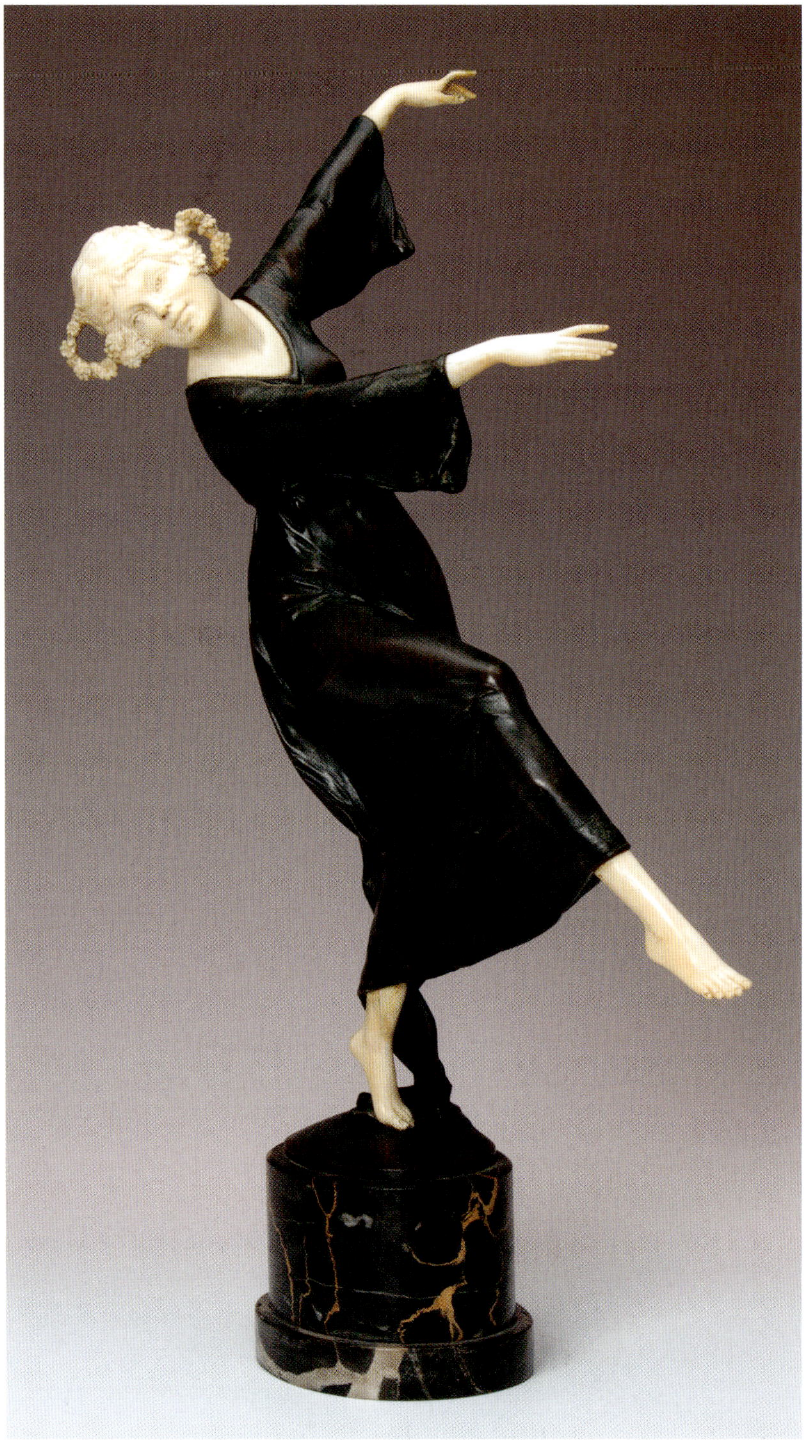

Dancer with Garlands
Bronze and ivory on marble base
Height: 46cm. (18in.)
PRIVATE COLLECTION

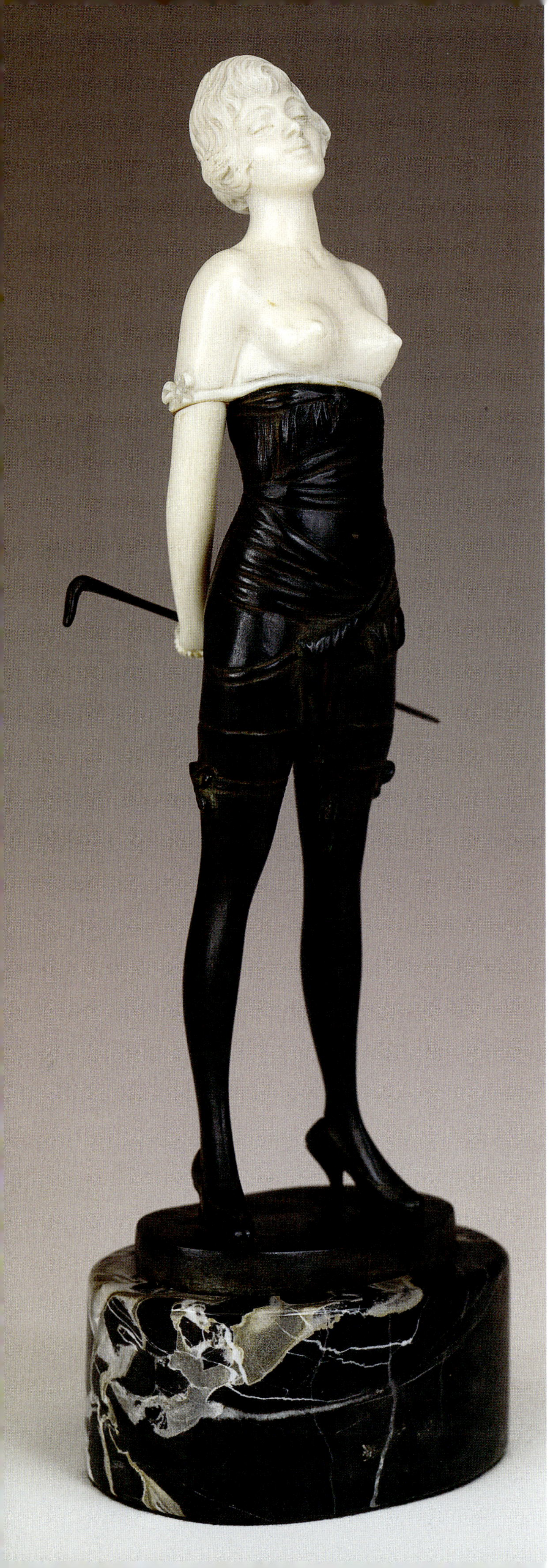

The Riding Crop
Bronze and ivory on marble base
Height: 30.5cm. (12in.)
S. AND J.S. COLLECTION

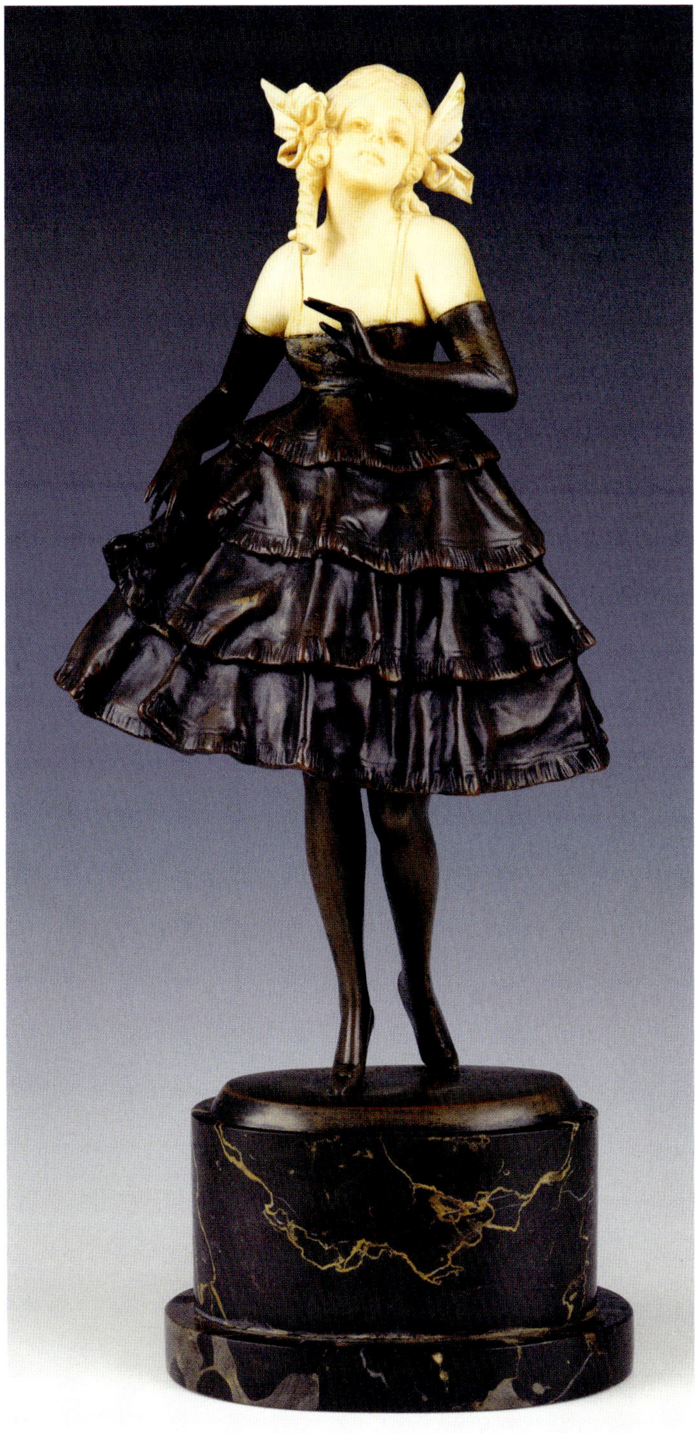

Indiscreet
Bronze and ivory on marble base
Height: 39.5cm. (15½in.)
PRIVATE COLLECTION

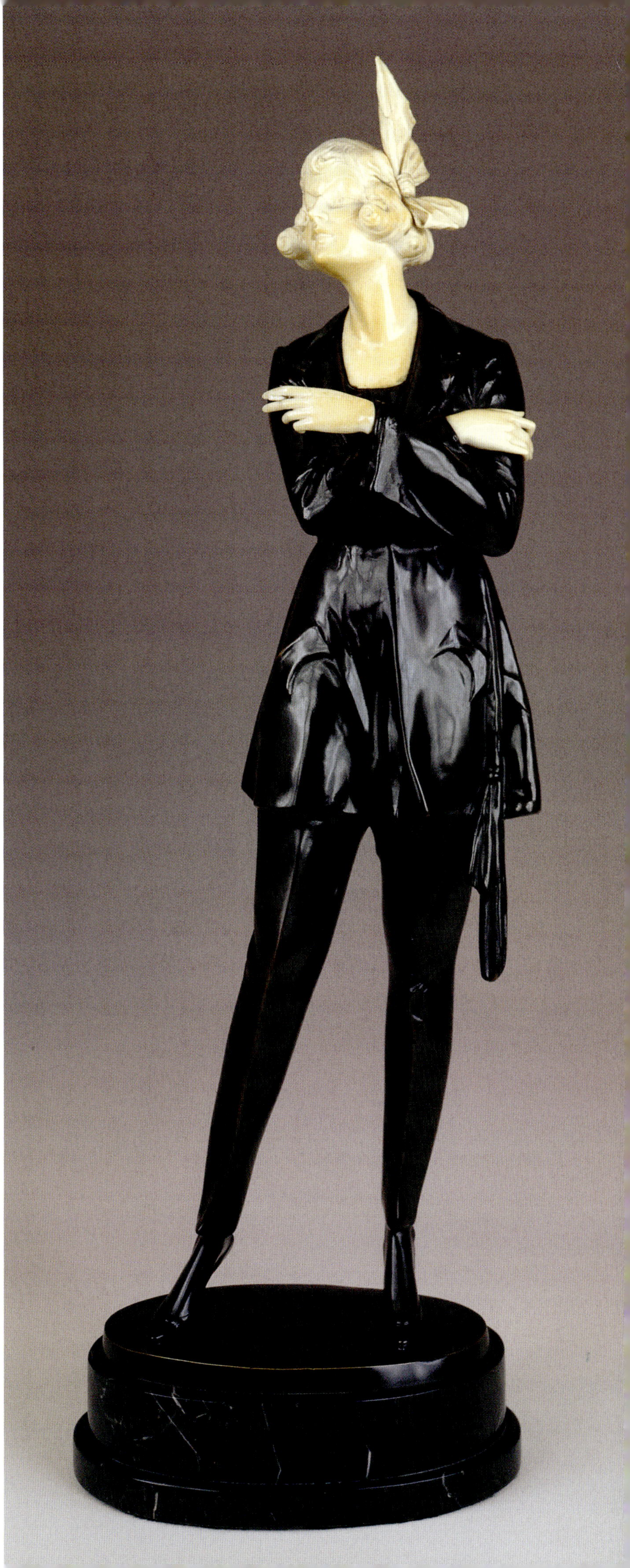

The Cigarette
Bronze and ivory on marble base
Height: 72cm. (28¼in.)
S. AND J.S. COLLECTION

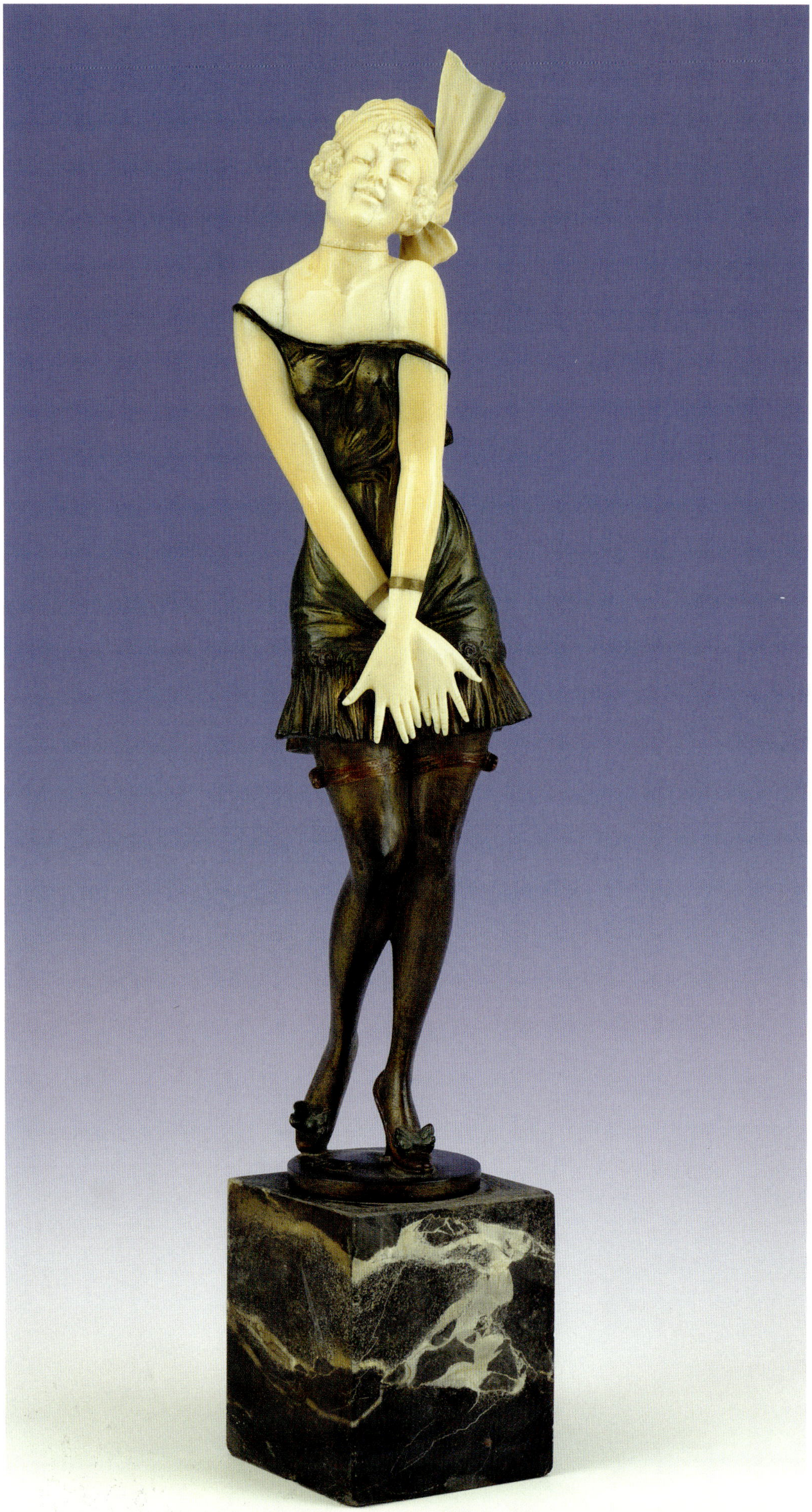

Young Woman in Chemise and Garters
Bronze and ivory on marble base
Height: 46.5cm. (18¼in.)
PRIVATE COLLECTION

Queen of the Broken Hearts
Bronze and ivory on marble base
Height: 66.5cm. (26¼in.)
PRIVATE COLLECTION

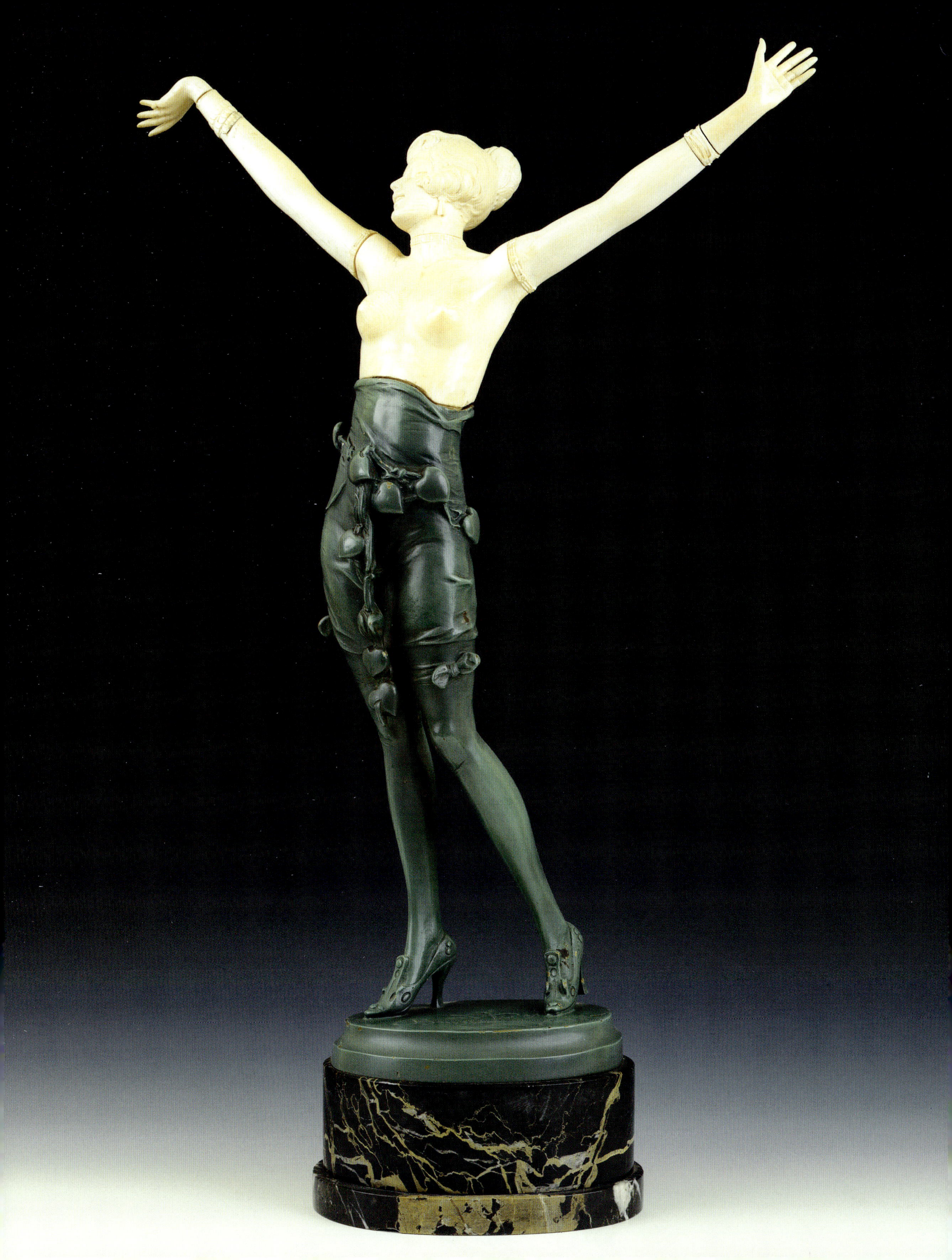

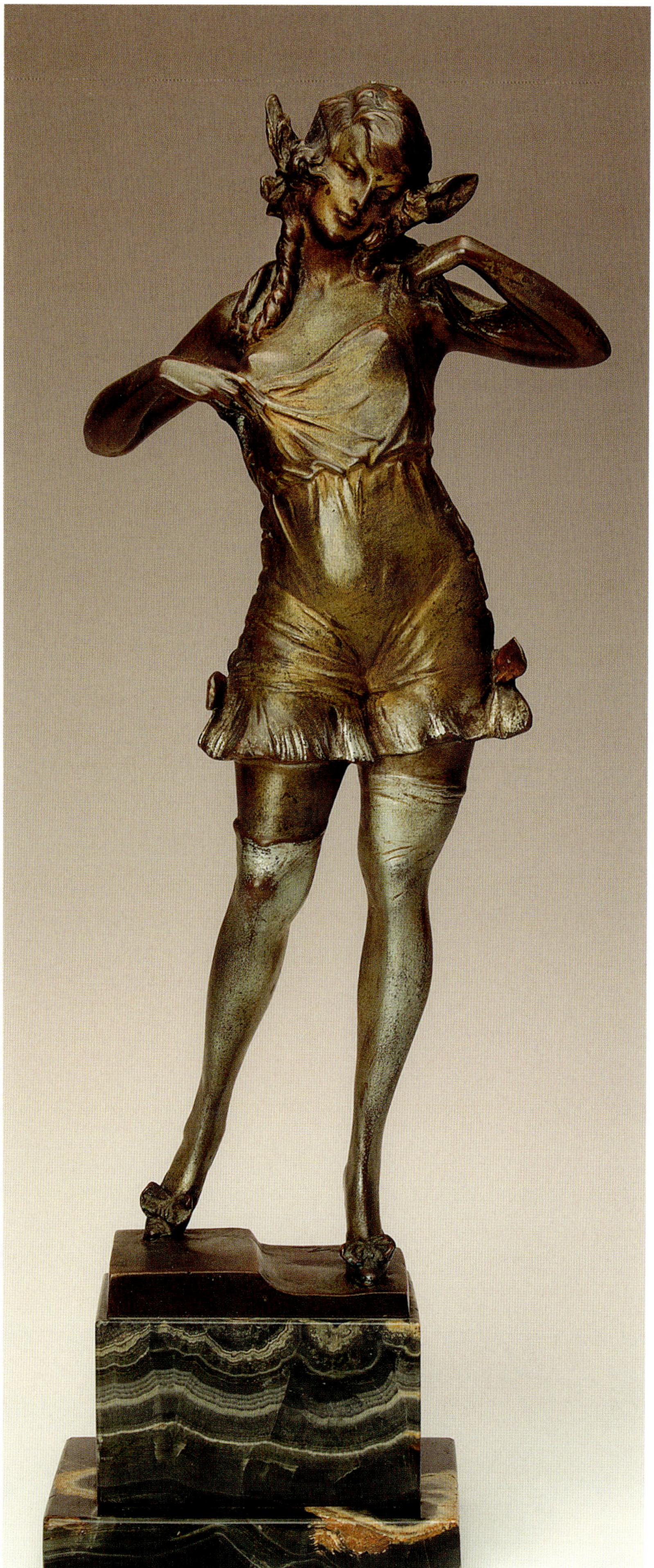

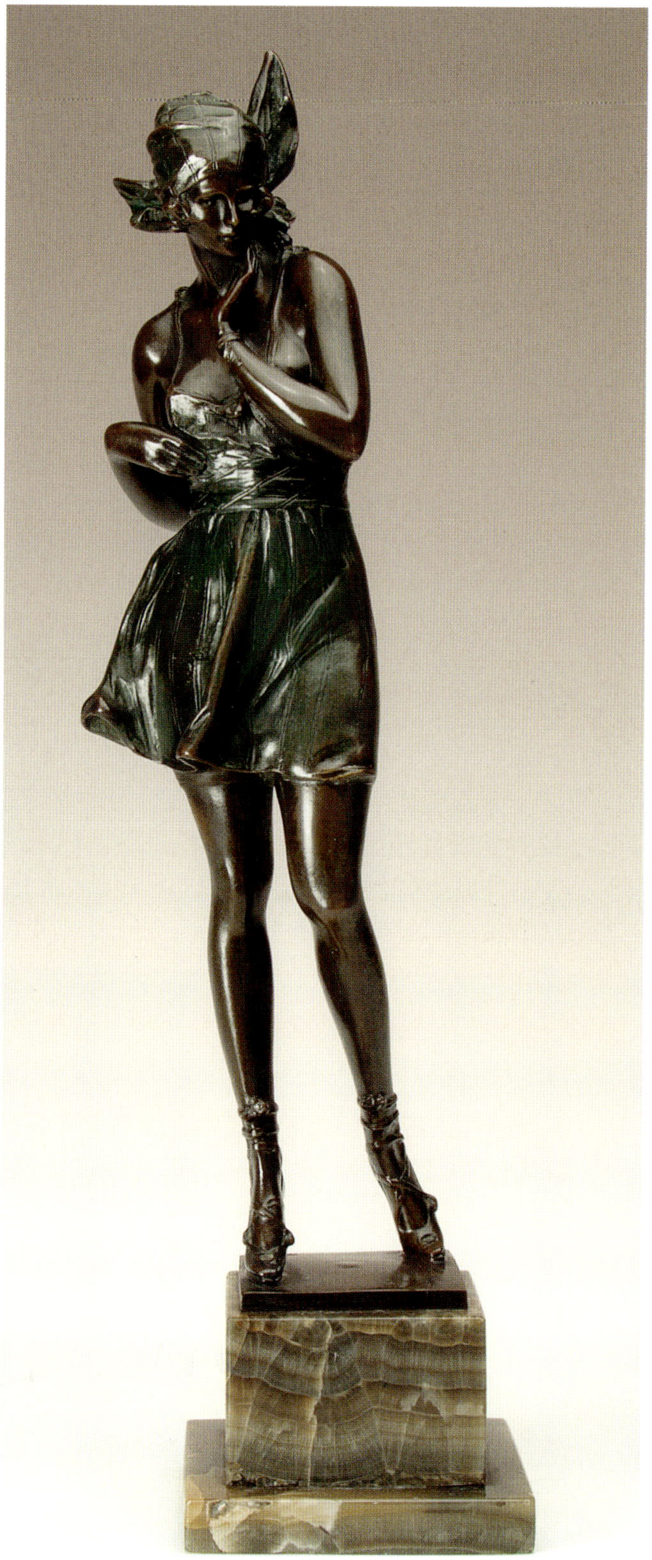

Bather
Bronze on marble base
Height: 39cm. (15¼in.)
DINO MENASCHE COLLECTION

Négligée
Bronze on marble base
Height: 39.5cm. (15½in.)
HEBERT GOMES COLLECTION

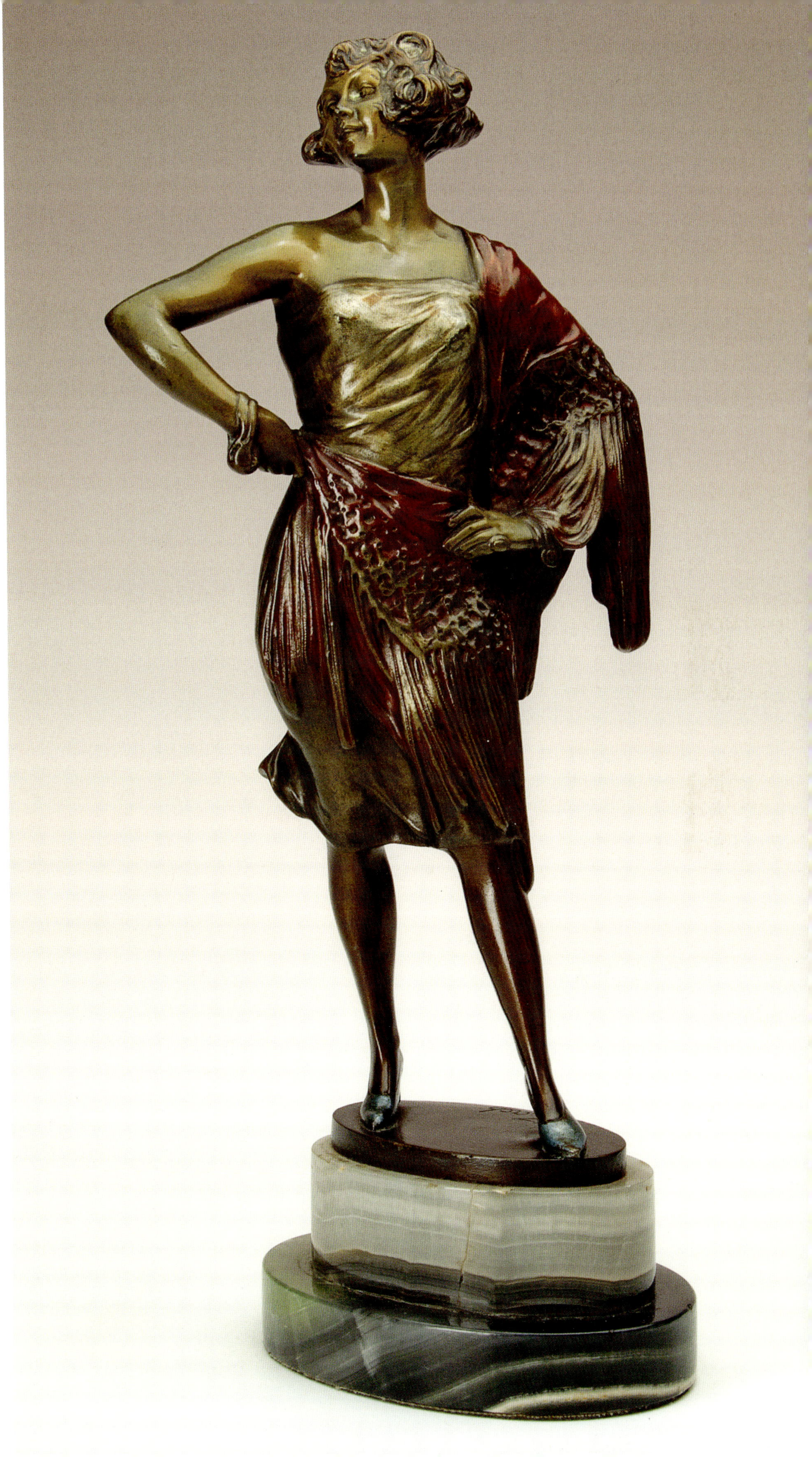

The Shawl
Bronze on onyx base
Height: 29.5cm. (11½in.)
DINO MENASCHE COLLECTION

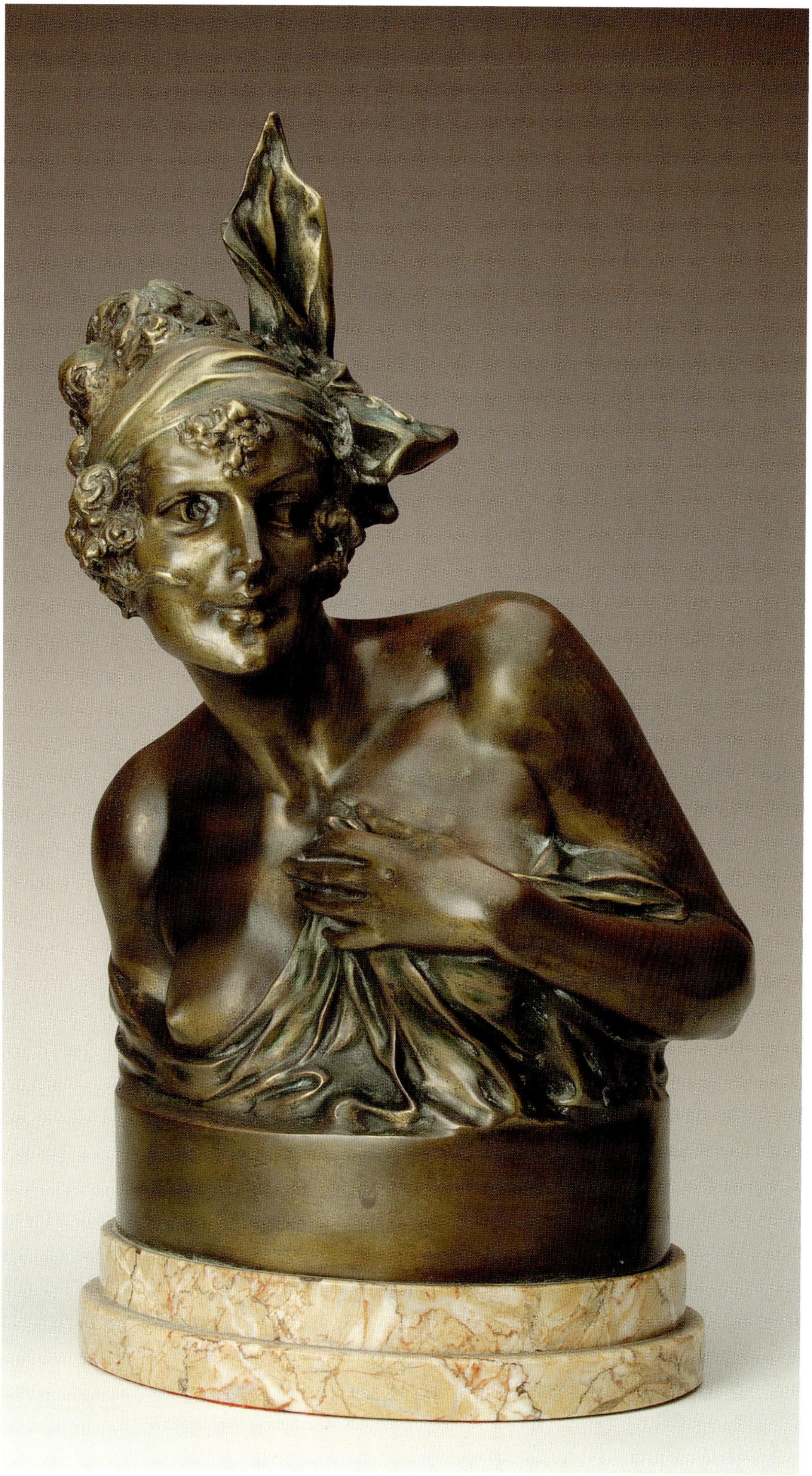

Eternal Beauty
Bronze on marble base
Height: 45cm. (17¾in.)
HEBERT GOMES COLLECTION

Maharanee and Maharajah
Bronze on marble base
Height: 42.5cm. and 47.5cm.
(16¾in. and 18¾in.)
HEBERT GOMES COLLECTION

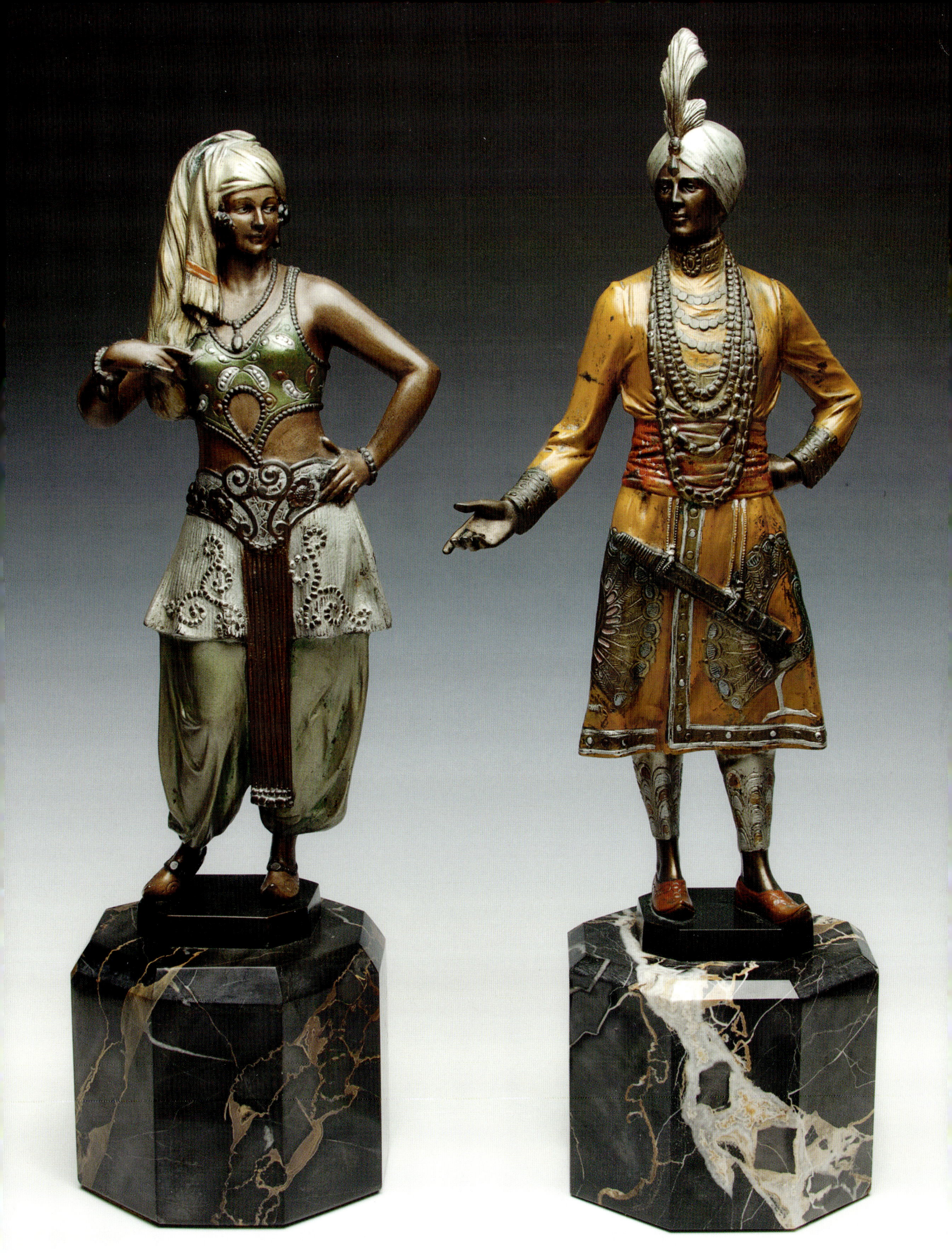

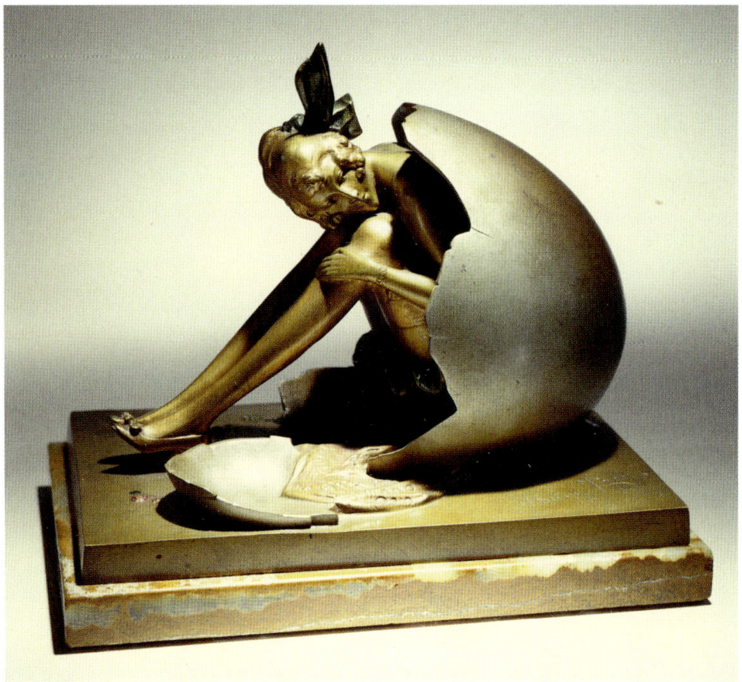

Maiden in Egg (Cholesterol)
Bronze on marble base
Height: 16.5cm. (6½in.)
PRIVATE COLLECTION

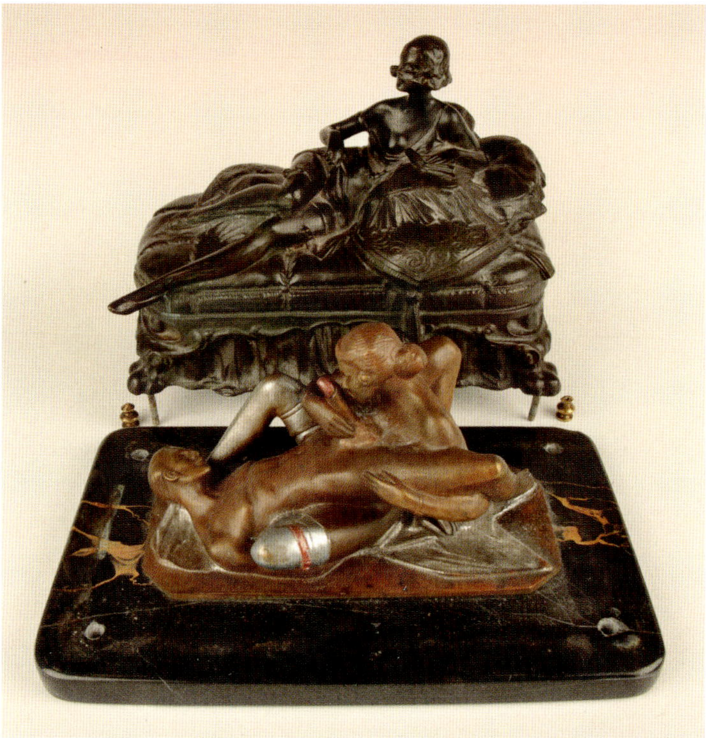

Arousal
Bronze on marble base
Height: 20cm. (8in.)
MICHAEL AND PESSI JAKOBOV

The Royal Embrace
Bronze on marble base
Height: 18cm. (7in.)
MICHAEL AND PESSI JAKOBOV

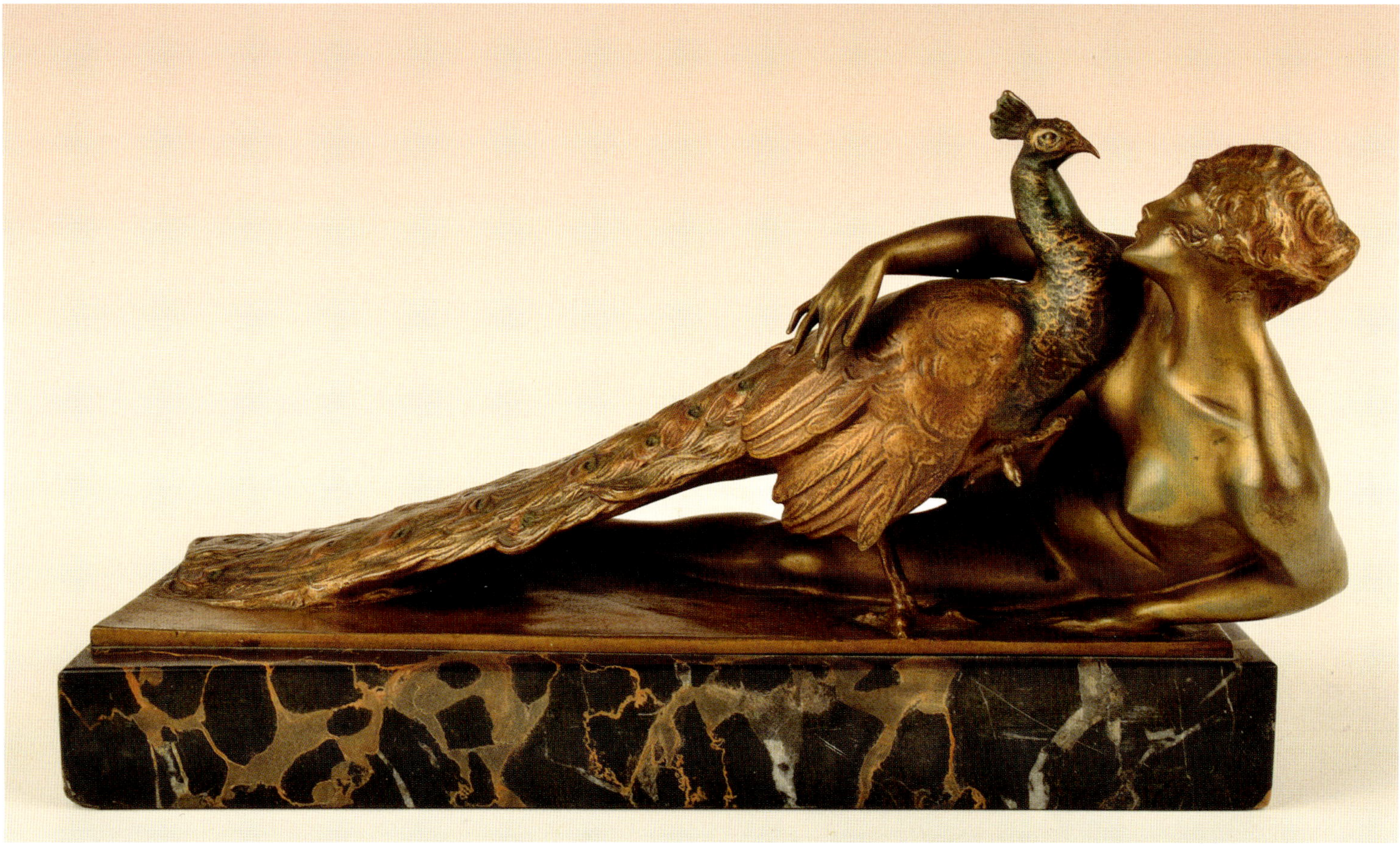

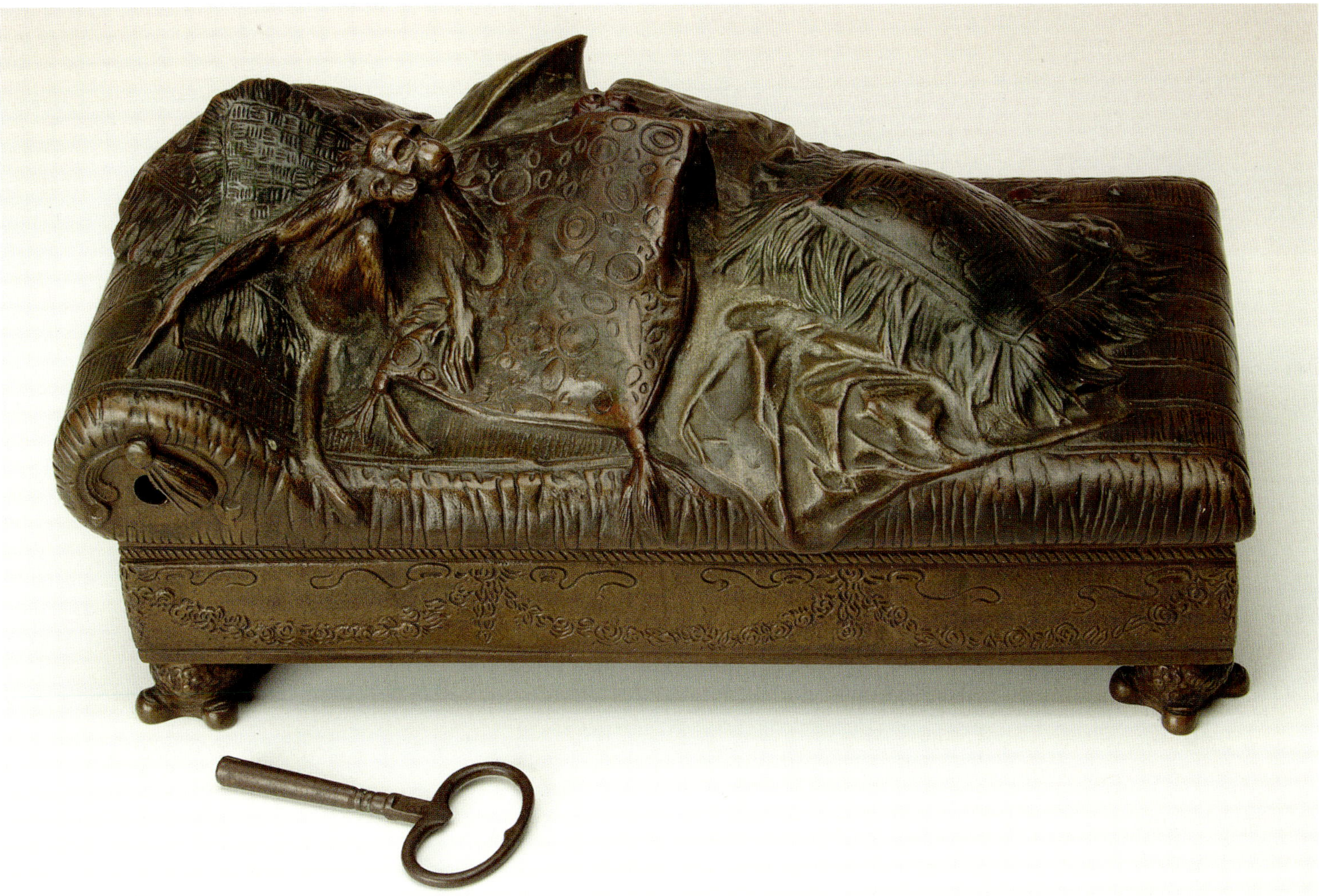

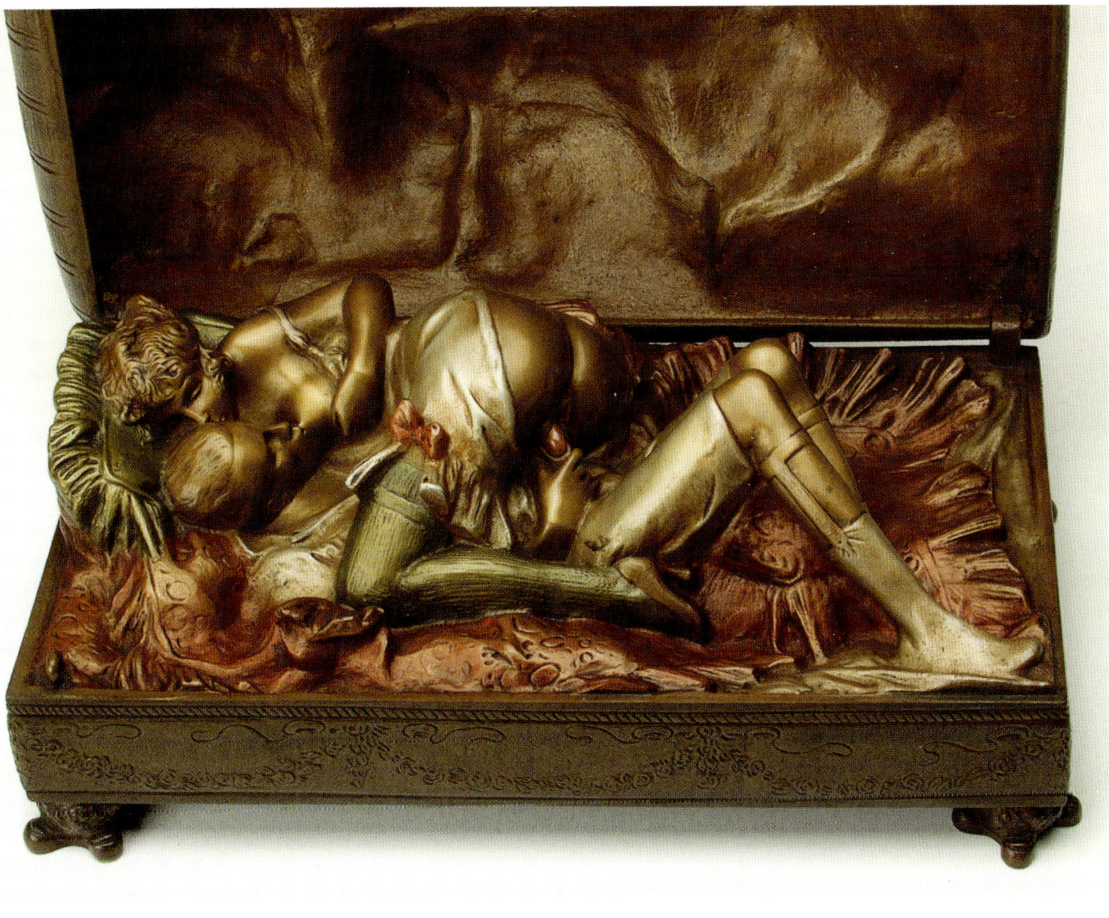

The Monkey's Secret
(shown closed and open)
Bronze
Height: 13.5cm. (5¼in.)
HEBERT GOMES COLLECTION

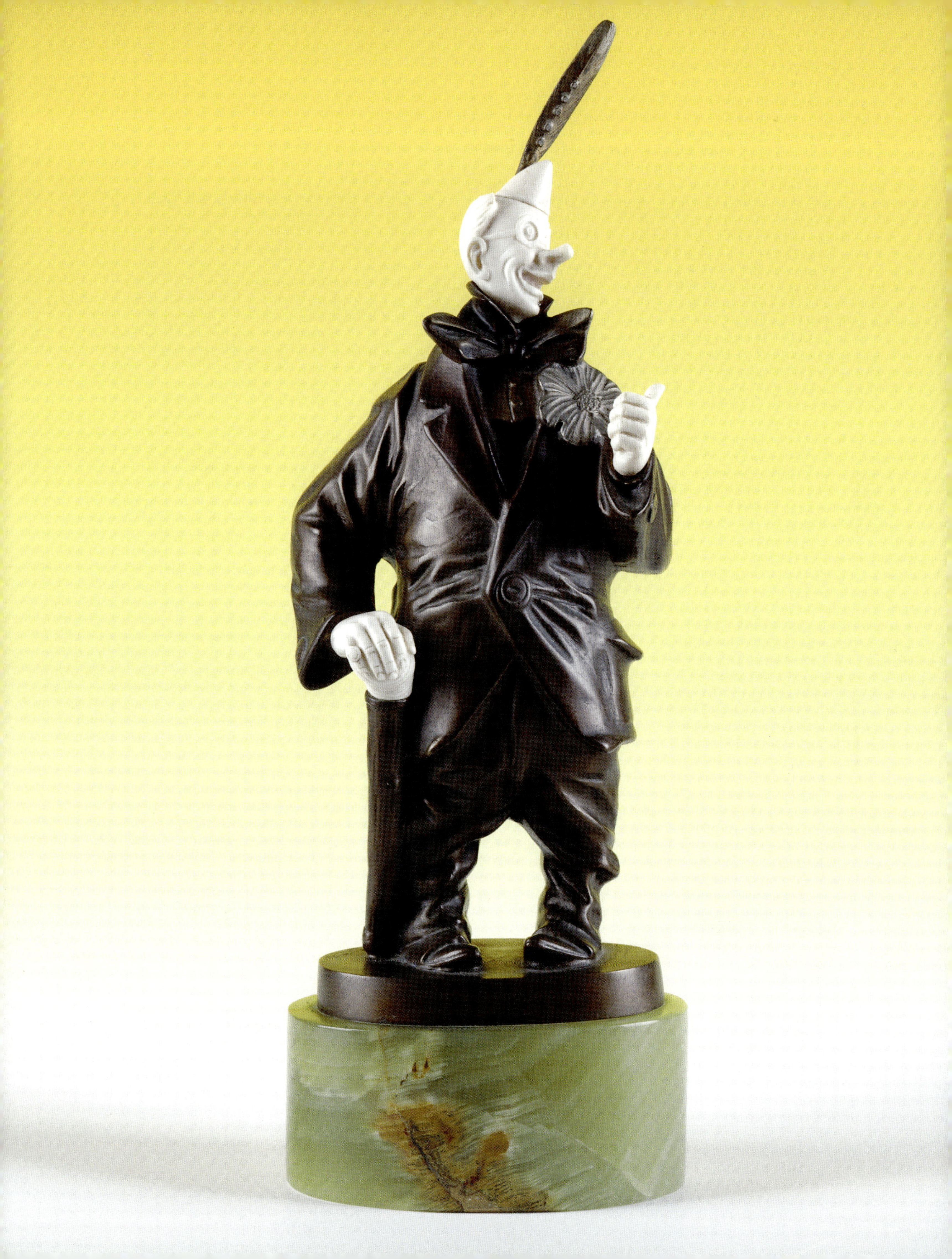

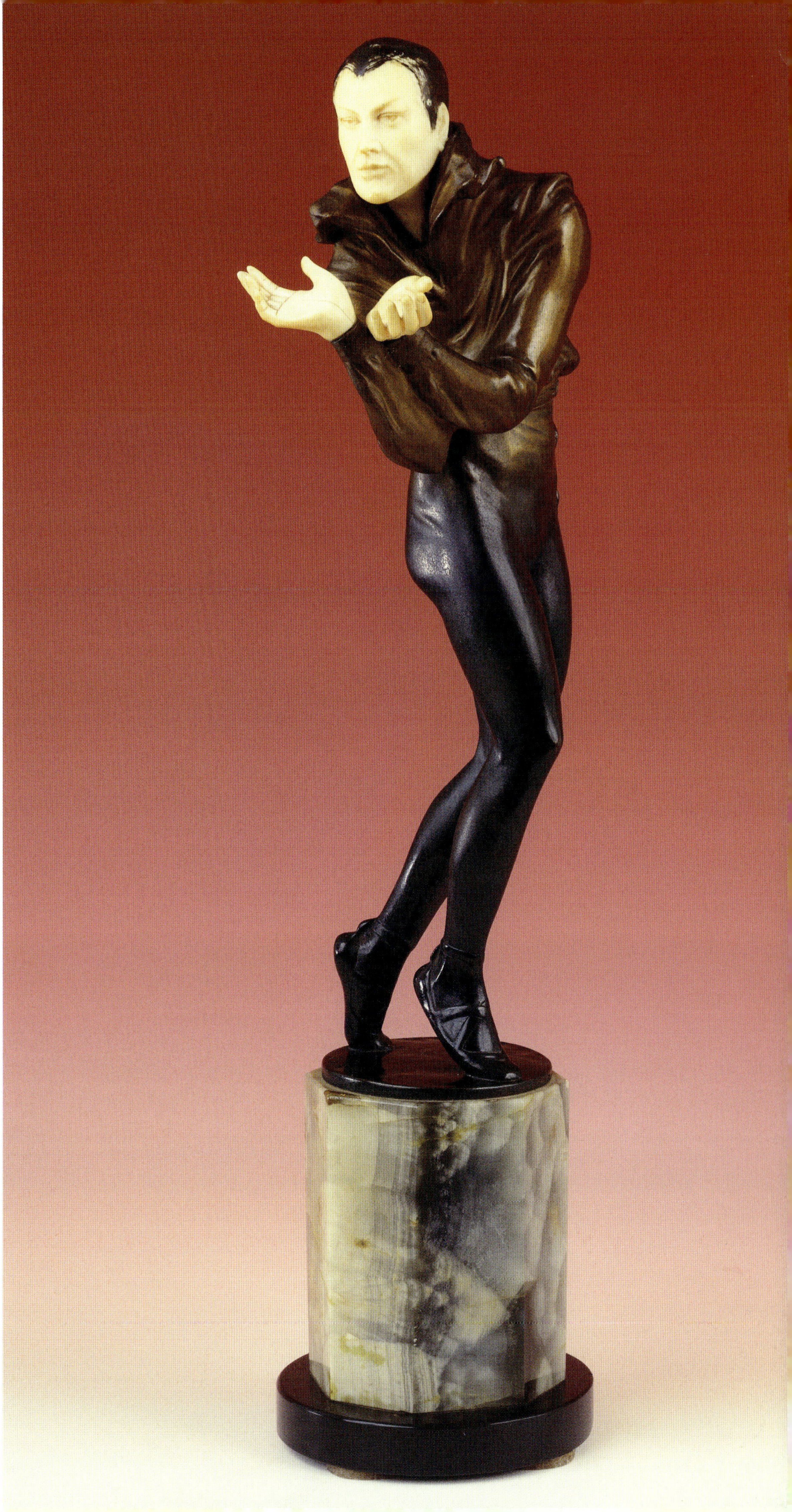

Clown with Plume
Bronze and ivory on onyx base
Height: 32cm. (12½in.)
HARRY JAROSCH COLLECTION, VIENNA

Dancer
Bronze and ivory on marble base
Height: 50cm. (19¾in.)
PRIVATE COLLECTION

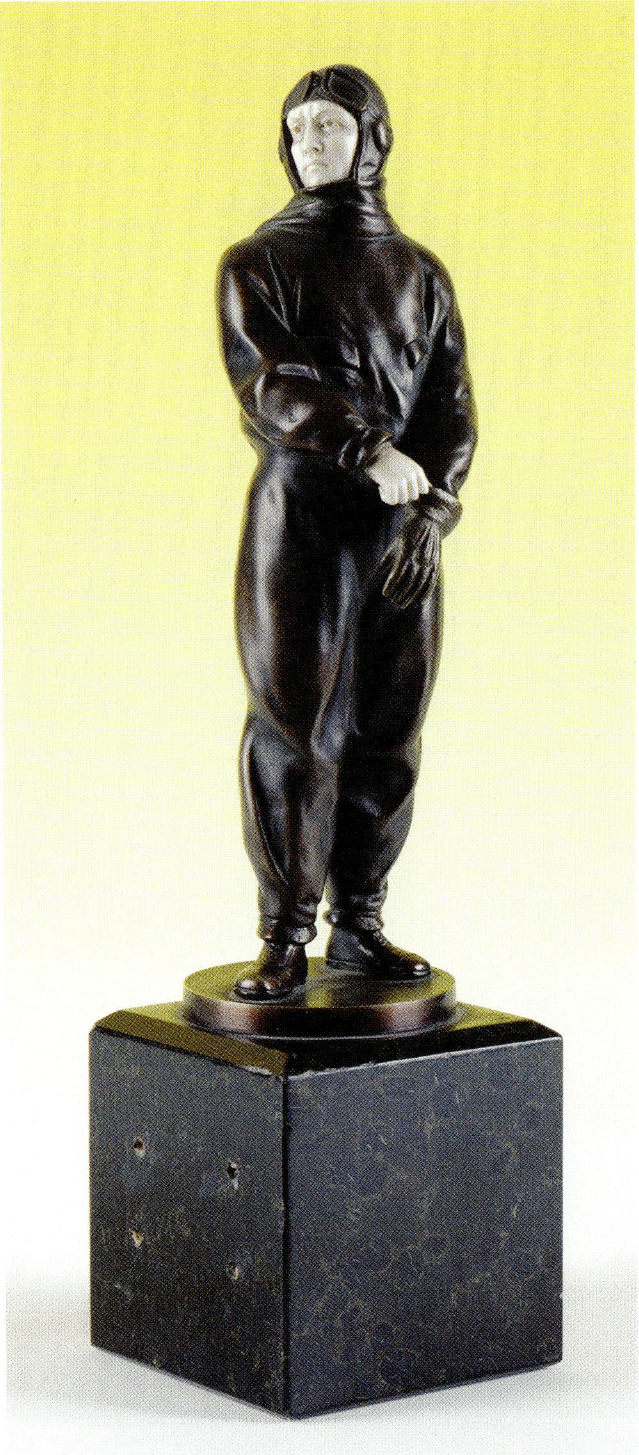

Pilot
Bronze and ivory on marble base
Height: 26cm. (10¼in.)
HARRY JAROSCH COLLECTION, VIENNA

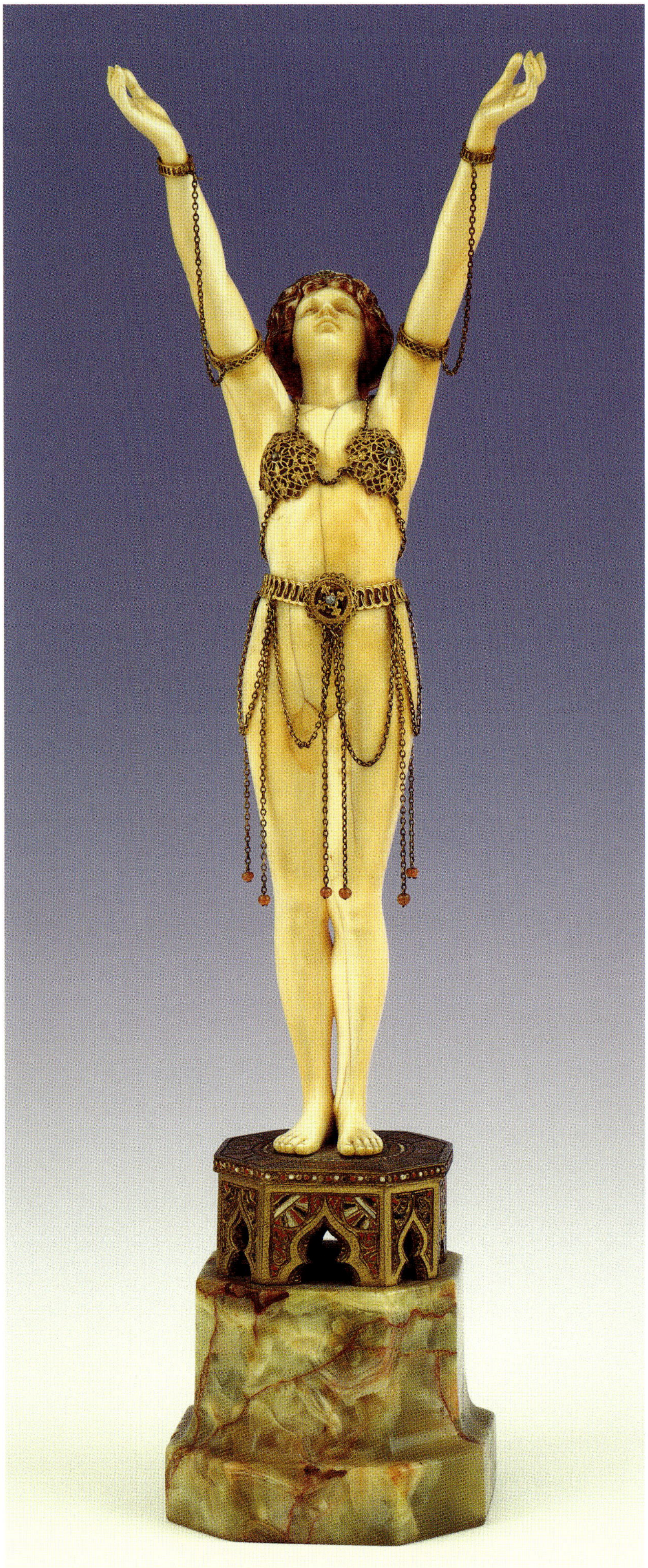

Harem Dancer
Bronze and ivory on onyx base
Height: 34.5cm. (13½in.)
PRIVATE COLLECTION

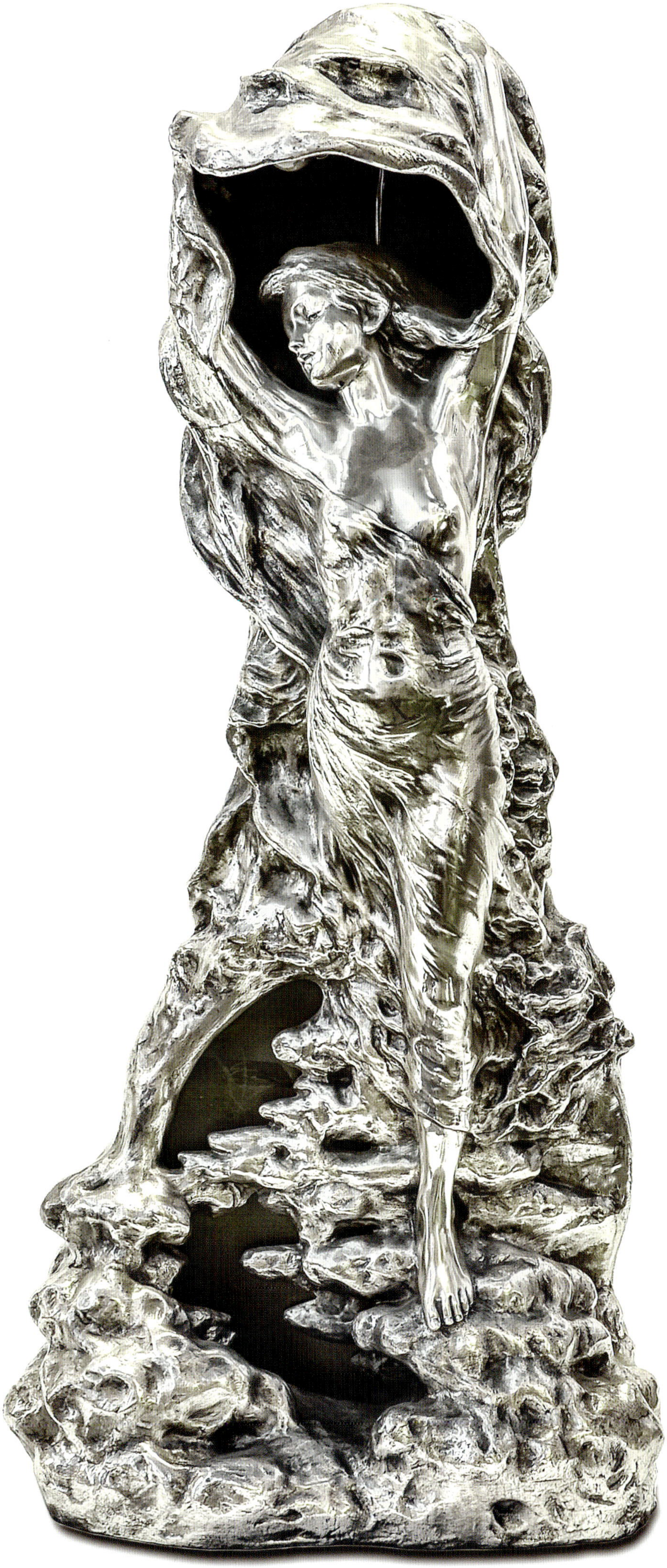

Goddess
Silvered bronze (mounted as a lamp)
Height: 72cm. (28¼in.)
PRIVATE COLLECTION

Nude with Drape
Bronze and ivory on marble base
Height: 19.5cm. (7¾in.)
DINO MENASCHE COLLECTION

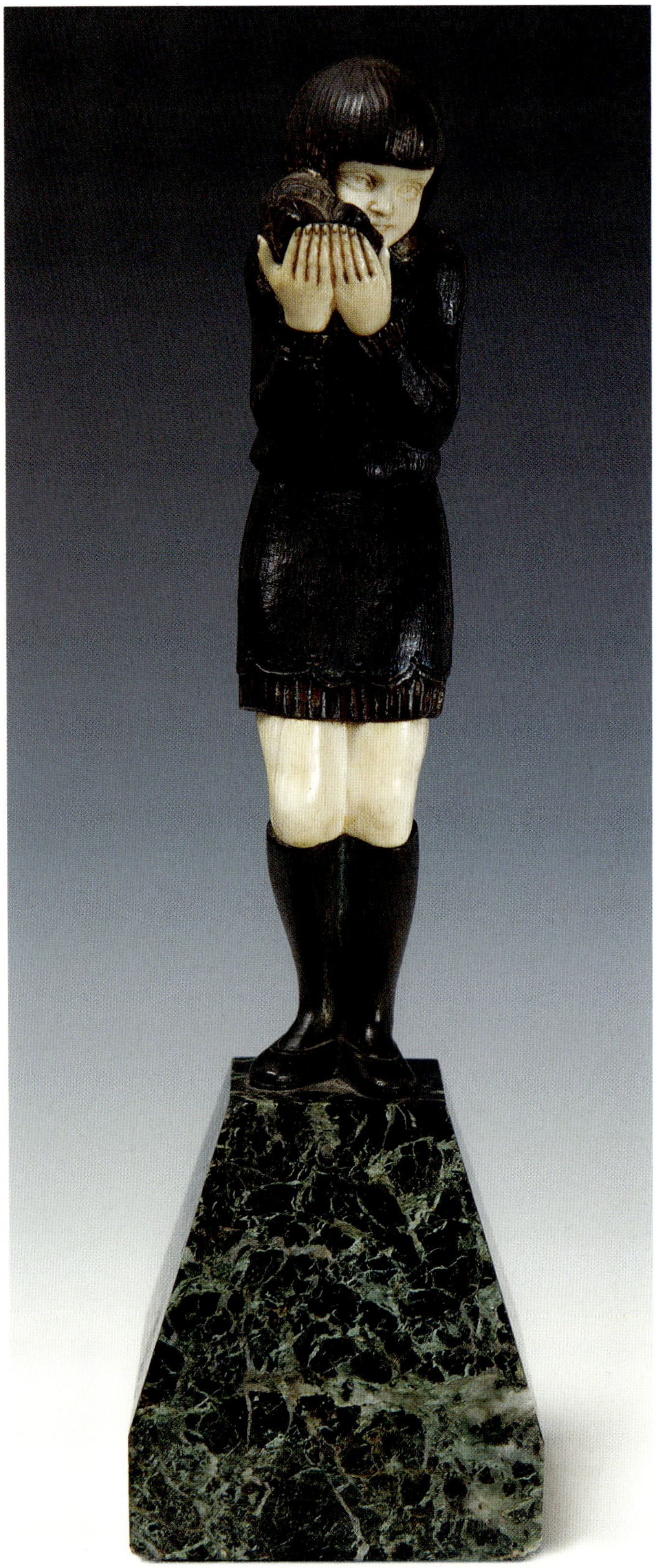

Small Offering
Bronze and ivory on marble base
Height: 27.5cm. (10¾in.)
PRIVATE COLLECTION

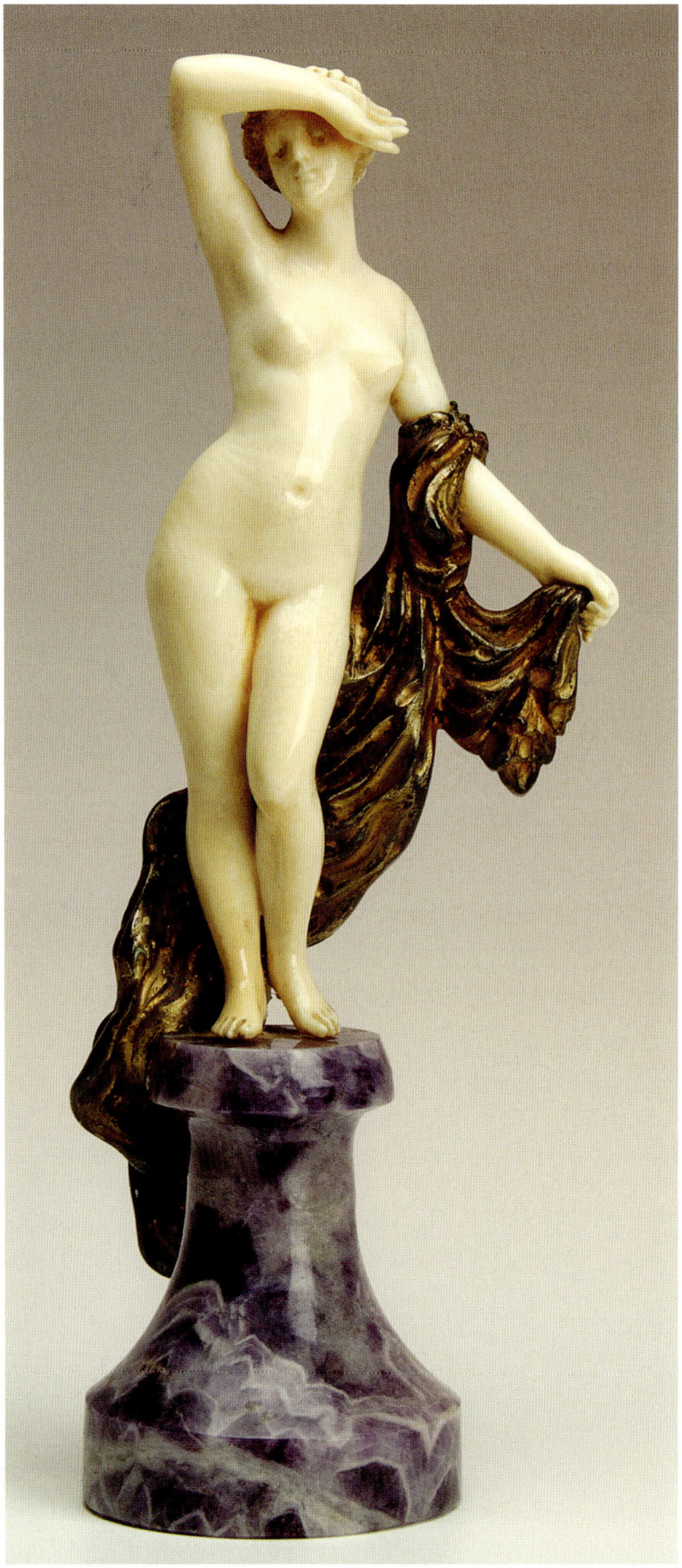

Maiden with Jars
Bronze, marble and ivory on a marble and onyx base (mounted as a lamp)
Height: 57cm. (22½in.)
PRIVATE COLLECTION

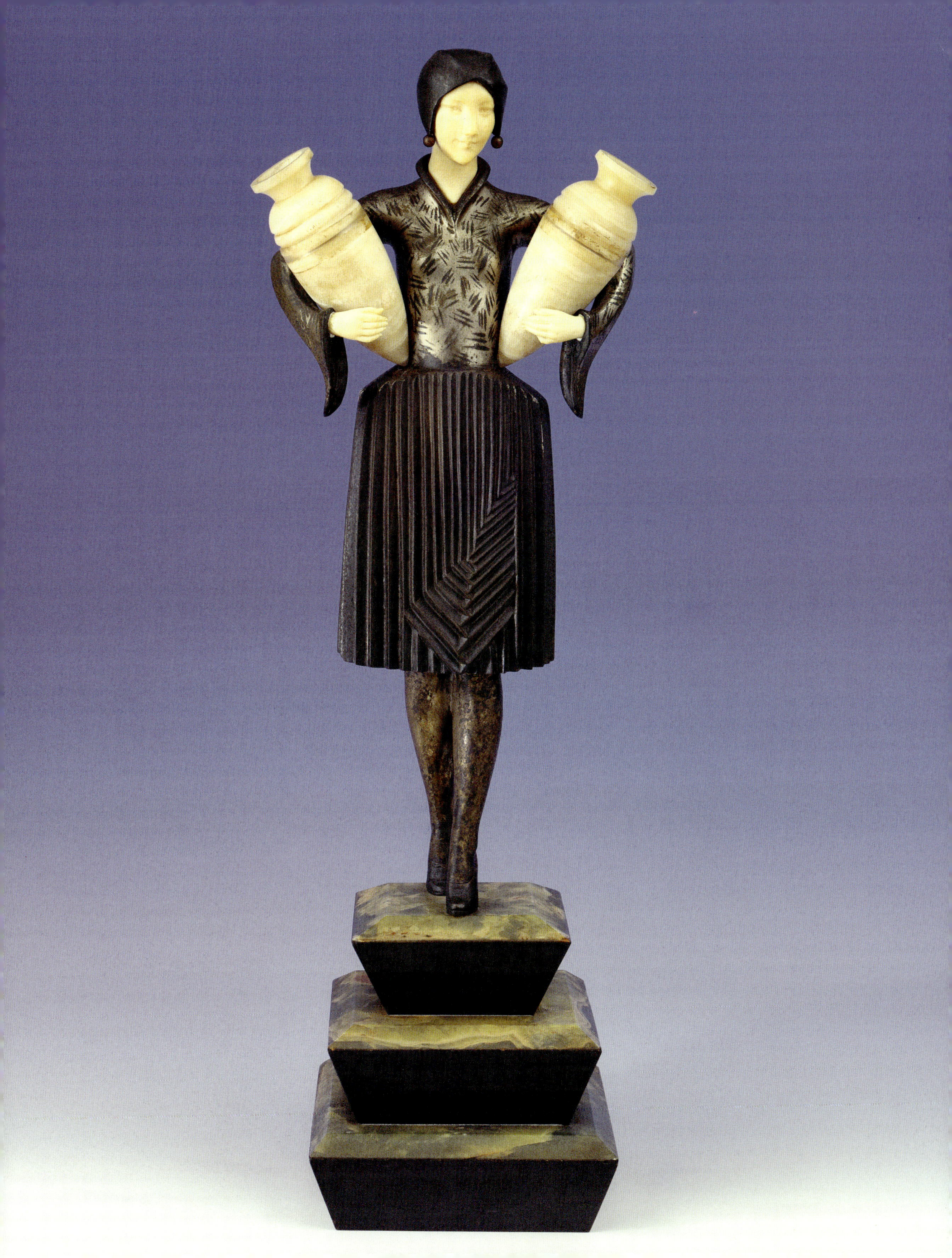

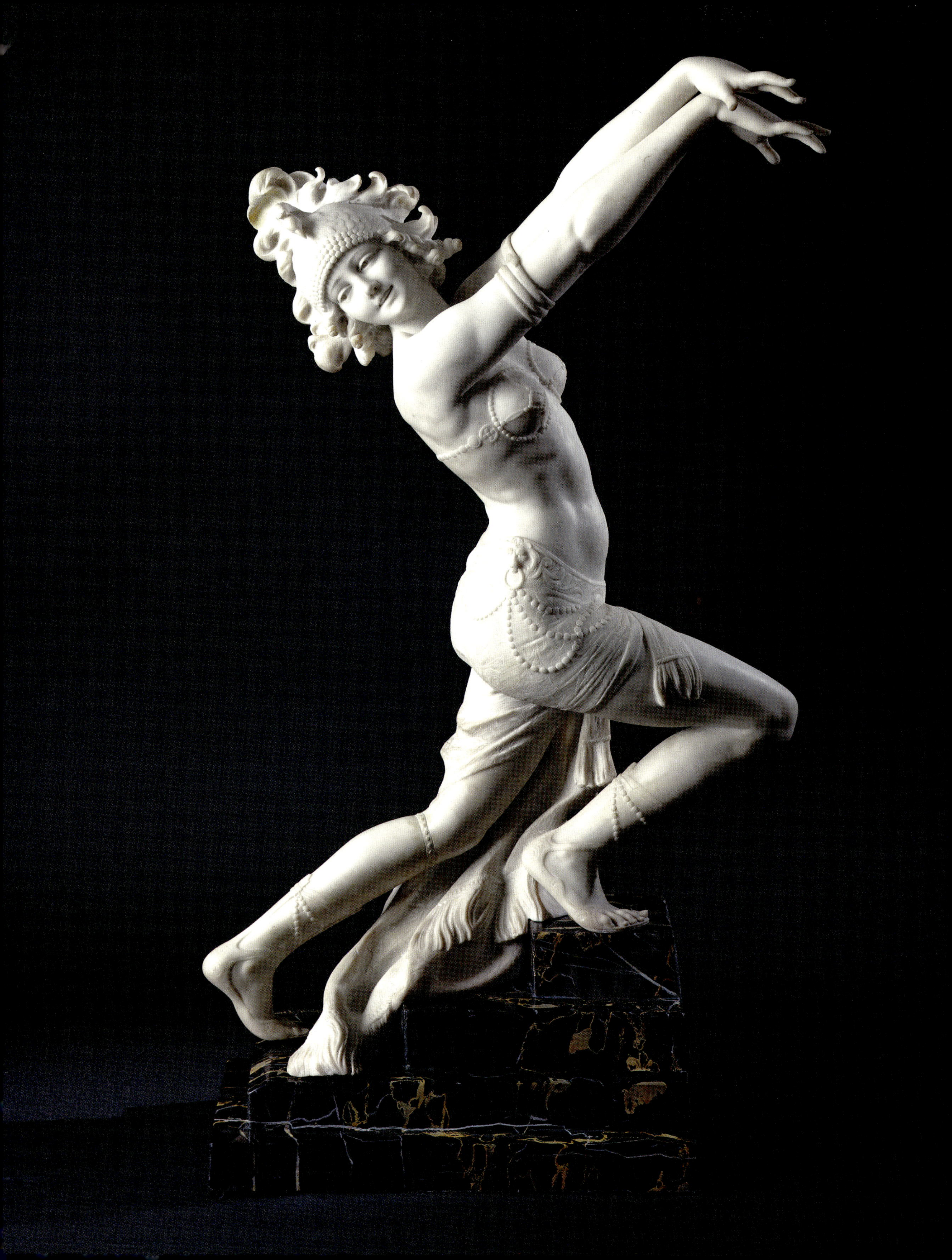

Eastern Dancer
Marble on marble base
PRIVATE COLLECTION

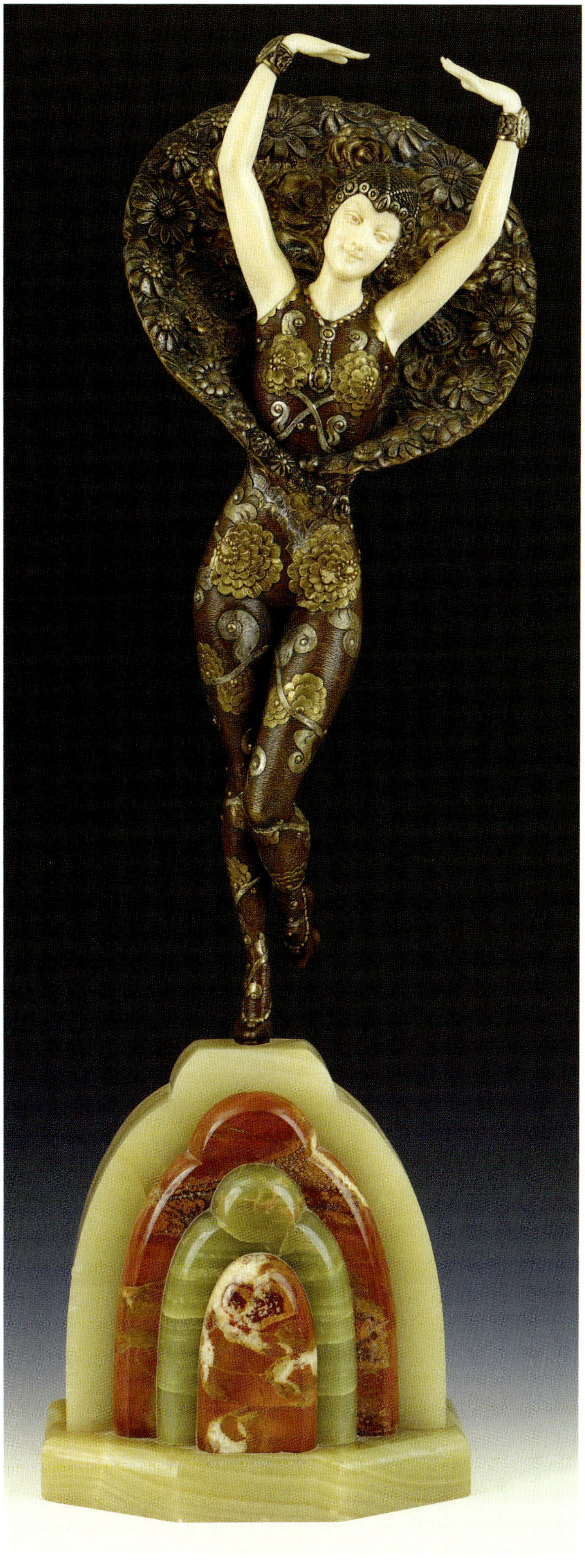

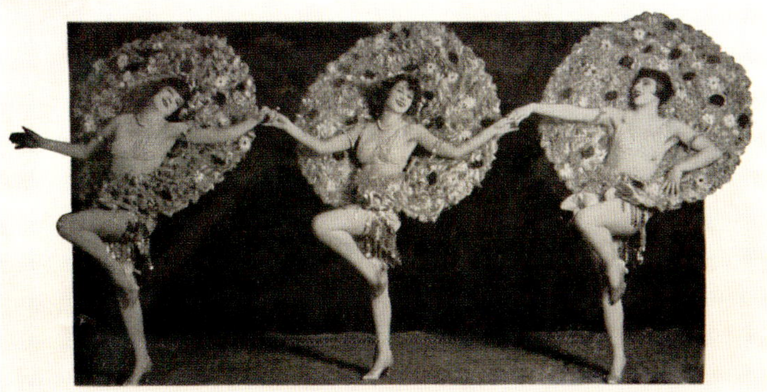

Chorus girls in a Paris Music Hall revue.

Floral Dancer
Bronze and ivory on marble and onyx base
PRIVATE COLLECTION

L.N
PARIS
J.L

L.N.J.L. CATALOGUE PAGES

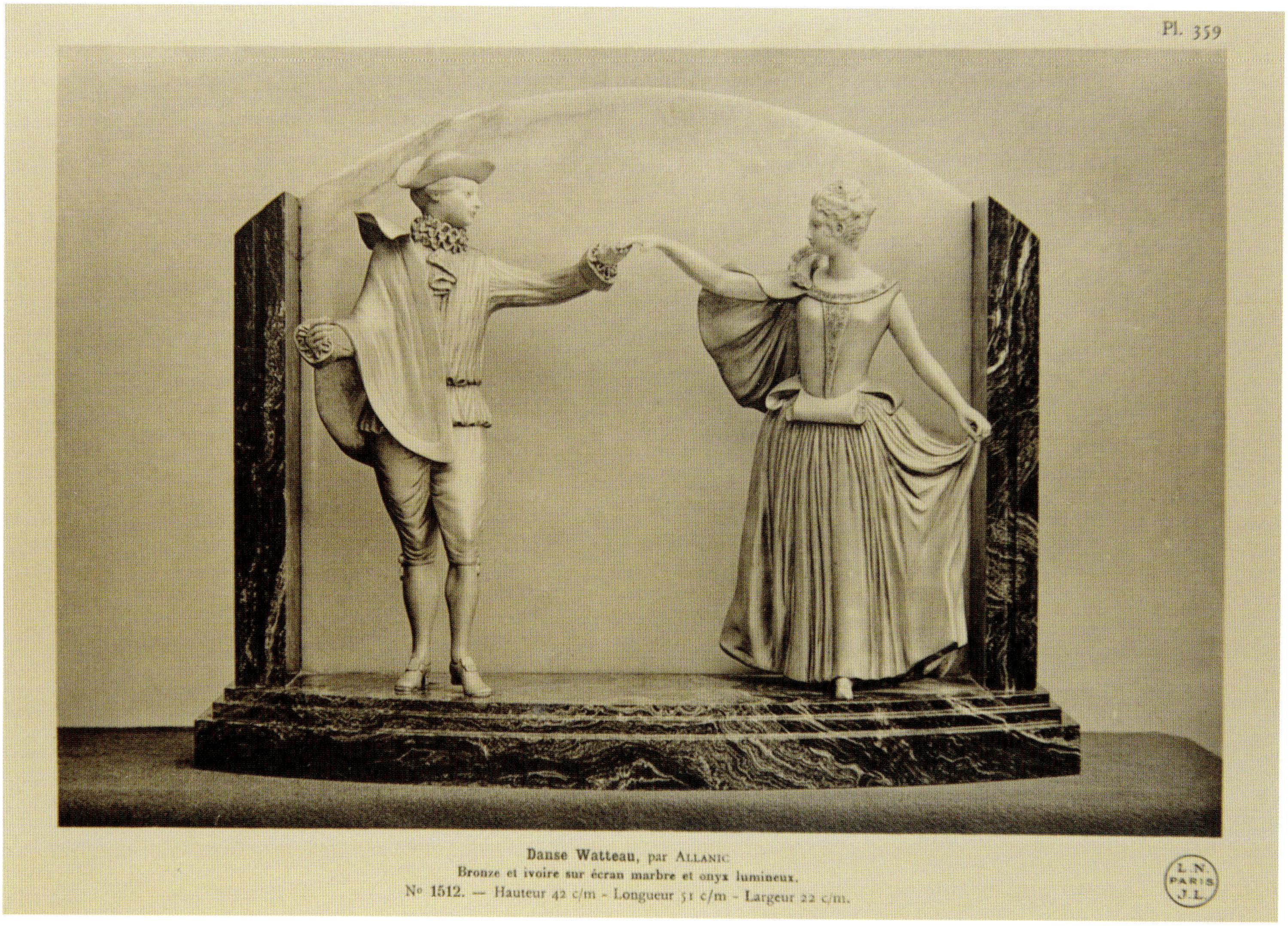

ALLANIC – Watteau Danse

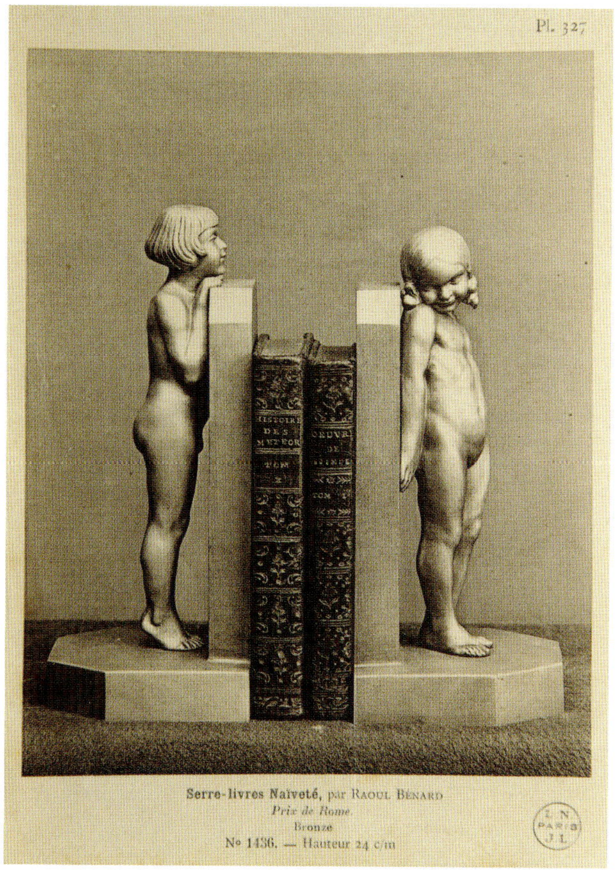

BÉNARD – Simplicity (bookends)

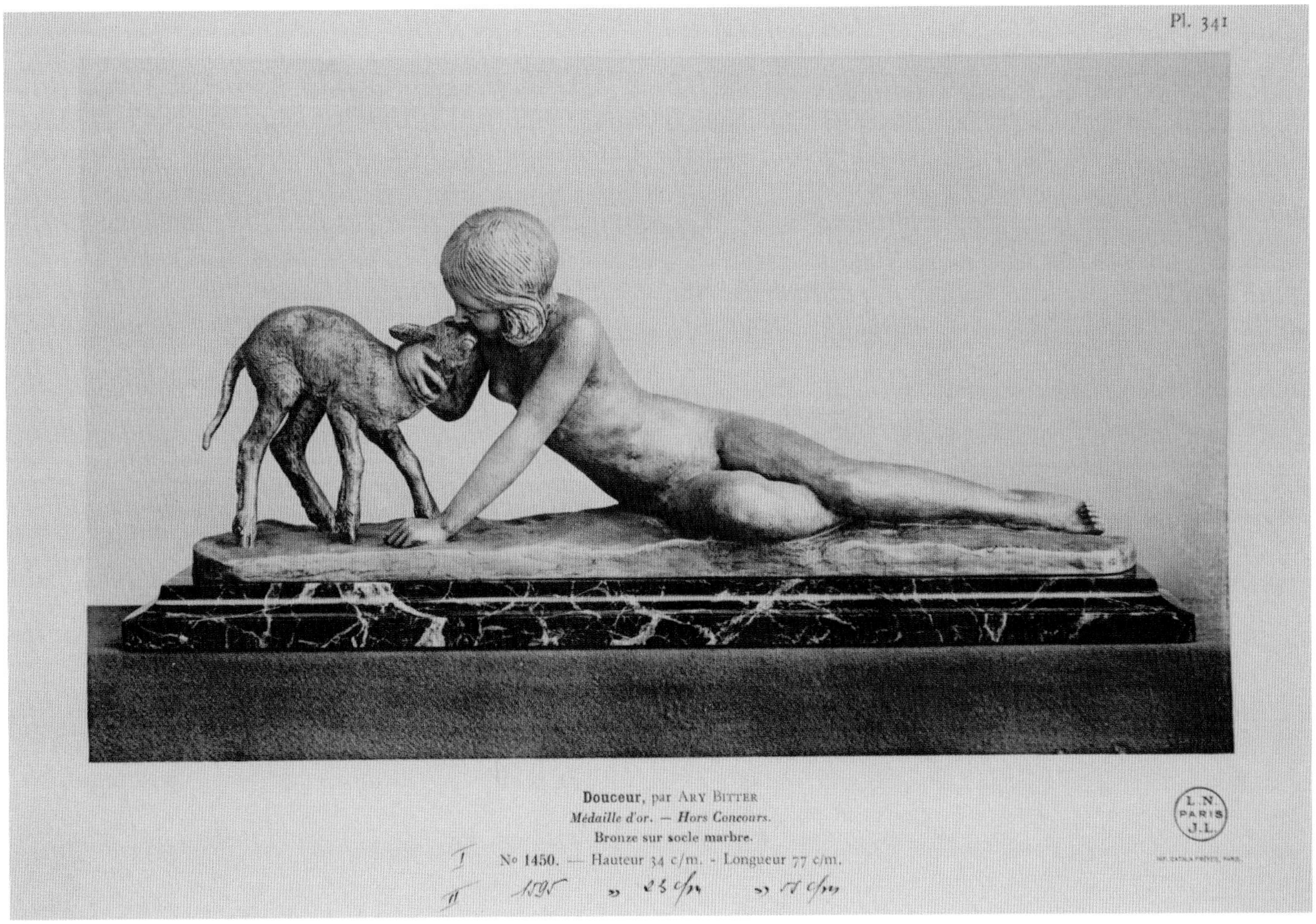

BITTER – Tenderness

BITTER – Chloé Seated

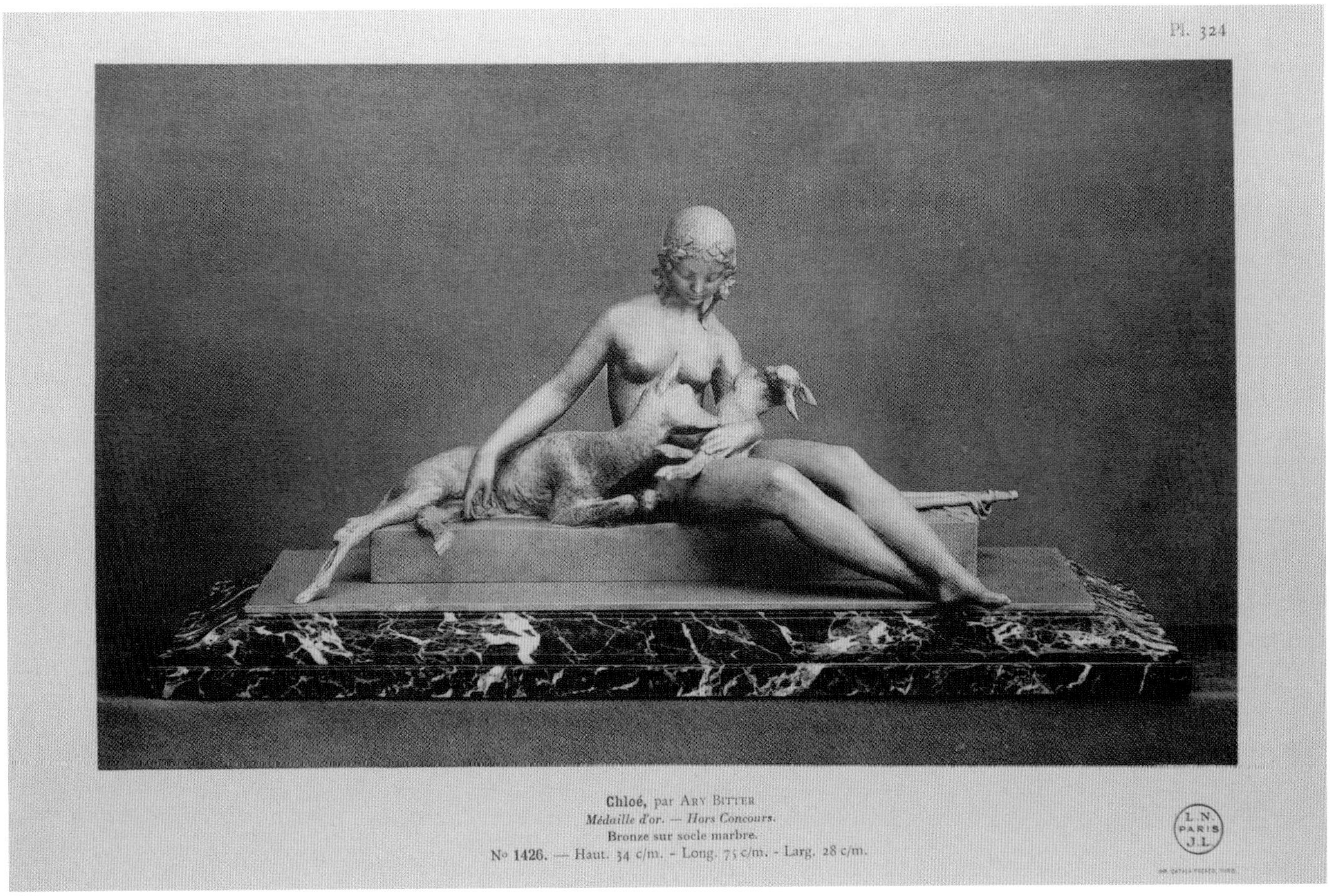

Pl. 325

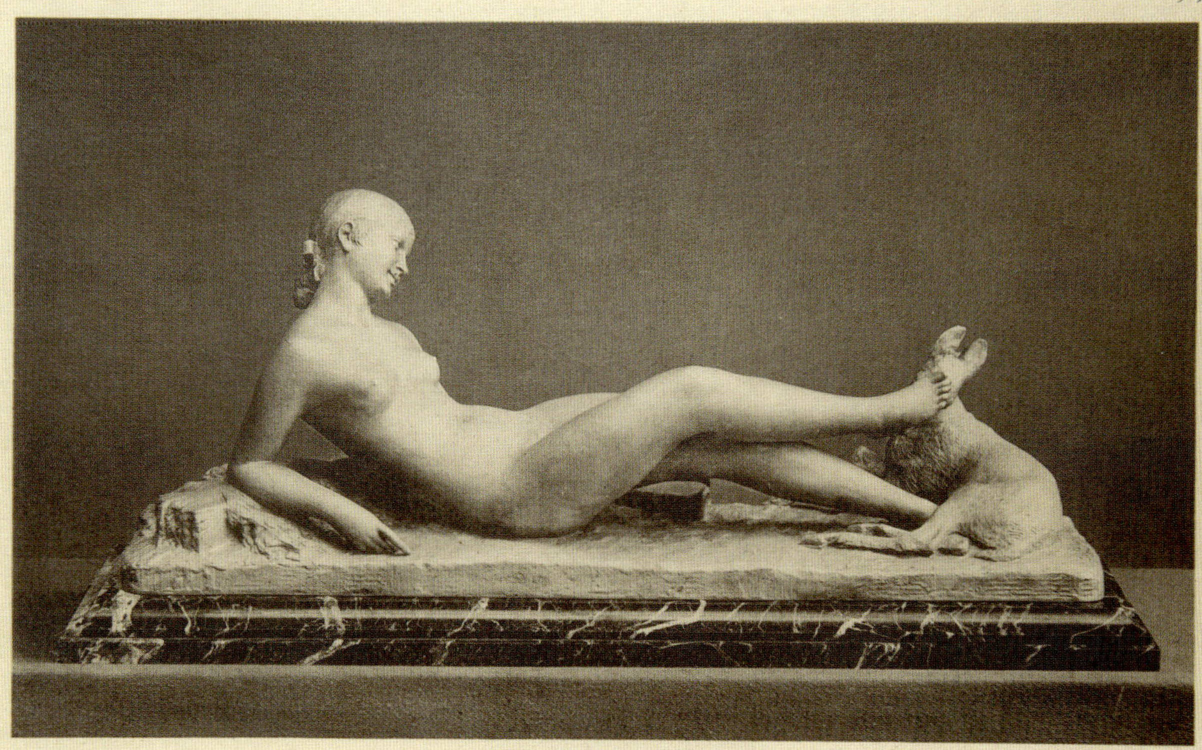

Chloé, par ARY BITTER. - *Salon 1927.*
Médaille d'Or - Hors Concours. — Bronze sur socle marbre.
N° 1419 — I. Haut. 34 c/m. - Long. 87 c/m. - Larg. 21 c/m.
N° 1440 — II. Haut. 22 c/m. - Long. 55 c/m. - Larg. 15 c/m.
N° 1441 — III. Haut. 15 c/m. - Long. 38 c/m. - Larg. 11 c/m.

L.N. PARIS J.L.

BITTER – Chloé Lying

BITTER – Unexpected Encounter

Pl. 330

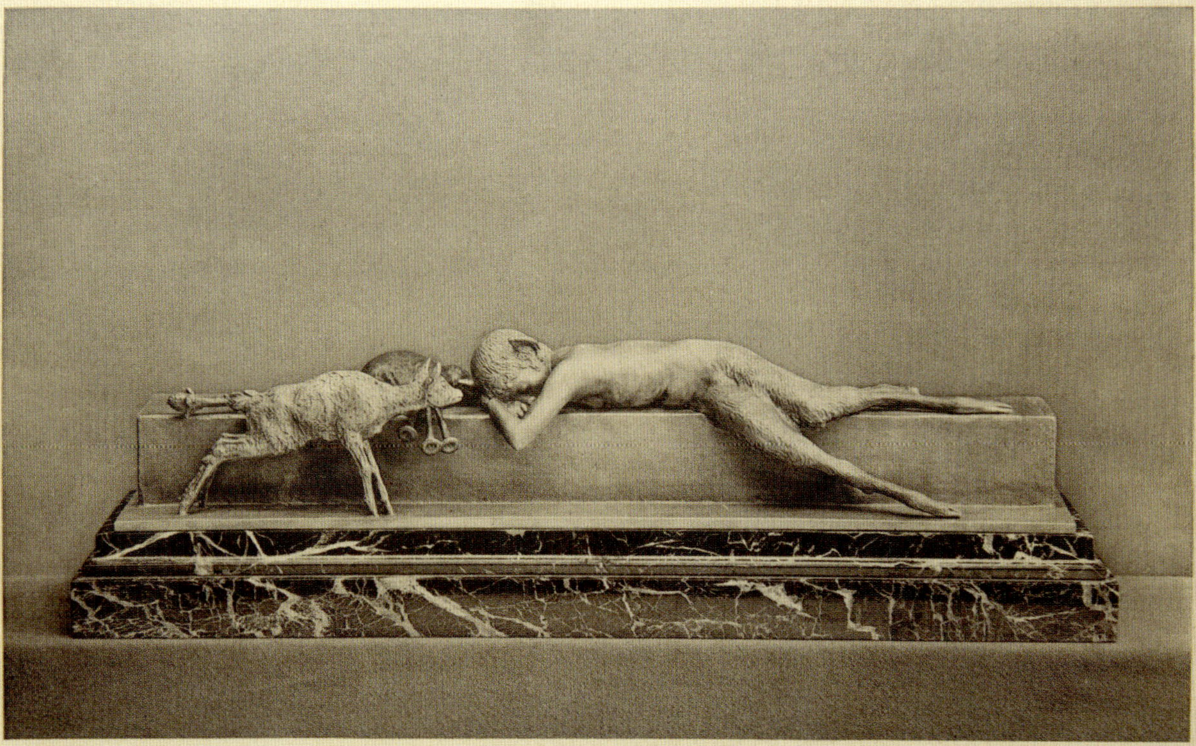

Rencontre inattendue, par ARY BITTER
Médaille d'Or - Hors Concours.
Bronze sur socle marbre.
N° 1442. — Dimensions : 23 × 84 × 19.

L.N. PARIS J.L.

Pl. 306

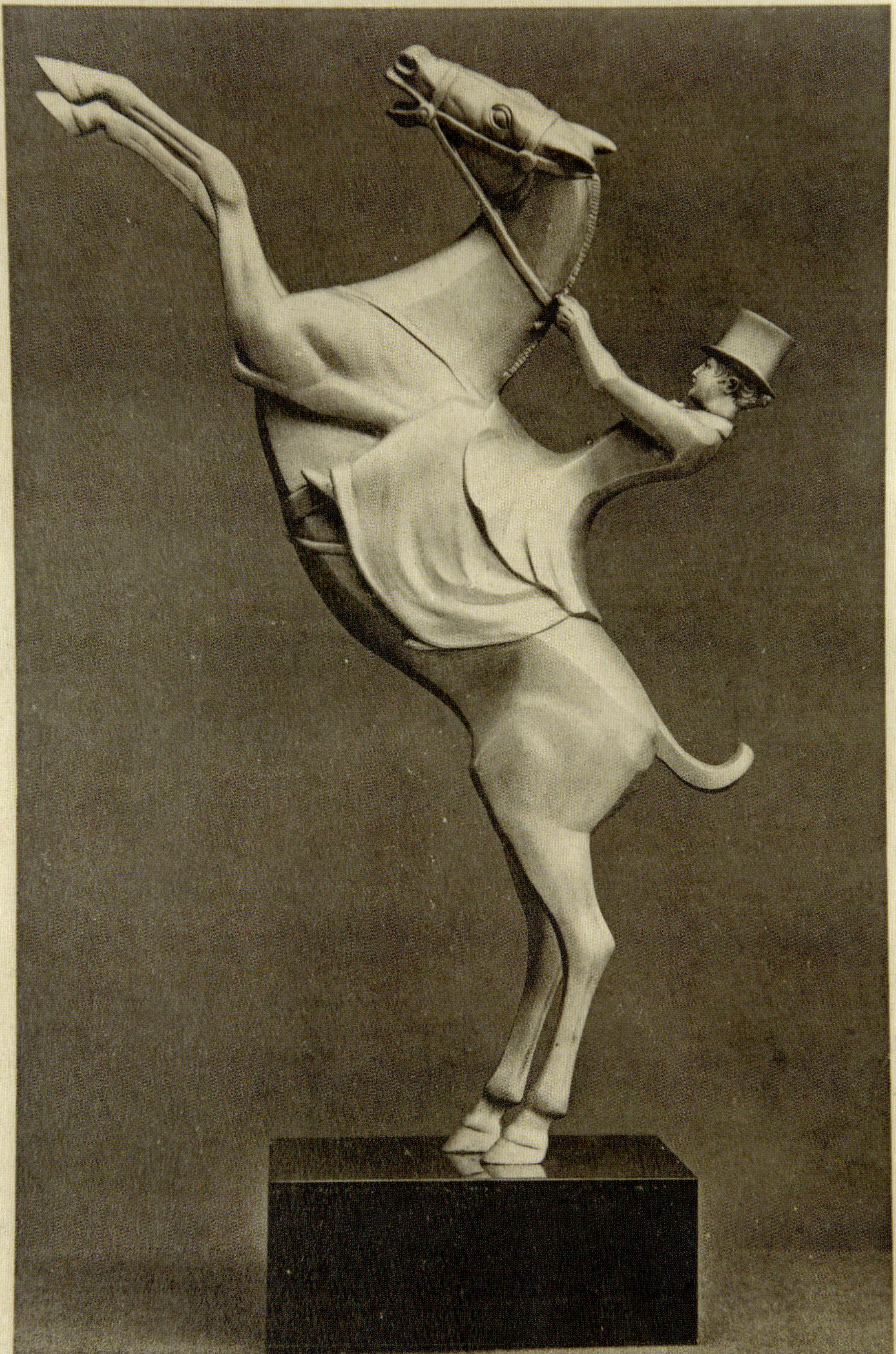

La Cabrade, par BOURAINE
Bronze argenté et ivoire sur socle marbre
N° 1367. — Hauteur 46 c/m.

L. N. PARIS J. L.

IMP. CATALA FRÈRES, PARIS

BOURAINE – Bucking

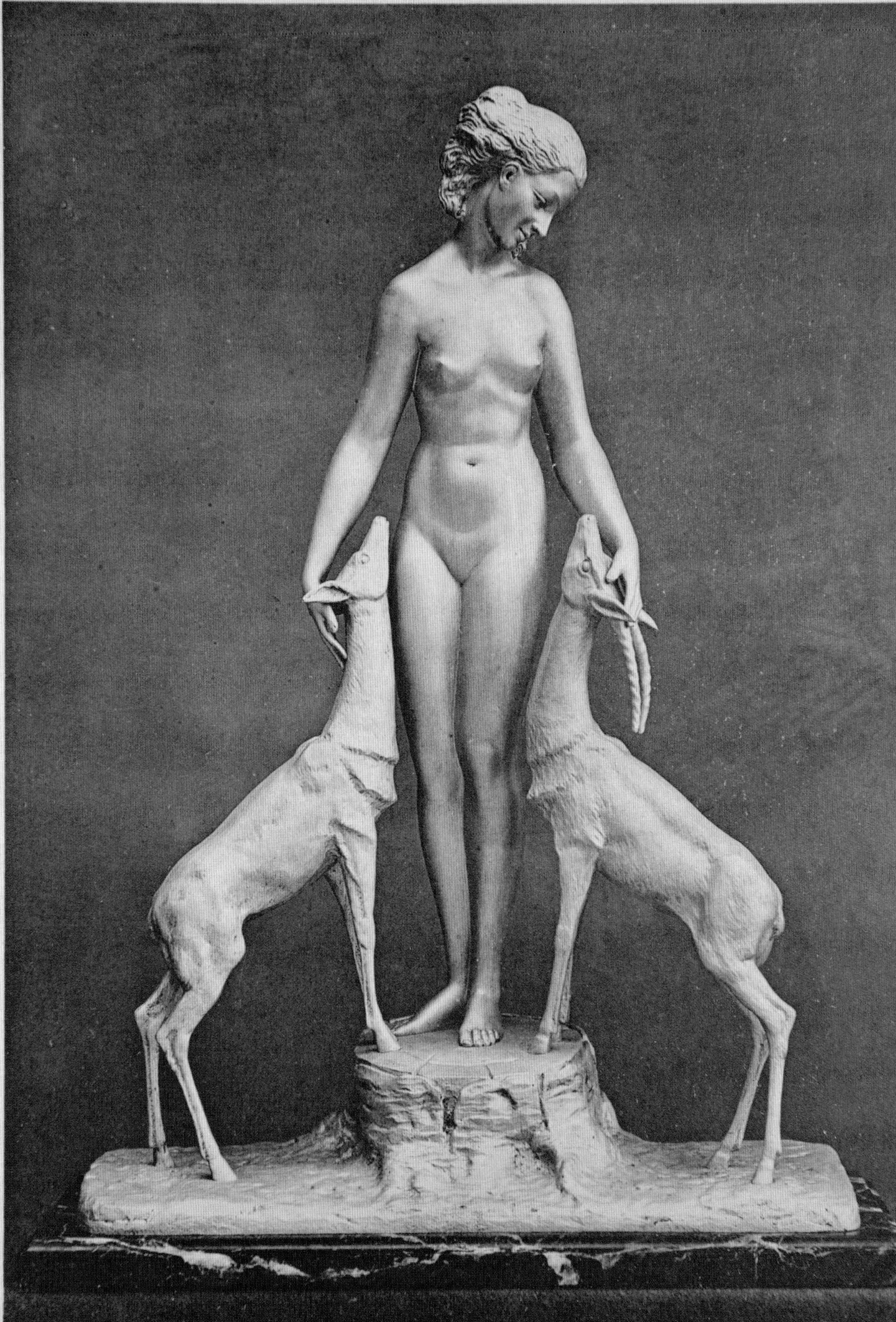

Jeune fille aux Gazelles, par Bouraine
Bronze sur socle marbre
N° 1383. — Hauteur 50 c/m - Largeur 40 c/m.

L. N.
PARIS
J. L.

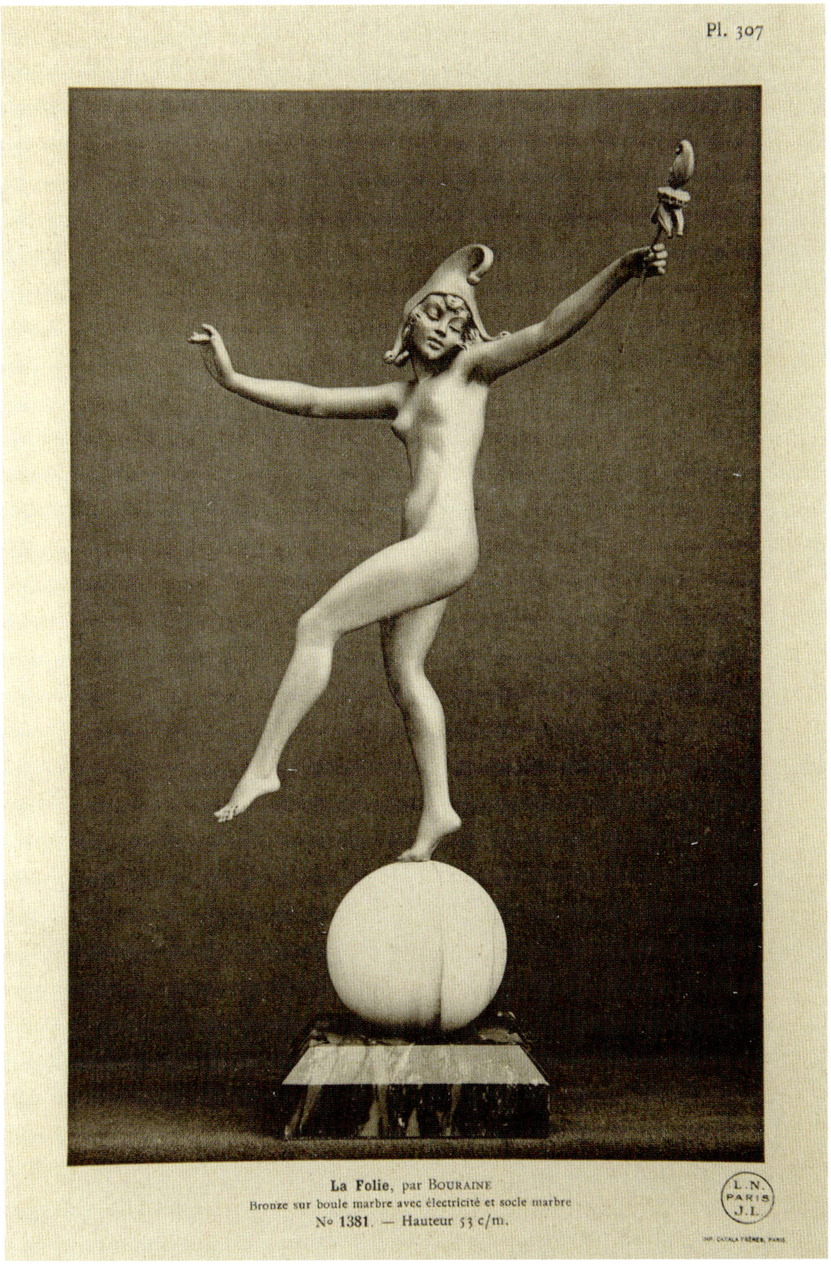

BOURAINE – Folly

BOURAINE – Pheasant

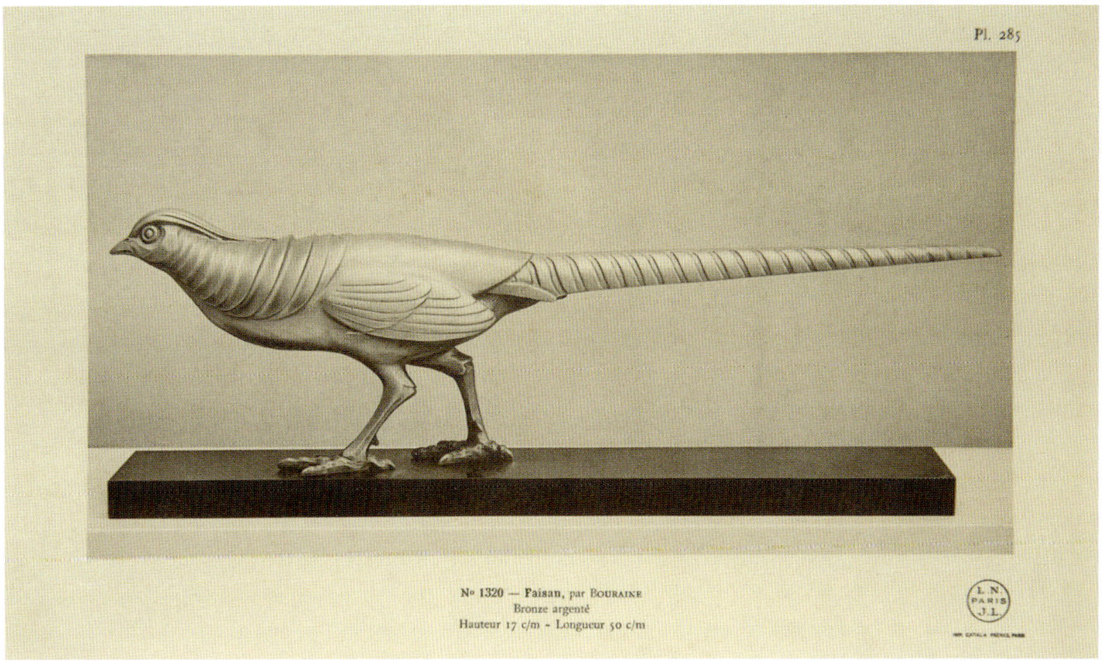

BOURAINE – Maiden with Gazelles

Pl. 292

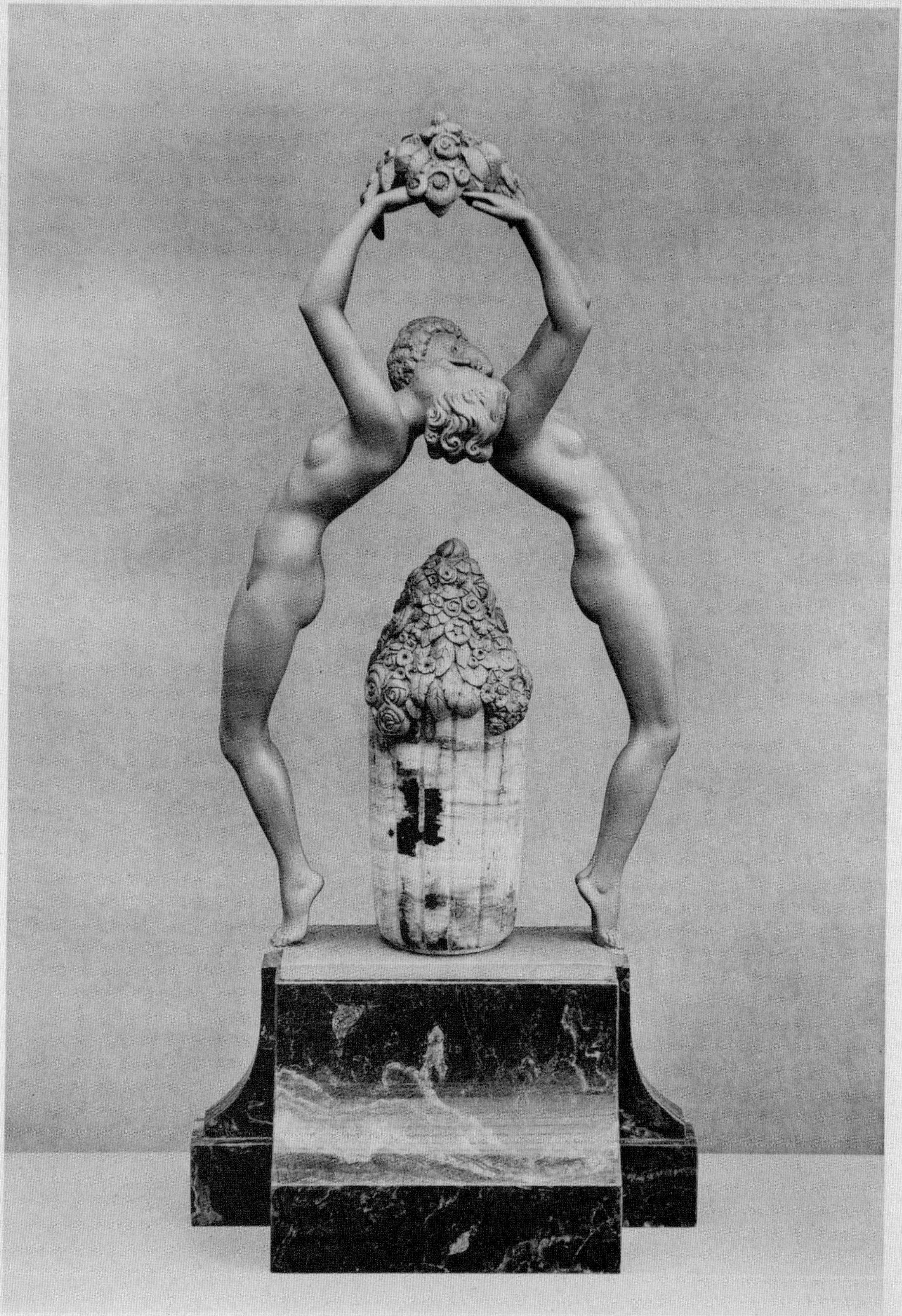

Floréal, par BOURAINE
N° 1296 — Bronze, vase et socle marbre
Hauteur 66 %m - Largeur 30 %m

L. N.
PARIS
J. L.

G. Boilan - imp. Paris

BOURAINE – Floral

Pl. 343

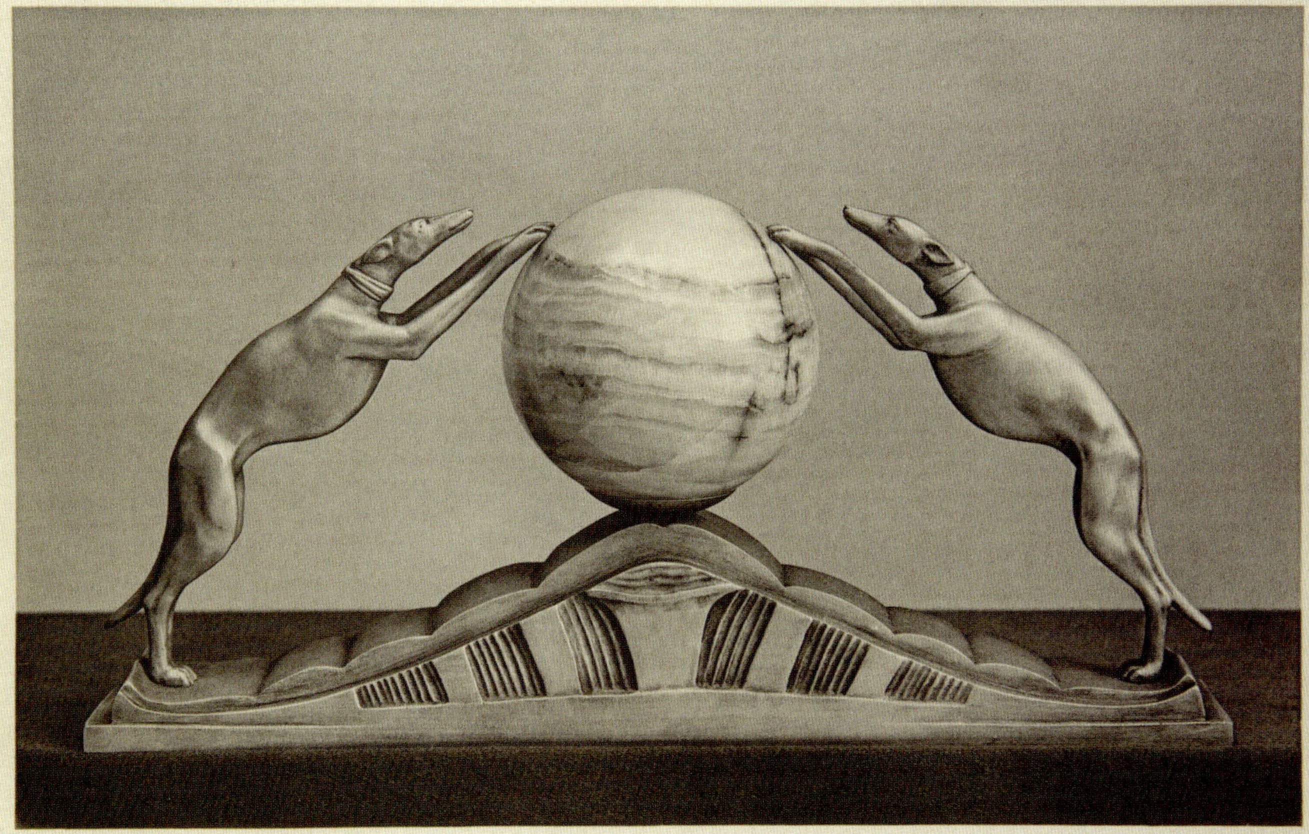

Jeu de Lévriers, par Ch. Breton
Bronze, boule lumineuse.
N° **1490**. — Hauteur 23 c/m. Longueur 46 c/m.

L.N. PARIS J.L.

BRETON – Hounds Play

Pl. 371

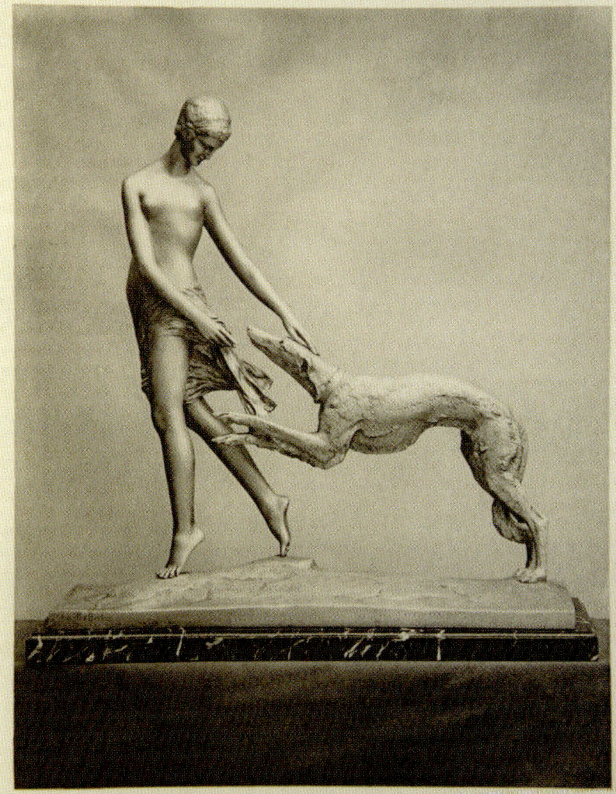

Jeunesse, par Ch. Breton
Salon A. F. 1928
Bronze argenté sur socle marbre.
N° **1540**. — Hauteur 63 c/m - Longueur 62 c/m - Largeur 20 c/m.

L.N. PARIS J.L.

BRETON – Youth

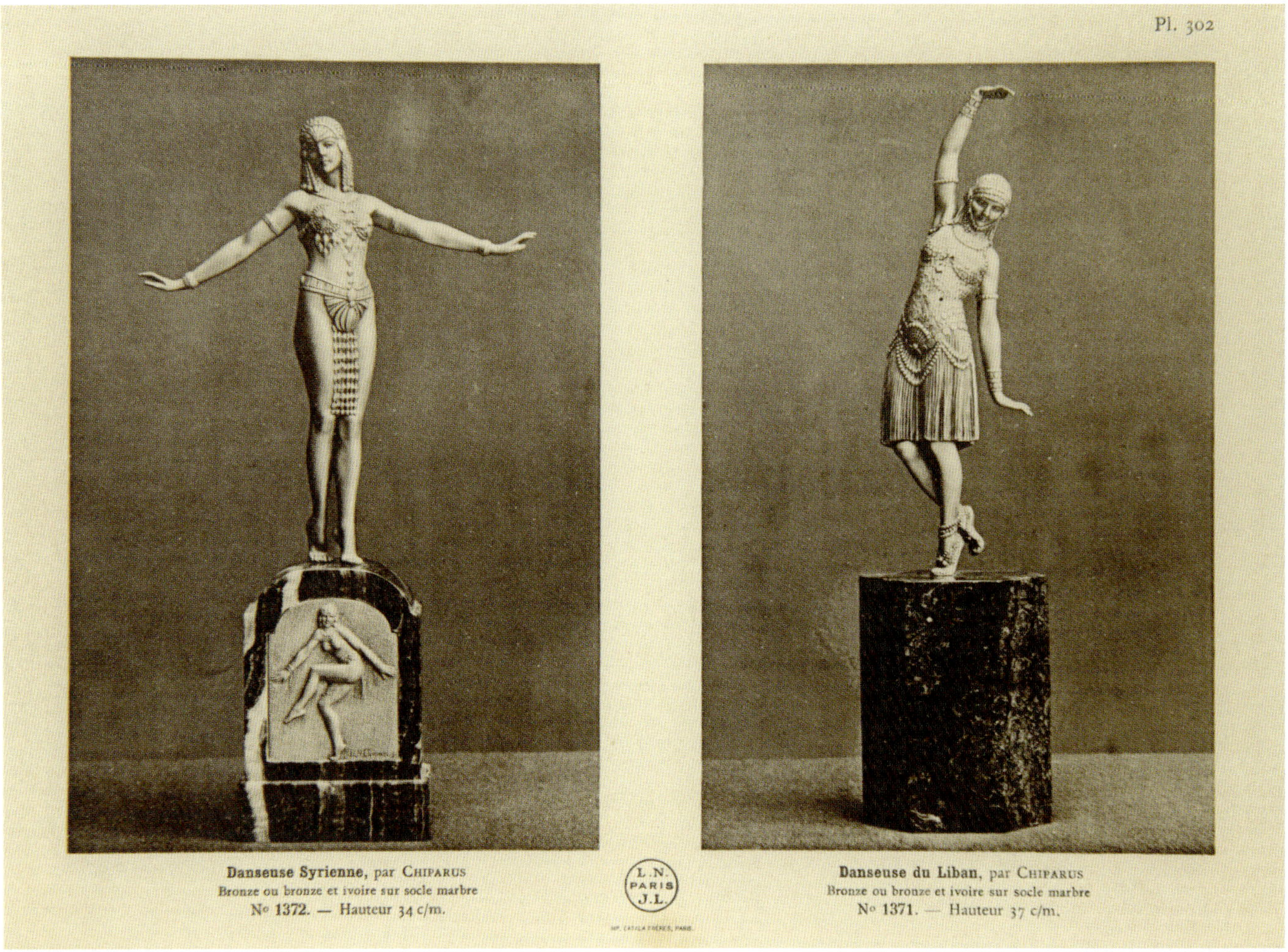

CHIPARUS – Syrian Dancer – Dancer of Lebanon

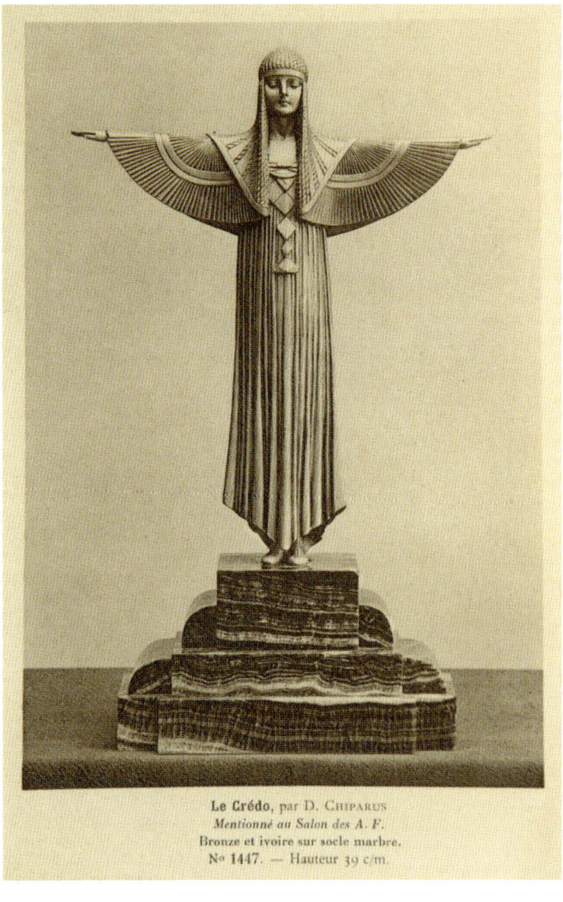

CHIPARUS – Credo

CHIPARUS – Finale

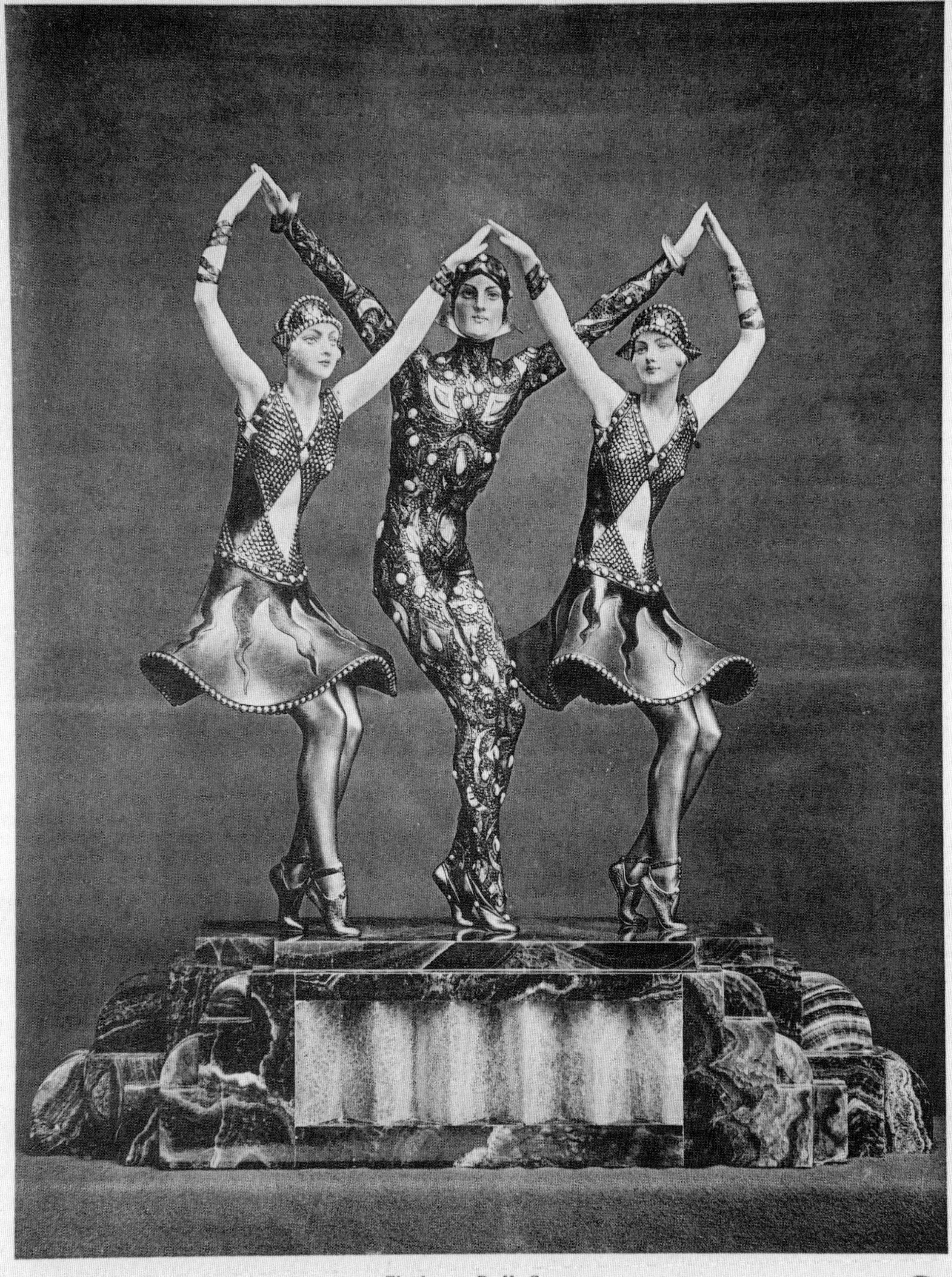

Finale, par D.-H. CHIPARUS
Bronze et ivoire sur socle marbre.
I N° 1556. — Hauteur 63 c/m - Longueur 58 c/m - Largeur 23 c/m
II N. 1609 » 41c/m » 38c/m.

L. N. PARIS J. L.

IMP. CATALA FRÈRES, PARIS

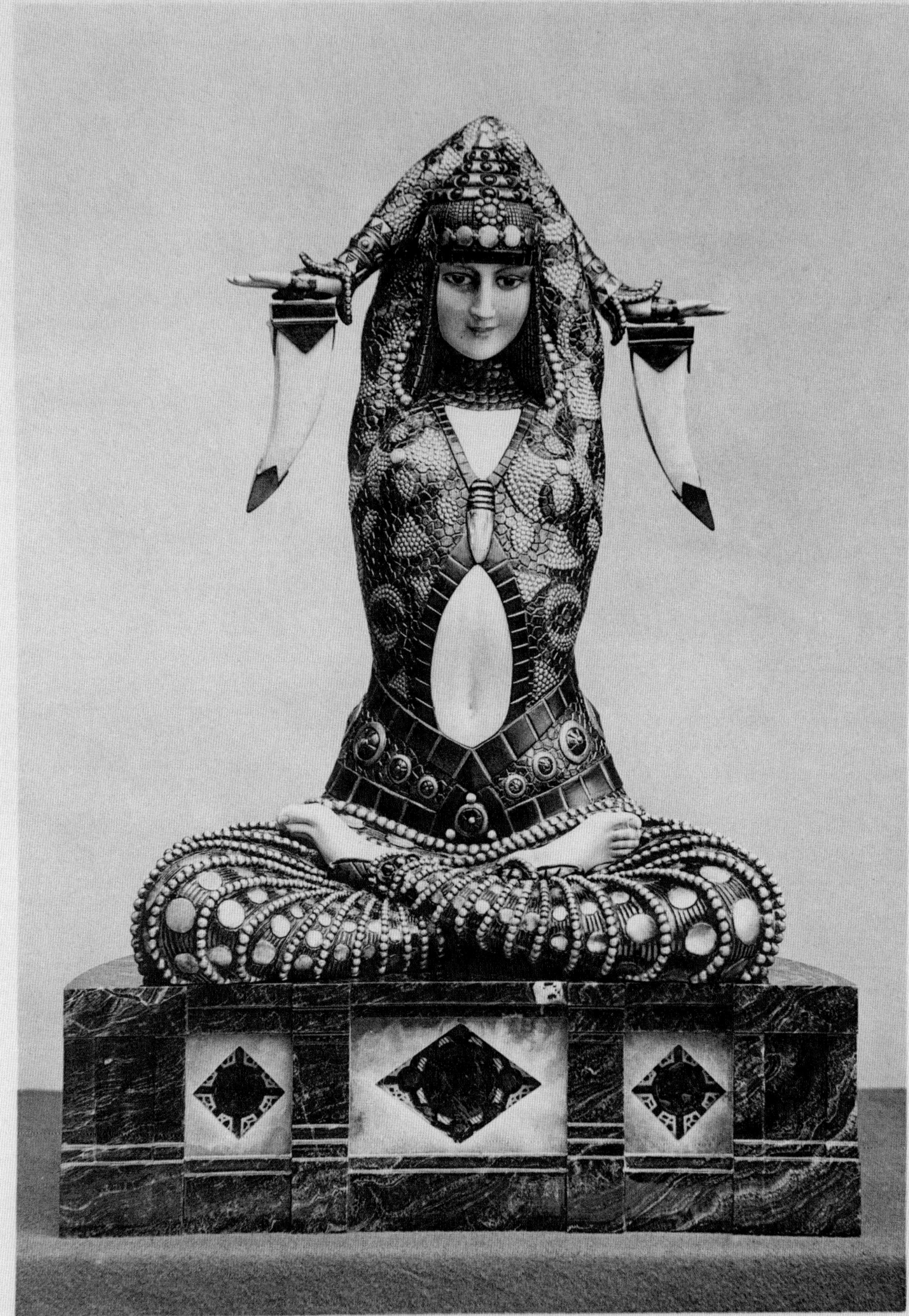

Civa, par D.-H. Chiparus
Mentionné, Salon des A. F.
Bronze et ivoire sur socle marbre lumineux.
No 1510. — Hauteur 55 c/m - Longueur 37 c/m - Largeur 27 c/m

L.N. PARIS J.L.

IMP. CATALA FRÈRES, PARIS.

CHIPARUS – Civa

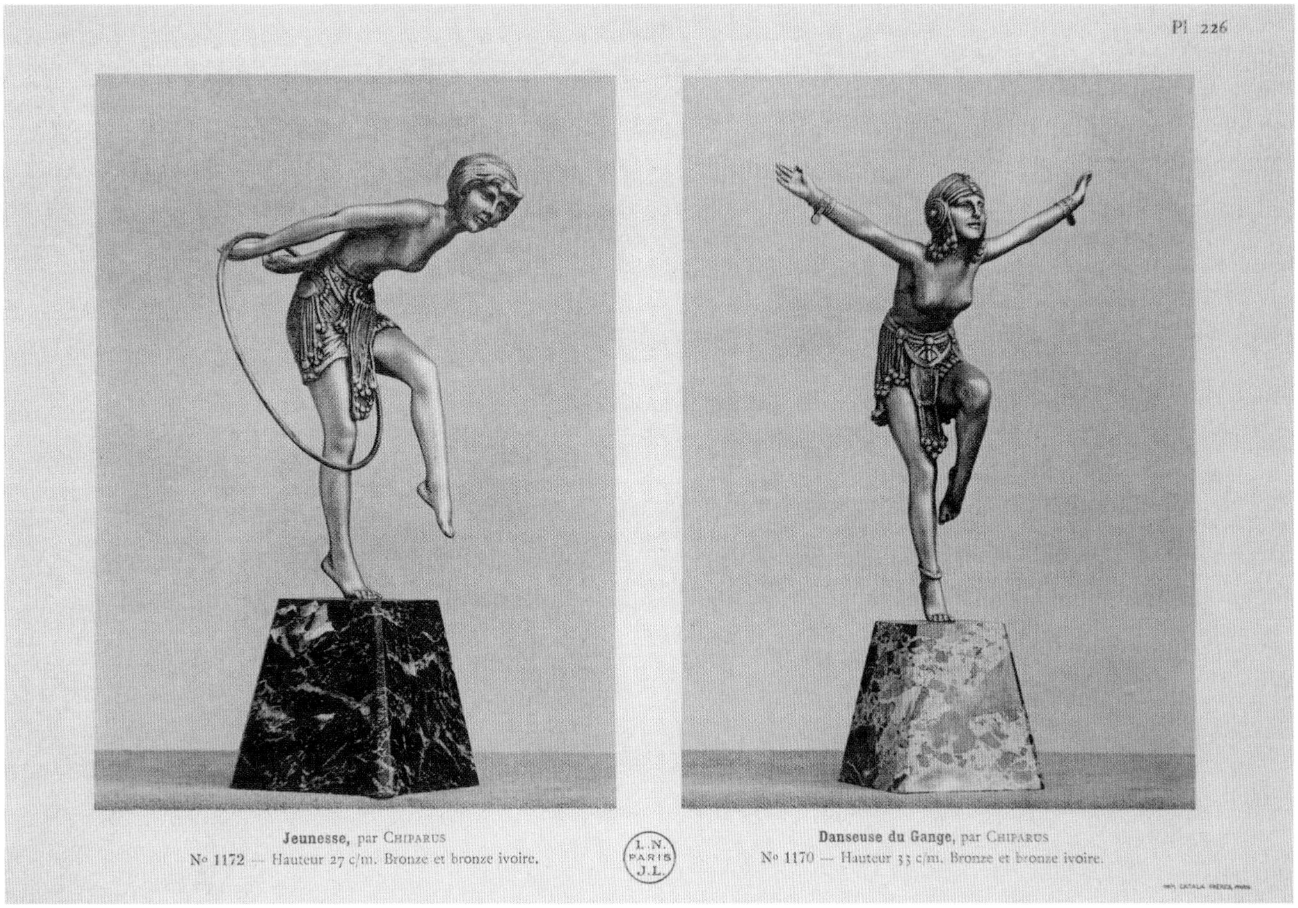

CHIPARUS – Young Girl – Dancer of The Ganges (Chain Dancer)

CHIPARUS – Dancer of Olynthus – Delhi Dancer

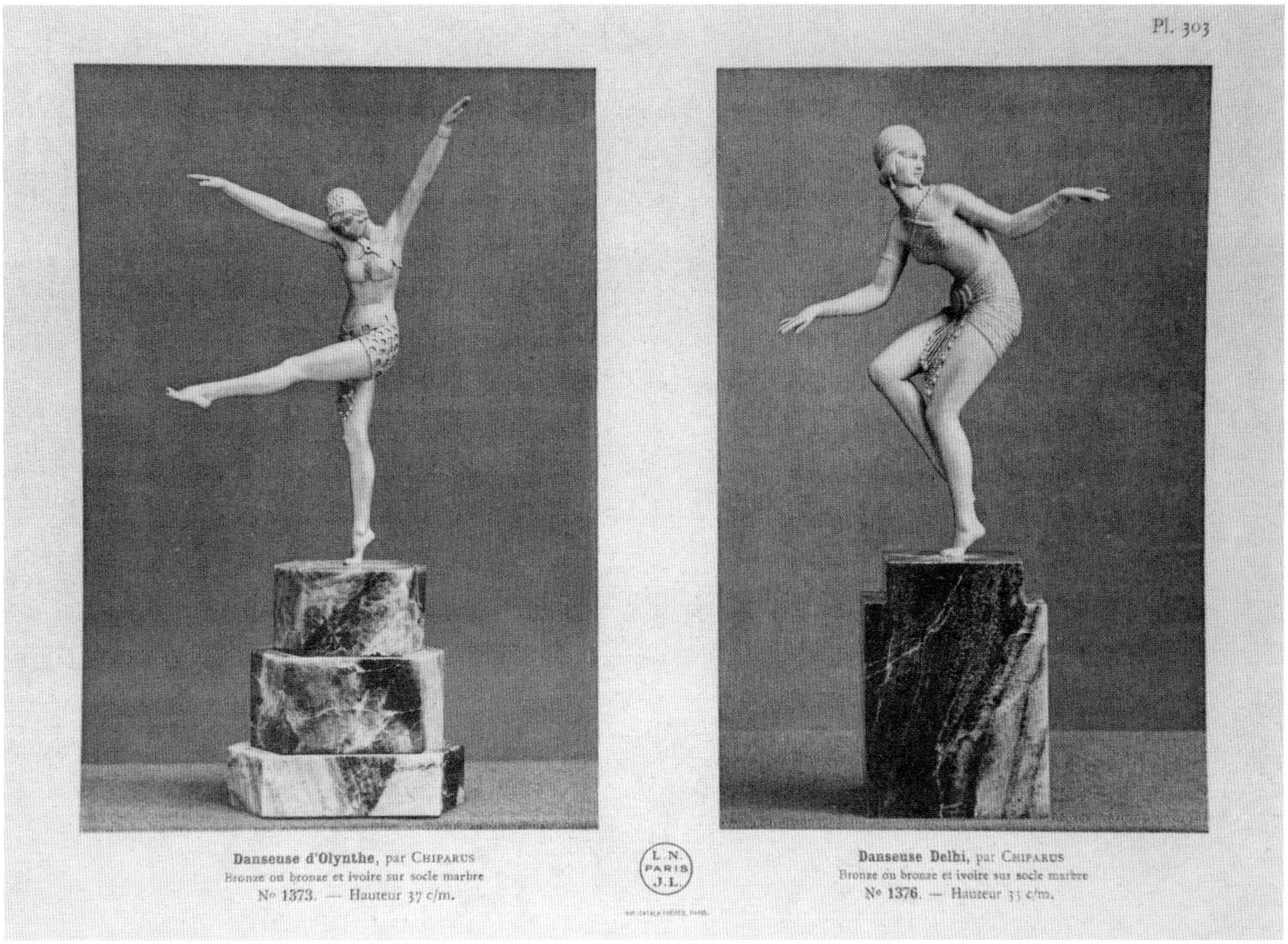

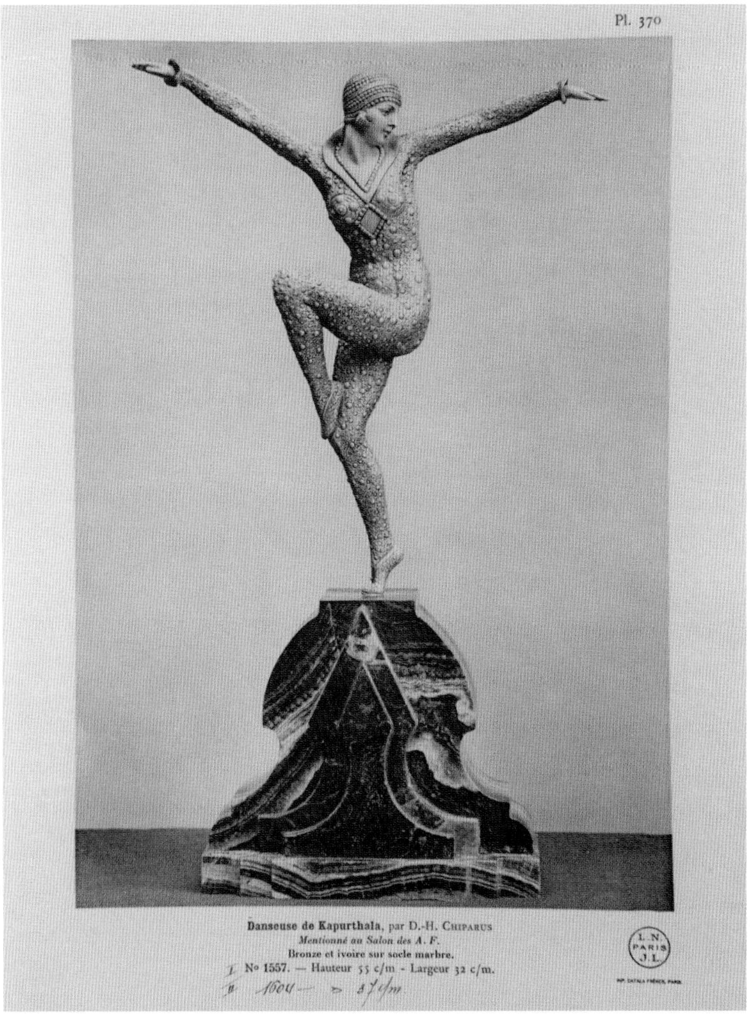

CHIPARUS – Dancer of Kapurthala

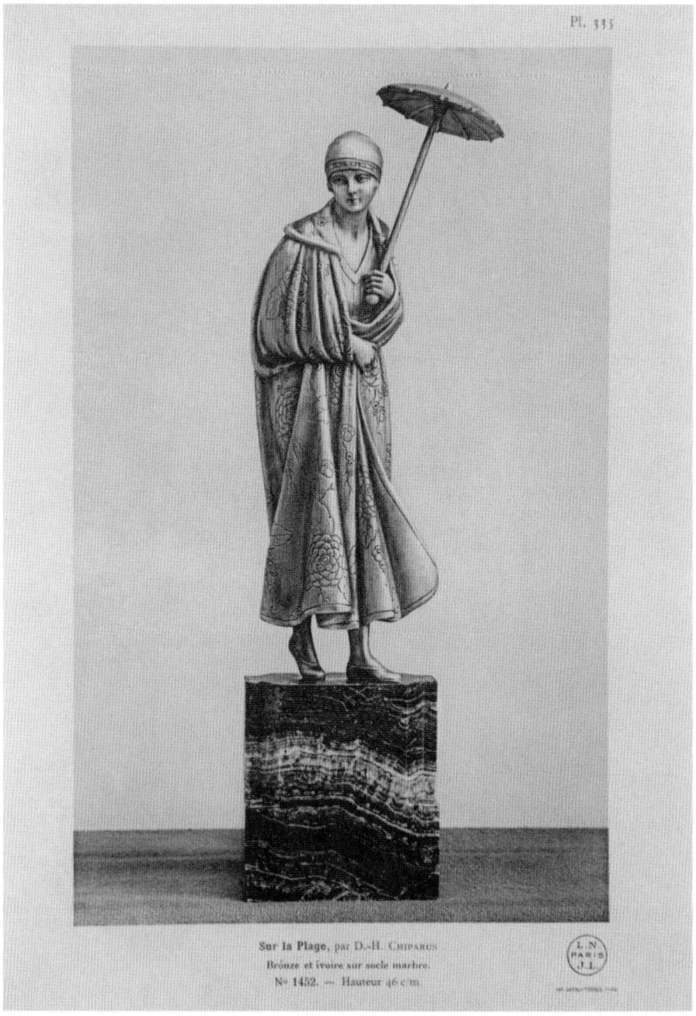

CHIPARUS – On the Beach

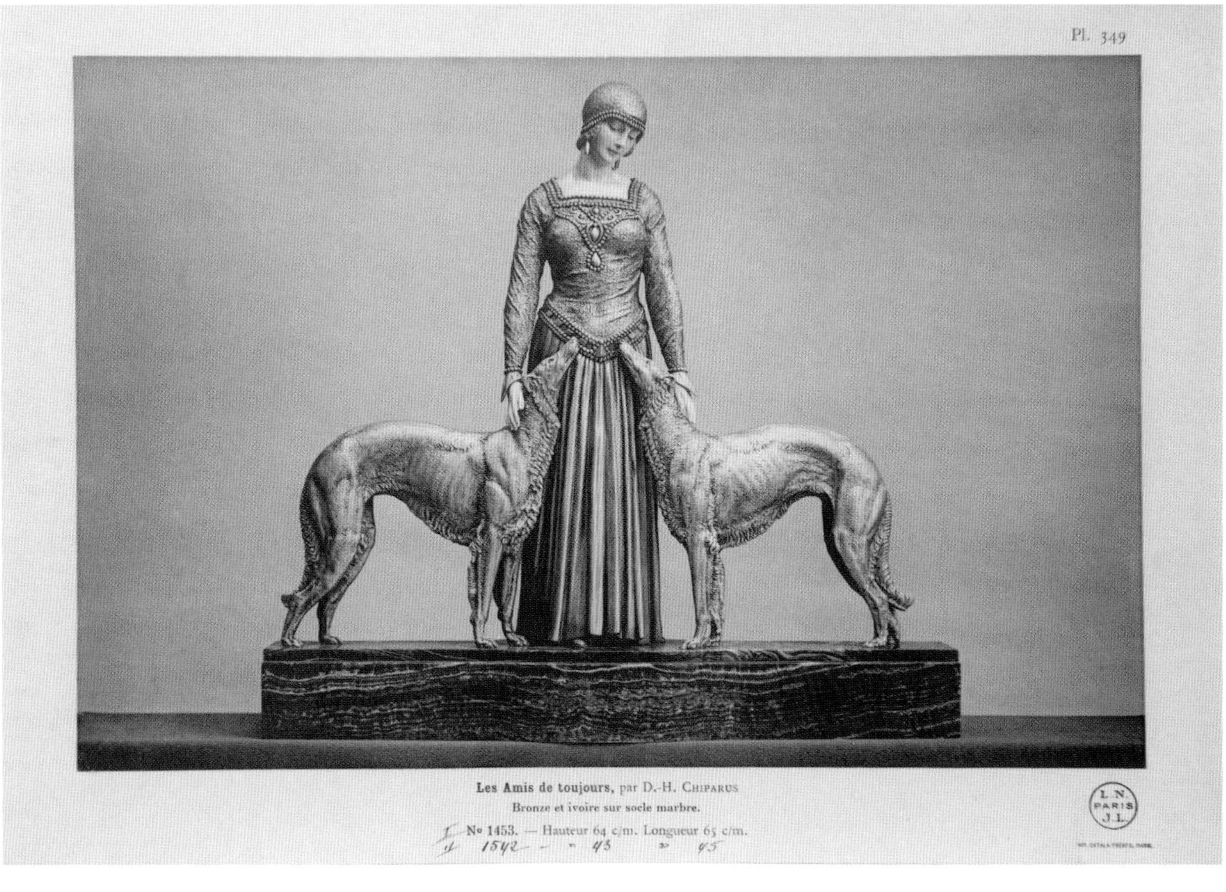

CHIPARUS –
Eternal Friends

Pl. 308

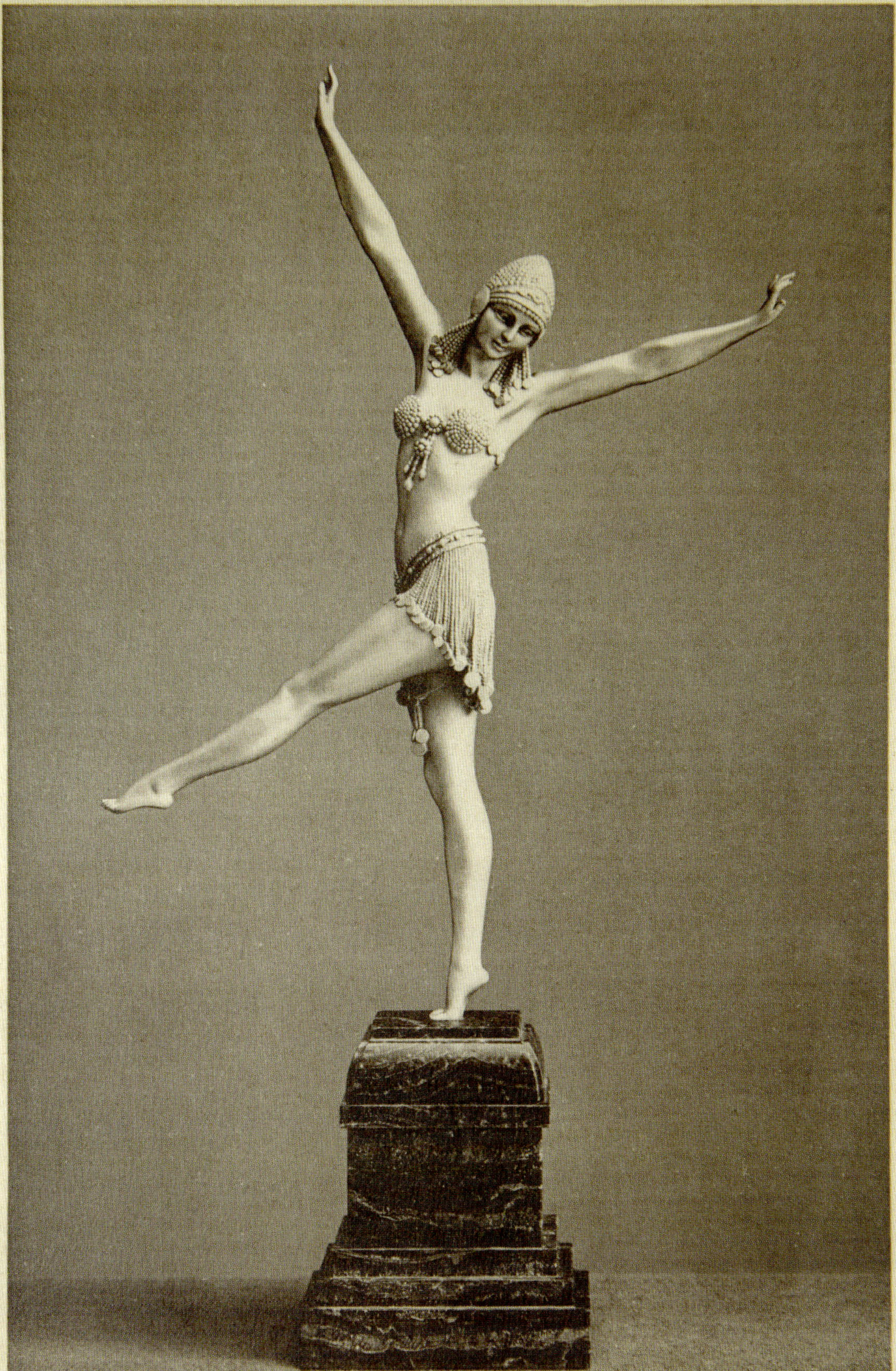

Danseuse de Palmyre, par CHIPARUS
Bronze sur socle marbre
I No **1377**. — Hauteur 67 c/m.
II 1395. — „ 44 c/m.
III 1593. — „ 33 c/m.

L.N. PARIS J.L.

IMP. CATALA FRÈRES, PARIS

CHIPARUS –
Dancer of Palmyra

Pl. 316

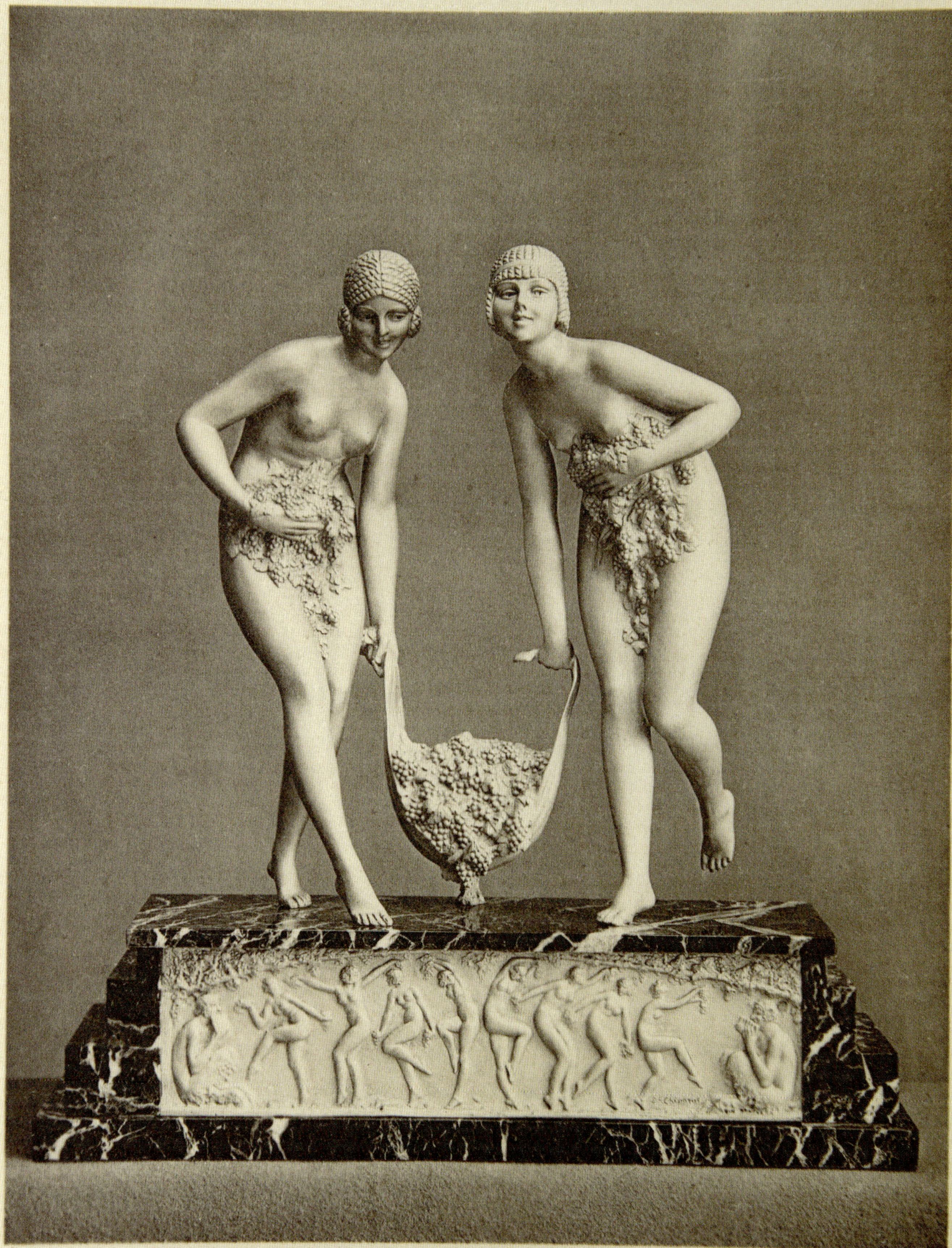

Vendanges juvéniles, par Chiparus

Bronze sur socle marbre avec applique bronze

N° 1318. — Hauteur 45 c/m - Largeur 42 c/m.

L.N.
PARIS
J.L.

CHIPARUS – Young Grape Harvesters

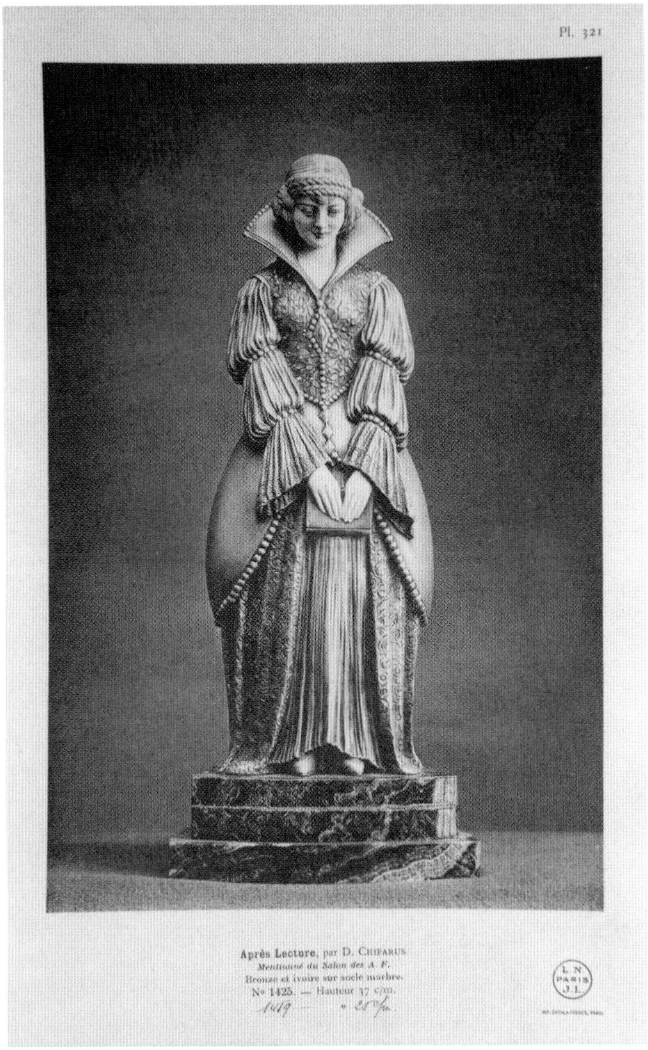

CHIPARUS – After Reading

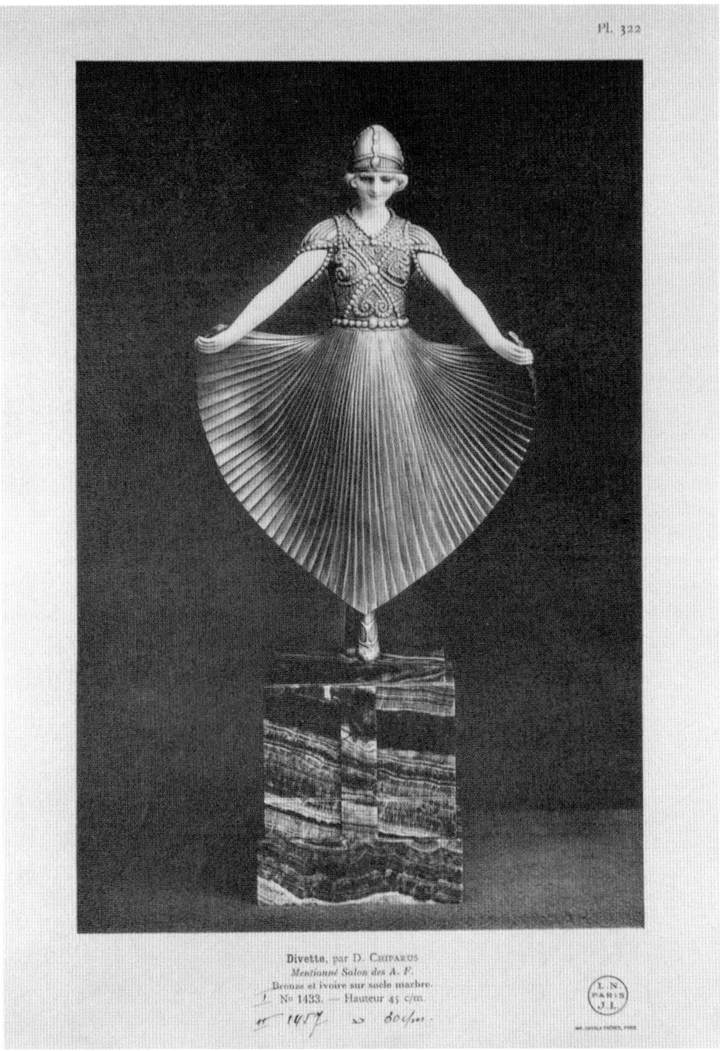

CHIPARUS – Actress

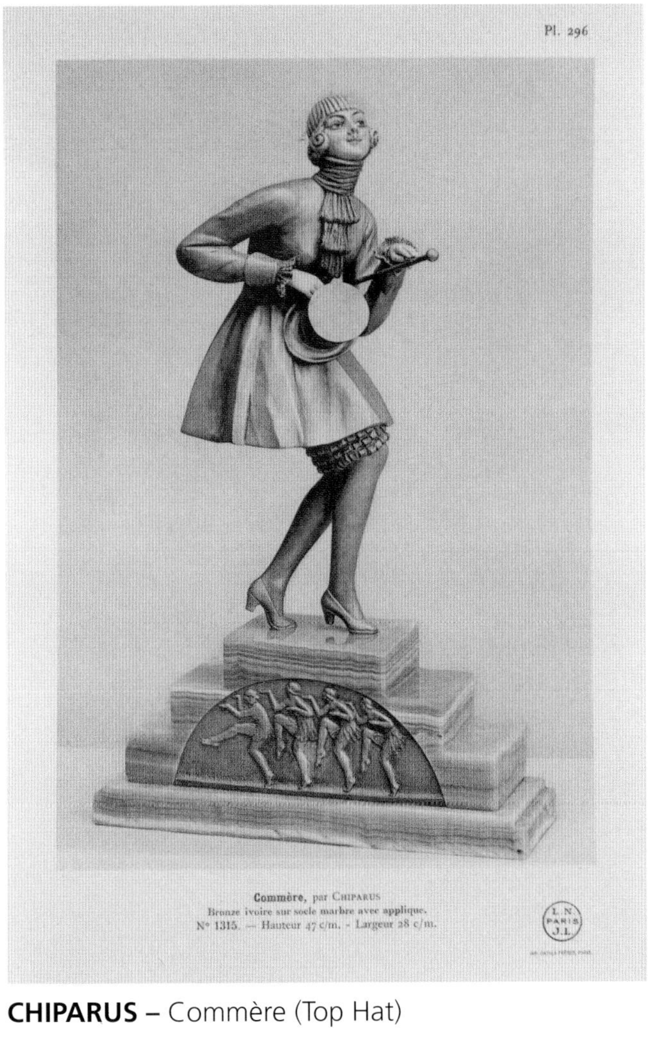

CHIPARUS – Commère (Top Hat)

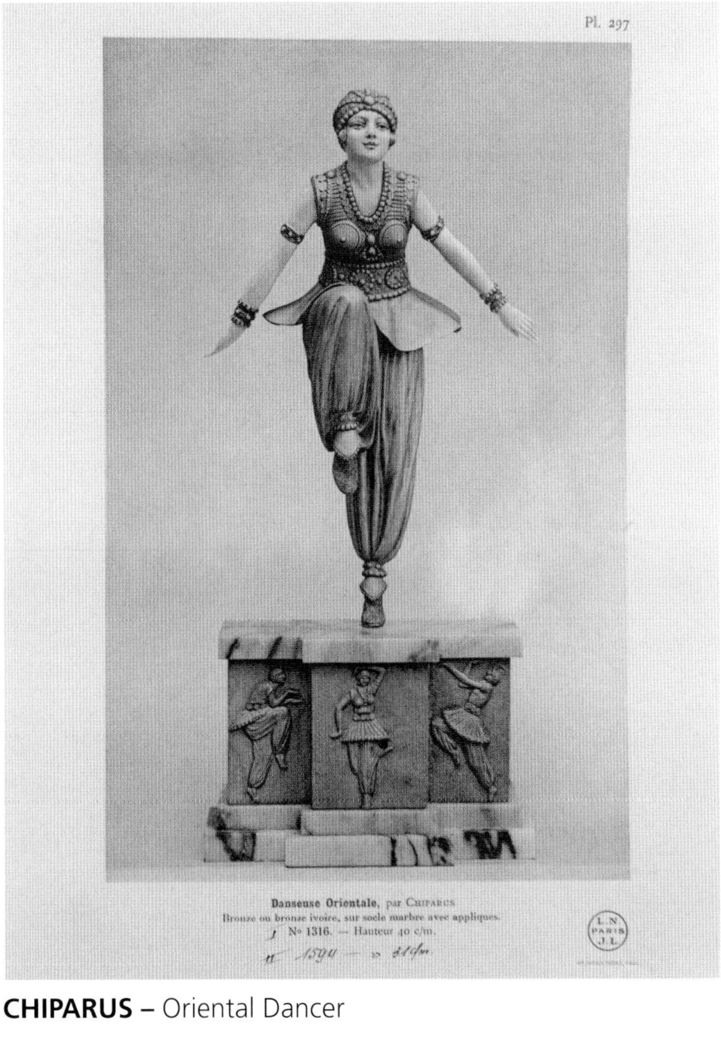

CHIPARUS – Oriental Dancer

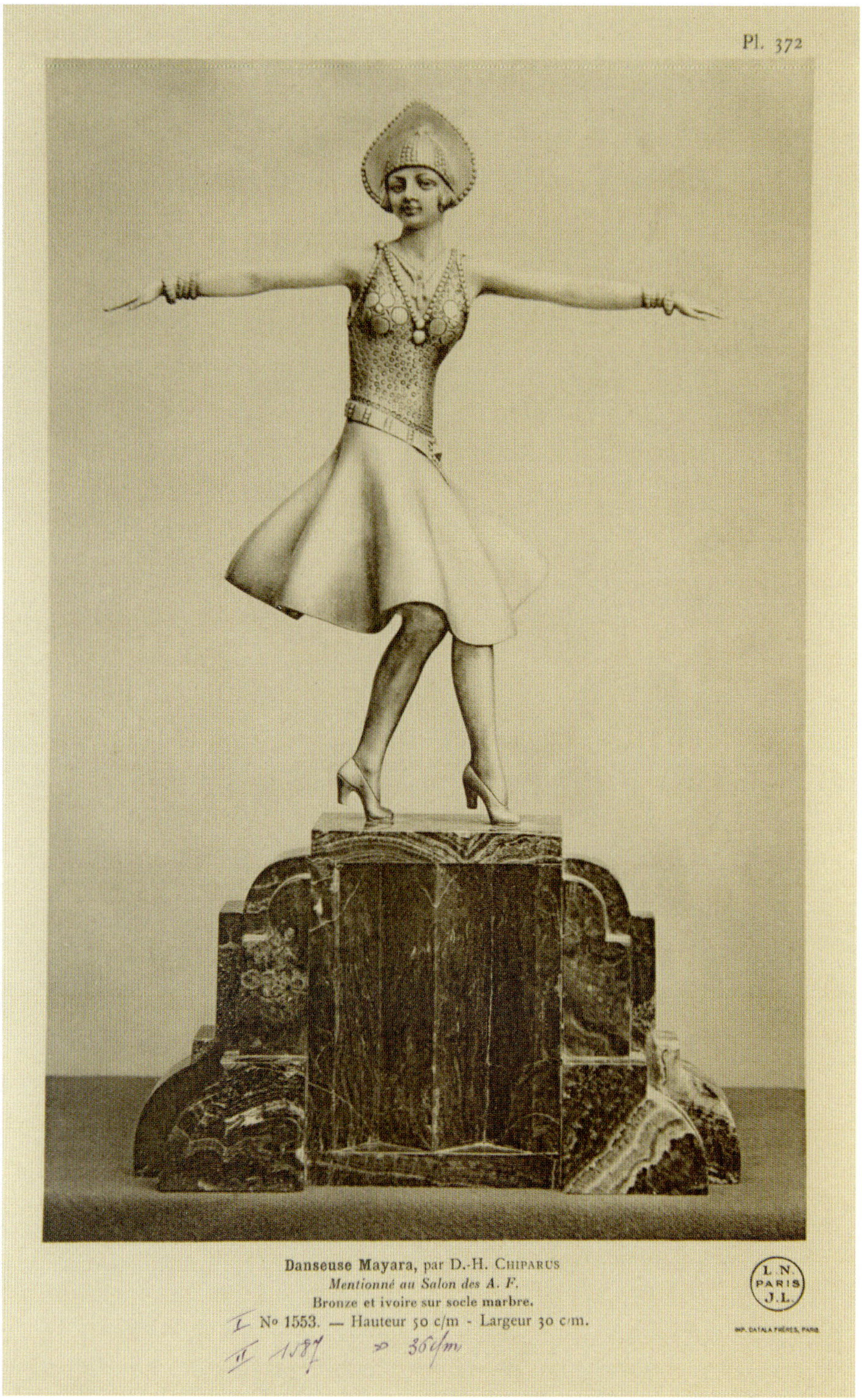

CHIPARUS – Hungarian Dancer

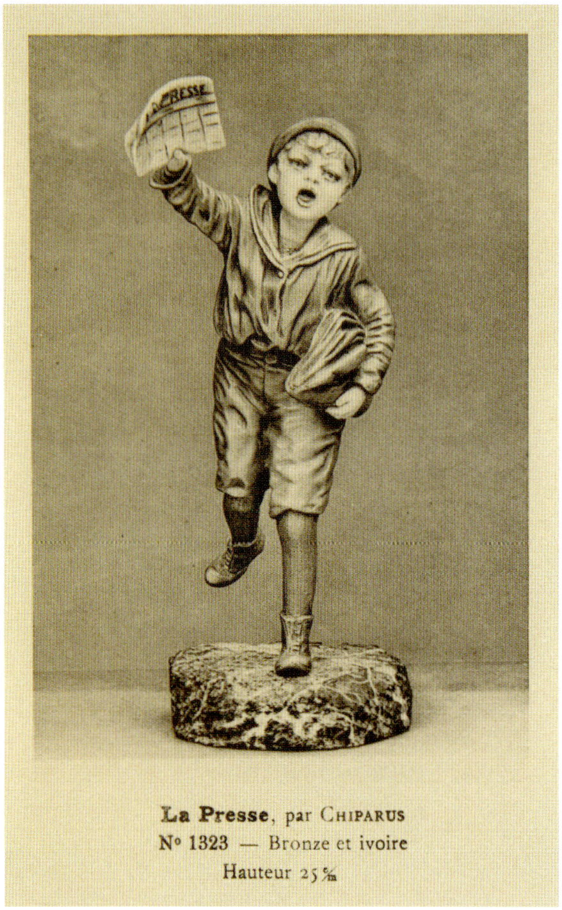

CHIPARUS – Press Boy

CHIPARUS – Indiscreet

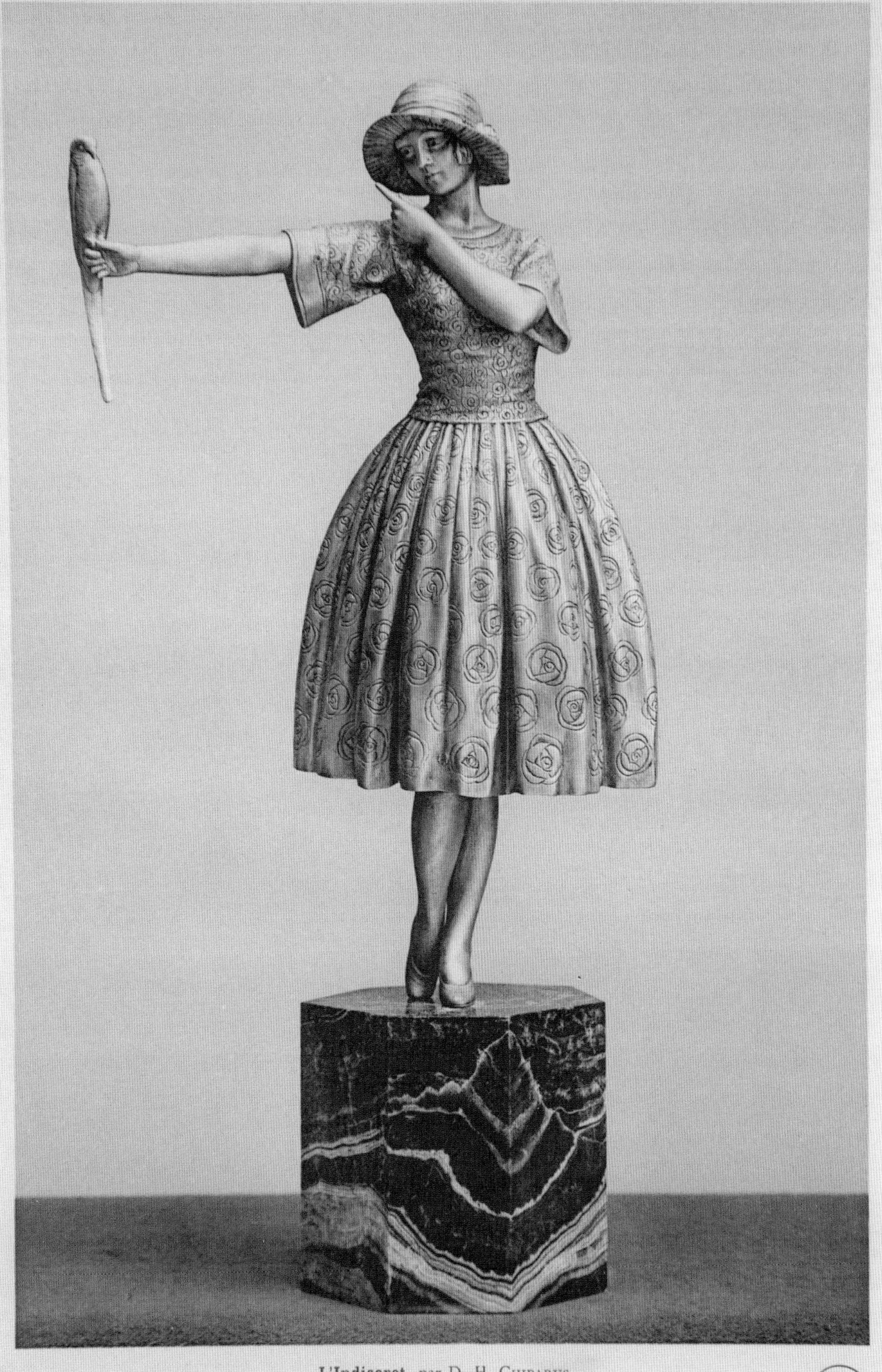

L'Indiscret, par D.-H. Chiparus
Mentionné, Salon des A. F.
Bronze et ivoire sur socle marbre.
I N° **1464.** — Hauteur 45 c/m.
II 1597 " 30 c/m.

L. N. PARIS J. L.

IMP. CATALA FRÈRES, PARIS

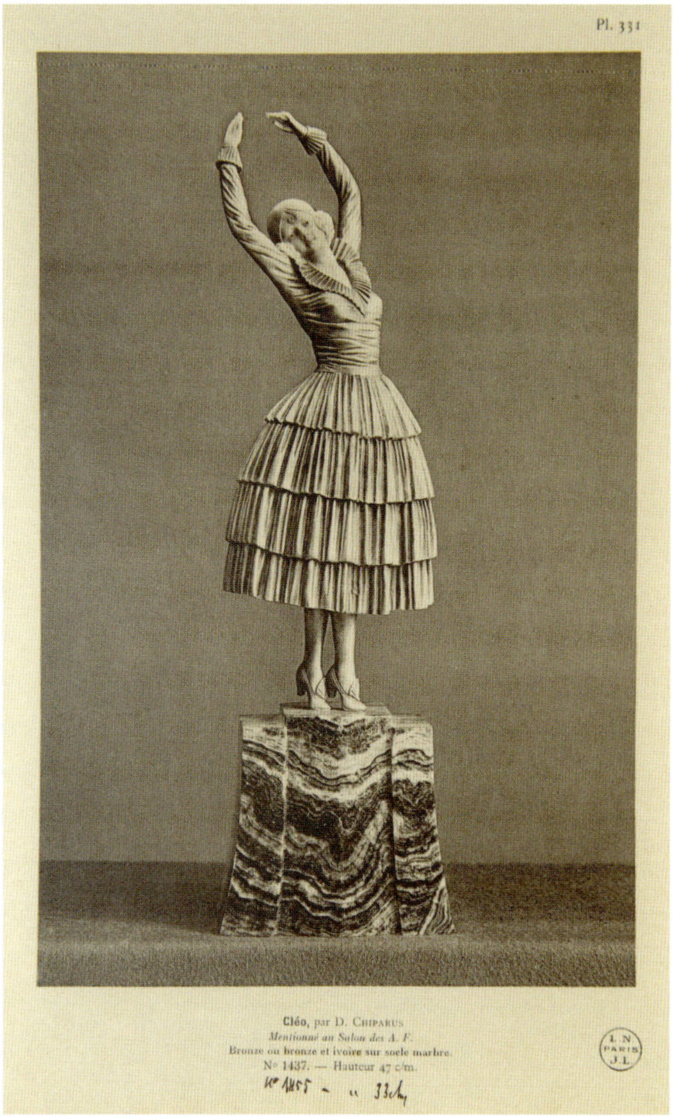

CHIPARUS – Cléo (Ballet Dancer)

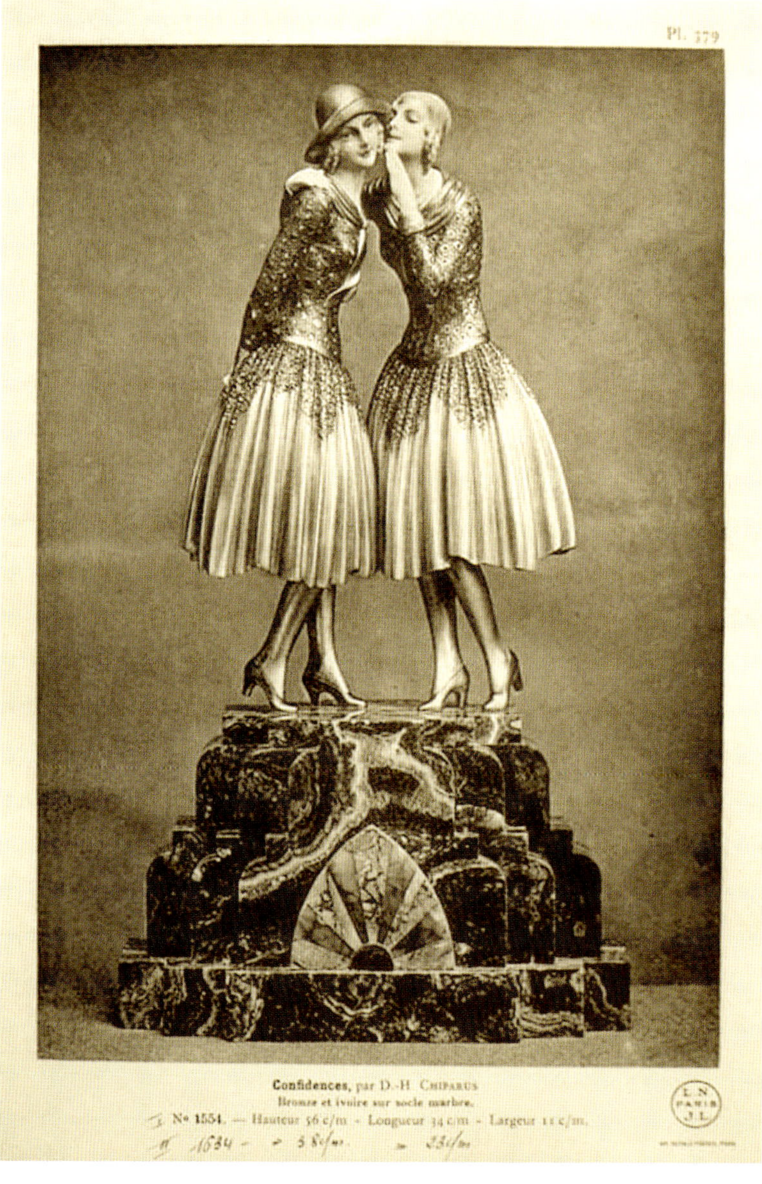

CHIPARUS – The Secret

Pl. 357

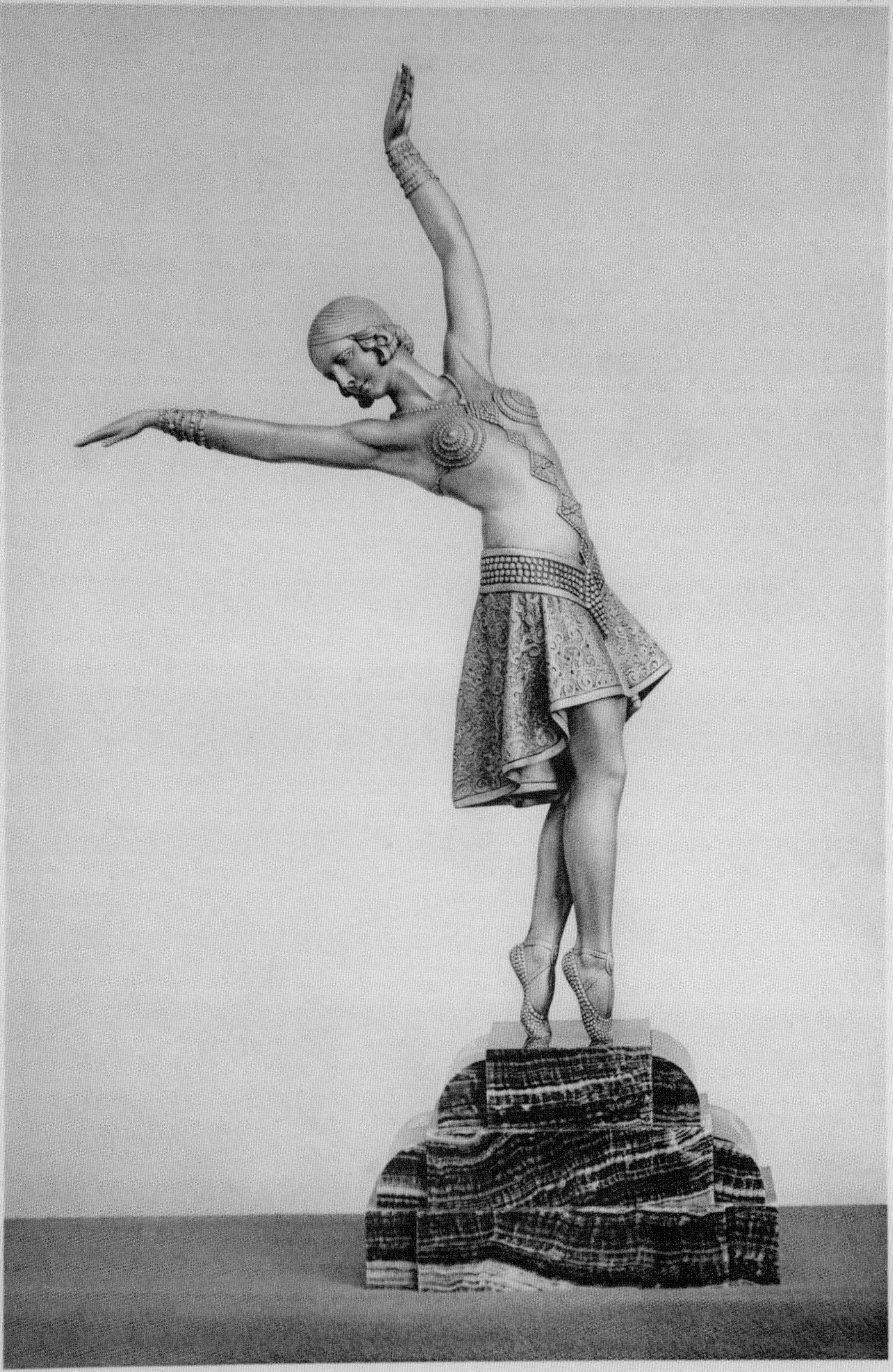

Vedette, par D.-H. Chiparus
Mentionné, Salon des A. F.
Bronze sur socle marbre.
N° 1487. — Hauteur 80 c/m.
1576 – „ 54 c/m.
1586 – „ 37 c/m.

L.N. PARIS J.L.

IMP. CATALA FRÈRES, PARIS.

CHIPARUS – Vedette

Pl. 363

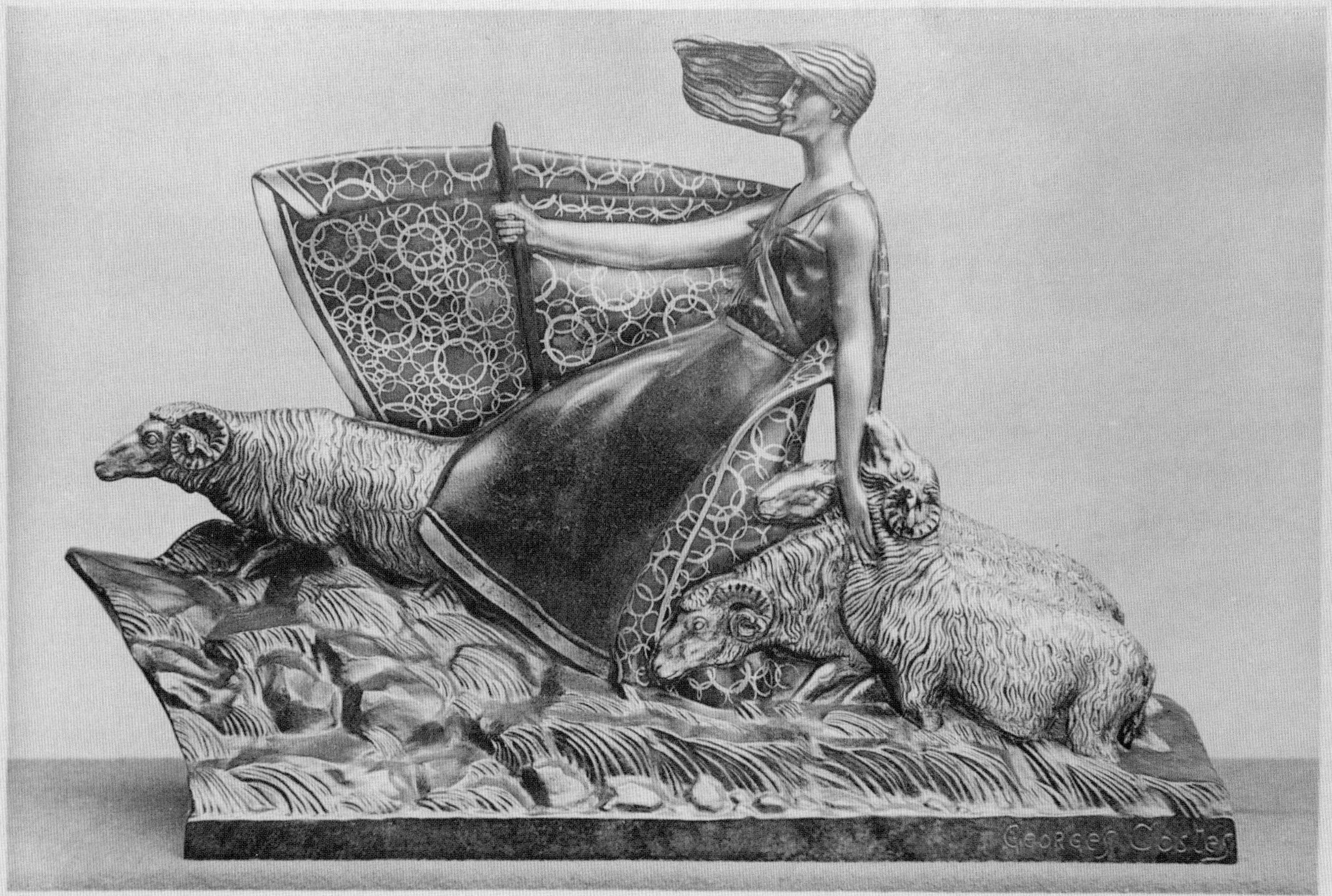

Vers la Montagne, par Georges Costes
Bronze gravé.
N° 1533. — Hauteur 35 c/m - Longueur 50 c/m - Largeur 12 c/m.

L.N. PARIS J.L.

IMP. CATALA FRÈRES, PARIS

COSTES – Towards the Mountain

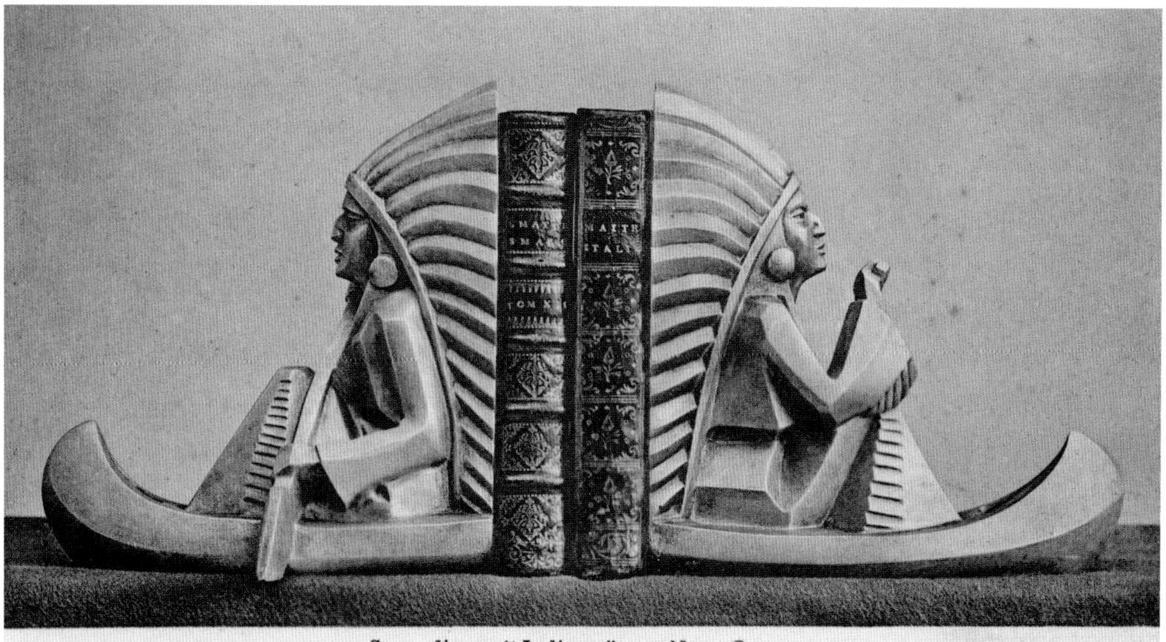

Serre-livres " Indiens ", par Noël Coulon
Bronze doré et argenté.
N° 1489. — Hauteur 19 c/m.

COULON – Indians (bookends)

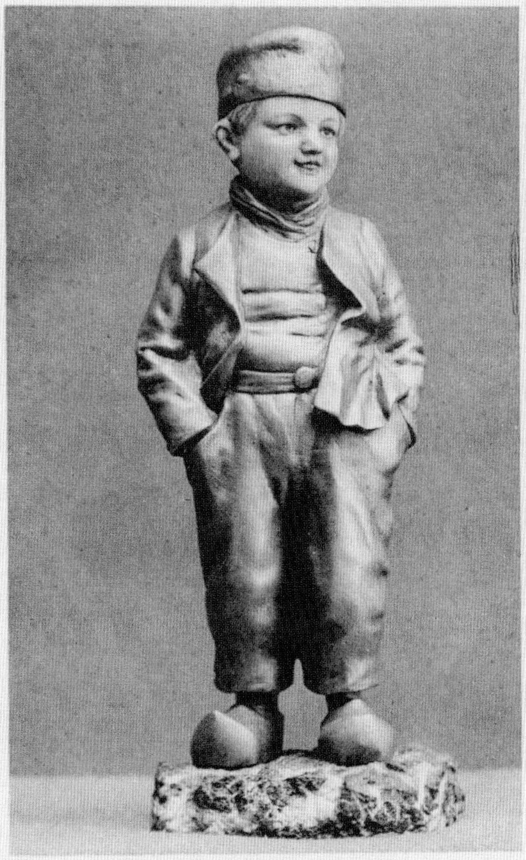

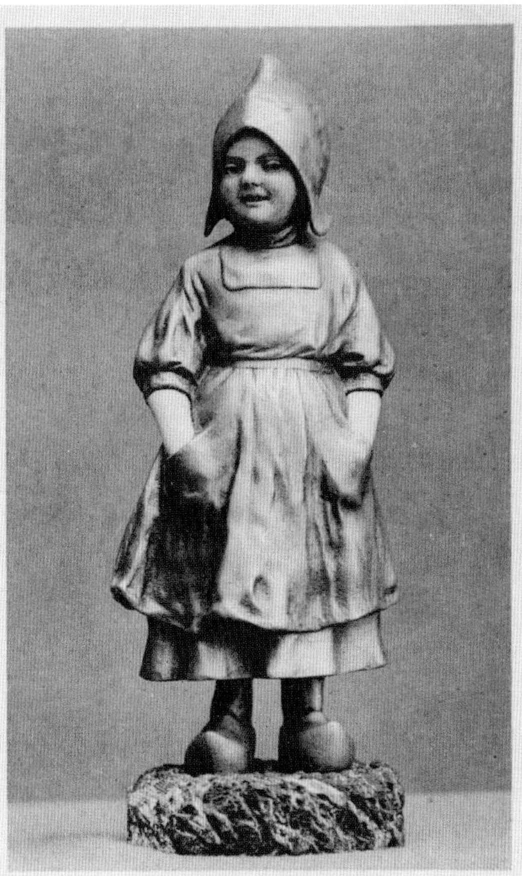

Jeune hollandais
par D'ASTE
Nº 966 — Hauteur 24 c/m.

Jeune hollandaise
par D'ASTE
Nº 967 — Hauteur 24 c/m.

D'ASTE – Dutch Boy – Dutch Girl

D'ASTE – See-Saw

Pl. 191

Balançoire, par D'ASTE
I Nº 949 — Hauteur 31 c/m., largeur 50 c/m.
II 1370 » 20 c/m » 33 c/m.

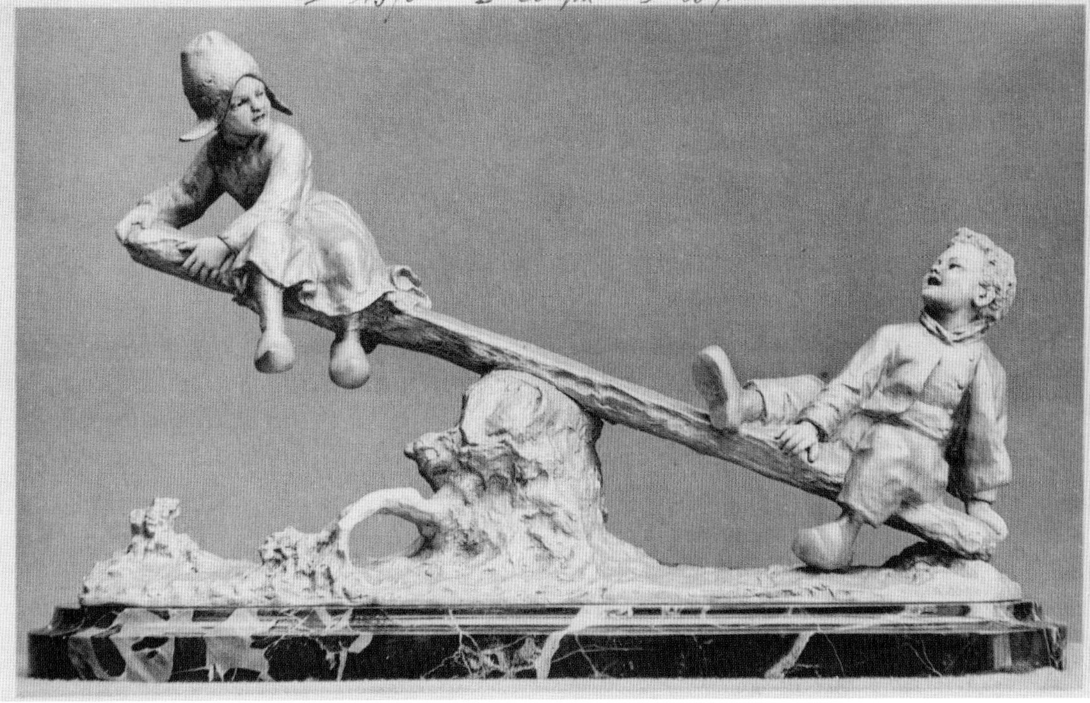

Pl. 287

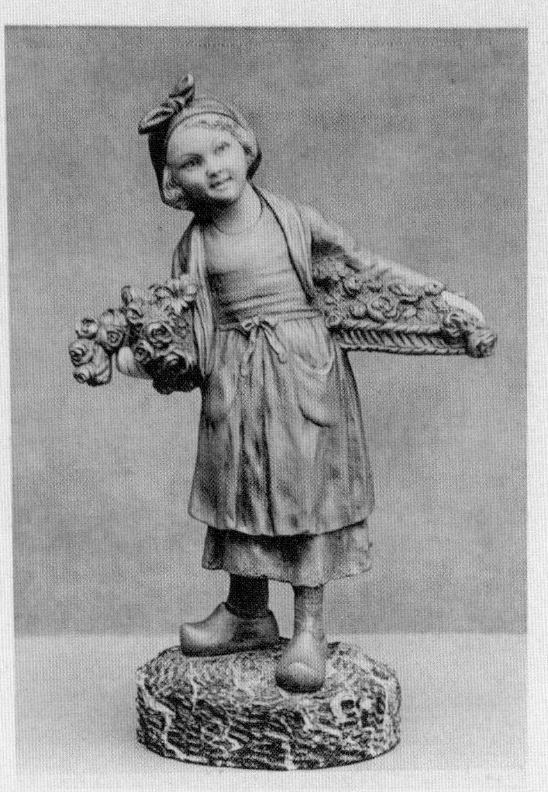

Petite fleuriste, par J. d'Aste
N° 1305 — Bronze et ivoire Hauteur 25 %

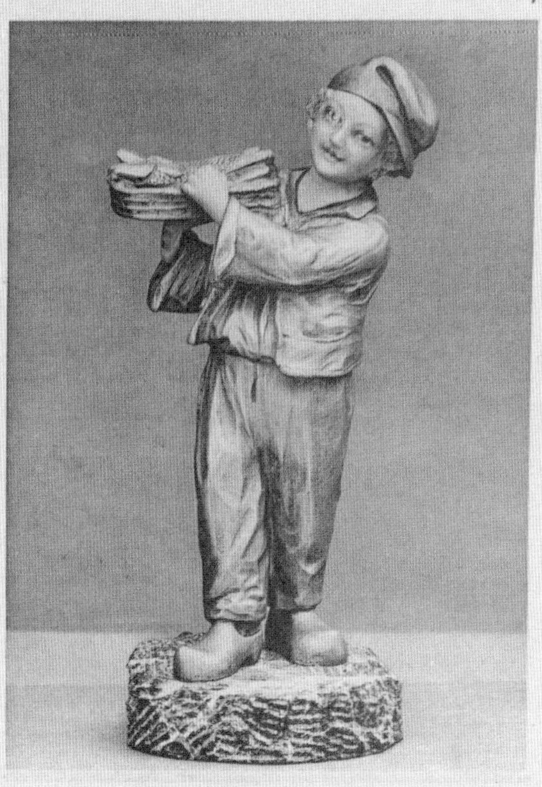

Petit pécheur, par J. d'Aste
N° 1304 — Bronze et ivoire Hauteur 23 %

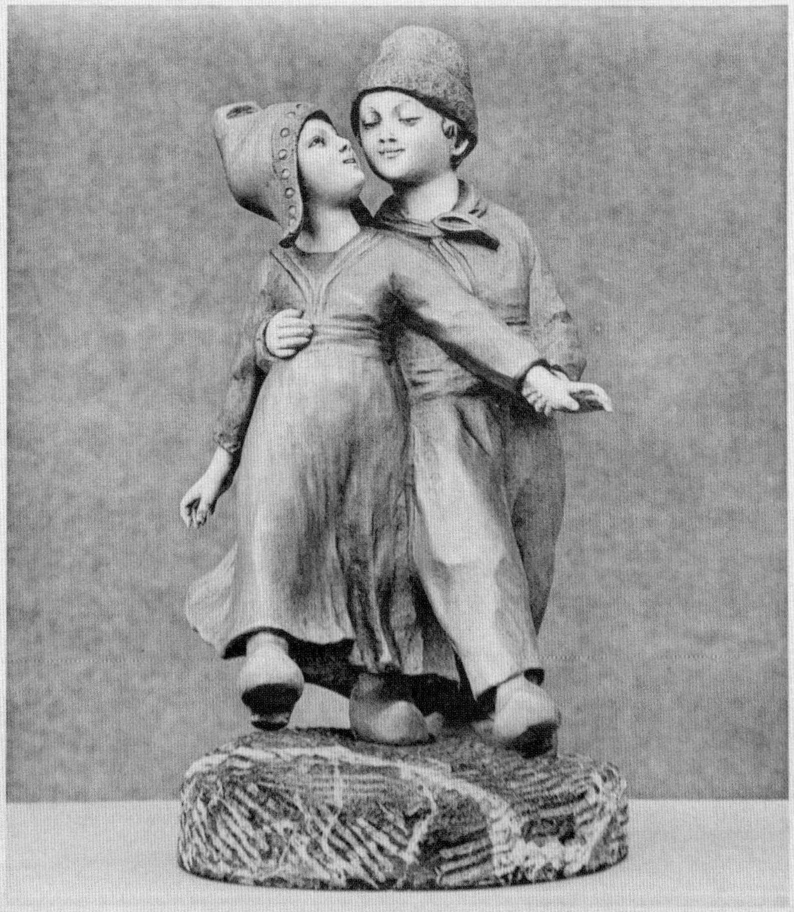

Danse enfantine, par J. d'Aste
N° 1319 — Bronze et ivoire Hauteur 24 %

L. N.
PARIS
J. L.

G. Bottan - imp. Paris

D'ASTE – Little Flower Seller

D'ASTE – Little Fisherman

D'ASTE – Childish Dance

D'ASTE – Young Girl with Hoop

Pl. 290

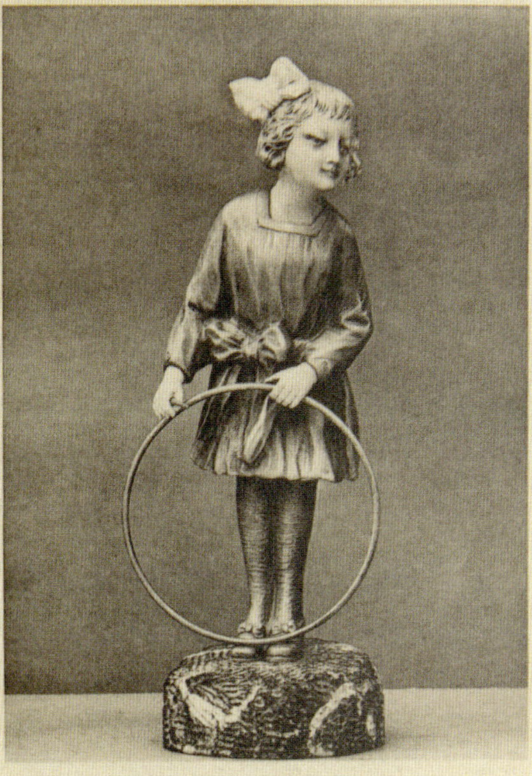

Fillette au cerceau, par J. d'ASTE
N° 1311 — Bronze et ivoire
Hauteur 22 c/m

D'ASTE – Dutch Dance

Pl. 289

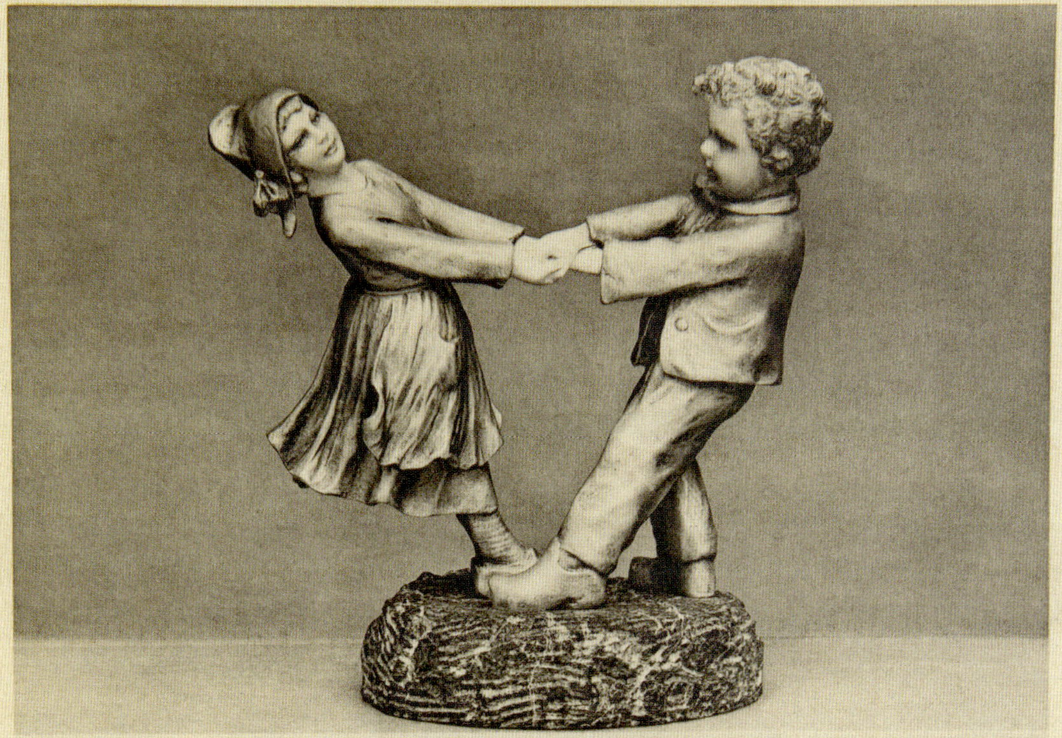

Tourbillon Hollandais, par J. d'ASTE
N° 1309 — Bronze et ivoire
Hauteur 20 c/m - Largeur 22 c/m

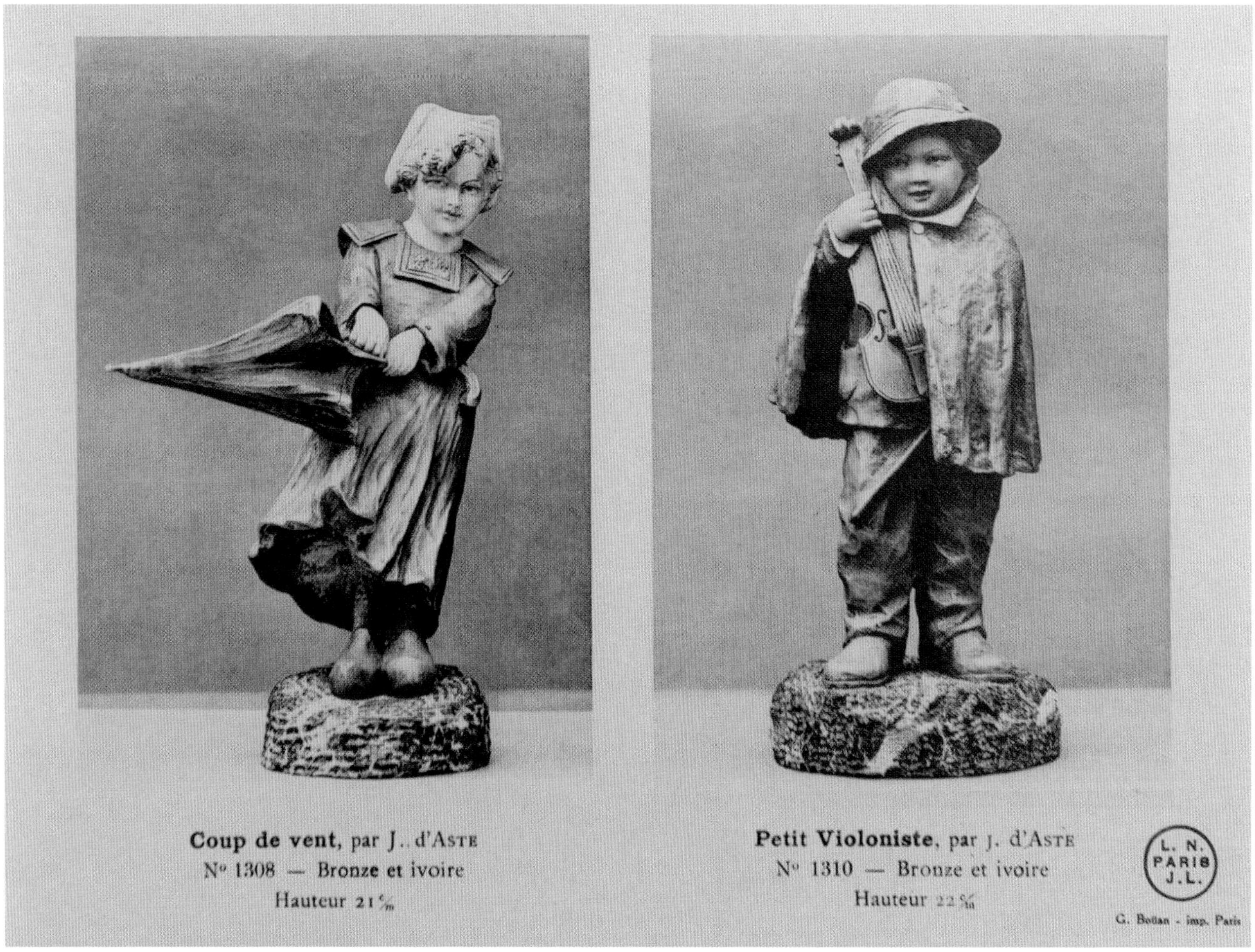

D'ASTE – Gust of Wind – Little Violinist

D'ASTE – At the Spring – Promises

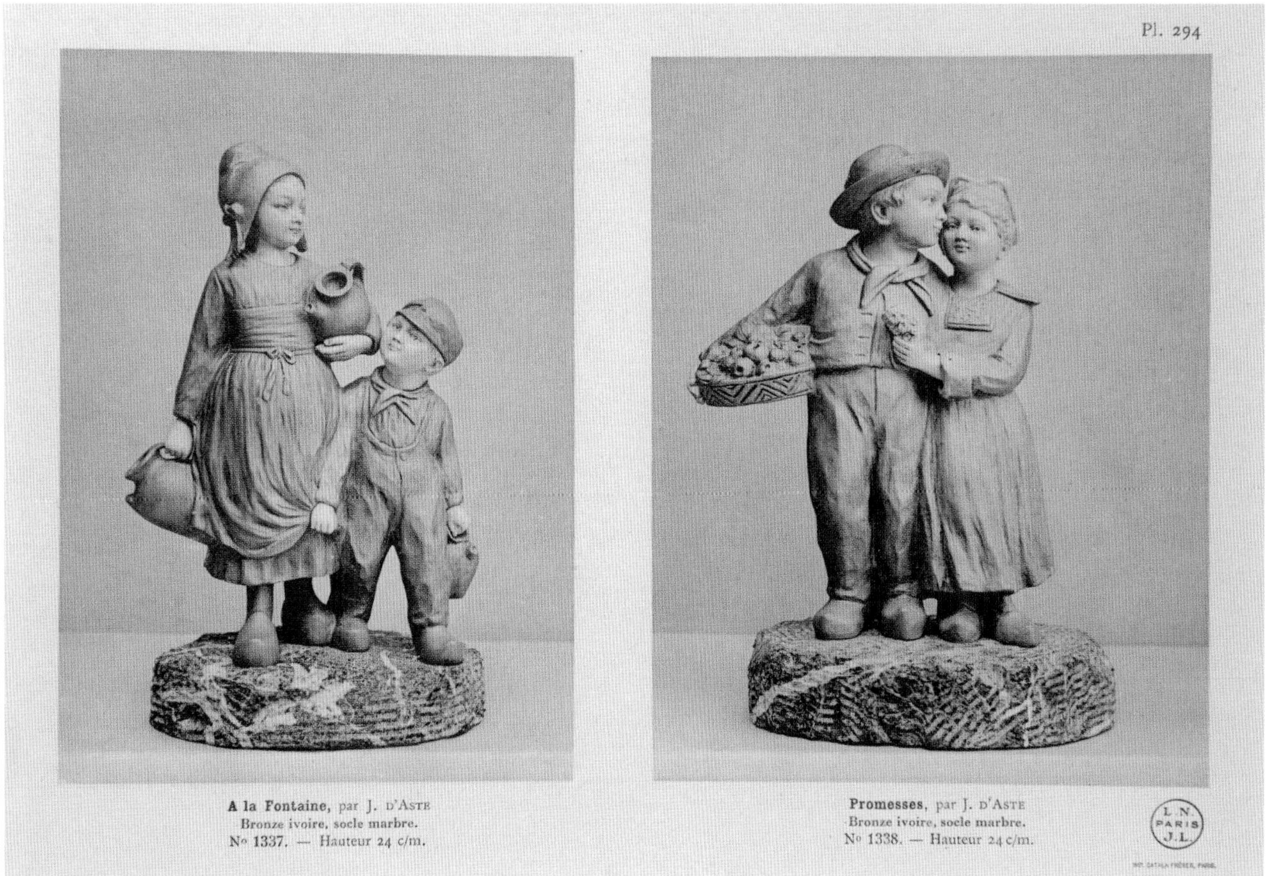

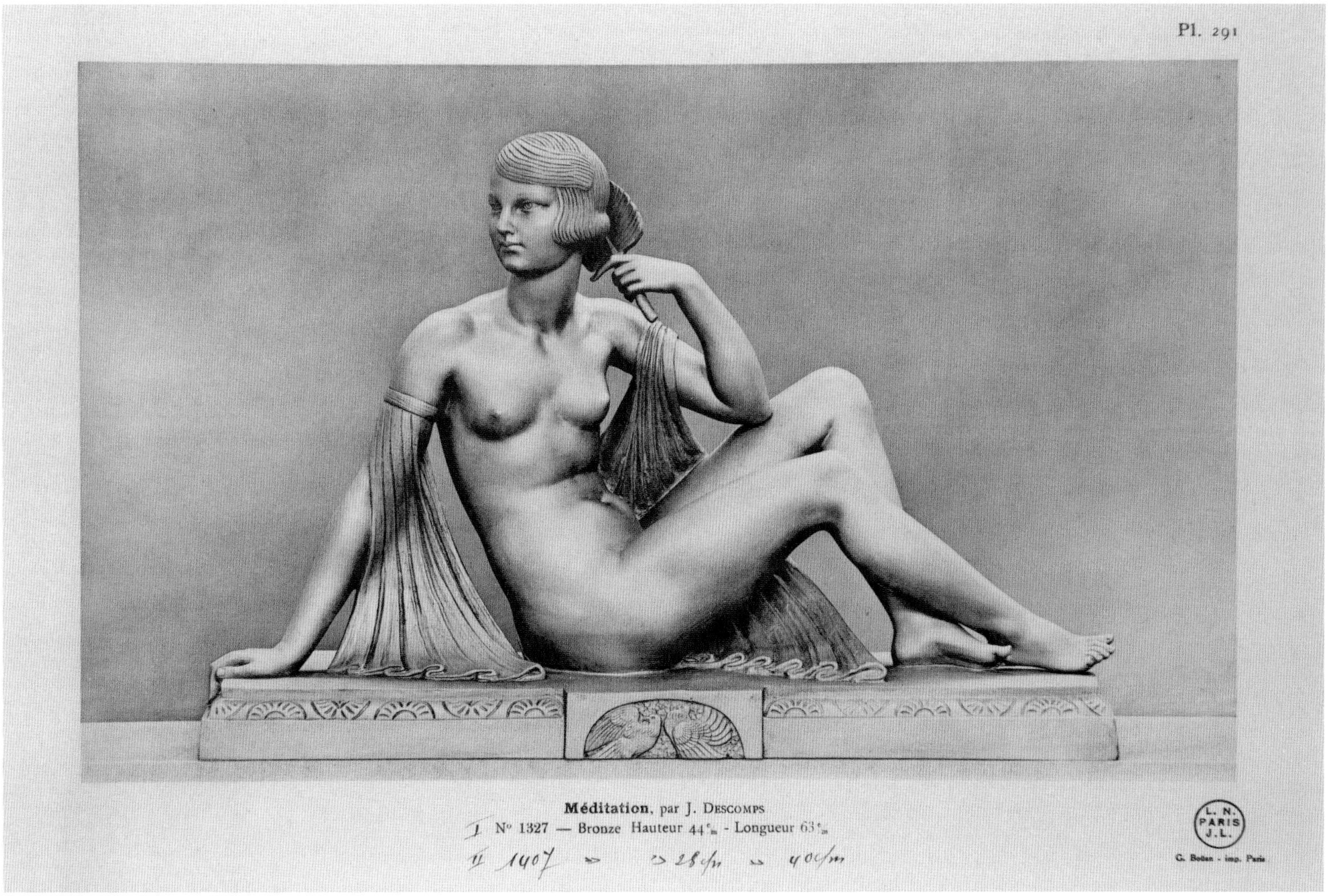

DESCOMPS – Meditation

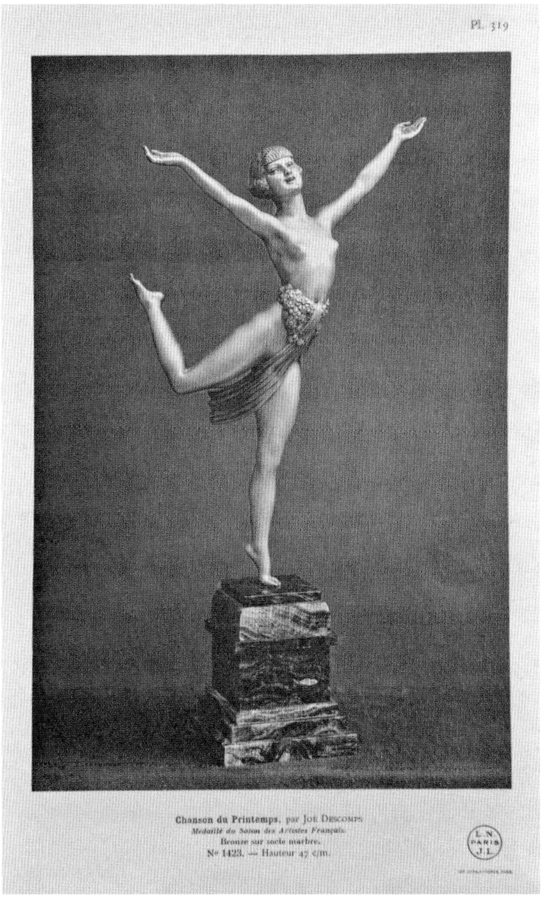

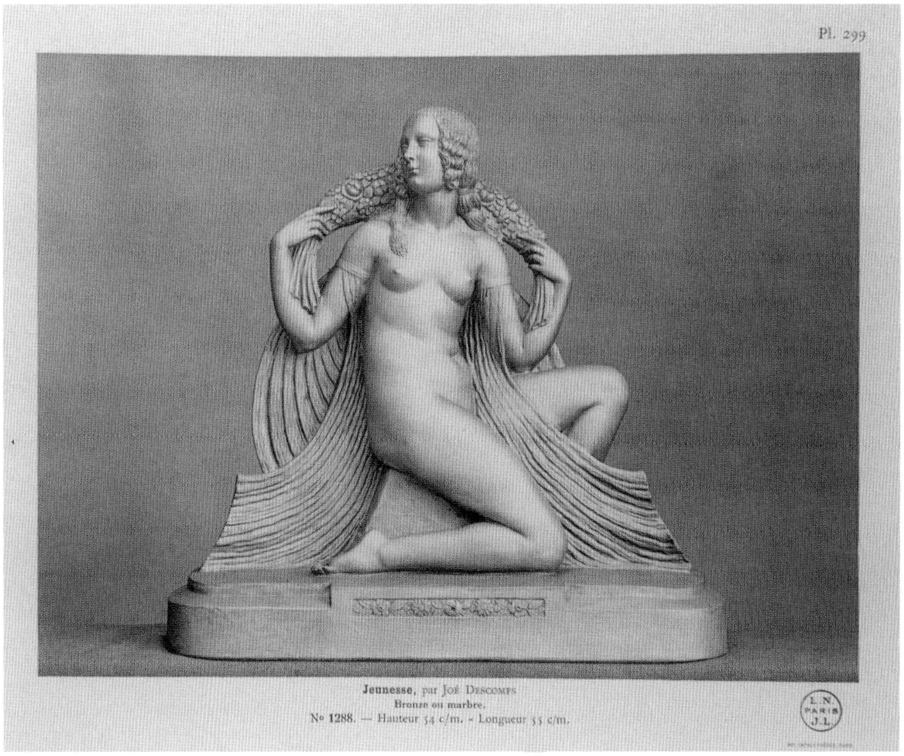

DESCOMPS – Youth

DESCOMPS – Spring Song

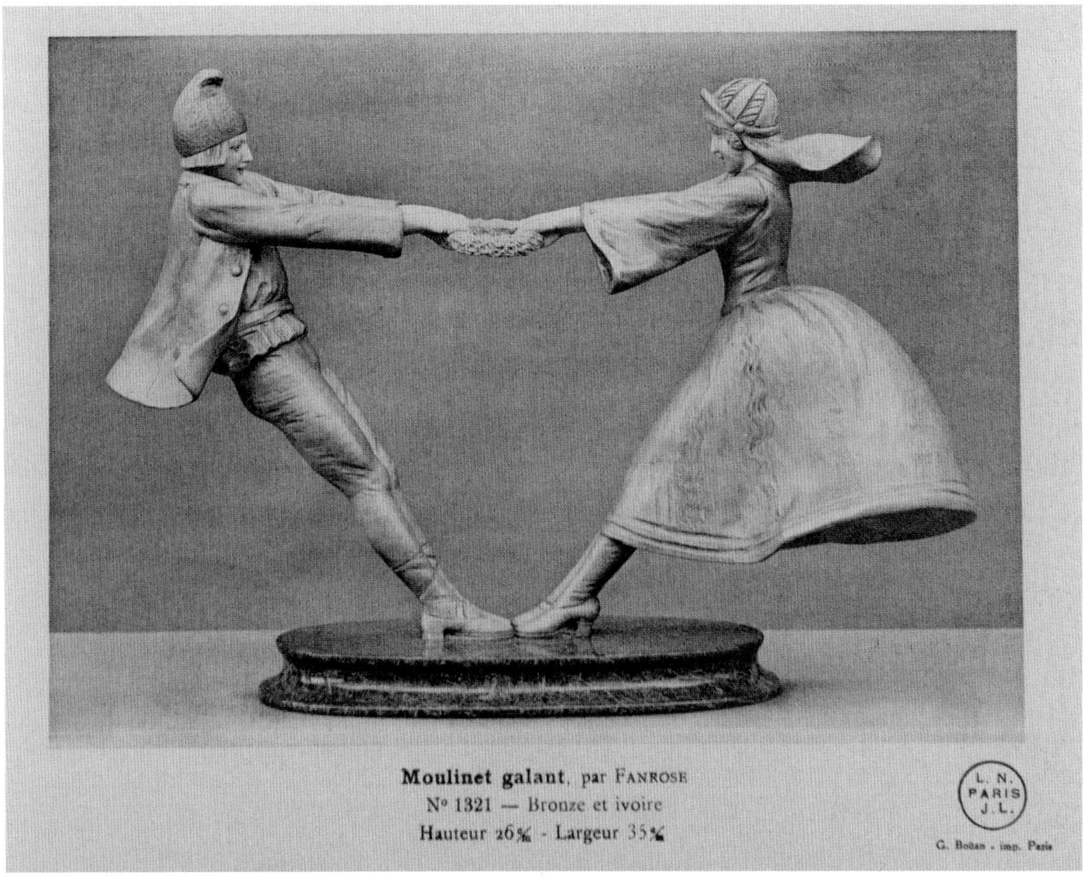

FANROSE – Amorous Twirl (Garland Dance)

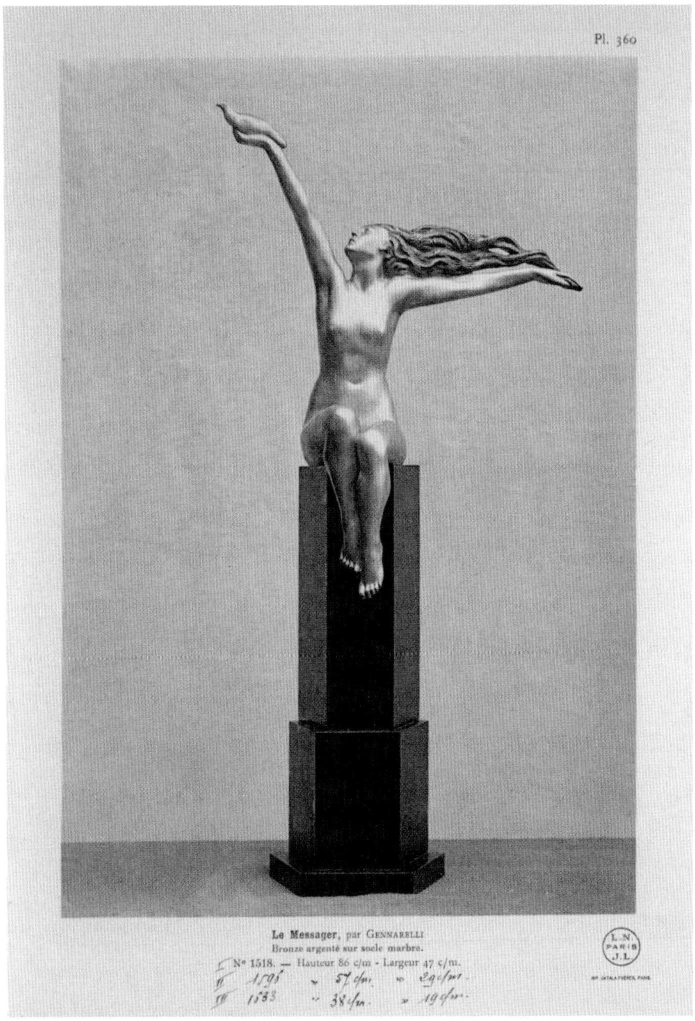

GENARELLI – Messenger

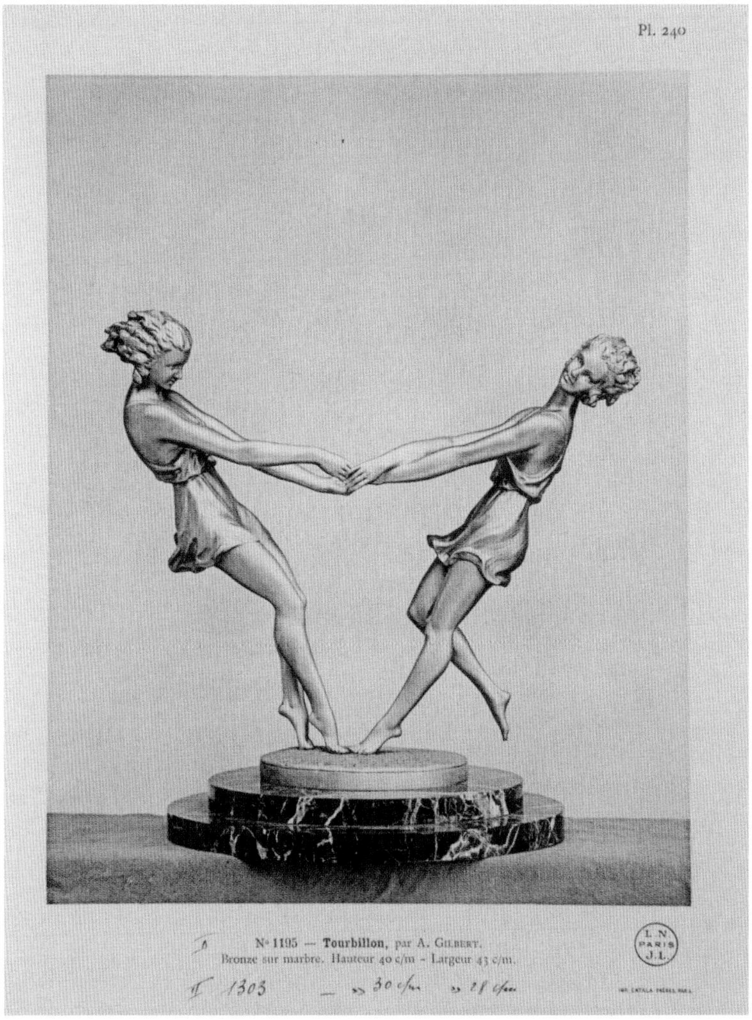

GILBERT – Whirling

Pl. 286

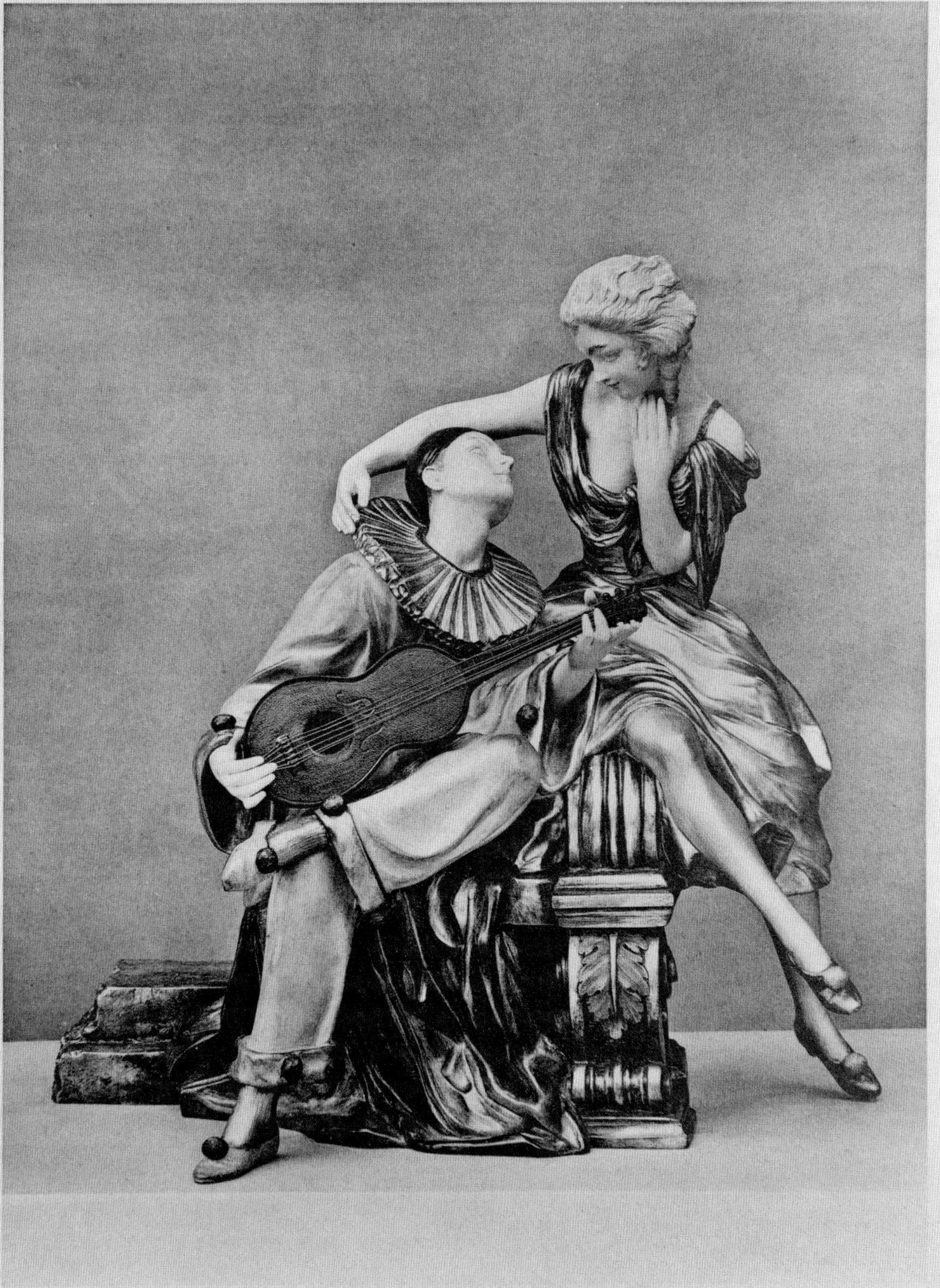

Romance, par A. GILBERT
N° 1254 — Bronze et ivoire
Hauteur 39 %m - Largeur 38 %m

L. N. PARIS J.L.

G. Boüan - imp. Paris

GILBERT – Romance

Pl. 265

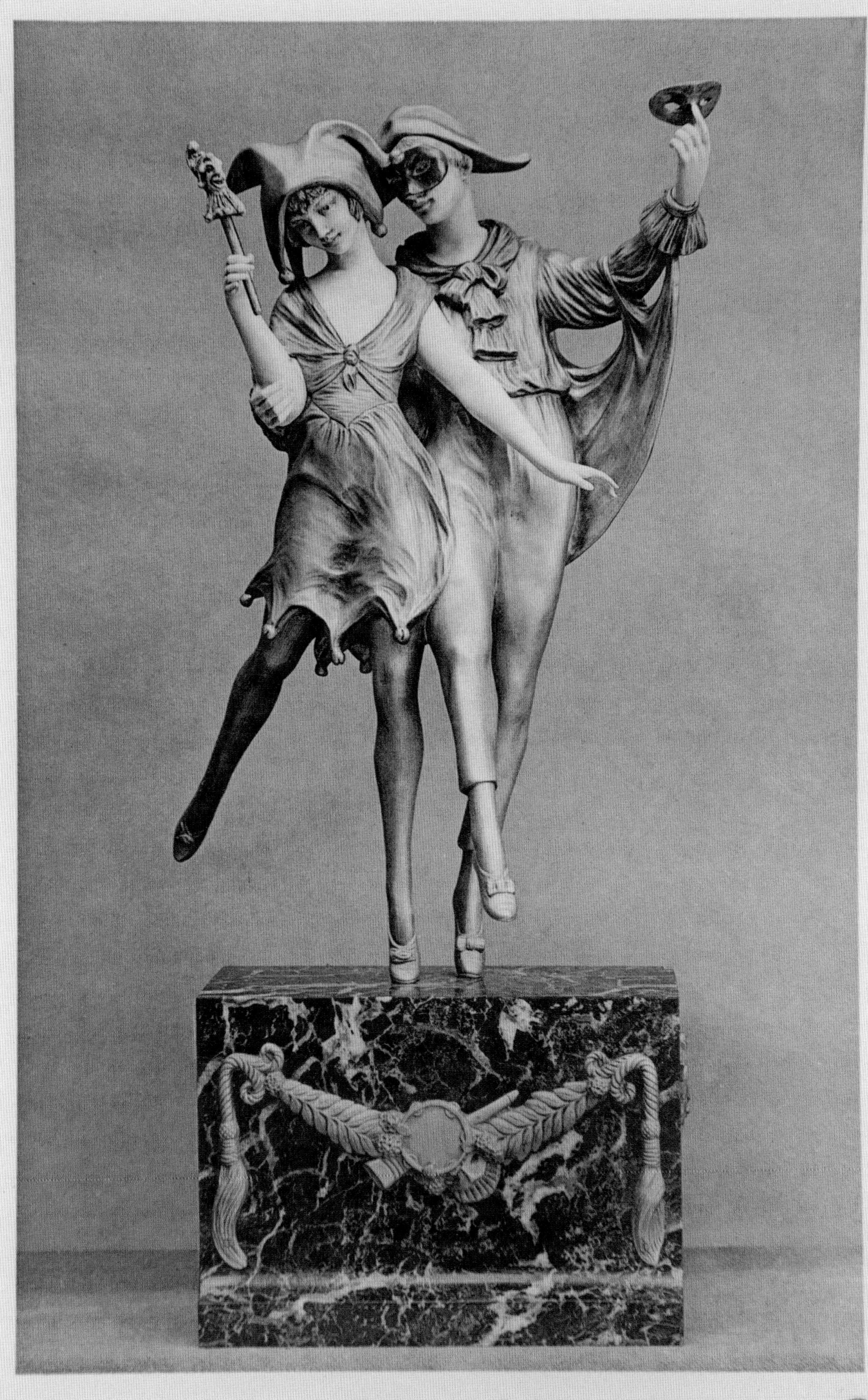

Séduction, par A. Gilbert
N° **1243** - Bronze et ivoire sur socle marbre avec appliques
Hauteur 56 c/m - Largeur 22 c/m

L.N.
PARIS
J.L.

IMP. CATALA FRÈRES, PARIS

GILBERT – Seduction

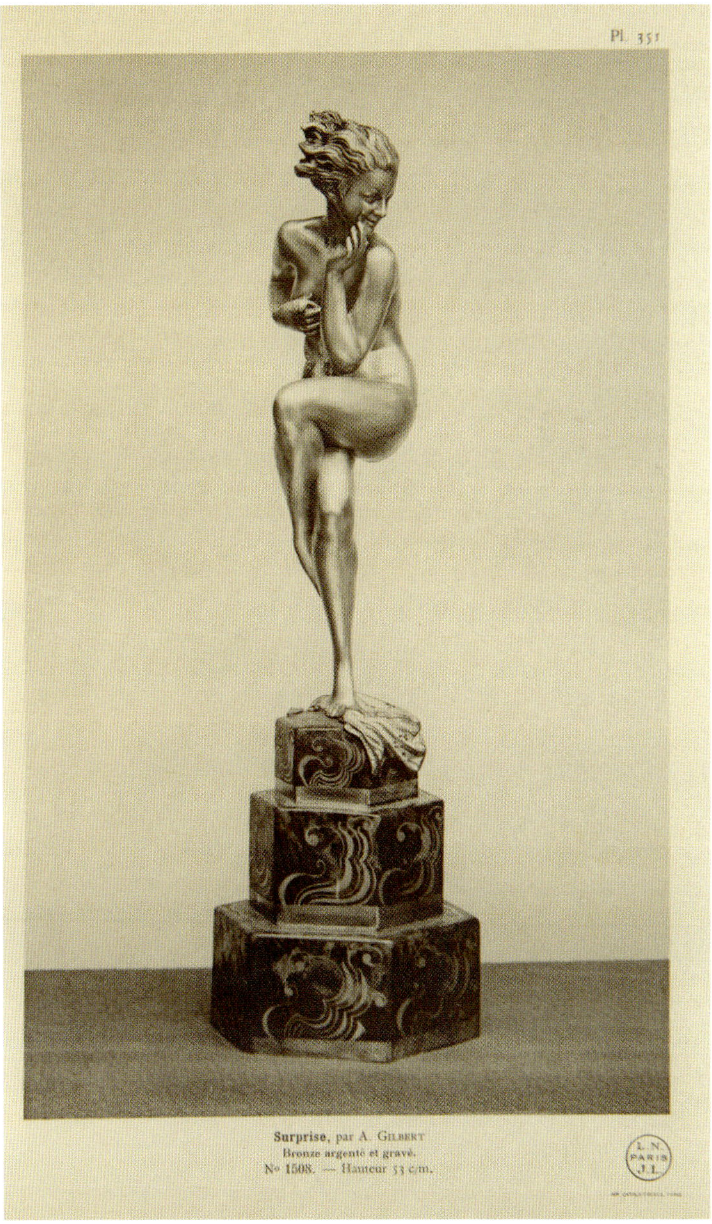

GILBERT – Surprise

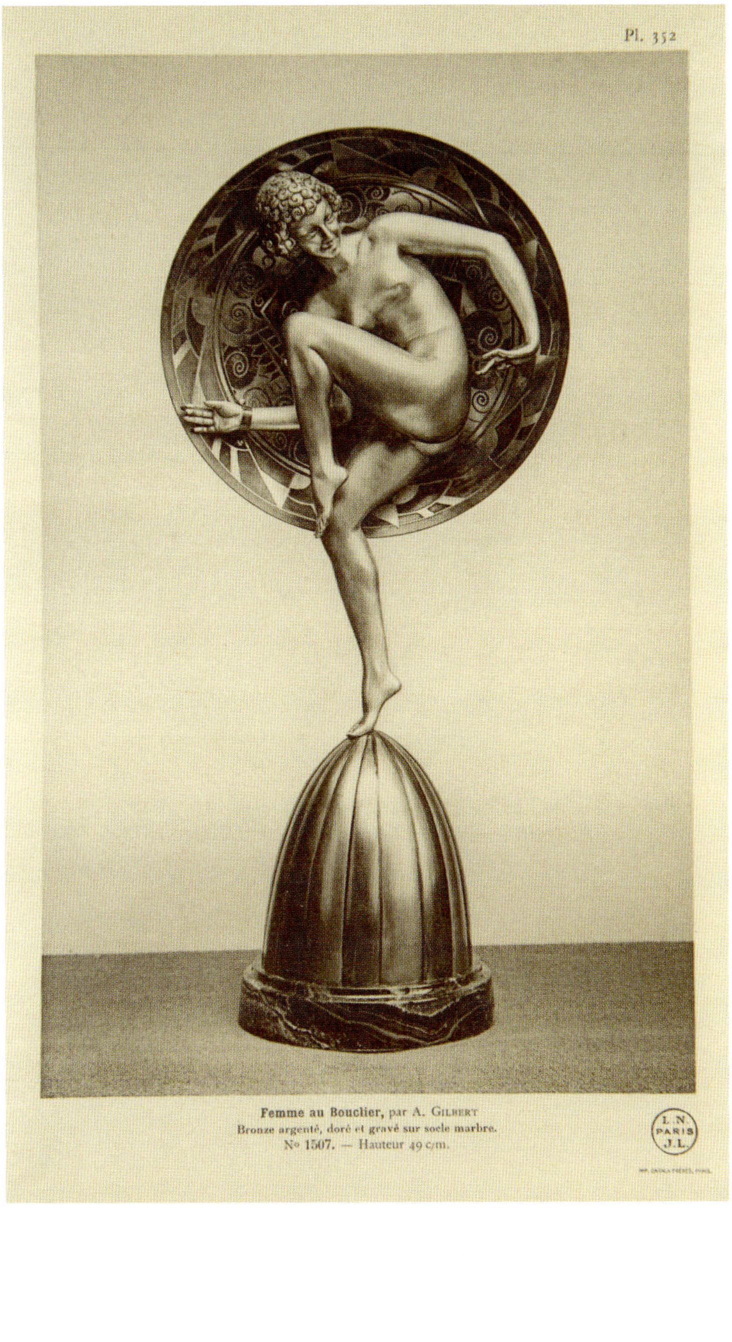

GILBERT – Woman in Shield

Pl. 255

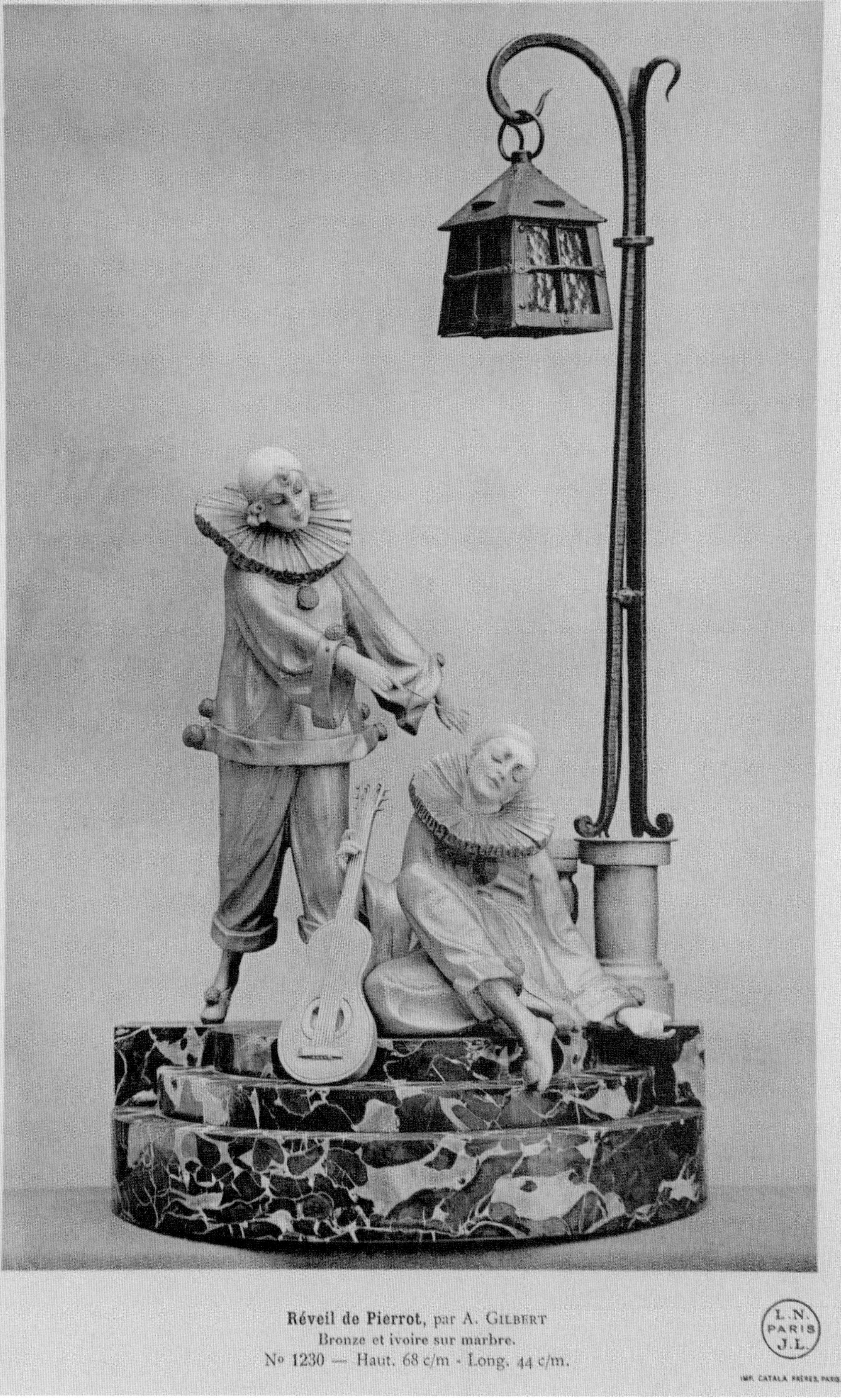

Réveil de Pierrot, par A. Gilbert
Bronze et ivoire sur marbre.
N° 1230 — Haut. 68 c/m - Long. 44 c/m.

L.N. PARIS J.L.

IMP. CATALA FRÈRES, PARIS

GILBERT – Pierrot's Awakening

Pl. 347

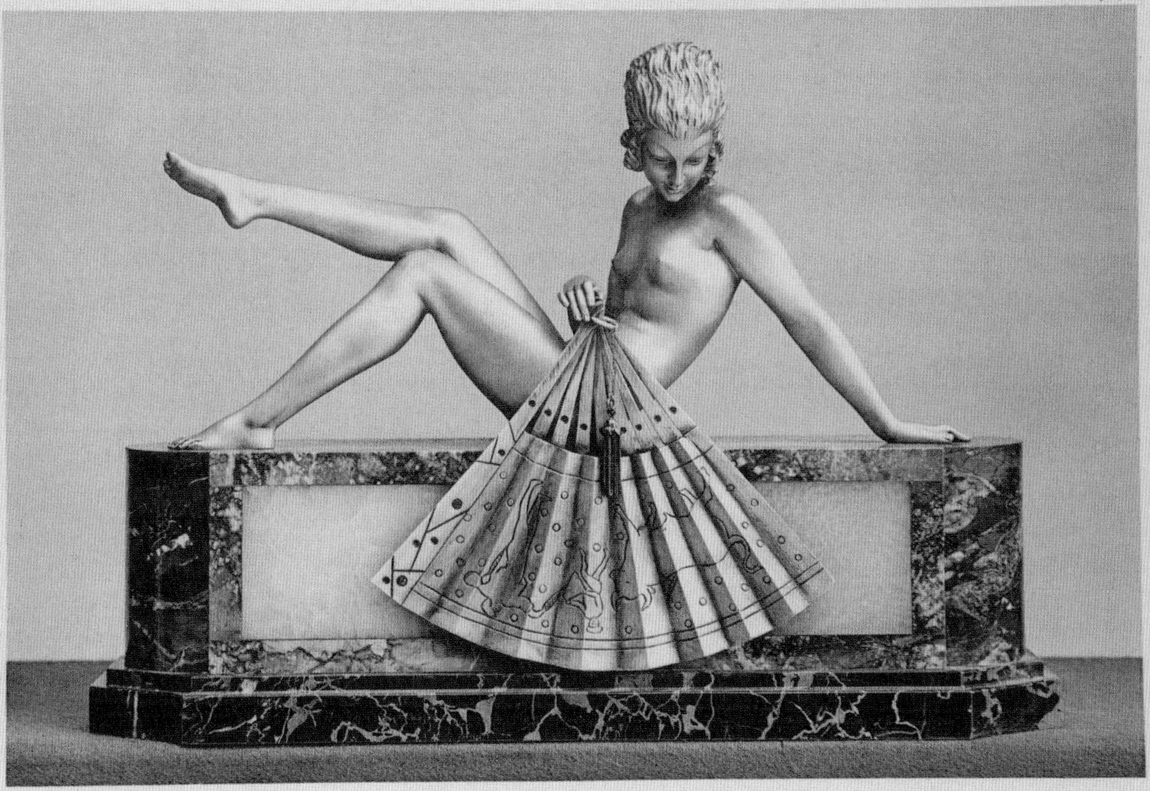

Femme à l'Éventail, par GILBERT
Bronze sur socle lumineux.
N° 1463. — Hauteur 32 c/m. Longueur 42 c/m.

L.N. PARIS J.L.

GILBERT – Maiden with Fan

GILBERT – Invitation to Ride

Pl. 358

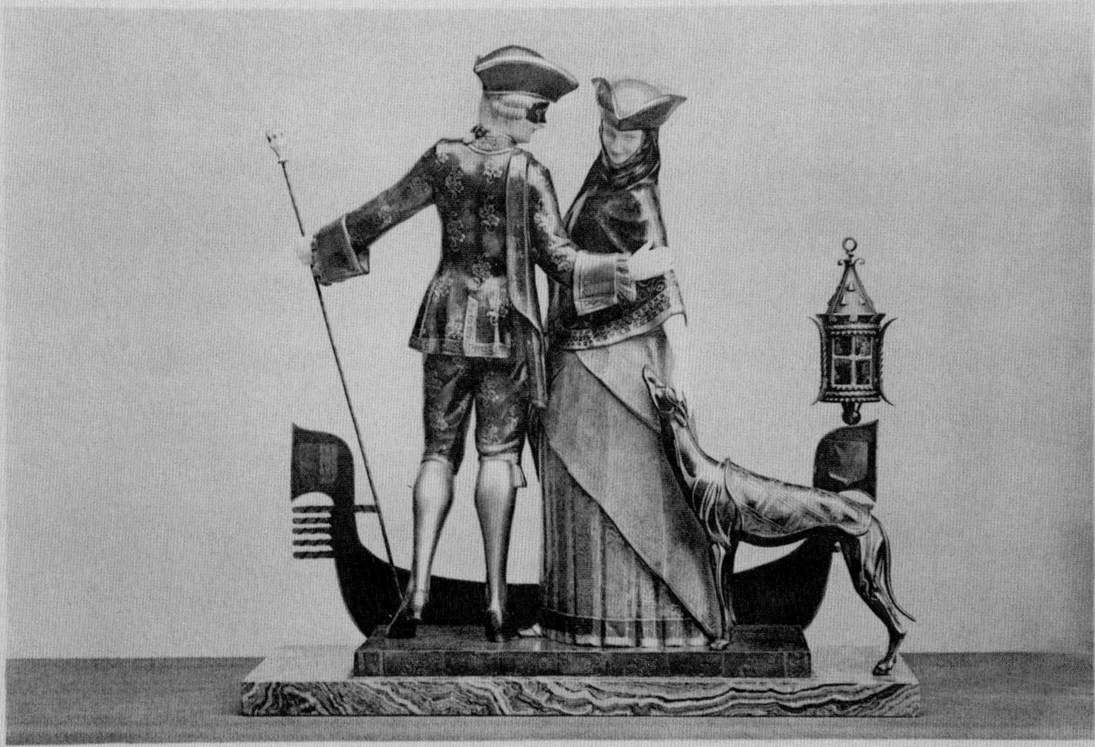

Invitation au Voyage, par A. GILBERT
Bronze gravé et ivoire sur socle marbre.
N° 1517. — Hauteur 62 c/m - Longueur 62 c/m - Largeur 26 c/m.

L.N. PARIS J.L.

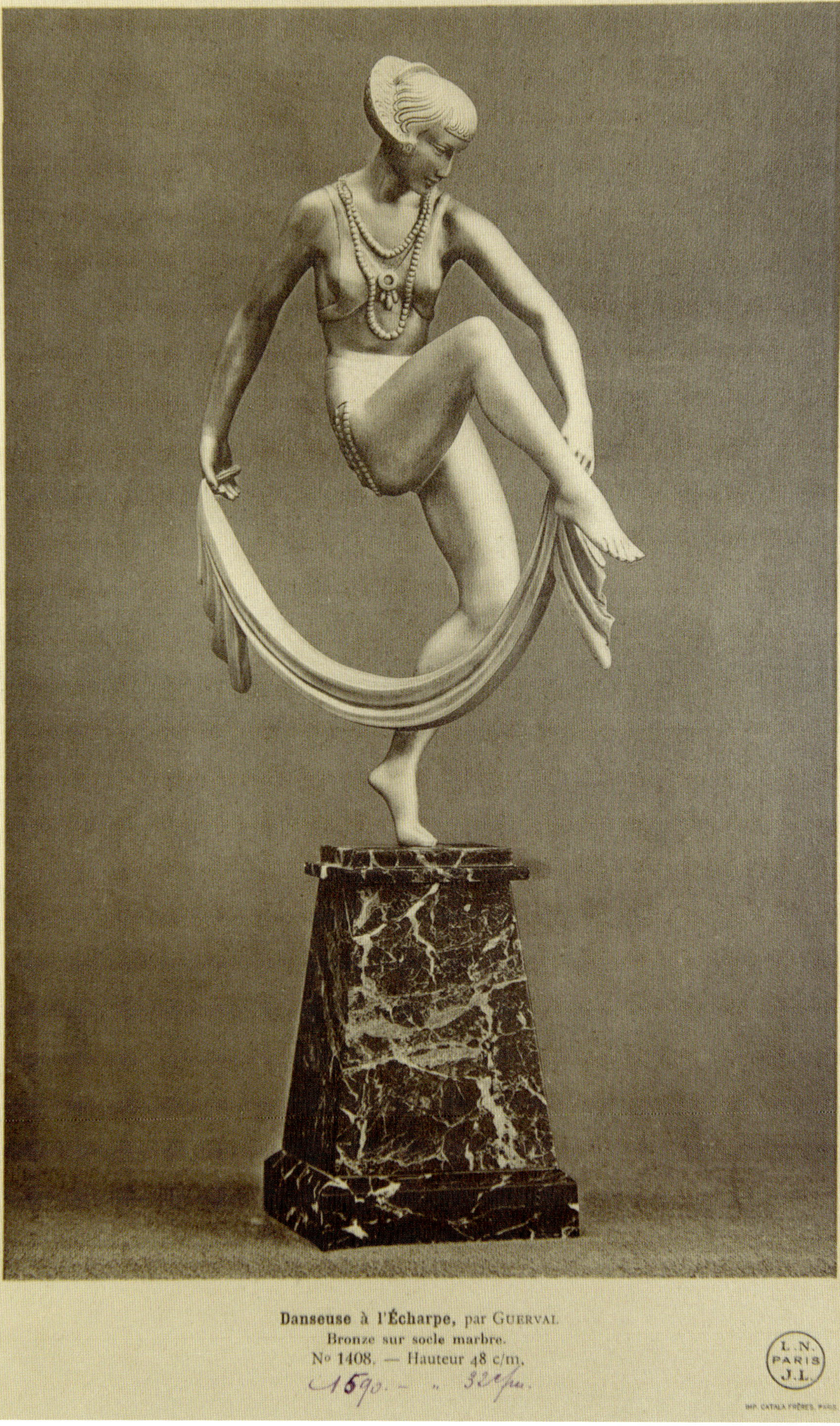

Danseuse à l'Écharpe, par GUERVAL
Bronze sur socle marbre.
N° 1408. — Hauteur 48 c/m.
1590.– „ 32c/m.

L. N. PARIS J. L.

IMP. CATALA FRÈRES, PARIS

GUERVAL – Scarf Dancer

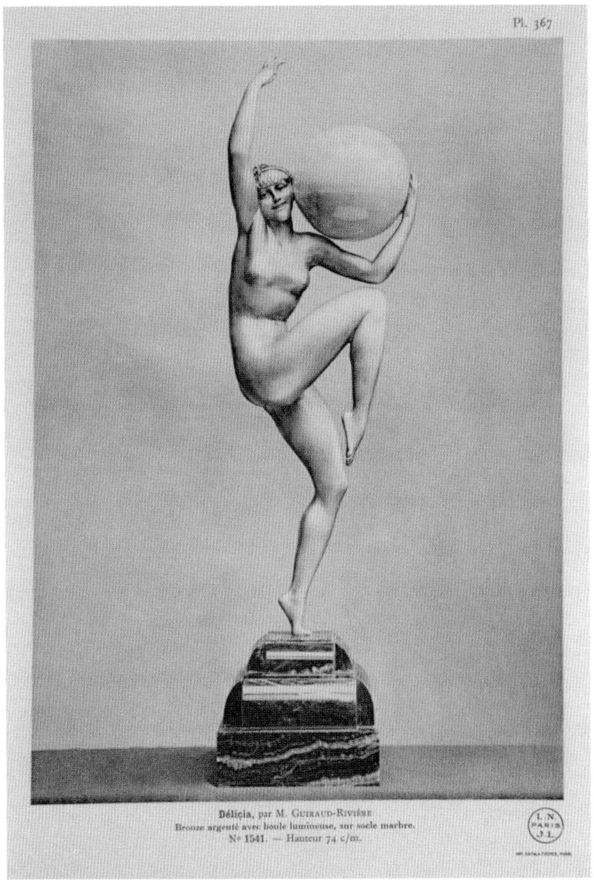

GUIRAUD-RIVIÈRE – Delicia

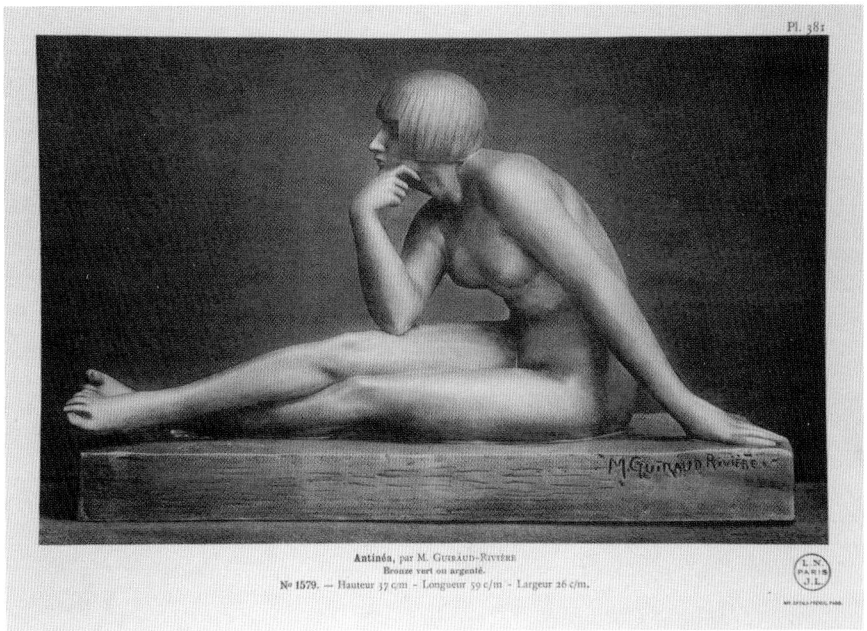

GUIRAUD-RIVIÈRE – Antinéa

GUIRAUD-RIVIÈRE – Charioteer

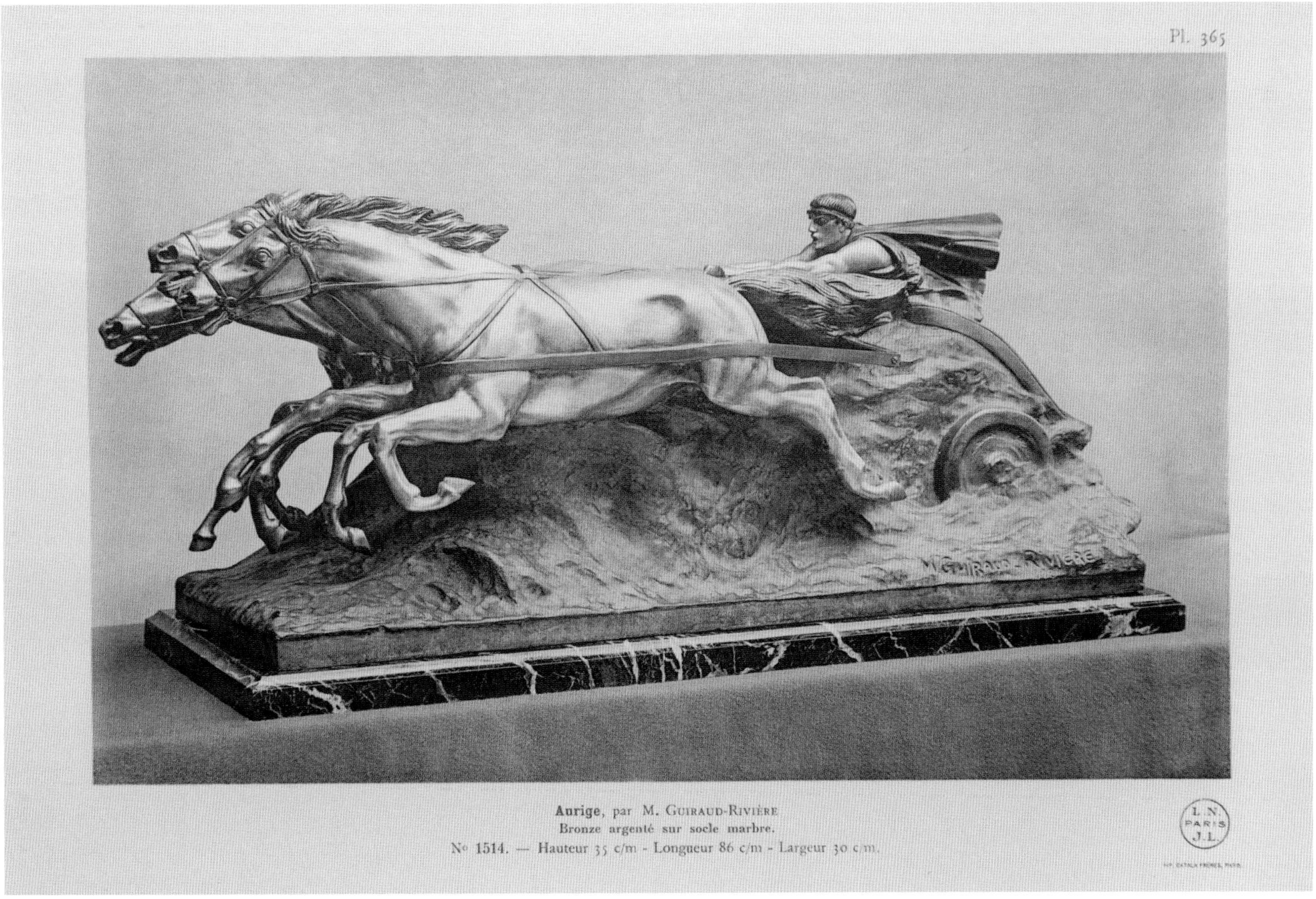

Pl. 340

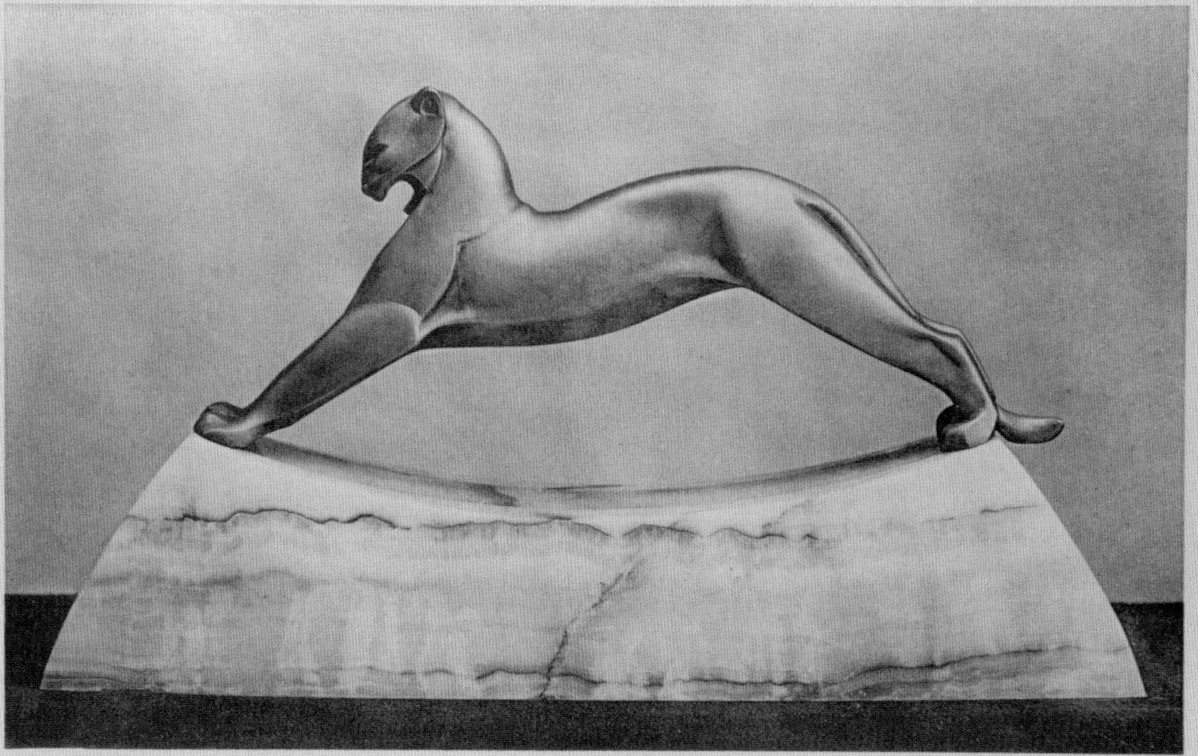

Panthère noire, par ALEX. KÉLÉTY
Bronze gravé sur socle avec électricité.
N° 1429. — Hauteur 28 c/m. - Longueur 51 c/m.

L.N. PARIS J.L.

KÉLÉTY – Black Panther

KÉLÉTY – Hunting Hounds

Pl. 329

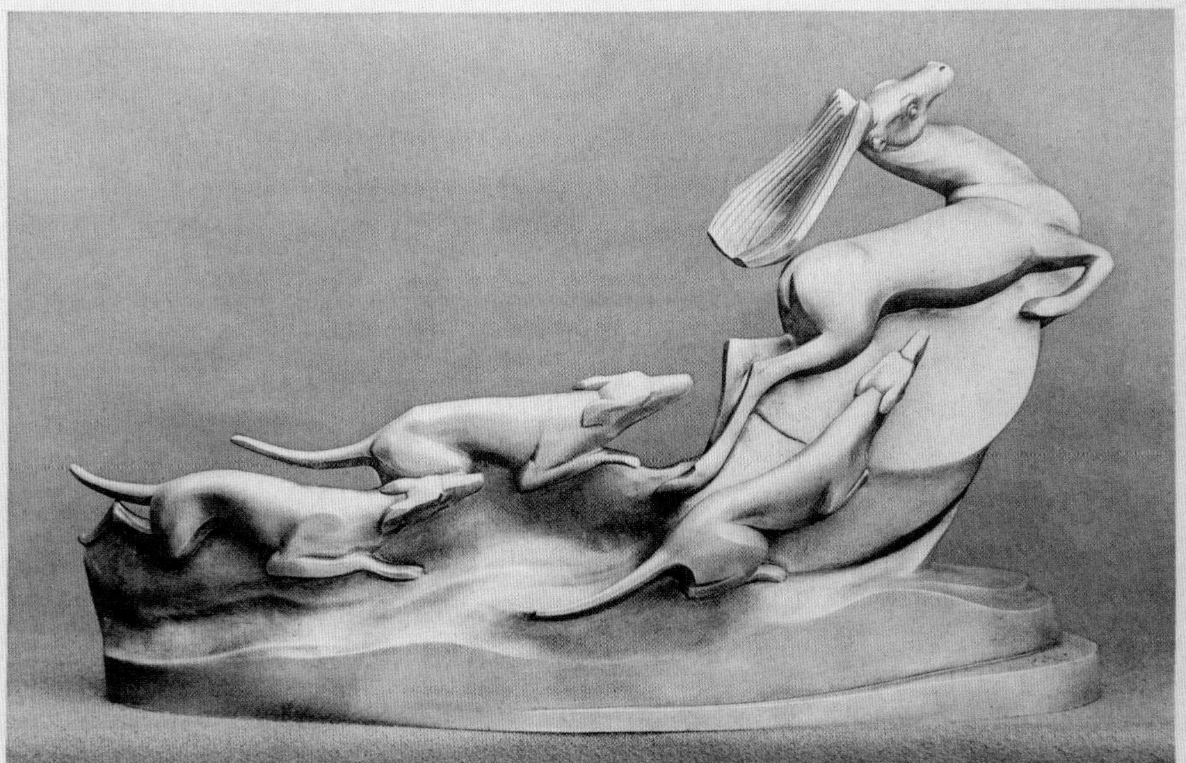

Chasse à courre, par ALEX. KÉLÉTY
Bronze argenté et bronze gravé.
N° 1446. — Hauteur 30 c/m. - Long. 50 c/m.

L.N. PARIS J.L.

Pl. 348

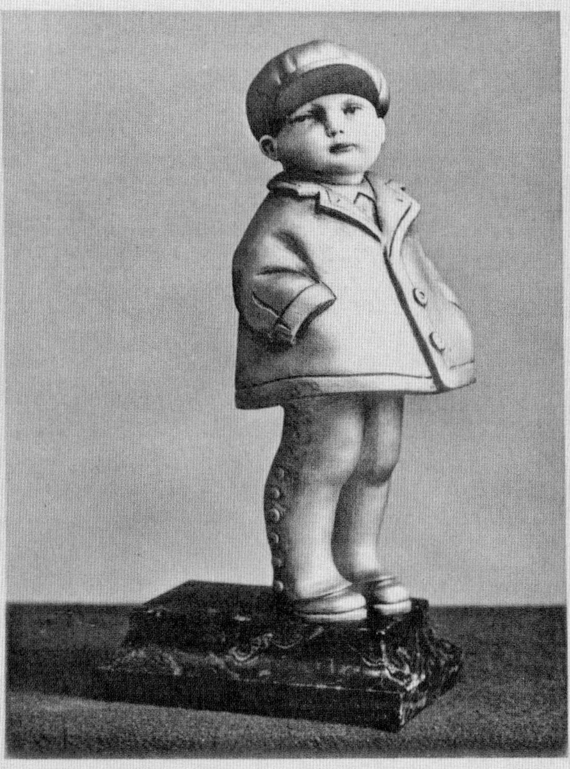

Freddy, par ALEX. KÉLÉTY
Bronze et ivoire sur socle marbre.
N° 1473. — Hauteur 23 c/m.

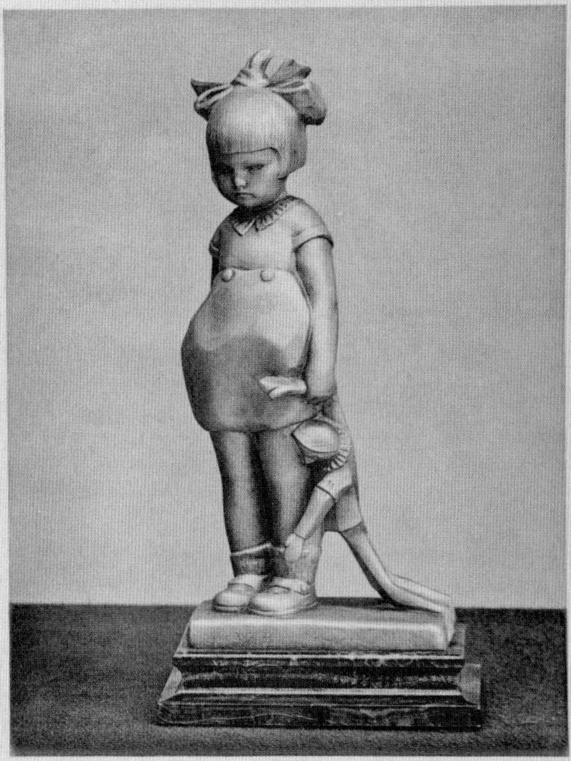

Polichinelle, par ALEX. KÉLÉTY
Bronze gravé sur socle marbre.
N° 1451. — Hauteur 27 c/m.

L.N. PARIS J.L.

IMP. CATALA FRÈRES, PARIS.

KÉLÉTY – Freddy – Polichinella

LAUREL – Farandole

Pl. 237

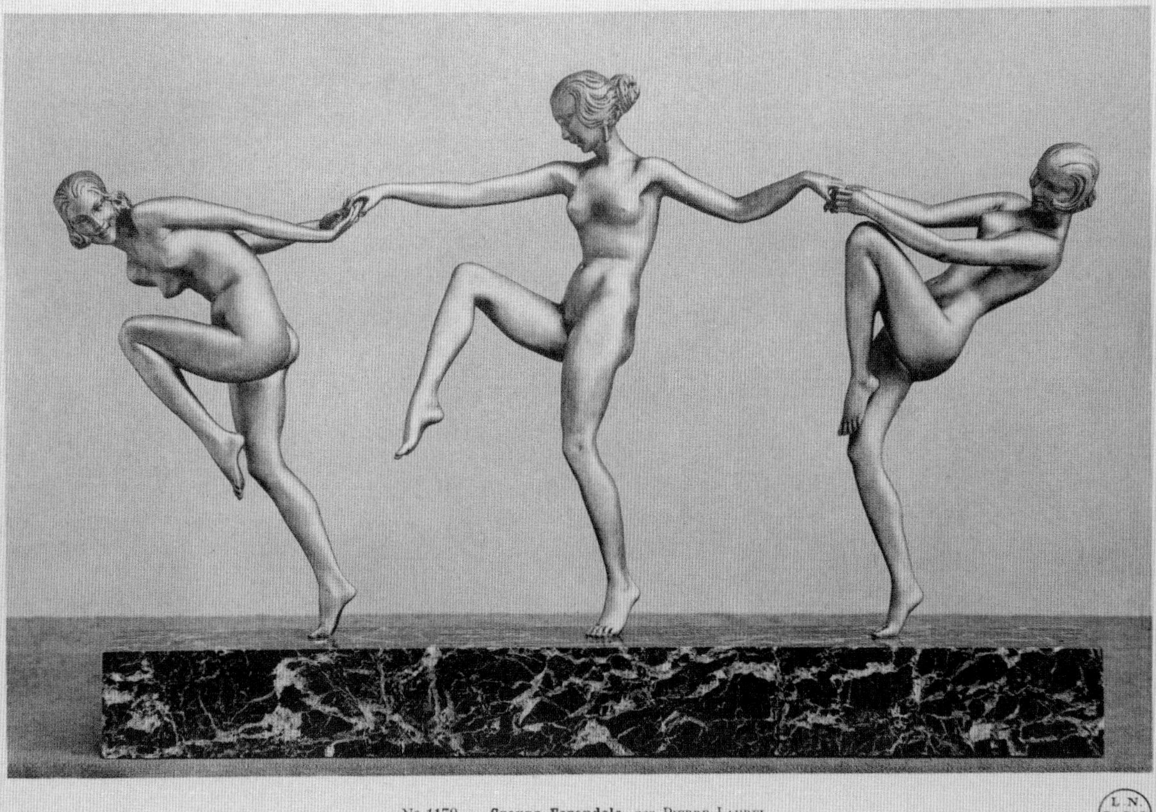

N° 1179 — **Groupe Farandole**, par PIERRE LAUREL
Hauteur 40 c/m. — Largeur 60 c/m.

L.N. PARIS J.L.

IMP. CATALA FRÈRES, PARIS.

Pl. 336

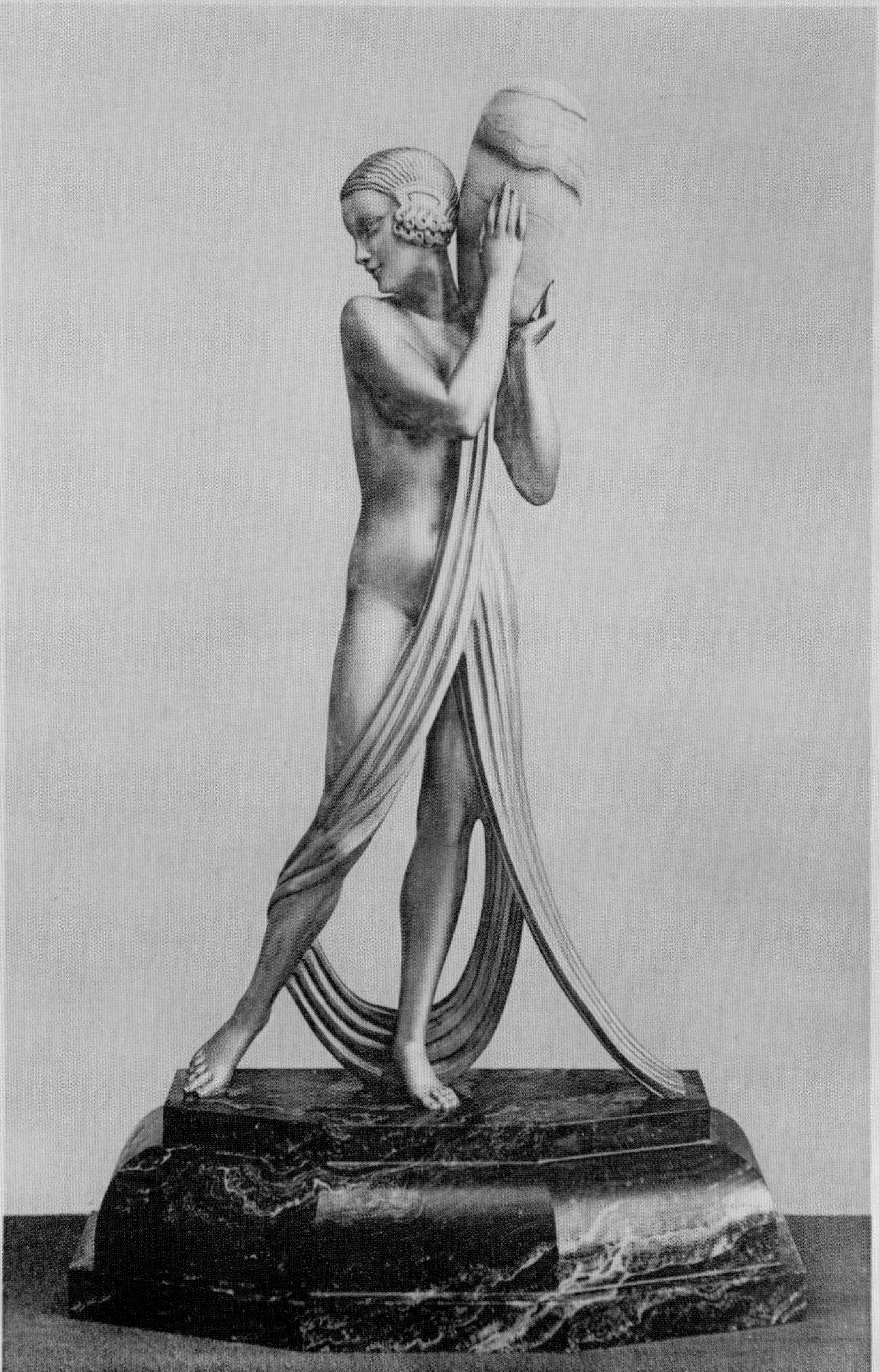

Danseuse au voile, par LAUREL

Bronze sur socle marbre et vase à l'électricité.

N° **1448.** — Hauteur 49 c/m.

L. N. PARIS J. L.

LAUREL – Veiled Dance

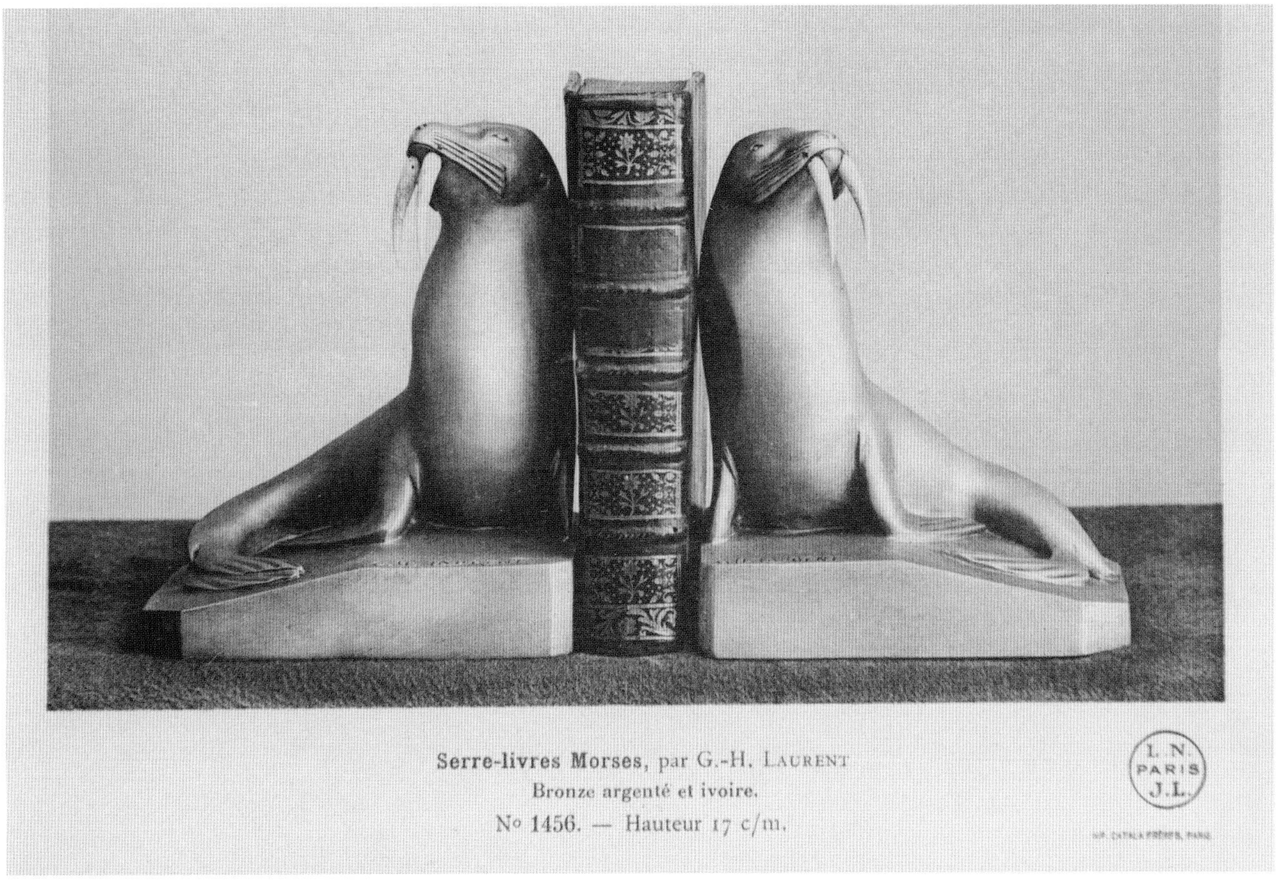

LAURENT – Walruses (bookends)

LAURENT – Crested Grebe (bookends)

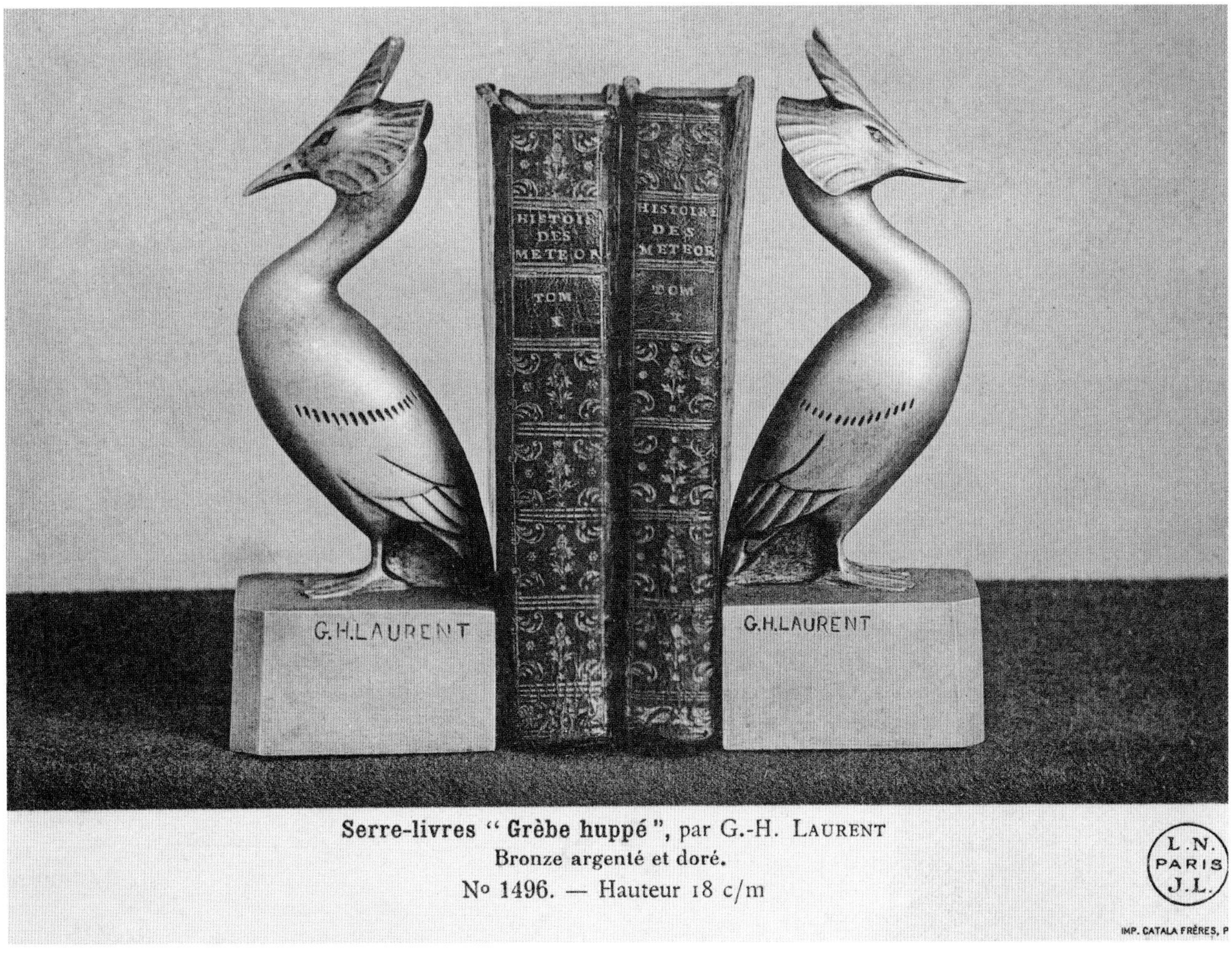

Pl. 374

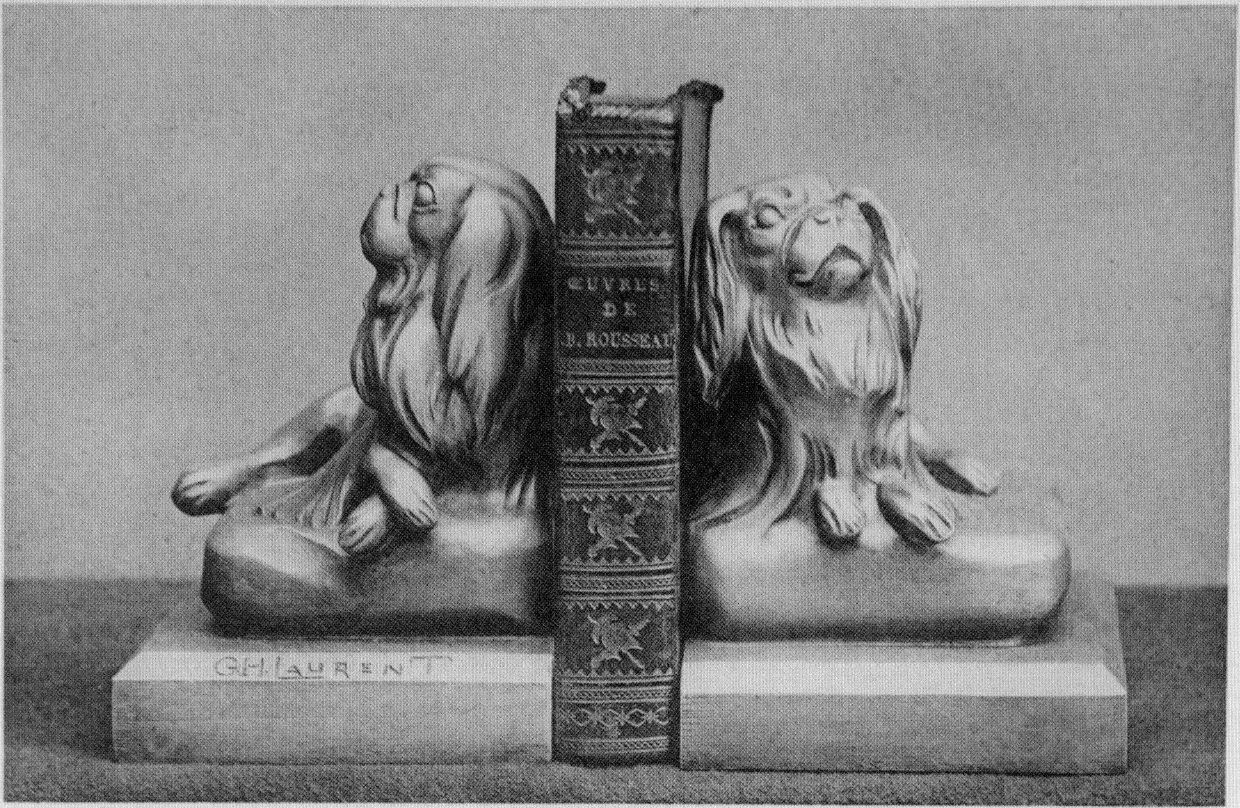

Serre-livres " Pékinois ", par G.-H. LAURENT
Bronze argenté.
N° 1565. — Hauteur 13 c/m

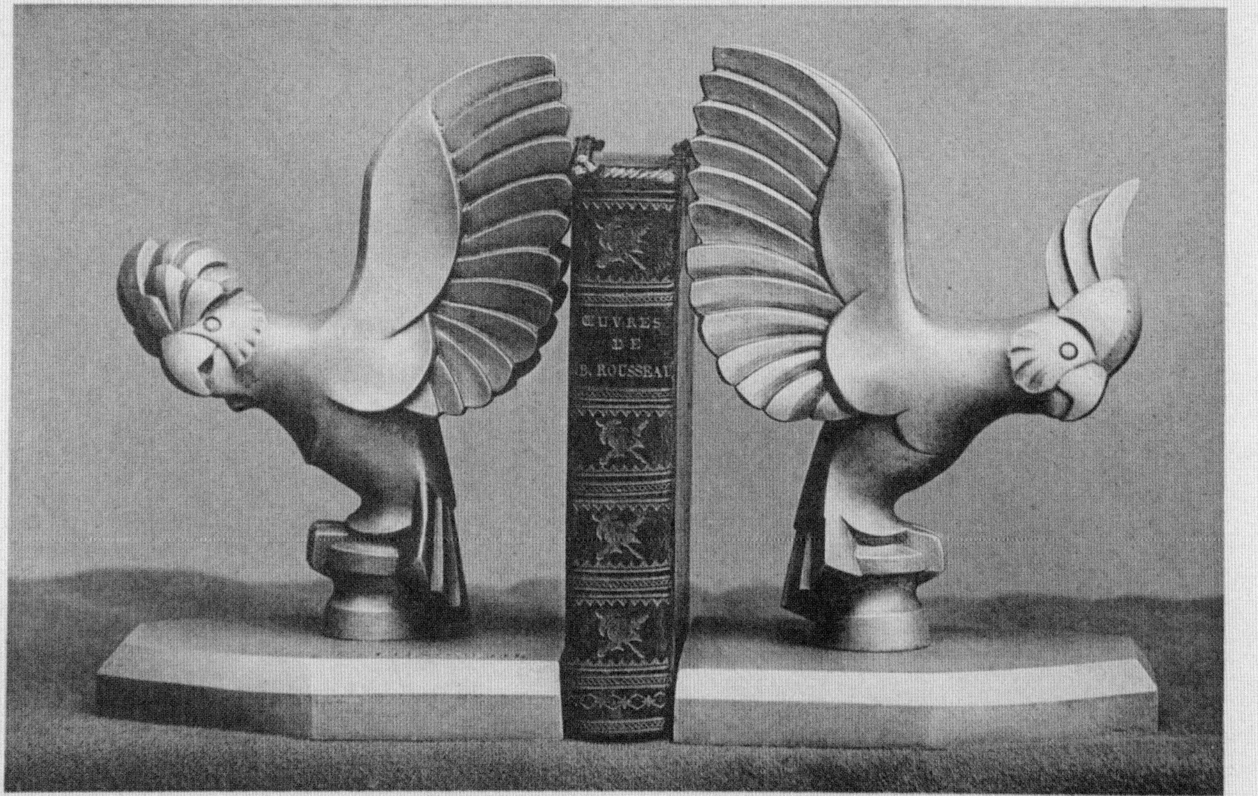

Serre-livres " Cacatoès ", par G.-H. LAURENT
Bronze argenté.
N° 1564. — Hauteur 17 c/m.

L.N. PARIS J.L.

IMP. CATALA FRÈRES, PARIS.

LAURENT – Pekinese (bookends) – Cockatoos (bookends)

Pl. 304

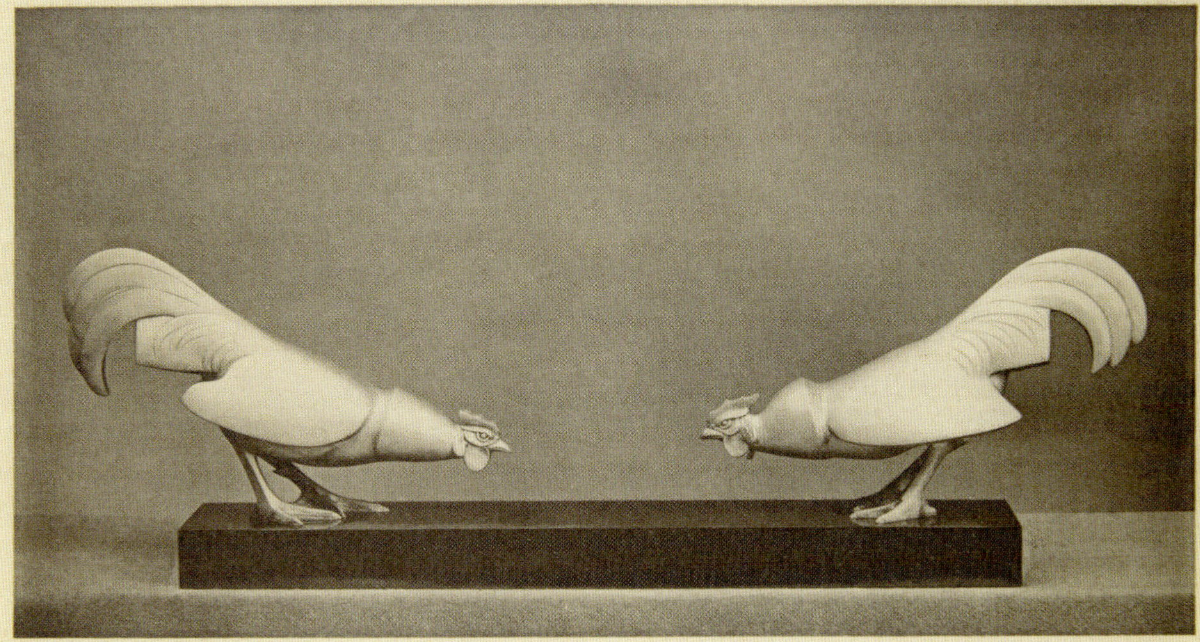

Combat de coqs, par Le Faguays
Bronze argenté sur socle marbre
N° 1339. — Longueur 70 c/m. - Hauteur 21 c/m.

LE FAGUAYS – Cock Fight

LE FAGUAYS – Modern Diana

Pl. 334

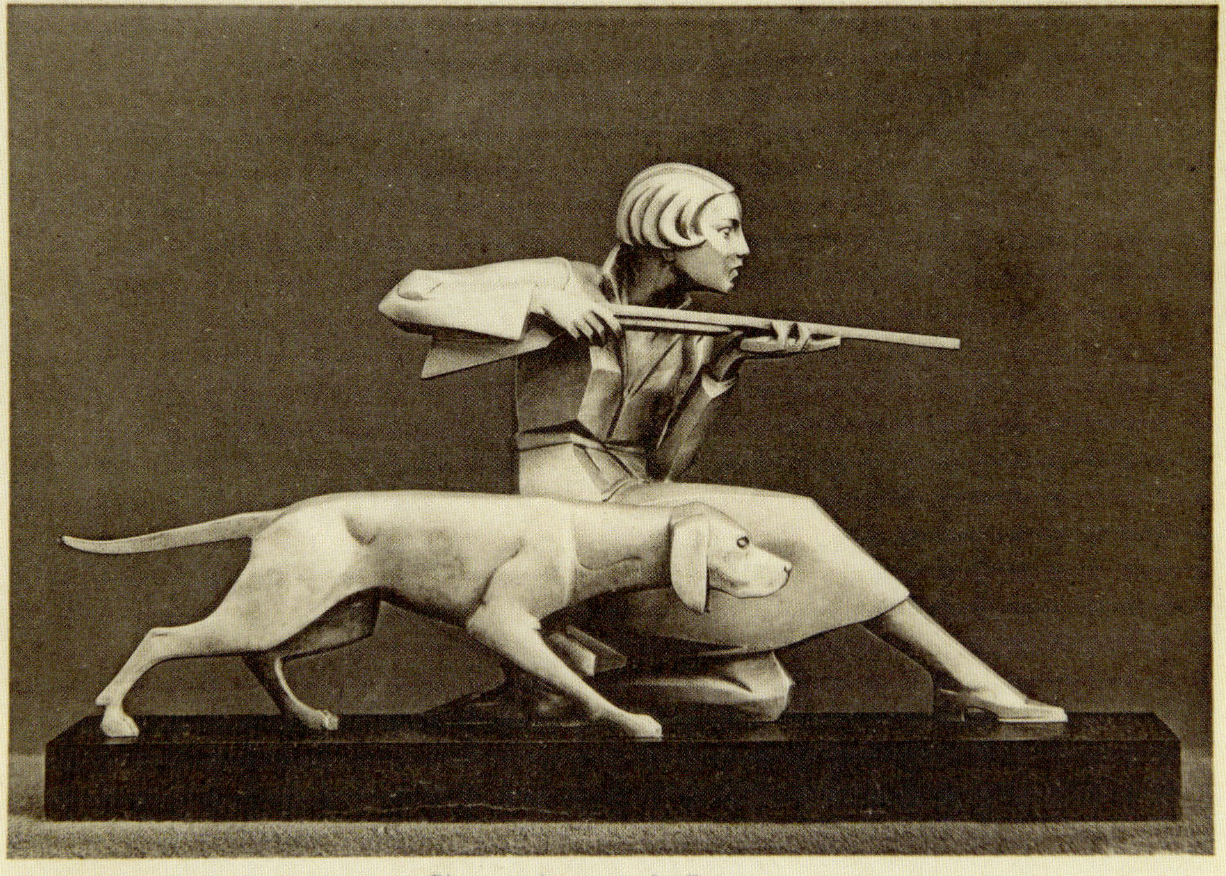

Diane moderne, par Le Faguays
Bronze argenté sur socle marbre.

Pl. 277

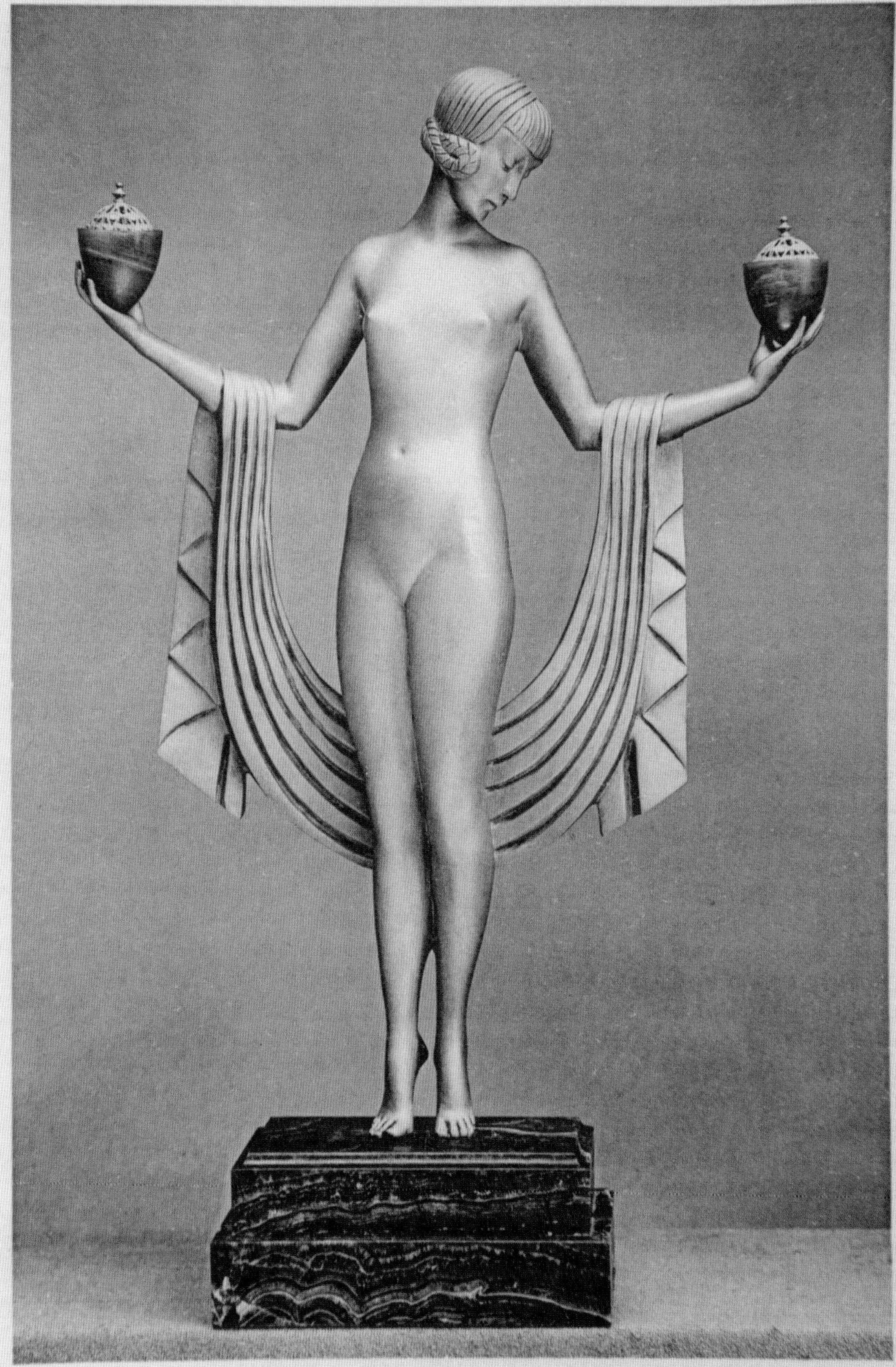

Vestale, par Le Faguays

I N° 1284 - Bronze sur marbre - Hauteur 52 c/m

II 1468 » » » » 36 c/m

L.N. PARIS J.L.

IMP. CATALA FRÈRES, PARIS

LE FAGUAYS – Vestal Virgin

Pl. 293

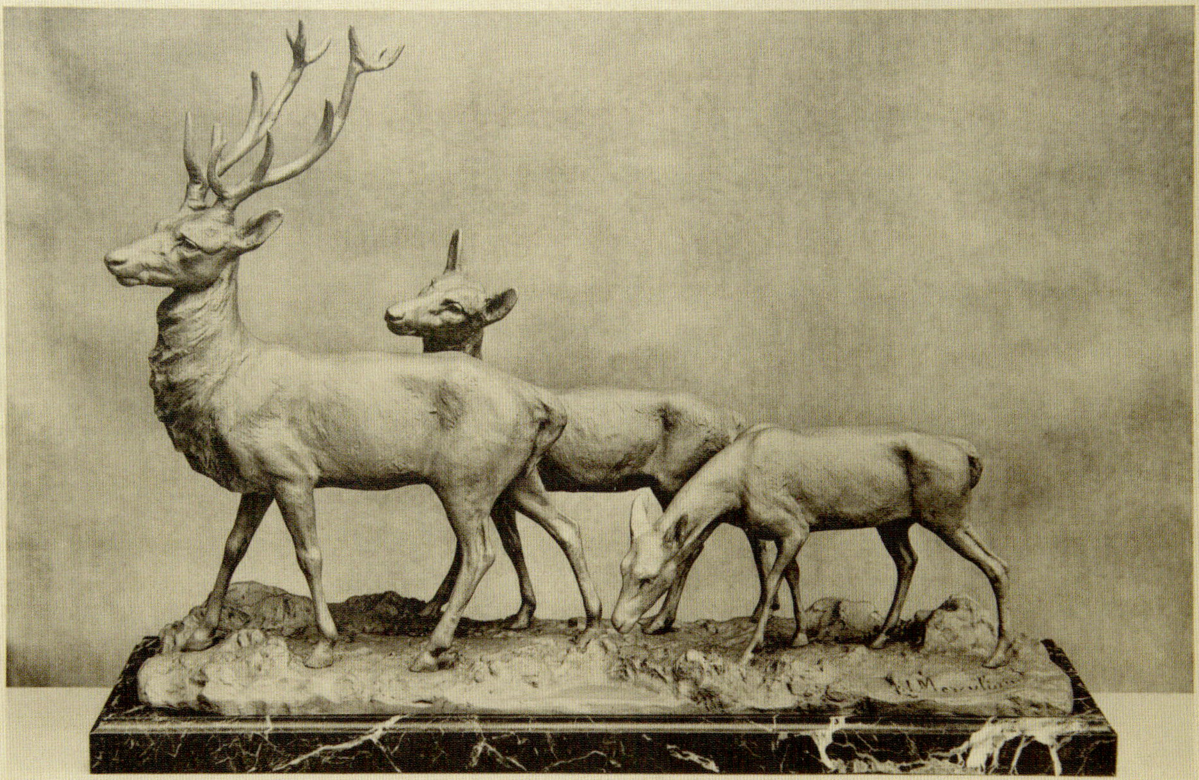

Cerf et biches, par MERCULIANO (Salon des Artistes Français 1926)
N° 1328 — Bronze sur socle marbre Hauteur 55 c/m - Longueur 76 c/m

L. N. PARIS J.L.

G. Bottan - imp. Paris

MERCULIANO – Stags

MORLON – Distraction

Pl. 378

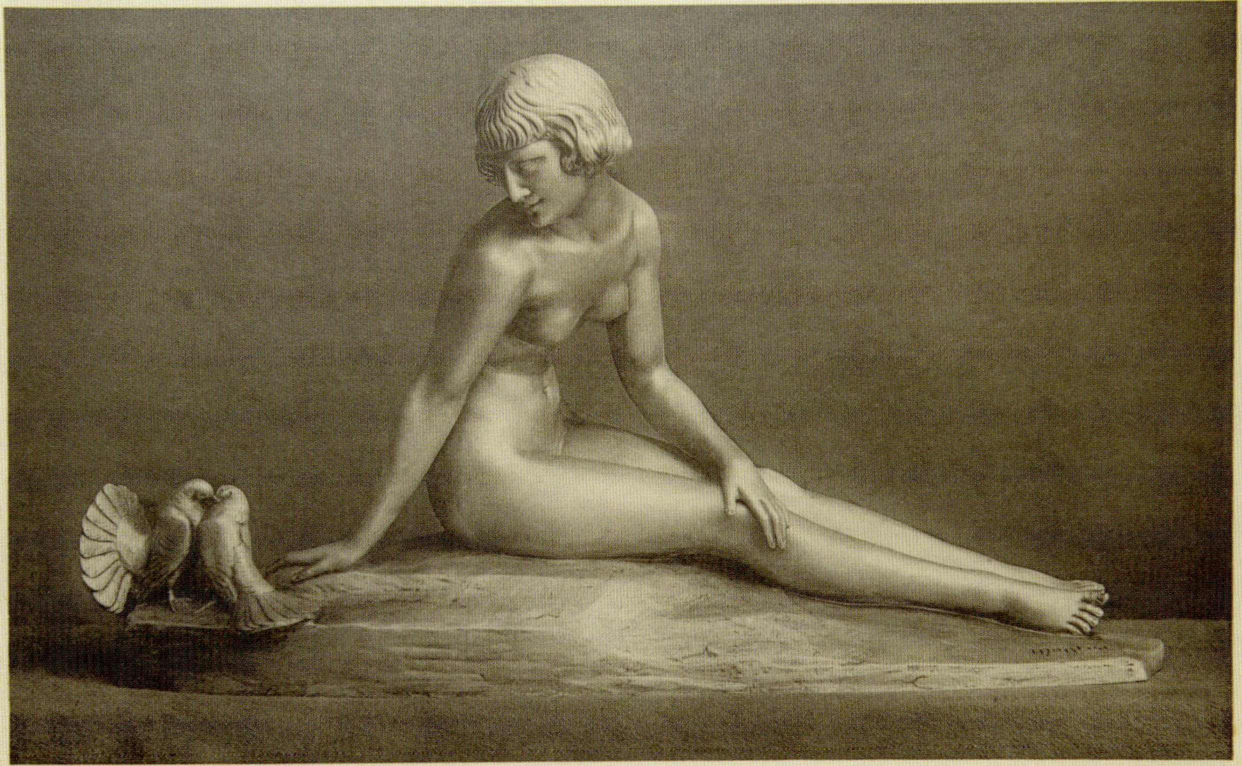

Distraction, par MORLON
Bronze argenté.
N° 1580. — Hauteur 35 c/m - Longueur 60 c/m - Largeur 19 c/m.

L. N. PARIS J.L.

IMP. CATALA FRÈRES, PARIS.

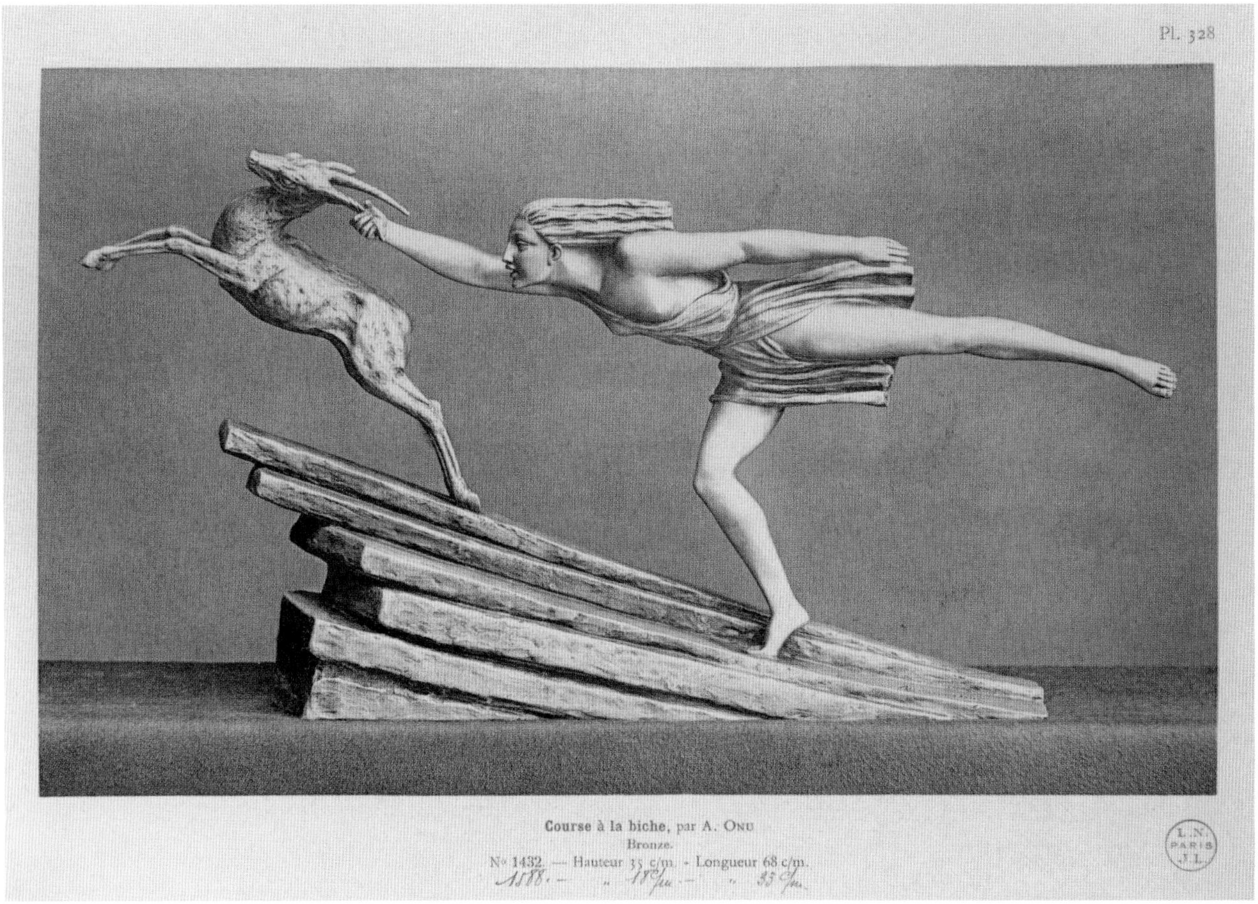

ONU – Chasing the Hind

PEYRE – Fun in the Sun

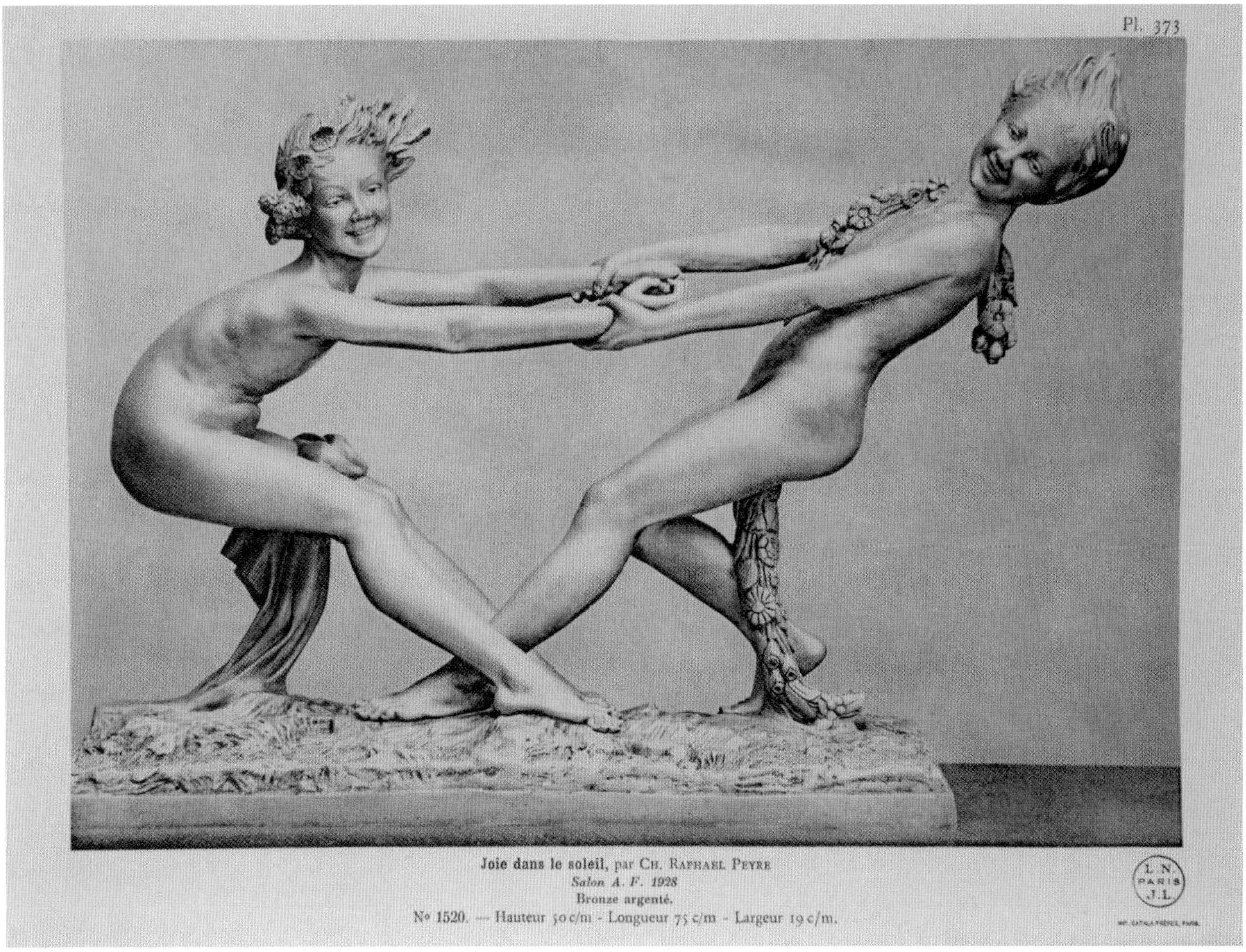

Pl. 369

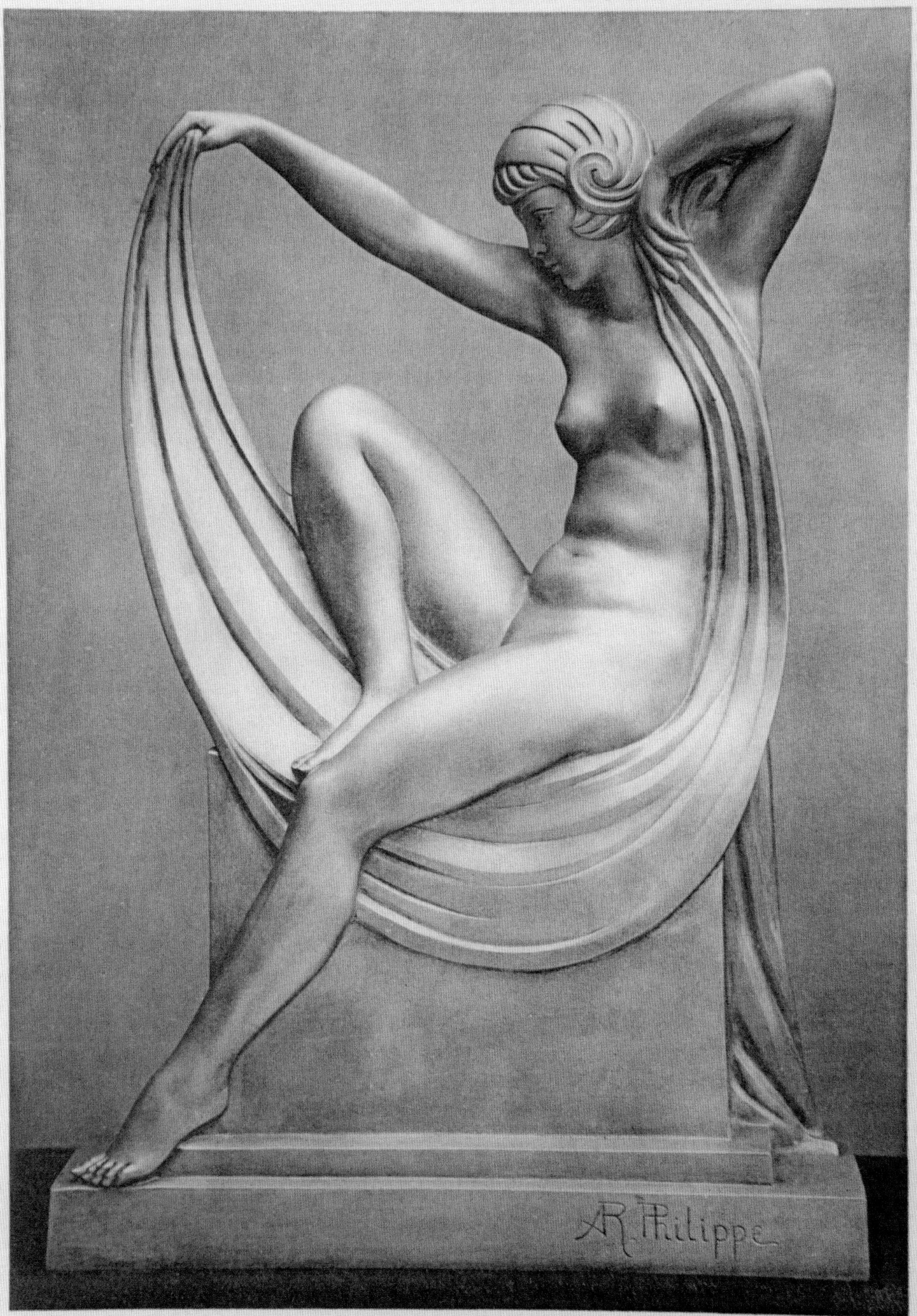

Avant le bain, par A.-R. PHILIPPE

Bronze argenté.

I **Nº 1570.** — Hauteur 53 c/m - Longueur 36 c/m - Largeur 11 c/m.

II 1621 » 35 c/m » 24 c/m

L.N. PARIS J.L.

IMP. CATALA FRÈRES, PARIS

PHILIPPE, A.R. – Before the Bath

Pl. 366

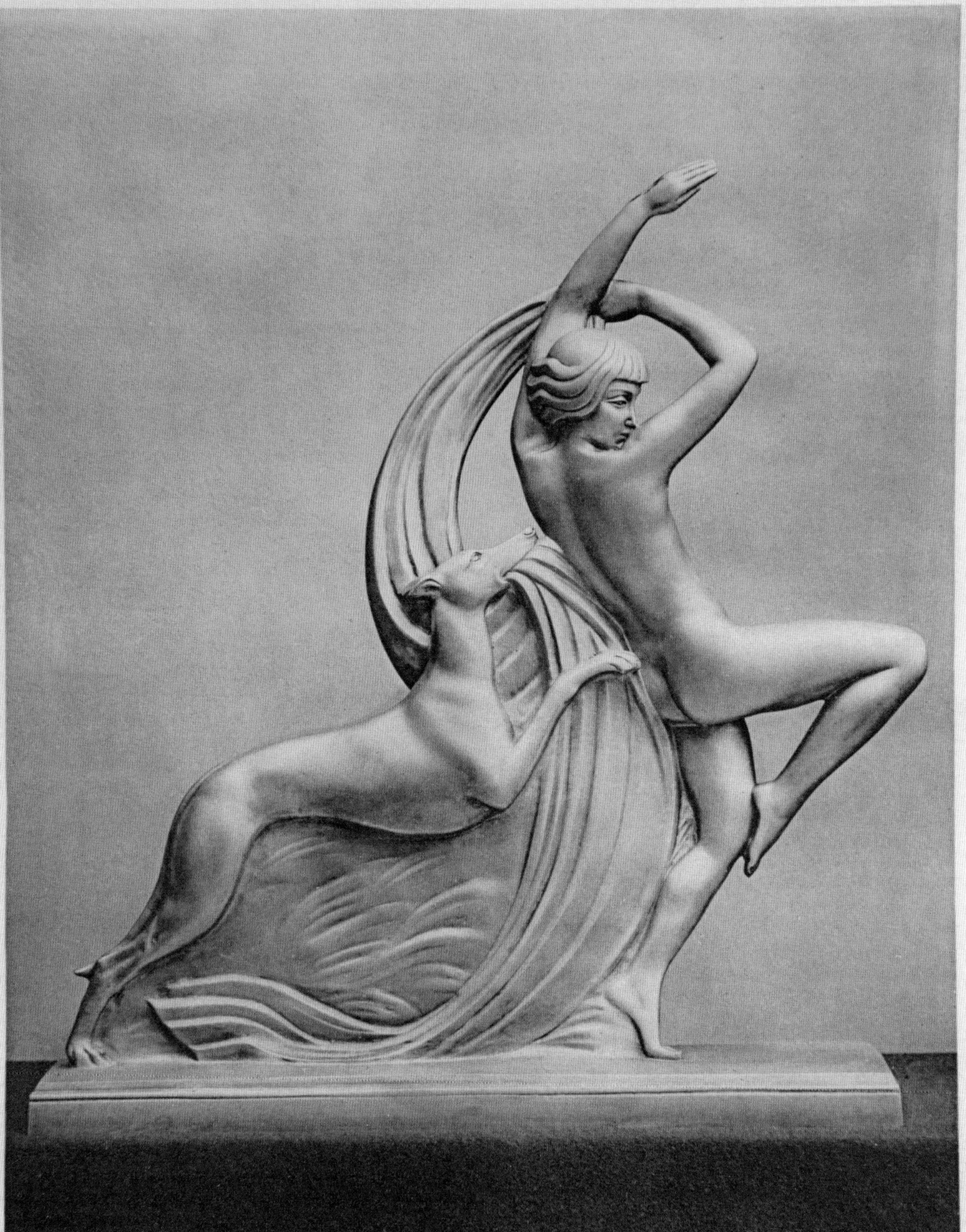

Danseuse au lévrier, par A.-R. PHILIPPE
Bronze argenté.
N° 1558. — Hauteur 57 c/m - Longueur 56 c/m - Largeur 10 c/m.

L.N.
PARIS
J.L.

IMP. CATALA FRÈRES, PARIS

PHILIPPE, A.R. – Dancer with Hound

Pl. 355

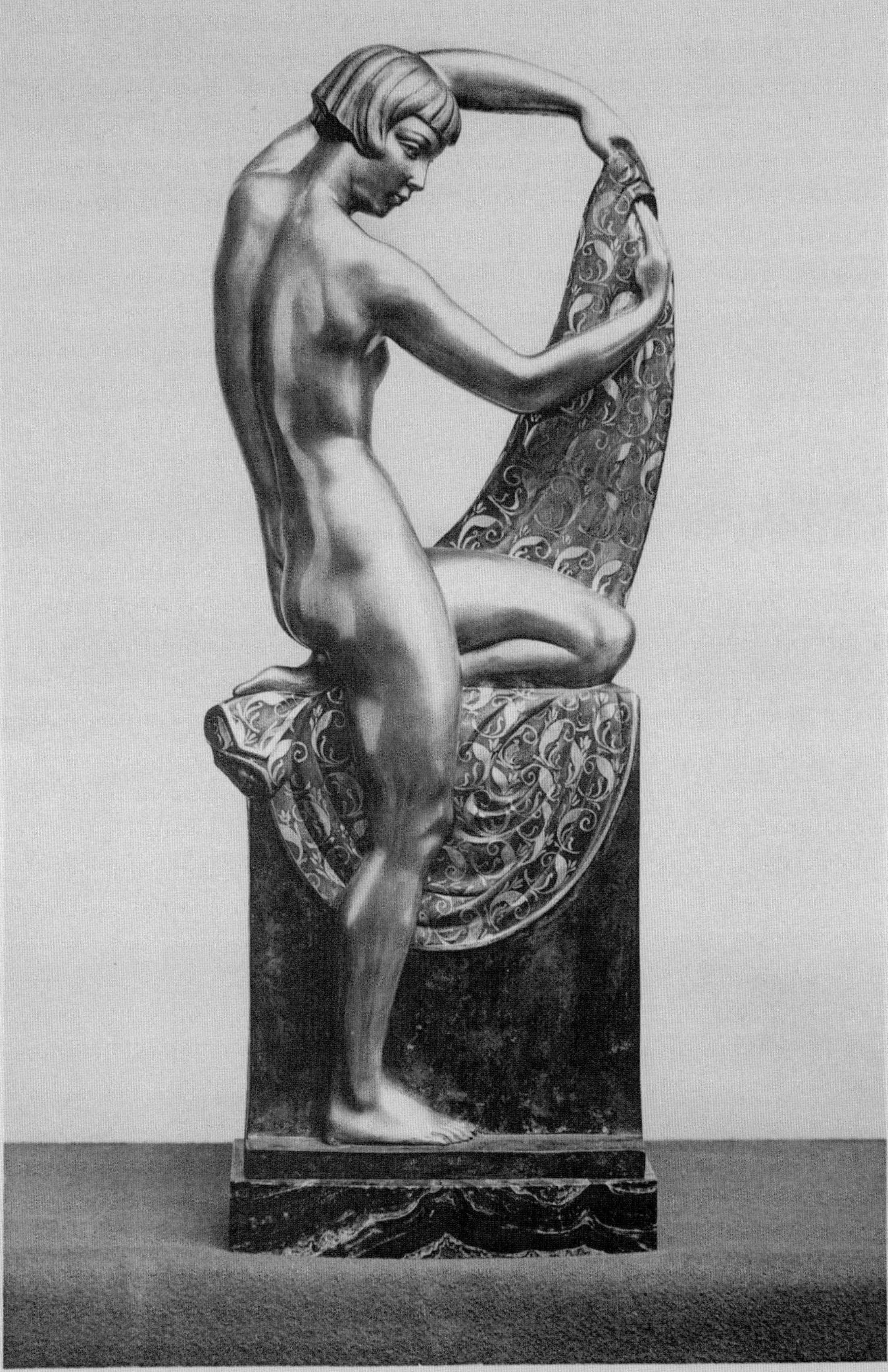

Baigneuse, par A.-R. PHILIPPE
Bronze argenté et gravé sur socle marbre.
I N° 1502. — Hauteur 49 c/m.
II 1573 ~ 30 c/m.

L.N. PARIS J.L.

IMP. CATALA FRÈRES, PARIS

PHILIPPE, A.R. – The Bather

Pl. 368

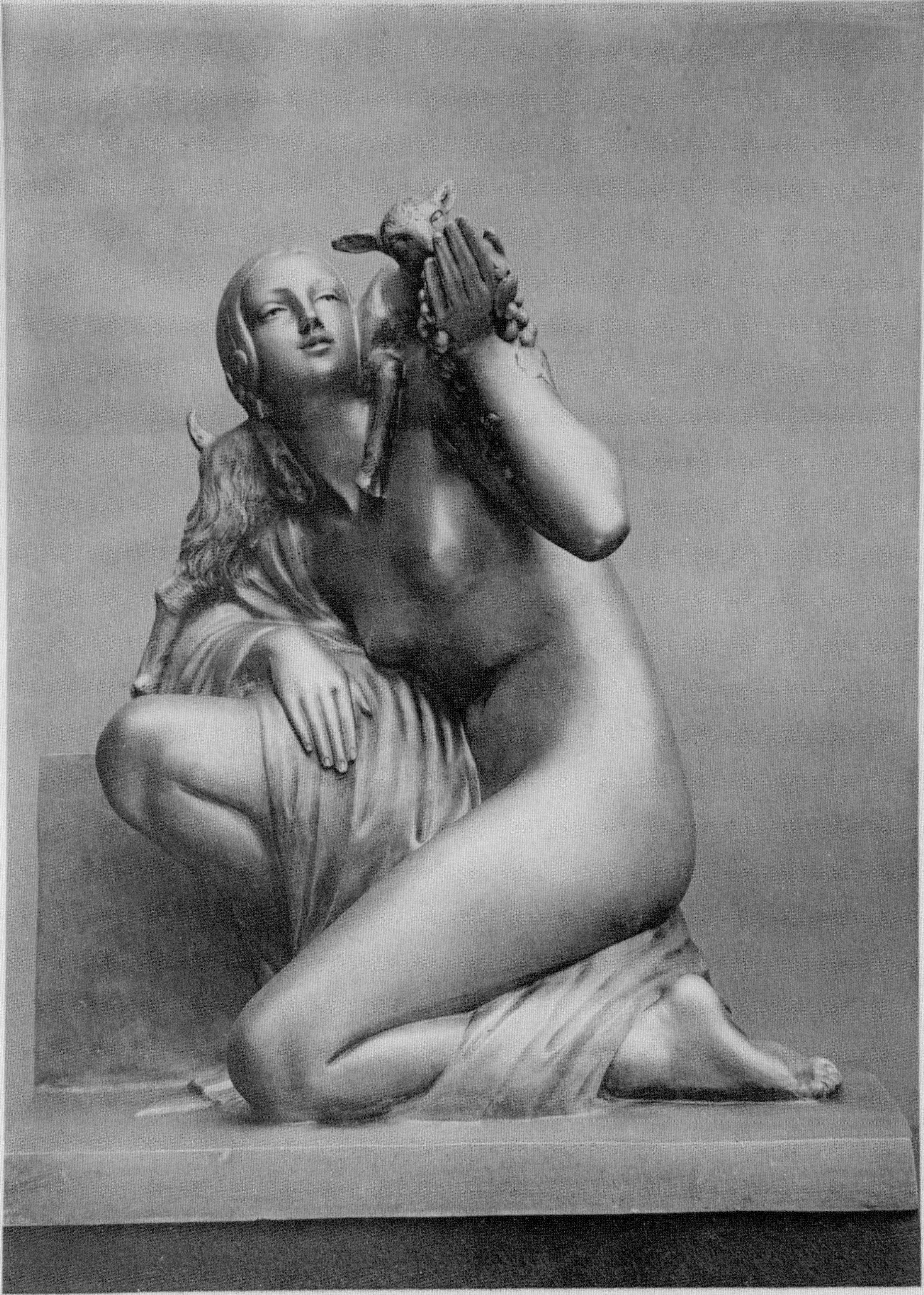

Jeux d'Automne, par FANNY ROZET

Bronze argenté.

No 1537. — Hauteur 48 c/m - Longueur 41 c/m - Largeur 24 c/m.

L.N. PARIS J.L.

IMP. CATALA FRÈRES, PARIS.

ROZET – Autumn Games

Pl. 354

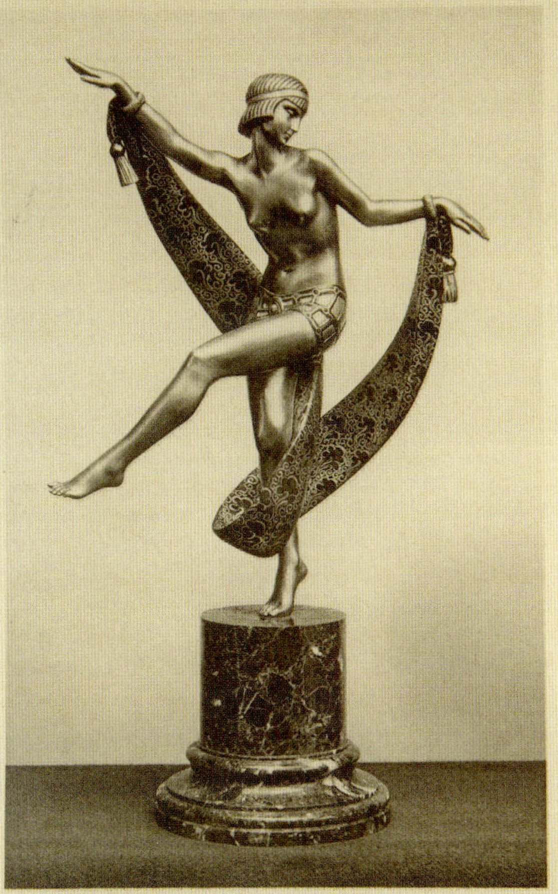

Pas de l'Écharpe, par FANNY ROZET
Bronze argenté et gravé sur socle marbre.
N° 1495. — Hauteur 47 c/m.

ROZET – The Scarf Dance

Pl. 337

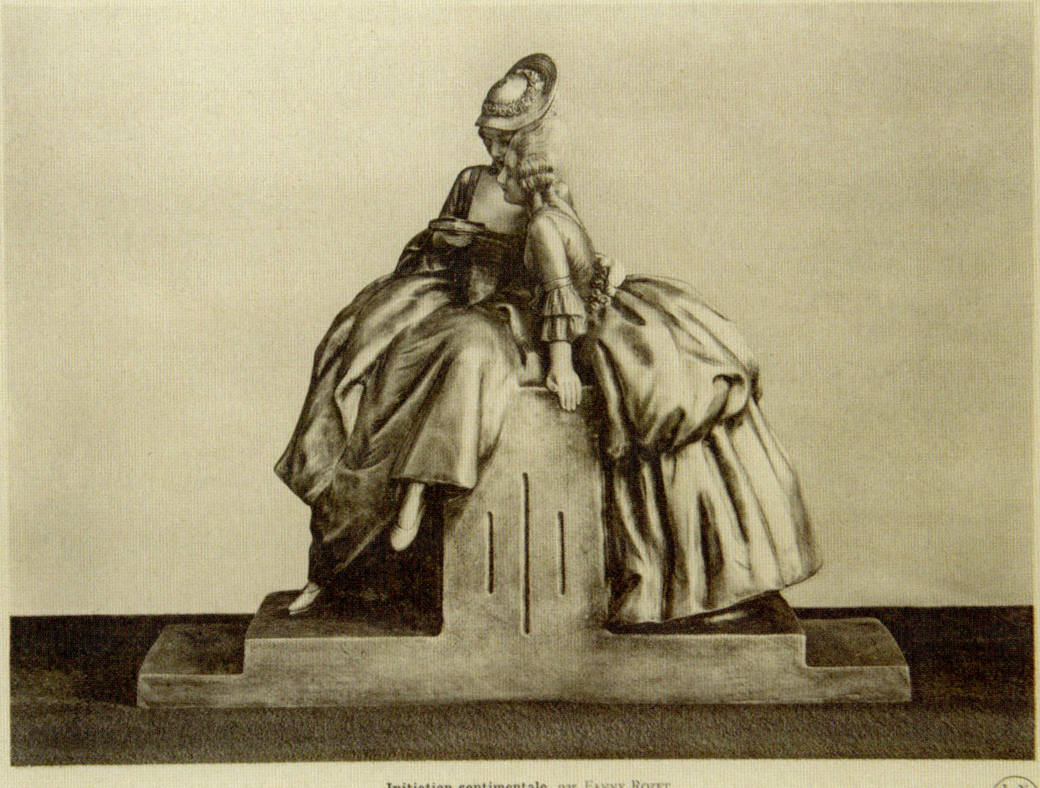

Initiation sentimentale, par FANNY ROZET
Salon des Artistes Français, 1927
Bronze et ivoire.
N° 1443. — Hauteur 31 c/m. - Longueur 36 c/m.

ROZET –
Sentimental Initiation

Pl. 350

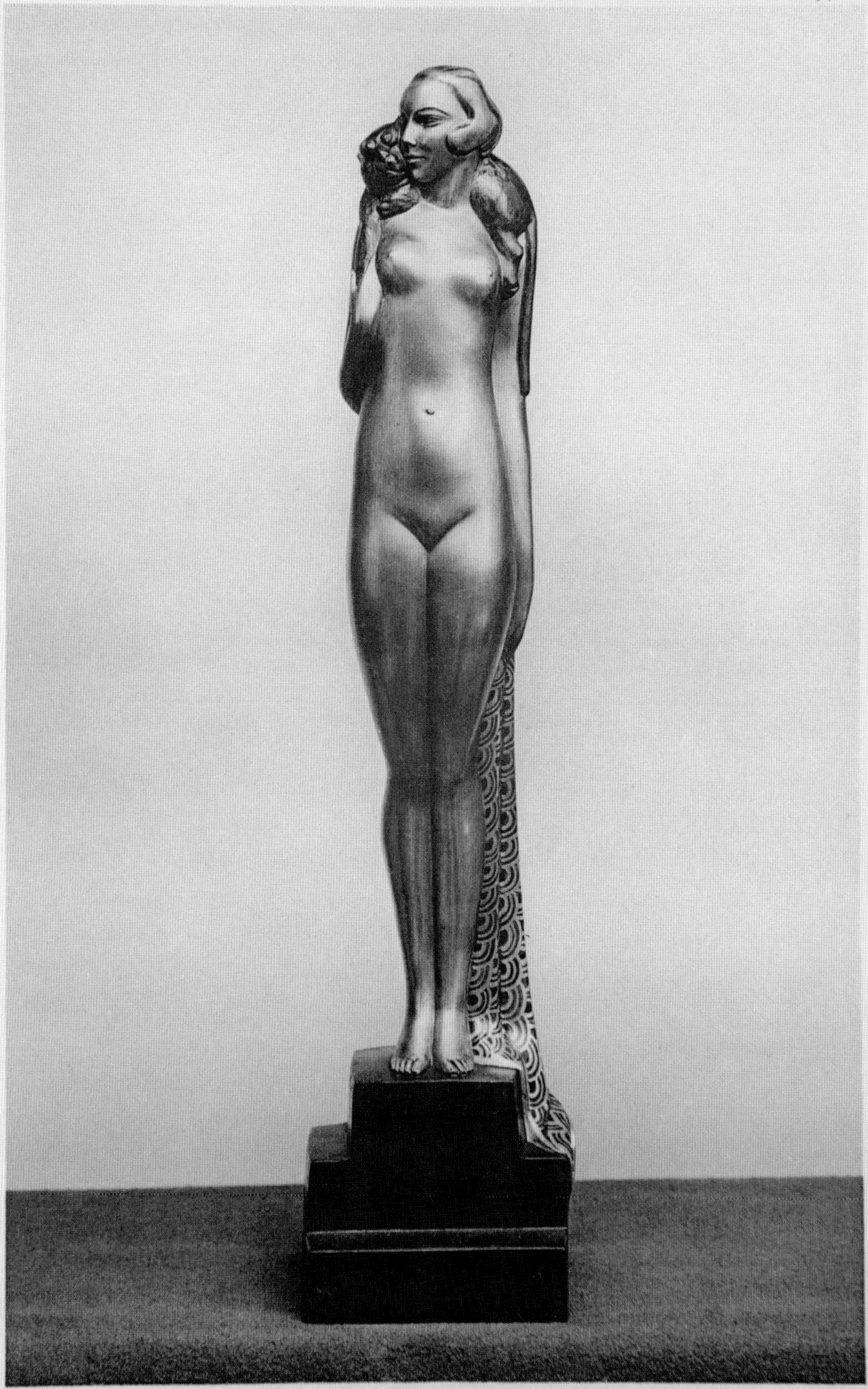

Petite Lionne, par M.-L. Simart
Bronze argenté et gravé.
N° 1491. — Hauteur 48 c/m.

L.N. PARIS J.L.

IMP. CATALA FRÈRES, PARIS.

SIMART – Young Lioness

Pl. 300

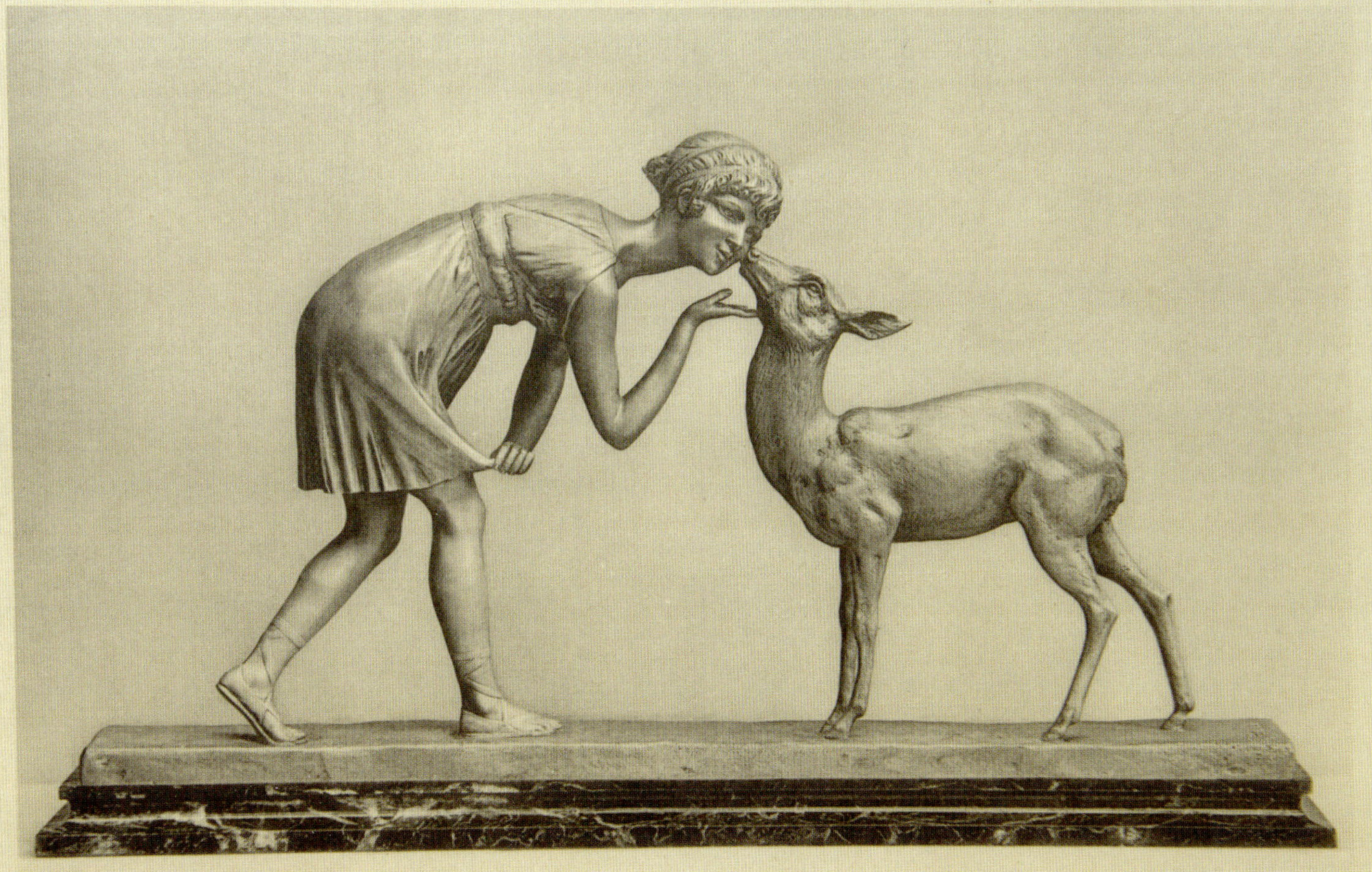

Caresse, par VERSCHNEIDER
Bronze sur socle marbre.
N° 1159. — Hauteur 35 c/m - Longueur 63 c/m

L.N. PARIS J.L.

VERSCHNEIDER – Caresses

Bibliography

Annuaire des Arts Décoratifs et Industriels Modernes [Art Deco directory]. Paris, 1924.

Arwass, Victor, *Art Deco Sculpture*. St. Martin's Press, New York, 1992.

Berman, Harold, *Bronzes, Sculptors and Founders 1800-1930*. Abage Encyclopedia, Abage, Chicago, 1974.

Brandt, Frederick R., *Late 19th and Early 20th Century Decorative Arts*. Virginia Museum of Fine Arts, Richmond, 1985.

Bret, David, *The Mistinguett Legend*. St. Martin's Press, New York, 1990.

Callender, Harold, *Fun Tomorrow, The Story of an Artist and a Way of Life*. Spiral Press, New York, 1953.

Catley, Bryan, *Art Deco and other Figures*. Antique Collectors' Club, Woodbridge, Second edition, 2003.

Chapman, Gary, *The Dolly Sisters, Icons of the Jazz Age*. Edditt Publishing, 2013.

Cordelier, Suzanne F., *La Vie Brève de la Argentina* [The Brief Life of La Argentina]. Librairie Plon, Paris, 1936.

Dahhan, Philippe, *Etains 1900* [Pewter]. Les Editions de l'Amateur, Paris, 2000.

Dinger, Brigitte, *Von Jugendstil bis Art Deco, Schönheit in Elfenbein* [From Art Nouveau to Art Deco, Beauty in Ivory]. Deutsches Elfenbein Museum [German Ivory Museum], Erbach, 1988.

Exposition International des Arts Décoratifs et Industriels Modernes, *Catalogue Général Officiel* [Official General Catalogue]. Paris, 1925.

Exposition International des Arts Décoratifs et Industriels Modernes, *Rapport Général* [General Report]. Librairie Larousse, Paris, 1927.

Faveton, Pierre, *Les Annees 20* [The 1920s]. Editions Messidor / Temps Actuels, Paris, 1982.

Forrest, Michael, *Art Bronzes*. Schiffer Publishing, Pennsylvania, 1988.

Higonnet, Patrice, *Paris – Capital of the World*. The Belknap Press, Cambridge, London, 2002.

Hillier, Bevis, *The World of Art Deco*, The Minneapolis Institute of Art. E.P. Dutton and Co., New York, 1971.

Kjellberg, Pierre, *Les Bronzes du XIXe Siècle* [Bronzes of the 19th Century]. Les Editions de l'Amateur, Paris, 1987.

Klein, Dan, *All Color Book of Art Deco*. Octopus Books, London 1974.

Mackay, James, *Sculptors in Bronze*. Antique Collectors' Club, Woodbridge, 1977.

Mann, Carol, *Paris Between the Wars*. The Vendome Press, New York, 1996.

Max le Verrier, *contemporary catalogue*, Paris.

Monneret, Jean, *Catalogue raisonné du Salon des Indépendants, 1884-2000*. Salon des Indépendants, 2000.

Neuwirth, Waltraud, 'Echte Bronzen' [Real Bronzes], *Argentor Musterbuch Nr.30 / Katalog B*. Selbstverlag Dr. Waltraud Neuwirth, Wien, 2007.

Panzetta, Alfonso, *Scultori Italiani Dell'Ottocento* [Italian Sculptors of the 19th Century]. Umberto Allemandi & C., Torino, 1994.

Quénioux, Gaston, *Les Arts Décoratifs Modernes* [Art Deco]. Librairie Larousse, Paris, 1927.

Richemond, Stéphane, *Terres cuites orientalistes et africanistes 1860-1940* [Oriental and Africa Terracotta 1860-1940]. Les Editions de l'Amateur, Paris, 1999.

Rose, Phyllis, *Jazz Cleopatra, Josephine Baker in her time*. Vintage Books, New York, 1989.

Sanchez, Pierre, *Dictionnaire du Salon d'Automne (1903-1945)*. De Jacob, Dijon, 2006.

Sanchez, Pierre, *Dictionnaire des Indépendants (1920-1950)*. De Jacob, Dijon, 2008.

Savinio, Alberto, *Isadora Duncan*, Franco Maria Ricci, Parma, 1978.

Verne, Henri and Chavance, René, *L'Art Décoratif Moderne en France* [Art Deco in France]. Librairie Hachete, Paris, 1925.

Vicario, Vincenzo, *Gli Scultori Italiani dal Neoclassicismo al Liberty* [Italian Sculptors from Neoclassicism to Liberation]. Il Pomerio, Lodi, 1994.

Wiser, William, *The Crazy Years – Paris in the Twenties*. Thames and Hudson, 1990.

Photographic Credits

Rainer Querfurth: p123 right, p147, p155, p165 right, p173, p174 left, p186, p187, p199 right, p201 left, p219, p240, p242 left.

John Dessarzin: p8, p10, p42, p45, p53, p54 left, p56 top, p57, p58 top right, p59, p60, p63 bottom, p70 bottom, p71 left, p72, p73, p74, p75, p76 top, p78, p79, p87, p90 bottom, p96, p97, p98, p99, p102, p104 right, p105, p106 left, p107, p108, p109 bottom, p110, p111 right, p117 right, p119, p121, p124, p126, p128, p129, p136, p137, p138, p139, p143, p144, p145, p150, p151, p152, p153, p156 left, p159, p166 bottom, p167, p169, p171, p174 right, p175, p180, p182, p189 top, p191, p192, p193, p194 centre and right, p195, p197, p200 left, p201 right, p202 top, p203 top right, p204, p205, p209, p210, p211, p212 left, p213 right, p214 top, p 216 left, p222 right, p230 left, p231, p232, p233, p238 top, p241, p242 right, p245, p246, p247.

Marcelo Ferrari: Spine, p2, p3, p30 top and centre, p38, p39, p40, p41, p43, p44, p46, p48, p49 top, p50, p58 bottom, p61, p62, p64, p67 top, p71 right, p76 bottom, p77 right, p82 bottom left, p86, p91, p92, p100, p101, p112, p114, p117 left bottom, p122, p125, p127, p130, p131, p132 left, p133, p134, p135, p140 bottom, p141, p142, p146 right, p156 right, p160, p165 left, p168, p170, p172, p177, p179, p183, p185 top, p188 right, p189 bottom, p190, p194 left, p196 left, p198, p199 left, p200 right, p203 top left, p208, p212 right, p213 left, p217, p218, p220, p221, p222 left top and bottom, p223, p224, p225, p226, p227, p229, p230 right, p234, p235, p236, p237, p239, p244 right.

Danilo Takano: Front cover, Back cover, p6, p47, p49 bottom, p51, p55, p58 top left p65, p66 left, p68 bottom, p69 left, p77 left, p80, p84, p85, p88, p89, p113, p118, p132 right, p140 top, p146 left, p154, p161, p176, p178, p181 right, p203 bottom, p206, p207, p215, p228, p244 left.

Federico Adrián Marino: p83, p90 top, p115, p157.

Lucía Picerno: p184.

Heidi Iro archives: p93, p94, p95.

Le Verrier Blanchet Collection: p158.

Beck-Lipsi Collection: p162, p136, p164, p166 top.

Maggie Strunk: p52 top, 238 centre and bottom.

José Dwek: p109 top, p120, p148.

Cláudio S. Moraes: p52 bottom.

Tatiana Boltiansky: p243.

Mariana Reveil: p67 bottom.

Dirk Visser: p12, p56 bottom, p70 top, p196 right.

Alex Daligand: p123 left.

Ali Elai: p106 right.

Robin Hill: p103.

Francisco Pinto: Author image.

Private archives: p116, p149.

Personal archives: p16, p17, p18, p19, p20, p21, p22, p23, p24, p25, p26, p27, p30 bottom, p31, p32, p33, p34, p35, p54 right, p63 top, p66 right, p68 top, p69 right, p81, p82 top and bottom right, p104 left, p111 left top and bottom, p117 left top, p181 left, p185 bottom, p188 left, p202 bottom, p214 bottom, p216 right, p247 left, p248.

Index

Page numbers in **bold** refer to illustrations